BEST AMERICAN SCREEN-PLAYS

· FIRST SERIES · COMPLETE SCREENPLAYS ·

EDITED BY SAM THOMAS

FOREWORD BY FRANK CAPRA

Crown Publishers, Inc.
New York

*This book is dedicated to
Margot Thomas,
who won her spurs long ago
as Best American Spouse.*

ACKNOWLEDGMENTS

I would like to express my thanks and appreciation to the following people—all of whom helped to bring this project to fruition: To Stan Belkin, general counsel of Warner Brothers, and Ms. Judith Singer of that legal department for their unfailing courtesies and cooperation. To my editor at Crown, Brandt Aymar, for his unwavering support, enthusiasm, and patience. To Ms. Sandra Gottlieb, director of business affairs at 20th Century-Fox; to Ron Tropp, former vice president of business affairs at Embassy, and Ms. Nancy Cushing Jones of Universal Pictures, Business Affairs for their courtesies and cooperation; and to Dr. Knudsen and Ray Holland of the University of Southern California's Doheny Library, Special Collections, for their kind assistance in making available to us a copy of *Meet John Doe*. And to all the numerous writers' agents, business managers, and other representatives who helped make this anthology possible, including my own agent, Ben Kamsler of H. N. Swanson & Co. — a hearty thank you.

Published by Crown Publishers, Inc., 225 Park Avenue South, New York, New York 10003 and simultaneously in Canada by General Publishing Company Limited.
CROWN is a trademark of Crown Publishers, Inc.
Manufactured in the United States of America

Library of Congress Cataloging-in-Publication Data
Main entry under title:
Best American screenplays.
1. Moving-picture plays. I. Thomas, Sam.
PN1997.A1B36   1986   812′.5′08   85-17091
ISBN 0-517-55542-5

10 9 8 7 6 5 4 3 2 1
First Edition

CONTENTS

iii

FOREWORD BY
FRANK CAPRA

Having guested some years back at Sam Thomas's class at UCLA on The Literature of the Screen, I was delighted when I heard from him regarding his new project, his anthology, *Best American Screenplays*.

I feel honored at his request to write a foreword for his work, the first book in almost a half century to offer the reader a full, varied, and excellent collection of screenplays published in their entirety.

As I have often said and been quoted as such in Mr. Thomas's introduction to my work *Meet John Doe,* ". . . Scriptwriting is the toughest part of the whole racket . . . the least understood and the least noticed."

I stand by that.

In my collaboration with all the fine writers who worked on my films, and by virtue of my own background as a writer before I became a director and producer of many of my own works, no one knows better than I how important the script is. My close collaboration with all these very talented screenwriters is a testament to that.

The time has, indeed, arrived, beyond question, for great screenplays to be read, admired, and considered as literature. I hope this will be the first of many such anthologies by Mr. Thomas paying homage to the great scripts of the cinema. Motion pictures will always have a need for fine writers, and I nurture the hope that the next fifty years of cinema will develop as fine a group of screenwriters as those who preceded them in my time.

INTRODUCTION

. . . It is the writer who is the dreamer, the imaginer, the shaper. He works in loneliness with nebulous materials, with nothing more tangible than paper and a pot of ink; and his theatre is within his mind. He must generate phantoms out of himself and live with them until they take a life of their own and become, not types, but characters working out their own destinies. If the ultimate film is to have any significant content, throwing some new glint of life on life, it is the writer who will have to create it. . . .
FROM DUDLEY NICHOLS, *20 Best Film Plays.**

1

Literature, as Christopher Morley once described it, is the most seductive, the most deceiving, the most dangerous of professions.

Since we are forthwith going to plunge into a discussion of literature, let me not deceive you, nor place you in any danger. But I do wish to seduce you, that is, to beguile you, not to lead you astray with the perhaps startling notion—at least for some of you—that it is decidedly time to recognize and acknowledge that the motion-picture screenplay, at its best, can and should be considered literature in the same sense as a great novel or a great drama.

To be more precise, if a novel or a play is greatly valued by us because it can stand the test of time as to content, beauty of form, and emotional effect, and thus can be read with enjoyment and satisfaction, so may a screenplay meet these criteria.

If we can esteem a great social novel of manners such as Thackeray's *Vanity Fair,* with its unforgettable character Becky Sharp, should we not consider the screenplay of *The Graduate* by Calder Willingham and Buck Henry, as adapted from the novel by Charles Webb, with their equally unforgettable Mrs. Robinson and Ben Braddock, as fine an admirable study and commentary on a culture? If we esteem Molière's *The Miser* and Rostand's *Cyrano de Bergerac* as classic plays, why should we not bestow similar accolades upon Julius J. Epstein, Philip G. Epstein, and Howard Koch for *Casablanca* and Steve Gordon's *Author,* which in time may be worthy of them as well.

There are palpable differences, certainly, among all these forms. But assuredly, when you consider them carefully and critically, the distinctions become, in essence, form and little else. And of these, the screenplay and the stage play are not as far apart as you might think. Of all the forms of literature, these two are most closely allied.

Although the stage play depends primarily on the word and the screenplay on visual projections, an important characteristic they share is that each is an incomplete work.

Just as the words, the settings, and the stage directions of a stage play need to be brought to life by actors, a director, and a performance, so does a screenplay. Both are incomplete in that sense.

Yet you will find almost total agreement that the stage play can be considered literature—to be read, admired, critically acclaimed, researched, annotated, and analyzed. Drama departments in high schools and in universities all over the world devote much time in their curricula in this fashion. The novel receives the same devoted attention, but not the screenplay as yet. I believe that it should if it meets with the criteria of a classic or great work.

What all great literature throughout the ages has in common is that it has always been concerned with ways to express the qualities of humaneness in man—qualities marked by consideration, sympathy, and compassion for other human beings and all living creatures on our planet—and, above all, with fervent pleas for human love amidst the upheavals, problems, and struggles of human life with its frailties and imperfections.

---

*Published by Crown Publishers, Inc., 1943

Before the advent of cinema, it took the best of poetry, prose, and drama—the combined effort of literature through centuries of time—to make clear to us that when we discover the balance, the fusion of mind and spirit we view as order and civilization, which causes human life to become productive and livable, that life, that order will always express the highest aspirations of our poets, our philosophers, our prophets, and through them our hopes for mankind.

So do the screenplay and cinema at their best.

It is undeniably true for many of us today in our American culture as reflected in our cinema and in our art that life is without meaning and of limited expectations, like a Poe suspense story in an atmosphere of gloom, doom, dread, and guilt—suspended by a thread above a gigantic open mass grave in this nuclear age. In that world man has no place in the universe; he is separated from a Supreme Being, be it a god-figure or a life-force, uncertain even of his physical and emotional qualities as a man or as a woman. A subject for dissection and experimentation by science, sociologists, psychologists, physiologists, and computers, trying to find out what makes man tick, as if we were ten-dollar quartz wristwatches or transistor calculators robotized with interchangeable mass-produced parts.

The diminishing of the condition of being human, as observed in all the critical moments of human history beginning with the plays of Euripides more than two thousand years ago and in the admonitions of the biblical prophets, emerges again and again in human society when it does not fulfill basic human needs. Man in his despair almost always turns to the demeaning of man.

In cinema, as in any literature, when this occurs, we sink to the debasing level of an effluence of works that violate and play false man's state of being human. This kind of cinema—no matter how well crafted or effective such glitzy or sleazy works may be— subjugates us and reduces us to the dark side of our nature, where we are portrayed as endless repetitions of mechanical characters without feelings. Human beings degenerated into cruel, savage, aggressive, and violent creatures—dehumanized beyond measure.

If then one of the pervasive themes in art of our time is the alienation of human life— ecological literature, if you will, in the larger sense that man has estranged himself from his true environment having polluted himself in the present marketplace of existence—it is also undeniably true that great films, and the writers and filmmakers who create them, have done as much or more with the tremendous audiences they reach to keep intact that image of man as a being whose humaneness and future depend on his achieving his highest aspirations.

In assessing broadly the more than half century of cinema we span in our anthology, it is notable, despite almost two decades of a spate of sleaze, that we are once again, as evidenced over the last few years, giving rise to a body of film that is intensely human.

Among these films are Robert Benton's *Kramer vs. Kramer*; Irving Ravetch and Harriet Frank, Jr.'s *Norma Rae*; Bo Goldman's *Melvin and Howard*; Alvin Sargent's *Ordinary People*; Ernest Thompson's *On Golden Pond;* James Brooks's *Terms of Endearment;* and John Briley's *Gandhi.*

Almost all of these films won Academy Awards for both Best Screenplay and Best Picture over this most recent span of time. All reflected a desire and purpose to unite man and nature in the fullest sense of mind and spirit and to give all the problems of their characters a humane face. It is significant that these films were accorded the Academy's highest honors almost one after the other.

There are signs too of a reborn romanticism in film in a rising rebellion in all art against technology and the computer age much in the manner that romanticism attacked science and the mechanical universe in the eighteenth century for its dehumanizing values born of that beginning Industrial Revolution.

This, despite the remarkable box-office successes of films that cater to the showy gadgets of present-day engineering marvels with blinking light panels, space wizardry, and comic book primitivism.

The Academy Award films cited a few paragraphs back most emphatically indicate that we are once again giving full attention in our film literature to the idea that man must be understood through man and that human consciousness is the key to reality. This literature is not the empty, adolescent and immature restatements of so-called realism cynically used; nor is it naturalism disguised as adult themes, hiding behind facile clichés like "telling it the way it is."

Therefore, what we will attempt to accomplish in this anthology, *Best American Screenplays,* is to singularize those screenplays that, after careful evaluation and scrutiny based on the criteria we have offered, we judge to be literature of the film. These are the screenplays that, in my estimation, have contributed a great deal to American art, culture, and craft in approximately the better part of this century, roughly from the late twenties and the founding of the Academy to the present, as developed from a course of study originated by me at the University of California at Los Angeles Extension more than a decade ago, entitled The Literature of the Screen.

What you have in these pages for your perusal and enjoyment are final screenplays in their entirety, complete in every detail save shot numbers, which are not critical to the screenplays and which have been omitted for your greater reading enjoyment. This should in no way inhibit the film buff or serious student from appreciating the work in question.

Some of you may ask, what about all those screen directions the writer uses in his screenplay? Surely you don't consider that "literary"? I respond, why not? It is part of the complete work. Do we demean a great drama because of its stage directions?

You will also take note that in a few instances some screenplays differ in some important details from the motion picture as filmed other than the usual small, colloquial changes in dialogue affected by performers and directions on the set. I will refer to those important differences in the short introductions preceding the screenplays in question. *Arthur, The Graduate,* and *Butch Cassidy and the Sundance Kid,* for example, were affected by such changes. This will undoubtedly be of strong interest to some of you.

Almost all of the works chosen for this premiere anthology, *Best American Screenplays,* First Series, have won either a nomination for an Academy Award or the Oscar itself for Best Screenplay. In many cases these scripts have won other prestigious awards as well—those bestowed by the Writers Guild of America and the New York Critics Circle.

To be more precise, *Best American Screenplays* should perhaps have been called *Among the Best American Screenplays,* when you consider that not every collection one chooses to put together can satisfy everyone, including this editor.

Some screenplays, for example, which I might have liked to include, such as Herman Mankiewicz and Orson Welles's *Citizen Kane*; Carl Foreman's *High Noon*; or Paddy Chayefsky's *Network*; and John Huston's *Treasure of the Sierra Madre*; as well as some of the works of Billy Wilder, had to be excluded because of difficulties in obtaining copyright clearances. These are screenplays that we admire and hope to include in subsequent anthologies.

Nonetheless, what we have selected for you and have included in this volume we deem to be of the highest quality and quite representative of a comprehensive first anthology that has been more than two arduous years in the making.

We are proud of our selections and, if you will allow us to say so, of our achievement in putting together this collection—the first on the subject in many decades, considering that John Gassner and Dudley Nichols's estimable pioneering anthology *20 Best Film Plays,* for which I have the highest regard, is now out of print and was published almost a half century ago, I hope and trust we can continue to follow in their footsteps. We feel that in *Best American Screenplays,* First Series, we present works eminently worthy of the accolade the Literature of the Screen.

In *All Quiet on the Western Front,* as written for the screen by George Abbott, Maxwell Anderson, and Dell Andrews and produced in 1930, we have an elegy to humanity and compassion in its heartfelt and numbing depiction of the horrifying carnage of modern mass warfare in World War I. It is the definitive work for all time on the dehumanizing effects of war on the young, who must do the fighting and dying—a mirror reflecting the effects of jingoism on the idealism of these German youths fresh from the schoolroom, presaging the disillusionment and false gaieties of the generation following their time in the 1920s, which lost and rejected that idealism.

In Robert Riskin's *Meet John Doe,* written in 1941, we have a warm, populist paean to the common man, a voice of cheer and hope in the wilderness of despair during America's worst depression years of the 1930s, with its abiding faith in the people and in democracy and in its message of courage, so typical of most of Mr. Riskin's films with the great Frank Capra.

In Lonne Elder III's *Sounder,* written in 1972, we have represented still another deeply resonated personal view of 1930 depression times. Here we have an intensely human study of a black family in the South, during their bleak, starvation-ridden days, trying to eke out a living with dignity from their sharecropper land. Simple in its warmth and in its depiction of close-knit family love, it focuses on the close relationship between a father and his young son. Though they suffer deeply, they sustain an abiding faith in education as a way of hope for the future as well as a way out of grinding poverty.

In *Casablanca,* as written for the screen by Julius J. Epstein, Philip G. Epstein, and Howard Koch in 1942, we do not have just an all-time, popular romantic tale that takes place during World War II but, in a way, a depression story as well. Mirrored in it are all the scars and blights inflicted on decent people during those difficult times of difficult choices that marred and blurred the struggle for democracy and decency against the dark and evil forces of Hitler and nazism. Personified by the character of Rick (Humphrey Bogart) and the film's Quisling character, Captain Reynaud (Claude Rains), the triumph of *Casablanca* is the underlying idealism in Rick winning out over his cynicism.

In David Newman and Robert Benton's *Bonnie and Clyde* written in 1966, we round out our overview of the great American depression of the 1930s in a special genre, the folk gangster story, an important part of this country's cinema. This film depicts a thread of violence that runs through so much of American life and history, the desperate way of life that has no end but death.

In William Goldman's *Butch Cassidy and the Sundance Kid* (1968), we may note the resemblance to *Bonnie and Clyde* in yet another film genre, the Western, depicting, in similar fashion, violence ending in sudden death. Both are in some fashion biographical; both are stylistically written and mounted as folk ballet. Both in their way reflect the self-doubting decade of the 1960s in America with its deepening dissatisfactions and distrust of our institutions, going back into this country's violent, unlawful past to find a distant mirror.

In *Rebel Without a Cause,* as written for the screen by Stewart Stern in 1955, and in *The Candidate,* written by Jeremy Larner in 1971, we have two further representations of the unease that afflicted America in the 1960s. *Rebel Without a Cause* anticipated a large-scale breakdown in the American family and the emergence of the teenager group as an important subculture in our country. It presaged the protests and dissatisfactions of the college campus and the concomitant adolescent explosion of street gangs and crime in the American urban scene of the sixties and seventies. *The Candidate* concerns itself with the disquiet of the decent American who runs for political office hoping to improve the lot of his fellow citizens and learns to his dismay of the compromises he must make in depending so slavishly and expensively on all the media and the people who manipulate it. It is a disturbing depiction of the blights of our modern election processes, particularly in television.

Calder Willingham and Buck Henry's *The Graduate* (1967) in its brilliant, satiric, comedic way, also reflects the unease expressed by the two works cited above.

In contrast, in *Miracle on 34th Street,* as written for the screen by George Seaton in 1947, when the American future was still bright and unclouded by nuclear dangers and there were no deep uncertainties in our country, we have a classic fairy tale, a charming motion picture that is genial, witty, original, and loving—a joy for both child and adult. This story reaches deep for feelings and human values and for the felicities of family love, friendship, companionship, and goodwill.

In *On Golden Pond,* as scripted by Ernest Thompson in 1980, we delve even deeper into the thicket of family and filial relationships with its profound hates and profound loves and find warmth, wit, and perception against a background of the trials of old age.

Rounding out our delightful comedies in this anthology, we have Steve Gordon's *Arthur (1980).* In *Arthur* we have a testament to the untimely death of this talented writer, Steve Gordon. The screenplay's scintillating wit and comedic verve serve its kooky characters so well that it very favorably reminds one of the best in the great tradition of Hollywood's zany comedies, linking it in no small way to Dudley Nichols and Hagar Wilde's *Bringing Up Baby* as directed by Howard Hawks and to films like *It Happened One Night,* another Robert Riskin and Frank Capra masterpiece.

All of these works reflect importantly on American society and culture during the roughly fifty-year span of time we cover in our anthology. From the heady, raucous, ritual-breaking days of the 1920s with its origins in the so-called liberating but destructive demise of the Victorian way of life after World War I, through the intense suffering of the depression years, through World War I with its own turbulence and soul-shocks amidst shattering revelations of the sick spirit of man vented in unprecedented hatreds and genocides, through the sobering and disquieting aftermath of this war culminating in the American Vietnam experience, through Mei Lei and Watergate with yet another round of fragmentation and even deeper shattering of American ideals and our view of ourselves. All of this represents more than a half century of swiftly moving events that severely tested our most cherished assumptions and beliefs.

To look back, by reading these screenplays, at those critical eras and vital moments in our own history that have shaped our epochal present is to give us through a special window in time a unique view that is exciting, revealing, and illuminating—an opportunity that is far more rewarding, in my opinion, than perusing most of the scholarly and pedantic overviews of this half century in American life.

To read these screenplays now, to savor their richness of humanity as well as their portents for the future in reexperiencing our past, is to realize that they have stood the test of time (with the natural exception, of course, of our more recent choices) as surely and completely as a master canvas by Rembrandt.

2

But before you dip into our anthology to begin with your favorite screenplay, may I suggest, for those of you who are unfamiliar with the screenplay form, that we take a bit more time so that we may enable you to read these scripts more fully and with more enjoyment.

For those readers who may initially find this literary form—given our training from early schooling to read prose or poetry rather than works designed for performance—we can, I trust, with just a small amount of preparation overcome this unfamiliarity.

To enjoy reading a motion-picture script as a final screenplay becomes a matter simply of becoming more literate in this form and of achieving an understanding of film grammar and the elements of the script more than anything else. This is not at all a difficult task, I assure you.

And so, let us now go into the basics of the shot, the cuts, the dissolves, the camera movements of cinema, and the components of the script.

To begin with, one may say that a film in essence is the sum total of all its visual elements, to which sound in all its aspects has been added.

I think that this can be grasped most quickly by offering an analogy between prose and the drama.

If a short story or a novel is considered to have as components of its grammar the word, the sentence, the paragraph, and the chapter; and the play correspondingly has the word, the sentence (as dialogue), the scene, and the act; then, in film grammar, we would correspondingly again have the shot, the scene, and the sequence.

The shot (or the word) then is the basic film unit. No matter how short or long it is, whether it lasts a second or thirty seconds, this is the fundamental entity of film language. And that is what we are defining and describing—film language, language in sight and time. You must grasp the fact that one shot, one word-sentence, as the case may be, one speech on the screen can actually represent, on some occasions, a correspondingly longer psychological or dramatic time far beyond its actual screen duration as one, two, or thirty seconds.

What this simply means is that the continuum of screen time is quite special, as you may appreciate, if you think about it.

To put it another way, one shot in a film that lasts, say, five seconds compared with an almost identical scene written for the stage, may very well have an impact dramatically and psychologically that might take the dramatist fully five minutes to accomplish the identical purpose in dialogue, and the film shot may have been achieved without having one word of dialogue in it. To compare it even further, it might take a novelist a full twenty pages of prose to accomplish the identical effect.

To continue, then, if the shot is the intrinsic unit of film, then the next large unit, the scene, usually consists of a series of shots filmed in the same location and during the same period of time elapsed but from different angles and camera positions.

Arrange a number of scenes together, and you logically have a film sequence loosely comparable to a dramatic act or to one or more chapters of a novel, sometimes referred to as part I and so on. In the earlier days of screenwriting, you would still find sequences literally in use. *All Quiet on the Western Front* was written in sequences from *A* through *J*. Today, such nomenclatures, or divisions, are not used in cinema.

Let us broaden the analogies further for the sake of clarity.

As in prose and drama, all of these film building-blocks in cinema structure are related to one another in techniques of flow, rhythm, continuity, and transitions of time and space.

Like the sentence and the paragraph, the first and most basic building-block in film grammar is the simple cut made by joining together two pieces of film comprising two or more shots.

To equal the transitions of time and place as envisaged by the novelist as chapter and the dramatist as scene or act, film uses the wipe, or dissolve, that is, going to film-black from one time and place and emerging in another time and possibly another place.

And, finally, if in prose we also have the comma, the period, the semicolon, the colon, the dash, and the exclamation point, to name most of the stalwarts of punctuation marks and movement in verbal and written grammar, so do we loosely have their counterparts in film as initially orchestrated and arranged by the writer in his dialogue and screen directions, and subsequently arranged, orchestrated, and juxtaposed by the film editor and director in their use of shot film angles and camera positions and the rhythm of these shots and scenes.

In D. W. Griffith's day and for a considerable time afterward, well into the fifties, audiences had no great difficulty in dealing with these basics of film grammar as described.

Within the last several decades, however, film grammar has taken a step forward and become more sophisticated, assisted no little by modern art, modern music, modern literature and modern technology. Today, for better or worse as the case may be, we have complicated as well as freed our film grammar from traditional restrictions in sound as well as sight, by the use of shock cuts, cuts out of sequence, jump cuts, instantaneous flashbacks, and the dismissal of the dissolve as choices. We now have at our command a whole new array of camera and microphone positions as the result of technical advances in both the lab and on the set, accompanied on occasion by a sometimes bewildering acceleration and fragmentation of shots, influenced no little by modern television commercials and the new genre of musical video shorts built around a song.

Arrange all these elements of film grammar as developed over the decades of cinema, orchestrate and juxtapose them creatively as envisioned by the screenwriter, the director, and the editor, and you have, in result, almost the entire creative range and process of filmmaking.

3

If you now have a working comprehension of film grammar, all that remains for us to enhance your enjoyment of these screenplays is to turn your attention briefly to the elements of the screenplay itself.

Of all the components that creatively enter into the full process of filmmaking, alongside that of film grammar and partaking of it, it is the comprehensive totality of the screenplay that is least understood even by the devoted filmgoer, certainly not out of lack of interest but for historic, aesthetic, and stylistic reasons stemming from misinformation and misunderstanding.

An investigation of what we mean by cinematic literacy is the key to this understanding.

For most of us as filmgoers, the experience of taking in a motion picture is much like going past an iceberg at sea or venturing through a cathedral, a supermarket, or a bedroom without having an opportunity to linger as much as we would like. To the untrained mind and eye, capturing only the impressionable stimuli and satisfactions or dissatisfactions of that visual journey, one sees, for the most part, only the thrust and outline of those structures, or their most outstanding embellishments captured as details—the components we see most easily, the visible portion.

What we do not see or note immediately is the whole of the structure: the substructures, the plans, the designs, the supports, and the total sense of form and content as a result. Therefore, to the untrained eye and mind, what goes unnoticed in film are the special qualities of writing, the arrangement of words and scenes, and the film knowhow (or grammar) qualities that give a script and a film its force, its character, and a great deal of its substance.

Because of this visual fact of life and optic physiology, because most of us see incompletely then, as a result, and are not educated to see wholly to overcome this physiological bias, we fall into cinematic illiteracy all too easily.

To become visually literate requires orientation and perception, as much or more than the Sunday pleasure driver who would like to drive his car in the Le Mans Grand Prix.

The truly literate filmgoer has to do more than use his eyes and his feelings in a surface manner. He has to use that sense of sight (and sound) with intelligence and sensitivity and discrimination. He has to have the capacity, in short, for judgment based upon input factors other than just that of physiological sight.

And this means he has to listen and to read with filmic literacy if he wishes to evaluate cinema with some substance rather than just express his likes or dislikes on viewing a film.

It is a necessity to read screenplays with intelligence and capacity if you are to judge writing value and weigh its contribution to a film. It is scant comfort to a screenwriter to be told that you enjoyed his film and just adored those catchy expressions of his, like . . . "If you want me, just whistle . . ." or "Come up and see me sometime . . ." or "Love is never having to say you're sorry . . ."

Any screenwriter, of course, does appreciate your informing him that you like his work. But he would be ever so much more appreciative if you understood what he was trying to say in that work. Even more if you could comment with clarity and perception about his skill in delineating a character, an event, or a historic truth.

If you took proper note of the epigraph for this introduction on the role of the screenwriter in film, which was so ably voiced by Dudley Nichols, whose impressive body of work (much of it with John Ford) includes *The Informer, Stagecoach,* and *The Long Voyage Home,* consider more completely and objectively now the craft and contribution to content of the superior screenwriter. Let us analyze those elements.

Perhaps one good way to begin would be to describe the work of the Writers Guild Arbitration panel.

As an ongoing member of this panel (until recently), I have on a number of occasions taken part in assisting the guild in judging the contesting of credits between two and sometimes three screenwriters.

Now if you realize that writing credits are the economic lifeblood of this craft, since they are the basis for residual payments and, of course, for professional prestige, you will understand that arbitration of credits is a pretty serious business.

What is a typical case for arbitration?

For example, Writer A has been succeeded by Writer B on a script. The Studio or Producer decides that Writer B's contribution to the final script as filmed is greater than Writer A's. Therefore, the Studio wishes Writer B's credit to appear before Writer A's on the film. Or, in another example, the Studio is of the opinion that Writer B's effort, on succeeding Writer A on the script, is so superior and has so transformed the scenario that Writer A should no longer be considered as a coauthor. The Studio thereby requests that Writer A's name be removed from the credits entirely and that Writer B receive full and sole credit.

Well then, how do you arbitrate such cases when Writer A feels that he has not been treated fairly and so appeals to the Guild? (It should be noted that the scripts so appealed never have the author's name on them, to ensure impartiality.) How do you judge?

Now you come to the crux of the problem. Is it simply a case of counting the number of lines of dialogue or pages contributed by Writer A versus the number of lines contributed to the script by Writer B?

Of course not. On surface appraisal, it might appear that this would be a fair procedure. But if, as we have tried to make clear to you, there is a totality of the screenplay to consider—both the visible and invisible portions—so that we can measure the chemistry, craft, content, and structure of the work in question, then we must go into additional criteria.

To accomplish this, one has to break the script down roughly to four elements—construction, style, characterization, and dialogue—and give them almost equal weight.

In the judgment, therefore, one has to consider the relative importance of all these contributions to a script as a unique experience for that script and that script alone, to weigh them as judiciously as possible and to comprehend fully all these elements as they come together in the complete totality of the screenplay itself. This is not always an easy task and is quite often in fact a perplexing one.

The important thing for you to remember, however, is that there are more elements to deal with in judging the worth of a script than just the visible portion—the screen directions and dialogue. Structure, construction, style, or point of view—the things you don't often see, as we have tried to demonstrate—also must be considered.

It may be instructive and illuminating for those of you who wish to take the time to make some of your own judgments as to the construction, style, characterization, and dialogue of some of the screenplays in this anthology. It would be very much worth your while.

Weigh, if you will, the screenwriter's creation of ideas, plot, and characters as exemplified in George Seaton's *Miracle on 34th Street*. Note the development of character in *Casablanca* and the point of view that gives a screenplay its style and uniqueness as exemplified in Lonne Elder's *Sounder*. Measure the ordering of dramatic scenes and the progression of those scenes to build climax and resolution as crafted by Robert Riskin in *Meet John Doe*. And last but not least, weigh the most visible aspect of the screenwriter's contribution to film—his dialogue as evidenced by Steve Gordon's *Arthur*, and Calder Willingham and Buck Henry's *The Graduate*. All of inestimable distinction.

When ordered in a master fashion, all of these components that enter into a screenplay give the director, the actor, and all the other contributors to the creative aspects of film the opportunity to use these words, these scenes, these sequences, and these characters to maximum advantage.

At this point, lest we might by assumption deprecate the role of the screenwriter-adapter who molds story material to film from other media, let us realize that this writer although he hasn't furnished original story and characters per se, still has to bring enormous skill and creativity to a work, depending on each individual situation. Above all, do not make the mistake of considering such a screenwriter a mere translator.

One case in point is the adaptation of *Casablanca* from an unproduced play that never saw the light of day on Broadway. Read the play and make your own judgment.

To further appreciate adapting skill and creativity in film writing, consider a few remakes of motion pictures. Compare the later Hollywood version to the Fritz Lang classic thriller *M* from his own screenplay in collaboration with his wife, Thea von Harbou, based on the true case of a compulsive child murderer in Düsseldorf; or the recent remake of *39 Steps* to Alfred Hitchcock's original version, adapted from the John Buchan novel by Charles Bennett. Compare the related screenplays.

Speculate if you will on what a Michael Curtiz would have accomplished as director of yet another version of *Casablanca,* from a different screenplay written by someone other than the very talented Julius J. Epstein, Philip G. Epstein, and Howard Koch. Or what a William Wyler might have accomplished with still another version of *Casablanca,* using the same beautifully crafted Epstein and Koch script.

This is fascinating conjecture, but not very practical, considering the cost of feature films these days. Compare these multimillion-dollar costs to the budget of a recording of Beethoven's Ninth Symphony, where we are able to compare different versions of the work by, say, a Leonard Bernstein, a George Szell, or a Zubin Mehta—or as many conductors (directors) as the market could bear. Suffice it to say, Beethoven, in each case, remains the composer of note.

Furthermore, to those who maintain that the real film, the heart of a work, is created in the editing room by the film editor or the director, who has control on the set and in the final cut, it must be stressed that the superior screenwriter anticipates much of what is shot on the soundstage and edited in the lab. Not necessarily only by his dialogue and construction, or by writing in an array of camera angles in his script (which he seldom does these days unless he is directing the film himself) but by the film grammar in his screen directions. In many cases, this talented screenwriter will include nonverbal images and specific movements in these directions that are fundamental to the development of the film if carried out. Screen and actor "business," if you will, that will often transcend dialogue in its effectiveness.

Thus, wit and epigram, comic antic and tragic comprehension by no means have to be verbal to be effective. In film at its best, any of these highly sought-after and desirable literary and theatrical values may be conveyed to an audience by means of symbols, signs, and behavior without a word of dialogue being written or uttered. To testify to that, one need only recall the famous last scene from *All Quiet on the Western Front* (whoever was responsible for it), where Paul, as portrayed by Lew Ayres, is shot by a sniper as he raises his head above his trench to reach for a butterfly, a bit of business that does not appear in the final screenplay.

All in all then, before his script gets to camera, the superior screenwriter, making full use of all the film grammar elements described herein within the crucible of his own creativity very often offers so much more beyond story and dialogue and construction.

It is in these areas of film grammar and construction that the creative distinctions of the superior writer and the superior director often become blurred and neglected. Many a fine screenwriter's contributions to the total effectiveness of a film are passed over or attributed to the director. And in some cases, of course, the contributions of the director are attributed to the screenwriter. But that is the exception, I believe. The weight of the evidence and the tendency to ignore construction and content on film for emphasis on the visual elements indicate that it is the screenwriter who suffers the most in this.

Orson Welles put this rather well in an interview published in *Sight and Sound* (December 1950), which is as valid and true today as it was then.

In referring to the writings of serious cinema journalists who, to him, seemed to start from an article of faith that "a silent picture was better than one with sound . . .," Mr. Welles went on to say:

> what I mean to say is that you [the journalist] always overstress the value of images. You judge films in the first place by their visual impact instead of looking for content. This is a great disservice to the cinema. It is like judging a novel only by the quality of its prose. I was guilty of the same sin when I first started writing for the cinema. It was the experience of film-making which changed my outlook. Now I feel that only the literary mind can help the movies out of that cul de sac into which they have been driven by mere technicians and artificers. That is why I think today the importance of the director in film-making is exaggerated, while the writer hardly ever gets the place of honor due him. . . . In my opinion the writer would have the first and last word in film-making, the only better alternative being the writer-director, but with the stress on the first word.

I feel certain Mr. Welles offered no blanket judgment of film journalists with that statement, as I do not in quoting him. Most reviewers, most critics of film, are quite capable in my judgment, but some are not.

But that is not the issue here. Let me put it into proper perspective with the plaint of one former distinguished film reviewer and critic, Mr. Leo Mishkin, who, indeed, earnestly wished and attempted to give the screenwriter his due as a creator whenever it was truly earned.

In a remarkable and candid letter to the *Newsletter* journal of the Writers Guild of America, West (February 1972), Mr. Mishkin, then the film critic of the *New York Morning Telegraph*, who had been ably writing about cinema for more than thirty-five years, had this to say:

> I was highly intrigued by the piece in the January *Newsletter* ("A Sour Note on Criticism," originally appearing in the *Hollywood Reporter's* anniversary edition with the caption "Film Criticism: How Writers Ignore Writers").
>
> The countervailing argument that prevailed over a period of years [Mr. Mishkin went on] was as observers, and without any knowledge of what took place in story conferences, on the set, or in the editing of the film, we could not justifiably say who was responsible for what in the picture we selected for awards. Where did the writer leave off and the director begin? Was that clever line of that actor in the original script, or did he think it up on the spur of the moment because the line in the script didn't sound right when he spoke it? Or was it something looped in afterwards because the producer of the movie wanted to establish a certain mood? How was the stupid critic to know?
>
> Like you (the screenwriter), I am getting pretty tired of those johnny come-lately, know-it-all critics who would sound off on anything and everything they see without any knowledge whatsoever of what took place before they saw it. One of those grievous misconceptions of what we like to think is a free democratic society is the idea that everybody is entitled to an opinion. To my own way of thinking, the only kind of opinion that is worth anything is one that comes from an informed and educated background in the field in which an opinion is being expressed.

To all those capable and sincere movie reviewers and critics out there working at their craft today who subscribe to Mr. Mishkin's judgment and who, like him, wish to evaluate the screenwriter's contribution to film justly and no more, I would like to offer a constructive suggestion, if I may.

It is simply that, whenever they view a film they consider distinctive and of notable merit, they should take the trouble to read the screenplays of those works thus singled out.

Let me illustrate.

On May 26, 1927, a *New York Times* film reviewer (he was nameless and had no byline) had this to say in part about the film he had just seen, *Seventh Heaven*, the script of which was to win the very first Academy Award for screenwriting (adapation) for Benjamin Glazer who adapted his scenario for the screen from the Broadway play by Austin Strong:

> Mr. Borzage, the director, revealed no little imagination in this work and sometimes when it is least expected. He has [Borzage] a happy way of setting forth a touch of comedy at the psychological moment. Take the moment when Papa Boule's [the taxi driver's] taxi

explodes. All that is left of the taxicab is the old-fashioned horn and Papa Boule brushing away a tear, despairing that "Eloise" [the taxi] died for France. . . .

Well, the point to be made here most explicitly—and I go so far back in time to the founding of the Academy of Motion Picture Arts and Sciences to show how long this has been going on—is that the reviewer in the *New York Times* attributed this creative and effective "piece of business" to the director, when, in accuracy and justice, it should have been credited to the screenwriter, Mr. Glazer.

It is clear in reading Mr. Glazer's screenplay that this scene concerning Mr. Boule, the taxi driver, and his cab—to singularize but one example—was created by him, not Mr. Borzage, the director. This scene is not in evidence in the play written by Mr. Strong, which was but a stage play, bound by the confines and limitations of that stage.

The taxicab, Eloise, used quite frequently in other scenes of the screen version of *Seventh Heaven,* became a character in Mr. Glazer's script as he wrote it. To accomplish that "touch of comedy" singled out by the reviewer, Mr. Glazer wrote in a number of episodes involving Eloise in Paris in the early part of the screenplay to build up to that touch of comedy and sentiment later on when the taxicab, as part of the famous taxicab army that rescued the French capital from the Boche, is blown up on the Marne battlefield by a shell during World War I.

Thus, what we are demonstrating here is that the screenwriter, Mr. Glazer, worked out a sequence of scenes involving Eloise so that it could pay off in dramatic and comedic terms.

Had this unknown and nameless *New York Times* reviewer taken the trouble to read Mr. Glazer's script (it is interesting that the regular film reviewer at the paper at that time, Mordaunt Hall, used to annoy studios and studio publicity men by insisting on reading scripts), he certainly would have been better prepared to assess Mr. Glazer's role in the creation of the filmic whole vis-à-vis Mr. Borzage.

This is in no way intended to demean Mr. Borzage's considerable contribution as the director of this charming and sentimental love story, which gained him an Academy Award as well, but only to give Mr. Glazer evenhanded credit for his own contribution and to help correct the record.

To correct these misunderstandings, I submit, would only be possible by the reviewers and critics reading those screenplays of notable merit. Not only would those film journalists be far better equipped to assess the screenwriter's contribution to the film in question—not so much as to determine whose contribution was greater, the writer or the director, but, more importantly, to enable him, the film journalist, to evaluate more intensely the vital writing elements and contents of a film, which is of even greater consequence.

There is not a single film—however banal and devoid of substance it might appear to be—that has not some content or meaning. Even the commonplace, the trite, and the cliché attest to certain beliefs, human myths, mores, rituals, and cultural patterns.

Mind you, I am not requesting that film journalists read *every* screenplay of *every* film they see but only of those they consider to have singular merit. Only in this manner can they be on relatively sure ground in trying to assess the screenwriter's contribution.

To be sure, there is no guarantee that this will be wholly effective. It may be difficult under the best of conditions, upon reading a "final screenplay," to judge the content or to weigh the relative contributions to the film of a writer or a director. To be as objective as possible and to be scrupulously fair, one must realize that by the time a script achieves the status of "final screenplay" and the studio puts the film into production based on that scenario, that script, by that time, has already probably had input not only principally from the writer but also from the director of the film and the producer, and ofttimes from the stars of the film itself, good or bad as that may be.

Nonetheless, what is important is that in reading these "final screenplays," each case should be judged on its own merits and with consideration of the worth of each script in the interests of high-quality film journalism, not so much the issue of who contributed more to a film, the writer or the director. The latter consideration could only be a relatively fruitless endeavor if it were given greater consequence.

In making this suggestion that the film journalist read plays of singular merit, I am aware of the probable logistic problem of getting scripts into the hands of these journalists at the proper time for deadline needs, even though, as far as the accessibility of the scripts is concerned, I have no doubt that the studios or the screenwriters themselves through their agents or the Writers Guild would be happy to comply with requests from legitimate film reviewers and critics on a regular basis.

More to the point, since writing these words, I have had occasion to discuss this with Charles Champlin, the very able arts editor and critic-at-large of the *Los Angeles Times,* and he has enthusiastically endorsed this proposal. I have put Mr. Champlin in touch with Allen Rivkin, public relations director of the Writers Guild, West. Mr. Rivkin has stated that his office will do its best to assist in obtaining screenplays from whatever source possible for Mr. Champlin and his staff at the *Times* or for any other accredited journalists in film who request them.

I fully hope and trust that this modest proposal, which is certainly not original with me, may be the beginning of a new era in communication in this area. I trust too that it will lead to greater understanding of the role and contribution of the screenwriter and, in doing so, will lead to a greater comprehension of the nature and content of film itself to the ultimate greater enjoyment of the reader of this and future anthologies. In essence, I believe that is what we are all interested in.

Mind you, nothing in these pages should be construed as an attempt to demean the role or the talents of the great film directors of cinema, a number of whom directed the very works you will be reading in this anthology. I stand second to none in my admiration for such luminaries as Frank Capra, John Ford, William Wyler, Billy Wilder, and John Huston, to name just a few.

Their fame is great enough and deserved enough that we do not have to diminish them or dim their luster in order to raise up the great screenwriter. We desire only to make you aware of the legitimate differences that have clouded the role and importance of the scenarist in film.

When you read the screenplays we have selected for you in this anthology, you be the judge.

As I leave you now, above all, keep before you—if you can imagine yourself an astronaut hovering high in the sky—the image of cinema as a great metropolis spread out before you in all its grandeur, with all its immense variety of structures—roofs, walls, domes, windows, turrets, sacristies, arenas, rooms, halls, and embellishments—all anchored to a common base or foundation . . . the script, without which nothing stands.

SAM THOMAS
Los Angeles, California
1986

ALL QUIET
ON THE WESTERN FRONT

Screenplay by George Abbott, Maxwell Anderson,
and Dell Andrews

PAUL	Lew Ayres
KATCZINSKY	Louis Wolheim
TJADEN	Slim Summerville
HIMMELSTOSS	John Wray
MULLER	Russell Gleason
DYING FRENCHMAN	Raymond Griffith
PAUL'S MOTHER	Beryl Mercer
KEMMERICH	Ben Alexander

Adaptation by Dell Andrews*
Dialogue by Maxwell Anderson and George Abbott
(Abbott Version, November 19, 1929)
Produced by Carl Laemmle, Jr., for Universal, Pictures, 1930
Directed by Lewis Milestone
Cinematography by Arthur Edeson
Music by David Broekman

---

* The Academy Award nomination for achievement for writing listed George Abbott first, then Maxwell Anderson and Dell
Andrews.

This classic war story of American cinema, based on the novel by Erich Maria Remarque, as adapted for film by George Abbott, Maxwell Anderson, and Dell Andrews and written in sequences unlike the screenplays of today, is known as the Abbott Version, a designation placed on the script itself in the title pages of the manuscript by Universal in November of 1929.

The late Maxwell Anderson, one of the contributors to the script, is of course well known as a playwright notable for such plays as *Winterset, Key Largo,* and *Mary of Scotland.*

The remarkable George Abbott, still alive and active at the writing of this introduction at the age of ninety-seven, wrote numerous plays and directed even a greater number on Broadway, one at a recent revival of *On Your Toes,* a successful musical, also written by him. What is even more remarkable about George Abbott is that his reputation is based primarily on the musical comedy not on the drama. He was coauthor with Richard Bissell of *The Pajama Game,* both for the stage and screen version, and he codirected the film with Stanley Donen and was also involved as codirector with *Damn Yankees,* among many other films.

All Quiet on the Western Front, as a novel, is much more grim than the script or the motion picture itself. Mr. Remarque's fine work has great impact in its directness and sparse simplicity. No false sentimentality, no patriotism, no slogans or cant here. The novel offers stark images of searing quality and visceral impact.

What the adapters of the novel accomplished in turning the book into a film of such enduring quality in their final scenario is quite good and evidences much skill. The novel would not have worked well as a motion picture as written, despite its vivid war scenes, given its episodic almost impressionistic quality and its fragmented poetic bursts of imagery, jumping from here to there in time. The sequences from *A* to *J,* as put together by Mr. Abbott and the other adapters, are most sound, creative in their structure, and have a climax-building effect that transcends the novel, fine as it is. As an example of the structure in the script, for those of you who might wish to compare the novel to the screenplay, note that the book opens with Paul (Lew Ayres) and his fellow teenage schoolmates, who had run off to war to enlist directly from their schoolroom, already veteran soldiers. In the beginning of the screenplay, on the other hand, we begin with their jingoistic schoolmaster in the schoolroom passionately inflaming the impressionistic teenagers with patriotism to get them to enlist for the *Vaterland.* This enables us to get the full cumulative impact of the transition of these innocent youths from peace to the horrors of trench warfare, the decimation of their numbers one by one and Paul's later return to the schoolroom to tell off his schoolmaster, still jingoistic to the end.

Worthy of note, Lew Ayres, now seventy-seven years old, was so affected by playing Paul, the idealistic young German student disillusioned by war, that he became a conscientious objector during World War II and served with distinction in the noncombatant Medical Corps.

Today, Mr. Ayres is still involved in fighting for peace through religion and is active in promoting a recently produced film on the great religions of the world.

All Quiet on the Western Front, as a motion picture—which won an Academy Award for the director, Mr. Milestone, as well as an award for the film as Best Picture—has to be a landmark film as one of the great antiwar motion pictures of all time. Its depiction of these young German students striving poignantly and agonizingly to retain their humanity in the dehumanizing, horrible life of the trenches is masterful on a personal note that denotes "war is hell." There has never been a film that more eloquently speaks for pacifism and the futility of war than this.

SEQUENCE "A"

SCENE 1-A

Medium shot of the corridor of the school: A janitor and his wife are sweeping. As they talk, the janitor opens one door and sweeps out, and then his wife opens the other and we see the street and the soldiers beyond.

JANITOR. Thirty-thousand!
WIFE. Huh, from the Russians?
JANITOR. No, from the French. Say, from the Russians, we capture more than that every single day.

SCENE 2-A

Ext. Semiresidential street in a German city. Day. A column of German soldiers with full equipment is marching toward the camera and close to it. Far in the background, more marching soldiers are seen, field kitchens, etc. All through this first sequence either to the eye or to the ear marching soldiers should be constantly in mind.

SCENE 3-A

Closer angle from the side of the troops shooting out of a store: Troops marching down the street. In the foreground are the backs of civilians who are watching the soldiers. Into the shot comes a BUTCHER *with an apron on. He calls.*

BUTCHER. Mr. Postman!

HIMMELSTOSS *turns.*

BUTCHER. War is war, and schnaps is schnaps—but business must go on—you didn't leave the mail yet this morning.

PETER *enters the scene, trying to get across the street. He smacks* HIMMELSTOSS *good-naturedly across the rear.*

PETER. Hello, Himmelstoss!
HIMMELSTOSS. Hello there, young man.
HIMMELSTOSS. I'm sorry but this is my last mail I deliver anyhow—
BUTCHER. What?
HIMMELSTOSS. Tomorrow I change uniforms.
BUTCHER. You are going in the army?
HIMMELSTOSS. I was called—I'm a sergeant in the reserve, you know.
PETER. Well, HIMMELSTOSS, when you get to Paris look out for those French girls.

PETER *sees his chance to duck across the street and runs.* HIMMELSTOSS *passes mail to* BUTCHER.

HIMMELSTOSS. There you are.

Waves to soldier.

HIMMELSTOSS. Good-bye, Henry. There's Schmitt! You know, the barber.

Calls: Good Luck!

BUTCHER. Well, Himmelstoss, I'll be called myself if it doesn't end in a few months. It will be though.
HIMMELSTOSS. I'm sure you're right, Mr. Meyer.
BUTCHER. Come Himmelstoss, let's have a schnaps for good luck.

A man passes, MEYER *says to him*

MEYER. Mr. Himmelstoss is going to war.
PASSERBY. That's the way to end it. Every man we can spare should be put in up at the front. That's right!

HIMMELSTOSS *and* MEYER *exit.*

Camera travels with the troops, as they march past HIMMELSTOSS *down to the corner and turn to the right. Then the camera trucks back through a schoolroom window and into a schoolroom.*

Dissolve to:

[*Editor's Note: From Scene 4-A through Scene 20-A* KANTOREK's *voice-over overlaps with screen directions.*]

SCENE 4-A

Int. schoolroom. In the foreground appears the profile of KANTOREK. *He is talking with enthusiasm. At first, his words are inaudible because of the noise of the military band, but as the band recedes, we hear him speak:*

KANTOREK. Now, my beloved class, that is what we must do—strike with all our power—give every ounce of strength to win victory before the end of the year. It is with reluctance that I bring this subject up again.

Camera swings around KANTOREK's *face to show the scholars he is addressing, while his voice continues. Close shot of* KANTOREK *as he continues to talk.*

KANTOREK VOICE (*continues*). You are the life of the Fatherland, you boys—you are the iron men of Germany. You are the heroes who will repulse the enemy when you are called upon to do so.

Pan shot of the boys as they sit and watch him as though fascinated. Camera travels from face to face as KANTOREK'S *voice continues.*

And I find myself wondering if it would not be better for you to repulse him before you are called?

Close shot of KANTOREK.

(Takes on a new tone)

It is not for me to suggest that any of you should stand up and offer to defend his country. But I wonder if such a thing is going through your heads? I know that in one of the schools the boys have risen up in the classroom and enlisted in a mass, and of course, if such a thing should happen here, you would not blame me for a feeling of pride. And why should you not, my young heroes? I look from face to face and I see doubt, I see confusion.

Pan shot of the classroom, Camera stops on KEMMERICH, *who is looking in front of him at* KANTOREK.

Dissolve to:

SCENE 5-A

Ext. train standing on a platform. Soldiers are looking out of the windows and waving good-bye to those on the platform. Camera trucks up to KEMMERICH'S *face seen at one of the windows. A woman is standing by the window. She is dressed in black—evidently she is his mother. When the train begins to move she sobs hysterically and clings to the window. The train starts. During this shot, we simultaneously hear* KANTOREK'S *voice.*

KANTOREK'S VOICE *(continues)*
Perhaps some will say you should not be allowed to go yet, that you are too young, that you have homes, mothers, fathers, that you should not be torn away. Are your fathers so forgetful of their Fatherland that they would let it perish rather than you? Are your mothers so weak that they cannot send a son to defend the land which gave them birth? No!

Dissolve to:

SCENE 6-A

Int. schoolroom. Close-up of KEMMERICH'S *face. It shows the struggle which is going on within him, as* KANTOREK'S *voice continues—*

KANTOREK'S VOICE
And after all, is a little experience such a bad thing for a boy?

Camera shifts to LEER *who is sitting nearby.*

Dissolve to:

SCENE 7-A

Street Corner.

KANTOREK'S VOICE *(continues)*
Is the honor of wearing the uniform something from which we should run? And if our young ladies glory in those that wear it, is that anything to be ashamed of?

Street Corner. LEER *is there waiting. A girl comes along whom he had evidently expected to meet. As he steps forward she shakes her head and points to a soldier in uniform coming into the scene from the opposite direction. She takes the soldier's arm and they go off together.* LEER *turns and looks about him. Camera swings in several directions showing soldiers with girls, then Camera swings back to* LEER. LEER *walking down the street in a very resplendent uniform, with a girl on either arm. At the end of the street, he stops and kisses each of the girls very passionately while* KANTOREK'S *voice continues:*

Dissolve to:

SCENE 8-A

Close shot of LEER. *He is looking up at* KANTOREK.

SCENE 9-A

Interior schoolroom: Camera pans from face to face, stopping on PETER.

KANTOREK'S VOICE *(continues)*
I know that you have never desired the adulation of heroes. That has not been part of my teaching. We have sought to make ourselves worthy and let acclaim come when it would. But to be foremost in battle is a virtue not to be despised.

SCENE 10-A

Cavalry Charge: An officer is leading the charge, his saber raised, in the fashion of old-time war prints. Two or three men fall and the officer drops from his horse. The men and horses become confused and a retreat is possible, until PETER, *his saber raised, and turning to one of his comrades, pushes to the front. Instantly, the charge is reorganized and sweeps on, led by* PETER.

Dissolve to:

KANTOREK'S VOICE *(continues)*
There is such a thing as being nurtured too long in peace. There is such a thing as becoming soft. A war puts iron into a nation! And if

iron turns out to be a bitter medicine, then it is our cup and we will drink it.

SCENE 11-A

Interior schoolroom: Close-up of PETER's *face highly excited and enthusiastic.*

KANTOREK'S VOICE *(continues)*
I would rather endanger myself. I would rather, single-handed, go forth and take the spears in my breast!

SCENE 12-A

Close-up of KANTOREK.

SCENE 13-A

Interior schoolroom. ALBERT's *face close up.*

Camera pans again, this time stopping on ALBERT's *face.* ALBERT *pretends to be listening to the subject but at the same time he is writing on a pad which lies before him on his desk.*

KANTOREK'S VOICE *(continues)*
It would not be courage, it would not be sacrifice; it would be a glorious victory to give the life of one old man for so much youth and brilliant promise!

Dissolve to:

SCENE 14-A

Pad on which ALBERT *is still writing. At the top of the page,* ALBERT *has written "Shall I Enlist"; on the left-hand side, "For," and "Against" on the right side. Under "For," he has set down:*
  1. No more classes.
  2. See Paris.
Under the heading "Against" he has written:
  1. Might get shot.
  2. Have to get up early.

KANTOREK'S VOICE *(continues)*
But this I cannot have. It is you who must go— I who must remain behind!

Back: As he finishes these writings, we see MULLER *lean into the scene, peer over his shoulder and snatch the paper away.* MULLER *busies himself reading* ALBERT's *notes. We see him writing and as he hands pad back to* ALBERT *and* ALBERT *reads, an insert of the pad shows* MULLER's *amendments. Opposite "See Paris," we see "Has been done before." By "Might Get Shot," we read "No loss." Near "Have to get up early," is "good." Around "No more classes" he draws a loop and an arrow to indicate that it should be in the other column under "Against."*

Back: from ALBERT's *close-up, the camera pans to* BEHM, *who is listening to* KANTOREK *intently, a worried expression on his face.*

Dissolve to:

SCENE 15-A

Impressionistic field of battle. BEHM, *in uniform, is seen terrified before an onrushing bayonet charge, a dozen bayonets coming toward his helmet. He throws up an arm before his eyes and turns away.*

KANTOREK'S VOICE *(continues)*
I believe it will be a quick way, there will be few losses, but if losses there must be—then let us remember the Latin phrase which must have come to the lips of many a Roman when he stood embattled in a foreign land: *"Dulce et decorum est pro patria moro."*

Dissolve to:

SCENE 16-A

Close-up BEHM's *face.* BEHM *slowly raises one arm as if to shield himself from something, then shakes himself free from the illusion and continues to listen.*

KANTOREK'S VOICE *(continues)*
Sweet and fitting it is to die for the Fatherland!

Dissolve to:

SCENE 17-A

Interior PAUL's *home. Long shot of* PAUL *sitting at his desk at home. He is writing and pauses in the middle of a sentence when the bugle sounds outside. (This bugle being, in fact, part of the band which is marching by.) He rises and stands torn between his work and the call to duty as* KANTOREK's *voice continues—*

KANTOREK'S VOICE *(continues)*
Some of you may have ambitions. I know of one young man who has great promise as a writer. And he has written the first act of a tragedy that would be a credit to one of the masters—

Dissolve to:

SCENE 18-A

Close-up PAUL's *face. Camera pans from face to face.*

KANTOREK'S VOICE *(continues)*
. . . and he is dreaming, I suppose, of following in the footsteps of Goethe and Schiller, and I hope he will. But now our country calls—the Fatherland needs leaders. Personal ambitions must be thrown aside in the one great sacrifice for your country.

SCENE 19-A

Long shot of boys.

KANTOREK'S VOICE *(continues)*

(Raising his voice)
It has given us all we are and without it, we are nothing. Walk into the woods. Do you love them? Why? Because they are German. Walk into the street and see the people and listen to the voices. Do you feel at home there? German street! German voices! Those things we dare not lose though it cost us our lives to save them! Here is a glorious beginning for your lives—the field, the field of honor calls you! Why are we here? You, Kropp, what has kept you back?

SCENE 20-A

Medium shot of group around PAUL.

You, Muller, you know how much you are needed! Ah, I see you look at your leader. And I, too, look to you, Paul Baumer, and I wonder what you are going to do?

The boys all turn to see what he will do. PAUL, *after a flash of indecision, rises with reckless enthusiasm.*

PAUL. I'll go.
OTHERS. I'll go—I'll go. Me, too! Count me in!

There is a general rush to jump up and volunteer. There is a great cheering and shouting. (ALMOST SCREAMING)

KANTOREK. Iron Men! The defenders of the Fatherland.

He counts them as they enlist.

SCENE 21-A

Medium shot of group and BEHM. *He is seated.*

CROWD. Come on, Behm. Come on, join up. Don't be a quitter.

BEHM *shakes his head. They pull him to his feet; he sinks back again. Another angle.* PETER *and* LEER *rush across the room and pull* BEHM *up.*

PETER. We're all going, everybody!

BEHM *turns his eyes helplessly towards* PAUL.

SCENE 22-A

Close shot of PAUL. PAUL *gesticulates his encouragement and enthusiasm, urges him to join the others.*

SCENE 23-A

Close shot of group and ALFRED. *He throws ink-well and shatters it against wall:*

ALFRED. No more classes!

SCENE 24-A

Long shot of room. All the students shout and throw books in the air—dashing ink-wells against the wall.

SCENE 25-A

Close shot of KANTOREK. *He is leaping about enjoying the orgy. He throws his own papers in the air with shouts.*

KANTOREK. For the Fatherland! Iron men—young heroes!

SCENE 26-A

Med. shot of group around BEHM. PAUL *has joined the persuaders.*

PAUL. Stick together, that's what we've got to do! Let's all stick together. Come on, Behm.

BEHM *rises.*

BEHM. All right, I'll go!

SCENE 27-A

Long shot of room. The excitement now passes all bounds. They then begin to march and out of the chaos comes a kind of order. KANTOREK *takes his place at the head.* PAUL, LEER *and* PETER *follow and the column of boys gradually forms as they march around the room, shouting and singing hysterically. They march out the door and the camera continues to show the wrecked room as we hear them marching and singing. They pass back close outside the windows and beyond them in the distance can be seen column after column of troops going off to war.*

Fade out.

SEQUENCE "B"

SCENE 1-B

German barracks—moving shot—day fade in: The boys from the class are walking in line, a corporal at the head of them. They carry uniforms rolled in bundles. MULLER *has his school books. They look about with bright-eyed eagerness, except for* BEHM *who trails in the rear. As they pass by a building, the practice field comes in view. We see squads drilling, men at bayonet practice etc. Camera moves up near* PAUL *who is in the front. He looks back and calls to the others jokingly.*

PAUL. Keep in line there, soldiers!

ALBERT. All right, General, anything you say.

PETER *gives* PAUL *the knee and there is a half scuffle. The company stops in front of a barracks. Closer shot of the* CORPORAL.

CORPORAL. Get into uniform ready to report. Fall out.

The CORPORAL *turns and walks away. The boys break up and tumble over each other in their eagerness to get into the barracks.*

SCENE 2-B

Int. close-up door in hall to barracks room revealing long view of room through doorway. ALBERT *enters, opens the door and goes a few steps into the room. The others scramble into the scene and enter the room.*

SCENE 3-B

Int. barracks room. The room is large and almost square—bunks arranged in pairs one above the other, with straw mattresses. Small stools beside them. Against the walls are lockers. In some of the windows parts of uniforms are hanging to dry. There is a gun rack at one end of the room. The boys crowd in, stop and look around.

SCENE 4-B

Row of bunks. The boys choose their bunks and rapidly start getting into their uniforms.

PETER. Boy, I bet this place'll get us in good condition.

KEMMERICH. We'll have to be, for the long marches.

PETER. I'm going to get in the cavalry and ride.

MULLER. No cavalry for me. The infantry's where you see the fighting. You'd be out guarding a barn or something while I'm capturing trenches. Me for the infantry. They're the backbone of the army, boy.

PETER. Where's the game, that's what I want to know?

PAUL. You don't get a gun for a long while.

PETER. If I am going to pop off a few enemies I have to have some practice.

MULLER. Bayonet drill, that's what I want— Zow! *(makes an imaginary thrust)*

ALBERT. You won a medal that time, boy.

MULLER. Medal! Say, in about a month, I'll be covered with them.

SCENE 5-B

Close-up of MULLER *and* KEMMERICH *on opposite lower bunks. While* MULLER *is lacing his leggings,* KEMMERICH *puts his boots on* MULLER'S *bunk.* MULLER *raises his head, sees the boots and tells* KEMMERICH:

MULLER. Keep your boots off my bed.

KEMMERICH. Son, it's an honor to have those boots on your bed. They're the best boots in the army. My uncle gave them to me. —Special imported leather. You don't expect me to put them on the floor?

MULLER. Put 'em anywhere you like, except on my bed. Put 'em under your pillow, or wear 'em for a watch charm, for all *I* care.

SCENE 6-B

Close-up of another group. LEER *has his complete uniform on and is dismally surveying himself. The sleeves of the coat are too long, the collar stands away from the nape of the neck a couple of inches. The trousers are baggy and far too big. The leggins hang loosely. He looks up at* PAUL.

SCENE 7-B

Close-up PRIVATE *on opposite side of room. The* PRIVATE *who is cleaning up calls out:*

PRIVATE. Attention!

SCENE 8-B

Close-up of the group. They are all startled and wheel toward the door.

LEER. Well, for the love of—. It's Himmelstoss!

PAUL *and* PETER *start out to greet him.*

SCENE 9-B

Close-up at door. HIMMELSTOSS *is standing rigidly.* PETER *enters scene and greets him:*

PETER. Hello, Himmie.

PAUL. Hello, Himmelstoss.

PETER. You didn't know you'd see me again so soon, did you?

They offer hands. HIMMELSTOSS *ignores both their hands, looks coldly at them.*

HIMMELSTOSS. Don't you see my rank?

PETER. Sure.

HIMMELSTOSS. Fall back!

Camera moves with HIMMELSTOSS *who advances into the room.*

SCENE 10-B

Semi-close-up including group and HIMMELSTOSS.

ALFRED. Gee! Himmelstoss, we certainly—

HIMMELSTOSS. What did you say?

ALBERT. I was going to say—

HIMMELSTOSS. Never mind.

ALBERT. What's eating you, Himmelstoss?

HIMMELSTOSS. When you address your superior officer, say "Sir."

PAUL. Oh, come on, Himmelstoss, we know you—take off the false whiskers.

HIMMELSTOSS gives PAUL a look to silence him.

Gee, I believe you mean it.

HIMMELSTOSS. You'll find out if I mean it.

PAUL. But only a few days ago—

PAUL shrugs and starts to walk away.

HIMMELSTOSS. *(speaking fiercely).* Silence! Come back here.

PAUL returns.

We'll get these false notions out of your heads! Line up!

SCENE 11-B

Longer view. The boys look at each other not knowing whether to obey him or not. HIMMELSTOSS snaps out:

HIMMELSTOSS. Get in some kind of a line, I say, and be quick about it.

The boys obey, bewildered by the sudden change. HIMMELSTOSS watches them narrowly. BEHM, who has been slowly dressing and has just put on his trousers and shoes, climbs down and stands with the others.

HIMMELSTOSS. *(Very sarcastically).* That's a pretty sight, that is. Have you ever heard of standing in line? You make a fine mess of it. Well, we'll learn how—we'll spend the day on that! And then, there'll be plenty of other things. You may be stupid but I'm used to that. Oh, I'll not neglect you. There isn't much to start with, but I'll do my best. I see that you've come here with a slight misunderstanding, but I'll correct that. You can forget what you've ever learned—you can forget what you've been and what you are.

He leans forward and shakes his finger under their noses.

I'll take the mother's milk out of you! I'll make you hard-boiled! I'll make soldiers of you or kill you! NOW SALUTE!

The boys are bewildered but click their heels together and assume rigid positions.

Fade out.

SCENE 12-B

Ext. a freshly ploughed field—rain. The rain has filled many of the furrows with water. HIMMELSTOSS' platoon, under full packs and with heavy rifles, is marched into the scene. They are dog-tired. Their feet drag through the mud and water.

HIMMELSTOSS. Halt! Mark time!

The platoon comes to an exhausted stop.

SCENE 13-B

Close-up KEMMERICH and BEHM. The effort of raising and lowering their feet is almost too much for them.

SCENE 14-B

Full front view of platoon. HIMMELSTOSS surveys the boys, then gives the order:

HIMMELSTOSS. Prepare to advance!

The boys obey the order.

Advance!

The platoon takes a few steps forward.

Lie down!

There is a moment of uncertainty, then the platoon lies in the mud.

HIMMELSTOSS. Up! Prepare to Advance! Advance! Lie down! Up!

The platoon drags itself through the drill. They are all covered with mud—miserable. HIMMELSTOSS walks beside them on dry land.

HIMMELSTOSS. Prepare to advance! Advance! Lie down! Crawl forward! Keep your face down!

He jams LEER's face into the mud. It is easier to crawl forward on their stomachs, but keeping their heads down fills their faces with mud.

Dissolve from 14-B. To interior barracks. HIMMELSTOSS in foreground with boys lined up each side of table for drill, a corporal enters doorway as HIMMELSTOSS is drilling. HIMMELSTOSS explains the change at Lohne.

HIMMELSTOSS. I have originated this drill to teach them how to go through the subway when they change trains at Lohne.

Dissolve to HIMMELSTOSS' bed. PAUL and ALBERT on. HIMMELSTOSS watches PAUL finish making bed. HIMMELSTOSS examines same critically and pulls bed to pieces again. Then orders PAUL to remake bed. HIMMELSTOSS exits. PAUL tells ALBERT:

PAUL. I have remade his bed fourteen times and each time he has some fault to find and pulls it to pieces.

Dissolve to:

Interior latrine. HIMMELSTOSS, *panning* ALBERT *and* MULLER, *tells them:*

HIMMELSTOSS. You will scrub this entire floor with this.

He then hands them a tooth brush. The boys start scrubbing.

Dissolve to:

Barracks grounds. HIMMELSTOSS *watching as* KEMMERICH, *and* PETER *police the grounds with hand brooms and dust pans.*

Dissolve to:

SCENE 15-B

Full view of the platoon.

HIMMELSTOSS. We shall have a little bayonet practice. All I have here is a light stick—wooden gun—charge me.

BEHM *lunges at him weakly.* HIMMELSTOSS *strikes him over the knuckles with his cane.*

HIMMELSTOSS. Harder! Charge me, strike!

As BEHM *charges again,* HIMMELSTOSS *cracks him on the wrist.* BEHM *stumbles and almost falls.*

Fall in!

BEHM *does so.* HIMMELSTOSS *watches him.*

SCENE 16-B

Close view of part of the platoon. The boys are glaring angrily at HIMMELSTOSS. BEHM *takes his place among them.*

HIMMELSTOSS. Baumer—step forward, let us see what you can do.

Paul looks at HIMMELSTOSS, *glad of the opportunity to mix with him. He exits quickly.*

SCENE 17-B

Full view of platoon. HIMMELSTOSS *is in the foreground.* PAUL *advances to him and stops.* HIMMELSTOSS *grins tauntingly:* PAUL *charges;* HIMMELSTOSS *fences with him and strikes his knuckles a hard blow.* HIMMELSTOSS *jeers at him:*

HIMMELSTOSS. Come, come—you act like an old man. Don't be afraid of hurting me! Run at me! Attack me!

PAUL *tries again.* HIMMELSTOSS *strikes his forearm a stinging blow.* PAUL *lunges desper-*

ately and is easily evaded. PAUL *charges, lunges furiously, only to be evaded, dodged, fenced off.* HIMMELSTOSS *wields the wooden rifle much faster than* PAUL *can possibly move the heavy gun, and as a consequence is cracked on the arms, shoulders and back until he is too tired to lift the gun again.* HIMMELSTOSS *steps away.*

HIMMELSTOSS. You see what you are, Baumer; you're a clumsy lout. You are as useless here as anywhere else. Fall in!

Paul takes his place.

About face! Forward by squads, march!

The platoon follows instructions and marches out of the scene, gladly relieved.

SCENE 18-B

Traveling scene of platoon marching. HIMMELSTOSS *marches near the front squad. He calls out:*

HIMMELSTOSS. Trail rifles, march at ease!

The boys can scarcely believe their ears. What has come over HIMMELSTOSS? *They trail their rifles and walk along with a little less fatigue.* HIMMELSTOSS *smiles.*

Sing!

HIMMELSTOSS *breaks into song. The boys join rather feebly.*

HIMMELSTOSS. Halt!

The boys stop with a command, he brings them to a front line.

HIMMELSTOSS. So we have no spirit today, we are in no mood for relaxation. Work is what we love. Good, back to work. Squads right, march.

The squads face about.

Dissolve to:

SCENE 19-B

A freshly ploughed field—same as before. The boys are going through the same evolutions.

HIMMELSTOSS. Prepare to advance! Advance! Lie down! Up! Prepare to advance! Advance! Lie down! Crawl forward!

Dissolve to:

SCENE 20-B

Traveling scene of platoon marching. The boys are again returning, each of them a moving mountain of mud.

HIMMELSTOSS. Sing!

The boys, weary as they are, sing heartily.

Dissolve to:

SCENE 21-B

The barracks yard—no rain—grey sky. Day. The ground is wet from recent rain. HIMMELSTOSS *marches his sixteen men to the front of the barracks, singing with all the force they can muster. They are covered with mud. They come into foreground and reach the door to their barracks.*

HIMMELSTOSS. Four hours to clean up. Inspection at three. Dismiss.

The boys break ranks and start to the fountain in the yard. They walk past to barracks, some going in as they pass.

SCENE 22-B

Trucking shot. Closer shot of one group of them as they walk.

MULLER. The swine. That means we got no time off. It'll take four hours to get ready for inspection.
PAUL. I'd like to know what's in his mind.
MULLER. He hasn't got any.
LEER. I'm going to cut him open and find out some day.
ALBERT. He's too thick skinned, he won't cut.
LEER. I'll get even with him, you wait—if it's the last thing I do—
PAUL. But I can't get it through my head how that mild little postman can suddenly become this worst bully in the world.
ALBERT. They all get to be bullies as soon as they get any power. They all bully each other, starting with the General and ending with us.
MULLER. Makes it nice for us.

They arrive at the fountain.

SCENE 23-B

Medium shot across fountain. The boys take off their clothes and bend over, facing Camera, to wash out mud. As they work, they talk.

PAUL. The day we volunteered, I couldn't have imagined that a braided postman was going to have more power over me than my parents, my teacher and all the books that were ever written.
KEMMERICH. We learned a lot since we left school I guess.
LEER. Yeh, we learned that what matters is not the mind but the boot brush, not intelligence but the system, not freedom but the drill.

PETER. We came in to fight—we wanted to be heroes—and they train us for heroism as though we were circus ponies.
LEER. Aw, shut up.
MULLER. Well, he's right; a shiny button is more important here than four volumes of Schopenhauer.
BEHM. Left wheel—right wheel jump to attention—parade march—click your heels. Salute!
PETER. I'm through with all that stuff—no more saluting!

As he finishes speaking an officer approaches. PETER *sees him and calls out:*

PETER. Attention.

The others snap to attention. The officer passes. The others turn slowly and look at PETER.

Fade out.

SCENE 24-B

Long view of training field near the barracks. Fade in: A Company of one-hundred-fifty men is being put through its paces on the field. In the foreground three officers, including the Captain, are watching the drill. As the men go through a wide wheeling movement, the outside group passes the Camera and shows us the faces of HIMMELSTOSS' *platoon.*

Dissolve to:

SCENE 25-B

Another section of the field. The manikins which are used for bayonet practice hang in a row. HIMMELSTOSS' *platoon is lined up in front of the manikins.*

HIMMELSTOSS. Fix bayonets! Prepare to charge! Charge!

With terrible and blood-curdling howl, four boys throw themselves forward as one man and drive their bayonets through the sacks.

SCENE 26-B

Medium shot of officers.

LIEUTENANT. Sounds like the real thing!
CAPTAIN. They do it as if they meant it, don't they?

HIMMELSTOSS' *platoon lines up in front of the Captain.*

CAPTAIN. Sergeant!

HIMMELSTOSS *comes forward.*

CAPTAIN. They're going up tomorrow. I recommend leave till twelve!

The boys' faces, rigid in line, brighten at this prospect.

SCENE 27-B

Medium shot of HIMMELSTOSS *and* OFFICERS.

HIMMELSTOSS *(Grimly)*. Very well, sir.

HIMMELSTOSS *salutes and retires.*

SCENE 28-B

Closeup PAUL *and* ALBERT. *They steal a side glance at each other at this news.*

SCENE 29-B

Longer view of field. HIMMELSTOSS *joins his platoon.*

HIMMELSTOSS. Left by squads—march!

The boys start to move.

Dissolve to:

SCENE 30-B

Ext. foot bridge over canal—near ploughed field. HIMMELSTOSS *leading his men.*

SCENE 31-B

Closeup of HIMMELSTOSS. *He is smiling craftily.*

SCENE 32-B

Long shot of men marching toward canal. HIMMELSTOSS *stands at one side.*

SCENE 33-B

Moving close shot of faces of PAUL, ALFRED *and* LEER. *They look ahead.*

SCENE 34-B

Long shot of canal ahead.

SCENE 35-B

Close shot of boys. They look at each other apprehensively

SCENE 36-B

Close shot of HIMMELSTOSS *in foreground. He is standing on bridge watching boys wade through canal. They go up to the waist in muck and mud.*

SCENE 37-B

Opposite side of canal—closer view. The boys reform ranks and pretend to march. They are furious at HIMMELSTOSS *for playing the dirty trick, though they say nothing.*

Dissolve to:

SCENE 38-B

Ext. entrance to barracks building. The boys are standing in line.

HIMMELSTOSS. *(Sarcastically)*. You are on leave till midnight. Dismiss!

The boys enter the building. HIMMELSTOSS *smiles craftily.*

Dissolve to:

SCENE 39-B

Interior barracks room—close-up group. The boys are hurriedly removing their soaking clothing. MULLER *throws a soggy coat violently to the floor.*

MULLER. That rat!

LEER. That shoots our leave.

Camera pans to another group. PAUL'S *muddy clothes are in a heap on the floor. He is holding his mud-covered shoes in his hand.*

PAUL. It'll take three hours to oil these shoes.

Camera pans to another group. ALBERT *is in his undershirt and trousers. He walks disgustedly to the window and stares out unseeingly.*

SCENE 40-B

Close-up ALBERT *at window. He suddenly straightens up as he sees someone below.*

SCENE 41-B

Long shot of HIMMELSTOSS *walking across yard.*

SCENE 42-B

Close shot ALBERT.

ALBERT. There goes the ape now—while we slave over this mud he goes off to have a few drinks.

The other boys enter the scene and look below. Camera pulls back showing large group.

LEER. Some day I'm going to take one smack at him—just one.

MULLER. Me too, that's my life work from now on.

PETER. Why only one? I'm going to take several—I might even kick him when he's down. I feel mean.

PAUL *has been thinking—formulating a plan. He starts to roll up a blanket and pillow. The others look at him wonderingly.*

ALBERT. What are you doing?

PAUL *looks around carefully and the others gather to hear what he has to say.*

PAUL. Sh!

SCENE 43-B

Ext. country lane—late evening. A hedge runs along the side of the lane and on the opposite side is a pile of stones, large enough to conceal two or three men. HIMMELSTOSS *comes along the lane, a little elevated and singing a German song. His figure is barely recognizable in the half light.* PAUL, MULLER *and* ALBERT *are concealed behind the pile of stones. The others are behind the hedge. As* HIMMELSTOSS *passes,* PAUL *leaps from behind him, throws a bed cover over his head and ties it around him so that he is unable to raise his arms. The singing stops. A light figure flies through the air and* ALBERT *alights on* HIMMELSTOSS' *shoulders, bearing him to earth.* HIMMELSTOSS *lets out a roar, but* ALBERT *instantly has his face in a pillow, muffling the sound. He holds* HIMMELSTOSS' *head in a viselike grip. The others rush in.*

SCENE 44-B

Ext. ditch near the road. The boys carry HIMMELSTOSS *in, see that he is tied securely and dump him into the mud of the ditch, his head just cut of the water.*

SCENE 45-B

Ext. country lane. Near ditch. HANS, *a private, is slowly coming toward the camera, whistling softly. A muffled cry is heard. The cry is heard again. The private is startled. He rushes forward to the ditch as he excitedly asks:*

PRIVATE. Who is it?

SCENE 46-B

Ext. ditch near road—close-up HIM- MELSTOSS. *The private runs into the scene as he repeats:*

PRIVATE. Who is it?

As he is about to stoop down, HIMMELSTOSS *groans:*

HIMMELSTOSS. Sergeant Himmelstoss.

PRIVATE *straightens up, surprised, then pleased. He lets out a long:*

PRIVATE. Oh-h-h-h-

Turns to walk way—thinks better of it. Turns back and kicks HIMMELSTOSS *further into the mud.*

Fade out:

SEQUENCE "C"

SCENE 1-C

Ext. railroad station in a German town near the front. Mid-day. Shoot from elevated position.

Fade in:

A train loaded with soldiers is slowly arriving in the immediate foreground. Just beyond it is a small railroad station. Each car has its own markings. The train stops. A confusion of orders is heard.

Fourth Company, fall in! To the right about march! Platoon halt!

The soldiers climb out, form into companies out of sight, then march into view and down a street that goes into the background. On the station platform are many cots, with wounded men on them. A motorcycle comes tearing from the background. Another company is formed and marches away.

The distant rumble of big guns is occasionally heard.

SCENE 2-C

Close-up of a section of marching troops. Akeley. Our boys from the school are seen passing, alert and on edge, silent, wide-eyed.

The drone of an airplane rapidly increasing in volume is heard.

All eyes are turned to the sky. The boys can see nothing and look quickly at each other.

SCENE 3-C

Airplane view of street. Troops and railroad station. Close-up of the trap that releases bomb. As the trap is opened, it reveals the scene and shows the bomb falling away into the distance.

SCENE 4-C

Long view of street toward railroad station. The street is filled with troops marching toward the camera. The bomb from the airplane lands on a building and explodes. The troops instantly scatter in all directions. The road is empty. As the smoke and dust clear away, a sharp command is heard:

Fall in! Fall in!

The troops reappear, form in line and resume marching.

Dissolve to:

SCENE 5-C

Ext. column of men moving along a country road. Rain. Night. A single star shell rises far in the distance, describing a parabola through the sky and lighting the faces of the men.

SCENE 6-C

Close-up group. Moving scene. PAUL *and the others are startled by the sudden light.*

SCENE 7-C

Ext. long shot looking down the street of a ruined village. Nite. A column of troops marches along the street and stops in front of a factory which is still intact. The order:

Halt!

is given. The troops stop.

SCENE 8-C

Int. factory. Close-up door. Shooting toward exterior. A private is leaning in the doorway. In the background the troops have stopped.

A SERGEANT'S VOICE. Second Company replacements, fall out!

The replacements leave the column. The Sergeant's voice continues:

SERGEANT'S VOICE. Here you are, Corporal.

The column starts moving. The private in the doorway turns and enters the factory.

SCENE 9-C

Int. small room in factory. The room has probably been used as a storeroom. The windows are heavily curtained. In one corner, on piles of straw, two Artillerymen are sleeping. In another corner, beside a charcoal fire, sit TJADEN *and* HAIL WESTHUS. *A couple of candles stuck in the necks of bottles throw grotesque shadows on the walls. The* PRIVATE *enters and says: to* TJADEN *and* WESTHUS:

PRIVATE. Here's some more—fresh out of the turnip patch.

He goes toward the artilleryman and flops on the straw. WESTHUS *and* TJADEN *look up as the recruits enter, a* CORPORAL *with them.*

THE CORPORAL. This is where you bunk.

He goes out. The recruits unload their packs and pick out places to sleep, gazing about curiously. PAUL *hesitates in front of a bunk, looks inquiringly about, then drops pack on the floor beside it.* WESTHUS *slowly gets up and goes to* PAUL.

SCENE 10-C

PAUL *is standing between two piles of straw near the wall.* WESTHUS, *a giant of a man with tremendous hands, enters, lifts* PAUL *by the waist and sets him aside.* PAUL *is astonished.* WESTHUS *points toward the wall and says:*

WESTHUS. My card.

PAUL *looks at the wall; it is covered with names, dates, addresses, etcetera.* PAUL *is puzzled.* WESTHUS *looks from* PAUL *to the wall, goes to it and points out a name.*

SCENE 11-C

Close-up of the wall. WESTHUS' *finger points to his name as voice is heard:*

WESTHUS. That's me—and this is where I live.

SCENE 12-C

Close-up PAUL *and* WESTHUS. *He points to the bunk.*

PAUL. Oh, I didn't know.
WESTHUS. You know now.
PAUL. Sure.
WESTHUS. All right.

WESTHUS *picks up a plate and goes back toward the fire.*

SCENE 13-C

Longer view. PAUL *and others in foreground.* WESTHUS *and* TJADEN *in background.* WESTHUS *goes to the fire and takes his former place. The boys are strangely silent.*

An occasional muffled reverberation from the big guns is heard.

ALBERT. Here's a bunk.
PAUL. Thanks.
BEHM. Say, when did we eat last?
PETER. Don't remind me. I was fine until you spoke.
MULLER. Where are we, anyway?
ALBERT. I don't know—the name on the railway station had been shot off.
PAUL. There must be something to eat somewheres—I'll ask those fellows.
PETER. Sure. You're acquainted with them.

PAUL *starts forward.*

SCENE 14-C

Medium shot of WESTHUS. *Others and fire.* PAUL *approaches.*

PAUL. Beg your pardon, Mr. Westhus, but we haven't eaten since breakfast and we thought maybe you could tell us what we ought to do about it.

WESTHUS. *(after a mumbled conversation with Tjaden).* My friend, here, thinks you ought to eat without further delay.

(They both laugh loudly.)

PAUL. What's funny?

TJADEN. This is a bad town to bring an appetite to soldier. We've been here since yesterday morning and we've been living on baled hay and razor blades.

PAUL. But we're willing to buy our food— where's the canteen?

The others laugh again— louder.

TJADEN. The only canteen in this region is out looking for supplies. Ever hear of Katzinsky?

PAUL. Who?

TJADEN. Katzinsky, he's out looking for food and if he finds any maybe you get to lick the dish, how do I know?

SCENE 15-C

Another angle showing boys crowding and listening.

PETER. Tell us where to look and we'll go too.

TJADEN. You wouldn't find nothing. With Kat it's different. It's a gift.

They all look uncomprehendingly at each other.

TJADEN. If that guy was left down in the middle of the ocean on a raft he'd shoot a buffalo within half an hour and serve it up with mashed potatoes on a white cloth.

Dissolve to:

SCENE 16-C

Ext. between two R.R. box cars. Night. KAT *comes up between the two cars. He stops abruptly, his nose wrinkles as he smells food!*

*(*KAT *has chevrons of a corporal.)*

SCENE 17-C

Int. box car. Rows of meat of all kinds are hanging from the roof. Also there are piles of all kinds of provisions.

SCENE 18-C

Close-up KAT *between cars. His eyes light up. He exits around to side of the car.*

SCENE 19-C

Ext. side of box car. A sentry is on duty before the open door of the car. KAT *passes slowly, glances at the sentry, who straightens and looks at him.* KAT *disappears around the corner of the car. The sentry relaxes. After a moment,* KAT

appears again and repeats the business. The sentry grows suspicious. As KAT *goes around the corner of the car, he increases the sentry's suspicions by looking back at him. The guard takes a step after him, stops and looks after him uneasily. While he still has his back turned,* KAT *re-appears again behind him. The sentry whirls around.* KAT *saunters past him, goes around the corner of the car, out of sight. The sentry can stand it no longer. He walks rapidly after him.* KAT *re-appears under the center of the car and quickly climbs into the open door. The sentry comes into the scene, pauses uncertainly, then goes to the end of the car.* KAT *appears in the doorway, a half filled gunny sack over his shoulder. He jumps lightly to the ground and starts walking. The sentry whirls around.* KAT *passes him, nods and starts away. The sentry suddenly calls out:*

SENTRY. Halt!

KAT *does the opposite. He dashes away. The sentry raises his gun and fires.*

SCENE 20-C

Ext. corner of shelled building. KAT *runs wildly around the corner.*

Dissolve to:

SCENE 21-C

Int. small room of factory. Night. KAT *comes in through the window with a sack, startling those in the room.* KEMMERICH *sees him and calls:*

KEMMERICH. Attention!

KAT *whirls, drops the sack and stands at attention, looking around for the officer.* TJADEN *and the others burst out laughing.* KAT *disgustedly throws the sack at them. He turns to the boys, then back to the others as he asks:*

KAT. What is this?

TJADEN. Volunteers for the future General Staff.

KAT *looks the boys over slowly, then says:*

KAT. Sometime I'm going to take one of you volunteers apart to find out what makes you leave school to get into the army.

KAT *notices they are standing at attention:*

KAT. At ease. Take your hands down. This is no parade ground. Hungry?

They all step forward.

KAT. Wait a minute! That's no invitation. Can you pay?

They all quickly start digging in their pockets for money.

KAT. Not money. That's just paper out here. Got any cigarettes, cigars, fresh fruit, cognac, toilet soap or chewing tobacco?

They begin to fish in pockets and hand him stuff. TJADEN *hauls the enormous chunk of meat out of the water as he asks:*

TJADEN. Hey, Kat, what's the idea? There ain't enough here for us.

SCENE 22-C

Med. shot of KAT. *He has an accumulation of goods before him. He turns to* TJADEN.

KAT. I wish you two would get bumped off. I'm tired of feeding you for nothing. Come and get it, boys.

He slaps them on the rear as they start toward the fire.

Dissolve to:

SCENE 23-C

A long shot of a lorry driving toward camera shoot from below. It pulls up opposite camera and is seen to be empty except for a driver and a CORPORAL. *The latter jumps out and enters building.*

SCENE 24-C

Int. of room. Medium shot. CORPORAL *enters and walks over to* KAT.

CORPORAL. You're rejoining the company tonight, Kat. Take these replacements with you. There's a lorry waiting outside.

KAT. Klant! Any more bad news?

CORPORAL. Yeh. You get the wiring duty tonight between twenty-seven and twenty-eight. Pick up the stuff at the Pioneer dump in the woods and restring the whole line.

KAT. Wiring duty with this bunch?

CORPORAL. That's right. It's quiet tonight and you can teach them a couple of things about shells.

KAT. I'd rather do it alone, if you don't mind. These babes get killed off too fast.

CORPORAL. I don't mind, but that's orders. The lorry's waiting.

KAT. I heard you.

The CORPORAL *goes out.* KAT *rises.*

KAT. *(To* TJADEN). Do you hear that?

TJADEN. I heard it. Last night I was too hungry to sleep and tonight when I got a belly full they think up wiring duty.

KAT. Grab your stuff, kindergarten, our taxi's burning money outside.

The boys begin to pack their things.

Dissolve to:

SCENE 25-C

Ext. full view of motor lorry. Night. Moving scene. The lorry is jammed with the men who were in the factory with the exception of the two artillerymen. The lorry rolls and lurches over a road full of holes. Beside the lorry is a stream of munition wagons going in the same direction. They joke with the men in the lorry, who answer back.

MUNITION WAGON DRIVER. Hey, how far is it to Paris?

WESTHUS. Follow us.

He jerks his thumb at the recruits.

SCENE 26-C

Close-up LEER, KAT *and the* DRIVER. *As the lorry rolls violently,* ALBERT *exclaims:*

ALBERT. Is that any way to drive?

KAT. Let him drive any way he wants—you're rather have a broken arm than a hole in your guts, wouldn't you?

SCENE 27-C

Full view of lorry passing the artillery lines. The guns emplacements are camouflaged with bushes against aerial observation. Now and then smoke rolls over the lorry, the guns roar and each time they do, the lorry staggers.

SCENE 28-C

Close-up group in lorry. KEMMERICH *is holding on with one hand. A concussion catches him off balance and blows him halfway across the truck. The boys pile against each other in confusion. Smoke from big guns rolls over the scene. They wet their lips with their tongues, tasting the acrid smoke. Plunging awkwardly against* PAUL's *shoulders.*

KEMMERICH. Excuse me.

KAT. That corporal was all wet. It isn't going to be so quiet tonight.

PAUL. How can you tell.

KAT. You'll tell after you've been here long enough.

TJADEN. The Tommies are firing already and it's only eleven o'clock.

WESTHUS. What's the matter with them? They're an hour early.

KAT. Their clocks must be fast.

The recruits listen to this in open-eyed wonderment, amazed at the callowness of the men. Three shells land beside the lorry. The burst of flames shoots across the fog, the shell fragments howl and drone. The recruits cry out, though none of them are hurt.

KAT. Listen, kids, we're going to string some wire. We pick it up at the dump and carry it up where we need it. You're going to see some shell fire, and you're going to be scared at first, but don't worry about that. When we come back I'll get you all some nice clean underwear. Now listen careful. The big shells you don't have to pay any attention to. They make the most noise—they go zoom! Plunk! and land about five miles behind the lines. The things to watch out for are the light ones. They don't give you much warning— they go zing! Poof! and when you hear that— dive—down with your face in the mud, or they'll knock you down. Keep your eyes on me and when you see me flop, you flop—only try to beat me to it. There may be shrapnel, too—that sounds like a street car turning a curve; when you hear that, get down. When in doubt stick to old mother earth. She's your best friend, take it from me—in fact, she's your only friend.

The distant, muffled roar of the guns becomes louder. BEHM *dodges back. The noise of a waggletop is heard approaching.*

KAT. Don't jump. That's a mortar. It'll go over.

The faces of all the boys have changed. In their blood a contact has shot home. Consciousness of the Front. In their veins, in their hands, in their eyes, is a tense waiting. A strange sharpening of the senses. Their bodies, with one bound are in full readiness. The lorry turns into a broken wood. The trees are shattered, tops of some are blown off, others are only stumps. They pass a soup kitchen, continue a short distance and finally stop. The soldiers start to unload.

SCENE 29-C

Ext. woods. Night close view of the lorry. The soldiers unload.

KAT. Fall in!

The boys line up. The lorry driver calls out:

DRIVER. Anybody going back?

The boys look at him. He turns to lorry and drives back the way he came, the boys looking after him longingly. They suddenly feel terribly alone.

KAT. All right, this way. Come on!

Snapping them into it. They start forward through the trees.

SCENE 30C

Road in woods. Night moving scene. The camera follows KAT *and his men as they march down the road. Mist and fog begin to envelop them. They turn a corner. Before them is a crossroads, the moon is shining. At the crossroads and the mist and smoke is breast high. Along the road, crossing in front of them, troops are marching. Their helmets gleam softly in the moonlight. Their bodies are hidden in the mist—just their heads and rifles stand out above it—nodding head, rocking carriers of guns. As* KAT's *men advance, the troops take shape. Coats, trousers, and boots appear out of the mist. They become a column. Guns and munition wagon follow, drawn by horses, whose backs shine in the moonlight.* KAT *and his men find an opening and pass through. As they move forward.*

The noise of the front grows louder and louder.

SCENE 31-C

Ext. Pioneer dump in woods. Night. The mist has thinned considerably. KAT *and his men march into the scene. Some of them load their shoulders with pointed and twisted iron stakes; others thrust smooth iron rods through rolls of wire. When they have the needed supplies, they start on.*

SCENE 32-C

Road through a woods. Night. Moving scene from behind KAT's *men. The ground becomes more broken. Some of the men stumble. It becomes darker—almost black. Out of the dark a voice is heard:*

THE VOICE. Look out, deep shell holes on the left! Mind, trenches!

The boys peer out, seeing nothing. They take cautious steps, moving more slowly. The line suddenly stops.

SCENE 33-C

Close-up PAUL *and* MAN *before him. As the man before him stops,* PAUL *bumps his face against the roll of barbed wire the man is carrying.* KAT's *voice is heard:*

KAT. Cigarettes and pipes out!

SCENE 34-C

Longer view from behind men. Moving scene. The men move on. They pass some shell-smashed lorries in the road. Suddenly they come out of the woods and stop. Before them is a graveyard and a shelled church. The crosses shine in the moonlight. Beyond is the Front. An uncertain red glow spreads along in the skyline from one end to the other. It is in perpetual movement, punctuated with bursts of flames from the muzzles of the batteries. Balls of light rise up high above it. Silver and yellow spheres are exploded and rain down in showers of white and green stars. French rockets go up which unfold a silk parachute to the air and drift slowly down. They light up everything as bright as day. Their light shines on the men, throwing their shadows sharply outlines on the ground. They hover for the space of a minute before they burn out. The thunder of the guns swells to a single heavy roar and then breaks up again into separate explosions. The dry bursts of the machine guns rattle. Above them the air teems with invisible swift movement, with howls, pipings and hisses. They are the smaller shells—and amongst them, booming through the night like an organ, go the great coal boxes and heavies. They have a horse, distant bellow and make their way high above the howl and whistle of the smaller shells. Searchlights begin to sweep the sky. They pick up a flock of wild geese flying in formation. At first the geese look like airplanes.

Dissolve to:

The geese flying.

Dissolve back to:

The scene as before. Searchlights still play across the sky. One of them pauses and quivers a little. Immediately a second one is beside it. A small insect is caught between them and tries to escape—an airplane. The airman is confused; is blinded and falls.

SCENE 35-C

Close view KAT and his MEN. Camera facing them. The men are awe-stricken by the sight and sound of the Front. KAT gives an unheard order and they march out of the scene.

Dissolve to:

SCENE 36-C

Open field and entrance to communication trenches. Moving scene. Night. KAT and MEN are moving across the field. The camera follows them to the entrance of the trench and down into it.

Dissolve to:

SCENE 37-C

Field and shell holes. Night. The MEN are driving in iron stakes, unrolling barbed wire, guiding entanglements.

SCENE 38-C

Close-up PAUL, BEHM, KEMMERICH, and KAT. They are unrolling wire—their hands cut and bleeding. KAT is instructing them. He looks toward the sky.

SCENE 39-C

Sky. Night. Miniature. Rockets go up, releasing parachutes, which in turn release green and blue stars.

SCENE 40-C

Long view of men at work. KAT and group in foreground. KAT is looking at the sky. He looks down and says:

KAT. Mighty fine fireworks if they weren't so dangerous
PAUL. (whispers). What does that mean?
KAT. Bombardment.

A shell lands quite some distance away. KAT dives to the ground.

KAT. Down! Down! Mother earth!

BEHM, who is slightly separated from the rest, is a little slow in doing this. Another shell lands near him and explodes.

SCENE 41-C

Close-up of BEHM. As the shell explodes, BEHM is knocked down. He jumps to his feet, blinded, and runs in circles, his hands to his eyes.

SCENE 42-C

In shell hole. The camera is placed in a shell hole. KAT, KEMMERICH, PAUL and a couple of others are in the foreground looking over the rim of the shell hole. In the background, BEHM, mad with pain, is crying hysterically. He runs, staggering, toward the enemy lines. He is shot down—and lies still. KEMMERICH, PAUL and the other recruits are horrified at their first sight of violent death. KEMMERICH cries out hysterically:

KEMMERICH. Behm! Behm! I'm coming Behm!

KEMMERICH goes temporarily insane. He starts out of the shell hole. KAT grabs for him—too late.

KAT. Come here—you crazy—that's the trouble with—
KEMMERICH. It's Behm! Don't you see? It's Behm!

KEMMERICH frees himself, gets out and runs to BEHM. The others watch in petrified silence. KEMMERICH picks up BEHM and starts back to-

ward the shell hole. He reaches it and lowers
BEHM *into it.* BEHM *is dead.*

SCENE 43-C

Close-up group around BEHM *and*
KEMMERICH. KAT *coldly says to* KEMMERICH:

KAT. Don't do that again. Do you want to
get killed?
KEMMERICH. *(madly).* It's Behm!
KAT. It's a stiff. It won't do you any good
nor anyone else—when I tell you to take to
cover, you do it. Come on—

He leads.

SCENE 44-C

Shell holes and wire entanglements. KAT *and
the others come from the shell hole and resume
work. Cries of the wounded fill the air, cries and
screams.*

TJADEN. Sounds like a couple of columns
over there got it in the neck.
KAT. Wounded horses.

*The men try to work, but as the firing dies
down, the cries of the horses grow louder. The
screaming seems to come from all directions.
The men cannot work. They stop to listen.*

DETERING. *(sick with horror).* It's horses all
right.

*Unable to control himself, he stands up and
yells:*

Shoot them, down, you—why don't you
shoot them?

SCENE 45-C

Close-up of group. KAT *answers quietly:*

KAT. They've got to look after the men
first.

SCENE 46-C

*Another section of shell holes seen thru
glasses. Stretcher bearers are gathering the
wounded. Near them, wounded horses are
dashing about. A shell bursts among them.*

SCENE 47-C

Group of KAT's *men.* DETERING *suddenly
throws his gun to his shoulder and aims.* KAT
hits it in the air.

KAT. Are you crazy?

DETERING *trembles and throws his rifle on the
ground. Perspiration has broken out on all of
them.*

SCENE 48-C

*Another section of shell holes seen thru
glasses. The stretcher bearers are moving off.
Soldiers run in. They shoot the horses, and
other horses that pass. A soldier goes down on
his knees, aims and fires. A horse slowly, hum-
bly, sinks to the ground. The cries cease.*

SCENE 49-C

Close-up group of KAT's *men. The men lower
their hands from their ears. Only one, long-
drawn dying sigh still hangs on the air.*
DETERING *walks up and down cursing:*

DETERING. Anybody that'd use horses in a
war ought to be cut up—ought to be skinned
alive—Damn 'em—what have they done?
What have horses got to do with this—
KAT. *(takes him by arm).* All right, keep
your shirt on—that don't do any good.

He turns to others.

Come on, boys, we're going back now.

They start to pick up things.

Dissolve to:

SCENE 50-C

*Exterior German trench—rain. The trench is
occupied by German soldiers who are moving
back and forth. In the background,* KAT *and the
group are coming toward it. A shell explodes in
the trench. Smoke and mud fill the air.* KAT *and
the others tumble into a shell hole.*

SCENE 51-C

Exterior shell hole—rain. KAT *and the others
tumble into the hole. After a moment* KAT *peers
over the edge toward the smoking trench in the
background, then turns back and says:*

KAT. You never know when you'll be safe,
do you? Those birds in a bomb-proof dugout
are blown to a sausage and we're here un-
protected and as safe as lice. Trust your luck,
that's all. Come on.

They follow him out of the hole.

Dissolve to:

SCENE 52-C

*Entrance to communication trench—other
end—night—moving scene. In the background
are the wire entanglements and shell holes. In
the foreground is the entrance to the trench. As
the men reach it and start down, the camera
pulls back.* KAT *is restless, looks quickly in all
directions.* TJADEN *asks him:*

TJADEN. What's the matter?
KAT. I wish I was back home.

PAUL. *(amazed).* Home?

TJADEN. *(explains).* Behind the lines.

WESTHUS. It won't last much longer.

KAT. *(nervously).* I don't know—I got a feeling it will.

The men trudge through the trench.

Dissolve to:

SCENE 53-C

Open field and graveyard—night. The graveyard is suggested in the foreground. As the men near it, all hell suddenly breaks loose behind them. The ground spurts rocks and flames. The noise swells, thunders, roars. KAT *yells:*

KAT. Cover! Cover! Take cover!

They all run wildly past the camera.

SCENE 54-C

Graveyard—woods in background—night. The men run over the foreground heading toward the trees. A cloud of flame shoots up before them. A second explosion throws three or four trees into the air—they crash to the ground. Escape is cut off. The shells begin to hiss heavy fire. The men scatter and disappear behind mounds in the graveyards. The night goes mad. Flames of the explosion light up the graveyard.

SCENE 55-C

Close-up PAUL *behind mound. Night-effect scene. He has his face buried in the earth hugging it. He cautiously raises his head and peers toward the woods, seen in the b.g. The ground between is a heaving mass—a surging sea. Daggers of flame from the explosions leap up like fountains. The air is filled with clods of earth. The woods is slowly vanishing.* PAUL *raises his arm a few inches. A shell-splinter rips off the sleeve. He quickly opens and closes his fist to determine the extent of the injury; it is not serious. A shell tears a large hole in the earth a few yards in front of him.* PAUL *decides to make a dash for it. He rises to a crouch, runs forward, spins around and falls into the hole as a fragment of shell hits him in the head.*

SCENE 56-C

Shell hole—close-up. PAUL *falls into the hole and lies still. A steel splinter has slashed into his helmet. His face is covered with mud. The roar of the explosion is deafening.*

SCENE 57-C

Section of cemetery—toward woods. A soldier crouches behind a mound in the foreground. Others are seen in the distance. Spurts of flame cast weird shadows. The earth is rolling, pitching, like an ocean in a storm. A

series of quick explosions—the woods vanish. An explosion in the foreground wipes out the mound with the crouching soldier—all that is left is a shell hole.

SCENE 58-C

Close-up of PAUL's *shell hole.* PAUL *is beginning to regain consciousness. He wipes the mud out of his eyes. Clods of earth, smoke, shell splinters, fill the air. Beside* PAUL, *where the explosion has torn away the earth, a corner of a shattered coffin is visible.* PAUL *feels his helmet, cautiously removes the splinter. He feels the soft earth before him, and without looking, begins to dig into it. He feels the wood of the coffin and crawls under it. The earth trembles from an explosion nearby. The body in the coffin slides partly out.* PAUL's *hand comes in contact with the cloth on the corpse. He feels an arm. Believing it to be one of his companions he calls out— and getting no answer, raises his head to see. His eyes open in horror. He starts to move away, but an avalanche of earth falls from above.* PAUL *moves closer to the corpse, pulling it over him for protection.*

SCENE 59-C

Open space in graveyard— PAUL's *shell hole in background.* KAT, KROPP *and another soldier are flattened out on the earth beside mounds in the foreground. The earth is heaving from the constant explosions. The air is heavy with smoke and mud. The shelling is too thick—they must take the chance of moving to a safer place.* KAT *calls to* ALBERT, *who doesn't hear him, touches him and motions for him to follow. As they crawl into the background, they pass the other soldier and motion for him to come along.*

SCENE 60-C

PAUL's *shell hole—close view.* PAUL *is in the foreground. A hand enters and clamps him on the shoulder.* PAUL *is terrified—had the dead man awakened. The hand shakes him. He turns his head and sees* KAT, *who crawls into the scene. Behind him are* ALBERT *and the other soldier, who crawls on beyond them. With a crash a black object falls near them—a coffin throw-up. It lands on the outstretched arm of the man who is crawling away. He cries out in pain.* KAT *and* PAUL *go up to him. They try to lift the coffin without exposing themselves above the level of the shell hole. It is too heavy. They pry up the loosened lid and toss out the corpse, which slides to the bottom of the hole. The soldier swoons.* ALBERT *helps them get the coffin off the man's arm.* KAT *takes a piece of the lid to make a splint. They all use their bandages* and strap the arm to it as the man regains consciousness.

(NOTE: During the above scene it gradually grows lighter.)

SCENE 61-C

Long view of graveyard–dawn. The shelling abruptly ceases. The earth settles down, the smoke clears away. The graveyard is a mass of wreckage. Coffins and corpses lie thrown about. Heads, then bodies, cautiously appear.

SCENE 62-C

Close view PAUL's *shell hole–dawn.* KAT's *head appears. He turns and calls to the others.* ALBERT *and* PAUL *climb out, supporting the wounded soldier. They have to step over a leg that has been torn clean off, the boot still on it. They stumble off hastily.*

SCENE 63-C

Long view of graveyard. PAUL, KAT, ALBERT *and the soldier are going toward what was formerly the woods, now only the stripped trunks of a few trees. Other men join them; less than half the number that came out. It begins to rain, the camera follows them. They come to an open grave and stop. In it lies a corpse, nearby are two coffins, the bodies partly exposed.*

KAT. The poor stiffs had to get killed once again, but we should thank 'em because each one that was flung up saved one of us.

They move around the bodies and exit.

Dissolve to:

SCENE 64-C

Close-up of lorry on road. Rain. The driver and two other men with forked sticks in their hands are waiting. The driver is stretched out on the running-board. KAT *and the group enter and clamber hastily into the lorry. The driver gets in, followed by the men with the sticks. Only about half the number of men are going back. The lorry drives off.*

SCENE 65-C

Close-up lorry. Rain. Moving scene. The lorry bumps through holes. The men rock to and fro in half sleep. There is plenty of room now. The men with the forked poles are in the front. They watch for telephone wires which hang crosswise over the road. They lift them over the heads of the soldiers as they call out:

MEN WITH POLES. Mind—wire— Mind—wire—

The soldiers dip their knees sleepily and straighten up again. Monotonously the lorry

sways, monotonously falls the rain, monotonously come the calls:

Mind—wire— Mind—wire—

An explosion sounds off the side of the road. The soldiers wince, their eyes open, become tense, their hands grasp the rail ready to leap over the side. There are no more explosions. They relax and doze again.

Mind—wire— Mind—wire—

Their knees bend, straighten again. They are half asleep.

Dissolve to:

SCENE 66-C

Ext. front of factory. Rain. Day. The second company is lined up. They are fresh and wide-awake. The lorry arrives. The soldiers pile out sleepily. As they start into the factory, a sergeant stops them.

SERGEANT. All right—this way. Fall in.

The recruits hesitate, then fall into line with the column.

SCENE 67-C

Close-up section of column. The recruits look around, sleepily, wonderingly. KAT *asks a soldier behind him:*

KAT. What's the idea? SOLDIER. Orders to march. KAT. Where? SOLDIER. The front. KAT. Oh, for the love of—

The tired recruits groan. An order is heard.

ORDER. Forward, march!

The column moves forward. The last of the line is the field kitchen.

Fade out.

SEQUENCE "D"

SCENE 1-D

Ext. battle field. Night. Fade in: There are explosions. All around, planes cross the sky. Searchlights.

SCENE 2-D

Int. dugout full view. Night. The boys are half sitting, half lying on their pallets. Some doze, others stare ahead with glazed eyes. PAUL, KAT, and WESTHUS *are sitting in the foreground try- ing to play skat.* TJADEN *and* DETERING *are nearby. They have a hard time keeping their minds on the game. Whenever there is a loud explosion lifting above the skat players, as well as all the others, wince involuntarily. The flash of the explosions can be seen through the open- ing into the trench.* WESTHUS *plays a card and starts to take the trick.* KAT *grabs his wrist.*

KAT. Hey, take your hands off that.
WESTHUS. Queen takes it.
KAT. If you think that's a queen, look again.
WESTHUS. It's a Jack.
KAT. *(Raking in the money).* Yeah.
WESTHUS. Honest—those cards look alike. It's too noisy.
KAT. Yeah. Your delicate nerves can't stand—

Breaks off suddenly and throws a stick.

SCENE 3-D

Close-up of KAT's *pack lying on floor. The stick descends on it and a rat runs out, disap- pearing into the corner.* KAT *pulls out a piece of bread, badly gnawed at one end.*

KAT. That was Oscar. The son of a—

With a knife he cuts off the bitten end and throws it into a corner.

SCENE 4-D

Group at card table as KAT *rejoins them.*

TJADEN. Don't be so snooty. You may wish you had that back. About two more days of this and the rat-bitten end of a hunk of bread will look just like a piece of angel food.
PAUL. It wouldn't keep up for two more days, would it?
KAT. Didn't I tell you this was going to be a bad one?
PAUL. I don't mind the days so much—it's keeping up all night that—
KAT. Two more days makes a week, kid, and then you can say you've been under fire.
WESTHUS. Not scared, are you?
PAUL. No, I was just asking that's all. Want to play some more?
WESTHUS. Do you?

There is a sudden louder roar. Everybody jumps and PAUL, *who is holding himself to- gether with difficulty, leaps to his feet. He controls himself and sits down again.*

PAUL. Sure, your deal.
KAT. Wait a minute.

He reaches under the table, picks up a boot, and with a backhand flip, sends it flying into a corner.

SCENE 5-D

Close-up of two rats in a corner. They are eating a piece of bread. A boot comes flying at them and they disappear. They reappear almost instantly and turn to the bread.

SCENE 6-D

Close-up group at table.

PAUL. You'd better get your boot before they eat that.
WESTHUS. *(Points to* PAUL, *pleased.)* He's all right.

KEMMERICH's *voice comes from outside the scene.*

KEMMERICH. It's Behm! It's Behm!

Everybody turns toward the voice.

SCENE 7-D

Close-up of KEMMERICH. *He is lying on a straw pallet—he is dreaming and talking in his sleep.*

KEMMERICH. It's Behm! Oh God! Can't you see it's Behm? He didn't want to come to war.

Half rises.

KEMMERICH. No, no, it isn't Behm, it isn't Behm! It's Kemmerich!

SCENE 8-D

Close-up group at table. HANS *is in the background.*

MULLER. Shut him up, can't you? It's bad enough here as it is

PAUL *goes toward* KEMMERICH.

SCENE 9-D

Close-up of KEMMERICH. PAUL *enters and kneels beside him.*

PAUL. Everything's all right, Franz, you're dreaming.

He shakes KEMMERICH, *who looks at him with wide eyes for a moment, then turns his face to the mattress and begins to sob.* PAUL *lays a hand on his shoulder.* KEMMERICH *turns back to* PAUL.

KEMMERICH. Was I saying something?
PAUL. I guess you were dreaming.
KEMMERICH. Yes, I was—I'm sorry.

SCENE 10-D

Full view of the dugout. Facing the entrance. A SERGEANT *enters.*

WESTHUS. Attention!
SERGEANT. Three men wanted for observer duty.

(He turns to PAUL*).*

Have you been out?
PAUL. No, sir.
SERGEANT. All right, you—and you—and you.

He points to PAUL, KEMMERICH *and* MULLER *in succession. They pick up their things and follow him as he turns to go.* KEMMERICH *is still dazed.*

SCENE 11-D

Ext. trench. Long view. Entrance to dugout in foreground. Night. Bombardment. Heavy shells and others of every calibre are falling thickly. The earth booms, the night roars and flashes. A shell tears up the parapet in the foreground, another lands in the trench and explodes with a hollow, furious blast. Only the observers are seen in the trench. All others have vanished. The earth is trembling from the force of the explosions. As the sergeant comes from the dugout followed by the others, a shell explodes in the embankment, throwing loose dirt over them. They exit.

SCENE 12-D

Ext. trench. Moving scene in trench. Night. Shooting toward the enemy lines, which are a rim of fire. The howling and flashing is terrific. The SERGEANT *rushes to an observer. He posts* MULLER *here and relieves the man on duty, then continues with* PAUL *and* KEMMERICH. *At the next post he leaves* PAUL, *then continues with* KEMMERICH. *They pass a machine gunner. Further on,* KEMMERICH *is posted. The man relieved staggers quickly away. The* SERGEANT *exits. The camera moves close to* KEMMERICH. KEMMERICH *is left alone—terrified, trembling with fear. Shells burst all around him. He looks around, wide-eyed, into the night. As far as he can see, the earth spouts fountains of mud and iron.*

Dissolve to:

SCENE 13-D

Ext. trench. Dawn. Long view. Gray day. Moving scene. The bombardment is stronger than it was the night before. The explosions of mines mingle with the gun fire—the most dementing convulsions of all—the whole region

where they go up becomes one grave. Clouds of smoke roll across the scene. The trench is almost gone. At many places, it is only eighteen inches high. It is broken by holes and craters and mountains of earth. Many of the upper layers of concrete over the dugouts are caved in. PAUL *is at his post in the foreground. His face is almost black with mud and powder smoke. He is weak from exhaustion and nervous strain. A relief man arrives.* PAUL *attempts to throw off his feelings.*

PAUL. Any food arrive?
THE RELIEF. Not yet. Couldn't get through. Even Kat had to turn back. A fly isn't small enough to get through such a barrage.

As he finishes speaking, KEMMERICH *enters, trembling so much he can barely walk. They start away, the camera following, and come to* MULLER, *whose condition is better—he is not as high-strung as* KEMMERICH. *They all exit toward the dugout,* PAUL *keeping close to* KEMMERICH *—worried by his looks.*

SCENE 14-D

Int. dugout. Dawn. The din of the explosions is deafening. The men are crouching against the walls—stony-eyed, mute, deadened by the strain. They pay no attention as PAUL, KEMMERICH *and* MULLER *enter.* MULLER *lies in a corner, and automatically opening his knapsack, starts nibbling on a crust of bread.* KEMMERICH *sits near him, his back to the wall. He can control himself no longer. He bursts into sobs.* PAUL *stands watching both of them—he feels helpless. He goes to* KAT *and sits down beside him.* BERTINCK *enters.*

BERTINCK. The barrage is worse. Men in two more dugouts gone but we'll make another attempt to bring up food by evening.

BERTINCK *exits.*

SCENE 15-D

Close-up PAUL, KAT *and* TJADEN. PAUL, *too, is shaking as he sits beside* KAT *and* TJADEN—*his nerves on edge. Their attention is called to an opposite corner.*

SCENE 16-D

Close-up another recruit. His face is haggard. He holds his hands over his ears and shivers with each concussion.

SCENE 17-D

Close-up of group. KEMMERICH *in background. The deadly tension—their bodies are like a thin skin stretched painfully over re-*

pressed madness. They dare not look at each other.

KAT. How about skat?

PAUL, WESTHUS and KAT sit down to play, but can't make it—they look up at each explosion. And each time, KEMMERICH starts up—he is beginning to break under the strain. KAT and PAUL keep an eye on him.

SCENE 18-D

Ext. trench. Entrance to dugout. Day. A shell lands in front of the dugout, burying it.

SCENE 19-D

Int. dugout toward entrance. The shell lands outside—the explosion completely blocks the entrance. KEMMERICH springs to his feet, screaming. He rushes toward the entrance and claws at the earth blocking it. KAT and PAUL try to hold him. KEMMERICH fights with them. His eyes roll crazily, his mouth is wet and pours out half choked words.

KEMMERICH LEAVE ME ALONE—let me out of here—I got to get out—let me out!

He breaks away from them, clutching at his throat. PAUL casts a quick glance at KAT. KEMMERICH claws frantically at the earth. He feels that he is suffocating in here. KAT drags him up and hits him on the jaw. KEMMERICH goes down to his knees. PAUL interposes between KAT and KEMMERICH.

PAUL. That's enough!
KAT. Don't stand there! Grab him! Hold him!

PAUL grips KEMMERICH and holds him so that KAT can hit him again. KAT lets KEMMERICH have another on the chin, which lays him out. They carry him to a corner. The others have watched, pale-faced. The incident has distracted their attention from themselves—they are more quiet now. PAUL is taking care of KEMMERICH.

SCENE 20-D

Ext. entrance to dugout. Day. Five men are shoveling the dirt from the entrance. They have it almost cleared away.

SCENE 21-D

Int. dugout. Toward entrance. KAT, PAUL and KEMMERICH in foreground. KEMMERICH has regained consciousness. He is calm now and looks around with clear eyes.

KAT. You all right now?
KEMMERICH. I think so. Paul,
(turning to PAUL).

I couldn't hold out any longer.

Light comes in through the entrance. It has been cleared. Suddenly the walls crack and ring out metallically under a direct hit. Rifles, helmets, earth, mud and dust fly everywhere. The walls reel. Sulphur smoke pours in. KEMMERICH and two other recruits, terrified, spring screaming to their feet. They rush toward the entrance. KAT and TJADEN stop the other two but KEMMERICH gets out. PAUL rushes after him.

SCENE 23-D

Ext. trench near dugout—reverse angle. PAUL and KEMMERICH in foreground. The others from the dugout are crouching in the entrance. As PAUL and KEMMERICH start toward the dugout, KAT and ALBERT come forward. They help KEMMERICH into the dugout.

SCENE 24-D

Int. dugout—toward entrance—day. KEMMERICH is brought in and put on the floor. Bandages are ready. They slit his trouser leg and bind the wound, which is above the knee.

PAUL. You're lucky, Franz. You're out of all this now—you're lucky.

PAUL wraps a blanket around KEMMERICH and PAUL and KAT carry him out.

KEMMERICH. Paul, I'm sorry I was such a fool!

SCENE 25-D

Close-up of muzzle of large French gun—day. The gun is one of the largest, a 30.5. The camera follows the muzzle up to position revealing a gray sky. The gun is fired—flame and smoke fill the screen. When the smoke clears away, the sky is black, it is NIGHT. The gun is fired again. The belch of flames is blinding.

SCENE 26-D

Int. dugout.—Night. Again the men are sitting and lying around mutely—staring into space—an atmosphere of despair. Outside is heard the deadly roar of the explosions. ALBERT jumps to his feet.

MULLER. If we're going to fight, why can't we fight? Why can't we go over? We'll go crazy staying here. Let's go after 'em—let's do something.

They are beginning to break under the strain of waiting.

TJADEN. Sit down. If that cook of ours had any guts, he'd send something through. He's so far back he can't hear the shooting.

KAT *creeps in through the entrance. He has one loaf of bread.*

TJADEN. Any luck?
KAT. You'll have to split this up among you.
ALBERT. We need water, too—
KAT. Yes, and dessert and feather beds to sleep on.

Shows him the pail—no water. The CORPORAL *puts down the bread and exits. They eye it hungrily and look at each other. Every one of them could eat all of it and not be half filled—yet they hold back.* KAT *takes the break, tears off chunks and passes it around. Now they do not nibble it, they are too hungry. They gulp it down. In a moment there is none left—and they're as hungry as before.*

SCENE 27-D

Ext. trench—night—heavy bombardment. A lone soldier, at a listening post, is in sight. The fury of the shelling has not abated. Suddenly from around the corner in the background hundreds of rats storm the trench, crawling over each other, trying to climb the walls, rushing into dugouts—many of them turn into a dugout entrance in the foreground.

SCENE 28-D

Medium shot of group inside dugout.

SCENE 29-D

An angle of the same, showing entrance to dugout: Everyone jumps to his feet, grabs rifles and spades and commences slaughtering the rats. Yells and indistinct curses fill the air. The madness and despair of many hours unloads itself in this outburst of action. The rats scream—weapons thud—faces are distorted. The rats are killed or driven out. Then men, in their fury of action, stop just in time to avoid attacking each other. Exhausted, they lie down to rest. Abruptly the roar of the bombardment ceases. The sudden silence is startling—for a moment, there is the deathlike silence of a tomb. Then they spring to their feet, startled, fearful. Outside cries are heard.

VOICES. They are coming over! Attack! Attack! They're coming over!

Instantly all is action. Hand grenades are pitched out of the entrance into the trench—helmets are put on. In a few seconds the dugout is empty.

SCENE 30-D

Ext. trench shooting toward enemy lines. Night. The entrance to the dugout is directly under the camera. A machine gun is just being placed in position. The men from the dugout pour out and stand ready. Orders are heard coming from all directions. In the open space before the trench the wire entanglements are seen, torn to pieces. The background is hidden by smoke and dust. The first French storm troops are seen advancing through the smoke. The artillery behind the trench is heard opening fire.

SCENE 31-D

Close-up German machine gun. The gunner is waiting—waiting for the enemy to get closer. Suddenly the gun barks rapidly, moving back and forth slowly.

SCENE 32-D

Ext. barbed wire entanglements. Night. The Frenchmen have reached the barbed wire. The rapid reports of the machine gun are heard. The Frenchmen are mowed down. Others come on, reach the wire and get through.

SCENE 33-D

Close-up at barbed wire. A Frenchman reaches the wire, stumbles—his hand grabs the wires.

SCENE 34-D

Close-up German artillery. The guns are being fired rapidly.

SCENE 35-D

Close-up Frenchman on barbed wire. An explosion blows his body away—only the hands are left clutching the wire.

SCENE 36-D

Int. trench close-up group. TJADEN, WESTHUS *and* PAUL *are throwing hand grenades. Others pass them the grenades with the strings already pulled.*

SCENE 37-D

Close-up PAUL. *He is rapidly throwing the hand grenades. He grabs another, raises his arm and holds it aloft as if petrified.*

SCENE 38-D

Close-up shell hole close to trench. The heads of three Frenchmen pop over the edge. The center one is the most advanced. His eyes are fastened on PAUL *in a gripping gaze.*

SCENE 39-D

Close-up PAUL. *He stands with upraised arm, fascinated by the eyes of the Frenchman. Another hand snatches the grenade from* PAUL'S *hand. He turns quickly toward* WESTHUS, *toward the Frenchman again.*

SCENE 40-D

Close-up three Frenchmen. They duck back into the shell hole just before an explosion goes off in front of them.

SCENE 41-D

Ext. trench—full view—toward French lines. A scene of action. The French are near. The Germans scramble out, fight furiously and are driven back across their own trench, fighting as they go—pulling wire cradles into the trench, leaving bombs in the trench with strings pulled. The French are advancing—they reach the trench, bombs explode—men fall—others come on.

SCENE 42-D

Another trench—behind first one—shoot from above. The Germans are retreating, backing, running, fighting, toward the foreground. They crouch behind every obstacle, throw grenades, fight furiously, desperately in a mad anger and relief from inaction. The French push on, drop; others come on. The Germans fight, filled with fear and madness. They reach the trench in the foreground which is manned and ready for the counter attack. The French come on. Machine guns, rifles, grenades, stop them. They waver, then start back. The barrage lifts and moves forward. The Germans rush from the trench, yelling madly.

SCENE 43-D

Ext. first trench from inside the trench shooting up. The French retreat over the trench, which has been blown to pieces, almost annihilated. The Germans enter, following them.

SCENE 44-D

Ext. shell hole between lines. Three or four wounded men lie in the hole—also a few dead ones. The French come through, followed by the Germans. The injured men clutch at all who pass, crying piteously for help, for relief, the tide sweeps over them.

SCENE 45-D

Ext. barbed wire entanglements. Planks are thrown over the entanglements. The French retreat over them; some who are caught on the wires are shot down, others get across. The Germans enter; some cross, others fall.

SCENE 46-D

Ext. French machine gun-nest—from above. The machine gun is pointed toward camera. Frenchmen stagger past. As they clear the gun commences to sputter. Germans rush in, fall, others come on. PAUL, KAT, WESTHUS,

DETERING throws a bomb. The machine gun stops. They rush foward.

SCENE 47-D

The French flee as the Germans rush in. KAT snatches the water container used for cooling the gun. He drinks thirstily; the others follow. They rush out.

SCENE 48-D

Ext. long view of French trench and dugouts. The few Frenchmen who are left in the trench are starting to retreat. A couple of explosions wipe them out. The Germans rush in.

SCENE 49-D

Close view in French trench. In the foreground is a Frenchman, dead, leaning against the wall of the trench. He collapses and falls out of sight. Frenchmen are retreating as PAUL, KAT and the others jump into the trench. They look around wildly, then dive into dugouts, KAT first. In a moment they re-appear carrying five tins of corned beef, a little butter, and two bottles of Cognac. As they start back toward their own lines, KAT grabs a loaf of bread that is partly hidden under the body of a dead Frenchman.

Dissolve to:

SCENE 50-D

Ext. German trench close view. PAUL, KAT and the others wearily drop into the trench. The dugout is demolished. They lie exhausted a moment, then fall upon the food they have brought back. KAT brings out the bread. One end of it is bloody. He cuts it off, then passes the rest around.

Dissolve to:

SCENE 51-D

Ext. trench listening post—close view of PAUL—moonlight. The ground is shiny, greasy, PAUL is on sentry duty. Beyond him can be seen the shell holes out of which the mist is creeping. It floats low over the ground. The front is quiet— a few parachute lights are in the sky. PAUL stares off across the shell holes as he wipes the moisture off his gun. Stretcher bearers are seen moving about among the shell holes.

SCENE 52-D

Ext. shell holes—moonlight. The mist floats out of a hole in the foreground, fat rats crawl in and out of the hole, in which are seen the dead bodies of men.

SCENE 53-D

View of battlefield— moonlight. Stretcher bears are going from body to body.

Fade out.

SEQUENCE "E"

—

SCENE 1-E

Close-up of huge pot of beans. A hand takes cover off and examines them with fork.

Two voices are heard. Meanwhile, the camera pans to a big rack full of sausage and past a table heaped with bread.

VOICES.

COOK. Why don't they get here?

ASSISTANTS. They're still asleep.

COOK. They slept twenty-four hours now.

ASSISTANT. I 'spose they was tired. Fighting is not so easy.

Camera pans up to show room and cooks

COOK. Well, it's a lot easier than cooking. I'll tell you that. Sleeping for a whole day and night, and meanwhile what happens to my dinner— I'd like to see one of them do my job for a while.

ASSISTANT. Here they come!

MULLER. How about it, Ginger?

SCENE 2-E

Showing MULLER *and a line of men waiting. In the background, other stragglers approach.*

MULLER. When you going to give us something to eat?

COOK. When you all get here.

(To assistant)

They think I'm going to stand here all day—one bunch and then another. Maybe I should serve it to them in their quarters, like officers.

The whole line begins to clatter spoons and pans. GINGER *goes to the front of the building.*

SCENE 3-E

Close-up group at entrance. The line of eighty men is forming in the background, GINGER, *looks out and asks stiffly:*

GINGER. What do you want?

KAT. Beans! You homely looking son of a frog's leg. What do you think we want?

GINGER.

(Looks down the line)

I'll feed you when you're all here.

TJADEN. We're all here now.

GINGER. Half the company's here. Do get the rest of them, wake 'em up.

KAT. I wish I could wake 'em up, but some is in dressing stations and some is pushing up daisies, and it'd be kind of a tough job.

SCENE 4-E

Close-up GINGER. *His mouth drops open— the facts stagger him. He counts the men and says:*

GINGER. Eighty men, and I've cooked for a hundred and fifty.

SCENE 5-E

Close shot of group.

WESTHUS. All right, we'll have enough for once. Come on, dish out.

TJADEN. You mean you cooked beans for one hundred fifty?

The COOK *nods.*

TJADEN. And you've got bread for one hundred fifty? And sausage for one hundred fifty?

The COOK *nods.*

TJADEN. And tobacco for one hundred fifty?

COOK. Everything. There's been a mistake. I should have been notified.

TJADEN. What a feast.

Makes a mental calculation.

TJADEN. Everyone gets—two issues.

KAT *elbows* TJADEN.

KAT. Get back in line, will you?

CROWD. Two issues; Double rations! Oh boy! (etc).

GINGER. Oh, no. Oh, no. that won't do! I can't give eighty men what's meant for a hundred and fifty!

KAT. Listen, you drew rations for the Second Company. All right, we're the second company—let's have it.

GINGER. I have my orders.

TJADEN. Kat's right.

(Forcing forward)

We're the Second Company and if only half of us comes back, that's our good luck. Dish out.

GINGER *starts to close the door in* KAT's *face.* KAT *rams his shoulder inside and the others push in with him. They thrust the door wide open and drag out* GINGER *among them.* KAT *continues holding* GINGER *by the collar of his coat.*

KAT. You're the yellowest baboon that ever wheeled a cook wagon, and you're scared of shells, and all we want is one little bit of back talk and we'll tear you up and eat you raw. You keep your kitchen so far behind the lines, we never get anything until it's cold and we're asleep. Now, you low down rat, give out, or we'll wreck the joint and help ourselves.

CROWD. *(all about).*

LIEUT. BERTINCK *enters.* MULLER *sees him and calls out.*

MULLER. Attention!

The company snaps to attention. BERTINCK *looks them over.*

BERTINCK. At ease. What's going on here?

PAUL *starts back to his place in line.* BERTINCK *has turned to him.* PAUL *stops and explains:*

PAUL. He's cooked for a hundred and fifty, sir, and he only wants to give us half.

BERTINCK. I see.

(Looks the men over, turns to cook.)

Serve the whole issue, the boys can do with it.

(Looks at the beans and adds)

Bring me a plate too.

BERTINCK *exits. The men jump about as they crowd forward and* GINGER *serves out beans recklessly.*

GINGER. All right, take it! Take it all! Take everything!

Dissolve to.

The eating gag. TJADEN *makes* ALBERT *stretch.*

SCENE 6-E

Open space near field kitchen close-up group. The men are lying flat on the ground, empty plates about them. All have cigarettes or cigars. KAT *is chewing tobacco. Only* TJADEN *and* PAUL *are still eating. They are sitting in the foreground, side by side.* TJADEN *finishes the last mouthful from his plate, which sits on top of the stack of four empties, and then, without missing a beat, continues to eat from* PAUL's *plate, which is about half full,* TJADEN *tries to give the illusion of eating from his own plate, while really eating from* PAUL's. PAUL *finally*

notices the theft and gravely hands his plate over to TJADEN.

PAUL. Don't mind me.

TJADEN. That's all right. Don't mention it.

TJADEN *accepts the plate.*

SCENE 7-E

Close-up KAT *and* WESTHUS. WESTHUS, *who has been lying supine, lifts himself slowly, picks up his plate and looks into it. He shakes his head, looks toward the kitchen, starts to rise, then thinks better of it and lies down again.*

KAT. There's more—go help yourself.

WESTHUS. It's too far.

SCENE 8-E

Close-up group.

PAUL. When are we going back to the front?

KAT. Tomorrow.

TJADEN. It's enough to take away a man's appetite.

PAUL. You know, fellows, if they're going to march us in again tomorrow, we ought to go see how Kemmerich is.

ALFRED. That's a good idea.

MULLER. How far's the dressing station?

KAT. About two miles.

MULLER. We could take his things to him.

PAUL. Gee, it seems rotten to think of anything happening to him—

ALFRED. The French certainly deserve to be punished for starting this war.

LEER. Everybody says it was somebody else.

TJADEN. Well how do they start a war?

ALBERT. One country offends another,

TJADEN. How could one country offend another? You mean there's a mountain in Germany gets mad at a field over in France?

ALBERT. Well, stupid, one people offends another.

TJADEN. If that's it, I shouldn't be here at all—and I don't feel myself offended!

KAT. It doesn't apply to tramps like you.

TJADEN. Good, I can be going home right away!

PAUL. You try it.

TJADEN. Me and the Kaiser felt just alike about this war. We didn't either of us want any war. I'm going home! He's there already!

MULLER. Somebody must have wanted it. Maybe it was the English. Oh, no. I know I don't want to shoot any Englishmen. I never saw one till I came up here—and most of them never saw a German till they came up here. They weren't asked about it.

HANS. It must be useful to somebody.

TJADEN. Not me and the Kaiser.

MULLER. I think maybe the Kaiser wanted a war.

KAT. I don't see that—he's got everything he needs.

MULLER. Well, he never had a war before. Every full-grown emperor needs one war to make him famous. That's history.

PAUL. General, too, they need wars.

MULLER. And manufacturers. They get rich.

ALBERT. I think it's more a kind of fever. Nobody wants it in particular, but then all at once, there it is. We didn't want it—the English didn't want it—and here we are fighting.

KAT. I tell you how the whole thing should be done. Whenever there is going to be a war you should rope off a big field and sell tickets and on the big day the kings and their cabinets should be put in the center dressed in their underpants and fight it out with clubs. Let the best country win.

PAUL *gets up laughing, and beckons to* MULLER *and* ALBERT *and* LEER *that it's time to go.*

MULLER *(Rising)*. The best thing is not to talk about the rotten business. We're going over and cheer up Kemmerich.

TJADEN. The Kaiser and me want you boys to be back in time to march tomorrow—don't forget.

The boys start away.

Dissolve to:

SCENE 9-E

Int. room in dressing station. Fade in. On a cot in the foreground lies KEMMERICH. *Only his body from the waist up can be seen. His face is wan, lined. His hands, which lie on the bed cover, are thin and bony. His eyes are expressionless. He is near the end. A door to a hall, in the background is opened. An orderly points to* KEMMERICH's *cot and exits.* PAUL, ALBERT, MULLER *and* LEER *enter.* PAUL *has a spray of cherry blossoms in his hand. They come down to the cot, greeting* KEMMERICH. MULLER *is carrying a bundle.* KEMMERICH's *eyes turn to them, otherwise, he cannot move. He attempts a smile. For a moment there is silence as they gaze at* KEMMERICH's *drawn face—they don't know what to talk about.* PAUL *says:*

PAUL. Hello, Franz.

KEMMERICH. Hello Paul.

MULLER. Hello, Albert.

PAUL. How they treating you, Franz?

KEMMERICH. All right, but they're robbers here—robbers. They stole my watch.

MULLER. I always told you nobody should carry a valuable watch.

The others look at MULLER—*looks which tell him to keep quiet.*

KEMMERICH. They took it while I was under the ether.

PAUL. You'll get it back.

LEER. You feel all right, do you?

KEMMERICH. Pretty good. But I have such a terrible pain—my foot—every toe on my right foot hurts.

SCENE 10-E

Close-up of the lower part of KEMMERICH's *body. They all look toward the lower part of* KEMMERICH's *body. Under the covers, the clear outline of only one leg is seen.*

SCENE 11-E

They immediately understand.

MULLER. But how can your foot hurt— when your leg's been—

He stops abruptly and winces with pain. PAUL *has kicked him on the shin.*

(Adds lamely)

I mean—that's funny—the toes hurt—huh?

SCENE 12-E

Close-up of KEMMERICH. *He is watching them. Suddenly he realizes:*

KEMMERICH. I know what you mean—I know—they cut my leg off—I know what you mean.

He turns his face away, half crying.

SCENE 13-E

Close-up of cot. KEMMERICH *is in foreground, others on the other side of the cot.* PAUL *and the others glare at* MULLER.

PAUL. You mustn't feel bad about it, Franz, lots of worse things could happen.

KEMMERICH *is quietly crying.*

KEMMERICH. I wanted to be a forester.

PAUL. You can still be a forester. They make artificial legs that are wonderful.

ALBERT. And you're through, too. You can go home. Think of that!

MULLER. We brought your things for you, see?

He holds out the bundle.

KEMMERICH. Put 'em under the bed.

MULLER *does so. He emerges from under the bed with* KEMMERICH's *boots.*

MULLER. Say Franz, these are wonderful boots of yours, do you know it?

(To the others)

Look at that leather, will you?
LEER. Say, that's slick, isn't it?

PAUL, LEER *and* ALBERT *also look at the boots—they all would like to have them.* MULLER *matches the sole to one of his own boots. They all feel the other one.* LEER *takes it and also matches it to his own boot.* MULLER *looks up, pleased.*

MULLER. I was just thinking, Franz, if you're not going to be using these—

SCENE 14-E

Close-up MULLER *and* KEMMERICH.

MULLER. Why don't you leave them with us?

KEMMERICH *shakes his head.*

MULLER. No?
KEMMERICH. I want to keep them.
MULLER. My boots give me terrible blisters. After all, what good are they to you now? I—

SCENE 15-E

Close-up feet of MULLER *and* PAUL. *The heel of* PAUL's *boot comes down on* MULLER's *toes.*

SCENE 16-E

Close-up group. MULLER *winces, looks at* PAUL, *and reluctantly puts the boots under the cot.* PAUL *turns to* KEMMERICH.
PAUL. Well, we'll be going, Franz—
KEMMERICH. Can't you stay a little longer?
PAUL. I'll come right back—

He motions for the others to get going. They file out.

SCENE 17-E

Int. hall. Close-up door to KEMMERICH's *room.* PAUL *and the others come thru the door, close it and stop.* MULLER *comes close to* PAUL, *hesitates a moment, then continues:*

PAUL. I'll meet you later.
MULLER. I'm sorry, Paul. I wouldn't do anything to hurt Franz. If I could help him, I'd—I'd walk barefoot—only—only—why should some orderly get those boots?
ALBERT. Muller is right.

PAUL. I understand. We're all alike out here. Only the facts are important to us. *(pause).* We get that way.

SCENE 18-E

Close-up at KEMMERICH's *cot—Akeley.*

PAUL *enters and sits beside* KEMMERICH, *who is sinking rapidly. The hollows in his forehead are deeper, his features sharper. The skeleton is working itself through. Wounded men are being brought into the room.*

KEMMERICH. Ask the doctor to come, will you, PAUL?

PAUL *gets up. The camera follows him.*

A doctor is just passing. PAUL *salutes and pointing to* KEMMERICH, *says:*

PAUL. He wants you.

The DOCTOR *glances at* KEMMERICH *then goes on.* PAUL *sits beside the bed again.*

KEMMERICH. Do you really think I'll ever get well?
PAUL. Of course.
KEMMERICH *(After a pause).* Do you really think so?
PAUL. Sure. Once you've got over the operation.

KEMMERICH *lapses within himself, then beckons to* PAUL *to come closer.* PAUL *leans over him,* KEMMERICH *whispers:*

KEMMERICH. I don't think so.

PAUL *straightens up—struggles for a way to encourage him. He stammers quickly:*

PAUL. Don't talk such nonsense. You'll be as good as new—they fix up worse things than that around here.

SCENE 19-E

Close-up KEMMERICH. *His eyes close. Tears roll out from under the lids.*

SCENE 20-E

Close-up PAUL *and* KEMMERICH. PAUL *is miserable. Orderly enters again, looks at* KEMMERICH *and goes away.* PAUL *takes out his handkerchief to wipe away the tears, but it is too dirty. He sits there too helpless to do anything.* KEMMERICH *is slowly shaking his head—it is no use. He knows the end is near.* PAUL *sinks down beside the cot on his knees.* KEMMERICH *groans and* PAUL *whispers:*

PAUL. Oh, God, this is Franz Kemmerich, 19 years old. He doesn't want to die. Let him not die.

KEMMERICH. Paul—
PAUL. *(Looking up)* Yes, Franz.
KEMMERICH. And here's a picture of me—
you could give that to my mother if you—
when you see her.

PAUL *calls:*

PAUL. Franz!

KEMMERICH *starts to sink rapidly.* PAUL *looks
at him, startled with horror. He gets up and
rushes away.* KEMMERICH *begins to gurgle.*

KEMMERICH. If you—find—my watch—
send it—home—

SCENE 21-E

Int. hall—near door. A DOCTOR *and an*
ORDERLY *are standing talking and smoking in
the foreground.* PAUL *rushes out of a background door, calling:*

PAUL. Doctor! Where's the Doctor?

He sees the DOCTOR *and runs down to him,
clutching him by his apron.*

PAUL. Come quick! Franz Kemmerich is
dying.

The DOCTOR *turns to* ORDERLY, *who is the one
who has been watching* KEMMERICH. *The*
DOCTOR *asks:*

DOCTOR. Which one is that?
ORDERLY. Amputated leg.
DOCTOR¡ *(Angrily)* I've amputated a dozen
legs today—
ORDERLY. Bed 26.
DOCTOR. You see to it!

He walks rapidly away. PAUL, *in a rage,
starts after him. The* ORDERLY *stops him, looks
toward the room where* KEMMERICH *is, then
starts toward it.* PAUL *follows. As they go
through the door.*

Fade out.

SCENE 22-E

*Ext. hospital door. Close-up. Moving scene.
Just the bottom of the door is seen. The door
opens,* PAUL'S *feet come into view. As he comes
down the steps, more of his body comes into
view, revealing* KEMMERICH'S *boots, which he
carries under his arm. He pauses a moment,
looking straight ahead. The wind blows his
hair—he breathes deeply and starts toward the
camera which pulls back to a full view and
continues moving with* PAUL. PAUL *feels the
surge of his life in his limbs. He gradually increases his speed until he is running. He passes*

*men who call to him, but he runs on,
unheedingly.*

Dissolve to:

SCENE 23-E

*Small room in a deserted French house full
view.* KAT *is asleep in one corner.* MULLER *is
reading a book, seated in the center of the room,
his feet on the table. The door bursts open and*
PAUL *rushes in and stands panting a minute.*
MULLER *leaps to his feet as he sees the boots.*

MULLER. He gave them to you after all.
PAUL. *(Nodding and passing them)*

PAUL *comes slowly down to the table and
sinks, panting, into a chair.* MULLER *takes the
boots, feels their softness and immediately
starts putting them on.*

PAUL. I saw him die, Muller—I didn't know
what it was like to die before.

MULLER *pauses and looks up at him.*

PAUL. And then I came outside and it felt so
good to be alive and I started in to walk fast
and I began to think of the strangest things
being out in the fields and everything like
that—and girls—I felt as if there were something electric running from the ground up
through me—and I started—and I began to
run hard and passed soldiers—and I heard
voices all about, but—

(Stops, dazed)

I ran and I ran and it seemed as if I couldn't
breathe enough air into me—and now I'm
hungry.

PETER *and* LEER *enter.*

PETER. Here's some mail. Ah, you got the
boots, eh?
LEER. One for you, PAUL.

He passes PAUL *a letter.*

MULLER. I've got a few things to eat—the
party is on me.

He gets food out of his pack.

PETER. *(Looking at boots)*

Those are a little too small for you, aren't
they?
MULLER. No, they feel fine.
PETER. They fit me much better than they
fit you.
MULLER. Have it your own way.
PETER. I don't wish you any bad luck, but if
anything should happen to you, I get the
boots, huh?

MULLER. *(His mouth full)*

Sure! But I'm here for duration, so don't get your hopes too high.

SCENE 24-E

Another angle— PAUL. *He is reading letter and begins to laugh.*

MULLER. What's the matter?

PAUL. I have a letter from our dear professor. He sends you all his best wishes.

ALBERT. I wish he was here.

PETER. What does he say?

PAUL. We are the hope of Germany—Iron Youth!

He looks at the boots. He says slowly,

Youth! that was long ago.

PAUL *exits.* MULLER *looks after him, gets up, stomps his feet into the boots.*

MULLER. I don't mind the war now—it'll be a pleasure to go to the front in boots like these. What boots! They can march me to the front any time they like now.

He walks up and down. Camera turns to his feet and holds it for

Dissolve to:

SEQUENCE "F"

———

SCENE 1-F

Ext. country road. Day. Moving scene. Close-up feet of marching soldiers. At the street, the camera is stationary. A column of troops is marching. As KEMMERICH'S *boots come into view, the camera moves with them, and then raises and reveals a close-up of* MULLER. *He is marching cheerfully. As he looks down at the boots, the camera drops back to a close-up of the boots.*

Dissolve to:

SCENE 2-F

Ext. muddy field. Rain. Day. Close-up feet of marching soldiers. Moving scene. KEMMERICH'S *boots are in the foreground. Behind them, can be seen a long line of marching feet, ploughing through the rain and mud.*

Dissolve to:

SCENE 3-F

Open field and shell holes. Snow. Day. Moving scene. Low camera setup. The ground is frozen. Some hand to hand fighting is seen. In

the foreground is MULLER, *wearing* KEMMERICH'S *boots. All that can be seen of him is his figure from the waist down. He is running across the field. His feet stumble, fall and lie still. From the opposite direction a mass of French troops enter and run over him.*

Dissolve to:

SCENE 4-F

Ext. day. Grass. Moving scene. Low camera setup. The camera stays with the feet of the marching troops and moves through them to the opposite side and reveals KEMMERICH'S *boots marching. Beyond them, can be seen the tops of fruit trees in full bloom. The camera moves up to reveal* PETER, *who is walking freely. The camera drops down to the boots again*

Dissolve to:

SCENE 5-F

The exterior trench. Mud. The trench is filled with men lined up waiting for the zero hour. In the foreground are KEMMERICH'S *boots. The heavy bombardment suddenly ceases. Commands are heard.*

Prepare to advance! Advance!

All the feet are seen going over the top. KEMMERICH'S *boots fall back into the empty trench and lie still.*

Dissolve to:

SCENE 6-F

Ext. village street. Day. Moving scene. KEMMERICH'S *boots are marching in time with others. The camera pulls back and reveals* ALBERT *wearing the boots. The camera pulls back still further till a company of men is seen. The command:*

Halt! Fall out!

is heard. There is a general scrimmage as the men break up and run to their billets, which are seen in the background. The men look tired, are dirty and mud-covered. Most have beards—of all lengths.

SCENE 7-F

Int. canteen. Day. Full view from behind the bar. Through the open door men are seen running in all directions. A crowd of them run into the canteen and up to the bar—a confusion of voices is heard:

Bear! Bear! Vin Blanc! Vin Rouge! Bis! Bis! Do I get a drink or not?

PAUL *and* KAT *and the rest of the gang succeed in getting their drinks.*

SCENE 8-F

Close-up corner of canteen near window.
PAUL *and* ALBERT *enter and sit on a bench
beside the window, through which a canal can
be seen. Their appearance has changed—they
are harder, their faces lined slightly, bearded,
muddy.* PAUL *raises his glass:*

PAUL. *(Wryly)* Happy days!
ALBERT. Oh, you have to get funny again.

They click glasses. As PAUL *starts to drink,
his eyes focus on a mirror and open wide,
startled.*

SCENE 9-F

*Close-up mirror on wall. In the mirror is the
reflection of a theater poster on the opposite
wall. All that can be seen of it is the slender
figure of a girl wearing a white dress, white
stockings and shoes with high heels. One hand
is resting on a railing, the other holds a floppy
straw hat. Behind her is a lake.*

SCENE 10-F

Close-up PAUL *and* ALBERT. ALBERT *notices*
PAUL's *rapt expression and he too looks in the
mirror. They both whirl and look toward the
poster, then get up and go toward it.*

SCENE 11-F

Close-up poster. PAUL *and* ALBERT *enter and
admire the girl. Beside her stands a man dressed
in white trousers, a blue jacket and a sailor's
cap.* PAUL *has a far away expression.*

PAUL. I'd forgotten there were any girls
like that.
ALBERT. There aren't.
PAUL. Just look at these thin shoes—she
couldn't march far in those.
ALBERT. Do you have to talk shop when
we're in such charming company? How old
do you think she is?
PAUL. About twenty-two—at the most.
ALBERT. No, no. That'd make her older
than us!

(With decision)

She's seventeen.

PAUL *nods, willing to be convinced.*

PAUL. A girl like that—that would be good,
eh, Albert?

ALBERT *shifts his gaze and looks at the man,
and resents his appearance.*

ALBERT. We wouldn't have much chance
with him around.

*He looks at his ragged, stained and dirty
uniform.* PAUL *also looks himself over, then at
the poster, and proceeds to tear off the man,
being very careful not to damage the girl. Now,
satisfied, they stand off and admire their handi-
work, relieved and pleased.* PAUL, *desiring to
touch her hair, reaches out a hand, but hesitates
as he notices how dirty it is. He turns to* ALBERT.

PAUL. We might take a bath and wash our
clothes.
ALBERT. She's a long way from here now—
that poster was put up four months ago—look
at that date. May—1917.

ALBERT *glances at the girl again.*

Here's to her, anyway.

ALBERT *agrees. They raise their glasses and
toast the girl.* ALBERT *says:*

ALBERT. All right—to all of 'em—
everywhere!

SCENE 12-F

Longer view of poster. PAUL *and* ALBERT
drink a toast to the girl. LEER *and* TJADEN *enter
and sit at a table in the foreground. They notice*
PAUL *and* ALBERT. TJADEN *looks closely at the
poster and remarks:*

TJADEN. Personally, I like 'em bigger
around.

LEER *leans over and whispers in* TJADEN's
ear. They both laugh. PAUL *turns to* ALBERT.

PAUL. Say, this conversation was on a high
moral plane up to now.
ALBERT. And now we do need a bath.

They put down their glasses and start away.
TJADEN *and* LEER *are amazed.*

TJADEN. A bath?
LEER. What for?

PAUL *and* ALBERT *stop and give the picture a
knowing look.*

PAUL. You wouldn't understand.

PAUL *and* ALBERT *exit.* TJADEN *and* LEER
exchange puzzled looks. TJADEN *gets to his feet.*

TJADEN. I think there's something doing. I
don't believe a bath'd do me any permanent
harm.

LEER *gets up.*

LEER. Lead on, Reckless.

As they hurry out, PAUL *and* ALBERT *are seen
through the window going toward the canal.*

After a moment LEER *and* TJADEN *come into view, running after them.*

SCENE 13-F

Ext. bank of canal long view. The small, nude figures of PAUL *and* ALBERT *can be seen diving into the canal as* LEER *and* TJADEN *run in and disappear behind a bush near the water.*

SCENE 14-F

Close-up PAUL *and* ALBERT *in the water. They are standing on the bottom of the canal; just their bodies from the waist up can be seen.* ALBERT *soaps himself, then tosses the cake to* PAUL, *who fails to catch it.* PAUL *dives for it as* LEER *and* TJADEN *swim into view.* PAUL *comes up. On the opposite bank three French girls walk into view on a cow-path that runs parallel to the canal. The boys see them.* LEER *calls:*

LEER. Hello. Come on in. Have a swim.

SCENE 15-F

Close-up of the French girls moving scene. They are not so young, nor so pretty. They wave to the boys. One of them, a slim brunette, laughs and does a few light steps on the bank as she walks along.

SCENE 16-F

Close-up boys in water. They are swimming along and gesticulating wildly as they call out:

BOYS. Ici! Ici! Je vous aime! Je t'adore! Ici maintenant!

SCENE 17-F

Full view— girls in foreground— boys beyond in water— moving scene. The girls wave in answer, then turn from them and continue walking. LEER *suddenly pretends to be drowning, throws up his hands, calls:*

LEER. Help! Help!

The girls pause.

SCENE 18-F

Close-up boys in water. LEER *goes under.* TJADEN *goes down and his feet appear, waving.* LEER *reappears, gurgling, and calls out:*

LEER. Oui, oui, si vous plait! Si vous plait!

SCENE 19-F

Close-up girls. They laugh and start away, turning off the path toward a house that is seen in the background through the trees.

SCENE 20-F

Close-up boys in water. They are disconcerted at their lack of success. TJADEN *gets an idea and swims rapidly away.*

SCENE 21-F

Close-up boys' clothes on edge of canal. The clothes are piled near a bush. Water is in the foreground. TJADEN *appears in the water, up to his waist. He reaches into his trousers pocket and brings out a sausage, then exits from the scene.*

SCENE 22-F

Canal— boys in foreground. On the bank the girls are quite away off. TJADEN *swims into the scene, gesticulating wildly with the sausage. The girls stop and come back, close to the water's edge. They are much interested, nodding and beckoning for the men to come over.* LEER *shakes his head and points up the canal.*

SCENE 23-F

Long view of foot bridge over canal. Sentries are posted on the bridge.

SCENE 24-F

Full view moving scene boys in foreground. LEER *beckons to the girls to come over. They shake their heads and point in the direction of the bridge. The men now tempt the girls by indicating all manner of foods, in pantomime.* TJADEN *almost drowns trying to demonstrate eating off plate with knife and fork. The women are now friendly and point to the little cottage among the trees.*

LEER. Ce soir?

(unintelligible rush of French, ending with)

Oui, oui, ce soir!

They raise their hands, put them together, rest their faces on them and shut their eyes. The slim brunette does a two-step. The Blonde twitters and makes a motion of eating. The boys nod eagerly. The girls disappear into the trees toward the house. They (boys) tread water and watch until the girls are seen entering the cottage. The boys are satisfied and in high spirits. They start to swim toward the opposite bank.

SCENE 25-F

Bank of canal. Reverse angle. A CORPORAL *is standing on the bank. The boys, who are turning to swim toward it, stop as they see the* CORPORAL.

CORPORAL. You fellows stay on this side or you'll get yourselves in a lot of trouble.

The CORPORAL *turns and exits into the bushes. The boys remain motionless for a moment, then start toward the shore.*

SCENE 26-F

Heavy foliage on bank of canal. The boys come into the scene from the water. The bushes are so thick that it hides them completely from the shoulders down. They talk as they dress:

ALBERT. I knew there was a catch to it.
TJADEN. I hate to disappoint those girls.
LEER. Yeah, Tjaden, that's tough on them.
PAUL. What could they do if they caught us crossing over—court martial?
TJADEN. Sure.
PAUL. Well, that ends that.

Dissolve to:

SCENE 27-F

Int. canteen. Close-up. Group. The four from the canal are telling their experiences to KAT.

TJADEN. Yes, she was. Oh! They were real swell kids, it's too bad—she liked me, too.
LEER. Which one liked you?
TJADEN. The blonde. She's a nice piece of work, that blonde.
ALBERT. They all liked Tjaden.
PAUL. Yes, that time he stuck his feet up—they fell for that!

TJADEN *beams, well satisfied with himself. An off-stage voice is heard calling:*

SERGEANT'S VOICE. Katzinsky! Is Katzinsky in here?

KAT *has his back toward the door.* TJADEN *starts to call out, to say that he is here, when* KAT *clamps a hand over his mouth, motioning for him to keep quiet. The* SERGEANT's *voice is heard again.*

Kat! Katzinsky!
KAT. I'm not in, see?

KAT *hunches lower over the table. The* SERGEANT *enters and stands beside him.* KAT *looks up.*

SERGEANT. You heard me.
KAT. That's right.
SERGEANT. You draw a guard duty job tomorrow morning. Report at daybreak with your platoon. There'll be a lorry waiting.
KAT. Where are we going?
SERGEANT. I don't know.
KAT. I'm supposed to get ten days' rest.
SERGEANT. Tell that to the captain.

The SERGEANT *exits. They are all disgusted. Their rest is shot.*

KAT. Well, I'm going to get drunk.

KAT *gets up and exits toward the bar.*

TJADEN. And I'm going to swim the canal tonight. The nerve of them, giving us guard duty when we're on leave. We'll all go, huh?
PAUL. There are only three girls.
TJADEN. I got the blonde. You all can fight for the other two.

TJADEN *pours himself a drink.* PAUL *glances at the others, then gets up and exits.* LEER *sees him go.*

SCENE 28-F

Close-up at counter. There is a man on duty. PAUL *enters.*

PAUL. Give me one of those sausages.

LEER *enters behind him, gets the idea and exclaims:*

LEER. You can't get away from me, you know. I'll take some sausage, too.
ALBERT. Listen, boys, there's only one way out of this—we've got to get Tjaden drunk!

Dissolve to:

SCENE 29-F

Close-up group at corner table. Night. A cognac bottle, nearly empty, is on the table. TJADEN *is almost "out". As he puts down an empty glass,* LEER *hands him a full one.*

LEER. That's yours, Tjaden.
TJADEN. I had mine.
PAUL. You're way behind.

TJADEN *looks a little bewildered. He looks at the others—all of them have a glass in their hands. He gulps down the liquor, smiles foolishly, his head resting on the table. The three others look at him a moment, then rise and tiptoe away.*

Dissolve to:

SCENE 30-F

Ext. bank of canal. Close-up. Ground. Night. Parts of uniforms fall into scene. Three pairs of bare feet are seen. In the foreground hands are stuffing sausage and bread into a pair of boots.

PAUL'S VOICE. I want the little brunette. She was flirting with me all along.
LEER'S VOICE. I'll take Tjaden's blonde—
ALBERT'S VOICE. Thanks for leaving me the one I wanted.

Hands pick up all of the boots. The feet exit toward the canal. After a moment.

SPLASHES ARE HEARD

As they dive in.

SCENE 31-F

Close-up in water. Water. The boys are swimming on their backs, holding their boots out of the water.

ALBERT. What if there's a major in with them?

LEER. Then we just beat it. He can try reading the regimental numbers on our birthday suits.

SCENE 32-F

Opposite bank and trees. Long view night. The three boys reach the bank and climb out. They take the provisions from the boots, put the boots on, then disappear among the trees.

SCENE 33-F

Ext. girls' cottage. Long view. Night. The boys are seen through the trees in the distance, approaching the house. The windows are shuttered but light gleams through the chinks. The boys before the door. LEER whistles softly.

SCENE 34-F

Ext. door. Close-up.

BRUNETTE. Qui va la?
LEER'S VOICE. Sh-sh-camerade!
PAUL'S VOICE. Bon ami!

The upper half of the door opens, revealing the three French girls framed in the opening. Their eyes open wide in shocked amazement as they stare at the boys, who are not seen. Then they burst into laughter and cling to each other as they sway back and forth.

SCENE 35-F

Reverse Angle. Shooting over the girls' shoulders. The lower half of the door conceals the naked bodies of the boys from the waist down. The girls, still laughing, put their hands over their eyes and turn away. The boys hold up the food stuff.

THE BRUNETTE. Un moment, un moment!

She runs out, followed by the others. The boys exchange looks—they're getting over all right. The girls reappear with clothing which they toss out to the boys, who start to put them on.

SCENE 36-F

Int. of the girls' house toward the door. Night. ALBERT enters first, in a short raincoat. PAUL follows him, similarly clad; LEER brings up the rear in a voluminous and highly colored kimono. The three boys approach a large dining table and put the food stuff on it. The women watch them smilingly, with an occasional burst of laughter at LEER's kimono. LEER takes advan-

tage of the situation to put his arm around the blonde when he sees her laughing at him. She continues to laugh against his shoulder.

SCENE 37-F

Close shot of TJADEN at table. He is asleep, lying on the table.

SCENE 38-F

Close-up of PAUL and the BRUNETTE. PAUL is extracting a large piece of liverwurst from a package. He does this very slowly. His eyes on the BRUNETTE's face. Her eyes are glued on the package and become ecstatic when she sees what it contains. PAUL very carefully cuts her a slice of liverwurst and holds it up to her. She lets her arms fall to her side and eats the piece out of his hand, smiling up at him.

SCENE 39-F

Close-up of ALBERT and GIRL. He builds a sandwich out of the contents of his pack, placing layer after layer of thin cut bread with meat and other ingredients, until the sandwich assumes tremendous proportions. ALBERT's girl watches him with delight and when he finally hands her the plate with the sandwich on it, takes the edge of the plate in both her hands, leans over and kisses him in thanks.

SCENE 40-F

Full view of moon. LEER's girl starts the victrola. LEER and the BLONDE do some marvelous steps which look especially funny in his kimono. The dance is climaxed by a kiss at one end of the room.

ALBERT *and his girl are seated in a chair near the wall.* PAUL *and the* BRUNETTE *have walked toward an open fireplace.*

SCENE 41-F

Close-up PAUL and the BRUNETTE. She leans against him, her head comes in contact with his cigarette case, which she takes out, and offers him a cigarette. He lights one for her and one for himself. She sits in a large chair and pulls him down at her feet. She strokes his hair.

BRUNETTE. La Guerre—grand malheur! Pauvres garcons!

PAUL *holds her arm tightly and presses his lips into the palm of her hand. Her fingers close around his face. She leans over him and he kisses her.*

SCENE 42-F

Close-up of the victrola. It runs down and finally stops.

Dissolve to:

SCENE 43-F

Int. close-up of a door. It is just closing—

Dissolve to:

SCENE 44-F

Int. another door. It is also just closing—

Dissolve to:

SCENE 45-F

Int. still another door. It is just closing—

Dissolve to:

SCENE 46-F

Close shot of TJADEN *as before. He gets off balance and falls on the floor with a clatter.*

TJADEN. No, I don't surrender—the cold steel, boys—give 'em the bayonet—

He struggles with those who are helping him to his feet. Then he realizes he is among friends.

I thought that Frenchman had me that time—I thought it was all up with the Kaiser and me.

In his befuddled groping he puts his hand in his pocket. It encounters sausage which he pulls out and looks at startled.

I got a date with a blonde and I can't think who.

SCENE 47-F

Ext. house. Night. The door opens and light streams out. A pair of boots appear— ALBERT's.

ALBERT. *(calling)* Paul!

SCENE 48-F

A nearly dark room. Just the vaguest silhouette is seen. Sound will perhaps tell us that PAUL *is sitting up in bed and the* BRUNETTE *is lying beside him.*

PAUL. *(calling).* Alright.

(then quietly)

They're waiting for me—Goodbye!
BRUNETTE. Oh, mon pauvre garcon.

She sits up and kisses him.

PAUL. What's your name.
BRUNETTE. Huh?
PAUL. Name—name—Camille, Georgette?
BRUNETTE. Oh, nom—Susanne.
PAUL. Susanne, I wish you could understand me—I wish I could tell you something.
BRUNETTE. Pauvre Garcon. C'est la Guerre.

PAUL. I'll never see you again, I know that—and I wouldn't even know you if I did, and yet I'll remember you always—forever. If you could only know how different this is from the women we soldiers meet—
SUSANNE. C'est la guerre.
PAUL. No, no, no! Not the war—You. That's what I'm talking about—you. It just seems as though all war and terror and grossness had fallen away from me. Like a miracle. Like something I never believed.
ALBERT. *(calling from below)*
Paul! Come on!
PAUL. *(calling)*
I'm coming.

PAUL *jumps out of the bed in bare feet and pulls on boots.*

SUSANNE. Pauvre garcon—pauvre enfant.

His boots clatter to the door and as he opens it, the shadows of the two bodies are shown against the wall for a moment, and then disappear as PAUL *runs down the stairs with a clatter.*

SCENE 49-F

Ext. door to house. Close-up. Night. Light streams out. Two pairs of feet, in boots, are seen. Inside, the feet of the girls can be seen. Another pair of boots follows and then a girl's bare feet inside. There are expressions of farewell.

GIRL'S VOICE. Bon soir! Bon soir!
BOY'S VOICE. We'll be all right.

The boy's feet exit.

SCENE 50-F

Ext. among trees. Night. The three men naked again, are making their way down to the water in the darkness. They stop suddenly, hearing a splash. They peer into the darkness.

SCENE 51-F

Close shot of KAT. *Floundering out of the water, naked in the half light. He carries the sausage in one hand. He stumbles forward toward the house.*

SCENE 52-F

Close shot of the three boys. Beyond them, KAT *is seen stumbling up the hill in a great hurry. They are exploding with an effort to restrain their laughter. Holding hands over their mouths they rock, rock with noiseless glee—they finally roll on the ground in absolute abandon and roar with laughter.*

Fade out.

SEQUENCE "G"

———

SCENE 1-G

Close shot of brand new, yellow, unpolished coffin. Camera moves to show other coffins. It pulls back to show a whole mountain of coffins. It swings over and discloses marching troops. Trucking up close to the troops we discover, KAT, PAUL, TJADEN *and* ALBERT.

PAUL. *(Glancing toward coffins)*

Take a look.

KAT. Huh?

He looks in the direction indicated.

SCENE 2-G

Long shot of coffins stacked against a shelled school house.

SCENE 3-G

Moving shot of KAT, PAUL *etc.*

PAUL. That's a good preparation for the offensive.
ALBERT. They're for us.
KAT. No coffin is going to get me.
TJADEN. I should say not. You'll be thankful if they slip a water proof sheet around your Aunt Sally of a carcass.

Dissolve to:

SCENE 4-G

Interior of dugout. Close-up of man's hand picking a louse out of a shirt.

TJADEN. This is a good invention just the same.

Camera pans to a boot polish can over a candle held by a wire. Camera pulls back and shows TJADEN *picking the lice from shirt and dropping them in can.* MULLER, PAUL, KAT, ALBERT, DETERING *and others are sitting around. Some repairing equipment— some hunting for lice— some eating.*

TJADEN. If you crack each separate louse, think of all the energy you use up.

Artillery fire is constantly heard. In the foreground our group is sitting around the lighted stump of a candle, their coats and shirts off, hunting for lice.

PAUL. When are we going over, Kat?
KAT. Tonight or in the morning.
WESTHUS. Tonight?

KAT. Take a look at Bertinck when you go by the dugout. Every time he puts on that old uniform, over we go. I've watched him.
PAUL. Has he got it on now?
KAT. He has.

(There is a faint groan among the boys)

WESTHUS. *(Rising)* I'd better get that strap fixed on my helmet.

He picks up a helmet. DETERING *rises, looks at him, then deliberately snatches the helmet out of his hand.*

DETERING. What are you doing with that?
WESTHUS. Hey, what's the joke?
DETERING. Will you let my helmet alone!
WESTHUS. Whose helmet? That's mine!
DETERING *(pointing to another helmet)*. There's yours, with the broken strap!
WESTHUS. All right. Don't fight a war about it.
DETERING. You wanted to hand me the broken strap, that's all!
WESTHUS. *(Drawing back his arm as if to strike)*. You're crazy!
KAT. Let him alone, Jaie!

He strikes WESTHUS, *who takes the blow without flinching, looks hard at* DETERING *and fails to strike back.* PAUL *and* KAT *drag* DETERING *away from* WESTHUS *and set him down near the wall. He makes no resistance, and begins to sob.*

WESTHUS. He's crazy.
DETERING. Well, what if I am?
KAT *(to Paul)*. What's the matter with him?
PAUL. *(To Kat)*

He got a letter today. He wants to get back to his farm.
KAT. We'd all like to get back, if it comes to that.
DETERING. A woman can't run a farm alone. That's no good, you know—no matter how hard she works. Here's the harvest coming round again—

DETERING *suddenly gets up and goes out, unable to control himself.*

ALBERT. I wonder what we'd do if it were suddenly peace time again?
LEER. It never will be again. Can't imagine it.
ALBERT. Well—but if it were, what would you do?
LEER. Clear out of this.
ALBERT. Of course, and then what?
LEER. Get drunk.
ALBERT. I mean seriously.
LEER. So do I.

TJADEN *(Holding up a driving band).* Well, I'd go looking for a Cinderella that could wear this for a garter, and when I found her, nobody'd see me for two weeks.

KAT. You might get drunk first, but after that everybody'd go back to what he was doing. Detering would go to his farm, Westhus would dig peat, I'd start making harness again. *(He takes out a photograph).* Ever see that? My old people. Damn lousy war!

PAUL. It's all very well for you to talk. You've got something to go back to. Wife, children, job. How about Leer, and Albert and me? What have we to go back to? — School?

KAT. Why not? You know everything already!

PAUL. That would be sweet, wouldn't it? Sitting down in front of Kantorek again. Leer, how many children had Charles the Bald?

ALBERT *(Pretending to be KANTEREK).* Yes, Leer. Discuss the three-fold theme of Wilhelm Tell? — and what was the purpose of the poetic league of Gottingen?

LEER. And what and why is cohesion?

PAUL. That's all rot, everything they teach you. What good is it after you've been out here? They never taught us anything really useful like how to light a cigarette in the wind — or make a fire out of wet wood — or bayonet a man in the belly instead of the ribs where it'd get caught.

LEER. Forget it. You'll be dead some day, so what's the difference?

SCENE 5-G

Ext. intersection of trench. Day.

(The distant sounds of artillery)

LEER *comes out of the dugout entrance in the background and comes toward the camera. As he nears the intersection* HIMMELSTOSS *comes into view in the cross section. Two young recruits precede him. They start to go straight ahead.* HIMMELSTOSS *stops and bellows at them. They come back into view, frightened, and start toward the camera.* LEER, *who has stopped, doubles up with laughter as he sees* HIMMELSTOSS. HIMMELSTOSS *turns toward him. The recruits stare open-mouthed.* LEER *turns and goes toward the dugout, holding his sides.* HIMMELSTOSS *follows him, after giving a curt order for the recruits to wait.*

SCENE 6-G

Int. of large dugout. LEER *comes through the entrance, still helpless with laughter. The others look up.* LEER *tries to talk, but cannot.*

PAUL. What's up?

LEER. Himmelstoss!

LEER *tries to explain, but for a while can only point to the entrance.* HIMMELSTOSS *enters.* PAUL, ALBERT *and* HANS *stare in amazement.*

PAUL. Himmelstoss! I'm beginning to think there *is* justice in the army.

HIMMELSTOSS. *(After looking them all over)* Well, well. So we are all here?

ALBERT. A bit longer than you, Himmel.

HIMMELSTOSS. Since when have we become so familiar? Stand up there — bring your heels together — all of you.

LEER. You take a run and jump at yourself.

HIMMELSTOSS. I command you, as your Superior Officer. Do you want to be court-martialled?

PAUL. I do. There's going to be a big attack any minute now, and I'd just love to get out of it.

HIMMELSTOSS. Will you obey my orders?

PAUL. It isn't customary to ask for salutes here — but I'll tell you what we'll do. We're going to attack a town that we tried to take once before. Many killed and many wounded. It was a lot of fun. This time you're going with us and if any of us stop a bullet before we die we'll come up to you, click our heels and ask stiffly, 'Please Sergeant Himmelstoss may we go?'

HIMMELSTOSS *backs up before* PAUL's *burning eyes. In confusion, he backs toward the entrance, turns and goes. A whistle is heard, men begin to file out of the dugout.*

Dissolve:

SCENE 7-G

Long shot of trench. With cannonading heard.

SCENE 8-G

Ext. second line German trenches — Evening. Fade in. The full company is lined up, ready to go over.

The barrage suddenly lifts. There is complete silence.

The men quickly pick up their weapons expectantly. BERTINCK *is seen holding a watch in his hand.* PAUL *and the others are in the foreground.* HIMMELSTOSS *is next to* PAUL, *who ignores him.* BERTINCK *gives a command.*

BERTINCK. Ready! Ready!

SCENE 9-G

Ext. first and second line German trenches full view evening. The first line trenches are in the foreground. Suddenly the men from the first trench pile out of it and into view. They run past the camera. The men from the second line pour out from their trench and run forward. Others run forward in the communication trench between the first and second line.

SCENE 10-G

Between the trenches is a low, barbed wire entanglement. PAUL *and* KAT *and others are at it, putting planks across it. Others from the second line are waiting to cross. As the planks are put in place, men cross, rush forward, jump into the first trench, climb out and run forward.* HIMMELSTOSS *is just climbing out of the second line trench.* PAUL *and the others run forward.*

SCENE 11-G

Ext. first line trench. Men from the second trench are leaping into this one, crawling out and going forward. PAUL *and* KAT *jump in and start to climb out. They are crowded back by others.* KAT *finds a spot and starts up. The others follow.*

SCENE 12-G

Cross section of trench. German troops are climbing over it and advancing. HIMMELSTOSS *arrives in a panic. He drops down to the bottom and holds his arm as though it were wounded.* PAUL *comes up and starts to go on when he spies* HIMMELSTOSS. *He stops and goes back for him.*

SCENE 13-G

Close shot. As PAUL *comes to him.*

PAUL. Get out!

SCENE 14-G

Close-up of HIMMELSTOSS. *Baring his teeth defiantly*

PAUL. *(From off scene)* Up! Get on with the others!

SCENE 15-G

Close shot of the two. PAUL *pulls* HIMMELSTOSS' *arm down to see if it is really injured.* HIMMELSTOSS *shows his guilt by backing away.* PAUL *grabs him and chokes him.*

PAUL. Get up, I say! You yellow rat. You stinking sneaking yellow rat. Let us do it, eh? Get up! Get up.

Bangs his head against embankment.

SCENE 16-G

Long shot of same. The CAPTAIN *and another wave of men arrive.*

CAPTAIN. Forward! Forward! Join in.

HIMMELSTOSS *snaps to attention and rushes to the attack.* PAUL *follows.*

SCENE 17-G

Ext. first line trench and shell holes. A hill is in the background, the top of it out of sight. The CAPTAIN *is running forward.* HIMMELSTOSS *is running like mad. He passes the* CAPTAIN *and runs toward the hill, up which the Germans are advancing.* PAUL *also follows the wave of the attack.*

SCENE 18-G

Ext. near top of hill. Long view. Reverse angle. The Germans are running up the hill, coming into view beneath the camera. In the background are shell holes and the trenches. Suddenly, from behind the camera, flames belch forth Flame throwers. The Germans hesitate, waver, then fall back.

SCENE 19-G

Ext. side of hill. Germans rush in from the left. Flame throwers come into view at the right. Also machine gunners get into action. The Germans are driven back; some fall.

SCENE 20-G

Close view in smoke and flames. Five or six Germans are seen in the flames. They crumple and fall.

SCENE 21-G

Ext. other side of hill. Germans rush in from the right. Flames stop them; also machine guns. The Germans retreat.

SCENE 22-G

Ext shell holes long view reverse angle. The Germans run over the foreground toward their trenches.

The roar of flames and the rapid fire of machine guns.

Many fall, others hide in shell holes.

SCENE 23-G

Close view at shell hole. KAT, ALBERT *and* LEER *run into the scene.* KAT *and* LEER *jump into the hole.* ALBERT *is shot in the leg. He stumbles and falls on the rim of the hole. He tries to crawl to the hole.* KAT *and* LEER *reappear, crawl to* ALBERT *and drag him into the trench with them.*

SCENE 24-G

Ext. PAUL'S *shell hole. Low set up. Water is at the bottom of the hole. Beyond the rim can be seen the clouds of smoke from the flames throwers.* PAUL *appears at the edge of the hole, hesitates a moment then jumps into it. He stares around wildly for a moment then peers over the rim of the hole toward the French lines.*

SCENE 25-G

Ext. long view foot of hill. The last few Germans run past the camera. Beyond them the French troops can be seen coming down the hill. Shells from the German artillery fall among them.

SCENE 26-G

Ext. PAUL's shell hole. PAUL sees the Frenchmen advancing and quickly slides to the bottom of the hole. He lies in the water up to his waist, his face buried in the mud, his body crumpled as if he were dead. His helmet on the nape of his neck.

SCENE 27-G

Long view PAUL's shell hole. The first line of French reach the hole, race around it and through it. Some step on PAUL as they pass.

SCENE 28-G

Close-up PAUL. He is lying half in the water. A Frenchman's feet run over him. After he has passed PAUL raises his head slightly and looks around fearfully. Terror of being caught helpless shows in his eyes. He swiftly pulls a small dagger from his belt. His eyes are alert. Although he sets his jaw grimly his eyes are filled with terror. He buries his hand with the knife under the mud. His forehead is wet, the sockets of his eyes damp. A spasm of fear sweeps over him.

SCENE 29-G

Shot of Frenchman. Running toward shell hole.

SCENE 30-G

Close shot of PAUL. He slumps down again as if dead.

SCENE 31-G

Medium shot of shell hole. The Frenchman running for shelter throws himself down on top of PAUL.

SCENE 32-G

Close-up PAUL. The Frenchman falls into the scene and lies half over PAUL. The Frenchman starts to rise again, but PAUL, with the frenzy of terror in his eyes whirls over and strikes desperately with his dagger, driving it again and again into the throat and chest of the Frenchman. Then PAUL leaps away from him.

SCENE 33-G

Longer view in shell hole. PAUL leaps away from the Frenchman, and watches him tensely, ready to strike another blow if the man makes a move to attack. The Frenchman, gasping for breath, becomes limp and collapses. PAUL, horrified by what he has done, cannot take his eyes from the soldier. The soldier moves, tries to rise, gasps and lies still.

SCENE 34-G

Close-up of PAUL. He sits back against the edge of the shell hole, his eyes fixed in horror on the object in front of him. Gradually, without knowing what he is doing, he begins to climb backward out of the shell hole, still looking at the Frenchman. There is constant machine gun fire and almost instinctively, PAUL tries out the situation by lifting his helmet above the edge of the shell hole with one hand, still keeping his eyes fixed in front of him. The helmet is knocked out of his hand almost instantly by a bullet. PAUL slips back, nearer to the bottom of the hole, recovers his helmet, puts it on, and sits still, continuing to watch his wounded enemy. The machine gun bullets make a network over his head, never ceasing. The stem of a sapling which grows on the edge of the shell hole just behind PAUL, is gradually eaten away by the fire and falls down the declivity past him. PAUL sees blood on his hand and is nauseated. He takes some earth and rubs the skin so that his hand is muddy and the blood cannot be seen. He hears the Frenchman gasp and looks quickly toward him.

SCENE 35-G

Close-up of the French soldier. He is groaning and gasping for breath. He moves a little and raises his head, but does not see PAUL. He is a young man, with a small pointed beard, soft, dark eyes, and black curly hair. He breathes easier now, but has not the strength to keep his head up. It falls to one side, helplessly resting on his bent arm. His other hand bloody from the wounds, rests on his chest. His gasping stops, he is still.

SCENE 36-G

Close-up PAUL. Believing the man is dead, PAUL shrinks further away from him, horrified by what he has done. He turns his head away, not wanting to look at him. But almost instantly his eyes open again. The man is gasping again. PAUL looks at him, then gets the thought that maybe he can help him—maybe he can save his life. He starts forward.

SCENE 37-G

Close view PAUL *and Frenchman moving scene.* PAUL *is in the foreground, his back to the camera. Beyond him is the French soldier. As* PAUL *crawls forward, the camera moves with him. He moves a few feet, stops and listens to the man, moves another foot, moves forward again. The camera goes past* PAUL *and close to the Frenchman as he opens his eyes. He sees* PAUL—*his eyes open in utter terror. His body lies still, but in his eyes there is an extraordinary expression of fright and terror. The eyes cry out, yell, all the life is gathered together in them for one tremendous effort to flee—gathered together there in a dreadful terror of* PAUL—*of death.*

SCENE 38-G

Close-up PAUL *and the soldier. He has stopped within a few feet of the soldier.* PAUL's *eyes are fastened on those of the soldier.* PAUL *is powerless to move. He whispers:*

PAUL. No—no—I won't hurt you—I want to help you.

The Frenchman continues to stare at him, uncomprehendingly. The hand drops away from his chest. The movement breaks the power of his eyes. PAUL *reaches out a hand and strokes the man's forehead. The soldier tries to shrink away, in his eyes is still more concentrated terror.*

PAUL. No—no, no, I tell you!

PAUL *unbuttons the man's tunic to find the wounds. The soldier's eyes lose their stare, the eyelids droop; the tension is past. The shirt is stuck and will not come away, it must be cut off.* PAUL *reaches for his knife. The Frenchman's eyes open, see the knife, and in them again comes demented fear.*

PAUL. I want to help you, don't you under-stand—it's all right, comrade—comrade—

The man understands the word, comrade, and relaxes slightly, although he continues to watch PAUL *who takes out his field dressing, cuts away the shirt, and places the dressing over the three wounds. The soldier's dry lips move,* PAUL *leans over to listen, then reaches for his water bottle. It is empty, pierced by a bullet. He turns and goes down toward the water.*

SCENE 39-G

Longer view in shell hole. PAUL *goes to the bottom of the hole and scoops up some water in his hands, returns to the Frenchman who gulps it down.* PAUL *returns for more. As he starts down the third time,*

Fade out.

SCENE 40-G

Int. PAUL's *shell hole. Night. Full view fade in. There is a light bombardment. Now and then the rapid fire of machine guns can be heard. Occasional star shells light up the scene.* PAUL *is on the opposite side of the shell hole, as far away from the dying man as he can get. The Frenchman groans, gasps, gurglings can be heard between the sounds of exploding shells. A star shell lights up the scene, casting weird, flickering shadows over the shell hole.*

SCENE 41-G

Close-up of the French soldier. He is near death. His breath comes in gasps. He groans and gurgles.

SCENE 42-G

Close-up of PAUL. *A slightly demented look is in his eyes. His face muscles twitch. The dying man is driving all reason from him. The gasping of the man roars in his ears.* PAUL *clasps his hands over them. To him the sounds seem louder. He snatches his hands away and cries out.*

PAUL. Stop that! You'll have to stop that! I can bear the rest of it, but I can't listen to that!

He makes a movement to get up, then sinks back again. He looks wildly for a way of escape. With a quick movement, PAUL *draws his dagger, looks toward the Frenchman, then with a gesture of revulsion throws it away. He turns away. He can look at the man no longer. In a frenzy he cries out:*

PAUL. Why do you take so long dying? You're going to die anyway.

He turns quickly toward the soldier:

No—no—I didn't mean that—you won't die—they're only little wounds—you'll get home—you'll be all right. You'll get home long before I will.

In his terrible anxiety to reassure the man he crawls quickly out of the scene.

SCENE 43-G

Close-up at the Frenchman. PAUL *crawls quickly into the scene. Death gleams in the man's eyes. He tries to speak, his throat is dry.* PAUL *goes out toward the water, and is back again instantly with his cupped hands full. He pours it down the man's throat, then goes back for more. The man gurgles, collapses. He is dead.* PAUL *returns and starts to give him the water, stops and listens for his breathing, then pours the water out of his hand. For a moment there is a complete silence.* PAUL *sinks down beside the dead man. Then again the rapid fire of machine guns and the heavier sounds of explosions are heard.* PAUL *turns to look at the soldier, and in* PAUL's *face all the rage, terror, hatred has gone. He commences to talk, low, intensely, pathetically:*

PAUL. I'm sorry I had to do it. I didn't mean it when I said I wished you were dead—I didn't want to kill you! I'm not a murderer—I'm not a murderer—

His voice breaks. He stares at the man, feeling that he must do something. He moves closer, props the man up again so that he lies comfortably, then closes the man's eyes. Then a desire to escape sweeps over him again. He backs out of the scene.

SCENE 44-G

Near edge of shell hole. PAUL *backs into the scene, still looking at the man, then turns and crawls to the top of the hole. He takes off his helmet and holds it up over the edge.*

SCENE 45-G

Ext. German trenches. Close view. A German machine gunner is looking toward the camera, out over the shell holes. He catches sight of something and begins to fire.

SCENE 46-G

PAUL's *shell hole. Close view.*

The rapid fire of the machine gun is heard.

The helmet is knocked out of PAUL's *hand and rolls away over the ground.* PAUL *ducks down a little lower. Again the demented expression shows in his face. He looks toward the Frenchman as a star shell lights up the scene.*

SCENE 47-G

Close-up of the French soldier. His head has fallen back. The eerie light of the star shell casts flickering shadows over his white face. His open eyes are turned toward PAUL.

SCENE 48-G

Close-up of PAUL. *The eyes of the Frenchman seem to accuse him. He stares at them, fascinated. He tries to turn away, but always looks back. In growing hysteria he cries out:*

PAUL. You know I can't run away, that's why you accuse me! I tell you I didn't want to kill you! I tried to keep you alive! If you jumped in here again I wouldn't do it. You see—when you jumped in here, you were my enemy—I thought of your hand-grenades, of your bay-

onet, of your rifle—and I was afraid of you! But you're just a man like me—and I killed you. Forgive me, comrade. If you have just a little breath left, say that for me—say you forgive me! No, no, you're dead! You can't tell me that! Dead! If you had only run two yards further to the left I wouldn't have killed you—you'd be alive now. Why don't they teach us in training school that you're just poor devils like us—and your mothers are just as anxious for you and you have the same fear of death and the same dying and the same agony!

(Tears come into his eyes)

Only you're better off than I am—you're through—they can't do any more to you now. You're better off—I've got to go on and kill—or be killed—and if I die, I'll have to die the way you did—and if I live, I'll have to remember the way you died—and you'll follow me and I'll have to think about you—because it was me that killed you! Oh, God! Why did they do this to us? We only wanted to live—you and I—why should they send us out to fight each other? Why should we be left all alone here—all alone with death? How could you be my enemy? If we threw away these rifles and these uniforms you could be my brother just like Kat and Albert. Take twenty years of my life—comrade, and stand up—take more—more—

Suddenly he goes toward the dead man.

SCENE 49-G

Close-up at French soldier. PAUL *enters and kneels beside him. Tears are streaming down his face. In great agitation he pours out more words:*

PAUL. You'll have to forgive me, comrade. I'll do all I can. I'll write to your parents—I'll write to—

PAUL *checks himself—maybe he is married—maybe he has children? With trembling hands he reaches into the man's tunic. He finds a pocket-book and starts to open it. Then fear grips him. If he opens it and he will see the man's name, and then he will never be able to forget him.*

PAUL. I can't do it—I can't—if I don't know who you are, I may be able to forget you—time will wipe out the memory of you—but if I learn your name it will always stand before me—accusing me—

He sways back and forth uncertainly—he tries to put the book back, but some emotion restrains him. The book falls from his hands. Some snapshots and letters fall out of it. PAUL *picks them up, one by one and looks at them. As he does so, sobs shake his body. Incoherently he starts to speak again:*

PAUL. I'll write to your wife—I'll write to her—she must hear it from me! I promise you she shall not want for anything—I will tell her everything I have told you—I will help her—and your parents too—only forgive me! Forgive me!

His head drops, he slides to the ground. Sobs rack his body. Slowly the sobbing ceases. He breathes regularly—he sleeps.

Fade out slowly.

SCENE 50-G

Fade in. Close view in shell hole. Night. PAUL *stirs in his sleep, looks around confusedly. He listens. The barrage has lifted. The machine guns have stopped firing—there is a deathlike silence. He is calmer now and in a daze looks at the French soldier, then away toward the German lines. Quickly he backs away, then crawls to the top of the shell hole.*

The camera follows him. He looks over the edge then crawls out of the scene.

SCENE 51-G

Ext. shell hole. PAUL *is worming his way carefully toward the German lines. A rocket goes up, lighting up the scene.* PAUL *is instantly quiet.*

SCENE 52-G

Ext. German trenches. Close view. The light from the rocket lights up the scene. An observer is seen dozing in his place, trying to keep his eyes open. Suddenly, to wake himself, he rises, stamps his feet and warms his arms in the Russian fashion. A pile of grenades lie at his feet. The light from the star shell fades out. The OBSERVER *hears a slight sound in No Man's Land and stands up to look. His attention is instantly riveted. He stoops for a grenade and stands holding it, looking out over the field.*

SCENE 53-G

Ext. shell holes. PAUL *is creeping slowly forward through the darkness. Only the dim outline of his body can be seen. His boots, scraping over the ground make a slight noise.*

SCENE 54-G

Ext. German French close-up of observer. Shooting over the OBSERVER's *shoulder, toward the shell holes.* PAUL *cannot be seen but the*

slight sound of his boots scraping over the earth can be heard

Suddenly the OBSERVER *throws the grenade.*

There is an explosion and a cry in the distance

KAT *and* LEER *run into the scene.*

KAT (*to* OBSERVER). What's the idea? Do you want to start things popping 'round here?

Three or four rifles crack in the distance.

KAT. There they go now! Fool! When they're asleep over there, let them sleep!
THE OBSERVER. I saw someone out there!
KAT. Where?
THE OBSERVER. Listen! I can hear him.
KAT (*listening*). It's one of our own.
LEER. Sure it is.
OBSERVER. Well, how could I—I?

KAT *leaves him and peers over the trench.* KAT *crawls over the edge of the trench followed by* LEER.

SCENE 55-G

Still night in No Man's Land. There is a little sporadic firing in the distance. KAT *and* LEER *are crawling toward* PAUL, *who is lying face downward. As they reach him,* KAT *whispers:*

KAT. Where's it got you?
PAUL. I don't know—
KAT. Take hold under his shoulder, Leer, we'll drag him back.

KAT *turns* PAUL *over slightly to get hold under his arm and sees his face.* PAUL *recognizes* KAT:

PAUL. Hello, Kat.
LEER. It's Paul!
KAT. It's a good job we came out here.

A rifle cracks

KAT *and* LEER *lie still for a moment, then begin to drag* PAUL.

KAT. Come on now—

They exit out of the scene.

Dissolve to:

SCENE 56-G

Int. Red Cross dugout. Night.

Dissolve in:

KAT *and* LEER *bring in* PAUL. ALBERT *who is lying on a stretcher, calls out:*

ALBERT. Paul, where did they get you?

PAUL *looks at* ALBERT, *surprised at seeing him here.*

PAUL. Right side—and you?
ALBERT. Left leg—above the knee.
KAT. Cut out the talk—both of you!

(He turns to Paul)

You've lost enough blood.

As a CORPORAL *commences removing* PAUL'S *clothes, Fade out:*

SCENE 57-G

Int. Red Cross dugout. Day.

Fade in: KAT *enters and goes to* PAUL *and* ALBERT.

KAT. Cheer up you fellows, they'll be sending you back within an hour.

ALBERT *seems relieved—* PAUL *continues staring straight before him, without changing expression.* KAT *watches him a moment then asks:*

KAT. Did you get any sleep, Paul?
PAUL. No! *(He looks up at Kat)* Kat, something terrible happened yesterday—I can't get it out of my mind—I stabbed a man—with my hands—stabbed him.
KAT. I know how it is, the first time. Never mind—The stretcher bearers will find him.
PAUL. He's dead, Kat—I watched him die!

All the horror of the death he watched shows in PAUL'S *eyes. He continues:*

PAUL. I killed him! I've got to send money—I promised it—I promised I'd send money—
KAT. What for?

PAUL'S *hysteria rises:*

PAUL. I've got to take care of his wife—and his parents—I killed him....
KAT. Don't be foolish, Paul. We've all had to kill people—we can't help it. That's what we're here for to kill or get killed. Look there for instance—

KAT *turns toward the door.* PAUL *follows the direction of* KAT'S *motion.*

SCENE 58-G

Ext. trench, through doorway. A SNIPER *is standing on the fire-step and looking over the parapet through telescopic sights. He sees someone out across the shell holes, aims and fires.*

(A distant cry is heard)

The SNIPER *turns around proudly and says to a man beside him:*

THE SNIPER. That's found a billet! Did you see how he leapt in the air?

SCENE 59-G

Int. Red Cross dugout. Close-up PAUL *and* KAT. PAUL *and* KAT *in the foreground. The* SNIPER *can be seen through the entrance beyond them.* KAT *turns to* PAUL:

KAT. What do you say to that?

(PAUL *nods)*

He's scored three hits today—if he keeps that up, he'll have a decoration for his buttonhole by this evening.
ALBERT. *(Interrupting)* Or be made Sergeant-Major.

For a while PAUL *is quiet.* KAT *sits down beside him. The horror dies out of* PAUL'S *eyes. The* LANCE CORPORAL *finishes bandaging his wounds and exits.* PAUL *turns to* KAT, *calm now:*

PAUL. I could never do it.
KAT. Just the same, it's very good for you to see it just now.
ALBERT. You don't need to lose any more sleep over your affair.
PAUL. It must have been because I had to be there with him so long—after all, war is war.

KAT *nods. Out through the entrance the* SNIPER *is aiming the rifle. It cracks out sharp and dry.*

Fade out:

SEQUENCE "H"

SCENE 1-H

Long shot of Red Cross train in motion. Night.

Dissolve to:

SCENE 2-H

Long shot hospital. Ambulances come up to front door.

SCENE 3-H

Close shot of stretchers full of wounded. Waiting to get in hospital. In the group are ALBERT *and* PAUL. *General noises of routine work are heard.*

ORDERLY *(in door)*. One more now.
NURSE. That one's next.

They take stretcher inside. Camera trucks up closer to PAUL *and* ALBERT.

ALBERT. Paul—
PAUL. Yes,
ALBERT. I've decided. I'm not going to be crippled. If they take my leg off, I'm going to croak myself. That's all.
SOLDIER. *(Lying near him)* Then stay awake, boy. Don't let 'em chloroform you, 'cause they'll put you on the chopping block and whack it off sure. That's easier than patching it up.
ALBERT. Paul—
PAUL. Yes, Albert—
ALBERT. How do you feel?
PAUL. My wounds burn terribly. Why don't they take us in?
SOLDIER. They ain't got any room. They have to wait 'till somebody dies.

A SERGEANT *passes near.*

ALBERT. Sergeant—

The SERGEANT *comes up to him.*

Here's a couple of cigars with belly bands—
SERGEANT. *(Smells of them)* Got any more like that?
ALBERT. Yes, a lot of them. And, my friend here has a handful, too—so, if you'll just see that we get put near each other when we get into the hospital, we'll give 'em to you.
SERGEANT. Sure, I'll take care of you.

Dissolve to:

SCENE 4-H

Long shot of interior hospital. SISTERS *are working there with* ORDERLIES. *They make up a couple of cots as* ALBERT *and* PAUL *are wheeled in on the trollies.*

SCENE 5-H

Close shot of PAUL *being lifted into cot.* SISTER LIBERTINE *seems alarmed about his condition and whispers to* ORDERLY *who nods.*

SCENE 6-H

Another angle showing ALBERT.

ALBERT. Sister—
SISTER L. In just a minute.

ORDERLY *comes up and gives* PAUL *hypodermic. Then she turns to* ALBERT.

ALBERT. Will you have a doctor see my leg right away?
SISTER. I'm sorry—you'll have to wait 'till morning.
ALBERT *(desperately).* Till morning?

SISTER. All the surgeons are busy now.
ALBERT. But, I may lose my leg.
SISTER. We're doing the best we can. There are many worse cases here than yours.

She makes him comfortable.

SCENE 7-H

A longer angle.

As the camera follows the doctor. We see an old lady sitting beside a cot, watching continuously a boy who lies there with half-closed eyes. SISTER LIBERTINE *approaches.*

SCENE 9-H

Close shot of the same.

SISTER. Your time's up.
LADY. Already?
SISTER. Yes. I'm sorry.

The old lady rises and goes. A man is heard singing a hymn.

SCENE 9-H

An angle taking in ALBERT. *A doctor passes.*

ALBERT. Doctor—

The doctor goes on without looking.

SCENE 10-H

Close up of the SOLDIER *singing. The* SOLDIER, *with a bandage around his head, is wildly singing a hymn. He stops—his mouth stays open—he gurgles and he's still.* ORDERLIES *enter, put his clothes on the trolley and wheel him out. As they exit, another trolley brings in a new occupant for the bed.*

SCENE 11-H

Medium shot of WACHTER. *The boy beside whose bed the old lady had been sitting. The* SISTER *leads a* DOCTOR *up to him.* DOCTOR *approaches, looks him over, and motions to the* ORDERLIES *to take him out.*

SCENE 12-H

Closer shot of PAUL *and* HAMMACHER *and a man by cot.*

HAMMACHER. See that?
PAUL. What's the matter?
HAMMACHER. Look!

SCENE 13-H

Shot of FRANZ WACHTER *being lifted to trolley. Camera pans to where* SISTER *is taking tunic from wall and follows her as she comes back and puts it across the man's knees. She picks up his other possessions and follows as they wheel him out. Another man is wheeled in and the nurses work at making the bed.*

SCENE 14-H

Closer shot of HAMMACHER *and* PAUL.

HAMMACHER. You've seen the last of him.

PAUL. How do you know?

HAMMACHER. They're taking him to the dying room.

PAUL. To what?

HAMMACHER. You'll never lay eyes on him again.

PAUL. Where they taking him?

HAMMACHER. The dying room.

PAUL. What's that?

HAMMACHER. When you're going to kick the bucket, they take you out of the way so's they can use the bed. They got a room down the end of the building—it's right next to where they keep the coffins and it saves a lot of trouble. We call it the dying room.

PAUL. *(Worked up over the idea)* But suppose you get well—

HAMMACHER. You never do.

PAUL. You might.

HAMMACHER. When they take you for that little ride I guess it's like telling you you're going to die and you do. You're too weak to care, anyhow. I've seen a lot of them wheeled out there and nobody's ever come back yet.

PAUL. They'll never get me.

SCENE 15-H

Another angle of ALBERT.

ALBERT *(Yelling)*. Can't I get a doctor? Can't I get a doctor?

PAUL. Don't do that, Albert.

ALBERT. My leg hurts.

PAUL. My side hurts. Doesn't do any good to yell about it.

ALBERT. I want a doctor.

The SERGEANT *approaches.*

SERGEANT. What's the matter, here?

ALBERT. Can't we get looked after?

SERGEANT. How'd you make out with those cigars?

ALBERT. They're under my pillow—but my leg's burning up—it's on fire.

SERGEANT. All right, I'm looking after you. If you just don't make so much noise. You two boys will be next.

ALBERT. *(Smiles back)* Oh!

SCENE 16-H

Close-up of SERGEANT'S *hand taking cigars from under* ALBERT'S *pillow.*

SCENE 17-H

Long shot of room. DOCTOR *and* ORDERLIES *approach.*

Fade out.

SCENE 18-H

Fade in:

Int. long corridor. Dawn. The faint light of dawn is coming through the windows. SISTER LIBERTINE, *with her head resting on her arms, is asleep at the desk in the foreground. Another* SISTER *enters, just coming on duty.* SISTER LIBERTINE *raises her head and smiles wanly as she says:*

THE SISTER. How has it been, Sister Libertine?

SISTER LIBERTINE. Pretty bad. Seven died in the wards. It's hard on the others when that happens.

In the background, other SISTERS *carrying prayer books, enter and open all doors to wards as they come toward the camera.* SISTER LIBERTINE *rises, picks up her Bible and says:*

SISTER LIBERTINE. I don't think I'll be much good at matins this morning.

She joins the other sisters who go through a doorway near the foreground.

SCENE 19-H

Int. small chapel in hospital. The SISTERS *enter, take their places and commence devotion, intoning the Litany.*

Intonation of the Litany.

SCENE 20-H

Int. ward close-up PAUL, ALBERT *and* HAMMACHER. *They are all sleeping lightly.*

The intonation of the Litany can be heard.

They all stir restlessly. PAUL *and* HAMMACHER *awaken first.*

PAUL. What's that?

HAMMACHER. Morning devotion. They always open the doors so we can get our share.

PAUL. Why should they wake everybody up? Be quiet out there.

SCENE 21-H

Longer view. Toward door. The group is in the foreground. A SISTER *appears in the doorway.*

HAMMACHER. Shut the door, will you, Sister?

THE SISTER. We're saying prayers—that is why the door is open.

PAUL. We want to sleep.

THE SISTER. *(Smiling).* Prayer is better than sleep—

ALBERT. *(Half awake)* I bet they cut it off.

PAUL. Now you see you've waked him— Shut the door!

SCENE 22-H

Close view of SISTER. *She is disconcerted, but answers sweetly:*

THE SISTER. But we are saying prayers for you, too.

PAUL. Shut the door, anyway!

The SISTER *disappears, smiling, leaving the door open.*

The Litany continues

PAUL *turns to* HAMMACHER:

PAUL. *(Coldly)* If you don't shut it, I'm going to let something fly! Do you hear? All right.

A bottle crashes up against the door. Singing stops. A swarm of SISTERS *appear in the doorway.*

THE SISTERS, *(In concert)* Oh! Oh! Oh! Oh! Boys! And when we're praying for you, too!

SCENE 23-H

Shot of boys—reverse angle.

PAUL & HAMMACHER. Shut the door! Shut the door!

SISTER. Here's the Inspector.

SCENE 24-H

Med. shot of doorway. The INSPECTOR *has joined the group of* SISTERS.

INSPECTOR. What's the matter?

ANOTHER SISTER. He threw a bottle.

INSPECTOR *starts forward.*

SCENE 25-H

Reverse angle. INSPECTOR *walks among the cots.*

INSPECTOR. What's the idea?

They remain quiet.

SCENE 26-H

Close-up group.

INSPECTOR. You fellows want to spend the rest of your time locked up? Who threw that bottle?

PAUL *is just about to speak but* HAMMACHER *gets ahead of him.*

HAMMACHER. I did.

Everybody looks at him. The INSPECTOR *makes a gesture of hopeless resignation and exits.*

SCENE 27-H

Long shot of INSPECTOR. *Going out door, shrugging shoulders helplessly.* SISTER *shuts door.*

SCENE 28-H

Close shot of PAUL, ALBERT *and* HAMMACHER. PAUL *looks at* HAMMACHER, *puzzled.*

PAUL. What made you say you did it?

HAMMACHER. They can't do anything to me—

PAUL. Why not?

HAMMACHER. I've got a shooting license.

PAUL. What do you mean?

HAMMACHER. Well, I got a crack in the head and they gave me a certificate to tell the world I was not responsible for my actions. Believe me, ever since then I've had a grand time.

SCENE 29-H

Close-up of ALBERT. *He tries to bend down to see if his leg is cut off, but is unable to move.*

ALBERT. Paul!

SCENE 30-H

Med. shot from across PAUL'S *cot toward* ALBERT.

PAUL. Yes? What is it, Albert?

ALBERT. They amputated, didn't they?

PAUL. No. You're imagining things.

ALBERT. It's just like Kemmerich said. My foot hurts—the toes hurt—and it's on that leg.

PAUL. Why don't you just forget it and go to sleep.

His eye catches someone approaching. He holds very still.

SCENE 31-H

Long shot front row showing PAUL. *Lady returning to her cot.* HAMMACHER *sees her and looks at the others. They watch her pityingly.*

SCENE 32-H

Close shot of old lady. She approaches cot. She looks and sees a strange face. For a moment she thinks her boy has been moved. She turns and looks at the other cots. Then she realizes. Her head bows, then she looks up. She goes.

SCENE 33-H

Close shot of SISTER LIBERTINE *standing in doorway. She sees the old lady and her face shows the pity she feels. Other* SISTERS *can be seen walking through hall.* SISTER LIBERTINE *walks toward the camera.*

SCENE 34-H

Another angle showing SISTER LIBERTINE *passing among the cots.*

SCENE 35-H

Closer shot taking in ALBERT.

ALBERT. Sister!
SISTER LIBERTINE. Yes?

(She comes to him)

ALBERT. I haven't seen myself—for a long while. Could you let me have a mirror?

SCENE 36-H

Closer shot of PAUL *as he lies with his face away from* ALBERT. *He registers surprise at what he has just heard and lies very still and alert. In the background, over his bed, we see* SISTER LIBERTINE *handing* ALBERT *the mirror.* PAUL *rolls over from time to time to watch* ALBERT.

SCENE 37-H

Close shot of ALBERT. ALBERT *taking the mirror.*

ALBERT. Thank you.

He looks at himself, the SISTER *turns to other duties. He glances around to see that she is gone and then tilts the mirror up to see if his leg has been amputated.*

SCENE 38-H

Med. with mirror showing that his leg is not under the covers.

SCENE 39-H

Close shot of ALBERT. *With a look of absolute despair, he turns the mirror with the jagged edge toward his throat and is about to make a slash at himself.*

SCENE 40-H

Med. shot from across PAUL'S *bed.*

PAUL. Albert!

He reaches over half out of his cot and grabs ALBERT'S *wrist.*

ALBERT. I don't want to live. I told you. I don't want to—let me go.
PAUL. Stop him! Albert! Don't!
HAMMACHER. What's the matter?
VOICES OFF SCENE. He's trying to kill himself!
VOICES OFF SCENE. What'd he do?
VOICES OFF SCENE. Where's the Sister?

SISTER LIBERTINE *has run to* ALBERT'S *cot and with the help of an* ORDERLY *takes the mirror away from him. While the confusion continues,* ALBERT *protests over and over that he wants to die. She turns gently to* PAUL *and helps him to get covered up again.*

SISTER. You shouldn't have moved like that. Get back, quickly!

Fade out.

SCENE 41-H

Fade in: Night.

Close-up of a bell ringing.

SCENE 42-H

Int. long view of hospital corridor. Night. The corridor is dimly lighted. The desk, in the foreground, is deserted. In the far background an orderly crosses. A bell near the desk rings often and long.

·SCENE 43-H

Close-up of a hand on bell. It can be heard ringing far off. Camera pulls back and shows PAUL *lying twisted in bed. He is holding his side with the other hand. He takes it away and it is bloody.*

SCENE 44-H

Another angle taking in ALBERT *and* PAUL.

HAMMERICH. Is that you ringing Paul?
PAUL. Yes.
HAMMERICH. Something gone wrong?
PAUL. I think I have a hemorrhage—and I've been ringing forever and nobody comes.
HAMMERICH. They're all asleep I guess, they had a terrible night. I'll yell.

(Shouts)

Hey, somebody, hey,

(Then quietly)

Are you sure you're bleeding?
PAUL. Yeah—the bandage has been wet for a long time.
VOICE. What's the idea, can't you let anybody sleep?
2D VOICE. The fellow's bleeding.
ALBERT. Is it you, Paul?

PAUL *looks around and hears sounds of other men who are awake. He calls out:*

PAUL. Can anybody make a light?
HAMMERACH. Some of you fellows by the door.
VOICE. Reach over can't you, Bill?

There is quite a general commotion.

SCENE 45-H

Close shot of door.

SISTER LIBERTINE. What is it?

SCENE 46-H

Longer shot taking in PAUL *and door.*

PAUL. I'm bleeding.

SISTER LIBERTINE *hurries to him, puts her hand on* PAUL's *bandages, then hurries out, her voice coming back to them:*

SISTER LIBERTINE'S VOICE. Why didn't somebody call me?

PAUL. I've been ringing half the night—confound it—I knew something was wrong—I've been ringing.

SISTER. *(Coldly)* Doctor. At once, please.

She re-enters with DOCTOR *and sleepy* ORDERLIES.

Dissolve to:

SCENE 47-H

A series of trick shots.

To indicate a hectic night operation. Close-up of ether can.

Inserts:

Close-up of bandages.

Close-up of hands holding PAUL *down.*

Close-up faces in masks.

Then a general topsy-turvy mix-up of all these things going in and out of focus.

Dissolve to:

SCENE 48-H

Long shot. Of the hospital ward with PAUL *lying in the foreground white and still. It is now morning. The* SISTERS *can be heard singing as before, but more faintly. The* DOCTOR *enters in the background and goes past the cots looking over the occupants. He approaches* PAUL *and pauses. He bends over to examine him more closely.*

SCENE 49-H

Close-up of PAUL. *He seems to have little life left.*

SCENE 50-H

Medium shot of the same. The DOCTOR *turns and gestures to the* ORDERLIES *to take him out.*

SCENE 51-H

Shot from above. Showing ORDERLIES *starting to lift* PAUL *out of bed.* PAUL *opens his eyes.*

PAUL. What are you doing?

ORDERLY. Just keep quiet, son.

PAUL. Where are we going? Sister, what are they doing?

SCENE 52-H

A side angle.

SISTER. Quiet.

PAUL. Where we going?

SISTER. We're going to change your bandages. That's all. Now lie still.

PAUL *sinks back and then turns his head to watch* SISTER LIBERTINE *as she walks toward wall.*

SCENE 53-H

Close shot of SISTER LIBERTINE. *Taking tunic from wall.*

SCENE 54-H

Reverse angle of PAUL.

PAUL. No.

ORDERLY. Lie still now.

PAUL. *(Becoming frantic)* No. I know what you're going to do.

ORDERLY. Quiet.

PAUL. You're taking me to the dying room. But I'm not going to die. I'm not going to die. I want to stay here.

SISTER. We're going to the bandaging ward.

PAUL. Then what do you want my tunic for? I know I've seen you take the others. I know.

DOCTOR. *(Brusquely)* Take him out.

PAUL. All right. I'll come back. I'll fool you. I don't want to die. I won't die. I won't die.

They take him out.

Fade out.

SCENE 55-H

Med. shot day. HAMMACHER, *dressed to leave hospital, stands beside* ALBERT's *cot.*

ALBERT. I guess I'd rather be alive with one leg, than not to be alive at all. I thought I wouldn't, but here I am.

HAMMACHER. Sure, sure, you'll get used to the idea. Say, suppose you was like me and likely to hit your best friend over the head with a bottle without knowing what you was doing. That's what you call real trouble.

ALBERT. Maybe you're all over it now.

HAMMACHER. Well, I feel pretty good. Hope you get out soon.

ALBERT. Yes, I feel pretty good too— *(lowers voice)* I've been all right for a week— only I don't want to go 'till I find what happened to Paul.

HAMMACHER. Now what's the use of kidding yourself—when they go in there they don't come back, that's all.

PAUL. *(Voice heard)* Albert.

SCENE 56-H

Med. shot of PAUL *riding in on trolley. Beaming with triumph.*

PAUL. Here I am. I told you I'd come back. I showed the damn doctor. They couldn't kill me. I didn't let them. I wouldn't die.

SCENE 57-H

A closer angle of PAUL *is wheeled up.*

ALBERT. *(In triumph at* HAMMACHER*)* He wouldn't come back, huh? He wouldn't come back.

HAMMACHER. *(To* PAUL*)* Glad to see you, kid.

PAUL. *(To orderly)* No, over here is where I live.

They good-naturedly wheel a cot next to ALBERT.

ALBERT. And, Paul, your leave came just after they took you away. You can go back home now.

PAUL. And you're all right, Albert?

ALBERT. Sure—I'm all right, but I won't need Kemmerich's boots any more, so you can have them.

Fade out.

SEQUENCE "I"

SCENE 1-I

Ext. close-up wheels and steps of European train. Day. Fade in. The wheels slow down and stop. The legs and feet of soldiers crowd off and rush away. KEMMERICH'S *boots come into view, pause, then go on.*

Dissolve into:

SCENE 2-I

Ext. street. Close-up boots. Moving scene. The boots are walking along. The camera pulls back to a full view of PAUL. *He is walking along, looking about reminiscently, his face lighting up as he recognizes familiar places. Dogs trot along the street. People whom he passes, and others standing in doorways, follow him with their gaze as he walks eagerly along, heavy laden, with his pack, rifle and full equipment.*

Dissolve to:

SCENE 3-I

Ext. front of PAUL'S *home. Day.* PAUL *enters and stops. His eyes wander quickly over the house, then he half runs up to the door, lifts the latch, and starts in.*

SCENE 4-I

Int. lower hall of PAUL'S *home. Toward exterior door.* PAUL *eagerly comes thru the door, closes it, and comes toward the camera. He stops and deeply breathes the familiar odors. Suddenly, as he fully realizes he is home, a flood of emotions sweep through him. His eyes dim with tears. He slowly goes past the camera.*

SCENE 5-I

Int. hallway, stairs to upper landing. PAUL *enters and starts slowly up the stairs, which creak as he goes up. He stops as he hears a door open on the upper landing. His sister,* ERNA, *comes to the upper railing and looks down, her eyes light up as she recognizes him.*

ERNA. Paul! Paul—

PAUL *doesn't look up. He lowers his head and takes off his helmet. After a moment he looks up.* ERNA *runs off.* PAUL *starts up again but stops as he hears a door opening and his sister's voice calling:*

ERNA'S VOICE. Mother, Mother, Paul's here!

SCENE 6-I

Close-up PAUL. *The sound of his sister's voice calling to his mother has made him powerless to move.*

He sways on his feet. His hands grip the rifle, his teeth clench. Against his will, tears stream down his face. He supports himself against the butt of his rifle and tries to call out, to laugh, to speak, but no words come. He stands there paralyzed, miserable and helpless to move.

SCENE 7-I

Longer view on stairs. ERNA *comes running down the stairs and starts to take* PAUL *in her arms but stops as she sees he is crying. Amazed she asks:*

ERNA. What's the matter, Paul?

PAUL. *(Shaking his head helplessly and trying to smile)* Nothing.

(They stare at each other for a moment, unable to believe this moment has really come)

I'm glad to be here, that's all.

He pulls himself together and goes up the stairs, his pack bumping against the banisters. ERNA *looks after him, then follows.*

SCENE 8-I

Upper landing, head of stairs. PAUL *comes up and leans his rifle in a corner. As he puts his pack and other equipment against the wall,* ERNA *enters and stands looking at him.*

PAUL'S MOTHER'S VOICE. Paul!

They both turn and look in the direction from which the voice came, the bedroom.

PAUL. Is she in bed?
ERNA. *(Nods)* She's ill.

PAUL *hesitantly goes toward the bedroom,* ERNA *following.*

SCENE 9-I

Int. bedroom, PAUL'S MOTHER'S. *At one side are windows, thru which comes a low light, flooding the bed. Near the bed is the door to the hall.* PAUL'S *mother is on the bed, trying to turn her head so as to see the door.* PAUL *and* ERNA *enter. She stops in the doorway while* PAUL *comes slowly to the bed and stands there. The upper part of his body in shadow. After a time he says:*

PAUL. Here I am, Mother.

SCENE 10-I

Close-up PAUL *and his* MOTHER. *She is anxiously searching his face. Fearfully she asks:*

PAUL'S MOTHER. Are you wounded?

After a moment's hesitation PAUL *answers:*

PAUL. No, Mother, I've got leave.

She relaxes, relieved, and reaches out her hand for his. PAUL *holds it. Tears of happiness run down her cheeks. She tries to make light of them:*

PAUL'S MOTHER. Here I lie now and cry instead of being glad.

She turns toward ERNA.

MOTHER. Erna, get down that jar of cranberries—

SCENE 11-I

Longer view, including ERNA. PAUL'S *mother turns back to him.*

PAUL'S MOTHER. You still like them, don't you Paul?
PAUL. Yes, Mother, I haven't had any for a long time.

ERNA *is smiling now—she exclaims:*

ERNA. We might almost have known you were coming—here I am making your favorite dish, potato-cakes.

She breaks off her speech. The mention of potato-cakes reminds her that they may be burning.

ERNA. They may be burning!

She dashes away toward the kitchen. PAUL *turns back to his mother as she says:*

PAUL'S MOTHER. Sit here beside me.

He pulls a chair closer and sits beside the bed.

SCENE 12-I

Close-up PAUL *and* MOTHER. *She takes his hand again and he can not help notice how white and sickly they are compared to his. Her eyes never leave his face. She murmurs softly:*

PAUL'S MOTHER. My Paul. My baby.

His grip tightens on her hand. He is happy but can say nothing. Everything he has wished for has happened. He has returned safely and now sits here beside his mother. But he can not feel at home—a sense of strangeness will not leave him. He feels a barrier standing between himself and his home. He looks around vaguely, struggling to feel he belongs here. The light has died from his mother's face—she senses his feelings and expresses them.

PAUL'S MOTHER. What's the matter, Paul? Has it been so long that we're strangers?

He attempts to shake off his feelings. He smiles and squeezes her hand again as he says:

PAUL. I've got some little presents for you, Mother.

He rises quickly and goes out.

SCENE 13-I

Int. hall, top of stairs. PAUL *enters and stops beside his pack. He turns and looks back toward the bedroom. He controls his emotions, picks up his pack and goes back toward his* MOTHER'S *room.*

SCENE 14-I

Int. MOTHER'S *bedroom.* PAUL *enters and starts to spread out the provisions he has in the pack—a whole Edam cheese, two loaves of* bread, three-quarters of a pound of butter, two tins of liver-sausage, a pound of dripping and a little bag of rice. He turns to his mother and says:

PAUL. I suppose you can make some use of these.

PAUL'S MOTHER. Paul, you've been starving yourself!

PAUL. Don't you believe it—These were extra.

He pauses.

PAUL. Is it pretty hard to get food here?

PAUL'S MOTHER. Yes, there isn't much. Do they give the soldiers plenty to eat?

PAUL smiles.

PAUL. We have enough.

He feels easier now that the tension is broken, and sits beside the bed again.

SCENE 15-I

Close-up PAUL and MOTHER. Suddenly fear for him grips her. She seizes his hand and asks falteringly:

PAUL'S MOTHER. Was it very bad out there, PAUL?

Into PAUL's eyes flashes all the horror he has seen and suffered—the fields of dead and dying—the lines of men mowed down—the pain and suffering of hospitals. She could never realize it—she must not know of it. He shakes his head.

PAUL. No, Mother, not so very. There's always a lot of us together, so it isn't so bad.

But she is not convinced—she continues anxiously:

MOTHER. You sure?

PAUL. Of course, I'm sure.

PAUL'S MOTHER. The Muller boy said it was terrible out there.

PAUL. Is Muller here now?

PAUL'S MOTHER. Yes, he was wounded.

PAUL. I know.

PAUL'S MOTHER. And he says that gas and all these new things are terrible.

PAUL smiles grimly:

PAUL. That's just talk. What about me? Ever see me looking better?

She smiles relieved, and believes him.

SCENE 16-I

Longer view, including door. ERNA enters and comes down to the bed.

ERNA. Hadn't I better go and tell father that Paul's home? If Paul could watch the things on the stove—

MOTHER. No, no, child—I'm getting up.

PAUL rises;

PAUL. I have to report to the District Commandent before six. I'll have to go before dinner.

MOTHER. Run along now and let me put my things on.

The mother starts to push back the covers. ERNA and PAUL go out.

Dissolve to:

SCENE 17-I

Ext. Street and front of PAUL's home. Day. PAUL comes out of the house and toward the camera.

SCENE 18-I

Ext. corner of street. Reverse angle. As PAUL is going toward the corner, a street car starts around it.

SCENE 19-I

Close-up wheels of street car. They are turning the corner and make a sound similar to that of a large shell approaching.

SCENE 20-I

Ext. street near corner. Close-up PAUL. Akeley shot. As he hears the screech of the wheels he throws himself to the pavement. The screeching of the car wheels stop. PAUL looks up, confused and bewildered, then sees where he is. He rises quickly and looks around, embarrassed, and hurries around the corner.

SCENE 21-I

Ext. around corner of street. PAUL hurries around the corner and passes a German MAJOR without seeing him. The MAJOR calls out loudly:

THE MAJOR. Hey, you!

PAUL stops.

THE MAJOR. Can't you salute?

PAUL. Sorry, Major, I didn't notice you.

THE MAJOR is furious. He roars:

THE MAJOR. Don't you know how to address an officer?

PAUL restrains an impulse to crash his fist into the MAJOR's fat face. He snaps to attention, clicking his heels:

PAUL. I did not see you, Herr Major.

THE MAJOR. Then keep your eyes open! What is your name?

PAUL. Paul Baumer.

THE MAJOR. What regiment?

PAUL. Fourth Regiment, Second Company.

THE MAJOR *continues to torment* PAUL, *who still stands at attention:*

THE MAJOR. Where are they?

PAUL. Between Langemark and Bixschoote.

THE MAJOR *is stupefied:*

THE MAJOR. Eh?

PAUL. I'm just arrived on leave.

THE MAJOR *becomes more furious than before:*

THE MAJOR. I see you think you can bring your front line manners here, huh? Well, we don't stand for that sort of thing here. We have discipline here!

He stares at PAUL, *then continues:*

THE MAJOR. Twenty paces backwards, double march!

PAUL *is mad with rage, but obeys the command. He doubles back, then marches up to the* MAJOR. *Six paces away he springs to a stiff salute and maintains it until he is six paces beyond.* THE MAJOR *barks out:*

THE MAJOR. About now! Halt!

PAUL *returns and stands at attention.* THE MAJOR's *attitude relaxes slightly:*

THE MAJOR. Let this be a lesson to you, Baumer. For once I will put mercy before justice. Now dismiss!

PAUL *whirls and turns back toward home.*

Dissolve to:

SCENE 22-I

Int. PAUL's *room. Day. In one corner, near a window, is his wooden bed. Against one wall is a small, brown leather sofa. In a corner is a small iron stove. Against another wall are book shelves filled with classics, moderns, periodicals, papers, school books badly thumbed. On the walls are drawings, etc. In another corner is a glass case filled with butterflies. In the center of the room is a small table on which is a vase of flowers.* PAUL *rushes in. He already has his tunic half off. He jerks the rest of it off and throws it in a corner, then starts to remove his shirt, placing various articles, including the things* KEMMERICH *gave him, on the dresser. He stops and looks at these things and decides to see* KEMMERICH's *mother as soon as he gets dressed. He then goes to a wardrobe and snatches down a civilian suit.*

SCENE 23-I

Int. bedroom of PAUL's *mother. She is out of bed and partly dressed. She hears* PAUL *in his room and calls to him.*

PAUL's MOTHER. Paul, is that you?

SCENE 24-I

Int. PAUL's *room. Close-up* PAUL. *He has his shirt off and is just about to remove his trousers. He stops and turns toward the door. The bandaged wound in his side can be seen. He keeps the anger out of his voice as he answers.*

PAUL. Yes, Mother.

SCENE 25-I

Int. bedroom of PAUL's MOTHER. *She hears his voice and smiles, adjusts her dress and starts out.*

SCENE 26-I

Int. PAUL's *room, toward door.* PAUL *has put on civilian trousers. He reaches for a shirt as the door opens and his mother enters.* PAUL *whirls so that she will not see the wound. He quickly puts on the shirt and turns to face her. She comes up to him, stops and looks at him as she happily says:*

PAUL's MOTHER. That's better, Paul—now you're my boy again.

PAUL *smiles and turns away to select a tie, but has some trouble tying it. The mother helps him. The outside door is heard opening and closing with a bang.*

PAUL's FATHER's VOICE. Where's Paul? Where's my soldier,

Footsteps are heard rushing up the stairs. PAUL *answers:*

PAUL. Here, Father, in my room.

His father rushes into the room, but stops short as he sees PAUL *in civilian clothes. Disappointment shows in his face as he asks:*

HERR BAUMER. But where's your uniform?

PAUL *points toward the corner:*

PAUL. It's over there.

ERNA *appears behind her father, then goes toward the kitchen.* HERR BAUMER *comes to* PAUL, *takes his hand and shakes it as he says:*

HERR BAUMER. It's good to see you again—

He hesitates and looks at the uniform, then continues:

HERR BAUMER. But why didn't you leave your uniform on—is it anything to be ashamed of? I wanted to show you off a bit!

He looks at PAUL *almost accusingly—* PAUL *has cheated him out of the glory of parading him before his cronies.* PAUL *answers quietly:*

PAUL. These clothes are more comfortable. Mother likes me better in these, too. I'll go around if you want but not in the uniform.

HERR BAUMER. Sure. Sure, just as you say.

Dissolve to:

SCENE 27-I

Long shot of beer garden.

SCENE 28-I

Medium shot of PAUL *and* HERR BAUMER *sitting at a table with three men.*

FIRST CITIZEN. How do you find it here now, Baumer? Do you miss the excitement.

PAUL. Not much.

FIRST CITIZEN. Well, well, you will find us not unintelligent here. We're behind the lines, but we know enough to honor the soldier who keeps on in spite of blood and death.

HERR MEYER *comes bustling back between the tables, and speaks to* HERR BAUMER.

HERR MEYER. Good afternoon, Mr. Baumer. Isn't this your son, Paul, here?

BAUMER. Yes, yes. This is Mr. Meyer, Paul.

MEYER *(shaking hands with him).* I'm glad to meet you, young man. Glad to meet you. And how are things out there? Terrible, terrible, eh? But we must carry on. And after all, you do at least get decent food out there. Naturally it's worse here—naturally. The best for our soldiers every time. That's our motto: Give the soldier the best. How's the spirit at the front now? Excellent, eh, excellent.

PAUL. About as usual.

MEYER. That's right. You'll find plenty of spirit in this town too. We haven't given up by a long way! We're just as determined as you are to see it through! You won't find many up there ready to quit, will you?

PAUL. Well, the boys wouldn't kick if it was over.

MEYER *laughs.*

MEYER. The soldier will have his little joke! But first you have to give the Frenchies a good licking, don't you? And before you're

through, you'll have the whole of Belgium, the coal areas of France and a slice of Russia.

PAUL. Do you think we need them?

MEYER. We must have them. Must have them! And if you boys want to come home, let me show you what must be done before you come home. Look, here is the line. It runs so—in a V—here is San Quentin. You can see for yourself you are almost through now. All right—shove ahead out there with your everlasting trench war-fare—smash through the johnnies—and then there will be peace!

PAUL. When you get in it, the war isn't the way it looks back here.

MEYER. Oh, shucks—shucks! You don't know anything about it. You know the details, yes—but this relates to the whole, and you can't judge that. You do your duty, you risk your lives—That deserves the highest honor. Every man of you ought to have the Iron Cross, but first of all the enemy line must be broken through in Flanders—and then rolled up from the top!

He blows his nose and wipes his beard.

MEYER. Completely rolled up they must be, from the top to the bottom—and then—to Paris! Yes, sir—then to Paris! And it's you who must do it, you and your comrades! We depend on you, we're lost without you!

Rising suddenly.

PAUL. I—I'll have to go. You'll excuse us. There's someone I must speak to.

PAUL *and his* FATHER *rise. The others at the table rise and bow.* PAUL *and his* FATHER *make their way through the tables. A* SOLDIER *sits at a table near the entrance.* PAUL *hurries toward him.*

SCENE 29-I

One of the tables. MULLER, *who has lost an arm, is seated alone, drinking. He is far gone in liquor.* PAUL *enters to him.*

PAUL. Muller! Muller!

He tries to rise.

MULLER. Well, if it isn't little old Paul!

PAUL. I heard you were here, Muller.

MULLER. Sit down, Paulie. I'm glad to see you. Let's get drunk.

PAUL

Agitated, taking his hand.

They don't know anything about it here, MULLER. They think we're heroes.

MULLER. We are. We're iron men, you haven't forgotten that.

PAUL. They think the war's great. They tell us to push on to Paris.

MULLER. Sure, that's the place for me. Let's both push on to Paris.

He gets up and whispers in PAUL's *ear. He slumps to his seat, laughing, and drops his head on his arm.*

MULLER. That's right. Push on to Paris!

PAUL's FATHER *enters and takes him by the arm.*

FATHER. Paul, I'm afraid you hurt Mr. Meyer's feelings. I think you ought to go back and—

PAUL. No.

FATHER. It's better to talk to a fine citizen like Mr. Meyer, than this fellow who's always drunk.

PAUL *controls himself with difficulty. He is about to answer rashly, instead he turns to* MULLER.

PAUL. I'll see you again, Muller.

MULLER. Sure. Met you in Paris.

PAUL. Come on, Father.

They go.

Fade out.

SCENE 30-I

Fade in.

Day. MOTHER's *room.* ERNA *is getting a blanket spread on bed to cover her* MOTHER.

ERNA. You had better lie down.

MOTHER. I don't want Paul to come back and find I'm sick again.

ERNA. He won't come back, Mother, not for a long while. He is gone to see Mrs. Kemmerich. Paul promised Franz, when he died, that he'd take a picture.

MOTHER. I don't think Paul likes it home.

ERNA. Oh, now, Mother.

MOTHER. I try to understand him, but each day he seems to get farther and farther away, and now his furlough is coming to an end.

ERNA. Not yet, Mother.

Coming to her.

MOTHER. I can't bear to think of his going away. I'll never see him again.

ERNA. Now, Mother.

Helps her down and covers her with blanket.

You lie down and keep quiet.

SCENE 31-I

Interior front room of KEMMERICH *home. Day. The room is small, over-furnished, and filled with bric-a-brac.* FRAU KEMMERICH, *a very fat woman of about forty-five, is sitting in a large rocking chair holding the picture of* KEMMERICH. *She is weeping wildly as she rocks back and forth rapidly.* PAUL *is facing her, sitting uncomfortably on the edge of a straight chair. On a small table near them are the things* KEMMERICH *gave him to give to his mother.* PAUL *is talking:*

PAUL. So I guess that's all, Frau Kemmerich.

He is relieved that the ordeal is over and gets up to go, but FRAU KEMMERICH *wails louder than before and motions for him to remain seated. Finally, she calms herself.*

FRAU KEMMERICH. Tell me, Paul, how did he die?

While she dabs at her eyes with a soggy handkerchief, PAUL *makes a quick decision:*

PAUL. He died instantly. He was shot through the heart.

FRAU KEMMERICH *stops rocking and leans closer to* PAUL *as she says very calmly:*

FRAU KEMMERICH. You lie, Paul. I know better. I have felt his anguish. Tell the truth! I want to know it! I must know it!

As she talks, she leans closer to PAUL, *who looks questioningly at her, puzzled that she should insist on knowing how* FRANZ *suffered. But he sticks to his resolve to console her.*

PAUL. No, I was beside him. He died at once.

FRAU KEMMERICH *sinks back into the chair. Fresh sobs rack her body. She mops her eyes with the handkerchief. She pleads with him:*

FRAU KEMMERICH. Tell me. You must tell me. I know you want to comfort me, but don't you see, you torment me far more than if you told me the truth? Tell me, how it was and even though it will be terrible, it will be far better than what I have to think if you don't.

PAUL *is growing impatient. Why is she so stupid as to insist on the details? What difference does it make how* FRANZ *died? What difference does it make how thousands died? They are all dead! But he cannot tell her. With slight impatience, he says:*

PAUL. He died immediately. He felt absolutely nothing at all. His face was quite calm.

FRAU KEMMERICH. Then, how did you get the picture?

PAUL. I'd promised him before, that if anything ever happened to him, I'd bring you the picture.

FRAU KEMMERICH *stops sobbing. Her eyes become calm, intense. She slowly rises to her feet. Her voice is tremulous as she asks:*

FRAU KEMMERICH. Will you swear it?

PAUL. Yes.

FRAU KEMMERICH. By everything that is sacred to you?

PAUL *almost laughs—what could be sacred to him now?*

PAUL. Yes. He died at once.

FRAU KEMMERICH. Are you willing to never come back yourself, if it isn't true?

PAUL. May I never come back if he wasn't killed instantaneously.

FRAU KEMMERICH, *controlling herself with difficulty.*

FRAU KEMMERICH. Thank you. Thank you, Paul.

Suddenly, her face breaks up and she goes to pieces, and cries to him accusingly:

FRAU KEMMERICH. Oh, but why are you living then, if he is dead? Why should you be living when Franz is gone? No, no, no, forgive me!

She throws herself, sobbing, on the floor in front of the chair.

FRAU KEMMERICH. You'd better go now, Paul. Forgive me if I don't look at you again! Oh, why should it be Franz? Why should it be Franz? Go now, go now! Oh, please go away!

Her shoulders shake with sobs. PAUL *rises, glad of the escape offered him, and quickly leaves the room.*

SCENE 32-I

Long shot of PAUL *hurrying down the street. As he comes down, he stops and looks back.*

SCENE 33-I

Another angle showing PAUL'S *school in the background. He hesitates, then turns in.*

SCENE 34-I

The corridor outside KANTOREK'S *classroom.* PAUL *walks tentatively along the hallway past several closed doors. The door to* KANTOREK'S *classroom is open.* PAUL *pauses, then steps forward so that he can see inside.*

SCENE 35-I

Looking in through the doorway of the classroom. KANTOREK *is standing in front of the class, speaking.*

KANTOREK. From the farms they have gone, from the schools, from the factories—they have gone blithely, happily, singing, ever forward, realizing that there is no other duty now but to save the Fatherland. The age of enlistment is now sixteen years, and though you are barely men, your country needs you for the greatest service a citizen can give—

SCENE 36-I

Close-up of PAUL'S *face, seen through the classroom door. Just as he is turning away.*

SCENE 37-I

The class room. KANTOREK *hurrying to the door to stop* PAUL.

KANTOREK. Baumer! Paul! You come at the right moment, Baumer! Just at the right moment!

SCENE 38-I

Looking toward the doorway of the classroom. KANTOREK *has caught* PAUL'S *shoulder and brings him into the room.* KANTOREK *is beaming with pride.*

KANTOREK. And as if to prove all I have said, here is one of the first to go—a lad who sat before me on these very benches, who gave up all to serve in the first year of the war, one of the iron youth who have made Germany invincible in the field! Look at him, bronzed and sturdy and clear-eyed—the kind of soldier everyone of you should envy!

He lays an arm around PAUL'S *shoulders.*

Paul, lad, you must speak to them, you must tell them what it means to serve your Fatherland!

PAUL. *(Embarrassed)* No, no. I can't say anything.

KANTOREK. You must, Paul. Just a word. Just tell them how much they're needed out there. Tell them why you went and what it means to you.

PAUL. *(Almost unable to speak)* I can't say anything.

KANTOREK. If you remember some deed of heroism, some touch of nobility, tell about it.

PAUL. Well, I can't tell you anything you don't know. We live in trenches out there, and we fight, and we try not to be killed, but sometimes we are—that's all—

KANTOREK. *(Pleading)* No, no, Paul—

EVANSTON TOWNSHIP HIGH SCHOOL

HALL PASS ONLY

Date: _Feb 18, 1997_

Time: _11:02_

Name: _Lila Freeman_

ID.#: _____

Counselor: _MiRC_

From: _Film crit +_
Screen plays

To: _Ch_

K. Berg
signature

AS-7 (6-83)

PAUL. (*Flaring up*) I've been there! I know what it's like!—

KANTOREK. But that's not what one dwells on, Paul, lad—

PAUL. I heard you in here reciting that same old stuff—making more iron men—more young heroes—and I tried to get away! You still think it's beautiful and sweet to die for your country, don't you? Well, we used to think you knew, but the first bombardment taught us better! It's dirty and painful to die for your country! When it comes to dying for your country it's better not to die at all. There are millions out there dying for their countries, and what good is it doing?

KANTOREK. Paul!

PAUL. You asked me to tell you why I enlisted and what it meant to me! I'll tell you! I enlisted because you thought you knew better than I did—and now I know you knew nothing, and you still know nothing! You're telling the same old lies at the same old stand! Go out and die, you say, but if you'll pardon me, it's easier to say go out and die than it is to do it—and it's easier to say it than to watch it happen!

A boy rises in the back of the room and a couple of boys hiss lightly.

KANTOREK. No, no, boys!

He calms the class by lifting a hand.

I am sorry, Baumer—but I must—

PAUL. (*Quietly*) It's no use talking like this—You won't know what I mean. Only it's a long while since we enlisted out of this classroom—so long I thought maybe the whole world had learned by this time—only now, they're sending babies, and they don't last a week. I shouldn't have come on leave. Up at the front, they don't tell lies. Up there, you're alive or you're dead—and that's all—and you can't fool anybody about that very long. And up there, we know we're lost and done for whether we're dead or alive. Three years we've had of it—four years—and every day a year and every night a century—and our bodies are earth and our thoughts are clay and we sleep and eat with death. And we're done for, because you can't live that way and keep anything inside you. I shouldn't have come on leave. I'll go back tomorrow. I've got four more days but I can't stand it here. I'll go back tomorrow.

KANTOREK *goes to* PAUL, *tries to put an arm around his shoulders and lead him from the room, but* PAUL *shakes him off and goes out, his*

eyes full of tears. There is a silence in the classroom after PAUL is gone.

KANTOREK. You must not think I did not understand your attitude, gentlemen. You were right to resent what Baumer said. But we must make allowances. Baumer has served well and has been through much. His state of mind is typical in those suffering from shellshock. But I am glad he spoke to us. For remember this, Baumer goes back tomorrow. No matter what he says, no matter what attitude he takes, in his heart he is a patriot, loyal and unswerving! Will you let him walk alone out of this classroom, will you let him go back into danger alone—this bronzed, stalwart figure, beautiful in his devotion, heroic against a flaming sky? Who will go with him?

A student rises.

STUDENT. I will, sir!

ANOTHER STUDENT. I will!

ANOTHER STUDENT. We'll all go!

The students begin to rise all over the room, crying "I will!"

KANTOREK. Thank God, thank God, for youth and courage! Now we shall win! Now, I know we shall win!

They shout and throw ink wells, and join in a general riotous celebration, repeating the earlier enlistment scene.

Fade out.

Fade in.

SCENE 39-I

PAUL'S *room again, late at night.* PAUL *opens a closet door, takes out his soldier's clothes and lays them out over a chair, ready for morning. He brings out his pack, looks to the buckles and sets it down beside his chair. This concluded, he takes off his civilian coat, holds it at arms' length, gives it a farewell glance and hangs it in the closet. He sits on the edge of the bed and begins to take off his shoes. He looks up.*

SCENE 40-I

Medium shot toward the door of PAUL'S *room.* FRAU BAUMER *stands there with a candle in her hand. She is looking at him. She comes forward through the door.*

SCENE 41-I

Medium close view of PAUL'S *bed. His mother enters the scene and sits beside him on the edge of the bed.*

PAUL. You should go back and get to sleep, Mother.

FRAU BAUMER. I can sleep enough when you're gone. Must you go tomorrow, Paul? Must you?

PAUL. Yes, Mother. The orders were changed.

FRAU BAUMER. I'll pray for you every day, and perhaps you can get a job that is not so dangerous.

PAUL. Yes, Mother. Perhaps I can get into the cook house—that can usually be done.

FRAU BAUMER. You do it, then. And if the others say anything—

PAUL. That won't worry me, Mother. Now you go back to sleep.

FRAU BAUMER sighs and does not reply. PAUL gets up and wraps the cover around her shoulders. She supports herself on his arm. She is in pain. PAUL goes with her out the door.

SCENE 42-I

In FRAU BAUMER's room. PAUL is tucking the cover about her.

PAUL. You must get well again, Mother, before I come back.

FRAU BAUMER. Yes, yes, my child.

PAUL. You ought not to send your things to me, Mother. We have plenty to eat out there. You can make much better use of them here.

He smooths her hair back from her forehead.

FRAU BAUMER. I have two sets of underwear for you—all wool—don't forget to put it in your pack.

PAUL. *(Kissing her)* No, I won't. Goodnight, Mother.

FRAU BAUMER. Goodnight, my child.

PAUL *goes out.*

Fade out.

SEQUENCE "J"

——

SCENE 1-J

A panorama of the battlefield. Far away is the Front and a light and sporadic cannonading is being carried on. The camera swings around past some dugouts and then shoots back toward the rear. A lone figure is approaching. As it grows closer, we see it is PAUL carrying rifle and pack. He looks around almost happily as he goes toward a dugout and enters.

Dissolve to:

SCENE 2-J

Interior of dugout. Medium shot of doorway. PAUL stands there looking around. KAT's voice is heard.

KAT. You don't need to pay any attention to the big ones. You can hear them coming a long way off—and they mostly go over.

SCENE 3-J

Reverse angle. KAT is sitting eating a piece of bread, and talking to some sixteen-year-old boys who are evidently new recruits.

KAT. But when you hear one that sounds like a trolley car going 'round a curve, just pretend you're an angle worm and get right down into the earth. She's your only friend.

SCENE 4-J

Close-up of PAUL. He is smiling happily at the familiar words.

PAUL. Hello, Kat.

SCENE 5-J

Medium shot to take in both men.

KAT. Huh!

He looks up.

Who is it?
PAUL. It's Paul.
KAT. Paul!

He comes forward. He stops in front of PAUL, greatly moved.

So you got back?

They shake hands.

SCENE 6-J

Close shot of TJADEN. He is coming forward from the rear of the dugout.

TJADEN. Me and the Kaiser didn't expect you so soon.

SCENE 7-J

Medium shot of group.

PAUL. Hello, Tjaden.

KAT. Now, confound it, it's like a war again.

TJADEN. Well, we'll end it quick now we got Paul back.

KAT. In all my useless existence I never was so glad to see anybody. Come on, let's go outside and talk.

They start out.

SCENE 8-J

Long shot showing the three men. Coming out of the dugout. They walk to some boxes at one side and sit.

SCENE 9-J

Close shot of the three men.

KAT. Have a good time?

PAUL. Pretty good—not very. Where's everybody.

KAT. You better not ask.

PAUL. Things are worse?

KAT. Our food is made of sawdust—whether you got bread or jam it's all the same thing—we're rotten with dysentery. The artillery's so worn out, they can't shoot over us any more. Our fresh troops are anemic boys who know nothing about war except how to die, nobody has any life. We know we're losing. Nobody says much about it but we all know it. We're just animals—that's all. We fight to stay alive. But I've got a feeling that I'm going to get mine just before the end.

TIADEN. He's been talking that way the last week.

KAT. Mark what I say, when they croak me, then you can know it's pretty nearly over.

TJADEN. Well, the Kaiser'n me's both going to come out of it safe. I got that all decided.

KAT. Was it nice back home?

PAUL. No. It's nicer where you've got somebody that understands you.

Dissolve to:

SCENE 10-J

Long shot of battleground. In the background is a ridge. In the foreground some soldiers are straggling toward the Front. They are the new recruits who had hissed PAUL in the schoolroom. Only very casual firing is heard. A figure comes over the ridge. It is PAUL. He carries a sack of provisions.

PAUL. *(Calling)* Hey!

A soldier turns.

SCENE 11-J

Closer shot as PAUL approaches the boy.

PAUL. I want you to take these provisions up to the Front.

BOY. What?

PAUL. I was taking food up to the Front when my partner got hit. I've got to carry him back.

BOY. Well, all right.

PAUL. Keep your ears open for shrapnel and if you hear it coming dive for the earth.

BOY. Yes, sir.

PAUL *turns and hurries back over the ridge. The boy looks at him for a moment, then shoulders bundle.*

SCENE 12-J

Close shot of shell hole on other side of ridge. KAT has just finished binding his leg. The bandage is already bloody. PAUL hurries up and joins him.

PAUL. Did you get the blood stopped?

KAT. It's all right.

PAUL. Let me tighten it. *He works on bandage.*

KAT. The war is over now. I told you I'd get it just before the end.

PAUL. *(Working on bandage)* How's that?

KAT. It's all right. What's the difference? If I was going to be hit, why couldn't I get it a year ago—two, three, four years ago.

PAUL. I didn't think we'd ever be separated, Kat.

KAT. One of those wooden-headed surgeons is likely to saw my leg off, mark me A-1, and send me back.

PAUL. No, you're out of it and it may last a long while, too.

KAT. I tell you it's over—as soon as I'm hit, it's over. I knew that. Gimme a cigarette.

PAUL. But we're going to see each other in peace time anyhow. We're going to get together later, aren't we?

KAT. Of course we are, kid.

PAUL. You're one person that I understand, Kat, and that understands me—we mustn't let this separate us. Now, we better go on.

KAT. Must, Paul, must

PAUL *takes KAT's good leg by the knee and gets KAT on his back again. They start.*

SCENE 13-J

Shot of a French sniper in a tree.

SCENE 14-J

Medium shot of PAUL carrying KAT, sweat pouring down his face as he hurries on. A bullet whines near. PAUL quickens his pace.

PAUL. I think I see stretcher bearers, Kat.

SCENE 15-J

Close shot over PAUL's shoulder showing KAT's face. There is a slight trickle of blood running down over the ear. KAT is dead.

SCENE 16-J

Close shot of PAUL.

PAUL. Say, we're lucky. Do you know it, Kat. 'Cause I couldn't carry you so very much farther. Do you hear, Kat? We're safe. If my wind will last till we get there.

They pass the camera.

SCENE 17-J

Shot from behind showing PAUL *staggering toward stretcher bearers. He half falls as he lets* KAT *down. Then he falls back, gasping for breath.*

SCENE 18-J

Closer shot of PAUL. *An orderly examines* KAT, *while another offers water bottle to* PAUL.

SCENE 19-J

Close shot of ORDERLY *examining* KAT.

ORDERLY. You might have caused yourself a lot of trouble.

SCENE 20-J

Close shot of PAUL *over* ORDERLY'S *shoulder.*

PAUL. Huh?
ORDERLY. He's stone dead.
PAUL. *(Shakes his head).* He was hit in the leg.
ORDERLY. And that's not all.
PAUL. He's fainted.
ORDERLY. Want to bet any money on it? I tell you he's dead.
PAUL. It isn't possible. Only a couple of minutes ago I was talking to him. He's fainted.

PAUL *rushes to the back of* KAT. *As he puts his hand under* KAT'S *head, he feels it wet and pulling his hand away, looks at it. It is covered with blood.*

SCENE 21-J

Close shot of ORDERLY *looking down.*

ORDERLY. You see—must have got hit in the back of the head while you was carrying him.

SCENE 22-J

Close shot of PAUL. *He stares into space like a doomed man.*

ORDERLY. Want to take his pay back and things?

PAUL *nods. The orderly's hands enter scene and pass the things to* PAUL.

ORDERLY. You two related, are you?

PAUL *shakes his head. He rises. He looks down at* KAT, *a last farewell look and then walks away, half stumbling like a drunken man.*

SCENE 23-J*

Shot of the French sniper adjusting telescope sighter. PAUL *has walked out into an open space, oblivious to his surroundings. He pauses. Across his face comes a vision of marching troops. They are German soldiers marching to "Die Wacht am Rhine." Another shadowy column comes from another angle, a column of French, marching to "The Marseillaise." Other columns march, and other anthems are merged into the music. The troops march toward a single point on the horizon and disappear into a common grave.* PAUL *is agitated in his dream. He calls out to stop the passing troops and finally leaps to his feet.*

PAUL. No, stop. No more! No more!

He stops abruptly and sinks down.

SCENE 24-J*

Shot from above. As he rolls over, a trickle of blood runs down his forehead. There is a smile of peace and calm on his face.

Dissolve to:

SCENE 25-J*

The sound of a typewriter and the printed report "ALL QUIET ON THE WESTERN FRONT," double-exposed across PAUL'S *face.*

Fade out.

Editor's Note.—As noted in my general introduction and as all of you who have seen the film know, the last scenes were changed to Paul's being shot by the French sniper as Paul reached for a butterfly above the trench parapet. I have not been able to determine who made this change.

MEET JOHN DOE

Screenplay by Robert Riskin

LONG JOHN WILLOUGHBY (JOHN DOE)	Gary Cooper
ANN MITCHELL	Barbara Stanwyck
D. B. NORTON	Edward Arnold
THE COLONEL	Walter Brennan
MRS. MITCHELL	Spring Byington
HENRY CONNELL	James Gleason
MAYOR LOVETT	Gene Lockhart
TED SHELDON	Rod La Rocque
BEANY	Irving Bacon
BERT HANSEN	Regis Toomey
MRS. HANSEN	Ann Doran
SOURPUSS SMITHERS	J. Farrell MacDonald
ANGELFACE	Warren Hymer
MAYOR HAWKINS	Harry Holman
SPENCER	Andrew Tombes
MANNETT	Pierre Watkin
WESTON	Stanley Andrews
BENNETT	Mitchell Lewis
CHARLIE DAWSON	Charles C. Wilson
GOVERNOR	Vaughn Glaser
DAN	Sterling Holloway
RADIO ANNOUNCER	Mike Frankovich
RADIO ANNOUNCERS AT THE CONVENTION	Knox Manning, Selmer Jackson, John B. Hughes
POP DWYER	Aldrich Bowker
MRS. BREWSTER	Mrs. Gardner Crane
MIKE	Pat Flaherty
ANN'S SISTERS	Carlotta Jelm, Tina Thayer
RED, OFFICE BOY	Bennie Bartlett
MRS. HAWKINS	Sarah Edwards
RADIO M. C.	Edward Earle
SHERIFF	James McNamara
MRS. DELANEY	Emma Tansey
GRUBBEL	Frank Austin
RELIEF ADMINISTRATOR	Edward Keane

MR. DELANEY	Lafe McKee
JOE, NEWSMAN	Edward McWade
BIXLER	Guy Usher
BARRINGTON	Walter Soderling
POLICEMAN	Edmund Cobb
MIDGET	Billy Curtis
LADY MIDGET	Johnny Fern
JIM, GOVERNOR'S ASSOCIATE	John Hamilton
GOVERNOR'S ASSOCIATE	William Forrest
FIRED REPORTER	Charles K. French
MAYOR'S SECRETARY	Edward Hearn
NEWSPAPER SECRETARY	Bess Flowers
ED, A PHOTOGRAPHER	Hank Mann
PHOTOGRAPHER	James Millican

And The Hall Johnson Choir

Screenplay by Robert Riskin,
based on a story by Richard Connell and Robert Presnell
Produced and directed by Frank Capra for Warner Bros., 1941
Art Director: Stephen Gooson
Music By Dimitri Tiomkin
Choral arrangements by Hal Johnson
Music Director: Leo F. Forbstein
Assistant Director: Arthur S. Black
Photography by George Barnes
Sound by C. A. Riggs
Edited by Daniel Mandell
Gowns by Natalie Visart
Special Effects by Jack Cosgrove
Montage Effects by Slavko Vorkapitch

This screenplay by Robert Riskin, based on a story by Richard Connell and Robert Presnell, which was nominated for an Academy Award in 1941, represents for Mr. Riskin and his longtime collaborator in film, director Frank Capra, a typical example of their work.

Highly populist, full of affection and hope for the common man and the forgotten men of the great American depression of the early thirties, Mr. Riskin's script has within it much of the tradition of the democratic and religious idealism stemming from the American Revolution through his literary antecedents Ralph Waldo Emerson and Walt Whitman. The idea is that the democratic man can achieve the ultimate if he stands together and works together with others, ready to extend a helping hand on a personal basis to his friend and neighbor.

Long John Willoughby as portrayed by Gary Cooper and as written by Mr. Riskin is that sort of model. The simplicity of his character and the directness of the script, with all the affection that it has for people—a hallmark, as we have noted in all of Mr. Riskin's work with Mr. Capra—gives the film extraordinary evangelical power. Some viewers might find this story naïve. But as we look back at this now, almost half a century later, its simple directness and idealism are not only refreshing but notable in our present era when the common citizen's capacity for indignation and participation in being neighborly is not at all common.

Particularly worthy of mention is Mr. Riskin's extraordinary collaboration with his director, Mr. Capra. Within the space of five years, Mr. Riskin won one Academy Award for *It Happened One Night* (1934) and two nominations for *Mr. Deeds Goes to Town* (1936) and *You Can't Take It With You* (1938), and Mr. Capra won three Oscars for his directing collaboration on these films.

On the occasion when Mr. Capra visited our class at U.C.L.A., the Literature of the Screen, to talk about his collaboration with Mr. Riskin, he offered these revealing comments:

> . . . scriptwriting is the toughest part of the whole racket . . . the least understood and the least noticed. Bob and I had a wonderful relationship first of all . . . and we liked each other too. . . .

> . . . I had a pretty good idea of visual effects from my Mack Sennett experience (gag writing) not jokes . . . visual effects. Bob had playwriting experience . . . but between the two of us . . . . I would sort of think ahead and think of the next sequence in terms of visual things . . . and then we'd discuss it. He'd walk and write and while he was writing then I would think ahead to the next sequence to try to figure it out. . . . what would happen with the relationships between the people . . . what it should be. Then I'd read what he wrote. I'd rewrite . . . he'd rewrite. It was a constant collaboration really on the part of the script. So much so that when I started shooting on the picture I never looked at the script because I knew every inch by heart. . . .

Close and extraordinary collaborations between master screenwriter and master director, it should be noted, most often produce masterful and extraordinary motion pictures. As mentioned earlier, blessed with screenwriter Dudley Nichols, John Ford went on to fashion one memorable film after another.

The list goes on and on.

Other than the credits noted above, Mr. Riskin, who passed away in 1955 at the age of fifty-eight, had a very successful career as a playwright in the 1920s before going to work at Columbia in 1931.

In his illustrious film career as a screenwriter, he also wrote *The Whole Town's Talking* (1935), *Lost Horizon* (1937), *Magic Town* (1947), which he also produced, and *Pocketful of Miracles* (1961), based on his *Lady for a Day* (1933), from which he adapted the former.

Ext. Bulletin Office—Sidewalk. Close-up: Of a time-worn plaque against the side of a building. It reads:

THE BULLETIN
"A free press for a free people."

While we read this, a pair of hands come in holding pneumatic chisel which immediately attacks the sign. As the lettering is being obliterated,

Dissolve to: Close-up: A new plaque on which the lettering has been changed to:

THE NEW BULLETIN
"A streamlined newspaper for a streamlined era."

Cut to: Int. Bulletin outer office. Full shot: Of a mid-western newspaper office.

Med shot: At a door at which a sign-painter works. He is painting CONNELL's *name on the door. It opens and a flip office boy emerges. The painter has to wait until the door closes in order to resume his work.*

Full shot: Of the outer office. The activity of the office seems to suddenly cease, as all eyes are centered on the office boy.

Med. shot—panning: With the office boy—who has a small sheet of paper in his hand. He walks jauntily to a desk, refers to his paper, points his finger to a woman, emits a short whistle through his teeth, runs a finger across his throat and jerks his thumb toward managing editor's office. The woman stares starkly at him while her immediate neighbors look on with sympathy. The office boy now goes through the same procedure with several other people. All watch him, terror written in their eyes.

Med. shot: Toward CONNELL's *office door where painter works. It opens and three people emerge. Two men and a girl. The girl is young and pretty. All three look dourful. The painter again has to wait for the door to shut before resuming his work. The two men exit. The girl suddenly stops.*

Close shot: Of the girl. Her name is ANN MITCHELL. *She stands, thinking, and then suddenly, impulsively, wheels around. Camera pans with her as she returns to* CONNELL's *office door, flings it open and disappears. The painter remains poised with his brush, waiting for the door to swing back. There is a slight flash of resentment in his eyes.*

Int. CONNELL's *office. Full shot:* CONNELL *is behind his desk on which is a tray of sandwiches and a glass of milk, half gone. Near him sits* POP DWYER, *another veteran newspaperman.* ANN *crosses to* CONNELL's *desk.*

CONNELL *(on phone)*. Yeh, D. B. Oh, just cleaning out the deadwood. Okay.

ANN *(supplicatingly)*. Look, Mr. Connell. . . . I just can't afford to be without work right now, not even for a day. I've got a mother and two kid sisters to . . .

Secretary enters. (Her name is Mattie.)

SECRETARY. More good luck telegrams.

ANN. Well, you know how it is, I, I've just got to keep on working. See?

CONNELL. Sorry, sister. I was sent down here to clean house. I told yuh I can't use your column any more. It's lavender and old lace! *(flicks dictograph button)*

MATTIE *(over dictograph)*. Yeah?

CONNELL. Send those other people in.

MATTIE *(over dictograph)*. Okay.

ANN. I'll tell you what I'll do. I, I get thirty dollars a week. I'll take twenty-five, twenty if necessary. I'll do anything you say.

CONNELL. It isn't the money. We're after circulation. What we need is fireworks. People who can hit with sledge hammers—start arguments.

ANN. Oh, I can do that. I know this town inside out. Oh, give me a chance, please.

She can get no further, for several people enter. They are cowed and frightened. ANN *hesitates a moment, then, there being nothing for her to do, she starts to exit. She is stopped by* CONNELL's *voice.*

CONNELL. All right, come in, come in! Come in! *(to Ann)* Cashier's got your check. *(back to others)* Who are these people? Gibbs, Frowley, Cunningham, Jiles—*(to Ann at door)* Hey, you, sister!

Ann turns.

CONNELL. Don't forget to get out your last column before you pick up your check!

ANN's *eyes flash angrily as she exits.*

Int. Outer Office. Med shot: ANN *storms out. The painter again has to wait for the door to swing back to him.*

Int. ANN's *office. Full shot:* ANN *enters her office and paces around, furious. A man in alpaca sleeve-bands enters. His name is* JOE.

JOE. You're a couple sticks shy in your column, Ann.

ANN *(ignores him)*. *muttering* . . . A rich slob like D. B. Norton buys a paper—and forty heads are chopped off!

JOE. Did you get it, too?

ANN. Yeah. You, too? Oh, Joe . . . oh, I'm sorry, darling . . . why don't we tear the building down!

JOE. Before you do, Ann, perhaps you'd better finish this column.

ANN. Yeah. Lavender and old lace!

Suddenly she stops pacing. Her eyes widen as a fiendish idea strikes her.

ANN. Wait, Joe—wait!

She flops down in front of her typewriter.

ANN. *(muttering).* Wants fireworks, huh? Okay!

She begins to pound furiously, her jaw set. Close-up: Of ANN. *Eyes flashing as she types.*

Close-up: Of JOE, *watching her. The wild look in her eye and the unnatural speed of her typing causes him to stare dumbly at her.*

Med. shot: ANN *bangs away madly. Finally she finishes. She whips the sheet out of the typewriter, hands it to* JOE.

ANN. Here.

As JOE *takes it,* ANN *begins to empty the drawers of her desk.*

Close-up: Of JOE *reading what* ANN *has written.*

JOE *(reading).* "Below is a letter which reached my desk this morning. It's a commentary on what we laughingly call the civilized world. 'Dear Miss Mitchell: Four years ago I was fired out of my job. Since then I haven't been able to get another one. At first I was sore at the state administration because it's on account of the slimy politics here we have all this unemployment. But in looking around, it seems the whole world's going to pot, so in protest I'm going to commit suicide by jumping off the City Hall roof.' Signed, A disgusted American citizen, John Doe.'"

JOE *pauses to absorb this.*

JOE *(continues reading).* "Editor's note . . . If you ask this column, the wrong people are jumping off roofs."

JOE *glances up toward* ANN, *in mild protest.*

JOE. Hey, Ann, this is the old fakeroo, isn't it?

Full shot: ANN *has just about accumulated all her things.* JOE *stares at her, knowing it's a fake.*

ANN. Never mind that, Joe. Go ahead.

JOE *shrugs, shakes his head, and exits.* ANN *stuffs her things under her arm and also goes.*

Int. Outer office: Med shot: Voices ad lib— "Awfully sorry you're not going." "Good-bye." (Laughing)

ANN *comes out. Suddenly, she stops, gets another idea, picks up a book from a desk, and reaches back to heave it.*

Med. shot: At CONNELL's *office door. The sign-painter has just finished* CONNELL's *name, and as he leans back, pleased, wiping his brushes, the book flies in. The painter lifts his head slowly, his wrath too great to find utterance.*

Dissolve to: Int. GOVERNOR JACKSON's *office: Close-up: Of two of* GOVERNOR's *ASSOCIATES.*

MAN *(reading newspaper).* ". . . .and it's on account of the slimy politics here that we have all this unemployment." *(agitated)* There it is! D. B. Norton's opening attack on the Governor!

2ND MAN. Why Jim, it's just a letter sent in to a column.

JIM. No, no. I can smell it. That's Norton!

While he speaks, the GOVERNOR *has entered.*

GOVERNOR. 'Morning, gentlemen. You're rather early.

MEN. 'Morning. 'Morning, Governor.

JIM *(pushes paper over to him).* Did you see this in the New Bulletin, Governor?

He emphasizes the word "new" cynically.

GOVERNOR. Yes. I had it served with my breakfast this morning.

2ND MAN. Jim thinks it's D. B. Norton at work.

JIM. Of course it is!

GOVERNOR. Oh, come now, Jim. That little item? D. B. Norton does things in a much bigger way . . .

JIM. It's his opening attack on you, Governor! Take my word for it! What did he buy a paper for? What did he hire a high-pressure editor like Connell for? He's in the oil business! I tell you, Governor, he's after your scalp!

GOVERNOR. All right, Jim. Don't burst a blood vessel, I'll look into it. *(flips button on dictograph)* Get me Spencer of the *Daily Chronicle*, please.

Dissolve to: Int. SPENCER's *office: Med. shot:* SPENCER *is on the telephone.*

SPENCER. Yes. Yes. I saw it, Governor . . . and if you ask me that's a phoney letter. Why, that gag has got whiskers on it. Huh? Okay, I'll get the mayor and maybe the Chamber of Commerce to go after them. *(into dictagraph)* Get Mayor Lovett on the phone!

Int. MAYOR's *office: Med shot: Of* MAYOR's *secretary.*

SECRETARY *(picking up phone).* Hello? Sorry, the Mayor's busy on the other phone.

Camera pans over to the MAYOR *who is fatuous and excitable.*

MAYOR *(into telephone).* Yes, I know, Mrs. Brewster. It's a terrible reflection on the city. I've had a dozen calls already.

SECRETARY *enters scene.*

SECRETARY. Spencer of the *Chronicle.*
MAYOR. Hold him. *(into phone)* Yes, Mrs. Brewster, I'm listening.

The SECRETARY *lays down the receiver.*

Dissolve to: Int. corner of a bedroom: Close shot: Of MRS. BREWSTER– *stout and loud. She is propped up in bed– a breakfast tray on her lap– the newspaper by her side.*

MRS. BREWSTER. As President of the Women's Auxiliary, I insist that this John Doe man be found and given a job. If something isn't done, I'll call a meeting of the whole Auxiliary—yes, and of the Junior Auxiliary, too. We'll hold a meeting and see—

Cut to: Int. MAYOR's *office: Med. shot: Of* MAYOR. *He lays the receiver down and we continue to hear* MRS. BREWSTER's *voice.* MAYOR *picks up* SPENCER's *phone.*

MAYOR. Yes, Yes, Spencer. Who? The Governor? Well, what about me? It's *my* building he's jumping off of! And *I'm* up for re-election, too!
MAYOR'S SEC'Y. Shh!
MAYOR *(to Secretary).* What are you doing? Get Connell at the *Bulletin! (to Spencer)* Why, he's liable to go right past my window, *(suddenly– to Sec'y– excitably)* What was that?!
SECRETARY. What?
MAYOR. Out the window! Something just flew by!
SECRETARY. I didn't see anything.
MAYOR *(semi-hysterical).* Well, don't stand there, you idiot. Go and look. Open the window. Oh, why did he have to pick on my building?

The SECRETARY, *telephone in hand, peers out window.*

MAYOR. Is there a crowd on the sidewalk?
SECRETARY. No, sir.
MAYOR. He may be caught on a ledge! Look again!
SECRETARY. I think it was just a sea-gull.
MAYOR. A sea-gull? What's a sea-gull doing around the city hall? That's, that's a bad omen, isn't it? *(picks up Mrs. Brewster's phone)*
SECRETARY. Oh, n-no, sir. The sea-gull is a lovely bird.
MAYOR *(into telephone).* I-it's all right, Mrs. Brewster. It was just a sea-gull. *(catches himself)* Er, nothing's happened yet! No, I'm watching. Don't worry. Ju-just leave it all to me!

The SECRETARY *holds out another phone. The* MAYOR *drops* MRS. BREWSTER's *phone again, and her voice is still heard.*

MAYOR *(into Spencer's phone).* Spencer, I'll call you back.

Secretary has gotten CONNELL *on the phone– hands phone to* MAYOR.

MAYOR. Hello! Connell! This is—*(to Secretary)* What are you doing? *(back to phone)* This is the Mayor.

Int. CONNELL's *office: Full shot:* CONNELL *is on the phone.* POP DWYER *is draped in a chair nearby.*

CONNELL. Yes, Mayor Lovett! How many times are you gonna call me? I've got everybody and his brother and sister out looking for him. Did you see the box I'm running?

He picks up the front page of the Bulletin; we see a four column box on the front page.

CONNELL *(reading).* "An appeal to John Doe. 'Think it over, John. Life can be beautiful,' says Mayor. 'If you need a job, apply to the editor of this paper . . .'" and so forth and so forth. . . . Okay, Mayor. I'll let you know as soon as I have something! What? . . . Well, pull down the blinds! *(he hangs up)*

The door opens and a man enters. His name is BEANY. *Walks fast, talks fast and accomplishes nothing. Outside, we see the painter trying once more to get his sign painted. He reaches in– and pulls the door to.*

BEANY. I went up to Miss Mitchell's house, boss. Boy, she's in a bad way.
CONNELL. Where is she?
BEANY. Hey, do you know something? She supports a mother and two kids. What do you know about that?
CONNELL *(controlling his patience).* Did you find her?

BEANY. No. Her mother's awful worried about her. When she left the house she said she was going on a roaring drunk. Er, the girl, I mean!

CONNELL (barking). Go out and find her!

BEANY. Sure. Hey, but the biggest thing I didn't tell you . . .

CONNELL picks up telephone.

CONNELL. Hello!. . . . Yeh?

BEANY. Her old man was Doc Mitchell. You know, the doc that saved my mother's life and wouldn't take any money for it? You remember that? Okay, boss, I'll go and look for her.

BEANY exits, knocking over an ash-stand.

CONNELL (into phone). Holy smokes, Commissioner. You've had twenty-four hours! Okay, Hawkshaw, grab a pencil. Here it is again. She's about five foot five, brown eyes, light chestnut hair and as fine a pair of legs as. . . .

The door opens, ANN stands there— CONNELL sees her.

CONNELL (into phone—staring at Ann) ever walked into this office.

Med. shot: At door. The sign painter is slowly beginning to lose patience. He again reaches in—pulls the door shut—glaring at ANN.

Close-up. Of ANN.

ANN (innocently). Did you want to see me?

Wider shot: CONNELL, without moving, stares at her.

CONNELL (quietly—sizzling). No. I've had the whole army and navy searching for you because that's a game we play here every day.

ANN. I remember, distinctly, being fired.

CONNELL. That's right. But you have a piece of property that still belongs to this newspaper. And I'd like to have it!

ANN. What's that?

CONNELL. The letter.

ANN. What letter?

CONNELL. The letter from John Doe.

ANN. Oh!

CONNELL. The whole town's in an uproar. We've got to find him. The letter's our only clue.

ANN (simply). There is no letter.

CONNELL. We'll get a handwriting expert to—(suddenly realizes what she has said) What!

He stares at her for a moment, flabbergasted—exchanges a look with POP—crosses to the back door—shuts it—then comes back to face her.

Close shot: ANN and CONNELL.

CONNELL. Say that again.

ANN. There is no letter. I made it up.

CONNELL looks at her a long moment and then up at POP.

CONNELL (repeating dully). You made it up.

ANN. Uh-huh. You said you wanted fireworks.

Wider shot: As he recovers from the shock, and then wheels on ANN again.

CONNELL. Don't you know there are nine jobs waiting for this guy? Twenty-two families want to board him free? Five women want to marry him, and the Mayor's practically ready to adopt him? And you. . . .

As CONNELL glares at her the door springs open and BEANY enters.

BEANY. I just called the morgue, boss. They say there's a girl there—

CONNELL. Shut up!

Close-up: Of BEANY. He is startled by this—and then stares pop-eyed as he sees ANN.

BEANY. Ann! Say, why didn't yuh—

CONNELL. Beany!

Med shot: At the door. The painter is beginning to grind his teeth. He pulls the door shut, viciously.

Wider shot: To include all.

POP. Only one thing to do, Hank. Drop the whole business quickly.

CONNELL. How?

POP. Run a story. Say John Doe was in here, and is sorry he wrote the letter and—

CONNELL (jumps in quickly). That's right. You got it! Sure! He came in here and I made him change his mind. "Bulletin editor saves John Doe's life." Why, it's perfect. I'll have Ned write it up. (into dictograph) Oh, Ned!

NED'S VOICE. Yeah?

CONNELL. I got a story I want yuh to—

ANN. Wait a minute!

She rushes over—snaps the dictograph off.

Med. shot: Of ANN, leaning on CONNELL'S desk.

ANN. Listen, you great big wonderful genius of a newspaperman!

ANN (continuing). You came down here to shoot some life into this dying paper, didn't you?

CONNELL *blinks under the attack.* POP *and* BEANY *move into the scene.*

ANN. Well, the whole town's curious about John Doe and, boom, just like that you're going to bury him. There's enough circulation in that man to start a shortage in the ink market!

CONNELL *(thoroughly bewildered)*. In *what* man!

ANN. John Doe.

CONNELL. What John Doe?

ANN. Our John Doe! The one I made up! Look, genius—Now, look. Suppose there *was* a John Doe—and he walked into this office. What would you do? Find him a job and forget the whole business, I suppose! Not me! I'd have made a deal with him!

CONNELL. A deal?

ANN. Sure! When you get hold of a stunt that sells papers you don't drop it like a hot potato. Why, this is good for at least a couple of months. You know what I'd do? Between now and let's say, Christmas, when he's gonna jump, I'd run a daily yarn starting with his boyhood, his schooling, his first job! A wide-eyed youngster facing a chaotic world. The problem of the average man, of all the John Does in the world.

Two shot: ANN *and* CONNELL. *Despite himself, he's interested in her recital.*

ANN. Now, then comes the drama. He meets discouragement. He finds the world has feet of clay. His ideals crumble. So what does he do? He decides to commit suicide in protest against the state of civilization. He thinks of the river! But no, no, he has a better idea. The City Hall. Why? Because he wants to attract attention. He wants to get a few things off his chest, and that's the only way he can get himself heard.

CONNELL. So?

Full shot: Of the whole group. BEANY *grins in admiration.* CONNELL *has leaned back in his chair, his eyes glued on* ANN.

ANN. So! So he writes me a letter and I dig him up. He pours out his soul to me, and from now on we quote: "I protest, by John Doe." He protests against all the evils in the world; the greed, the lust, the hate, the fear, all of man's inhumanity to man.

Arguments will start. Should he commit suicide or should he not! People will write in pleading with him. But no! No, sir! John Doe will remain adamant! On Christmas Eve, hot or cold, he goes! See?

She finishes, takes a deep breath—awed, and at the same time proud of her accomplishment.

Close shot: Of CONNELL. *He just stares at* ANN.

CONNELL *(after a pause—quietly)*. Very pretty. Very pretty, indeed, Miss Mitchell. But would you mind telling me who goes on Christmas Eve?

ANN. John Doe.

CONNELL *(loses control—screams)*. What John Doe?

ANN *(screams right back)*. The one we hire for the job, you lunkhead!

There is silence for a moment.

CONNELL *(breaking silence—speaks with a controlled patience)*. Wait a minute. Wait a minute. Lemme get this through this lame brain of mine. Are you suggesting we go out and hire someone to say he's gonna commit suicide on Christmas Eve? Is that it?

ANN *(nodding)*. Well, you're catching on.

CONNELL. Who, for instance?

ANN. Anybody! Er, er—Beany'll do!

Close-up: BEANY. *He is petrified.*

BEANY. Why sur— Who? Me? Jump off a— Oh, no! Any time but Christmas. I'm superstitious.

Full shot: BEANY *backs away from them—and when he gets to the door—makes a dash for it.*

Int. outer office: Med. shot: At door. As BEANY *comes dashing out, he almost upsets the painter from the stool. When the door is shut, the name of "Connell" which he has been printing is all smudged over. The painter stares at it, helplessly for a second, and then—unable to stand it any more, rises, throws his brush violently to the floor—after completely smearing the sign himself.*

Int. CONNELL's *office: Full shot:*

CONNELL *(sighing)*. Miss Mitchell, do me a favor, will you? Go on out and get married and have a lot o' babies—but stay out o' newspaper business!

POP. Better get that story in, Hank, it's getting late.

ANN *(to* CONNELL*)*. You're supposed to be a smart guy! If it was raining hundred dollar bills, you'd be out looking for a dime you lost some place.

CONNELL. Holy smokes! Wasting all this time listening to this mad woman.

He crosses to his desk just as NED *enters from the back door.*

NED. Look, Chief! Look what the *Chronicle* is running on John Doe. They say it's a fake!

CONNELL *turns sharply.*

Close-up: Of ANN. *She was just about giving up, when she hears this—and her eyes brighten alertly.*

Med. shot: At CONNELL's *desk.* CONNELL— *reading the paper—becomes incensed.*

CONNELL. Why, the no-good—low-down—*(reading)* "John Doe story amateur journalism. It's palpably phoney. It's a wonder anyone is taking it seriously." What do yuh think of those guys!

ANN *has walked into scene while* CONNELL *is reading.*

ANN. That's fine! That's fine! Now fall right into their laps. Go ahead. Say John Doe walked in and called the whole thing off. You know what that's going to sound like on top of this!
CONNELL *(doesn't like Ned hearing all this).* That's all, Ned. Thank you.

NED, *puzzled, exits.* CONNELL *comes away from his desk and walks around.*

CONNELL *(fighting spirit).* "Amateur journalism", huh? Why, the bunch of sophomores! I can teach them more about—

But he is interrupted by the front door being flung open. On the threshold stands BEANY.

BEANY. Hey, boss. Get a load of this.
CONNELL *(joins him in the doorway).* What?
BEANY. Look!

Med. shot: Over their shoulders. In the outer office are a large group of derelict-looking men. Some standing—some sitting—some leaning. It looks like the lobby of a flophouse had been transplanted.

Close shot: Beany and Connell.

CONNELL. What do they want?
BEANY. They all say they wrote the John Doe letter.

Med. shot: POP *and* ANN *have walked over and also peer out.*

CONNELL *(amused, turns).* They all wrote the letter?

ANN *pushes* CONNELL *aside—talks to* BEANY.

ANN. Tell them all to wait.

She shuts the door and turns to CONNELL.

ANN. Look, Mr. Connell—One of those men is your John Doe. They're desperate and will do anything for a cup of coffee. Pick one out and you can make the *Chronicle* eat their words.

Close-up: Of CONNELL. *A broad smile slowly spreads over his face.*

CONNELL. I'm beginning to like this.

Med. shot: POP *looks worried.*

POP. If you ask me, Hank, you're playing around with dynamite.
CONNELL. No, the gal's right. We can't let the *Chronicle* get the laugh on us! We've got to produce a John Doe now. *(muttering)* Amateur journalism, huh! *(starts for door)* I'll show those guys.
ANN. Sure—and there's no reason for them to find out the truth, either. *(significantly)* Because, naturally, *I* won't say anything.

CONNELL *turns sharply, stares at her a moment puzzled, then grins.*

CONNELL *(grinning).* Okay, sister, you get your job back.
ANN. Plus a bonus.
CONNELL. What bonus?

Close-up: Of ANN. *She takes the plunge. She is a little frightened at her own nerve, but she is going to brazen it out.*

ANN *(tries to drop it casually).* Oh, the bonus of a thousand dollars the *Chronicle* was going to pay me for this little document. You'll find it says, er: "I, Ann Mitchell, hereby certify that the John Doe letter was created by me—"

Med. shot: As she speaks, she gets the "little document" out of her bag, hands it to CONNELL *who glares at her, takes the paper and starts to read. Ann leans over his shoulder.* POP *peers over his other shoulder.*

CONNELL. I can read. I can read!
ANN. Sorry.

She backs away. CONNELL *continues reading her confession.*

CONNELL. So you think this is worth a thousand dollars, do you?
ANN *(very carelessly).* Oh, the *Chronicle* would consider it dirt cheap.
CONNELL. Packs everything, including a gun. *(flings paper on desk)* Okay, sister, you've got yourself a deal. Now let's take a look at the candidates. The one we pick has gotta be the typical average man. Typical American that can keep his mouth shut.

POP. Show me an American who can keep his mouth shut and—I'll eat him.

CONNELL *(opens door).* Okay, Beany, send 'em in one at a time. *(he steps back and rubs his hands in anticipation)*

Wipe to: Montage: Half a dozen different types of hoboes appear—and in each instance ANN *shakes her head, negatively.*

Wipe to: Close shot: Of a TALL CHAP, *head hanging shyly.*

Two shot: Of ANN *and* CONNELL. *They are impressed.*

Full shot: ANN *and* CONNELL *exchange hopeful glances and begin slowly walking around the new candidate.*

Close-up: Of TALL CHAP. *He feels awkward under this scrutiny.*

Wider shot: CONNELL *stops in his examination of the man.*

CONNELL. Did you write the letter to Miss Mitchell?
TALL CHAP *(after a pause).* No, I didn't.

ANN, CONNELL *and* POP *evince their surprise.*

CONNELL. What are you doing up here then?
TALL CHAP. Well, the paper said there were some jobs around loose. Thought there might be one left over.

They study him for a second, then ANN *walks over close to him.*

Two shot: ANN *and* TALL CHAP.

ANN. Had any schooling?
TALL CHAP. Yeah, a little.
ANN. What do you do when you work?
TALL CHAP *(slight pause).* I used to pitch.
ANN. Baseball?
TALL CHAP. Uh-huh. Till my wing went bad.
ANN. Where'd you play?
TALL CHAP. Bush leagues mostly.
Med. shot: To include the rest of them. They have their eyes glued on his face. ANN *is very much interested.*

CONNELL. How about family? Got any family?
TALL CHAP *(after a pause).* No.
CONNELL. Oh, just traveling through, huh?
TALL CHAP. Yeah. Me and a friend of mine. He's outside.

CONNELL *nods to the others to join him in a huddle. He crosses to a corner. They follow.*

Close three shot: They speak in subdued voices.

CONNELL. Looks all right—
ANN. He's perfect! A baseball player. What could be more American!
CONNELL. I wish he had a family, though.
POP. Be less complicated *without* a family.
ANN. Look at that face. It's wonderful. They'll believe *him.* Come on.

Close-up: Of TALL CHAP. *He is a strange, bewildered figure. He knows he is being appraised, but doesn't know why. He fingers his hat nervously and looks around the room. Suddenly he is attracted by something.*

Close-up: Of tray of sandwiches on CONNELL's *desk.*

Close-up: Of TALL CHAP. *He swallows hard. His eyes stare at the sandwiches hungrily.*

Med. shot: Over his shoulder. Shooting toward the huddling group. It breaks up. They walk toward him.

Med. shot: Another angle.

CONNELL. What's your name?
TALL CHAP. Willoughby. John Willoughby, Long John Willoughby they called me in baseball.
ANN. Er, would you, er, would you like to make some money?
JOHN. Yeah, maybe.

NOTE: Henceforth in this script he shall be referred to as JOHN DOE.

ANN. Would you be willing to say you wrote that letter—and stick by it?
JOHN. Oh, I get the idea. Yeah, maybe.

There is an appraising pause, and CONNELL *again signals them to join him in a huddle. They exit to their corner.*

Close-up: Of JOHN. *His eyes immediately go to the sandwiches.*

Close-up: Of tray, with sandwiches and milk, on desk.

Close-up: Of JOHN. *His eyes rivetted on tray. He glances, speculatively, over toward them and then back to the tray.*

Med. shot: Of the huddled group.

ANN. That's our man. He's made to order.
CONNELL. I don't know. He don't seem like a guy that'd fall into line.

ANN (*it's significant to her*). When you're desperate for money, you do a lot of things, Mr. Connell. He's our man, I tell you.

Suddenly, they are startled by a loud thud; they all look around sharply.

ANN. He's fainted! Get some water quickly!

As all three rush to him

CONNELL. Hurry up, Pop.
ANN. Oh.
CONNELL (*to John*). Right here. Sit down.
JOHN. Huh?
ANN. Are you all right?
JOHN. Yeah, I'm all right.

Dissolve to: Int. ANN's *office. Close-up: Of* JOHN—*sitting at* ANN's *desk, just completing a meal—and still eating voraciously.*

Camera draws back and we find another bindle-stiff sitting beside JOHN, *packing food away in silence. He is the friend* JOHN *referred to. He is much older and goes by the name of* COLONEL.

Camera continues to pull back revealing ANN *who sits nearby, watching them sympathetically.*

Close shot: JOHN *and the* COLONEL. *They continue eating.* JOHN *glances up and catches* ANN's *eye. He smiles self-consciously.*

Close-up: Of ANN. *She, too, smiles warmly.*

Med. shot: They continue to eat silently.

ANN. How many is that, six? Pretty hungry, weren't you?
COLONEL. Say, all this John Doe business is batty, if yuh ask me.
ANN. Well, nobody asked yuh.
COLONEL. Trying to improve the world by jumping off buildings. You couldn't improve the world if the building jumped on you!
JOHN (*to Ann*). Don't mind the Colonel. He hates people.
ANN. He likes you well enough to stick around.
JOHN. Oh, that's 'cause we both play doo-hickies. I met him in a box car a couple o' years ago. I was foolin' around with my harmonica and he comes over and joins in. I haven't been able to shake him since.

Full shot: Suddenly, he starts to play the overture from "William Tell." The COLONEL *whips out an ocarina and joins him.* ANN *stares, amused. The door opens and* CONNELL *and* BEANY *barge in, followed by half a dozen photographers.*

CONNELL. All right, boys, here he is.

ANN (*jumping up*). No, no, no! You can't take pictures of him like that—eating a sandwich—and with a beard!

She waves the photographers out, and shuts the door.

CONNELL. But, he's gonna jump off a building!
ANN. Yes, but not because he's out of a job. That's not news! This man's going to jump as a matter of principle.
CONNELL. Well, maybe you're right.
ANN. We'll clean him up and put him in a hotel room—under bodyguards. We'll make a mystery out of him. (*suddenly*) Did you speak to Mr. Norton?
CONNELL (*nods*). Thinks it's terrific. Says for us to go the limit. Wants us to build a bonfire under every big shot in the state.
ANN. Oh, swell! Is that the contract? (*seeing paper in* CONNELL's *hand*)
CONNELL. Yes. (*sees the* COLONEL) What's he doing here?
ANN. Friend of his. They play duets together.
CONNELL. Duets? But can we trust him?
ANN. Oh!
JOHN. I trust him.
CONNELL. Oh, you trust him, eh? Well, that's fine. I suppose he trusts you, too?
ANN. Oh, stop worrying. He's all right.
COLONEL (*insulted*). That's—
CONNELL. Well, okay. But we don't want more than a couple o' hundred people in on this thing. Now the first thing I want is an exact copy of the John Doe letter in your own handwriting.
ANN. I got it all ready. Here.
CONNELL. Well, that's fine. Now I want you to sign this agreement. It gives us an exclusive story under your name day by day from now until Christmas. On December twenty-sixth, you get one railroad ticket out of town, and the *Bulletin* agrees to pay to have your arm fixed. That's what you want, isn't it?
JOHN. Yeah, but it's got to be by bone-setter Brown.
CONNELL. Okay, bone-setter Brown goes. Here, sign it. Meanwhile, here's fifty dollars for spending money. That's fine. Beany!
BEANY. Yeah, Boss?
CONNELL. Take charge of him. Get him a suite at the Imperial and hire some bodyguards.
ANN. Yeah, and some new clothes, Beany.
BEANY. Do you think we better have him de-loused?
CONNELL. Yeh, yeh, yeh.
BEANY. Both of 'em?

CONNELL. Yes, both of 'em! But don't let him out of your sight.

ANN. Hey, Beany, gray suit, huh?

BEANY. Yeah.

CONNELL. Okay, fellows.

ANN. Take it easy, John Doe.

JOHN *and the* COLONEL *follow* BEANY *out.*

CONNELL *(turns to Ann).* And you! Start pounding that typewriter. Oh, boy! This is terrific! No responsibilities on our part. Just statements from John Doe and we can blast our heads off.

ANN *(interrupting).* Before you pop too many buttons, don't forget to make out that check for a thousand.

CONNELL *(grimaces).* Awwwww!

Dissolve to: Int. Living-room of suite.

Full shot: The door opens and BEANY *enters. He is followed by* JOHN *and the* COLONEL. JOHN *glances around, impressed. The* COLONEL *looks glum.*

Med. shot: At door. As JOHN *exits scene into the room, tailed by the unhappy* COLONEL. BEANY *beckons someone out in the corridor.*

BEANY. Okay, fellas.

Three bruisers stand in the doorway.

BEANY. Now, lemme see. You sit outside the door. Nobody comes in, see. You two fellas sit in here.

As they reach for chairs,

Cut to: Med. shot: JOHN *is pleased as his gaze wanders around the room.*

JOHN. Hey, pretty nifty, huh?

COLONEL. You ain't gonna get me to stay here.

JOHN. Sure, you are.

COLONEL. No, sir. That spot under the bridge where we slept last night's good enough for me.

While he speaks, JOHN *has managed to get a glimpse of himself in a mirror—admiring his new suit.*

BELL HOP. Hey, what'll I do with this baggage?

BEANY. Aw, stick 'em in the bedroom.

COLONEL. Gimme mine. I ain't staying! You know we were headed for the Columbia River country before all this John Doe business came up. You remember that, don't yuh?

JOHN. Sure. I remember. . . . Say, did your ears pop coming up in the elevator? Mine did.

COLONEL. Aw, Long John. . . . I tell you— it's no good. You're gonna get used to a lotta stuff that's gonna wreck you. Why, that fifty bucks in your pocket's beginning to show up on you already. And don't pull that on me neither! *(as John brings out harmonica)*

JOHN. Stop worrying, Colonel. I'm gonna get my arm fixed out of this.

Wider shot: As BEANY *enters scene with box of cigars.*

BEANY. Here's some cigars the boss sent up. Have one.

JOHN'S *eyes light up.*

JOHN. Hey, cigars!

He grabs one and stuffs it in his mouth.

BEANY *(to Colonel).* Help yourself.

COLONEL. Naw.

JOHN *flops into a luxurious chair—and immediately* ANGELFACE *holds a light up for his cigar.* JOHN *looks up, pleased.*

JOHN. Say, I'll bet yuh even the Major Leaguers don't rate an outfit like this.

ANGELFACE *(hands him a newspaper).* Here. Make yourself comfortable. *(turns to the Colonel)* Paper?

COLONEL *(sharply).* I don't read no papers and I don't listen to radios either. I know the world's been shaved by a drunken barber and I don't have to read it.

ANGELFACE *backs away, puzzled.*

COLONEL *(crosses to John).* I've seen guys like you go under before. Guys that never had a worry. Then they got ahold of some dough and went goofy. The first thing that happens to a guy—

BEANY. Hey, did ya get a load of the bedroom?

JOHN. No.

BEANY *beckons to him to follow, which* JOHN *does with great interest.*

Int. bedroom: Full shot: As BEANY *and* JOHN *puff luxuriously on their cigars and examine the room.*

COLONEL *(in doorway).* The first thing that happens to a guy like that—he starts wantin' to go into restaurants and sit at a table and eat salads—and cup cakes—and tea—*(disgusted)* Boy, what that kinda food does to your system!

JOHN *pushes on the bed and is impressed with its softness.*

COLONEL. The next thing the dope wants is a room. Yessir, a room with steam heat! And curtains and rugs and 'fore you know it, he's all softened up and he can't sleep 'less he has a bed.

Close-up: Of BEANY. *He stares, bewildered, at the* COLONEL.

Wider shot: JOHN *turns and crosses to window.*

JOHN *(as he goes)*. Hey, stop worrying, Colonel. Fifty bucks ain't going to ruin me.

COLONEL. I seen plenty of fellers start out with fifty bucks and wind up with a bank account!

BEANY *(can't stand it any more)*. Hey, whatsa matter with a bank account, anyway?

COLONEL *(ignoring him)*. And let me tell you, Long John. When you become a guy with a bank account, they got you. Yessir, they got you!

BEANY. Who's got him?

COLONEL. The heelots!

BEANY. Who?

JOHN *(at the window)*. Hey There's the City Hall tower I'm supposed to jump off of. It's even higher than this.

BEANY. Who's got him?

COLONEL. The heelots!

Close-up: JOHN *opens window and leans out.*

Close-up: Of BEANY. *His eyes pop; he's petrified.*

Med. shot: JOHN *stretches far out of the window, and quickly bounces back.*

JOHN. Wow!

At the same time BEANY *springs to his side and yanks him back.*

BEANY. Hey, wait a minute! You ain't supposed to do that till Christmas Eve! Wanta get me in a jam?

JOHN *(twinkle in his eye)*. If it's gonna get you in a jam, I'll do you a favor. I won't jump.

He exits to the living room.

Int. living room: Full shot: As JOHN *enters, flicking ashes from his cigar, grandly, the* COLONEL *leaves the doorway, still pursuing his point.*

COLONEL. And when they get you, you got no more chance than a road-rabbit.

BEANY *(dogging the* COLONEL*)*. Hey. Who'd you say was gonna get him?

JOHN. Say, is this one of those places where you ring if you want something?

BEANY. Yeah. Just use the phone.

The thought of this delights JOHN.

JOHN. Boy! I've always wanted to do this!

He goes to the phone.

BEANY. Hey, Doc, look. Look, Doc. Gimme that again, will yuh? Who's gonna get him?

COLONEL. The heelots!

BEANY. Who are they?

Two shot: The COLONEL *finally levels off on* BEANY.

COLONEL. Listen, sucker, yuh ever been broke?

BEANY. Sure. Mostly often.

COLONEL. All right. You're walking along—not a nickel in your jeans—free as the wind—nobody bothers you—hundreds of people pass by in every line of business—shoes, hats, automobiles, radio, furniture, everything. They're all nice, lovable people, and they let you alone. Is that right?

Close-up: Of BEANY—*nodding his head, bewildered.*

COLONEL'S VOICE. Then you get hold of some dough, and what happens?

BEANY *instinctively shakes his head.*

Two shot: The COLONEL *takes on a sneering expression.*

COLONEL. All those nice, sweet, lovable people become heelots. A lot of heels. *(mysterioso)* They begin creeping up on you—trying to sell you something. They got long claws and they get a strangle-hold on you—and you squirm—and duck and holler—and push 'em away—but you haven't got a chance—they've got you! First thing you know, you own things. A car, for instance.

BEANY *has been following him, eyes blinking, mouth open.*

COLONEL. Now your whole life is messed up with *more* stuff—license fees—and number plates—and gas and oil—and taxes and insurance—

Close shot: Of the LUGS *at the door. One of them listens with a half-smile on his face. The other, more goofy, looks bewildered. He has been listening—and now, slowly rises, ears cocked, frightened by the harrowing tale. Camera retreats before him—as he slowly walks nearer to* BEANY *and the* COLONEL. *Meantime, we continue to hear the* COLONEL'S *voice.*

COLONEL'S VOICE. . . . and identification cards—and bills—and letters—and flat tires—and dents—and motorcycle cops—and traffic tickets and court rooms—and fines—and lawyers—

Wider shot: The LUG *steps up directly behind* BEANY—*and the two horrified faces are close together—both staring at the* COLONEL.

COLONEL. And a million and one other things. And what happens? You're not the free and happy guy you used to be. You gotta have money to pay for all those things—so you go after what the other feller's got—*(with finality)* And there you are—you're a heelot yourself!

Close shot: Of the two heads of BEANY *and the* LUG. *They continue to stare, wide-eyed, at the* COLONEL.

Wider shot: As JOHN *approaches the* COLONEL.

JOHN *(smiling)*. You win, Colonel. Here's the fifty. Go on out and get rid of it.
COLONEL *(as he goes)*. You bet I will! As fast as I can! Gonna get some canned goods—a fishing rod, and the rest I'm gonna give away.
ANGELFACE *(aghast)*. Give away?
JOHN *(calling)*. Hey. Get me a pitcher's glove! Got to get back into practice.
ANGELFACE. Say, he's giving it away! I'm gonna get me some of that!
BEANY. Hey, come back here, yuh heelot!

The COLONEL *has just reached the door when it flies open and Ann comes in with photographer* EDDIE—*she sees* JOHN *all dressed up.*

ANN. Hello there. Well, well! If it isn't the man about town!
EDDIE. All set, Ann?
ANN *(coming out of it)*. Huh? Oh, yes. Let's go. *(she backs away)* Now, let's see. We want some action in these pictures.
JOHN. Action?
ANN. Um-hum.

JOHN *winds up in pitching pose—his left leg lifted up high.*

EDDIE. That's good.
ANN. No, no, no. This man's going to jump off a roof.
EDDIE. Oh.
ANN. Here. Wait a minute. Let me comb your hair. Sit down. There. That's better.

Close shot: She combs his hair—straightens his tie—etc. He inhales the fragrance of her hair and likes it—winks to the others. She poses JOHN's *face and looks it over.*

ANN. You know, he's got a nice face, hasn't he?
ANGELFACE. Yeh—he's pretty.

JOHN *gives him a look and starts to get up slowly.*

ANN. Here. Sit down! *(to* ANGELFACE*)* Quiet, egghead! *(back to* JOHN*)* All right, now, a serious expression.
JOHN *(laughing)*. Can't. I'm feeling too good.
ANN. Oh, come on, now. This is serious. You're a man disgusted with all of civilization.
JOHN. With all of it?
ANN. Yes, you're sore at the world. Come on, now.
JOHN. Oh, crabby guy, huh?

He tries scowling.

ANN. Yeah. No, no! *(laughing)* No! No, look. You don't have to *smell* the world! *(the men laugh)*
JOHN. Well, all those guys in the bleachers think—
ANN. Never mind those guys. All right, stand up. Now let's see what you look like when you protest.
JOHN. Against what?
ANN. Against anything. Just protest.
JOHN *(laughing)*. You got me.
ANN. Oh, look. I'm the umpire, and you just cut the heart of the plate with your fast one and I call it a ball. What would you do?
JOHN *(advances toward her)*. Oh, yuh did, huh?
ANN. Yes!
JOHN. Why can't you call right, you bone-headed, pig-eared, lop-eared, pot-bellied—
ANN. Grab it, Eddie, grab it!

Eddie takes the picture.

A Montage: Of Newspaper inserts featuring John Doe's picture.

"I protest against collapse of decency in the world."
"I protest against corruption in local politics."
"I protest against civic heads being in league with crime."
"I protest against state relief being used as political football."
"I protest against County Hospitals shutting out the needy."
"I protest against all the brutality and slaughter in the world."

Close-up: Superimposed over all of the above is a circulation chart—showing the circulation of the Bulletin *in a constant rise.*

Dissolve to: Int. GOVERNOR's *study: Med. shot: The* GOVERNOR *paces furiously. In front of him are several associates.*

GOVERNOR. I don't care whose picture they're publishing. I still say that this John Doe person is a myth. And you can quote me on that. And I'm going to insist on his being produced for questioning. You know as well as I do that this whole thing is being engineered by a vicious man with a vicious purpose—Mr. D. B. Norton.

As he finishes saying this, Dissolve to: Ext. D. B.'s *estate:*

Close-up: Of D. B. NORTON. *Camera pulls back and we find him on horseback.*

Reverse long shot: We discover that he is watching the maneuvers of a motorcycle corps who are in uniform. They are being drilled by TED SHELDON.

Med. shot: As a groom rides toward D. B.

GROOM. Mr. Connell and Miss Mitchell are at the house, sir.

D. B. Oh, they are? All right, come on. *(clicking)*

Dissolve to: Int. D. B.'s *study: Med. shot—panning: As* ANN, D. B. *and* CONNELL *enter and cross to* D. B.'s *desk.*

ANN *(as they walk)*. Personally, I think it's just plain stupidity to drop it now.

They reach D. B.'s *desk and stop.*

ANN. You should see his fan mail! Thousands! Why, it's going over like a house afire!

Close-up: Of D. B. *He studies her a moment before he turns to* CONNELL.

D. B. What are you afraid of, Connell? It's doubled our circulation.

Wider shot: To include all three.

CONNELL. Yeah, but it's got everybody sore. Ads are being pulled—the Governor's starting a libel suit—what's more, they all know John Doe's a phoney—and they insist on seeing him.

ANN. Well, what about it? *Let* them see him! We'll go them one better. They can also hear him. *(to* D. B.) You own a radio station, Mr. Norton. Why not put him on the air?

Close-up: Of D. B. *He admires her fight.*

CONNELL's VOICE. Watch out for this dame, D. B. She'll drive you batty!

ANN. Ohh!

Wider shot: To include all three.

CONNELL. Look. We can't let 'em get to this bush-league pitcher and start pumping him. Good night! No telling what that screwball might do. I walked in yesterday—here he is, standing on a table with a fishing pole fly-casting. Take my advice and get him out of town before this thing explodes in our faces!

ANN. If you do, Mr. Norton, you're just as much of a dumb cluck as he is! Excuse me.

CONNELL *(to Ann—hotly)*. No, you've got yourself a meal ticket and you hate to let go.

ANN. Sure, it's a meal ticket for me. I admit it, but it's also a windfall for somebody like Mr. Norton who's trying to crash national politics. *(she turns to* D. B.) That's what you bought the newspaper for, isn't it? You wanta reach a lotta people, don't you? Well, put John Doe on the air and you can reach a hundred and fifty million of 'em. He can say anything he wants and they'll listen to him.

Close-up: Of D. B. *Fascinated by* ANN.

Wider shot: CONNELL *stares at her derisively.* D. B. *is completely absorbed.*

ANN. Let's forget the Governor, the Mayor and all small fry like that! This can arouse national interest! If he made a hit around here—he can do it everywhere else in the country! And you'll be pulling the strings, Mr. Norton!

Close-up: Of D. B. *His eyes have begun to light up with extensive plans.*

Wider shot: D. B. *continues to study* ANN *with deep interest. Then he turns to* CONNELL.

D. B. Go down to the office and arrange for some radio time.

CONNELL *(protesting)*. Why, D. B., you're not going to fall for—

D. B. *(interrupting sharply)*. I want it as soon as possible.

CONNELL *(shrugging)*. Okay. I just came in to get warm, myself. Come on, let's go.

He starts out. ANN *picks up her bag, prepared to follow* CONNELL.

D. B. Er, don't you go. I want to talk to you.

CONNELL *goes.* ANN *waits, somewhat nervously.*

D. B. *(when* CONNELL *is gone)*. Sit down.

Med. two shot: ANN *and* D. B. D. B. *studies her for a moment.*

D. B. . . . Er, this John Doe idea is yours, huh?

ANN. Yes, sir.

D. B. How much money do you get?

ANN. Thirty dollars.

D. B. *(probingly).* Thirty dollars? Well, er, what are you after? I mean, what do you want? A journalistic career?

ANN. Money.

D. B. *(laughs).* Money? Well, I'm glad to hear somebody admit it. Do you suppose you could write a radio speech that would put that fellow over?

ANN. Oh, I'm sure I can.

D. B. Do it, and I'll give you a hundred dollars a week.

ANN. A hundred dollars!

D. B. That's only the beginning. You play your cards right and you'll never have to worry about money again. Oh, I knew it.

ANN'S *eyes brighten with excitement. They are interrupted by the arrival of* TED SHELDON, *in uniform.*

D. B. *(to* TED*).* Hello. Whenever there's a pretty woman around, er— *(laughing)* This is my nephew, Ted Sheldon, Miss Mitchell.

ANN. How do you do.

TED. How do you do!

D. B. All right, Casanova. I'll give you a break. See that Miss Mitchell gets a car to take her home.

TED. Always reading my mind, aren't you?

ANN *(laughing).* Thank you very much for everything.

D. B. And, Miss Mitchell—I think from now on you'd better work directly with me.

ANN. Yes, sir.

They exit. D. B. *walks to the door, a pleased expression on his face.*

Close-up: Of D. B. *His face wreathed in a victorious smile.*

Fade-out.

Fade-in. Int. ANN'S *living room: Close shot: Of* ANN. *She sits at a typewriter reading something she has written. Suddenly, impulsively, she yanks the sheet out of the machine and flings it to the floor. As she rises, camera pulls back. We find the floor littered with previously unsuccessful attempts to get the speech written. For a moment,* ANN *paces agitatedly, until she is interrupted by a commotion.*

Med. Shot: At door. ANN'S *two sisters,* IRENE *and* ELLEN, *aged nine and eleven—and dressed in their sleeping pajamas, dash in, squealing mischievously. Camera pans with them as they rush to* ANN *and leap on her.*

ANN. Oh! Hey! Oh, hey! I thought you were asleep!

ELLEN. We just wanted to say good night, Sis.

They embrace and kiss her.

ANN. Oh, oh! Oh, you little brats! You're just stalling. I said good night!

Med. shot: At door. ANN'S MOTHER *appears in the doorway. She is a prim little woman— her clothes have a touch of the Victorian about them— her hair is done up in old-fashioned style, her throat is modestly covered in lace.*

MOTHER *(above the din).* Come, come, come, children. It's past your bedtime.

ELLEN. Oh, all right.

MOTHER. Go on!

ELLEN. Come on, Pooch! Come on, come on.

MOTHER. Now, keep Pooch off the bed.

The CHILDREN *exit, squealing.* ANN'S MOTHER *goes to* ANN'S *desk and searches for something.*

ANN. Stick a fork through me! I'm done. I'll never get this speech right.

MOTHER. Oh, yes you will, Ann dear . . . you're very clever.

ANN. Yeah, I know. What are you looking for?

MOTHER. Your purse. I need ten dollars.

ANN. What for? I gave you fifty just the other day.

MOTHER. Yes, I know, dear, but Mrs. Burke had her baby yesterday. Nine pounds! And there wasn't a thing in the house—and this morning the Community Chest lady came around and—

ANN. And the fifty's gone, huh? Who's the ten for?

MOTHER. The Websters.

ANN. The Websters!

MOTHER. You remember those lovely people your father used to take care of? I thought I'd buy them some groceries. Oh, Ann, dear, it's a shame, those poor—

ANN. You're marvelous, Ma. You're just like Father used to be. Do you realize a couple of weeks ago we didn't have enough to eat ourselves?

MOTHER. Why, yes, I know, dear, but these people are in such need and we have plenty now.

ANN. If you're thinking of that thousand dollars, forget it. It's practically all gone. We owed everybody in town. Now, you've just gotta stop giving all your money away.

Her MOTHER *looks up, surprised at her tone.*

Close-up: ANN *realizes she has spoken sharply to her* MOTHER *and immediately regrets. Her face softens.*

Med. shot: As ANN *crosses to her* MOTHER— *and places an arm around her shoulder, tenderly.*

ANN. Oh, I'm sorry, Ma. Oh, don't pay any attention to me. I guess I'm just upset about all this. Gee whizz, here I am with a great opportunity to get somewhere, to give us security for once in our lives, and I'm stuck. If I could put this over, your Mrs. Burke can have six babies!

MOTHER. Do you mean the speech you're writing?

ANN. Yeah, I don't know. I, I simply can't get it to jell! I created somebody who's gonna give up his life for a principle, hundreds of thousands of people are gonna listen to him over the radio and, unless he says something that's, well, that's sensational, it's just no good!

MOTHER. Well, honey, of course I don't know what kind of a speech you're trying to write, but judging from the samples I've read, I don't think anybody'll listen.

ANN. What?

MOTHER. Darling, there are so many complaining political speeches. People are tired of hearing nothing but doom and despair on the radio. If you're going to have him say anything, why don't you let him say something simple and real, something with hope in it? If your father were alive, he'd know what to say.

ANN. Oh, yes, Father certainly would.

MOTHER. Wait a minute . . .

ANN. Huh?

MRS. MITCHELL *crosses to a desk, finds a key and unlocks a compartment.* ANN *watches her, curiously.*

Close shot: MRS. MITCHELL *extracts a diary from the compartment, which she handles very tenderly.*

Camera pans with her as she goes back to ANN.

MOTHER. That's your father's diary, Ann.

ANN. Father's. . . . I never knew he had a diary.

MOTHER. There's enough in it for a hundred speeches, things people ought to hear nowadays. You be careful of it, won't you dear? It's always helped keep your father alive for me.

ANN *(holds* MOTHER'S *hand to her cheek).* You bet I will, Ma.

Her mother abruptly leaves.

Close-up: ANN *turns her attention to the diary. As she opens it, her eyes sparkle expectantly. She becomes interested in the first thing she sees.*

Dissolve to: Int. corridor of hotel.

Med. shot: At door of JOHN'S *suite. A crowd of people are around the door trying to crash it. The* LUG *on guard stands before the door.*

LUG. Wait a minute. John Doe don't wanta sign no autographs.

INQUIRER. Well, what does he do all day?

LUG. What does he do all day? He's writin' out his memories!

Cut to: Int. living room

Med. shot: BEANY *is on the telephone. He is apparently weary from answering them all day.*

BEANY. Sorry, lady. You can't see Mr. Doe. He wants to be alone. No, no, he just sits around all day and commutes with himself.

Camera swings around to JOHN. *He stands in the middle of the floor, his pitcher's glove on, playing an imaginary game of ball. He winds up and throws an imaginary ball.*

Close-up: Of the COLONEL. *He wears a catcher's mitt— and smacks it as if he just caught the ball.*

BEANY *(umpiring).* St—rike!

COLONEL. I don't know how you're gonna stand it around here till after Christmas.

Full shot: At the door are the two LUGS, *watching the imaginary ball game. The* COLONEL *takes a couple of steps over home plate, and throws the "ball" back to* JOHN *who picks it up out of the air.*

COLONEL *(as he steps back behind the plate).* I ain't heard a train whistle in two weeks.

He crouches on his knees— and gives JOHN *a signal.*

COLONEL. I know why you're hangin' around—you're stuck on a girl—that's all a guy needs is to get hooked up with a woman.

Close shot: Of JOHN. *He shakes his head, and waits for another sign. When he gets it, he nods. He steps onto the mound— winds up and lets another one go. This is apparently a hit, for his eyes shoot skyward, and he quickly turns— watching the progress of the ball as it is flung to first base. From his frown we know the man is safe.*

Close shot: Of ANGELFACE *and* MIKE. ANGELFACE *is seriously absorbed in the game.* MIKE *leans against the wall, eyes narrowed, a plan going on in his head.*

ANGELFACE *(seriously)*. What was that? A single?

Close-up: Of JOHN.

JOHN *(explaining)*. The first baseman dropped the ball.

Close-up: Of ANGELFACE.

ANGELFACE *(shouting at "firstbaseman")*. Butterfingers! *(back to John)* That's tough luck, Pal.

Med. shot: JOHN *disregards him completely. He is too much absorbed with the man on first. He now has the stance of a pitch without the windup.*

COLONEL. When a guy has a woman on his hands—the first thing he knows his life is balled up with a lot more things—furniture and—

Close shot: Of JOHN. *He catches the "ball"— gets into position— nods to his catcher—raises his hands in the air, takes a peek toward first base— and suddenly wheels around facing camera, and whips the "ball" toward first base. Almost immediately his face lights up.*

Close-up: Of ANGELFACE.

ANGELFACE. Did you get him?

Close-up: Of JOHN. *He winks.*

BEANY *(umpiring)*. You're out!

Full shot: JOHN *flips the glove off his hand so that it dangles from his wrist— and massages the ball with his two palms.*

ANGELFACE. That's swell! What's this—the end of the eighth?

JOHN. Ninth!

He steps into the "pitcher's box".

Wider shot: Just as they take their positions, the LUG, *from outside, partly opens the door.*

LUG. Hey, Beany! There's a coupla lugs from the *Chronicle* snooping around out here!

BEANY *immediately comes from background.*

BEANY. Come on, Angelface!

As they reach the door, the LUG *speaks to* ANGELFACE.

LUG. What's the score, Angelface?
ANGELFACE. Three to two—favor of us.
LUG. Gee, that's great!

Close-up: Of JOHN. *He has heard this and grins mischievously. He starts winding up for another pitch.*

Close-up: Of MIKE. *He looks around mischievously, then turns to* JOHN.

MIKE. You've got swell form. Must have been a pretty good pitcher.

Wider shot: JOHN *is just receiving the ball.*

JOHN. Pretty good? Say, I was just about ready for the major leagues when I chipped a bone in my elbow. I got it pitchin' a nineteen-inning game!
MIKE. Nineteen!
JOHN. Yep. There was a major league scout there watching me, too. and he came down after the game with a contract. Do you know what? I couldn't lift my arm to sign it. But I'll be okay again as soon as I get it fixed up.
MIKE *(picks up newspaper— sighing)*. That's too bad.
JOHN. What do you mean, too bad?
MIKE *(pretending distraction)*. Huh? Oh, that you'll never be able to play again.
JOHN. Well, what are you talking about? I just told you I was gonna get a—
MIKE. *(interrupting carelessly)*. Well, you know how they are in baseball—if a guy's mixed up in a racket—
JOHN *(walking over)*. Racket? What do you mean?
MIKE. Well, I was just thinking about this John Doe business. Why, as soon as it comes out it's all a fake, you'll be washed up in baseball, won't you?
JOHN. Y-yeah. Gee, doggone it, I never thought about that. Gosh!
MIKE. And another thing, what about all the kids in the country, the kids that idolize ball players? What are they gonna think about you? *(shakes his head)*

Close shot: Of the COLONEL. *He has dropped his glove—flopped into a chair— and has taken out his ocarina.*

JOHN'S VOICE. Hey, did you hear that, Colonel?

The COLONEL *nods, disinterestedly, and begins to play.*

Wider shot: JOHN *ponders his dilemma for a second.*

JOHN. I gotta figure some way out of this thing!

COLONEL. The elevators are still runnin'.

MIKE (*carelessly*). I know *one* way you can do it.

JOHN. How?

MIKE. Well, when you get up on the radio, all you have to do is say the whole thing's a frame-up. Make you a hero sure as you're born!

John thinks this over, but something troubles him.

JOHN. Yeah, but how am I gonna get my arm fixed?

MIKE. Well, that's a cinch. I know somebody that'll give you five thousand dollars just to get up on the radio and tell the truth.

COLONEL (*eyes popping*). Five thousand dollars?

MIKE. Yeah. Five thousand dollars. And he gets it right away. You don't have to wait till Christmas.

COLONEL. Look out, Long John! They're closing in on you!

JOHN (*ignores* COLONEL). Say, who's putting up this dough?

MIKE. Feller runs the *Chronicle*. (*takes it out of his pocket*) Here's the speech you make—it's all written out for you.

JOHN *takes it.*

Close-up: Of the COLONEL.

COLONEL (*eyes heaven-ward*). Five thousand dollars! Holy mackerel! I can see the heelots comin'. The whole army of them!

MIKE. It's on the level.

Close-up: Of JOHN.

Dissolve to: Int. broadcasting station:

Close shot: TELEPHONE OPERATORS.

1ST GIRL. No, I'm sorry. Tickets for the broadcast are all gone. Phone the Bulletin.

2ND GIRL. Sorry. No more tickets left.

Med. shot: Crowd chattering—they recognize JOHN DOE *coming in.*

Close shot: At a side door in broadcasting station. As the COLONEL *and* MIKE *take their places.*

Int. office in broadcasting station: Full shot: JOHN *is led by* BEANY *into the office. They are immediately followed by several photographers.*

BEANY. Here he is.

ANN. Hello, John. All set for the big night? Swell!

PHOTOGRAPHER. Turn around.

2ND PHOTOGRAPHER. One moment—hold it! Now stand still, Mr. Doe.

ANN. Okay, Beany, take them outside.

Two shot: JOHN *and* ANN.

ANN. Now, look, John. Here's the speech. It's in caps and double-spaced. You won't have any trouble reading it. Not nervous, are you?

JOHN. No.

ANN. Of course not. He wouldn't be.

JOHN. Who?

ANN. John Doe. The one in there. (*pointing to speech*)

BEANY. Hey, don't let your knees rattle. It picks up on the mike!

ANN. Oh, Beany! You needn't be nervous, John. All you have to remember is to be sincere.

Wider shot. Man pokes his head in.

MAN. Pick up the phone, Miss Mitchell. It's for you.

ANN (*takes phone*). Hello? Yes, Mother. Oh, thank you, darling.

Full shot: While she speaks on the phone, MRS. BREWSTER *barges in, accompanied by two other ladies.*

MRS. BREWSTER. Oh, there he is, the poor, dear man! Oh, good luck to you, Mr. Doe. We want you to know that we're all for you. The girls all decided that you're not to jump off any roof at all. Oh, we'll stop it!

ANN *completes the phone call—crosses to* MRS. BREWSTER.

ANN. Sorry, ladies. Mr. Doe can't be bothered now. He's gotta make a speech out there, and—

While she gets them out— MIKE *slips into the room.*

Close shot: MIKE *and* JOHN.

MIKE. Have you got the speech I gave you?

JOHN (*taps breast pocket*). Yeah.

MIKE. Now, look. I'll give this money to the Colonel just as soon as you get started. We'll have a car waiting at the side entrance for you.

JOHN. Okay.

Full shot: ANN *turns away from the door.*

ANN (*to* MIKE). How'd you get in here?

MIKE. Huh? Oh, I just came in to wish him luck.

ANN. Come on, out. Out! *(turning to John).* Mother says good luck, too. John, when you read that speech, please, please believe every word of it. He's turned out to be a wonderful person, John.

JOHN. Who?

ANN. John Doe, the one in the speech.

JOHN. Oh. Yeah.

ANN. You know something? I've, I've actually fallen in love with him.

Full shot: They are interrupted by the arrival of CONNELL. *He is accompanied by several photographers—and a beautiful girl in a bathing suit. A banner across her front reads: "Miss Average Girl".*

CONNELL. All right, there he is, sister. Now, come on—plenty of oomph!

The GIRL, *all smiles, throws her arm around* JOHN's *shoulder—and strikes a languid pose. The flashlights go off.*

ANN. What's the idea?

CONNELL. No, no, no. That's too much!

PHOTOGRAPHER. One moment, please.

ANN. This is no time for cheap publicity, Mr. Connell!

CONNELL. Listen. If that guy lays an egg, I want to get something out of it. I'm getting a *Jane* Doe ready!

ANN *(trying to get rid of them).* That's fine, honey. Now, get out!

While there is this confusion, the COLONEL *pushes in and stands in the doorway.*

COLONEL. How're you doin'?

CONNELL *(calls to Beany outside).* All right, Beany—bring 'em in!

While CONNELL *speaks, two* MIDGETS *push the* COLONEL *out of the way and enter the room. The* COLONEL *glances down—and nearly jumps out of his skin.* BEANY *follows them in.*

COLONEL. Holy smoke! A half a heelot!

BEANY. There you are, Boss, just like you ordered. Symbols of the little people.

CONNELL. Okay. Get them up.

BEANY *lifts them up and places them, one on each of* JOHN's *arms. The flashlights go off.*

ANN. This is ridiculous, Mr. Connell! Come on, give him a chance. The man's on the air!

While she speaks, she tries to shove the photographers out.

BOY MIDGET *(to girl midget).* Come on, Snooks—you better bail out.

GIRL MIDGET *(coquettishly).* Goodbye, Mr. Doe!

BEANY *lifts her off—and* ANN *pushes them all out—just as the* STAGE MANAGER *reappears.*

STAGE MANAGER. Better get ready. One minute to go!

Two shot: JOHN *and* ANN. ANN *turns quickly to* JOHN.

ANN. Wow! One minute to go, and the score is nothing to nothing! Now, please, John, you won't let me down, will you? Will you? Course you won't. If you'll just think of yourself as the real John Doe.

Listen. Everything in that speech are things a certain man believed in. He was my father, John. And when he talked, people listened. They'll listen to you, too.

Funny—you know what my mother said the other night? She said to look into your eyes— that I'd see Father there.

STAGE MANAGER. Hey—what do you say?

ANN. Okay! We're coming. Come on!

ANN. Now, listen, John. You're a pitcher. Now, get in there and pitch! *(kisses his cheek)* Good luck.

For a moment he just stares at her, under a spell. Then, turning, he exits. After a second of watching him, ANN *follows.*

STUDIO OFFICIAL. Give him room, let him through. Come on.

Int. broadcasting stage: Med. shot: Camera retreats in front of JOHN *and the official, as they leave the office and proceed to the microphones. Everyone stares curiously at* JOHN—*whispering to each other.*

Med. shot: Shooting through glass partition, toward control booth. We see the two men at the board. They glance nervously at their watches— then at the clock on the wall.

Close shot: Of ANN. *She has taken a position at a table near the mike. Next to her sits* CONNELL. ANN *watches* JOHN *with intense interest.*

The COLONEL *has followed* JOHN *up to the microphone.*

COLONEL *(to John).* Hey. Let's get out o' here. There's the door right there.

M.C. Hey, what're you doing here?

COLONEL. That's what I'd like to know!

M.C. Come on, out. Out.

JOHN. Say, he's a friend of mine.

ANN *(at John's elbow)*. Never mind. Let him alone. He's all right. I'll be right over there pulling for you.

JOHN *starts to follow* ANN *away from mike.* ANN *leads him back to mike again.*

ANN. No, John—over here.
2ND M. C. Stand by.

Med. shot: At door. The COLONEL *surreptitiously tries the door, to see that it opens readily. Standing near him is* BEANY *and the others.*

Med. shot: Group around SPENCER. *They wait expectantly. Their eyes sparkling with excitement.*

SPENCER. Phone the *Chronicle.* Tell 'em to start getting those extras out.

Med. shot: Toward control booth. The man with the earphones on has his hand up ready to give the signal. He listens a moment, then abruptly drops his hand.

Close-up: The man near the announcer throws his hand up as a signal to someone off scene

Med. shot: An orchestra in a corner. The conductor waves his baton—and the orchestra blasts out a dramatic fanfare.

Close shot: ANNOUNCER *and* JOHN. ANNOUNCER *holds his script up and the moment the music stops he speaks dramatically:*

ANNOUNCER *(rapid-fire)*. And good evening, ladies and gentlemen. This is Kenneth Frye, speaking for *The New Bulletin.* Tonight we give you something entirely new and different. Standing beside me is the young man who has declared publicly that on Christmas Eve he intends to commit suicide, giving as his reason—quote: "I protest against the state of civilization." End quote. Ladies and gentlemen, the *New Bulletin* takes pleasure in presenting the man who is fast becoming the most talked-of person in the whole country, JOHN DOE!

The man next to him waves his hand—there is an outburst of music.

A flash: Of ANN—*she looks at* JOHN *intently.*

Med. shot: Group around BEANY. *They all applaud, except for* MIKE *and the* COLONEL. MIKE, *with his hand hanging down, nudges the* COLONEL.

Close shot: Of their hands meeting and we see the envelope change hands. Camera pans up to the COLONEL's *face which is twisted into a miserable grimace.*

Close-up: Of JOHN. *He glances around, uncertainly.*

Close shot: Of MIKE *and the* COLONEL. MIKE *elbows the* COLONEL *to throw his signal. The* COLONEL *looks toward* JOHN *and nods his head.*

Close shot: Of JOHN. *He catches the* COLONEL's *signal and quickly his hand goes to his pocket. Just as he is about to bring it out, his hand pauses. He turns and looks at* ANN.

Close-up: Of ANN. *A warm, pleading look in her eyes.*

Med. shot: Around JOHN. *He is still staring at* ANN, *when the* ANNOUNCER *reaches over and nudges him—pointing to the mike.* JOHN *snaps out of it—turns his face to the mike—pushes the paper back in his pocket—and starts reading* ANN's *speech.*

JOHN *(reading speech)*. Ladies and gentlemen: I am the man you all know as John Doe. *(clearing throat)* I took that name because it seems to describe—because it seems to describe *(his voice unnatural)* the average man, and that's me. *(repeats, embarrassedly)* And that's me.

Med. shot: The COLONEL *and* MIKE. *The* COLONEL *realizes* JOHN *is not going to make* SPENCER's *speech, and his face breaks into a broad grin. He takes* MIKE's *hand and slaps the envelope into his palm. Over the shot we hear* JOHN's *voice.*

JOHN'S VOICE. Well, it *was* me—before I said I was gonna jump off the City Hall roof at midnight on Christmas Eve. Now, I guess I'm not average any more. Now, I'm getting all sorts of attention, from big shots, too

Med. shot: To include JOHN *and* ANN.

Med. shot: Around SPENCER, *as* MIKE *enters to him and hands him envelope.*

MIKE *(whispering)*. We've been double-crossed!

SPENCER *stares at the envelope, frothing at the mouth.*

SPENCER. We have! 171239

Med. shot: Featuring JOHN *and* ANN.

JOHN. The Mayor and the Governor, for instance. They don't like those articles I've been writing.

Suddenly they are startled by SPENCER's *voice.*

SPENCER'S VOICE. You're an imposter, young fella! That's a pack of lies you're telling!

Quick flashes: Of reaction from audience, CONNELL *and others.*

SPENCER. Who wrote that speech for you? (*pointing accusing finger at* JOHN)

CONNELL. Beany, get that guy!

Med. shot: Around SPENCER. *It is as far as he gets. Several attendants,* BEANY *among them, have reached him and start throwing him out.*

Cut to: Int. D. B. NORTON's *study: Med. shot:* D. B. *and* TED SHELDON *are listening to* JOHN's *speech over the radio.* D. B. *is astonished at the disturbance in the program.*

D. B. (*recognizing the voice*). That's Spencer!

Cut to: Int. broadcasting stage:

Close shot: Of ANNOUNCER.

M.C. Ladies and gentlemen, the disturbance you just heard was caused by someone in the audience who tried to heckle Mr. Doe. The speech will continue.

Med. shot: Featuring JOHN *and* ANN.

JOHN. Well, people like the Governor (*laughing—ad libs*) People like the Governor and that fella there can—can stop worrying. I'm not gonna talk about them.

ANN *smiles admiringly.*

Close-up: Of JOHN. *He is becoming strangely absorbed in what he is saying.*

JOHN. I'm gonna talk about us, the average guys, the John Does. If anybody should ask you what the average John Doe is like, you couldn't tell him because he's a million and one things. He's Mr. Big and Mr. Small. He's simple and he's wise. He's inherently honest, but he's got a streak of larceny in his heart. He seldom walks up to a public telephone without shoving his finger into the slot to see if somebody left a nickel there.

Close-up: Of ANN. *Her eyes are glued on* JOHN.

JOHN'S VOICE. He's the man the ads are written for. He's the fella everybody sells things to. He's Joe Doakes, the world's greatest stooge and the world's greatest strength. (*clearing throat*) Yes, sir. Yessir, we're a great family, the John Does. We're the meek who are, er, who are supposed to inherit the earth. You'll find us everywhere. We raise the crops, we dig the mines, work the factories, keep the books, fly the planes and drive the busses! And when a cop yells: "Stand back there, you!" He means us, the John Does!

Cut to: Int. D. B.'s *study:*

Med. shot: D. B. *and* TED *listen near the radio.* TED's *eyes flash angrily.*

TED. Well, what kind of a speech is that? Didn't you read it?

D. B. *stops him with a gesture of his hand. He doesn't want to miss a word.*

Cut to: Int. broadcasting stage:

Med. shot: Toward JOHN.

JOHN. We've existed since time began. We built the pyramids, we saw Christ crucified, pulled the oars for Roman emperors, sailed the boats for Columbus, retreated from Moscow with Napoleon and froze with Washington at Valley Forge! (*gasping*) Yes, sir. We've been in there dodging left hooks since before history began to walk! In our struggle for freedom we've hit the canvas many a time, but we always bounced back!

Med. shot—panning: Around audience—to get a variety of interested faces.

JOHN'S VOICE. Because we're the *people* —and we're tough!

Close-up: Of JOHN.

JOHN. They've started a lot of talk about free people going soft—that we can't take it. That's a lot of hooey!. . . . A free people can beat the world at anything, from war to tiddle-de-winks, if we all pull in the same direction!

Med. shot: To include radio announcer and other radio officials. Their interest centered on JOHN.

JOHN. I know a lot of you are saying "What can I do? I'm just a little punk. I don't count." Well, you're dead wrong! The little punks have always counted because in the long run the character of a country is the sum total of the character of its little punks.

Int. D. B.'s *study. Med. Shot.* D. B.'s *expression of disturbance has vanished. It is now replaced by one of thoughtfulness and interest. He looks off toward the foyer, and impulsively goes in that direction.*

Cut to:
Int. foyer.

Med. shot: D. B. *crosses to a pantry door and pushes the swinging door open slightly.*

Int. pantry: Med. shot: All we can see through the slightly open door is one side of the room. Clustered around the radio on a table are all the household help. They listen, fascinated.

Int. foyer: Closeup of D. B. *His eyes begin to brighten with an idea. Meantime, over the foregoing shots,* JOHN's *voice has continued.*

JOHN's VOICE. But we've all got to get in there and pitch! We can't win the old ball game unless we have team work. And that's where every John Doe comes in! It's up to him to get together with his teammate!

Cut to: Int. broadcasting station:

Med. shot: Closeup: Of JOHN.

JOHN. And your teammates, my friends, is the guy next door to you. Your neighbor! He's a terribly important guy, that guy next door! You're gonna need him and he's gonna need you . . . so look him up! If he's sick, call on him! If he's hungry, feed him! If he's out of a job, find him one! To most of you, your neighbor is a stranger, a guy with a barking dog, and a high fence around him.

Med. shot: Somewhere in audience.

JOHN's VOICE. Now, you can't be a stranger to any guy that's on your own team. So tear down the fence that separates you, tear down the fence and you'll tear down a lot of hates and prejudices! Tear down all the fences in the country and you'll really have teamwork!

Med. shot: Around BEANY *and the* LUGS. *They, too, are interested.*

JOHN's VOICE. I know a lot of you are saying to yourselves: "He's asking for a miracle to happen. He's expecting people to change all of a sudden." Well, you're wrong. It's no miracle. It's no miracle because I see it happen once every year. And so do you. At Christmas time! There's something swell about the spirit of Christmas, to see what it does to people, all kinds of people . . .

Close-up: Of ANN. *Her eyes go from* JOHN *to the audience—as she watches their reaction.*

Full shot: Shooting toward audience over JOHN's *shoulder.*

JOHN. Now, why can't that spirit, that same warm Christmas spirit last the whole year round? Gosh, if it ever did, if each and every John Doe would make that spirit last three hundred and sixty-five days out of the year, we'd develop such a strength, we'd create such a tidal wave of good will, that no human force could stand against it.

Close-up: Of JOHN. *He has become visibly affected by the speech himself.*

JOHN. Yes, sir, my friends, the meek can only inherit the earth when the John Does start loving their neighbors. You'd better start right now. Don't wait till the game is called on account of darkness! Wake up, John Doe! You're the hope of the world!

He has finished—but does not move. He drops his head to conceal the moisture in his eyes.

Close-up: Of ANN. *She, too, remains seated. Her moist eyes riveted on* JOHN.

Med. long shot: Of Audience. There is no outburst of applause. All continue to stare forward, emotionally touched.

Med. shot: Of ANN. *She runs over to John.*

ANN. John! You were wonderful!

Med. shot: Of the audience. They too realize it is over—and gradually they rise and applaud him wildly, and the radio station rings with cheers.

Med. shot: JOHN *and* ANN. JOHN *stares at* ANN, *then turns to* COLONEL.

JOHN *(as he reaches* COLONEL). Let's get out of here.

They exit through the door at which the COLONEL *has been on guard.*

COLONEL. Now you're talking!

Med. shot: At side door. The COLONEL *opens it, and a little crowd of autograph hounds wait for* JOHN.

COLONEL. Gangway, you heelots!

They push their way to a taxi waiting at the curb.

Close-up: Of ANN. *She stares at them leaving, follows and tries to stop them, but her efforts are unsuccessful.*

Dissolve to: Ext. under a bridge: Med. shot: JOHN *and the* COLONEL *are in a secluded spot. The lights of the city can be seen in the distance. The* COLONEL *is building a fire.*

COLONEL. I knew you'd wake up sooner or later! Boy, am I glad we got out of that mess.

Close-up: Of JOHN. *He reaches around and pulls his pitcher's glove out of his back pocket, and starts pounding his fist into it.*

JOHN. I had that five thousand bucks sewed up! Could have been on my way to old Doc

Brown! *(imitates Ann)* "You're a pitcher, John," she said, "Now go in there and pitch! *(self-beratingly)* What a sucker!

Wider shot: To include the COLONEL, *who has quite a mound of twigs built, under which he lights a match.*

COLONEL. Yeah, she's a heelot just like the rest of them. It's lucky you got away from her.

JOHN. What was I doin' up there makin' a speech, anyway? Me? Huh? Gee, the more I think about it the more I could. . . .

COLONEL. Tear down all the fences. Why, if you tore one picket off of your neighbor's fence he'd sue you!

JOHN. Five thousand bucks! I had it right in my hand!

Dissolve to: Int. D. B.*'s study: Close-up:* D. B. *on telephone.*

D. B. What do you mean, he ran away? Well, go after him! Find him! That man is terrific!

Dissolve to: Ext. a box car (process). Close shot: Of JOHN *and the* COLONEL. *They play a duet on their instruments.*

Fade out:

Fade in: Ext. a small town street—day: Med. shot: As JOHN *and the* COLONEL *come from around a corner. Camera pans with them as they enter "Dan's Beanery".*

Int. DAN's *Beanery: Full shot: They enter and flop down on stools. Half a dozen other customers are present.*

Med. shot: Kids dancing to phonograph.

COLONEL. Jitterbugs.

Close shot: JOHN *and the* COLONEL.

JOHN. Yeh. Say, how much money we got left?

COLONEL. Four bits.

JOHN. Better make it doughnuts, huh?

COLONEL. Yeh.

DAN. What'll it be, gents?

JOHN. Have you got a coupla steaks about that big and about that thick? *(measuring)*

COLONEL. Er, yeh, with hash-brown potatoes and tomatoes and—and apple pie and ice cream and coffee—

DAN. And doughnuts! I know. Hey, Ma! Sinkers, a pair!

MA'S VOICE. Sinkers, a pair, coming up.

COLONEL. Glad he took the "T" out of that.

JOHN *(sees something off—nudges the Colonel).* Hey look!

*Long shot: Shooting from their view through the store window. In the street outside, a delivery wagon is passing. On its side is a sign reading "*JOIN THE JOHN DOE CLUB*".*

Int. DAN's *beanery: Close-up:* JOHN *and the* COLONEL.

COLONEL. Join the John Doe Club.

JOHN. John Doe Club?

Close shot: Of the WAITER *standing near the coffee urn. From back of it he has taken a local paper—on the front page of which is* JOHN's *picture. The* WAITER *looks at it and then turns his head to* JOHN.

Two shot: JOHN *and the* COLONEL. *They turn and see the waiter watching them peculiarly.*

COLONEL. Oh-oh.

Wider shot. As the WAITER *approaches them.*

WAITER. Are you John Doe?

JOHN *lowers his head.*

COLONEL. Who?

WAITER *(pointing to paper).* John Doe.

COLONEL. You need glasses, buddy.

WAITER. Well, he's the spittin' image of—

COLONEL. His name's Willoughby.

DAN. Oh!

JOHN. Long John Willoughby *(takes glove out of pocket).* I'm a baseball player.

COLONEL. Sure.

DAN *(eyes brightening).* Oh, no. I'd know that voice anywhere. You can't kid me! You're John Doe! Hey, Ma! Ma! That's John Doe!

MA. John Doe?

DAN. Yeah. Sitting right there, big as life.

CUSTOMER. Who'd you say it was?

DAN. John Doe! The big guy there! Picture's in the paper!

JOHN *gives the* COLONEL *the office and they hastily exit. Several customers, who had gathered around, now evince interest.* DAN *identifies* JOHN *as* JOHN DOE, *and the people follow* JOHN *out into the street.* DAN *hastily seizes the phone.*

DAN. Hey, Operator? Dan's Beanery. Look. Call everybody in town. John Doe was just in my place. Yeh. He ordered doughnuts.

Long shot: Shooting out of window toward street. We see JOHN *and the* COLONEL *as they hurry away, being followed by the crowd which is gradually growing larger. . . . as we see people crossing the street to get to them—*

TOWNSPEOPLE. There he is! John Doe!

There he is! Come on!
Gotta see John Doe!

Dissolve to: Ext. sidewalk: Med. shot: Millville City Hall. The sidewalk is crowded with people. Those near the entrance are trying to force their way in. MAYOR HAWKINS *guards the door.*

MAYOR HAWKINS. I know, you all voted for me and you're all anxious to see John Doe. We're all neighbors, but my office is packed like a sardine box.

GIRL. What does John Doe look like, Mr. Mayor.

MAYOR HAWKINS. Oh, he's one of those great big outdoor type of men. No, you can't see him.

MAYOR *notices one member of the crowd particularly.*

MAYOR HAWKINS. You didn't vote for me the last time. Shame on you—get off my front porch! *(turning)* Mr. Norton come yet? He should of been here fifteen minutes ago. Oh, there he comes now. Now, everybody on your dignity. Don't do anything to disgrace us. This is a little town, but we gotta show off

Wider shot: Of curb. From off-scene we hear the wail of sirens, and as the crowd on the sidewalk turn they see two motorcycle cops drive in, followed by a limousine.

Two shot: ANN *and* D. B.

ANN. Better let me talk to him.

D. B. All right, but present it to him as a great cause for the common man.

ANN *nods as they start toward building. Camera pans with them as the cops break through the curious mob.*

Med. shot: MAYOR HAWKINS *endeavors to assist them,*

MAYOR HAWKINS. Ah, here he comes! Give him room down there! Give him room, folks! How do you do, Mr. Norton! I'm the Mayor—

COP *(to Mayor).* Come back here!

MAYOR HAWKINS *(to cop).* Let me go, you dern fool! I'm the Mayor! Mr. Norton! I, I'm Mayor Hawkins. Your office telephoned me to hold him.

Int. City Hall: Med. shot: As they walk toward MAYOR'S *office.*

D. B. *(to Mayor Hawkins).* Well, that's fine. How is, he?

MAYOR. Oh, he's fine. He's right in my office there. You know, this is a great honor having John Doe here, and you too. Haven't

had so much excitement since the old city hall burned down. *(chuckling)* People were so excited, they nearly tore his clothes off. *(turns to secretary)* Oh, Matilda darling, phone the newspapers. Tell them Mr. Norton is here. Step right inside, Mr. Norton—my office is very comfortable here, Mr. Norton. Just had it air-conditioned. Gangway, please. Make room for Mr. Norton. Gangway, gangway. Here he is, Mr. Norton, well taken care of. The neighbors are serving him a light lunch.

Int. MAYOR'S *office. Full shot:* JOHN *and the* COLONEL *are surrounded by a room full of people, including the* SHERIFF *in full uniform and several policemen.* JOHN *sits at the* MAYOR'S *desk, which is filled with edibles.* D. B., ANN *and the* MAYOR *enter.* JOHN, *upon seeing* ANN, *gets to his feet.*

ANN. Hello, John,

JOHN. Hello.

D. B. Mister Mayor, if you don't mind, we'd like to talk to him alone.

MAYOR. Why, certainly, certainly. All right, everybody, clear out.

They all start to shuffle out—the MAYOR *excitedly egging them on.*

MAYOR'S WIFE. Quit pushing.

MAYOR. Don't argue with me here. Wait till we get home.

WIFE. Don't you push me around like that! Even though I'm your wife, you can't push me around—

MAYOR. Ohhhh!

They all shuffle out, and D. B. *shuts the door.* JOHN *watches him, doesn't like his proprietary manner.*

JOHN. Look, Mr. Norton, I think you've got a lot of nerve having those people hold us here.

D. B. There's nobody holding you here, Mr. Doe. *(laughing)* It's only natural that people —

JOHN. Well, if there's nobody holding us here, let's get going. Incidentally, my name isn't Doe. It's Willoughby.

ANN *(gets in front of him—pleads).* Look, John. Something terribly important's happened. They're forming John Doe Clubs. We know of eight already and they say that there's going—

JOHN *(interested despite himself).* John Doe Clubs? What for?

ANN. Uh-huh. To carry out the principles you talked about in your radio speech.

JOHN *(regains his former attitude).* I don't care what they're forming. I'm on my way and I don't like the idea of being stopped either.

ANN. Oh, but you don't know how big this thing is. You should see the thousands of telegrams we've received and what they're saying about you.

JOHN. Look, it started as a circulation stunt, didn't it?

ANN. Uh-huh . . .

JOHN. Well, you got your circulation. Now, why don't you let me alone?

ANN. Oh, it started as a circulation stunt, but it isn't any more. Mr. Norton wants to get back of it and sponsor John Doe Clubs all over the country. He wants to send you on a lecture tour.

JOHN. Me?

ANN. Uh-huh.

D. B. Why, certainly. With your ability to influence people, it might grow into a glorious movement.

JOHN. Say, let's get something straight here. I don't want any part of this thing. If you've got an idea I'm going around lecturing to people, why you're crazy! Baseball's my racket, and I'm sticking to it. Come on, Colonel, let's get out of here.

ANN. John!

The beaming COLONEL *starts to follow him to the door. When they get there, the door suddenly flies open and a crowd of townspeople push their way in—with the* MAYOR *and the* SHERIFF *trying to hold them back.*

MAYOR. Please, please! I just got rid of one crowd.

WOMAN. Oh, but please, Mr. Mayor, tell him the John Doe Club wants to talk to him.

Close-up: Of D. B. *He gets an idea. These people might influence* JOHN.

D. B. Let them in, Mr. Mayor. Let them come in.

Full shot: As the MAYOR *and the* SHERIFF *back away.*

MAYOR. Okay, folks, but remember your manners. No stampeding. Walk slow, like you do when you come to pay your taxes.

Med. shot: Of the group. They shuffle forward grinning happily. Those in the rear rise on tiptoes for a better look. The men doff their hats as they come forward.

Med. shot: Of JOHN, *the* COLONEL, ANN *and* D. B. JOHN *glances around nervously. The* COLONEL *is worried.*

Med. shot: Of the townspeople. They just stand there, awkwardly, some grinning sheepishly, others staring at JOHN. *Finally someone nudges a young man in the foreground and whispers.*

SOMEONE. Come on, Bert.

BERT. Okay. All right, give me a chance.

WOMAN *(making room for him).* Come right in.

Wider shot: As the group around JOHN *wait expectantly.*

BERT *(clearing throat).* My name's Bert Hansen, Mr. Doe. I'm the head soda jerker at Schwabacher's Drug Store.

Close shot: Of BERT—*as he plunges into his story.*

BERT. Well, sir, you see, me and my wife, we heard your broadcast, and we got quite a bang out of it, especially my wife.

Wider shot: To include JOHN *and the others.*

BERT. Kept me up half the night saying "That man's right, honey. The trouble with the world is—nobody gives a hoot about his neighbor. That's why everybody in town's sore and cranky at each other."

And I kept saying, "Well, that's fine, but how's a guy gonna go around loving the kind of neighbors we got? Old Sourpuss for instance!" *(laughing)*

You see, Sourpuss Smithers is a guy who lives all alone next door to us. He's a cranky old man and runs a second-hand furniture store. We haven't spoken to him for years. I always figured he was an ornery old gent that hated the world cause he was always slamming his garage door and playing the radio so loud he kept half the neighbors up. *(laughing)*

Close-up: Of BERT.

BERT. Well, anyway, the next morning I'm out watering the lawn and I look over and there's Sourpuss on the other side of the hedge straightening out a dent in his fender and, er, my wife yells to me out of the window. She says, "Go on. Speak to him, Bert." And I figured, well, heck, I can't lose anything—so I yelled over to him "Good morning, Mr. Smithers." He went right on pounding his fender, and was I burned! So I turned around to give my wife a dirty look and she said, "Louder, louder. He didn't hear you." So, in a voice you could of heard in the next county, I yelled, "Good morning, Mr. Smithers!"

Med. shot: Featuring JOHN *and* BERT. JOHN
is very interested.

BERT. Well, sir, you coulda knocked me
over with a feather. Old Sourpuss turned
around surprised like, and he put on a big
smile, came over and took my hand like an
old lodge brother, and he said, "Good morning, Hansen. I've been wanting to talk to you
for years, only I thought you didn't like me."
And then he started chatting away like a
happy little kid, and he got so excited his eyes
begin waterin' up.

*Med. shot: Of a group of neighbors. They
smile sympathetically.*

BERT'S VOICE. Well, Mr. Doe, before we got
through, I found out Smithers is a swell egg,
only he's pretty deaf, and that accounts for all
the noises.

Wider shot: To include BERT, JOHN *and
others.*

BERT. And he says it's a shame how little we
know about our neighbors, and then he got an
idea, and he said, "How's about inviting
everybody some place where we can all get
together and know each other a little better?"
Well, I'm feeling so good by this time, I'm
ripe for anything.

Close shot: Of ANN *and* D. B. *They listen,
amused and excited.*

BERT. So Smithers goes around the neighborhood inviting everybody to a meeting at
the school house and I tell everybody that
comes in the store, including Mr. Schwabacher, my boss. *(laughing)* Oh, I'm talking
too much.

Med. shot: JOHN *and* BERT.

BERT. Well, I'll be doggoned if over forty
people don't show up. Course, none of us
knew what to do, but we sure got a kick out of
seeing how glad everybody was just to say
hello to one another.

BERT'S WIFE. Tell him about making Sourpuss chairman, honey.

BERT. Oh, yeah. We made Sourpuss chairman and decided to call ourselves The John
Doe Club. And, say, incidentally, this is my
wife. Come here, honey.

His WIFE *comes forward and stands beside
him.*

BERT. This is my wife, Mr. Doe.

MRS. HANSEN *nods her head shyly—and* JOHN
*acknowledges the introduction by a half wave of
his hand.*

WIFE. How do you do, Mr. Doe . . . Er,
Sourpuss is here, too.

BERT *(turns around)*. Oh, is he?

WIFE *(pointing)*. Uh-huh.

Med. shot: Of a group around SOURPUSS. *He
is as described, except when he smiles, his
whole face warms up. Those around him push
him forward. At first he looks bewildered, then,
understanding, he starts toward* BERT, *grinning
sheepishly.*

Med. shot: Around BERT—*as* SOURPUSS
comes forward.

BERT. This is Sourpuss. Er, excuse me. Er,
Mr. Smithers, Mr. Doe.

SOURPUSS. Th-that's all right. If you didn't
call me Sourpuss, it wouldn't feel natural.
(laughing)

There are snickers from the background.

BERT. Well, anyway, I—I guess nearly
everybody in the neighborhood came, except
the DeLaneys. The DeLaneys live in a big
house with an iron fence around it and they
always keep their blinds drawn, and we always figured that he was just an old miser that
sat back counting his money, so why bother
about inviting him? Until, er, Grimes, the
milkman spoke up and he said, er, "Say,
you've got the Delaneys all wrong." And then
he tells us about how they cancelled their
milk last week, and how, when he found a
note in the bottle he got kinda curious like
and he sorta peeked in under the blinds and
found the house was empty. "If you ask me,"
he says, "they're starving."

SOURPUSS. Old man Delaney has been
bringing his furniture over to my place at
night, one piece at a time, and selling it.

Close shot: Of JOHN. *Profoundly impressed
by this.*

Wider shot: BERT *clears his throat.*

BERT. Yeah. And, well, sir, a half a dozen of
us ran over there to fetch them and we got
them to the meeting. What a reception they
got. Why, everybody shook hands with them
and made a fuss over them, and, well, finally,
Mr. and Mrs. Delaney just sat right down and
cried.

He smiles, embarrassed, and JOHN, *as well
as the others, clear their throats.*

SOURPUSS. And then we started to find out
about a lot of other people.

BERT. Yeah, sure. Er, you know Grubbel,
for instance.

BERT'S WIFE. Grubbel's here. See? *(pointing)*

BERT. Yeah. That's—that's him. Of course, you don't know Grubbel, but he's the man that everybody figured was the worst no-account in the neighborhood because he, he was living like a hermit and nobody'd have anything to do with him. Er, that, that is until Murphy, the postman told us the truth. "Why, Grubbel," he says, "he lives out of garbage cans because he won't take charity. Because it'd ruin his self-respect," he says.

BERT'S WIFE. Just like you said on the radio, Mr. Doe.

SOURPUSS. Well, sir, about a dozen families got together and gave Grubbel a job watering their lawns. Isn't that wonderful? And then we found jobs for six other people and they've all gone off relief!

BERT. Yeh. Er, and my boss, Mr. Schwabacker made a job in his warehouse for old man Delaney—

WIFE. And he gave you that five dollar raise.

BERT. Yeah! Wasn't that swell! *(laughing)*

Med. shot: Around MAYOR HAWKINS. *He steps forward.*

MAYOR. Why, Bert, I feel slighted. I'd like to join but nobody asked me.

Med. shot: Around BERT *and* SOURPUSS.

SOURPUSS. Well, I'm sorry, Mayor, but we voted that no politicians could join.

BERT'S WIFE. Just the John Does of the neighborhood. Cause you know how politicians are. *(becomes embarrassed)*

Close-up: Of the MAYOR—*completely deflated.*

SOURPUSS. Yeah. . . .

Med. shot: Around JOHN. *As they smile, amused at the* MAYOR's *discomfiture.*

Med. shot: Around BERT. *He looks over at* JOHN, *hesitates a moment, and then speaks.*

BERT. Well, er, the reason we wanted to tell you this, Mr. Doe, was to, to give you an idea what you started. And from where I'm sitting, I, I don't see any sense in your jumping off any building.

GROUP. No!

SOURPUSS. No!

BERT. Well, thank you for listening. Goodbye, Mr. Doe. You're a wonderful man and it strikes me you can be mightly useful walking around for a while.

Close-up: Of JOHN. *Deeply touched. Shifts awkwardly, unable to say anything.*

Med. shot: As D. B. *and* ANN *watch his face to see the effect.*

GROUP. Well, goodbye.

SOURPUSS. Goodbye Mr. Doe.

BERT *has turned to go, and the rest follow suit. They all shuffle silently out.*

Med. shot: Of an old couple who remain looking up at JOHN, *as those around them leave. The old lady takes the old man's arm and starts toward* JOHN. *Camera pans with them until they reach him.*

OLD LADY. I'm Mrs. Delaney, Mr. Doe. . . . and God bless you, my boy. *(she gently kisses his hand)*

The two OLD PEOPLE *leave.*

Close-up: Of JOHN. *He swallows a lump in his throat. He watches the old people until they have left, then with a quick glance at his hand—and self-consciously in front of the others, stuffs his hand into his pocket.*

Full shot: As they all watch him, without speaking. JOHN *runs his hand through his hair, stealing a fleeting glance at the others, and grins awkwardly.*

Close shot: Of D. B. *as he signals to the* MAYOR *and the* SHERIFF, *who have remained, to leave.*

Med. shot: Of the MAYOR *and the* SHERIFF, *who receive the signal and discreetly exit.*

Full shot: They wait for JOHN *to speak, but* JOHN *begins walking around, profoundly thoughtful.*

Close-up: Of the COLONEL *watching him, concerned.*

Two shot: Of D. B. *and* ANN. *Their eyes glued on him, expectantly.*

Full shot: JOHN *still paces, disturbed by clashing emotions. He stops, glances at the door, a soft, thoughtful expression in his eyes. Then, as his thought shifts, he runs his left hand over his pitching arm.*

JOHN. Gee, whizz—I'm all mixed up—I don't get it. Look, all those swell people think I'm gonna jump off a building or something.

He looks toward the door.

JOHN. I never had any such idea. Gosh! A fella'd have to be a mighty fine example himself to go around telling other people how to—Say, look, what happened the other night was on account of Miss Mitchell, here. She wrote the stuff.

ANN *walks over to* JOHN.

Two shot: ANN *and* JOHN. *She faces him, looking up into his face.*

ANN. Don't you see what a wonderful thing this can be? *(softly)* But we need *you*, John.

Close-up: Of the COLONEL. *He stares at* JOHN, *sees him weakening, and grimaces disgustedly.*

Wider shot: The COLONEL *watches* JOHN *as he continues to turn it over in his mind.*

COLONEL *(suddenly).* You're hooked! I can see that right now.

They all look up, startled.

COLONEL. They got you. Well, I'm through. *(crosses to door—stops, turns)* For three years I've been trying to get you up to the Columbia River country. First, it was your glass arm. Then it was the radio. And now it's the John Doe clubs. Well, I ain't waiting another minute.

He opens the door and when he sees the townspeople still gathered outside, he yells to them.

COLONEL. Gangway, you heelots!

He pushes his way out.

JOHN *(calling).* Hey, Colonel! Wait a minute!

He starts after the COLONEL, *but when he gets to the door, the townspeople surge toward him and block his way.*

JOHN. Hey, Colonel!
CROWD. Oh, please, Mr. Doe—

Close-up: Of JOHN.

JOHN *(calling futilely).* Hey, Colonel!

He tries to peer over the heads of the townspeople who go on chattering. There is a trapped look on JOHN's *face.*

Two shot: D. B. *and* ANN. *They exchange victorious glances:*

Dissolve to: Int. office of headquarters. Close shot: Of large map of the U.S. over the top of which we read: "John Doe Clubs." There are a dozen pegs scattered over the map, indicating where the clubs are. We hear D. B.'s *voice.*

Camera draws back and we find D. B. *talking to a group of men in front of him.*

D. B. I want you personally to go along with John Doe and Miss Mitchell and handle the press and the radio.

CHARLIE *(an experienced promoter).* Me?
D. B. Yes. I don't want to take any chances. And Johnson?

JOHNSON. Yes, D. B.

D. B. Your crew will do the mop up job. They'll follow John Doe into every town, see that the clubs are properly organized and the charters issued.

CHARLIE. Right.

D. B. There are only eight flags up there now. I want to see that map covered before we get through!

Med. shot: D. B. *is still speaking as camera moves down to the map again, which constantly remains a background for the montage following. As the montage proceeds, pegs begin to appear in abundance on the map.*

A montage: Accompanied by a fanfare of music.

1. *Flashes of banners reading:*
   "JOHN DOE COMING"— "JOHN DOE TONIGHT"
   "GOODBYE JOHN DOE, CALL AGAIN"
2. *Close-ups of* JOHN *speaking—superimposed over long shots of audiences of various types.*
3. *Flashes of* ANN *typing.*
4. *Flashes of sheets of paper being ripped out of a tyewriter.*
5. *Flashes of* JOHN *on the radio—with* ANN *by his side.*
6. *Flashes of people listening.*
7. *Flashes of people applauding.*
8. *Series of signs being nailed up:* "JOHN DOE CLUB—BE A BETTER NEIGHBOR."
9. *Superimposed shots of* JOHN *and* ANN *riding in trains, planes and automobiles.*
10. *Against stock shots of these cities, the names zoom up to the foreground of Kansas City, Chicago, Buffalo, Washington, Baltimore, Philadelphia, New York.*
11. *Superimpose map over the above titles, showing the states they are in being covered with pegs.*
12. *A picture of* JOHN DOE *on front page of* Time *magazine, with a caption under it reading:* "MAN OF THE HOUR."
13. *Conference Room.*
    Speaker: This has been growing like wildfire! If they only made demands, but the John Does ask for nothing!
14. *A man sits at a desk on which is a nameplate reading: "Relief Administrator."*

Man: People are going off relief! If this keeps up, I'll be out of a job!"

15. *Stock shot— of Capitol Hill.*

16. *Corner of a club smoking room. A group of legislators— some sit— some stand. The room is filled with smoke.*

    MAN: *As soon as he gets strong enough, we'll find out what John Doe wants! Thirty every Thursday— sixty at sixty— who knows what!*

17. *Insert: sign reading:* DEMOCRATIC HEADQUARTERS. *A man reports to the boss behind the desk.*

    Man: I'm sorry, boss. They just won't let anybody talk politics to them. It's, it's crazy.

18. *Insert: Sign reading:* REPUBLICAN HEADQUARTERS. *A man at a desk talks to several in front of him.*

    Man: We've got to get to them! They represent millions of voters!

Dissolve to: Insert: Of Map. Nearly every state in the union have pegs in them, varying in volume. Camera pulls back and we find the map is on a stand near a door, the sign on which we see in reverse. It reads: "OFFICE OF JOHN DOE HEADQUARTERS."

Int. JOHN DOE *headquarters. Med. shot:* D. B. *standing behind his desk, speaking to a group of people in front of him. We recognize the* MAYOR, *and the President of the Chamber of Commerce. Representatives of several other branches of the City Administration are also present.* CONNELL *sits near* D. B.— *scrutinizing him thoughtfully. On the other side of* D. B. *is* TED SHELDON.

D. B. I tell you, ladies and gentlemen, this thing has been nothing short of a prairie fire. We've received so many applications for charters to the John Doe Clubs we haven't been able to take care of them.

MAYOR LOVETT. I'd hate to have that many pins stuck in me!

Group laughs.

D. B. This John Doe convention is a natural. It's gonna put our city on the map. Why, over twenty-four hundred John Doe clubs are sending delegates. Can you imagine that? You, Mr. Mayor, will be the official host. You will make the arrangements for decorating the city, parades and a reception for John Doe when he gets home! And—don't wear your high hat!

MAYOR LOVETT *(disappointed)*. No high hat?

D. B. No high hat. And from you, Connell, I want a special John Doe edition every day

until the convention is over. *(dismissing them)* And now, if you will please just step into the outer office and look your prettiest because there are photographers there to take pictures of this committee.

They start to exit. The MAYOR *is full of excitement.*

MAYOR. Don't worry, D. B. Everything'll be taken care of!

D. B. Good.

COMMITTEE WOMAN. Isn't it all too wonderful?

The group, chattering, exit into outer office.

PHOTOGRAPHER'S VOICE *(from the outer office)*. Oh, Mr. Mayor, would you step right in the front row, please? Will you ladies get close to him? That's it!

Close-up: Of CONNELL. *To inter-cut with above speech. He has been watching* D. B.— *deeply disturbed about something.*

Wider shot: All have left except CONNELL, TED, *and* D. B. CONNELL *rises from his chair— with a deep sigh.*

CONNELL *(shaking his head)*. Well, I don't get it.

D. B. Huh? Get what?

CONNELL. Look, D. B. I'm supposed to know my way around. You spent a fortune on the John Doe movement. This convention's gonna cost plenty.

D. B. *(annoyed)*. Well?

CONNELL. Well, I'm stuck with two and two—but I'm a sucker if I can make four out of it. *(cocking his head)*. Where do *you* come in?

D. B. Why—uh— *(suddenly smiles)* Why, I'll have the satisfaction of knowing that my money has been spent for a worthy cause.

Close-up: Of CONNELL. *He stares at* D. B. *a moment. He realizes he has been told to mind his own business.*

Two shot: CONNELL *picks up his hat.*

CONNELL. I see. I'd better stick to running the paper huh?

D. B. I think maybe you'd better had. And Connell—I'd like to have the John Doe contract, all the receipts for the money we have advanced him and the letter Miss Mitchell wrote, for which I gave her a thousand dollars.

CONNELL. Yes. Sure.

CONNELL *leaves.*

Dissolve to: Int.: A hotel living room—night. Full shot: ANN's *luggage is packed and ready to be taken out. She stands near a desk stuffing papers into a manuscript case. She seems lost in worried thought. The door opens as* CHARLIE, *high pressure exploitation man, enters.*

CHARLIE. Well, we leave for the airport in half an hour. Is that Johnny-boy's room? I'd better hustle him up!

ANN. He'll be ready on time. He's packing now.

CHARLIE. Ah, good! *(crosses to Ann)* Did you see his picture on the cover of *TIME*?

ANN. Yeah.

CHARLIE *drops the magazine on the desk in front of her.* ANN *glances at it, unenthusiastically.* CHARLIE *goes to a table where there are several bottles of coca-cola and starts to pour himself a drink.*

CHARLIE. I gotta give you credit, Annie-girl. I've handled a good many big promotions in my time . . . everything from the world's fair to a channel swimmer, but this one has certainly got me spinning. And now a John Doe Convention! Wow! Say! If you could only get him to jump off the City Hall roof on Christmas Eve, I'd guarantee you half a million people there.

ANN. Charlie!

ANN *is lost in troubled thought.*

CHARLIE'S VOICE. Huh?

ANN *(nods toward door).* What do you make of him?

Two shot: CHARLIE *and* ANN.

CHARLIE. Who, Johnny-boy?

ANN *nods.*

CHARLIE. Well, I don't know what angle you want, but I'll give it to you quick. Number one, he's got great yokel appeal; but he's a nice guy. Number two, he's beginning to believe he really wrote that original suicide letter that you made up. Number three, he thinks that you're Joan of Arc or something!

Close-up: Of ANN. *This is definitely troublesome to her.*

ANN *(hoarsely).* Yeah, I know.

Wider shot: ANN *walks away—pacing perturbedly.*

CHARLIE. Number four, well, you know what number four is. He's nuts about you. Yeah, it's running out of his ears.

ANN *runs her hand through her hair. Suddenly she wheels around to* CHARLIE.

ANN. You left out number five. We're all heels, me especially.

She returns to her packing. CHARLIE *watches her a second.*

CHARLIE. Holy smoke!

They are interrupted by a knock on the door.

ANN *(calling).* Come in.

JOHN *enters, carrying a suitcase.*

JOHN. I'm all packed.

CHARLIE *(starts out).* Good. I'll go and get Beany-boy.

JOHN *(kidding him).* Okay, Charlie-boy!

CHARLIE. Huh? *(laughing)*

CHARLIE *winks good-naturedly and exits.* JOHN *turns to* ANN, *who concentrates on her packing.*

Med. shot: He looks at ANN *with great interest, and walks toward her, camera panning with him.* ANN *feels him coming, but does not turn.*

JOHN *(after a pause).* Can I help you pack?

ANN. No, thank you.

JOHN *wanders over to a chair and sits on the edge—watching her.*

Close-up: Of ANN. *She is conscious of his eyes on her and fumbles with her packing. Finally she turns.*

Close-up: Of JOHN. *He stares at her, a warm smile on his face.*

Close-up: Of ANN. *She becomes self-conscious and resumes her packing.*

Med. shot: JOHN.

JOHN. Do you care if I sit down out here?

ANN. No.

A broad smile appears on JOHN's *face.*

JOHN *(laughing).* You know, I had a crazy dream last night. It was about you.

ANN. About me?

JOHN *(laughing).* Sure was crazy. I dreamt I was your father.

Close-up: Of ANN. *The fact that he has seen himself in the image of her father disturbs her. She turns slowly.*

Two shot: JOHN *clears his throat nervously.*

JOHN. There was, there was something I was trying to stop you from doing. So, er, so I got up out of bed and I walked right through the wall here, right straight into your room. *(laughing)* You know how dreams are.

ANN *stares at him—fearful of the trend his dream is taking.*

JOHN. And there you were in bed. *(quickly apologizing)* But you—you were a little girl. You know—about ten.

He pauses and recalls the scene.

JOHN. And very pretty, too. So, I, I shook you, and the moment you opened your eyes, you hopped out of bed and started running like the devil, in your nightgown.

You ran right out the window there. And you ran out over the tops of buildings and roofs and everything for miles, and I was chasing you. *(laughing)* And all the time you were running you kept growing bigger and bigger and bigger—and pretty soon you were as big as you are now. You know—grown up. And all the time I kept, I kept asking myself, "What am I chasing her for?" And I didn't know. *(laughing)* Isn't that a hot one? Well, anyway, you ran into some place, and then I ran in after you and—and when I got there, there you were getting married.

Close-up: Of JOHN. *He suddenly becomes aware he is treading on sensitive grounds.*

JOHN *(awkwardly)*. And the nightgown had changed into a beautiful wedding gown. You sure looked pretty, too. *(laughing)* And then I knew what it was I was trying to stop you from doing.

Close-up: Of ANN. *She, too, begins to feel uncomfortable—not quite knowing how to handle it.*

Two shot: JOHN *glances at her.*

JOHN. Dreams are sure crazy, aren't they?

ANN *smiles, noncommittedly.*

JOHN. Well, would you like to know who it was you were marrying?

ANN *(forced lightness)*. Well, a tall handsome Ubangi, I suppose.

JOHN. No, not that bad. It was that fella that sends you flowers every day. Er, what's his name? Mr. Norton's nephew.

Close-up: Of ANN. *She recognizes the significance in this.*

ANN *(quietly)*. Ted Sheldon.
JOHN. Yeah, that's the one.

ANN *turns back to her packing.*

Wider shot: JOHN *starts to chuckle.*

JOHN. But here's the funniest part of it all. I was the fella up there doing the marrying. You know, the Justice of the Peace or something . . .

ANN. You were? I thought you were chasing me.

JOHN. Well, yes, I was. But I was your father then, see? But the real me, John Doe, er, that is, Long John Willoughby, I was the fellow up there with the book. You know what I mean?

ANN *(amused)*. I guess so. Then what happened?

JOHN. Well, I took you across my knee and I started spanking you.

ANN *turns and stares at him, eyes widening.*

JOHN *(quickly explaining)*. That is, I didn't do it. *(correcting himself)* I mean, I did do it, but it wasn't me. You see, I was your father then. Well, I laid you across my knee and I said: "Annie, I won't allow you to marry a man that's, that's just rich, or that has his secretary send you flowers. The man you marry has got to swim rivers for you! He's got to climb high mountains for you! He's got to slay dragons for you! He's got to perform wonderful deeds for you! Yes, sir!"

BEANY *enters and stands back of him, listening.*

And all the time, er, the guy up there, you know, with the book, me, just stood there nodding his head and he said, "Go to it, Pop, whack her one for me, because that's just the way I feel about it, too."

So he says, "Come on down here and whack her yourself." So I came down and I whacked you a good one, see? And then he whacked one—and I whacked you another one, and we both started whacking you like . . .

He demonstrates by slapping his knees, first with one hand and then with the other. Suddenly he becomes aware of BEANY *and stops, embarrassed.*

BEANY *(interrupting)*. Well, if you're through whacking her, come on, let's get going. *(to bell boys)* Okay, fellows, right in here. *(to* JOHN) You go out the side entrance. There's a bunch of autograph seekers out front. We'll be down with the bags in a minute. Come on! *(speaking to boys)* Don't make a government project out of this!

The bell boys have lifted her luggage and all exit.

Close-up: Of JOHN. *He has been left with his proposal unfinished.*

Dissolve to: Int. airport lunchroom—night. Med. shot: Scene opens with BEANY *entering airport lunchroom to end of counter at which* CHARLIE *is seated.*

CHARLIE. How're you, Beany?

BEANY. When does our plane take off again.

CHARLIE. In a couple of minutes.

Camera moves down counter to pick up JOHN *and* ANN *at table. They sit silently for a moment. We hear the strains of music from a "juke" box.*

JOHN *(after a pause)*. H-how many people do you think we've talked to already, outside the radio, I mean?

ANN. I don't know. About three hundred thousand.

JOHN. Three hundred thousand? What makes them do it, Ann? What makes them come and listen and, and get up their John Doe Clubs the way they do? I've been trying to figure it out.

ANN *(in an effort to disillusion him)*. Look, John—what we're handing them are platitudes. Things they've heard a million times: "Love thy neighbor," "Clouds have silver linings," "Turn the other cheek." It's just a —

JOHN *(sincerely)*. Yeah, I've heard them a million times, too, but—there you are. Maybe they're like me. Just beginning to get an idea what those things mean.

ANN *is deeply concerned. She watches him, helplessly.*

JOHN *(continuing)*. You know, I never thought much about people before. They were always just somebody to fill up the bleachers. The only time I worried about them was if they—is when they didn't come in to see me pitch. You know, lately I've been watching them while I talked to them. I could see something in their faces. I could feel that they were hungry for something. Do you know what I mean?

ANN *nods.*

JOHN. Maybe that's why they came. Maybe they were just lonely and wanted somebody to say hello to. I know how they feel. I've been lonely and hungry for something practically all my life.

ANN *forces a smile. The moment threatens to become awkward—until they are saved by the pilot's voice.*

PILOT. All aboard, folks!

They suddenly snap out of their mood—and as they rise:

Fade out.

Fade in: Int. D. B.'s *dining room. Full shot: As* D. B., ANN *and* TED SHELDON *enter and cross to table.* ANN *starts to sit and notices a fur coat flung over the back of the chair.*

ANN. Oh, somebody else sitting there?

D. B. No, no, no—that's your seat.

TED. And this is your coat.

ANN. Mine?

D. B. A little token of appreciation.

ANN *pauses a moment, glances toward* D. B. —*while* TED *throws the coat over her shoulders.*

ANN *(glances into a mirror)*. Oh! Oh, it's beautiful, D. B. Well—I don't quite know what to say . . .

D. B. Well, don't say anything at all. Just sit down.

Close-up: Of ANN. *She sits down, picks up her serviette—and something she sees suddenly makes her look with surprise at* D. B.

Camera pans down to a jewel box which had been under the serviette.

Camera pans back to ANN. *She glances up at* D. B. *somewhat bewildered.*

ANN. Oh!

D. B. Go ahead, open it, open it.

ANN *opens the box and holds up a lovely diamond bracelet. Her eyes dance.*

ANN. Oh! Oh, it's lovely!

TED. And a new contract goes with it.

Wider shot: D. B. *and* TED *exchange satisfied glances.* ANN *admires the bracelet on her wrist—and then turns to* D. B., *looks directly at him.*

ANN *(shrewdly)*. Well, come on, spring it! You've got something on your mind.

D. B. *laughs.*

ANN. Must be stupendous.

Wider shot: As D. B. *roars with laughter.*

D. B. You know, that's what I like about her. Right to the point, like that! All right, practical Annie, here it is.

He leans forward. ANN *waits.* TED *watches her face.*

Two shot: ANN *and* D. B.

D. B. Tomorrow night, before a crowd of fifteen thousand people, and talking over a nation-wide radio hook-up, John Doe will announce the formation of a third party.

ANN *(eyes widening)*. A third party?

D. B. Yes. The John Doe Party.

Wider shot: TED *watches* ANN, *expectantly.*

D. B. Devoted entirely to the interests of all the John Does all over the country. Which means, practically ninety per cent of the voters. He will also announce the third party's candidate for the presidency. A man whom he, personally, recommends. A great humanitarian; the best friend the John Does have.

ANN *(In an awed whisper)*. Mr. D. B. Norton!

D. B. *verifies her guess by leaning back, a pleased grin on his face, his huge chest expanded.*

D. B. Yes.

ANN *looks from one to the other, a little awed by the size of the project.*

ANN *(on her breath)*. Whow!

Dissolve to: Int. broadcasting booth—ball park—night. Med. shot: The place is a bee-hive of activity. Announcers walk about with "mikes" in their hands—all speaking at once—as they describe the scene below.

Close shot: Of N.B.C. ANNOUNCER.

N.B.C. ANNOUNCER. And although the opening of the convention is hours off, the delegates are already pouring into the ball park by the droves, with lunch baskets, banners and petitions, asking John Doe not to jump off any roof. . . .

Camera pans over to KNOX MANNING.

KNOX MANNING. It is still a phenomenal movement. The John Does, or the hoi polloi as you've heard people call them, have been laughed at and ridiculed but here they are, gay and happy, having travelled thousands of miles, their expenses paid by their neighbors, to come here to pay homage to their hero, John Doe.

Camera pans over to JOHN B. HUGHES.

JOHN B. HUGHES. And in these days of wars and bombings, it's a hopeful sign that a simple idea like this can sweep the country, an idea based on friendliness, on giving and not taking, on helping your neighbor and asking nothing in return. And if a thing like this can happen, don't let any of our grumbling friends tell you that humanity is falling apart.

This is John B. Hughes, signing off now and returning you to our main studio until nine o'clock when the convention will officially open.

Dissolve to: Int. ANN'S *living room. Med. shot: At Door.* ANN'S MOTHER *opens it and* JOHN *stands on the threshold. He has a small box of flowers in his hand. Water drips from his hat.*

MRS. MITCHELL. Oh, John. Come in.

JOHN. Say, I'm kinda—it's raining out a little—

MRS. MITCHELL. That's all right.

Wider shot: MRS. MITCHELL *lays his hat down somewhere. John takes a few steps inside the room, not quite knowing what to do.*

MRS. MITCHELL *(turning to him)*. It's good to see you. Sit down.

JOHN *(mumbles)*. Thanks.

He sits on the edge of a chair, still clinging to the little box. Then holds box out awkwardly.

JOHN *(awkwardly)*. It's for Ann . . .

MRS. MITCHELL *(taking the box)*. Oh, how nice! Thank you very much.

JOHN. Flowers.

MRS. MITCHELL. I'm terribly sorry she isn't here.

JOHN. She isn't?

MRS. MITCHELL. No, she just left. I'm surprised you didn't run into her. She went over to Mr. Norton's house.

JOHN. Oh!

MRS. MITCHELL. Did you want to see her about something important?

JOHN. Yeah. I, uh, well . . . No. It'll wait.

JOHN *(suddenly)*. Say, he's a nice man, isn't he? Mr. Norton, I mean. He's, er, he's done an awful lot for the—

Close-up: Of MRS. MITCHELL. *She watches him, amused.*

Wider shot: JOHN *is still struggling to find conversation.*

JOHN. Well, I guess I'll see her at the convention later.

MRS. MITCHELL. Yes, of course. I'll see that she gets the flowers.

He rises and looks around for hat on the floor and back of the chair.

JOHN. Thanks. Good night, Mrs. Mitchell.

MRS. MITCHELL *(finds his hat and gives it to him)*. Good night, John.

Close-up: Of JOHN. *He starts away and suddenly stops, speculatively. He glances out of the corner of his eye toward* MRS. MITCHELL.

JOHN (*going back to her*). Say, Mrs. Mitchell, I, er, I'm kinda glad Ann isn't here. You see, I was, I came over here hoping to see her alone and kinda hoping I wouldn't, too. You know what I mean? There was something I wanted to talk to her about. But, well, I—It'll wait, I guess. Good night.

Close-up: Of MRS. MITCHELL. *She begins to sense what is on his mind, and her face becomes serious.*

Close-up: Of JOHN. *He smiles helplessly. Starts toward door.*

MRS. MITCHELL'S VOICE. Good night, John.

Two shot: JOHN *and* MRS. MITCHELL. *He stares at her a second.*

JOHN (*suddenly*). Say, look, Mrs. Mitchell, have you ever been married? (*catches himself*) Oh, sure you have. (*grins sheepishly*) Gosh! That's pretty silly! I guess you must think I'm kinda batty!

JOHN *shakes his head at his own stupidity.*

JOHN (*can't get over it*). Well, I guess I'd better be going at that!

He bows again, and starts for the door. When he gets there, he is stopped by MRS. MITCHELL'S *voice.*

MRS. MITCHELL'S VOICE. John. My husband said: "I love you. Will you marry me?"
JOHN (*whirls*). He did? What happened?
MRS. MITCHELL. I married him.

JOHN *comes right back to her.*

Two shot: JOHN *and* MRS. MITCHELL.

JOHN (*full of excitement*). Oh, yeah. That's what I mean. See? It was easy as all that, huh?
MRS. MITCHELL. Uh-huh.
JOHN. Yeah, yeah, but look, Mrs. Mitchell, you know I, I love Ann and it's gonna be awfully hard for me to say it because, well, you know, she's so wonderful, and, well, the best I ever was was a bush-league pitcher.

Close-up: Of JOHN.

JOHN. And you know, I think she's in love with another man, the one she made up. You know, the real John Doe. Well, that's, that's pretty tough competition.

Two shot: JOHN *and* MRS. MITCHELL. *She is terribly fond of* JOHN *and deeply sympathetic.*

JOHN. I bet you he'd know how to say it all right. And me, I, I get up to it and around it and in back of it, but, but I never get right to it. Do you know what I mean? So the only

chance I've got is, well, if somebody could kinda give her a warning sort of, sorta prepare her for the shock!

MRS. MITCHELL. You mean you'd like me to do it, huh?
JOHN. Well, I was thinking that—Yeah, you know, sort of break the ice.

Close-up of MOTHER. *She doesn't know how she can, with her present strained relationship with* ANN, *but* JOHN'S *sincerity touches her.*

MOTHER. Of course I will, John.

Two shot: JOHN'S *face lights up, gratefully.*

JOHN. Gee whizz! Thank you, Mrs. Mitchell. (*grabs her hand*). Gee, you're—uh—you're okay!

He exits from scene—but almost immediately he is back. He plants a kiss on her cheek and goes.

Cut to: Ext. sidewalk. Front of ANN'S *apartment. Med. Shot: An automobile stands at the curb, in front of which is* BEANY. *Also waiting, are four motorcycle policemen.*

BEANY (*to the other men*). This John Doe meeting is gonna be one of the biggest things that ever happened.

As JOHN *appears in the doorway of the apartment house, he pretends to throw a baseball at them.*

BEANY. Why, they're coming from all over; trains, box cars, wagons—(*sees* JOHN) look out!

Med. shot: (reverse angle). As BEANY *holds the door open for* JOHN.

JOHN Hello, bodyguards! Hey, had your dinner yet?
BODYGUARD. Not yet.
JOHN. Well, look. No. Go ahead and have your dinner. I'll—

He is about to enter the car when a voice from off-scene stops him.

CONNELL'S VOICE. Wait a minute, John.

Camera pans over to a taxicab which has just driven in. CONNELL *hands the driver a bill and walks, rather unsteadily toward* JOHN.

Med. shot: Around BEANY'S *car.* CONNELL *ambles into scene.*

JOHN. Hello, Mr. Connell.
CONNELL. Hiyah, John. (*broad wink*). John, I want to have a little talk with you. (*lurches—John holds him up*) What's, what's the matter—are you falling? Come here.

Takes his arm to lead him off.

BEANY *(protesting).* Hey, Boss.

CONNELL. Oh, quiet, quiet, quiet. *(to John)* Say, tell me something, did you, did you read that speech you're gonna make tonight?

JOHN. No, I never read the speeches before I make them. I get more of a kick out of it that way.

CONNELL *(wisely).* Uh-huh. That's exactly what I thought. Beany, go on down to the office, tell Pop to give you the speech. There's a copy on my desk.

BEANY *(protesting).* Gee whizz, Boss, you know Mr. Norton told me not to leave him, not even for a minute.

CONNELL *(shooing him away).* Go on, go on, go on. And we'll be at Jim's Bar up the street.

He points in the general direction and again takes JOHN's *arm.* JOHN *watches him, rather amused to see* CONNELL *off his milk diet, and allows himself to be led away.*

Wipe to: Int. A bar room. Close shot: In a corner booth, JOHN *and* CONNELL *sit, close together, drinks in front of them.* JOHN's *drink has remained untouched.* CONNELL *is just taking a long swig. From off-scene we hear the strains of an old-fashioned torch ballad, coming from an automatc piano.*

CONNELL *(after a pause).* You're a nice guy, John. I like you. You're gentle. I like gentle people. Me? I'm hard—hard and tough. *(shakes his head—disparagingly)* I got no use for hard people. Gotta be gentle to suit me. Like you, for instance.

JOHN *smiles, amused at him.* CONNELL *starts to light his cigarette, which is bent. He holds the match up, but it never reaches the tip of the bent cigarette. He puffs, satisfied.*

CONNELL. Yep, I'm hard. But you want to know something? I've got a weakness. You'd never guess that, would you? Well, I have. Want to know what it is?

JOHN *nods.*

CONNELL. The Star Spangled Banner. *(looks directly at John)* Screwy, huh? *(turns back to his glass)* Well, maybe it is. But play the "Star Spangled Banner"—and I'm a sucker for it. It always gets me right here—*(thumps his diaphragm)* You know what I mean?

Close-up: Of JOHN. *His face has become serious.*

JOHN. Yeah. *(points to back of neck)* It gets me right back here.

Two shot: JOHN *and* CONNELL. CONNELL *speculates about this with his head cocked.*

CONNELL. Oh, back there, huh? *(shrugs, dismissing it)* Well, every man to his own taste.

JOHN *smiles at him.* CONNELL *tries lighting his bent cigarette again—with the same result—while* JOHN *watches, amused.*

CONNELL. You weren't old enough for the first world war, were you?

JOHN *starts to answer, but* CONNELL *goes right on.*

CONNELL. Course not. Must have been a kid.

He pours JOHN's *drink into his own glass.*

CONNELL. I was. I was just ripe. And rarin' to go. *(takes drink)* Know what my old man did when I joined up? He joined up too.

Close-up: Of JOHN. *He finds himself intensely interested.*

CONNELL'S VOICE. Got to be a sergeant.

Two shot: JOHN *and* CONNELL.

CONNELL *(as he raises his glass).* That's a kick for you. We were in the same outfit. Funny, huh?

Close-up: Of CONNELL. *He lifts his glass to his lips, and without drinking, lowers it.*

CONNELL *(voice lowers).* He was killed, John.

Close-up: Of JOHN. *His face enveloped in an expression of sympathy.*

Two shot: CONNELL *stares down at the glass which he revolves between his palms.*

CONNELL. I saw him get it. I was right there and saw it with my own eyes.

Without glancing at JOHN, *he lifts the glass and drains it.*

CONNELL *(turns to* JOHN). Me? I came out of it without a scratch. Except for my ulcers. Should be drinking milk. *(picks up his glass)* This stuff's poison.

As he holds up his glass, he realizes it is empty.

CONNELL *(yelling to bartender).* Hey, Tubby!

BARTENDER'S VOICE. Yes, Mr. Connell?

CONNELL *(indicates the empty glass)*. Whadda you say?

TUBBY. All right.

Close shot: JOHN *and* CONNELL. CONNELL *looks around guardedly, to make certain he is not overheard.*

CONNELL *(confidentially)*. Yessir. I'm a sucker for this country. *(gets a little sore about it)* I'm a sucker for the Star Spangled Banner—and I'm a sucker for this country. *(taps table with his middle finger)* I *like* what we got here! I like it! *(emphasizes each point)* A guy can *say* what he wants—and *do* what what he wants—without having a bayonet shoved through his belly.

Med. shot: As he leans back and nods his head, satisfied he made his point.

CONNELL. Now, that's all right, isn't it?

JOHN. You betcha.

The BARTENDER *comes in with drink and departs.*

CONNELL. All right. And we don't want anybody coming around changing it, do we?

JOHN *shakes his head.*

JOHN. No, sir.

Two shot: JOHN *and* CONNELL.

CONNELL. No, sir. And when they do I get mad! I get b-boiling mad. And right now, John, I'm sizzling!

JOHN *looks at him, puzzled.*

CONNELL. I get mad for a lot of other guys besides myself—I get mad for a guy named Washington! And a guy named Jefferson—and Lincoln. Lighthouses, John! Lighthouses in a foggy world! You know what I mean?

JOHN *(huskily)*. Yeah, you bet!

CONNELL *takes a drink and looks at* JOHN *a moment before he speaks.*

CONNELL *(leans on the table)*. Listen, pal—this fifth column stuff's pretty rotten, isn't it?

JOHN. Yeah. It certainly is.

CONNELL. And you'd feel like an awful sucker if you found yourself marching right in the middle of it, wouldn't you?

JOHN *glances up sharply.*

CONNELL. And you, of course you wouldn't know it because you're gentle. But that's what you're doing. You're mixed up with a skunk, my boy, a no-good, dangerous skunk!

JOHN's *resentment vanishes—and is replaced by puzzlement.*

JOHN. Say, you're not talking about Mr. Norton, are you?

Two shot: JOHN *and* CONNELL.

CONNELL *(emphatically)*. I'm not talking about his grandfather's pet poodle!

CONNELL *again makes an effort to light his bent cigarette—and again is unsuccessful.*

JOHN. You must be wrong, Mr. Connell, cause he's been marvelous about the John Doe Clubs.

CONNELL *(sarcastically)*. Yeah? *(suddenly)* Say, you're sold on the John Doe idea, aren't you?

JOHN. Sure.

CONNELL. Sure. I don't blame you. So am I.

Close-up: Of CONNELL.

CONNELL *(sincerely)*. It's a beautiful miracle. A miracle that could only happen in the good old U.S.A. And I think it's terrific! What do you think of that! Me! Hard-boiled Connell! I think it's plenty terrific!—*Two shot: John is rather pleased to hear him say this.*

CONNELL. All right! Now, supposing a certain unmentionable worm, whose initials are D. B., was trying to use that to shove his way into the White House. So he could put the screws on, so he could turn out the lights in those lighthouses. What would you say about that? Huh?

JOHN. Nobody's gonna do that, Mr. Connell. They can't use the John Doe Clubs for politics. That's the main idea.

CONNELL. Is that so? Then what's a big political boss like Hammett doing in town? And a labor leader like Bennett? And a lot of other big shots who are up at D. B.'s house right now? Wolves, John, wolves waiting to cut up the John Does! *(snorting)* Wait till you get a gander at that speech you're gonna make tonight!

JOHN. You're all wet. Miss Mitchell writes those speeches and nobody can make her write that kind of stuff.

CONNELL *(cynically)*. They can't, huh? *(then barking)* Who do you think writes 'em? My Aunt Emma? I *know* she writes them.

Close-up: Of JOHN. *His jaw stiffens, angrily.*

CONNELL's VOICE. And gets a big bonus for doing them, too. A mink coat and a diamond bracelet.

JOHN *glares at him, his rage mounting.*

Close-up: Of CONNELL. *Unaware of* JOHN's *wrath.*

CONNELL. Don't write 'em? Why, that gold-grabbin' dame would double-cross her own mother for handful of Chinese yen!

JOHN (*in an outraged outcry*). Shut up! If you weren't drunk I'd—

Simultaneously his hand comes in and grabs the startled CONNELL *violently by his shirt front, lifting him out of his seat. Camera pulls back to include* JOHN—*who towers over* CONNELL.

Wider shot: JOHN *is still holding* CONNELL, *glaring down at him, enraged, when* BEANY *runs into the scene.*

BEANY (*holding out the envelope*). Hey, Boss! Here's the speech, Boss.

Suddenly he sees what's happening, and stares open-mouthed.

BEANY. Hey!

Med. shot: As JOHN *pushes* CONNELL *back into the seat, snatches the envelope from* BEANY, *and exits.*

CONNELL. Go on and read it, John, and then start socking!

Wider shot: As JOHN *exits from place.* BEANY *suddenly realizes he has gone—and chases after him.*

BEANY. Hey, wait a minute, Mr. Doe!
CONNELL. . . . .Tubby?
BEANY'S VOICE. Yes, sir?
CONNELL. Better bring me a glass of milk.

Close-up: Of CONNELL. *He stares at his unlighted cigarette—grimaces unhappily.*

CONNELL (*mumbling*). I'm smoking too much.

He grinds out the unlighted cigarette in the tray.

Dissolve to: Int. D. B.'s *dining room. Close shot: Of* D. B., *who is at head of table, talking on phone.*

D. B. (*into telephone*). . . . Yes, Charlie? You've got everything all set? Fine! Has John Doe been taken care of? Good! How many people do you think will be there?

A pleased expression comes over his face.

D. B. Fifteen thousand? Oh my, that's fine. Now, listen, Charlie, as soon as John Doe stops talking about me, I want you to start that demonstration. And make it a big one, you understand?

As D. B. *hangs up,*

Wider shot: Including TED SHELDON.

TED. Don't worry about that, D. B. My boys are there. They'll take care of it.

D. B. (*into telephone*). What? yes, I'll be there fifteen minutes after I get your call.

Camera draws back as he speaks. We see that dinner has been concluded. His listeners, besides TED *and* ANN, *are half a dozen distinguished looking men, some with cigars stuck in their mouths, others sip from champagne glasses.* ANN *sits to* D. B.'s *right.*

Cut to: Int. foyer: Med. shot: At D. B.'s *front door. A butler is opening the door for* JOHN.

BUTLER. Why, Mr. Doe. . . .
JOHN. Where are they?
BUTLER. In the dining room, sir.

JOHN *strides toward the dining room. Camera pans with* JOHN, *who is dripping wet, as he crosses the foyer until he comes within sight of the open door of the dining room.* JOHN *stops.*

Cut back to: Int. D. B.'s *dining room. Wider shot:* D. B. *addressing the group at the table.*

D. B. Well, gentlemen, I think we're about ready to throw that great big bombshell—
SOMEONE'S VOICE. Yeah, well it's about time.
D. B. Even a conservative estimate shows that we can count on anywhere between ten and twenty million John Doe votes. Now, add to that the labor vote that Mr. Bennett will throw in . . .

He indicates BENNETT *who nods, importantly.*

D. B. . . . and the votes controlled by Mr. Hammett and the rest of you gentlemen in your own territories—(*emphatically*) and nothing can stop us!

Close-up: Of ANN. *She seems distressed. She apparently has been listening to things that have caused her considerable anxiety.*

Wider shot: WESTON *leans forward and speaks to* D. B.

WESTON. As I said before, I'm with you—providing you can guarantee the John Doe vote.
D. B. Don't worry about that.
BENNETT. You can count on me under one condition. Little Bennett's gotta be taken care of!

D. B. Didn't I tell you that everybody in this room would be taken care of? My agreement with you gentlemen stands!

BARRINGTON. I'm with you, D. B., but I still think it's a very daring thing we're attempting!

D. B. These are daring times, Mr. Barrington. We're coming to a new order of things. There's been too much talk going on in this country.

ANN *glances up at* D. B.*, a startled look in her eyes.*

Close shot: D. B.*'s audience beams with satisfaction as he continues.*

D. B. Too many concessions have been made! What the American people need is an iron hand!

WESTON. You're right!

BENNETT. That's true. You're quite right, D. B.!

D. B. Discipline!

GROUP. Quite right! Exactly!

There are cries of: "Hear, hear!" and applause.

Close up: Of ANN. *She is completely seized by panic—and although she attempts applauding, it is feeble.*

Med. shot: Shooting through open door toward dining room. Prominently in view is ANN, *still lost in troubled thought.* D. B. *is still on his feet.*

D. B. And now—*(lifting champagne glass)* may I offer a little toast to Miss Ann Mitchell—the brilliant and beautiful lady who is responsible for all this!

The men rise.

Close-up: Of JOHN. *His mouths screws up bitterly*

JOHN *(quiet contempt).* That's a swell bracelet you're wearing.

He leaves her, abruptly.

Int. dining room: Full shot: JOHN *enters and looks the men over appraisingly as he goes toward* D. B. *They all stare at him.*

D. B. John—*(concerned)* Why aren't you at the convention?

JOHN *doesn't answer.*

D. B. Is there anything wrong?

JOHN *(after a pause).* Oh, no. Nothing's wrong. Everything's fine! So there's gonna be a new order of things, huh? Everybody's

gonna cut himself a nice, fat slice of the John Does! *(turns toward* D. B.*)* You forgot one detail, Mr. Big Shot—you forgot me, the prize stooge of the world. Why, if you or anybody else thinks he's gonna use the John Doe clubs for his own rotten purpose, he's gonna have to do it over my dead body!

D. B. Now, hold on a minute, young man! Hold on! That's—rather big talk! I started the John Doe clubs with my own money and I'll decide whether or not they're being properly used!

JOHN. No you won't! You're through deciding anything!

D. B. *cannot believe his ears.*

JOHN. And what's more, I'm going down to that convention and I'm gonna tell those people exactly what you and all your fine-feathered friends here are trying to cook up for them!

He looks up at ANN—*and starts tearing the speech in his hand.*

JOHN *(strongly).* And I'll say it in my own words this time.

He flings the torn paper toward ANN—*and starts out.*

HAMMETT AND OTHERS. Stop him, somebody! He'll ruin us, D. B.!

Med. shot: At Door. As JOHN *reaches it,* TED *steps up in front of him.*

TED *(menacingly).* Wait a minute, young feller—my uncle wants to talk to you.

D. B. *walks up to* JOHN.

D. B. Listen to me, my son! Before you lose your head completely, may I remind you that I picked you up out of the gutter and I can throw you right back there again! You've got a nerve accusing people of things! These gentlemen and I know what's the best for the John Does of America, regardless of what tramps like you think!

Get off that righteous horse of yours and come to your senses. *You're* the fake! We believe in what we're doing! You're the one that was paid the thirty pieces of silver! Have you forgotten that? Well, I haven't!

You're a fake, John Doe, and I can prove it! You're the big hero that's supposed to jump off tall buildings and things! Do you remember? What do you suppose your precious John Does will say when they find out that you never had any intention of doing it? That you were being paid to say so? You're lucky if they don't run you out of the country!

Why, with the newspapers and the radio stations that these gentlemen control, we can kill the John Doe movement deader than a doornail, and we'll do it, too, the moment you step out of line! Now, if you still want to go to that convention and shoot your trap off, you go ahead and do it!

Full shot: D. B. *leaves* JOHN *and returns to his chair.* JOHN *stares at him, unbelievingly.*

Close shot: Of JOHN.

JOHN (*after a pause*). Do you mean to tell me you'd try to kill the John Doe movement if you can't use it to get what you want?
D. B.'S VOICE. You bet your bottom dollar we would!
JOHN (*cynically*). Well, that certainly is a new low. I guess I've seen everything now.

Wider shot: As JOHN's *lips curl up contemptuously and he steps up to the table.*

JOHN (*throwing his hat on the table*). You sit there back of your big cigars and think of deliberately killing an idea that's made millions of people a little bit happier! An idea that's brought thousands of them here from all over the country, by bus and by freight, in jallopies and on foot—so they could pass on to each other their own simple little experiences.

Close-up: Of ANN. *Her eyes light up happily.*

JOHN'S VOICE. Why, look, I'm just a mug and I know it. But I'm beginning to understand a lot of things. Why, your type's old as history. If you can't lay your dirty fingers on a decent idea and twist it and squeeze it and stuff it into your own pocket, you slap it down! Like dogs, if you can't eat something, you bury it!

Close-up: Of JOHN. *His voice is pleading.*

JOHN. Why, this is the one worthwhile thing that's come along. People are finally finding out that the guy next door isn't a bad egg. That's simple, isn't it? And yet a thing like that's got a chance of spreading till it touches every last doggone human being in the world—and you talk about killing it!

Full shot: They listen to him—unmoved.

JOHN. Why, when this fire dies down, what's going to be left? More misery, more hunger and more hate. And what's to prevent that from starting all over again? Nobody knows the answer to that one, and certainly not you, with those slimy, bolloxed-up theories you've got! The John Doe idea may be the answer, though! It may be the one thing capable of saving this cockeyed world! Yet you sit back there on your fat hulks and tell me you'll kill it if you can't use it!

Well, you go ahead and try! You couldn't do it in a million years, with all your radio stations and all your power! Because it's bigger than whether I'm a fake! It's bigger than your ambitions! And it's bigger than all the bracelets and fur coats in the world!

Wider shot: ANN *runs to* JOHN.

ANN (*sincerely*). You bet it is, John!

JOHN *starts to exit.*

Med. shot: Shooting toward door.

JOHN (*turning to them*). And that's exactly what I'm going down there to tell those people!

As JOHN *reaches door,* TED SHELDON *jumps in front of him.*

Close shot:

TED. Wait a minute, you ungrateful rat! My Uncle's been too good to—

While he speaks, JOHN *looks down at the fist clutching his shirt, and then, with a suddenness that startles* TED, *he steps aside and clips* TED *on the jaw.* TED's *knees buckle and he goes down.* JOHN *exits.*

Wider shot: As several men rush to TED's *assistance.* D. B. *does not move.*

MAN. He's getting away!
ANN. John!

Ext. entrance to D. B.'s *house: Med. shot: As* JOHN *hurries out. He goes by half a dozen members of* TED SHELDON's *motorcycle troops who wait around to escort* D. B. *to the convention.*

Int. Dining room: Full shot: The room is full of commotion. ANN *is running out of the room, going after* JOHN. *Several men bend over* TED. D. B. *glares toward door, his face hardening.* HAMMETT *is barking at him.*

D. B. *reaches under the table, lifts up two phones. Hands one to* HAMMETT.

D. B. Get the *Bulletin*!

He, himself, dials the other phone.

ANN. John!
BARRINGTON. I've always told you, D. B. you're playing with dynamite!
D. B. (*calling to men*). Don't let that girl get away!

The butler rushes out.

WESTON. Before he gets through tonight he'll ruin us all!

BENNETT. You've got to stop him, D. B.!

D. B. I'll stop him! I'll stop him cold! Don't worry, I've been ready for this!

Cut to: Ext. D. B.'s *entrance—at gate. Med. shot: As* ANN *runs alongside* JOHN.

ANN. John! Oh, John, please listen to me! Please—I can explain everything, John. I didn't know what they were going to do! Let me go with you, John! John, please!

JOHN *gets into taxi—slams door—* ANN *runs beside cab as it starts off.*

JOHN. Go ahead, driver! Ball park!

ANN. John, please let me go with you! Please, John!

Several troopers grab ANN.

TROOPER. Mr. Norton wants to see you.

ANN. Oh!

As the men get a firmer grip on her and ANN *fights to get loose: Cut to: Int.* D. B.'s *study: Med. shot:* D. B. *is on the phone. The others pace around, perturbedly.* HAMMETT *has the second phone in his hand.*

D. B (*into phone*). Listen to me, Mayor Lovett, you do as I say. I want them both arrested. You tell the police department to pick up Connell. I've got the girl here.

HAMMETT (*holds out phone*). I've got the *Bulletin!*

D. B (*hotly*). I don't care what you charge them with! If you're worried, let them go in the morning, but keep them in jail over night!

He hangs up the receiver. Grabs another phone from HAMMETT.

D. B. Hello, *Bulletin?* Put Pop Dwyer on.

Dissolve to: Ext. entrance to ball park: Med. shot: Over the entrance gate a huge banner reads:

WELCOME TO
JOHN DOE CONVENTION

People come from all directions and pour through the gates. Some carry umbrellas over their heads, others have their coat collars turned up. Women hold newspapers over their heads to protect their hats. It is a misty, drizzling rain.

Ext. ball park: Long shot: (shooting from ANNOUNCER'S *view): Down at the Speaker's platform which has been erected on "Home Plate." On it, in the rear, is a brass band. In front of it is a speaker's table, over which dan-*

gles the microphone of a public address system. Attached to the table are several microphones with names of broadcasting stations on them.

Med. shot: Shooting toward audience. They sing: "The Battle Hymn of the Republic".

Med. shot: Toward people seated in grandstand. They join in the singing.

Another angle: Toward a third section. They also pick up the song.

Long shot: Taking in as many as possible. Everyone sings, and the volume has risen considerably.

Med. shot: Shooting down an aisle. A stream of people take up the song, as they march to their seats.

Med. shot: At entrance to Park. Crowds are coming in—and they, too, begin singing. They are also joined by the policemen posted at the gates.

Med. shot: A second entrance to Park. Another crowd is entering, also singing.

Med. shot: Of BERT *and* SOURPUSS *in the foreground of a group on platform, all of whom sing.* BERT *has a large rolled-up scroll in his hand.*

Close-up: Of the COLONEL. *Sitting in a corner somewhere, looking around speculatively, with a stubborn mental reservation that they are still all heelots.*

Several close shots: Of small groups—with their wet faces held high, singing lustily, eyes sparkling.

Long shot: Shooting from the platform down toward the audience. The song finally comes to a climax—and immediately, lusty cheering starts, as they see JOHN *coming on platform.*

Med. shot: Toward Platform. JOHN *goes to the microphone of the public address system.*

JOHN. Listen, ladies and gentlemen!

Before he can go any further, the band strikes up the strain of " AMERICA" *and immediately the large assembly begins singing it.*

Close-up: Of JOHN. *As his lips form the words. His expression is solemn.*

Various shots: Of groups, singing.

Long shot: As people sing. Finally the song is ended, and an enthusiastic cheer is emitted by the crowd.

Med. shot: On platform. JOHN *again steps toward the microphone and makes another effort to speak, but the* CLERGYMAN *places a detaining hand on his arm.*

CLERGYMAN. Just a moment, John. We begin with a short prayer.

Longer shot: Shooting over the heads of the audience toward the platform in the background. Gradually the cheering subsides.

CLERGYMAN *(speaking into public address system).* Quiet, please. Ladies and gentlemen—let us have a moment of silent prayer for the John Does all over the world . . . many of whom are homeless and hungry. Rise, please. Everybody rise.

The CLERGYMAN *and* JOHN, *standing next to him, immediately bow their heads.*

Long shot: Shooting toward audience. As far as the Camera eye can see, heads are bowed in prayer. The reflection on the wet umbrellas creates a strange and mystic light.

Several close shots: Of small groups—in silent prayer.

Close-up: Of the COLONEL. *Rather grudgingly, he has his head lowered.*

Close-up: Of JOHN. *His eyes are shut—his face wreathed in an expression of compassion.*

Med. shot: At press section. They, too, bow respectfully. The reporters are quiet for the first time.

Ext. street: Long shot: Directly in front of entrance to ball park. A stream of news trucks pull up, filled with newsboys—they immediately alight.

Ext. street: Med. shot: In front of another entrance. More trucks arrive—packed with newsboys.

Ext. street: Med. shot: Shooting toward entrance. As an army of newsboys, each carrying a stack of newpapers, run toward us yelling:

NEWSBOYS. Extry, extry! Read all about it!

Med. shot: Toward another entrance. Another swarm of newsboys dash in, also shouting.

NEWSBOYS. Extry! John Doe a fake!

Long shot: Of audience with their heads still bowed. Slowly, they begin turning around, puzzled, as from all directions and down every aisle, boys are running, waving papers in the air.

NEWSBOYS *(shouting).* Here you are! John Doe a fake! Read all about it! John Doe movement a racket!

Close shot: Of JOHN. *He looks up, terror-stricken.*

Med. shot: At press section. Great excitement prevails here.

ANNOUNCER (JOHN B. HUGHES). Newsboys! Hundreds of yelling newsboys are swarming into the park like locusts! They're yelling, "John Doe's a fake! Fake!"

Med. shot: Of audience. As newsboys are distributing papers to the baffled people.

NEWSBOYS. Here you are! No charge! John Doe a fake!

Med. shot: Of a second group. Some already have papers and peer, unbelievingly, at the headlines. Others grab papers from newsboys' hands.

MAN *(reading).* "Federal investigation urged by Chamber of Commerce."

Med. shot: Speaker's platform. SOURPUSS *and* BERT, *reading paper.*

SOURPUSS. How could he be a fake? *(laughing)*
BERT. It must be some kind of a gag.
SOURPUSS. A what?
BERT. A gag. A gag!

Ext.: Somewhere inside ball park: Long shot: We hear the shrieking of sirens and almost immediately a limousine, escorted by Sheldon's motorcycle troops, pulls up. Directly behind it is a string of cars.

Med. shot: The door of the limousine flies open and D. B. *comes out. He immediately heads for the platform.*

Camera pans over and we see troopers pouring out of the cars with TED SHELDON *directing them.*

TED. Come on, come on, step on it! Step on it! Step on it! You all know your places now, so let's get going! Wait for the signal!

Med. shot: DRUNK *with a balloon. He holds balloon up to* TED, *getting in* TED's *way.*

DRUNK. Hey, mister, will you autograph my balloon?
TED. Sure! *(and breaks balloon).*
TROOPER. *(pushing drunk aside).* Gangway!

Ext.: Park. Med. shot: At Speaker's platform. JOHN *is in front of the microphone trying to*

*make himself heard over thousands of voices,
all speaking at once.*

JOHN. Ladies and gentlemen! This is exactly what I came down here to tell you about
tonight. Please, if you'll all just be quiet for a
few minutes I can explain this whole thing to
you. As you all know, this paper is published
by a man by the name of D. B. Norton. . . .

*Med. shot: Shooting towards audience.
Down an aisle stalks* D. B., *his hand waving in
the air.*

D. B. *(shouting).* Don't listen to that man!
He's a fake!

*Camera pans with him as he hurries down the
aisle to the platform—all eyes turned toward
him.*

Close-up: Of JOHN. *As he stares at* D. B.
approaching, too flustered to know what to do.

Med. shot: Toward platform. As D. B. *runs up
the few steps and proceeds to the microphone,
troopers clearing the way for him.*

TROOPER *(drags John from mike).* Stand
back!

D. B. Wait a minute! Everybody wait a minute! Wait a minute, ladies and gentlemen! My
name is D. B. Norton . . . you all know me! I
accuse this man of being a faker! We've been
taken for a lot of suckers! And I'm the biggest
of the lot!

I spent a fortune backing this man in what I
believed to be a sincere and worthy cause,
just as you all did! And now I find out it's
nothing but a cheap racket! Cooked up by him
and two of my employees for the sole purpose
of collecting dues from John Does all over the
country!

JOHN *breaks away from the troopers and gets
to the mike.*

JOHN. That's a lie!

D. B. It's not a lie! Nickels and dimes! To
stuff into their own pockets! You can read all
about it in the newspapers there!

JOHN. That's a lie! Listen—don't believe
what he says! . . .

D. B. *(over-lapping above speech).* Let go of
me! This man had no intention of jumping off
of the top of a building! He was paid to say so!
(turning to John) Do you deny that?

JOHN. That's got nothing to do with it!

D. B. *Were* you paid for it—or weren't you?

JOHN. Yes! I was paid! But the—

D. B. *(over-lapping above speech).* And what
about the suicide note? You didn't write that,
either!

JOHN. What difference does that make?

D. B. *Did* you write it—or didn't you?

JOHN. No, I didn't write it, but—

D. B. Ah, you bet your life you didn't! You
look in your papers, ladies and gentlemen,
and you'll find Miss Mitchell's signed confession that she was the one that wrote it!

JOHN. Listen, folks, it's a fact that I didn't
write the letter, but this whole thing started—

D. B. There! You see? He admits it! You're
a fake, John Doe! And for what you've done to
all these good people—they ought to run you
out of the country—and I hope they do it!

*He leaves the platform—followed by his
troopers.*

Several shots: Of groups as they stare at
JOHN, *silent and stunned, waiting for him to
speak.*

*Full shot: The whole park full of people wait
in breathless anticipation. From somewhere in
the distance we hear a single voice of a man.*

VOICE. Speak up, John! We believe you!

*Med. shot: Under the platform. We see sev-
eral of* D. B.'s *troopers pulling at the cables of
the public address system.*

Close shot: Of JOHN. *He speaks into the
microphone.*

JOHN. Please listen, folks! Now that he's
through shooting off his face, I've got a couple of things to tell you about—

*Close shot: Under the platform. One of the
troopers disconnects the public address system
by cutting the cable.*

Close-up: Of JOHN. *He realizes the loud
speaker is dead, and looks around helplessly.*

Med. shot: Somewhere in audience TED
SHELDON *directs troopers.*

TED. Come on! The rest of you get in here
and riot! Break this crowd up! Come on!

*Med. shot: Of a group of John Does. They
still stare uncertainly. Suddenly, the head of one
of* SHELDON's *troopers appears—and cupping
his hands over his mouth, he yells toward
platform.*

TROOPER. John Doe's a fake! Boo!
Boooooo!

Long shot: From ANNOUNCER's *view. Shooting toward audience. The crowd is all yelling at
once now.*

Med. shot:

ANNOUNCER. I'm sorry, folks, but we can't hear him any more. Something's gone wrong with the loudspeaker.

Med. shot: Of JOHN. *Trying to talk over microphone.*

JOHN. Say, they can't hear me! The thing's not working! *(shouts)* Ladies and gentlemen! Look—this thing's bigger than whether I'm a fake—*(turns to* BERT*)* Look, Bert, you believe me, don't you?
BERT *(cynically)*. Sure, I believe you. Walking my legs off digging up five thousand signatures for a phoney!

Suddenly, nervously, he begins tearing up the petition in his hand.

BERT. Well, there you are, Mr. Doe! *(flinging crumpled petition at him)* Five thousand names asking you not to jump off any roof!

He turns to leave.

Close shot: Of SOURPUSS, *who, heartbroken, stops* BERT.

SOURPUSS. It makes no difference, Bert—the idea's still good. We don't have to give up our club!
BERT *(harshly)*. Yeah? Well, you can have it!

He exits.

Long shot: From ANNOUNCER'S *view. Crowd is yelling wildly.*

ANNOUNCER. They're starting to throw things!
2ND ANNOUNCER. Somebody's going to get hurt!

Close-up: Of JOHN. *He looks helplessly down at the hostile crowd.*

Int. police station: Full shot: ANN *and* CONNELL *are surrounded by several policemen. A sergeant sits at his desk, on which is a radio.* ANN'S *face is haggard and desperate as she listens to the radio announcer.*

ANNOUNCER. I'm afraid it'll be John Doe. Listen to that mob!

Unable to stand it any longer, ANN *suddenly jumps out of her seat.*

ANN. I've got to get to him!
OFFICER. Sorry, lady—I can't let you out.
ANN *(sobbing)*. Oh, let me go! Let me go to him! Oh, please, please let me go! They're crucifying him! I can help him!

OFFICER. Sorry, sister. We got orders to hold you.
ANN. Orders from who? Can't they see it's a frameup?

She is still desperately struggling to get free—when her mother comes hurrying in.

MRS. MITCHELL. Ann, darling!
ANN. Oh, Mother! They won't let me go! They won't let me go!

The police release her and she throws herself into her mother's arms.

Ext.: ball park. Close shot: Of JOHN. *He still attempts to get himself heard.*

JOHN. Listen, folks! You gotta listen to me, everybody!

Med. shot: Of a group of John Does.

A MAN *(yelling toward* JOHN*)*. Back to the jungle, you hobo!
2ND MAN *(disgustedly)*. Just another racket!
JOHN'S VOICE. Stick to your clubs!
MAN *(shouting)*. We've been fed baloney so long we're getting used to it!

Close shot: Of JOHN. *He disregards the missiles that fly around his head.*

JOHN *(supplicatingly)*. The idea is still good! Believe me, folks!. . . .

Ext.: ball park. Med. long shot: Toward platform. The crowd pushes menacingly around the platform, with policemen struggling to control them. JOHN *still stands there, pathetic and helpless. Missiles of all kinds fly into the scene. The members of the band are scrambling off the platform—as well as the others, until John is left alone.*

Long shot: Shooting toward audience. They still boo and yell.

Med. shot: Of the COLONEL. *Fearful for* JOHN, *he starts pushing his way through the crowd toward him.*

Med. shot: Of a group of people. Suddenly a woman reaches into a lunch basket she carries and takes out a tomato.

WOMAN *(shouting)*. You faker!

She reaches back to throw the tomato.

Close-up: Of JOHN. *His voice is gone. His eyes are glassy. He is making one last effort to speak.*

JOHN *(hoarsely)*. Listen. . . John Does . . . *(weakly)* You're the hope of the world . . .

As if in challenge to that statement, the tomato flies in and strikes him on the forehead. It seems to stun him. He remains motionless, staring before him with sightless eyes. The red smear of the tomato trickles down his face.

Med. shot: Of the COLONEL, *amidst the crowd. He sees* JOHN *hit and winces. Then, setting his jaw, he pushes people violently aside, trying to reach* JOHN.

Med. shot: On platform. JOHN *stares futilely before him. The* COLONEL *reaches his side and glancing sympathetically up at his face, starts to lead him off the platform. A squadron of policemen also rush to his rescue and precede* JOHN *and the* COLONEL.

Trucking shot: Down the aisle—as police disperse the crowd who boo and threaten JOHN *from the sidelines.*

Close shot: Of JOHN. *He is oblivious of the jeering, shouting mob—and of the wet newspapers flung in his direction.*

Med. shot: At dug-out exit—as the police finally manage to get him safely out of the park.

Med. shot. ANNOUNCER'S *booth.*

JOHN B. HUGHES. The police finally manage to get him out of the park! If that boy isn't hurt, it'll be a miracle!

Int.: police station. Med. shot: ANN *and her mother sit on a bench. A policeman is in the background.* ANN *stares into space. Her mother has an arm around her.*

ANNOUNCER'S VOICE. Ladies and gentlemen, this certainly looks like the end of the John Doe movement.

A policeman snaps the radio off.

CONNELL *(lifts glass of milk).* Well, boys, you can chalk up another one to the Pontius Pilates.

Two shot: ANN *and her mother.*

ANN *(sobbing).* I should have been there. I could have helped him. *(desolately)* He was so all alone!

Her MOTHER *draws* ANN *consolingly to her, and lays her head on her breast.*

Dissolve to:

Ext.: a highway. Med. shot: Of BERT'S *car on the way home.*

Int.: car. Close shot: BERT *and* SOURPUSS. *They both look depressed. After a silence,* SOURPUSS *speaks.*

SOURPUSS *(throatily).* A lot of us are going to be mighty ashamed of ourselves after tonight. We certainly didn't give that man much of a chance.

They lapse again into silence. BERT *stares grimly at the road.*

Dissolve to: Ext.: Clearing under the bridge. Close-up: Of JOHN. *He sits on a rock, his head bent low, tears streaming shamelessly down his cheeks. Camera draws back and we find the* COLONEL *before the fire, boiling water in a small tin pan.*

COLONEL'S VOICE. Have some more coffee, Long John?

JOHN. No, thanks, Colonel.

JOHN *lifts his eyes skyward, stares profoundly, a curious expression over his face.*

Dissolve to: A Montage. Long shot: Of JOHN, *a lonely figure, walking dejectedly. As he walks, faces begin to appear one by one, to taunt him. Their accusing voices are heard:*

WOMAN'S VOICE. Faker!

MAN'S VOICE. Racketeer!

2ND VOICE. Liar!

3RD VOICE. Cheat!

4TH VOICE. Imposter!

5TH VOICE. Why don't you jump!

GIRL'S VOICE. Christmas Eve at midnight! *(she laughs, sneeringly)*

Dissolve to: Another shot: Of JOHN *walking, his expression immobile. Over the shot appear several scenes through which* JOHN *has lived:*

1. BERT *shaking hands with him, saying:*

BERT. You're a wonderful man, Mr. Doe.

2. MRS. DELANEY *kissing his hand and saying:*

MRS. DELANEY. May God bless you, my boy.

3. ANN *in Broadcasting Station, kissing him:*

ANN. Now, get in there and pitch!

4. D. B. *issuing his tirade at* JOHN:

D. B. You're a fake, John Doe, and I can prove it! You're the big hero that's supposed to jump off tall buildings and things. you remember? What do you suppose your precious John Does will say when they find out that you never had any intention of doing it— that you were being paid to say so?

5. *Again the girl who laughed appears:*

GIRL. Christmas Eve at midnight?

And again she laughs sneeringly.

Dissolve to: Ext.: City Hall tower—night. Long shot: It is a picturesque scene of the City Hall outlined in silhouette against the sky. A peaceful mantle of snow silently descends upon it. Over the shot we hear the plaintive voices of children singing "Holy Night."

Dissolve to: Ext.: Outside of D. B.'s *house: Med. shot: Outside* D. B.'s *Study—through window. A group of eight young carolers sing "Holy Night." It is a continuation of the music from previous scene.*

Cut to: Int. D. B.'s *study. Med. shot: In the dimly lit room, we see the lonely figure of* D. B., *as he stands near a window staring out, meditatively. The voices of the children singing Christmas carols are faintly heard.*

Close-up: Of D. B. *He peers into the night, enveloped by disturbing thoughts. After a moment, he takes out his watch and glances at it. Then, as if annoyed by his own apprehension, he shoves it violently back into his pocket.*

Camera retreats in front of him as he crosses, determinedly, to a humidor, takes a cigar and shoves it into his mouth. Just as he is about to light it, he becomes aware of the singing, and cocks his head, listening.

Wider shot: As he drops the match and the unlighted cigar—and starts toward door. Just then the BUTLER *comes through.*

BUTLER. Merry Christmas, sir.
D. B. Oh. Merry Christmas.

D. B. *hands him a bill and nods toward the children. The* BUTLER *exits.*

Close-up: Of D. B. *Staring out into space moodily. We hear the voices of the children saying, "Thank you, sir! Merry Christmas!"* D. B.'s *mouth screws up, unhappily. It is far from a "merry" Christmas. It is a very lonely, conscience-stricken one.*

Dissolve to: Int.: Police station. Med. shot: A SERGEANT *sits in front of his desk. Opposite him is a* POLICEMAN. *Their rummy game has been interrupted by a phone call which the* SERGEANT *is now answering.*

SERGEANT. Who? John Doe? Is that screwball still around? *(laughing)*
POLICEMAN (with disgust). Aw, that dame's been callin' all day.
DESK SERGEANT. Sure, sure, I know. Yeah. At midnight, huh? Okay, lady. We'll have the place surrounded with nets.

He hangs up the phone—twirls his finger at his temple, shrugs—and reaches for a card.

Cut to: Int: ANN's *bedroom. Close shot:* ANN *is in bed. She looks wan. Her hand still rests on the phone.*

Camera pulls back to reveal a doctor by her side and her mother at the foot of the bed. They watch her—concerned.

ANN. Oh—they're laughing at me!

Impulsively, ANN *picks up the receiver and starts dialing again.*

DOCTOR'S VOICE. You're a sick girl, Ann. You'd better take it easy.
MRS. MITCHELL. Whom are you calling now? You called that number not ten minutes ago!
ANN *(into phone).* Hello. Mr. Connell? Have you seen him yet? Have you—

Cut to: Int.: Corridor of City Hall. Med. shot: Toward a telephone booth. CONNELL *speaks into the phone.*

CONNELL. Now listen, Ann—he can't possibly get in without our seeing him. I'm watching the side door and the Colonel's out front, so stop worrying.

Int.: ANN's *bedroom. Close shot:*

ANN. Thank you.

She hangs up the receiver, despairingly. Then, suddenly, she jumps out of bed and runs to a clothes closet—grabbing a coat and scarf.

MRS. MITCHELL. Why, Ann!. . . .
DOCTOR. Ann, don't be foolish!

Dissolve to: Insert: The City Hall Tower clock registers 11:45.

Cut to: Ext.: Highway. Med. shot: BERT's *car driving in the snow.*

Int.: Car. Full shot: BERT HANSEN *drives. In the car with him are his wife,* SOURPUSS *and several others.*

BERT *(complainingly).* If this isn't the craziest, the battiest, the looniest wild goose chase I ever heard of!
MRS. HANSEN. Oh, shut up, Bert. Sourpuss is right.
BERT. Yeah? Well, if he is, I'm a banana split!
SOURPUSS. That man is gonna be on that roof. Don't ask me how I know. I just know. And you know it as well as I do.

BERT. Sure, sure. I'd like to believe in fairy tales, but a guy that's a fake isn't gonna jump off any roof.

MRS. HANSEN. I don't think he was any fake—not with that face. And, anyway, what he stood for wasn't a fake.

BERT. Okay, honey, okay.

Cut to: Int.: Main floor corridor City Hall. Full shot: It is vast and empty, except for a colored porter, scrubbing.

Med. shot: At entrance. As ANN enters from outside. Determinedly, she starts toward elevators.

Close shot: At Elevator. ANN pushes button impatiently. She feels weak, and has to brace herself to stay on her feet. Suddenly, she is startled by the COLONEL's voice.

COLONEL. Elevators ain't running.

Camera pans over to the COLONEL, who sits on the stairs, next to the elevator.

Med. shot: ANN walks over to him, her face lighting up hopefully.

ANN. Colonel!

COLONEL. You shouldn't have gotten out of bed, Miss.

ANN. Has he been here?

COLONEL. No.

ANN. Have you seen him?

COLONEL *(sadly)*. I ain't seen him for a week.

ANN. Where's Connell?

COLONEL. He's watching the other door.

ANN. Oh. Gee, you're swell! Oh.

ANN *stares at him a moment, then, impulsively, she starts to pass him to go up the stairs,*

COLONEL *(grabs her)*. No sense in going up there! I been here for hours. He ain't here!

ANN *(pulls away from him)*. Oh, let me go, will you!

COLONEL *(calling after her)*. Now, that's crazy. It's fourteen floors!

But ANN vanishes. The COLONEL shakes his head and resumes his post.

Med. shot: At entrance. As the MAYOR, followed by D. B., HAMMETT, and the others, enters. Camera pans with them as they go toward elevator.

Med. shot: They arrive at the elevator. The MAYOR takes out his keys and unlocks the elevator door.

Close shot: Of the COLONEL. He watches them, puzzled. Can't figure out what they are doing here.

Cut to: Insert: Of elevator dial—as the light flicks on to number 14, indicating 14th floor. Camera pans down to elevator door, which opens and the men come out.

MAYOR. This is as far as the elevator goes. We've got to walk up to the tower.

He indicates the stairway.

Cut to: Wider shot: As they cross to stairway, silently.

Dissolve to: Ext.: City Hall roof. Full shot: The men enter. They glance around searchingly—and then slowly move toward the edge of the parapet.

Closer shot: The men look obviously self-conscious. No one speaks for a while.

BENNETT *(breaking the silence)*. That tramp is probably full of Christmas cheer and asleep in some flop house.

There is again silence. After a few minutes, the MAYOR speaks.

MAYOR. Let's go. I've got to decorate my tree.

Cut to: Int.: Corridor—14th floor. Med. shot: Outside Men's Washroom. JOHN comes out, and as camera pans with him, he proceeds to letter chute next to elevator. We see that it is the top of the chute, and from the elevator being there, we know it is the 14th floor. JOHN drops the letter into the chute.

Ext.: City Hall roof. Full shot: The place is silent except for occasional scraping of feet as several of the men move around. They continually refer to their watches. Finally, D. B. gives up impatiently.

D. B. Well, I give up. I don't know what gave us the idea that he—he'd attempt anything like this.

WESTON. I guess you're right. I'm afraid the joke's on us. Let's go.

D. B. I hope nobody finds out we've been here.

They all start to exit, when suddenly D. B. stops. He puts his hand out, and they all stop to listen. They hear footsteps, and back into the shadows.

Med. shot: Shooting toward stairs. JOHN appears around the bend and mounts the last few steps.

Med. shot: Of the huddled group. They watch breathlessly. In the darkness, their eyes dominate the scene.

Med. shot: Over their shoulders. As JOHN, *expressionless, his cigarette in his hand, crosses to the parapet, and looks out. He takes a puff of his cigarette and exhales the smoke.*

Med. shot: Of the huddled group. The MAYOR *is for stepping forward, but* D. B. *with an extended hand stops him, indicating for them to wait and see what happens.*

Close-up: Of JOHN. *He takes the envelope out of his pocket and examines it.*

Close shot: Of the group. Their eyes glued on him tensely.

Close shot: Of JOHN. *He stares at the envelope.*

Insert: Of envelope. On it is written: "TO JOHN DOES EVERYWHERE".

Close-up: Of JOHN. *He replaces the envelope in his pocket.*

Int.: Tower. Close shot: The group. Their eyes riveted on JOHN. *They feel the moment has come. Several of them glance toward* D. B.

Wider shot: To include them all, and JOHN. *He drops his cigarette on the ground, and, bending over, crushes it with his foot. Just as he straightens out again,* D. B. *speaks.*

D. B. *(restrained voice).* I wouldn't do that if I were you, John.

Close-up: Of JOHN. *As he turns sharply, startled. He stares blankly at the five people.*

Med. shot: Of the group. They move slightly forward and stop.

D. B. It'll do you no good.

Close-up: Of JOHN. *He continues to stare at them, strangely.*

Wider shot: To include them all.

D. B. The Mayor has policemen downstairs with instructions to remove all marks of identification you may have on your person. You'll be buried in Potter's Field and you will have accomplished nothing.

Close shot: Of JOHN. *After a moment, he speaks.*

JOHN *(in a sepulchral voice).* I've taken care of that. I've already mailed a copy of this letter to Mr. Connell.

Med. shot: Of the group. Amazed that he thought of this. They feel themselves helpless. D. B. *tries taking an authoritative tone.*

D. B. *(his throat is dry).* John, why don't you forget this foolishness?

He steps forward as he speaks.

JOHN *(quickly—threateningly).* Stop right where you are, Mr. Norton, if you don't want to go overboard with me.

Close-up: Of JOHN's *face. His eyes have a wild, maniacal look in them.*

Close-up: Of D. B. *He stares into* JOHN's *eyes and a terrified expression covers his face.*

Wider shot: As D. B. *instinctively backs up.*

JOHN *(throatily).* I'm glad you gentlemen are here. You've killed the John Doe movement, all right, but you're going to see it born all over again. Now, take a good look, Mr. Norton

Int.: Landing to tower. Med. shot: As ANN *practically has to pull herself up to the last step. Her face is wet from fever and exhaustion.*

ANN *(an outcry).* John!

Int.: Tower. Full shot: As everyone, startled by the outcry, turns. ANN *staggers into scene.*

ANN *(crying).* John!

She rushes and throws her arms around him.

ANN *(muffled sobs).* Oh, John, darling. No! No!

Close shot: JOHN *and* ANN. *He stares down at her, blankly.* ANN *clutches him, her head buried in his shoulder.*

ANN *(muffled sobs).* I won't let you. I love you, darling.

Med. shot: Of the group. They remain motionless, watching.

Close shot: JOHN *and* ANN. *She emits wracking sobs, then lifts her eyes up to him.*

ANN *(in a desperate plea).* John. Please, John, listen to me. We'll start all over again, just you and I. It isn't too late. The John Doe movement isn't dead yet.

Suddenly she becomes conscious of the others present, and she turns her head.

Camera pans over to what she sees. The group of men watching, silently.

Camera pans back to ANN. *Her eyes widen slowly. She looks from them to* JOHN *and back*

again, and her face takes on an excited, breathless look, as the reason for their being there becomes comprehensible to her.

ANN *(excitedly)*. See, John! It isn't dead, or they wouldn't be here! It's alive in *them*. They *kept* it alive. By being afraid of it. That's why they came up here.

Close shot: ANN *and* JOHN. *He continues to stand with his hands at his sides, looking at her, while she clings to him desperately. While she speaks, he turns his face from her and stares at the men.*

ANN. Sure, it should have been killed before. It was dishonest.

Close-up: Of JOHN. *He is staring strangely at the group of men—as slowly, gradually, the curtain is being lifted from his clouded brain.*

ANN'S VOICE. But we can start clean now. Just you and I. It'll grow again, John. It'll grow big. And it'll be strong, because it'll be honest!

Close-up: Of ANN. *Her strength is fast ebbing away. She clings to* JOHN *more tenaciously.*

ANN *(last bit of effort)*. Oh, darling, if it's worth dying for, it's worth living for. Oh, please, John. . . .

She looks up at his face, seeking some sign of his relenting—but she finds none.

Close-up: Of ANN, *who still clinging to him, lays her cheek on his chest—and lifts her eyes heavenward.*

ANN *(a murmured prayer)*. Oh, please, God—help me!

Flash: Of the men—as they stare transfixed, waiting breathlessly

Med. shot: At Entrance. BERT, SOURPUSS *and others appear—having run up the stairs breathlessly. Their eyes are filled with apprehension.* CONNELL *and the* COLONEL *are with them. When they see the scene before them, they stop, awed.*

Close-up: Of ANN. *Suddenly she stares before her—as a divine inspiration comes to her. Her eyes light up with a wide, ecstatic fire.*

Two shot: ANN *and* JOHN. ANN *turns and glances up at* JOHN'S *face.*

ANN *(tensely)*. John!

She takes his face in her two hands and turns it to her.

ANN. John, look at me. You want to be honest, don't you? Well, you don't have to die to keep the John Doe idea alive! Someone already died for that once! The first John Doe. And He's kept that idea alive for nearly two thousand years.

Close shot: BERT, *his* WIFE *and* SOURPUSS. *The cynical expression on* BERT'S *face begins to soften.*

ANN'S VOICE *(with sincere conviction)*. It was He who kept it alive in *them*—and He'll go on keeping it alive for ever and always! For every John Doe movement these men kill, a new one will be born!

Two shot: ANN *and* JOHN. JOHN *remains grimly unmoved.* ANN *continues.*

ANN *(ecstatically)*. That's why those bells are ringing, John! They're calling to us—not to give up—but to keep on fighting! To keep on pitching! Oh, don't you see, darling? This is no time to give up!

Several flashes: (To intercut with ANN'S *speech)—One of* BERT; *his* WIFE; CONNELL; D.B.

Med. shot: Toward ANN *and* JOHN. ANN'S *strength is slowly waning.*

ANN. You and I, John, we can—*(suddenly)* No, John, if you die, I want to die, too! *(weakly)* Oh, I love you so—

Her strength leaves her—and as her eyelids slowly shut, she collapses limply at his feet.

Med. shot: Of BERT'S *group, as they react to this.* BERT *stares, profoundly moved.*

Med. shot: JOHN *and* ANN—*as he stares bewildered, at* ANN *at his feet. Mechanically, he reaches down and lifts her in his arms.*

BERT'S VOICE. Mr. Doe . . .

JOHN *vaguely becomes aware of* BERT'S *presence and glances toward him.*

Med. shot: BERT, *his* WIFE *and* SOURPUSS.

BERT *(his voice choked—haltingly)*. You don't have to—Why, we're with you, Mr. Doe. We just lost our heads and acted like a mob. Why, we . . .

BERT'S WIFE *(jumping in)*. What Bert's trying to say is—well—we need you, Mr. Doe. There were a lot of us didn't believe what that man said.

Close-up: Of JOHN—*as he listens to her, expressionless.*

WIFE'S VOICE. We were going to start up our John Doe Club again whether we saw you or not.

Med. shot: BERT, *his* WIFE *and* SOURPUSS.

WIFE. Weren't we, Bert?

BERT *nods.*

WIFE. And there were a lot of others that were going to do the same thing. Why, Mr. Sourpuss even got a letter from his cousin in Toledo, and . . .

SOURPUSS *(joining—eagerly).* Yeah, I got it right here, Mr. Doe!

Close-up: Of JOHN. *The bewildered look in his eyes has vanished. It is now replaced by an expression of softness and understanding.*

WIFE'S VOICE *(choked).* Only—only it'll be a lot easier with you. Please—please come with us, Mr. Doe!

JOHN *remains standing, thoughtful.*

Med. shot: Of BERT's *group. They all look supplicatingly at him.*

Close-up: Of JOHN. *He stares at* BERT's *group and, shifting his gaze, looks at* D. B. *and his crowd. Then, turning back to* BERT, *his eyes*

light up and something of a warm smile appears on his face.

Full shot: As JOHN, *having decided on his course, starts forward with* ANN *in his arms. The church bells chime loud and victoriously.*

Med. shot: Around BERT. *Their eyes brighten ecstatically as* JOHN *walks toward them. They all speak at once.*

BERT'S GROUP *(ad-lib).* Mr. Doe!
She'll be all right!
We've got a car downstairs . . .

They follow JOHN *out, chattering excitedly. Only* CONNELL *and the* COLONEL *remain.*

Close-up: Of CONNELL. *He glares at* D. B. *defiantly.*

Close-up: Of D. B. *awe-stricken by the scene he has witnessed.*

Med. shot: CONNELL *and the* COLONEL.

CONNELL *(to* D. B.*—defiantly).* There you are, Norton! The people! Try and lick that! Come on, Colonel.

They exit, arm in arm, as the music swells— suggesting emergence from darkness and confusion to light and understanding.

Fade out.

CASABLANCA

Screenplay by

Julius Epstein, Philip G. Epstein,

and Howard Koch

RICK	Humphrey Bogart
ILSA	Ingrid Bergman
LASZLO	Paul Henreid
CAPTAIN RENAULT	Claude Rains
MAJOR STRASSER	Conrad Veidt
FERRARI	Sydney Greenstreet
UGARTE	Peter Lorre
SAM	Dooley Wilson
ANNINA	Joy Page

Screenplay by Julius Epstein, Philip G. Epstein, and Howard Koch
adapted from the play *Everybody Comes to Rick's* by Murray Burnett and
Joan Allison
Produced by Hal Wallis for Warner Brothers, 1942
Directed by Michael Curtiz
Edited by Owen Marks
Music by Max Steiner
Song, "As Time Goes By," written and composed by Herman Hupfeld

In reading *Casablanca* by Julius Epstein, Philip G. Epstein, and Howard Koch, written in 1942 in the heart of the World War II years, as adapted from an unproduced play *Everybody Comes to Rick's* by Murray Burnett and Joan Allison, it is fascinating to note how enduring the popularity of this work is.

First, regard the expert craftsmanship with which this work is written. Note how quickly, effortlessly, and richly the tone of the story and the times are set in the early scenes . . . the tragic lot of the war refugees in Nazi-dominated Casablanca and their hope for a precious visa to take them to liberty . . . the roundup by the Vichy police . . . the tragic attempts by the refugees to flee . . . the pickpocket . . . the Austrian couple . . . the hope for freedom represented by the plane . . . all accomplished within a few beginning pages of the screenplay. A striking example of the screenwriter's filmic craft, merging exposition with action.

Note, similarly, the key use of the theme song "As Time Goes By," written and composed by Herman Hupfeld. One usually thinks of a theme song as a catchy tune and lyric that will sell records and thereby help the picture as well. But in *Casablanca,* the song as used (it was not actually written for the picture) plays a most important role, almost a rich minor character if you will. It is not only effective as an aural bit of sentiment but as a bridge, a theme, and a running commentary of Rick's past, poignant love affair with Ilsa. It also serves as a flashback key of effectiveness, enabling the viewer to go back in time to Rick and Ilsa in Paris. It is not often a song plays such an important role in film.

Let me also call your attention to the Victorian, or what we would call in America, the genteel tradition of the story. In 1942 one would hardly expect to find an almost unabashed Victorian piece. Yet if you think of the tenets of this tradition—love, duty, responsibility, and sacrifice, not to mention honor—note, if you will, how Rick as written and as played by Humphrey Bogart, fulfills all these Victorian qualities. Under that shell of cynicism, he only pretends to be looking out for himself. You will perceive this early in the script when Ugarte (Peter Lorre) is apprehended for his theft of the letters of transit, and Rick makes the point that he will stick his neck out for no one. But then take note how he plays "Sir Lancelot" later on in the story when it really counts to save the lovely refugee girl Annina from Captain Renault's (Claude Rains) clutches; and, more importantly, what Rick does for love, honor, and sacrifice when he sends Ilsa (Ingrid Bergman), the woman he loves, off with her husband, Laszlo, to safety with the letters of transit so Laszlo can go on fighting against the evil forces of the world, as represented here by nazism.

The Epstein brothers contributed to the editing of this film, which enabled *Casablanca* to really get itself together for public showing—a contribution which is somewhat unusual for writers to make. In his illuminating visit to our class at UCLA on the Literature of the Screen to discuss *Casablanca,* among other of his works, on one occasion, Julius Epstein related to us his experience in writing that now-memorable war film. Writing just ahead of the shooting of the film by director Michael Curtiz, on almost a day-to-day basis, Julius Epstein and his brother, soon after they created the ending of the film while taking a ride in Julius's convertible up Sunset Boulevard, went to a preview of *Casablanca*. The audience at that preview did not buy the ending entirely—the scene where Rick shoots and kills the Nazi major, Strasser, who was trying to prevent Laszlo and Ilsa from flying off to safety from the airport. In that scene, Captain Renault, on viewing the body of the Nazi major on the ground, immediately called for "the rounding up of the usual suspects" in that version of the film at that preview.

On mulling over the audience's lukewarm reception to the film at that preview, Julius and his brother, Philip, suddenly realized that, as shot, the ending of the film had Captain Renault out of character in all too quickly calling for "the rounding up of the usual suspects" to save Rick. This was all wrong for the captain, who was portrayed as an opportunist throughout the film, always weighing his own interests first. At the suggestion of the brothers Epstein, this scene was changed slightly before the picture went into general release. The change allowed for a series of cuts between the captain and Rick to show the captain making up his own mind whether he should save Rick or not . . . and Rick's reaction to his life hanging in the balance . . . and then came Renault's "round up the usual suspects." This, thus, created some suspense in character and made the scene and the ending work far better. The rest was history.

Born in New York in 1909 and educated at Penn State, Julius J. Epstein began his professional career as a radio publicist. In 1939 he entered into a long and valuable collaboration with his brother, Philip (born 1912, now deceased), which lasted until 1958. Julius Epstein's films include (alone and in collaboration) *Four Daughters* (1938), *The Man Who Came to Dinner*

(1941), *Arsenic and Old Lace* (1944), *The Last Time I Saw Paris* (1954), and *The Tender Trap* (1955).

Howard Koch, co-scenarist with Julius and Philip Epstein on *Casablanca,* was born in New York City in 1902. After graduating from Columbia law school, he began writing plays in the twenties. Among his radio scripts is Orson Welles's famous *War of the Worlds* production. Among his other film credits are *Sergeant York* (co-scenarist, 1941) and *Mission to Moscow* (1943).

Fade in. Long shot: Revolving globe. As the globe revolves it becomes animated—Long lines of people (in miniature) stream from all sections of Europe—to converge upon one point on the tip of Africa. Over this animated scene comes a voice of a Narrator.

NARRATOR. Refugees—streaming from all corners of Europe towards the freedom of the New World—all eyes turned toward Lisbon, the great embarkation point—But not everybody could get to Lisbon directly—so a Refugee Trail sprang up—

Dissolve to:

Animated map, which illustrates the trail as the NARRATOR *mentions the points,*

NARRATOR *(continuing).* Paris to Marseilles—across the Mediterranean to Oran—Then by train—or auto—or foot—across the rim of Africa to Casablanca in French Morocco—

Dissolve to:

Relief map of Casablanca, showing the ocean on one side and the desert on the other. The voice of the NARRATOR *comes over.*

NARRATOR. Here—the fortunate ones through money—or influence—or luck—obtain exit visas and scurry to Lisbon—and from Lisbon to the Americas—But the others—wait in Casablanca—and wait—and wait—

As the NARRATOR'S *voice fades away—*

Camera zooms to:

Close shot: relief map of Casablanca. A street on the map.

Dissolve to:

Full shot: Glass shot, old Moorish section of city. Day. At first only the turrets and rooftops are visible against a torrid sky. In the distance is a haze-enveloped sky. The camera pans down the facades of the Moorish buildings to a narrow, twisting street crowded with the polyglot life of a native quarter. The intense desert sun holds the scene in a torpid tranquillity. Activity is unhurried and sounds are muted . . . Suddenly the screech of a siren shatters the calm. Veiled women run screaming for shelter. Street vendors, beggars and urchins melt into doorways. A police car speeds into the shot and pulls up before an old-fashioned Moorish hotel—flophouse would be a better word for it.

Cut to:

Int. corridor of this decrepit hotel. Native French police officers run up the steps, crash into the doors of the various rooms, come out—dragging frightened refugees.

Cut to:

Close shot: Door, as one police officer flings it open. The shadow of a man hanging by a rope from a chandelier is seen on the wall. The officer slams the door shut.

Street corner. Two other policemen have stopped a white civilian and are talking to him.

1ST POLICEMAN. May we see your papers, please?
CIVILIAN *(nervously).* I—I don't think I have them—on me.
1ST POLICEMAN. In that case, we'll have to ask you to come along.
CIVILIAN *(patting his pockets).* It's just possible that I—Yes, here they are.

He brings out his papers. The 2nd policeman examines them.

2ND POLICEMAN. These papers expired three weeks ago. You'll have to—

Suddenly the CIVILIAN *breaks away, starts to run wildly down the street. The camera trucks with him. From off scene we hear the* POLICEMAN *shout "Halt!"—But the* CIVILIAN *keeps going. A shot rings out, the man falls.*

The camera pans to a—

Med. close shot. JAN *and* ANNINA BRANDEL *are huddled in a doorway, the dazed and frightened spectators to this casual tragedy. They are an Austrian couple, very young and attractive, thrust by circumstances from a simple country life into an unfamiliar hectic world.* ANNINA'S *hand clutches her husband's arm as their eyes follow the* POLICE *who are examining the victim.*

Cut to:

JAN *and* ANNINA. *They both speak with a Central European accent. At this moment the police car sweeps past them on its way back.* JAN *takes his wife by the hand.*

JAN. The Prefecture must be this way.

They start off in the direction taken by the police car.

AN INSCRIPTION: *"Liberté, Egalité, Fraternité," carved in a marble block along the roofline of a building.*

The camera pans down the facade, French in architecture, to the high-vaulted entrance over which is inscribed: "Palais de Justice." Cam-

era continues to pan down to the entrance. A queue of people of all ages and nationalities overflow from inside the building and down the steps. The camera pans over the line of waiting people extending into the square. We pick up a babel of languages with only a few recognizable words such as "visa," "Monsieur le Prefect," "Portugal," "a hundred francs," etc. Suddenly the attention of the people is attracted toward the street.

The Square (from the angle of the waiting line). The square is typically French in its landscaping and architecture. This is the center of the modern city of Casablanca. The police car is just pulling up to the curb in front of the Prefecture. A policeman opens the grated door at the back of the car and a nondescript assortment of refugees begin to pour out.

Sidewalk café on one side of the square. A middle-aged English couple are standing in front of their table for a better view of the commotion in front of the Prefecture. A dark-visaged European smoking a cigarette leans against a lamp post a short distance away. He is watching the English couple more closely than the scene on the street.

ENGLISHWOMAN. What on earth's going on there?

DARK EUROPEAN *(walking over to the couple).* Pardon, Madame . . . have you not heard?

ENGLISHMAN. We hear very little—and we understand even less.

DARK EUROPEAN. Two German couriers were found murdered in the desert. *(with an ironic smile)* The . . . unoccupied desert.

Int. front of the Palais de Justice (from the angle of the cafe) as the refugees are unloaded from the police car.

DARK EUROPEAN'S VOICE *(over scene)* This is the customary roundup of refugees, liberals and . . . *(as a young blonde girl—the last to leave the car—is herded with the others in front of the Prefecture)* Of course, a beautiful young girl for M'sieur Renault, the Prefect of Police.

The sidewalk café.

ENGLISHWOMAN *(puzzled)* I don't understand.

DARK EUROPEAN. As usual, the refugees and the liberals will be released in a few hours. *(smiling slightly)* The girl will be released later.

ENGLISHWOMAN *(horse-faced and past middle age)* Why, a woman isn't safe in this wretched place!

DARK EUROPEAN *(shrugging)* To get out of Casablanca they say one needs two dollars for an exit visa and two hundred for the Prefect. Unless, of course, one is a beautiful young girl. The rich and the beautiful sail to Lisbon. The poor are always with us.

ENGLISHWOMAN. Dreadful . . .

DARK EUROPEAN. Unfortunately, along with these unhappy refugees the scum of Europe has gravitated to Casablanca. Some of them have been waiting years for a visa. *(puts his arm compassionately around the Englishman)* M'sieur, I beg of you, watch yourself. Take care. Be on guard. . . .

ENGLISHMAN *(rather taken aback by this sudden display of concern)* Er—er—thank you. Thank you very much.

DARK EUROPEAN. Not at all *(raises his hat politely)* Bon jour, Madame. Bon jour, M'sieur.

He walks out of the shot. The ENGLISHMAN, still a trifle disconcerted by the EUROPEAN'S action, looks after him, mopping his brow with his pocket handkerchief.

ENGLISHMAN *(restoring his pocket handkerchief)* Friendly chap, wasn't he?

As he pats his breast pocket there is something lacking. He opens his coat, feels inside.

ENGLISHMAN. Silly of me . . .

ENGLISHWOMAN. What, dear?

ENGLISHMAN. Leaving my wallet in the hotel room . . .

He closes his coat, then suddenly he looks off in the direction of the departing dark EUROPEAN, the clouds of suspicion gathering. But now, overhead, the drone of a low-flying airplane is heard. Heads look up.

Airplane flying overhead—its motor cut for a landing.

Plane. Showing the swastika on its tail.

Trucking shot. Along the waiting line of refugees outside the Palais de Justice. Their upturned gaze follows the flight of the plane. In their faces is revealed one hope they all have in common—and the plane is the symbol of that hope. The camera stops at the last of the line far out on the street, just as JAN and ANNINA appear and take their places at the very end. Their eyes also follow the droning plane.

ANNINA. Perhaps tomorrow we shall be on the plane. *(wistfully)* Jan, is it true that in America you can travel a thousand miles without a visa?

JAN *(smiles at his wife with superior knowledge)*. Annina, you and your fairy tales . . .

Dissolve to:

Airport. The plane is swooping down—past a neon sign on a building on the edge of the airport. The sign reads: "RICKS."

Group shot. CAPTAIN LOUIS RENAULT, *a French officer, appointed by Vichy as Prefect of Police in Casablanca, stands chatting with other officers. He is a handsome, middle-aged Frenchman, debonair and gay, but withal a shrewd and alert official. Around him are clustered the German Consul,* HERR HEINZE, *a young Italian officer,* CAPTAIN TONELLI, *and* RENAULT's *aide,* LIEUTENANT CASSELLE. *Behind them is a detail of French native soldiers. The officers watch the approaching plane as it taxies toward them. The German and Italian detach themselves from the group and walk toward the place where the plane will stop. The German walks briskly a step ahead of the Italian, who appears to be making an effort to catch up.*

The plane with the swastika over the door. When the door is opened, the first passenger to step out is a large German wearing heavy, horn-rimmed spectacles. He is bland-faced, with a perpetual smile that seems more the result of a frozen face muscle than a cheerful disposition. On any occasion when MAJOR STRASSER *is crossed, the smile melts and the expression hardens into iron.* HERR HEINZE *steps up to him with upraised arm.*

HEINZE. Heil Hitler.
STRASSER *(with a more relaxed gesture)*. Heil Hitler.

They shake hands.

HEINZE *(in German)*. It is good to see you again, Major Strasser.
STRASSER *(in German)*. Thank you, thank you.

The Italian steps up with elaborate good will.

TONELLI. Captain Tonelli, at your service sir.
STRASSER. That is kind of you.
TONELLI. Our staff is anxious to cooperate—

But he gets no farther than that. STRASSER *turns away to greet* RENAULT *and* CASSELLE, *who have come into the shot.* HERR HEINZE *makes the introduction.*

HEINZE *(in English)*. May I present Captain Renault, Police Prefect of Casablanca . . . Major Strasser.

The two shake hands.

RENAULT *(courteously—but with just a suggestion of mockery underneath his words)*. Unoccupied France welcomes you to Casablanca.
STRASSER *(in perfect English—beaming on the Frenchman)*. Thank you, Captain. It is very good to be here.
RENAULT. Major, may I present my aide, Lieutenant Casselle.

CASSELLE *does not offer to shake hands. They merely salute and bow.* RENAULT *leads* STRASSER *toward the edge of the airfield, where their cars await them.* HEINZE *and* CASSELLE *follow, with the Italian captain left to bring up the rear.*

Trucking shot. RENAULT *and* STRASSER *walking toward the cars.*

RENAULT *(again the suggestion of a double-edged inference)*. You may find the climate of Casablanca a trifle warm, Major.
STRASSER. Oh, we Germans must get used to all climates—from Russia to the Sahara. *(suddenly the smile fades and the eyes harden)* But perhaps you were not referring to the weather.
RENAULT *(sidesteps the implication with a smile)*. What else, my dear Major?
STRASSER *(casual again)*. By the way, the murder of the couriers—what has been done?
RENAULT. Realizing the importance of the case, my men are rounding up twice the usual number of subjects.

Again STRASSER *looks at him sharply.*

HEINZE. Captain Renault means that the round-up is a blind. We already know who the murderer is.
STRASSER. Good. Is he in custody?
RENAULT. There is no hurry. Tonight he will come to Rick's. *(indicating the cafe at the airport's edge)* Everybody comes to Rick's.

HEINZE *shrugs to indicate that he can do nothing with* RENAULT.

STRASSER. I have already heard about *this* café—and also about M'sieur Rick himself.

As they arrive at the car—

Dissolve to:

Int. Prefecture of Police. RENAULT's *office.* RENAULT, STRASSER, HEINZE *and other offi-*

cials are standing around a table on which some papers are lying.

RENAULT. All the plans are made. Guards at all the doors, windows—two men on the roof—there is no chance of escape.

Cut to:

Door as it opens and a NATIVE POLICEMAN *enters.*

NATIVE POLICEMAN *(saluting).* Captain Renault—

RENAULT *(to* STRASSER *and the others).* You will excuse me for one moment—

He walks towards the door.

Cut to:

Med. shot at door. The NATIVE POLICEMAN *has left it slightly ajar. Through the opening two beautiful women can be seen standing down the hall. When* RENAULT *comes into the scene the* NATIVE POLICEMAN *whispers to him.* RENAULT *looks through the opening at the two women.*

RENAULT: *(thoughtfully).* Which one? *(sighs).* Oh well, tell the dark one to wait in my private office and we'll go into the visa matter thoroughly.

NATIVE POLICEMAN. Yes, Captain.

He starts away.

RENAULT *(taking another quick look down the hall).* And it wouldn't hurt to have the other one leave her address and phone number.

Cut to:

Med. shot. STRASSER *as* RENAULT *comes in the scene.*

RENAULT. Now—where were we?

STRASSER *(annoyed).* Don't you think, Captain Renault, that with so much important work to be done you could devote a little less time to personal matters?

RENAULT *(shrugging).* Well—you like war; I like women. We are both very good at our jobs.

STRASSER. I think the German viewpoint is a much healthier one.

RENAULT. You are probably right, Captain Strasser. At least with your work you get a lot of fresh air.

STRASSER *shakes his head. It is hopeless to argue with* RENAULT.

STRASSER. Now—the real reason for my visit. Has Victor Laszlo arrived yet?

HEINZE. This afternoon from Oran.

RENAULT. With a very beautiful young woman. Otherwise, he traveled light.

STRASSER. This is not a laughing matter. Laszlo *must not leave* Casablanca. That isn't very complicated, is it? Have I made myself clear?

RENAULT *(that blandness again).* Oh, Captain Strasser is extremely simple.

STRASSER *looks at him. Just how did he mean that?*

STRASSER *(looking at* RENAULT *closely).* It is well known that he is prepared to offer a fabulous bribe for an exit visa.

RENAULT. I am prepared to refuse it.

But he sighs a sigh which shows that it must have been quite a struggle.

STRASSER. Do you know where Laszlo is staying?

RENAULT. We even know the time he intends to bathe. *(starting for the door).* Now, if you will excuse me—there is a problem across the hall I must go into—

STRASSER. I would like to talk to Laszlo.

RENAULT *(glancing at himself in a mirror next to the door).* Undoubtedly he will be at Rick's. Or have I mentioned that before?

And, satisfied with his appearance, he starts across the hall.

Dissolve to:

*Electric sign "*RICK'S*". Night.*

Camera pans down to:

Couple entering RICK'S *thru the revolving door. From the café we hear sounds of music and laughter.*

Cut to:

Int. RICK'S. *An expensive and chic night club which definitely possesses an air of sophistication and intrigue. The camera pans around the room, soaking in the atmosphere.*

A woman, just past the first blush of youth, is singing to the accompaniment of a four-piece orchestra.

The piano is a small, salmon-colored instrument on wheels. There is a negro on the stool, playing. He is dressed in bright blue slacks and sport shirt.

About him there is a hum of voices, chatter and laughter. The occupants of the room are varied. There are Europeans in their dinner jackets; their women beautifully begowned and bejeweled. There are Moroccans in silk robes. Turks wearing fezzes. Levantines. Naval of-

ficers. Members of the Foreign Legion, distinguished by their kepis—

Across the room, stretching the entire length of the wall, is a tremendous, resplendent bar.

The camera dollies from the piano to the bar. As the camera passes the various tables we hear a babel of foreign tongues. Here and there we catch a scattered phrase or sentence in English— "I have an idea for a little business in Brazil—" *A very beautiful young woman at another table is being nostalgic. She is saying to an elderly male admirer:* "It used to take a Villa at Cannes, or the very least, a string of pearls—"

As the camera nears the bar we see a man staring hopelessly into space. His companion is trying to cheer him up, but the man says tonelessly, "I'll never get out of here—I'll die in Casablanca." *From the table next to the bar there is a burst of feminine laughter.*

Now we are at the bar.

Cut to:

Med. shot. Russian bartender, a huge, jovial looking person. He wears a silk smock. He hands a drink to a customer, with the Russian equivalent of "Bottoms Up." *Then he calls out to a passing waiter.*

RUSSIAN BARTENDER. Carl—

The WAITER *stops, turns, walks to the bar. He is a small, mild-mannered man with spectacles.*

CARL. Yes, Fydor—
FYDOR *(heavy Russian accent).* Carl, my frien'— *(he hands him a huge sheaf of bar checks).* You will make the computations, plees? I am so busy—

CARL *just glances quickly through the checks, then hands them back to Fydor.*

CARL *(German accent).* Two hundred and seventy-eight francs. You undercharged on the last check.
FYDOR *(gratefully, as* CARL *walks away).* Thank you, my frien', thank you—*(to the customer; with great admiration for* CARL*).* All in his head, like an adding machine—Three books he wrote on mathematics—astronomy—the greatest professor in the whole University of Leipzig.
CUSTOMER *(turning to look at* CARL *in the distance).* Really? Is that so?
FYDOR *(nodding vehemently).* And the mos' vonderful t'ing of all—he's not a bad waiter!
CUSTOMER. And what did you do before you came here?

FYDOR *(sadly).* I was the Czar's favorite sword swallower—Whenever he felt depressed—*(leaning closer to customer).* Tell me, my frien', do you think there's a future in America for a sword swallower?

CARL, *tray in hand, walking up to a private door, over which a burly man stands guard.*

CARL *(to the burly man).* Open up, Abdul.
ABDUL *(respectfully, as he opens the door).* Herr Professor.

CARL *goes in.*

Cut to:

Long shot. Int. gambling room as CARL *comes in. The camera takes in the activity at the various tables, then—*

Cut to:

Med. shot at baccarat table. A woman hands a check to the dealer. He, in turn, turns around and hands it on to a tuxedoed overseer who looks at the check, then at the woman.

OVERSEER *(to woman).* Just one minute, please.

He walks toward a table.

Cut to:

Close shot. A man's hand holding a drink. We see the OVERSEER'S *body come into the scene. His hand places a check on the table. The other man's hand picks up the check. Obviously, the man is studying the check. Then his hand comes into the scene and on the back of the check, in pencil, it writes:*

"Okay— RICK"

The OVERSEER'S *hand takes the check as—*

The camera pulls back to:

Med. shot. RICK *sitting at the table alone. He just sits staring at the drink. There is no expression in his eyes. He is a complete dead pan.* RICK *is an American of indeterminate age.*

Cut to:

Table. Two women and a man. The women are glancing off scene at RICK'S *table, fascinated.* CARL *is in the scene, preparing Turkish coffee.*

WOMAN *(to* CARL*).* Will you ask Rick if he'll have a drink with us.
CARL. Madame, he never drinks with customers unless he invites them to his table.
2ND WOMAN *(disappointedly; glancing towards* RICK*).* What makes saloon-keepers so snobbish?

MAN (*to* CARL; *holding out a bill*). Perhaps if you told him I ran the second largest banking house in Amsterdam . . . ?

CARL (*shaking his head*). That wouldn't impress Rick. The leading banker in Amsterdam is now the pastry chef in our kitchen.

He takes the bill from the man's hand and walks away. Camera pans with him, disclosing:

Med. shot. RICK. *He is glancing towards the open door and indicating that the person seeking admittance is not to be let in.*

There is a commotion at the door. A voice with a German accent is heard shouting.

GERMAN VOICE. Of all the nerve! Who do you think—

RICK *gets up, and with no change of expression, walks across the floor to the door, camera trucking with him.*

Cut to:

Ext. door. A red-faced German is protesting to ABDUL.

GERMAN. I know there's gambling in there! I . . .

The door opens, RICK *comes out.*

RICK (*coldly*). Yes?

Cut to:

Entrance to RICK'S *as* UGARTE *comes in. He is a small, thin man with a nervous air. If he were an American he would look like a tout. He looks interestedly in the direction of* RICK *and the* GERMAN.

Cut to:

Med. shot RICK *and* GERMAN.

GERMAN (*waving his card*). I've been in every gambling room between Honolulu and Berlin and if you think I'm going to be kept out of a saloon like this, you're very much mistaken.

RICK *just looks at him calmly, takes the card out of the* GERMAN'S *hand.*

RICK (*tearing up the card*). Your money's good at the bar.

CARL, *tray in hand, comes out of the gambling room, walks right between the* GERMAN *and* RICK.

CARL. S'cuse me.

GERMAN (*to* RICK). Why—what—Do you know who I am?

RICK (*coldly*). I do. You're lucky the bar's open to you.

He turns away from the sputtering GERMAN, *catches the negro's eye at the piano. The negro, who while still playing, has been watching the by-play, winks at* RICK. RICK *acknowledges the wink with some friendly gesture. It isn't quite a smile, but it is probably the closest thing to a smile that* RICK *can manage. Anyway, it establishes the fact that as far as* RICK *is concerned, the negro is a privileged person.*

RICK *goes back into the bar.*

Cut to:

Med. shot. At table in gambling room as RICK *comes into the scene. A moment later* UGARTE *follows him into the scene.*

UGARTE (*with the manner of a man who curries favor*), M'sieur Rick.

RICK (*barely looking at him*). Hello, Ugarte.

RICK *sits on a stool at the end of the bar.* UGARTE *follows him. There is nobody near them.*

UGARTE (*fawning*). Watching you just now with the Deutches Bank, one would think you had been doing this all your life.

RICK (*stiffening*). What makes you think I haven't?

UGARTE (*vaguely*). Oh, nothing. When you first came to Casablanca, I thought—

RICK (*coldly*). Yes?

UGARTE (*fearing to offend* RICK, *laughs*). What right have I to think? (*hastily changing the subject*). Too bad about those German couriers, wasn't it?

RICK (*indifferently*). They got a break. Yesterday they were just two German clerks; today they're the Honored Dead.

UGARTE (*shaking his head*). You will forgive me for saying this, M'sieur Rick, but you are a very cynical person.

RICK (*shortly*). I forgive you.

BARTENDER *coming into scene with two drinks, which he sets before the men.*

UGARTE (*his eyes lighting up*). Oh, Rick— you are going to drink with me?

RICK. No.

UGARTE (*sadly*). You despise me, don't you?

RICK (*indifferently*). If I gave you any thought, I probably would.

UGARTE. You object to the work I do. But think of the poor refugees who must rot in this place if I did not help them. Is it so bad that through ways of my own I provide them with exit visas?

RICK *(staring at his drink)*. For a price, Ugarte, for a price.

UGARTE. Yes—but those poor devils who cannot meet Renault's price, I get it for them for half. Is that so parasitic?

RICK *turns to look at* UGARTE.

RICK. I don't mind a parasite. I object to a cut-rate one.

UGARTE. Well, after tonight I am through with the whole business. Rick, I am leaving Casablanca.

RICK. Who did you bribe for your visa? Renault or yourself?

UGARTE *(ironically)*. I found myself much more reasonable. *(he takes envelope from his pocket, taps it on his hand)*. Do you know what these are? Something that not even you have ever seen—*(lowers his voice)*. Letters of Transit signed by Marshall Weygand. They cannot be rescinded or questioned.

RICK *looks at him, then holds out his hand for the envelope*.

UGARTE. In a moment. Tonight I will sell these for more money than even I ever dreamed of. Then—farewell to Casablanca. Rick—I have many friends in Casablanca, but because you despise me you're the only one I trust. Will you keep these Letters for me?

RICK. For how long?

UGARTE. Perhaps an hour, perhaps longer.

RICK *(taking them)*. I don't want them here over night.

UGARTE. No fear of that. Waiter—

Cut to:

Med. shot. WAITER *coming into the scene.*

UGARTE *(to* WAITER*)*. Any messages for me?

WAITER. No, M'sieur.

UGARTE. I am expecting some people. If anyone asks for me, I will be here.

The WAITER *nods, leaves.* UGARTE *turns to* RICK.

UGARTE. Now, Rick, I hope you are more impressed with me. Excuse me, I go to share my good luck with your roulette wheel.

He starts across the floor.

RICK. Wait a minute—

UGARTE *stops.* RICK *comes up to him.*

Cut to:

Close shot. RICK *and* UGARTE. RICK'S *voice is barely audible.*

RICK. I heard a rumor that those German couriers were carrying Letters of Transit.

UGARTE *doesn't reply for a moment.*

UGARTE. Yes—I heard that rumor, too. Poor devils.

RICK *looks at* UGARTE *steadily.*

RICK *(slowly)*. You're right, Ugarte. I am a little more impressed with you.

UGARTE *smiles and almost swaggers toward the gambling table.* RICK *starts for the door.*

Cut to:

Med. shot. Café. SAM *is playing and singing the "Knock Wood" number, accompanied by the orchestra. The café is in semi-darkness. The spotlight is on* SAM, *and every time the orchestra comes in on the "Knock Wood" business, the spotlight swings over to the orchestra.*

Cut to:

Med. shot. RICK *as he makes his way from the gambling room to* SAM *on the floor.*

Cut to:

Med. close shot at piano. RICK *comes into shot, and during one of the periods when the spotlight is on the orchestra,* RICK *slips the Letters of Transit into the piano, then exits towards the bar.*

Cut to:

Med. shot at bar. RICK *comes in and watches* SAM *in his number.*

Cut to:

Close shot at small table. FERRARI. *He sees* RICK *at bar, exits in his direction.*

Cut to:

Med. shot at bar. RICK. FERRARI *comes into shot.*

FERRARI *(as he comes up to* RICK*)*. Hello, Rick.

RICK. 'Lo, Ferrari. How's business at the Blue Parrot?

FERRARI. Fine—but I would like to buy your café.

RICK. It's not for sale.

FERRARI. You haven't heard my offer.

RICK. It's not for sale at any price.

FERRARI *sighs.*

FERRARI. What do you want for Sam?

RICK. I don't buy or sell human beings.

FERRARI. Too bad. That's Casablanca's leading commodity. In refugees alone we could make a fortune if you would work with me through the Black Market.

RICK. Suppose you let me run my business and you run yours.

FERRARI. Suppose we ask Sam? Maybe he'd like to make a change?

RICK. All right, suppose we do. Let's speak to him.

NEGRO *at piano. He has just finished his number. He gets up, starts to wheel his piano towards the center of the floor.* RICK *and* FERRARI *come up to him.*

RICK. Sam—Ferrari wants you to work for him at the Blue parrot.

SAM. Ah likes it fine here.

RICK. He'll double what I pay you.

SAM. Ah ain't got time to spend what ah makes here.

RICK. Sorry, Ferrari.

RICK *looks at Ferrari, smiles, shakes his head; then he winks at Sam. Ferrari exits.*

Cut to:

Med. shot at long bar in café proper. YVONNE *is sitting on a stool, drinking brandy.* FYDOR, *who is looking at her with lovesick eyes, is filling her tumbler.*

FYDOR. The boss' private stock. Because— Yvonne—I loff you.

YVONNE *(morosely).* Oh, shut up.

FYDOR *(fondly).* For you, Yvonne, I shot opp.

RICK *saunters into the scene, leans against the bar next to* YVONNE. *But he pays no attention to her. She looks at him bitterly, without saying a word.*

Cut to:

Med. shot. SAM *is in the midst of a number.*

Cut to:

Med. shot. RICK *and* YVONNE. *As only* SAM *is spotlighted at the piano,* RICK *and* YVONNE *stand in the gloom.* YVONNE, *who has never taken her eyes off* RICK, *finally blurts out:*

YVONNE. Where were you last night?

RICK. That's so long ago. I don't remember.

Pause.

YVONNE. Will I see you tonight?

RICK *(calmly).* I never plan that far ahead.

YVONNE *turns, looks at* FYDOR, *extends her glass to him. As* FYDOR *is about to fill the glass* RICK *turns, stops him with a gesture.*

RICK. She's had enough.

YVONNE. Pay no attention to him, Fydor. Fill it up.

FYDOR *hesitates, looks at* RICK.

FYDOR *(putting the bottle down).* I loff you, Yvonne, but he pays me.

YVONNE *wheels on* RICK *with drunken fury.*

YVONNE. I'm sick and tired of having you—

RICK. Fydor, call a taxi.

FYDOR. Da, Boss. *(he walks toward the café entrance).*

RICK *(taking* YVONNE *by the arm).* Come on, we're going to get your coat. You're going home.

YVONNE. Take your hands off me—

He pulls her along toward the hall door.

Street in front of RICK'S. FYDOR *stands at the curb signalling a cab. Finally one pulls up.*

Ext. RICK'S *(shooting toward the entrance).* RICK *and* YVONNE *come out of the café. He is putting a coat over her shoulders. She is objecting violently.*

YVONNE. Who do you think you are, pushing me around. I'm a lady. I sang in America. I've been married twice.

RICK *(to* FYDOR—*as he and* YVONNE *approach the waiting cab).* You'd better go with her, Fydor, to be sure she gets home.

FYDOR. Da, Boss.

One on each arm, they help YVONNE *in the cab.* FYDOR *follows her in.*

RICK. And Fydor.....(FYDOR *looks out through the window).* Come right back.

FYDOR *(his face falling).* Da, Boss.

The cab starts off

Trucking shot. RICK *as he walks back toward the café entrance.*

RENAULT'S VOICE *(Over scene).* How extravagant you are—throwing away women like that. Some day they may be very scarce.

RICK *turns toward the voice.*

A table on the café terrace. RENAULT *is sipping some brandy. His eyes are amused.* RICK *walks into the shot.*

RICK. Hello, Louis.

RENAULT. I think now I shall pay a call on Yvonne—maybe get her on the rebound, eh?

RICK *(as he takes a seat at the table).* When it comes to women, you're a true democrat.

RENAULT *laughs, pours* RICK *a drink. There is the sound of a plane warming up on the adjacent air field.* RICK *looks in the direction of the sound.* RENAULT *follows his gaze.*

Med. shot. Transport plane in the full glare of the floodlights, standing poised on the runway, its motor racing, ready for the takeoff.

Cut to:

Med. shot. RICK *and* RENAULT. RICK *is still looking steadfastly at the plane.*

RENAULT. The plane to Lisbon—*(looks at* RICK *shrewdly).* You would like to be on it?
RICK *(curtly).* Why? What's in Lisbon?
RENAULT. The Clipper to America.

RICK *doesn't answer; looks at the plane warming up, but his look isn't a happy one.*

RENAULT. I have often speculated on why you do not return to America. Did you abscond with the church funds? Did you run off with the President's wife? I should like to think you killed a man. It is the romantic in me.
RICK *(still looking at the plane—sardonically).* It was a combination of all three.
RENAULT. And what in Heaven's name brought you to Casablanca?

The plane's motors grow louder.

RICK. My health. I came to Casablanca for the waters.
RENAULT. Waters? What waters? We are in the desert.
RICK. I was misinformed.

RENAULT *shakes his head but can say nothing for the plane is speeding down the runway. Its lights shine on the faces of* RICK *and* RENAULT. RICK *cannot take his eyes from the plane. Now it leaves the ground and passes almost directly over them. He watches the plane until its lights disappear into the distance.*

Med. shot. A CROUPIER *so identified by the green visor over his eyes, comes into the scene.*

CROUPIER. Excuse me, M'sieur Rick, but a gentleman inside has won ten thousand francs. The cashier would like some money.
RICK *(not at all perturbed).* I'll get it from the safe.
CROUPIER. I am humiliated, M'sieur Rick. I do not understand how—
RICK. It's all right, Emil. Mistakes will happen.

RICK *and* RENAULT *both rise. As they start toward the door, a French and an Italian officer come out, arguing violently on some political subject. As they meet* RENAULT *they both come*

to attention and salute; then move on, still arguing. RICK *and* RENAULT *start in.*

RENAULT. Rick, there is going to be some excitement here tonight. We are going to make an arrest in your café.
RICK *(not at all excited).* Again?

Cut to:

Int. Café as RICK *and* RENAULT *come in.*

RENAULT. This is no ordinary arrest. A murderer, no less.

Cut to:

Close shot. RICK *as his eyes react. Involuntarily they glance toward the gambling room.*

Cut to:

Med. shot. RICK *and* RENAULT. *They are starting for the steps alongside the bar.*

RENAULT *(who has caught the look).* If you are thinking of warning him—don't put yourself out. He can't possibly escape.
RICK *(starting up the steps).* I stick my neck out for nobody.
RENAULT. A wise foreign policy—

There is a drink at the end of the bar waiting to be picked up by a WAITER. RENAULT *takes the drink as he starts upstairs after* RICK. *The* WAITER *turns around—no drink.*

RENAULT *(up the steps—drink in hand).* You know, Rick, we could have made this arrest earlier in the evening at the Blue Parrot—

RICK *enters a room on the landing.*

Cut to:

Int. RICK'S *office as he comes in, followed by* RENAULT.

RENAULT. —But out of my high regard for you we are staging it here. It will amuse your customers.
RICK *(opening a door).* Our entertainment is enough.

Cut to:

Med. shot at door to a small, dark room off the office, where the safe is kept. RICK *goes in, starts to open the safe.* RENAULT, *drink in hand, leans against the door jamb.*

RENAULT. Ricky, we are to have an important guest tonight—Major Strasser of the Third Reich—no less. We want him to be here when we make the arrest. A little demonstration of the efficiency of my administration.
RICK. I see. And what's Strasser doing here? He hasn't come all the way to Cas-

ablanca to witness a demonstration of your efficiency.

RENAULT. Perhaps not.

RICK. Louis, you have something on your mind. Why don't you spill it?

RENAULT (admiringly). You are very observant. As a matter of fact, I wanted to give you a word of advice.

RICK. Yes?

RENAULT. There are many exit visas sold in this café, but we know that you have never sold them. That is the reason we permit you to remain open.

RICK (amiably). I thought it was because we let you win at roulette.

RENAULT. Yes, that is another reason . . . My dear Rick, there is a man who has arrived in Casablanca on his way to America. He will offer a fortune to anyone who will furnish him with an exit visa.

RICK. Yes? What man?

RENAULT. Victor Laszlo.

RICK. Laszlo here in Casablanca!

RENAULT (watching Rick's reaction). Ricky, this is the first time I have ever seen you so impressed.

RICK (casual again). Laszlo has succeeded in impressing half the world.

RENAULT. And it is my duty to see that he does not impress the other half. (now intensely serious). Rick, Laszlo must never reach America. He stays in Casablanca.

RICK. It'll be interesting to see how he manages.

RENAULT. Manages what?

RICK. His escape.

RENAULT. But I just told you—

RICK. Stop it, Louis. He escaped from a concentration camp, didn't he? The Nazis have been chasing him all over Europe.

RENAULT (grimly). This is the end of the chase.

RICK. Ten thousand francs says it isn't.

RENAULT. Is that a serious wager?

RICK. I just lost ten thousand francs. I'd like to get it back.

RENAULT. Make it five thousand. I am only a poor corrupt official. (RICK nods). Done. No matter how clever he is, he still needs an exit visa—or I should say, two.

They start out of the room and down the steps, camera trucking with them.

RICK. Why two?

RENAULT. He is traveling with a lady.

RICK. He'll take one.

RENAULT. I think not. I have seen the lady. And if he did not leave her in Marseilles, nor in Oran, he will not leave her in Casablanca.

RICK. Maybe he's not as romantic as you.

RENAULT. It does not matter—one or two— romanticist or not—there is no exit visa for him.

RICK. Louis, where did you get the idea I might be interested in helping Laszlo?

RENAULT. Because, my dear Ricky, I suspect under that cynical shell, you are at heart a sentimentalist. (RICK breaks into a laugh). Laugh if you will, but I happen to be familiar with your record. You fought with the Ethiopians against Italy, and you risked your neck with the Loyalists in Spain—

RICK (casually). Well—there wasn't much doing in Paris at the time. (anxious for a change of subject). Apparently you are determined to keep Laszlo here.

RENAULT. I have had my orders.

RICK. I see. Gestapo spank.

Med. shot. RENAULT. They are down now. As he speaks he faces the huge mirror over the bar.

RENAULT. You over-estimate the influence of the Gestapo, Ricky. We do not interfere with them and they do not interfere with us. In Casablanca I am master of my fate. I am captain of my—

He stops short as in the mirror he sees the reflection of CAPTAIN STRASSER as he comes into the café.

Med. shot. RICK and RENAULT.

RENAULT (hurriedly). Excuse me, Ricky—

He hurries towards STRASSER. RICK looks in the mirror, sees whom RENAULT is hurrying toward, smiles cynically. The CROUPIER, who has been waiting, comes into the scene.

RICK (handing the money to the CROUPIER). There you are.

CROUPIER (with grim determination). It shall not happen again, m'sieur!

He hurries away. RICK picks up a drink from the bar.

Café. RENAULT is walking with CARL.

RENAULT. Carl, see that Herr Strasser gets a good table—close to the ladies.

CARL. I have already given him the best, M'sieur! (sadly). . . . Knowing he is German and would take it anyway.

The Café as they enter from the hall. RENAULT beckons to a NATIVE OFFICER who is apparently waiting for the word. He approaches and salutes.

RENAULT (in a low voice). Take him quietly. Two guards at every door.

NATIVE OFFICER. Yes, sir.

He salutes and starts toward the door of the gambling room. The camera travels with RENAULT, *who walks to a table on one side of the cafe where* STRASSER *and* HEINZE *are seated. At the adjoining table are some German officers.* STRASSER *beams as* RENAULT *approaches the table.*

RENAULT. Good evening, gentlemen.
STRASSER. Good evening, Captain.
HEINZE. Won't you join us?
RENAULT *(sitting down)*. Thank you. It is a pleasure to have you here, Major.
STRASSER. A very interesting club.
RENAULT. Especially so this evening. *(low voice)*. In just a minute you will see the arrest of the man who murdered your couriers.

Cut to:

Close shot. UGARTE *at the roulette table in the gambling room. Piled in front of him is a huge stack of chips. He is having a run of luck and his eyes are feverish as they follow the marble that is bouncing on the wheel. The marble stops on number 13. Exultantly* UGARTE *reaches for the chips which the* CROUPIER *shoves on the table. But just then another hand closes onto* UGARTE'S *arm. A look of terror crosses his face.*

NATIVE OFFICER'S VOICE *(over scene)*. You will come with me, Senor Ugarte.
UGARTE *(in a low voice)*. Allow me to cash my chips.

The NATIVE OFFICER *nods, follows* UGARTE *to the* CASHIER.

The CASHIER'S *booth. The* CASHIER *pays* UGARTE *the amount of his chips.* UGARTE *thrusts the money in his inside coat pocket. As his hand comes out of the pocket, it grips a small revolver, pointed at the* NATIVE OFFICER. *The* OFFICER *makes a jump for* UGARTE, *and the gun goes off. The* OFFICER *clasps his shoulder. A woman screams. People at the gambling tables duck for cover.* UGARTE *runs toward the hallway.*

Quick flashes.

(a) RICK *crossing the floor of the cafe, turns abruptly toward the door to the gambling room.*

(b) A woman in a booth jumps to her feet, looks in the direction of the sound.

(c) A man at the bar is lifting his glass to drink. Abruptly he puts the glass down.

(d) The music stops as SAM'S *hands hold on the piano keys.*

(e) CARL, *behind the bar, flashes an expectant look toward* STRASSER'S *booth.*

(f) RENAULT, STRASSER *and* HEINZE *all jump to their feet.*

Hallway between the rooms. UGARTE *rushes into the hallway as* RICK *appears from the opposite direction.*

UGARTE. Rick, help me!
RICK *(low voice)*. Don't be a fool. You can't get away.
UGARTE. Hide me. Do something. You're in this, too. You have the Letters of Transit—

Before he can finish, RENAULT, STRASSER, HEINZE *and others rush in from behind* RICK. *Other police officers appear from the gambling room, grab* UGARTE. *Without a word, Rick pushes his way through the group to the cafe.*

MAN *(half kiddingly, half in earnest)*. When they come to get me, RICK, I hope you'll be of more help.
RICK. I stick my neck out for nobody.

The Cafe. RICK *comes out on the floor. An air of tense expectancy pervades the room. A few customers are on the point of leaving.* RICK *speaks in a very calm voice.*

RICK. I'm sorry there was a disturbance, but it's all over. Everything's all right. *(glances toward his piano player)*. Sam...

At the piano. Sam nods, begins to play.

SAM. Oh' Noah, what'd he do? *(he shouts at the audience)*. C'mon, folks—*(he starts again)*. Oh' Noah, what'd he do?

He waits and plays the next phrase.

Full shot. Taking in several tables. There is a half-hearted response from the people.

THE PEOPLE. Ol' Noah, what'd he do?
SAM *(grinning, playing louder and faster)*. Dat's right. He built a floatin' zoo.

Tables. The people, under SAM'S *spell again, join in and sing. The gloom is somewhat lifted. We pan over various tables, picking up all types of people during the course of the song.*

STRASSER'S *table. The song is finished and the excitement has quieted down.* RENAULT, STRASSER *and* HEINZE *are now back at their table. The* HEADWAITER *is taking their order.*

STRASSER. ...Champagne, and a tin of caviar—very cold.
RENAULT. Let me recommend Veuve Cliquot twenty-six, Major.
WAITER. Very well, sir.

He goes out of the shot.

RENAULT *(calls to* RICK, who is off scene).
Oh, Rick...

RICK *walks into the shot.*

RENAULT. Rick, this is Major Heinrich
Strasser of the Third Reich.
STRASSER. How do you do.
RENAULT. And you already know Herr
Heinze.

RICK *nods to* STRASSER *and* HEINZE.
STRASSER. Please join us, Herr Rick.

RICK *sits down beside* HEINZE, *facing*
RENAULT *and* STRASSER.

RENAULT *(changing the subject).* Rick, we
are very honored tonight. Major Strasser is
one of the reasons why the Third Reich enjoys
the reputation it has today. *(* RICK *nods).*
STRASSER *(smiles).* You repeat "Third
Reich" as though you expected there to be
others.
RENAULT. Personally, I will take what
comes.

The WAITER *appears with drinks, begins to
open the bottles and pour during the ensuing
conversation.*

STRASSER. Do you mind if I ask you a few
questions? Unofficially, of course.
RICK *(shrugging).* Make it official, if you
like.
STRASSER. What is your nationality?

RICK *looks at him a moment before replying.*

RICK *(poker face).* I'm a drunkard.

STRASSER *looks closely at him.*

Close shot. RENAULT.

RENAULT. That makes Rick a citizen of the
World.

Med. shot, RICK, RENAULT *and* STRASSER.

RICK. I was born in New York, if that'll
clear things up any.
STRASSER *(to* RICK—*very amiably).* I under-
stand you came here from Paris at the time of
the Occupation.
RICK. That seems to be no secret.
STRASSER. Are you one of those people who
cannot *imagine* the Germans in their beloved
Paris?
RICK. It's not particularly *my* beloved Paris.
HEINZE *(slight laugh).* Can you imagine us
in London?
RICK. When you get there, ask me.

STRASSER *(digging into the caviar).* How
about New York?
RICK. There are certain sections of that city
I would not advise you to try to invade.
STRASSER. Who do you think will win the
war?
RICK. I haven't the slightest idea.
RENAULT. Rick is completely neutral about
everything. And that takes in the field of
women, too.

STRASSER *takes a little black book from his
pocket, riffles through the pages.*

STRASSER *(to* RICK). You weren't always so
carefully neutral. We have a complete dossier
on you. *(reads).* 'Richard Blaine, American.
Age thirty-seven. Cannot return to his country.'—*(looks up from book).* The reason is a
little vague. We also know what you did in
Paris—(RENAULT, *very curious, tries to look
over* STRASSER'S *shoulder).* Also, Herr Blaine,
we know why you left Paris.

RICK *reaches over, takes the book from*
STRASSER'S *hand.*

STRASSER. Don't worry. We are not going to
broadcast it.
RICK *(looking in the book).* Are my eyes
really brown?
STRASSER. You will forgive my curiosity,
Herr Blaine. The point is, an enemy of the
Reich has come to Casablanca and we are
checking up on anyone who can possibly be
of help to us.
RICK. My interest in Victor Laszlo's
staying or going—*(with a glance toward*
RENAULT)—is only a sporting one.
STRASSER. In this case, you have no sympathy for the fox?
RICK. Not particularly. I understand the
hounds' point of view, too.
STRASSER. Victor Laszlo published the
foulest lies in the Prague newspapers until the
very day we marched in, and even after that
he continued to print scandal sheets in a
cellar.
RENAULT. One must admit he has great
courage.
STRASSER. Also, he is very clever. Three
times he slipped through our fingers. In Paris
he continued his activities. We intend not to
let it happen again.
RICK *(rises with a slight smile).* You'll excuse
me, gentlemen. Your business is politics.
Mine is running a cafe.
STRASSER. Good evening, Herr Blaine.

RICK *walks out of the shot, toward the gambling room.*

RENAULT. You see, you have nothing to worry about Rick.

STRASSER *(His eyes following the direction* RICK *has gone).* Perhaps...

Cut to:

Med. shot at another table. The dark-appearing foreigner we had seen in the opening sequence is busily engaged with a middle-aged prosperous looking man.

DARK FOREIGNER *(his arms thrown solicitously around the other man).* I beseech you, my friend—be on guard. Take care. Use every precaution.

SAM *at piano. He is idling away at something sentimental. The people at the tables have resumed their chatter. As he plays* SAM *glances casually around. Suddenly, as his eyes look toward the entrance, his playing falters, then stops altogether.*

Med. shot the Cafe. (Shooting toward the entrance). We see what SAM *is staring at. A couple has just come in and we recognize them as* VICTOR LASZLO *and his companion whose face we saw in the car window outside of* UGARTE's *hotel. She wears a simple white gown. Her beauty is such that people turn to stare. The* HEADWAITER *comes up to them.*

HEADWAITER. Yes, M'sieur.

LASZLO *(in quiet, even tones).* I reserved a table. Victor Laszlo.

Closeup. BERGER *looking intently at* LASZLO.

Close shot. The WOMAN— *who has been looking around casually. When she sees* SAM, *her face registers a startled surprise for just an instant.*

HEADWAITER'S VOICE *(over scene).* Yes, M'sieur Laszlo. Right this way.

Close shot. SAM. *He sees her looking at him, turns his gaze away, resumes his piano playing.*

Trucking shot. Group—as the HEADWAITER *takes them to a table. Although they pass right by the piano and the woman, (who is later to be identified as* ILSA LUND), *looks directly at* SAM, *the latter with a conscious effort keeps his eyes on the keyboard.* ILSA *smiles slightly. Camera stops on* SAM. *After she has gone out of scene,* SAM *steals a look in her direction.*

At LASZLO's *table. The* HEADWAITER *seats* ILSA *and goes out of shot.* LASZLO *takes the chair opposite. He surveys the room with a sweeping glance.*

LASZLO. I see no one of UGARTE's description.

ILSA. Victor, are you sure we should have come here—so in public?

LASZLO. There is often a greater safety in what appears to be a risk.

MAN'S VOICE *(off scene).* Excuse me, but you look like a couple who are on their way to America.

A small blond man, later identified as BERGER, *walks into scene.*

LASZLO. Well?

The man reaches into his vest pocket, brings out a ring with a large aquamarine stone.

BERGER. You will find a market there for this ring. I am forced to sell it at a great sacrifice.

LASZLO. Thank you, but I hardly think—

BERGER. Then perhaps for the lady. The ring is quite unique.

He holds it down to their view, begins to twist the stone, which is apparently screwed into the setting.

Insert. The ring in BERGER's *hand. The stone comes loose in his fingers. In the setting underneath, on a gold plate, is a faint impression of the Lorraine Cross of General De Gaulle.*

LASZLO'S VOICE. Yes, I am *very* interested.

The table.

BERGER. Good.

LASZLO *(lower voice).* What is your name?

BERGER. Berger...And at your service, sir.

ILSA *(looking o.s., gives* LASZLO *a signal).* Victor!

LASZLO *(to* BERGER, *low voice as he comprehends the signal).* Meet me in a few minutes at the bar *(in a louder voice, obviously for the benefit of someone off scene).* I do not think we want to buy the ring. But thank you for showing it to me.

BERGER *takes the cue. He sighs, puts the ring away.*

BERGER. Such a bargain. But if that is your decision—

He bows and turns away. Camera pans. As he walks away, he brushes by CAPTAIN RENAULT *and* MAJOR STRASSER, *who are approaching the table. They glance sharply at* BERGER *as he passes. Then* RENAULT *beams as camera pans back with them to the table.*

RENAULT. Welcome, welcome—welcome to Rick's.

LASZLO. You welcomed us this afternoon at the airport, Captain.

RENAULT. I welcome everyone everywhere. When I die, I expect to be of great help to St. Peter. May I present Major Strasser...Mademoiselle Ilsa Lund—and M'sieur Victor Laszlo.

The German bows, but there is not the slightest recognition from either ILSA *or* LASZLO. RENAULT *and* STRASSER *wait to be asked to seat themselves. But* LASZLO *is plainly blocking their approach to the table.*

LASZLO. I am sure you will excuse me if I am not gracious...but you see, Major Strasser...I am a Czechoslovakian.

STRASSER. You *were* a Czechoslovakian— now you are a subject of the German Reich.

LASZLO. I am on French soil. What is it you want of me?

STRASSER. Merely to discuss some matters arising from your presence on...French soil.

LASZLO. This is hardly the time or the place...

STRASSER *(hardening).* Then we shall state another time and another place. Tomorrow at ten, in the Prefect's office. With Mademoiselle.

LASZLO *(turns to* PREFECT). Captain Renault, I am under your authority. Is it *your* order that we come to your office?

RENAULT *(amiably).* Let us say it is my request. That is a much more pleasant word.

LASZLO. Very well.

He bows and turns back to the table, where he sits next to ILSA. RENAULT *and* STRASSER *walk out of the shot. At this moment the wall lights are going down, as the floor show is about to begin.*

The dance floor. A MASTER OF CEREMONIES *stands in the spotlight.*

MASTER OF CEREMONIES. And now, ladies and gentlemen, we continue the evening's entertainment with that sensational South American chanteuse, Senorita Andreya.

The girl appears in the spotlight, a guitar strapped over her shoulders. As she acknowledges the introduction, there is a scattering of applause from the audience.

The table. LASZLO *and* ILSA.

LASZLO. Strasser...This time they *really* mean to stop me.

ILSA. Victor, I am afraid for you.

LASZLO. We have been in difficult places before.

He puts a hand over hers. ILSA *smiles back at him, but her eyes are still troubled.*

LASZLO. I will find out what Berger knows. If you see anyone watching me, remember his face. We must learn who are our enemies and who are our friends.

ILSA *nods.* LASZLO *rises, starts toward the end of the bar, which is on the far corner of the cafe.*

Pan shot—that follows LASZLO *across the room in the comparative darkness. Though most people watch the singer, some heads turn.*

ILSA—*from the table, watches him anxiously.*

At the bar. BERGER—*is sipping a drink. Over scene we hear the sound of the Spanish entertainer.* LASZLO *walks into the shot, casually takes a place at the bar next to* BERGER.

LASZLO *(to* FYDOR). A champagne cocktail, please.

FYDOR. Yes, M'sieur.

As FYDOR *moves down the bar to make the cocktail,* LASZLO *takes out a cigarette.* BERGER *leans over to give him a light.*

BERGER *(low voice).*...I recognize you from news photographs, M'sieur Laszlo.

LASZLO. In a concentration camp, one is apt to lose a little weight.

BERGER. We read five times that you were killed in five different places.

LASZLO *(smiles wryly).* As you see, it was true every time...Thank the good Lord you found me, Berger. I am looking for a man by the name of Ugarte. He is to help me.

BERGER *(shakes his head silently).* M'sieur Laszlo, Ugarte cannot even help himself. He is under arrest for murder. He was arrested here tonight.

LASZLO *(absorbs the shock quietly).* I see.

BERGER *(with intense devotion).* But we who are still free will do all we can. We are organized, M'sieur—underground like everywhere else. Tomorrow night there is a meeting. If you would come—

He stops as he sees a gendarme move into scene in b.g.

At the table. ILSA. RENAULT *moves into scene behind her, unnoticed until he speaks.*

RENAULT. Mademoiselle...

ILSA *is startled, but she covers up with a smile.*

ILSA. Captain Renault...

RENAULT. Does the cold blanket of inhospitality also cover me?

He gestures toward the chair by her side, plainly indicating that he would like to sit down with her.

ILSA. Since we are in Casablanca under your protection, Captain...

She nods toward the chair. Her manner is friendly, but reserved.

RENAULT. Thank you.

As he sits down, he gestures to a hovering waiter.

RENAULT *(to waiter)*. Your best champagne, and put it on my bill.

ILSA. No...please...

RENAULT *(shooing the waiter away)*. It is a little game we play. They put it on my bill, I tear the bill up. It is most convenient.

Off scene the song finishes and there is some applause. The lights come up.

From their perspective the songstress acknowledges the applause and leaves. SAM *wheels out his piano.*

At the table ILSA *is looking off at* SAM.

RENAULT. Mademoiselle, I was informed you were the most beautiful woman ever to visit Casablanca. That is a gross understatement.

ILSA. You are very kind. What a lovely uniform, Captain.

RENAULT *(pleased)*. I have a uniform for every occasion—*(significantly; on the make, definitely)* Every occasion *(indicates his medals, which cover his entire breast in a row)*. What do you think of my medals?

ILSA. One of them is out of line.

RENAULT. That is the one I really earned. It should be a little conspicuous.

ILSA *laughs. At the sound, off scene, of* SAM's *piano, she looks off again.*

Med. shot. SAM *at piano—as he plays, he steals a nervous glance in* ILSA's *direction, looks away again.*

At table. ILSA *looks back at* RENAULT.

ILSA. Captain, the boy who is playing the piano...somewhere I have seen him.

RENAULT. Sam? He came here from Paris with Rick.

ILSA. Rick? Who is he?

RENAULT *(smiles)*. Mademoiselle, you are in Rick's. Well, Rick is...

ILSA *(with an air of being casual, but pursuing her own line of inquiry)*. Is what?

RENAULT. He is the kind of man that...Well, if I were a woman and I...*(tapping his chest)* were not around, I would be in love with Rick. But what a fool I am! Talking to a beautiful woman about another man!...

The GENDARME *(who appeared in b.g. of scene at bar between* LASZLO *and* BERGER*) enters scene during the above beside* RENAULT *and waits to catch his attention.* RENAULT *looks up, annoyed.*

GENDARME. Mon Capitaine...

RENAULT *(annoyed)*. What is it?

GENDARME *(to* ILSA*)*. Excuse-moi...

He stoops and whispers something in RENAULT's *ear.*

RENAULT *(annoyed—low voice)*. Not now, fool.

GENDARME. But, mon Capitaine...*(to* ILSA*)*. Excuse-moi...*(whispers again)*.

RENAULT *(gives up, rises with a sigh)*. Will you excuse me? I'll only be a moment.

ILSA *(with a little smile)*. I shall try to live until you return.

RENAULT *doesn't quite know how to take this, but decides to take it as a compliment. He bows and exits scene, the* GENDARME *following. As soon as they have gone,* ILSA *looks off scene and calls....*

ILSA. Sam....

Angle past ILSA *to* SAM. SAM *looks up, startled.* ILSA *motions him to come over.* SAM *hesitates—starts to wheel the piano over.*

Close shot. At table—as SAM *wheels in the piano. On his face is that funny fear. And to tell the truth,* ILSA *herself is not as self-possessed as she tries to appear. There is something behind this, some mysterious, deep-flowing feeling.*

ILSA. Hello, Sam.

SAM. Hello, Miss Ilsa. I never expected to see you again.

ILSA. It's been a long time. A lot of the Seine has flowed under the Pont-Neuf since then.

SAM. Yes, Miss Ilsa. A lot of water under the bridge.

He sits down and is ready to play.

ILSA. Some of the old songs, Sam.

SAM *begins to play a number. He is nervous, waiting for anything. But even so, when it comes he gives a little start....*

ILSA. Where's Rick?

SAM *(evading)*. I don't know. Ain't seen him all night.

ILSA *gives him a tolerant smile.* SAM *looks very uncomfortable.*

ILSA. When will he be back?

SAM. Not tonight no more. He ain't coming. He went home.

ILSA. Does he always leave so early?

SAM. He never—I mean—*(desperately)*. He's got a girl up at the—Blue Parrot—He goes there all the time...

ILSA. Sam, you used to be a much better liar.

SAM. Leave him alone, Miss Ilsa. You're bad luck to him.

ILSA *(softly)*. Sam, play it once for old time's sake.

SAM. I don't know what you mean, Miss Ilsa.

ILSA. Play it, Sam. Play "As Time Goes By."

SAM. I can't remember it, Miss Ilsa!

Of course he can. He doesn't want to play it. He seems even more scared.

ILSA. I'll hum it for you. *(starts to hum).*

He begins to play it very softly.

ILSA. Sing it, Sam.

SAM. I don't know the words!

ILSA *(softly she feeds him the first line, speaking it)*. 'You must remember this......'

—and SAM *picks it up, singing:*

"You must remember this,
A kiss is still a kiss,
A sigh is just a sigh....."
Etc., etc.

Entrance to gambling room. RICK—*comes swinging out. He has heard the music and he is livid.*

RICK. What the—! Sam, I've told you—!

He stops abruptly, stops speaking and stops moving.

From his perspective SAM *and* ILSA—*at the piano.*

Closer angle. SAM *and* ILSA. SAM *looks over his shoulder at* RICK *and stops playing.* ILSA *knows why even before she turns and looks. She knows who she'll see when she turns. She turns slowly. She isn't breathing much.*

Closeup. RICK—*isn't breathing at all. It's a wallop, a shock. For a long moment he just looks at her and you can tell what he is thinking.*

He starts moving forward, his eyes riveted on her. Camera trucks ahead of him, keeping him in closeup as he moves across the cafe.

Reverse angle. Trucking shot, moving in the direction he is going, straight for the piano. ILSA *is looking directly at* RICK, *too.* SAM *is plainly terrified. He puts his stool on top of the piano and with a plaintively accusing...*

SAM. Now you've done it!

—he wheels the piano quickly away. ILSA *doesn't notice. She still looks at* RICK.

(A couple of intercuts.)

RENAULT *and* LASZLO *are approaching from the bar.*

Cut to:

Group shot. At table RENAULT *moves into scene with* LASZLO, *arm in arm.*

RENAULT *(to* ILSA). See what I have found for you—a wandering escort.

She doesn't seem to have heard, and RENAULT *looks off in the direction she is looking.*

RENAULT. Well, you were asking about Rick and here he is.

Side angle. Group—as RICK *moves into scene.*

RENAULT. Ricky, my dear friend, here are some nice people. I have the honor of introducing—

RICK. Hello, Ilsa.

ILSA *(under her breath)*. Hello, Rick.

She offers her hand and he takes it.

RENAULT. You know each other? *(no answer from either)*. Well, then, do you also know

ILSA. This is Mr. Victor Laszlo.

She says it in a funny way—as if she's frightened to say it and yet would rather say it herself than have someone else. RICK *measures* LASZLO *with a look, then looks at* ILSA *and smiles. You would say there is some mockery in the way he smiles.*

LASZLO. One hears a great deal about Rick in Casablanca.

RICK *(looks back at him)*. And about Victor Laszlo everywhere.

LASZLO. Won't you join us for a drink?

RICK. I'll join you. I never drink unless I'm alone.

LASZLO *(with a laugh as they sit)*. Well, that is a new turn on the old phrase—'Drink alone and like it'. *(he is making conversation)*. This is a most interesting cafe—I congratulate you.

RICK. And I congratulate you.

LASZLO. What for?

RICK. Oh—your work. *(why does he look at* ILSA?)

LASZLO. Thank *you*. I try.

RICK. We all try. You succeed.

RENAULT. I can't get over—you two. She was asking about you earlier, Rick, in a way that made me extremely jealous.

ILSA *(to* RICK). I wasn't sure you were the same. Let's see, the last time we met....

RICK. Was it "La Belle Aurore"?

ILSA. How nice. You remembered! But of course—that was the day the Germans marched into Paris.

RICK. Not an easy day to forget, was it?

ILSA. No.

RICK. I remember every detail—the Germans wore gray, you wore blue.

LASZLO. Ilsa, I don't wish to be the one to say it—but it's late.

RENAULT *(glancing at wristwatch)*. So it is. And we have a curfew here in Casablanca. It would never do for the Chief of Police to be caught drinking after hours and have to fine himself.

LASZLO *(signalling the waiter)*. I'm afraid we're almost the last ones left. I hope we haven't overstayed our welcome.

RICK. Not at all. *(he takes the check from the* WAITER*)*

LASZLO. Oh, please, I'd rather....

RICK. Tonight's on me.

RENAULT. Another precedent broken. This has been a most interesting evening. *(they all rise)*

LASZLO *(to* RICK *as he helps* ILSA *on with her wrap)*. I'd like to come back.

RICK. Do that.

ILSA *(extending her hand to* RICK*)*. Will you say good night to Sam for me?

RICK. I will.

ILSA. There's still nobody in the world who can play "As Time Goes By" like Sam.

RICK. He hasn't played it for a long time.

A pause. ILSA *smiles*.

ILSA. Good night.

RICK *and* LASZLO *nod good night to each other*. LASZLO *and* ILSA *start to the door*, RENAULT *with them*.

Close shot. RICK—*watches them go*. RENAULT *can be heard saying*....

RENAULT'S VOICE. I'd better get you a cab—this time of night—gasoline rationing—

The revolving door is heard turning.

Ext. Café. The three—come out. RENAULT *walks through shot to the curb and is heard to blow his whistle.* LASZLO *lights a cigarette, speaks very casually...*

LASZLO. A very puzzling fellow, this Rick. Just what sort is he?

ILSA *doesn't look at him. With an effort she keeps her voice steady.*

ILSA. I really can't say. I met him in Paris. We were acquaintances...

A cab is heard to draw up. ILSA *moves forward out of shot.* LASZLO *follows her.*

Camera pans up to the sign "RICK'S".

Dissolve to:

The sign—now dark—illuminated only as the revolving beacon from the airport strikes it.

Int. Rick's. The customers have all gone. The house lights are out. RICK *sits at a table. There is a jigger glass of Bourbon on the table directly in front of him—and another glass empty on the table before an empty chair. Near at hand is a bottle from which this one drink, exactly, has been poured.* RICK *just sits, staring at the drink. His face is entirely expressionless.*

During the following scene the beacon continues its gyration, picking up first one and then the other in its sweep around the room. (The effect should be to create a mood of unreality that will make the flashback a plausible device.)

SAM *comes in. He stands hesitantly before* RICK.

SAM. Boss—*(no answer, as* RICK *drinks)*. Boss—!

RICK *(not looking at* SAM*)*. Yes?

SAM. You goin' to bed, Boss?

RICK *(filling his glass)*. No. Not right now.

SAM *looks at* RICK *closely, realizes* RICK *is in a grim mood.*

SAM *(lightly, trying to kid* RICK *out of it)*. You plannin' on goin' to bed in the near future?

RICK. No.

Pause.

SAM. You evah goin' to bed?

RICK. No.

SAM *(still trying)*. I ain't sleepy neither.

RICK. Good. Have a drink.

SAM. No. Not me.

RICK. No? Then don't have a drink.

SAM. Boss, let's get out of here.

RICK *(emphatically)*. No, sir. I'm waiting for a lady.

SAM *(earnestly)*. Please, Boss, let's go. There's nothin' but trouble for you here.

RICK. She's coming back. I know she's coming back.

SAM. Boss, we'll take the car and drive all night. We'll get drunk. We'll go fishin' and stay away until she's gone.

RICK. Shut up and go home.

SAM *(stubbornly)*. No, suh. I'm stayin' right here.

SAM *sits down at the piano, starts to play softly. Suddenly* RICK *bursts out —*

RICK *(really drunk now)*. They grab Ugarte and she walks in. That's the way it goes. One in, one out — *(pause. He thinks of something)*. Sam —

SAM *(still playing)*. Yeah, Boss?

RICK. Sam — if it's December, in Casablanca, what time is it in New York?

SAM. My watch stopped.

RICK *(drunken nostalgia)*. I bet they're all asleep in New York. I bet they're asleep all over America — *(with sudden vehemence)*. Of all the gin joints in all the towns in all the world she walks into mine —! *(irritably to* SAM*)*. What the — are you playing?

SAM *(who has been improvising)*. A little somethin' of my own.

RICK. Well, stop it. You know what I want to hear.

SAM. No, I don't.

RICK. Play it. You played it for her and you can play it for me.

SAM. I'm not sure I —

RICK. Play it!

SAM *starts to play "As Time Goes By."*

Cut to:

Close shot. RICK. *He pours a drink as* SAM *plays. From his expression we know that he is thinking of the past.*

(Montage and flashback).

Dissolve to:

Flashbacks:

Paris.

Dissolve to:

(The following are superimposed on backgrounds of stock shots).

Champs Elysees on a spring day.

RICK *is driving a small, open car slowly along the boulevard. Close beside him, with her arm linked in his, sits* ILSA.

Dissolve to:

Excursion boat on the Seine. Night.

An orchestra is playing French music. By themselves, at the rail of the boat, stand RICK *and* ILSA. *They are transported by the night, by the music, by each other.*

Dissolve to:

Int. RICK'S *Paris apartment.*

ILSA *at window fixes flowers.* RICK *opens champagne.* ILSA *joins him.*

RICK. Who are you really? What were you before? What did you do? What did you think?

ILSA. We said "no questions."

RICK. Here's looking at you, kid.

They drink.

Int. swank Paris Café. RICK *and* ILSA *dancing*

Int. ILSA'S *Paris apartment.* RICK *and* ILSA *on.*

ILSA. A franc for your thoughts.

RICK. In America they'd only bring a penny...it'd be about all they're worth, I guess.

ILSA. I'm willing to be overcharged — come on — tell me.

RICK. I was just wondering.

ILSA. Yes?

RICK. Why I was so lucky — why I should find you waiting for me to come along.

ILSA. Why there is no other man in my life?

RICK *nods.*

ILSA. Well, that's easy. There was. He is dead.

RICK. I'm sorry. We said "no questions." I'll never ask another.

ILSA. This should be answer enough.

She kisses him.

The street. Stupefied people are staring from their windows, into the street below. The camera comes to rest on a loud-speaker wagon, around which is clustered a group of frightened French people. A harsh German voice is barking out the tragic news of the Nazi push toward Paris. Parisians are being told how to act when the conquerors march in.

Two shot. RICK *and* ILSA.

RICK. Nothing will stop them now. Wednesday—Thursday at the latest—they'll be in Paris.

ILSA *(frightened)*. Richard, they'll find out your record. It won't be safe for you here.

RICK *(smiles)*. I'm on their blacklist already—their roll of honor.

Dissolve to:

A small café in the Montmartre. Sign over the café: "La Belle Aurore"

Dissolve to:

SAM *playing at the piano, "As Time Goes By," blending in with the background music. He looks happily over his shoulder.*

Pull back to:

Med. shot. SAM *at the piano playing "As Time Goes By."* ILSA *is leaning on the piano, listening. Nobody else is in the room—everyone being in the street, listening to the loudspeaker.* ILSA's *attitude, as she listens, is very distraught. There is evidently something on her mind—and it isn't all concerned with the war.*

ILSA *(trying to shake off her mood)*. Sam—all the—how do you call them?—'hot' piano players say they never took a lesson in their lives. Of course, you never did, did you, Sam.

SAM *(gravely)*. Studied twelve years. Juilliard Foundation, New York.

ILSA *(wryly)*. Well—all the best theories are going under these days.

RICK, *bearing a champagne bottle and glasses, comes into the scene. His manner is wry, but not the bitter wryness we have seen in Casablanca.*

RICK. Henri wants us to finish this bottle and then three more. *(pouring)*. He says he'll water his garden with champagne before he lets the Germans drink any of it.

He hands a glass to ILSA *and* SAM.

SAM *(looking at his glass)*. This sorta takes the sting outa bein' Occupied, doesn't it, Mister Rick?

A shout is heard from the people in the street. RICK *and* ILSA *look at each other, then hurry to the window.*

Cut to:

Med. shot at open window as RICK *and* ILSA *come into the scene. The loudspeaker is blaring in German.*

RICK. My German's a little rusty. . . .

ILSA *(sadly)*. It's the Gestapo. They say they expect to be in Paris tomorrow. They are telling us how to act when they come marching in.

They are silent, depressed.

ILSA *(smiling faintly)*. With the whole world crumbling we pick this time to fall in love.

RICK *(with an abrupt laugh)*. Yeah. Pretty bad timing. *(looks at her)*. Where were you ten years ago?

ILSA *(trying to cheer up)*. Ten years ago? Let's see. . .*(thinks)*. Oh, yes. I was having a brace put on my teeth. Where were you?

RICK. I was looking for a job.

Pause. ILSA *looks at him tenderly.*

ILSA. Rick—Hitler or no Hitler, kiss me.

RICK *takes her in his arms, kisses her hungrily. While they are locked in an embrace the dull boom of cannons is heard.* RICK *and* ILSA *separate.*

ILSA *(frightened, but trying not to show it)*. Was that cannon fire—or just my heart pounding?

RICK *(grimly)*. That was the new German 75. And, judging by the sound, about thirty-five miles away—*(another booming is heard—* RICK *smiles grimly)*. And getting closer every minute.

Ext. Montmartre Street. From angle of ILSA *and* RICK *through window. Crowd collected around loudspeaker.*

Med. shot. SAM *coming into the scene.*

SAM. Dem Germans'll be here mighty soon. Dey'll come lookin' fer you. . .There's a price on your head.

ILSA *reacts to this worriedly.*

RICK *(drily)*. I left a note in my apartment. They'll know where to find me.

SAM *shrugs helplessly, goes.* ILSA *looks at* RICK.

ILSA. It's strange, Rick—I really know so very little abut you.

RICK. I know very little about you—just the fact that you had your teeth straightened.

ILSA. Don't joke, Rick. You are in danger. You must leave Paris.

RICK. *We* must leave.

ILSA *(without looking at him)*. Yes, of course—we. . .

RICK. The train for Marseilles leaves at five. I'll pick you up at the hotel at four-thirty.

ILSA *(quickly)*. No, not at the hotel. I have things to do in the city before I leave. I'll meet you at the station.

RICK. All right. The Gare de Leon at a quarter to five. *(a thought strikes him)*. Say—why don't we get married in Marseilles?

ILSA *(evasively)*. That's too far ahead to plan...

RICK *(happy, excited at the thought of leaving with* ILSA *)*. Yes, that is too far ahead. I wonder if the engineer on the train could marry us?

ILSA *(laughing nervously)*. Oh, Rick...

RICK. Why not? The Captain on a ship can. It doesn't seem fair...

Suddenly ILSA *starts to cry softly.*

RICK. Ilsa—what's the matter?

ILSA *(controlling herself)*. Nothing, darling. It's just that I—I love you so much and I hate the Germans so much. It sort of—*(stops, looks at* RICK *)*. Oh, Rick—it's a crazy world—anything can happen—If you shouldn't get away—If—if something should keep us apart—Wherever they put you—wherever I'll be—I want you to know—*(she can't go on—she lifts her face to his)*. Rick—*(he kisses her gently)*. No. Kiss me as though—as though it were the last time.

He looks into her eyes, then kisses her—as though it were the last time. Over the scene SAM *is again playing "As Time Goes By."*

Dissolve to:

The clock over the Gare de Leon. The hands stand at three minutes to five. A teeming rain spatters against the roof of the building.

Trucking shot. The camera moves along the station platform, where a crowd of bedraggled refugees stand shivering in the cold rain.

There is a hectic, fevered excitement evident in the faces we pass. This is the last train from Paris! The camera stops on RICK, *who is glancing at his watch, then up at the clock. It is two minutes before train time. Rain is pouring over his head and shoulders, but he seems not to notice. Suddenly* SAM *appears with an envelope clasped in his hand.*

RICK. Where is she? Have you seen her?

SAM. She done checked out of the hotel, Boss. But this here note came just after you left.

RICK *grabs the letter. He fumbles as he tries to open it. The envelope fights him. At this moment the train pulls into the station. There is a hubbub among the crowd. Finally* RICK *gets the envelope open, stares down at the letter.*

Insert. The letter which reads:
"Richard:
I cannot go with you or ever see you again. You must not ask why. Just believe that I love you. Go, my darling, and God bless you.
Ilsa."

SAM'S VOICE *(frantically—over scene)*. Boss, dat's de las' call. Boss, do you hear me? Hurry up. De train...

The raindrops pour down the letter, smudging the writing. The train gives a long, mournful whistle.

Dissolve to:

Special effects shot with the hour-glass changing into the drink. Camera pulls back and moves up to a closeup of RICK. *He stills stares at the drink. There is no sound of music now, utter silence.* SAM *has gone home. The circle of light passes over* RICK's *face and sweeps out of scene and only by a flicker on his face do we follow the light around the room.*

The next time it passes, RICK's *eyes are caught by the light and his head turns, following it. Camera pans with the light. The circle reaches the door.* ILSA *is standing in the doorway. Camera remains on her. The circle passes on and in the darkness it is hard to tell that she is still there.*

RICK *is staring at the doorway. It is probable that at first he thinks it is imagination that is playing a trick on him. The light sweeps over him again. His expression hardens.*

ILSA *at the doorway in the darkness.*

ILSA. Rick.

As she starts forward, the light passes over her. Her face is eager and pleading.

Table. RICK *gets half to his feet as she enters scene. The light sweeps by.*

RICK. We closed up at one o'clock.

ILSA. I came back. I had to talk to you.

Her manner is a little uncertain, a little tentative—but with a quiet determination beneath it.

RICK. I saved my first drink to have with you *(reaches for bottle)*.

ILSA. Not tonight.

She sits down in the chair before the empty glass. Her eyes are searching his face, but there is no expression on it except a cold and impassive one. He sits down, too, and reaches for his glass and half-gestures with it toward her.

RICK. Mind if I?

ILSA. No...

RICK. *Especially* tonight.

He drains his glass and, reaching for the bottle, pours himself another drink. She watches this with a look which says that she wishes he wouldn't drink tonight.

RICK. Why did you have to come to Casablanca? There are other places.

ILSA. I wouldn't have come if I had known that you were here. Believe me, Rick, that's the truth, I didn't know.

RICK. Funny about your voice. How it hasn't changed. I can still hear it—'Rick dear, I'll go with you anyplace. We'll get on a train together and we'll never stop. All my life, forever more—!'

ILSA. Please don't. *(she watches as he takes another drink).* I can understand how you feel.

RICK. And funny about your looks. *They*'ve changed a little. At least from that first day. And the other days.—How long was it we had, honey?

ILSA. I didn't count the days.

RICK. All hail the happy days! *(takes another drink)* When there were no questions asked, and faith was something all in one piece—

ILSA. Please. Rick.

RICK. Mostly I remember the wow finish. A guy standing on a platform, and the last train about to pull out, and Sam pushing him to get on—and the guy just standing there with a comical look on his face, because his insides had been kicked out by a pair of French heels.

ILSA *(after a pause).* Can I tell you a story, Rick?

RICK. Has it got a finish, honey, has it got a twist?

ILSA. I don't know the finish yet.

RICK. Maybe one will come to you as you go along.

ILSA. It's about a girl who was very young. She had just come to Paris from her home in Oslo. At the house of some friends she met a man—a very great and good man. They became friends—he became her teacher. She had been brought up very provincially, and he opened up for her a whole beautiful world of knowledge and thoughts and ideals. Everything she ever knew or ever became was because of his goodness. And she looked up at him and worshipped him with a feeling she supposed was love—

RICK *(definitely interrupting).* I heard a story once. In fact, I've heard a lot of stories in my time. They went along with the sound of a tinny piano in the parlor downstairs. "Mister, I met a man when I was only a kid", they'd always begin.

ILSA, *shuddering, gets up.*

ILSA. I'll go now.

RICK *(as she walks away).* I guess neither one of our stories was very funny. *(then in a moment he adds)* But you might tell me just who it was you left me for. Was it Laszlo—or were there others in between—or aren't you the kind that tells?

ILSA *tears in her eyes. She stops in the doorway, looks back at him, then she turns and walks out.*

RICK *his head slumps over the table. Gradually his body sags over the table. The glass tips over, spilling its contents over the cloth.*

Fade out.

Fade in.

Int. RENAULT's *office. Day.* STRASSER *is with* RENAULT.

STRASSER. I strongly suspect that Senor Ugarte left the Letters of Transit with Herr Blaine. I would suggest you search the Cafe immediately and thoroughly.

RENAULT. If Rick has the Letters, he is much too smart to let us find them there.

STRASSER. You give him credit for too much cleverness. My impression was that he's just another blundering American.

RENAULT. Quite so. But we mustn't underestimate American blundering *(innocently).* I was with them when they 'blundered' into Berlin in 1918.

STRASSER *looks at him.*

STRASSER. As to Herr Laszlo, we want him watched twenty-four hours a day.

RENAULT *(reassuringly).* It may interest you to know that at this very moment M'sieur Laszlo is on his way to the Prefecture.

Cut to:

Ext. Prefecture of Police. People are packed around the entrance. LASZLO *and* ILSA *make their way through the jam.*

Dissolve to:

Med. long shot shooting from in back of the desk, toward the door as it is opened by the NATIVE OFFICER, *who ushers in* LASZLO *and* ILSA. *Both* RENAULT *and* STRASSER, *in the f.g., rise, facing the couple as they walk toward them.* RENAULT *moves forward to offer* ILSA *his hand.*

RENAULT. I am delighted to see you both.

ILSA. Thank you, Captain.

LASZLO *bows to both men, but offers to shake hands with neither.*

RENAULT. Mademoiselle, may I present Major Strasser?

STRASSER. It is a pleasure, Fraulein.

ILSA *bows to* STRASSER *as* RENAULT *offers her a chair.*

RENAULT *(extending his hand)*. How nice to see you. Did you have a good night's rest?

LASZLO *(shaking hands)*. Very good, thank you.

RENAULT *(looking at him solicitously)*. You look a little tired. Didn't you sleep well?

LASZLO. Very well, thank you.

RENAULT. That's strange. No one is supposed to sleep well in Casablanca.

He laughs.

LASZLO *(briefly)*. I think it would be best if we proceed with the business.

STRASSER *(now as cold as* LASZLO*)*. Very well, M'sieur Laszlo, we will not mince words. You are an escaped prisoner of the Reich. So far you have been fortunate in eluding us. You have reached Casablanca—it is my duty to see that you stay in Casablanca.

LASZLO. Whether or not you succeed in fulfilling your duty is, of course, problematical.

STRASSER. Not at all. Captain Renault's signature is necessary on every exit visa.

LASZLO. I am perfectly aware of the Captain's official duties.

STRASSER *(turns to* RENAULT*)*. Captain, would you think it is possible that M'sieur Laszlo will receive a visa?

RENAULT. I am afraid not. I regret, M'sieur.

LASZLO *(casually)*. Well, perhaps I shall like it in Casablanca.

STRASSER. And Mademoiselle?

ILSA. You need not be concerned about me.

LASZLO *(prepares to rise)*. Is that all you wish to tell us?

STRASSER *(smiles)*. Do not be in such a hurry, M'sieur Laszlo. You have all the time in the world. You may be in Casablanca indefinitely.... *(suddenly leans forward, speaks intently)*. Or you may leave for Lisbon tomorrow. On one condition.

VICTOR. And that is?

STRASSER *(leaning forward, speaking intently)*. You know the leader of the Underground Movement in Prague, in Paris, in Amsterdam, in Brussels, in Oslo, in Belgrade, in Athens...

LASZLO. Yes—even in Berlin.

STRASSER. Even in Berlin. If you will furnish me with their names and their exact whereabouts—you will have your exit visa in the morning...

RENAULT *(tongue in cheek again)*. And the honor of having served the Third Reich!

LASZLO. Before France fell I was in a German concentration camp for a year. That is honor enough for a lifetime.

STRASSER. You will give us the names?

LASZLO. If I didn't give them to you in the concentration camp where you had more "persuasive methods" at your disposal, I certainly won't give them to you now *(the passionate conviction in his voice now revealing the crusader)*. And what if you track down these men and kill them? What if you murdered all of us? From every corner of Europe hundreds of men—thousands—would rise up to take our places. Even Nazis cannot kill that fast.....

STRASSER. M'sieur Laszlo, you have a reputation for eloquence which I can now understand. But in one respect you are mistaken. You said the enemies of the Reich could all be replaced. But there is one exception—*no one could take your place* in the event anything...er...unfortunate should occur to you while you were trying to escape.

LASZLO. You will not dare to interfere with me here. This is still Unoccupied France. Any violation of neutrality will reflect on Captain Renault.

RENAULT. M'sieur, in so far as it is in my power....

LASZLO. Thank you.

RENAULT. By the way, last night you evinced an interest in Senor Ugarte.

LASZLO. Oh, no. I don't believe I had ever heard of him before.

RENAULT *(slyly)*. Ah—my mistake—What made me think you had—

LASZLO *(very casual)*. Well—now that we're here—a man who murdered two Germans—I wouldn't mind having a few words with him.

STRASSER *(wryly)*. You would find the conversation a trifle one-sided. *(pause)* Senor Ugarte is dead.

LASZLO *and* ILSA *look at each other.*

ILSA. Oh.

RENAULT *(picking up the papers on his desk)*. I am making out the report now—*(coming around the desk)*. We haven't quite decided yet whether he committed suicide or died trying to escape.

LASZLO *(after a pause)*. You are quite finished with us?

STRASSER *(bows)*. For the time being.

As ILSA *and* LASZLO *leave, the young officer comes in. When the door has closed on* ILSA *and* LASZLO:

RENAULT *(to young officer)*. Undoubtedly their next step will be to the Black Market. *(significantly)* You will—
YOUNG OFFICER. Yes, Captain. By the way—another visa problem has come up.
RENAULT *(happily, as he looks at himself in the mirror)*. Show her in.

Dissolve to:

Full shot. The black market. A cluttered Arab street of bazaars, shops and stalls. All kinds and races of people are milling about the merchandise which native dealers have on outdoor display. Both men and women are dressed in tropical clothes. The canopies over the stalls give them some protection from the scorching sun. On the surface, the atmosphere is merely languid, but there is the sinister undercurrent of illicit trade.

The camera moves along the row of stalls toward a disreputable building at the head of the Market. Over the entrance of the building is a faded sign: Blue Parrot Café.

Over scene we hear the hypnotic sound of a single flute. During its progress through the marketplace, the camera picks up the following fragmentary scenes:

(a) An American is inquiring of a food vendor:

AMERICAN. Can you tell me when the bus from Tangiers will arrive?
VENDOR *(shrugs)*. Who knows, M'sieur? There are sandstorms, sabotage—*(smiles significantly)*—and customs officials.

The American looks a little confused by this answer. The camera moves on to—

(b) A rug stall. The dealer is holding up a small Persian rug in an effort to sell it to an English couple.

ENGLISHWOMAN *(doubtfully)*. But are you sure this is perfectly legal?
DEALER. Madame, there is no rug in my shop that has not been smuggled in legally. You see, the authorities have been—

The camera moves on close to the Blue Parrot Café. Near the entrance—

(c) A Frenchman and a native are talking together in low tones.

NATIVE....But M'sieur, we would have to handle the police. That is a job for Senor Ferrari—

Cut to:

Entrance to Blue Parrot. SENOR FERRARI *comes out, looks impatiently up and down the street.*

Cut to:

Med. shot. The two Americans.

1ST AMERICAN. That's Senor Ferrari. He's pretty near got a monopoly on the Black Market here.

Cut to:

Med. shot. SENOR FERRARI. *He is about to go back into the café when* ANNINA *and* JAN *walk up to him.*

JAN. Excuse me—you are Senor Ferrari, are you not?
FERRARI. Yes?
JAN. We were told that you might be able to help us?

FERRARI *looks at them a moment before answering.*

FERRARI. Come in.

He leads the way into the Blue Parrot.

Dissolve to:

Close shot. FERRARI. *His huge frame is rolling with laughter.*

FERRARI. Five hundred francs for an exit visa....

The camera pulls back to reveal JAN *and* ANNINA *standing like frightened children before* FERRARI *in his private office.*

FERRARI. Young man, in Casablanca five hundred francs will buy you a pound of sugar, but not an exit visa.
ANNINA. But, Senor Ferrari, that is all we have left. What can we do?
FERRARI *(shrugs)*. Perhaps if you had a talk with Captain Renault—
ANNINA *(her lips tight)*. We have already talked with him.

She takes her husband's arm, preparatory to leaving.

FERRARI. I am sorry. That is all I can suggest.

The camera pans with them as they walk to the door.

Cut to:

Int. Blue Parrot Café much less pretentious than RICKS. *The bar is well populated, but there are only a few people at the tables.* RICK *comes into the scene, walks towards* FERRARI. *He is waring his usual dead pan.*

Cut to:

Med. shot outside door to office. As RICK *comes into the scene, the door opens and* FERRARI *comes out, ushering out* JAN *and* ANNINA, *who look very downhearted.*

FERRARI *(patting* ANNINA's *shoulder).* There—don't be too downhearted. Perhaps you can come to terms with Captain Renault.

JAN. Thank you very much, Senor.

He leads ANNINA *away.* RICK *watches the couple as they move toward the door. Then he walks in the direction of* FERRARI.

Med. shot. SENOR FERRARI. RICK *walks into the shot.*

RICK. Hello, Ferrari.

SENOR FERRARI *turns around, pleased to see* RICK.

FERRARI. Good morning, Rick.

RICK. I see the bus is in. I'll take my shipment with me.

FERRARI. No hurry. I shall have it sent over. Have a drink with me.

RICK. I never drink in the morning. And every time you send my shipment over, it's a little short.

FERRARI *(chuckling).* Carrying charges, my friend, carrying charges...*(pulling out a chair).* Here—sit down. There's something I want to talk over with you, anyhow. *(*RICK *sits down—* FERRARI *hails a waiter).* The Bourbon...*(to* RICK—*sighing deeply).* The news about Ugarte upset me very much.

RICK. You're a fat hypocrite. You don't feel any sorrier for Ugarte than I do.

FERRARI *(eyes* RICK *closely).* Of course not. What upsets me is the fact that Ugarte is dead and no one knows where those Letters of Transit are.

RICK *(dead pan).* Practically no one.

FERRARI. If I could lay my hands on those Letters, I could make a fortune.

RICK. So could I. And I'm a poor businessman.

FERRARI. I have a proposition for whoever has those Letters. I will handle the entire transaction, get rid of the Letters, take all the risk—for a small percentage.

RICK. And the carrying charges.

FERRARI *(smiling).* Naturally there will be a few incidental expenses—*(looking at* RICK *squarely).* That is the proposition I have for whoever has those Letters.

RICK *(drily).* I'll tell him when he comes in.

FERRARI. Rick—I'll put my cards on the table. I think you know where those Letters are.

RICK *(shrugging).* Well, you're in good company. Renault and Strasser probably think so too. I came here to give them a chance to ransack my place.

FERRARI. Rick—don't be a fool. Take me into your confidence. You need a partner—

But RICK *isn't listening to him. He is looking through the open door in the direction of the linen bazaar.*

Cut to:

Long shot. Linen Bazaar. ILSA *and* LASZLO *have paused there in front of the linen bazaar.* LASZLO *leaves* ILSA *and is walking toward the Blue Parrot Café.*

Cut to:

Med. shot. RICK *and* SENOR FERRARI.

RICK *(interrupting* FERRARI, *gets up).* Excuse me. I'll be getting back.

FERRARI *nods, takes a long drink. Camera trucks with* RICK *as he walks toward the door, where he meets* LASZLO *coming in.* LASZLO *stops, addresses him politely.*

LASZLO. Good morning...

RICK *(with a jerk of his head, not pausing).* Senor Ferrari is the fat gent at the table.

He continues out of shot. LASZLO *looks after him with a puzzled expression.*

Med. shot. A linen stall—where ILSA *is examining a napkin which an Arab vendor is endeavoring to sell. There is a sign on the counter by the display which reads: "700 francs". From* ILSA's *manner it is apparent that she is aware of* RICK's *approach and is pretending to be absorbed in the article to escape his notice.*

ARAB....You will not find a treasure like this in all Morocco, Mademoiselle. Only seven hundred francs.

RICK *comes into shot.*

RICK. You're being cheated.

ILSA *takes a split second to compose herself. When she turns to* RICK, *her manner is politely formal.*

ILSA. It doesn't matter, thank you.

ARAB. Ah—the lady is a friend of Rick's? For friends of Rick's we have a small discount. Seven hundred francs, did I say? You can have it for two hundred.

Reaching under the counter, he takes out a sign reading: "200 francs" and replaces the other sign with it.

RICK. I'm sorry I was in no condition to receive visitors when you called on me last night.

ILSA. It doesn't matter.

ARAB. Ah! For *special* friends of Rick's we have a *special* discount.

He replaces the second sign with a third which reads: "100 francs."

RICK. Your story left me a little confused. Or maybe it was the Bourbon.

ARAB. I have some tablecloths—some napkins—

ILSA. I'm really not interested.

ARAB. Only one moment—*(hurriedly exits).*

There is a small silence between ILSA *and* RICK. *She pretends to examine the goods on the counter.*

RICK. Why did you come back? To tell me why you didn't show up at the railway station?

ILSA *(quietly).* Yes.

RICK. Well, you can tell me now. I'm reasonably sober.

She looks at him quietly.

ILSA. I don't think I will, Rick.

RICK. Why not? After all, I was stuck with one railroad ticket. I think I'm entitled to know.

ILSA *(slowly).* Last night I saw what has happened to you. The Rick I loved in Paris—I could tell him. He'd understand—*(pause. Her eyes cloud).* But the Rick who looked at me with such hatred in his eyes—who snarled at me—*(shakes her head).* I'll be leaving Casablanca soon. We'll never see each other again. We knew very little about each other when we were in love in Paris. If we leave it that way, perhaps when we think of each other—we'll remember those red letter days—not Casablanca—not last night—

RICK *(his voice low but intense).* Did you run out on me because you couldn't take it? Because you knew what it would be like—hiding from the police—sneaking around corners—running away all the time?

ILSA. You can believe that if you want to.

RICK. Well, I'm not running away any more. I'm settled now—above a saloon, it's true—but—*(ironically).* Walk up a flight. You'll find it worth your while.

ILSA *shakes her head.*

RICK. All the same, you'll come to me. Some night—you'll lie to Laszlo—you'll be there!

ILSA *(tight-lipped).* No, Rick. You see, it happens that Victor Laszlo is my husband.

RICK *stares at her.*

ILSA. And has been for some time. — *(pause)* Even when I knew you in Paris.

She walks away into the café towards LASZLO *and* FERRARI. RICK *stares after her—then exits scene in the opposite direction. The Arab rushes back, his arms loaded. He stops in consternation, looks from side to side, anguished.*

ARAB. Lady!—Rick!—

He puts his burden on the counter, and, with a sad headshake, puts away the sign "100 francs" and replaces it with the original, "700 francs".

Cut to:

Int. café. LASZLO, SENOR FERRARI *and* ILSA. FERRARI *is helping* ILSA *into a chair.*

FERRARI. I was just telling M'sieur Laszlo that unfortunately, I am not able to help him.

ILSA *(troubled).* Oh.

LASZLO *(to* ILSA*).* You see, my dear, the word has gone around, I am a marked man.

FERRARI *(to* ILSA*).* As leader of all illegal activities in Casablanca, I am an influential and respected man, but it would not be worth my life to do anything for M'sieur Laszlo. You, however, are a different matter.

LASZLO. Senor Ferrari thinks it might just be possible to obtain an exit visa for you.

ILSA. You mean—for me to go on alone?

FERRARI. And *only* alone.

LASZLO. I will stay here, Ilsa, and keep on trying. Perhaps in a little while. . .

FERRARI. We might as well be frank, M'sieur. It will take a miracle to get you out of Casablanca. And the Germans have outlawed miracles.

ILSA *(to* FERRARI*).* We are only interested in two visas, Senor.

LASZLO. Please, Ilsa. We mustn't be hasty.

ILSA *(firmly).* No, Victor.

FERRARI *(getting to his feet).* Excuse me. I will be at the bar.

He bows and goes.

LASZLO. Ilsa, I won't let you stay here. You must get to America. And believe me—somehow—I'll get out—I'll join you. . .

ILSA (*slowly*). Do you really want me to go on alone, Victor? Do you really want to stay here—without me? (*pause*).

LASZLO (*honestly*). No.

ILSA. Very well then, the subject is closed. We'll have a drink and go back to the hotel.

LASZLO. No, Ilsa, you must listen to me...

ILSA (*interrupting*). Victor—if the situation were different—if I had to stay and there were only a visa for you—would you take it?

LASZLO *hesitates*.

LASZLO (*not very convincingly*). Ye-es, I would.

ILSA *smiles faintly*.

ILSA. I see. When I had trouble getting out of Lilles, why didn't you leave me there? And when I was sick in Marseilles and held you up for two weeks and you were in danger every minute of the time—why didn't you leave me then?

LASZLO (*with a wry smile*). I meant to, but something serious always held me up. My— my laundry was late coming back—or there was a cinema I wanted to see...

ILSA (*smiling at him fondly*). We'll just forget about the drink. A pack of American cigarettes—and we'll go home.

LASZLO (*reaches over, puts his hand over hers*). I love you very much, Ilsa.

ILSA (*affectionately*). That makes me feel very good.

LASZLO. I also need you very much.

ILSA. And that makes me feel very important.

LASZLO (*smiling faintly*). Don't tell anyone. Leaders of the Underground are not supposed to be in love.

ILSA (*smiling*). Your secret is safe with me. (*she gets up*). Ferrari is waiting for our answer.

Med. shot. FERRARI at bar talking to the bartender.

BARTENDER (*shaking his head*). Three of our silver shakers were stolen last night.

FERRARI (*not disturbed*). Hassid El Bey, most likely. Go over there later and buy them back. Not more than fifty francs though.

ILSA *and* LASZLO *come into the scene.*

LASZLO. We've come to a decision. For the present we'll go on looking for two visas. Thank you very much.

FERRARI (*his manner indicating it is hopeless*). Well—good luck. But be careful—(*a flick of his eyes in the direction of the bazaar*). You know you're being shadowed?

LASZLO (*not turning*). Of course. It becomes an instinct.

FERRARI (*shrewdly—looking at* ILSA). I observe that you in one respect are a very fortunate man...M'sieur I am moved to make one more suggestion—Why, I do not know. Because it cannot possibly profit me, but...have you heard about Senor Ugarte and the Letters of Transit?

LASZLO. Something.

FERRARI. Those Letters were not found on Ugarte when they arrested him.

LASZLO (*after a moment's pause*). Do you know where they are?

FERRARI. Not for sure, M'sieur. But I will venture a guess—that Ugarte left those Letters with M'sieur Rick.

ILSA's *face darkens.* LASZLO *quietly observes.*

LASZLO. Rick?

FERRARI. He is a difficult customer, that Rick. One never knows what he will do, or why. But it is worth a chance.

LASZLO (*starts to rise*). Thank you very much.

They all get up.

ILSA. And for your coffee, Senor— (*bravely*). I shall miss that when we leave Casablanca.

FERRARI (*bows*). You were gracious to share it with me. Good day, Mademoiselle.... M'sieur.

LASZLO. Good day.

FERRARI *walks toward the entrance of his cafe. Camera trucks with* ILSA *and* LASZLO *as they start down the marketplace.*

LASZLO. Always Rick.

He watches ILSA *out of the corner of his eye as they go along.*

Dissolve to:

Ext. RICK's. *Night. The* DARK EUROPEAN *is entering the cafe, his arm around a prosperous male tourist.*

DARK EUROPEAN (*solicitously*). Put yourself in my hands. There are vultures in there— vultures—Be on guard—

Cut to:

Med. shot at bar. FYDOR *is gazing intently at a slip of paper. He has many bottles lined up in front of him—and as he looks at the slip of paper he mixes ingredients.* CARL *comes into the scene.*

CARL. Two brandies for the Leuchtags, please.

FYDOR *(not even looking at him)*. Bottle's down de bar. Halp yourself. I'm too busy.

CARL. Too busy?

FYDOR *(nodding)*. A Yenkee gave me dis recipe for American drink. In two or t'ree years I will be in America, please Heaven— so I'm prectisink.

CARL *(reaching for the brandy bottle)*. What is the name of the drink?

FYDOR *(peering very closely at the slip of paper)*. It sounds vunderful—*(reading with difficulty)*. Meecky—Feen—Dere are co-int'nly some strange things in it.

CARL. Sounds good. When you perfect it— try it out on me.

He walks away.

Cut to:

Med. shot the LEUCHTAGS *at table. They are a middle-aged couple.* CARL *comes into the scene with the brandy.*

MR. LEUCHTAG. Carl—have a brandy with us.

MRS. LEUCHTAG *(beaming with happiness)*. To celebrate our leaving for America tomorrow.

CARL *(pouring)*. Thank you very much. I thought you would ask me, so I brought the good brandy.

MR. LEUCHTAG. Frau Leuchtag and I are speaking nothing but English now.

MRS. LEUCHTAG. So we should feel at home ven ve get to America.

CARL *(handing them the drinks)*. A very wise idea.

MR. LEUCHTAG *(raising his glass)*. To America.

MRS. LEUCHTAG *and* CARL *repeat* "To America". *They clink glasses and drink.*

MR. LEUCHTAG *(proudly, to display his good English, addresses his wife)*. Liebchen—what watch?

MRS. LEUCHTAG *(glancing at her wrist watch)*. Ten watch.

MR. LEUCHTAG *(surprised)*. Such much?

CARL *(reassuringly)*. You will get along beautifully in America.

Cut to:

Med. shot, the bar. RICK *and* RENAULT.

RICK. That was some going-over your men gave my place this afternoon. We just got it cleaned up in time to open.

RENAULT. I told Strasser we would not find the Letters here. But I told my men to be especially destructive. You know how that impresses Germans. *(pours himself a drink)*. Rick—have you got those Letters of Transit?

RICK *looks at him a moment.*

RICK *(steadily)*. Louis—are you Pro-Vichy or Free French?

RENAULT *(promptly)*. Serves me right for asking a direct question. The subject is closed.

Cut to:

Med. shot. RICK *and* RENAULT. RICK *is gazing at* YVONNE *and a German officer approaching the bar.*

RICK. I see Yvonne has gone over to the enemy.

RENAULT. Who knows? In her own way she may constitute an entire second front—*(out of the corner of his eye he sees* ANNINA *approaching—he gets up)*. I think it is time for me to flatter Captain Strasser a little. See you later, Rick. *(he strolls away)*.

Med. shot at bar. YVONNE *and* OFFICER.

GERMAN OFFICER *(arrogantly—to* CARL*)*. French seventy-fives.

YVONNE *(somewhat tight already)*. Pick up a whole row of 'em, Carl—*(indicating on the bar with her hand)*—starting here and—

GERMAN OFFICER *(cutting in)*. We will begin with two.

In the background one of the French officers makes a remark which causes laughter from his group. We do not catch the words, but the remark is very evidently directed at the GERMAN OFFICER *and his French companion. The* GERMAN OFFICER *turns toward the group, his face very red.*

GERMAN OFFICER *(clipping his words)*. Will the gentleman who made that remark kindly repeat it?

A French officer steps out from the group.

FRENCH OFFICER *(drunk enough to be reckless)*. I made it. And what I said is none of your business.

GERMAN OFFICER. I will make it my business—

The GERMAN OFFICER *raises his fist and the* FRENCH OFFICER *prepares to defend himself. There are exclamations from the people nearby.* RICK *walks into the shot between the two men, addresses the German.*

RICK. I don't like disturbances in my place. Either lay off politics or get out.

Cut to:

STRASSER'S TABLE. RENAULT, STRASSER *and the other* GERMAN OFFICERS *have settled back in their chairs.*

STRASSER. . . . You see, Captain, the situation is not as much under control as you believe.

RENAULT. My dear Major, we are trying to cooperate with your government. But we cannot regulate the feelings of our people.

STRASSER (*eyes him closely*). Captain Renault, are you entirely certain which side you're on?

RENAULT. Frankly, I have no conviction, if that is what you mean. I blow with the wind, and the prevailing wind is blowing from Vichy.

STRASSER. And if it should change?

RENAULT (*smiles*). Surely the Reich does not admit that possibility?

STRASSER. We are concerned about more than Casablanca. We know that every French province in Africa is honeycombed with traitors just waiting their chance—waiting, perhaps, for a leader.

RENAULT (*casually, as he lights a cigarette*). A leader like. . . . Laszlo?

STRASSER (*nods*). I have been thinking. It is too dangerous if we let him go. It may be too dangerous if we let him stay.

RENAULT (*thoughtfully*). I see what you mean. . . .

Cut to:

Cashier's booth in the gambling room. ANNINA *is emptying her bag of bills, which she lays on the counter.*

ANNINA. Two hundred francs worth, please.

The Cashier hands out the chips, takes in the bills. The camera trucks with ANNINA *as she crosses to the roulette table, where* JAN *is bending over the spinning wheel.* ANNINA *watches breathlessly over his shoulder. The wheel stops. The* CROUPIER *takes in the chips.* JAN *wipes his forehead.*

JAN. Black again. . .

ANNINA (*handing him the chips*). This is all we have, Jan. Do you think we should?

JAN (*bitterly*). We might as well have nothing as two hundred francs.

He begins to scatter the chips recklessly over the board. ANNINA *looks at him for a moment,* comes to a silent resolve, and walks toward the hallway.

Cut to:

Med. shot. ANNINA. *She stops, looks in* RICK'S *direction, steels herself to approach him. Then, her mind made up, she makes her way to his table, camera trucking with her.*

ANNINA. M'sieur Rick. . .

RICK. Yes?

ANNINA. Could I speak to you—just for a moment?

RICK *looks at her.*

RICK. How did you get in here? You're under age.

ANNINA. I came with Captain Renault.

RICK (*cynically*). I should have known.

ANNINA. My husband is with me, too.

RICK. He is? (*looks over to where* RENAULT *is seated*). Captain Renault is getting broad minded. (*to* ANNINA). Sit down.

ANNINA. Thank you.

RICK. Drink? Ah, of course not—Mind if I. . . ?

ANNINA. Oh, no—(*nervously as* RICK *pours himself a drink*). M'sieur Rick—what sort of man is Captain Renault?

RICK (*shrugging*). Like any other man. . . (*pause*). Only more so.

ANNINA. I mean—is he trustworthy?—Is his word. . . ?

RICK. Just a minute. Who told you to ask me that?

ANNINA. He did. Captain Renault did.

RICK. I thought so. (*pause*). Where's your husband?

ANNINA (*wryly*). At the roulette table—trying to win enough for our exit visas. Of course he is losing.

RICK *looks at her closely.*

RICK. How long are you married?

ANNINA (*simply*). Six weeks. (RICK *nods*). We came from Bulgaria. Things are very bad there, M'sieur. A devil has the people by the throat. So Jan and I, we. . . we did not want our children to grow up in such a country.

RICK (*wearily*). So you decided to go to America.

ANNINA. Yes. But we do not have much money, and travel is so difficult and expensive M'sieur. It took much more than we thought to get here. Then Captain Renault sees us and he is so kind. He wants to help.

RICK. I'll bet.

ANNINA. He tells me that he can get an exit visa for us. But...*(again she hesitates)*. But we have no money.

RICK. Does Renault know?

ANNINA. Oh, yes.

RICK. And he is *still* willing to give you an exit visa?

ANNINA. Yes, M'sieur.

RICK *looks down at his drink for a moment.*

RICK. And you want to know...?

ANNINA. Will he keep his word, M'sieur?

RICK *(still looking at his drink)*. He always has.

There is a silence.

Cut to:

RICK *and* ANNINA. ANNINA *is very disturbed.*

ANNINA. M'sieur, you are a man. If someone loved you...very much, so that your happiness was the only thing in the world that she wanted and...she did a bad thing to make certain of it, could you forgive her?

RICK. No one has ever loved me that much.

ANNINA. But, M'sieur, if he never knew...if the girl kept this bad thing locked in her heart...that would be all right, wouldn't it?

RICK *(harshly)*. You want my advice?

ANNINA. Oh yes, M'sieur, please.

RICK. Go back to Bulgaria.

ANNINA. M'sieur Rick—If you knew what it means to us to be able to leave Europe—to get to America...*(pause)*. But if Jan should find out—He is such a boy. In many ways I am so much—so much older than he is.

RICK *(getting up—noncommittally)*. Well—everyone in Casablanca has a problem. Yours may work out. Excuse me.

Cut to:

Close shot. ANNINA. *She looks down at the tablecloth, her lips are trembling.*

ANNINA *(tonelessly)*. Thank you—M'sieur Rick.

She gets up. Exits.

Cut to:

Med. shot, RICK *dead-pan, as usual, walking among the tables. He stops short as he sees someone entering.*

Cut to:

Med. shot at revolving door. ILSA *and* LASZLO *have just come in.* RICK *comes up to them.*

RICK. Good evening.

LASZLO. Good evening. You see, we are here again.

RICK. I take that as a great compliment to Sam. *(to* ILSA*)*. I suppose to you Sam means Paris of—well—happier days.

ILSA *(quietly)*. Indeed, he does. Could we have a table very close to Sam.

LASZLO *(who has been looking around)*. And as far from Captain Strasser as possible.

RICK. Well, the geography might be a little difficult to arrange—*(snaps his fingers for the* HEADWAITER*)*.

Cut to:

Close shot. ILSA *as* RICK *confers with the* HEADWAITER *she looks at* RICK *intently.*

Cut to:

Full shot, RICK *and* ILSA, LASZLO *and the* HEADWAITER.

HEADWAITER *(to* ILSA *and* LASZLO*)*. Right this way, if you please—

LASZLO *(to* RICK*)*. Thank you very much.

RICK *(to* ILSA*)*. I'll have Sam play "As Time Goes By." I think that's your favorite number?

ILSA *(smiling)*. It is. Thank you.

She follows LASZLO *to their table.* RICK, *camera following, walks to* SAM, *bends over, whispers something to him.*

SAM *shakes his head, but starts to play "As Time Goes By."*

RICK *looks in* ILSA's *direction, but she seems to be paying no particular attention.* RICK *saunters toward the gambling room.*

Cut to:

Int. gambling room as RICK *comes in. He looks towards the roulette wheel.* JAN *and* ANNINA *are there. Two players walk away from the table.* JAN *and* ANNINA *are alone there.*

Cut to:

Med. shot at roulette table. JAN's *eyes are tragic. As* RICK *comes into the scene, the* CROUPIER *is saying to* JAN:

CROUPIER. Do you wish to place another bet, M'sieur?

JAN. No thank you—*(he juggles the two remaining chips in his hands wryly)*. We can't leave without tipping, can we, Annina?

She just looks at him, dumb with misery.

RICK *(to the* CROUPIER*)*. I'll take over the wheel. *(to* JAN; *dead-pan)* Have you tried twenty-four tonight?

JAN *looks at* RICK, *then at the two chips in his hand. Pause. He puts the two chips on twenty-four.*

RICK *spins the wheel.*

Cut to:

Close shot. JAN *looking straight ahead.*

Cut to:

Close shot. CROUPIER *looking at* RICK.

Cut to:

Close shot, CARL *in the background, looking at the wheel, fascinated.*

Cut to:

Full shot at wheel. It stops spinning.

RICK *(calling out).* Twenty-four.

The CROUPIER *pushes a pile of chips onto the number.* JAN *reaches for it.*

RICK *(not even looking at* JAN*).* Leave it there.

JAN *hesitates.* ANNINA *looks at* RICK.

ANNINA *(to* JAN*).* Leave it there.

JAN *withdraws his hands. In the background,* CARL *draws a little closer.* RICK *spins the wheel. Nobody speaks while it spins. When it stops* RICK *calls out.*

RICK. Number twenty-four.

In the background CARL *gasps. The* CROUPIER *shoves a pile of chips towards* JAN.

RICK *(to* JAN*).* Now, take it—and don't ever come back.

In the background the last two customers are seen walking out. One of them is complaining to CARL.

CUSTOMER. Had terrible luck tonight. You sure this place is honest?

CARL *(fervently).* As honest as the day is long!

ANNINA *(to* RICK; *all choked up).* M'sieur Rick, I—

She kisses him and exits towards JAN—*at cashier's desk.*

Close two shot. JAN *and* ANNINA *at Cashier's desk.*

ANNINA. He is an American, Jan. You see, America *must* be a wonderful place.

ANNINA *and* JAN *hurry from the room.*

Cut to:

Close two shot. RICK *and* CROUPIER.

RICK *(to* CROUPIER*).* How were the receipts tonight?

CROUPIER *(drily).* Well—a couple of thousand less than I thought they would be.

RICK *smiles slightly and exits towards bar.*

Int. hallway leading to bar. RICK *enters from gambling room.* CARL *comes up to* RICK *as they walk towards the bar.*

CARL *(solicitously).* May I get you a cup of coffee, M'sieur Rick?

RICK. No, thanks.

CARL. I wish to tell you that it is a privilege to work for you. I will tell Fydor. Nothing exciting ever happens at the bar.

Med. shot, RENAULT, ANNINA *and* JAN *in a corner near the bar,* JAN *is pressing the bills upon him.*

RENAULT. No, no, not here. Come to my office in the morning. We'll do everything business-like.

JAN. We'll be there at six.

RENAULT. I'll be there at ten. *(smiling broadly, but insincerely).* How happy I am for both of you. Still—it's very strange that you should have won—*(he looks off).*

Cut to:

Med. shot, RICK *at the bar.*

Cut to:

Full shot. RENAULT, ANNINA *and* JAN.

RENAULT *(seeing* RICK*).* Well, perhaps not so strange after all—Run along, now. I'll see you in the morning.

ANNINA. Thank you so much, Captain Renault.

She and JAN, *beaming with happiness, go off.* RENAULT *looks after her, regretfully. Then he walks towards* RICK.

Cut to:

Med. shot RICK *pretending not to do so, he is glancing in* ILSA's *direction.* RENAULT *comes up to him.*

RENAULT. As I suspected, you're a rank sentimentalist.

RICK. Why?

RENAULT *(chidingly).* Why do you interfere with my little romances?

RICK *(sarcastically).* Put it down as a gesture to love.

RENAULT *(good-naturedly).* I forgive you this time. However, I will be in tomorrow night with a breath-taking brunette. It will make me very happy if she loses.

He smiles, walks into the gambling room.

Cut to:

Med. shot. FYDOR *and* CARL *whispering together.* FYDOR *looks towards* RICK *with great admiration. Then, with giant strides he moves towards* RICK, *camera trucking with him. He reaches* RICK.

FYDOR *(grandly).* You haf done a beyootiful t'ing!

And he takes RICK'S *face between his two huge paws and plants a resounding kiss on* RICK'S *forehead. Then, before the astonished* RICK *can recover, he walks back to the bar with huge strides.*

RICK *(recovering).* Why, you Russian—!

He swears under his breath.

Cut to:

LASZLO *approaching* RICK.

LASZLO. M'sieur Blaine, may I discuss something confidential with you?
RICK *(still angry at* FYDOR*).* This is certainly my night for hearing confidences.
LASZLO. I won't take much of your time. Is there some place private—?
RICK *(nodding towards it).* Come up to my office.

As they start up—

Quick dissolve to:

Int. RICK'S *office.* RICK *is seated at his desk.*

RICK. There's no use our fencing around. You've come about those Letters of Transit, haven't you?
LASZLO. I have.
RICK. It seems to be the general impression in Casablanca that I have those Letters.
LASZLO *(looking at him very steadily).* Have you?
RICK. I don't want to do anything to either bolster or dispel that impression.

Pause.

LASZLO. Suppose we proceed under the assumption that you have the Letters?
RICK *(shrugging).* Go ahead.
LASZLO. You must know that it's very important I get out of Casablanca.
RICK. Why you more than any of the other thousands who are stuck here?
LASZLO *(simply).* Whether Victor Laszlo, the man, gets out is not important at all. But it's my privilege to be one of the leaders of a great movement. You know what I have been doing. You know what it means to the work—to the lives—of thousands and thousands of little people that I be free to reach America and continue my work.
RICK. I'm not interested in world events. I'm a saloon-keeper. Politics are for grown-ups.
LASZLO *(looking at him closely).* That wasn't always your attitude.
RICK *(lighting a cigarette).* Wasn't it?
LASZLO. My friends here in the Underground tell me that you have quite a record. You ran guns to Ethiopia. You fought against the Fascists in Spain.
RICK. I was well paid on both occasions.
LASZLO. Yes—but the winning side would have paid you better. Isn't it strange that you always happened to be on the side of the under-dog?

RICK *thinks a moment.*

RICK. As I always say, I am a poor business man.
LASZLO. Are you enough of a business man to appreciate an offer of a hundred thousand francs?
RICK. I appreciate it—but I don't accept it.
LASZLO. I'll raise my offer to two hundred thousand francs.
RICK. If you offered me a million francs—or three francs—my answer would be the same.
LASZLO. I see. You intend using the Letters yourself some day?
RICK. Not at all. *(bitterly)* I'm much too comfortable here to travel.
LASZLO. Then you are saving them for someone else?
RICK. No. I may even put a match to them some day.
LASZLO. Then I don't understand. There must be some reason why you won't let me have them.

From the cafe we hear the sound of male voices raised in song. RICK *gets up.*

RICK. There is. I suggest that you ask your wife.

LASZLO *looks at him, puzzled.*

LASZLO. I beg your pardon?
RICK. I said—ask your wife.
LASZLO. My wife!

The sound of the male singing grows louder.

RICK. Yes *(hears the singing).* Who's singing that?

He goes out, leaving LASZLO to stare after him.

Cut to:

Int. cafe two German officers, beer mugs in hand, are standing by the piano, singing the "Wacht am Rhine." SAM, looking very uncomfortable, is accompanying them. Everybody in the room is looking at them. Suddenly SAM stops playing.

SAM (to the officers). Dat's all I know of dat song.

An officer swears at SAM in German, grabs SAM and lifts him off the stool. A German officer sits at the piano. The officers resume their singing.

Cut to:

Med. shot at bar. A French officer starts forward. FYIXOR leans forward quietly and lays a restraining hand on his arm.

Cut to:

Med. shot RICK on steps. He listens to the officers sing—his expression deadpan. LASZLO has come out of the room. His lips are very tight as he listens to the song.

Cut to:

Crane shot over the room. The room grows deadly quiet. STRASSER is on his feet, singing too. As the camera passes the DARK EUROPEAN we see that he is singing the "Wacht am Rhine" too. But nobody else in the room is. RENAULT has come in from the gambling room, and stands by the door. We can't tell from his expression what he is thinking.

Cut to:

Full shot German officers at the piano. The officers singing the song.

Cut to:

Pan shot as LASZLO crosses floor to the orchestra.

Cut to:

Med. shot LASZLO as he reaches orchestra. He asks SAM something.

LASZLO. Play it!

SAM looks towards the steps—toward RICK.

Cut to:

Close shot RICK. He nods almost imperceptibly.

Cut to:

Med. shot SAM and LASZLO and orchestra as they start to play the first few bars—

Cut to:

Med. shot, YVONNE and German officer. She jumps to her feet.

YVONNE (singing). "Allons enfants de la patrie—"

Cut to:

Full shot, SAM, orchestra and LASZLO.

LASZLO (singing with YVONNE). "Le jour de gloire est arrive—!"

Someone in the back of the room adds his voice. A woman joins in. A French officer steps defiantly forward and stands beside LASZLO.

Cut to:

Full shot, room as others stands at their tables, singing the "Marseillaise"

Cut to:

Close shot, RICK his expression hasn't changed.

Cut to:

Close shot, RENAULT is smiling faintly but we still can't tell what he thinks.

Cut to:

Full shot. Room. Everyone has gathered together and is singing. The German officers at the bar, and STRASSER at his table, are very conspicuous because they are so alone. The singing grows more fervent.

CHORUS. Contre nous de nos tyrannie...

Others now join in from all parts of the room—guests, waiters, bartenders, native police, etc. The chorus swells. By now the German song can scarcely be heard.

Med. shot. The German Officers. For a few moments they try to compete with the other end of the room, but it's no use. The German song is smothered under La Marseillaise. One by one they stop singing, stare out resentfully toward the tables.

Close shot. The DARK EUROPEAN. He has edged away from the Germans. He is now singing La Marseillaise as fervently as he did the German song.

Close shot. RICK his expression hasn't changed.

Close shot. RENAULT *at door to gambling room. He is smiling faintly, but we can't tell what he thinks.*

Full shot. Throng as they sing. Their faces are aglow.

Med. shot, ILSA *singing at the table.* ILSA *glances proudly at* LASZLO.

Full shot singing people. The music swells as the song is finished on a high, triumphant note.

Close shot. YVONNE *her face exalted. She deliberately faces the alcove, where the Germans are watching. She shouts at the top of her lungs.*

YVONNE. Viva La France. Vive La Democracie.

At Orchestra platform, several French officers surround RICK, *offering him a drink.*

Med. shot. STRASSER, *his looks are not pleasant. He strides across the floor towards* RENAULT, *camera trucking with him. He reaches* RENAULT—*who is standing outside the door to the gambling room.*

STRASSER *(under his breath to* RENAULT). You see what I mean? If Laszlo's presence in a cafe can inspire this unfortunate demonstration, what more will his presence in Casablanca bring on. As a warning retaliation I advise that this place be shut up at once.

RENAULT *(innocently).* But everybody seems to be having such a good time.

STRASSER. Much too good a time. The place is to be closed.

RENAULT. But I have no excuse to close it.

STRASSER *(snapping).* Find one.

RENAULT *thinks a moment, then he blows a loud blast on his whistle. The room immediately grows quiet. All eyes turn toward* RENAULT.

RENAULT *(loudly).* Everybody is to leave immediately! This cafe is closed until further notice!

An angry murmur starts among the crowd.

RENAULT. Clear the room at once!

RICK *comes quickly up to* RENAULT.

RICK. What's the idea? You can't close me up. On what grounds?

RENAULT *throws open the door to the gambling room.*

RENAULT *(pointing inside with a dramatic gesture).* I am shocked—*shocked* to find that there is gambling going on in here!

RICK *(at a loss at this display of nerve).* Well, I'll be—

The CROUPIER *comes out of the gambling room and up to* RENAULT.

CROUPIER *(handing* RENAULT *a roll of bills).* Your winnings, sir.

RENAULT *(putting the bills in his pocket).* Thank you very much. *(turns to the crowd again)* Everybody out at once!

Cut to:

Med. shot. ILSA *at table.* STRASSER *enters. His manner is heavily cordial. During this scene the cafe is gradually emptying. The scene should be played at a suspenseful, fast tempo.*

STRASSER. . .Fraulein, there is something I must warn you about.

ILSA *motions to a chair.* STRASSER *bows and sits down. She looks at him questioningly.*

STRASSER. It is not safe for Herr Laszlo to stay in Casablanca.

ILSA. This morning you implied it was not safe for him to leave.

STRASSER. That is also true. Except for one destination. *(leans closer to her)* To return to Occupied France under a safe conduct from me.

Full shot, room as the crowd, prodded on by gendarmes, starts streaming out. They are murmuring disappointedly.

Cut back to:

Med. shot. ILSA *and* STRASSER *at table.*

ILSA *(with intensity).* And of what value is that? You may recall what German guarantees of security have been worth in the past.

STRASSER. There are only two other alternatives for him—neither of them pleasant.

ILSA. What are they?

STRASSER. It is possible the French authorities will find a reason to put him in the concentration camp here. That, I assure you, would be no improvement on the one he escaped from.

ILSA. And the other alternative?

STRASSER. My dear Fraulein, perhaps you have already observed that in Casablanca human life is cheap—and German money plentiful. . . .

She looks at him, understanding what he means. He bows and exits as LASZLO *arrives at the table.*

Cut to:

Med. shot. ILSA *and* LASZLO. LASZLO *is helping her on with her wrap. They start out.*

ILSA. What happened with Rick?
LASZLO *(looking at her closely).* We'll discuss it later. Come—

Bar as people are hastily downing their drinks, and leaving. One of the German officers addresses FYDOR.

GERMAN OFFICER. Think I'll have a quick one before I go. What's that you're mixing?
FYDOR *(looking at the slip of paper).* Some new drink—
GERMAN OFFICER. I'll have it.

He reaches over, takes it, drinks it. Then he throws some change on the bar, starts out, camera trucking with him. After a few steps a glazed expression comes into his eyes. He clutches convulsively at his stomach. He is running hell-bent for the door, as we—

Dissolve to:

Int. dark hotel room. A door is heard to open and then the light is switched on, revealing ILSA *and* LASZLO *as they enter the room.* ILSA *takes off her wraps while her husband walks over to the window and starts to draw the shades. There are no words spoken—and we sense a tension between the two.* ILSA's *eyes follow him, but* LASZLO *apparently takes no notice. He looks out of the window.*

Long shot man across street—standing in the doorway of a house.

Int. hotel room at window. ILSA *enters to* LASZLO, *stands close beside him.*

LASZLO *(as he draws the shade).* Our faithful friend is still there.
ILSA. Victor, please don't go to the Underground meeting tonight.
LASZLO *(soberly).* I must *(adds with a smile)* And besides, it isn't often that a man has the chance to display heroics before his wife.
ILSA. Don't joke, After Strasser's horrible threats tonight—Victor, I'm frightened!
VICTOR *(with another quiet smile).* To tell you the truth, my dear, I am frightened, too. So shall I remain hiding here in a hotel room in that unpraiseworthy condition—or shall I carry on the best I can?
ILSA. Whatever I would say, you'd carry on.
LASZLO. Since our friend Rick has refused us there is little alternative, as I see it.

ILSA *turns away to conceal her emotion. She sits on the edge of her bed.* LASZLO *follows her*

with his eyes. He is looking at her steadily and thoughtfully—but in no way antagonistically.

LASZLO. One would think that if sentiment wouldn't persuade him, the money would.
ILSA *(ill at ease, trying to keep her voice steady).* Did he—Did he give any reason?
LASZLO. He suggested that I ask you.
ILSA. Ask *me?*

He walks across to her and looks down at her.

LASZLO. He said— "ask your wife." I don't know why he said that.

ILSA *finds it impossible to look at him. She looks away.* LASZLO *turns off the light switch, making the room dark except for the dim light that comes from the shaded windows.*

LASZLO. Our friend outside will think we have retired now. That is what I want him to think. I will go in a few minutes.

He sits down on the bed beside her. A silence falls between them. It grows strained. Finally—

LASZLO *(quietly).* Ilsa—?
ILSA. Yes?

Pause.

LASZLO. Ilsa—when I was in the concentration camp—were you lonely in Paris?

Their faces are barely visible in the darkness.

ILSA. Yes, Victor. I was.
LASZLO *(sympathetically).* I know how it is to be lonely—*(pause; very quietly).* Is there anything you want to tell me?

Close shot. ILSA *in the darkness. Her lips tremble as she controls herself.*

ILSA *(very low).* No, Victor—there isn't.

Silence. Then....

VICTOR'S VOICE. I love you very much, my dear.
ILSA *(barely able to speak).* Yes. Yes, I know. Victor—Whatever I do, will you believe that—that—
LASZLO. You do not even have to say it. I will believe.

Med. shot. The two. After a moment he gets up.

LASZLO *(quite cheerfully).* Well—our friend must be convinced I'm sound asleep. *(bends down, kisses her cheek)* Good night, dear.
ILSA. Good night, dear.

He walks out of scene. She watches him, then....

ILSA. Victor!—

She gets up and exits after him.

Med. shot. The two at the door. He is just opening it. ILSA *enters to him. In the slit of light from the partially opened door, we can see her face, which is strained and worried.*

LASZLO. Yes, dear?

She hesitates. After a pause....

ILSA *(in a tone which suggests this is not what she has been tempted to say).* Please be careful.

LASZLO. Of course.

He kisses her on the forehead and goes out the door. She stands there for a few seconds, then crosses to look out of the same window as before.

Long shot. The figure in the doorway—has gone.

Hotel room. ILSA—*watches for a moment longer.*

Long shot. A wall in back of hotel. LASZLO's *figure is visible against the wall, going down the narrow street.*

Hotel room. ILSA—*leaves the window and crosses the room to the place she dropped her wrap. She puts it on. Then, after a second's pause, she walks to the door and goes out.*

Dissolve to:

Int. RICK's *office.* RICK *and* CARL—*are bent over ledgers.* CARL *is very busy figuring.*

CARL *(looking up).* Well—you are in pretty good shape, Herr Rick.

RICK. How long can I afford to stay closed?

CARL. Two weeks—maybe three.

RICK *(gets up).* Maybe we won't have to. A bribe has worked before. In the meantime, everyone stays on salary.

He walks to the door.

CARL. Oh, thank you, Herr Rick. Fydor will be very happy to hear it. I owe him money.

RICK *(at door).* You lock up, Carl.

CARL. I will. Then I am going to the meeting of the—

RICK *(interrupting).* Don't tell me where you're going.

CARL *(with a smile).* I won't. Good night, Herr Rick.

RICK. Good night, Carl.

He goes out.

Cut to:

Balcony outside office. RICK—*walks toward his apartment.*

Cut to:

Int. RICK's *apartment. It is dark. The door is opened by* RICK, *letting in some light from the hall. A figure is revealed in the room.* RICK *lights a small lamp. There is* ILSA *facing him, her face white but determined.* RICK *pauses for a moment in astonishment.*

RICK. How did you get in?

ILSA. The stairs from the street.

RICK. I told you this morning you'd come around—but this is a little ahead of schedule. *(with mock politeness)* Won't you sit down?

ILSA *(as she takes the chair).* Richard, I had to see you.

RICK. So I'm Richard again? We're back in Paris. I've recovered my lost identity.

ILSA. Please...

RICK *(lights a cigarette).* Your unexpected visit isn't connected by any chance with the Letters of Transit? *(*ILSA *remains silent).* It seems while I have those letters, I'll never be lonely.

ILSA *(looks at him steadily).* Richard, you can ask any price you choose. You can impose any condition you want. But you must give me those Letters.

RICK. I went all through that with your husband. It's no deal.

ILSA. I know how you feel about me, and I don't blame you. But I'm asking you to put your feelings aside for something more important.

RICK. Do I have to hear again what a great man your husband is? And what an important Cause he's fighting for?

ILSA. It was your Cause, too. In your own way, you were fighting for the same thing.

RICK. Well, I'm not fighting for anything any more—except myself. I'm the only Cause I'm interested in now.

A pause. ILSA *deliberately takes a new approach.*

ILSA. Richard, we loved each other once. If those days meant anything at all to you—

RICK *(harshly).* I wouldn't bring up Paris if I were you. It's poor salesmanship.

ILSA. Please listen to me. If you knew what really happened. If you knew the truth—

RICK *(cuts in).* I wouldn't believe you, no matter what you told me. You'll say anything now, to get what you want.

ILSA *(her temper flaring—scornfully).* You *want* to feel sorry for yourself, don't you? With so much at stake, all you can think of is your own feeling. One woman has hurt you, and you take your revenge on the rest of the world. You're a coward, and— *(breaks)*. Oh, Richard, I'm sorry. But *you're* our last hope. If you don't help us, Victor Laszlo will die in Casablanca.

RICK. What of it? I'm going to die in Casablanca. It's just the spot for it. Now, if you— *(he stops short as he looks closely at* ILSA*)*.

Close shot. ILSA. *She is holding a small revolver in her hand.*

ILSA. All right. I tried to reason with you. I tried everything. Now I want those Letters.

Close shot. RICK. *For a moment, a look of admiration comes into his eyes.*

Med. shot. ILSA *and* RICK.

ILSA. Get them for me.

RICK. I don't have to. *(reaching into his inner pocket)* They're right here.

He has the Letters in his hand.

ILSA. Put them on the table.

RICK *(shaking his head)*. No.

ILSA. For the last time, put them on the table.

RICK. You'll have to kill me to get them. If Laszlo—if the Cause means so much, you won't stop at anything...Well, go ahead, shoot. You'll be doing me a favor.

Close shot. ILSA. *She rises, still pointing the gun at* RICK. *Her finger rests on the trigger. It seems as if she is summoning nerve to press it. Then, suddenly, her hand trembles and the pistol falls to the table. She breaks up, covering her face with her hands.* RICK *walks into the shot, stands close to her. Suddenly, she flings herself into his arms.*

ILSA *(almost hysterical)*. Richard, I tried to stay away. I thought I would never see you again...that you were out of my life. The day you left Paris, if you knew what I went through! How much I loved you...how much I still love you—

Her words are smothered as he presses her tight to him, kisses her passionately. She is lost in his embrace.

Fade out.

Int. RICK's *apartment. A little while later. Close shot on a table before a couch. There is a bottle of champagne on the table and two half-filled glasses. We hear* ILSA *talking as the camera pans to her and* RICK. *She is gazing into space as she talks.* RICK *is listening intently, but not looking at her.*

ILSA...We were married three weeks when Victor got word they needed him in Prague. Just a two-line item in the paper, "Victor Laszlo apprehended. Sent to concentration camp." The months went by. Then came a rumor that he was dead. *(she pauses for a moment)* I was lonely before, but now I had nothing left—not even hope. *(she puts her hand on his)* Until I met you.

RICK. But why didn't you tell me all this?

ILSA. Victor made me promise to keep our marriage a secret. I knew his plans and his friends. If the Gestapo found out I was his wife, Victor felt it would be dangerous for me and for those working with us...I kept my promise.

RICK. Then you got word he escaped?

ILSA. You remember there was a telephone call? *(*RICK *nods)* A friend of Victor's. They were hiding him in a freight car on the outskirts of Paris. He was sick and he needed me. I didn't tell you because you wouldn't have left Paris—and they would have caught you. So...well, you know the rest.

RICK. It's still a story without an ending. *(looks at her directly)* What about now?

ILSA *(simply)*. I'll never have the strength to go away from you again.

RICK. And Laszlo?

ILSA. Richard, you'll help him now, won't you? You'll see he gets out? *(*RICK *nods)*. Then he'll have his work—all the things he's been living for.

A pause.

RICK. All except one. He wouldn't have you.

ILSA. I can't fight it any more. I ran away from you once. Some morning I may wake up to find that you've gone, and if it lasts fifty years or ten days I know there'll be more heartache in it than happiness. I don't know what's right any longer. You'll have to think for both of us, Richard—for all of us.

RICK *(takes her in his arms)*. I've already made up our minds.

ILSA *(in a whisper)*. I wish I didn't love you so much.

She draws his face down to hers.

Ext. alley. LASZLO *and* CARL *making their way through the darkness toward* RICK's. *The headlights of the speeding car sweep toward them and they flatten themselves against a wall to avoid detection. The lights move past them and they continue down the alley.*

Quick dissolve to:

Int. RICK's. LASZLO *and* CARL *enter and cross toward the bar, out of breath from their exertion.*

CARL. I think we lost them, Herr Laszlo.

LASZLO. I'm afraid they caught some of the others.

Cut to:

Int. RICK'S *apartment.* RICK *and* ILSA *as they hear voices below.* RICK *crosses to the door.*

Med. shot RICK *at the door upstairs.* ILSA *standing just in back of him. Her expression shows her anxiety for* LASZLO. *She makes a move as if to come out on the balcony but* RICK'S *arm bars her way.*

RICK *(low tone).* He's all right. Keep out of sight and leave it to me.

She withdraws behind the door as RICK *walks out to the balcony railing.*

Full shot. Café.

RICK. What's happened?

Both CARL *and* LASZLO *look up.*

CARL *(excitedly).* Herr Rick, the police break up our meeting! We get away so close a shave like this. *(indicates with his fingers the tiniest margin)*

RICK. Come up here, Carl.

CARL, *who is just about to pour a drink, looks up wonderingly, then puts the bottle down and starts toward the stairway.*

CARL. Yes, I come.

RICK *(to* CARL, *as he comes up the stairs).* I want you to put out the light at the rear entrance. It might attract the police.

CARL. But Fydor always puts out that light before...

RICK *(cutting in).* Tonight he forgot.

Med. close shot. The balcony where RICK *stands, as* CARL *climbs into the shot.*

RICK *(low voice—jerks his head toward the door).* Miss Lund. I want you to take her home.

CARL'S *eyes grow enormous but he asks no questions.*

CARL. Yes, Herr Rick.

As CARL *goes to the door,* RICK *starts downstairs.*

Cut to:

Med. close shot. LASZLO *in front of the bar. He is wrapping one of the small bar towels around a cut in his wrist.* RICK *comes into the shot, looks questioningly at the injured hand.*

LASZLO. It's nothing. Just a little cut. We had to get through a window.

He buttons his cuff down over the towel to hold it in place as RICK *walks in back of the bar, picks up a bottle of whiskey and pours a drink.*

RICK. This might come in handy.

He shoves the glass across the bar to LASZLO.

LASZLO. Thank you.

LASZLO *takes it in a swallow.* RICK *is now pouring one for himself.*

RICK. Don't you ever wonder if it's worth all this? *(*LASZLO *looks at him, puzzled).* I mean what you're fighting for?

LASZLO. We might as well question why we breathe. If we stop breathing, we die. If we stop fighting our enemies, the world will die.

RICK. What of it? Then it'll be out of its misery.

LASZLO. Do you know how you sound, M'sieur Rick? Like a man trying to convince himself of something that in his heart he doesn't believe. Each of us has a destiny. For good or for evil. It is our...Letter of Transit, M'sieur Rick, from birth to death. Neither we nor the world will be *allowed* to die until we have reached our destination.

RICK *(drily).* I get the point.

With the bottle in his hand, RICK *starts around toward the front of the bar,* LASZLO'S *body turning as he presses* RICK *closely.*

LASZLO. I wonder if you do. I wonder if you know that you're trying to escape from yourself and that you'll never succeed. What you're meant to do will follow you wherever you go. That is what I mean by your destiny.

RICK *looks at* LASZLO *for a moment, then sits down at a table and begins to pour himself another drink.*

RICK *(ironically).* You seem to know all about my "destiny."

LASZLO. You see, M'sieur Rick, I know a good deal more about you than you suspect. I know, for instance, that you are in love with a woman.

RICK *has lifted his glass to drink. He puts it down, stares at* LASZLO, *who stands facing him from the bar.*

LASZLO. I can sense that more easily because I also love a woman. *(smiles just a little)* It is perhaps a strange circumstance that we should be in love with the same woman.

RICK *straightens up in his chair, watches* LASZLO *closely.* LASZLO *walks over to the table.*

LASZLO. I knew there was something between you and Ilsa the first evening I came in this place. But don't let that knowledge distress you. No one is to blame. I demand no explanation. I ask only one thing.

He sits down. Their eyes hold across the table.

LASZLO. You have the Letters of Transit. You will not give them to me. It seems this time there may be no way out for me. I want my wife to be safe...M'sieur Rick, I ask you as a favor to use the Letters to take her away from Casablanca.

RICK *looks at* LASZLO *incredulously.*

RICK. You love her that much?

LASZLO. Apparently you think of me only as the leader of a Cause. Well, I am also a human being and...*(looks away for a moment, then quietly).* Yes, I love her that much.

At this moment there is a sharp knock on the front door of the café, followed by the entrance of several gendarmes. RICK *and* LASZLO *rise as a* FRENCH OFFICER *walks into the lighted area, addresses* LASZLO.

FRENCH OFFICER. M'sieur Laszlo, you will come with us. We have a warrant for your arrest.

LASZLO. On what charge?

FRENCH OFFICER. Captain Renault will discuss that with you later.

LASZLO *looks at* RICK *who smiles ironically.*

RICK. It seems "destiny" has taken a hand.

In dignified silence LASZLO *crosses to the* POLICE OFFICER. *Together they walk toward the door.* RICK'S *eyes follow them, but his expression reveals nothing of his feelings.*

Dissolve to:

Int. RENAULT'S *office.* RICK *and* RENAULT.

RENAULT....If we can prove at the trial that he was at the meeting, we will have grounds to hold him.

RICK. You haven't any actual proof, and you know it. (RENAULT *shrugs)* You might just as well let him go now.

RENAULT. Ricky, I would advise you not to interest yourself too much in what happens to Laszlo. If by any chance you were to help him escape—

RICK *(cutting in).* What makes you think I'm interested?

RENAULT. Because one: You have bet ten thousand francs that Laszlo *will* escape. Two: You have the Letters of Transit...Now don't bother to deny it...And then you might do it

simply because you don't like Strasser's looks. As a matter of fact, I don't like them either.

RICK *(grins).* They're all excellent reasons...Yes, I have the Letters, Louis. But I'm using them myself. I'm selling out my place and leaving Casablanca on tonight's plane...the last plane.

RENAULT. What!

RICK. And I'm taking a friend with me. *(smiles)* One you'll appreciate.

RENAULT. What friend?

RICK. Ilsa Lund. *(an amazed incredulity is written on* RENAULT'S *face)* That ought to rest your fears about my helping Laszlo escape. He's the last one I want to see in America.

RENAULT *(shrewdly).* But I still don't understand. You did not come here to tell me that. You have the Letters of Transit. You can fill in your name and Miss Lund's and leave any time you please. Why are you still interested in what happens to Laszlo?

RICK. I'm not. But I *am* interested in what happens to Ilsa and me. We have a legal right to leave—that's true. But it's been known that people have been held in Casablanca in spite of their legal rights.

RENAULT. Why should we want to hold you?

RICK. Ilsa is Laszlo's wife. She knows a good deal that Strasser would like to know...

RENAULT. I see.

RICK. Louis, I'll make a deal with you. If you could get Laszlo on a real charge—one you could actually hold him on—would that be a feather in your cap?

RENAULT. It most certainly would. Germany...*(corrects himself).* Vichy would be grateful.

RICK. Then release him and he at my place a half hour before the plane leaves. I'll arrange for Laszlo to come for the Letters of Transit. That will give you criminal grounds to make the arrest. In catching the whale, two small fish will slip through your fingers. To the Germans that will only be a minor irritation.

RENAULT *(puzzled).* There's something I don't understand about this business. Miss Lund—she's very beautiful, yes—But you're not that way about women. How do I know you will keep your end of the bargain?

RICK. I'll make the arrangements with Laszlo right now in the visitors' pen.

RENAULT. Ricky, I will miss you. Apparently you're the only one in Casablanca that has even less scruples than I.

RICK *(drily).* Thanks... *(he rises).* Oh, by the way, call off your watchdogs after you let him go. I don't want them around this afternoon. I'm taking no chances, Louis—even with you.

Quick dissolve to:

Int. vistors' pen. There is the wire netting that separates the visitors from the prisoners. RICK *is seated on his side. There is nobody else in the room. Then a door opens and a guard leads* LASZLO *into the room. As* LASZLO, *looking coldly at* RICK, *seats himself, the guard leaves the room.*

Cut to:

Med. shot. RICK *and* LASZLO *facing each other across the netting.*

RICK *(sotto voce).* I haven't much time. I've bribed a release for you.

LASZLO *(looking at him closely).* Thank you—

RICK. I've decided to let you have the Letters of Transit—*(*LASZLO *stares at him)*—for a hundred thousand francs.

LASZLO. Very well.

RICK. Better get down to my café a few minutes before the Lisbon plane leaves.

LASZLO. They'll shadow me.

RICK. I've taken care of that.

RENAULT *in his office listening over sort of a dictaphone.*

LASZLO'S VOICE. *(coming through).* And Ilsa?

There is a pause. RENAULT *strains his ears.*

RICK'S VOICE. Bring her with you all ready to leave.

RENAULT *smiles broadly.*

Cut to:

Med. shot. RICK *and* LASZLO.

LASZLO *(gratefully).* M'sieur Rick—

RICK *(curtly).* Skip it. This is strictly a matter of business. *(he gets up and walks out).*

Dissolve to:

Int. MARTINEZ' *office long shot.* RICK *and* MARTINEZ *at table. As the camera moves up to them we hear* MARTINEZ *saying:*

MARTINEZ. Shall we draw up papers, or is our handshake good enough?

RICK *(getting up).* It's certainly not good enough. But being I'm in a hurry, it'll have to do.

MARTINEZ *(shaking hands, sighs enviously).* Oh—to get out of Casablanca—to go to America...You are a lucky man.

RICK. Oh, by the way—my agreement with Sam's always been he gets twenty-five percent of the profits. That still goes.

MARTINEZ. I happen to know he gets ten percent. But he's worth twenty-five.

RICK. And Abdul and Carl and Fydor—they stay with the place, or I don't sell.

MARTINEZ. Of course they stay. Rick's wouldn't be Rick's without them.

RICK. So long. *(he walks to the door, stops, turns).* Don't forget, you owe Rick's a hundred cartons of American cigarettes.

MARTINEZ. *(smiles).* I shall remember to pay it to myself.

RICK *walks off.*

Dissolve to:

Med. shot. Plane at airport. Night. A crew of workmen are giving it the last-minute inspection. Fuel is being pumped into its tanks. On the fuselage is painted:

LISBON—CASABLANCA

As camera moves across field—

Dissolve to:

Ext. RICK'S. *On the door a huge placard is pasted. It reads:*

CLOSED
By Order of The Prefect of Police.

Dissolve to:

Med. shot at front door as RICK *comes into scene and opens the door to admit* RENAULT.

RICK. You're late.

RENAULT. I was informed when Laszlo was about to leave the hotel, so I knew I would be on time.

RICK. I thought I asked you to tie up your watchdogs.

RENAULT. Laszlo will not be followed here. *(looks around the empty café, sighs).* This place won't be the same without you, Ricky.

RICK. It'll be all right, Louis. I've arranged with Martinez. You'll still win at roulette.

RENAULT *smiles.*

RENAULT. Is everything ready?

RICK *(tapping his breast pocket).* I have the Letters right here.

RENAULT. Tell me, Rick—when we searched the place, where were they?

RICK. In Sam's piano.

RENAULT. Serves me right for not being musical!

The sound of a car pulling up is heard.

RICK. They're here. Hide in my office.

As RENAULT *walks toward the office—*

Ext. Café. LASZLO *is paying the cab driver.* ILSA *is walking toward the entrance.*

LASZLO *(to cab driver).* Take the luggage to the airport.

Int. café at door. RICK *is opening it to admit* ILSA. *She goes into his arms.*

Close shot. ILSA *and* RICK. *Her intensity reveals the strain she is under.*

ILSA. Victor thinks I'm leaving with him. Haven't you told him?

RICK. Not yet.

ILSA. But it's all right, isn't it? You were able to arrange everything?

RICK. Everything.

He kisses her—as he once kissed her in Paris. She looks at him with a vaguely questioning look. He gently disengages himself.

Full shot. The Café as LASZLO *comes in.*

LASZLO. M'sieur Blaine, I don't know how to thank—

RICK *(cutting him short).* There's no time for that. You won't have any trouble in Lisbon, will you?

LASZLO. No. That is all arranged.

RICK. Good *(takes out the Letters).* Here are the Letters. Signed in blank. You'll just have to fill in the names.

He hands them to LASZLO, *who takes them gratefully.*

LASZLO. M'sieur Blaine, I—

RENAULT'S VOICE *(over scene).* Victor Laszlo!

They wheel toward the office door.

Med. shot. RENAULT *coming down the steps.*

RENAULT. Victor Laszlo, you are under arrest...

Med. close shot. ILSA *and* LASZLO *both caught completely off guard, and speechless. They turn toward* RICK. *Horror is in* ILSA'S *eyes.*

RENAULT'S VOICE *(over scene)*...on a charge of accessory to the murder of the couriers from whom those Letters were stolen.

He walks into the shot, notices their bewildered expressions.

RENAULT. Oh, you are surprised about my friend Rick? The explanation is quite simple. Love, it seems, has triumphed over virtue.

Obviously, the situation delights RENAULT. *He is laughing as he turns toward* RICK. *Suddenly the laugher dies in his throat.*

Full shot. Favoring RICK. *In* RICK'S *hand is a gun, which he is levelling at* RENAULT.

RICK. Nobody is going to be arrested, Louis. Not for a while yet.

RENAULT *(staring open-mouthed for a moment).* Have you lost your mind, Rick?

RICK. Yes. Sit down over there.

RENAULT *hesitates.*

Close shot. ILSA *as her belief in* RICK *comes back.*

Full shot. Favoring RICK *and* RENAULT.

RENAULT *(walking toward* RICK). Put that gun down.

RICK *(not retreating a step).* Louis, I wouldn't like to shoot you. But I will if you take one more step.

RENAULT *halts for a moment and studies* RICK. *Then he shrugs.*

RENAULT. Under the circumstances, I will sit down.

He walks to a table, sits down and reaches into his pocket.

RICK *(sharply).* You will keep your hands on the table...away from your pistol pocket.

RENAULT *(taking out a cigarette case).* I suppose you know what you are doing, but I wonder if you realize what this means?

RICK. Perfectly. But we'll have plenty of time to discuss that later.

LASZLO. There won't be any trouble at the airport, will there?

RENAULT *(sighing).* I'm afraid not. *(reproachfully, to* RICK). Call off your watchdogs, you said!

RICK *takes a phone on a long cord, slides it across the table to* RENAULT.

RICK. Just the same, call the airport and let me hear you tell them. And remember—I've got this gun pointed right at your heart.

RENAULT *(as he dials).* That is my least vulnerable spot. *(into phone)* Hello, airport?—Captain Renault calling from Rick's Café. There'll be two Letters of Transit for the Lisbon plane. There's to be no trouble about them.—Good.

Cut to:

Med. shot. STRASSER *on phone in German consulate.*

STRASSER *(jiggling receiver violently).* Hello...hello...What was that?...

He hangs up the receiver momentarily, presses a buzzer on his desk, then again lifts receiver.

STRASSER. Get me the Prefecture of Police. *(to officer entering door).* My car, quickly! OFFICER *(saluting).* Zu Befehl, Herr Major.

The officer exits; STRASSER resumes on the telephone.

STRASSER. This is Major Strasser...Have a squad of police meet me at the airport at once. At once! Do you hear?

Hanging up the receiver, and grabbing his cap, he hurriedly exits.

Dissolve to:

Long shot. Airport. Night. In the far b.g. the beacon atop of the radio tower slowly resolves its light, dimmed by a heavy fog. In the middle b.g. the outline of the Transport plane is barely visible. Near its open door stand a small group of people, attaches, etc.

A car pulls up near the open door of the hangar in the f.g.

Med. shot. A uniformed orderly is at the telephone near the hangar door.

ORDERLY. Hello, radio tower...Lisbon plane taking off in ten minutes...Thank you.

He hangs up, crosses toward the car.

Med. shot at car. The Orderly salutes smartly as he recognizes Renault alighting from the car. The latter is closely followed by Rick, hand in pocket, still covering RENAULT with a gun. LASZLO and ILSA come from the rear of the car.

RICK *(indicating ORDERLY).* Louis, could you spare this man to help locate the luggage? RENAULT *(bows ironically).* Certainly, Ricky. Anything you say.

He nods curtly to the orderly, who escorts LASZLO off in the direction of the plane. RICK takes the Letters of Transit out of his pocket, hands them to RENAULT.

RICK. If you don't mind, Louis, you fill in the names. *(smiles).* That will make it even more official. RENAULT. You think of everything.

He takes out his pen, spreads the papers on the fender of the car.

RICK *(quietly).* The names to fill in are Mr. and Mrs. Victor Laszlo.

Both ILSA and RENAULT look at RICK with astonishment.

ILSA. But why *my* name, Richard? RICK *(still watching RENAULT).* Because you're getting on that plane. ILSA *(dazed).* But I...I don't understand. What about you?... RICK. I'm staying here to keep Captain Renault company till the plane leaves. ILSA *(as RICK's intention fully dawns on her).* No, Richard, no!...What's happened to you? Last night we said...

Close shot. RICK.

RICK. Last night we said a good many things. We meant them then—just as we meant them once in Paris. But the minute that plane leaves the ground and you're not with him, you'll regret it.

Med. shot.

RICK. Do you have any idea what you've got to look forward to here? Nine chances out of ten we'd both land in the concentration camp. Is that right, Louis? RENAULT *(as he finishes countersigning the papers).* I'm afraid Major Strasser will insist...

Cut to:

Long shot STRASSER's car speeding toward the airport.

Cut back to:

Med. shot. We pick up ILSA in the middle of a speech.

ILSA. ...And what about you? You'll still be here— RICK *(more entreaty in his tone).* I'll be all right, Ilsa. You've done that for me. You've given me back my—myself. And we'll always have that to remember. A few moments that were ours. But if we're honest, we know that's all we've got a right to. ILSA *(wavering a little).* You're just saying that, Richard, to make me go— RICK *(cutting in).* Maybe I am. But what difference does it make? What good are words now? Inside of us we both know you belong with Victor. You decided that once. This time it's my turn. Maybe you'll hate me for it now, but you'll be thankful the rest of your life.

At this moment LASZLO walks into the shot. ILSA stands hesitating. RICK cuts in before she can speak.

RICK. Laszlo, there's something you should know before you leave.

LASZLO (*sensing what is coming*). M'sieur Rick, I do not ask you to explain anything.

RICK. But I'm going to, anyway. It might make a difference to you later. You said you knew about Ilsa and me.

LASZLO. Yes.

RICK (*his voice more harsh, almost brutal*). She tried everything to get them. But nothing else worked. She did her best to convince me she was still in love with me. That was all over long ago, but for your sake she pretended it wasn't—and I let her pretend.

ILSA. Richard!

She makes a move toward RICK.

RICK. No! (*indicating* RENAULT). Don't step in front of him. That's just what he's waiting for.

RENAULT (*wryly*). And I thought I was forgotten.

LASZLO. It is time to go, Ilsa.

Close shot. ILSA *as she looks at* RICK *for the last time. She speaks under her breath.*

ILSA. God bless you, Richard.

She turns, runs toward the plane.

Med. shot as LASZLO *comes up to* RICK. *In his hands are the Letters of Transit.*

LASZLO. M'sieur Rick, thank you for these (*significantly*). And for everything.

There's a moment's pause as the two men look at one another.

LASZLO. And welcome back in the fight (*they shake hands*). This time your side will win.

He turns and goes out of the shot toward the plane.

Two shot. RICK *and* RENAULT. RENAULT *regards* RICK *triumphantly.*

RENAULT. Ricky, I was right! You *are* a sentimentalist!

RICK. What are you talking about?

RENAULT. What you just did for Laszlo. And that fairy tale you invented to send Ilsa away with him. I know women, my friend. She went, but she knew you were lying.

RICK. Anyway, thanks for helping out.

RICK's *face reveals nothing. With his free hand he takes out a cigarette and lights it.*

RENAULT. I suppose you know this is not going to be pleasant for either of us...and especially for you. I have to arrest you, of course.

RICK. When the plane leaves, Louis.

RENAULT *shrugs.*

Long shot. Airport miniature. The plane's motors roar. It slowly taxis down the field.

Med. shot near hangar. A car comes speeding down the roadway toward RICK *and* RENAULT *and screams to a stop.*

Close shot. RICK *and* RENAULT. RENAULT *makes a move toward the car.*

RICK (*in a low voice*). Stay where you are, Louis.

Medium shot. STRASSER *alights from the car and runs toward* RENAULT.

STRASSER. What was the meaning of that phone call?

RENAULT. Victor Laszlo is on that plane.

He nods off down the field.

Long shot. Airport (miniature). The plane has reached the far end of the field, it is turning around, preparatory for the take-off run.

Med. shot near hangar. STRASSER *is dazed for a moment, then recovers.*

STRASSER. Why do you stand there? Why don't you stop him?

RENAULT. Ask M'sieur Rick.

STRASSER *makes a step toward the telephone which is visible just inside the hangar door.* RICK *pulls revolver from his pocket and points it at* STRASSER.

RICK. Keep away from that phone!

STRASSER *stops in his tracks, looks at* RICK, *sees that he means business.*

STRASSER (*steely*). I would advise you not to interfere with an officer of the Third Reich!

RICK. I'm a true neutral. I was willing to shoot Captain Renault...and I'm willing to shoot you.

Long shot airport (miniature). The plane speeds down the field and starts to rise from the ground.

Med. shot near hangar. STRASSER *watches the plane in agony. His eyes dart toward the telephone.*

Close shot. RENAULT. *He watches fascinated.*

Med. shot. RICK *and* STRASSER. STRASSER *runs toward the telephone.*

Close shot at telephone. STRASSER *desperately grasps the receiver.*

STRASSER *(into phone).* Hello...Hello...

RICK'S VOICE *(over scene).* Put down that telephone!

STRASSER *(into phone).* Give me the Radio Tower.

Med. shot. RICK *and* STRASSER.

RICK. Put down that phone or I'll shoot.

STRASSER, *his one hand with the receiver, pulls out a pistol with the other hand and shoots quickly at* RICK. *The bullet misses its mark.* RICK *now shoots at* STRASSER, *who crumples to the ground.*

Med. shot. RICK *and* RENAULT. RENAULT *continues to stare off scene.* RICK *watches upward, as the sound of the plane becomes fainter.*

Long shot sky. The Transport grows smaller in the distance.

Med. shot near hangar. RICK *continues to stare aloft. At the sound of a car approaching, both men turn.*

Long shot a police car speeds in and comes to a stop near RENAULT. *Four police hurriedly alight.*

Close shot. RENAULT *looking at* RICK.

Close shot, RICK *as he returns* RENAULT'S *gaze. His eyes are expressionless.*

Full shot. The gendarmes run to RENAULT. RENAULT *turns to them.*

RENAULT. Major Strasser has been shot *(pauses as he looks at* RICK *then to the gendarmes:)* Round up the usual suspects...

GENDARME *(saluting).* Yes, Captain.

He leads the other gendarmes off. The two men look at one another.

RICK. Thanks, Louis.

RENAULT *(lights a cigarette).* Ricky, until this affair dies down, it might be just as well for you to disappear from Casablanca. I understand there's a Free French garrison over at Bravvaville. If you're interested, I might be induced to arrange your passage.

RICK *(smiles).* My Letter of Transit? *(his eyes following the plane, which is now receding into the distance).* I could use a trip...But it doesn't make any difference about our bet, Louis. You still owe me the ten thousand francs.

Fade out.

The end.

MIRACLE ON 34TH STREET

Screenplay by George Seaton

KRIS KRINGLE	Edmund Gwenn
DORIS WALKER	Maureen O'Hara
FRED GAILEY	John Payne
SUSAN WALKER	Natalie Wood
JUDGE HARPER	Gene Lockhart
MR. SAWYER	Porter Hall
CHARLIE HALLORAN	William Frawley
THOMAS MARA	Jerome Cowan
MRS. HARPER	Thelma Ritter

Screenplay by George Seaton, adapted from an
original story by Valentine Davies
Produced by William Perlberg for Twentieth Century-Fox, 1947
Directed by George Seaton
Cinematography by Charles Clarke & Lloyd Ahern
Music by Cyril Mockridge

This classic American comedy fantasy, which was produced in 1947, is notable for winning two Academy Awards for writing. For George Seaton's Best Screenplay and Valentine Davies's Best Original Story.

The film also received a nomination for Best Picture, which was won that year by *Gentlemen's Agreement*.

George Seaton, who had a distinguished career as a screenwriter, and as a director and producer as well, was born in 1911. In 1933 he came to Hollywood from New York during the depression and became a junior writer at MGM—most happy to be earning a salary of seventy-five dollars a week. Honing his skill as a screenwriter, Mr. Seaton went on to write films like *Country Girl,* for which he also won an Academy Award, adapting it from Clifford Odets' play. Like many a writer who became a director "to protect his material," as George used to put it, he also had great success in that craft, directing not only *Miracle on 34th Street,* but also *Country Girl* (which he also coproduced), and *Teacher's Pet,* and *Airport,* among others.

It is interesting to note that some of the screen's greatest films have come about as a result of the director and the writer being one. To wit: George Seaton, John Huston, and Billy Wilder.

For those of you who wish to observe more closely the writer-director at work in the creative process—with the assistance of the film editor, of course—compare the final screenplay to the completed film as exhibited and note the small but important changes and deletions for smooth climax rhythm in the last few scenes.

An amiable gentleman, who was very well liked and active in the industry, George served as president of the Writers Guild West for a time, and as president of the Academy as well. He always found time among his busy activities to be a guest at my classes at UCLA, the Literature of the Screen, to give students the benefit of his experiences, and he was an inspiration to all who knew him.

What can one say about this classic, *Miracle on 34th Street,* that hasn't already been said about this charming fairy tale? This is no children's story, necessarily, for like many such works of rich imagination, it is an adult classic as well, to be enjoyed by audiences of all ages. A brilliant comedy, with a court scene that is as imaginative and rich in humor and mirth as any written for the screen, the ending came hard for George and Valentine Davies, who both worked on it from the beginning—their first collaboration. They did not have an ending at first, and, as George tells it, they "both deliberately painted themselves in a corner without having the court scene climax of the post office sending over all those letters to prove that Kris was indeed Santa Claus." Nonetheless, they worked it out in time and it was a masterful touch.

One incident I would like to share with you concerning this picture, and more particularly about "comedy," considering the masterful job Edmund Gwenn did in playing the difficult role of Kris Kringle just perfectly, is George Seaton's account of the actor's passing away. George was present, standing in the doorway of Gwenn's hospital room as he came to visit the actor, who was a good friend. Calling affectionately to Gwenn, who was in bed and full of tubes, George said: "It must be hard, Teddy. . . ." Gwenn responded: "But not as hard as playing comedy..." And he died ten seconds later. George himself passed away in 1979.

Fade in. Ext. New York Street—Day—Close shot. Front window of small, side-street shop. Inside we see a WINDOW DRESSER *creating a display for the coming Christmas season. The cotton snow, the tiny pine trees and the sleigh are all in place. He is now placing the figure of Santa Claus into the sleigh. The* WINDOW DRESSER *glances up. His eyes widen.*

Int. store window— WINDOW DRESSER's *angle. Looking through the window is a man who is the living, breathing incarnation of Santa Claus. He has the white beard, the pink cheeks, the fat tummy and all—and what's more, his name is* KRIS KRINGLE. *He is dressed in suit and overcoat and carries a cane which hangs nattily over his arm. He smiles at the* WINDOW DRESSER *it is a friendly, jolly smile.*

Angle on WINDOW DRESSER. *He smiles weakly in return and then gets back to his work. There is a quick tap on the window.*

Angle—shooting toward window, past WINDOW DRESSER *in f.g. As the* WINDOW DRESSER *looks up,* KRIS *begins to talk but due to the glass pane between cannot be heard. The* WINDOW DRESSER *cups a hand to his ear and* KRIS *speaks louder—but still nothing is heard. Now the old gent pantomimes for the* WINDOW DRESSER *to open the front door—he has to tell him something very important.*

Ext. Street—Shooting past KRIS *toward store window. The* WINDOW DRESSER, *a little annoyed, stops his work and climbs out of the store window. Camera moves with the old fellow as he makes his way to the front door. Presently the door is unlocked and the* WINDOW DRESSER *appears.*

WINDOW DRESSER. I'm sorry, the store isn't open today and I—

KRIS. Oh, I don't want to buy anything—and I'm sorry to interrupt your work but I just wanted to tell you you were making a rather serious mistake.

WINDOW DRESSER *(not understanding).* Huh?

KRIS. With the reindeer, I mean. You were putting Prancer where Blitzen should be and Dasher should go on my right-hand side.

The WINDOW DRESSER *begins to ease back slowly and uneasily.*

WINDOW DRESSER. He—he should, huh?

KRIS. Oh, yes. And another thing—Donner's antlers have four points instead of three—but I don't suppose anybody would notice that except me.

WINDOW DRESSER *(starting to close the door nervously).* No—no I don't suppose so. Well—goodbye—thanks—

KRIS *(gaily).* Not at all—glad I could help. Goodbye.

KRIS *exits happily, camera holding on the closed door. The* WINDOW DRESSER *looks after the old man and his furrowed forehead asks, "Who the hell was that?"*

Dissolve to:

Ext. Central Park—Day—Angle—Path approaching reindeer pen—Trucking shot— KRIS. *He walks along the path with a firm, sure, happy stride. In his hand he carries some carrot tops. His pace slackens as he looks off almost affectionately.*

Angle in front of reindeer pen.

Shooting past a kid and his father at bars in f.g. In b.g. we see the reindeer shyly clustered at the rear of the pen. The ten-year-old is trying desperately to get the reindeer to come forward and eat some peanuts from his hand.

KID. Here reindeer, here reindeer—

HIS FATHER. It's no use, Jimmie, reindeer are too shy—they're afraid of people. Come along, son—

They start out.

Angle on KRIS. *He smiles as he comes closer.*

Close shot: A couple of the reindeer. They lift their heads and look off.

Full shot—Pen—Shooting through bars. The reindeer come trotting toward camera.

Another angle, as KRIS *approaches bars from one side, the reindeer from the other. As* KRIS *speaks to them as you would do to a favorite dog or cat, he feeds them carrot tops and reaches through bars and pats them. The reindeer are not the slightest bit afraid—we hope.*

KRIS. Hello, boys and girls! It's good to see you. Sorry I couldn't get over on Sunday but I was awful busy. *(scratching them with his cane)* There! Does that feel good? Say, I think you've put on a little weight. John been treating you all right—?

KRIS *stops speaking as he becomes conscious of the faint sound of "Jingle Bells" being played by a brass band. He decides to investigate. He gives the reindeer the last of the carrot tops.*

KRIS. I'll see you later. *(he starts out)*

Dissolve to:

Angle sidewalk—Corner of Central Park West and 77th St. A crowd, held back by a rope, is "ohing" and "ahing" at something off. KRIS *pushes through to f.g. and looks off smiling.*

Long shot—77th Street. The Macy Christmas parade is preparing to start on its annual trek through Manhattan. We see floats, giant inflated figures on story-book characters, a band, etc. It is a scene of great confusion—people rushing around making last minute changes, the band noodling on their instruments, the wind whipping the big balloons around, shouting, complaining, etc. In f.g. is the Santa Claus float.

Out.

KRIS, *as he surveys this last-mentioned float with the eyes of a critic. He nods approval—then suddenly he frowns.*

Angle at float. The MACY SANTA CLAUS, *all bedecked in his fur-trimmed red outfit, is having great difficulty cracking his long whip. At the moment he's got it wound all around his arm. Disgustedly he starts down from float.*

KRIS, *feeling that he must come to the man's aid, starts out.*

Angle at float, as MACY'S SANTA CLAUS *climbs down.* KRIS *enters shot. His manner is charming—he only wants to help.*

KRIS *(politely).* Allow me, sir.

KRIS *takes the whip and lets fly with it in a most experienced manner. The end cracks smartly just an inch above the farthest reindeer's ear.*

KRIS *(a golf pro correcting a bad swing).* You see, it's all in the wrist—and, of course, you must follow through.

THE MACY SANTA, *although it's hard to notice at first glance due to all the whiskers, is plenty mulled.*

MACY'S SANTA *(in high-pitched amazement).* Is za' so?

KRIS. It's just like throwing a ball—if you—

KRIS *stops short as he realizes. He sniffs a couple of times and confirms his suspicions.*

KRIS *(horrified).* You've been drinking!

MACY'S SANTA *(to himself).* 's cold. Man's gotta do somethin' to keep warm.

KRIS *(angrily).* You ought to be ashamed of yourself! Don't you realize there are thousands of children lining the streets waiting to see you—children who've been dreaming of this moment for weeks! You're a disgrace to

the tradition of Christmas and I refuse to have you malign me in this fashion!

He climbs down from the float out of the scene.

MACY'S SANTA *(to himself).* 's cold. Man's gotta do somethin' to keep warm.

Angle sidewalk, as KRIS *enters angrily. He speaks to a costumed* CLOWN *with baggy pants.*

KRIS. Who's in charge of this parade?!
CLOWN *(trying to keep his pants from falling off).* If you find out let me know—these pants are going to fall off right in the middle of Columbus Circle.

Camera moves with KRIS *as he continues along sidewalk. He meets a young lady dressed as* DRUM MAJORETTE.

KRIS. Pardon me, could you tell me who's in charge here?
MAJORETTE *(pointing off).* Yes—Mrs. Walker. There she is down there.

KRIS *mumbles a "thanks" and starts off.*

Out.

Group, featuring DORIS WALKER, *a handsome, well-dressed, efficient-looking young lady. She is checking off personnel on a pad as she instructs them where to go.*

DORIS. Float number six. You walk behind the band. Float number three.

At this moment, MR. SHELLHAMMER, *a harried, excited gentleman, hurries in.*

SHELLHAMMER. Miss Walker, something's got to be done. Rub a dub dub just isn't big enough. We can get the Butcher and the Baker in, but the Candlestick Maker—
DORIS. I'm sorry, Mr. Shellhammer, but that's not my department. I've got enough to do taking care of the people. Float number four.
SHELLHAMMER. Oh, dear! And I was hoping this— *(he exits)*

At this moment KRIS *enters from the opposite direction.*

KRIS. Mrs. Walker?

DORIS *mumbles a "yes" and turns to see* KRIS. *Thinking he is the Santa Claus that should be on the float, she lights into him.*

DORIS. What do you mean taking your costume off? Now get dressed and get back—*(a good look and she sees she's wrong)* Oh—I'm sorry—I thought you were our Santa Claus.

KRIS *(furiously)*. Your Santa Claus is intoxicated!

DORIS *(the last straw)*. Oh, no—don't tell me.

KRIS. It's shameful! How can you be so negligent as to allow a man—

But DORIS *doesn't want to listen. She dashes out, followed by* KRIS.

Angle at float—Shooting down toward side-walk. MACY'S SANTA CLAUS *in f.g. gaily singing "Jingle Bells." He shivers a bit—then, still singing, he sneaks his hand under the lap robe and takes out a pretty well-killed pint bottle. At this moment* DORIS, *followed by* KRIS, *hurries in.*

DORIS *(furious; taking bottle)*. Put that down! What do you mean by drinking?! You know it's not allowed.

MACY'S SANTA. 's cold. Man's gotta do somethin' to keep warm.

KRIS *(weighing his cane in his hand threateningly)*. I'll warm you up! I ought to take this cane and—

DORIS *(just as mad)*. And I ought to *(she wants to fire him but she can't)* Somebody get some coffee—lots of it—and black!

An underling who has been looking on mumbles, "Yes, Mrs. Walker" and hurries out.

MACY'S SANTA *(calling after him)*. Black with a little cream. *(to* DORIS*)* Wake me up when the parade starts.

He reclines on the side of the float to catch a few winks. DORIS *shakes him—then gives up.*

*Close shot—*DORIS. *She shuts her eyes in pain and defeat. Then suddenly they pop open and she looks quickly to her right.*

KRIS—DORIS's *angle.*

KRIS. Shameful! Absolutely shameful!

*Two shot—*DORIS *and* KRIS. *In the excitement she had forgotten about* KRIS.

DORIS *(anxiously)*. Could you be Santa Claus? Have you had any experience?

The question strikes KRIS *as rather droll—even in his anger he is forced to smile.*

KRIS *(tolerantly)*. A little.

DORIS. You've got to help me out—please!

KRIS. Madam, I am not in the habit of substituting for spurious Santa Clauses—*(a pause; then)* However—the children must not be disappointed. I'll do it.

As DORIS *sighs a relieved "Thank you"—*

Dissolve to:

Central Park West—Day—Angle at corner of 77th Street—Long shot, with the band playing, the parade is turning onto Central Park West. The Santa Claus float is last in line.

Out.

Angle—77th Street. DORIS WALKER, *weary and glad that it's finally on its way, stands looking after the parade. A motorcycle with sidecar pulls up at the curb.* SHELLHAMMER *is in the bathtub.*

SHELLHAMMER. He's wonderful. He's the best we've ever had—and he didn't need any padding!

DORIS. What?

SHELLHAMMER. Padding, padding—he didn't even need padding. Where did you find him?

DORIS *(she still can't believe it)*. I just turned around and there he was.

SHELLHAMMER. Well, I'm glad you turned around—I mean I'm glad he was there. Just think if Mr. Macy had seen—*(a hushed tone)* the other one.

DORIS. Just think if Mr. *Gimbel* had seen the other one.

The thought of it makes SHELLHAMMER *shudder.*

SHELLHAMMER. Are you going to ride in a motorcycle or a car?

DORIS. Subway. I'm going home and get in a hot tub—and I might stay right there until *next* Thanksgiving.

SHELLHAMMER. But you really should see the parade—you've worked so hard on it.

DORIS. If I want to, which I doubt, I can see it from the roof of my apartment.

In reaching for one of her gloves, DORIS *takes from her pocket the whiskey bottle she had confiscated from the Santa Claus.*

SHELLHAMMER. Oh, that's right—you live down by—*(sees bottle)* Why, Mrs. Walker—!

The motorcycle pulls out of scene. DORIS *smiles as she looks at the bottle.*

Series of production shots of parade, as it comes down Central Park West. After we have shown the excitement and magnitude of this parade—

Dissolve to:

Angle—Central Park West—Front of apartment building. We hear the sounds of the parade off screen. DORIS *enters shot. She stops before entering building and looks off.*

Central Park West— DORIS's *angle—Long shot—Shooting past the backs of people in f.g. The parade is passing.*

Angle— DORIS. *She sighs, glad it's over, and enters the building.*

Lap dissolve to:

DORIS's *apartment—Day—Angle at door. It opens and* DORIS *enters. We pan her across the combination living-dining room as she takes off her coat. It is a small apartment. The living room is a reflection of* DORIS—*modern, in good taste, neat—but rather cold.*

DORIS *(calling as she crosses).* Susan! Susan!

The door to the kitchen swings open and CLEO, *the colored maid, pokes her head out.* CLEO *is definitely* not *a hundred and eighty pounds of "How Y'all, honeychile"—she is pleasant, trim and intelligent.*

CLEO. She's watching the parade, Mrs. Walker.

DORIS *(puzzled).* Oh? Where—with whom?

CLEO. That Mr. Gailey who lives in the front apartment.

DORIS. Oh, yes.

CLEO *(indicating window).* I've been keeping an eye on her.

DORIS. She'll see everything from there—that's the fifty yard line.

CLEO. He's very fond of Susan. When he asked me—I didn't think you'd mind.

DORIS *(crossing to window).* Well—I guess it's all right.

DORIS *at window—Shooting past her. Being a back apartment, the windows open onto an airway—directly across are the rear windows of the front apartment. The shades are up so that we can see a man and small girl in the living room of the front apartment.* DORIS *raps on the window and calls "Susan" a couple of times. They do not hear her.*

Another angle—Near window. DORIS *in f.g.,* CLEO *behind.*

DORIS. I guess my parade's making too much noise. *(she steps away from window)*

CLEO *(smiling).* Susan left a definite order for you to go in and say hello.

DORIS *(taking off her hat).* All right—I'll go in for a minute.

Int. front apartment—Angle at front window (process). FRED GAILEY *and* SUSAN *are sitting on the window seat watching the parade.* FRED *is an easy-going, likeable, comfortable person in his middle thirties. He is drinking a cup of coffee.* SUSAN *is six. She is healthy and intelligent—perhaps too much so for her age. Although she's pretty, she lacks that very important ingredient that makes a six-year-old an attractive, vital human being—there is no gaiety about her, no fun.* FRED *seems far more excited at seeing the parade than* SUSAN.

FRED. Look at the big baseball player!

SUSAN. He was a clown last year. They just changed the head and painted him different—my mother told me.

FRED. Wow! He's really a giant, isn't he?

SUSAN *(a very literal person).* Not really. There are no giants, Mr. Gailey.

FRED. Maybe not now, Susie—but in olden days—*(* SUSAN *shakes her head)* Well, what about the giant that Jack killed?

SUSAN. Jack who?

FRED. Jack—er—Jack—and the bean stalk.

SUSAN *(blankly).* I never heard of that.

FRED. Oh, you must have—you've just forgotten. It's a fairy tale.

SUSAN *(not much respect for them).* Oh, one of those. I don't know any fairy tales.

FRED. You mean your mother or father never read you any?

SUSAN *(shakes her head).* My mother thinks they're silly. I don't know whether my father thinks they're silly or not. I never met my father. You see, my father and mother were divorced when I was a baby.

FRED *is a bit startled at her almost adult manner. He quickly changes the subject.*

FRED. Well—that baseball player looks like a giant to me.

SUSAN. People sometimes grow very big but that is abnormal.

FRED *is taken aback again.*

FRED. Your mother tell you that, too?

SUSAN *nods as she looks out at the parade. The doorbell rings.* FRED *rises, his eyes still fastened on this too-advanced youngster.*

Angle at door, as FRED *enters and opens it.* DORIS *stands in the doorway.*

DORIS. How do you do—I'm Susan's mother.

FRED. Yes, I know. Susie's told me quite a bit about you—won't you come in?

DORIS *(entering).* Thank you.

FRED. I'm Fred Gailey.

DORIS. Yes, I know—Susan's told me quite a bit about *you,* too. *(exiting)* Hello, dear—

Angle at window—(process).

SUSAN. Hello, Mother.

DORIS *enters and gives* SUSAN *a big hug and kiss.*

FRED *(entering scene).* Would you like a cup of coffee? You must have frozen standing out—

DORIS. Oh, don't bother—I'm—

FRED. No bother—it's all ready.

DORIS. Well, in that case, thanks— *(* FRED *exits; to* SUSAN *)* What do you think of my parade?

SUSAN. It's much better than last year.

DORIS. I hope Mr. Macy agrees with you.

Int. Kitchenette.

Angle FRED *as he pours a cup of coffee. This room is a compact kitchen—breakfast nook combination. Living room is seen in b.g. through open door.*

FRED *(calling).* Sugar? Cream? Both? Neither?

DORIS *(coming to kitchen in f.g.).* Just one sugar, please. This is very kind of you, Mr. Gailey. *(she has reached Fred and takes coffee)* And I want to thank you for being so kind to Susan. Cleo tells me you took them to the Zoo yesterday.

FRED *(pouring a cup for himself).* That's right—but I must confess that was part of a deep-dyed plot. I'm fond of Susie, very fond of her—but I also wanted to know you—I read somewhere that the surest way to meet the mother was to be kind to the child. It worked.

During the above they have seated themselves at the breakfast table.

DORIS *(smiling).* What a horrible trick!

SUSAN *is now heard calling from the living room. She doesn't speak with any childish excitement but rather in the manner of "Here Comes Malicious."*

SUSAN. Here comes Santa Claus!

DORIS *closes her eyes and sinks back in her chair—just the thought of it was too much.*

DORIS *(calling back).* Don't ever mention the name!

SUSAN. He's better than last year's—at least this one doesn't wear glasses.

DORIS *(to* SUSAN *).* This one was a last minute substitute—the one I hired, I fired.

SUSAN. Why?

DORIS. Remember how the janitor was last New Year's?—Well, he was worse.

SUSAN *(understanding).* Oh.

FRED *is a bit taken aback by this adult conversation between mother and child.*

FRED. I see she doesn't believe in Santa Claus either. *(* DORIS, *drinking her coffee, shakes her head)* No Santa Claus, no fairy tales, no fantasies of any kind, is that it?

DORIS. That's right—I think we should be realistic and completely truthful with our children—and not let them grow up believing in a lot of myths and legends—like Santa Claus for example.

Having finished her coffee, DORIS *rises and goes into the living room.*

Int. Living room—Angle at window. DORIS *enters.*

DORIS *(to* SUSAN *).* Well, that's the last float, dear. Come along.

SUSAN. The acrobats were good.

DORIS. At those prices, they should be. *(to* FRED *)* Thanks again for the coffee.

They start for the hall door, camera panning.

SUSAN. And thank you for inviting me in.

FRED. It was a pleasure, Susie.

SUSAN. Mother, I was thinking—we've got such a big turkey for dinner and there are only two of us, couldn't we invite Mr. Gailey, couldn't we?

DORIS. Well, dear, I—

FRED *(to* DORIS *).* Oh, please, don't even think about it—I—

SUSAN. It's an awful big turkey.

Angle at door, as they stop.

DORIS. It's not that, dear—but I'm sure Mr. Gailey has other plans.

SUSAN. No he hasn't, have you?

FRED *(to* DORIS *).* To be perfectly honest and truthful with the child I must say I haven't any plans but I don't want to interfere—I think I better—

SUSAN *(to* DORIS *).* Please, Mother, please—

DORIS *(in a spot).* Well—er—I—

SUSAN *(to* FRED *).* Did I ask all right?

Caught, FRED *closes his eyes.* DORIS *utters an amazed "humph" as she stares at him.*

SUSAN. Didn't I ask all right, Mr. Gailey?

FRED. That all depends. *(he looks inquiringly at* DORIS*)*

DORIS *(smiling)*. Dinner's at three o'clock.

FRED *(kneeling beside* SUSAN*)*. Susie, you asked just right. *(gives her a pat)* See you at three.

DORIS *and* SUSAN *exit ad libbing "Goodbye," "See you later."* FRED *throws in a "thanks" or two and closes the door. Satisfied with his progress,* FRED *starts back into the living room.*

Dissolve to:

Ext. Times Square–Day–Long shot, as the Macy parade winds through the Square.

Angle– SHELLHAMMER *in motorcycle bathtub. It slows up and stops at the curb.*

Closer shot– SHELLHAMMER *at curb. He overhears a couple of mothers talking excitedly.*

1ST MOTHER. Did you see him?! He waved right at Johnny!

2ND MOTHER. He's wonderful! The best one I've ever seen. We must take the children down to meet him at the store.

SHELLHAMMER *is delighted and he can't resist the opportunity.*

SHELLHAMMER *(to the women)*. Yes! And while you're there you can do your shopping.

The motorcycle pulls out and the mothers look at each other rather surprised.

Dissolve to:

Ext. Macy's Dept. Store–34th St. at 7th Ave.–Day–Long shot. The parade is over and KRIS, *on the marquee platform, is speaking, via loudspeaker, to the half-million people crowded into 34th Street.*

Closer shot–marquee. KRIS *is making whatever speech the boys at Macy's will write for him. In b.g. we see the second floor windows of Macy's.*

Int. second floor Macy's–(process). In f.g. we see SHELLHAMMER *at a desk speaking on phone. In b.g. on platform we see* KRIS, *his back to us, at microphone.*

SHELLHAMMER. —I tell you, Mrs. Walker, he's marvelous! Everybody's crazy about him and so is Mr. Macy.

Int. DORIS's *living room.* DORIS, *dressed in a robe and hair piled on top of her head, looks like she just stepped out of the bath. She stands in f.g., phone in hand. In b.g. we see* SUSAN *playing the piano.* DORIS *waves a quieting hand*

and SUSAN *stops.* DORIS *listens for a moment, then speaks.*

DORIS. Well, hire him by all means . . . it's perfectly all right with me—in fact, it'll save me a frantic search in the morning.

SHELLHAMMER *at phone–(process).*

SHELLHAMMER. All right—then I'll take care of it as soon as he gets through. Oh, you'll love him. I just know with that man on the throne my department will sell more toys than it ever has—he's a born salesman. I just feel it.

DORIS *at phone.* SUSAN *in b.g. has her hands poised above the keyboard waiting for her mother to hang up.* DORIS *listens, rather bored—*

DORIS. Yes . . . yes . . . yes—we'll talk about it in the morning. Goodbye.

The moment the receiver is down, SUSAN *starts playing.*

Dissolve to:

Int. Macy's Department Store–Just inside entrance to employees' locker room–Day. It is the next morning and employees are filing in, ad libbing about their Thanksgiving Day dinners, etc. SHELLHAMMER *hurries in. He carries a typewritten sheet of paper. He looks around, then starts out.*

Angle–At row of lockers. KRIS, *dressed in his own outfit, is seated on a stool pulling on his boots. The costume he has worn in the parade hangs nearby. The locker room boy stands talking to* KRIS. ALFRED *is seventeen, innocent-looking, rotund and hails from Flatbush Avenue.*

ALFRED. —Gee, dat sure is an elegant costume

KRIS. Yes, I've had it for years—and years.

ALFRED. Sure makes a bum outta the one they gave you. But even dat one is better'n the one I wear.

KRIS. You, Alfred—?

ALFRED *(self-conscious but rather proud)*. Yeah—I play Santa Claus over at the "Y" near our block, see. Started about tree years ago, see—dey hadda costume but it din have no paddin'—so since I carried my own paddin' around wid me I got the job, see.

KRIS. You enjoy impersonating me!

ALFRED. Aw, yeah—I get a big boot otta it—givin' packages to the lill kids and watchin' dere faces get that Crizmas look allova sudden—makes me feel kinda good and important.

During above SHELLHAMMER *is seen coming from b.g.*

SHELLHAMMER *(as he comes to f.g.).* There you are, there you are. Good morning. My, what a striking costume! Now before you go up on the floor I just want to give you a few tips on how to be a good Santa Claus.

KRIS *(smiling; tolerantly).* Go right ahead.

SHELLHAMMER. Well, here's a list of toys we have to *"push"*—you know, things that we're overstocked on. Now you'll find that a great many children will be undecided as to what they want for Christmas—when that happens you immediately suggest one of these items. Understand?

KRIS *(with a slow, angry nod).* I certainly do.

SHELLHAMMER *doesn't notice* KRIS's *attitude. He rushes on.*

SHELLHAMMER. Good. Now you memorize that list and when you're finished come up to the seventh floor—I'll be waiting for you.

SHELLHAMMER *turns, walks to b.g. and disappears around the corner.* KRIS *stares at the list for a moment, then disgustedly begins tearing it into small pieces.*

KRIS. Imagine! Making a child take something he doesn't want just because *he* bought too many of the wrong toys! That's what I've been fighting against for years—the way they commercialize Christmas!

ALFRED. Yeah—dere's a lot of bad isms floatin' aroun' dis world but da woist is commoishallism. Make a buck, make a buck! Even in Brooklyn it's the same—don' care wha' Crizmas stan's fer—jus' make a buck, make a buck! *(Kris starts to hang up the other costume)* Don' bodder. I'll puddit away fer you.

KRIS *mumbles a "thank you" and now he doesn't quite know what to do with the torn bits of paper in his hand.*

ALFRED. Jes trow 'em on da floor, I get tired jes sweepin' up dust—sweepin' up something like *dat* makes me feel like I'm accomplishin' sompin! *(Kris drops the paper)* Thanks.

As ALFRED *starts sweeping,* KRIS *exits.*

Dissolve to:

Int. Seventh floor Macy's Department Store— Day—Long shot—Shooting past line of children and parents toward Santa Claus' dais in b.g.

Closer shot—Santa Claus' dais. KRIS, *at the moment, has on his lap a boy of five. The*

mother, her back to us, is in the f.g. KRIS is happy and having the time of his life—and his happiness is sincere, not the feigned good nature of the run-of-the-mill Santas.

KRIS.—ah, yes—Peter's a fine name. And what do you want for Christmas, Peter?

PETER. I wanna—I wanna—*(then in one breath)* I wanna fire engine just like the big ones only smaller that's got real hoses that squirt real water and I won't do it in the house just in the backyard. *(crossing his heart)* I promise.

In f.g. we see the MOTHER's *hand waving gingerly to attract* KRIS's *attention.* KRIS *glances up.*

Reverse angle on MOTHER—*shooting past* KRIS. *Although her voice is not heard, she mouths the following plainly enough to be understood.*

MOTHER. No, no—I've looked everywhere—can't find it.

Three shots— KRIS, PETER *and* MOTHER.

KRIS. Well, Peter—I can tell you're a good boy—you'll get your fire engine.

The MOTHER *is amazed at this double cross and* PETER *is delighted.*

PETER *(crawling from his lap).* Oh, thank you—thank you very much—*(to his mother with great superiority)* You see, I told you he'd get me one.

The MOTHER *smiles sweetly but inwardly she is furious.*

MOTHER. Yes, dear—now you wait over there. *(acidly)* Mommy wants to thank Santa Claus, too.

Camera closes in as the mother moves toward Kris.

MOTHER *(sotto voce; angrily).* What do you mean by saying a thing like that? I told you I couldn't find one—I've looked all over— they're just not making that kind of fire engine.

KRIS *(kindly).* You don't think I would have said that unless I was sure, do you? You *can* get them—*(consulting a notebook)* —at the Acme Toy Company at 246 West 26th Street. And they're only eight-fifty—a wonderful bargain.

The MOTHER *is so amazed she can't speak. She just stares dumbfounded.* KRIS *proudly holds up his little black book.*

KRIS. I keep track of the toy market pretty closely. Does that surprise you so?

MOTHER. It's not that so much but—but what really bowls me over is that *Macy's* is sending me to *another store*.

KRIS. Well, the only important thing is to make the children happy and whether Macy or somebody else sells the toy doesn't make any difference. Don't you feel that way?

MOTHER. Yes—but I never dreamed that Macy's did.

KRIS *(definitely)*. As long as I'm here they do.

Wipe to:

Same setup. Now a different woman is leaning over as KRIS *speaks quietly.*

KRIS.—you'll find just what you want at F. A. O. Schwarz's—six seventy-five.

Wipe to:

Same setup. A man has taken the woman's place.

KRIS. Bloomingdale's has exactly what the little girl wants—two forty-nine—but for Johnny's wagon I'd suggest you get it here— we have the best wagons in town.

Wipe to:

Same setup. A third woman is now listening.

KRIS.—go to Stern's on 42nd Street—they have them and they're worth every penny.

Int. Santa Claus floor—Day. SHELLHAMMER *is walking across the floor. He looks off toward* KRIS. *Deciding to see how the old man is doing, he happily starts to walk over.*

Angle at rear of dais. As SHELLHAMMER *approaches and stands eavesdropping.* KRIS *or the children cannot be seen in the shot—however,* KRIS's *voice is heard.*

KRIS's VOICE.—oh yes we have skates and they're very good—(SHELLHAMMER *smiles*) — but they're not quite what your boy wants— (SHELLHAMMER *frowns*) —I'd suggest that you go to Gimbel's, they have exactly what you're looking for.

At the mention of Gimbel's, SHELLHAMMER *immediately goes into a state of shock. He stands rigid, dumbfounded—sending customers to their arch rival Gimbel is too much for the human mind to comprehend. He begins to tremble and mutter "Gimbel's" unbelievingly to himself. Now, as the full impact of it all hits him, he moves forward with murder in his heart.*

Angle—Dais. KRIS *and a woman in f.g.* SHELLHAMMER *is seen coming around the corner of dais menacingly.* SHELLHAMMER *is all set to commit Santacide but realizes it's impossible in front of so many witnesses. He stalks off, frustrated and angry.*

Angle— SHELLHAMMER *walking—Trucking shot. He is still muttering "Gimbel's" to himself furiously. Now the character of the* MOTHER *(we have seen previously with* KRIS*) stops him.*

MOTHER. Pardon me, but the guard over there said I was to speak to you. You the head of the toy department?

SHELLHAMMER *(he hasn't got time)*. Yes, madam, but at the moment I'm—

MOTHER *(going right on)*. I want to congratulate you and Macy's on this new stunt you're doin'. *(*SHELLHAMMER *looks puzzled)* Imagine sending people to other stores—I—I don't get it. It's—it's—

SHELLHAMMER *(weakly)*. It certainly is.

MOTHER. You said it. To think that a big store like this puts the spirit of Christmas ahead of the commercial—it's—it's wonderful! I never done much shopping here but believe me from now on I'm a regular Macy customer!

Wipe to: Int. Toy Department. Two women are talking to SHELLHAMMER. *We see the toy department in b.g.*

1ST WOMAN.—if you knew the time and energy we mothers spend looking for just the right toy—

2ND WOMAN.—and your Santa Claus tells us where to get it just like that—it's marvelous—just marvelous!

1ST WOMAN. I can't tell you how grateful I am—but I can certainly show you. Outside of Tommy's scooter, which I'm going to get at Gimbel's, I'm going to do every other bit of my Christmas shopping right here!

SHELLHAMMER *has listened to this with growing puzzlement.*

Wipe to:

Int. SHELLHAMMER's *office—Two shot.* SHELLHAMMER *behind his desk. A middle-aged Southern woman stands talking to him.*

WOMAN.—ah tell you this new policy of yoh's is so helpful and friendly it's almost Southern. Of course down home everybody is helpful and friendly but I nevah expected to find it in New York City. An' I just wanted to tell you and thank you.

SHELLHAMMER *rises and mutters a be-wildered "Thank you" in return. The woman heads for the door. She exits and as she does,* SHELLHAMMER'S *secretary enters, closing the door behind her.*

SECRETARY. There are six more women out there who'd like to thank you.

SHELLHAMMER *(so confused).* Not now. I've got to think this thing over.

SECRETARY. Well, personally, I think it's a wonderful idea, too.

SHELLHAMMER. *You* think so and *those* women think so—but the point is will Mr. Macy think so.

Dissolve to:

Int. Santa Claus floor—Day—Angle—Shooting from dais toward line of children.

In the immediate f.g. are SUSAN *and* FRED. SUSAN *is singularly unexcited at the prospect of meeting Santa Claus.*

SUSAN. This seems awfully silly, Mr. Gailey.

FRED. Well—I thought as long as we were in the store you might as well say hello to him.

SUSAN. Why?

FRED. Because maybe when you talk to him you'll feel differently about Santa Claus.

SUSAN *shrugs—still thinks this whole business is pretty foolish.*

Angle—Shooting toward dais, as KRIS *waves goodbye to a little boy. Being next in line,* FRED *sort of helps* SUSAN *up toward* KRIS.

KRIS *(lifting her up on his lap).* Well—young lady—what's your name?

SUSAN *is not the least excited. She speaks politely and in a very honest, straightforward manner.*

SUSAN. Susan Walker. What's yours?

KRIS *and* FRED *are a bit startled by this most practical and direct reply.*

KRIS. Mine? Kris Kringle—I'm Santa Claus.

SUSAN *smiles tolerantly as if she were the adult and they were the children.*

KRIS. You don't believe that, do you?

SUSAN *(shaking her head).* You see my mother is Mrs. Walker, the lady who hired you. But I must say you're the best-looking one I've ever seen—your whiskers aren't loose at the sides.

KRIS. That's because they're real—just like I'm really Santa Claus. *(*SUSAN *looks at the beard skeptically)* Go ahead—pull it.

SUSAN *reaches up slowly and gives the beard a tug and is rather surprised that it isn't a fake. She glances at* FRED, *beginning to wonder a little. She still disbelieves—but wonders.*

Angle—Near entrance to floor—Trucking shot. DORIS, *some papers in her hand, is crossing toward some offices. She is looking toward the crowd of children. Presently her pace slackens as she sees* SUSAN *and* FRED.

*Long shot—Dais—*DORIS'S *Angle. We see* SUSAN *in* KRIS'S *lap.*

DORIS. *Annoyed, she starts toward dais.*

*Angle—Dais—*KRIS, FRED *and* SUSAN.

KRIS. —now what would you like me to bring you for Christmas?

SUSAN. Nothing—thank you.

KRIS. Oh, now you must want something.

SUSAN. Whatever I want my mother will get for me—if it's sensible and doesn't cost too much, of course. *(*DORIS *enters)* Hello, Mother.

DORIS. Hello, dear. *(curtly)* Hello, Mr. Gailey. Come along, Susan, I think you've taken up enough of this gentleman's time. *(helping her down).*

They start out, followed by FRED.

*Three shot—Trucking—*DORIS, SUSAN *and* FRED.

FRED. The explanation for all this is very simple. Cleo's mother sprained her ankle; she had to go home; she asked me if I'd bring Susan down here to you—

DORIS *(cutting in).* Yes, I know—Cleo called me. I've been wondering where you were.

FRED. Well—we—we thought as long as we were here we might as well say hello to Santa Claus.

DORIS *glances at* FRED—*she knows it wasn't* SUSAN's *idea.*

SUSAN. He's a nice old man, Mother—and those whiskers are real, too!

There is a note of excitement in the child's voice that DORIS *doesn't care for.*

DORIS *(to* SUSAN*).* Yes—many men have long beards like that, dear. Susan, would you mind sitting here for a moment? I'd like to talk to Mr. Gailey.

SUSAN. All right.

As SUSAN *sits on a bench* DORIS *and* FRED *exit.*

Angle at side near rug department, as they enter.

FRED *(he knows he's in for it; with feigned darkness).* I shouldn't have brought Susie to Santa Claus, huh?

DORIS *(good-naturedly).* Now you're making me feel like the proverbial stepmother.

FRED. I'm sorry—it's just that I couldn't see any great harm in merely saying hello to the old gent.

DORIS. But I think there *is* harm. I tell her Santa Claus is a myth. You bring her down here, she sees thousands of gullible children and meets a very convincing old man with real whiskers. This sets up within her a harmful mental conflict. What is she to think? Whom is she to believe?

Ext. Cubicle. Angle at chair where SUSAN *was seated. It is empty. Camera swings over and we see the child walking slowly, tentatively toward the dais.*

Trucking shot— SUSAN, *as she continues moving hesitantly. She* is *in a mental conflict. Her intellect tells her it's silly—and then, she wonders. Presently the side of the dais comes into view and* SUSAN *stands to listen.*

Angle at dais. KRIS *in f.g.,* SUSAN *in b.g.* KRIS *has just said goodbye to a little boy and now a* WOMAN *and* GIRL *step forward.*

KRIS. Hello, there, young lady—what's your name?

WOMAN. I'm sorry—she doesn't speak English. She's Dutch—she just came over.

Close-up—the GIRL. *She's a blonde with beautiful eyes that are rather sad. She smiles the smile of a youngster who hasn't had much to be happy about.*

MOTHER'S VOICE. She's been living in an orphans' home in Rotterdam ever since—well—

Angle at dais.

MOTHER. We've adopted her. I told her you wouldn't be able to speak to her—but—but when she saw you in the parade she said you *were* Sinterklaas, as she calls you, and that you *could* talk to her. I didn't know what to do, I—

KRIS, *smiling, has already turned toward the girl.*

KRIS. Hallo! Ik ben bly dat je gekomen bent.

Close-up— GIRL. *Her big eyes open even wider. She wants to laugh, cry, shout and run all at the same time.*

GIRL *(moving toward* KRIS). O! U bent Sinterklass! Ik wist het wel.

Angle at dais, as the GIRL *climbs up on his lap.*

GIRL. Ik was zeber dat U het zou begrypen.

KRIS. Natuurlyk. Zed me maar wat je zou willen hebben van Sinterklaas.

GIRL. Niets. Ik heb van alles. Ik wil alleen maar by deze lieve dame zyn.

Close-up—The WOMAN. *Frankly, she is amazed—and undoubtedly will do all her shopping at Macy's from now on. Over this comes the sound of the Dutch clambake between* KRIS *and the* GIRL.

Close-up— SUSAN. *Here, too, is a most surprised young lady—but a quiet surprise. It has made a great impression on her—and she stands wondering.*

Two shot— DORIS *and* FRED.

DORIS. —and by filling them full of fairy tales they grow up considering life a fantasy instead of a reality. They keep waiting for Prince Charming to come along and when he does he turns out to be—.

Even though she's talking about SUSAN, *the above has a first person singular ring to it which doesn't escape* FRED.

FRED. We were talking about Susie, not you.

DORIS *is a little flustered and realizes she is up against someone who can see right through her.*

DORIS. —well—well whether you agree or not I must ask you to respect my wishes regarding Susan. She's *my* responsibility and I must bring her up as I see fit.

As DORIS *exits,* FRED *mumbles an "Okay." He looks after her a moment. Bit by bit he's beginning to understand this girl.*

Dissolve to:

Int. Doris's office—Day—Two shot— DORIS *and* SUSAN. SUSAN *is seated and* DORIS *is pacing. Evidently* DORIS *has been trying to talk some sense into the child.*

SUSAN.—yes, I see what you mean, Mother, but when he talked Dutch to that girl he was so—

DORIS. Susan—I speak French but that doesn't make me Joan of Arc. What I'm trying to explain to you is—*(there is a knock at the door)* Come in.

The door in b.g. opens and KRIS *pokes his head in.*

KRIS. They said you wanted to see me, Mrs. Walker.

DORIS. Yes—please come in.

KRIS *(to* SUSAN *as he enters)*. Hello, there—good to see you again.

SUSAN. It's nice to see *you*.

KRIS. You're awfully lucky, Mrs. Walker. That's a lovely little girl you have there.

DORIS *(impatiently)*. Thank you—and Susan's the reason I asked you to drop down—she's a little confused and maybe you can help to straighten her out.

KRIS. Be glad to.

DORIS. Would you please tell her that you're not *really* Santa Claus—that there actually *is* no such person.

KRIS. I'm sorry to disagree with you, Mrs. Walker, but not only *is* there such a person but here I am to prove it.

DORIS. No, no—you misunderstand. I want you to tell the truth. What is your name?

KRIS. Kris Kringle. *(more interested in* SUSAN*)*. I'll bet you're in the first grade.

SUSAN. Second.

DORIS *(getting a little annoyed)*. I mean your *real* name.

KRIS. That *is* my real name. *(to* SUSAN*)*. Second grade!

SUSAN. It's a progressive school.

DORIS *has gone to the door.*

Angle at door—Shooting past DORIS. *We see secretary in b.g. at desk.*

DORIS. Could I have this gentleman's employment card, please?

Two shot— KRIS *and* SUSAN.

KRIS. That hat is very cute. Where did you get such a lovely outfit?

SUSAN *(as if everyone ought to know)*. Macy's! We get ten per cent off.

DORIS *enters the shot, disturbed at being totally ignored.*

DORIS. Please don't feel that you have to keep pretending for Susan's benefit—she's an intelligent child and always wants to know the absolute truth.

KRIS. Good—because I always tell the absolute truth. *(back to* SUSAN*)*. Now about your school, what's the name of your teacher?

During the last DORIS *fumes and the door is heard to open.*

SECRETARY'S VOICE. Here it is, Mrs. Walker.

DORIS *exits from scene.*

Angle at door. As DORIS *takes card secretary exits.* DORIS *looks at card—her eyes pop.*

Insert—Card. It reads:
NAME: KRIS KRINGLE

ADDRESS: BROOK'S MEMORIAL HOME
         126 Maplewood Dr.,
         Great Neck, LONG ISLAND

AGE: As old as my tongue and a little bit older than my teeth.

Back to scene. DORIS *doesn't have to read any further. She is suddenly struck with the horrifying thought that the man is nuts. Gingerly she goes back to* SUSAN, *camera panning.*

DORIS. Susan, dear—you go in and talk to Miss Adams for a few minutes—I'll be right with you.

SUSAN *(getting up)*. All right. *(to* KRIS*)*. Goodbye.

KRIS. Goodbye, young lady—hope to see you again.

SUSAN. Thank you—I hope so too.

SUSAN *exits.* DORIS *manages to keep her distance from* KRIS.

DORIS. I'm sorry, Mr.—er—
KRIS. Kringle.

DORIS *can't get herself to say the name.*

DORIS. I'm sorry but we're going to have to make a change.

KRIS *(puzzled)*. Change?

DORIS. Yes—the Santa Claus we had two years ago is back in town and I feel we owe it to him to—

KRIS *(in all innocence)*. Have I done something wrong?

DORIS. No—no—but—*(the inter-office communicator buzzes;* DORIS *flips a switch)* Yes?

WOMAN'S VOICE ON MACHINE. Mr. Macy wants to see you immediately.

DORIS's *heart sinks as she flips the key. So* MACY *knows too.*

DORIS. Please sit down. I'll be right back and sign your pay voucher.

DORIS *makes a circular path to the door and exits.* KRIS's *eyes follow her—he's really puzzled. What could he have possibly done to be discharged.*

Dissolve to:

Int. Outer Macy office—Day. Angle as DORIS *comes across room.*

SECRETARY. Go right in, Mrs. Walker—Mr. Macy's waiting.

Camera pans as DORIS *crosses in front of us and goes to a door marked "Mr. Macy—Private." She opens door, affording us a view of* MACY's *office. We see* MACY *standing behind his desk. Six or seven men are listening.*

MACY *(as door opens).* —the effect that this will have on the public is—*(seeing Doris).* Oh—come in, Mrs. Walker—

Int. MACY's *office—Angle* MACY *at desk.* MR. MACY, *nearing sixty, is businesslike, pleasant, enthusiastic.*

MACY. —I've been telling these gentlemen of the new policy you and Mr. Shellhammer initiated—

Reverse angle. Group listening—as DORIS *comes to f.g. She doesn't know what he's talking about.*

MACY'S VOICE. I can't say that I approve of your not consulting the advertising department first but in the face of this tremendous response on the part of the public—I can't be angry with you.

During the above DORIS *is completely at sea.* SHELLHAMMER, *who stands next to her, flashes her one of those "I'll explain later" looks.*

Macy at desk.

MACY. Now to continue, gentlemen. I admit that on the face of it this plan sounds idiotic and impossible. Imagine—Macy's Santa Claus sending customers to Gimbel's!

Close-up— DORIS, *as this news hits her!*

MACY'S VOICE. But, gentlemen, you cannot argue with success.

MACY *as he runs his hands through a stack of messages on his desk.*

MACY. Look at this! Telegrams, messages, telephone calls—the Governor's wife, the Mayor's wife. Over five hundred thankful parents expressing undying gratitude to Macy's. Never, in my entire career, have I seen such a tremendous and immediate response to a merchandising policy.

Camera pulls back as MACY *walks around his desk.*

MACY. And I'm positive that if we expand our policy we will expand our results as well. Therefore, from now on not only will our Santa Claus continue in this manner but I want *every* sales person in this store to do precisely the same thing.

Flash of group listening. This is unheard of and they are amazed.

MACY'S VOICE. If we haven't got exactly the article the customer wants—

MACY. *Moving shot as he walks amongst the gathering, driving home points first to one and then another.*

MACY. —we'll send him where he *can* get it. No high-pressuring and forcing a customer to take something he really doesn't want. We'll be known as the helpful store, the friendly store, the store with a heart, the store that places public service ahead of profits!—and consequently we'll make more profit than ever before. *(Camera pans him to the door as he continues)* Now I don't want to keep you any longer—it's late, we're all tired and we want to get home for dinner—so we'll continue first thing in the morning.

Angle at door. MACY *has opened the door and the group starts to file out.*

MACY. In the meantime you boys get together and figure out the best way to promote this thing.

There goes their dinner—and their evening. Nevertheless they manage to muster up cheerful "Yes, sirs" and "Goodnights" as they exit. Now DORIS *and* SHELLHAMMER *start out.*

MACY. I want to thank you two again—and in your Christmas envelopes you'll find a more practical expression of my gratitude.

DORIS *and* SHELLHAMMER. Thank you, Mr. Macy.

MACY. And tell that Santa Claus I won't forget him either. *(a sudden thought).* Say— we don't want to run any chance of losing him—might as well put him under contract— we can find something else for him to do during the rest of the year.

DORIS *pales and walks out weakly.*
SHELLHAMMER *utters a rather obsequious "Yes, Mr. Macy" and follows.*

Ext. Macy's office, as they come out. MACY *closes door. Camera trucks with them.* DORIS *walks as if in a trance.*

SHELLHAMMER *(excitedly).* Imagine, a bonus! He just assumed it was our idea so I *(noticing* DORIS's *blank expression)* What's the matter?

DORIS *(weakly).* I fired him.

SHELLHAMMER. Who?

DORIS. Santa Claus.

SHELLHAMMER *(in a high soprano).* What?

DORIS. He's crazy. He thinks he *is* Santa Claus.

SHELLHAMMER. I don't care if he thinks he's the Easter Bunny, you've got to get him back.

DORIS. But he's insane, I tell you. We'll just have to hire somebody else and have him do the same thing.

SHELLHAMMER. Oh, no, no. You heard what Mr. Macy said—we've *got* to keep him.

DORIS. But what if he should have a sudden fit or something? No, no—I better tell Mr. Macy

SHELLHAMMER *(stopping her).* But maybe he's just a *little* crazy, like painters or composers or some of those men in Washington. We can't be sure until he's been examined! If you fire him and then we find out he wasn't *really* crazy—Mr. Macy will have *us* examined—*and fired.*

DORIS *(thoughtfully).* I suppose we should be sure. We could have Mr. Sawyer talk to him.

SHELLHAMMER. Of course! He's a psychologist! That's what he's paid for—to examine employees! Now until we get his report we won't say a word.

DORIS. I'll get in touch with him right away. *(she starts out)*

SHELLHAMMER. But first get that Santa Claus back—the examination won't be worth a thing without the patient.

Dissolve to:

Int. Doris's office—Day—Two shot—Doris and Kris.

DORIS. *(sweetly).* —it was just because I felt we owed it to him but Mr. Macy suggested we find something else for the other Santa Claus and keep you on by all means.

KRIS. Well—thank you. That's mighty good news.

DORIS. Then you'll be here in the morning, then?

KRIS. I certainly will! You see, Mrs. Walker, this is quite an opportunity for me. For the last fifty years or so I've been getting more and more worried about Christmas. It seems we're all so busy trying to beat the other fellow in making things go faster and look shinier, and cost less, that Christmas and I are sort of getting lost in the shuffle.

DORIS *is not interested, but at least she'll try to talk him out of it to end the conversation.*

DORIS. Oh, I don't think so. Christmas is still Christmas.

KRIS *(shakes his head).* Christmas isn't just a day—it's a frame of mind—and that's what's been changing. That's why I'm glad I'm here—maybe I can do something about it. And I'm glad I met you and your daughter—you two are a test case for me.

DORIS *(puzzled).* We are?

KRIS. Yes—you're sort of the whole thing in miniature. If I can win you over, then there's still hope. If not—I guess I'm through. *(starts for door)* But I'm warning you I don't give up easily. Goodnight.

DORIS. Goodnight. *(remembering)* Oh—Mr. Kringle. The first thing tomorrow morning will you report to Mr. Sawyer's office, please.

KRIS. Sawyer?

DORIS. Yes—he'll give you a little examination. We do it with all our employees.

KRIS *(not to be fooled).* A mental examination?

DORIS *(in a spot).* Well—it's—er—

KRIS *(not disturbed in the least).* Oh, I don't mind. I've taken dozens of them and never failed one yet. Know them by heart. *(now Kris rattles off a test)* How many days in the week? Seven! How many fingers do you see? *(he holds up four)* Four! Muscular-coordination test. *(he stands with arms extended and touches the tip of his nose first with a finger of his right hand, then his left)* No damage to the nervous system. Who was the first President of the United States? George Washington. Who was the vice-president under John Quincy Adams? Daniel D. Tompkins—and I'll bet your Mr. Sawyer doesn't know that! *(smiling as he exits)* Goodnight!

DORIS, *as she looks after him thoughtfully. She picks up his employment card, glances at it, then lifts the receiver on phone.*

DORIS *(on phone).* Miss Adams—get me the Brooks Memorial Home in Great Neck—it's a home for old people—that's right. I want to speak to the doctor in charge.

Fade out:

Fade in. Int. Mr. Sawyer's Office—Day—Close shot—Sawyer behind desk, as he jots down his findings. Around fifty, he has sharp features which seem to emphasize his self-importance. His speech is clipped and biting. Like a great many nervous people he has the habit of tugging at his left eyebrow with his free hand.

SAWYER. How many days in the week?

Angle— KRIS, *seated across desk. He is dressed in his street clothes, his hat and cane on his lap. In spite of* SAWYER'S *manner* KRIS *is pleasant and cooperative.*

KRIS *(pleasantly).* Seven.

Two shot:

SAWYER. Who was the first President of the United States?
KRIS. George Washington.
SAWYER. How much is three times five?
KRIS. You asked me that before—*(just being helpful)* You'll find the answer right there at the bottom of the—

It is obvious SAWYER *has forgotten—nevertheless, he'd never admit it.*

SAWYER *(tugging at his eyebrow).* I'm conducting this examination. How much is three times five?
KRIS. Same as it was before—fifteen. You're rather nervous, aren't you, Mr. Sawyer? Do you get enough sleep?
SAWYER. My personal habits are of no concern to you!
KRIS *(friendly).* I'm sorry—it's just that I hate to see anyone so tied up in—

SAWYER *interrupts by thrusting three fingers in front of* KRIS.

SAWYER. How many fingers do you see?
KRIS. Three. *(then he takes Sawyer's hand to look more closely)* You bite your nails, too.

SAWYER *quickly pulls his hand away, angrily.*

SAWYER. Now I want you to stand with your feet together and your arms extended, then I want you—
KRIS *(rising).* The muscular coordination test? Surely, be glad to.

KRIS *begins to touch his nose with the tips of his fingers expertly.*

KRIS *(as he does it; genuinely interested)* You know—sometimes the cause for nervous habits like yours is not obvious. Often they're the

result of an insecurity. Are you happy at home, Mr. Sawyer?

This is too much for SAWYER.

SAWYER. That will be all, Mr. Kringle—the examination is over. You may go.

KRIS *answers with a friendly "Thank you," picks up his hat and cane and starts.*

SAWYER *(indicating private door).* You can go out that way. *(then like most insecure people he can't resist the chance to show how secure he is)* And it may interest you to know I've been happily married for twenty-six years.
KRIS *(pleased).* Oh—I'm delighted to hear it. Goodbye. *(he exits)*

SAWYER *at desk. He picks up phone and buzzes his secretary.*

SAWYER *(on phone).* Get me Mrs. Walker.

Int. Outer office. SECRETARY *at desk.*

SECRETARY. Yes, sir. And your wife is on six-seven-two—she says it's very important.

Int. SAWYER'S *Office—* SAWYER *at desk. Angrily he flips up the proper key and starts right in.*

SAWYER. Agnes, how many times have I told you not to bother me at the office—No! Not a penny! I give you a liberal allowance and it's up to you to run the house on it! If that fat, stupid brother of yours would get a job you wouldn't have to be pestering me all the time! *(he slams down the receiver, flips another key and picks up phone again)* Mrs. Walker, I'd like to talk to you right away about this Kringle fellow.

Int. DORIS'S *office.* DORIS *is at the phone. Angle also includes* SHELLHAMMER *and* DR. PIERCE *seated nearby.*

DORIS. Come right in. Dr. Pierce from the Brooks Home is here and it would be a good time to settle the whole matter. *(she hangs up)* Sorry, Doctor, but that was Mr. Sawyer, the gentleman I was telling you about.
DR. PIERCE. Oh, yes—
DORIS. I can't tell you how much we appreciate your giving us your time, Doctor—
DR. PIERCE. Not at all. As a matter of fact, I was going to call *you* today. I had a feeling along about now you people would be *wondering* about Kris.

The door opens and MR. SAWYER *enters.*

DORIS. Dr. Pierce—Mr. Sawyer.

The two men exchange greetings. SAWYER *turns to* DORIS.

SAWYER. Mrs. Walker—after giving this man a comprehensive examination, it is my considered opinion he should be dismissed immediately.

DORIS *(she was afraid of this)*. Really? He failed to pass the examination?

SAWYER. —er—yes.

DR. PIERCE. He didn't answer the question correctly?

SAWYER. Well—yes, he did—but there was a complete lack of concentration. He kept changing the subject—he was even questioning *me*. I don't think there's any doubt about it—he should be placed in a mental institution.

DR. PIERCE. I don't agree, Mr. Sawyer. People are only institutionalized to prevent them from harming themselves or other people. Mr. Kringle is incapable of either. His is a delusion for good—he only wants to be friendly and helpful.

SHELLHAMMER *(hoping his word will add some weight)*. That's what I feel, too.

DR. PIERCE. There are thousands of people walking around with similar delusions—living perfectly normal lives in every other respect. A famous example is that fellow—er—I can't think of his name—but for years he has insisted he's a Russian prince. There's been all kinds of evidence to prove him wrong, but nothing has shaken his story. Is he in an institution? No—he owns a famous restaurant in Hollywood and is a highly respected citizen.

SAWYER *(pompously)*. Dr. Pierce, I have made a great study of abnormal psychology. I have found from experience that when a fixed delusion is challenged, the deluded is apt to become violent.

DR. PIERCE. I'm afraid, I have to disagree again, Mr. Sawyer. If you tell Kris that there is no Santa Claus I grant you he will argue the point but he will not become violent.

SAWYER. His whole manner suggests aggressiveness—Look at the way he carries that cane—he's never without it!

DR. PIERCE. I know Kris always carries a cane—but surely you are not implying he would use the cane as a weapon!

SAWYER *realizes it is useless to discuss the matter with* DR. PIERCE. *Becoming more pompous, he turns to* DORIS.

SAWYER. Mrs. Walker, naturally I cannot discharge this man—that is up to you—but you asked for my opinion and I have given it to you. So when he exhibits his latent maniacal tendencies—which I assure you he will—please realize the responsibility is completely yours.

SAWYER *turns on his heel and exits. They all look after him.*

DR. PIERCE *(smiling)*. Speaking of delusions—!

DORIS. Now we're right back where we were.

SHELLHAMMER. No, we're not! After listening to Dr. Pierce I feel perfectly confident.

DORIS. But if anything happens you won't be blamed—I will.

DR. PIERCE. Mrs. Walker, nothing's going to happen. Please don't feel that what I have said was prompted by my affection for Kris. My specialty is geriatrics—(SHELLHAMMER'S *questioning eyes cause him to add)*—the treatment of the diseases of old age—I've had quite a bit of experience and *I* assure you Kris has no—*(with mock seriousness)*—"latent maniacal tendencies."

It's a big decision and DORIS *thinks it over.*

DR. PIERCE. You probably want to discuss this with Mr. Shellhammer, so I'll be on my way. May I see Kris?

DORIS. Why certainly, Doctor. *(rising)* Use the employees' elevator—It's much quicker.

SHELLHAMMER. The same one you came up on.

DR. PIERCE *(trying to get his bearings)* Let's see—I'm a little twisted—

DORIS *(crossing)*. Here—I'll show you—

Int. Outer office, as DR. PIERCE, DORIS *and* SHELLHAMMER *pass through and exit.*

SHELLHAMMER. I want to thank you again, Doctor—*(pointedly, hoping it will sway* DORIS*)* You've made me feel much easier. *I* haven't a doubt in the world about Kris any more.

Int. Corridor outside DORIS'S *office, as they enter.* DORIS *is still giving it plenty of thought. Camera moves ahead of them as they walk down corridor.*

DORIS *(trying to reach a conclusion)*. How long have you known Kris, Doctor?

DR. PIERCE. Not too long—he wandered into the home about eight months ago, looked the place over, and said, "It'll do"—and just stayed.

DORIS. Did he ever tell you his real name?

DR. PIERCE. No—but I rather think it's Kris Kringle. *(the others look amazed)* I mean—I think the family name was Kringle and a couple of foolish parents called him Kris. You've met "cute" people like that, haven't you? *(grimacing at the thought)* I once knew a girl called *Olive Tree*.

DORIS. But if this delusion is based on a desire to be young again—why does he identify himself with a figure of old age—Santa Claus?

DR. PIERCE *(smiling–shaking his head)*. Santa Claus is *immortal*—he goes on and on.

SHELLHAMMER. Maybe that's why Mr. Kringle is so anxious to keep the spirit of Christmas alive.

DR. PIERCE. Exactly! If it disappears—so does Santa Claus, and Kris' symbol of immortality is gone.

SHELLHAMMER *(surprised)*. You mean I was right?

The DOCTOR *nods.*

SHELLHAMMER *(proudly)*. Well—!

DORIS. I don't want to deprive him of the chance to earn a little money—I'm sure he can use it—but you understand my position, Doctor. If there's the slightest possibility of his becoming violent or even getting into trouble I couldn't—

SHELLHAMMER. But what possible trouble could he get into?

DORIS. All that's got to happen is for a policeman to ask him his name—big argument—whisttt—Bellevue.

They have reached the elevator and stop.

DR. PIERCE. Well, you can prevent that very simply. There must be someone here at the store who could rent a room out to him—then they could go to and from work together. I'd just as soon he didn't take that long train ride out to Great Neck twice a day.

SHELLHAMMER. That would solve everything. If someone were with him they could steer him away from any trouble.

DORIS *(thoughtfully)*. You mean sort of take custody of him—*(the Doctor nods)* Would he agree to that?

The elevator door behind them opens.

DR. PIERCE. I'll talk to him—I'm sure he will.

DORIS. In that case, tell him he can stay.

DR. PIERCE *(stepping into elevator)*. Good. Thank you—

DORIS. It's the seventh floor. And thanks again.

The elevator door closes. They start walking back, camera trucking.

SHELLHAMMER. I'm sure you've made a wise decision. Now let's see—do you know anybody who could rent him a room?

DORIS *(nods)*. You.

SHELLHAMMER *(hedging)*. Well—er—

DORIS. You son's away at school—what about his room?

SHELLHAMMER. Well—uh—I don't mind—be glad to—but I'm positive Mrs. Shellhammer wouldn't care for the idea. *(suddenly)* Say! I have a thought. We always have martinis before dinner. I'll make them double strength tonight—I'm sure after a couple of them she'll be more receptive to the idea.

DORIS. But Kris finishes work at five-thirty—what about in-between time?

SHELLHAMMER. You take him home to dinner and I'll call you as soon as my wife's plas . . . feeling gay.

DORIS. Oh, no—I—

SHELLHAMMER *(peeved)*. Really, Mrs. Walker! If I'm willing to have my wife have a big headache in the morning, the least you can do is have a little headache tonight.

DORIS *(amused)*. All right.

They walk out of shot—

Dissolve to:

Int. DORIS' *kitchen–night.* DORIS *and* FRED *are working in the tiny kitchen preparing dinner.*

DORIS. Cleo's mother *would* have to have a sprained ankle today of all days.

FRED. Very inconsiderate of her. But I don't think I'm doing such a bad job.

DORIS. You're doing a very good one and I don't think I thanked you enough for coming to dinner—I just couldn't see Susan and me sitting down alone with him.

FRED. I suppose I should be insulted being here in the sole capacity of a buffer—but I'm not. As a matter of fact I hope he comes to dinner often.

DORIS *(definitely)*. He won't.

FRED. Why not? He's a completely fantastic, delightful and unselfish human being, and they're as rare as dinosaurs these days.

DORIS. And consequently he represents a world that doesn't exist. Therefore he's a bad influence on a child who's growing up in the world as it *does* exist.

FRED *pushes the swinging door, which leads to the living room, open a trifle and peers out.*

FRED. He doesn't look like such a bad influence.

Angle—At door. Shooting past FRED *in f.g. Through the crack we see* KRIS *and* SUSAN *across the living room.*

Int. Living room—Two shot— KRIS *and* SUSAN. *She is in pajamas and robe, and is lying on floor crayoning a color book.*

KRIS. —and what sort of games do you play with the children here in the apartment building?

SUSAN. I don't play much with them—they play silly games.

KRIS. They do?

SUSAN. Like today they were in the basement playing Zoo and all of them were animals. When I came down, Homer—he was supposed to be the Zoo Keeper—he said, "What kind of an animal are you?" And I said, "I'm not an animal, I'm a girl," and he said, "Only animals allowed here—goodbye," so I came upstairs.

KRIS. Well, why didn't you tell him you were a bear or a lion?

SUSAN. Because I'm *not* a bear or a lion.

KRIS. But the other children were only children and they were pretending to be animals.

SUSAN. That's what makes the game so silly.

KRIS. I don't think so. It sounds like a wonderful game to me. Of course, in order to play it, you've got to have an imagination. Do you know what the imagination is?

SUSAN. That's when you see things and they're not really there.

KRIS. Well-ll—that can be caused by other things, too. No—to me The Imagination is a place all by itself, a separate country. You've heard of the British nation and the French nation—well, this is The Imagination. It's a wonderful place. (SUSAN *looks very skeptically at him*) How would you like to be able to make snowballs in the summertime or drive a big bus down Fifth Avenue? How would you like to have a ship all your own that makes daily trips to China and Australia? (SUSAN *is still skeptical, but interested*) How would you like to be the Statue of Liberty in the morning and in the afternoon fly south with a flock of geese?

SUSAN *stares disbelievingly for a moment—but then, not wanting to run the risk of missing out on anything, nods ever so slightly.*

KRIS. It's very simple—of course, it takes practice. Now the first thing you do is learn how to pretend. The next time Homer says, "What kind of an animal are you?"—you tell him you're a monkey.

SUSAN. But I don't know how to be a monkey.

KRIS. Sure you do. Now just bend over a little—

Int. Kitchen. DORIS *is draining the water off some vegetables and* FRED *is examining the meat in the broiler.*

FRED *(lightly).* —on the contrary, Haislip, Haislip, MacKenzie, Sherman and Haislip have been very good to me—but being an exceptional lawyer I want to open my own office.

DORIS *(handing him a glass of milk).* Would you put this at Susan's place, please.

FRED *(starting out).* I think you can take the meat out—looks done.

Int. Living room—Angle at kitchen door. As FRED *enters and looks off.*

Two shots—Kris and Susan—Fred's angle. SUSAN *is giving a pretty good imitation of a monkey. Her tongue, tucked under her upper lip, gives the facial characteristics—and with a bent right arm she is scratching herself.*

KRIS. There—that's better. *(seeing* FRED *off).* We're just having our first lesson in pretending.

Three shot.

KRIS *(winking at* FRED*).* And we're doing quite well, too.

SUSAN *(looking at her imitation in a mirror).* Gee! That's good!

Close shot— FRED. *He studies the two for a moment. He can see that* KRIS *could be a wonderful influence on* SUSAN. *An idea strikes him. He glances quickly toward the kitchen, then back to* KRIS. *He puts milk on table. Camera pans him to* KRIS.

FRED. Mr. Kringle, Mrs. Walker just mentioned that they're trying to find a room for you here in town.

KRIS. That's right. Dr. Pierce doesn't like me to make that long trip every day.

FRED. Well—I was just thinking—I'm all alone in my apartment—twin beds—plenty of room—if you'd like to come in I'll be only too happy to have you.

KRIS *(pleased).* Now that's awfully nice of you—

FRED. You could ride down to work and back every day with Mrs. Walker and—

KRIS *(thoughtfully).* Yes—give me a chance to really talk things over with her and besides I—

He glances off.

Angle— SUSAN *at mirror, still entertaining herself as a monkey.*

Two shot— KRIS *and* FRED. KRIS *wants to be close to this child too.*

KRIS. —I could see Susan now and then. Mr. Gailey—it's a deal.

The phone rings. FRED *starts for phone.*

FRED *(as he crosses)*. Good. We'll drive out after dinner and get your things. *(picks up phone)*. Hello. . . . Oh, yes—just a moment. *(camera pans* FRED *toward kitchen door)* Mrs. Walker! Mr. Shellhammer—

At this moment DORIS *comes through the swinging door carrying a couple of serving dishes filled with vegetables. She puts them down on the set table and anxiously answers the phone.*

DORIS. Hello—hello, Mr. Shellhammer—

Int. SHELLHAMMER'S *living room—Night—Close shot—* SHELLHAMMER *at phone.*

SHELLHAMMER. Yes—just a moment—Mrs. Shellhammer would like to talk to you—*(then quietly)* I made the martinis triple strength—she feels wonderful!

Camera pans as SHELLHAMMER *carries the phone, which has a long cord, across the room.*

SHELLHAMMER. Here you are, pet.

Now the couch, with Mrs. Shellhammer on it, comes into view. She is feeling just too, too marvelous for words. Her constant smile is happy, contented and charming—her voice mellow and musical.

MRS. SHELLHAMMER. —why we'd just *loooove* to have Santa Claus stay with us. I think it would be simply *chaaaaarming*.

DORIS *at phone.*

DORIS. —Oh, so do I, Mrs. Shellhammer—just a moment, please—*(she covers receiver; speaks to* KRIS*)* It's Mrs. Shellhammer.

Group shot.

DORIS. They have a lovely room and they'd be only too happy if you'd stay with them.
KRIS. Oh, that's very sweet of them. Please thank them very much but I'm going to stay with Mr. Gailey.
DORIS *(dumbfounded)*. Mr. Gailey?

DORIS *flashes a murderous glance at* FRED, *who smiles weakly and heads for the kitchen.*

FRED. I—I'd better get the meat.
DORIS *(to* KRIS—*trying her best)* But the Shellhammers are much closer to the store—it would be so convenient

KRIS. I know, but I like to be near the Park—besides I wouldn't want to hurt Mr. Gailey's feelings.

Close shot: DORIS *is dead and she knows it. Dully she speaks into the phone.*

DORIS. Mrs. Shellhammer, I'm sorry but he's made other arrangements. *(a pause during which* DORIS *is only half listening. She stares at the kitchen door)* What?—Oh—*(she glances at the phone)* And a Happy New Year to *you*, Mrs. Shellhammer. *(she hangs up, then unenthusiastically)* Dinner is ready.

Int. Kitchen. FRED *holds a platter on which are six steaks. Knowing he's going to catch hell, he glances upward in supplication and then starts out.*

Int. Living room—Table in f.g.—Kitchen door in b.g. DORIS *is throwing ocular daggers at* FRED *as he enters and sets the platter on table.* KRIS *and* SUSAN *are seating themselves.*

SUSAN. Hmmmm! Steak!
FRED. Well, not exactly. It's venison—a friend at the office gave it to me.
DORIS. If you don't like it I've got eggs for you.
SUSAN. But what is it?
DORIS. Venison. Deer meat.
KRIS *(quietly)*. May I have eggs, too? Venison—you understand. I—just—couldn't.
FRED *(it dawns on him)*. Oh, I'm sorry—

Dissolve to:

Int. SUSAN'S *bedroom—Night. Angle at bed.* SUSAN *is in bed—* KRIS *sits on the edge.* SUSAN *is chewing bubble gum.*

KRIS. —but there must be *something* you want for Christmas. Something you haven't even told your mother about.

SUSAN *just looks up at him. Her big eyes reveal that there is* something—*but she's not quite sure whether she can take* KRIS *into her confidence or not.*

KRIS. Why don't you give me a chance?

SUSAN *studies him for another moment then eases out of bed and starts across the room, camera panning. She goes to a small dresser,* opens one of the drawers and digging way down to the bottom where secret things are kept, she pulls out a folded piece of paper. Camera pans her back to KRIS. She hands it to him. KRIS unfolds it.

Insert— Paper in KRIS' *hands. It is a page out of a magazine like House Beautiful and shows a photograph and floor plan of a charming colonial bungalow. The soiled edges and deep creases reveal that it has been unfolded and gazed at many, many times.*

Back to scene.

SUSAN *(quietly).* That's what I want for Christmas.

KRIS. You mean a doll's house like this.

SUSAN *(shaking her head).* A real house. (KRIS *is amazed).* If you're really Santa Claus you can get it for me—and if you can't you're only a nice man with a white beard like Mother says.

KRIS. Now wait a minute, Susie, just because every child can't get his wish, that doesn't mean there isn't a Santa Claus.

SUSAN *(disappointed; climbing back into bed).* That's what I thought you'd say.

KRIS. But don't you see, some children wish for things they couldn't possibly use—like real locomotives or B-29's—

SUSAN. But this isn't like a locomotive or a B-29.

KRIS. It's awful big for a little girl like you. What could you possibly do with a house like this?

SUSAN. Live in it with my mother.

KRIS *is a bit taken aback at her sincerity.*

KRIS. But you've got this lovely apartment.

SUSAN. I don't think it's lovely. I want a backyard with a swing and a

KRIS *is really struck and silent.* SUSAN *stops and studies him for a moment then reaches for the paper he holds.*

SUSAN. I guess you can't get it, huh?

KRIS *(pulling paper back).* I didn't say that.

He looks into her big eyes. He can't disappoint this child. It's obvious this house means everything to her.

KRIS *(quietly).* Well—it's a tall order but I'll do my best. May I keep this picture? (SUSAN *nods)* Goodnight, Susie.

SUSAN. Goodnight, Mr. Kringle.

KRIS *leans over and kisses her and starts out, camera holding on* SUSAN. *The moment the door is heard to close,* SUSAN, *mechanically and*

preoccupied, reaches over and pulls something out of the drawer of the night table. It is a glass half filled with water. Into it she deposits her bubble gum and then replaces the glass in the drawer of the night table.

Dissolve to:

Ext. Brooks Memorial Home—Night. It is a former private mansion. A sign in f.g. reads:

HENRY S. BROOKS MEMORIAL HOME

Dissolve to:

Int. KRIS' *room—Night.* KRIS *is just finishing packing his belongings, talking to* DR. PIERCE *as he does.* FRED *is at the mantle examining the many knickknacks that make* KRIS' *room look like a child's conception of Santa's workshop.*

KRIS. —and don't forget to let me know how Mr. Riddle's operation comes out.

DR. PIERCE. I'll call you as soon as it's over. Well, Kris—I've got to run—so good luck—

KRIS *(dismissing it).* Thank you—I won't say goodbye—after all, I'll be back in a month.

FRED. Goodbye, Doctor—glad to have met you.

DR. PIERCE. Glad to have met *you.*

FRED *(holding up a gadget).* Did you make this, Kris?

KRIS *(nodding).* Hmm—hmmm—Mrs. Mansfield wanted one for Christmas so I— *(then suddenly)* Say—you haven't told me what *you* want for Christmas. What would you like me to bring you?

DR. PIERCE *(smiling tolerantly).* An X-ray machine—we've needed one here for years but the Board seems to feel that new drapes and rugs are more important.

KRIS. X-ray machine. All right, Doctor, you shall have it.

DR. PIERCE *(laughing).* If I get an X-ray machine, I'll know you're Santa Claus, too.

KRIS *smiles his jolly smile.*

KRIS. You'll see—

DR. PIERCE *laughs a "goodbye" and exits.*

Dissolve to:

Int. Corridor Brooks Home—Night. KRIS *and* FRED *stand at the door.* FRED *carries a couple of suitcases. A lot of elderly people are gathered around ad libbing goodbyes. A couple of women are weeping.*

KRIS. Now don't cry, Jenny—I'll see you all Christmas morning.

ELDERLY FAT MAN (*yelling above the ad libs*). If you can get any size 46 shorts at Macy's for me, Kris—grab them.

KRIS. I'll get 'em for you wholesale, Ben.

They all laugh and KRIS *and* FRED *exit.*

Dissolve to:

Int. FRED'S *coupe—Night—(process).*

FRED. —then the moment they graduated he developed a strong aversion to work and a great affinity for the bottle.

KRIS. Oh, that's too bad.

FRED. Then just after Susie was born he walked out one day and she hasn't heard a word from him since.

KRIS. And like a lot of other women she's determined not to give anybody a chance to hurt her again.

FRED (*nodding*). She's crawled into an armadillo shell loaded down with a lot of bitter and cynical ideas and she won't come out even for a minute. Worse than that though, she's dragged Susie in with her.

KRIS. You're rather fond of Mrs. Walker, aren't you?

FRED. Frankly, I'm in love with her—and I think if I could just crack that shell maybe she'd be in love with me. If she'd just break down and have a good cry and admit she's lonely—

During the above KRIS *has been casting a sidelong glance at* FRED—*he's happy* FRED *feels as he does. It's going to make his task much easier.*

Disolve to:

Int. FRED'S *bedroom—Night.* KRIS, *dressed in a nightshirt, is in f.g. cleaning out the pockets of his jacket.* FRED *can be heard brushing his teeth in the bathroom.* KRIS *takes out the picture of* SUSAN'S *house. He looks at it.*

Flash—Insert. The picture of the house.

Back to scene. KRIS *smiles impishly—he starts to go to work on his plan. He adopts a casual tone.*

KRIS. —uh—it's a nice place you've got here.

FRED'S VOICE. And was I lucky to *get* it.

KRIS (*fishing*). You—you like living in Manhattan?

FRED (*entering during following*). Oh, it's all right. Of course, someday I'd like to get a house out on Long Island—not a big place. Just one of those "Junior Partner" deals around Manhasset.

KRIS. Yes—I know the kind you mean. One of those colonial bungalows.

FRED. That or a Cape Cod—

Angle— KRIS. *Satisfied that everything is fine so far, he starts his missionary work. Camera pans him as he crosses, back of* FRED, *toward bed.*

KRIS. —uh—you know I think you're right about Mrs. Walker. A little—er—effort on your part she might crawl out of that shell. Take her to the theatre, to dinner—

FRED. I've tried. She's too busy with her job.

KRIS. Well, try a little harder. Those two are a couple of lost souls and it's up to us to help them. I'll take care of Susie if you take care of her mother.

FRED (*turns off wall light and starts for the bed*). It's a deal.

KRIS. All ready? (*he reaches to turn off bedside light*).

FRED. Oh no, you don't. I'm not going to be cheated this way. All my life I've wondered and now I'm going to find out. (KRIS *is puzzled*) I'm going to learn the answer to a question that has troubled the world for centuries. Does Santa Claus sleep with his whiskers inside or out?

KRIS *smiles, lies back and places his beard on top of the sheet.*

KRIS. Always sleep with them out. Cold air makes them grow.

FRED. Thank you. Now I can sleep peacefully. Goodnight.

He turns off the light. KRIS *mumbles a goodnight in the darkness.*

Fade out.

Fade in.

Int. Macy's Advertising Dept.—Day—Long shot. Along the back wall a number of tables have been placed end to end, making one tremendously long one. Behind this stand a dozen girls a few feet apart. In front of each is a stack of full pages clipped from the daily papers. They are working in the assembly line technique with each girl adding her particular page as an album is passed along table.

Close shot at long table—Moving shot, of an album large enough to hold a full page of a newspaper. Already it contains several such pages. Now a girl's hands come into shot and place on the top a page ad from Wanamaker's. The hands push the album to the next pair of hands which contribute a page announcing the bargains to be found at Klein's. The next girl augments the pile with a Sterns' ad and so we follow it, seeing Sak's, Gimbel's, Sterns', Bloomingdale, Hammacher-Schlemmer, Mac-Creery's, all represented. Finally, the last pair of hands puts the cover of the album in place. On it is printed R. H. MACY & CO.—SHOPPING GUIDE FOR THE CONVENIENCE OF OUR CUSTOMERS.

Dissolve to:

Int. Main Floor—Macy's—Day—Close shot— Advertising album on counter.

SALESMAN'S VOICE.—yes, I know exactly what you want. We don't carry that brand but I think Gimbel's does—let me see—

During the above the salesman's hand enters shot and starts to open album. As it does, we pan up to—

Two shot. Salesman and customer (separated by counter). Behind them we see as long a shot as possible of Macy's main floor. While the salesman finds the proper page the customer, a lady, can't believe her eyes—so she takes out her glasses and glances at the printing on the cover of the album.

SALESMAN. Yes—here it is. I thought I noticed it before. Two-ninety-eight—looks like an exceptional bargain.

CUSTOMER *(a little dazed).* Yes—yes—it does. Thank you.

The salesman mumbles a "Not at all" as the customer, still bewildered, starts away.

Dissolve to:

Ext. Macy's Day Long shot, featuring the big sign: "MACY'S." After establishing the sign camera pans down Broadway and stops at the entrance of another department store a block farther south. The large neon sign reads: "GIMBEL'S."

Dissolve through to:

Int. Mr. Gimbel's Office—Day—Full shot. MR. GIMBEL, *a handsome, kindly gentleman of about sixty, is talking to half a dozen men who are seated about the room. At the moment* MR. GIMBEL *is rather angry.*

MR. GIMBEL.—why didn't one of *you* think of this idea. It's the greatest good-will policy I've ever heard of! Every shopper in New York City suddenly thinks Macy is a benevolent spirit, thinking only of the welfare of the public. *(pointing to himself)* And what does that make Gimbel? Nothing but a profiteering money-grubber! Well, two can play at this game! From now on if we haven't got what the customer wants, send him over to Macy's!!

Dissolve:

Ext. Gimbel's—Day—Long shot. Featuring GIMBEL'S *sign. Camera pans back up Broadway to* MACY'S.

Dissolve to:

Insert—Magazine in DORIS's *hands. It is opened to The Talk of the Town page of the New Yorker, featuring the following quatrain under the familiar heading: "Notes and Comments." It reads:*
The millennium is here
And here's the symbol.
Gimbel loves Macy
And Macy loves Gimbel.

Int. DORIS's *apartment—Day—Two shot—* DORIS *and* FRED. DORIS *is reading the verse to herself. She smiles as she finishes and hands magazine back to* FRED.

DORIS. It's very funny.

FRED. It's the clarion call of a new era. Why if Macy can love Gimbel and vice versa, agreement in the U.N. is child's play.

During the following, DORIS *clears the table of the luncheon dishes, going back and forth to the kitchen.*

DORIS. Wait'll Macy and Gimbel find out that it's costing them business—it'll stop.

FRED. But that's just the point. They're making more than they ever have.

DORIS. I think you and *The New Yorker* are confusing benevolence with inflation

FRED. Then why did all the other stores follow suit?—because they weren't getting the business. And it says here the policy's beginning to spread all over the country. And just think, Kris started the whole thing.

DORIS. It's amazing how a silly idea like that'll catch on.

FRED. I don't think it's silly at all. Kris is right—we've all become too cynical and selfish. It's about time we—

DORIS *(cutting in).* Please, not on Sunday. I hear that going to work and coming home every day Monday through Saturday.

FRED. And you're not impressed?

DORIS *(sarcastically).* Oh, of course I am. He's convinced me in six easy lessons that the world is just a *dandy* place! No matter what the newspapers say, everybody can love everybody. All it takes is a little trust and blind faith. Just do what he says and you'll be happier than you've ever been—

SUSAN *and a half dozen boys and girls of her age come busting into the apartment. All except* HOMER, *who is the Zoo keeper, are animals.* HOMER *is herding them into their proper imaginary cages.*

HOMER. Come on there, you lion—get over there! And *(to* SUSAN*)* —Monkey, you belong over here.
DORIS. What *is* this?

Full shot.

SUSAN *(with plenty imagination)*. Our other Zoo burned down. It was terrible! The flames were as high as mountains! Some of us were burned alive! We just had to find a new Zoo!
DORIS. Well, I—
SUSAN. Oh, please, Mother—we're having so much fun. Please—
DORIS. Well—don't get too excited.

This is enough of an answer for the children. HOMER *takes over.*

HOMER. All right—all animals in their cages.

The kids, as different animals, get under tables, behind chairs, etc.

Angle— SUSAN. *She is behind a ladder-back chair, pretending to be a monkey. Evidently she has practiced—she is quite good and having a wonderful time.*

Angle— DORIS. DORIS *is looking off toward* SUSAN *with mixed emotions. These fantasies are against everything* DORIS *has taught her—and yet the child seems more alive, more enthusiastic than she ever has been.* FRED *appears behind* DORIS. *He looks off toward* SUSAN *and then down at* DORIS. DORIS *is coming around—he's sure of it.* DORIS *turns suddenly to go back into the kitchen and notices that* FRED *has been watching.*

Int. Kitchen, as DORIS *enters and goes to sink. She is a bit self-conscious at being caught. She does her best to cover up, not being capable of admitting that* KRIS's *influence on the child might be a good one.*

DORIS. Now she'll be having nightmares for weeks.
FRED *(quietly)*. But she'll be having a lot of fun in the daytime.

DORIS *silently plunges into the dishes.* FRED *tries to hide an amused smile as he hands her a dish.*

Fade out.

Fade in.

Int. Seventh Floor Macy's—Long shot. The floor is deserted except for a few guards and KRIS *who, at the moment, is coming toward camera calling cheery "goodnights" to the guards. When he reaches f.g., he sees someone off. Camera pans him to* FRED *who stands waiting.*

KRIS. Hello, Fred! Good to see you.
FRED *(a little down)*. Hello, Kris.

KRIS *awaits some news from* FRED *which isn't forthcoming.*

KRIS. Well?
FRED *(shakes his head)*. Do you know anybody who can use two good seats for "Annie Get Your Gun"?
KRIS. She's working again tonight, huh?

FRED *nods and the two start for escalator.*

FRED. This saving her soul and winning her heart at the same time is all right but I can't do it if she's going to spend all of her time loving R. H. Macy and Company.
KRIS. Have you made *any* progress?
FRED. Well, I call her Doris and she calls me Fred, but that's as far as it's gone.

They get on the escalator.

Dissolve to:

Int. Second floor, as KRIS *and* FRED *come off the escalator and walk to the next section, which eventually takes them to the main floor. The camera rides the escalator with them.*

KRIS. You know I think this working every night is just a defense. I think she's lonely and miserable—and I think she's *afraid* to be alone with you for fear she'll break down and admit it.
FRED. Could be. Well—we'll try again tomorrow night. You want to see the show?
KRIS *(thoughtfully)*. No, thanks—not tonight.
FRED. I'll turn the tickets in. Why don't we have dinner together and then go home and play a game of chess?
KRIS *(wisely)*. So you're going to be my caretaker again tonight, huh?
FRED *(not too convincingly)*. Oh, no. I just thought that—

They have reached the main floor.

KRIS *(smiling).* I might get into trouble. All right—you go tell her not to worry—I'll meet you at the locker room in ten minutes.

FRED *exits.* KRIS *looks after him a moment then starts away.* MR. SAWYER *approaches.*

KRIS. Hello, Mr. Sawyer.

MR. SAWYER *grunts an unhappy "Hello."*

KRIS. How are your nails coming along?

KRIS *leans forward to look but* SAWYER *angrily pulls his hand away and stalks out of scene.*

Dissolve to:

Insert—Wrist watch. The time is 6:35.

Int. corridor outside employees' locker room. FRED *is looking at his watch. Several male employees file out but no* KRIS. FRED *is puzzled. He enters the locker room.*

Int. Locker room, as FRED *enters.* ALFRED, *the locker boy, stands by the bulletin board.*

FRED. Pardon me, have you seen Mr. Kringle?

ALFRED. Oh, Kris left already—must be twenty minutes ago. Went out the back door.

Worried, FRED *hurries out.*

Dissolve to:

Int. DORIS' *Office—Night.* DORIS *is dialing a phone with one eye on a telephone book.*

FRED. —I guess he just got tired of being looked after like a child. He wanted to assert himself.

DORIS. That's what I'm afraid of. *(on phone)* Psychiatric ward, please.

FRED. Who are you calling?

DORIS. I thought I'd start with Bellevue.

FRED. But he hasn't had time to—

DORIS. Hello—has anybody been brought in by the name of Kris Kringle? He says he's Santa Claus.

Int. Bellevue. A young interne sits at a desk (just a set piece).

INTERNE. I can offer you a Robin Hood, two Napoleons and a Rasputin, but no Santa Claus.

Dissolve to:

Int. DORIS' *Office—Night.* FRED *is at the phone. He mumbles a discouraged "Thank you" and hangs up.*

FRED. That makes four police stations, three hospitals and the Zoo—it's no use. All you can do is keep your fingers crossed.

DORIS. But if he gets into any kind of trouble the papers are sure to pick it up. Then what happens?

FRED. It's not your fault. Don't worry—they won't fire you for it.

DORIS. I'm not worried about myself. I'm thinking about Kris.

FRED *(pleasantly surprised).* Isn't that a little out of character for you? Getting sentimental about an eccentric old man?

DORIS. It's not a question of sentiment. It's just that he's—he's—*(she can't find the words)*

FRED. Yes—I know just what you mean. I feel the same way.

DORIS *grabs her hat and coat almost angrily. She's weakened and she's annoyed with herself for doing it. She starts for the door.* FRED *follows, smiling.*

Int. SUSAN's *bedroom—Night.* SUSAN *is in bed,* KRIS *sits on the edge.* CLEO *is at the door.* SUSAN *is chewing bubble gum. They ad lib good nights as* CLEO *exits.*

KRIS. How would you like me to sing a little goodnight song?

SUSAN. If you want to.

KRIS. Doesn't your mother sing to you at night?

SUSAN. No—why should she?

KRIS. No reason—I just think it's kind of nice.

KRIS *starts to sing a simple nursery rhyme. During this* SUSAN *is blowing a big bubble. Presently* KRIS's *singing peters out as he stares fascinated at the big bubble.*

Dissolve to:

Int. SUSAN's *bedroom—Night—Close shot—* KRIS. *He is now chewing a piece of bubble gum.*

KRIS *(ready).* Here goes.

He starts to tongue the gum into position.

Out.

Close shot— SUSAN. *She doesn't want to discourage him so she doesn't say anything. However, a little frightened of what might happen, she runs her fingers over her own chin as if saying, "Watch out for the beard." Now her eyes grow wider as the bubble evidently be-*

comes larger. Presently a look of panic comes over her—then a pop is heard. SUSAN *closes her eyes almost in pain.*

Dissolve to:

Int. FRED'S *bedroom—Night—Close-up.* KRIS *in nightgown—shooting into a mirror. With comb, tweezers, brush, cleaning fluid, etc., he is working hard to get the bubble gum out of his whiskers. A door is heard to open.*

Int. FRED'S *living room.* FRED *has just entered the apartment. Puzzled at seeing lights on, he looks around and listens. A few "ouches" are heard froom the bedroom.*

FRED *(starting).* Kris?

Int. Bedroom. Shooting past KRIS *at mirror.*

KRIS. Hmmm?

FRED *hurries in.*

FRED. We've been looking all over for you. Where have you been?

KRIS. Where you haven't been looking. *(wisely)* So you had a little time alone together, huh?

Now it dawns on FRED.

FRED. So that's it!

KRIS *(nodding).* Now go tell her you found me and that'll give you a little *more* time together. *(Fred smiles and starts to leave)* But before you do, let me give you a word of advice. *(Fred bends a serious ear)* If you ever grow a beard, never chew bubble gum.

As FRED *starts out—*

Dissolve to:

Int. DORIS' *apartment—Night. A doorbell is heard to ring. Presently* DORIS *enters from the bedroom and crosses to door. She is putting a robe on as she crosses.*

Angle at door, as DORIS *opens it, revealing* FRED *in hall.*

FRED. Well, I found out where he is—he's in all kinds of trouble.

DORIS *(fearing the worst).* Oh, no!

FRED *(pointing toward his apartment).* He's got bubble gum in his whiskers.

DORIS. You mean he was—Why didn't he answer the phone?

FRED. It seems he's playing cupid as well as Santa Claus.

DORIS *(baffled).* What?

FRED. He feels we're two rather nice people and we should spend more time together. He knew we'd go looking for him.

DORIS *is a little embarrassed.*

DORIS. Well—I'm glad he's all right. *(starts to ease door closed)*

FRED. Where do you want to look for him tomorrow night?

DORIS. Tomorrow night?

FRED. Oh, he's going to keep disappearing, I promise you—unless, of course, he sees we can get together on our own occasionally. *(*DORIS *is skeptical)* So if you don't like the idea of touring the police stations you better ask me in for a cup of coffee.

DORIS *is undecided. Finally she opens the door wider and* FRED *steps in. As they move into the living room,* SUSAN *is heard mumbling and moaning in her sleep.* DORIS *listens briefly at the hall door.*

FRED. Sounds like somebody's dreaming.

DORIS. And I don't wonder. Kris has been filling her with bean stalks and giants and— *(starting for kitchen)* Would you like a sandwich?

FRED. No, thanks—just a cup of coffee.

DORIS *exits into the kitchen.* FRED *walks over to the window and peeks out.*

FRED'S *apartment window—* FRED'S *angle.* KRIS'S *head is visible above the sill.*

Int. DORIS' *apartment—Angle at window.* FRED *smiles.*

Dissolve to:

Int. DORIS' *apartment—Angle at table.* DORIS *and* FRED *are sitting, having coffee.* DORIS *is looking out of the corner of her eye toward* KRIS.

DORIS. Is Peeping Tom still there? *(*FRED *glances; then nods)* Now I know what to get him for Christmas—binoculars.

There is a sudden frightened, piercing scream from SUSAN. FRED *and* DORIS *rush out of the room.*

Int. SUSAN'S *room. Shooting past* SUSAN *in bed. Door in b.g. The room is dark.* SUSAN, *half asleep, half awake, is crying fearfully. The door opens, the light is switched on and* DORIS, *with* FRED *a step behind her, starts for the bed.*

SUSAN. Uncle Fred, Uncle Fred!

FRED *comes to the bed and takes* SUSAN *in his arms.*

FRED. Now, now, Susie—it's all right. It was only a dream—it's all over.

SUSAN *(clinging to him desperately)*. Uncle Fred, Uncle Fred!

Close shot—DORIS *near door. She has stopped when* FRED *went to the bedside. She looks off at the two, deeply disturbed. In a moment of fear and insecurity her daughter has called out for a comparative stranger rather than herself. It's hard to take and it hurts. Over this we hear* FRED's *and* SUSAN's *voices.*

FRED'S VOICE. Now there's nothing to worry about, Susie—it didn't really happen—it was just a dream.

SUSAN'S VOICE. I was way down, down—and I couldn't get out.

Another angle. FRED *and* SUSAN *in f.g.,* DORIS *in b.g.*

FRED *(comforting her)*. Well, you're out now, Susie—and we're all here.

SUSAN. I was at the bottom—I was reaching, reaching, but there was nobody there to grab my hand.

During the above DORIS *has started forward, then checks herself.*

Close shot—DORIS.

FRED'S VOICE. Well, you lie down and we'll talk about something else.

During the above DORIS *turns and quietly starts to leave the room.*

Another angle. FRED *and* SUSAN *in f.g.,* DORIS *walking toward door in b.g. As he eases the child back into the bed* FRED *turns, expecting to now hand the situation over to* DORIS. *He sees her exiting. He realizes that this has hit her rather hard.*

Int. Corridor, as DORIS *walks toward living room.*

Int. SUSAN's *room.* FRED *starts to quiet* SUSAN *down by singing to her. He sings a popular tune with a "Goodnight" angle—something perhaps like "Japanese Sandman." During this, it is obvious that* SUSAN *is worried about that moment when she will be left alone again.*

SUSAN *(as* FRED *sings)*. You'll leave the light on, won't you, Uncle Fred? (FRED *nods as he sings; then, after a moment)* You won't close the door, will you? (FRED *shakes his head)*

Int. Living room. The sound of FRED's *singing comes over.* DORIS *sits—she is doing a lot of*

thinking. For the first time her shell seems to have collapsed around her. She is genuinely and femininely worried and a little frightened.

Dissolve to:

Int. Living room—Angle at corridor. FRED, *coming quietly from* SUSAN's *room, stops as he looks off toward* DORIS.

DORIS—FRED's *angle. Even though her face is not visible,* FRED *can see that the experience has had its effect on* DORIS. *Her posture, her back, her shoulders reveal her mood.*

Angle—FRED. *The situation has had its effect on him, too. He finds himself in the odd position of having been proven correct but not liking it. There is no satisfaction in his victory. Sympathetically he starts toward* DORIS.

Angle—DORIS *at window. At the sound of his footsteps crossing the room,* DORIS's *body straightens as she quickly crawls back into her shell of reserve. She is determined not to let anyone notice her own insecurity.*

Another angle, as FRED *enters. He stands behind* DORIS *who doesn't turn.*

FRED *(quietly)*. She's sleeping now. (DORIS *doesn't speak;* FRED *is warm, sincere, and now tries his best to bolster her)* I'm sorry, Doris—but I wouldn't attach too much significance to her calling for me instead of you—After all, it's—it's only natural for a child, especially a little girl, when she's frightened to—to want the protection of a man. It has nothing to do with your relationship with her and with insecurity and—after all, she was half asleep—I—I probably was in her dream so she just called out—

DORIS *turns, showing not a trace of having been shaken.*

DORIS *(casually)*. Probably. Would you like another cup of coffee?

FRED *is a bit surprised at this obvious, almost childish refusal to become emotional.*

FRED. Yes—yes, thanks.

DORIS *exits. Camera holds on* FRED *for a moment as he looks after her. He's puzzled and sorry for her. Camera pans him to* DORIS *at the table.*

FRED *(as he crosses)*. I wish you'd spill some coffee or accidentally break one of those cups.

He has reached DORIS. *She turns questioningly.*

FRED. Because when we don't let ourselves become emotional over big things very often a little, trivial thing, splits us wide open and what you need is a good cry.

DORIS. I've never found that tears help any situation.

FRED *(kindly).* Why don't you give them a chance? I don't mean just about Susie. I'll bet you haven't cried since—well, for years. You've been defiant and determined not to give in to your emotions. It won't work, Doris.

DORIS *seems impervious to any words—but maybe not as much so as she would like* FRED *to believe. She serves the coffee.*

DORIS. Sugar?

FRED. Please. Some day you're going to admit that this defiance and independence hasn't been as satisfying as you'd like everyone to think, and when that happens somebody's going to have to help you—*(tenderly)* and I'd like to be that person. But I can't, nobody can, as long as you—

During the last part of the above, DORIS *has started to sit to drink her coffee. In so doing she has snagged her stocking. She looks down horrified—*

DORIS. Look at that! My best nylons!

This is one of those trivial things FRED *has spoken about—yet it starts the tears going—tears that have been overdue for a long, long time.* FRED, *almost happy at her weeping, embraces her. With her head on his shoulder, she cries copiously.*

FRED *(quietly; tenderly).* That's it, darling—let it go. Don't try to hold it back. Let it go.

And she does.

Angle at FRED's *window—Close-up—* KRIS, *as he looks across the airway and sees them in each other's arms. He is as happy as is humanly possible.*

Int. FRED's *living room.* KRIS, *in his nightshirt, gets up from the window and fairly dances around.*

Fade out.

Fade in.

Int. 7th floor Macy's—Day—Entrance to Santa Claus department. A standing sign blocks the doorway. It reads:

WILL BE BACK IN
A LITTLE WHILE—
I'M FEEDING MY
REINDEER—
SANTA CLAUS

Angle near Santa Claus throne. History is being made— MR. MACY *is shaking hands with* MR. GIMBEL! KRIS *stands between the two, an arm around the shoulders of each. At least a dozen photographers are recording for posterity the most important handshake since Grant and Lee called off the Civil War at Appomattox. There are no children present.*

Three shot— MR. MACY, MR. GIMBEL, KRIS. *They hit a pose and hold it, then, feeling that that was the last one—*

GIMBEL. Now we'll take some at *my* store.

MACY. Of course, of course—but just a moment. I have something I'd like to give our friend here. *(he takes a check out and hands it to* KRIS*)* Just a little something to show my appreciation for everything you've done.

KRIS *(his eyes pop at the amount).* Thank you—Mr. Macy—that's very kind of you.

MR. GIMBEL *can't help but take a sidelong gander at the amount. He, too, is impressed.*

GIMBEL *(to* MACY*).* Never thought you were that generous. *(to* KRIS*)* That's a bit of money—what are you going to do with it?

KRIS. Well, there's a friend of mine—a doctor—he's been very kind to me. He needs an X-ray machine.

MACY. I don't think that's going to be enough.

GIMBEL *(almost aggressively).* I'll make up the difference.

MACY *(to* KRIS*).* Buy it through the store and you can get twenty percent off.

GIMBEL *(proudly).* I can get it for cost.

MACY. Cost?

KRIS *(smiling).* "Nobody, but nobody, undersells Gimbel's."

The two men laugh good-naturedly.

Dissolve to:

Int. Macy's cafeteria—Long shot—Day. KRIS, *carrying a tray, enters shoot. Camera pans him as he crosses to* ALFRED, *the pudgy locker-room boy, who sits dejectedly staring out the window.*

KRIS. Well, Alfred, how about a game of checkers after lunch?

ALFRED. Leave us not, today, Kris—I don' feel like it.

KRIS (worried, sitting). What's the matter, Alfred?

ALFRED. Nothin', nothin'—

KRIS. Something is wrong—now what is it?

ALFRED (ashamed of it). Well—'member I was tellin' you I liked to dress up as Sanna Claus on Crizmas over at the "Y" and give out packages to the young kids? (Kris nods) Well, I was tellin' that to Mr. Sawyer, see, and he says dat's very bad.

KRIS. Sawyer? You mean— (he bites his nails in a nervous imitation)

ALFRED. Dat's the one—(impressed) he's a psy-psychologist, y'know.

KRIS (darkly). Yes, I know. Why is it bad—does he say that?

ALFRED. Oh sure—he says dat guys who dress up like Sanna Claus, see, and give presents away do it because when dey was young dey musta did somethin' bad, and dey feel guilty about it, see, so now dey do somethin' dey think is good to make up fer it, see. It's what he calls a—a guilt complex.

KRIS tries to control his anger.

KRIS. How old are you, Alfred?

ALFRED. Seventeen.

KRIS. Seventeen! Doesn't seem to me like you've had much time to be guilty of anything except overeating.

ALFRED. It's nothin' to laugh about, Kris. It's pretty serious, he says.

KRIS. That's a lot of rubbish, Alfred—and don't listen to it.

ALFRED. Oh, he knows what he's talkin' about—he's been studyin' that stuff for a long time.

KRIS (all right, he'll reason it out for him). What's the basis of this guilt complex you're supposed to have—does he say?

ALFRED. Well, he ain't found out yet—it's probably way down inside of me someplace, see—maybe somethin' that happened to me when I was a baby, he says. It takes time, but he'll do it, he says.

KRIS. You mean, you're going to him again —

ALFRED. Oh sure—I go every day for a little while durin' my lunch hour, see. He don' soak me nuttin'—he's doin' it fer free 'cause I'm an interestin' case, see.

KRIS (controlling his growing anger). What else has he found wrong with you, Alfred.

ALFRED. Well—he says 'cause I dinn go to school very far I feel inferior. Dat's annuder reason I like bein' Sanna Claus, he says, 'cause I'm putting somethin' over on dese young kids. It makes me feel smarter than dey

are, see. An' makes my ego feel better or sumpin'.

KRIS. Anything else?

ALFRED. No—just that I hate my fodder. I dinn know it but he says I do. You know, it's kinda funny—he tole me when I found out all dese things I'd feel better—but I don't—I feel kinda dirty inside knowin' I got all those complexes. An' I worry about 'em at night when I should be sleepin'.

KRIS. And he sees you every day?

ALFRED. Yeah—I just sit in a chair and say anythin' dat comes into my head—

KRIS. Excuse me, Alfred. (quietly furious, rising) A few things have just come into my head and I want to say them to Mr. Sawyer.

He starts away ready to commit murder.

Dissolve to:

Int. SAWYER's Office—Day. SAWYER is at his desk writing. His hat and umbrella are on the corner of the desk. He looks up as the door is heard to burst open.

SAWYER. What do you mean bursting into my—

Angle— KRIS. He leaves the door open. Camera pans him to desk.

KRIS (evenly). Are you a licensed psychiatrist?

SAWYER. I've studied psychology for many years. What business is it of yours?

KRIS. I have great respect for psychiatry and great contempt for meddlers who go around practicing it. You have no more right to analyze Alfred than a dentist has to remove a gall bladder.

SAWYER. I beg your pardon!

KRIS. Your job here I understand is to give intelligence tests. You ought to be horse-whipped—taking a normal, impressionable boy like Alfred and filling him up with complexes and phobias!

SAWYER. I think I am better equipped to judge that than you are.

KRIS. Just because the boy wants to be good and kind to children you tell him he has a guilt complex!

SAWYER. Having the same delusion, you couldn't possibly understand. The boy is definitely maladjusted and I'm helping him.

KRIS. Maladjusted! You talk of maladjustment?! It looks to me as if the patient is running the clinic here!

SAWYER. How dare you! Leave this office immediately!

KRIS. Now either you stop analyzing Alfred or I'm going to tell Mr. Macy what a contemptible, malicious fraud you are!

SAWYER. Get out before I have you thrown out!

Angle— KRIS— shooting past SAWYER. Outer office visible through open door in b.g.

KRIS *(quieting down)*. There's only one way to handle a man like you—you won't listen to reason, you're heartless, you have no humanity—

SAWYER *leans across the desk rather threateningly.*

SAWYER. Are you going to leave?!

KRIS. Yes, there's only one way to handle your kind.

KRIS *quickly picks up the umbrella from the corner of the desk and as if putting a period to the conversation conks* SAWYER *on the head.* SAWYER *falls back into the chair and* KRIS *exits out the private door into the hall. As he strikes* SAWYER, DORIS *and* SHELLHAMMER *can be seen entering outer office in b.g. They see the action, but* KRIS *cannot see them. They rush in.*

Angle— SAWYER— In chair. The blow has stunned him, but that's all— however, when he sees DORIS *and* SHELLHAMMER *approach he fakes unconsciousness.*

Wider angle. As DORIS *and* SHELLHAMMER *reach him they are ad libbing, "What happened?" "Are you hurt?" "He's unconscious." etc.*

Dissolve to:

Int. Examination room— Macy Hospital— Day. SAWYER *is lying on a table.* DORIS *and* SHELLHAMMER *stand by. Throughout the following, the nurse swabs a good-sized lump on his forehead.*

SAWYER. —we were merely talking, but the moment I mentioned Santa Claus—the moment I attacked his delusion he became violent. I told you he had latent maniacal tendencies, well—*(pointing to his head)* I think this proves it!

SHELLHAMMER *(nervously)*. Maybe we'd better have Dr. Pierce give him another examination.

SAWYER *(disgustedly)*. Dr. Pierce! He doesn't know anything about this sort of thing. He's a general practitioner!

SHELLHAMMER *(to* DORIS*)*. You must admit, this is rather serious. Perhaps we had better get a competent psychiatrist.

DORIS. But he's taken dozens of those tests and always passes a hundred percent.

SAWYER *(sarcastically)*. In view of this— *(the bump again)* it's possible his condition has changed!

SHELLHAMMER *(to* DORIS*)*. I don't think we can take any chances—really I don't. And I can't see any harm in it. If he passes the test he can return to work immediately—and if he doesn't—well, it's better we find out.

DORIS *(hates to admit it)*. Yes—I suppose so.

SAWYER. And you better have the examination right away before he tells Mr. Macy—er—before Mr. Macy finds out.

SHELLHAMMER. Oh, yes—oh my, yes. *(to* DORIS*)*. You explain to Mr. Kringle—after all, you're a friend of his and—

DORIS. I won't do it—I *can't* do it. I've grown very fond of him and this would be like coming out and telling him I thought he was insane.

SAWYER *(the bump once more)*. Well, you don't call this acting *normal,* do you?!

DORIS. Of course I don't! But neither are thousands of other old people! This is going to hurt him deeply and I don't want to be the one to do it!

She rushes out to keep from crying—

Dissolve to:

Int. 7th Floor— Macy's— Day— Long shot. Angle at entrance to Santa Claus department, shooting toward KRIS *on throne— kids are lined up in front. Into f.g. walk* SAWYER *and* SHELLHAMMER, *stop and look off.*

Reverse angle— Two shot— SAWYER *and* SHELLHAMMER.

SAWYER. Just a minute—if he sees me or if you mention the word "psychiatrist" it's more or less attacking his delusion again. He's apt to become violent.

SHELLHAMMER. But in front of the children—oh, no—that would be terrible.

SAWYER. You better get him out of the store on some other pretext. Then, once outside, I'll explain it to him—

SHELLHAMMER *(a little nervously)*. All right—if you think that it's better that way.

He exits. Camera holds on SAWYER *for a moment, rather smug about the whole thing.*

Angle— KRIS *on throne. He is just saying goodbye to a child.* SHELLHAMMER *enters.*

SHELLHAMMER *(with forced gaiety)*. Oh, Kris—Mrs. Walker wanted me to tell you that we're going to take some publicity pictures this afternoon down—down at the City Hall—you and the Mayor.

KRIS. Oh, good—like to meet him. Few things I'd like to talk over. *(then remembering)* But I just made an appointment with Mr. Macy at four o'clock—want to talk to him about something.

SHELLHAMMER. Oh, you'll be back in plenty of time. Now there's a car waiting for you downstairs and—it's starting to drizzle—I'll get your coat.

KRIS. Thanks. Be right with you—just want to take care of a few of these kiddies first—

Angle— SAWYER *at entrance. Rather pleasd with himself, he reaches over and takes the standing sign (which reads,* WILL BE BACK IN A LITTLE WHILE—I'M FEEDING MY REINDEER—SANTA CLAUS) *and puts it in the center of the entrance way. He exits.*

Dissolve to:

Ext. Macy's—Employees' entrance—Day. We are shooting through the windows of a limousine. A chauffeur is at the wheel. From the building in f.g. come KRIS *and another man. As they get into the car we see* SAWYER *exit from building, hurry to car and get into the front seat.*

Int. Car—Back seat (process). KRIS *is a bit surprised at seeing* SAWYER.

Front seat—(process).

CHAUFFEUR. Where to?
SAWYER. Bellevue.

Back seat—(process). KRIS, *shocked, starts to move toward the door. The man beside him holds his arm very firmly.* KRIS *sinks back into the seat as the car pulls away. He is dazed and bewildered.*

KRIS *(quietly).* Did she know about this?
SAWYER'S VOICE. Yes—we all discussed it.

Close-up— KRIS. *He sits stunned and deeply hurt.*

Dissolve to:

Ext. Bellevue Hospital—Day—Long shot. We see the limousine pull up in front. As SAWYER, KRIS *and the man alight and start for the building—*

Dissolve to:

Int. Doctor's office—Day—Close shot— KRIS *(process). He is seated in a chair staring dully ahead—dispirited, broken; he seems like a tired old man for the first time. Behind him is a*

window, *heavily screened, and through it we see the East River and Manhattan beyond.*

DR. ROGERS. Who was the first President of the United States, Mr. Kringle?

KRIS *is thinking only of* DORIS *and doesn't even hear the question. He mutters to himself.*

KRIS. How could she do it?

Angle—Two doctors. DR. ROGERS *at a desk, the other stands.*

DR. ROGERS *(not understanding).* What did you say?

Three shot. KRIS *becomes aware that someone is speaking to him. He turns his head toward the doctor and mumbles something that sounds like "What?"*

DR. ROGERS. I asked you a question, Mr. Kringle. Who was the first President of the United States?

KRIS *is about to answer—then stops.*

Close shot— KRIS. *He is thoughtful for a moment. He glances over his shoulder at the view out the window—then after another second of deliberation he turns to the doctor.*

KRIS. The first president? Calvin Coolidge.

Group shot. The doctors exchange a glance. DOCTOR ROGERS *makes a note on a form in front of him.*

DR. ROGERS. How much is two times five?
KRIS *(counting on his fingers).* Eight.
DR. ROGERS *(after again making a notation).* How many days in the week, Mr. Kringle?
KRIS. That all depends on whether it's leap year or not.

As the doctors exchange another sympathetic look—

Dissolve to:

Insert—Office door—Day. It is the typical double door setup of a large tenant. The lettering reads:

HAISLIP, HAISLIP, MacKENZIE,
SHERMAN AND HAISLIP
Attorneys-at-Law

Then under somewhere on the list of a half dozen associates is the name, Frederick M. Gailey.

Dissolve through to:

Int. Fred's office—Day. It is a small junior partner's office. FRED *is behind his desk spouting some legalistic language into a dictaphone. The telephone rings.*

FRED *(lightly into dictaphone).* Excuse me— the telephone's ringing. *(he hangs up dictaphone; answers phone)* Hello—yes—yes, we *(a little worried)* share an apartment together . . . Bellevue!? . . . What happened, is he—

Int. DR. ROGERS' *office—Bellevue—Day—Angle* DR. ROGERS *at phone.*

DR. ROGERS. He's quite comfortable—he'll be with us for a few days and he was wondering if you'd bring over his personal things— yes—yes—In view of his examination I'm afraid I'll have to recommend commitment— yes, I know—but I'd rather discuss it with you in person, Mr. Gailey.

Int. FRED's *office.* FRED *at phone.*

FRED. I'll be right over, Doctor.

Deeply worried, he hangs up and starts out.

Dissolve to:

Int. Psychiatric patient's sitting room—Day. Angle at door, as FRED *and a nurse enter. The nurse indicates* KRIS *offscreen.*

FRED. Thanks.
NURSE. I'll take these.

FRED *hands over the small bag of* KRIS's *belongings. Camera pulls ahead of* FRED *as he crosses the room. It is sparsely furnished. He walks past a dozen or so patients, all dressed alike in hospital bathrobes. They are playing cards, reading—some are just thinking. Presently he arrives beside* KRIS, *who sits in a chair.*

FRED. Hello, Kris.
KRIS *(quietly).* Hello, Fred.

FRED *doesn't quite know how to get into the subject—he finally jumps in with both feet.*

FRED. Why did you do it, Kris? *(*KRIS *is silent)* You deliberately failed that examination, didn't you? *(*KRIS *nods)* Why?

KRIS *has done a lot of thinking—and he speaks calmly with no bitterness, as if expounding a theory.*

KRIS. Why? Because the last few days I've had great hope—I had a feeling Doris was beginning to believe in me—and now I find out she was just humoring me all the time.
FRED. But I just talked to her on the phone—she didn't know anything about this

taking pictures with the Mayor—that was Sawyer's idea.
KRIS. I'm glad of that. But why didn't *she* come to me and explain the whole thing?
FRED. She didn't want to hurt you.
KRIS *(nodding).* But only because I was a nice, kind old man and she felt sorry for me.
FRED. That's not true.
KRIS *(nodding).* Yes, it is. She had doubts and that's why she was—just sorry. If *you'd* have been dragged off here instead of me, she wouldn't have been sorry, she'd have been furious. Belief makes you mad—doubt makes you sorry.
FRED. All right, she had doubts. Why not? She hasn't really believed in anything for years. You can't expect her to suddenly—
KRIS *(going on).* It's not just Doris. There's Mr. Sawyer. He's contemptible, dishonest, selfish, deceitful, vicious—yet he's out there and I'm in here. He's called normal, I'm not. Now what makes him normal?—because he conforms to a pattern, because he thinks and acts like the great majority? So we've got a world full of Sawyers—and if that's normal, I don't want it. That's why I answered the questions incorrectly.
FRED. But you can't just think of yourself. What happens to you matters to a lot of other people. People like me who believe in what you stand for—and people like Susan who are just beginning to. You can't quit—you can't let them down.
KRIS. I suppose I shouldn't. *(thoughtfully)* You really think there's any hope?
FRED. I don't know—but I *do* know that it's not impossible to change the norm. In Henry the Eighth's time everybody used to eat with his hands—it was normal. If you did it today they'd send you to a psychiatrist. Who knows, maybe some day the Sawyers'll be in here instead of out there.
KRIS *(after a moment's decision).* You're right! I'm ashamed of myself. Even if we can't win—we can go down swinging. *(he starts for door)* Let's get out of here.
FRED. Wait a minute. Not so fast. You're forgetting your examination—you flunked it—but good.
KRIS *(remembering).* Oh, yes—that's right. I said Calvin Coolidge was the first President. I can imagine what they must think of me for saying that. Why he wasn't even President when he was President. *(then dismissing it)* Well, you'll get me out of this—you'll think of something.
FRED. It's not going to be so easy.
KRIS. For you it will be. I believe you're the greatest lawyer since Darrow.

FRED. Now just a second—you're putting me in an awful spot!

KRIS. I believe in you and you can't let me down.

FRED *starts to argue further, but he realizes* KRIS *has thrown his own words right back at him. He picks up his hat.*

FRED. I'll do everything I can—so long, Kris. *(he exits)*

Dissolve to:

Int. MACY's *office—Night.* MACY *stands over* SAWYER, *who is seated, reading the riot act.*

MACY. Dangerous, my foot! And I don't care if he failed ten examinations. You had no right to do it! Now you get the case dropped tomorrow or you might have another lump to match that one!

SAWYER *mumbles a weak "Yes, sir."*

Dissolve to:

Int. JUDGE HARPER'S *Outer Office—Day—Insert—A thick sheaf of legal papers tucked under a man's arm. Across the top page in large type is printed:* LUNACY REPORT. *Below this, after* Subject *is typed* KRIS KRINGLE. *Camera pulls back and we see it is held in the hands of* MR. THOMAS MARA, *a brisk and rather dapper Assistant District Attorney. He is speaking to* SAWYER.

SAWYER *(panicky),* —and Mr. Macy would rather drop the whole thing right now.

MARA *(shaking his head).* It's too late. Can't be done. Kringle's been examined by psychiatrists of a city hospital. It has to go through the regular routine now.

A door to the JUDGE's *chambers in b.g. opens and a* CLERK *comes in.*

CLERK. Judge Harper will see you now, Mr. Mara.

MARA *says "Thanks" and exits.* SAWYER *is rather sick.*

Int. JUDGE HARPER's *chambers—Angle at desk. He holds the papers as if waiting to offer them to someone, as the camera continues back we see to whom.* JUDGE HENRY X. HARPER *is a plump man in his middle fifties. He sits at his large, ornate desk.* MARA *enters shot.*

HARPER. Hello, Mr. Mara.

MARA. Hello, Judge. All of us at the District Attorney's office were pleased to hear the good news. *(Harper mutters a questioning* "Hmm?")* I mean your being put up for re-election.

HARPER *(pompously).* Yes, Mr. Mara, my party has done me that honor, and I have accepted.

MARA *hands the* JUDGE KRIS's *report.*

HARPER. What's this?

MARA. Just some routine commitment papers.

HARPER *(leafing the pages)* Age unknown. An old man, is he?

MARA. Very old, Your Honor.

The JUDGE *turns another page and sighs.*

HARPER. I suppose I'll have to read all this.

MARA. You can take my word for it, Judge. It's cut and dried. This fellow calls himself Kris Kringle. He thinks he's Santa Claus!

The JUDGE *utters an "Oh, oh," and quickly reaches for his pen. As he does, there comes a sharp knock on the door. The Judge looks up, pen in hand.*

HARPER. Come in!

Angle at door, as a bespectacled court clerk in a black alpaca coat enters.

CLERK. A Mr. Gailey to see you, Your Honor. He represents Mr. Kringle.

HARPER. *He looks puzzled.*

HARPER *(resignedly).* Better show him in. *(he puts the pen back)*

Angle toward door, as FRED *enters briskly with a pleasant smile.*

FRED. Your Honor, there seems to be undue haste in this case. I wish to protect my client's rights, as I'm sure you do.

As FRED *walks toward the desk, camera pulls back to include the other two.*

HARPER *(hastily).* Of course, of course—!

FRED. If Your Honor please, I request a formal hearing to which I may bring witnesses—

HIS HONOR *looks reproachfully at* MARA.

HARPER. I thought you said this was cut and dried?

MARA. That's what I was told. I didn't know anything about a protest . . .

HARPER *glances through the papers before him thoughtfully.*

FRED. Of course you may sign the commitment papers now if you wish, Your Honor—but I shall bring in a habeas corpus this afternoon.

HARPER. There's no point in signing them. We'll have a hearing. Three o'clock—er—(*looks at calendar*) Monday afternoon.

FRED *ad libs a "Thank you, Your Honor," and starts out.*

Int. JUDGE HARPER'S *outer office, as* FRED *comes out, passes through and exits into the corridor.* SAWYER, *who sits in b.g., watches him worriedly. Presently* MARA *comes out. He stops to pick up hat and coat and puts them on.*

SAWYER. That man—I heard him say something about Mr. Kringle before—who is he?

MARA (*irritated*). His name's Gailey—Kringle's lawyer. Probably grabbed the case to get some cheap publicity.

SAWYER(*horrified*). Publicity! Oh, we can't have that, Mr. Mara. We *must* avoid publicity! I—I—

SAWYER *thinks his best chance is with the other lawyer. He hurries out.*

Dissolve to:

Int. Court House lobby—Day, as SAWYER *comes out of an elevator. He looks up and down. Finally he spots* FRED *off and exits quickly.*

Angle—Another section of lobby. FRED *in f.g., has stopped to light a cigarette.* SAWYER *can be seen hurrying toward us from b.g. He reaches* FRED *and turns on an ingratiating smile.*

SAWYER. Er—Mr. Gailey—my name's Sawyer. I represent Mr. Macy.

FRED *deliberately blows out the match—then looks* SAWYER *over. He speaks lightly but with an unmistakable tone of contempt.*

FRED. So you're Sawyer.

SAWYER. Yes—now regarding this Kringle matter—we're very anxious to avoid publicity of any kind. If you would agree to let this matter go through—er—quietly—I'm sure we could find some generous way of expressing our appreciation.

FRED'S *contempt has grown considerably in the last moment.*

FRED (*toying with him*). Sounds very interesting—

SAWYER(*hopefully*). Then you'll cooperate?

FRED (*going on*).—very interesting. Publicity—I'm glad you mentioned it. In order to win this case I'm going to need public opinion and plenty of it and publicity's the way to get it. Thanks again.

Camera pans FRED *away from a bewildered* SAWYER *to a door marked* COURT REPORTER'S ROOM. FRED *enters.*

Angle— SAWYER. *He'd even raise his wife's allowance to get out of this one.*

Dissolve to:

Series of Inserts.
(A) *Newspaper clipping in type of the* New York Times. *A small one-column head reads:*

MACY'S SANTA HAS
LUNACY HEARING

Kris Kringle, the jolly old Santa Claus who has enthralled thousands of children . . . etc.

(B) *Larger clipping, two-column head in type of* New York World Telegram:

DOCTORS DOUBT SANITY OF SANTA
WHO LAUNCHED GOOD WILL CAMPAIGN

The man who believes in the Christmas spirit is not in his right mind according to a report filed by alienists at Bellevue Hospital . . . etc., etc.

(C) *Two-column head with one column cut of* KRIS, *in type of the* New York Daily News:

KRIS KRINGLE KRAZY?
KOURT KASE KOMING
"KALAMITY!" KRY KIDDIES.

Dissolve to:

Int. JUDGE HARPER'S *living room.*

HARPER. I don't see what they're making such a fuss about—after all he's an—

As he says this the camera has continued to pull back and we see that he is in his living room. The modest furnishings reveal that he is an honest judge. Across the room is CHARLIE HALLORAN, *a short, paunchy politician.* CHARLIE *is chewing his cigar.*

HALLORAN (*cutting in*). How you been feeling lately, Harry? You look kind of run down.

HARPER (*surprised*). Me? I'm fine, Charlie. Never better.

HALLORAN (*shaking his head*). Go see the Doc. Take a few weeks off. Go fishin'—go huntin'—go anywhere.

HARPER. Why should I?

HALLORAN (*coming to the point*). This Kringle case is dynamite, Harry. Let some judge handle this that isn't comin' up for re-election.

HARPER. I can't do that.

HALLORAN. Listen, Harry. I'm no legal brain trust. I don't know a habeas from a corpus.

He walks up to the JUDGE *and jabs a finger into his chest emphatically.*

HALLORAN. But I know politics. That's *my* racket. I got you elected, didn't I? And I'm trying to get you re-elected.

HARPER. Certainly, Charlie. Don't misunderstand me. I appreciate all you—

HALLORAN (*cutting in*). And I'm telling you—get off this case.

HARPER. But why?

HALLORAN. Because you're a regular Pontius Pilate before you start—that's why. If you handle it you'll be every little kid's villain and their parents will hate you, too—and they won't vote for you.

HARPER. I don't believe it! I'm an honest man, and certainly nobody is going to hold it against me for doing my duty as I see it.

He stops as two kids, TERRY, *aged seven, and* ALICE, *aged five, dressed in pajamas and wrappers, hurry into the room calling, "Grandma." "Grandma, we're ready." Camera pans them to a door leading to a room off living room. As they reach it,* MRS. HARPER, *gray and pleasant, enters through door. They swarm all over her, kissing, hugging and saying, "Goodnight, Grandma."*

MRS. HARPER. Goodnight, Terry. Goodnight Alice. Now *straight to bed*. I promised your mother you'd be in bed by eight o'clock and it's way past that.

TERRY. Aren't you coming up?

MRS. HARPER. I'll be up in a minute and tuck you in—now scoot.

The kids start back across the room. As they pass the JUDGE *he starts toward them with outstretched arms in anticipation of his hug and kiss. The children merely give him a cold stare and leave without a nod.* HARPER *turns indignantly to his wife.*

HARPER. A fine way to treat their grandfather! No hug—no kiss—no anything!

MRS. HARPER (*starting back toward the kitchen; coldly*). I don't blame them! Any man who puts Santa Claus on trial for lunacy!

JUDGE HARPER *stands there amazed.*

HALLORAN (*dryly*). See what I mean?

As HARPER *looks after his wife thoughtfully—*

Dissolve to:

Int. Courtroom—Day—Long shot. Shooting past empty judge's bench in f.g. Everybody is in his place, seemingly waiting for HARPER *to appear. Being a hearing, not a trial, there is no jury. About twenty spectators are scattered about. Three or four reporters and a couple of sob sisters sit in the first row, resting their pads and pencils on the broad railing which divides them from the court.*

Angle— FRED *and* KRIS *at Plaintiff's table.* FRED *is getting some papers in order—* KRIS *is looking around.* FRED, *suddenly remembering something, reaches in his pocket and takes out a ring box, opens it and shows it to* KRIS.

KRIS. Oh—that's a beautiful one! When are you going to ask her?

FRED. Tonight.

KRIS (*as he continues examining it*). Oh—she'll like this—

Angle—Prosecution's table. MARA, *an assistant and* SAWYER *are present.*

SAWYER (*to* MARA—*rather nervously*). How—how long do you think this'll take?

MARA (*sourly; sorry he ever got roped in on it*). Maybe a week.

SAWYER. A week! But that seems impossible—all that has to be done is—

MARA (*interrupting; impatiently*). Look. You don't think that lawyer's going to be stupid enough to let him admit anything, do you? He's naturally going to deny everything—then I'll bring witnesses and he'll bring witnesses and—

During the above speech the Bailiff's voice has been heard calling out, "All rise!" and MARA *has risen, as has everyone else in the shot.*

Angle—Toward JUDGE's *bench.* JUDGE HARPER, *in his robes, emerges from his chambers and goes to the bench. As he does, the* BAILIFF *drones in a rapid monotone:*

BAILIFF. Trial Term, part III. Mr. Justice Harper presiding. All those having business with this Court, draw near and ye shall be heard.

Angle—Shooting toward MARA, *as he steps to the bench.*

MARA. In the matter of Kris Kringle, Your Honor—(HARPER *nods*) The commitment papers are before you. If your Honor please, I should like to call the first witness. *(His Honor nods again;* MARA *turns to* KRIS) Mr. Kringle, will you take the stand?

Angle at FRED'S *table.* KRIS *rises slowly and exits toward the witness stand.*

HARPER. *He glances at someone in audience.*

CHARLIE HALLORAN—*in audience. The politician returns a sour look.*

Angle—Witness box, as KRIS *enters and sits. He looks at the judge and gives him a very merry smile and a nod.*

KRIS. Good morning, Your Honor.

HARPER. *He reacts, returning the greeting in dignified surprise. He studies* KRIS *keenly. He certainly doesn't seem to be the senile old man in the report. He glances down at the papers and then at* KRIS *again, a ray of hope in his face. Over this comes the clerk's monotone:*

BAILIFF. Do you swear to tell the truth, the whole truth and nothing but the truth, so help you God?
KRIS *(his right hand raised).* I do.

He sits.

Group shot, to include the JUDGE *and* MARA, *who stands in front of* KRIS, *about to examine him.*

HARPER. Before you begin, Mr. Mara, I want to explain to the witness that this is a hearing, not a trial. *(he turns to* KRIS) Mr. Kringle, you do not have to answer any questions against your wishes or even testify at all.
FRED *(in b.g., as he rises).* We have no objections, Your Honor.
KRIS. I'll be glad to answer any questions that I can.

HARPER *nods to* MARA, *who turns to* KRIS.

MARA. What is your name?
KRIS. Kris Kringle.
MARA. Where do you live?

KRIS. That's what this hearing will decide.

This brings a suppressed wave of chuckles from the spectators. The JUDGE *looks surprised and pleased as he glances out at the spectators and bangs his gavel.*

Courtroom—from JUDGE'S *angle. The newspapermen and women are laughing and writing.* KRIS *has scored a point.*

HARPER. *Smiling, he looks toward* KRIS *with much relief. This man is certainly far from senile.*

HARPER. A very sound answer, Mr. Kringle.

Angle toward witness box. MARA *is icy as he faces* KRIS. *He asks the next question, knowing the answer will be in the negative.*

MARA. Do you believe that you are Santa Claus?
KRIS. Of course!

A stunned silence. MARA *is startled by this admission.* FRED *alone seems unperturbed.* HIS HONOR *looks worried.* MARA *recovers quickly. He gives* KRIS *a smile of sympathy, as if to a pathetic child. The hearing is over as far as he is concerned. He turns to the judge with an air of finality.*

MARA. The State rests, Your Honor.

He walks to his table and sits down.

HARPER. *Amazement and anxiety are written all over his face as he glances out toward* CHARLIE HALLORAN.

HALLORAN. *He returns* HARPER'S *look, shaking his head sadly as if he were saying "I told you so!"*

Angle toward witness stand. FRED *is now on his feet, still calm and smiling.*

HARPER *(hopefully).* Well, Mr. Gailey, do you wish to cross-examine the witness? I believe he was employed to *play* Santa Claus. Perhaps he did not understand the question.
KRIS *(sharply).* I undertood the question perfectly, Your Honor!

HIS HONOR *looks unhappy.*

FRED. No further questions at this time.

He nods to KRIS, *who bows to the* JUDGE *and leaves the stand, returning to his seat at* FRED'S *table. As he does so:*

HARPER *(to* FRED, *his tone dejected).* In view of this statement, do you still wish to put in a defense, young man?

FRED. I do, Your Honor. I am fully aware of my client's opinions. In fact, that is the entire case against him. All those complicated tests and reports boil down to this: Mr. Kringle is not sane because he believes himself to be Santa Claus.

HARPER *(sadly).* An entirely logical and reasonable assumption, I'm afraid.

FRED. It would be if the clerk here or Mr. Mara or I believed that we were Santa Claus.

MARA *(half rising). Anyone* who thinks he's Santa Claus is not sane—!

FRED *(to the judge).* Not necessarily. You believe yourself to be Judge Harper, and nobody questions your sanity, Your Honor, because you *are* Judge Harper.

HARPER *(looking at* FRED *as if he suspected an insult).* I know all about myself, young man. Mr. Kringle is the subject of this hearing.

FRED. Yes, Your Honor—and if he is the person he believes himself to be—just as you are—then he is just as sane.

HARPER *(impatiently).* Granted—but he isn't.

FRED. Oh, but he *is,* Your Honor!

HARPER *(angrily).* Is *what*?

FRED. I intend to prove that Mr. Kringle *is* Santa Claus.

The JUDGE *and* MARA *react in amazement. From the spectators comes a roar of excitement.*

Courtroom—Full shot. Reporters are dashing for the phones. Flash bulbs are popping. Everybody is talking to everybody else at once. As HIS HONOR *raps his gavel vainly for order,*

Dissolve to:

Int. DORIS's *living room—Night—Angle at hall door. The bell is heard ringing.* DORIS, *carrying a newsaper, enters and opens door.* FRED, *a few newspapers under his arm, enters.*

FRED. Hello—sorry I'm late. *(he kisses her)* Get your coat. I reserved our regular table at Luigi's. We're going to have a little celebration.

DORIS. What are we celebrating?

FRED *(extending the newspapers and speaking in the manner of a newsboy).* Read all about it! Gailey throws a bombshell into New York Supreme Court.

DORIS *(holding up her paper—darkly).* Oh, I read that.

FRED *(taking his paper and crossing to couch).* I haven't seen this one. Front page, huh? Good.

DORIS *(following him).* You're not serious about this.

FRED *(as he sits).* Of course I am.

DORIS. But you can't possibly prove that he's Santa Claus.

FRED *(as he reads).* Why not? You saw Macy and Gimbel shaking hands. That was impossible but it happened.

DORIS. Honestly, Fred, I—

FRED. It's the best defense I can use. Completely logical—completely unexpected—

DORIS *(sitting next to him).* And completely idiotic—What about your bosses Haislip and MacKenzie and the rest of them? What do they say?

FRED. That I'm jeopardizing the prestige of an old established law firm, and that either I drop this impossible case or they will drop me. I beat them to it—I quit.

DORIS. Fred, you didn't.

FRED. Of course I did. I can't let Kris down. He needs me and all the rest of us need him.

DORIS. Look, darling, he's a nice old man and I admire you for wanting to help him, but you've got to face facts and be realistic. You can't throw your career away because of a sentimental whim.

FRED. I'm *not* throwing my career away.

DORIS. If Haislip feels that way so will every other law firm in town.

FRED. I'm sure they will. Then I'll open my own office.

DORIS. And what kind of cases will you get?

FRED. Probably a lot of people like Kris who are being pushed around. That's the only fun in law anyway. And if you believe in me, have faith in me, I promise you everything will—

DORIS *rises.* FRED *looks after her. He now rises and goes to her.*

FRED. You *don't* have any faith in me, do you?

DORIS. It's not a question of faith—it's just common sense.

FRED. Faith is believing in things when common sense tells you not to. Don't you see—it's not just Kris that's on trial, it's everything he stands for—kindness and joy and love and all the other intangibles—

DORIS *(losing patience).* Oh, Fred, you're talking like a Boy Scout. You're living in a realistic world and those lovely intangibles of yours are attractive but not very profitable. You don't get ahead that way.

FRED. That all depends on what you call "getting ahead." Evidently you and I have different definitions.

DORIS *(angrily)*. The last few days we've talked about some wonderful things. Now you go on an idealistic binge; give up your job; throw away all security, and you expect me to be happy about it.

FRED. Yes. I guess I expected too much. Someday, Doris, you're going to find out that your way of facing this realistic world just doesn't work, and when you do don't overlook those *lovely intangibles*—you'll discover they're the only things that are worthwhile.

He picks up his hat and exits.

Out

Angle—Shooting past DORIS, *windows in b.g. Across the airway we see* FRED *close the Venetian blinds, shutting off our light source.*

Close shot— DORIS, *in darkness. Presently the trace of a sob is heard—*

Dissolve to:

Int. MARA's *apartment—Night.* MRS. MARA *is wrapping Christmas packages with the help of* TOMMY, *a six-year-old, who is having trouble with some Scotch tape.* MARA *sits in a nearby chair surrounded by papers. He throws one down disgustedly and rises.—*

MARA. These reporters make me look like a sadistic monster who likes to drown cats and tear wings off of butterflies. This old man is—

MRS. MARA *jumps in quickly.*

MRS. MARA. Oh, Tommy—run in and get Mother's scissors, will you? They're in the bedroom. *(Tommy exits—then she continues; laying down the law)* I don't want you to discuss this case in front of him—it would break his heart. And while we're on the subject, I agree with the reporters—Mr. Kringle seems to be a nice old man and I don't see why you have to keep persecuting him.

MARA *(trying not to explode)*. Firstly, I am not persecuting him—I am *prosecuting* him and secondly, I like the old man, too, and I wish I had never gotten into this but it's too late now and there's nothing I can do about it. This is up to the State of New York and I'm just their duly appointed legal representative. Kringle has been declared a menace

to society by competent doctors. It is my duty to protect the State of New York and see that he is put away and no matter what they say about me, *I've got to do it.*

MRS. MARA. Sometimes I wish you were a butcher or a plumber.

MARA. If I lose this case, it's more than possible you will *get* your wish!—No, whether I like it or not, I got to put the old man away.

He slumps in the chair, dejectedly.

Dissolve to:

Ext. Elevators, Court Bldg.

ALFRED. Hello, Kris.

Dissolve to:

*Int. Courtroom—Day—Full shot. Shooting from behind witness box. The spectators' section is much fuller now. A row of tables for the press, which is now full, has been placed along the railing. On them printed signs read "*RESERVED FOR THE PRESS*". In immediate f.g. we see the back of a man as he is being sworn in. Now he sits and* FRED *steps forward.*

FRED. Your name?

Angle—Witness box—Shooting past FRED. *The witness is* MR. MACY.

MR. MACY. R. H. Macy.

FRED. Mr. Macy, if you recognize the gentleman seated there—*(he points to* KRIS*)*

KRIS. *He smiles and nods to Macy.*

FRED'S VOICE.—will you tell us who he is?

Angle at witness box— MACY *and* FRED.

MACY. Kris Kringle.

FRED. Your employee, is he not? *(*MACY *nods).* Do you believe him to be truthful?

MACY. Yes.

FRED. Do you believe him to be sound of mind?

MACY. *(The honor of R. H. Macy & Co. is at stake).* I certainly do!

MARA *jumps up and comes toward the witness box.*

MARA *(in a deliberate, stern voice)*. Mr. Macy, you are under oath. Do you really believe that this man is Santa Claus?

Close-up— MACY. *He hesitates. He is in a hell of a spot—and we can see what he is think-*

ing. For superimposed over his face comes a three-column headline, saying:

MACY ADMITS HIS SANTA CLAUS A FRAUD

Thousands of Children Take
Business Elsewhere

Then it fades out again. MR. MACY *gulps.*

MACY. Well—he gives every indication of—

MARA'S VOICE. I asked you, Mr. Macy—do you really believe that this man is Santa Claus.

Now superimposed over MACY'S *face comes another flash. It is a shot of four or five-year-old faces. They are standing on the curb watching* KRIS *pass in the Thanksgiving Day Parade. Their expression is one of complete faith and belief. It fades out.* MACY *makes up his mind.*

MACY *(without a doubt).* I do!

Full shot.

FRED *(quickly).* That is all.

There is a murmur from the spectators. As MACY *steps down in evident relief, a few flash-bulbs go off*

THE JUDGE. *He looks pleased as he raps the gavel and glances off at* HALLORAN.

HALLORAN. *He nods hopefully.*

Press section. MACY'S *testimony has caused a mild furor. The boys have a story already. They are delighted.*

MACY. *As he returns to his seat he passes* SAWYER. *He gives him a ferocious glare.*

MACY. You're fired.

Over these shots we hear MARA *saying, "Your Honor," trying to be heard above the commotion in the court. By now it is quiet.*

Angle—At bench.

MARA. Your Honor, I object to this testimony. It is ridiculous, irrelevant and immaterial. Mr. Gailey is making a circus out of this court. There is no such person as Santa Claus—and everybody knows it.

There is a subdued murmur of disagreement from the spectators.

FRED. Your Honor, I submit that this is purely a matter of opinion. Can Mr. Mara offer any proof that there is *no* Santa Claus?

MARA *(growing hotter).* No—and I do not intend to! This is no nursery. This is the New York State Supreme Court. I will not waste this court's time with such childish nonsense.

FRED *(calmly).* Mr. Mara seems to have appointed himself the judge here, Your Honor. He is now ruling on what testimony I may introduce.

MARA. Your Honor, I demand an immediate ruling from this court: Is there or is there not a Santa Claus?

JUDGE HARPER. *He looks very unhappy.* MARA *has won, he fears. He coughs judiciously, stalling for time. Then he glances out at* HALLORAN.

HALLORAN. *He is frantically shaking his head and gesturing toward the* JUDGE'S *chambers.*

JUDGE HARPER. *He nods to* HALLORAN. *Then he looks down at* FRED *and* MARA.

HARPER. The Court will take a short recess to consider this matter.

Dissolve to:

Int. JUDGE'S *Chambers—Day. The* JUDGE *is seated.* HALLORAN *is pacing the room furiously, chewing his cigar.*

HALLORAN. I don't give a hoot in Harlem what you do with old whisker-puss—but if you go back in there and rule that there is no Santa Claus, you better start looking for that chicken farm right now. We won't be able to even put you in the primaries.

HARPER *(very much distressed).* But, Charlie—listen to reason. I'm a responsible judge. I've taken an oath. How can I seriously rule there *is* a Santa Claus?

HALLORAN *is fit to be tied but he suppresses any outburst. He speaks calmly, sarcastically.*

HALLORAN. All right—go on back and tell 'em that the New York State Supreme Court rules that there's no Santa Claus. It's all over the papers. The kids read it and they don't hang up their stockings. So what happens to all those toys that were supposed to be *in* the stockings—nobody buys 'em. You think the toy manufacturers are going to like that? So they have to lay off a lot of employees— union employees. Now you got the C.I.O. and the A.F. of L. against you. They're gonna love you for it—*and* they're gonna say it with votes. And the department stores are going to love you, too—and the Christmas card makers and the candy companies. Oh, you're going to be an awful popular fellow! And what about the Salvation Army? They got a Santa Claus on every corner. They take in a fortune! *(he draws a deep breath)* Henry, I'm telling you, if you rule there's no Santa Claus, you can count on getting just two votes—your own and that District Attorney's out there.

HARPER. *He shakes his head sadly and raises a single finger.*

HARPER. The District Attorney's a Republican.

He rises and starts for the door.

Dissolve to:

Courtroom—Full shot. Bailiff calls: "All rise," as JUDGE HARPER *sweeps majestically to the bench and sits. There is silent tension in the room.*

HARPER. *He looks about and clears his throat.*

HARPER. Before making a ruling, this Court has consulted the highest authority available.

He glances at HALLORAN.

Flash— HALLORAN. *Chewing his cigar, he smiles.*

HARPER.

HARPER. The question of Santa Claus seems to be largely a matter of opinion. Many people firmly believe in him. Others do not. The tradition of American justice demands a broad and unprejudiced view of such a controversial matter. This Court, therefore, intends to keep an open mind. We shall hear evidence on either side.

Courtroom—Full shot. There is a buzz of reaction. MARA *jumps to his feet. He looks at* FRED *with great scorn.*

MARA. Your Honor, the burden of proof for this ridiculous contention clearly rests with my opponent. Can he produce any evidence to support his views?

FRED *(rising).* If Your Honor please, I can. *(His Honor nods)* Will Thomas Mara please take the stand?

MARA *(startled).* Who—me?

FRED *shakes his head, turning to the spectators' section.*

FRED. Thomas Mara, *Junior.*

Angle at aisle. THOMAS MARA, JR.—*a bright, cheerful, seven-year-old boy—breaks away from his mother and starts eagerly down the aisle.*

MARA. *He gives his wife an accusing look which says, "How come?"*

MRS. MARA, *a well-dressed young woman. She returns his look with a shake of her head which denies all responsibility. She holds up a subpoena with a large gold seal on it, and shrugs.*

Full shot. TOMMY *is eagerly climbing into the witness chair.* FRED *stands near him.* HARPER *raises his eyebrows.* MARA *is nonplussed. He doesn't know whether to protest or not.*

FRED. You know the difference between telling the truth and telling a lie, don't you?

TOMMY. Gosh, everybody knows you shouldn't tell a lie—'specially in Court!

Subdued laughter.

FRED. Do you believe in Santa Claus, Tommy?

TOMMY *(with a violent nod of his head).* Sure I do. He gave me a brand new Flexible Flyer sled last year—and this year I wrote him that I—

FRED *(cuts him off with a smile).* And what does he look like?

TOMMY *(pointing unerringly at Kris).* There he is sitting there!

MARA *(very feebly).* Your Honor, I protest.

HARPER *(shaking his head).* Overruled.

FRED. Tell me, Tommy, why are you so sure there *is* a Santa Claus?

TOMMY *(indignantly).* Because my Daddy told me so. Didn't you, Daddy?

There is a roar of laughter. HARPER *grins broadly as he bangs his gavel.*

FRED. And you believe your Daddy, don't you, Tommy? He's a very honest man.

TOMMY. 'Course he is! My Daddy wouldn't tell me anything that wasn't so! Would you, Daddy?

FRED. Thank you, Tommy.

TOMMY *gets down from stand.*

MARA'S VOICE *(protesting).* Your Honor—!

HARPER *looks in his direction.*

Angle— MARA. *He stops short as he looks off at his son.*

Angle— KRIS. *As* TOMMY *passes* KRIS's *table, he says in a very loud whisper:*

TOMMY. Don't forget. A real "uffishill" football helmet.

KRIS *nods and winks.* TOMMY *scoots up the aisle.*

Angle— MARA. *He looks after the kid. He's a District Attorney but he's a father, too.*

Angle in aisle. MRS. MARA *stands waiting for* TOMMY *who enters. The two look off toward* MARA. *The mother's look is one of: "If you break this kid's heart I'll never talk to you again."*

Angle— MARA, *as he looks toward them. He might be able to let down the State of New York—but not his son. He turns to the* JUDGE.

MARA. Your Honor, the State of New York concedes the existence of Santa Claus.

Angle

MRS. MARA *and* TOMMY. *Satisfied, and rather proud of her husband, she leads the child out. The spectators in the shot are talking excitedly. The gavel is heard pounding.*

Angle at bench, as MARA *steps forward.*

MARA. But in so conceding we ask of Mr. Gailey to cease presenting personal opinion as evidence. The State could bring in hundreds of witnesses with opposite opinions, but it is our desire to shorten the hearing rather than prolong it. I therefore demand that Mr. Gailey now submit *authoritative proof* that Mr. Kringle is *the one and only* Santa Claus.

HARPER *(glumly)*. Your point is well taken, Mr. Mara. I'm afraid I must agree.

He glances anxiously out at HALLORAN.

HALLORAN. *He is the picture of "I told you so" again.*

Full shot—The JUDGE *looks down at* FRED.

HARPER. Mr. Gailey, are you prepared to show that Mr. Kringle is Santa Claus, on the basis of competent authority?

FRED. *He rises slowly and reluctantly. "Authoritative proof" was something he was hoping to avoid.*

FRED. Not at this time, Your Honor. I ask for an adjournment until tomorrow.

Full shot.

HARPER. This Court stands adjourned until three o'clock tomorrow afternoon.

Angle— FRED *and* KRIS. *Spectators rising in b.g.* FRED *is completely discouraged. He pats* KRIS *affectionately but sadly on the back.*

Angle—last row. DORIS *sits looking off toward* FRED. *People tenderly, sympathetically exit in front of her. She rises slowly. We see* ALFRED *and* SHELLHAMMER *waiting in the aisle.*

ALFRED *(defeated)*. Well—I guess that's that.

DORIS *(almost fighting mad)*. There's a way, Alfred—there's got to be!

Dissolve to:

Int. Hallway—Night—Angle at door of DORIS's *apartment. As* DORIS *approaches it, key in hand, the door suddenly flies open and half a dozen children come tearing out.* DORIS *jumps aside to avoid a collision. The kids ad lib "So long!" "Goodbye, Susie!" "See ya tomorrow!" Etc.* SUSIE *stands in the doorway shouting last minute plans.*

DORIS. *She reacts to this, looking at* SUSAN *with a mixture of wonder and pleasure. She certainly is a different child—alive, excited, gay.*

Reverse angle. Shooting from inside apartment. SUSAN *holds the door open as* DORIS *enters.*

SUSAN *(her eyes still sparkling)*. Hello, Mother. You know what? We played apartment house. Homer was the superintendent, Nancy was the elevator man and I was the exterminator!

DORIS *(laughing)*. You were?

She comes into room, camera pulling back ahead of her. She drops into a chair with a sigh of exhaustion and removes her hat.

DORIS *(calling)*. Hello, Cleo—!
CLEO. 'Evening, Mrs. Walker!

SUSAN *walks toward her solemnly.*

SUSAN. Mother, is Mr. Kringle coming over tonight?
DORIS. No, I'm afraid not.
SUSAN. But he hasn't been here for so long. Won't he come *soon*?

DORIS *(her hands on* SUSAN's *arms)*. He may never be able to come again.

SUSAN *(upset)*. Why not?

DORIS. It's hard to explain, dear. You see they're having—well—sort of a trial about him.

SUSAN *(incredulous)*. You mean like for a murder? Has he done something wrong?

DORIS. No—no! It's not that kind of a trial, dear. It's only because he says he's Santa Claus.

SUSAN. But he *is* Santa Claus, Mother. I just have a feeling.

DORIS. Some people don't believe that, so that's why they're having this—

SUSAN *(cutting in)*. But he's so kind and nice and jolly. He's not like anyone else. He *must* be Santa.

DORIS *(half to herself)*. I think perhaps you're right, Susie.

SUSAN. Is Mr. Kringle sad now, Mother?

DORIS. I'm afraid he is, dear. I'm sure he misses you and—

SUSAN. Then I'll write him a letter! Right now!

Dissolve to:

Insert—Letter—In DORIS's *hands. Pencilled in childish printing we see:*

"—to tell you that I believe all you told me and everything will turn out fine. I hope you are not sad.

　　　Yours truly,
　　　　Susan."

Int. DORIS's *living room—Night—Angle at desk.* DORIS *is reading it. She smiles warmly—then, on a sudden impulse, starts to add a note.*

Insert—Letter. As DORIS's *pen adds at the bottom:*

"I believe in you, too.
　　Doris."

Back to scene. She folds the letter and places it in an envelope, which she seals as she rises and walks to the door.

Hallway—Reverse angle, as DORIS *opens the door and comes out, letter in hand. She walks to a glass mail chute a few steps down the hall, starts to put the letter in it.*

Close shot—Letter in DORIS's *hand. We see it has a Special Delivery stamp and has "*KRIS KRINGLE*" in Susan's printing. As* DORIS *drops it in and it slips down the chute,*

Dissolve to:

Letter on Conveyer—Traveling shot—Night. As the letter moves along the conveyer we see that SUSAN *has addressed it:*

　　KRIS KRINGLE
　　NEW YORK COUNTY COURT HOUSE
　　CENTER AND PEARL STREETS
　　NEW YORK CITY

A hand reaches in and picks up letter.

Int. Main Post Office—Night—Angle at sorting racks. AL GOLDEN *holds the letter in his hand. He wears a green eyeshade and an old sweater over a collarless shirt. Next to him is* LOU SPOLETTI, *also busy sorting mail. The Christmas rush is on. The place is cluttered with bulging mail bags. Al glances at the letter then does a "take."*

AL. Here's a new one! I've seen 'em write to Santa Claus— "North Pole"— "South Pole"—and every other way. But here's a kid writes to: "Kris Kringle, New York County Court House!" Can you beat that?

LOU. The kid's right! They got him on trial down there. He claims he's Santa Claus and the D.A. claims he's nuts. *(taking a folded newspaper from back pocket)* Here—read it! Right on the front page.

AL *glances at the paper but only for a second. A thought strikes him.*

AL *(reflectively)*. Lou—how many Santa Claus letters we got in the dead letter office?

LOU *(disgustedly)*. I d'know—must be fifty thousand of 'em. Bags and bags all over the joint and more comin' in every day.

AL *(smiling almost impishly)*. Be nice to get rid of 'em, wouldn't it, Lou?

LOU. Yeah but—*(suddenly he sees what* AL *is driving at)* Gees, Al—that's a wonnerful idea! You mean—

AL. I mean why should we be boddered with this stuff! Get a couple of trucks up here—big ones—right away! Load 'em with all the Santa Claus mail we got. Deliver it all to Mr. Kringle down at the Court House. Let somebody else worry about it—

LOU *has started away calling, "Joe! Harry!" And Al happily starts singing "Jingle Bells."*

Dissolve to:

Int. Courtroom—Day—Full shot. The courtroom is packed to the eaves now. Bailiffs guard the doors and standees line the walls. There are two rows of tables for the Press and all are occupied. The bench is empty and the room buzzes with subdued conversation.

Angle— FRED's *table.* KRIS *in f.g. He is reading* SUSAN's *letter. The open envelope is on the table in front of him.* FRED *enters rather glumly, brief case in hand.*

FRED. 'Morning, Kris.

KRIS *glances up from the letter to return a cheery greeting, then looks at it again.*

FRED. I'm afraid I've got bad news for you, Kris. I've tried every way to get some competent authority—I wired the Governor, the Mayor, but—

KRIS *(indicating the letter).* This means more to me than all the Governors and Mayors in the world.

Angle— MARA's *table in f.g,* KRIS *and* FRED *at table in b.g.* MARA *looks over toward* FRED, *who sits rather discouraged, then turns confidently to an assistant.*

MARA. It's all over, George—look at him—he hasn't got a thing.

Dissolve to:

MARA *and his assistant sit down and out of shot. Camera holds and we see a bailiff come up to* FRED, *tap him on the shoulder and speak to him. We are too far away to hear anything but the bailiff's arms seem to tell us that he is talking about a big pile of something. Puzzled,* FRED *gets up wearily and starts out with bailiff.*

Dissolve to:

Full shot—Court—Shooting past judge. MARA *is addressing the court.* FRED *is not present—but during the following he enters from rear and comes down aisle to his table.*

MARA. —the defense has yet to bring in one concrete piece of evidence to substantiate this preposterous claim. Not one competent authoritative proof that this man is Santa Claus. In view of these facts and especially since today is Christmas Eve and we are all anxious to get to our homes, I ask you that you sign the commitment papers without further delay.

Angle at bench.

HARPER *(in a hopeless tone, as if he already knew the answer).* Mr. Gailey, have you anything further to offer?

FRED *(raising a book in his hand).* Yes, I have, Your Honor. I should like to submit the following facts in evidence. It concerns the

Post Office Department, an official agency of the United States Government.

The JUDGE *looks puzzled. He can't imagine where this is leading, but he'll give* FRED *every chance.*

FRED. The Post Office Department was created by the Second Continental Congress on July 26, 1776. The first Postmaster-General was Benjamin Franklin.

People begin to perk up a little. MARA *looks very annoyed.*

FRED. The Post Office Department is one of the largest business concerns in the world. Last year, under Robert Hannegan, it did a gross business of $1,112,877,174.00.

MARA *(jumping up).* Your Honor, I'm sure we're all gratified to know that the Post Office Department is doing so nicely. But it hardly has any bearing on this case.

FRED. It has a great deal, Your Honor. If I may be allowed to proceed.

HARPER *(grasping at any straw).* By all means, Mr. Gailey

FRED. The figures which I have quoted indicate an efficiently run organization. Furthermore, the U. S. Postal Laws and Regulations make it a criminal offense to wilfully misdirect mail—or intentionally deliver it to the wrong party. Consequently the department uses every precaution possible.

MARA *(jumping up again).* Your Honor, the State of New York is second to none in its admiration of the Post Office Department. It is efficient, authoritative and prosperous. We are happy to concede all of Mr. Gailey's claims.

FRED. For the record?

MARA *(nodding).* For the record. Anything to get on with this case.

FRED. Then, Your Honor, I wish to introduce these pieces of evidence.

He hands three letters to the CLERK *who stamps them.*

CLERK. Exhibits "A," "B," "C,"

FRED *(holding them up).* I have here three letters, Your Honor. They are simply addressed to "Santa Claus"—no other address whatsoever. Yet these letters have just now been delivered to Mr. Kringle by bona fide employees of the Post Office. I offer this, Your Honor, as positive proof that a competent Federal authority—

He hands the letters to the judge, who takes them happily.

MARA *(on his feet again)*. Three letters, Your Honor, are hardly "positive proof." I understand the Post Office receives thousands of such letters every year.

FRED. I have further exhibits, Your Honor, but I hesitate to produce them.

MARA *(his voice rich with sarcasm)*. We'd all like to see them, I'm sure!

HARPER *(impatiently)*. Yes, indeed. Just bring them in, Mr. Gailey. Put them on the table there.

FRED *(with a shrug)*. Very well, Your Honor.

He beckons toward the rear door.

Angle—rear door. The bailiff acknowledges the signal, opens the door and at least ten court attendants, each carrying a mail sack, start parading down the aisle.

Flashes of KRIS. *He reacts in amazement at the vast amount of mail he has received.*

MARA. *He is not very happy as he sees the procession of mail bags. He glances anxiously at the* JUDGE.

HARPER. *He looks off toward* HALLORAN *hopefully.*

HALLORAN. *He is looking at* HARPER *and grinning from ear to ear.*

CLERK's *desk. As the attendants begin to empty the mail sacks on the desk. The clerk is snowed under by the avalanche.*

Angle near bench.

FRED. Your Honor—every one of these letters is addressed to Santa Claus. The Post Office has delivered them. The Post Office is a branch of the Federal Government. Therefore, the United States Government recognizes this man, Kris Kringle, as the one and only Santa Claus.

HARPER. *He bangs for order with his gavel. This is the out he has been waiting for.*

HARPER. Since the United States of America believes this man to be Santa Claus, this Court will not dispute it. Case dismissed!

Full shot. There is pandemonium. Flash bulbs are popping. Legmen are rushing up the stairs. FRED *and* KRIS *are surrounded by people.*

Two shots— KRIS *and* FRED. *They are happily shaking hands. People are slapping them on the back and congratulating them. Reporters are begging for statements.* KRIS *hurriedly* picks up his hat and coat. He fights his way toward the judge, who is rising to leave.

Full shot.

KRIS. Thank you very much, Your Honor, and a Merry Christmas to you!

HARPER. Thank you, Mr. Kringle. Same to you.

KRIS *slips away and out a side door.*

Rear of courtroom. DORIS *rises from her seat and moves toward the aisle. As she reaches it she hesitates—looking toward* FRED.

FRED—DORIS's *angle. He is still surrounded by well-wishers.*

DORIS. *She wants to go and offer her congratulations, too. She starts down toward the front—then stops as two reporters block her path. One is handing the other a $10 bill.*

FIRST REPORTER. You win, Eddie. Here you are. I never thought Gailey would pull it off. That letter gag was smart as—

SECOND REPORTER. It wasn't just the letters. You've got to hand it to the guy. He believed in Kringle right from the start. And before he was finished, he had all the rest of us believing in him, too!

DORIS *hears this—reacts. The point hits home. She turns and follows the rest of them out of the room.*

Lap dissolve to:

Ext. Court House—Day, as DORIS *comes out. She stops by one of the huge pillars to turn up her collar. She hears a "Psst!" She looks.*

Angle at pillar— KRIS *pokes his head around.*

KRIS. I got your note. It made me very happy.

DORIS. I'm glad, Kris.

KRIS. We're having a big Christmas party at the Brooks' home tomorrow morning. We'll have breakfast and a beautiful tree and—I'd like to have you and Susan.

DORIS. Oh, we'd love to. I can't think of anyone I'd rather spend Christmas with. Would you like to come to dinner tonight?

KRIS *(hurriedly)*. Tonight? I can't. It's Christmas Eve— *(with a knowing wink)* Goodbye.

KRIS *scoots away.* DORIS *stands there smiling. As she turns and moves on.*

Dissolve to:

Ext. Brooks' Memorial Home—Day—Long shot. We see DORIS *and* SUSAN *walking up the path.*

Dissolve through to:

Int. Living Room—Brooks' Home—Day— Long shot. It is a large, narrow room and at the moment it is deserted. In the f.g. is a large Christmas tree with presents all around it. Now the double doors at the far end of the room are opened by KRIS *and another Santa Claus and people begin to pour in—inmates of the home, friends, etc.* SUSAN *manages to sneak to the front of the crowd and rushes toward us and the tree. On her hands and knees she crawls amongst the presents, looking frantically for a particular one. She moves out of scene.*

Angle at back of room. KRIS *stands introducing the other Santa Claus to* MR. MACY

KRIS. Have you met my assistant, Alfred?

And sure enough it's ALFRED, *the locker-room boy, with no trace of a guilt complex.*

ALFRED *(overwhelmed—almost frightened).* Mr. Macy!

Angle near Christmas tree. Coming toward us is DR. PIERCE. *He seems like a man walking in a trance. His eyes are riveted on something off to the left. As he moves in that direction, camera slides over and presently an X-ray machine comes into view between camera and* DR. PIERCE. *The doctor is not excited—he is too moved and surprised. If he were a woman he'd cry. He runs his hand over it almost affectionately, then glances at the card. At this moment* KRIS *comes up behind him. The* DOCTOR *speaks quietly, haltingly.*

DR. PIERCE. Kris—all I can say is—the State Supreme Court declared you to be Santa Claus—and personally and professionally I agree with them.

KRIS *smiles, puts* PIERCE *on the shoulder and is about to speak when he notices something across the room. The smile fades. Camera slides with him as he crosses the room. Here we find* SUSAN *sitting disillusioned, defiant, impasssive—and yet her eyes are moist.* DORIS *sits next to her. They do not notice* KRIS *approaching.*

DORIS.—but, darling, there are *lots* of presents there for you.
SUSAN. Not the one I wanted. Not the one Mr. Kringle was going to get for me.
DORIS. What was that?

SUSAN. It doesn't matter. I didn't get it. I knew it wouldn't be here but I thought there would be a letter or something telling me—
KRIS *(stepping toward them).* I don't suppose you even want to talk to me.

SUSAN *looks at him coldly, distrustfully.*

DORIS. It's something about a present that—
KRIS. Yes—yes—I know. I tried my best, Susie, but—
SUSAN. You couldn't get it because you're not Santa Claus—that's why. You're just a nice old man with whiskers like my mother said and I shouldn't have believed you.

Two shot— DORIS *and* SUSAN.

DORIS. I was wrong when I told you that, darling. you *must* believe in Mr. Kringle— and keep right on doing it. You must have faith in him.
SUSAN *(baffled).* But he didn't get me the— that doesn't make sense, Mommy.
DORIS *(more to herself).* Faith is believing in things when common sense tells you not to. *(it's too deep for* SUSAN—*she mutters a puzzled "huh?")* I mean—just because things don't turn out the way you want them to the first time you've still got to believe in people. I found that out.

KRIS. *He is proud of* DORIS.

Three shot. SUSAN *is thinking it over. She is not to be won over too easily.*

SUSAN *(resignedly).* You mean it's like that "if at first you don't succeed, try, try again"?
DORIS. Yes.
SUSAN *(disgustedly).* I thought so.

Dissolve to:

Int. Corridor near front door—Brooks' Home—Day. A lot of guests are saying "good-bye" to the elderly inmates. FRED *puts on his coat, camera pans him a few feet to* DORIS *who has several packages. Their attitude has that tinge of formality that generally follows a split-up.*

FRED. May I drive you home?
DORIS. Thanks.

KRIS *enters holding a piece of paper.*

KRIS. Now if you go this way you'll miss a lot of traffic—I wrote it all down—you see you go down Maplewood until you—

Angle— SUSAN*—near door. She stands holding a doll and other presents, waiting for* DORIS. *She is mumbling to herself.*

SUSAN. I believe, I believe—it's silly, but I believe.

Dissolve to:

Int. FRED's *car—(process)—Day.* SUSAN *sits next to the window. We see a residential section.* DORIS *holds* KRIS's *directions.*

DORIS. This must be the turn here—*(looks)*—that's right—Ashley. *(the car turns)* Now you go straight for four blocks—

Close-up— SUSAN. *She is mumbling almost inaudibly, "I believe, I believe." She glances out of the window—her eyes widen and she shrieks:*

SUSAN. Stop! Uncle Fred, stop!

Int. Car—Three shot. FRED, *not knowing what's up, slams on the brakes.*

SUSAN. Stop! Stop!

Before anyone can even think, SUSAN *starts to open the door and starts out.*

Ext. Car. As SUSAN *gets out* DORIS *is heard yelling, "Susan, what's the matter?" But the child waits for nothing. Camera pans her as she rushes up the walk of a house and now the house comes into view. It is practically identical to the one she has always wanted. On the lawn is a "*FOR SALE*" sign.* SUSAN *tries the door. It is open and she disappears into the house.*

Angle at car, as DORIS *and* FRED *come out. Completely bewildered, they hurry after* SUSAN *(camera panning) and calling.*

Int. house, as DORIS *and* FRED *enter. The house is empty and shows evidence of recently departed tenants. A broken umbrella, a torn hat, crushed packing boxes are scattered about.*

DORIS. Susie! Susie!
FRED. Where are you?
SUSAN'S VOICE. I'm upstairs!

DORIS *(starting for stairs)*. Come down here this minute! You know you shouldn't be running around in other people's houses—you know better than—

SUSAN *comes rushing down the stairs. She seems to have wings—she's so excited and thrilled.*

SUSAN. But this is my house, Mommy—the one I asked Mr. Kringle for!
DORIS. Now, Susie, darling—!
SUSAN. It is—it is—I know it is! My room upstairs is just like I knew it would be. Oh, you were right, Mommy—*(to* FRED*)* Mommy told me if things don't turn out just right the first time you still got to believe. And I kept believing—and you were right Mommy—Mr. Kringle *is* Santa Claus. *(she rushes out)*
DORIS. Where are you going?
SUSAN'S VOICE. To see my swing.

During the above FRED *has just been looking at* DORIS.

FRED. You told her that?

DORIS *doesn't answer.* FRED *takes her in his arms.*

FRED. The house seems to be for sale. We can't let her down.

DORIS, *starting to cry, clings harder to* FRED.

DORIS. In my heart I never doubted you, Fred—it was just my silly common sense—
FRED *(lightly)*. Well, it even makes sense to believe in me now. After all, I must be a good lawyer. I take a little old man and legally prove to the world that he's Santa Claus. Now you know that—

FRED *stops suddenly and he notices something off. He nudges* DORIS *and points.*

Angle—near fireplace. Leaning in the corner is a cane, a common cane but just like the one KRIS *always carried.*

Two Shot— FRED *and* DORIS.

DORIS. Oh, no—it must have been left by the people who moved out.
FRED *(not sure)*. Maybe—and maybe I didn't do such a wonderful thing after all.

Fade out.

REBEL WITHOUT A CAUSE

Screenplay by Stewart Stern

JIM	James Dean
JUDY	Natalie Wood
PLATO	Sal Mineo
JIM'S FATHER	Jim Backus
JIM'S MOTHER	Ann Doran
BUZZ	Corey Allen
JUDY'S FATHER	William Hopper
JUDY'S MOTHER	Rochelle Hudson
GOON	Dennis Hopper
RAY	Edward Platt
MIL	Steffi Sidney
NEGRO WOMAN	Marietta Canty
JIM'S GRANDMA	Virginia Brissac
HELEN	Beverly Long
LECTURER	Ian Wolfe
CRUNCH	Frank Mazzola
GENE	Robert Foulk
COOKIE	Jack Simmons
HARRY	Tom Bernard
MOOSE	Nick Adams
CHICK	Jack Grinnage
CLIFF	Clifford Morris

Produced by David Weisbart
Directed by Nicholas Ray
Screenplay by Stewart Stern
Adaptation by Irving Shulman
From a story by Nicholas Ray
Director of Photography Ernest Haller, A.S.C.
Art Director Malcolm Bert
Music by Leonard Roseman
Film Editor William Ziegler, A.C.E.
Sound by Stanley Jones
Set Director William Wallace
Costumes Designed by Moss Mabry
Dialogue Supervisor Dennis Stock
Makeup Supervisor Gordon Bau, S.M.A.
Assistant Directors Don Page and Robert Farfan

In this cinematic study of troubled children on the American scene of the fifties, we have a noteworthy juvenile near-tragedy with revealing and important insights—not in the Greek classic sense but in quite Freudian terms and full of Oedipal material. This is a story of abandonment and terror but also of self-discovery and reconciliation, and like *The Graduate*, it is an examination of the innocence of youth but from an entirely different direction, of course.

In Stewart Stern's most able screenplay, as in the story by the director, Nicholas Ray, which won him a nomination for an Academy Award that year in 1955, we are presented with a leading character, the seventeen-year-old Jim, brilliantly portrayed by the late James Dean, seeking love and direction from his father, who is a weak role model. Here we have a microcosm and archetype of the rebellious, troubled youth of America, which was to arise with great force a decade later, far beyond the problems of the young in this motion picture.

These are nice kids, troubled kids, but still of a generation that obeyed the law. They were polite and they tried to be close to their parents.

A warm, psychologically sound story of decent youth, written with sympathy and empathy for the young. The question Jim asks of his father, "What can you do when you have to be a man?" when he is in trouble and seeks advice, is an eternal query of children that resonates again and again in filial relationships—an eternal question that always needs answering.

Mr. Stern, the talented screenwriter of *Rebel Without a Cause*, was born on March 22, 1922, in New York City and was educated at the University of Iowa. After a career as a stage actor, he began writing for films and TV after his stint of duty in the infantry during World War II. His screen credits include *The Rack* (1956); *The Outsider* (1962); *The Ugly American* (1963); and *Rachel Rachel* (1968).

CAST OF CHARACTERS

JIM'S FAMILY

JIM'S GRANDMA   A chic, domineering woman in her sixties who has made her son Frank dependent upon her for every breath he takes. She is the irritant in the household—the silent ruler—the silent enemy of Frank's marriage.

JIM'S FATHER   Frank is an unfeathered man who has never been able to have fun. He is anxious to be a real father to Jim, but has never learned how.

JIM'S MOTHER   Tense and immature, she has never found the husband she married. Upset by the presence of her mother-in-law, mated with an ineffectual and joyless man, she takes out her disappointment on him and on her son.

JIM   The angry victim and the result. At seventeen he is filled with confusion about his role in life. Because of his "nowhere" father, he does not know how to be a man. Because of his wounding mother, he anticipates destruction in all women. And yet he wants to find a girl who will be willing to receive his tenderness.

JUDY'S FAMILY

JUDY'S FATHER   A junior partner in a law firm. Boyish, attractive and debonair. Because he is frightened by the adolescence of his daughter, Judy, his only recourse is to criticize her.

JUDY'S MOTHER   Self-centered and frightened by the coming of middle-age. She feels that Judy's blossoming youth is threatening her wifely position as the desirable object of the husband's attentions.

JUDY   The victim and the result. At sixteen, she is in a panic of frustration regarding her father—needing his love and suffering when it is denied. This forces her to invite the attention of other men in order to punish him.

BEAU   Judy's brother. Because he is very young he is a danger to nobody and thus will grow up happily—certain of the love of his father who feels comfortable in giving it.

PLATO   Son of a divided family—an absent father and a traveling mother—he feels himself the target of desertion. At fifteen he wants to find a substitute family for himself so that he need no longer feel cold, and especially a friend who will supply the fatherly protection and warmth he needs and cannot find.

BUZZ   A sado-masochistic boy of seventeen, who acts out aggressively his idea of what a man should be in order to hide his real sensitivities and needs. He was probably rejected by both parents and must constantly court danger in order to achieve any sense of prestige or personal worth.

THE KIDS

HELEN
CRUNCH
MOOSE
GOON
CHICK
COOKIE
MIL   All searching for recognition in the only way available to them; all suffering from unfulfilled hungers at home; all creating an outside world of chaos in order to bear the chaos they feel inside. They are soldiers in search of an enemy.

NEGRO WOMAN   The maid supplied by Plato's absent mother to attend to his needs.

GUIDE   At Planetarium and a father in his own right.

LECTURER   At Planetarium.

RAY   A sympathetic Juvenile Officer

GENE   Another Juvenile Officer.

ALSO: Policemen, Adults, Other Rebels, Three Mexican Children, Victim of a stomp gang.

Fade in. A deep night sky. Matte shot. Camera searches slowly upward through the heavens and the silver tone of a bell is heard sounding the strokes of midnight.

On the final note of the bell, camera is full on the Milky Way and there it rests, just long enough for a burst of Easter singing to arise. The hymn is sung by the crude, unmatched voices of children. Camera pans down to include:

Spire of a church. Camera continues its downward pan as the singing continues and we pass a window beyond which is the source of the singing. Camera pans off window to show—

Long shot. City. Night. Suddenly revealed— crisp and sparkling with lights. Camera pans down and over:

A lonely street full of parked cars. The singing diminishes but a thread of it remains. A car has just parked. The headlights snap off. A MAN *emerges whistling the same melody and pulls some gifts from the front seat. He slams the door and starts down the street in the direction of a house with bright windows. He must pass an empty lot full of rusty grass and litter which lies in darkness between two street lights.*

As the MAN *walks by the lot, still whistling, a* GROUP OF FIGURES *rises silently from the grass, figures who have been lying in concealment until now. They step noiselessly onto the pavement and follow the* MAN. *At the sound of their boots the whistling stops. The* MAN *glances behind him and sees the figures walking after him, filling the pavement. A street light shows them to be boys and girls and all quite young. The* MAN *moves on more swiftly and the sound of their pursuit increases. He begins to run toward the lighted house and the following steps run too. Suddenly he stops under the next street light and turns to face the figures. They are upon him and around him quickly. Nobody speaks for a moment, then one of the boys grins. His name is* BUZZ. *He is big and filled with an awareness of his own masculinity.*

BUZZ *(friendly, cool).* That was pretty what you were whistling. Whistle some more.

The MAN *whistles a nervous phrase, trying to make a joke of the situation which he doesn't understand.*

BUZZ *(continuing; suddenly).* You got a cigarette?
MAN. Oh, I think so—

The MAN *fumbles in his pocket, finds a pack and drops it in his nervousness. The* FIGURES *wait until he picks it up. He offers one to* BUZZ.

MAN *(continuing).* Filter tips.
BUZZ *(smiling—encouraging).* You smoke it. Smoke it, Dad.

Smiling uncertainly, the MAN *puts the cigarette in his mouth.* BUZZ, *still smiling, takes out a packet of wooden matches.*

BUZZ *(continuing).* I'll light it for you, Dad.

BUZZ *ignites a match and holds it near the Man's face for a second, searching it. Then he ignites the whole box under his nose. The* MAN *shrieks, and his packages fall.* BUZZ *slaps him sharply, his smile gone.*

The camera pans away as the figures enclose him, and holds on a small mechanical monkey which has dropped from its wrappings. It begins to dance madly on the pavement, then runs down. The feet of the figures scatter past the unmoving monkey. Then camera rises to show that the man has disappeared. There is a moment of awful stillness, then we see a boy coming down the street alone. He is quite drunk, and he slips once. This is JIM, *a good-looking kid of seventeen with a crew-cut and wearing a good suit. The spilled packages on the pavement stop him. He bends down to see what they are and picks up the mechanical monkey from the wreckage. He smiles and winds it up. He sets it on the sidewalk and sits down. He watches it dance for a moment, happily. A siren is heard distantly, growing louder.* JIM *pays no attention to it as he winds the monkey again and releases it for its dance.*

SUPERIMPOSE TITLE: "REBEL WITHOUT A CAUSE" STARRING— *as siren rises piercingly close, and* JIM *looks up, we:*

Dissolve to:

Close shot. Throbbing light of police car. Night. The siren screaming wildly, then dying. The sound of brakes. Camera moves to reveal the police car stopped at the entrance of a Precinct Station. Two officers dismount, bearing between them the struggling JIM. *They bear him up the steps and in through the double doors.*

Inside precinct station. (Reception area). A large open space onto which several corridors converge. In the middle is a Sergeant's desk, really a quadrangular counter in the center of which the SERGEANT *stands. There are a few glass-walled interviewing rooms which open off the area, and several benches lining the walls. The scene is one of confusion, activity and waiting. Phones ring. The arrested pass in custody of officers. Present among others at* JIM's *entrance are:* JUDY, *who is blonde and sixteen. She sits on a crowded bench wearing an expression of downcast bitterness. On a bench across the way from her are three remarkably dirty little Mexican children without shoes or socks. The oldest is a* BOY *of four who is protecting his little* SISTER *who in turn mothers an infant crying on the bench beside her. Standing at a corner of the desk is a docile, undersized*

boy of fifteen named JOHN "PLATO" CRAWFORD.
He is shivering. With him is a large NEGRO
WOMAN, *his maid.* JIM *comes through the
doors and is led to the desk. One of the officers
presents a brief report to the* SERGEANT, *who
examines it.*

SERGEANT. Mixed up in that beating on
Twelfth Street?

OFFICER. No. Plain drunkenness.

SERGEANT. This says he was picked up
there.

OFFICER. They had him on the carpet for
an hour at Headquarters. He's clear. Plain
drunkenness.

SERGEANT. Young squirt. All right—You
want to lean him against something? Stand
him over there.

The officer leads JIM *to* JUDY'S *bench and
stands him against the wall beside it.*

JIM *is frisked, a look of prayer on his upturned face. The* OFFICER *finds the toy monkey
in his pocket and would take it, but when* JIM
asks to keep it, the OFFICER *hands it back and
moves away. Another officer enters and leads
the prisoner who is sitting next to* JUDY *into
another room.* JIM *sits beside her. He smiles at
her but receives only a chilling look. He winds
the monkey up and sets it dancing on the floor,
but she is not amused. Camera pans to show
others reacting to the monkey with pleasure.
We see* PLATO *look up and smile a little. Camera stops on the* MEXICAN CHILDREN *who are
smiling too. A bald* JUVENILE OFFICER *named*
GENE, *squats before them, smiling.*

GENE. You going to tell me your name
now?

The little boy shakes his head.

LITTLE BOY (*touching* GENE'S *bald pate*).
Where's your hair?

GENE. It's all gone.

LITTLE BOY. Did you get a haircut?

GENE. No—it just fell out!

LITTLE BOY (*sympathetically*). Aw—

GENE *laughs as another Juvenile Officer enters and pauses to look at the children. His
name is* RAY.

RAY. What gang does *he* belong to?

GENE. Give him a couple of years.

RAY. Where's your mamma, honey?

LITTLE BOY. I don't know.

RAY *and* GENE *exchange looks, then* RAY
moves across to JUDY—*camera following. He
looks down at her, consults the file in his
hand.*

RAY. JUDY—we're ready for you now.

JUDY (*a mumble*). He hates me.

RAY. What?

JUDY. He hates me.

She rises. RAY *leads her to one of the glass-
walled offices. Camera moves with them.* JIM
watches them go.

RAY. What makes you think he hates you,
JUDY?

JUDY. I don't think. I *know*. He looks at me
like I'm the ugliest thing in the world. He
doesn't like my friends—he—(RAY *leads her
into the office*).

Inside small office as JUDY *comes in,* RAY
*following. He indicates a chair for her while
he sits down behind a desk*

JUDY. He doesn't like anything about
me—he calls me—he calls me—

*She starts to cry. She doesn't hide it, but
keeps wiping the tears with the palms of her
hands.*

RAY. He makes you feel pretty unhappy?

JUDY (*crying*). He calls me a dirty tramp—
my own father!

RAY. Do you think your father means that?

JUDY. Yes! I don't know! I mean maybe he
doesn't mean it but he acts like he does.
We're altogether and we're going to celebrate Easter and catch a double bill. Big
deal. So I put on my new dress and I came
out and he—

RAY. That one?

JUDY. Yes—he started yelling for a handkerchief—screaming. He grabbed my face
and he rubbed all my lipstick off—he
rubbed till I thought I wouldn't have any lips
left. And all the time yelling at me—that
thing—the thing I told you he called me.
Then I ran out of the house.

RAY. Is that why you were wandering
around at one o'clock in the morning?

JUDY. I was just taking a walk. I tried to
call the kids but everybody was out and I
couldn't find them. I hate my life. I just hate
it.

RAY. You weren't looking for company,
were you?

JUDY. No.

RAY. Did you stop to talk to anyone, Judy?
(*she is silent*). Do you enjoy that?

JUDY. No. I don't even know why I do it.

RAY. Do you think you can get back at
your Dad that way? I mean sometimes if we
can't get as close to somebody as we'd like
we have to try making them jealous—so

they'll have to pay attention. Did you ever think of that?

JUDY. I'll never get close to *anybody*.

RAY. Some kids stomped a man on Twelfth Street, Judy.

JUDY. You know where they picked me up! *Twelfth* Street! I wasn't even *near* there!

RAY. Would you like to go home if we can arrange it? *(no answer. RAY addresses WOMAN OFFICER).* Did you notify the parents?

WOMAN OFFICER. She wouldn't give me their number.

RAY. What's your number, Judy? We'll see if your Dad will come and get you. *(JUDY looks up hopefully).* Unless you really don't want to go home. *(silence).* Would you rather stay here?

Camera moves close on JUDY. She looks up and speaks very quietly.

JUDY. Lexington 05549.

The wail of a siren is heard. JUDY looks off through the glass wall toward JIM. RAY is heard dialing.

Med. shot. JIM's bench. JIM sits with his head back, eyes closed. As the siren mounts louder, JIM opens his mouth and imitates it—a long, forlorn wail.

Med. shot, PLATO and NEGRO WOMAN. PLATO smiles faintly and moves out toward JIM, NEGRO WOMAN following. Camera pans with them. PLATO sits by JIM. She stands over them. JIM's wailing continues.

Med. shot. JIM, PLATO, NEGRO WOMAN. An OFFICER moves into shot.

OFFICER. Hey!

JIM continues for a moment.

OFFICER *(continuing).* Hey! That's enough static out of you.

JIM. Want me to imitate a stupid cop?

OFFICER. Cut it out now. I'm warning you.

JIM. Yes, ma'am.

The OFFICER moves out. The NEGRO WOMAN bends over PLATO who is shivering violently.

NEGRO WOMAN. You shivering, John? You cold?

PLATO shakes his head. JIM notices him.

JIM. Want my jacket?

PLATO looks up at JIM.

JIM *(continuing).* You want my jacket? It's warm.

PLATO wants it but shakes his head "no."

Full shot. JUDY's office. RAY and JUDY seated as before. JUDY is still gazing through the glass.

RAY. Your mother will be down in a few minutes, Judy—

JUDY *(clearing).* What?

RAY. Your mother will be down in a few minutes.

JUDY *(startled).* My *mother*?

RAY signals to a WOMAN OFFICER just outside and leads JUDY to the door.

Outside door as RAY turns JUDY over to the WOMAN OFFICER.

RAY. She's being called for.

JUDY. You said you'd call my *father*.

RAY. Goodbye, Judy. Take it easy.

JUDY doesn't answer. RAY goes back inside as camera leads the WOMAN OFFICER and JUDY past JIM's bench. Camera stops on JIM, PLATO and the NEGRO WOMAN. JIM stares at JUDY and whistles but gets no reaction. GENE enters and comes to the NEGRO WOMAN.

GENE. John Crawford?

NEGRO WOMAN. Yes, sir.

GENE. Come with me, John.

PLATO rises and goes with GENE, the NEGRO WOMAN following. JIM is alone. He closes his eyes, throws his head back and gives another siren wail as camera moves close on his face.

VOICE OF JIM'S MOTHER *(o.s.).* Jim!

JIM looks up suddenly, scared. Then he smiles mysteriously and staggers to his feet.

Low angle. Tight three. JIM's parents and grandma framed in the doorway, frozen. They are all dressed in evening clothes. The MOTHER is a very chic but rather hard-faced woman. The FATHER is an unfeathered man. The GRANDMA is the smallest, also very chic and very bright-eyed.

Med. shot. JIM as he faces them.

JIM. Happy Easter.

Tight shot. The family.

MOTHER. Where were you tonight? They called us at the club and I got the fright of my life!

Silence.

FATHER. Where were you tonight, Jimbo?

Close shot. JIM. He says nothing.

Close shot. FATHER laughing uncomfortably.

Med. shot. JIM.

JIM. You think I'm funny?

JIM *turns suddenly and walks to the glass wall of the office behind which* PLATO, *the* NEGRO WOMAN *and* GENE *are visible. He looks through the glass partition which separates him from* PLATO.

JIM *(continuing).* Why didn't you take my jacket?

Inside office. JIM *is seen through the glass. He moves away.* PLATO *is still shivering, cracking his knuckles.*

GENE. Do you know why you shot those puppies, John? *(silence).* Is that what they call you or do you have a nickname?

PLATO *(a murmur).* Plato.

NEGRO WOMAN. You talk to the man nice now, Hear? He's going to help you.

PLATO. Nobody can help me.

GENE. Can you tell me why you killed the puppies, Plato?

PLATO. No, sir. I just went next door to look at them like I always do. They were nursing on their mother and I did it. I guess I'm just no good?

GENE. What do you think's going to happen, you do things like that?

PLATO. I don't know. End up in the electric chair?

GENE. Where did you get the gun?

PLATO. In my mother's drawer.

NEGRO WOMAN. She keep it to protect herself, sir. She scared without a man in the house.

GENE. Where's your mother tonight, Plato?

PLATO. She's away.

NEGRO WOMAN. Seems like she's always going somewhere. She got a sister in Chicago and she go for the holiday. She says her sister is all the family she has.

GENE. Where's your father?

PLATO *is silent.*

NEGRO WOMAN. They not together, sir. We don't see him in a long time now.

GENE. Do you hear from him, son?

PLATO *looks up as* JIM *and his family move into the next office.* JIM *smiles at* PLATO, *who returns it feebly, then looks away—embarrassed.*

GENE. You know if the boy ever talked to a psychiatrist?

PLATO *(smiling a bit).* Head-shrinker?

NEGRO WOMAN *(laughing).* Oh, Mrs. Crawford don't believe in them!

GENE. Well maybe she better start.

Other office. JIM, *his parents,* GRANDMA *and* RAY *are gathered in the small room.* JIM *is humming* THE RIDE OF THE VALKYRIES *to himself as if he had absolutely no interest in what is happening around him.* RAY *suspects this is something more than mere disinterest, so lets the humming go on, in order to discover its real purpose.* GRANDMA *watches everything like a tennis match, reacting with soft little sounds of terror or astonishment or sympathy. No one pays any attention to her. For a moment no one talks.* RAY *watches* JIM *as he hums. Then the* FATHER *shakes his head and looks up.*

FATHER. I don't see what's so bad about taking a little drink.

RAY. You don't?

FATHER. No. I definitely don't. I did the sa—

RAY. He's a minor, Mr. Stark, and it looks to me like he had more than a little drink.

FATHER *(chuckling).* Say, listen—

MOTHER *(to* JIM: *in intimate, half-humorous disapproval).* Jim—don't hum.

JIM *merely rolls his eyes at her, then away—but continues his humming.*

FATHER. I guess I cut pretty loose in my day too.

MOTHER. Really, Frank? When was that?

FATHER. Listen—*can't you wait till we get home?*

RAY. Whoa! Whoa! I know you're a little upset but—

FATHER. Sorry.

RAY. What about you, Jim? Got anything to say for yourself? *(*JIM *stops humming and shrugs).* Not interested, huh? *(*JIM *shakes his head).*

MOTHER. Can't you answer? What's the matter with you anyhow?

FATHER. He's just loaded, honey.

MOTHER. I was talking to *Jim.*

FATHER *(to* RAY). Let me just explain to you—we just moved here, y'understand? The kid has no friends yet and—

JIM. Tell him why we moved here.

FATHER. Hold it, Jim.

JIM. You can't protect me.

FATHER *(to* JIM). You mind if I *try*? You have to slam the door in my face? *(to* RAY). I try to get to him—what happens? *(to* JIM). Don't I give you everything you want? A bicycle—you get a bicycle. A car—

JIM. You buy me many things. Thank you.

FATHER. Not just buy! You hear all this talk about not loving your kids enough. We give you love and affection, don't we? *(silence;* JIM *is fighting his emotion but his eyes grow wet).* Then what is it? I can't even touch you anymore but you pull away. I want to understand you. Why'd you get drunk? You must have had a reason. *(JIM stares straight ahead, trying not to listen).* Was it because we went to that party? *(silence).* You know what kind of drunken brawls those parties turn into—it's no place for kids.

MOTHER. A minute ago you said you didn't care if he drinks.

GRANDMA. He said a *little* drink.

JIM *(exploding).* You're tearing me apart!

MOTHER. What?

JIM. Stop tearing me apart! You say one thing and he says another and then everybody changes back—

MOTHER. That's a fine way to behave!

GRANDMA *(smiling).* Well you know who he takes after!

RAY. Outside, Jim. Come outside.

RAY *pushes him out the door firmly, and into office vacated by* PLATO *and* GENE.

RAY. Excuse us a minute?

FATHER *(very overwrought).* Sure. Sure.

GENE's *office.* RAY *and* JIM *alone.*

JIM. Someone should put poison in her epsom salts.

RAY. Grandma?

No answer. JIM *turns away from* RAY.

JIM. Get lost.

RAY. Hang loose, boy. I'm warning you.

JIM. Wash up and go home.

RAY. Big tough character. You don't kid me, pal. How come you're not wearing your boots?

Suddenly JIM *flings himself at* RAY *who deftly flips him past and drops him near the desk.*

RAY *(continuing).* Too bad you didn't connect. You could have gone to Juvenile Hall. That's what you want, isn't it?

JIM. No.

RAY. Sure it is. You want to bug us till we have to lock you up. Why?

JIM. Leave me alone.

RAY. No.

JIM. I don't know why—!

RAY. Go on—don't give me that. Someone giving you hard looks?

JIM. I just get so—*(fighting tears).* Boy, sometimes the temperature goes way up.

RAY *(suddenly gentle).* Okay. Okay. Let it out. *(JIM starts crying).* You feel like you want to blow your wheels right now?

JIM. All the time! I don't know what gets into me—but I keep looking for trouble and I always—I swear you better lock me up. I'm going to smash somebody—I know it.

RAY. Try the desk.

JIM *smashes his fist against it, letting loose for a moment.* RAY *watches, then sits near him.*

RAY. That why you moved from the last town? 'Cause you were in trouble? You can talk about it if you want to—I know about it anyway. Routine check.

JIM. And they think they are protecting me by moving.

RAY. You were getting a good start in the wrong direction back there. Why did you do it?

JIM. Mess that kid up?

RAY *just nods.*

JIM *(continuing).* He called me chicken.

RAY. And your folks didn't understand?

JIM. They never do.

RAY. So then you moved?

JIM. They think I'll make friends if we move. Just *move* and everything'll be roses and sunshine.

RAY. But you don't think that's a solution.

JIM *is silent; he picks at his nails.*

RAY *(continuing).* Things pretty tough for you at home?

JIM. She eats him alive and he takes it. *(*JIM *stares at his family through hole in door).* What a zoo!

RAY. What?

JIM. A zoo. He always wants to be my pal, you know? But how can I give him anything when he's—I mean I love him and I don't want to hurt him—but I don't know what to do anymore except maybe die.

RAY. Pretty mixed up?

JIM. If he could—

RAY. "If he could" what? You mean your father?

JIM. I mean if he had the guts to knock Mom cold once I bet she'd be happy and I bet she'd stop picking. They make mush out of him. Just mush. One thing I know is I never want to be like him.

RAY *(interrupts).* Chicken?

JIM. I bet you see right through me, don't you? *(*RAY *shrugs).* How can anyone grow up in this circus?

RAY. You got me, Jim—but they do. Want some water?

JIM *(as* RAY *gets a cup of water from cooler).* Boy—if I had one day when I didn't have to be all confused and ashamed of everything—or I felt I belonged some place.

RAY *(giving him water).* Here. Look, will you do something for me? If the pot starts boiling again, will you come and see me before you get yourself in a jam? Even if you just want to talk—come in and shoot the breeze. It's easier sometimes than talking to your folks.

JIM. Okay—

RAY. Any time—day or night. You calmed down enough to go back now?

JIM *(smiling).* You serious?

RAY smiles and opens the door.

RAY's *office as* JIM *comes towards his* MOTHER *and forces himself to kiss her.*

JIM. I'm sorry.
MOTHER. All right, darling.

She rises and takes his arm. They start out through the door into the hall, followed by GRANDMA *and* FATHER.

GRANDMA *(to* RAY*).* This was all very unfortunate, but he made a mistake and he's sorry—so we're not going to have any more trouble. He's always been a lovely boy—

JIM. Lovely! Grandma—if you tell another lie you're going to turn to stone.

RAY. Luck, Jim. Don't forget.

FATHER *(offering* RAY *three cigars).* Have some cigars.

RAY. No thanks, I don't smoke.

FATHER. Go on—Give 'em to your friends.

RAY. No—thanks very much, Mr. Stark.

MOTHER. Frank he doesn't want any.

JIM *grins at* RAY *who nods. They all leave.* RAY *looking after them, shakes his head and lights a cigarette. We see* JIM *and his family pass through the main door. Waiting to enter, in the custody of some uniformed police, are* BUZZ *and the kids we saw at the opening, sullen and truculent. As they march into the lobby and* JIM *grows smaller in the distance, the music comes up and out.*

Fade out.

Fade in.

Low angle. Alley. Morning. A rabbit comes running down the alley followed by a group of young kids, screaming with pleasure. As camera pans with the group, the littlest, a boy of five, stops near us looking after the disappearing group. The shouts of the children wane.

JUDY *rushes out from a backyard beyond him. She is carrying school books and a bag-lunch. She wears a polo coat against the winter wind.*

JUDY *(yelling).* Beau!

The boy, who is her brother, BEAU, *looks up but doesn't move.* JUDY *stops at her gate. A car careens down the alley, past him.*

Long shot. JUDY *and* BEAU *seen through a window in* JIM's *house.* JIM *is in f.g. looking out through the curtains. He smiles.*

JUDY *(yelling).* What are you trying to do, get yourself killed?

BEAU *(laughing).* Yes!

VOICE OF JIM'S MOTHER. Your eggs are on the table, dear.

JIM *turns from window and passes camera*

Full shot JIM's *dining room. The* MOTHER *is just setting a plate of eggs at* JIM's *place. The* FATHER *is seated, drinking coffee and looking at the newspaper.* GRANDMA *comes in from kitchen.* JIM *is neatly dressed in tie, tweed jacket and slacks.*

MOTHER. Sit down and eat—you'll be late.

JIM *(approaching table).* It'd stick in my throat, Mom. I'm nervous or something—

GRANDMA. It's a wonder we don't all have TB or some other terrible disease after living in all those smoky cities!

MOTHER. Well, drink your milk anyhow.

GRANDMA *(muttering).* There aren't so many factories here.

FATHER. Mother—

JIM *(still standing; he drinks).* You make any sandwiches?

FATHER. My first day of school, mother'd make me eat and by golly I could never even swallow till recess—

MOTHER *(bringing bag of lunch from buffet).* There's nothing to be nervous about. Here's peanut butter and meat loaf—*(* JIM *makes a mouth-stuck-together-with-peanut-butter sound).*

GRANDMA. What did I tell you? Peanut butter!

MOTHER. Well, there's a thermos of orange juice and some apple-sauce cake in the wax paper to wash it down.

GRANDMA. I baked that!

JIM *(he kisses her cheek).* 'Bye, Mom.

MOTHER. Goodbye, dear.

FATHER *(rising).* So long, young fella. Knock 'em dead, like your old man used to!

JIM. Sure—*(he gets to the door and turns)*. You know something? I have a feeling we're going to stay here.

FATHER. And listen—watch out about the pals you choose—Know what I mean? Don't let them choose you—

But JIM *is on his way out.*

Full shot. JIM's *backyard as* JIM *comes out of the kitchen door into the early sunshine.*

JUDY's VOICE. Come out of the alley, Beau! This is the last time I'm going to call you.

JIM *blinks, pauses and sees* JUDY. *He takes off his tie and puts it in his pocket. Then he starts across the backyard, camera panning with him to:*

Full shot. The Alley with JIM *coming out his gate,* JUDY *and* BEAU *visible beyond. He stops again.*

JUDY. Beau! All right—go to school alone!

She starts down the alley. BEAU *skips after her and starts tightrope-walking the gutter gravel.*

JIM *(calling)*. Hey!

JUDY *glances at him briefly, but continues.* JIM *follows a few yards, but on his side of the alley.*

JIM *(continuing)*. Hey, didn't I see you before some place?

JUDY *ignores him, but something self-conscious happens to her walk.* JIM *runs across the alley.*

Med. shot. JUDY *stopping as* JIM *enters.* BEAU *tight-rope walking on down the hill.*

JIM. Hi. I saw you before.
JUDY. Bully for you.
JIM. You don't have to be unfriendly.
JUDY. Now that's true!
JIM *(smiling)*. See?
JUDY. "Life is crushing in on me."
JIM *(smiling)*. "Life can be beautiful." Hey, I know where it was.
JUDY. Where what was.
JIM. Where I saw you. *(no answer)*. Everything going okay now? *(no answer)*. You live around here?
JUDY *(relieved)*. Who lives?
JIM. See, I'm new.
JUDY. Won't mother be proud.
JIM. You're really flipped—aren't you.

JUDY *looks up a little surprised.*

JIM *(continuing)*. Where's Dawson High School?

JUDY. You going there?
JIM. Yeah—why—
JUDY. Dig the square wardrobe!
JIM *(defensively)*. Yeah. So where's the high school?
JUDY *(softer)*. University and 10th—Want to carry my books?

An auto horn, stuck, in the distance.

JIM. I was just getting my car. I could take you.

The horn approaches, loud.
JUDY. The kids take me.
JIM. Oh.

Another angle. JIM *and* JUDY *as the car, horn blowing, wheels into view above them and comes careening into the alley.* JUDY *sees it and moves a step away from* JIM.

JUDY. I'll bet you're a real yo yo.
JIM. A what?
JUDY *(yelling over horn)*. Goodbye! See you!
JIM *(yelling)*. I'm not so bad.

JUDY *is moving toward the car.*

Med. shot. Car full of kids as it comes to a jolting stop near JUDY. *The boys wear suede coats, leather jackets, black peggers, boots. Their clothing is not uniform—it is the air they assume which is uniform: swaggering, self-conscious, piratical. Someone is always combing his hair. The driver is* BUZZ, *whom we recognize as the leader of the stomp gang we met on Easter. He wears a leather jacket. With him are* CHICK, *a slight bespectacled lad;* CRUNCH, BUZZ's *first lieutenant;* COOKIE, *a hanger-on;* GOON, *a character; and the girls* HELEN *and* MILLIE. *The kids are screaming as* BUZZ *jams on the brakes.* JUDY *comes forward.* JIM *hangs back.*

BUZZ. Stella-a-a-a!

JUDY *comes to them quickly, smiling.*

JUDY. Steady Marlon!
BUZZ. Wanna make the colored lights go around and around?

JUDY *and* BUZZ *kiss ardently and without love.* JIM *goes for his car.*

BUZZ *(looks after* JIM *then at* JUDY*)*. What's that?
JUDY. A new disease.
BUZZ *(a little suspicious)*. Friend of yours?
JUDY. I'm glad they let you out.
BUZZ. Nobody chickened.
JUDY. I heard about it. You're lucky he lived.

BUZZ. They always live.

During this JIM *has gotten his car and has driven up.*

JIM. Where's University and 10th?
JUDY *(pointing right)*. That way!
CHICK *(pointing left)*. That way!
BUZZ *(pointing up)*. That way!

Simultaneously

The kids laugh wildly. The radio blares. JUDY *lays her head on* BUZZ's *shoulder and his arm goes around her as the car zooms away.* JIM *looks after them a moment, then follows.*

Dissolve to:

Close shot. Bicycle rack. Wheels spin in, one after another and drive straight into their slots. As the nearest bike moves in:

Med. shot. PLATO *just getting off his motor scooter. He comes forward, passes camera which pans with him then stops – as the school is suddenly revealed. Music starts with a crash and keeps mounting through the following.* PLATO *sighs and moves away from us to join the parade of students filling the Main approach.*

Parking lot as cars scream into their places noisily. JIM *gets out of one and comes forward. A motorcycle roars by, just missing him.* JIM *stares off and starts to move as camera pans with him to:*

Another angle. School. Another crash of music. JIM *moves toward the parade.*

Full shot. Mid-way down main approach. A number of kids pass, gossiping happily as they greet each other for the first time since vacation. Camera searches over them and stops upon our special group moving toward us BUZZ, JUDY *and the rest, all abreast. Others must park at their passage or be elbowed out of the way, staring resentfully, but not daring to challenge the group's priority.* PLATO *runs forward, past them.*

Door from within bouncing from hand to hand as students enter. PLATO *moves through the door and disappears in a milling of kids.* JUDY *enters with her group and moves on with them.*

Med. shot. Monitor (inside corridor). The Monitor is an athletic letter-sweater boy with an arm brassard that bears the letters "HC". Kids pour past him. JIM *enters.*

JIM. Hi—can you tell we where I go? I'm just starting here.

MONITOR *(pointing at brassard)*. Mr. Bassett's office—203. He'll tell you where your home room is—
JIM. Thanks a lot.

JIM *moves out.*

Angle shot. Corridor. Shooting past a row of steel lockers. The clash and slam of doors as kids throw in coats, pull out books and primp for the day ahead. PLATO *comes to his locker, which is the nearest, and opens it.*

Full shot. Corridor. JIM *moves toward us from the distance. Crowded at the entrance to a classroom in f.g. are* JUDY *and her pals. They are sneaking a smoke, passing the cigarette from one cupped hand to another. As* JIM *comes near,* JUDY *sees him. So do the others. They fold their arms across their chests and whistle "We are the girls of the institute" – all but* JUDY. JIM *glances at her and continues on past camera. A bell starts ringing crazily over the music.*

Close shot. PLATO. *He is straightening his tie in the mirror. Above it, pasted to the locker door, is a still of Alan Ladd. In the mirror we can see* JIM *moving past.* PLATO *sees him too. He wheels around and stares.*

PLATO *(to himself)*. Hi.

The strident music of the students diminishes. The ringing of the bell stops. There remain only JIM's *footsteps.*

Long shot. JIM *moving off down the corridor.* PLATO *is in f.g. looking after him. He slams his locker and starts after* JIM, *moving at the same speed and hovering near the wall. The footsteps of the two boys echo stonily. They are alone.* JIM *stops at a bulletin board near a bend in the corridor.* PLATO *stops too.*

Bulletin board. JIM *looking at the notices.* PLATO *drifts in several yards away and hangs near the wall watching* JIM *who doesn't see him.* JIM *reads:*

Insert: Bulletin board, "Attention All Juniors and Seniors" – Planetarium field trip – 2 pm – Sharp!"

Another angle. JIM *and* PLATO *as* JIM *turns from bulletin board and starts away.*

PLATO *(clearing his throat)*. Hi.
JIM. Hi there.
PLATO. You remember me?
JIM. No. I don't think so—
PLATO. I'm sorry—I made a mistake.

JIM *starts toward camera as* PLATO *after another look, turns in the opposite direction and walks away from us, smashing his fist against the wall as he goes.* JIM *stops, full in camera. His face clouds, trying to remember. He turns full around to look after* PLATO, *then turns back and continues on his way. The footsteps fade.*

Dissolve to:

Full shot. Planetarium seen from the parking lot—a great dome crowns it—the city lies below. Camera picks up JIM's *car maneuvering through the crowded lot. In b.g. a few other late-comers are dashing up steps to Planetarium.* JIM *drives into a small lot behind observator, parks, then runs to observatory entrance.*

Full shot. Lobby as JIM *runs through, opens door of theater and passes inside.*

Long shot. Sky full of stars seen past JIM's *head. Darkness. This is not our sky. It is a replica of it projected onto the dome of the Planetarium. The stars slide their tentative ways in an ever-changing pattern. One of them is much larger than the rest and increases in size as we watch. Music of the spheres is heard—a high threatening tremulo.*

LECTURER'S VOICE. For many days before the end of our earth people will look into the night sky and notice a star, increasingly bright and increasingly near.

JIM *looks around for a seat and passes down aisle. Seen beyond him is the projector, moving slowly, its great dumb-bell head sparkling with pin-points of light.* JIM *takes a seat in front row.* PLATO, *in the row behind him, moves over a seat to be nearer. They exchange looks.*

Full shot. Normal students watching intently.

LECTURER'S VOICE. As this star approaches us, the weather will change. The great polar fields of the north and south will rot and divide, and the seas will turn warmer.

Low angle. LECTURER. *A dry, elderly man in a stiff white collar. He is seated at a desk, the light from the reading lamp spilling upward onto his face.*

LECTURER. The last of us search the heavens and stand amazed. For the stars will still be there, moving through their ancient rhythms.

Angle shot. Students. Some watching, some taking notes. An OLD LADY TEACHER *in f.g. taps the heads of two kids in the row before her. They stop their whispering. She smiles at them.*

LECTURER'S VOICE. The familiar constellations that illuminate our night will seem as they have always seemed, eternal, unchanged

and little moved by the shortness of time between our planet's birth and its demise.

Med. shot. PLATO *staring upward.*

LECTURER'S VOICE. Orion, the Hunter.

PLATO *looks off.*

Med. shot. JIM *(from* PLATO's *angle).* JIM *is seated in the row ahead of* PLATO. *His lips are parted as he looks up.*

JIM. Boy!
PLATO *(leaning forward).* What?
JIM *(surprised).* Once you been up there, you know you been some place!
LECTURER'S VOICE. Gemini, the Twins.

Two shot. JUDY *and* BUZZ. BUZZ *has his arm around her. He is nuzzling her ear. She is blandly watching the dome.*

LECTURER'S VOICE. Cancer, the Crab.

BUZZ *pokes* JUDY *who looks at him. He curves his wrist toward her, opening and closing his first two fingers like the pincers of a crab.*

BUZZ. I'm a crab!

She laughs. So do the others.

Med. shot. JIM *(*PLATO *behind). Seen from* JUDY's *angle.* JIM *turns at the sound of the laughter, and smiles.*

LECTURER'S VOICE. Taurus, the Bull.
JIM *(in good imitation).* Moo!

He waits for approval.

Angle shot. JUDY, BUZZ *and group (seen from* JIM's *angle). He is in f.g. They are staring at him. Nobody laughs.*

CRUNCH *(flat).* Yeah, moo.
BUZZ. Moo. That's real cute. Moo.
GOON. Hey, he's real rough—
CRUNCH. I bet he fights with cows.
BUZZ. Moo.

They turn from him. JIM *withers and looks front.* JUDY *smiles a little and looks away so the others cannot notice her amusement.*

LECTURER'S VOICE. Sagittarius and Aries— all as they have ever been.

PLATO *leans in and touches* JIM's *shoulder, lightly at first, then harder.* JIM *turns to him.*

PLATO. You shouldn't monkey with him.
JIM. What?
PLATO. He's a wheel. So's she. It's hard to make friends with them.
JIM. I don't want to make friends.

He turns back, unhappy at having revealed himself.

Another shot. JUDY, BUZZ, CRUNCH. JIM *seen in b.g. The kids are whispering among themselves and pointing at* JIM, *who looks up and notices. He is getting uncomfortable.*

LECTURER'S VOICE. And while the flash of our beginning has not yet traveled the light years into distance—

Full shot. The dome. The star rushes nearer, looming larger and larger. The music rises in tension and volume.

LECTURER'S VOICE. Has not yet been seen by planets deep within the other galaxies, we will disappear into the blackness of the space from which we came.

Two shot. JIM *and* PLATO *staring upward, cringing back into their seats as the light on their faces increases. Music is up loud.*

Full shot. The dome seen past PLATO's *head. The heavens grow brighter as the star plummets near. Music at crescendo.*

LECTURER'S VOICE. Destroyed as we began in a burst of gas and fire.

The sky is blasted by a wild flush of light. Music reaches explosion. The stars appear again.

Moving shot. Faces of normal kids watching seriously—very impressed.

LECTURER'S VOICE *(continuing)*. The heavens are still and cold once more. In all the complexity of our universe and the galaxies beyond, the Earth will not be missed.

Med. shot. JIM *and* PLATO *looking up.*

LECTURER'S VOICE. Through the infinite reaches of space, the problems of Man seem trivial and naive indeed. And Man, existing alone, seems to be an episode of little consequences.

PLATO *ducks his head down on the back of* JIM's *chair.* JIM *looks at him.*

LECTURER'S VOICE. That's all. Thank you very much.

The lights go on. The rustle and confusion of kids stretching after sitting too long. Scattered applause. JIM *rises and ruffles* PLATO's *hair.*

JIM. Hey, it's over. The world ended.

PLATO *looks up at him.*

PLATO. What does he know about Man alone?

Med. Shot. LECTURER *as he reaches over and turns a dial. "Morning Song" by Grieg comes on softly.*

Low angle. OLD LADY TEACHER *rising. She stares around at the bustling students and claps her hands sharply, but the noise is barely heard above the tumult.*

TEACHER *(shrill)*. May I have your attention? May I please have your attention? Classes will meet at the busses outside. May I have your attention? *(to herself)*. The heck with it.

She picks up her coat and bag.

Planetarium parking lot. School busses and autos, some new and some heaps, are parked in f.g. Beyond is the dome of the Planetarium. Kids mill about, some already driving off in their cars. One bus, already full, pulls past camera.

Med. shot. Front of bus seen from within. Driver in f.g. Kids swarm up the steps and enter. PLATO *is among them, but keeps looking back for* JIM. PLATO *boards the bus and pauses near the driver to peer through windshield. His face clouds.*

Long shot. JUDY *and group. Seen from* PLATO's *angle through windshield. They are standing idly in a loose line near* BUZZ's *car. They are looking back toward Planetarium.*

Med. shot. Front of bus, seen from within. PLATO *turns suddenly and pushes his way past the kids who are boarding.*

PLATO. Excuse me. Excuse me.

Full shot. Parking lot. Bus in f.g. Beyond it JUDY *and the group are visible.* PLATO *squeezes out.*

MALE TEACHER. JOHN, where you going?
PLATO. I forgot something. I'll get a hitch.

PLATO *moves quickly past the teacher who climbs in. The door slams, the bus moves away.* PLATO *stops and looks after it. The last cars are clearing the lot. Only* JIM's *and* BUZZ's *remain.* PLATO *looks at the small, waiting group.*

Med. shot. The group seen from the rear. PLATO *in the distance facing them.*

BUZZ. What you looking at?

Med. shot. PLATO *wild-eyed with fear.*

PLATO. Nothing.

He runs off, camera panning with him. His goal is the Planetarium Entrance, visible beyond. He races toward it frantically.

Med. shot. The group looking off after
PLATO. BUZZ, *nearest camera, pulls a switch-*
knife from his pocket and pops the long blade
open. JUDY *stares at it, then looks up at* BUZZ
apprehensively. CRUNCH *sits down on the*
bumper and lights a cigarette.

Display lobby. Planetarium as PLATO *rushes*
in, out of breath, stops and looks around. In
distance he sees JIM *leaning over the pendulum*
pit, smoking quietly. PLATO *doesn't move.* JIM
hasn't even looked up.

PLATO (*screaming as if he were yelling*
"*Fire!*"). What's your name!
JIM. Jim. What's yours?
PLATO (*a little quieter*). Plato. It's a
nickname.

JIM *nods.* PLATO *goes over to him, camera*
following, until they are close together, both
leaning over the rail.

PLATO. Listen, I told you not to fool with
them. Now they're waiting for you.
JIM. I know. That's why I came back.
PLATO. You scared?
JIM. I just don't want trouble.
PLATO. He has a knife.
JIM. I saw it. Gee, look at that thing swing,
will you? Do you think it never stops?
PLATO. No. It's perpetual motion.
JIM. Oh, I bet some little guy comes in here
at night and pushes it. Go-go-go!

PLATO *walks cautiously to the door and starts*
outside, camera following.

Long shot. Kids (corner of Observatory) with
PLATO *leaning out of door, seeing them, pulling*
back quickly.

Inside display lobby as PLATO *pulls back*
through the door. JIM *seems to have disap-*
peared. PLATO *stares around frightened.*

PLATO. Jim?

JIM *is looking at another exhibit whose me-*
chanical voice is heard.

JIM. I'm here.
PLATO (*coming to him*). They're still there!
(JIM *nods. They watch the exhibit a while*
longer). Jim—Do you think when the end of
the world comes it'll be at night?
JIM. No. In the morning. (PLATO *looks up*
questioning. JIM *smiles and shrugs*). I just have
a feeling.

They start moving, camera leading.

PLATO. If you don't want trouble, I know a
place we can go—(JIM *looks up at him*). It's a
big mansion and we could sneak around there

and they wouldn't even know. You could be
safe—

They turn a corner quickly.

Doors to balcony (from inside) as JIM *and*
PLATO *come to them from behind camera, fling*
the doors open and step outside.

Balcony as JIM *and* PLATO *come onto it, lean*
on the parapet. PLATO *points off.*

PLATO. There it is.

High long shot. Mansion. (Matte). It is fall-
ing into elegant ruin, casting long afternoon
shadows on the great lawns and promenades.

Closeup PLATO *looking urgently at* JIM.

PLATO. Should we go?

Two shot. JIM *and* PLATO. PLATO'*s back is to*
us. JIM *looks past him and sees something.*

JIM (*quietly*). The shadows are getting long.

PLATO *turns to look too.*

Long high shot. Parking lot, JIM'*s car is*
where he left it. Into the driveway, like logs
driven before a sea, the shadows of the waiting
kids appear and advance until the kids them-
selves come into view. They pause there a mo-
ment, then look up.

HELEN (*smiling*). Le soleil tombe dans la
mer.

Laughter. The kids scatter along the wall at
the foot of the balcony stairs. BUZZ *goes to*
JIM'*s car, knife in hand, and stands silently.*

Low angle. Two shot. JIM *and* PLATO *staring*
down from balcony parapet. At last JIM *moves*
out past camera.

Low angle. Long shot. JIM *and* PLATO. JUDY
in f.g. The two boys walk down the stairs. Cam-
era pans with them as they reach parking lot
level and start walking past other members of
the group.

Traveling shot. JIM *and* PLATO *coming*
forward.

Dolly shot. BUZZ *from* JIM'*s angle. As camera*
moves in toward BUZZ *standing alone at the car,*
he suddenly bends down and slashes JIM'*s tire.*
Camera stops. There is the hiss of air escaping.
BUZZ *straightens and smiles past camera.*

Close shot. JIM *inhaling sharply in shock and*
suppressed anger.

Full shot over JIM'*s car. Group in b.g. motion-*
less. JIM *and* PLATO *approach the car.* JIM *stops*

and looks down. BUZZ *stands smiling and puts away the knife.*

Close shot. Rear wheel. The tire slashed, the wheel rests on the ground.

Full shot. Car. Shooting between group and BUZZ *toward backs of* JIM *and* PLATO, *who are looking down at car which rests on its rims.* JIM *turns and moves toward group. He stops, looks from one to the other and smiles nervously. Then he looks straight at* BUZZ.

JIM *(wearily).* You know something?
BUZZ. What?
JIM *(reproachfully).* You watch too much television.

Med. shot. The group and JIM. JUDY *has come to* BUZZ, *stands on the wall above him.*

BUZZ. Hey, he's real abstract and different.
JIM. I'm cute, too.

Suddenly GOON *starts clucking softly like a chicken. One by one the others pick it up.* BUZZ, *the last, crows. Silence.*

Med. shot. The group and JIM.

JIM. Meaning me?
BUZZ. What?
JIM. Chicken?

The group gives a quick, short laugh.

Med. shot. JIM *as he takes off his glasses, smiles. Shakes his head disapprovingly.*

JIM. You shouldn't call me that.

Close shot. PLATO *watching anxiously.*

Med. shot. BUZZ *with* JUDY *watching above him.* JIM *enters shot until he is close to* BUZZ's *face. He looks up at* JUDY. *Camera closes in until we are tight on the three. The heads are nearly touching.*

JIM *(softly to* JUDY). You always at ringside? You always travel in this rank company?

BUZZ *clutches* JIM's *hair and jerks his head up. He cracks* JIM *smartly across the face with the palm of his hand.*

Close shot. JUDY *looking at* JIM. *Her eyes clear in recognition.*

Another angle. The group and JIM *as* JIM *tears free and comes at* BUZZ, *slugging. But* BUZZ, *with a laugh, leaps onto the parapet and turns, the knife in his hand again.* JIM *stops short. The group and* PLATO *move in around him.*

JIM. I thought only punks fought with knives.

BUZZ. Who's fighting? This is the test, man. It's a crazy game.
HELEN. Les jeux de courage!

Close-up. CRUNCH. *He is smiling. His arms are around the shoulders of the kids who flank him.*

CRUNCH *(wetting his lips).* Machismo. Machismo.

Med. shot. Group.

JIM. Machismo?
BUZZ. Somebody find him a knife.

Close shot. PLATO *seen between heads of* MIL *and* COOKIE. COOKIE *holds up a switch knife and tosses it over into the circle.*

PLATO. Jim!

Full shot. Circle as the knife falls at JIM's *feet.* JIM *stoops and picks up his weapon, then faces* BUZZ. *Then he springs his blade.*

BUZZ. You know the action? No cutting. Just sticking—jab real cool.

BUZZ *hops from the parapet. They begin stalking each other.* BUZZ *slides his knife from hand to hand trying to hypnotize* JIM. *Suddenly he pokes out and pricks* JIM's *shirt. The group sighs "Ole!"* JIM *makes no effort at self defense. Silence.* BUZZ *pricks* JIM *again, "Ole!"*

BUZZ *(as he maneuvers).* What you waiting on, Toreador? I thought you wanted some action!

JIM *cuts out half-heartedly.*

BUZZ. Big brave bull. Hah! Toro! Hah! Hah!
GOON. Moo!
BUZZ. Come on—Fascinate us. Impress us. What's happening? Let's go!
JIM. I don't want trouble.
BUZZ *(furious suddenly).* You crud chicken! You're wasting our time! *(viciously, he slaps* JIM *across the face.* JIM *lashes out and misses.* BUZZ *hops back).* Yeah—that's pretty close. How about a little closer, Toreador? Cut off a button and you get to join the club!

Outside entrance of parking lot. A uniformed GUIDE *of middle-age stares past camera. Cries of "Ole," are heard in the distance.*

GUIDE *(turning).* Mr. Minton! Mr. Minton! Trouble!

The LECTURER *appears running. He stops short at what he sees, and blinks in the sunlight.*

GUIDE. Look. There's your audience.

LECTURER. Oh, I don't think so. From the school?

Inside circle. JIM *is covered with sweat and about to drop. He is getting the worst of it, still refusing to defend himself.*

Close shot. PLATO. *He is looking on in despair.*

GROUP. Ole! Ole!

Suddenly, with a cry, PLATO *pushes through.*

Inside circle as PLATO *comes through. His eyes are wild. He holds a tire chain in his hand.*

MIL. BUZZY! Look out! He's got a chain!
BUZZ *(smiling as he sees* PLATO*).* Hey! Chicken Little!

BUZZ *trips* PLATO *quickly and kicks him while he's down.* CRUNCH *grabs the chain.*

JIM. All right—you want it, you got it!

Suddenly JIM *transforms. He bores forward expertly—pricks* BUZZ *again and again. Cries of Ole greet him.* BUZZ *is surprised.*

Full shot. Group. We hear only the breathing of the combatants. Beyond we see the GUIDE *approaching swiftly. The* LECTURER *trails at a safe distance.*

Closeup. CRUNCH. *He looks up. His smile fades.*

CRUNCH. Honk. Let's split.

Group as they look off and see the GUIDE *and* LECTURER *approach.* BUZZ *and* JIM *are both breathing hard.* PLATO *is getting to his feet.*

BUZZ. Split for what? Couple old poop-heads?

He folds up his knife and puts it away. So does JIM.

JIM. You satisfied or you want more?
BUZZ. How 'bout you? Say the word and you're cold, Jack—you're dead.
JUDY. Buzzie—we better get out of here.
BUZZ. What's eating you, Judy? You want him alive?
JIM. Where can we meet?
BUZZ. Know the Millertown bluff?
COOKIE. The bluff, Buzz! That's dangerous up there.
BUZZ. Draw him a picture, Chicken Little. Eight o'clock. Cookie, you call Moose and get a couple cars. We're going to have us some real kicks. Little chickie-run. You been on chickie-runs before?
JIM. Sure—that's all I do.

The GUIDE *bursts in among them. The* LECTURER *remains on the fringe.*

GUIDE. All right—all of you—start moving!
JUDY. You mean l'il ol' us? What's the matter with the nice man?
GUIDE. Don't clown with me.
BUZZ. Why'nt you go suck on something sweet?
GUIDE. You think you're tough? I got a son twice your size and I can still handle him.
LECTURER. Don't lose control, Mr. Jamison. I think if we just explain—
GUIDE. Explain to *these*? They think they own the world!
CRUNCH. The world is round!
MIL. The world is flat!
COOKIE. All the world's a stage!

There is wild laughter from the kids as they close around the GUIDE *and start edging him away, up the steps toward the Planetarium balcony.*

THE KIDS. The world goes round the sun! Goodbye proud world!
I got the world on a string!
The world's my oyster!
Hey! A fish-eater! Brain food.

They are gone. The LECTURER *looks after them then comes to* JIM. JIM *looks down at his shirt. There are spots of blood.* PLATO *opens it, spits on a handkerchief and starts to wipe the blood away.*

LECTURER *(smiling wanly: to* JIM*).* Sometimes the world is too much with us, isn't it, son? What was the disturbance?
JIM. Nothing.
LECTURER. You're bleeding. Are you all right?
JIM. I scratched my mosquito bites. I'm fine. *(*LECTURER *hesitates).* I'm fine—*thanks*!

LECTURER *goes.* JIM *impatiently closes his shirt.*

PLATO. Are you really going to meet them?
JIM. Who knows. Plato?
PLATO. What?
JIM. What's a chickie-run?

Dissolve to:

Downstairs hall. JIM's *house. A single light is burning.* JIM *steals in from the kitchen, peers cautiously into the living room, then starts up the stairs. A crash is heard above.* JIM *stops, undecided whether to go or stay, then moves quickly up the stairs, no longer trying to be quiet.*

Upper hall. JIM'S *house as* JIM *rises into view at the top of stairs. He sees a figure on hands and knees mopping something off the rug. Leak-light from the staircase dims details. An apron is tied around the figure's waist and its bow sticks bravely up in the air.*

JIM. Mom?

The figure straightens and turns around, smiling. It is the FATHER. *He is neatly dressed in his business suit but wears a Mary Petty apron.*

FATHER. Hya, Jimbo.

JIM *leans against the wall, shaking his head and trying not to laugh. The* FATHER *laughs unhappily, trying to make it all seem a joke.*

FATHER. You thought I was Mom?
JIM. Yeah!
FATHER. It's just this get-up. The girl's out and I was bringing Mom's supper.
JIM *(giggling).* And you dropped it?
FATHER *(laughing too).* Yeah! Shh!
JIM. That's funny!
FATHER. I better clean this up before she sees it.

He starts dabbing among the spilled dishes with a wet cloth. JIM *watches him.*

JIM. Let her sec. What could happen. *(the* FATHER *continues dabbing).* Dad—*(the* FATHER *looks up at him).* Dad—don't. Don't.

JIM *touches his* FATHER'S *elbow, bringing him to his feet. They look at each other a moment then* JIM *goes to his bedroom. The* FATHER *goes back to mopping up the mess.*

Inside JIM'S *room as he comes in, shuts the door and throws himself miserably on his bed. He writhes as if the pain he feels were physical. Outside, radios are heard in the night—tuned to different stations. He feels under his jacket and holds up his hand to the moonlight. There is blood on it. He reaches up and takes his alarm clock and is setting it as camera glides to his window and holds over the rooftops.*

Full shot. JUDY'S *backyard. Moonlight.* JUDY *stands near camera looking up at the moon. The radios seem louder out here. One breaks through.*

ANNOUNCER. Time now for the seven o'clock news. Friends, the next time you go shopping.

VOICE OF JUDY'S FATHER *(o.s.).* Judy.

She wheels around.

Long shot. The FATHER *standing erect on back porch, silhouetted against a window.*

FATHER. What are you wishing for, Judy?

Med. shot. JUDY. *She hasn't moved.*

JUDY *(softly).* I wasn't wishing. I was looking at the moon.

Full shot. Backyard featuring the FATHER. *We see him now as a tall and handsome man. There is something boyish and appealing about him.*

FATHER *(singing lightly).*
"Man in the Moon, how came you there—
Up in the sky where you are shining—
Floating so high in the frosty air—?
Oh, say—Man in the Moon!"—

JUDY *comes forward, stands below him on the step. Her look is adoring.*

JUDY *(astonished).* How did *you* know that?
FATHER. We used to sing it in school. *(he smiles).* Don't look at me with such horror. They had schools in those days.
JUDY. But the same song. I think it's fantastic!
FATHER. We were romantic then too—
JUDY. Are you and Mom home tonight?
FATHER. No. Why?
JUDY. Nothing, only it'd be nice to spend an evening together for a change.
FATHER. With *us* old creeps? Come on, we have to eat.
JUDY *(rising).* Daddy—*(he looks at her).* Good evening.
FATHER. Hi.

He turns away and goes into the house. She hesitates and then follows. Something in the moods has changed. He has neglected to hold the door for her.

Dining room. JUDY'S *house as the* FATHER *comes to the head of the table and takes his seat. Three places are set.* JUDY *follows. She stands above his chair, looking down at him as he drinks his tomato juice.*

JUDY *(quietly, afraid).* Didn't you forget something?
FATHER. What?

JUDY *doesn't answer, but leans down and kisses him quickly on the lips.*

FATHER *(continuing; shocked).* What's the matter with you?

JUDY *freezes, frightened. He collects himself a little.*

FATHER *(continuing).* You're too old for that kind of stuff, kiddo. I thought you stopped doing that long ago.

JUDY *(very hurt).* I didn't want to stop.

The mother enters briskly from another part of the house—an attractive, brittle woman of thirty-five.

MOTHER. Didn't want to stop what?

FATHER. Nothing.

JUDY. I was talking to Dad.

FATHER. I didn't kiss her so it's a big thing.

MOTHER *(calling to kitchen).* Bertha! You can serve the souffle! *(to* FATHER*).* Fish souffle. *(to* JUDY*).* You don't have to stand there, darling. Drink your tomato juice.

JUDY *slides into her chair reluctantly and unfolds her napkin.*

JUDY. I guess I just don't understand anything.

FATHER. I'm *tired*, Judy. I'd like to change the subject.

JUDY. Why?

FATHER. I'd like to, that's all. Girls your age don't do that. You need an explanation?

JUDY *(very low).* Girls don't love their father? Since when? Since I got to be sixteen?

She half-rises to kiss him again.

FATHER. Stop it now! Sit down!

Suddenly the FATHER *slaps her. Even as he does it he is as stunned as* JUDY. *The mother stops eating. She has never seen such a display and is shocked. He tries to control himself by buttering a piece of bread. There is a terrible silence into which* BEAU *enters in his pajamas. He runs to his* FATHER'*s chair, then halts—looking from face to face. The* FATHER *puts an arm around him, hugs him almost savagely.*

FATHER *(thickly).* Hi, rascal.

BEAU *(hushed).* Hi.

JUDY *rises, weeping.*

JUDY. May I please be excused?

She starts out. The FATHER *rises and follows after her.*

FATHER *(softly).* Hey, Hey, Glamorpuss. I'm sorry.

She leaves the room, interrupting the joke he was going to make. He turns back to the table and sits down. The MOTHER *rises and comes to him.*

FATHER *(continuing).* I don't know what to do. All of a sudden she's a problem.

The mother stands behind his chair. She tips his head back against her body and kneads his neck and shoulders.

MOTHER. She'll outgrow it, dear. It's just the age.

BEAU *(in a sudden burst).* The atomic age!

The door slams.

MOTHER *(kissing her husband's hair).* It's the age when nothing fits.

Inside JIM's *room. We see him lying on his bed as before. His eyes are open. The alarm clock goes off.* JIM *starts as if shot, then stops the wild ringing. The time is seven-forty-five. He makes no move to leave the bed. There is a light tap on the door, then it opens and the* FATHER *is there, seen in light from the hall and still wearing the apron.*

FATHER. You awake?

JIM. Yes.

FATHER. Listen—I took a steak out of the freezer. I thought we could have a real old-fashioned stag party—just the two of us, what do you say?

JIM. I'm not hungry *(the* FATHER *turns away).* Hey—I want to ask you something.

FATHER *(happily).* Shoot, Jimbo.

JIM. Suppose you knew that you had to do something very dangerous—where you have to prove something you need to know—a question of honor. Would you do it?

FATHER *(laughing).* Is there some kind of trick answer?

JIM. What would you do, Dad?

FATHER *(evading).* I wouldn't do anything hasty. Let's get a little light on the subject.

The FATHER *turns on the light and looks at* JIM *who is now sitting on the edge of the bed. He removes his jacket and the bloody shirt is revealed. The* FATHER *stares.*

JIM. Blood.

FATHER. How'd that happen! What kind of trouble you in?

JIM. The kind we've been talking about. Can you answer me now?

FATHER. Listen—nobody should make a snap decision—This isn't something you just—we ought to consider all the pros and cons—

JIM. We don't have time.

FATHER. We'll make time. Where's some paper. We'll make a list and if we're still stuck then we ought to get some advice—

He goes out, to the study next door. JIM *rises.*

JIM. What *can* you do when you have to be a man?

FATHER. Well, now—

JIM. Just give me a direct answer! *(pause).* You going to stop me from going, Dad?

FATHER. You know I never *stop* you from anything. Believe me—you're at a wonderful age. In ten years you'll look back on this and wish you were a kid again.

JIM. Ten years? Now, Dad—I need an answer now!

FATHER. I just want to show you how foolish you are. When you're older you'll laugh at yourself for thinking this is so important—

During this, JIM *has kicked off his shoes and put on his boots and jacket and goes out.*

Living room featuring stairs. JIM *comes running down the stairs and out the kitchen door.*

FATHER'S VOICE. Jim? Will you listen? You can't go out till we—Jim!

The FATHER *comes down the stairs, goes to the front door and calls:*

FATHER. Jim? Jim!

He goes to kitchen door, calls again, gets no answer, comes back into the living room, sees he is still wearing the apron. He rips it off and throws it down—then starts for the stairs.

Dissolve to:

The Plateau. Moonlight. Wind shrieks over the exposed plateau, which is several hundred yards long. It cuts into the darkness like the prow of a ship and ends in empty air. A dozen cars are scattered about, defining a sort of runway in the center. There are twenty kids present, but very little talk. Most of them belong to BUZZ'S *group but there are a few whom we have not met before. They stand in small clots, murmuring and smoking. The atmosphere is strung tightly, like the moments before a dawn attack. In b.g. near the cliff's edge, are two cars of similar make and model. They face away from camera toward the edge of the plateau. There are no headlights anywhere . . . blackout conditions.*

MOOSE, *a boy in a leather jacket and cheap yachting cap stands guard between the cars, his back to us. His hands are on his hips. His legs are spread. Some girls drift in.*

Another angle. Plateau featuring PLATO *as he wanders through the crowd searching for* JIM. *He passes* BUZZ'S *car where* BUZZ, JUDY *and the rest are eating hamburgers. They have all changed into fighting wardrobe.*

BUZZ *(calling out).* Hey, Chicken-Little. *(*PLATO *stops).* Where's Toreador? He beg off?

PLATO. He's not scared of you.

BUZZ *(laughing).* Yeah? *(to* GOON*).* Goon! You seen that adolescent type anywheres?

COOKIE. He won't show.

GOON. Well, you going to wait all night? I'm getting nervous, man! We got to *do* something!

CRUNCH *(looking off).* Hey, Buzz!

BUZZ. What?

COOKIE. Over there.

BUZZ *snaps on the spotlight again and swings it off.*

Full shot. JIM'S *car as* JIM *gets out and* PLATO *runs to him.*

JIM. How'd *you* get here?

PLATO. I hitched.

JIM. Boy, I bet you'd go to a hanging.

PLATO. My personality's showing again. Should I leave?

JIM. No. It's okay.

BUZZ *enters.*

BUZZ. Come on. Let's see what we're driving. *(*JIM *gets out;* PLATO *starts to follow).* Just him.

JIM. Stay there.

The two boys move away. PLATO *looks after them, hurt, then goes to side of* JUDY *and stands.*

Dolly shot. JIM *and* BUZZ *as they come forward*

BUZZ. What you say your name was?

JIM. Jim Stark.

BUZZ. Buzz Gundersen.

JIM. Hi.

BUZZ. Glad to meet you.

They shake hands briefly as they walk. They come to MOOSE *and stop.*

MOOSE. Got some goodies for you, Buzzie-boy.

BUZZ. Flashlight?

MOOSE *produces one and hands it to* BUZZ *who goes to one of the guarded cars, motioning* JIM *to come, too.*

Closer shot. BUZZ, JIM *and* MOOSE *seen as hood is raised, revealing their faces beneath it.* BUZZ *explores the motor with the flashlight.*

BUZZ. Looks good.

MOOSE. Clean as a whistle. They both got plenty breeze.

BUZZ. Look good to you?

JIM. Sure. It's fine.

BUZZ. Okay.

He closes the hood. Group moves across to other car.

JUDY *and* PLATO. *The other kids are behind them.* JUDY *looks to see that their attention isn't on her, then speaks quietly to* PLATO.

JUDY. Is he your friend?
PLATO. Yes. My *best* friend.
JUDY. What's he like?
PLATO. Oh, I don't know. You have to get to know him. He doesn't say much but when he does you know he means it. He's sincere.
JUDY. Well, that's the main thing—don't you think so?
PLATO. Maybe next summer he's going to take me hunting with him—and fishing. I want him to teach me how and I bet he won't get mad if I goof. His name's Jim. It's really James but he likes Jim more. *(laughing).* People he really likes—he lets call him "Jamie."
JUDY. Want to finish my hamburger? I only took a bite.
PLATO. Okay.

Full shot. Guarded cars. JIM *is close in f.g. at wheel of his car.* BUZZ *is beyond, at wheel of his. Both boys are gunning their engines, listening critically.* JIM *lets his idle.*

JUDY, GOON *and group. They watch in silent anticipation.* PLATO *starts away from them.*

Traveling shot. PLATO *hurrying away from the group. He stops, looking off.*

JIM *and* BUZZ. PLATO *in distance.*

BUZZ. Better try the doors. Jump out. *(*JIM *opens his door).* No—quick, man! You got to break quick.

JIM *shuts his door and tries again. So does* BUZZ. *Then both boys walk forward to the edge. Neither says a word.* BUZZ *puts his hand on* JIM's *shoulder.*

High angle. The edge of the bluff (process). JIM *and* BUZZ *are directly below us. Under them the plateau falls steeply away in a sheer drop of a hundred feet to the ocean below.*

Two shot. JIM *and* BUZZ. JIM *is staring below. He is beginning to perspire. He lights a cigarette. Without taking his hand from* JIM's *shoulder,* BUZZ *borrows the cigarette from his lips, takes a drag and hands it back.* JIM *takes another puff then tosses it into the abyss.*

BUZZ *(quietly).* This is the edge, boy. This is the end.
JIM. Yeah.
BUZZ. I like you, you know?
JIM. Buzz? What are we doing this for?
BUZZ *(still quiet).* We got to do *something.* Don't we?

Long shot. JIM *and* BUZZ *with* PLATO *in f.g.* JIM *and* BUZZ *appear to him as two close friends. Suddenly they break and go, without speaking further, to their cars. They back up to the opposite end of the plateau, headlights dark.* PLATO *follows them with his gaze.*

Group shot. GOON *and others looking up as the cars glide by.*

Med. shot. JUDY *waiting as* BUZZ *and* JIM *move into starting position next to her.* JUDY *goes to* BUZZ. JIM *is in b.g.—looking on.*

JUDY. Feel okay?
BUZZ. Give me some dirt.

She bends out of sight for a moment as BUZZ *goes on talking, then hands him the dirt. He rubs it into his palms.*

BUZZ. Hey, Toreador! She signals. We head for the edge. The first guy who jumps—chicken! *(*JUDY *and* BUZZ *kiss, without much interest).* What's happening?
JUDY. Good luck, Buzz.

She starts out, without kissing him again.

JIM *(calling softly).* Judy.

Med. shot. JIM's *car as* JUDY *comes to him.*

JIM. Me too.

She looks at him a moment then bends and hands him some dirt. Their heads touch for an instant.

JIM. Thank you.

She breaks the look and hurries away.

Long shot. The cars. They are lined up in two rows—headlights facing each other. JUDY *comes into shot. When she gets near camera, she stops and turns back to face them.*

BUZZ. Hit your lights!

Suddenly the headlights of all the cars come on full.

Reverse shot. JUDY. *She is in the center of the glare. Behind her we see the other kids filing out of their cars, hurrying toward the edge of the bluff. The sound of the two motors revving then dying and revving again.*

Inside JIM's *car.* JIM *grips the wheel firmly, relaxes his hands to rub his palms together and crack his knuckles. He grips the wheel again. Steps on the accelerator, winding his engine into a roar. He lets up, looks tensely at—*

BUZZ *in his car. His chin juts forward. He lets go of the wheel, starts to comb his hair.*

Slow pan shot. Spectators staring off at the cars. A boy has his arm around the girl in front of him, his cheek against hers. Both are looking off. Some of the kids smoke. All are involved in the blasting of engines.

PLATO *among the spectators near edge of the bluff. He is chewing his lip. Camera pans down to show that the fingers of both his hands are tightly crossed.*

Close shot. JUDY *staring tensely into the glare. Suddenly she raises her hands high above her head.*

Close shot. JIM *sweating it out. He leans forward, squinting, ready.*

Close shot. BUZZ. *He puts his comb between his teeth and clamps it hard. He settles himself for the run.*

Long shot. Plateau. The cars are in close, seen from the rear. JUDY *is a small distant figure, arms stretched high. The exhaust blasts. Now she drops her arms. The cars leap ahead.*

Med. shot. JUDY. *She whirls to see the cars snap by, then begins running up the center of the plateau between the lines of spectators.*

Full shot. Spectators. Shooting over their shoulders as the cars approach and scream past.

Pit shot. Cars. As they approach, gaining speed, and thunder over the camera.

Inside JIM'S *car. (Process). He is tense.*

Inside BUZZ'S *car. (Process). His hands hard on the wheel. The comb is still between his teeth. He begins edging toward the door on his left.*

Moving close shot. JUDY *biting hard on her finger, as she runs forward.*

Close shot. PLATO. *Both hands cover his mouth. The fingers are still crossed.*

Inside JIM'S *car. (Process). As he edges to his left. He is driving with one hand. He opens the door, gets set for his jump.*

Inside BUZZ'S *car. (Process). He reaches for the door handle and misses. As he raises his arm to reach again, the strap of his windbreaker sleeve slips over the handle. He looks down in panic, then back at the drop ahead. He tugs but cannot get the sleeve loose.*

Closeup. PLATO *staring. He shuts his eyes tight and keeps them shut.*

Shooting at backs of the two cars as they race through the row of lights toward the edge.

Inside JIM'S *car. (Process). His face is soaked. He looks once toward* BUZZ—*then ahead. His eyes widen in fear. He shoves left and flings himself forward, and out.*

Outside JIM'S *car as he sprawls forward—into camera.*

Inside BUZZ'S *car. (Process).* BUZZ *leans way forward now. He seems to rise in his seat. His mouth opens and the comb falls out.*

Full shot spectators staring in disbelief. Suddenly a youth ducks his face into the neck of his girl friend so he cannot see. At the same instant—

CROWD *(in a single breath).* Oh!

Rear view. Edge of the bluff as the two cars go over. There is NO human sound.

Close shot. JIM *as he stops rolling.*

BUZZ'S *car in flight. (Special effects). The car soars through the night, the vehicle of a terrible journey.*

Med. shot. BUZZ. *(Process). Surprise has gone. He rides lightly on the thrill of his last moment—then suddenly, his face twists in a spasm of protest and loss.*

The kids staring at his flight.

JIM *unaware of the disaster—glad he made it.*

Low angle. Edge of the bluff. With headlights blazing, both cars dive down.

Med. shot. JUDY *standing frozen as the spectators shove past and around her.*

Wide angle. Edge of the bluff as spectators swarm to it, stand looking down.

JIM *on hands and knees, trying to rise. Legs rush by him, knock him onto his face.*

Long shot. (Special effects). Both cars plunge into the ocean below.

JIM *at edge of bluff. He is pushing through spectators.*

JIM *(a harsh whisper).* Where's Buzz! Where's Buzz!

PLATO *working his way through the crowd.*

PLATO *(calling).* Jim! Jim!

CRUNCH. CRUNCH *looks up as he hears* JIM'S *repeated cry.* JIM *enters behind him, continuing blindly on his way.*

CRUNCH *(tight fury).* Down there! Down there is Buzz!

JIM *looks over the edge.*

Rear view. Spectators. A siren wail approaches. The kids wheel and scatter, panicking past the camera.

Close shot. MOOSE. *Looks at* JIM. *Runs.*

Close shot. GOON. *Turns. Runs.*

Med. shot. JIM *seen between legs of hurrying kids. The siren and the pounding of their feet on the hard turf.* JIM *is sitting on the edge of the bluff.* PLATO *rushes in, stops short as he sees him.*

PLATO. Come on, Jim! We got to get out of here!

JIM *doesn't move.* PLATO *grabs his arm and yanks.*

PLATO. Get up! Get up! Come on!

JIM *stands.* PLATO *pushes him.*

PLATO. Go on! Move!

They start away, PLATO *still pushing from behind.*

Med. shot. JUDY. *She is standing alone in the wind on the emptying plateau.* JIM *and* PLATO *move past in the distance.* JIM *sees her and stops.*

Close shot. JUDY. *She is shuddering violently but there are no tears. She seems not to see or hear or be aware of anything around her.*

Full shot. JIM *and* PLATO *watching* JUDY. JIM *moves toward her, camera panning with him and leaving* PLATO *behind.* JIM *stands before* JUDY *until she notices him. He shakes his head for all the sorrow he feels, but no words come. Tentatively he offers her his hand. After a moment, she takes it. She knows only that help is being offered and that she will accept it with trust.* JIM *leads her away toward the car.*

Dissolve to:

High long shot. JIM'S *street. Night. There is no movement anywhere. In the houses bordering the street a few lights still burn.* JIM'S *car approaches out of distance and slows when it reaches the alley.*

Med. shot. JIM'S *car as it slows and stops.* JIM, JUDY *and* PLATO *in the front seat.* JUDY *has the door open before the car even stops. She is shaking, agitated and withdrawn.*

JUDY *(hardly audible).* This is fine—

She gets out and starts away, leaving door open.

JIM *(calling quietly).* Judy. Will you be okay?

PLATO *looks at him.* JUDY *hesitates.* JIM *raises a hand to her in a shy farewell. She smiles vaguely, then hurries away from them.*

Near JIM'S *backyard (alley).* JIM *and* PLATO.

JIM. I got to go in. You better get home too. *(he touches* PLATO*).* Hey—what?

PLATO. Why don't you come home with me? I mean nobody's home at my house—and I'm not tired, are you? I don't have many—people I can talk to.

JIM. Who has?

PLATO. If you want to come we could talk and then in the morning we could have breakfast like my dad used to—*(he pauses—then excitedly as though an idea had suddenly struck him).* Gee . . . if you could only have been my father . . . we could . . .

JIM *(interrupting).* Hey . . . you flipped—or something? You better take off . . .

PLATO *(suddenly, pleasantly).* O.K. G'night. I got to pick up my scooter. See you tomorrow.

JIM. Yeah.

PLATO *turns, walks up the alley to the street.* JIM *goes into his kitchen door.*

Hallway. JUDY'S *house. Three doors open onto it: one is closed—this is* JUDY'S *room:—another, leading into* BEAU'S *room is open, but the room beyond is dark; the third, also open, reveals the bedroom of* JUDY'S *parents. As* JUDY *comes into the hallway, the parents, who are reading in their beds, look up.* JUDY *hesitates, then starts toward her own room.*

BEAU'S VOICE *(quietly).* Hello, little cute sister.

JUDY *stops.* BEAU *appears at his door in white pajamas, a small ghost.* JUDY *looks at him.*

BEAU. Hello, darling, baby-pie, glamorpuss, sweetie—

JUDY *touches* BEAU'S *head and tries to smile.*

FATHER *(calling from his bed).* Beau! You belong in bed!

BEAU *flees.* JUDY *turns without another glance at her parents, and opens the door of her room.*

Inside bedroom of JUDY'S *parents. As* JUDY *slams her bedroom door o.s., the* FATHER *reacts. Perhaps, he wishes she had given him a chance to say goodnight. The* MOTHER, *who uses reading glasses, looks up at the slam. Then she looks over at her husband, shrugs when she catches his gaze, and goes back to her magazine.*

Inside JIM's *living room. The television is on, but only a hum comes from it, and the screen is a flickering gray. The* FATHER *sits lumpily in a chair by the fireplace, still dressed but with his collar open. The sound of* JIM's *step in the dining room makes him open his eyes. Fear of facing his son makes him shut them again. The boy comes in, a bottle of milk in his hand. Seeing his* FATHER *there, he stops short—his impulse is to flee. Instead he comes in and looks down at the sleeping man whose eyelids, fluttering in the* FATHER's *masquerade of sleep, make him seem to be having a dream.* JIM *is torn between his desire to leave and his need to speak. He turns off the television quietly, then lies down on the couch across the way. He mumbles the things he would say to his* FATHER *and the answers he feels he would get. The old man opens his eyes once, sees the boy there, head banging upside down from the couch. Then he shuts them again.*

*Upside down long shot. Room (*JIM's *viewpoint). Suddenly, inverted in his vision, the* MOTHER *appears at the head of the stairs, in bathrobe and nightgown. She pauses a moment, then runs down crying:*

MOTHER. He's home! You're home! You're all right!

The camera rights itself suddenly.

JIM *as he completes his turn, pulling his head up and sitting.*

FATHER *as he pretends to awaken with a start.*

Full shot, room as the MOTHER *hurries to* JIM, *holds him, inspects him, kisses him.*

MOTHER. What happened, darling. We were so worried. I was going to take a sleeping pill, but I wouldn't till I knew you were home.

JIM. I have to talk to someone, Mom. I have to talk to you both. And Dad this time you got to give me an answer.

FATHER. Go ahead.

JIM. I'm in terrible trouble.—You know that big high bluff near Miller-town Junction?

FATHER. Sure—there was a bad accident there. They showed the pictures on T.V.

JIM. I was in it.

MOTHER. How!

JIM. It doesn't matter how. I was driving a stolen car—.

MOTHER. Do you *enjoy* doing this to me or what—

JIM. Mom—I'm not—

MOTHER. And you wanted him to make a *list*!

FATHER. Will you let him tell it!

JIM. She never wants to hear. She doesn't care!

MOTHER. I guess when I nearly died giving birth to you—that shows how much I don't care!

FATHER. Just relax, please relax!

JIM. I told you Dad, it was a question of honor. They called me chicken—you know, chicken! I had to go or I would never have been able to face any of those kids again. So I got in one of these cars and a boy called Buzz got in the other. We had to drive fast and jump before the cars went over the edge of the bluff. I got out okay but Buzz didn't. He was killed.

MOTHER. Good Lord!

JIM. I can't keep it to myself any more—

FATHER. Well, just get it off your chest, son.

JIM. That's not what I mean. I've never done anything right. I've been going around with my head in a sling for years . . . I don't want to drag you into this but I can't help it. I don't think I can prove anything by going around pretending I'm tough any more, so maybe you look like one thing but you still feel like another.

FATHER. You're absolutely right!

JIM. Are you listening to me? You're involved in this! I want to go to the police and tell them I was mixed up in this thing tonight?

FATHER. You what?

MOTHER. No!

FATHER. Did anyone see you there? I mean did they get your license number or anything?

JIM. I don't think so—

FATHER. Well—

MOTHER. What about the other boys—Do you think they'll go to the police?

JIM. What's that got to do with it?

MOTHER. Why should you be the only one.

FATHER. Look Jim. Far be it from me to tell you what to do, but there's—

MOTHER. Are you going to preach now? Are we going to have a sermon?

FATHER. I'm just explaining what *you* mean! You can't be an idealist all your life! Nobody thanks you for sticking your neck out!

MOTHER. That's right!

JIM. Except yourself!

FATHER. Will you wait a minute?

JIM. You don't want me to go.

MOTHER. No! I don't want you to go to the police! There were other people and why should you be the only one involved!

JIM. But I *am* involved! We're all involved, Mom! A boy was *killed*! I don't see how we can get out of that by pretending it didn't happen!

FATHER. You know you did wrong. That's the main thing, isn't it?

JIM. No! It's nothing! Just nothing! You always told me to tell the truth. You think you can just turn that off?

MOTHER. He's not saying that! He's saying don't volunteer!

JIM. Just tell a little white lie?

FATHER. You'll learn as you get a little older, Jim.

JIM. I don't want to learn that!

MOTHER. Well, it doesn't matter anyhow—because we're moving.

JIM. No! You're not tearing me loose any more.

FATHER. This is news to me! Why are we moving?

MOTHER. Do I have to spell it out?

JIM. You're not going to use me as an excuse again, Mom. Every time you can't face yourself you want to move and you say it's because of me or the neighborhood or some other phony excuse. Now I want to do one thing right and I'm not letting you run away. *(silence)*. Dad?

FATHER. Son—this is all happening so fast—

JIM. You better give me something, Dad. You better *give* me something fast. *(he stops as he sees the emptiness in them)*. Mom?

MOTHER. Jimmy, you're very young—and a foolish decision now could wreck your whole life.

JIM. Dad—answer her—aren't you going to stand up for me? *(the FATHER is mute, helpless . . . Suddenly JIM screams)* Dad? *(he leaps at his FATHER, dragging him to his feet, hands at the man's throat)*.

MOTHER. *Stop it! You'll kill him! Jim! Do you want to kill your father?*

Suddenly JIM loosens his hands and rises. He looks swiftly at each of them—moves a few steps toward the door, looks back at them again—then rushes out of the house. The parents stand frozen.

Dissolve to:

Outside Precinct Station. JIM's car comes to a stop at the curb. JIM gets out and approaches the flight of steps leading up the entrance. A bare bulb on either side is the only illumination. As he mounts the first step, the double doors above him swing open revealing several people. JIM stops short. So do they.

Low angle. CRUNCH, MOOSE and their parents. JIM's back in f.g. The boys stare down at him.

High angle. JIM (from the boys' point of view) as he stares up at them. MOOSE's father takes his arm and starts him down the stairs, the others moving too.

MOOSE. Let go of me—

MOOSE'S FATHER. You want a good crack in the mouth?

JIM *starts forward up the steps.* CRUNCH *grabs him.*

CRUNCH. This place appeal to you or something?

They move down the steps as JIM breaks away and continues up. He goes through the doors.

Inside doors as JIM comes through and stops. He looks back through the glass. We see the group reach the curb where their cars are parked. There is a brief discussion which we cannot hear, then CRUNCH and MOOSE move off to MOOSE's car. JIM turns back. He looks worried as he passes camera.

Med. shot. CRUNCH and MOOSE. They stop at MOOSE's car and look back at the entrance. The parents are seen beyond them, getting into their cars. CRUNCH is near tears with anger.

CRUNCH. What's he going to pull—

MOOSE. Nothing, Crunch. They picked him up like the rest of—

CRUNCH. You see any cops?

MOOSE'S FATHER. *(yelling)*. You monsters start home. We're going to—

MOOSE. Yeah. Yeah.

MOOSE'S FATHER. We're following you so better get there.

CRUNCH. *You see any cops?*

MOOSE. No—

CRUNCH. He's going to cheese, I tell you. *Nobody* arrested him!

MOOSE. I think I should go home.

CRUNCH. No. We're going to bring him down.

MOOSE. CRUNCH—my father's—You going to kill him?

CRUNCH *(crying)*. You clean out of your head? Come on!

CRUNCH *gets into the car.* MOOSE *follows. They gun the motor and throw the car into a sharp U-turn. MOOSE's FATHER jumps into his car. He steps on the starter but nothing happens—just the empty whirring, over and over. Finally it starts, but the boys have gone.*

Inside Precinct Station. Juvenile division. A desk sergeant is writing in the record book. Facing him across the desk and handcuffed to an officer is a young hoodlum, very different in appearance from the kids we have met—a typical duck-tail 'cat'.

SERGEANT *(spelling)*. W-O-J-T-what?

HOODLUM. O-W-I-C-Z. Wojtowicz. What's the matter, man? That's the craziest name in town! It swings!

JIM. Excuse me—but—You know where I can find—I mean I don't remember his last name—

SERGEANT. Look—can't you see I'm writing?

HOODLUM *(combing his duck-tail)*. Man, this cat never stops. He just keeps going like Big Jay at a session!

OFFICER. Shut up.

HOODLUM. He's writing a book about me—

SERGEANT. What I could write about you they wouldn't print.

JIM. I think his first name's Ray—I have to see him. It's very important.

SERGEANT. What's the charge?

OFFICER. Assault with a deadly weapon.

JIM. Listen—

SERGEANT *(annoyed)*. He's not here. He's not at Juvenile Hall. I don't know where he is. He's out on a call and he'll be out all night. How old are you?

JIM. My parents know I'm out. They know I'm here.

SERGEANT. Come back tomorrow.

JIM. I'll wait for him.

SERGEANT. Why don't you come back tomorrow, son? *(to hoodlum)*. Ever been booked before?

JIM turns away, notices a phone on the wall—puts in a coin, asks for a number.

Bedroom of JUDY's *parents. Through an open door we hear a radio playing—a late disc-jockey show for teenagers in which numbers are dedicated by request.* JUDY's MOTHER *and* FATHER *are in bed,* FATHER *has phone in his hand.*

FATHER. Who wants her? Who? Jim who? Never heard of you.

He hangs up phone, looks at his wife. She rolls over in bed. The FATHER *turns off the bed lamp, then sits up, worried in the dark.*

JUDY's *bedroom. It is her radio we have heard. She turns off light, opens the door a crack, and looks out toward her parent's room.*

Dissolve to:

Traveling shot. PLATO. *He is coming up the walk to his house. When* PLATO *has come a few feet, somebody whistles.* PLATO *and camera stop. Short, quiet whistles come from the box-wood and shrubbery on both sides of the walk.* PLATO *turns and starts to run, camera following. He gets to his door, tries the key, but in his panic it will not go into the lock. Suddenly a hand reaches in and jerks him around.* CRUNCH *stands above him.* GOON *closes in from the other side. All very tense and hotted up!*

PLATO. What do you want!

CRUNCH. You know what we want. We want your friend.

GOON. We got eyes for him.

PLATO. Listen, you guys ought to go home. The cops are cruising every—

GOON. Where does he live?

PLATO *reaches up swiftly and rings the bell.* GOON *grabs him.* CRUNCH *cracks him.*

CRUNCH. You better tell us and I'm not kidding.

PLATO. My old man's got a gun.

GOON. His old man's got a gun. What do you think of that! *(he drives a hard blow at* PLATO's *belly). Your friend talked—(he belts him again).* Now *you* talk! Talk!

The door opens and the NEGRO WOMAN *is there.* CRUNCH *sends* PLATO *spinning into the house past her. He falls.*

NEGRO WOMAN *(yelling)*. What you doing! What you doing to him! You clear out of here 'fore I call the police! *(she swings at* CRUNCH *who faces her, challenging).* Clear out. Go on! Go on now!

MOOSE. Let's go, CRUNCH.

They turn and move past camera. PLATO *gets up off the floor. We hear the sound of a heap starting. The* NEGRO WOMAN *closes the door.*

Inside PLATO's *foyer as* NEGRO WOMAN *bolts the door.*

NEGRO WOMAN. Why you like to mix with bad boys like that? Why you get in trouble all the—

PLATO. I have to go out. I have to warn him.

He starts up the stairs. She follows him heavily.

NEGRO WOMAN. You not going anywhere! You staying home while your mama's away.

Bedroom of PLATO's *mother, a lacy affair with imported dolls on the pillows.* PLATO *rushes in, opens the drawer of the night-table and pulls out a gun. He checks to see that it is loaded. The* NEGRO WOMAN *appears in the door and stares at him, turns on the light which illuminates the bed-lamp.*

NEGRO WOMAN. John! What you doing with that! You leave that be! Put it down before you hurt yourself. Hear me?

But PLATO *moves past her and out of the room. She turns after him.*

NEGRO WOMAN *(continuing)*. John! You stay home! John! John!

The slam of a door is heard below.

Dissolve to:

JIM's *garage. Night.* JUDY *waiting inside.* JIM's *car pulls in, a radio going softly. He turns the motor off and is about to turn off the radio when we hear the announcer:*

ANNOUNCER. Coming up now another request—this time from the boys down at Anna's Pizza Paradise—A new arrangement of a great oldie in rhythm and blues. Jim, this is dedicated to you—from Buzz.

JIM *stares at the radio, then turns it off.*

Another angle.

JUDY. They'll be looking for you.

JIM. They saw where I jumped! I didn't chicken! What do I have to do—kill myself?

JUDY. It doesn't matter to them.

JIM. You were looking for me, weren't you?

JUDY *(a small voice)*. No—I was just—maybe—

JIM. I tried to call you before.

JUDY. I thought so.

JIM. Want some milk? *(*JUDY *comes forward).* That's all I can do when I'm nervous. Drink milk. Here—have a slug.

She shakes her head. He takes a sip.

JIM. You still pretty upset?

JUDY. I'm numb *(she is shuddering a little).*

JIM. You cold?

JUDY. Even if I'm near a fire, I'm cold. I guess just about everybody's cold.

JIM. I swear, sometimes, you just want to hold onto somebody! Judy, what am I going to do? I can't go home again.

JUDY. Neither can I.

JIM. No? Why not? *(no answer).* You know something? Sometimes I figure I'll never live to see my next birthday. Isn't that dumb?

JUDY. No.

JIM. Every day I look in the mirror and say, "What? You still here?" Man! *(they laugh a little).* Hey! You smiled! *(she shakes her head—beginning to warm to him).* Like even today. I woke up this morning, you know? And the sun was shining and everything was nice. Then the first thing that happens is I see

you and I thought this is going to be one terrific day so you better live it up, boy, 'cause tomorrow maybe you'll be nothing.

JUDY. I'm sorry I treated you mean today. You shouldn't believe what I say when I'm with the kids. Nobody acts sincere.

JIM. Why'd you get mixed up with them? You don't have to prove anything.

JUDY. If you knew me you wouldn't say that.

JIM. I don't think you trust anybody, do you?

JUDY. Why?

JIM. I'm getting that way, too.

JUDY *(she looks at him).* Have *you* ever gone with anyone who—

JIM. Sure. Lots of times.

JUDY. So have I. But I've never been in love. Isn't that awful?

JIM *(smiling).* Awful? No. It's just lonely. It's the loneliest time.

She looks up. He kisses her forehead.

JUDY. Why did you do that?

JIM. I felt like it.

JUDY. Your lips are soft when you kiss.

JUDY *rises.*

JIM. Where you going?

JUDY. I don't know, but we can't stay here.

JIM. Where can we go? I can't go back into that zoo.

JUDY. I'm never going back.

JIM. Listen! I know a place! PLATO showed me before. An old deserted mansion near the planetarium *(he rises).* Would you go with me? *(she hesitates).* You can trust me, Judy.

JUDY. I feel as if I'm walking under water.

They start out.

Dissolve to:

Inside bathroom. JIM's *house. The water is running in the sink and* JIM's *father is fixing a stomach settler. Gradually he grows aware of a heavy pounding which insinuates itself above the splash of water. The* FATHER *pauses, then turns off the tap. The pounding continues.* JIM's MOTHER *appears at the bathroom door. She is seen in the mirror tying her robe.*

MOTHER. Frank? I'm frightened.

FATHER. What's that pounding?

MOTHER. I don't know. First I thought it was Jim but—

FATHER. He's home. I heard the car.

MOTHER. Are you going down there?

FATHER. Look—just relax, will you? *(the pounding ceases).* See? It stopped.

MOTHER. I still think you should go down.

He goes out of the bathroom, into the hall.

Foyer. JIM'S *house as the* FATHER *comes down the stairs, turning on the light as he comes. He reaches the door and pauses. The* MOTHER *stops midway down the stairs.*

FATHER *(through the door).* Who's there? *(silence).* Anyone there?
MOTHER *(low; at balustrade).* Open it.

The FATHER *opens the door and looks up sharply.*

Close shot. Door. FATHER'S *head in f.g. as he stares at it. Nailed to the door by its outstretched wings, its head hanging in an attitude of crucifixion, is the freshly killed carcass of a chicken. Low whistles are heard from outside. The* FATHER, *frightened, looks out into the night.*

Full shot. Front lawn and street. Shooting over the FATHER'S *head. The whistling continues.*

FATHER *(hoarsely).* Who's out there?
VOICE. Where's your son?
FATHER. What?
ANOTHER VOICE. Where's your baby boy gone to, Daddy? We want him.

Suddenly the FATHER *slams the door and rushes past us into the house.*

Full shot. Foyer as the FATHER *rushes to the bottom of the stairs.*

FATHER. Look in his room! *(the* MOTHER *disappears).* Jim! Jim!

The FATHER *dashes into the living room, then into the hall again and down through the kitchen door.*

Back yard as the FATHER *comes out. He closes the door quietly and calls in a low voice:*

FATHER. Son?

He stares around the yard, then hurries to the garage. JIM'S *car is missing. He looks up suddenly.*

Reverse shot. JUDY'S FATHER *seen across the alley wall. He is standing in his own back yard.*

JUDY'S FATHER. Is anything wrong? I'm your neighbor.

Med. shot. JIM'S FATHER. *He smiles feebly.*

JIM'S FATHER. Oh, no, thanks. I just wanted to—to be sure my garage was closed.

JIM'S FATHER *closes his garage door and walks back toward his house.*

JIM'S MOTHER'S VOICE. Is he there?
JIM'S FATHER. No, honey. No, he's not here.

He starts for the house again after a quick look in the direction of JUDY'S FATHER.

Full shot. JUDY'S *back yard.* JUDY'S FATHER *watches* MR. STARK *disappear, then . . .*

JUDY'S FATHER *(softly).* Judy?

The alley by JIM'S *house.* PLATO *drives up on scooter. He checks the garage, sees* JIM'S *car is gone, is about to take off in confusion, hears door slam in* JIM'S *back yard, shuts off engine, fixes tie, combs hair, goes in the fence gate to* JIM'S *back yard.*

Full shot. JIM'S *back yard.* JIM'S FATHER *is coming toward him.* JIM'S FATHER *and* PLATO *simultaneously say:*

FATHER. What are you doing?
PLATO. Where's Jim?
FATHER. I don't know. Do you—do you know where he is?
PLATO. No. No, I don't.

Closeup. PLATO *remembers about the mansion—then almost to himself:*

PLATO. I know where—

Back to full shot. FATHER *and* PLATO.

PLATO. Hope I didn't bother you. Goodnight.

He runs to scooter.

FATHER. Hey, come back here. Who are you?

Dissolve to:

Split screen montage. It begins with a telephone ringing alone in the corner of the screen. As camera moves back we see that the phone is in an office at Juvenile Hall. RAY *is standing by, trying to make sense out of the incoming reports.*

The other part of the screen lights up and becomes:

Bedroom of PLATO'S MOTHER *where the* NEGRO WOMAN *is speaking hysterically into the phone.*

Bedroom of JUDY'S *parents. The* FATHER *is on the phone.* BEAU *has awakened and is crying. His* MOTHER *tries to divert him.*

JIM'S *bedroom.* JIM'S FATHER *sits disconsolately on the bed, the phone in his hand. He is talking earnestly.*

*During this the sound of the telephone ring-
ing has increased to become the sound of many
and this has been submerged in a deep rising
riot of sirens whose wail mounts higher and
higher until:*

Dissolve to:

*Full shot. Planetarium. Moonlight. A lone
siren wails in distance. Aside from this, all is
very still. Camera pans past the dome and settles on an isolated mansion set high on a hill
nearby. Stone balustrades drop down to sunken
gardens where the grass has gone to seed
around a waterless fountain.*

*Closer shot. Mansion. Night. A Mediterra-
nean villa with a large domed solarium which is
connected to the main building by a low enclosed arcade. A crash and the falling of splin-
tered glass is heard.*

*Long shot. Promenade. Shooting through pil-
lars of the main entrance portico, down the long
promenade outside arcade. Two figures, seen in
the distance, are disappearing through a window. Camera trucks down promenade until it
reaches a broken window through which* JIM *is
just disappearing. When he gets inside, he
reaches back and takes his leather jacket which
has been spread on the sill to protect them from
splinters, shakes it out and puts it on. Running
footsteps are heard approaching.* JIM *looks out
nervously.* PLATO *bursts in, out of breath.*

PLATO. Jim!
JIM. Who's that!
PLATO. It's me!
JIM. How'd you find me? What's
happening?
PLATO. They're looking for you!—
JIM. Yeah?
PLATO. Everybody! Crunch and Goon and
everybody! I think they're going to kill you.
JIM. We know.
PLATO. They think you told the police on
them. They—who's in there?
JIM. Judy.
PLATO. Help me in!

JIM *gives* PLATO *a hand over the windowsill.*

Inside arcade. JIM *and* JUDY *are seen in an
entering shaft of moonlight.* PLATO *hits the floor
and disappears into darkness.*

JIM. Hey where'd you go?
PLATO. I'm here. Shut up.
JIM. Come out come out wherever you are!
PLATO. Shut up. Are you nuts?
JIM. No. I'm scared.

*A match flares and lights a candle on an
antique Spanish candelabra.* PLATO *is revealed
bending over it. He lights the other candles
through the following:*

PLATO. We're safe here. I hope. *(he holds up
the candelabra).* What do you think?
JIM *(gazing around).* Wow! Well now—there-
then!

*His wonderment is justified. The floor of the
arcade is marble and there are marble benches
and neo-Roman busts lining the walls.*

PLATO. Isn't it crazy?
JIM. Wowee ow wow! Let's take it for the
summer.
JUDY. Oh, Jim!
JIM. No—come on. Should we rent or are
we in a buying mood, dear?
JUDY *(laughing).* You decide, darling. Re-
member our budget.
PLATO. Don't give it a thought. Only three
million dollars a month!
JUDY. Oh, we can manage that! I'll scrimp
and save and work my fingers to the
bone . . .
JIM. Why don't we just rent it for the
season?
JUDY. You see, we've just—oh, *you* tell
him, darling. I'm so embarrassed I could die!
JIM. Well—we're newlyweds.
JUDY. There's just one thing. What about—
PLATO. Children? Well, we really don't encourage them. They're so noisy and troublesome, don't you agree?
JUDY. Yes. And so terribly annoying when
they cry. I just don't know what to do when
they cry, do you dear?
JIM. Of course. Drown them like puppies.
JUDY. See, we're very modern.
PLATO. Shall I show you the nursery? It's
far away from the rest of the house. If you
have children—Oh I hate the word!—or if
you decide to adopt one—they can carry on
and you'll never even notice. In fact, if you
lock them in you never have to see them
again, much less talk to them.
JUDY. *Talk* to them! Heavens!
JIM. Nobody *talks* to children! They just tell
them one thing and mean another.
PLATO. It's wonderful that you understand
so well—and so young too! You know the
most wonderful feature about the nursery?
JIM. What?
PLATO. There's only one key.
JIM. We'll take it!
PLATO. Come on!

PLATO *leads them away from us down the
arcade, the candelabra casting wild shadows*

on the walls. *They are laughing as they disappear through the glass doors at the end and their laughter echoes stonily.*

Dissolve to:

Med. shot. A street and an alley. Night seen through the windshield of a police car. Its radio is on low. Two officers are in the front seat. One of them drinks coffee from a container. Suddenly MOOSE'S *heap moves past on the street ahead. In it are* MOOSE, GOON *and* CRUNCH.

Full shot. The street as MOOSE'S *heap continues up the empty street. The police car slides out of the alley where it has been concealed, and follows at a distance. Its headlights are off.*

Close shot, CRUNCH, GOON *and* MOOSE *(Process). They are in the front seat of* MOOSE'S *heap.*

MOOSE. What time is it?
CRUNCH. Hang loose. We got all night.
MOOSE. That maid saw us. She could identify us too.
CRUNCH. You still want to go home, Moose?
MOOSE. No.
CRUNCH. Then shut your mouth before your guts run out!
GOON. *What* guts?

Dissolve to:

Inside glass solarium. A swimming pool lies at the center. There is no water in it. Framing the pool is a flagstone walk with marble benches spotted here and there. The great glass room had once been planted thickly with tropical foliage. But now what palms and lianas remain are withered and dead with lack of care. At the edge of the pool, near the deep end, a blanket has been spread and a candelabra burns upon it. In its mysterious light our three kids are revealed: JIM, *bouncing precariously at the end of the diving board;* JUDY *on the blanket nearby;* PLATO *on the pool's bottom. All three are laughing hysterically when suddenly* JIM *starts to lose his balance.*

JIM *(yelling).* Quick! Fill the pool! *(he falls in.* PLATO *rushes to him).* Let's see how long we can stay under.
PLATO. Man, you're schizoid!
JIM *(in another outburst of laughing).* I'm what? What?
JUDY. You can't talk underwater!
JIM *(gargling).* I bet you hear everything I say!
PLATO *(gargling).* Isn't he schizoid?
JIM *(gargling).* Hey! How 'bout that!

They laugh again. JIM *swings up the ladder and goes to* JUDY. PLATO *follows.*

PLATO. Haven't you noticed your personality splitting?
JIM. Not lately.

They all sit on the blanket.

JIM. How do you know so much about this junk, Plato?
PLATO. I had to go to a head-shrinker. I only went twice though. My mother said it cost too much, so she went to Hawaii instead.

JIM *lies back with his head in* JUDY'S *lap. She strokes his hair and smiles at him.* PLATO *looks away.*

JIM. No. Seriously. What's your trouble?

PLATO *hesitates a moment, then leans back, cuddling between the two of them.*

PLATO. I don't know but whatever it is, it's gone now. I mean I'm happy now. Here *(*JIM *puts his arm under* PLATO'S *chin).* I came here before.
JIM. When was that?
PLATO. When I was here? When I ran away, I used to run away a lot but they always took me back.
JIM. Who?
PLATO. Mom and Dad. I used to be in my crib and I'd listen to them fight.
JIM. You remember that far back? Boy, I can't even remember yesterday.
JUDY. Plato, where's your father now?
PLATO. He's dead. He was a hero in the China Sea.
JIM. You told me he's a big wheel in New York!
PLATO. I did? Well, he might as well be dead. What's the difference?
JUDY. It's all right
JIM. Sure.

PLATO *closes his eyes.* JUDY *hums a lullaby as she strokes* JIM'S *lips with a finger. He snaps at it. Then he kisses her hand, looks at her palm. They whisper.*

JIM *(continuing).* You have a long life-line.

She takes his palm and examines it.

JUDY. So have you.

She kisses it, holds her cheek against it.

JIM. Ever been in a place like this before?
JUDY. Not exactly. It's certainly huge.
JIM. How many rooms do you think there are?
JUDY. I don't know.

JIM. Should we explore?

She looks at PLATO. JIM *shrugs—tests to see if the boy is awake, but there is no reaction.*

Carefully, they crawl to their feet. JIM *supporting* PLATO's *head with his hands as they do so.* JIM *takes the other blanket and covers* PLATO *with it.* JUDY *kneels on the other side and tucks it in. They look at each other across him and smile. Then suddenly* JUDY *bends down and kisses* PLATO's *cheek very softly.* JUDY *and* JIM *rise.*

JIM *takes a candle from the candelabra and leads* JUDY *along the edge of the pool to the glass doors beyond. Silence except for their footfalls on the flagstone. In the distance we see the doors open and the couple pass through. When they close again, a sob come from* PLATO.

High angle closeup. PLATO *lying as they left him, but his eyes are open and he is crying. Camera booms up as* PLATO *throws off the blanket and looks after them. Camera booms higher until he is revealed as a small and lonely figure sitting by himself. The pool echoes his weeping.*

Dissolve to:

Inside library. Mansion. Night. The door opens slowly and JIM *appears with the candle.* JUDY *lingers at the door. The flickering light reveals a formerly lavish room, panelled in oak. There is a tapestry couch, empty bookcases, some dim portraits, a leather table and several chairs around a great stone fireplace.*

JIM. Hey! Will you look at *this* room! *(he looks behind him).* Judy?

She comes forward. JIM *drips wax on the table-top and sticks the candle on it. His hand shakes.* JUDY *sits on the couch.*

JIM *(continuing).* Want to read any books? Take your pick! *(he sits beside her).* Isn't this the craziest?
JUDY. Hi.
JIM. Hi.

He takes her hand. She looks at him and smiles.

JIM *(continuing).* What?
JUDY. Your hand's all wet and it's shaky. *(she kisses it).* You're so funny.
JIM. Why?
JUDY. I don't know—you just are. Leaving a light for Plato. That was nice.
JIM. Maybe he's scared of the dark.
JUDY. Are you?

JIM *snuffs out the candle. They are left in moonlight. A pause.*

JIM *(singing).*
Here we are—
out of cigarettes—
Junior's in the nurs'ry—
See how late it gets—
JUDY. You don't need to do that.
JIM. There's something I should tell you, Judy.
JUDY. I know already. We don't have to pretend now.
JIM *(laughing).* What a relief!

He leans back, relaxed at last. She snuggles close to him.

JUDY. Is this what it's like to love somebody?
JIM. You disappointed?
JUDY *(mussing his hair).* Funny Jimmy. You're so clean and you—this is silly.
JIM. What?
JUDY. You smell like baby powder.
JIM. So do you.
JUDY. I never felt so clean before.
JIM. It's not going to be lonely, Judy. Not for you and not for me.
JUDY. *I love somebody.* All the time I've been looking for someone to love me and now—I love somebody. And it's so easy. Why is it easy now?
JIM. It is for me too.
JUDY. I love you, Jim. I really mean it.

She kisses his lips gently and looks into his face. He returns the kiss. Their arms go around each other.

JIM. I mean it too.

He kisses her again—

Full shot. Road near Planetarium. MOOSE's *heap crawls up and turns left. A moment later, the police car appears and does likewise—still holding its distance.*

Full shot. The mansion as MOOSE's *heap moves past on the road below. Suddenly it stops.*

Inside MOOSE's *heap.* CRUNCH *looks off, curious.*

GOON. What you stopping for?
CRUNCH. You scam a car up there?
MOOSE. So what?
CRUNCH. Nobody's lived in that hunk of junk for five-six years.

He switches on the spotlight. It illuminates JIM's *heap.*

CRUNCH. Well, what do you know! I feel a kick coming on!

He turns off all the lights and gets out. The others follow.

Med. shot. Police car. It has halted. One of the officers gets out and draws his gun. The other makes radio contact in a low voice:

OFFICER. This is Unit 17. Unit 17.

RADIO. Come in, Unit 17.

OFFICER. We just zeroed three kids in a heap. Crest Drive and Observatory. Looks like house-breaking. Send us some help. They may be armed. Over.

Close shot. PLATO asleep on the blanket. Only a single candle burns in the candelabra. The same low whistles heard earlier come from all around him and rise in volume. Suddenly his eyes open. He doesn't move, but he has come suddenly awake.

Low shot. PLATO lying in f.g. Next to his face are a pair of booted feet. He looks up. Camera pans up to show CRUNCH. He is smiling. He holds a tire chain in his hand which he swings.

CRUNCH. Good morning.

Full shot. The swimming pool. GOON and MOOSE are behind CRUNCH. They too are armed with tire chains. They all laugh. PLATO rolls away from them and runs toward the deep end of the pool.

CRUNCH. Moose! Take the steps! Goon! The other side.

The boys run to their assigned places. PLATO sees no exit. He flings himself down the ladder and into the pool. He feints this way and that, the boys responding as if they were fencing. CRUNCH swings down the ladder and his boots make a loud report as they hit the pool. MOOSE advances down the steps at the shallow end. GOON climbs onto the pool bottom at the opposite side. The feinting continues, wordlessly, as the circle closes around PLATO. The only sounds are the stamping of their boots as they try to distract him from side to side, and the animalistic grunts they make to scare him. Suddenly PLATO sees an opening and plunges past MOOSE, pushing him over, and stumbles up the steps.

CRUNCH. Come on! Let's make it!

They stream out of the pool after PLATO. He reaches the glass doors first, streaks through, and bangs them shut behind him.

Traveling shot. Arcade. PLATO's face is visible only when the moonlight strikes him through the passing windows. The sound of running steps behind him.

Full shot. Main room. A pattern of moonlight on the bare floor as PLATO dashes in and through it. He falls over a piece of furniture and comes scurrying in to camera, wheels around on hands and knees to face the door. The boys plunge into the moonlit square and stop. PLATO tries not to breathe. A match is struck. CRUNCH looks around, but can see nothing. That match goes out. The boys start up the stairs, whispering. Immediately, PLATO crawls forward, under the piano. He hears a murmur of voices from behind the oak door of the library—next to the piano. He moves to it stealthily.

Close shot, PLATO at door listening through it, on hands and knees. His confusion mounts. He shakes his head to clear it. Then, suddenly he rises and tries the knob. The door is locked. He beats on it.

PLATO. Save me!

The boys run across the room. As they hit the moonlit square, PLATO spins and fires. Somebody drops and starts moaning. JIM opens the door.

PLATO *(shrieks).* What you run out on me for! What you leave me alone for?

JIM. Plato!

There is a rush of boys coming forward.

PLATO *(with hate).* I don't want you for my father!

JIM. Your *father!*

PLATO *fires at JIM. JIM leaps at PLATO with a cry and knocks him down.*

JIM *(continuing; in rage).* You crazy nut! You crazy, crazy nut!

PLATO *(screaming).* Get away from me!

He rolls away from JIM and runs to the main door.

JUDY. Jim!

Main door, from inside. PLATO falls upon it, fumbles with the bolt and swings the door wide. He steps out into the waning moonlight and we see him running down the lawn. JIM rushes into the doorway and stops short.

Full shot. Mansion. The OFFICERS are moving away from us toward it. PLATO runs wildly toward them.

OFFICER *(sharply).* Halt!

PLATO *stops, confused.*

OFFICER *(continuing).* Come here.

JIM *runs out on the promenade and starts over the balustrade.*

JIM. Plato!

Close shot. PLATO. *His face is working desperately in growing panic.*

OFFICER'S VOICE. Come here, son.
PLATO. No!
JIM'S VOICE. Plato!
OFFICER'S VOICE. Just walk over here quietly now—and there won't be any trouble.

PLATO *runs out.*

Close shot. JIM *as he screams.*

JIM. Plato!

Full shot. Main doorway as JUDY *rushes out, followed by* GOON *and* MOOSE. *They all stop dead at the balustrade.*

JUDY. Jim! Watch out!

Reverse shot. Lawn. JIM *seen in f.g.* PLATO *bolting toward the woods in the direction of the planetarium. The officers have both hit the ground in the distance. They fire again.* JIM *hesitates a moment, then rushes after* PLATO. *The officers fire again.*

Moving shot. JIM *as he runs after* PLATO.

Med. shot. OFFICERS *as they rise to their feet.*

FIRST OFFICER. Take the house! I'll head him off.

Full shot. Front of mansion. JUDY *flies down the stairs and rushes past camera.*

OFFICER'S VOICE. Halt! Halt!

Prowl car. Another part of town (Process). RAY *is driving.* JIM'S *father is beside him. The mother is in the back seat.*

RADIO. —located at Summit Drive—the Planetarium.

RAY *(snapping on mike).* The planetarium? One kid inside—five housebreaking in area. Will proceed. *(turning to* JIM'S *parents).* There are some kids in trouble—you'll have to go with me.
FATHER. Perfectly all right.

Edge of woods as JIM *hurtles in from the open ground beyond. He stumbles against a tree and sinks down.*

JIM *(yelling).* Plato!

Traveling shot in the woods as PLATO *rushes through the moonlit trees, sobbing.*

JIM'S VOICE *(distant).* Plato!

Med. shot. JIM *at the base of a tree. He is whimpering, shaking his head.* JUDY *crashes through the brush and drops beside him.*

JUDY. Did he hit you?

She is on the verge of hysteria.

JIM. No!
JUDY. We have to go back!
JIM. No! I got to find him.

He starts to rise.

JUDY. After he tried to shoot you?
JIM. He didn't mean it—we shouldn't have left him. He needed us.
JUDY. He needed you, maybe. So do I.

There is a sound of distant gunfire. Both kids freeze.

JIM. He needs you too. Come on.

JUDY, *breaking into a run, follows after him through the brush.*

JUDY. You should have heard him talk about you tonight. Like *you* were the hero in the China Seas.
JIM. Sure. He was trying to make us his family.
JUDY. They're killing him!

JIM *runs ahead blindly and disappears in the trees.* JUDY *rushes after him a few steps, then stops.*

JUDY *and* JIM *running.*

PLATO *running.*

The planetarium. Moonlight. Shooting from the bridle path and panning to the building. PLATO *reels in and goes to the front door.*

Med. shot. Door to planetarium. PLATO *clutches the handle. The door is locked. He whimpers once in frustration.*

Med. shot. Policeman running up same path PLATO *has followed.*

PLATO *at door to planetarium. He smashes the glass with his gun and dives through.*

Inside planetarium as PLATO *lands. He is cut and bleeding.*

OFFICER'S VOICE. Come out of there.

PLATO *wheels and skitters backward across the floor of the observatory on his hands and knees until he comes to the door of the planetarium theater.*

Reverse shot. Main entrance. Seen from inside. The OFFICER *in b.g.,* PLATO *in f.g. The* OFFICER *appears in the entrance, then moves quickly to one side to be less of a target. He reaches in to unlatch the door.*

OFFICER. You're making it tough on yourself, kid. Come out quietly now. You didn't kill anybody yet.

PLATO *fires at him, then opens the door of the planetarium theater and runs inside. The door swings shut behind him.*

Outside planetarium. The OFFICER *is hugging the outside wall. Another siren wails and a spotlight catches the* OFFICER *who runs out into the light.*

OFFICER *(running).* Need a little help here!

Full shot. Parking lot as the CHIEF'S *car wheels to a stop. It is followed by a civilian car and a cab.*

CHIEF'S *car.*

CHIEF. We heard firing. He get anybody? You alone?

OFFICER. We got a cookaboo inside. He wounded some kid earlier.

CHIEF. How'd he get in?

OFFICER. Smashed the front door.

CHIEF. Any other entrance?

OFFICER *(leaving).* Down in back.

Med. shot. Bushes bordering planetarium as JIM *climbs through them and stops short, staring in amazement.* JUDY *is in b.g.*

Full shot. Parking lot. JIM *seen in f.g. hiding in the screen of leaves. Beyond we see the full activity—the crowd, the cars, searchlights playing on the planetarium entrance, police moving in under direction of the* CHIEF.

CHIEF *(loud on speaker)* Silence. Please maintain silence. Keep back and stay off the pavements. Keep back and stay off the pavements. There will be emergency vehicles coming through. This warning is for your own protection.

RAY'S *prowl car come in.* JIM'S *parents climb out, curious.* RAY *hurries to consult with an officer who briefs him, then hurries to the chief's car.*

Parking lot. Several patrol cars now line the parking lot. The NEGRO WOMAN *in her nightgown and overcoat pushes forward from a cab and accosts an* OFFICER.

NEGRO WOMAN. What's going on?

OFFICER. I don't know, lady. Some kid's in trouble. Stand back, please.

NEGRO WOMAN. I got to know. My boy run off tonight. He had a gun with him, too.

Med. shot. CHIEF'S *car as* RAY *hurries in.*

CHIEF. Hello, Ray—Know anything about this?

RAY. As much as you do—Loan me your mike, will you?

CHIEF *(handing it to him).* Help yourself.

RAY *(into mike).* I am addressing the boy in the planetarium. I am speaking to the boy inside. This is RAY FRAMEK from the Juvenile Division—

Close-up JIM *as he reacts to* RAY'S *name. He rises and looks off.*

RAY'S VOICE *(over speaker).* You are now surrounded. You are surrounded by many armed police. Whoever you are, drop your weapon and come outside.

Med. shot. JIM'S FATHER *standing by* RAY'S *car, gazing off with interest. His wife comes out and stands beside him, looks at him questioningly.*

RAY'S VOICE *(over speaker).* Come outside. Clasp your hands over your head and come outside quietly—

The FATHER'S *gaze has traveled over the scene. Suddenly he sees his son followed by* JUDY, *run into the planetarium.*

MOTHER. Frank!

FATHER. Stay here *(he goes over to* RAY). That was my son!

RAY. You sure?

FATHER. I think I know my son.

The FATHER *moves behind the crowd, camera trucking with him, until he reaches the bushes at the edge of the parking lot and stops, gathering himself. Meanwhile* RAY'S *voice continues over:*

RAY'S VOICE *(over speaker).* Jim Stark! I'm addressing Jim Stark. Nobody will harm you or your friends if you follow these instructions. We are here to protect you. Drop your guns and come outside. Nobody will hurt you if you do as I say—

The FATHER *starts forward along the bushes as if stalking game. Each step is carefully placed and quiet, but his heart tugs him along like a kite dragging an anchor.*

CHIEF. Officers! Another boy and girl just ran into the planetarium. We do not know if they are armed. Hold your positions until further instruction.

Inside planetarium as JIM *comes dashing in, spins around, staring.* JUDY *follows. A siren is heard outside growing shrill.*

CHIEF'S VOICE *(over speaker)*. Ambulance. Ambulance is coming through. Clear a passage. Will you people make way there?

Floodlights strike the door and illuminate the lobby dimly.

JIM *(softly)*. Plato?

Silence. JIM *moves cautiously to the door of the planetarium theater.* JUDY *hangs back. Another siren is heard approaching. More floodlights strike the door.*

JIM *(continuing—calling softly)*. Plato? Plato, you in there? *(silence)*. Hey, I'm going to open the door now. You'll be able to see me and you can shoot me if you want, but just remember one thing, Plato—You're my friend. That means a lot to me. *(he opens the door slowly)*.

Inside theater. Darkness except for the splash of light from the door where JIM *stands in silhouette. He lets the door close. Blackness.*

JIM. Plato?
PLATO. I'm here.
JIM. Boy, I'm blind as a bat! You got a match? I'm going to break my neck in here. Where are you?
PLATO. I've got a gun.
JIM. I know. Light a match, will you? *(PLATO obeys)*. That's swell. How are you?
PLATO. I'm fine.

Another siren is heard outside. JIM *has reached the lecturer's desk and, just as the match goes out, he throws a switch. The stars appear on the dome and the projector starts its slow revolution.*

PLATO. You think the end of the world will come at nighttime, Jim?
JIM. No. At dawn.
PLATO. Why?
JIM. I just have a feeling. Where are you?
PLATO. Here.
JIM. Well, stop hiding and stand up. I can't talk to you if I don't see you. *(JIM waits. Nothing happens)*. Hey, look at the stars, Plato. Stand up and look at the stars.

Plato rises from behind a row, then JIM *continues:*

JIM. That's fine. *(JIM approaches slowly)*. I'm not going to hurt you.
PLATO. Why did you run out on me?
JIM. We didn't run out. We were coming right back.
PLATO. You sure?
JIM. Sure I'm sure. Judy's waiting. You ready to come out now?

A siren is heard.

PLATO. No.
JIM. I promise nothing'll happen if you do. *(silence)*. You want my jacket? It's warm.

JIM *takes off his jacket and holds it out to* PLATO.

PLATO. Can I keep it?
JIM. What do *you* think? *(JIM gives him the jacket—PLATO puts it on)*. You want to give me your gun now, Plato?
PLATO. My gun?
JIM. In your pocket. Give it to me.
PLATO. I need it.
JIM. You trust me, don't you? Just give it to me for a second.

PLATO *hands him the gun.* JIM *removes the cartridges and puts them in his pocket.*

PLATO. You promised to give it back.
JIM. Friends never break promises, do they? *(gives him back the gun)*. Okay. Here. Now listen. There are a lot of people outside and they all want you to be safe. You understand that? They said I could come in and bring you out.
PLATO. Why?
JIM. They like you. Okay?
PLATO. Come on!

JIM *opens the door for* PLATO, *then follows him out.* JUDY *joins them.*

JUDY. Hi, Plato!
PLATO. Hi.

Observatory as JIM, JUDY *and* PLATO *come to the entrance.* PLATO *sees an* OFFICER.

PLATO. Who's that?
JIM. Just a guard.
PLATO. I shot at one of them.
JIM. But you didn't hurt anybody.

Outside observatory as PLATO *and* JIM *come forward into the early dawn.* PLATO *stops and looks off, scared.*

Slow pan shot. The crowd. It has grown enormously. Silence. There are armed officers everywhere—all waiting, alert.

Med. shot. NEGRO WOMAN. *Her eyes are moist. Her lips move in silent prayer.*

Med. shot. JIM's *parents. The* FATHER *looking on anxiously. The* MOTHER *is crying against the car.*

Med. shot. JIM *and* PLATO.

PLATO. Those aren't my friends. Make them go away.

JIM *(tense; calling past camera).* Ray! Will you tell these guys to move back?

Suddenly PLATO *bolts.* JIM *wheels after him.*

JIM *(yelling).* Plato! Don't be a fool!

Full shot. Planetarium as PLATO *dashes to the stairway leading to the balcony.*

JIM'S FATHER *and* MOTHER. *Their faces reflect panic as they see* PLATO *running in* JIM'S *coat.*

MOTHER. It's Jim!

Full shot. Balcony. Shooting down the stairs as PLATO *rushes up.* JIM *closes behind him. Camera pans with* PLATO *as he climbs the ladder to the ledge of the small dome.* JIM *stops at the foot of the ladder.*

JIM. Plato!
PLATO. Keep away from me! I don't believe you anymore!

He raises the gun as if to shoot JIM. *An* OFFICER *drops to one knee and fires a shot at* PLATO.

Full shot. Small dome. PLATO *drops like a stone to* JIM'S *feet.*

Close-up. JIM.

JIM *(screaming—wildly). But I've got the bullets!* The gun was empty!

Close shot. NEGRO WOMAN *as she screams, a handkerchief in her mouth.*

Close shot. JUDY. *She sobs once and runs up steps.*

Med. shot. JIM *staring down at* PLATO.

JIM. Plato? *(he crouches over* PLATO). Plato, Hey, Jerkpot!

There is nothing. He rises and faces the crowd, shaking his head in wonder and reproach.

JIM *(quiet).* What did you have to do that for?

Full shot, the roof. Parents and Officers. The NEGRO WOMAN *is hysterical.* RAY *shoves past her, followed by* JIM'S FATHER *and* MOTHER. *They rush toward camera.*

Ambulance crew. They spring into action, arrive with stretcher.

The balcony. JIM *is at* PLATO'S *side. A couple of* OFFICERS *rush forward to take* JIM. *The* FATHER *comes in and pushes them aside.*

FATHER. Let him alone! He's *mine*! I'll take care of him!

RAY, *who has witnessed this, motions to the officers.*

RAY. It's all right! It's all right!

The FATHER *stares down at* JIM *for a moment. Then he kneels beside his son, puts his coat over* JIM'S *shoulders. He speaks very gently.*

FATHER. For a minute . . . that jacket . . . I thought . . . *(breaks off, then).* You couldn't help it, son. *(reaches out, gently, but firmly).* You did everything a man could do.

He takes JIM *by the elbow and starts to bring him to his feet. The boy suddenly resists, and remains kneeling.*

FATHER. Stand up, Jim. I'll stand up with you. Let me *try* to be as strong as you want me to be.

A faint hope appears in the boy's face. He no longer resists as the FATHER *helps him to rise. But he still keeps his back to him. The ambulance attendants start putting* PLATO *on a stretcher.* JIM *moves, as if to stop them, but the* FATHER *still holds his shoulders.*

JIM. He depended on me.
FATHER. And you can depend on me, son. Trust me. Whatever comes we'll face it together, I swear.

JIM *feels, for the first time, the love and security he has always wanted. He clutches at his* FATHER, *crying unashamedly. The* FATHER'S *arms envelop him.* PLATO, *through his death, has helped these two find each other.*

Close shot. JUDY *and* RAY *watching.*

Low angle. NEGRO WOMAN *as she bends over* PLATO'S *body.*

NEGRO WOMAN *(as they lift* PLATO *onto litter).* This poor baby got nobody. Just nobody.

As he is carried past her, she follows.

Balcony stairs. From below as JIM, *supported by his* FATHER, *comes down.* RAY *is behind them. They pause for a silent meeting with the* MOTHER *at foot of the stairs. She kisses* JIM *and starts wiping his tears away, but he is weeping soundlessly and it does no good.*

JIM *looks back up at the dome. The ambulance attendants are bearing* PLATO'S *litter down the last few stairs, followed by the* NEGRO WOMAN.

Group. The ambulance attendants come down the last few stairs followed by the NEGRO WOMAN. JIM *steps forward suddenly and adjusts the blanket covering* PLATO. JUDY *comes to*

JIM's *side. The litter passes camera and we
hold on two shot of* JIM *and* JUDY, *seen against
the lightening sky.*

JIM *(to* JUDY, *half to himself).* He was always
cold.

JUDY *moves to* JIM *and touches his arm
lightly. He looks down at her.*

Med. shot. The group. JIM's *arm is around*
JUDY *as he leads her, firmly, towards his*
MOTHER *and* FATHER. *His voice is warm, brimming with the new found pride he takes in his
parents as he introduces* JUDY *to them.*

JIM. Mom—Dad—this is my friend. Her
name is Judy.

*The parents nod warmly and smile at her. She
smiles shyly in response, happy at being accepted. There is a warmth emanating from the
tight little group. Changes have happened to
them. Old things have been shed and a new start
has been made. Camera booms—pulls back
high to:*

High general shot. Planetarium, JIM *and*
JUDY, FATHER *and* MOTHER *threading their way
through the crowd as the camera continues to
pull back.*

Fade out.

The end.

BONNIE AND CLYDE

Screenplay by David Newman and Robert Benton

CLYDE BARROW	Warren Beatty
BONNIE PARKER	Faye Dunaway
C. W. MOSS	Michael J. Pollard
BUCK BARROW	Gene Hackman
BLANCHE	Estelle Parsons
FRANK BRYCE	Denver Pyle
MALCOLM MOSS	Dub Taylor
VELMA DAVIS	Evans Evans
EUGENE GRIZZARD	Gene Wilder

Screenplay by David Newman and Robert Benton
Produced by Warren Beatty for Warner Bros., 1966
Directed by Arthur Penn
Director of Photography: Burnett Guffey, A.S.C.
Art Director: Dean Tavoularis
Film Editor: Dede Allen
Sound by Francis E. Stahl
Set Decorator: Raymond Paul
Special Effects: Danny Lee
Costumes designed by Theadora Van Runkle
Special Consultant: Robert Towne
Music composed by Charles Strouse
Production Manager: Russ Saunders
Assistant to the Producer: Elaine Mich
Script Supervisor: John Dutton
Makeup created by Robert Jiras
Miss Dunaway's Makeup by Warner Bros. Cosmetics
Flatt & Scruggs "Foggy Mountain Breakdown" courtesy Mercury Records
Men's Wardrobe: Andy Matyasi
Women's Wardrobe: Norma Brown
Hair Stylist: Gladys Witten
Assistant Director: Jack N. Reddish

Winner of the Writers Guild 1967 awards for both Best Written Original Screenplay and Best Written American Drama, and nominated in 1967 by the Academy for Best Story and Screenplay written directly for the screen, this screenplay by David Newman and Robert Benton has already become something of a classic. Stylistically, this film, in dealing with the criminal lives of the legendary Bonnie and Clyde, as choreographed and composed by the authors and the director, Arthur Penn, has the sound, look, and appearance of a fugue, a tone poem, a folk ballet.

We have in America a whole genre of gangster films, some of which are folk legends, like this one and the likes of *Jesse James* and, of course, *Butch Cassidy and the Sundance Kid,* which appears elsewhere in this anthology as a Western. The classic gangster film, for example, *Little Caesar* and *Public Enemy*, which also deals with this period, but in urban America, occupies itself primarily with the pursuit of power in the tradition of the American robber barons of big business. The latter was quasi-legal, of course, while the former was wholly illegal and involved ruthless killing in the pursuit of that power. In *Bonnie and Clyde* there is no pursuit of power. Their life is not glamorous. They never have any real money to speak of, no legion of minions doing their bidding. Their lives are pathetic, actually, and you know they are headed for extinction.

They are also without excuse about their awareness of their crimes and the sure knowledge that they will pay for them. They are responsible for what they do. Folk legends do not make excuses of insanity or diminished capacity before the bar of justice. Some of the pathos of the story—in fact, the larger part of it—hinges on Bonnie's wish toward the end, when retribution is closing in, that she and Clyde could start all over again if they had the chance—without crime. But Clyde will have none of that. He would do what they did differently, that's all, so they would not be caught. He never had any wish to go into any other line of work. In the scene where he and the dispossessed farmer shoot up the farm sign and the windows of the farmhouse from which the farmer had just been evicted by a bank, Clyde, the son of a sharecropper, who shares in the farmer's hatred of the bank—an endemic feeling among many of those who worked the soil during the depression—tells the farmer with some pride, "We rob banks."

Bonnie, who's twenty-one, and Clyde, twenty-two, in this time of their lives, are arrested adolescents in a very real sense. Their spree of crimes are a lark for a while, punctuated with violence. After the moving scene of Bonnie with her mother at a visit toward the end of the film, the inevitability of their demise drawing close becomes stronger and stronger and the feeling of dread is well shared by the audience. Bonnie is almost destroyed in the scene with her mother, and she is pitiful after that.

Though the violence of the film is shocking at times, I do not have the feeling that violence has been used exploitively. It is well integrated with the story itself and in that light justifiable. This pair cannot be called heroes by any stretch of the imagination. You feel pain here for these alienated adolescents and some sorrow but not repugnance. If nothing else, this picture succeeds in mirroring some of the alienation, bitterness, and ignorance of that depression era and some of its children. In some ways it is akin to what *Rebel Without A Cause* represented for the fifties, and it presaged what would come in the sixties. A well-realized film and an excellent script.

David Newman, coauthor of *Bonnie and Clyde,* was born on February 4, 1937, in Logan, Utah, and began in films when he was sixteen as an MGM office boy. He later became a magazine writer and an editor as *Esquire* until he teamed up with Robert Benton. Their partnership lasted from 1966 to 1972; they wrote several plays and screenplays together.

Robert Benton was born on September 29, 1932, in a small town near Dallas. Prior to his partnership with Mr. Newman, he also worked on *Esquire,* as an art director. It was after they wrote the Broadway play *It's a Bird . . . It's a Plane . . . It's Superman* that they collaborated on *Bonnie and Clyde*. Mr. Benton's other credits include *What's up, Doc?* (cowriter); *The Late Show* (writer-director); and *Kramer vs. Kramer* (1979) (writer-director), for which he won an Academy Award as scenarist.

Note: The character named *Ivan* has been changed to *Malcolm*. The character named *Hamer* has been changed to *Bryce*.

CAST OF CHARACTERS

CLYDE BARROW	Young, dapper, reckless.
BONNIE PARKER	Blonde, somewhat fragile, intelligent in expression.
C. W. MOSS	1931 version of a rock-'n-roll hood; blond, surly, and not very bright.
BUCK BARROW	Clyde's older brother, a chubby, jovial, simple, big-hearted man.
BLANCHE	Buck's wife; a young housefrau, no more and no less, inclined to panic.
SHERIFF	
FRANK BRYCE	Tall, strong, contemptuous of almost everyone and particularly women and criminals; some hidden evil in him sometimes shows in his face.
MALCOLM MOSS	C. W.'s father; a fat farmer with gray hair, shrewd and cunning.
BONNIE'S MOTHER	A fragile, weepy old woman.
BONNIE'S SISTER	
BONNIE'S UNCLE	
EUGENE GRIZZARD	A Texas undertaker, about 30 years old.
VELMA DAVIS	Grizzard's sweetheart, a little younger.
MR. WEEKS	A real estate agent in Joplin, Missouri.
GROCERY	
DELIVERY BOY	In Joplin.
HAWKINS	A Missouri bank guard.
BANK CUSTOMER	A snooty, middle-aged matron.
A BANK TELLER IN MINEOLA	
A BANK OFFICIAL IN MINEOLA	
SHERIFF	
PETE SMOOT	A typical Iowa small-town Sheriff.
BILLY	Smoot's young deputy, cold, intense and humorless.
BANK TELLER IN A SMALL TEXAS TOWN	
AN ELDERLY GROCERY CLERK	
A MASSIVE, MUSCULAR BUTCHER	
A POLICEMAN IN HOSPITAL	
A SHORT-ORDER COOK	
A HAMBURGER-STAND COUNTERMAN	
AN OKIE FAMILY IN LOUISIANA	
FARMER IN TEXAS	A 45-year-old man.
DAVIS	An old Negro sharecropper.
WOMAN WITH BABY	Texas farmer's family.
CHILD	
A FISHERMAN	With a string of catfish.

ALSO: Police, townspeople, and other incidental characters in Texas, Missouri, Oklahoma, Kansas, Iowa, Louisiana.

———

The film begins with two title cards introducing the central characters, executed in the style of similar cards used to begin the serials of the late 1930's. The title cards show a photograph of the character looking straight ahead, posed against the plain white background. The words appear at the bottom of the frame. The frame should be smaller than 1:85-1.

TITLE CARD 1:
BONNIE PARKER, *who was born in Rowena, Texas, 1910, and moved with her large family to West Dallas. In 1931 she worked as a waitress in a cafe before meeting* CLYDE BARROW *and beginning her career in crime.*

TITLE CARD 2:
CLYDE BARROW, *who was born in Telco, Texas, 1909, to a family of sharecroppers. As a young man he became a small-time thief and was apprehended after robbing a gas station. He served two years in the penitentiary for armed robbery and was released on good behavior in 1931.*

Cut to:

CREDITS: BONNIE AND CLYDE
CREDITS *should be simple and absolutely silent. No music should occur in the film until where first indicated in the script.*

———

Fade in. Int. Bedroom. Close-up of BONNIE PARKER. *Day. Blonde, somewhat fragile, intelligent in expression. She is putting on make-up with intense concentration and appreciation, applying lipstick and eye make-up. As the camera slowly pulls back from the closeup we see that we have been looking into a mirror. She is standing before the full-length mirror in her bedroom doing her make-up. She overdoes it in the style of the time: rosebud mouth and so forth. As the film progresses her make-up will be refined until, at the end, there is none.*

The camera pulls back and continues to move very slowly throughout the first part of this scene. As the camera continues to move away, we see, by degrees, that BONNIE *is naked. Her nudity is never blatantly revealed to the audience, but implied. That is, she should be "covered" in various ways from the camera's P.O.V., but the audience must be aware of her exposure to* CLYDE *later in the scene. This is the only time in the film that she will ever be this exposed, in all senses of the word, to the audience. Her attitude and appraisal of herself here are touched with narcissism.*

The bedroom itself is a second-story bedroom in a lower-class frame house in West Dallas, Texas. The neighborhood is low income. Though the room reveals its shabby surroundings, it also reveals an attempt by BONNIE *to fix it up. Small and corny* objets d'art *are all over the tops of the bureaus, vanity tables, etc. (Little glass figurines and porcelain statuettes and the like.)*

BONNIE *finishes admiring herself. She walks from the mirror and moves slowly across the room, the camera moving with her, until she reaches the screened window on the opposite wall. The shade is up. There are no curtains. She looks out the window, looking down, and the camera looks down with her.*

Ext. Bedroom. BONNIE'S *P.O.V. Day. Over her shoulder, we see the driveway leading to the garage connected to the house. There is an old car parked in the driveway, its windows open. We see a man walking up the driveway, somewhat furtively. He is a rather dapper fellow, dressed in a dark suit with a vest, a white collar, and a straw boater. It is* CLYDE BARROW. *Obviously, he is about to steal the car. He looks it over, checking around him to make sure no passers-by are coming. He peers inside the front window to see if the keys are in the ignition. He studies the dashboard.* BONNIE *continues watching, silently. Finally she calls out.*

BONNIE. Hey, boy! What you doin' with my mama's car?

Ext. Driveway. Day. CLYDE, *startled, jumps and looks to see who has caught him. Obviously frightened, he looks up and his face freezes at what he sees.*

Ext. Window. CLYDE'S *P.O.V. Day. We now see what he is looking at: at the open window, revealed from the waist up, is the naked* BONNIE. *She looks down, an impudent half-smile on her face. She doesn't move or make any attempt to cover herself.*

Ext. close-up of CLYDE—*Day—whose face changes from astonishment to an answering smile of impudence. (Seeing what he has, he realizes that this girl is clearly not going to scream for the police. Already they are in a little game instigated by* BONNIE, *sizing each other up, competing in a kind of playful arrogance. Before they speak, they have become coconspirators.)*

Close-up of BONNIE, *still smiling. Finally she speaks.*

BONNIE. Wait there!

Int. Bedroom. Day. Running from the window, she flings open a closet and grabs a dress, and shoes. She slips on the shoes, and flings the dress on, running out the door as she does. The camera tracks with her, moving as fast. As she runs down the stairs she buttons up the dress.

Ext. Driveway. Day. She flies out the door, slamming it behind her, runs off the porch (all this has been one continuous movement since she left the window, in great haste) and continues quickly into the driveway. Four feet away from CLYDE, *she stops on a dime. They stand there, looking at each other, smiling the same challenge. For a few seconds, no one speaks, then:*

BONNIE *(putting him on)*. Ain't you ashamed? Tryin' to steal an old lady's automobile.

CLYDE *(with the same put-on)*. I been thinkin' about buyin' me one.

BONNIE. Bull. You ain't got money for dinner, let alone buy no car.

CLYDE *(still the battle of wits going on)*. Now I got enough money for cokes, and since it don't look like you're gonna invite me inside—

BONNIE. You'd steal the dining room table if I did.

CLYDE *(he moves from his spot)*. Come to town with me, then. How'd that be?

BONNIE *(starting to walk onto the sidewalk)*. Goin' to work anyway.

Ext. Street. Moving shot. Day. The camera tracks. It is a hot Texas afternoon, all white light and glare. As they walk the block to town in this scene, their manner of mutual impudence is still pervading.

CLYDE. Goin' to work, huh? What do you do?

BONNIE. None of your business.

CLYDE *(pretending to give it serious thought)*. I bet you're a . . . movie star!

(thinks) No . . . A lady mechanic? . . . No . . . A maid?—

BONNIE *(really offended by that)*. What do you think I am?

CLYDE *(right on the nose)*. A waitress.

BONNIE *(slightly startled by his accuracy, anxious to get back now that he is temporarily one-up)*. What line of work are you in? When you're not stealin' cars?

CLYDE *(mysteriously)*. I tell you, I'm lookin' for suitable employment right at the moment.

BONNIE. What did you do before?

CLYDE *(cooly, knowing its effect)*. I was in State Prison.

BONNIE. State *Prison*? *(she shows her surprise)*

CLYDE. Yeah.

BONNIE *(herself again)*. Guess *some* little old lady wasn't so nice.

CLYDE *(tough)*. It was armed robbery.

BONNIE *(sarcastically)*. My, my, the things that turn up in the driveway these days.

They reach the corner and turn. They are on:

Ext. Main Street. Day.—a small-town street of barber shops, cafes, groceries, etc. At the moment, it is deserted. They continue walking down the empty street. CLYDE *looks the place over. Tracking.*

CLYDE. What do y'all do for a good time around here, listen to the grass grow?

BONNIE. Guess you had a lot more fun up at State Prison, huh?

CLYDE *laughs, enjoying her repartee. They continue walking. At a hydrant,* CLYDE *stops.*

CLYDE *(showing off, but seriously)*. See this loot? *(pointing at his right foot)* I chopped two toes off of it. With an axe.

BONNIE *(shocked)*. What? Why?

CLYDE. To get off the damn work detail, that's why. *(stopping)* Want to see?

BONNIE *(a lady of some sensitivity)*. No! . . . *(turning cute)* I surely don't intend to stand here and look at your dirty feet in the middle of Main Street.

They continue walking in silence past a few stores, each planning what next to say.

BONNIE. Boy, did you really do that?

CLYDE. Yeah.

BONNIE. You must be crazy.

Dissolve to:

Ext. Gas station. Day. Gas station up the block. BONNIE *and* CLYDE *are seen leaning against the soft drink chest, their profiles silhouetted by the bright sun. They are drinking cokes. As they begin to talk, the camera moves in closer to them.* CLYDE *takes off his hat and rubs the cold coke bottle across his forehead.* BONNIE *watches him.*

BONNIE. What's it like?

CLYDE. Prison?

BONNIE *(very interested)*. No, armed robbery.

CLYDE *(he thinks it a silly question)*. It's . . . I don't know . . . it isn't like anything.

BONNIE *(thinking she's heard proof that he's a liar)*. Hah! I knew you never robbed no place, you faker.

CLYDE *(challenged)*. Oh, yeah? *(studies her, then makes up his mind to show her)*

Close-up. Gun. Day. He reaches in his jacket and pulls out a gun. The camera moves to a closeup of the gun, glinting in the sunlight.

Ext. Street. Day. The camera pulls back to show BONNIE *looking at it with fascination. The weapon has an immediate effect on her. She touches it in a manner almost sexual, full of repressed excitement.*

BONNIE *(goading him on)* Yeah, well you got one all right, I guess . . . but you wouldn't have the gumption to use it.

CLYDE *(picking up the challenge, proving himself)*. You just keep your eyes open.

Ext. Little grocery store across the street. Day. The camera remains just behind BONNIE'S *shoulder so that throughout the following scene we have* BONNIE *in the picture, looking at what we look at.*

CLYDE *goes into the little store. We remain outside with* BONNIE *watching. For a minute nothing happens. We can barely see what is going on in the store. Then* CLYDE *comes out, walking slowly. In one hand he holds the gun, in the other a fistful of money. He gets halfway to* BONNIE *and smiles broadly at her, a smile of charm and personality. She smiles back. The moment is intense, as if a spark has jumped from one to the other. Their relationship, which began the minute* BONNIE *spotted him in the driveway, has now really begun.* CLYDE *has shown his stuff and* BONNIE *is "turned on."*

Suddenly the old man who runs the grocery store comes running out into the street, completely dumbfounded. He stands there and says nothing, yet his mouth moves in silent protest. CLYDE *points the gun above him and fires. It is the first loud noise in the film thus far and it should be a shock. The old man, terrified, runs back into the store as fast as he can.* CLYDE *quickly grabs* BONNIE's *hand. The camera swings with them as they turn and begin to run down the street. A few yards and the stores disappear entirely. The landscape turns into that arid, flat and unrelieved western plain that begins where the town ends.*

Ext. Store. At the edge of town. Day. A car is parked at the back of the store. As soon as they reach it, CLYDE *motions and* BONNIE *gets in.* CLYDE *runs to the front, lifts up the hood and crosses the wires to make it start. As he stands back,* BONNIE *calls to him:*

BONNIE. Hey, what's your name, anyway?
CLYDE *(he slams the hood).* Clyde Barrow.

He runs over to the door, opens it, shoves her over, and starts up the engine. The entire sequence is played at an incredibly rapid pace.

BONNIE *(loud, to make herself heard over the gunning motor).* Hi, I'm Bonnie Parker. Please to meet you.

Ext. Road. Day. VROOM! The car zooms off down the road, doing 90. The fast country breakdown music starts up on the sound track, going just as fast as the car.

Ext. Car. Day. The car, still speeding, further down the road. We zoom down and look in the rear window. CLYDE *is driving, we see from behind.* BONNIE *is all over him, biting his ear, ruffling his hair, running her hands all over him—in short, making passionate love to him while he drives. The thrill of the robbery and the escape has turned her on sexually.*

Ext. Car. Another angle. Day. The camera pulls back and above the car. The car starts to go crazy in a comical fashion, manifesting to the audience just what is happening to the driver controlling it. The car swerves all over the road. The car comes to a sudden halt. The car starts again. It swerves this time almost right off the road. The car comes to a sudden halt. The car starts again. It swerves this time almost right off the road before it straightens out. It jumps and jerks. Another car comes down the road the other way and CLYDE's *car swerves so much as to make the other guy drive right off the road into the dirt. It is almost Mack Sennett stuff, but not quite that much.*

Int. Car. BONNIE *and* CLYDE. *Day.* BONNIE *grabs the wheel and turns it sharply.*

Ext. Car. Day. It hairpins off the road onto a shoulder beneath some trees.

Int. Car. BONNIE *and* CLYDE—*Day—still settling to a stop.* BONNIE *and* CLYDE *appear to be*

necking heavily now, punctuated by BONNIE's *squeals of passion as she squirms and hops about like a flea, trying to get to* CLYDE. *The floor gear-shift is keeping their bodies apart, however. In exasperation,* BONNIE *takes the gear shift and shoves it forward out of their way. She plunges onto* CLYDE, *burying him from view.*

BONNIE *(kissing, biting)*.. . . You ready? . . .
CLYDE *(muffled, laughing)*. . . . Hey, wait . . .
BONNIE *(giggling herself).* Aren't you ready? Well, *get* ready!

BONNIE *has obviously touched him. With savage coquetry she tears into her clothes and his.*

BONNIE *(muffled).* C'mon, honey, c'mon, boy . . . let's go . . . let's . . .
CLYDE *(muffled).* Hey . . . hey, wait a minute . . . quit that now, cut it out. *(sharply)* I said, *cut it out*!

He shoves her rudely away, slamming her into the far car door. Suddenly it looks as if they've been fighting. Both unbuttoned and unglued, they stare silently at one another, breathing heavily. CLYDE *gets out of the car, clearly shaken. Despite the fact that he may have encountered this situation many times before, it's one that no twenty-one-year-old boy in 1932 is sophisticated enough to dismiss easily with bravado.*

BONNIE *remains seated in the car. She seems terribly vulnerable. She fumbles about for a cigarette, too confused to figure out what didn't happen.* CLYDE *turns back and reaches through the car window from the driver's side, lighting it for her.* BONNIE *casts* CLYDE *a fishy stare, then accepts the light.*

CLYDE *(trying to be casual, even insouciant).* Look, I don't do that. It's not that I can't — *(his voice cracks, the match burns his fingers, and he bangs his head onto roof of car, and he goes right on)* — it's just that I don't see no percentage in it. I mean there's nothin' *wrong* with me, I don't like boys.

BONNIE *doesn't know what she thinks, and* CLYDE *is trying to gauge her reaction— whether she feels rejected or repelled. In fact, it's both—along with a little latent fascination.*

BONNIE *(finally, spitting out smoke).* Boy . . . boy . . . boy . . .
CLYDE *(a little annoyed).* Boy, what?
BONNIE. Your advertising is dandy. Folks'd just never guess you don't have a

thing to sell. *(a little afraid)* You better take me home, now.

CLYDE *(getting back into car)*. Wait!

BONNIE. Don't touch me!

She gets out of car, leaving CLYDE *draped across the front seat, reaching after her.*

CLYDE *(almost shouting)*. If all you want's stud service, then get on back to West Dallas and stay there the rest of your life!

This stops her. Now CLYDE *pours it on, with an almost maniacal exuberance that becomes more controlled as he gets control of* BONNIE.

CLYDE. But you're worth more'n that, a lot more, and you know it, and that's why you come along with me. You could find a lover boy on every corner in town and it doesn't make a damn to them whether you're waiting on tables or picking cotton, so long as you cooperate. But it does make a damn to me!

BONNIE *(turning, intrigued)*. Why?.

CLYDE. Why? Because you're different! You're like me and you want different things.

BONNIE *is hooked now.*

CLYDE *(continuing)*. You and me travelin' together, we could cut clean acrost this state, and Kansas, too, and maybe dip into Oklahoma, and Missouri or whatnot, and catch ourselves highpockets and a high-heeled ol' time. We can be somethin' we could *never* be alone. I'll show you . . . when we walk into the Adolphus Hotel in San Antone', you wearin' a silk dress, they'll be waitin' on you and believe me, sugar, they're gonna know your last name.

He stops, having begun to woo her to something more intense than a casual, physical coupling.

BONNIE. When'd you figure that all out?

CLYDE. First time I saw you.

BONNIE. How come?

CLYDE *(intensely, with real honesty)*. 'Cause you may be the best damn girl in Texas.

Close-up. BONNIE.

BONNIE. Who are you, anyway?

Cut to:

Int. Roadside cafe. BONNIE *and* CLYDE. *Day.* BONNIE *and* CLYDE *seated in booth, now C.U.* CLYDE. *The sound track bridges the scene: the question that* BONNIE *has just asked is now suddenly rebutted by* CLYDE, *as he points a finger at her.*

CLYDE *(not answering her, preferring to lead the conversation)*. I'll tell you about you.

He loves doing this and he does it well. The more he envisions BONNIE's *life, the more instinctively accurate he becomes. She grows more and more fascinated, like a child watching a mind reader.*

CLYDE. Lessee . . . You were born somewheres around East Texas . . . got a big old family, right? . . . You went to school, of course, but you didn't take to it much 'cause you was a lot smarter than everybody else anyway. So you just quit. Now . . . *(thinking, playing it for all it's worth)* . . . When you were sixteen . . . no, seventeen, there was a guy who worked in . . . uh . . .

Pull back taking in BONNIE, *favoring* CLYDE.

BONNIE. *(fascinated)*. Cement plant—

CLYDE. Right, Cement plant. And you liked him 'cause he thought you was just as nice as you could be. You almost married that guy, but then . . . you thought, no, you didn't think you would. So you got your job in the cafe . . . *(getting closer to home now, hitting them right in there)*. And every morning you wake up and you hate it. You just hate it. And you get down there and you put on your white uniform—

BONNIE *(enthralled)*. Pink.

CLYDE. And the truck drivers come in to eat greasy burgers and they kid you and you kid them back, but they're *stupid* and *dumb*, boys with big tattoos all over 'em, and you don't like it . . . And they ask you for dates and sometimes you go . . . but you mostly don't, and all they ever try is to get into your pants whether you want to or not . . . and you go home and sit in your room and think, *when* and *how* will I ever get away from this? . . . And now you know.

BONNIE *is half-mesmerized by his talk. A waitress comes with their food. A cheap, gaudy dame, she has spit curls on each temple in the style of the times.* CLYDE *looks at her and at* BONNIE, *who also wears spit curls. As soon as the waitress leaves:*

CLYDE *(pointing at her hair)*. Change that. I don't like it.

Without a word of protest, BONNIE *immediately reaches in her bag and takes out a mirror. She holds it up and with the other hand, brushes back her spit curls into her hair. She never again wears them. When she has pushed them back she looks at* CLYDE *for his approval. He nods his okay. She smiles, puts back her mirror and begins to eat her food. She's ravenously hungry and eats with total concentration on her plate.* CLYDE *doesn't touch his food, just watches* BONNIE *eat for a minute.*

CLYDE. God, you're a knockout.

Ext. Roadside cafe. Day for Dusk. CLYDE *and* BONNIE *emerge from the cafe into the early evening. They move toward the car they have stolen. Just beyond sits a newer model car.* BONNIE *is surprised to see* CLYDE *head toward the newer car.*

BONNIE. Hey, that ain't ours.
CLYDE. Sure it is.
BONNIE. But we came in this one.
CLYDE. Don't mean we have to go home in it.

She walks amazed around the new car and gets in beside him. He turns the key and they pull away from the cafe.

Int. Abandoned farm house. A wide shot of the parlor living room. Day. The room is bare. In the middle BONNIE *is waking, having slept on a couple of car seats covered with an old piece of tattered blanket. There are windows behind her. She looks about bewildered.*

BONNIE. Clyde . . .

She starts to panic and runs to the window.

BONNIE *(continuing).* Clyde . . .

At another window CLYDE *appears.*

CLYDE. Hey, lady.
BONNIE *(chagrined at her fear).* Where you been keeping yourself?
CLYDE. Slept out by the car.
BONNIE. Oh . . . These accommodations ain't particularly deluxe.
CLYDE. No . . . If they're after us, I want the first shot. Come on, you got some work to do.

BONNIE *moves to the door and out of the house.*

Ext. Farm house. Front yard. Day. On the door is a sign which reads:

Insert:

PROPERTY OF MIDLOTHIAN CITIZENS BANK —TRESPASSERS WILL BE PROSECUTED.

Wide angle. Across fence. Day. On the dilapidated picket fence six old bottles have been placed. As BONNIE *joins* CLYDE *he turns and fires six quick shots. The bottles disappear.*

BONNIE. You're good.
CLYDE. The best.
BONNIE. And modest . . .
CLYDE. Come on. Got you all set up over here.

Wider angle. They move around to the side of building where CLYDE *points to a tire hanging by a rope from a tree. He means that to be* BONNIE's *target. He hands her a gun.*

CLYDE. Set her spinnin'.

BONNIE *fires. She misses.*

CLYDE. Again. Come down slow with it . . .

BONNIE *fires again and hits the tire. She smiles and blows the smoke from the barrel in pride and self-mockery.*

CLYDE. Ain't you something? I tell you I'm going to get you a Smith and Wesson, it'll be easier in your hand. Now try it again once . . .

BONNIE *sights. As she is about to fire, a man appears around the corner of the building. A* FARMER. *She fires and hits the tire.*

FARMER. Heighdo.

CLYDE *whirls at the sound. He grabs gun from* BONNIE *because his is empty. He aims at* FARMER.

FARMER *(frightened).* No sir . . . no sir. You all go right ahead.

CLYDE *watches him warily.*

FARMER *(continuing).* Used to be my place. Not any more. Bank took it.

CLYDE *and* BONNIE *start to move toward the farmer. All three move around to the front of the building. At a distance we see an Okie car loaded with belongings. A* WOMAN *with a* BABY *in arms sits in front. A smaller* BOY *stands outside the car.*

FARMER. Yessir, moved us off. Now it belongs to them. *(He points at the foreclosure sign.)*

BONNIE. Well, that's a pitiful shame.

CLYDE *shakes his head sympathetically. He loads the empty gun.*

FARMER *(bitterly).* You're damned right, ma'm.

He looks up to see an OLD NEGRO *who has come from a distant shack and now stands near* CLYDE'S *car.*

FARMER *(nodding toward Negro).* Me and him put in the years here. Yessir. So you all go right ahead. We just come by for a last look.

He stands a moment looking at the house and then turns toward his family in the car. CLYDE *and* BONNIE *look after him.* CLYDE *spins and fires three fast shots into the fore-closure sign. The* FARMER *stops and turns, looking at* CLYDE. CLYDE *offers the gun to the farmer. He looks at it, then accepts it. He slowly takes aim at the sign and fires. It pleases him. He looks at* CLYDE *and* BONNIE *who smile.*

FARMER. You all mind?

BONNIE *and* CLYDE *are puzzled.*

FARMER. Hey, Davis! Come on over here.

The NEGRO *moves toward them. Now* BONNIE *understands. She takes the second gun from* CLYDE *and hands it to* DAVIS. DAVIS *looks from* BONNIE *to the* FARMER *and toward the house. The* FARMER *fires again. This time at a window. He nods to* DAVIS. DAVIS *slowly raises the gun and fires at another window. It shatters and they can't keep from laughing. The* FARMER *returns the gun as does* DAVIS.

FARMER *(continuing).* Much obliged.

He extends his hand. CLYDE *shakes it.*

FARMER. Otis Harrison. And this here's Davis. We worked this place.
CLYDE *(formally).* Miss Bonnie Parker. And I'm Clyde Barrow.

Across FARMER'S *car. Wide shot. Day. The* FARMER *turns and moves toward his people.* DAVIS *moves toward his shack.* CLYDE *and* BONNIE *in the b.g.*

Close angle. BONNIE *and* CLYDE.

CLYDE *(continuing)* We rob banks.

BONNIE *turns quickly to look at* CLYDE. *He smiles and nods.*

Fade out.

Fade in. Ext. A long, country road. Day. A car is driving down it. It is the next day. BONNIE *is driving,* CLYDE *beside her.*

Int. Car. Day.

CLYDE. You just stay in the car and watch and be ready. *(he is playing it cool, knowing*

she is scared. He thinks he's James Cagney) Okay now? *(he hands her a gun from the glove compartment)* You just be ready if I need you.

BONNIE'S *hands are tense on the wheel. Her face shows how nervous she is now that the time has come.*

CLYDE. Scared?
BONNIE. No.

They drive in silence.

CLYDE. What are you thinkin' about?
BONNIE. Nothin'.

Ext. Business street of a little town. Day. We are still in the car. BONNIE *pulls over and stops by the bank.* CLYDE *is frozen in his seat. We can see that, for all his talk, he is scared, too.*

BONNIE. What are you waitin' for?

That gets him. CLYDE *throws the door open and jumps, practically dives out the door. The camera follows his motion right inside the bank, tracking very fast.*

Int. Bank #1. Day. Something is very screwy here. The bank is dark, the TELLER *is half asleep over his books.* CLYDE *approaches, thrusts the gun at him.*

CLYDE *(with a swagger).* This is a stickup. Just take it easy and nothin' will happen to you. Gimme the money.
TELLER *(looking up with no fear, his voice calm and conversational).* Heighdy.
CLYDE *(nonplussed at this).* Gimme the money!
TELLER. What money? There ain't no money here, mister.
CLYDE *(totally befuddled at the turn of events).* What do you mean there ain't no money? This here is a bank, ain't it?

The camera pans around the bank. We see that it is empty, dusty and shuttered.

TELLER. This was a bank. We failed three weeks ago.
CLYDE *(furious).* What? What??

In a rage, he goes behind the partition, grabs the teller and pushes him ahead with the gun. CLYDE *is fuming. He forces the teller out the front door.*

Ext. Bank #1. Day—showing BONNIE *in the car. She is terrified as she sees* CLYDE *and the* TELLER *coming at her. She doesn't understand what is happening.*

CLYDE *(shoving the teller forward).* Tell her! Tell her!

TELLER *(acting like a man who has had his sleep interrupted by lunatics)*. As I was tellin' this gentleman, our bank failed last month and ain't no money in it. I sure am sorry.

BONNIE'S *reaction is one of hysterical relief and appreciation of what's funny in the situation. She laughs uproariously, she can't stop laughing. This makes* CLYDE *madder than ever. He shoves the teller to the ground.*

Int. Car. Day. Completely humiliated, CLYDE *gets in the car, shoving* BONNIE *over. She is still laughing.* BONNIE *starts the car.* CLYDE *points his gun out the window.*

Close shot. Bank window—whereon is lettered: ASSETS-$70,000.

Int. Car. CLYDE *and* BONNIE. *Day. Angle to include bank window.* CLYDE *aims and puts a bullet through each of the zeros. We see each zero shot through. Then the entire window hangs there for a second and suddenly crashes. On the soundtrack,* BONNIE'S *laughter.*

Cut to:

Int. Car. Day—still driving. BONNIE *has still not fully recovered from her mirth, but is quieting down because she sees that* CLYDE *is really mad and can't be pushed too far.*

CLYDE *(steaming)*. We got $1.98 and you're laughin'.

She tries to stop.

Ext. Street. Day. The car pulls down another street of shops in another little hick town. A grocery store ahead.

Int. Car.

CLYDE. Keep it running.

Int. Grocery store. Day. There is an old CLERK *behind the counter, and standing in the b.g., almost out of our vision, is a* BUTCHER— *an enormous giant of a man.* CLYDE *steps up to the counter.*

CLYDE. Give me a loaf of bread, a dozen eggs and a quart of milk.

The CLERK *gets the order and puts it in a bag. He rings open the cash register preparatory to asking* CLYDE *for the money.* CLYDE *pulls his gun.*

CLYDE. This is a stickup. I'll take all the money in that drawer now.

He reaches over the counter into the cash drawer and grabs the bills. He smiles. Suddenly looming beside CLYDE *is the* BUTCHER, *brandishing a meat cleaver. Camera looks up at this formidable sight as the cleaver comes crashing down, missing* CLYDE *and sticking in the wooden counter. He grabs* CLYDE *around the chest in a bear hug and actually lifts him off the ground. The struggle is in silence.* CLYDE *is terrified, fighting wildly to get free. The gun in* CLYDE'S *hand is pinned, because the man has* CLYDE'S *arm pinned to his thigh.* CLYDE *tries to raise the barrel at an upward angle to shoot, finally he is able to do so. He fires. The bullet enters the* BUTCHER'S *stomach. The* BUTCHER *screams, but reacts like a wounded animal, more furious than ever. He still holds* CLYDE *in a fierce hug, staggering around the store, knocking into shelves and spilling cans.* CLYDE *is hysterical with fear. He shoots the* BUTCHER *again. The* BUTCHER *falls to his knees, but still he doesn't release* CLYDE. *In a panic,* CLYDE *drags the man to the door, trying to get out.*

Ext. Grocery store. Day. BONNIE *sees* CLYDE *and the* BUTCHER *holding his legs. She is terrified.* CLYDE *drags him out on the street. The* BUTCHER *won't let go.* CLYDE, *in real panic, aims the gun at his head and fires. Click. Out of bullets. In blind fury, he pistol-whips the* BUTCHER'S *head with two terrific swipes. Finally the* BUTCHER *lets go. Hysterical,* CLYDE *jumps away and leaps into the car on the other side.* BONNIE *still at the wheel.*

CLYDE. Get the hell out of here!

They drive off at top speed.

Int. Car. Day. CLYDE *is shaken. He speaks haltingly, panting; trying to get control of himself.*

CLYDE. Damn him, that big son of a bitch . . . He tried to kill me . . . I ain't got eyes in back of my head . . . I didn't want to hurt him. It wasn't a real robbery . . . Some food and a little bit of dough. I'm not against him. Damn!

Ext. Speeding car. Day. The car is speeding down an open road. Suddenly it begins to buck and cough. There is something wrong with the motor.

Close shot. C. W. MOSS. *Ext. Filling Station. His cherubic cheeks are puffed up as he blows into the fuel lines of* CLYDE'S *car. There is a distinctly flat sound.*

Reaction: CLYDE *and* BONNIE. CLYDE *stands by the hood.* BONNIE *remains seated in the car.* CLYDE *is covered with sweat and grease— clearly he has gotten in his licks on the engine without success. Neither he nor* BONNIE *seems impressed by the noise* C. W. *is making.*

Another angle. c. w. — *as he screws back the fuel line and moves between* BONNIE *and* CLYDE *to the ignition, turning the engine over. It purrs beautifully.* CLYDE *is astonished.*

CLYDE. *What was wrong, anyway?*

c. w. (*moving back to screw on gas cap*). Air bubble — clogged the fuel line.

c. w. *now stands between* BONNIE *and* CLYDE.

c. w. (*continuing*). I just blowed her away.

CLYDE *still can't get over it.*

CLYDE. You just blowed it away.

c. w. *belches. He is embarrassed before* BONNIE.

c w. 'Scuse me, ma'm . . . Anythin' else I can do for you?

CLYDE *nods vigorously, looking across* c. w.*'s back to* BONNIE. BONNIE *gets the message.*

BONNIE. Well . . . I'm not sure . . . (*she looks around*) Say, them little red things there stickin' up? Are they gas pumps?

c. w. (*he's not too bright*). Sure.

BONNIE. Isn't that interesting? How does that there gasoline get in my little old car?

c. w. (*trying to be helpful*). Well, y'see, there's this tank underground, and the gas comes up this tube into the pump and into your car, M'am.

BONNIE. My, you're a smart fellow. You sure know a lot about automobiles, don't you?

c. w. (*he has no idea he's being toyed with*). Yeah, I do.

BONNIE. Well, would you know what kind of a car this is?

c. w. (*touching it*). Yeah, it's a Chevrolet 8-cylinder coupé.

BONNIE. No, no.

c. w. Sure it is.

BONNIE. No, this is a *stolen* Chevrolet 8-cylinder coupe.

c. w. *jerks his hand off it as if he touched a hot stove.*

CLYDE (*getting in the conversation*). You ain't scared, are you? (*to Bonnie*) I believe he is. What a pity. We sure coulda used a smart boy who knows such a great deal about automobiles. (*suddenly business-like, to C. W.*) You a good driver, boy?

c. w. (*getting quite confused*). I guess so.

CLYDE (*pretending to cool on him*). No, I don't think so. He's better off here . . .

BONNIE. What's your name, boy?

c. w. C. W. Moss.

BONNIE. What's the C. W. for?

c. w. (*reluctantly*). Clarence Wallace.

BONNIE. I'm Miss Bonnie Parker and this is Mr. Clyde Barrow. We . . . rob . . . banks. (*C. W. reacts with wide eyes*)

CLYDE (*swiftly, testing his mettle*). Ain't nothing wrong with that, is there, boy?

c. w. (*nervously*). Uh, nope —

BONNIE. (*with a put-on sigh*). No, he ain't the one.

CLYDE. Unless, Boy, you think you got enough guts for our line of work?

c. w. (*affronted in his dumb way*). What do you mean? I served a year in the reform school.

BONNIE. Oh, a man with a record!

CLYDE (*laughs*). Now look here, I know you got the nerve to short-change old ladies who come in for gas, but what I'm askin' you is have you got what it takes to pull bank jobs with us?

BONNIE. Mr. C. W. Moss?

c. w. (*anxious to prove himself*). Sure, I could. Sure I could. I ain't scared, if that's what you think.

CLYDE. Prove it.

c. w. *walks away from the car. Camera remains where it was. We see him walk inside the gas station office, open the cash drawer, close it and come out. He emerges with a fistful of money. He walks over to* BONNIE's *window, sticks his hand inside and drops the money on her lap. We see the bills flutter down. Not a word is spoken.* BONNIE *moves over into the middle.* c. w. *opens the door and gets in behind the wheel. For a moment we see them all sitting there, each smiling their little smile.* CLYDE *starts to hum a hillbilly tune quietly. The sound track picks it up (banjo and violin, etc.) and as the music swells, they drive off down the road.*

Int. Hospital room. Day. A small room with a bed. On it, covered by a sheet which humps like a mountain over his enormous stomach, is the BUTCHER. *His head is propped up on a pillow and he sips a liquid through a bent glass straw. Camera is on the left side of the head of the bed, seeing the* BUTCHER *in a three-quarter profile. On the opposite side of the bed stands a uniformed patrolman who is in the act of flashing mug-shot photos for the* BUTCHER *to identify his assailant. The lawman holds a stack of them in front of them, swiftly changing the cards like a grade-school teacher with her flash cards. At each picture, the* BUTCHER *grunts negatively and goes on sipping from his glass straw. One picture, two, three go by. The fourth picture is a mug shot of* CLYDE. *Again the* BUTCHER *grunts 'no,' without hesitation. As the next picture comes into view, we*

Dissolve to:

Ext. Motel. Night—on a painted wooden sign, lit by one attached light, which reads: "MOTOR COURT".

Int. Room in Motor Court. Night—in darkness. Camera is close on BONNIE. *She is awake and restless. O.S. comes the measured snoring that we will think comes from* CLYDE. BONNIE *raises up and kneels over Clyde. She needs him. Clyde seems to snore on. Camera drops between them and we see that the snoring actually comes from* C. W. BONNIE *drops back on her pillow. We cut close on* CLYDE. *He is awake.*

Int. Cafe. Day. BONNIE, CLYDE *and* C. W. *seated in a booth in a cafe. The Waitress brings the food and serves everybody. We see* C. W. *With great concentration, as he does everything by relating to the immediate action he happens to be involved with, he takes the sugar shaker and begins methodically sprinkling sugar over all his food. He sugars the meat, the beans, and the beets.* BONNIE *and* CLYDE *watch this performance with first, amazement and second, disgust. They can't believe what they see.*

BONNIE *(incredulously).* C. W., what are you doing? *Why* do you do that?

C. W. *(beginning to eat it).* Why not?

BONNIE. It's just disgusting, that's why.

C. W. *(chewing).* Not to me it ain't.

BONNIE. But . . . but it makes everything sweet!

C. W. Yeah, I know.

With a resigned expression, BONNIE *turns away and begins to eat. Suddenly a look of consternation crosses* C. W.*'s face.*

C. W. Damn! No mayonnaise!

He gets up and goes down to the counter on the other end of the restaurant, out of our vision, apparently planning to put mayonnaise over the sugar. The minute he is out of earshot, BONNIE *gets* CLYDE'*s attention.*

BONNIE. Clyde, why does he have to stay in the same room as us?

CLYDE *seems not to have heard the question. He takes up the sugar shaker and spreads a thin field of sugar on the dark table surface. He will sketch his plan in the sugar.*

CLYDE. Lemme show you about tomorrow.

He begins to sketch.

BONNIE. Why?

CLYDE. Now C. W.'ll be waitin' right outside in the car. Here is the teller's cage. Four of them and over here the desks and what have you . . .

BONNIE. Why, Clyde . . .

CLYDE. Hmmm??

BONNIE. In the same room with us?

CLYDE. Hell, where else? Ain't gonna spread out all over the state . . .

The harshness of his tone concerns him and he recovers with a smile.

CLYDE *(continuing).* Not yet, anyway. Now, the door to the bank is here now. You cover me from there.

BONNIE *(takes his hand to her face).* Just that I love you so much.

CLYDE. You're the best damn girl in Texas.

C. W. *comes back with the mayonnaise; looks at the table.*

C. W. Hey, you spilled the sugar.

Three shot.

CLYDE *(eating).* The layout for tomorrow up in Mineola.

C. W. Mineola? Gosh, that's four, five hundred miles from here!

CLYDE. So what? We take U.S. 85 to Willis Point, don't you know, and cut over on State Highway 28 at Kaufman, keep on goin' till we hit the farm-to-market road that connects to 105 and that's right up by Mineola. On a Saturday afternoon . . .

Ext. Small Kansas town. The car driving into a small Kansas town. It is Saturday afternoon, sunny. The streets are filled with people, cars, wagons. C. W. *is driving,* BONNIE *is in front with him,* CLYDE *is in the back.* C. W. *looks scared to death at the idea of robbing a bank. The car pulls up in front of the bank, double-parked.* BONNIE *and* CLYDE *get out.*

Ext. Car. Day.

CLYDE. Keep it running.

BONNIE *and* CLYDE *enter bank.*

Int. Bank #2. Day. Cut to the interior of the bank. BONNIE *and* CLYDE *come in, assume the classic positions—she at the door where she can cover the bank,* CLYDE *at the first teller's cage.*

CLYDE *(in a very quiet voice).* This is a stickup.

TELLER. What?

CLYDE. This is a stickup.

This time everyone in the bank hears it. The people gasp and pull back. CLYDE *slowly edges toward the door and prods* BONNIE *forward. She carries a paper sack.* CLYDE *motions her to go from cage to cage and get all of the money.* BONNIE *begins doing so, while* CLYDE *keeps his gun trained on everybody. We see* BONNIE *get the money from the first teller, the second teller, then . . .*

Ext. Small town street. Day. A car parked in a tight spot has just pulled out.

Close-up C. W. *Day—who suddenly looks delighted to see a parking space.*

Ext. car—street. Day. Immediately he methodically begins to back in. It's a tight spot and he has to cut the wheel, pull forward, cut some more, pull back and so on. The scene, for the audience, should be nervous and funny.

Cut to:

Int. Bank #2. Day. Inside the bank, BONNIE *and* CLYDE *have filled the sack. They run out the door, the camera tracks with them.*

Ext. Small town street. Day. They run for where the car was, but it isn't there. Then they see C. W. *has parked it.*

Int. car. Day.

CLYDE. Let's go! Let's go!

C. W. *suddenly realizes what a stupid thing he's done.*

Ext. Car. Street. Day. C. W. *tries to shoot out of the parking spot, but he can't. He has to go through the business of backing up, cutting the wheel and all of it. The scene is one of pure pandemonium and chaos.*

Int. Car.

CLYDE. Come on! Get it out!

Ext. Car. Day. A policeman arrives and begins firing at car. C. W. *gets the car halfway out of the spot, scraping fenders in the process, and the car is almost out when suddenly a face looms up at the window—a dignified, white-haired, celluloid-collared man, obviously a bank official who has leaped onto the running board. His screaming can barely be distinguished from all the noise.*

MAN. Stop!

CLYDE *fires through the window.*

Close-up (special effects). The face of the man explodes in blood. Then he drops out of sight.

Ext. Car. Day. The car shoots off down the road, doing ninety. Police are firing at the escaping car; BONNIE *and* CLYDE *are shooting out the back window;* C. W. *is almost having a nervous breakdown at the wheel.*

Ext. Street. A movie house. Day. A police car that had been chasing CLYDE *and* BONNIE's *car comes down the street. It is obvious that the cops have lost them. They are searching the street for a sign of* CLYDE's *car. They pass a movie house whose marquee reads: "*GOLDDIGGERS OF 1933*". They slow for a moment, decide that is not a probable place to look. They drive off.*

Int. Movie house. Wide across audience at screen. The opening musical sequence of "Golddiggers" is on the screen. Ginger Rogers sings "We're In The Money". Among the audience we cannot make out our three people. It is a small audience and thinly dispersed.

Tight shot at audience. Camera pans the audience while on the track we hear the music of the song. First of our group who becomes visible is C. W. *He is staring at the screen and eating bites from a candy bar in each hand. Camera pans further and we see that* CLYDE *is in the row behind* C. W. *and a few seats to one side.* CLYDE *is nervous and keeps watching the entrance doors. He is in a rage. He shifts in his seat.*

CLYDE. Boy, you gotta be poor in the head. You . . .! Count of you I killed a man. Murder . . . you too.

Shot from behind CLYDE. *Shooting toward screen.*

CLYDE *(continuing).* Dumb ass stupid.

C. W. *turns to* CLYDE *and nods agreement. This infuriates* CLYDE *even more. He slaps the back of* C. W.'s *head.*

CLYDE. Ever do a dumb thing like that again, I'll kill you boy!

Angle at BONNIE. *She has been watching the movie; is now disturbed by the noise. She turns back to* CLYDE *from her seat on the aisle.*

BONNIE. Ssshh! If you boys want to talk why don't you go outside?

She smiles at her joke and turns back to the screen to the movie which she is obviously enjoying enormously.

Int. Cheap motel bathroom. Close-up
BONNIE. *Day. On the right of the screen, f.g.,*
BONNIE *stands at the sink fixing her make-up
in the mirror. The make-up has become more
conservative. On the left, further back, is a
bathtub and in it sits* C. W. *His head and knees
peek over the gray, soapy water. He is engaged
with his usual single-minded concentration, in
washing himself, carefully scrubbing his arms,
not a thought in his head.* BONNIE *finishes her
make-up and regards herself quizzically, tilting
her head to look at herself at different angles.
She is smoking a cigarette, and really, studying
herself.*

BONNIE. What do you think of me, C. W.?
C. W. Uh . . . well, you're just fine, I
guess. Uh, well, course you're a real good
shot . . . and . . . uh . . . well, sometimes
you look pretty as a painting.

Camera stays with BONNIE *during all this,
watching her look at herself as she listens to*
C. W.'s *evaluation. She has a narcissistic concern at the moment and as she hears him enu-
merate her values, she thinks about each in
turn and decides yes, that's true.*

C. W. Hey, uh, Bonnie . . . could you get
me that washrag there?

Responding automatically, BONNIE *turns
and walks to a towel rack, pulls the washcloth
off and starts toward* C. W. *when suddenly she
stops with a smile on her face and a sudden
motion. Teasingly, she holds the washcloth out
at arm's length.*

BONNIE *(coyly)*. Why'nt you come get it?
C. W. *(not even realizing what's on her
mind)*. Huh?
BONNIE *(wiggling the washcloth like a bull-
fighter's cape)*. Whyn't you come get it, C.
W.?

Suddenly C. W. *looks mortally embarrassed
as he realizes what that would entail.*

C. W. Aw, Bonnie, come on, gimme it.

BONNIE *tries another tack. She begins sauntering over slowly, teasingly, still holding out
the treasured washcloth.*

BONNIE *(pertly)*. All right, I'll bring it
myself.

As she moves closer to the tub, C. W. *realizes that she will be able to peer down into the
tub and see him and he frantically reaches up
with one hand and yanks the washcloth into the
tub, causing a great splash.* BONNIE, *somewhat the victim of the splash, jumps back and
away. Recovering her composure, she looks at*

C. W. *who is slunk down in the tub like a gross
September Morn. She has tried him and he has
failed; she realizes now that he was no choice
for her, no real man, even if he might perform
sexually. He is a lump. This irritates her; his
very presence is demeaning to herself and*
CLYDE.

BONNIE *(irritated with herself for even
thinking of such a thing)*. You simpleton,
what would you do if we just pulled out some
night while you was asleep?
C. W *(trying to give the right answer, but
obviously faking it)*. Oh, I wouldn't know
what to do. But you wouldn't do that. You
couldn't now.

BONNIE *realizes, with some weariness, the
inevitable truth of what he's said; thus resigned, she says patronizingly:*

BONNIE. That's right, C. W. We'll always
be around to take care of you.

*Pointedly, she throws her cigarette in his
bath-water, "Sssssssss". She turns and leaves
the bathroom, slamming the door behind her.*

*Int. Bedroom. Camera goes with her into
the connecting bedroom.* CLYDE *is sitting on
the edge of the bed cleaning the guns and oil-
ing them. He is quiet and preoccupied and
takes no note of* BONNIE's *present condition.
The moment she enters, he looks up.*

CLYDE *(quietly)*. Bonnie, I want to talk to
you. Sit down. BONNIE *sits, a little taken off
balance by his serious manner. But she listens
quietly.*

CLYDE *(continuing)*. This afternoon we
killed a man and we were seen. Now nobody
knows who you are yet, but they're going to
be after me and anybody who's runnin' with
me. Now that's murder now and it's gonna
get rough. *(*BONNIE *nods.* CLYDE *continues
speaking carefully and gently.)* Look, I can't
get out, but right now you still can. You say
the word and I'll put you on the bus to go
back to your Mother. 'Cause you mean a lot
to me, honey, and I ain't going to make you
run with me. So if you want, you say the
word.

BONNIE, *moved by his offer, has tears in her
eyes.*

CLYDE *(as he pauses)*. Why? We ain't
gonna have a minute's peace.

BONNIE *doesn't like him in this mood. She
tries to josh him out of it.*

BONNIE. Oh, pshaw.

CLYDE (*trying to make her see the serious-ness of it*). Bonnie, we could get *killed.*

BONNIE (*death has no reality for her*). Who'd wanna kill a sweet young thing like me?

CLYDE (*amused in spite of himself*). I ain't no sweet young thing.

BONNIE. Oh, Clyde, I can't picture you with a halo, and if you went to the other place you'd rob the Devil blind, so he'd kick you right back to me.

Close-up. CLYDE—*touched deeply, realizes that this was a lovely thing to say to him.*

Int. Motel bedroom. They kiss. They are near the bed on which are some guns that CLYDE *has been cleaning. The kiss moves toward real love making. They are on the bed and push the guns aside. Some fall to the floor.* CLYDE *breaks the embrace after it has reached a high pitch. He moves away from the bed toward the window.* BONNIE *follows him and embraces him from the rear. They are miserable.* BONNIE *frees him and returns to the bed. She falls on it face down. A gun presses into her face.* CLYDE *sits in the window, the light silhouettes him. He turns his face toward the glass and rests his head on the window pane.* BONNIE *turns to him from bed. She smiles a comforting smile at him. She rolls over onto her back. The gun is now under her head and moves it. She sits up and gestures to* CLYDE. *He remains at the window. She stares at him. She looks toward the bathroom. She looks back at* CLYDE. *She is moved and pained for him. She touches her cheek with the gun and waits for him to be able to look at her. Finally he does. Her look eases him and he almost smiles.*

Int. BUCK's *car. Day. Shot of little fuzzy doll tied by a white shoestring to the rear-view mir-ror of a car. The car is moving; the doll is bouncing up and down. In the front seat are* BUCK *and* BLANCHE BARROW. BUCK *is a jovial, simple, big-hearted man. A little chubby, given to raucous jokes, knee-slapping and broad re-actions. He is, in many ways, the emotional opposite of his brother. It doesn't take much to make him happy.* BLANCHE, *his wife, is the direct opposite of* BONNIE. *She is a housefrau, no more and no less, not terribly bright, not very ambitious, cuddly, simpering, madly in love with* BUCK *and desirous of keeping their lives on the straight and narrow. As the scene begins we hear and then see* BUCK, *driving, singing "The Great Speckled Bird."* BLANCHE *is sitting next to him looking at a movie maga-zine, appearing fairly miserable.*

BUCK (*singing*).

"What a beautiful thought I am thinking
Concernin' that great speckled bird,
Remember his name is recorded
on the pages of God's Holy word . . ."

BLANCHE. All right, now you did foolish things as a young man, honey-love, but you went and paid your debt to society and that was right. But now you just gettin' back in with the criminal element.

BUCK. Criminal element! This is my *brother,* darlin'. Shoot, he ain't no more criminal than you are, Blanche.

BLANCHE. Well, that ain't what I heard.

BUCK. Now word of mouth just don't go, darlin', you gotta have the facts. Shoot. Why he and me growed up together, slept and worked side by side. (*laughing*). God, what a boy he was!

BLANCHE. He's a crook.

BUCK (*chidingly*). Now you stop bad-mouthin' him, Blanche. We're just gonna have us a little family visit for a few weeks and then we'll go back to Dallas and I'll get me a job somewheres. I just ain't gonna work in your Daddy's church—That's final. (*laughing it off, singing*)

"What a beautiful thought I am thinking
Concernin' that great speckled bird . . ."

Cut to:

Ext. Cabin. The front of the motel. Day. BUCK's *car drives up to the cabin, honking the horn wildly. The door of the cabin opens and* CLYDE *comes running out. He is overjoyed to see his brother.* BUCK *jumps out of the car, equally delighted. They hug each other.*

CLYDE (*hugging him*). Buck!
BUCK. Clyde! You son of a bitch!

They laugh happily and begin sparring with each other, faking punches and blocking punches—an old childhood ritual. There is a great feeling of warmth between the two broth-ers. CLYDE *is more outgoing than we have ever seen him before.*

CLYDE. How's ma? How's sister?

BUCK. Just fine, just fine. Send their best to you.

CLYDE (*patting Buck's stomach*). Hey, you're fillin' out there. Must be that prison food.

BUCK. Hell no! (*laughing*) It's married life. You know what they say, it's the face powder that gets a man interested, but it's the baking powder that keeps him at home. (*he explodes with laughter and so does Clyde, who loves Buck's jokes*) Hey! you gotta meet my wife.

Hey, honey, c'mon out here now and meet my baby brother.

Camera swings to car. We see BLANCHE *still sitting there, her face obscured by the glint of sun on the windshield. Slowly, she gets out of the car, still carrying the movie magazine.*

BLANCHE *(suspiciously, quite the grand lady).* Howdy-do.

CLYDE *(shaking her hand).* Howdy-do. It's real nice to know you.

BUCK *beams with pleasure, thinking they must like each other.* BONNIE *comes out of the cabin, standing on the steps. The screen door slams behind her.*

Close-up. BONNIE. *Day—expressionless, looking it all over.*

Ext. Cabin. BUCK *and* CLYDE *notice nothing of this.* BUCK *bounds over to* BONNIE, *all jollity.*

BUCK *(grabbing her).* Well! You must be Bonnie! Now I hear you been takin' good care of the baby in the family. Well sis, I'm real glad to meet you! *(he hugs her;* BONNIE *just lets herself be hugged).* Say . . . *(breaking the hug)* I'd like you to meet my wife, Blanche.

BONNIE *(stiffly).* Hello.

BLANCHE *(stiffly).* Hello.

There is an awkward pause. Suddenly the screen door opens and C. W. *comes out, dressed in his long underwear.* BLANCHE *can hardly stand it.*

CLYDE. Everybody, this is C. W. Moss. C. W., my brother Buck and his wife, Blanche.

C. W. *(friendly).* Heighdy, y'all.

He pumps BUCK'S *hand vigorously and then goes to* BLANCHE. *With his characteristic one-track intensity, he decides to act just as friendly as he can with* BLANCHE, *ignoring the fact that he's standing there in his underwear.* BLANCHE, *however, is not ignoring it.*

C. W. Well how do, Mrs. Barrow. Or can I call you Blanche? I sure am pleased to meet you. *(shaking her hand; Blanche is slowly going crazy with mortification)* Did you have a hard time findin' us here in this neck of the woods? Well, you sure picked a good day for it. Say, you got a *Screenland* there! Any new photos of Myrna Loy? She's my favorite picture star.

BLANCHE *is starting to edge over to* BUCK *in sheer panic at this strange, young man in his BVD's, but* C. W. *takes no notice of it.*

BLANCHE *finally grabs* BUCK'S *arm.* BONNIE *watches it all, smirking.*

BUCK. Hey, lemme get the Kodak!

BUCK *goes to his car and gets a folding Brownie camera.*

CLYDE *(lighting up a cigar).* Hey, C. W., go put your pants on. We're gonna take some pictures.

BUCK. Y'all hear about the guy who thought Western Union was a cowboy's underwear?

BUCK *and* CLYDE *and* C. W. *laugh heartily.* C. W. *goes into the cabin.* BUCK *pushes* BLANCHE *and* CLYDE *together, posing them for a picture.*

BUCK. Lemme get one of my bride and my brother.

BLANCHE *(getting kittenish, and overdoing it).* Buck! Don't take my picture *now.* I'm just a mess from drivin' all day.

BUCK. Oh honey, now you look real fine.

BONNIE *watches* BLANCHE'S *behavior with hardly-veiled disgust.* BUCK *snaps the picture as* BLANCHE *is just about to move out of it.*

BLANCHE *(with unbecoming girlish outrage).* Did you take my picture? Oh Buck! I declare—

BUCK *laughs and goes to* BONNIE, *takes her by the arm and moves her next to* CLYDE *and* BLANCHE. *He lines them up, steps back and takes their picture.* CLYDE *is the only one smiling.*

CLYDE *(pulling out his gun and posing like a movie tough).* Hey, Buck, get one of this.

BUCK *does.*

BUCK *(giving Clyde the camera).* Clyde, you do one of me and my missus.

He puts his arm around BLANCHE. CLYDE *takes the picture.*

CLYDE *(throwing her a challenge).* Let me take one of Bonnie.

BONNIE *grins at him and responds with amused arrogance.*

BONNIE *(she yanks the cigar from Clyde's mouth, smokes it and poses).* Okay.

CLYDE *snaps the picture. Everyone but* BLANCHE *laughs.* C. W. *comes out dressed.*

BUCK *(drawing Clyde aside).* Hey, brother, let's you and me do a little talkin'.

CLYDE *(handing C. W. the camera)*. Here, C. W., take the girls' picture.

Int. Cabin. Day. They walk into the cabin. Camera goes with them. Bedroom is dark, shades pulled down. There is an aura of boys' clubhouse secret comaraderie in the following scene:

BUCK *(as soon as the door is shut; conspiratorially)*. It was you or him, wasn't it?

CLYDE. Huh?

BUCK. That guy you killed. You had to, didn't ya?

CLYDE *(they are protecting each other)*. Yeah, he put me in a spot, so I had to. He didn't have a Chinaman's chance.

BUCK. But you had to—

CLYDE. Yeah. I had to.

BUCK *(like two kids keeping a secret from Mom)*. Don't say nothin' to Blanche about it.

CLYDE. Hey, that time you broke out of jail, *she* talk you into goin' back?

BUCK *(it is obvious he had hoped Clyde hadn't known about it)*. Yeah, you hear about that?

CLYDE. I won't say nothin' to Bonnie about it.

BUCK. I appreciate it.

CLYDE. Yeah . . . say, what d'ya think of Bonnie?

BUCK. She's a real peach.

There is now a long pause—a lull in the conversation, as if they asked each other all the questions and are now out of things to say. It is too much for BUCK, *the natural enemy of silence, who suddenly claps his hands together and bursts out animatedly:*

BUCK. Boy, are we gonna have us a good time!

CLYDE *(matching his merriment)*. We surely are!

BUCK. Yessir! *(a pause, then:)* What are we gonna do?

CLYDE. Well, how's this—I thought we'd all go to Missouri. They ain't lookin' for me there. We'll hole up someplace and have us a regular vacation. All right?

BUCK. No trouble, now?

CLYDE. No trouble. I ain't lookin' to go back to prison.

BUCK. Hey, what's this I hear about you cuttin' up your toes, boy?

CLYDE *(ironically)*. That ain't but half of it. I did it so I could get off work detail— breakin' those damned rocks with a hammer day and night. Sure enough, next week I got paroled. I walked out of that god-forsaken jail on crutches.

BUCK. Shoot—

CLYDE. Ain't life grand?

Ext. Road. Day. We see the two cars, one behind the other, driving down a main road.

Int. First car. Day. CLYDE *is driving,* BUCK *sits next to him. No one else is in the car.*

BUCK. And the doc, he takes him aside, says, "Son, your old mama just gettin' weak and sickly layin' there. I want you to persuade her to take a little Brandy, y'know, to pick her spirits up." "Why, doc," he says, "you know my mamma is a teetotaler. She wouldn"t touch a drop." "Well, I tell you what," the doc says, "why don't you bring her a fresh quart of milk every day from your farm, 'cept you fix it up so half of it's Brandy and don't let on!" So he does that, doctors it up with Brandy, and his mamma drinks some of it. And the next day he brings it again and she drinks some more—and she keeps it up every day. Finally, one week later, he brings her the milk and don't you know she just swallows it all down, and looks at her boy and says, "Son, whatever you do, *don't sell that cow!*"

CLYDE *and* BUCK *explode in laughter.*

Int. Second car. Day. At the top of the laugh, cut to the int. of the second car, riding right in back of them. The atmosphere is completely unlike the cozy and jolly scene preceding. We have dead silence. BONNIE *is driving, smoking a cigarette, grim.* BLANCHE—*seated as far away as she can get from* BONNIE *without falling out of the car—makes a face at the cigarette smoke, rolls down the window for air.* C. W.'s *in the back seat, just staring.*

Cut to:

Ext. Garage apartment. Day. A residential street in Joplin, Missouri, showing a garage apartment above a double garage. Camera sees BUCK *talking to a dapper gent with keys in his hand.* BUCK *pays him. The man tips his hat and walks off.* BUCK *gestures and Clyde drives a car into the driveway.* C. W. *follows, driving* BUCK's *car with* BLANCHE. CLYDE *stops beside* BUCK. BUCK *leans into* CLYDE's *car and says:*

BUCK. I give him a month's rent in advance. We're all set. Let's get inside.

CLYDE *calls back to* C. W. *in the following car.*

CLYDE. Pull up and unload the stuff.

BUCK *(on the running board of moving car)*. Honey-love, I'm taking you into our first home.

BLANCHE *giggles. The two cars pull up before the garage and the people start to descend.*

Int. Garage apartment. Day. A winded BUCK *enters and puts down* BLANCHE. *As others behind him carry in their things and disperse throughout apartment.*

BLANCHE. Oh look, it's so clean, Buck. And a Frigidaire . . . not an icebox!

BUCK. He give me the grocery number.

He goes to the phone.

BUCK *(continuing)*. Lemme see, eh 4337 . . . Operator . . . please ma'm, may I have 4337 . . . if you please?

BLANCHE. Oh . . . they got linoleum on the counter. Ain't that clever!

BUCK. Hello, Smitty's grocery . . . I'd like to order a mess of groceries. Oh yeah . . . eh 143 Hillsdale Street. Lessee, about 8 pounds of porkchops, 4 pounds of red beans . . . a can of Chase and Sandborn . . . uh.

BLANCHE. Oh, isn't this something, Daddy!

BUCK. Sshh. Uh . . . quart of milk . . . uh 8 bottles of Dr. Pepper and that's it, I guess. No . . . no. Uh . . . a box of Rice Krispies . . . Bye now.

Cut to:

Int. Living room. Day. Open on BONNIE *and* CLYDE. *He is cleaning guns. She is watching something off screen. We hear a clicking sound.*

BLANCHE *(o.s.)*. My, you need a haircut, Daddy. You look like a hillbilly boy.

A look of disgust crosses BONNIE'S *face.* CLYDE, *who has been watching her, smiles. The clicking sound increases suddenly.*

BUCK *(o.s.)*. Gotcha!

BLANCHE *whoops. Camera cuts to see that* BUCK *and* C. W. *are playing checkers and* BUCK *has just beaten him.*

C. W. Again.

BUCK. Boy, you ain't never gonna beat me but you keep tryin' now.

He starts to set up the game again.

BLANCHE. Jest like an ol' man. Plays checkers all the time and doesn't pay any attention to his poor lonely wife.

She ruffles his hair again.

BUCK. Cut it out now, honey. I'm gonna teach this boy a lesson he'll never forget.

Camera cuts to BONNIE, *watching with disgust. Then slowly, a wicked little smile edges across her face. She watches for a moment more, then she rises and with the most ingenuous look she can muster up, beckons to* CLYDE *to follow her into the bedroom. A little puzzled,* CLYDE *follows.*

Int. Bedroom. BONNIE *closes the door and immediately begins fussing with* CLYDE'S *hair, doing a scathing imitation of* BLANCHE. *Though her miming expresses her irritation at being closeted with the Barrow menage, it is also a peach doing an imitation of a lemon— and it is disarmingly sensual . . . Indeed the mimicry allows* BONNIE *to be physically freer with* CLYDE, *and allows* CLYDE *to respond without anxiety, without self-consciousness. We should have the distinct—if momentary—feeling that* CLYDE *could suddenly make it with* BONNIE.

BONNIE *(doing an unmerciful imitation)*. Oh, Daddy, you shore need a haircut. You look just like a little old hillbilly boy, I do declare. *(she has her other hand toying with the buttons on his shirt, her hand slipping under, fluttering across his bare chest)* Oh mercy me, oh my stars!

CLYDE *laughs, and* BONNIE *tugs at the shirt—she kneels on the bed over* CLYDE, *who quite easily drapes across it.*

BONNIE *(a little louder)*. Oh, Daddy! Yore such a slowpoke!

She's letting her hair fall loose, its golden ends brushing up and down CLYDE'S *body.*

CLYDE *(amused, but cautionary)*. Hush up a little. They're in the next room.

BONNIE *(a mock-pout, but with an edge to it)*. Shoot, there's always somebody in this room, the next room and ever' other kind of room.

CLYDE *has his arm around* BONNIE, *and she's almost draped across him—but in the direction of the length of the bed, so their bodies almost form a crooked cross. She digs an elbow into his stomach.*

CLYDE. Oof! . . . now that ain't no nice way to talk about my brother.

BONNIE *(imitating Blanche again with baby talk)*. I ain't talking about your brother.

Suddenly BONNIE *straightens up to a kneeling position again, and cocks her head. When she speaks now it is with a simple plaintiveness.*

BONNIE. Honey, do you ever just want to be alone with Me? *(sensing Clyde's sensitivity to the sexual implication)* I don't just mean like *that* . . . I mean do you ever have the notion of us bein' *out* together and alone, like at some fancy ball, or, I don't know, where we walk in all dressed and they announce us and it's fancy and in public, but we're alone somehow. We're separate from everybody else, and they know it.

CLYDE *looks up to* BONNIE, *affectionately. He runs his hand carelessly down her body.*

CLYDE. I always feel like we're separate from everybody else.

BONNIE *(it's terribly important to her).* Do you, baby?

Suddenly there is a ring at the door. BONNIE *and* CLYDE *freeze.*

Int. Living room. BONNIE *and* CLYDE *run out into the living room, camera going with them.*

BONNIE *(to all).* Quiet! I'll get it.

BONNIE *goes down the stairs and reaches the front door.*

BONNIE. Who is it?
VOICE. Groceries, M'am.

Ext. Garage apartment. She opens the door. A young man is there with the two big sacks of groceries.

BONNIE. How much?
YOUNG MAN. Six dollars and forty-three cents.

BONNIE *pays him and goes to take the bags from him.*

YOUNG MAN. Here, M'am, them bags is heavy. Let me carry 'em up for you.
BONNIE *(curtly).* No thanks, I'll take 'em.

She takes the heavy bags and hefts them up and turns and walks up the stairs. They are obviously very heavy for her. Closeup the delivery boy's face, looking puzzled at this behavior. BONNIE *reaches the top steps, and voices are heard.*

BUCK'S VOICE. What was it?
CLYDE'S VOICE. Quiet. Open the door.
BONNIE. C'mon, c'mon . . .

Close-up. The DELIVERY BOY. *A look of suspicion comes across his face.*

Dissolve to:

Int. Garage apartment. Close-up of BONNIE *—seated in the living room.*

BONNIE *(reading from a pad; in a recital voice).* It's called "The Ballad of Suicide Sal." *(she pauses for effect; then begins:)*
"We each of us have a good alibi
For being down here in the 'joint';
But few of them really are justified
If you get right down to the point.
You've heard of a woman's glory
Being spent on a downright cur'."
BUCK'S VOICE: *(o.s.)* You write that all by yourself?
BONNIE. You want to hear this or not?

As she reads, the camera pans around the room picking out everyone's reaction. CLYDE *is looking and listening seriously.* BUCK *is grinning.* C. W. *is blank.* BLANCHE *is in the kitchen cooking.*

BONNIE.
"Still you can't always judge the story
As true, being told by her.
Now 'Sal' was a gal of rare beauty,
Though her features were coarse and
    tough—"
BUCK. Yeah, I knew her. She was cockeyed and had a hare-lip and no teeth!

BONNIE *flashes him a look that could kill. He shuts up fast. She continues:*

BONNIE.
"Now 'Sal' was a gal of rare beauty,
Though her features were coarse and
    tough;
She never once faltered from duty
To play on the 'up and up'."

Still listening, CLYDE *gets up from his chair and walks slowly past the living room windows. The camera angled slightly above him, sees down the street. We see two police cars quietly pulling up. One of them parks sideways in the driveway to block escape from the garage, the other stays on the street.* CLYDE *turns and looks out the window.*

BONNIE *(o.s. as we see out the window).*
"Sal told me this tale on the evening
Before she was turned out free,
And I'll do my best to relate it
Just as she told it to me—"

CLYDE *(seeing it).* It's the law.

(NOTE: The three major gun battles in this film of which this is the first, each have a different emotional and cinematic quality. The quality for this Joplin debacle is chaos, hysteria, extremely rapid movement and lots of noise. The audience should be assaulted. From the moment CLYDE *cries out, and throughout all the following action,* BLANCHE, *in blind*

panic, screams hysterically. The scream persists through the gunfire, never lessening on the soundtrack. Its effect should be at first funny to the audience, then annoying, and finally terrifying.

As soon as CLYDE *calls out,* BLANCHE *drops the frying pan on the floor and begins screaming. Camera cuts back to the living room. Everyone else leaps into action. Guns begin blazing from everywhere; we rarely see who is shooting at whom.)*

Ext. Garage apartment. Day. The police, we see in outside shot, are lined up in the street, firing. There are about ten of them.

Int. Garage apartment. Day. The gang runs down the stairs into the garage—we follow them with a hand-held camera tracking rapidly.

Ext. Street. Day. BLANCHE, *however, in utter panic, just runs right out the front door, and begins running down the quiet residential street, going nowhere, anywhere.*

Ext. Garage apartment. Day. BUCK, *crouching, shooting with one hand, gets the garage door open. A policeman fires.* BUCK *fires back and the cop falls dead in the street.* BUCK, *firing, dashes to the police car blocking their escape and releases the hand brake.* CLYDE, BONNIE *and* C. W. *leap into their car, gun the motor, still shooting madly. Two more police fall dead or wounded. One policeman is hurled through a fence by the blast of a sawed-off shotgun.* BUCK *jumps into the car with the others. They now begin to bump the police car with their car. The police car picks up speed as they push it and it tears into the street right at the group of firing police. The gang's car turns into the street in a hail of bullets and takes off down the street toward the running* BLANCHE. BONNIE *and* CLYDE *are in front;* BUCK *and* C. W. *in the back seat firing back at police. The car pulls alongside the wildly running* BLANCHE; *the back door is flung open and in almost the style of a cartoon, two hands reach out and lift her off her feet and pull her into the car. They speed away.*

Cut to:

Int. Car. Day. The inside of the car, still speeding. BLANCHE *is hysterical.* C. W. *is still firing out the window. The pursuing police car's driver is shot and the car crashes into a tree. The gang is not being pursued now, but* CLYDE *is driving at 90.* BLANCHE *is moaning and crying.* BONNIE, *in front, turns around furiously.*

BONNIE. Dammit, you almost got us killed!

BLANCHE *(crying).* What did I do wrong? I s'pose you'd be happier if I got shot.

BONNIE *(at her bitchiest).* Yeah, it would of saved us all a lot of trouble.

BLANCHE. Buck, don't let that woman talk to me like that!

BUCK *(caught in the middle of a bad situation, knowing Blanche is wrong, but trying to soothe her).* You shouldn't have done it, Blanche. *(quietly, cont.)* It was a dumb thing to do.

BLANCHE *(switching tactics).* Please, Buck, I didn't marry you to see you shot up! Please, let's go! Let's get out of here and leave. Make him stop the car and let us out!

BUCK *(still quietly).* Can't. I killed a man. We're in this now.

BLANCHE *(loud and shrill).* Please! Please!

BONNIE *(exploding).* Shut up! Just shut up your big mouth! At least do that, will ya, just shut up.

CLYDE. Cut it out, Bonnie.

BONNIE *is affronted.* BLANCHE *continues sobbing.*

BONNIE *(curtly).* Stop the car. I want to talk to you.

Without a word, CLYDE *stops the car.*

Ext. Roadside. Day. BONNIE *and* CLYDE *get out and walk fifteen feet away from the car. Both are irritated and touchy. Camera follows them.*

CLYDE *(coldly).* What is it?

BONNIE. Get rid of her.

CLYDE. Can't do that. She's Buck's wife.

BONNIE *(snapping her words).* Get rid of both of them then.

CLYDE. Why? What's the matter with you anyway?

BONNIE. *She's* what's the matter with me, a damn stupid back country hick without a brain in her head. *(contemptuously)* She ain't nothin' but prunes and proverbs.

CLYDE *(really pissed-off at Bonnie).* What makes you any better? What makes you so damn special? You're just a West Dallas waitress who spent half your time pickin' up truck drivers!

This hits home with BONNIE. *He has said the unforgivable.*

BONNIE *(raising her voice).* You talk to me like that! Big Clyde Barrow, just the same as your brother, an ignorant uneducated hillbilly. *(with deadly archness)* Only special thing about you is your *peculiar* ideas about lovemakin'—which is no love makin' at all.

CLYDE *stiffens. The two of them stand silent and tense, almost quivering with anger. They have stripped each other raw.* CLYDE *turns and looks back at the car. Everyone is waiting, watching them. He breathes a deep sigh, like a man counting to 10 to hold his temper.*

CLYDE. Look, Bonnie—

He can't finish.

Close. BONNIE. *She drops her head into her hand for a moment, comes up a little more relaxed. She looks at* CLYDE *and her eyes reflect the realization of the pain she has inflicted on him. She softens.*

BONNIE. Clyde . . . honey . . . I didn't mean all that, honey. Blame it on all that shootin', I just felt so bad . . . . sure enough . . . Clyde?

CLYDE. Okay . . . Okay, hon . . . let's get movin' . . .

He turns and begins walking back to the car. BONNIE *walks alongside him. On the few steps back, she regains all her dignity and acts aloof from the others waiting for her. She reaches the car.* CLYDE *opens her door for her and she gets in like a great lady. He walks around to his side, gets in, and they drive off.*

Wide shot. Ext. Car. Day. A very wide shot. We see CLYDE's *car driving along a wooded road. For a moment that is all we see, then we should become aware that far in the distance another car is following* CLYDE's.

Close. Rural mail box. On the opposite side of the road, CLYDE's *car swings across the road and* CLYDE, *who is driving, snatches a newspaper which protrudes from the box and hands it into the car. They drive out of the shot. Camera holds and soon the following car enters the shot. The man driving is a Texas ranger. He drives slowly. He drives out of the shot.*

Int. CLYDE's *car.* BUCK *is reading from the paper.*

BUCK (*jubilantly*). Hey, y'all, listen to this here: Law enforcement officers throughout the Southwest are frankly amazed at the way in which will-of-the-wisp bandit Clyde Barrow and his yellow-haired companion, Bonnie Parker, continue to elude their would-be captors. Since engaging the police in a gun battle on the streets of Joplin Missouri and slaying three of their number. . . .

BLANCHE. Oh, Lord . . .

We notice CLYDE *is wincing.*

BUCK. . . . the Barrow gang has been reported as far West as White City, New Mexico, and as far north as Chicago. They have been credited with robbing the Mesquite Bank in the aforementioned White City, the J. J. Landry Oil Refinery in Arp, Texas, the Sanger City National Bank in Sanger, Indiana, and the Lancaster Bank in Denton, Texas on three different occasions. In addition to these robberies, the fast travelling Barrows have been rumored to have had a hand in the robbing of two Piggly Wiggly stores in Texas, and one A & P store in Missouri, though Chief Percy Hammond, who first identified Clyde Barrow's brother, Buck, as a member of the gang, expressed some doubt that these last robberies were committed by the Barrow Gang alone.

BONNIE. Go on.

C. W (*finally*). Clyde, we ain't goin' to see a restroom for another thirty miles. Why don't you just stop here?

CLYDE *looks relieved.*

Ext. Wooded area. Day. He pulls the car to a stop, gets out and goes off into the woods. We watch him vanish behind the trees.

Int. Car. BUCK *still scanning the newspaper.*

BUCK (*with a laugh*). Hey now, here's something! Listen here: Lone Cop Arrests Two Officers In Hunt For Barrow. Police Officer Howard Anderson's heart turned faster than his motorcycle when he forced to the side of the road a roaring black V-8 sedan in which were three men and a blond-headed woman yesterday afternoon.

Everybody laughs. As BUCK *continues to read, his voice remaining on the soundtrack.*

Ext. Car. The camera goes outside the car and pulls back, way back, to reveal a police car quietly driving up behind the car. The car stops a good distance away and one man gets out, the only occupant of the car. He is tall, dressed in the uniform of the Texas Ranger. He draws his gun and slowly approaches the car from the rear. On the soundtrack BUCK's *voice continues; as we see all this taking place.*

BUCK. When he saw several machine guns in the car he was certain he'd caught Clyde Barrow, Bonnie Parker, and maybe Buck Barrow and the third unidentified member of the gang. It took a lot of telephoning and explaining to convince the motorcycle cop that his captives were two highway patrolmen and a blonde-haired stenographer from the Highway Patrol—. Haw! Haw! *(everybody busts up with laughter)*

In the meantime, on screen, the lawman is slowly approaching the back of the car. Suddenly, cut to shot of CLYDE *coming out of the woods, behind the lawman. His gun is tucked in his pants. In a second, he sees what is happening.* BUCK's *voice is continuing:*

BUCK. Anderson was held up as an example for every other Texas peace officer today. "That was a mighty brave thing," explained Highway Patrol Chief L. C. Winston.

CLYDE *whips out his gun. The following scene is played exactly like a classic fast-draw in an heroic Western.*

CLYDE. Sheriff!

BRYCE *spins around. Both men fire instantaneously, but* CLYDE *has the draw on him, and the aim. The gun goes flying from the* SHERIFF's *hand. A really razzle-dazzle display of grandstand marksmanship from Clyde.*

Immediately the gang leaps from the car and surrounds the man, guns drawn.

C. W. Boy! What a shot, Clyde!
BUCK. Sweet Jesus, I never seen shootin' like that!

The gang grabs the man and takes his handcuffs from his belt. CLYDE *makes him lean on the car's hood, arms extended, legs spread, while he frisks him. In general, everyone is excited over the capture.* BONNIE *takes the sheriff's gun and delicately places it on the radiator grill like an object d'art.*

CLYDE *(examining the man's wallet, really surprised).* Well, now, getta load of this. I want y'all to know we are in the custody of Cap'n Frank Bryce, and Frank here is a Texas Ranger.

Rev. angle across hood—so BRYCE's *face, not visible to* CLYDE *or anyone else behind him, is in foreground. His gnarled, powerful hands tremble slightly on the hood, as tho they might crinkle the metal like so much tissue paper. His eyes stare toward camera relentlessly, unblinking, but without passion. They are shark's eyes. They have witnessed much carnage, devoured it, and are still wide open for more.*

C. W. Sure 'nough, Clyde?
BUCK. Say there, peacemaker, I believe you got your spurs all tangled up. You're in *Missouri,* you know that?

CLYDE *has been going thru the man's credentials. Not so pleasantly:*

CLYDE. You didn't know you was in Missouri?
C. W. He's lost, this here Texas Ranger.

CLYDE *claps* BRYCE's *hands behind his back, handcuffs him, spins him around.*

CLYDE *(a little pissed).* —he ain't lost . . . them banks are offerin' extra reward money fer us, and Frank figured on easy pickin's, didn't you? *(he suddenly knocks Bryce's hat off)* Didn't you?

BRYCE *flinches involuntarily.* BUCK *suddenly grows wary at* CLYDE's *mood.* CLYDE *leans into* BRYCE, *looking up.*

CLYDE. —Now you ain't hardly doin' your job, Texas Ranger. You oughta be home lookin' after the rights of poor folks, not out chasin' after us.

He suddenly hefts BRYCE's *huge bulk onto the fender.*

BUCK *(trying to be casual).* Easy there, Clyde. Why take it so personal.
CLYDE *(to Bryce).* Reg'lar laws is one thing. But this here *bounty* hunting, we got to discourage that.

BLANCHE *looks very uncomfortable. She starts to say something, but* BUCK *intervenes.*

BUCK. Like how, Clyde?—

A tense moment. CLYDE *can't think of anything right away.*

C. W. *(trying to be helpful).* Shoot him.

BONNIE *shoots* C. W. *an angry glance—it's just what the gang doesn't want.*

C. W. *(trying again).* . . . hang him? . . .

Reaction— BONNIE *carefully gauging the moment to intervene.*

BONNIE *(suddenly).* —uh-uh. Take his picture.

CLYDE's *not sure he's heard right. Neither is* C. W.

C. W. Take his picture?
BONNIE *(pointedly ignoring C. W., brightly).* Then we'll let the newspapers have it—so's everyone can see Captain Frank Bryce of the Texas Rangers with the Barrow gang—*(moving demurely to Bryce)*—and all bein' just as friendly as pie.
BUCK *(grasping possibilities immediately).* . . . yeah, yeah . . .

BONNIE *(continuing right on, coyly picking up Bryce's gun from grill)* —why we 'bout the friendliest folks in the world. Texas Ranger waves his big ol' gun at us, and we just welcome him like he's one of our own.

CLYDE *(grinning widely).* Buck, get the Kodak!

BUCK *(relieved and excited).* Hot dog!

CLYDE *(to Bryce).* We're mighty proud to have a Texas Ranger in the family.

BRYCE *is obviously not pleased with this turn of events. Following dialogue is overlapped, ad-libbed, etc. A sense of mounting glee at the kind of vengeance they are going to exact.*

New angle. BUCK *is fiddling with the camera, setting up the shot with* CLYDE. BUCK's *following speech should be heard, b.g., to* CLYDE's *speech below it.*

BUCK.. . . keep him set on the hood, there . . . more to the sun, like that . . . yeah . . . when all his ranger friends see this . . . I bet he's gonna *wish* he was *dead!*

CLYDE *(to Bryce).* . . . see what come o' your *mischief?* . . . not doin' your *job?* Down in Duncanville last year poor farmers kept the laws away from us with shot guns . . . you're s'posed to be protectin' them from *us,* and they're protectin' *us* from *you. (giggling)* —don't make sense, do it?

BUCK. C'mon, now, Clyde, you and Bonnie first. Move into him, right close, right friendly.

CLYDE. All righty. *(to Bryce, whose hands are tied, hemmed in by them both)* Don't move, now, hear?

CLYDE *grandly puts an arm on* BRYCE's *shoulder,* BONNIE, *looking up admiringly from the other side.* BUCK *takes the picture.* BONNIE *immediately hops onto the hood, next to* BRYCE.

BONNIE. How's this? "Captain Bryce and new found friend."

She coyly loosens his tie, tousles his hair, and plants a big kiss on him while still ogling camera.

CLYDE.. . . yeah, yeah . . . quick, Buck, get it . . .

BUCK.. . . I'm gettin' it, I'm gettin' it.

Quite suddenly, BRYCE, *whose simmering intensity we should be more sensitive to than the gang is, spits on Bonnie.* BONNIE *half-screams in disgust, but* CLYDE *is on top of* BRYCE *in a flash, half-strangling on his own fury. He pulls* BRYCE *off the fender by the handcuffs, spinning him around crazily like a* lasso. BRYCE *is literally ricocheted off the car by the force, and, with* CLYDE *hanging on by the cuffs, plummets down the embankment to the sandy beach below, both men falling, spinning.* BRYCE *rises shakily. He tries to walk away.* CLYDE *grabs him again by the handcuffs and hurls him out into the water.* BRYCE *smacks into a tree stump poking out of the shallows and goes down.* CLYDE *is on top of him.*

Meanwhile, BUCK *has rushed down into the water, tries to pull* CLYDE *off* BRYCE.

BUCK *(frantic).* I got the picture. I got the picture . . .

CLYDE *(oblivious).* Lemme be, lemme be . . .

BRYCE *reaches the surface and* CLYDE *tries to throw him into deeper water. He hitches* BRYCE *over a moldy skiff, knocking aside one of the oars.* BUCK *upends* BRYCE *into the skiff and kicks it spinning.* CLYDE *picks up an oar and hurls it like a boomerang, ass over end at the skiff. It kicks up a spray.*

BUCK *(holding tightly to Clyde, yelling).* I got the PICTURE!

Reaction. CLYDE *waist deep, breathing heavily.*

CLYDE.. . . All right, all right . . . *(to Bryce, yelling)* WE GOT YOU . . . HEAR? . . . REMEMBER . . . YOU . . . YOUR FACE . . . WE GOT IT . . . WE GOT YOU . . . WE GOT YOU . . . WE GOT YOU . . .

BRYCE, *battered and handcuffed, stares back with mindless malice from the lazily spinning skiff to the hysterical spectre of* CLYDE, *screaming his madness across the water.*

Dissolve:

Int Bank. Inside the bank. In contrast to the previous inept bank robbery scene, this one goes admirably well, the gang performing slickly and without a hitch. As they enter, dripping wet, CLYDE *makes a general announcement to everyone in the bank.*

CLYDE. This is the Barrow gang. *(the people turn and freeze)* Everybody just take it easy and nobody will get hurt.

CLYDE *covers the door.* BONNIE *and* BUCK *go to the tellers' cages and get money.* BUCK *goes inside, emptying out the cash drawers. Cut to* BONNIE *filling the sack.*

Cut to a close-up of a burglar alarm button. Slowly a hand crawls up the wall and a finger slowly moves to push the button. When the finger is about one inch away, suddenly a gun appears in the frame and gently taps the hand away. The camera pulls back to reveal BUCK *smiling at a lady teller.*

BUCK. Don't do nothin' silly now.

Cut to CLYDE *standing near the door, training his guns on the entire bank. A farmer stands a few feet away, some bills clutched in his hand.*

CLYDE. That your money or the bank's?
FARMER. Mine.
CLYDE. Keep it, then.

Across the floor, the bank guard in the corner takes advantage of CLYDE'S *distraction to go for his gun.* CLYDE *spots it and fires a shot that just knocks the bank guard's hat off without harming him.*

CLYDE *(to the guard, who has practically frozen in fear)*. Next time I'll aim a little lower.

They finish robbing the bank. They start to exit. Near the door stands a guard with his hands raised. He wears sun glasses of the period. As they leave BUCK *snatches the sun glasses from the guard's head.*

BUCK. Get a good look at us! We're the Barrow boys.

Ext. Bank. Day. The gang runs wildly into the street where the car waits, motor running. As they leap into car, BUCK *throws the sun glasses into* BLANCHE'S *lap.*

BUCK. Happy birthday.

They zoom off. Shots are heard. BONNIE, BUCK *and* CLYDE *begin firing at the bank guards who are pursuing them. The guards fire back.*

Close-up. BLANCHE *sitting in the back seat with her fingers stuck tightly in her ears, eyes shut, trying to overcome her panic. A funny image, but one that also awakens pity. The next sequence is carried out in cross-cutting.*

Cut to:

The street in front of the bank. Police car pulls up and the excited crowd gestures in the direction of the departed gang. The siren starts.

Cut to:

Int. Gang car. Day. The siren heard now in the far distance.

BUCK *(to C. W. at the wheel)*. Kick it in the pants, C. W.

CLYDE. We got to make that state line!
C. W. *(driving like a wild man, but adlibing loudly)*. Can't get more'n this out of a Plymouth!

Cut to:

Int. Bank. The gang has left a legacy of celebrity behind. We see the bank guard whose hat was shot off being interviewed by a reporter. He is seated in a chair, his shirt open at the collar and a woman teller is fanning him.

BANK GUARD *(enjoying the limelight)*. Then he saw me goin' for my gun. Clyde Barrow himself, I mean. And suddenly I was starin' into the face of death!
WOMAN TELLER. Tsk, tsk.

A photographer steps in.

PHOTOGRAPHER. Just look this way, Mr. Hawkins.

The bank guard hurriedly buttons up his collar and smiles as the flashbulb goes off.

Cut to:

Ext. Gang car. Still speeding along, the siren more distant.

Cut to:

Int. Bank. The bank president and a policeman are posing for that classic picture where both stand flanking a bullet hole in the wall and point proudly at it. The flashbulb goes off.

Cut to:

Int. Police car. Two men in police uniforms following BONNIE *and* CLYDE.

FIRST POLICEMAN. Step on it, Randolph. We gotta catch 'em 'fore they reach the state line!

Cut to:

Int. Bank. FARMER *is describing* BONNIE *and* CLYDE *to passersby who dote on him as though he'd just had contact with a portion of the true cross.* FARMER *is aware of his position.*

FARMER. Clyde? . . . he looked like, well he looked real . . . clean . . . and Bonnie, she's too much a lady ever to be caught with a cigar in her mouth . . . I don't care *what* you heard before. I *saw 'em* right here, not twenty minutes ago . . .*(gravely)* —and all's I can say is, they did right by me, and I'm bringin' me a mess of flowers to their funeral.

Cut to:

Int. Gang's car. Car slows up perceptibly as CLYDE *says:*

CLYDE. Okay, relax. We're in Oklahoma now. Slow down.

Cut to:

Int. Police car.

FIRST POLICEMAN. Turn around. Don't waste no more gas.

SECOND POLICEMAN (*a young eager beaver type*). Ain't we gone to catch 'em?

FIRST POLICEMAN. Hell, they're over the State line. That's out of our jurisdiction.

SECOND POLICEMAN. Why don't we get 'em anyway?

FIRST POLICEMAN. I ain't gone to risk my life in Oklahoma. That's their problem.

Cut to:

Ext. Car. Now the gang's car is seen traveling down a long, narrow country road surrounded by cornfields.

Cut to:

Ext. Roadside by woods. Day. They get out, taking the various bags of money with them, and dump the lot on the hood. There is not an impressive amount of money.

CLYDE (*disappointed*). Hell. That ain't much, is it?

BUCK (*commiseratingly*). Times is hard.

CLYDE. Well, let's get to it.

He begins dealing and splitting the money out on the hood of the car, as they gather around.

CLYDE. This is Clyde Barrow. (*lays down a bill*) Buck Burrow . . , (*lays down a bill*) Bonnie Parker . . . C. W. (*goes back to the first again and lays out another round*) Clyde, Buck . . . Bonnie . . . C. W. Clyde, Clyde again . . . Buck . . . Bonnie . . . C. W.

BUCK *and* BLANCHE *stand watching.* BLANCHE *looks fretful. She nudges* BUCK *and whispers to him.* BUCK *whispers something back to her. Meanwhile,* CLYDE'S *counting still goes on.*

CLYDE. Bonnie . . . C. S. . . . Clyde . . .

BUCK (*very ill at ease in this position he has been forced into*). Um . . . eh . . . Clyde?

CLYDE. Hah?

BUCK *is clearly embarrassed.*

BUCK. Uh, Clyde . . . well . . . what about Blanche?

Everyone reacts with stunned amazement at BLANCHE'S *nerve in wanting to get her cut.*

BONNIE (*incredulous*). WHAT?

BLANCHE *sees she has to rise to her own defense, and she rises to the occasion with spirit and verve.*

BLANCHE. Well, why not? Say I earned my share! Same as everybody. I coulda got killed same as everybody, and I'm wanted by the law same as everybody. Besides I coulda got snake bit sleepin' in them woods every night! (*building it up*) I'm just a nervous wreck and that's the truth. And I have to listen to sass from Miss Bonnie Parker all the time. I deserve mine!

Close. BUCK. *Day—looking at* CLYDE, *his face full of weak smiles and embarrassment at his wife.*

CLYDE (*with a sigh*). Okay . . . okay . . . hold your horses, Blanche. You'll get your share.

BONNIE *is livid but says nothing.* CLYDE, *the leader has decided.* C. W. *looks indignant, like a hog who's just been given a bath.* CLYDE *begins counting all over again in near silence.*

BUCK. Married a preacher's daughter and she still thinks she's takin' the collection.

Everyone now laughs, but BLANCHE. CLYDE *continues counting.*

BUCK (*to Blanche*). Well, don't spend it all in one place now, hear?

BONNIE. She'll be doin' right well to spend it at all.

BONNIE *turns and ambles away from the car. After a moment* CLYDE *stops counting and moves after her. He's prepared for a fight, stands behind* BONNIE'S *arched back trying to gauge the degree of hostility there.*

CLYDE. Bonnie?

No answer.

CLYDE (*a little defensive*). Look, Bonnie, I've said it and I guess I'll keep sayin' it before we're thru—Blanche is Buck's wife and Buck is *family.*

He waits expectantly.

BONNIE (*finally, utterly without malice*). — she's such a silly-Billy . . .

BONNIE *looks plaintively to* CLYDE,

BONNIE. *My* family could use some of that money.

CLYDE. Them laws have been hangin' round your mamas house 'til all hours, Bonnie. It's just too risky to go there.

BONNIE *(exploding)*. Well, where *can* we go? We rob the damn banks, what else do we do?

CLYDE *cannot really answer. Suddenly* C. W. *starts yelling:*

C. W. CLYDE! CLYDE! CLYDE!

CLYDE *flinches at the sound.* C. W. *comes bounding over, as rude an assault on their sensibilities as he can be.*

CLYDE *(wincing as they are nose to nose).* I hear you, C. W.

C. W. This ol' heap's gushin' oil! We got to swipe us another set of wheels right away, or we won't get anywhere. Look here.

He reaches down under the pan of the car and scoops a gooey handful of slick black oil which he holds before their faces.

C. W. See?

CLYDE *nods slowly. He looks back to* BONNIE. *He sees.*

Dissolve:

Ext. Suburban street. A residential neighborhood on a suburban street. A rather well-to-do neighborhood. The camera is up on a porch of a white frame house, looking toward the street. On the porch, sitting in the swing in the left f.g. are a MAN *and a* WOMAN. *She is about twenty-nine, he is about thirty-six. He is sitting with his back to us, embracing the* WOMAN. *They are spooning, making low, loving murmurs.*

WOMAN. Oh, now . . . now, dear . . .
MAN. Mmmm . . . sweet thing . . .

We see in the distance two cars parked in front of the house. His and hers. Suddenly we see another car drive up (BONNIE *and* CLYDE*) and somebody gets out. Then the whole gang gets out, ditches the one car and gets in one of the parked cars. All the while the couple on the porch is busy spooning. The car begins to roll slowly into the street. The* WOMAN *notices.*

WOMAN. Say, isn't that your car, Eugene?
MAN *(still nuzzling her).* Mmmmmm . . . huh? *(he looks, leaps from the swing)* That's my car! Hey!

The MAN *and* WOMAN *run down the front steps and front walk to the second car. They jump in and take off, giving chase.*

Int. Car. Day. The WOMAN *is driving (it's her car). The* MAN *is furious.*

EUGENE. I'll tear 'em apart! Those punks! Steal a man's car right out from under him! Wait till I get my hands on those kids, Velma, I'll show 'em!

They continue driving, furious, the man cursing and muttering. We see through their windshield the other car way in the distance.

VELMA. What if they have guns, Eugene?
EUGENE *(realizing the possibility, he suddenly stops being mad and turns chicken).* We'd better get the police and let them handle this.

VELMA. Right.
EUGENE. Turn around and let's get back to town. We'll go get the sheriff.

They are by now on a narrow dirt road and the WOMAN *has to execute a U-turn. It takes her about seven cuts to turn the car around in the narrow space. They start back to town.*

Cut to:

Int. BONNIE *and* CLYDE'S *car.* BUCK *looks out the rear window.*

BUCK. They stopped chasin' us. They turned around.

Close-up. CLYDE *grinning mischievously.*

CLYDE. Let's take 'em.

BUCK *and* C. W. *laugh appreciatively at the reversal.* CLYDE *turns the car around. He performs the U-turn in the same narrow space in one, swift, smooth, beautiful turn.*

Cut to:

Int. The other car. VELMA *looks in the rear view mirror and sees that now she is being chased.*

VELMA. Oh, my Lord, they're comin' after us.
EUGENE *(in a panic).* Step on it, Velma, step on it!

Close-up. Accelerator. VELMA *jams it down to the floor. The car speeds.*

Ext. Road. The chase. Day. BONNIE *and* CLYDE'S *car gaining on them, gaining on them, gaining on them and finally overtaking them, coming up and ahead, forcing them to the side of the road.*

Med. shot. The MAN *and* WOMAN'S *car. Terrified, they roll up their windows, lock their doors and huddle together.*

Ext. Road. The Barrow gang piles out of their car and walks over, having a merry time. They surround the car and press their faces against the window, flattening their features, making menacing gestures at the shaking pair inside. We see this from the point of view of the MAN and WOMAN inside the car. CLYDE pulls out a gun, makes as if to shoot, but he is kidding. They all laugh uproariously, especially BUCK who is delighted with CLYDE's prank. All of this we see in pantomime from inside the trapped car.

Ext. Car.

CLYDE. C'mon, get out! Get out of there, I said.

They come out, hands held high, shaking with fear. They have practically turned to jelly.

CLYDE *(ordering them into the other car)*. Get in here.

Int. Other car. Day. They get in and the gang gets in. Seven people are now jammed inside. CLYDE drives, BONNIE next to him, C. W. next to her. In back, BLANCHE, then EUGENE with VELMA (of necessity) sitting on his lap, and then BUCK As will be seen, the reason the Barrows have kidnapped the couple is simply that they wanted company. Living as they do, seeing only each other day after day they long for diversion and new faces. So the atmosphere in the car will shortly change to one of friendliness and jollity, and it will get progressively more so in the series of cuts which advance the time. As the car starts up at the beginning, however, the MAN and WOMAN are terrified.

BUCK. What's your names?
EUGENE *(hesitantly)*. I'm Eugene Grizzard.
VELMA. I'm Velma Davis.

BUCK *(just as friendly as he can be)*. Well, howdy! We're the Barrow gang. That there is Clyde drivin' and I'm Buck.

The MAN and WOMAN almost faint from fear; clutch at each other. The gang all laugh at this. VELMA and EUGENE begin to realize that they are not going to get hurt and that the Barrows are friendly to them.

BONNIE. Look, don't be scared, folks. It ain't like you was the law. You're just folks like us.
EUGENE *(agreeing over-enthusiastically)*. Yeah, yeah, that's the truth.
CLYDE. I expect you been readin' about us.

The MAN and the WOMAN answer simultaneously with what they think is the right thing to say under the circumstances.

EUGENE. Yes.
VELMA. No.

They glare at each other.

EUGENE *(meaningfully)*. Yes, Velma, we have too.
BONNIE *(laughing at the contretemps)*. Well, you two must be in love, I bet.

EUGENE *and* VELMA *blush, get shy for a second. BONNIE smiles.*

BUCK *(gleefully, clapping his hands)*. Well, when you gonna marry the girl, boy?

Everyone chuckles heartily.

Cut to:

Int. Car. Later—still driving, same positions, but some time has elapsed. The atmosphere is now completely convivial and the captives are enjoying their new friends. As the scene starts, BUCK is finishing his joke.

BUCK. So then she drinks her milk down again, every drop. And she looks over at her son and says, "Son, whatever you do, *don't sell that cow!*"

The couple laughs with great amusement, but everyone else in the car doesn't laugh—this is the tenth time they've heard the joke.

Cut to:

Int. of car—getting on toward evening. All are thoroughly relaxed and chatting.

BONNIE *(to Velma)*. How old are you, honey?
VELMA. Thirty-three.

A sudden look of surprise registers on EUGENE's face.

Int. of car. Night. It is now night. Everyone inside the car is eating. Apparently they stopped somewhere along the way for food. In the crowded interior, it is like a party—food is being passed back and forth, laughter and gaiety, increasing warmth between the couple and the Barrows. The car has become a little society on wheels, dashing through the black night down the highway. Inside there is a small world of happiness and fun.

BUCK *is unpacking the food and passing sandwiches and drinks around the car.*

VELMA. Now I ordered some French fries, didn't I?

BUCK *(passing her some)*. Yeah, here you go.

CLYDE. Take it easy on those French fries, Velma. Ain't that right, Eugene?

EUGENE *(studying his hamburger)*. This isn't mine. I ordered mine well done. Who's got the other hamburger?

Close-up. C. W. *who has already taken a bite of the other one.*

C. W. Oh, is this supposed to be yours?

He extends the bitten burger out to EUGENE.

Full shot.

EUGENE. That's okay, forget it.

CLYDE *laughs at this.*

BUCK *(chewing)*. Haw! I sure am havin' a good time! How 'bout you folks? Ain't you glad we picked you up?

CLYDE *(laughing)*. Hey, maybe y'all ought to join up with us.

That idea strikes everyone as being very amusing.

EUGENE *(laughing)*. Ha! Wouldn't they be surprised back home to hear that?

VELMA. Yeah. What would Martha and Bill say if they heard that? *(she roars with laughter)*

EUGENE. Lordy! They'd throw a fit! *(roars with laughter)*

BONNIE *(laughing)*. What do you *do*, anyway?

EUGENE *(as his laugh begins to fade)*. I'm an undertaker.

Suddenly everyone freezes. A shudder, as if the cold hand of death had suddenly touched the occupants of the car. The atmosphere changes to cold, deadly, fearful silence in exactly one second. It is a premonition of death for the Barrows, and they react accordingly, BONNIE *especially.*

Close-up. BONNIE.

BONNIE *(tautly, in a flat voice)*. Get them out of here.

Ext. Road. Night. The car brakes to a sudden stop. The rear door is opened, the MAN *and* WOMAN *flung out into the darkness. The car drives off into the lonely night.*

From this point on, the audience should realize that death is inevitable for the Barrow gang, that it follows them always, that it waits anywhere. It is no longer a question of whether death will come, but when it will.

Ext. Woods. Morning. Moving with CLYDE *he tears through the brush, snagging his clothes, calling* BONNIE'S *name.* CLYDE'S *search is so desperate here that for a moment we might think he is fleeing from something rather than looking for something.*

In a moment he emerges onto the road. The car, with C. W. *driving, and* BUCK *and* BLANCHE *beside him, is patrolling slowly up ahead of him.*

CLYDE *spots it and runs toward it. Hold at this angle until he catches up with it and leaps onto the running board.*

Moving shot. Car. Morning. CLYDE, *now on the running board, his head poked into the car, his face apple red and sweating.*

CLYDE *(breathing heavily)*.. . . see anythin', Buck?

BUCK *is shocked at his brother's desperation, but makes no overt comment on it.*

BUCK. —not yet, boy.

CLYDE *(with an edge of paranoia, as if the three of them might be withholding something from him)*. —and *nobody* saw her leave, or heard anythin' *(almost a threat)*. . . C. W. . . .?

C. W. *is frightened at seeing Daddy* CLYDE *so upset, swerves the car.*

CLYDE *(exploding)*. —watch the damn road!

BUCK *(calmly)*. —not unless you did, Clyde.

Ext. Car. Moving shot. Day. CLYDE *gets the point. For the very first time we see* CLYDE, *the leader, helpless as he hangs onto the running board.*

CLYDE *(lamely)*.. . . Well, where do you think she could've gone? . . . Buck? . . . Buck?

BUCK *(amazed and a little frightened)*. Jesus, I don't know . . .

CLYDE *looks helplessly at his brother, then drops off the running board and continues on foot, running along, scanning the fields—the car keeping up beside him as he runs and we truck before both car and* CLYDE.

Angle on car through windshield. Reaction shot. Day. BUCK *turning to* BLANCHE, *shrugging his shoulders, speechless.*

Reverse angle through the windshield. Day—at CLYDE, *who has suddenly seen something begins gesticulating wildly, almost—from car's POV, a little comically.*

CLYDE. There! There! There!

He starts running off into a cornfield.

Another angle—picking up CLYDE *as he kicks his way into the cornfield, knees pumping high, knocking down the stalks. He stops and picks up the stocking he had spotted, takes it and moves on.*

Still another angle as CLYDE *has picked up a freshly beaten trail through the cornfield. He picks up one of* BONNIE'S *scarves, now. As he runs on, he clears a knoll and* BONNIE, *her yellow hair unmistakable even at this distance, comes into view. She's far off in the cornfield, stalking off, looking neither to right nor left, carrying a brown paper sack that has split, from which she has occasionally lost clothing.* CLYDE *screams,* "BONNIE." *She apparently doesn't hear.*

Angle on cornfield. Day. As CLYDE *gets closer.* BONNIE *herself suddenly breaks into flight, the paper bag splitting completely, the remaining clothes spilling out. There is a real chase where they each try to get the advantage.* CLYDE *is so exhausted from his run that he has real trouble cornering her as they maneuver up and down the rows of corn. Finally* CLYDE *catches her.*

Extreme close-up. BONNIE & CLYDE. *Day. As they tumble into the stalks of corn, mowing them down.*

BONNIE. Leave me alone! Leave me alone!
CLYDE *(holding her, kissing her frantically).* Hey . . . hey, hey, baby, hey, Bonnie, hey baby . . . *(calming her down).* . . . Hey, hey now . . . just where did you think you were goin'? . . .

BONNIE *doesn't answer.*

Up angle. POV CLYDE. *As he's momentarily distracted by* BUCK'S *laughter as he's in the cornfield picking up* BONNIE'S *clothing.* CLYDE *waves an impatient it's-all-right-wave. He turns back to* BONNIE *who he still holds tightly.*

CLYDE *(still frantic).* —Huh, Bonnie? Where? Where?
BONNIE. I don't know! You're hurting me, I was just scared is all . . . and my mama's been on my mind, and she's gettin' so old . . .

BONNIE *hesitates, beginning to feel a little foolish now.*

CLYDE. Boy, don't ever leave without sayin' somethin'. You really scared me, Bonnie.

BONNIE. But I mean it, though. I want to see my mama. Please, Clyde.

Two shot. BONNIE *and* CLYDE. *Day.*

CLYDE *(enormously relieved, kissing her).* Okay, sweetheart.

Dissolve to:

Ext. Side of a road. Very long shot. Day—of three or four cars parked on the side of a road in Texas. A light rain is falling. There are a lot of people gathered around, but the sound is an indistinct mixture of talk, laughter, etc.
There follows a quick montage of cuts which isolate specific moments in the family reunion, thereby implying the entire tone of the proceedings. The sense of family pervades.

Montage. BONNIE *and* MOTHER. BONNIE'S *mother, an old woman, grabs her and hugs her and cries.*

Montage. BONNIE, CLYDE, MAN. *A man, an uncle perhaps, stands with* BONNIE *and* CLYDE, *arms around them both, hugging them to his sides tightly.*

Montage. BONNIE *and sister.* BONNIE'S *sister hands them a scrapbook of clippings.*

SISTER. Here you arc, we been cuttin' and pastin' everything we could find about you in the papers.

CLYDE, BONNIE, BUCK *and* BLANCHE *all look at the scrapbook. We see a page of it, showing newspaper articles with the photographs the gang took back at the motel.*

BUCK. Hey look, here's that one I took of you, Clyde. That came out just fine!

Montage. BONNIE, CLYDE, MAN. BONNIE *and* CLYDE *are posing for a comic snapshot. A silly looking male relative is posing, pointing a gun at them. They have their hands in the air and are grinning broadly. (The effect should be funny and simultaneously frightening.)*

Montage BUCK, SMALL BOY. BUCK *is sitting with a little four-year-old on his knee, bouncing him up and down and singing. Both are having a fine time.*

BUCK *(singing).* Oh, Horsey! keep yer tail up, keep yer tail up, keep yer tail up, Oh, Horsey! keep yer tail up, Why don't you make it rise.

Montage—C. W. A hand off camera thrusts a sandwich at C. W. *He opens the bread to see what's inside it, then eats it.*

Montage— BONNIE & SISTER. BONNIE *sits stock-still while her sister gives her a permanent in the back seat of a car. Her sister pauses, setting down the curling iron. She strokes* BONNIE'S *yellow head with her hand, as though she were a wild animal that had paused long enough to be petted.* BONNIE *turns to see her sister's expression. They embrace.*

Montage—Family picnic—Favoring CLYDE, MOTHER & BONNIE. CLYDE, *in his best theatrical manner has been playing host in the sand pile, perhaps using some sort of towel across the arm or around the middle. The party is beginning to break up now as used paper plates and crumpled napkins are blowing across the sand and the group is finishing up on Eskimo pie.*

BONNIE'S UNCLE *(rising)*. Where y'all headed from here?

CLYDE *(right back)*. I don't know, what y'all got in mind? At this point we ain't headin' *to* anywhere, we're just runnin' *from*.

CLYDE *laughs, in fine spirits.*

Reaction— BONNIE. *She doesn't.*

BONNIE'S SISTER'S VOICE. C'mon, down, Little Tom! We're goin' home. Little Tom? Mathew, fetch Little Tom.

BONNIE. Don't go yet, Mama.

UNCLE'S VOICE *(cutting in)*. C'mere, c'mere you little corn roller.

Wide angle. As Uncle sweeps up the laughing little Tom.

Reaction— BONNIE. BONNIE *turns with increased urgency to her* MOTHER, *who, having been hefted to her feet by* BONNIE'S *sister, has turned to* CLYDE, *who gives her a big, boyish hug.*

MOTHER. . . . you know, Clyde, I read about y'all in the papers and I'm jes' scared.

BONNIE *(to Clyde)*. Sugar, make mama stay a while yet.

CLYDE *(ignoring Bonnie, as does Mother, ebulliently, even joshing)*. Now Mrs. Parker, don't y'all believe what you read in the papers! That's the law talking there. They want us to look big so's they'll look big when they catch us.

He knows he's stumbled onto the wrong thing, but he bounces right along—it's his style.

CLYDE. —and they can't do that. Why, I'm even better at runnin' than robbin' banks— aw shoot, if we done half the stuff they said we did, we'd be millionaires, wouldn't we, old sugar. *(he turns to Bonnie who continues*

to stare at her Mother) And I wouldn't risk Bonnie here just to make money, uncertain as times are. Why one time I knowed of a job where we could of made $2000 easy, but I saw the law outside and I said to myself, why Bonnie could get hurt here. So I just drove right on and let that money lay.

He waits for a response, as does BONNIE. BONNIE'S MOTHER *smiles, a little abstractedly.*

MOTHER. . . . Maybe you know the way with her, then. I'm just an old woman and I don't know nothin . . .

She trails off, looking nowhere in particular. CLYDE *takes her reaction to mean that he's overwhelming her with his confidence, and continues to pour it on.*

CLYDE. We'll be quittin' this just as soon as the hard times is over, Mother Parker, I can tell you that. Why me and Bonnie were just talkin' the other day and we talked about when we'd settle down and get us a home, and Bonnie said, "I couldn't bear to live morn'n three miles from my precious mother." Now how'd you like that, Mother Parker?

BONNIE'S MOTHER *has undergone a funny sort of transformation during* CLYDE'S *speech— as if something had suddenly come into focus before the old woman's eyes.*

MOTHER. Don't believe I would. I surely don't. *(to Bonnie)*. You try to live three miles from me and you won't live long, honey. *(to Clyde)* You'd best keep runnin' and you know it, Clyde Barrow. *(matter of fact)* Bye, baby.

She hugs BONNIE *who can barely respond. We move in for a closeup of* BONNIE *as her various relatives, young and old come by to squeeze, kiss and hug her with a chirpy little chorus of Bye, Bonnie! Bye, Bonnie, bye, bye, bye.*

Dissolve:

Ext. Platte City Motel. Platte City, Iowa. Day. Hold on the outside long enough to see the unusual structures: two little motel cabins connected by two identical garages, an entirely symmetrical structure.

Int. Platte City Motel Bedroom. With BONNIE. *Day—as she tries, against heavy odds, to file and trim her nails in a corner of the room. The odds are;* CLYDE *on a uke, b,g.,* BUCK, *and* BLANCHE—*gathered around* C. W. *who sits in the only stuffed chair in the room. Their o.s. raucousness is clearly shattering to* BONNIE *who, at a key moment in the* scene, ends up spearing her cuticle with a file, spurting a little blood and a lot of temper.

Other angle. CLYDE—BUCK—BLANCHE—C. W. *Day. A naked lightbulb (the lampshade has been removed) glares down on* C. W.'s *chest—where a pair of bluebirds have been tattooed with a rococo flourish.* BUCK *and* BLANCHE *are vastly amused—rather* BLANCHE *takes delight in* BUCK's *delight.*

BUCK. How long have ya had it?

C. W. *(like some docile animal submitting to inspection).* —just got it.

BUCK *(to Blanche, who stares fascinated as one of C. W.'s pectoral muscles contracts and the wings flutter).* Touch it, honey! Go on!

BLANCHE *squeals with amusement.* BUCK *takes* BLANCHE's *hand and places it on the bluebirds.*

BLANCHE *(titillated with delight).* Oh, no, Daddy! No!

Reaction BONNIE. *Day—as the file digs into her cuticle on* BLANCHE's *squeal. With barely controlled rage:*

BONNIE. What are you all doin'?

Int. Motel bedroom. Group shot. Fav. BONNIE. *Day.*

C. W. *(insensitive to Bonnie's stare).* Playin' with my tattoo, Bonnie.

BONNIE. Well, why don't you all go play with it somewhere else?

New angle. Motel bedroom. Day.

BLANCHE. What's bothering her?

CLYDE *(sees something coming).* Not now, Blanche.

BUCK *(who doesn't want to be victimized by Bonnie's temperament).* What's bothering her, Clyde?

BONNIE *(exploding).* I said go somewhere else!

She picks up the first three objects she can find on the dresser and hurls them—an ashtray, a Gideon Bible, and a flower pot—at the little group. The pot goes shattering into the wall. Everyone ducks.

CLYDE *(straightening up, matter-of-fact).* Bonnie's hungry, C. W. I saw a chicken place a few miles back. Who all wants to go get some food?

Int. Motel bedroom. Group shot. Day.

BLANCHE *(rising from her chair, a little shaken at Bonnie's outburst).* I sure do. I'm plenty tired of sittin' around here anyway.

BUCK *(not making a move to get up).* You can't drive, honeylove.

C. W. *(reluctantly).* I'll go.

CLYDE *makes a face to* BONNIE *pretending there's something going on between* C. W. *and* BLANCHE. BONNIE *tries to keep from being amused.* C. W. *moves out with* BLANCHE. BUCK *rises to go next door.*

C. W. What's everybody want?

CLYDE. Just five chicken dinners, and get somethin' for dessert.

BUCK. See if they got peach ice cream. *(he grins and pats his stomach).*

All finally exit, leaving BONNIE *and* CLYDE *alone.*

Ext. Car and street. Dusk. C. W. *and* BLANCHE *go out. We go with them. They get in the car and drive off.* BUCK *enters his cabin.*

Int. Motel bedroom— BONNIE *and* CLYDE. *Dusk.* CLYDE *reaches her, and for a moment both stare with fanatic intensity at each other,* BONNIE *trying desperately to keep a straight face. They are nose to nose, unblinking.* CLYDE *gives her a big raspberry, waggling his fingers in his ears like a kid. She laughs.*

BONNIE. I hate you all.

CLYDE. I hate y'all, too.

BONNIE. No, I *really* hate you.

She turns away from him, wilts onto the bed.

BONNIE *(eyes brimming).* Oh, baby, I've got the blues so bad . . .

CLYDE *moves behind her, begins to massage her back. There is something very delicate about the way he touches her; it suggests* CLYDE's *sensitivity to her mood rather than any degree of physical intimacy.*

CLYDE. Bonnie? . . . is it your mama, what your mama said?

BONNIE. What mama? . . . she's just an old woman now . . . I have no mama . . .

BONNIE *rolls over on her back, stares up at* CLYDE, *tears splaying across her face from the move.*

BONNIE *(quietly).* . . . so funny . . . I thought when we first went out, we were really goin' *somewhere* . . . but this is it— we're just *goin'*, huh?

She has addressed this last directly to CLYDE, *but there is nothing rhetorical about it—it is a real question.* CLYDE *doesn't answer for a moment. Then:*

CLYDE. Do you care about where we're goin'?

BONNIE *clearly finds this hard to say:*

BONNIE. Not as long as you care about me.
CLYDE *(quite simply)*. Why I love you, sugar.

It's the first time he's said it to her, and BONNIE *is overwhelmed. She wraps her arms around* CLYDE'S *middle, and snuggles into him, like a child. Neither we nor* CLYDE *can see* BONNIE'S *face now, and her voice is muffled by his chest.*

BONNIE'S VOICE. —enough to die with me, baby? . . . 'cause I think that's where we're goin' . . . I surely do.

CLYDE *is both touched and amused by the plea. He strokes her head lightly. Really meaning it.*

CLYDE. —wherever.

Dissolve:

Int. Car. BLANCHE, *her tense and agitated self growing increasingly more so lately, lights a fresh cigarette off the butt of the one she has been smoking.*

C. W. *(conversationally)*. You sure smokin' all the time lately.
BLANCHE *(quick to take offense, snaps)* So what?
C. W. Nothin'.

BLANCHE, *sick of it all, drops her head in her hand with a sigh.*

BLANCHE. Oh, God . . .

C. W. *looks at her, finally decides to say something that occurs to him.*

C. W. Whyn't you go back home to your papa?
BLANCHE *(it's been her dream)*. Oh, if I could! If I could just do that one thing! Oh, there's no tellin' why this all happened. I was a preacher's daughter.
C. W. What church is your pa affiliated with?
BLANCHE *(much more interested in talking about herself)*. Baptist . . . oh, and he thought the world of Buck, my daddy did, even knowing that Buck was serving time in jail. He forgave him for that 'cause he paid his debt to society.
C. W. We were Disciples of Christ.

Dissolve to:

Int. Fried chicken cafe. The camera remains stationary in this scene, in this position. A lunch counter sweeps down the center of the screen. We are at one end of the counter. In the f.g., a DEPUTY *sits drinking coffee, absorbed in his cup. In the b.g., at the other end of the counter, by the Exit door,* BLANCHE *and* C. W. *are being handed their order by the counterman.*

BLANCHE. Hey, C. W., I ain't got my money. Give me some, will you?

The DEPUTY *turns his head and looks over there.* C. W. *opens his jacket to reach in his pocket for money. As he opens his coat, his gun is clearly seen tucked in his pants. Camera zooms in to tight close-up of gun.*

Close shot. DEPUTY—*his face tense. Sound of door closing shut, as* C. W. *and* BLANCHE *leave.*

DEPUTY *(to counterman)*. Get Sheriff Smoot on the phone.

Dissolve to:

Int. Platte City Motel room—Night. On C. W.'s *moonlit chest and face, tattooed bluebirds heaving and occasionally snoring in the night. Behind him the room is dimly lit by flickering candles that are placed out of sight on the floor. The shapes in the room—the bed is gutted and only the box mattress remains— dresser, lamp shades, etc., are grotesque in the flickering light. O.s. sounds of* BONNIE *and* CLYDE, BONNIE *giggling and* CLYDE *whispering something we can't quite hear.*
Move across the room toward the gutted bed. More giggling from the floor beneath the box mattress—for a moment it should appear as if something perversely sexual may be going on between BONNIE *and* CLYDE.

BONNIE'S VOICE. Ready?
CLYDE'S VOICE *(a little embarrassed)*. Aw Bonnie—
BONNIE'S VOICE *(coaxing)*. C'mon!

CLYDE's *arm wielding a Tommy gun, clears the bed. With the muzzle,* CLYDE *knocks the swivel mirror on the dresser overhead, bringing* BONNIE *and* CLYDE *into view.*

Closer angle mirror— BONNIE *and* CLYDE. *Night.* BONNIE *lies stiff as a statue on the white mattress, impeccably dressed for her funeral. Candelabras made of empty beer bottles lie at her head and feet.* BONNIE's *hands and face are powdered and painted a waxen white. She wears a garish silk bow in her hair which is, for this occasion, curled like a little girl's.*

CLYDE *sits up, beer bottle in one hand, Tommy gun in the other, derby hat cocked—and just a little unsure of the whole thing. He takes a swig—* BONNIE *stops him, trying terribly hard not to change her position.*

BONNIE. Lie down now, honey.
CLYDE. I've done enough!

Angle on mirror— BONNIE *and* CLYDE. *Night.*

BONNIE *(with patience, to a child).* You *have* to lie down . . . it's the only way we can tell what we'll look like together.

She giggles again, more than a little gassed herself. CLYDE *clamps a big cigar between his teeth and abruptly lies down beside her.* CLYDE *is both amused and annoyed.*

CLYDE *(staring up at himself talking with cigar clenched between his teeth).* Whatta you think?
BONNIE *(It suddenly strikes her).* That's not the right tie!
CLYDE *What?*
BONNIE *(rising, weaving a little).* You can't wear polka-dots on an occasion like this.
CLYDE. Well what—
BONNIE. Stripes. Don't go away now.

She weaves her way over to the dresser, takes a swig from a bottle there herself, checks her makeup, and returns with the tie. Holding against his chest to try it out she almost falls into him. CLYDE *steadies her.*

BONNIE. Perfect.

She tries to tie it for him, and clearly has trouble with the knot.

CLYDE. OK, o.k. If we're gonna do this, at least I can tie it myself. Lie down before you fall down.

Int. Motel bedroom— BONNIE *and* CLYDE. *Night. She does, with some play-acting, exaggerated obeisance to* CLYDE's *command—reaching up at the last moment like a zombie and snatching an artificial flower from* BLANCHE's *hat which still lies on the dresser.* CLYDE *lies down now. They look into the mirror again.*

CLYDE *(grudgingly).* Better?
BONNIE. Much.

This tickles CLYDE *despite himself and he laughs—* BONNIE *begins to sing to him—performing for both* CLYDE *and her own image in the mirror—like some hoydenish vaudevillian. During the course of the song she will rise and*

take CLYDE *with her who finally joins in when they tip-toe over and begin to serenade* C. W.

BONNIE *and* CLYDE *(to the lugubrious strains of the Death March).*
"Did you ever think when a hearse went by,
That someday you or I may die?
They'll wrap you up in a big white sheet
and bury you down just about six feet.
The worms crawl in, the worms crawl out,
The worms play penuckle on your snout.
Your eyes fall in, your teeth fall out,
Your face turns green and the pus runs out.

During this last they have been hovering over C. W.'s *twitching face, like a couple of tipsy ghouls, whisper-singing into his ears.* C. W. *finally blinks, doesn't even bother to look at them.*

C. W. *I'm* gonna die if I don't get some sleep. Quit singing that.

Reaction— BONNIE *and* CLYDE. *Night. They smile, go back and lie down. Looking at their images:*

BONNIE. All right, shut your eyes now.
CLYDE *(playing along with her).* No, you first.
BONNIE. One for the money.
CLYDE. Two for the show.
BONNIE. Three to get ready—
CLYDE *and* BONNIE. Four to Go.

As they approach four we should feel that somehow when they shut their eyes, they really will die. They shut them on GO, *and screen goes black.*

Ext. Platte City Motel. Night. Ranged across the lawn are six police cars, loaded with peace officers. Four men come out and, guns drawn, walk cautiously over to the room on the right— BUCK *and* BLANCHE's.

Int. Platte City Motel. BUCK's *cabin. Night. There is a knock on the door. They sit bolt upright in bed. Before* BUCK *can say anything,* BLANCHE *puts her hand over his mouth to shut him up.*

BLANCHE *(calling out).* The men are on the other side.

Ext. Platte City Motel. Night. The four lawmen, among them the DEPUTY *from the cafe, edge their way across the lawn, past the first garage, past the second. Before they reach the door of* BONNIE *and* CLYDE's *cabin, the window smashes and there are blasts of gunfire. One cop is hit and falls, the others run back to the cars for cover.* BONNIE *and* C. W. *are at the window, firing steadily.*

CLYDE—*running into the garage to get the car. They must escape. All they can do is escape, and all they have is that one car in the closed garage.*

Outside. Two of the lawmen fall to the ground, shot. As the remaining two run back for cover, we see a blinding light rolling up in a space between the six cars. It is an armored truck, with mounted guns and spotlight, advancing toward the cabin.

Inside the armored truck. Two men in the seat. Sounds of gunshots coming from everywhere, piercing light. From inside the truck, we suddenly see the windshield shattered from bullets fired by BONNIE *and* C. W. *The driver is hit, and he slumps over the wheel. His body hits the horn, which starts blasting and continues throughout the battle. The other man, quickly, ducks under the dashboard for protection.*

Inside the garage. CLYDE *standing by the car. He holds the Browning Automatic. The garage door is shaking from the impact of bullets, shattering. His gun already firing (automatic clip) before he gets there,* CLYDE *in a crouch runs to the garage door, flings it up, and runs back inside the car. Now the door is open and he can get the car out. One hand on the wheel, one hand shooting, he rolls the car out onto the driveway. The battle is raging from all sides.*

Ext. Street. The car stops. CLYDE *keeps shooting. The door of the cabin flies open and* BONNIE *and* C. W. *come charging out, guns blazing away.* C. W. *fires the Thompson submachine gun,* BONNIE *fires two pistols with automatic clips. They run in a crouch, trying to get inside the car in front of their door. They make it.*

Camera pans across the motel to the other door. It opens, BUCK *and* BLANCHE *come out, holding a double bed mattress in front of them for protection. This makes their running awkward—the mattress is heavy.* BLANCHE *carries the front end,* BUCK *the back with one hand, the other firing his gun. They get halfway to the car and then* BUCK *is hit, shot in the head. He falls to the ground;* BLANCHE *and the mattress fall too since she has lost balance. Both are under the mattress.*

CLYDE *dashes out of the car and drags* BUCK *into the back seat.* BLANCHE *follows, hysterical. All guns on all sides are still firing. They*

fling themselves into the car and from a standing start, the car starts out at 60 mph down the driveway. One of the lawmen stands blocking the way with a double-barreled rifle, but the car keeps coming, about to run him down. He jumps out of the way and fires at the side. The glass cracks and we see BLANCHE *fling a hand to her face, which is bloody. A piece of glass has lodged in her eye. We hear her scream. The horn is still blasting.*

Int. The car swerving madly. CLYDE *manages to keep it on the road. They drive away.*

Ext. Street. The police run back to their cars to give chase, calling out to each other, unable to believe that the gang could possibly have gotten away.

Int. Car. Night, as it is speeding down the highway. Crazy, mad hillbilly music on the soundtrack. Packed inside this car right now is more sheer human misery and horror than could be believed. It is hell in there, hell and suffering and pain. The car is a complete mess. C. W. *is sobbing. Everyone is hysterical.* BLANCHE *is shrieking with pain and concern for* BUCK. BUCK *is alternating between groaning and passing out completely.* BONNIE *is yelling at everybody to shut up. Only* CLYDE, *driving with both hands clenched on the wheel, is silent. The car is doing 90.*

Ext. Suburban street. Night. The car from the outside, a half hour later. They have eluded the police. They are barreling down the road at top speed on a nice suburban street with proper homes. It is the middle of the night, utter silence. CLYDE *stops the car, points to a car in a driveway—it is a beautiful, shiny new and expensive automobile.* C. W. *runs out, runs up the driveway, peers inside, gets in, quietly backs it down the driveway and pulls behind the gang's bullet-riddled getaway car. Suddenly they both zoom off down the road together.*

Int. of the new car. Night. C. W. *driving alone. He is crying, mumbling, wiping his eyes and nose with one hand while he controls the wheel with the other.*

Ext. Ring of firs. Night. A wide field in the country. This is Dexter, Iowa. It is quiet. We see, in a long shot that takes in everything, that this is a meadow surrounded by a ring of trees, a dense forest that circles them. The meadow, however, is large.

The two cars drive into the middle of the field, headlights on. They stop and the Barrow gang gets out. They are in horrible shape—we can finally have a look at them. Half-dressed in their pajamas, bloody, dirty, in tatters. Those that can stagger out do so, others are carried. A far shot of all this.

Closer shot. Moving closer to them, we see CLYDE *and* C. W. *lay* BUCK *down on the ground.* CLYDE *begins to administer to his wounds as best he can, mostly just wiping him off.* BUCK *is semi-conscious. All are in a semi-daze.* BLANCHE *falls to her knees, still clutching her eyes. She is totally hysterical.*

BLANCHE. Oh, God, please help us! Dear Father in Heaven, get us out of this and Buck will never do another bad thing in his life! *(she continues moaning, praying, sobbing)*

BONNIE *walks over to the group, looking at* BUCK. C. W. *goes over to her. Two shot—* BONNIE *and* C. W.

C. W. He ain't got a chance. Half his head blown off.

Camera pulls back to take in BLANCHE.

BLANCHE. My eyes! *(she SCREAMS)* God, I think I'm blind. *(in the headlights)* . . . light hurts so bad . . .

BONNIE *walks over to the car and comes back with the sunglasses* BUCK *had given* BLANCHE. *Moving her out of the glare, she helps* BLANCHE *put them on.* BONNIE *now has an arm around* BLANCHE, *and* BLANCHE *shivers into* BONNIE *gracefully.* BONNIE *is a little repelled by* BLANCHE, *but comforts her out of genuine feeling for her.*

BLANCHE *(clinging).* Please, please get us to a doctor! Tell Clyde to get us to a doctor. We'll die here.

BONNIE *(helping with glasses).* —here, hon'.

BONNIE *looks silently up to* CLYDE. CLYDE *is looking dumbly down at his mangled brother.*

BLANCHE *(going on).* Clyde, Clyde, please get us to a doctor.

Though BLANCHE *cannot see it,* CLYDE *has knelt down to the side of* BUCK, *taking* BUCK'S *hand and with his other hand has begun smoothing* BUCK'S *hair back, away from the wound.*

BLANCHE. He's your brother!

BONNIE *(gently, knowing* CLYDE *will not and cannot answer* BLANCHE*).* Buck can't be moved, now, hon'.

BLANCHE'S *answer to this is hysterical sobbing, burying herself into* BONNIE, *mumbling*

half-coherent, muffled prayers between the sobs.

With BUCK *and* CLYDE.

BUCK *(weakly).* Clyde? . . . Clyde? . . .
CLYDE. Right here, boy.
BUCK. I believe I lost my shoes . . . maybe the dog hid 'em. . . . *(he lapses into unconsciousness again)*

CLYDE *has begun to cry a little, continues to smooth back* BUCK'S *hair with ritualistic regularity.*

Wide angle. Night. Camera pulls away, way back to wide shot of the entire field, showing the group in the center of the darkness, lit by the headlights.

Match dissolve into early dawn, camera still on the wide shot. The field is lighter, though the trees still loom blackly around it. The two cars, one almost a shattered wreck, the other bright and shiny and new, are parked in the center. The sky is light, but the trees cast a dark shadow on the field. The gang is just sitting around. BLANCHE *weeping next to* BUCK, C. W. *sitting on the running board of a car, staring.* BONNIE *standing and smoking.* CLYDE *still with* BUCK.

All is quiet.

Ext. Woods. Day. From the edge of the woods, a man in a white shirt emerges from behind a tree. The camera swings abruptly to get him. He calls out to the gang.

MAN. Surrender!

It is a total surprise. BONNIE, CLYDE *and* C. W. *all grab their guns and fire several shots; they are not firing the big guns now, but the pistols. The man lingers there for a moment— he looks strange, white, luminous, like an apparition—and then he vanishes into the woods. Silence, long enough to make you think it was perhaps an illusion.*

Then there is a volley of gunfire—a noise so large as to be almost an impossible sound— coming from the woods, all around, everywhere. A ring of little white puffs of smoke emerge from the woods; from every tree a puff of smoke. The camera pans in a circle. Behind every tree is a man with a gun. There are at least 150 people out there—peace officers, farmers with hunting rifles, kids with squirrel guns, everyone who wanted to come along and catch BONNIE *and* CLYDE. *Their number is so large because this time they want no possibility of the gang making what seemed by them supernatural escapes.*

From this point on, the sound of guns is unnaturally muffled on the sound track. We hardly hear them at all . . . it is like a dream.

Without a word, all of the gang including the half-dead BUCK *making his final effort, scramble for the nearest car. They run, throughout this battle, crouched, like animals—their only thought, to get away, to escape. To fight it out would be ludicrous.*

From the moment the Barrows start in motion, there is shooting again from the edge of the woods. We see them scrambling towards the car, in an extreme long shot, surrounded by the ring of smoke.

Cut to:

Int. of the car. All of them inside. CLYDE *is at the wheel.*

Cut to:

Ext. Car. Med. Long shot of the car moving. The sound track goes to complete silence. We see the car looking for an avenue of escape. It veers toward a tree, a man steps out from behind the tree and fires, the car jerks and veers toward another tree, again a man steps out and fires and so on. The car performs its eccentric dance, all in utter silence (no sound of the motor, nothing). The film should have the feeling of slow motion, as the car swerves and loops along the edge of the woods. Not once do any of the Barrows fire back. Another man steps out and aims.

Int. Car. Close-up. CLYDE. *At the wheel— shot in the arm. He grabs his arm in pain, loses control of the wheel.*

Cut to:

Ext. Car—out of control (still silent). It smashes into a tree stump. The picture stops, freezes for three beats. We hold the image of the moment of crash, with pieces of metal crumpling and flying into the air, suspended there by the stop-film.

Cut to:

Int. Car. Sound partly up again, but never at its realistic volume. From inside the smashed car, we peer out the window across the field and see the other car. The thought strikes the audience at the same time it strikes the gang— they must *get to that car.*

Med. shot of the second car, sitting in the field, shining in the sun. The lawmen also realize what must be done—cut off this escape. Though BONNIE, CLYDE *and the others are heading toward it, they suddenly train all their fire on the car rather than the gang.*

The car fills the frame of the screen. Bullets begin to hit it. It starts to quiver under the impact. For the next minute, we see the car die in front of our eyes. We see the beautiful machine fall to pieces—windows smash, tires torn apart, body riddled. The death of the car is as painful to watch as the willful death of a human being. The execution is paced deliberately to show the ritualistic tempo of the destruction.

Ext. Woods. The camera pulls back, way back and slightly above everything to reveal the entire field. On the left of the screen, BONNIE, CLYDE *and* C. W. *are scrambling toward the edge of the woods. In the center* BUCK *and* BLANCHE *have taken cover behind a fallen log. In the foreground, police begin to emerge from the woods. The camera zooms rapidly in with them toward* BUCK. BLANCHE *is screaming.*

BLANCHE. Don't kill him! Don't kill him! He's dying!

BUCK *is making a last feeble attempt. The zoom continues past* BUCK *until it comes tight on his hand, holding a gun. As the zoom shot reaches the hand, a lawman's foot steps on his hand.* BUCK *falls over. He dies.* BLANCHE *screams.*

BLANCHE. Don't die, Daddy, Don't die!

She goes berserk. Five men, one hardly a teen-ager, grab her and hold her as she writhes and cries. She is still wearing the sunglasses.

Cut to:

Ext. woods and stream. BONNIE, CLYDE *and* C. W. *Day. They have reached the edge of the woods. Camera tracks with them as they run. From all around come the sounds of the posse. The three get in through the pines and come finally to a deep stream. They jump in and start across, running awkwardly in chest-deep water. They are half way across when the police appear on the bank behind them, shooting.*

Close-up. BONNIE. *Day— as she is struggling through the water. A bullet hits her in the shoulder. We must see this bullet clearly, we must see it go in her flesh so that we can feel it.*

Tight close-up of BONNIE's *face as she screams. It is the first time she has been hurt, and the scream is pure animal pain. She cries out.*

Ext. Stream and cornfield. Day. CLYDE, *who has almost reached the other side, comes back and gets her. He drags her out of the water and into a cornfield that starts growing on the op-*

posite bank, C. W. *helping. He half-carries, half-runs with her into the cornfield, as the field gets deeper and thicker.*

They stop for a second.

CLYDE *(panting, to Bonnie).* Saw . . . saw a farm . . . up ahead . . . gotta get . . . a car . . .

He starts to give over the wounded BONNIE *to* C. W.

BONNIE. Baby, no . . .

But CLYDE *has not heard this last. Working on pure adrenaline now, he struggles onward. Camera tilts up slightly so we can see* CLYDE *as he essays his way toward a farmhouse with a car in the distance. After a few moments he disappears and we can hear only the cracking of the stalks as that sound too diminishes.*

Full shot. Cornfield. Day. Silence.

Close. C. W. *and* BONNIE. *Obviously some time later. They both lie prostrate in the field, listening.* C. W. *licks his lips.*

C. W. Maybe—
BONNIE. Shhh!

They wait for another long moment, picking up only the tiniest sounds.

BONNIE *(finally).* Oh, no.
C. W. *(nervously).* What? What?
BONNIE *(as though it were the most logical thing in the world).* I can't die without Clyde. I just can't.

C. W. *looks at her as if she's gone crazy. After another moment the corn begins to tremble, and we hear the o.s. sound of an approaching car.*

With C. W. *Day—tentatively lifting his head up to clear the corn stalks. With him we see the car looming larger, bearing down on us, splitting the corn stalks. The car finally comes to a stop a few feet in front of* C. W. BONNIE *is on her feet, and* CLYDE *tumbles out of the car, practically before it's stopped, sweeping* BONNIE *into him. For a moment both are on their knees a few feet from the running board of the car, simply holding onto each other and not moving.*

C. W. *(tugging at both of them frantically).* C'mon! C'mon! C'mon!

Abrupt cut:

Int. Car. About a half hour later. Day. They have gotten away, but are still escaping. C. W. *is driving. He is bare-chested.* CLYDE *is beside him in front, his arm bleeding. He falls in and*

out of consciousness. BONNIE *is stretched out in back. Her shoulder has been bandaged with* C. W.*'s shirt. She is unconscious.*

Int. Car. Late Day. CLYDE *comes half-awake and looks over at* C. W.

CLYDE. Head out, C. W.
C. W. *(determinedly).* I'm goin' home to my daddy's farm.

Dissolve to:

Ext. Road with campsite. The same evening. C. W. *is driving down the road, hell for leather. Nearing a campsite, where there are about six Okie cars and pick-up trucks all loaded down, with a number of poor families seated around a campfire, cooking.* C. W. *jams on the brakes. He gets out, looking totally exhausted.*

Reaction shot. The faces of the Okies, looking at this sudden presence in their midst.

Back to C. W.

C. W. *(about to drop).* Can y'all spare me a little water?

Ext. Campsite. Full shot. One man, the leader of the group, dips a cup of water and approaches C. W. *suspiciously. He comes close enough to make* C. W. *reach out for the water, but withholds it from him.*

MAN. Who are you, boy?
C. W. Name's Moss.

This seems to be enough for the man, who gives him the water. As C. W. *gulps it down, the man begins to circle the car, peering into it suspiciously. Suddenly he starts and his eyes open wide.*

MAN *(in really hushed and reverent tones).* It's Bonnie Parker and Clyde Barrow.

He stands there struck dumb, staring. Those of the others who have heard him begin to come over. Without a word they move quietly to the car and stare in.

Int. Car. BONNIE *is out in the back seat;* CLYDE *is semi-conscious in the front seat. He looks up through half-closed eyes.*

Ext. Car. We see a woman pour a bowl of soup at the campfire and bring it to C. W. *He accepts it.*

A man rolls a cigarette and lights it. Then, very gingerly, as if afraid to really touch him, he reaches through the window and places it in CLYDE'S *lips. It hangs there,* CLYDE *unable to drag on it or remove it.*

Children peer through the back window.

C. W. *finishes his cup of soup. He hands it and the cup of water back to a woman in the crowd.*

Quietly, moving together, the Okies step back. C. W. *walks to the driver's seat, gets in and shuts the door. He starts up the car.*

The people push a bit closer for a last look. CLYDE, *unable to do more, nods his head in a barely perceptible gesture by way of saying "thank you" to the people. The cigarette is still dangling from his lips.*

The car moves off. A YOUNG BOY *pulls on his* FATHER'S *shirt.*

BOY. Who was they, Pa?
MAN. That was Bonnie and Clyde, the bank robbers.

A woman, nearby, smiles sweetly.

Dissolve to:

Ext. Moss Farm. Middle of the night. The car pulls up outside the slightly ramshackle farm of MALCOLM MOSS, C. W.'s *father, in Arcadia, Louisiana. It sits, for a moment, in the dark. Then* C. W. *honks the horn. A few seconds pass, and the porch light comes on.* OLD MAN MOSS *comes out in his pajamas and peers into the darkness. He is a fat man with gray hair.*

MALCOLM. Who's there?
C. W. *(calling back).* Daddy?
MALCOLM. Who's there? Who is it?
C. W. It's C. W. It's Clarence.
MALCOLM. Clarence!

He runs down the steps, down the path to his son. They greet each other, hugging for a second, looking each other over.

MALCOLM. God, it's good to see you, boy!

He holds C. W. *at arm's length to study him, and suddenly he scowls at something he sees by the light of the porch.*

MALCOLM. What's that on your chest?
C. W. *(puzzled)* Huh? *(realizing what he means)* It's a tattoo . . . I'm in trouble. I'll tell you about it later. My friends are hurt. Help me get 'em in.

MALCOLM *goes to car and looks inside for a moment. He walks back to* C. W.

MALCOLM. Jesus, what happened to them? You in trouble, son?
C. W. Yeah. That's Clyde Barrow and Bonnie Parker. *(reaction from Malcolm)* We been shot. Help me get 'em inside. We gotta help 'em.

They go to the car and drag the unconscious BONNIE *out and begin carrying her up to the house.*

MALCOLM. Why'd you get yourself marked up? A tattoo! What in hell made you do a damn fool thing like that?

They reach the house.

C. W. C'mon, Pa, open the door.

Int. Sheriff's office in Dexter. Day. Although the scene begins with a full-screen close-up of a newspaper clipping with a photo, it is just a blurry-gray, crowded scene of BLANCHE'S *capture. Really impossible to make anybody out in the crowd. Camera stays on photo as we hear voice over of two men talking: a sheriff and his deputy.*

BILLY. I was in the bunch that took 'er. See here? Can you make me out? Here I am, see here, right behind Joe Boyd here.
PETE. Sure enough, Billy, is that your head there?

Camera pulls away. BILLY, *a young deputy—cold, intense, humorless and square, carefully folds up the clipping and puts it in his wallet.*

BILLY. Still can't figure how we let them other two get away.
PETE *(an older, more genial type).* Yeah, seems as how nobody can get 'em somehow.
BILLY *(sullen).* Yeah . . . well, maybe this boy'll be the one to do it, this Hamer guy. Boy, if he can't do it, Sheriff, ain't nobody but the whole U.S. Army can do it.
PETE *(with a new note of enthusiasm, gets up and walks to the window—turning to Billy).* You hear he quit the Rangers on account of Texas got that woman governor. Said he wouldn't work under no woman.
BILLY *(respectfully).* Yeah, that's somethin' all right. Say, how many they say he shot anyway in his day?
PETE. Sixty-five they say.
BILLY. Son of a sea-cook!

The door opens. We see, full shot and then fast close-up FRANK HAMER. *It should be a complete shock to the audience—this is the man kidnaped by the gang earlier and partially destroyed by* BONNIE.

HAMER *is dressed in his Ranger outfit and hat, and again he has that quality of sinister frenzy beneath his calm manner. His attitude toward these lawmen is sheer condescension, friendly only out of convention, really superior* and contemptuous of lesser workers in his field.

HAMER *(with politeness arising from condescension).* Excuse me, am I in the right place? Is this Sheriff Smoot?

PETE *and* BILLY *jump up from the chairs and walk over to* HAMER, *hands extended. They are quite impressed by meeting in the flesh.*

PETE *(mispronouncing his name).* Frank *Hammer.* I sure am pleased to meet you! *(shakes his hand)*

HAMER. *Ha*mer.

Ext. Moss farm. Close shot newspaper. Day. A coil of rope snaps into and through the paper, splitting it and revealing C. W.'s *startled face.* CLYDE *strides the porch angrily, snapping the rope.*

BONNIE *and* MALCOLM *are seated along with* C. W. *Though* BONNIE *has her arm supported by a sling and* CLYDE *has his shoulder bandaged, it is evident by* CLYDE's *heady indignation and* BONNIE's *attentiveness that both are well on the way to recovery.*

CLYDE *(still snapping rope).* FLED? What do they mean, fled? How in the nama God could I leave my brother to die when he was already dead when I left him? *(livid)* He was shot in too many pieces to pick off the ground! *Fled* . . . what do they know, the papers or the police? . . .

Suddenly he moves upon MALCOLM *with enormous intent, as if by pounding the point home to the one relative stranger among them, he will justify it all.* MALCOLM *momentarily flinches, then listens with intense deference.*

CLYDE. Why, while we were all lyin' around *here,* near *dead,* they had us holdin' up the Grand Prairie National Bank! They hung that one on us just for luck, I guess.

CLYDE *shakes his head, still thinking this over. Abruptly, to* BONNIE, *with deadly seriousness:*

CLYDE. Tell you what. Soon's we get well, we're gonna *take* that bank!

He breaks into a wicked grin, but then reels, catching himself on the porch railing. He's obviously dizzy from exertion and anger. BONNIE *starts—then sees* CLYDE *is in control.*

CLYDE *(remarking on his own dizziness).* Whoooooooo, boy . . . *(kneeling, to Bonnie)* They don't know nothin'—do they, sugar? BONNIE *(assuring him).* You did all you could, hon'. Nobody coulda done more.

C. W. *has been studying hard on the torn paper, b.g. Suddenly:*

C. W. Hey. How come I'm always called the "Un-identified sus-spect?"

Group shot. Porch. C. W. *has trouble with this last phrase.* BONNIE *laughs. This picks up* CLYDE's *spirits once more.*

CLYDE *(to* C. W.*).* You can just thank your lucky stars that's *all* you are. So long's they don't have your last name, you're home safe. MALCOLM *(toadying to Clyde, talking to Clarence).* Mr. Barrow's lookin' out for your interests, boy.

C. W. *(impressed).* Oh. . . . Hey, Pa, how you like havin' a coupla big deals stayin' with you?

MALCOLM *(friendly as can be).* Ain't that somethin' for me?

CLYDE *(back in good mood, expansive).* Well now, you been real nice to us, and I tell you what, let us pay you forty dollars for your hospitality, what do you say?

MALCOLM *(protesting vehemently).* No, no, no. I don't want your money. I'm just pleased to have your company. Any friend of my boy's . . .

C. W. *(abruptly).* Hey, Pa, let's have supper. I'm hungry.

MALCOLM *(smiling).* Yeah . . . okay, Clarence . . . *(to Clyde)* You're welcome here, now you know that.

Int. Moss house. They go into the house. Camera goes with them. As soon as they are out of earshot from BONNIE *and* CLYDE, MALCOLM *turns on* C. W. *displaying an entirely different demeanor from the one he presented outside.*

MALCOLM *(indicating tattoo which flutters through* C. W.'s *open shirt).* You look like trash, boy, marked up like that. Cheap trash.

C. W. *(protesting).* Bonnie says it looks good.

MALCOLM. Bonnie, what does she know. She's just cheap trash herself. Look what they do to you, and you don't ever get your name in the paper—just *pictures* put on your skin, by "Bonnie and Clyde"—*(more to himself)*—why they're a coupla kids.

C. W. But, Daddy—

MALCOLM. I'm just glad your ma ain't alive to see that thing.

C. W. *peeks at it, peering down at his chest, trying to bring the bluebirds into focus, puzzled.*

C. W. I don't see what's so bad about it . . .

Int. Hospital. Med. shot of the room. Seated in a soft chair, looking directly at us, is BLANCHE BARROW. *Her eyes are completely covered with a white bandage. She wears a hospital gown. The room is white and bright.*

Med. shot. HAMER *in the doorway. The nurse leaves. He reaches in his pocket and pulls out a white handkerchief. He puts it over his mouth to disguise his voice, afraid she will remember it from the kidnap. Quietly, almost on tiptoes,* HAMER *walks over to* BLANCHE. *He gets inches away from her face. She still doesn't know he is there.*

HAMER *(quietly, but suddenly, his voice muffled by the handkerchief).* Blanche Barrow.

She starts to her feet, then adjusts to his presence. She is a bit panicked. BLANCHE *is now a defeated human being. Her voice and manner bespeak great weariness, sorrow and still a touch of her old high-strung hysteria. But most of that is gone now, like everything else that was really vital in her life.*

BLANCHE. What? What? Who is it?
HAMER *(in a monotone, a relentless questioner).* You know your husband's dead.
BLANCHE *(her voice flat and expressionless).* I know.
HAMER. You're going to prison.
BLANCHE. I know it.
HAMER. Where's the rest of 'em?
BLANCHE. I don't know.
HAMER. Where's the rest of 'em?
BLANCHE. I just don't know. I don't know.
HAMER. How'd you get in with them?
BLANCHE *(starting slow, but warming up to the subject, she begins to talk and talk for the sake of airing her troubles).* I didn't mean to. I didn't. Buck said we was just goin' to visit, we wouldn't be doin' no robbin' and stealin', and then we went to Joplin and all of a sudden they started shootin'. *(hysteria begins to creep into her voice as she relives it all)* And we run off, God, I was scared. And then it was run all the time, and I wanted to go, I begged to go, but Clyde and Bonnie and C. W.—
HAMER *(seizing on it).* C. W. C. W. who?
BLANCHE. C. W. Moss.

Fade out:

Fade in:

Ext. Car on the Moss farm. A dirt path near the barn. Day. It is pouring rain, middle of the

afternoon, BONNIE *and* CLYDE *are inside the car, sitting. They have lived so much in cars that they tend to still spend much of their time in it rather than in a room. There they are themselves.*

Int. Car. BONNIE *is in the back seat, her legs wrapped in a plaid blanket, writing poetry. She looks like Elizabeth Barrett Browning. With one essential difference—her arm is in a sling and she is wearing bandages on the shoulder.* CLYDE *is in the front seat, reading a newspaper. He is also partially bandaged. On the dashboard is a box of ginger-snaps which he eats while he reads. They look domestic.*

CLYDE. Want a ginger-snap, Bonnie?
BONNIE *(busy, absorbed).* No, hum-umm. *(then she realizes his nice gesture and smiles warmly at him)* But thanks anyway, Clyde. *(she takes it all in, her situation, and looks content and cozy)* It's real nice here, just the two of us like this.

CLYDE *(more interested in his paper).* Uh-huh. *(something in the paper catches his interest)* Look here, honey, remember this?

He holds up the paper; there is one of the photos from the motel, the one showing BONNIE *smoking. She looks up at it with mild interest.*

BONNIE. Yeah, at the motel.
CLYDE *(studying the picture).* You sure don't resemble that no more.

Close-up BONNIE. *She doesn't. She has become totally fragile, the essence of herself. She is writing on a pad.*

CLYDE *and* BONNIE.

CLYDE. What you writin' this time?
BONNIE *(intensely).* I'm writing a poem about us. I'm writing *our* story.
CLYDE *(this appeals to his ego).* Oh, are you? Let's hear it. If it's good, I'll mail it in to the Law and it'll be printed in all the papers again.
BONNIE. Just let me finish this line.

She does so. CLYDE *munches a cookie.*

BONNIE *(continuing).* Okay, here it is.

Close-up. BONNIE—*as she reads intensely. At the beginning of this montage, the camera remains on her face. Behind her we see the rain on the window.*

BONNIE *(reading).*

"The Story of Bonnie and Clyde"

You've heard the story of Jesse James—
Of how he lived and died:
  If you're still in need
  Of something to read
Here's the story of Bonnie and Clyde.

Now Bonnie and Clyde are the Barrow Gang
I'm sure you all have read
  How they rob and steal
  And those who squeal
Are usually found dying or dead.

They call them cold-hearted killers;
They say they are heartless and mean;
  But I say this with pride,
  That I once knew Clyde
When he was honest and upright and clean.

But the laws fooled around,
  Kept taking him down
  And locking him up in a cell,
Till he said to me,
  "I'll never be free
So I'll meet a few of them in hell."

The road was so dimly lighted;
There were no highway signs to guide;
  But they made up their minds
  If all roads were blind,
They wouldn't give up till they died.

Cut to:

Int. Police station. Day. The manuscript is lying on the police blotter. HAMER *picks it up and and continues reading it. He reads it in a halting way:*

HAMER.
The road gets dimmer and dimmer;
Sometimes you can hardly see;
  But it's fight man to man,
  And do all you can,
For they know they can never be free.

From heartbreak some people have suffered;
From weariness some people have died;
  But take it all in all,
  Our troubles are small,
Till we get like Bonnie and Clyde.

Close-up of a newspaper page. The poem is printed all the way down the length of one column. On the sound track, BONNIE'S *voice picks up the recitation:*

BONNIE'S VOICE: (O.S.)
If a policeman is killed in Dallas,
And they have no clue or guide;
  If they can't find a fiend,
  They just wipe their slate clean
And hang it on Bonnie and Clyde.

Int. Car. Close-up of BONNIE. *Day. The day is sunny as we see it through the car window. She continues reading, but now she reads it directly from the newspaper:*

BONNIE.
If they try to act like citizens
And rent them a nice little flat
  About the third night
  They're invited to fight
By a sub-gun's rat-tat-tat.

Some day they'll go down together;
They'll bury them side by side;
  To few it'll be grief—
  To the law a relief—
But it's death for Bonnie and Clyde.

BONNIE *finishes the poem, as camera pulls back slightly to show that it is a different day, different clothes and the bandages are gone. As she stops, she has an expectant and somewhat self-satisfied look.*

Close-up of CLYDE. *His eyes are wide, his mouth open, his face shows surprise and delight and he is on the verge of a giant laugh.*

CLYDE *(in gleeful wonder).* Damn! That's me!

A great laugh comes bursting from him. Camera widens to take in BONNIE. *She is both startled and delighted by his response.*

CLYDE *(continuing).* In that poem!

BONNIE *giggles.*

CLYDE *(continuing; it is all starting to come out now—his realization that he has made it, that he is the stuff of legend, that he is an important figure).* A sub-gun's rat-tat-tat! *(he begins to laugh loudly).* Right in the paper!

Close-up BONNIE. *Now laughing too, with a great feeling of joy.*

Two shot. BONNIE *and* CLYDE.

CLYDE. Jesse James! You hear 'bout old Jesse, now you goin' to hear 'bout Clyde!

He puffs up with air and explodes like a steam valve.

CLYDE *(continuing).* Pshhhhhh!

He grabs BONNIE *and chuckles delightedly.*

CLYDE *(continuing).* Damn, Bonnie! You musta been one hell of a waitress!

Close-up. BONNIE—*laughing, her eyes filled with tears.* CLYDE'S *hand wipes them away.*

Two shot.

CLYDE *(shaking his head back and forth like a puppy, just so much glee in him that he can't hold it)* Oooooh, that Clyde! That's my boy, that Clyde!

He looks at her with love and delight, hugs her tightly.

CLYDE. Bonnie . . . *(she hugs him back)* The Poem of Bonnie and Clyde!

BONNIE *(laughing at the mistake, happy).* The *Story*.

CLYDE. The *Story* of Bonnie and Clyde! Oh, child, you really did tell that story!

He pulls her to him, his face inches away from hers, about to kiss her. She is waiting, expecting. . . . Suddenly, he lets out one wild laugh almost into her mouth.

He kisses her. She kisses back. They are chuckling, giggling. They grow more ardent; they pull back and laugh again. They begin to make love.

Ext. Arcadia street. Ice cream parlor. Day. Bright afternoon. Camera across the street from an ice cream parlor. Sign above it: "EVA'S HAND-PACKED ICE CREAM". A large plate glass window fronts the store, and through it we can see the people inside seated at tables and booths. Prominent in our vision is MALCOLM MOSS, seated, facing camera. He is seated across from another man, but we see him from the back.

MALCOLM *is obviously doing a lot of talking and then some hard listening; gesticulating and looking disturbed. After a bit of this, he rises from the table and begins walking toward the door. The other man rises and turns. We now see that it is FRANK HAMER.*

MALCOLM *and* HAMER *come out onto the sidewalk, squinting in the sunlight.* MALCOLM *mimes some social pleasantries by way of saying "goodbye", but* HAMER'S *face shows no emotion or recognition of the gesture. He turns and walks away, walking out of the frame.*

MALCOLM *stands where he is, in front of the ice cream parlor. By the expression on his face, we can see that he is rather disturbed by what he has heard and that he is still grappling with the problem.*

Dissolve to:

BONNIE *and* CLYDE. *They lie where they were with one difference—they are now wrapped in the blanket.* CLYDE'S *pants are wadded up and tangled with his shoes at the base of the blanket.*

CLYDE *(chuckling, apparently quite pleased).* Damn! . . . damn . . . damn!

He casts a sidelong glance to BONNIE, *wanting some sort of overt reaction from her. She's just smiling slightly.* CLYDE'S *underlying anxiety begins to surface.*

CLYDE *(not looking at her).* Hey, listen, Bonnie, how do you feel?

BONNIE *(watching him steadily, her slight smile growing).* Fine.

CLYDE. I mean you feel like you're s'posed to feel after you've uh . . .

BONNIE. Just.

CLYDE *(doesn't know what the fuck to say, desperately wants her approval).* Well, that's good, ain't it. Reason I ask is, I uh . . . Well, I figger it's a good idea to ask. I mean how else do I tell if I did it the way . . .

BONNIE *(stopping him, with great warmth).* Hey. You done just perfect.

CLYDE *looks at her for the first time, tremendously relieved. He can see she means it. Now his buoyancy, utterly, unchained breaks through:*

CLYDE. I did, didn't I? I mean I did, I really did. I did it, I did, I mean this was my first time and it was just like rollin' off a log when it comes right down to it, it was easy, I mean I didn't even have to try . . .

Lovingly, laughing, altogether overwhelmed with himself, CLYDE *pulls* BONNIE *into him. He kisses her, wants to make love again, but then pulls back and keeps chattering at sixty miles a minute. He's waited twenty-three years to talk about this, and he's got the perfect audience.*

Dissolve to:

Int. Kitchen. Moss farm. Twilight. After dinner. There are four empty plates, but only C. W. *and* MALCOLM *in the kitchen.* C. W. *is scraping the bottom of a wilted "EVA'S HAND-PACKED ICE CREAM" carton.* MALCOLM *studies his son's quiet intensity in this direction for a moment, then moves very close, whispers when he speaks. (Note: It might be possible to see* BONNIE *and* CLYDE *through a small window in the kitchen that would overlook a screened-in front porch. In the salmon-colored twilight, with the screen filtering a little like a scrim,* BONNIE *and* CLYDE, *together on the porch, can look a little unreal, as if they are already in the legendary past.)*

MALCOLM *(whispering).* Boy, they expect you to go downtown with 'em tomorrow?

C. W. *(out loud, licking his ice cream)* Who?

MALCOLM *(raising his own voice, infuriated by his son's obtuseness).* Bonnie and Clyde!

. . . *(He slaps the carton out of* C. W.*'s hands; whispering again)* Bonnie and Clyde.

C. W. Sure, I always go with them.

MALCOLM *thinks hard about this.*

MALCOLM. . . .better go then, you better go, better go . . . *(forcing* C. W. *to sit at table)* —but when they get back in the car to come on home, *don't get in with them.*

C. W. *(genuinely puzzled).* Why, Daddy?

MALCOLM. You just listen to your Pa fer once! Cain't you do that? *I'm yore Daddy, I'm* your kin, not Clyde.

C. W. *(still confused).* Well, what should I tell 'em? "I can't get back in the car with you?"

MALCOLM *is ready to kill— his son's obtuseness and his fear of* CLYDE *is whipping him into a quiet frenzy.*

MALCOLM *(squeezing* C. W.*'s arm).* No, you tell them *nothin',* hear? *(hesitates, then)* I made a deal and got you off with a coupla years!

C. W. *(a piercing treble).* Made a deal with who, Daddy?

MALCOLM *hauls off and whacks* C. W. *across the top of his head with the flat of his hand, then momentarily holds his hand over* C. W.*'s mouth.*

MALCOLM *(we can see his own fear).* . . . the law. Just don't get back in that car. *(eyeball to eyeball)* And whatever you do, don't let onto them, hear?

C. W. *suddenly smiles, as if he knew something.*

C. W. *(expletive).* Whew!. . . . You think them laws are gonna catch Bonnie and Clyde in town?

C. W. *returns to the ice cream carton—* MALCOLM *lets him, figuring he better find out what he can.*

MALCOLM. What do you think, Clarence?

C. W. *(matter of fact).* They ain't gonna catch 'em. Don't matter whether I let on or not.

MALCOLM *(playing along).* Mebbe. Just you be off'n the streets of that town when they go to get in their car.

C. W. *(looking directly at Malcolm).* Nobody catches Clyde. Clyde's got a sense, don't you know that, Daddy? Nobody catches Clyde.

MALCOLM *knows better, but for just a moment he stares at his son, fearing that maybe* C. W., *for all his limitations, has a sense about* CLYDE*'s sense.* C. W. *has finished with the carton and*

crumples it, licking the last remnants of cream off his fingers.

Int. Bedroom. Moss farm. Night. BONNIE *and* CLYDE*'s bedroom, the middle of that night. Both are wide awake, lying on opposite sides of the double bed. Both are staring into the night, disquiet.*

CLYDE *(suddenly).* Bonnie? Bonnie, will you marry me?

There is a silent gasp from BONNIE, *a barely perceptible stiffening. Then she talks in a voice falsely formal, still staring up at the ceiling.*

BONNIE. How could I do that, Clyde? You know it's impossible. We'd have to go to a Justice of the Peace and the Justice of the Peace is a lawman. We couldn't even take out a license.

CLYDE *(with a chuckle).* Hey now, you sound like you been givin' it some thought on your own.

BONNIE *(with a grim irony, her voice getting more and more emotional).* Oh no, I never gave it thought. I haven't thought about it at least ten times a day, I haven't thought about it every minute of my life since I met you. *(suddenly her voice cracks into tears)*

She flings herself violently across the bed and buries herself into CLYDE*'s chest, her knees drawn up, her head tucked down into him, her body shaking with sobs.*

CLYDE *(a bit startled by this, attempting to hold her, awkwardly, and placate her. He puts his arm around her).* Bonnie . . . are you crying, honey?

BONNIE *nods yes and slowly gets control over her tears.*

BONNIE *(her face still buried in* CLYDE*'s chest, she whispers).* Clyde, why do you want to marry me?

CLYDE *thinks a minute and then grins.*

CLYDE *(in an attempt to be humorous).* To make an honest woman out of you.

BONNIE *is silent.*

BONNIE *(finally, in a voice charged with anticipation and dream).* Clyde . . . what would you do, what would you do if some miracle happened and we could walk out tomorrow morning and start all over again, clean, with no record, with nobody after us?

CLYDE *thinks about it a minute.*

CLYDE. Well . . . I guess I'd do it all different. First off, I wouldn't live in the same state where we pull our jobs. We'd live in one state and stay clean there, and when we wanted to take a bank, we'd go to another state . . . and . . .

Suddenly he realizes that he has said the worst thing he could have said, that it was not the answer BONNIE *wanted to hear. He looks down at her, his voice anxious.*

CLYDE (*continuing*). Bonnie?

She is silent.

CLYDE. Bonnie . . .

She is silent.

CLYDE. Hey, Bonnie?

But she does not answer.

Ext. Roadside. Early morning. We see MALCOLM *jacking up the back wheel of his pickup truck which is parked on the side of the road in a wooded area.*

Cut to:

Ext. Arcadia street. Mid-morning. A street in Arcadia. The car is parked. BONNIE *and* CLYDE *walk towards the car carrying big bags of groceries and supplies and put them inside.*

CLYDE (*looking around*). What happened to C. W.?
BONNIE. He stopped off in that hardware store to get light bulbs for his daddy.

CLYDE *opens the door of the driver's seat and sits down.*

Int. Car. Arcadia street. Day.

CLYDE. Boy, my feet are sweatin'.

He takes off his shoes.

BONNIE (*kidding around*). You plannin' to drive with your shoes off?
CLYDE. Sure, why not?

He reaches in his shirt pocket and takes out his sunglasses. As he goes to put them on, one of the lenses falls out.

CLYDE. Damn!

He puts them on.

BONNIE (*laughing*). You gonna wear 'em?
CLYDE. Sure, drive with one eye shut.

BONNIE *gets in the car, rummages around in one of the bags and pulls out something wrapped in tissue paper. She unwraps it and puts it up on the dashboard, displaying it. It is a little porcelain shepherdess holding a crook in her hand, worth about thirty cents.*

BONNIE (*admiring it*). Isn't that the prettiest thing, hon? Just look here, you can see every little fingernail on her hands.

She shows him.

CLYDE. It is a pretty thing, honey.

CLYDE *turns on the radio and gets some hillbilly music. They are singing "Little Church in the Valley." He beats time on the steering wheel, getting a little impatient.* BONNIE *puts her shepherdess away and begins looking in the grocery sack.*

BONNIE. We got any peaches? I sure could go for a peach right now.

She burrows in the bag and comes out with a peach. She takes a big bite. The juice drips down the side of her mouth. She looks beautiful.

CLYDE (*he stops drumming his fingers, suddenly has an idea*). Why'n't we do it tomorrow?
BONNIE. Do what?
CLYDE. Tomorrow's Sunday, ain't it? We could drive all night and be on that golf course tomorrow morning!
BONNIE. You sure you feel up to it?
CLYDE (*enthused*). Yeah, why not? (*now feeling anxious and excited, he is impatient to move*) Where is that boy? He's gone too long.
BONNIE (*humming to the radio*). He'll be here. (*holding the peach to him*) You take a bite, hon.
CLYDE (*getting worried*). No, it's takin' too long. What if something happened?
BONNIE. Nothin' happened.
CLYDE (*more urgently*). Go take a look, see what's keepin' him.

Not too delighted with the chore, BONNIE *goes off. We remain with* CLYDE, *getting anxious. The music plays on.* BONNIE *comes back, hurriedly, now anxious herself.*

BONNIE. He ain't there.

CLYDE *jumps into action, slams his door.*

CLYDE. C'mon, let's go.

BONNIE *gets in. They drive off.*

Int. Store. Close-up C. W. *Day—hiding inside a store, peering out through a curtained window at them driving away. His expression is disturbed; his face half in shadow.*

Ext. Road. Day. BONNIE *and* CLYDE'S *car coming down the road. Camera sees from* CLYDE'S *P.O.V.* MALCOLM *standing in the road, waving him down. The pickup truck, its back jacked up, is parked beside him on a shoulder of the road.*

Int. Car. Day.

BONNIE. What's wrong?
CLYDE. I don't know.

Ext. Road. CLYDE *reaches the spot, pulls off the road and stops the car. He gets out. Camera pulls back.* CLYDE *talks to the old man,* BONNIE *stays in the car. Cut to a shot down the trench of the law, tense.*

Suddenly, a truck loaded with chickens comes riding down the road from the opposite direction. HAMER *sees it from a long way away and realizes that he cannot afford to let anything pass between him and his quarry. He decides the time is now. He leaps up from the trench and yells at* CLYDE.

HAMER. Barrow!

The OLD MAN *dives under his truck to hide. The shooting starts.*

We see the chicken truck. Two men in the front seat. They see ahead of them an incredible shooting match and, in terror, they jam on the brakes and leap out of the truck. They run as fast as they can into the meadow, away from the trouble.

The gun fight takes just seconds during which law fires eighty-seven shots at BONNIE *and* CLYDE, *giving them absolutely no chance. The sound is rapid, deafening.*

At no point in the gun fight do we see BONNIE *and* CLYDE *in motion. We see, instead, two still photographs cut into the sequence: one of* CLYDE, *half out of the car, taking careful dead aim with his gun, just as he did in the teaching scene; one of* BONNIE, *in terror, a pack of cigarettes in her hand clutched tight, looking as fragile and beautiful as she can be.*

The noise stops at once. Utter silence. It has been a massacre. BONNIE *and* CLYDE *never had a chance to return the gunfire. We see the car, a complete shambles. We never see* BONNIE *and* CLYDE *dead, though for a moment we discern their bodies slumped in the car.*

The camera pulls above the car until it is on a level with the opposite side of the road. Then, slowly, the six lawmen stand up in the trench. On the faces of the five deputies, horror and shock at what they have just done. HAMER, *however, registers no emotion. His face is a blank. He lights a cigarette. Slowly, slowly, the five men begin to edge closer to the car to see the result. Music, the wild country breakdown music, begins on the sound track.*

Before they reach the car, the camera swings away from them, past them, and zooms out and above into the meadow where the two truck drivers are standing—tiny, distant figures.

The truck drivers begin to walk toward the camera, coming back to the road to see what happened. They get closer and closer to the camera until they have reached a middle distance and, as they continue to walk at us, it is—

THE   END

Cut to black.

THE GRADUATE

Screenplay by

Calder Willingham and Buck Henry

BEN BRADDOCK	Dustin Hoffman
MRS. ROBINSON	Anne Bancroft
ELAINE ROBINSON	Katherine Ross
MR. ROBINSON	Murray Hamilton
MR. BRADDOCK	William Daniels
MRS. BRADDOCK	Elizabeth Wilson

Screenplay by Calder Willingham and Buck Henry,
based on the novel by Charles Webb
Produced by Mike Nichols—Lawrence Turman Productions for UA/
Embassy, 1967
Produced by Lawrence Turman
Directed by Mike Nichols
Cinematography by Robert Surtees
Music by Dave Grusin
Songs by Paul Simon

Written by Calder Willingham and Buck Henry as adapted from the splendidly conceived novel by Charles Webb, this screenplay, as well as the motion picture itself, was nominated for an Academy Award in 1967. It also won the Writers Guild Award for that year as Best American Comedy.

The Graduate, in a general way, can be bracketed with *Rebel Without a Cause,* in that both focus on the growing-up process of American youth, each mirroring a time of teenage unease and questioning of traditional roles in family relationships, the former in a comedic way of course, just as the latter is quite serious.

The adaptation by Mr. Willingham and Mr. Henry is quite good. Although the novel reads almost as a screenplay itself in its terseness, sequence, and style, the script truly enhances it. Its satirical aspects are sharpened.

As a comment on sexual mores and the hypocrisy of familial relationships of our times — particularly during the sixties, with its expanded license — the film reminds me of one of Molière's plays in a way, and that is a well-deserved compliment, in my opinion. Calder Willingham and Buck Henry do indeed attack corruption in family life, as represented by the Braddocks and the Robinsons. Like Molière in his works, their attacks are sharp, on the mark, and penetrating. Their sense of ridicule in *The Graduate* compares favorably with the French master. Coming closer to American literature, one can also find echoes of Mark Twain in the style of the film.

But unlike Molière, their work is not savage. The characters in *The Graduate,* that is to say, the parents of Ben and Elaine, can hardly be considered representative of all American families, nor do we come away, after viewing the film, with the feeling that the Braddocks and the Robinsons are thoroughly and completely corrupted. Bumbling, yes. Cynical to a degree, yes, in the person of Mrs. Robinson. Yet, despite Mr. and Mrs. Robinson's opposition to Ben's marriage to their daughter, if we can hazard a guess, I think they would come around to accepting Ben as their son-in-law eventually.

But that is still not the real point. The fun of the script and the movie is. The bumbling innocence of Ben and the cynical sexual sophistication of Mrs. Robinson give the film a brilliance in wit and humor that really engages us. The seduction scene, in the hotel, in my opinion, is a classic that will be well remembered always.

One can see, all in all, why this was a very popular film for the youth at the time the film appeared. *The Graduate* makes us understand why so many of our young at that time rose in the marketplace against the hypocrisies of adults whose institutions they began to question, doubt, and rail against. In that sense, the film mirrors that situation very well. The innocence of Ben and Elaine in that context, which I find believable, works very well as counterpoint to the corruptibility of their parents, beautifully so, and with great skill.

You will also note some differences between the screenplay and the film-as-shot that are worth mentioning. Toward the conclusion of the film, when Ben is pursuing Elaine at Berkeley, changes have been made and accomplished skillfully to quicken and improve the rhythm of the film so as not to delay its sense of climax, particularly in the scenes between Ben and Elaine. Compare the screenplay in these scenes with the film as completed for exhibition.

Here is a word about the backgrounds of Mr. Willingham and Mr. Henry.

Calder Willingham was born on December 23, 1922, in Atlanta, Georgia. He was educated at the Citadel and at the University of Virginia in the early forties. Mr. Willingham's first novel, published in 1947, *End as a Man,* was made into a motion picture in 1957 as *The Strange One.* In that same year, Mr. Willingham collaborated on the screenplay of *Paths of Glory* with Stanley Kubrick and Tim Thompson.

Buck Henry, born Buck Henry Zuckerman in 1930, in New York City, was educated at Dartmouth. In 1960 he joined The Premise, the Off-Broadway improvisational theater group, then moved to Hollywood where he began writing comedy material for "That Was the Week That Was." He also wrote the pilot for the "Get Smart" series with Mel Brooks. In 1978 he made his debut as a director, collaborating with Warren Beatty on *Heaven Can Wait,* for which both achieved a nomination for an Academy Award.

Ext. Amphitheater—Day shot—Helicopter's P.O.V.—Moving through clouds. The clouds separate and, far below, we can see a giant outdoor amphitheater. There is no sound but the wind. As we move closer to the amphitheater, we can hear snatches of words and phrases as though from a public address system.

Ext. amphitheater—Podium—Day—Shot of BEN *in cap and gown, standing in front of a microphone. The wind is blowing. He has to hold on to the papers from which he is reading.*

Ext. amphitheater—Shot of audience—Day. Thousands of expressionless students are sitting there.

Ext. amphitheater—Shot of podium—Day.

BEN.—and today it is right that we should ask ourselves the one most important question: What is the purpose of these years, the purpose for all of this demanding work, the purpose for the sacrifices made by those who love us? Were there *not* a purpose, then all of these past years of struggle, of fierce competition and of uncompromising ambition would be meaningless. But, of course, there is a purpose and I must tell it to you. I ask you to remember this purpose always and I pledge that I shall endeavor to carry it with me forever.

Shot—Amphitheater audience—Day. Staring at him impassively.

Intercut between shots of impassive students, seated, watching; of BEN *standing alone on the huge amphitheater stage; of close-ups of* BEN *speaking; of loudspeakers; of wind-blown papers on the podium.*

Ext. podium of amphitheater—Day.

BEN *(continuing)*. The purpose, my fellow graduates—the purpose is—

He stops, trying to think of the word. Close-up— BEN. *He begins to sweat.*

Shot—Amphitheater audience, watching.

Shot—Podium of amphitheater. BEN's *hands searching through the pages of his speech. The pages begin to blow away in the wind.*

Shot—Amphitheater audience—Day—staring.

Shot—Podium of amphitheater—Day.

BEN.—there is a reason, my friends, and the reason is—

Close-up— BEN. *He is in a panic. He looks up from his papers at the audience.*

Shot—Amphitheater—Day. The audience is gone.

Shot—Podium of amphitheater—Day.

BEN.—the reason is—the purpose is—

Sound of the wind becoming the roar of an aircraft coming at us through the air.

Shot—Amphitheater—Day. Huge and empty. Sound of aircraft.

CAPTAIN'S VOICE. Ladies and gentlemen, we are about to begin our descent into Los Angeles—

Sound of a sonic boom.

Cut to:

Int. plane—Close-up— BEN—*Night. His eyes open suddenly.*

CAPTAIN'S VOICE. The sound you have just heard is the landing gear locking into place. The Los Angeles weather is clear and the temperature is a pleasant 72. We do not expect any traffic delay and will make our four hour and eighteen minute flight plan smack on the nose. We enjoyed having you on board and look forward to seeing you again in the near future.

Shot. Pull back slowly from a close-up of a television screen with snow on it to reveal a long row of television sets along the ceiling of the aircraft. There is snow on all of them.

Reverse angle. Pull back from the close-up of BEN *to reveal a row of passengers, staring straight ahead, their headsets on.* BEN *turns and looks out of the window.*

Ext. Los Angeles—From the air—Night. Los Angeles, at night, its lights stretching endlessly in every direction.

Sound—Muzak and the Stewardess' landing speech.

Start of main titles.

Under titles:

STEWARDESS' VOICE. Ladies and gentlemen please fasten your seat belts in preparation for the landing and observe the no smoking sign. After we land, you will notice an increase in the sound level as the thrust of the engines is reversed to help reduce forward speed.

Int. airport—Moving sidewalk—Night. BEN *and the other passengers on the automatic sidewalk.*

MAN'S VOICE. Your attention, please! American Airlines Flight Number 4, 21 Club service, non-stop to New York is now leaving from Gate Number 40. All aboard, please.

Int. airport—Conveyor belt—Night. Shot of BEN's *suitcase on the conveyor belt.*

Int. airport—Moving sidewalk—Night shot of BEN *on the moving sidewalk.*

MAN'S VOICE. Please hold handrail and stand to the right. If you wish to pass, please do so on the left.

The man's voice repeats its message.

Int. airport baggage pickup section—Night shot— BEN's *suitcase comes off the first conveyor belt, through the metal gates, and slides down the ramp to the baggage pickup section.*

WOMAN'S VOICE. Mr. Justin. Mr. George Justin! Will you please come to the information counter.

Int. airport—Automatic doors—Night shot of BEN *walking through the automatic doors.*

Int. airport—Baggage pickup section—Another angle— BEN—*Night. He picks his suitcase up from the revolving baggage belt.*

Ext. airport—Shot—From outside the automatic doors—Night—that lead to the street.

RECORDED VOICE. Your attention, please. Parking in this area is limited to three minutes only. Please do not leave your car unattended.

We can see BEN, *carrying his suitcase, turn toward us, wave in our direction, walk toward us. The automatic doors whoosh open ahead of him as he walks into us with a smile.*

Final title.

Fade out.

Int. BEN's *room—Night—Closeup—* BEN. *His eyes are open and he is trying to remember something. There are the sounds of many people talking and laughing in other rooms. A radio nearby plays music. After a while, there is the sound of a door opening. The sounds of the people talking are louder.* MRS. TERHUNE's *voice can be heard among them.*

MRS. TERHUNE'S VOICE. —associate editor of the college newspaper in his junior year— managing editor in his senior year—

The sound of the door closing. MRS. TERHUNE's *voice and the voices of the other guests fade down.* MRS. TERBUNE's *voice can be*

heard with varying clarity through the remainder of the sequence.

After a few minutes, there is the sound of a light switch being snapped and light, as though from an overhead fixture, falls across BEN's *face. He does not move.*

After a few moments, there is the sound of the radio being snapped off.

MR. BRADDOCK'S VOICE. What's the matter?

BEN's *mouth opens a little bit and closes again.*

MR. BRADDOCK'S VOICE. The guests are all downstairs, Ben. They're all waiting to see you.
BEN. Look, Dad—could you explain to them that I have to be alone for a while?
MR. BRADDOCK'S VOICE. These are all our good friends, Ben. Most of them have known you since—well—practically since you were born.

BEN *has not moved. Now the bed on which he is lying moves as though someone has sat down upon it next to him.*

MR. BRADDOCK'S VOICE. What is it, Ben?

The camera begins to pull back slowly.

BEN. I'm just—
MR. BRADDOCK. —worried?
BEN. Well—
MR. BRADDOCK. About what?
BEN. I guess—about my future.
MR. BRADDOCK. What about it?
BEN. I don't know. I want it to be—
MR. BRADDOCK. To be what?
BEN *(quietly).* Different.

As BEN *says this, the door to the bedroom opens and* MRS. BRADDOCK *looks in.*

MRS. BRADDOCK. Is anything wrong?
MR. BRADDOCK. No! No—we're just on our way downstairs!

MR. BRADDOCK *gets off the bed and goes to a chair and picks up* BEN's *jacket which is lying across it.*

MRS. BRADDOCK. The Carlsons are here.
MR. BRADDOCK *(to* MRS. BRADDOCK*).* They are? *(to* BEN*). Come on.*

MR. BRADDOCK *puts the jacket on* BEN.

MRS. BRADDOCK. They came all the way from Tarzana. Now let's get cracking.
MR. BRADDOCK. It's a wonderful thing to have so many devoted friends.

They move out of the door, MR. BRADDOCK *steering* BEN.

Int. halls and stairway—Night. PHIL *and* MIMI CARLSON *are coming up the stairs as the* BRADDOCKS *are moving down.*

MR. CARLSON. Hey—there's our award winning scholar.

MRS. CARLSON. We're all very proud of you, Ben.

BEN. Thank you, Mrs. Carlson.

MR. CARLSON. Is that the new car out there? The little red Wop job?

MR. BRADDOCK. That's Ben's graduation present.

MR. CARLSON *(putting his arm across* BEN'S *shoulder).* Won't have much trouble picking them up in that, will you?

BEN. Sir?

MR. CARLSON. The girls. The *chicks.* The— the teeny boppers.

MRS. CARLSON. I think Ben has gotten beyond the teeny bopper stage—haven't you, Ben?

MRS. CARLSON *gives* BEN *a broad wink.* BEN *tries to smile and return the wink politely.*

BEN. Yes, ma'am.

The reach the hall at the bottom of the stairs.

BEN. Excuse me—I think I'd just like to check something on the car for a minute—

BEN *moves to the front door and opens it.* MR. LOOMIS *steps into the house and grabs* BEN'S *hand.*

MR. LOOMIS. Here's the track star himself. How are you, track star?

BEN. Just fine, Mr. Loomis.

MR. LOOMIS *closes the door and pushes* BEN *back down the hall.*

MR. LOOMIS. I want to get a drink and then I want to hear all about that thing you won. That Hopperman award.

BEN. Helpingham.

MR. LOOMIS. Helpingham! Right! Now you wait right here.

MR. LOOMIS *turns and goes into the dining room.* BEN *moves back to the stairway as three ladies come out of the living room. One lady takes* BEN'S *right hand, another lady his left, the third fingers the front of his jacket.*

LADY 1. BEN—we're all so proud of you.

LADY 2. Proud, proud, proud, proud, proud.

LADY 3. What are you going to do now?

BEN. I was going to go upstairs for a minute—

LADY 3. No—I meant with your future.

LADY 2. With your life.

BEN. Well—that's a little hard to say—

MR. MCQUIRE *appears behind* BEN.

MR. MCQUIRE. Ben!

BEN *(to the ladies).* Excuse me. *(he turns around).* Mr. McQuire.

MR. MCQUIRE *(overwhelmed with pride).* Ben.

BEN. MR. McQuire.

MR. MCQUIRE *takes* BEN'S *arm and steers him down the hall toward the back of the house and out through the back door.*

Ext. BRADDOCK *backyard and pool area— Night. The pool is eerily lit. There are four people standing and talking, drinks in their hands, at the back of the yard.*

MR. MCQUIRE. Come with me for a minute. Ben—I want to say one word to you—just one word—

BEN. Yes, sir.

MR. MCQUIRE. Are you listening?

BEN. Yes I am.

MR. MCQUIRE *(gravely).* Plastics.

They look at each other for a moment.

BEN. Exactly how do you mean?

MR. MCQUIRE. There is a great future in plastics. Think about it. Will you think about it?

BEN. Yes, I will.

MR. MCQUIRE. Okay. Enough said. That's a deal.

MR. MCQUIRE *turns and walks back into the house. The people at the other end of the yard look toward* BEN.

WOMAN #1. Here he is now. Here's Ben.

BEN. Excuse me just a minute—

BEN *goes into the house through the back door.*

Ext. BRADDOCK *backyard and pool area— Night. We can see through the windows of the house,* BEN *making his way through people trying to stop him and speak to him as he goes through rooms, up the stairs and to his room.*

Sound of a door slamming.

Int.—Ext. BEN'S *room—Night.* BEN *stands with his back against the door. The sounds of the party downstairs and, as* BEN *walks across the room to a window, the sound of the wind.*

Shot—Long shot (location). Over BEN *to pool area and people below.*

Sound of the door opening. BEN *turns.* MRS. ROBINSON *enters the room.*

MRS. ROBINSON. Oh, I guess this isn't the bathroom, is it?
BEN. It's down the hall.

They stand for a moment, looking at each other.
MRS. ROBINSON. How are you, Benjamin?
BEN. Fine, thank you—Mrs. Robinson. The bathroom is down at the end of the hall.

MRS. ROBINSON *moves into the room.*

MRS. ROBINSON. Such a pleasant room.
BEN. Look, Mrs. Robinson, I don't mean to be rude but—

MRS. ROBINSON *takes a cigarette from her purse and lights it.*

MRS. ROBINSON. Is there an ashtray in here?
BEN. No.
MRS. ROBINSON. Oh—I forgot. The track star doesn't smoke.

She blows out the match and puts it down carefully on the bedspread. BEN *picks up a wastebasket, walks over to the bed, picks up the match and puts it in the wastebasket.*

MRS. ROBINSON. Is it a girl?
BEN. Is *what* a girl?
MRS. ROBINSON. Whatever it is you're upset about.
BEN. Oh—no. I'm just sort of disturbed about things.
MRS. ROBINSON. In general.
BEN. That's right.

There is a long pause.

MRS. ROBINSON. Well—congratulations.
BEN. Thank you.

MRS. ROBINSON *moves out of the room and re-enters.*

MRS. ROBINSON. Benjamin, I want to ask you something.
BEN. What?
MRS. ROBINSON. Will you take me home?
BEN. What?
MRS. ROBINSON. My husband took the car. Will you drive me home?

BEN *reaches into his pocket and hands* MRS. ROBINSON *a set of car keys.*

BEN. Here—you take it.

MRS. ROBINSON *looks at him.*

BEN. Do you know how to work a foreign shift?

MRS. ROBINSON *shakes her head.*

BEN. You don't?
MRS. ROBINSON. No *(there is a pause).*
BEN. Let's go.

She throws the keys to him. He catches them.

Cut to:

Ext. BRADDOCK *house—Night. Shooting through the open front door.* MR. BRADDOCK *is talking to the* TERHUNES *at the door.* BEN *and* MRS. ROBINSON *come down the hall.*

BEN. Dad—Mrs. Robinson needs a ride home. I'll be right back.

MR. BRADDOCK *pats* BEN *on the shoulder.* MRS. ROBINSON *is walking ahead through the front door.*

MRS. ROBINSON *(as she passes the camera).* Wonderful party.

Cut to:

Ext. ROBINSON *house—Night. The car comes to a stop in the* ROBINSON *driveway. They sit for a moment.*

MRS. ROBINSON. Thank you.
BEN. Right.

She doesn't move. BEN *gets out and goes around to her side and opens the door.*

MRS. ROBINSON. Will you come in, please?
BEN. What?
MRS. ROBINSON. I want you to come in till I get the lights on.
BEN. What for?
MRS. ROBINSON. Because I don't feel safe until I get the lights on.

They move to the door. She takes out her key and opens the door.

Int. ROBINSON *hall and sunroom—Night.*

MRS. ROBINSON. Would you mind walking ahead of me to the sun porch. I feel funny about coming into a dark house.
BEN. But it's light in there now.
MRS. ROBINSON. Please.

BEN *turns and walks down the hall. They enter sunroom.*

MRS. ROBINSON. What do you drink? Bourbon?
BEN. Look, Mrs. Robinson—I drove you home. I was glad to do it. But I have some things on my mind. Can you understand that?

She nods.

MRS. ROBINSON. Yes.
BEN. All right, then.
MRS. ROBINSON. What do you drink?

He looks at her.

MRS. ROBINSON. Benjamin—I'm sorry to be this way, but I don't want to be alone in this house.
BEN. Why not?
MRS. ROBINSON. Please wait till my husband gets home.
BEN. When is he coming back?
MRS. ROBINSON. I don't know.

She pours herself a drink.

MRS. ROBINSON. Drink?
BEN. No.

She hands him a drink. There is a pause.

BEN. Are you always this much afraid of being alone?
MRS. ROBINSON. Yes.
BEN. Well, why can't you just lock the doors and go to bed?
MRS. ROBINSON. I'm very neurotic.

She turns on the phonograph. Sound of phonograph.

MRS. ROBINSON. May I ask you a question?

BEN *looks at her.*

MRS. ROBINSON. What do you think of me?
BEN. What do you mean?
MRS. ROBINSON. You've known me nearly all of your life. You must have formed some opinion.
BEN. Well—I've always thought that you were a very—nice—person.
MRS. ROBINSON. Did you know I was an alcoholic?
BEN. What?
MRS. ROBINSON. Did you know that?
BEN. Look—I think I should be going—
MRS. ROBINSON. Sit down, Benjamin.
BEN. Mrs. Robinson—if you don't mind my saying so—this conversation is getting a little strange. Now I'm sure that Mr. Robinson will be here any minute and—
MRS. ROBINSON. No.
BEN. What?
MRS. ROBINSON. My husband will be back quite late.

They look at each other. BEN *is half standing.*

MRS. ROBINSON. He should be gone for several hours.

She takes a step toward him. He puts his hand up and retreats around the other side of the chair.

BEN. Oh my God.
MRS. ROBINSON. Pardon?
BEN. Oh no, Mrs. Robinson, oh no.
MRS. ROBINSON. What's wrong?
BEN. Mrs. Robinson, you didn't—I mean you didn't expect—
MRS. ROBINSON. What?
BEN. I mean—you didn't really think that I would do something like that.
MRS. ROBINSON. Like what?
BEN. What do you think?
MRS. ROBINSON. Well I don't know.
BEN. For God's sake, Mrs. Robinson, here we are, you've got me into your house. You give me a drink. You put on music, now you start opening up your personal life to me and tell me your husband won't be home for hours.
MRS. ROBINSON. So?
BEN. Mrs. Robinson—you are trying to seduce me.

There is a pause. She looks at him.

BEN (*weaker*). Aren't you?
MRS. ROBINSON. Why no. I hadn't thought of it. I feel rather flattered that you—
BEN. Mrs. Robinson, will you forgive me for what I just said?
MRS. ROBINSON. It's all right.
BEN. It's not all right, it's the worst thing I've ever said to anyone.
MRS. ROBINSON. Sit down.
BEN. Please forgive me. Because I like you. I don't think of you that way. But I'm mixed up.
MRS. ROBINSON. All right. Now finish your drink.
BEN. Mrs. Robinson, it makes me sick that I said that to you.
MRS. ROBINSON. We'll forget it right now. Finish your drink.
BEN. What is wrong with me?
MRS. ROBINSON. Have you ever seen Elaine's portrait?
BEEN. Her portrait?
MRS. ROBINSON. Yes.
BEN. No.
MRS. ROBINSON. We had it done last Christmas. Would you like to see it?
BEN. Very much.

We move with MRS. ROBINSON *and* BEN *out of the sunroom, into the hall, up the stairs and along the hall to the doorway to* ELAINE'S *room.*

Int. ELAINE's *room—Night.* BEN *moves into the room and looks up at the portrait.*

BEN. Elaine certainly is an attractive girl, isn't she?

In the b.g. MRS. ROBINSON *watches him.*

BEN *(looking at the portrait).* I can't remember her as having brown eyes.

MRS. ROBINSON. Benjamin?

BEN. Yes?

MRS. ROBINSON. Will you come over here a minute?

BEN. Over there?

MRS. ROBINSON. Yes.

BEN. Sure.

MRS. ROBINSON. Will you unzip my dress?

He steps back.

MRS. ROBINSON. I think I'll go to bed.

BEN. Oh. Well, goodnight.

MRS. ROBINSON. Won't you unzip my dress?

BEN. I'd rather not, Mrs. Robinson.

MRS. ROBINSON. If you still think I'm trying to seduce you—

BEN. No, I don't. But I just feel a little funny.

MRS. ROBINSON. Benjamin— you've known me all your life.

BEN. I know that. But I'm—

MRS. ROBINSON. Come on.

She turns her back.

MRS. ROBINSON. It's hard for me to reach.

BEN *reaches forward and pulls the zipper down.*

MRS. ROBINSON. Thank you.

BEN. Right.

BEN *walks toward the door.*

MRS. ROBINSON. What are you so scared of?

BEN. I'm not scared, Mrs. Robinson.

MRS. ROBINSON. Then why do you keep running away?

BEN. Because you're going to bed. I don't think I should be up here.

MRS. ROBINSON *lets her dress fall to the floor.*

MRS. ROBINSON. Haven't you ever seen anybody in a slip before?

BEN. Yes, I have—

He looks up at the portrait of ELAINE.

BEN. But I just—Look—what if Mr. Robinson walked in right now?

MRS. ROBINSON. What if he did?

BEN. Well, it would look pretty funny, wouldn't it?

MRS. ROBINSON. Don't you think he trusts us together?

BEN. Of course he does. But he might get the wrong idea. Anyone might.

MRS. ROBINSON. I don't see why. I'm twice as old as you are. How could anyone think—

BEN. But they would! Don't you see?

MRS. ROBINSON. Benjamin—I'm not trying to seduce you. I wish you'd—

BEN. I know that. But please, Mrs. Robinson. This is difficult for me.

MRS. ROBINSON. Why is it?

BEN. Because I am confused about things. I can't tell what I'm imagining. I can't tell what's real. I can't—

MRS. ROBINSON. Would you like me to seduce you?

BEN. What?

MRS. ROBINSON. Is that what you're trying to tell me?

BEN. I'm going home now. I apologize for what I said. I hope you can forget it. But I'm going home right now.

BENJAMIN *walks out of the door and down the hall. The camera pushes with him to the door. We see the entire stairway and part of the downstairs hall.* BEN *gets to the stairs and starts down.*

MRS. ROBINSON'S VOICE. Benjamin?

BEN. Yes.

MRS. ROBINSON'S VOICE. Will you bring up my purse before you go?

BEN. I have to go now. I'm sorry.

MRS. ROBINSON *walks into the hall. Her back is to us. She is holding her dress in front of her.*

MRS. ROBINSON. I really don't want to put this on again. Won't you bring it up?

BEN. Where is it?

MRS. ROBINSON. On that chair in the hall.

She walks out of the shot.

BEN. Mrs. Robinson?

MRS. ROBINSON'S VOICE. I'm in the bathroom.

BEN. Well here's the purse.

MRS. ROBINSON'S VOICE. Could you bring it up?

BEN. Well I'll hand it to you.

BEN *starts back up the stairs.*

BEN. Come to the railing and I'll hand it up.

MRS. ROBINSON'S VOICE. Benjamin—I am getting pretty tired of all of this suspicion. Now if you won't do me a simple favor I don't know what.

BEN *appears as he slowly climbs the stairs.*

BEN. I'm putting it on the top step.

MRS. ROBINSON'S VOICE. For God's sake, Benjamin, will you stop acting that way and bring me the purse?

BEN *gets to the top of the stairs, and starts slowly down the hall.*

BEN. I'm putting it here by the door.

MRS. ROBINSON'S VOICE. Will you bring it in to me?

BEN. I'd rather not.

MRS. ROBINSON'S VOICE. All right. Put it in the room where we were.

BEN. Right.

Int. ELAINE'S *room—Night.* BEN *walks quickly into* ELAINE'S *room, crosses to the bed and puts the purse down. As he starts to turn back, he looks up at* ELAINE'S *portrait. There is a movement reflected in the glass of the portrait. He turns quickly.* MRS. ROBINSON, *naked, is shutting the door to the bedroom behind her.*

BEN. Oh God.

She smiles.

BEN. Let me out.

She turns the lock on the door.

MRS. ROBINSON. Don't be nervous.

BEN. Get away from that door.

MRS. ROBINSON. I want to say something first.

BEN. Jesus Christ!

MRS. ROBINSON. Benjamin—I want you to know I'm available to you. If you won't sleep with me this time—

BEN. Oh my God.

MRS. ROBINSON. If you won't sleep with me this time, Benjamin, I want you to know you can call me up any time you want and we'll make some kind of arrangement.

BEN. Let me out!

MRS. ROBINSON. Do you understand what I said?

BEN. Yes. Yes. Let me out!

MRS. ROBINSON. Because I find you very attractive and any time—

There is the sound of a car in the driveway outside. BEN *leaps at the door, pushes* MRS. ROBINSON *aside, struggles with the lock, gets the door open, runs into the hall and down the stairs.*

Int. sunroom—Night. BEN *rushes into the sunroom and sits down. Sound of footsteps on the driveway outside.* BEN *jumps up, gets the glass he had been drinking from and sits down again. Sound of the front door opening and closing.*

MR. ROBINSON'S VOICE. Is that Ben's car in front?

BEN *(jumping up).* Yes, sir!

Footsteps approach the sunroom. MR. ROBINSON *enters.*

BEN. I drove—I drove Mrs. Robinson home. She wanted me to drive her home so I—I drove her home.

MR. ROBINSON. Swell. I appreciate it.

BEN. She's upstairs. She wanted me to wait down here till you got home.

MR. ROBINSON. Standing guard over the old castle, are you?

BEN. Yes, sir.

MR. ROBINSON. Congratulations.

BEN. Thank you.

MR. ROBINSON *reaches for* BEN'S *glass.*

MR. ROBINSON. Here. It looks like you need a refill.

BEN. Oh no. I've got to go.

MR. ROBINSON. Is anything wrong? You look a little shaken up.

BEN. No. No—I'm just—I'm just a little worried about my future. I'm a little upset about my future.

MR. ROBINSON *takes the glass from him.*

MR. ROBINSON. Come on. Let's have a nightcap together.

MR. ROBINSON *turns his back to* BEN *to mix the drinks.*

MR. ROBINSON. Scotch?

BEN. Bourbon.

MR. ROBINSON *turns and hands him the drink.*

BEN. Thank you very much, sir.

MR. ROBINSON. Ben—how old are you now?

BEN. Twenty. I'll be twenty-one next week.

MR. ROBINSON *(taking out a cigarette).* That's a hell of a good age to be.

BEN. Thank you.

MR. ROBINSON. I wish I was that age again. Because, Ben—

BEN. Sir?

MR. ROBINSON. You'll never be young again.

BEN. I know.

MR. ROBINSON. Ben, can I say something to you?

BEN. What?

MR. ROBINSON. How long have we known each other now?

BEN *shakes his head.*

MR. ROBINSON. How long have you and I known each other? How long have your Dad and I been partners?

BEN. Quite a while.

MR. ROBINSON. I've watched you grow up, Ben.

BEN. Yes, sir.

MR. ROBINSON. In many ways I feel as though you were my own son.

BEN. Thank you.

MR. ROBINSON. So I hope you won't mind my giving you a friendly piece of advice.

BEN. I'd like to hear it.

MR. ROBINSON. Ben—I think—I think you ought to be taking it a little easier right now than you seem to.

BEN *nods.*

MR. ROBINSON. Sow a few wild oats. Take things as they come. Have a good time with the girls and so forth.

MRS. ROBINSON *enters the room. She is now wearing the dress she wore earlier.* BEN *starts to get up.*

MRS. ROBINSON. Don't get up.

BEN *sits.*

MR. ROBINSON. I was just telling Ben here he ought to sow a few wild oats. Have a good time while he can. You think that's sound advice?

MRS. ROBINSON *nods.*

MRS. ROBINSON. Yes, I do.

BEN. I've got to go.

He stands. MR. ROBINSON *stands up with him.*

MR. ROBINSON. You have yourself a few flings this summer, I bet you're quite a ladies' man.

BEN. Oh no.

MR. ROBINSON. What? You look like the kind of guy that has to fight them off. *(to* MRS. ROBINSON*).* Doesn't he look to you like the kind of guy who has to fight them off?

MRS. ROBINSON. Yes, he does.

They start out of the sunroom.

Int. ROBINSON *hall—Night.*

MR. ROBINSON. Oh say—Elaine gets down from Berkeley on Saturday.

BEN. Oh yes.

MR. ROBINSON. Ben—I want you to give her a call.

BEN. I will.

MR. ROBINSON. Great.

MR. ROBINSON *opens the front door and* BEN *goes out.*

Ext. ROBINSON *house—Night. Shooting over the car toward the house.* BEN *comes toward the car.* MRS. ROBINSON *appears in the doorway; the light behind her makes it difficult to see her face.*

MRS. ROBINSON. Benjamin?

BEN. Yes.

MRS. ROBINSON. Thank you for taking me home.

BEN *nods.*

MRS. ROBINSON. I'll see you soon, I hope.

BEN *continues to walk toward us.*

MR. BRADDOCK's VOICE. Ladies and gentle-men—your attention, please—for this after-noon's feature attraction.

Cut to:

Ext. BRADDOCK *backyard and pool area—Day. The sun shines brightly. Standing and sit-ting around the pool are* MR. *and* MRS. BRADDOCK, *their friends* MR. *and* MRS. ARNOLD, *and the Arnold children,* PETER *and* LOUISE, *who are eight or nine. Watching from across the fence on one side of the house: the young girl from next door and her boy friend. Across the fence on the other side of the house: a quartet of adults, formally dressed as though for a cocktail party, holding drinks and watching. One of them holds a baby. The* BRADDOCKS, *the* ARNOLDS *and their children are dressed in Cali-fornia Contemporary Sport Style: the adults in styles infinitely too young for them, the children in styles infinitely too old for them.*

MR. BRADDOCK *stands alone at the end of the pool near the house. The others are grouped, more or less, at the other end.* MR. BRADDOCK *is hamming it up.*

Shot— MR. BRADDOCK.

MR. BRADDOCK. Hey, over there—I mean you! Your attention, please!

MR. BRADDOCK *has moved over by one of the windows of the house, the window into the kitchen. He speaks quickly—in a fake sotto voce—towards the window.*

MR. BRADDOCK. Are you ready in there, feature attraction?

BEN's VOICE. Could I speak to you for a second, Dad?

MR. BRADDOCK. Now I'm going to ask for a big round of applause to bring this boy out here—wait a minute—let me amend that—to bring this young man out here—because to-day he is twenty-one years old—

MR. ARNOLD *(his hands like a megaphone)*. Let's get on with the show!

MR. BRADDOCK. Just hang on a minute because I have a few words to say—

MR. ARNOLD. You always do.

They laugh; MRS. ARNOLD *makes a face at* MR. ARNOLD *as he grinningly acknowledges the response to his snappy comeback.*

BEN'S VOICE. Dad—could we just talk about this for a second?

MR. BRADDOCK *(to the window)*. I can't hold them much longer, Ben. You better get out here.

BEN'S VOICE. I'd like to discuss this.

MR. BRADDOCK *(to his audience)*. This boy—I'm sorry—this young man—is soon to continue his education as a Frank Halpingham Award Scholar—but before he does—

MR. BRADDOCK *darts back to the window.*

MR. BRADDOCK. —before he does—*(to the window)*. You're disappointing them, Ben. You're disappointing them.

BEN'S VOICE. Dad—can you listen—

MR. BRADDOCK *(meaning it)*. I'll give you ten seconds. *(back to the people)*. He is going to give us a practical demonstration of what I feel safe in saying is a pretty exciting birthday present—and it better work or I'm out over two hundred bucks—so let's hear it for—

MR. BRADDOCK *moves to the screen door and pushes it open. It slams against the wall inside.*

MR. BRADDOCK. —Benjamin Braddock!

Int. BRADDOCK *breakfast kitchen—shot down the hall—Day. At the back of the hall, inside the house, stands* BEN, *dressed in a full length skin diver's wet suit, flippers on his feet, the oxygen tank strapped to his back, the mask pushed up his forehead, the air hose dangling. He holds a spear gun in his hand.*

The people applaud.

Ext. BRADDOCK *backyard and pool area—Day—Shot from* BEN'S *POV.*

The people in the backyard. His father stands just outside the screen door.

MR. BRADDOCK. Folks—this remarkable young man is going to perform for you some spectacular and amazing feats of daring in water that is over six feet deep—

BEN'S *arms come into view and pull the mask down.*

We are now looking through the mask as we move forward down the hall. Everything is slightly distorted through the glass. BEN'S *hand comes up again with the breathing apparatus in it.*

Sound: the rhythmic pumping of air, obliterating the sound of the people around the pool who seem to be applauding and chattering noiselessly.

We move out of the door and toward the pool. MR. BRADDOCK *is running back and forth, clapping his hands and delivering his now soundless pitch.*

We move down the steps and into the shallow end of the pool. MR. BRADDOCK *is moving along the side of the pool, motioning toward us to come down to the deep end. He joins* MR. ARNOLD *at the far end of the pool. They both begin to motion us toward them.*

We get to the deep end of the pool. MR. BRADDOCK *signals us with his hand to go under. He kneels down by the edge of the pool and reaches out with his hand and pushes us under. He has a big smile.*

We surface again and pan around for a last look. The figures, through the slightly distorted glass of the mask of MRS. ARNOLD *and* MRS. BRADDOCK, *watching and smiling; the neighbors on each side of the house, looking over their fences and laughing and pointing;* MR. ARNOLD *nodding encouragement and talking;* MR. BRADDOCK *on his knees, smiling and trying to reach out far enough to push us under. We go under and sink to the bottom of the pool.*

Ext. BRADDOCK *backyard and pool area—Day. Overhead shot (helicopter POV). Looking down on the pool, on* BEN'S *black suited body at the bottom and the people standing around the pool, looking down into it.*

Pull up and up and up, until there are thirty houses below us, with their owners, swimming, playing, eating, cooking, reading, dancing, sunbathing, constructing and gardening around thirty pools. Sound of BEN'S *breathing apparatus, fading into the sound of the wind.*

Hold for a few seconds, then:

Sound of a dime dropping into a pay phone and dialing.

Dissolve to:

Int. Taft Hotel Lobby—Night—Close-up— BEN. *In a phone booth. The booth is in the entrance area of the hotel between the lobby and the driveway.* BEN *holds the receiver to his ear. Sound of phone ringing.*

MRS. ROBINSON'S VOICE. Hello.

BEN. I don't quite know how to put this—

MRS. ROBINSON'S VOICE. Benjamin?

BEN. Look—I was thinking about that time after the party—

MRS. ROBINSON'S VOICE. Where are you?

BEN. —and I was wondering if I could buy you a drink or something—

MRS. ROBINSON'S VOICE. Where are you?

BEN. Uh—The Taft Hotel.

MRS. ROBINSON'S VOICE. Did you get a room?

BEN. No. Now I know it's pretty late and if you'd rather—

MRS. ROBINSON'S VOICE. Give me an hour.

BEN. What?

MRS. ROBINSON'S VOICE. I'll be there in an hour.

Sound of her phone hanging up. BEN *hangs up slowly. He stands up in the booth, looks around, moves about uncomfortably for a few moments, removes his jacket and carrying it folded across his arm in front of him, leaves the phone booth and crosses to the doors that lead to the main lobby. As he is about to go in, the doors open and a group of very old people start coming out, filling the doorway and moving very slowly, muttering to each other and helping each other out of the door and down the steps.* BEN *holds one of the doors open for them and stands politely to one side. As they get through,* BEN *starts to move inside. At that moment, a dozen young people, dressed as though for a high school dance, push him to one side and move past him into the lobby. He moves back against the other door, holding it open and allowing them to go in first. He smiles politely and they pay no attention to him at all. He follows them into the lobby. They move toward the front desk and he moves with them. One of the boys at the front of the group leans in and says something to the clerk behind the desk.*

The clerk points across the lobby and says something to him. There are the sounds of an orchestra playing somewhere. The group of young people passes by the desk and BEN *moves in behind them. He pauses at the desk and looks apprehensively at the hundreds of pigeon holes against the wall with the room numbers painted under them and the keys dangling suggestively.*

ROOM CLERK. Can I help you, sir!

BEN. What? Oh—no—I'm just—

He points vaguely in the direction of the other young people.

ROOM CLERK. Are you here for an affair, sir?

Terror and disbelief start in BEN's *eyes. He looks helplessly at the clerk.*

BEN. What?

ROOM CLERK. The Singleman party, sir?

BEN. Oh—yes. The Singleman party.

ROOM CLERK. It's in the main ballroom.

BEN. Ahh—thank you.

BEN *backs off and turns and starts across the lobby. He puts on his jacket as he goes. He gets to the entrance to the main ballroom. He pauses at the door, looks in.*

What he sees: People dancing, talking, sitting, etc. He turns back toward the lobby. He stops.

What he sees: The room clerk across the lobby watching him.

BEN *flashes a huge smile and points in toward the ballroom as though to express his joy at finding the* SINGLEMAN *affair inside, then turns back and enters the ballroom.*

Int. Ballroom—Night. As BEN *steps inside.*

VOICE. Hello.

BEN *turns. Four people stand in a row. Official greeters, they are:* MRS. SINGLEMAN, MR. SINGLEMAN, MISS DEWITTE *and a twelve year-old boy—* JEFFREY, *dressed formally and they are smiling with great determination.*

BEN. Hello.

It is the older lady who has said hello.

MRS. SINGLEMAN. You must be one of the Porters.

She grasps BEN's *hand and shakes it.*

BEN. No—actually I'm not—

MRS. SINGLEMAN. I'd like you to know my sister, Miss DeWitte—

MISS DEWITTE, *who, from the looks of things, always has been and always will be,* MISS DEWITTE, *takes* BEN's *hand.*

MISS DEWITTE. How do you do?

BEN. How do you do, MISS DEWITTE?

MRS. SINGLEMAN—and my husband, MR. SINGLEMAN—

BEN *finds himself shaking the twelve-year-old boy's hand.*

BEN *(apologetically).* Oh—sorry—

JEFFREY SINGLEMAN. Fine, thank you.

MRS. SINGLEMAN. That's Jeffrey, of course.

BEN *switches to* MR. SINGLEMAN's *hand.*

BEN. Of course.
MR. SINGLEMAN. I didn't get your name, sir.
BEN. Benjamin Braddock, sir.

MRS. SINGLEMAN *looks at a seating list she has been holding.*

MRS. SINGLEMAN. Braddock—Braddock?
BEN, Yes, but I'm afraid—
MRS. SINGLEMAN. I'll find your table in a moment. Braddock, Not Braniff? We have a Braniff.
BEN. No—actually I'm just looking for a friend.
MRS. SINGLEMAN. I'm afraid I don't understand.
BEN *(backing off)*. I'm not with your party—I'm sorry.
MR. SINGLEMAN. Hey—I don't get it.

BEN *is backing out.*

MISS DeWITTE. I've enjoyed meeting you, Mr. Braniff.
MRS. SINGLEMAN. Angela—please!

BEN *backs out of the ballroom.*

Int. Hotel lobby—Night. BEN *crosses the lobby, passing people going in and out of the hotel. He stops at the entrance to the Veranda Room:*

Int. Veranda Room—Night. This is a large room with a bar and many tables along the windows that look out over the hotel grounds. It is quite dark and cool inside and there are no more than a dozen people seated around.

The camera stays at the door as BEN *walks into the room and crosses to the far end where he sits down at a table by the window.*

Push in toward BEN *as he sits there. Muzak is playing.*

Cut to:

Angle on BEN *sitting smoking.*

Cut to:

New angle on BEN *sitting.*

Cut to:

New angle on BEN *sitting drinking.*

Cut to:

Angle on BEN. *In the door to the lobby in the b.g. is* MRS. ROBINSON. *She pauses, looks into the room, sees* BEN *and starts toward him.* BEN *is looking out the window. He does not see her approach.*

MRS. ROBINSON. Hello, Benjamin.
BEN. Oh. Hello. Hello.

He rises quickly.

MRS. ROBINSON. May I sit down?
BEN. Of course.

He pulls out a chair, for her.

MRS. ROBINSON. Thank you.

They sit down.

MRS. ROBINSON. How are you?
BEN. Very well. Thank you.

BEN *tries to smile then looks out the window, then down at the center of the table.*

MRS. ROBINSON. May I have a drink?
BEN. A drink? Of course.

BEN *looks toward a passing waiter and raises his hand. The waiter pays no attention.* BEN *looks back at* MRS. ROBINSON *apologetically.*

BEN. He didn't see me.
MRS. ROBINSON. Waiter!

For a moment, the noise in the room seems to recede. The WAITER *stops in his tracks, turns toward them. The* WAITER *moves to their table. The noise in the room comes back. The* WAITER *looks at* MRS. ROBINSON.

MRS. ROBINSON. I will have a martini.
WAITER NO. 1. Yes, madam.

The WAITER *moves away.* BEN *watches him go.*

MRS. ROBINSON. You don't have to be so nervous, you know.
BEN. Nervous. Well, I am a bit nervous. I mean it's—it's pretty hard to be suave when you're—

He shakes his head.

MRS. ROBINSON. Did you get us a room?
BEN. What?
MRS. ROBINSON. Have you gotten us a room yet?
BEN. I haven't. No.
MRS. ROBINSON. Do you want to?
BEN. Well—I don't. I mean I could. Or we could just talk.
MRS. ROBINSON. Do you want me to get it?
BEN. You? Oh no. No. I'll get it.
MRS. ROBINSON. Do you want to get it now?
BEN. Now?
MRS. ROBINSON. Yes.
BEN. Well—I don't know.
MRS. ROBINSON. Why don't you get it.
BEN. Why don't I get it? Well—I will then. *(he stands up)*. If you'll excuse me.

BEN *walks out of the Veranda Room and into the lobby.*

Int. Hotel lobby—Night. BEN *walks to the front desk and stands there.*

ROOM CLERK. Yes sir?
BEN. A room. I'd like a room, please.
ROOM CLERK. A single room or a double room?
BEN. A single. Just for myself, please.
ROOM CLERK. Will you sign the register, please?

He pushes the card and a pen toward BEN. BEN *writes his name on the card and then stares at it for a moment, crumples it up and fills out a second card.*

ROOM CLERK. Is anything wrong, sir?
BEN. What? No. Nothing.
ROOM CLERK *(taking a key from behind the counter).* Do you have any luggage, Mister— *(looks at registration card).* Gladstone?
BEN. Luggage. Yes. Yes. I do.
ROOM CLERK. Where is it?
BEN. What?
ROOM CLERK. Where is your luggage?
BEN. Well it's in the car. It's out there in the car.
ROOM CLERK. Very good, sir. I'll have a porter bring it in.
BEN. Oh no.
ROOM CLERK. Sir?
BEN. I mean I'd—I'd rather not go to the trouble of bringing it all in. I just have a toothbrush. I can get it myself. If that's all right.
ROOM CLERK. Of course.

BEN *reaches for the key.*

ROOM CLERK. I'll have a porter show you the room.
BEN. Oh. Well actually, I'd just as soon find it myself. I just have the toothbrush to carry up and I think I can manage it myself.
ROOM CLERK. Whatever you say, sir.

He hands BEN *the key.*

BEN. Thank you.

Int. Veranda Room—Night. MRS. ROBINSON *sits, patiently and calmly. Her face betrays absolutely nothing as she stares ahead of her and sips her martini.*

WAITER NO. 1. Mrs. Robinson.

She looks up. A WAITER *is standing next to the table with a telephone.*

MRS. ROBINSON. Yes?

The WAITER *plugs the phone into the wall socket next to the table and hands her the receiver.*

MRS. ROBINSON. Thank you.

The WAITER *nods and leaves.*

MRS. ROBINSON *(into phone).* Hello.
BEN'S VOICE. Mrs. Robinson?
MRS. ROBINSON. Yes?
BEN'S VOICE. It's Benjamin.
MRS. ROBINSON. Yes?
BEN'S VOICE. Benjamin Braddock.
MRS. ROBINSON. Benjamin—where are you?
BEN'S VOICE. Can you look through the glass.

MRS. ROBINSON *turns in her chair and looks through the glass into the lobby.*

Int. Lobby—Phone Booth—Night—What she sees. BEN *is in the phone booth in the lobby no more than twenty feet away.*

BEN'S VOICE. Can you see me now?
MRS. ROBINSON. Yes, I can.

Int. Lobby phone booth—Night. Over BEN's *shoulder, we can see his face reflected in the glass door and, through it,* MRS. ROBINSON *sitting in the Veranda Room.*

Intercut phone conversation.

BEN. I got a single room.
MRS. ROBINSON. That's fine.
BEN. But there's one thing. The desk clerk seemed to be a little bit suspicious. I mean—I don't know what their policy is—but—
MRS. ROBINSON. Well—do you want to go up first?
BEN. Yes. I think that would be good.
MRS. ROBINSON. I'll be up in five minutes.
BEN. Well—goodbye then—
MRS. ROBINSON. Benjamin.
BEN. Yes?
MRS. ROBINSON. Isn't there something you want to tell me?
BEN. To tell you?
MRS. ROBINSON. Yes.
BEN. Well—I want you to know how much I appreciate this—really—
MRS. ROBINSON. The number.
BEN. What?
MRS. ROBINSON. The room number, Benjamin. I think you ought to tell me that.
BEN. Oh? You're absolutely right. Absolutely. It's 512.
MRS. ROBINSON. Thank you.
BEN. You're welcome. Well—I'll see you later, Mrs. Robinson.

He hangs up.

Int. lobby—Phone booth—Shot— BEN. *He leaves the phone booth and walks back into the main lobby.*

Int. hotel lobby—Night. As he passes the desk, on his way to the elevator, he starts to pat his breast pocket.

BEN. I've got it.

The DESK CLERK *looks up.*

BEN. I say I've got it.
CLERK. Sir?
BEN. The toothbrush. I got it all right.
CLERK. Very good, sir.
BEN. Yes. Well—goodnight.
CLERK. Goodnight, sir.

BEN *walks out of shot.*

Int. hotel corridor—Night. BEN *leaves elevator, walks down corridor to hotel room and opens door.*

Int. hotel room—Night. BEN *closes the door behind him and leans with his back against it for a few moments looking at the room. The only light is that coming in the window.*

BEN *turns on the light switch on the wall near the door. The room blazes with the light from three lamps and an overhead fixture. He turns the switch off. He crosses to the bathroom.* BEN *steps in and turns on the light.*

Int. hotel room—Night. BEN *steps out, moves to the window. We see the pool area through the window.* BEN *closes the blinds.*

There is a knock on the door. BEN *crosses to the door and opens it.*

MRS. ROBINSON. Hello, Benjamin.
BEN. Hello, Mrs. Robinson.

MRS. ROBINSON *moves to the bureau and puts her purse and gloves on it. She looks at herself in the mirror for a moment, then turns slowly, looking at the room, finally ending on* BEN'S *face. She steps toward him.*

MRS. ROBINSON. Well?

He clears his throat and then he kisses her.

BEN. Well.
MRS. ROBINSON. Benjamin.
BEN. Yes?
MRS. ROBINSON. I'll get undressed now. Is that all right?
BEN. Sure. Shall I—I mean shall I just stand here? I mean—I don't know what you want me to do.
MRS. ROBINSON. Why don't you watch?

BEN. Oh—sure. Thank you.

She takes off her jacket.

MRS. ROBINSON. Will you bring me a hanger?
BEN. What?
MRS. ROBINSON. A hanger.

BEN *opens the closet door.*

BEN. Oh—yes. Wood?
MRS. ROBINSON. What?
BEN. Wood or wire? They have both.
MRS. ROBINSON. Either one will be fine.
BEN. Okay.

He brings her a hanger. She puts her jacket on it.

MRS. ROBINSON. Will you help me with this, please?

She turns her back.

BEN. Certainly.

He undoes the zipper at her neck.

MRS. ROBINSON. Thank you.
BEN. You're welcome.

She turns and looks at him. He backs away.

MRS. ROBINSON. Would this be easier for you in the dark?
BEN. Mrs. Robinson—I can't do this.
MRS. ROBINSON. You what?
BEN. This is all terribly wrong.
MRS. ROBINSON. Benjamin—Do you find me undesirable?
BEN. Oh no, Mrs. Robinson. I think—I think you're the most attractive of all my parents' friends. I mean that. I find you desirable. But I—for God's sake, can you imagine my parents? Can you imagine what they would say if they just saw us here in this room right now?
MRS. ROBINSON. What would they say?
BEN. I have no idea, Mrs. Robinson. But for God's sake. They brought me up. They've made a good life for me. And I think they deserve better than this. I think they deserve a little better than jumping into bed with the partner's wife.
MRS. ROBINSON. Are you afraid of me?
BEN. No—but look—maybe we could do something else together. Mrs. Robinson— would you like to go to a movie?
MRS. ROBINSON. Can I ask you a personal question?
BEN. Ask me anything you want.
MRS. ROBINSON. Is this your first time?
BEN. Is this—what?

MRS. ROBINSON. It is, isn't it? It is your first time.

BEN. That's a laugh, Mrs. Robinson. That's really a laugh. Ha ha.

MRS. ROBINSON. You can admit that, can't you?

BEN. Are you kidding?

MRS. ROBINSON. It's nothing to be ashamed of—

BEN. Wait a minute!

MRS. ROBINSON. On your first time—

BEN. Who said it was my first time.

MRS. ROBINSON. That you're afraid—

BEN. Wait a minute.

MRS. ROBINSON. —of being—inadequate— I mean just because you happen to be inadequate in one way—

BEN. INADEQUATE!

Long pause.

MRS. ROBINSON. *(starting to dress).* Well—I guess I'd better—

BEN. Don't move.

He slams the bathroom door shut. The light in the room disappears.

Fade out.

Fade in.

Ext. BRADDOCK *backyard and pool area— Day. The midsummer sun beats down on the* BRADDOCK *swimming pool and on* BEN *who lies on a rubber raft in the middle of the pool.* BEN *wears dark glasses, is deeply tanned, and holds a beer can in one hand.*

Sounds: teenagers yelling and swimming in nearby pools; a radio playing rock and roll; a television set tuned to a ball game.

Dissolve to:

Closer shot— BEN *drifting.*

Dissolve to:

Closer angle on BEN *drifting.*

Dissolve to:

Close shot— BEN. *Sound of the back door closing.* BEN *opens his eyes and moves his head slightly.*

What he sees. MR. BRADDOCK *is passionately stoking a barbecue fire.* MRS. BRADDOCK *is going toward him from the house, carrying some ominously large thing wrapped in tinfoil.*

Shot— BEN. *He rolls off the raft and swims to the end of the pool. He climbs out, walks to the back door, takes his shirt from a chair and starts*

to put it on as he opens the back door and goes through.

Int. special set—Taft hotel room. BEN *has just shut the door to the bathroom behind him. He is wearing his shirt, buttoned, and no trousers.*

Pan with BEN *as he walks across the room past* MRS. ROBINSON *who is standing in front of the bureau taking off her bracelet and watch. He moves to a chair and sits.*

He picks up a cigarette from an ashtray on a table next to the chair. MRS. ROBINSON *moves in to* BEN, *kneels in front of him and starts to unbutton his shirt.*

He takes the cigarette out of his mouth.

Int. special set— BRADDOCK *den and dining room—Night shot—New angle. We now see behind* BEN *the door that leads from the* BRADDOCK *den, in which* BEN *is sitting. In the dining room,* MR. *and* MRS. BRADDOCK *are sitting, having their dinner, looking through the doorways toward* BEN. BEN *stands, crosses back to the door to the den and shuts it.*

Int. BRADDOCK *den—Night—Reverse. On* BEN's *back as he returns to the chair and sits. A television set, facing the chair, is on.* BEN *picks up a can of beer and drinks from it. An animated cartoon is playing on the television set.* BEN *watches it.*

Reverse. BEN's *face, watching. Push in to close-up of his face.*

Reverse. Close-up of television set and cartoon.

Reverse. BEN *watching.*

Reverse. Close-up test pattern.

Cut to:

Int. Taft hotel room—Night. Close-up BEN *watching. Pull back and we are in the Taft hotel room.* BEN *is sitting on the bed, leaning against the headboard, watching the television set which is on a stand facing the bed.*

Sound of the hum of the test pattern.

Pull back to a wide shot of the room, lit only by the light from the television set. MRS. ROBINSON *walks into the shot, half dressed. She passes between* BEN *and the television set and goes out of frame.* BEN *continues to stare at the set.*

Sound of a zipper being pulled up.

MRS. ROBINSON *appears again and passes the other way.*

Sound of bracelets being put on.

MRS. ROBINSON *passes back the other way again.*

Sound of clothing being put on and a purse being snapped closed. MRS. ROBINSON, *now fully dressed and carrying her purse, passes through again and, without looking at* BEN, *goes to the door of the hotel room, opens it and exits.*

Int. BEN's *room—Close-up—*BEN—*Day. Sound of door closing. Follow* BEN *as he gets up and moves to the windows of what is now his bedroom in the* BRADDOCK *house. He opens the closed blinds over the window. The sun is bright outside. His bathing suit is on the window sill. He takes the suit and puts it on. He moves to the bedroom door, opens it and goes out.*

Ext. BRADDOCK *backyard and pool area— Day. We see* MRS. BRADDOCK *in the kitchen.* BEN *comes through the back door, moves to the pool and dives in. The raft floats in the center of the pool.*

Shot—Underwater. BEN *swims toward us the length of the pool.*

Shot—At the waterline. BEN *surfaces and, in one movement, pulls himself up on the raft and—*

Cut to:

Int. Taft hotel room—Night—lands on top of MRS. ROBINSON *on the bed. He stays on top of her for a moment.*

MR. BRADDOCK'S VOICE. Ben—what are you doing?

BEN *turns toward us and looks.*

Cut to:

Ext. BRADDOCK *backyard and pool area— Day shot—POV of* BEN *on raft.* MR. BRADDOCK *standing by the side of the pool. The sun is behind him.*

BEN's VOICE. Well—I would say that I'm just drifting.

Cut to:

Shot— BEN *on raft.*

BEN—here—in the pool.
MR. BRADDOCK. Why?
BEN. Well—it's very comfortable—just to drift here.
MR. BRADDOCK. Have you thought about graduate school?
BEN. No.

MR. BRADDOCK. Would you mind telling me then—what were those four years of college for? What was the point of all that hard work?
BEN. You got *me*.
MR. BRADDOCK (*trying unsuccessfully to control himself*). Now listen, Ben. I think it's a very good thing that a young man—after he's done some very good work—should have a chance to relax and enjoy himself, and lie around, and drink beer and so on. But after a few weeks I believe that person would want to take some stock in himself and his situation and start to think about getting off his ass.

MRS. BRADDOCK *steps in beside* MR. BRADDOCK.

MRS. BRADDOCK. The Robinson's are here.

MR. ROBINSON *steps in beside the others. They blot out the sun.*

MR. ROBINSON. Hi, Ben. What are you doing with yourself these days?
BEN. Oh—not too much. Taking it easy.
MR. ROBINSON. That's what I'd do if I could. Nothing wrong with that. Hey Ben, Elaine's coming down from Berkeley soon. I want you to call her up this time.
BEN. I will.
MR. ROBINSON. Because I just think you two would hit it off real well together.

MRS. ROBINSON *steps in beside them. (A long pause).*

MRS. BRADDOCK. Say hello to Mrs Robinson, Benjamin.

Shot— BEN.

BEN. Hello, Mrs. Robinson.
MRS. ROBINSON. Hello, Benjamin.

Dissolve to:

Int. BEN's *bathroom—Night.* BEN, *halfway dressed to go out, in slacks, shirt and tie, sits in a chair. The door opens and* MRS. BRADDOCK *enters.*

MRS. BRADDOCK. Can I talk to you a minute, son?
BEN. Sure.
MRS. BRADDOCK. Benjamin? I'm going to ask you something but you don't have to tell me if you don't want.
BEN. What?
MRS. BRADDOCK. Well I'm going to ask you what you do when you go off at night.
BEN. When I go off?
MRS. BRADDOCK. You don't have to tell me if you don't want.
BEN. No, I do. I want to tell you.

There is a pause.

BEN. I drive around.

MRS. BRADDOCK. What else?

BEN. Nothing else.

MRS. BRADDOCK. Well you don't drive around from midnight until noon the next day, Benjamin.

BEN. Oh, no.

MRS. BRADDOCK. Then what do you do? Do you meet someone?

BEN. Meet someone?

She nods.

BEN. Why did you say that?

MRS. BRADDOCK. Well this is your business, Benjamin (she starts toward the door). I don't want to play games with you.

BEN. No wait. Wait.

She stops.

BEN. I don't meet anyone, mother, but why did you say that?

MRS. BRADDOCK. Benjamin, I'm not going to pry into your affairs, but I'd rather you didn't say anything at all than be dishonest. Goodnight, son.

BEN. Well, wait.

She looks at him.

BEN. You think I'm being dishonest?

She nods.

BEN. Well why do you—why do you think that?

MRS. BRADDOCK. Because I know you don't drive around for twelve hours.

BEN. Oh. Well, I don't. Shall I tell you what I do?

MRS. BRADDOCK. Not if you don't want to.

BEN. I do.

MRS. BRADDOCK. But I don't want you to make up something.

BEN. I'm not. But I'm— I'm not very proud of what I do. I usually get kind of drunk. I usually drive over to Los Angeles and go to some bars and get kind of drunk. Then I take a hotel room. So I won't have to drive home on the freeway. I mean it kind of scares me to drive home after—

MRS. BRADDOCK. Goodnight, Benjamin.

BEN. You believe me, don't you?

MRS. BRADDOCK. No.

BEN. You don't?

She shakes her head.

BEN. But I want you to. Please. Please will you believe me.

Shot— MRS. BRADDOCK.

MRS. BRADDOCK *(she exits)*. Goodnight.

BEN'S VOICE. Wait a minute.

Cut to:

Int. Taft hotel room—Night—Shot— BEN. MRS. ROBINSON's *hands are undoing his necktie.* BEN *is dressed as in previous scene, plus a jacket.*

BEN. Wait a minute *(he pushes her hand away)*. Sit down a minute.

MRS. ROBINSON *looks at him and raises her eyebrows.*

BEN. Will you please sit down a minute.

MRS. ROBINSON *walks to the bed and sits. She reaches down to take off a shoe.*

BEN. Will you leave that shoe on for a minute. Please.

She straightens up.

BEN. Now—do you think we could say a few words to each other first this time?

MRS. ROBINSON. If you want.

BEN. Good. I mean are we dead or something?

MRS. ROBINSON. Well I just don't think we have much to say to each other.

BEN. All we ever do is come up here and throw off the clothes and leap into bed together.

MRS. ROBINSON. Are you tired of it?

BEN. I'm not. No. But do you think we could liven it up with a few words now and then?

MRS. ROBINSON. What do you want to talk about?

BEN. Anything. Anything at all.

MRS. ROBINSON. Do you want to tell me about some of your college experiences?

BEN. Oh my God.

MRS. ROBINSON. Well?

BEN. Mrs. Robinson If that's the best we can do let's just get the god-damn clothes off and—

She reaches for her shoe.

BEN. Leave it on! Now we are going to do this thing. We are going to have a conversation. Think of another topic.

MRS. ROBINSON. How about art.

BEN. Art. That's a good subject. You start it off.

MRS. ROBINSON. You start it off. I don't know anything about it.

BEN. Oh.

MRS. ROBINSON. Don't you?

BEN. Yes I do. I know quite a bit about it.

MRS. ROBINSON. Go ahead then.

BEN. Art. Well what do you want to know about it.

She shrugs.

BEN. Are you interested more in modern art or more in classical art.

MRS. ROBINSON. Neither.

BEN. You're not interested in art?

MRS. ROBINSON. No.

BEN. Then why do you want to talk about it?

MRS. ROBINSON. I don't.

BEN *nods and looks at the rug.*

MRS. ROBINSON. Can I take off my clothes now?

BEN. No. Think of another topic. Tell me what you did today.

MRS. ROBINSON. Do you really want me to?

BEN. Yes I do.

MRS. ROBINSON. I got up.

BEN *starts shaking his head.*

MRS. ROBINSON. Do you want to hear it or not?

BEN. Yes. But you might try and spice it up with a little originality.

MRS. ROBINSON. I got up. I ate breakfast and went shopping. During the afternoon I read a novel.

BEN. What one.

MRS. ROBINSON. What?

BEN. What novel did you read.

MRS. ROBINSON. I don't remember.

BEN *nods.*

MRS. ROBINSON. Then I fixed supper for my husband and waited until—

BEN. There!

MRS. ROBINSON. What?

BEN. Your husband! Mrs. Robinson! There's something we could have a conversation about.

MRS. ROBINSON. Him?

BEN. I mean everything. I don't know anything about how you—how you work this. I don't know how you get out of the house at night. I don't know the risk involved.

MRS. ROBINSON. There isn't any.

BEN. There's no risk?

She shakes her head.

BEN. How do you get out of the house?

MRS. ROBINSON. I walk out.

BEN. You walk right out the door.

She nods.

BEN. What do you say to him?

MRS. ROBINSON. He's asleep.

BEN. Always?

MRS. ROBINSON. Benjamin, this isn't a very interesting topic.

BEN. Please. Now tell me. How do you know he won't wake up sometime and follow you.

MRS. ROBINSON. Because he takes sleeping pills. He takes three sleeping pills every night at ten o'clock.

BEN. But what about the noise from the car. What if—

MRS. ROBINSON. The driveway's on my side of the house.

BEN *(smiling).* We're talking.

MRS. ROBINSON. What?

BEN. We're talking, Mrs. Robinson. We're talking.

MRS. ROBINSON. Calm down, Benjamin.

BEN. Now let's keep going here.

MRS. ROBINSON. Can I undress and talk at the same time?

BEN. Right.

MRS. ROBINSON. Thank you.

BEN. Now. You say the driveway's on your side of the house. So I guess you don't sleep in the same room.

MRS. ROBINSON. We don't.

BEN. So you don't—I mean I don't like to seem like I'm prying but I guess you don't sleep together or anything.

MRS. ROBINSON. No we don't.

BEN. Well how long has this been going on.

MRS. ROBINSON *(looking at the ceiling for a moment).* About five years.

BEN. Oh no. Are you kidding me?

MRS. ROBINSON. No. I'm not.

BEN. You have not slept with your husband for five years?

MRS. ROBINSON. Now and then. He gets drunk a few times a year.

BEN. How many times a year.

MRS. ROBINSON. On New Year's Eve. Sometimes on his birthday.

BEN. Man, is this interesting.

MRS. ROBINSON. Is it?

BEN. So you don't love him. You wouldn't say you—

MRS. ROBINSON. We've talked enough, Benjamin.

BEN. Wait a minute. So you wouldn't say you loved him.

MRS. ROBINSON. Not exactly.

BEN. But you don't hate him.

MRS. ROBINSON. No, Benjamin. I don't hate him. Unhook my blouse.

BEN *(unhooking her blouse).* Well how do you feel about him, then?

MRS. ROBINSON. I don't.

She nods and takes off her blouse.

BEN. Well you loved him once, I assume. When you first knew him.

MRS. ROBINSON. No.

BEN. What?

MRS. ROBINSON. I never did, Benjamin. Now let's—

BEN. Well, wait a minute. You married him.

She nods.

BEN. Why did you do that?

MRS. ROBINSON (*taking off her stockings*). See if you can guess.

BEN. Well I can't.

MRS. ROBINSON. Think real hard, Benjamin.

BEN. I can't see why you did, unless...you didn't *have* to marry him or anything, did you?

MRS. ROBINSON. Don't tell Elaine.

BEN. Oh no. You had to marry him because you got pregnant?

MRS. ROBINSON. Are you shocked?

BEN. Well I never thought of you and Mr. Robinson as the kind of people who...

MRS. ROBINSON. All right. Now let's get to bed.

BEN. Wait a minute. Wait a minute. So how did it happen?

MRS. ROBINSON. What?

BEN. I mean do you feel like telling me what were the circumstances?

MRS. ROBINSON. Not particularly.

BEN. Was he a law student at the time?

She nods.

BEN. And you were a student also.

MRS. ROBINSON. Yes.

BEN. At college.

MRS. ROBINSON. Yes.

BEN. What was your major?

MRS. ROBINSON. Why are you asking me all this?

BEN. Because I'm interested, Mrs. Robinson. Now what was your major subject at college?

MRS. ROBINSON. Art.

BEN. Art?

She nods.

BEN. But I thought you—I guess you kind of lost interest in it over the years then.

MRS. ROBINSON. Kind of.

BEN. Well how did it happen?

MRS. ROBINSON. What?

BEN. You and Mr. Robinson.

MRS. ROBINSON. How do you think.

BEN. I mean did he take you up to his room with him? Did you go to a hotel?

MRS. ROBINSON. Benjamin, what does it possibly matter?

BEN. I'm curious.

MRS. ROBINSON. We'd go to his car.

BEN. Oh no. In the car you did it?

MRS. ROBINSON. I don't think we were the first.

BEN *thinks for a moment.*

BEN. What kind of car was it?

MRS. ROBINSON. What?

BEN. Do you remember the make of the car?

MRS. ROBINSON. Oh my God.

BEN. Really. I want to know.

MRS. ROBINSON. It was a Ford, Benjamin.

BEN (*jumping up*). A Ford! A Ford! God-damnit, a Ford! That's great!

MRS. ROBINSON. That's enough.

BEN. So old Elaine Robinson got started in a Ford.

There is a pause.

MRS. ROBINSON. Don't talk about Elaine.

BEN. Don't talk about Elaine?

MRS. ROBINSON. No.

BEN. Why not?

MRS. ROBINSON. Because I don't want you to.

She walks to the bed.

BEN. Well why don't you?

She pulls the bedspread down. BEN *begins to remove his jacket.*

BEN. I wish you'd tell me.

MRS. ROBINSON. There's nothing to tell.

BEN. Well why is she a big taboo subject all of a sudden?

MRS. ROBINSON *uncovers one of the pillows.*

BEN. Well—I guess I'll have to ask her out on a date and find out what's—

MRS. ROBINSON. Benjamin, don't you ever take that girl out.

BEN *looks at her.*

MRS. ROBINSON. Do you understand that?

BEN. Well look. I have no intention of taking her out.

MRS. ROBINSON. Good.

BEN. I was just kidding around.

MRS. ROBINSON. Good.

BEN. But why shouldn't I?

MRS. ROBINSON. I have my reasons.

BEN. Then let's hear them.

MRS. ROBINSON. No.

BEN. Let's hear your reasons, Mrs. Robinson. Because I think I know what they are.

She pulls the covers down.

BEN. I'm not good enough for her to associate with, am I? I'm not good enough to even talk about her, am I?

MRS. ROBINSON. Let's drop it.

BEN. We're not dropping it. Now that's the reason, isn't it? I'm a dirty degenerate, aren't I? I'm not fit to—

MRS. ROBINSON. Benjamin?

BEN. I'm good enough for you but I'm too slimy to associate with your daughter. That's it, isn't it? ISN'T IT?

MRS. ROBINSON. Yes.

BEN. You go to hell. You go straight to hell, Mrs. Robinson. Do you think I'm proud of myself? Do you think I'm proud of this?

MRS. ROBINSON. I wouldn't know.

BEN. Well, I am not.

MRS. ROBINSON. You're not.

BEN. No sir. I am not proud that I spend my time with a broken-down alcoholic!

MRS. ROBINSON. I see.

BEN. And if you think I come here for any reason besides pure boredom, then you're all wrong.

She nods.

BEN. Because—Mrs. Robinson this is the sickest, most perverted thing that ever happened to me. And you do what you want but I'm getting the hell out.

MRS. ROBINSON. Are you?

BEN. You're goddamn right I am.

He starts putting on his shirt. She sits on the edge of the bed and watches him.

MRS. ROBINSON. That's how you feel about me.

He nods.

MRS. ROBINSON. That I'm a sick and disgusting person.

BEN. Now don't start this.

MRS. ROBINSON. What?

BEN. Don't start acting hurt.

MRS. ROBINSON. Don't you expect me to be a little hurt?

BEN. Mrs. Robinson, you lie there and tell me I'm not good enough for your daughter.

MRS. ROBINSON. Did I say that?

BEN. In so many words.

She shakes her head.

MRS. ROBINSON. Benjamin, I want to apologize to you if that's the impression you got.

BEN. Well two minutes ago you told me I wasn't good enough for your daughter. Now you say you're sorry I got that impression.

MRS. ROBINSON. I didn't mean it. I don't think you'd be right for each other. But I would never say you weren't as good a person as she is.

BEN. You wouldn't.

MRS. ROBINSON. Of course I wouldn't.

MRS. ROBINSON *walks to the closet.*

BEN. What are you doing?

MRS. ROBINSON. Well it's pretty obvious you don't want me around any more.

BEN. Well look—I was kind of upset there. I'm sorry I said those things.

MRS. ROBINSON. If that's how you feel—

BEN. But it's not.

MRS. ROBINSON *(smiling at him).* That's all right. I think I can understand why I'm disgusting to you.

BEN. Oh no. Look—I like you. I wouldn't keep coming here if I didn't like you.

MRS. ROBINSON. But if it's sickening for you—

BEN. It's not! I enjoy it! I look forward to it. It's the one thing I have to look forward to.

MRS. ROBINSON. You don't have to say that.

BEN. Well I wouldn't. I would never say it if it wasn't true.

MRS. ROBINSON. May I stay then?

BEN. Yes. Please. I want you to.

MRS. ROBINSON. Thank you.

BEN. Well don't thank me, because I want you to.

There is a long pause.

MRS. ROBINSON. But you won't ever take out Elaine, will you? I want you to promise me that.

There is another pause.

BEN. Look. Why the hell did you bring this up. It never occurred to me to take her out.

MRS. ROBINSON. Then give me your word you won't.

BEN. This is absurd.

MRS. ROBINSON. Promise me, Benjamin.

BEN. All right, for Christ's sake. I promise I will never take out Elaine Robinson.

MRS. ROBINSON. Thank you *(pause).* Benjamin—

BEN. Let's not talk about it. Let's not talk at all.

At opposite sides of the room, without looking at each other, they begin to take off their clothes.

Fade out.

Fade in.

Int. BRADDOCK *kitchen—Day.* BEN *sits at the table, eating his breakfast and looking at the back of a cereal box.* MR. *and* MRS. BRADDOCK *are there.*

MR. BRADDOCK. Elaine's back from school. I think it might be a nice gesture if you asked her out.

BENJAMIN *looks at his father for a moment, then continues eating and reading.*

Cut to:

Int. BEN's *room—Day.* BEN *is lying on his bed.* MRS. BRADDOCK *stands in the doorway.*

MRS. BRADDOCK. Don't you think that she's a terribly attractive girl sweetheart? Because I think she's one of the prettiest girls I've ever seen.

BEN *gives a small whimper.*

Cut to:

Ext. BRADDOCK *backyard and pool area— Day.* BEN *is lying face down on his raft in the middle of the* BRADDOCK *pool. The sun shines down. His diving mask is on over his eyes. His face is in the water, looking down at the bottom of the pool.* MR *and* MRS. BRADDOCK, *in their bathing suits, are in the pool, paddling around* BEN. *During the entire conversation they continue to swim around and around the raft, trying to talk and keep their heads above the surface.*

MR. BRADDOCK. It's pretty embarrassing. I really don't know what to tell Mr. Robinson. It's awkward and strained for me every time he suggests that you call up Elaine.
BEN. Next time he suggests it, I'll tell him I have no intention of ever calling her up in my life.
MR. BRADDOCK. I guess she's not good enough for you, is that it?
BEN. Look—Elaine Robinson and I do not get along.
MR. BRADDOCK. How do you know? You haven't seen her since high school. I guess your evenings, whatever you do with them, are just too valuable.
BEN. That has nothing to do with it—
MR. BRADDOCK. I guess I'll just tell Mr. Robinson that you're just too busy every evening—doing God knows what—
MRS. BRADDOCK. Don't go on like this. Now if Benjamin absolutely refuses to take her out—
BEN. I do.
MRS. BRADDOCK. —then I'll simply invite all the Robinson's over for dinner on Thursday.

Shot— BEN. *He slides off the raft and goes underwater.*

Shot— BEN *underwater. His hair streaming up, his eyes open.*

Cut to:

Int. special set BRADDOCK *dining room— Night. The dining room is one tenth its normal size. At a table for two are seated, jammed in against each other, the three* ROBINSONS *and the three* BRADDOCKS. ELAINE's *back is to us.* BEN *is at the other end of the table, facing us. The* ROBINSONS *and the* BRADDOCKS *sit along the sides.* MRS. ROBINSON *is next to* BEN, *everyone is eating, looking down at their places. After a few moments* BEN *throws his head back and starts to scream. As he continues to scream, everyone looks at him except* MRS. ROBINSON *who continues to eat calmly without looking up.*

Cut to:

Ext. BRADDOCK *backyard and pool area— Day.* BEN *surfaces and pulls himself up on the side of the pool.*

BEN. I'll go call Elaine now.

MR. *and* MRS. BRADDOCK *cling exhausted to the raft and try to smile at each other.*

Sound. Ding dong of the ROBINSON *door chimes.*

Cut to:

Ext. and int. ROBINSON *front door, hall and sunroom—Night. The door opens.* MR. ROBINSON *stands there with a huge smile.*

MR. ROBINSON. Well, Braddock—it's about time you got around to this. Come on in. I'm afraid the young lady isn't quite ready yet—

MR. ROBINSON *turns toward the sunroom.* MRS. ROBINSON *is sitting there.*

BEN. Hello.
MR. ROBINSON. What would you say to a short one? Bourbon still your drink?
BEN. Yes.

MR. ROBINSON *hands him drink.*

MR. ROBINSON. I'll see if she's ready.

MR. ROBINSON *exits.*

Shot— BEN *and* MRS. ROBINSON. *Note: Following dialogue played simultaneously.*

BEN. Hey listen—this was not my idea. It was my father's idea.
MRS. ROBINSON. Benjamin—I thought I made myself perfectly clear about this.
BEN *(whispering urgently).* Look, we'll go out to dinner and have a drink and I'll bring her back. Because it was either that or a din-

ner party for the two families. And I'm afraid I couldn't quite handle that, if you don't mind. I have no intention of ever taking your precious daughter out again in her life. So don't get upset about it.

MRS. ROBINSON. But I am. I'm extremely upset about it, Benjamin.

MR. ROBINSON'S VOICE (*from hall*). Hey—there she is. Miss America—that's who it is. It's definitely Miss America.

ELAINE'S VOICE. Daddy—can you fix this? The clasp is broken I think.

MR. ROBINSON'S VOICE. I'll do it—I'll do it.

ELAINE'S VOICE. Is Ben here?

MR. ROBINSON'S VOICE. He's in the lanai having a chat with your mother.

MR. ROBINSON *and* ELAINE *enter.*

ELAINE. Hello.
BEN. Hello.

Close-up— MRS. ROBINSON.

MR. ROBINSON'S VOICE. Well—I want you to keep your wits about you tonight. You never know what tricks Ben picked up back there in the East.

Lap dissolve to:

Ext. Freeway—Night. Shot— BEN *and* ELAINE *in* BEN's *car. From the back.* BEN *leans forward slightly, pushing the car recklessly in and out of the traffic.* BEN *is wearing dark glasses.*

ELAINE. You're living at home now. Is that right?

BEN. Yes.

ELAINE. Do you know what you're going to do?

BEN. No.

ELAINE. Are you going to graduate school?

BEN. No.

He leans on the horn. The car directly ahead of him does not move to the right. BEN *jerks his car over to the right, swerves around the car ahead, jamming his horn down, and swerves back into the outside lane, giving the driver of the other car an angry look as he passes him.* ELAINE *holds on to the dashboard to keep her balance.*

ELAINE. Do you always drive like this?
BEN. Yes.

Cut to:

Int. Restaurant—Night. A drab, almost deserted room with formally dressed WAITERS. BEN *and* ELAINE *are seated at a table.*

BEN. Do you want some dinner?

ELAINE. I'd love some.

A WAITER *moves forward toward them.*

BEN. Bring a menu.
WAITER #2. Dinner for two, sir?
BEN. No. Just for her.

The WAITER *moves away.*

ELAINE. Aren't you eating?
BEN. No.
ELAINE. Why not?
BEN. If it's all right with you, I'm not hungry.

The WAITER *returns with a menu.*

ELAINE. I've changed my mind. Thank you.

Cut to:

Ext. Sunset Strip—Night—Shots. BEN *and* ELAINE *walking on the strip.*

Ext. Strip joint—Night. BEN *pushes through the people crowded in around the entrance. Without turning around, he waits for* ELAINE *who has difficulty following him. As she gets to him, he starts forward again. He starts up the stairs.* ELAINE *is just behind him.*

Cut to:

Int. strip joint—Night. Seedy, ugly, three quarters filled. A tuxedoed hood leads them through the tables to a table directly under the stage on which a stripper is in the process of removing her dress. There is one chair facing the stage, the other with its back to and up against the stage. BEN *sits down in the chair facing the stage.* ELAINE *stands for a moment, unsure.*

BEN. Sit down.

ELAINE *sits in the chair with her back to the stage. She folds her hands on the table and looks down at them.* BEN *takes a pair of dark glasses out of his pocket and puts them on. The two chairs are slightly angled toward each other so that* BEN *can look up at the stage without looking directly at* ELAINE.

BEN. Why don't you watch the show?

The stripper is reflected in BEN's *glasses.*

ELAINE. Benjamin—do you dislike me for some reason?
BEN. No—why should I?
ELAINE. I don't know.

Shot—Across BEN—*the stripper. She is down to a tasseled bra and g-string. She is twirling the tassels.*

BEN. You're missing a great effect here.

ELAINE *turns around, looks at the stripper and turns back.*

BEN. How do you like that?

ELAINE *doesn't answer.*

BEN. Could you do it?
ELAINE. No.

The stripper sees ELAINE *look. The stripper smiles toward* BEN *and walks toward his table, twirling the tassels as she walks.* BEN *smiles as he watches her approaching.*

The stripper moves directly behind ELAINE's *chair. The spotlight from the back of the house falls onto* ELAINE's *face. As it does,* ELAINE *puts her hand up to shield her eyes.*

The stripper slides a finger into her mouth, wets it and holds it up in the air. The music stops and a drum roll starts. The stripper bends over ELAINE's *head and begins swinging the tassels so that they rotate in front of* ELAINE's *face.*

Shot— BEN. *He leans forward slightly to watch the action. The swinging tassels are reflected in his glasses.*

The drum roll gets louder and faster. The tassels swing more frantically.

Shot— ELAINE. *She pulls her hand down from in front of her eyes.*

Shot— BEN. *With* ELAINE's *face reflected in his glasses.*

Shot— ELAINE. *Through* BEN's *glasses.* ELAINE's *face seen darkly but fully for the first time. The tassels swing in front of it. Tears start out of her eyes.*

Shot— BEN. *He reaches up to remove the glasses.*

Shot— ELAINE. *As the glasses come off and her face is seen in the harsh spill from the spotlight. The tears are running down her face. Only her eyes are crying as she looks straight at* BEN.

Shot— BEN. *With his glasses off, he watches her. He reaches forward and puts his hand in the way of the tassels.*

STRIPPER. Hey!

Some of the customers start to boo. BEN *rises, takes* ELAINE's *arm and leads her toward the exit.*

Cut to:

Ext. strip joint—Night. The entrance to the strip joint. ELAINE *runs to the bottom of the steps. The Sunset Strip sidewalk outside is crowded with people moving back and forth.* BEN *follows her. She pushes through the crowd on the sidewalk.* BEN *catches her and holds her arm.*

BEN. Elaine—I'm sorry.

ELAINE *leans against the side of the building and pulls her arm away.*

ELAINE. Will you take me home now?
BEN. I'm sorry I took you in there.
ELAINE. I think I'd better go home now please.
BEN. But, Elaine—
ELAINE. Where is the car?
BEN. I just want to tell you something.

BEN, *facing her, keeps moving from side to side, trying to get her to look at him. She keeps looking away.*

ELAINE. I want to go home.
BEN. But could I just tell you this one thing?
ELAINE. What?
BEN. This whole idea—this date and everything. It was my parents' idea. They forced me into it.
ELAINE. Oh—that's very nice of you to tell me.
BEN. No. What I mean is—that's why I've been acting this way. I'm not like this. I hate myself like this.

She starts to cry. People on the sidewalk are looking at them. She turns away from them. BEN *moves away from them.* BEN *moves around in front of her.*

BEN. Listen—could you stop crying, please?
ELAINE. No, I couldn't.
BEN. But could you try?
ELAINE. No.

She brings both hands up to her face. BEN *looks at her for a few moments in agony. Then, very determined, he takes her wrists in his hands and pulls them away from her face. She looks up startled. She starts to give a little cry but before she can he is kissing her. She closes her eyes.*

He brings his fists, containing her hands, up to the side of her face. He opens his hands against her face, freeing her hands. Her hands move slowly to his wrists and hang on. After a while she pulls away, turning her head slightly to one side.

BEN. Elaine—

He starts to pull her head back.

ELAINE. Not here. Not here.

Dissolve to:

Ext. Drive in restaurant—Night. BEN *and* ELAINE *are sitting in the car in a drive-in restaurant. There are trays hooked into windows alongside of both of them. They are eating and drinking furiously.*

BEN. I've had this feeling—ever since I've graduated—this—kind of compulsion that I have to be rude all the time. Do you know what I mean?

ELAINE. Yes, I do.

He looks at her.

BEN. It's like I've been playing some kind of—game—but the rules don't make any sense to me—

She is watching him carefully.

BEN—they're being made up by all the wrong people—no—I mean no one makes them up, they seem to have made themselves up.

A car with a couple of teenagers has driven up in the slot on their right. Its radio is tuned into a rock and roll station and it is playing loudly. BEN *leans across* ELAINE *and speaks through the window to the kid behind the wheel.*

BEN. Say—I wonder if I could request you to turn that down a little?

The kid turns the radio up. BEN *and* ELAINE *roll their windows up.*

Series of shots. From outside of car. BEN *is talking with great animation—* ELAINE *is watching him. They are both eating as* BEN *talks, telling* ELAINE *a story. Their windows are rolled up.*

Sounds: Cars gunning their engines; horns honking; radios playing; waitresses yelling orders; customers yelling at waitresses; kids laughing and talking from car to car; motorcycles driving in and out; traffic.

Cut to:

Ext. ROBINSON *house—Night. The car coasts silently to a stop in front of the* ROBINSON *house. The radio plays quietly.* BEN *turns it off. They sit there for a long time without saying anything,* BEN's *hand touching her shoulder. It is very quiet.*

ELAINE. Well—maybe I'd better go in.

He nods. They continue to sit there for another long moment.

ELAINE. Would you like to come in? I could make some coffee.

BEN. No, I mean—I wouldn't want to wake anyone up.

ELAINE. We won't. Let's go inside.

BEN. Wait a minute.

ELAINE. Is anything wrong?

BEN. No—I was just thinking—look—it's still early—we could do something—go somewhere else.

ELAINE. All right.

He starts the car immediately and drives away from the house.

Int. BEN's *car—Night.* BEN *is driving.*

ELAINE. Where are we going?

BEN. I'm trying to think of where there's a place to have a drink around here.

ELAINE. Isn't there one in the Taft Hotel?

There is a squeal of tires as BEN *almost drives off the road.*

ELAINE. What *is* the matter?

BEN. Nothing. I'm just wondering if they have a bar or not. I mean let's go see. Let's go see if they do or not.

Cut to:

Int. Taft Hotel lobby—Night. BEN *and* ELAINE *enter the lobby and stand just inside the door. They start in a few steps.*

BEN. Listen, Elaine—it seems to me that there isn't a bar in here. I mean—as far as I know.

ELAINE. Of course there is. Look—The Veranda Room—right there.

One of the car parkers passes them on his way out.

CAR PARKER. Good evening.

Camera begins to pull up and away. A bellboy passes them.

BELLBOY. Hello, how are you, sir?

The room clerk smiles at them.

ROOM CLERK. Good evening, Mr. Gladstone.

BEN *and* ELAINE *stop a few feet into the center of the lobby. The camera pulls back to a high overhead shot revealing many people moving back and forth in the lobby, passing* BEN *and* ELAINE.

VOICE #1. Hello again.

VOICE #2. Hi, Mr. Gladstone. How are you this evening?

ELAINE. Benjamin—

BEN. Let's get out of here, Elaine. Let's go somewhere else.

ELAINE. Benjamin—do they know you?

BEN. Of course not.

VOICE #3. Good evening, sir.

VOICE #4. Mr. Gladstone—how are you?

He moves her toward the door.

BEN. Come on, Elaine. We're leaving.

Cut to:

Ext. Taft Hotel. BEN *brings* ELAINE *through the door to the porch.*

ELAINE. Ben—what's happening? Who is Mr. Gladstone?

BEN. I don't know. They must think I look like this guy Gladstone.

Pan with them as they start down the steps. Coming up the steps toward them is MISS DEWITTE, *on the arm of another elderly lady.*

MISS DEWITTE. Hello, Mr. Braniff.

Sound: Car starting noisily.

Cut to:

Ext. Taft Hotel driveway—Night. BEN *and* ELAINE *in his car. He takes his hand off the ignition, jams on the accelerator and drives the car speedily for twenty-one feet and jams on the brakes. He turns off the ignition and the lights. He puts his head down on the steering wheel. He lifts his head.*

BEN. Elaine—I like you. I like you so much. Do you believe that?

She nods.

BEN. Do you?

ELAINE. Yes.

BEN. You're the first—you're the first thing for so long that I've liked. The first person I could stand to be with.

She takes his hand.

BEN. I mean my whole life is such a waste. It's just nothing. I'm sorry. I'll take you home now.

He turns the key in the ignition and starts the car.

ELAINE. Benjamin—are you having an affair with someone?

He freezes with his hand still on the key.

ELAINE. I'm sorry.

He turns off the engine.

ELAINE. I'm sorry. That is not my business.

BEN. It just happened. It was just this thing that happened along with everything else. Can you understand that?

She nods.

ELAINE. Was she married or something?

BEN. Yes.

ELAINE. With a family?

BEN. Yes. She had a husband and a son.

ELAINE. Did they ever find out?

BEN. No.

ELAINE. And it's all over now.

BEN. Yes.

ELAINE. I'm glad.

He starts the car and drives out.

Ext. ROBINSON *house—Night—Shot—* BEN *and* ELAINE *at front door.*

BEN. Can we do something tomorrow?

ELAINE. All right.

BEN. During the day? We'll go for a drive or something.

ELAINE. Okay.

BEN. You sure you really want to?

ELAINE. Yes.

BEN. Because I wouldn't want you to do it unless you really wanted to!

ELAINE. I do.

BEN. You do?

ELAINE. Benjamin—I really do.

Dissolve to:

Ext. street no. 1—near ROBINSON *house—Day shot—Int.* BEN's *car—* BEN *driving. It is raining. On the seat beside* BEN *is a package. From the way it is wrapped, we can tell it is a gift.* BEN's *right hand is on it as he drives. The radio is playing. Past* BEN *and through the windshield as the* ROBINSON *house comes closer and closer. The front door of the* ROBINSON *house opens and* MRS. ROBINSON *comes out, dressed in a housecoat, and, in four or five fast steps, reaches the car, opens the door on the passengers' side and climbs in.* BEN *moves the package over onto his lap.*

MRS. ROBINSON. Drive down the block.

BEN. Mrs. Robinson—I have a date with Elaine. We're going for a drive.

MRS. ROBINSON (*looking at him for the first time*). Do *exactly* what I say.

BEN *starts the car forward down the driveway.*

Another angle— BEN *and* MRS. ROBINSON. *As they drive.*

BEN. Now it seems to me—

MRS. ROBINSON. Listen to me very carefully, Benjamin. You are not to see Elaine again. *Ever.* Those are my orders. Is that clear?

BEN *stops the car in front of a house halfway down the block.*

BEN. Mrs. Robinson—

MRS. ROBINSON. I can make things quite unpleasant.

BEN. How?

MRS. ROBINSON. In order to keep Elaine away from you—I am prepared to tell her everything.

BEN. I don't believe you.

MRS. ROBINSON. Then you'd better start believing me.

BEN. Mrs. Robinson, don't wreck it. I'm asking you please not to wreck it.

MRS. ROBINSON. Go home now.

BEN. I just don't believe you would do that.

MRS. ROBINSON *looks at him for a moment.*

MRS. ROBINSON. Try me.

There is a pause while BEN *looks at her expression. Then he grabs the keys out of the ignition, opens the door on his side and jumps out of the car, carrying the package.*

Track with BEN *as he runs up the street and up the driveway toward the* ROBINSON *house.* BEN *gets to the front door.*

BEN *(as he goes through the door).* Elaine!

Int. ROBINSON *halls, stairs, door to* ELAINE'S *room—Day.* BEN *runs in.*

BEN. Elaine?

ELAINE'S VOICE. Benjamin?

BEN. I'm coming up.

ELAINE'S VOICE. I'm not dressed yet.

BEN *runs up the stairs. He still carries the package.* BEN *gets to the top just as Elaine comes out of the door to her bedroom. She is wearing a skirt and slip and carrying one shoe.*

ELAINE. Benjamin—I said I wasn't dressed—

BEN *pushes her back into her room.*

Int. ELAINE'S *room—Day.*

ELAINE. What's the matter?

BEN. You've got to go over the back fence and I'll meet you on the corner.

ELAINE. Benjamin—what's happening?

BEN. Hurry up. Put your shoes on.

BEN *turns and looks.*

Shot—Over BEN'S *shoulder.* MRS. ROBINSON *is just entering the house.*

BEN. *No.*

He turns around.

New angle. ELAINE *is standing in the doorway watching him. She still holds the shoe in her hand.*

BEN. Why aren't you ready?

ELAINE. Because I want to know what's happening.

Sound of MRS. ROBINSON'S *footsteps in the hall below.*

BEN. There isn't time!

Int. ELAINE'S *room—Day.* BEN *pulls* ELAINE *around behind the open door. They stand in the angle formed by the door and the wall as though they are hiding from someone.* MRS. ROBINSON'S *footsteps can be heard coming up the stairs.*

BEN. Elaine—I have to tell you something.

He holds her against the wall in the corner.

ELAINE. What is it?

BEN. That woman—

ELAINE. What?

BEN. That woman. The older woman.

ELAINE. You mean the one who—

BEN. The married woman—it wasn't just *some* woman—

MRS. ROBINSON'S *footsteps can be heard coming down the hall.*

ELAINE. What are you telling me?

The footsteps stop.

Angle—Close on ELAINE. *Back in the corner.* MRS. ROBINSON'S *face appears in the crack in the door at* ELAINE'S *shoulder.* ELAINE *looks from* BEN'S *face to the crack through which she can see her mother's eyes staring.*

ELAINE. Benjamin, will you please just tell me what this is all about.

She looks back at BEN, *then back at her mother's face again.* MRS. ROBINSON'S *eyes watch her through the crack in the door.* ELAINE *looks away.*

ELAINE. Oh—no.

BEN *backs up.*

BEN. Elaine.

ELAINE. Oh my God—

Moving along the wall as though to keep as far from BEN *as possible,* ELAINE *moves away from the door.*

BEN. Please.

ELAINE *walks a few steps toward the other side of the room then turns back toward* BEN. *The tears are starting out of her eyes.*

BEN. No—don't cry—
ELAINE. GET OUT!
BEN. Don't cry. *(holds the package out to her.)*
ELAINE. Get out of here.

She moves toward him as though to hit him. He backs into the hall. ELAINE *slams the door shut.*

ELAINE *(holding the door).* Get out!

Int. ROBINSON *hall—Day.* MRS. ROBINSON *stands at the end of it, looking at* BEN.

MRS. ROBINSON *(calmly).* Goodbye, Benjamin.

Shot— BENJAMIN. *He looks at her in horror. He starts to back down the hall toward the stairs, holding the package against his chest.*

Int. special set— ROBINSON *hall—Day—Shot—Pulling back from* MRS. ROBINSON.

She is standing there, perfectly calm. She gets further and further away as though it is a very long hall in a very bad dream.

Fade out.

Fade in.

Int. BEN'S *room—Night.* BEN *sits cross-legged on his bed in the dark, his back against the fishtank, smoking.*

Dissolve through to:

Ext. ROBINSON *house—Day.* BEN *drives by in his car. He looks at the house.*

Dissolve to:

Int. BEN'S *room—Day.* BEN *dressed differently, stands by the window overlooking the backyard. Over his shoulder, we can see* MR. BRADDOCK *down by the pool, dressed in a sweater, cleaning the pool with a long-handled scoop.* MR. BRADDOCK *looks up at* BEN'S *window.* BEN *moves aside.*

Dissolve to:

Ext. ROBINSON *house—Day.* BEN *is standing behind a tree watching the* ROBINSON *house. In the driveway of the* ROBINSON *house,* ELAINE *is getting into the* ROBINSON *car.* MR. ROBINSON *is putting* ELAINE'S *luggage into the car.* MRS. ROBINSON *stands at the door.* MR. ROBINSON *gets into the car and starts it. The car drives down the driveway and down the street.*

Dissolve to:

Int. BEN'S *room—Night.* BEN, *dressed differently again, sits in a chair by his desk. He is writing. On the piece of paper is written: DEAR ELAINE, ELAINE, ELAINE, ELAINE, and her name several dozen times. He stops and looks up.*

Dissolve to:

Int. BRADDOCK *kitchen—Day. It is early morning. We see a swinging door pushed open to reveal:* MR. BRADDOCK, *dressed in a bathrobe, standing at the kitchen counter by the window through which we can see an orange tree.* MR. BRADDOCK *is pouring orange juice from a Minute Maid container.* BEN *stands inside door.*

MR. BRADDOCK. Say that again.

BEN. I'm going to marry Elaine Robinson.

MR. BRADDOCK *starts to smile.*

MR. BRADDOCK. Well—well—well—

He almost giggles as he crosses to BEN *and takes his hand to shake it.* MRS. BRADDOCK *appears in the doorway.* BEN *is shaking his father's hand.*

MRS. BRADDOCK. What's happening?
MR. BRADDOCK. Ben says he and Elaine are getting married.
MRS. BRADDOCK. I don't believe it.
MR. BRADDOCK. That's what he says. Right?
BEN. I'm going up to Berkeley today.
MRS. BRADDOCK. Oh, Ben—this is so—exciting—
MR. BRADDOCK. Come on, let's call the Robinsons. We've got something to celebrate.
BEN. No. I think you'll want to wait on that.
MRS. BRADDOCK. They don't know?
BEN. No—they don't.
MRS. BRADDOCK. Well—when did you decide all this?
BEN. About an hour ago.
MR. BRADDOCK. Wait a minute. You talked to Elaine this morning?
BEN. No. She doesn't know about it.
MR. BRADDOCK. She doesn't know that you're coming up to Berkeley?
BEN. No. Actually—she doesn't know about us getting married yet.
MRS. BRADDOCK. When did you two talk this over?
BEN. We haven't.
MRS. BRADDOCK. You haven't?
MR. BRADDOCK. Ben—this whole idea sounds pretty half-baked.

BEN. No—it's not. It's completely baked. It's a decision I've made.

MRS. BRADDOCK. But what makes you think she wants to marry you?

BEN *picks up his suitcase, walks to the door and turns.*

BEN. She doesn't. To be perfectly honest, she doesn't like me.

Dissolve to:

Ext. road no. 1 to Berkeley—Day. BEN *driving his car (left to right).*

BEN'S VOICE *(over).* Dear Elaine—I am now visiting Berkeley, after growing somewhat weary of family life. I have been meaning to stop by and pay my respects but am not entirely certain just how you feel about seeing me after the incident involving myself and your mother. It was certainly a serious mistake on my part but not serious enough. I hope—

The last part runs down like a record on an old gramophone.

Cut to:

Ext. road no. 2—to Berkeley—Day. BEN *driving his car (left to right).*

BEN'S VOICE *(over).* Mr. and Mrs. G. L. Robinson take great pleasure in announcing the wedding of their daughter...

It runs down.

Cut to:

Ext. gas station—Day. BEN'*s car is being gassed up. It is a huge gas station with dozens of pumps and many neon lights.* BEN *runs to a series of vending machines. He pushes quarters into them, receiving cigarettes, a sandwich, an apple, a cup of coffee. Balancing them all carefully, he runs back to the car, climbs in, puts his purchases on top of the dashboard, hands the attendant a bill and drives off.*

Cut to:

Ext. road no. 3 to Berkeley—Day. BEN *driving (left to right) and eating.*

BEN'S VOICE *(over).* Honey—I'm home.
ELAINE'S VOICE *(over).* Hi—Sweetheart.
BEN'S VOICE *(over).* Where are the kids?
ELAINE'S VOICE *(over).* Oh—they're having a wonderful time—spending the day at Mother's—she's teaching them to...

It runs down.

Ext. road no. 4 to Berkeley—Day. BEN *driving (left to right).*

BEN'S VOICE *(over).* Dear Mom and Dad. You may have wondered why Elaine and I haven't written in such a long time, but the postal system here in Greenland isn't the most efficient. Life among these wonderful natives...

It runs down.

Cut to:

Ext. road no. 5 to Berkeley—Day. BEN *driving (left to right).*

MAN'S VOICE *(over).* Do you, Benjamin Braddock take this woman, Mrs. Robinson, for your Mother-in-law, to love, cherish and...

It runs down.

Cut to.

Ext. toll booth on the Oakland Bridge—Day. BEN *barely stops as he hands the change out the window of the low-slung sports car and up to the toll taker.*

Cut to:

Ext. Oakland Bridge—Day. BEN *driving over bridge (left to right).*

MRS. ROBINSON'S VOICE *(over).* Benjamin— you and Elaine have made such a wonderful marriage. I often laugh when I remember those nights at the Taft.
BEN'S VOICE *(over).* Yes—how long ago that all seems.
MR. ROBINSON'S VOICE *(over; chuckling).* I'll never forget how peeved I was when I first...

It runs down...

Pan the car past us and hold on it as it disappears in the distance.

Dissolve to:

Int. Wendell Hall reception area—Dusk. Close on BEN *as he comes through the door. Move with him as he wanders around the commons room which is filled with students. Girls singing, couples necking; a man with a heavy knapsack.* BEN *walks to a lady receptionist no. 1, who sits at a reception desk.*

LADY RECEPTIONIST NO. 1. May I help you?
BEN *(too loudly).* Elaine Robinson.
LADY RECEPTIONIST NO. 1. Yes?
BEN *(clearing his throat).* Elaine Robinson. Does she live here?

The Receptionist runs her pencil along a list of names under the glass top of her desk. She finds it.

LADY RECEPTIONIST NO. 1. Three-oh-eight. Shall I call her for you?

The RECEPTIONIST's *hand moves to the receiver of a phone on the desk.* BEN *looks at her hand for several seconds. He takes a step backward. Her hand starts to lift the receiver.* BEN *moves backward, puts his hand up as though to stop her and shakes his head, speechlessly.*

Shot—The RECEPTIONIST. *Looking at* BEN.

Shot— BEN. *Move with him as he moves past the students toward the door.*

Dissolve through to:

Ext. campus—Dusk. Pan around campus in a circle, ending on a closeup of BEN, *standing in the middle of the deserted campus, looking around, lost.*

Dissolve through to:

*Int. rooming house hall and stairs—Night— * BEN *and* MR. MCCLEERY. *From the bottom of the stairway, shooting up.* MR. MCCLEERY *is the landlord of the rooming house. They are climbing a flight of stairs,* MR. MCCLEERY *first, then* BEN, *carrying his suitcase.*

MR. MCCLEERY. You a student?
BEN. Not exactly.

MR. MCCLEERY *stops and turns.* BEN *almost runs into him.*

MR. MCCLEERY. What's that?
BEN. I said—not exactly—no.
MR. MCCLEERY. What are you then?
BEN. Well—I'm just sort of traveling through.

MR. MCCLEERY *takes a couple of steps up,* BEN *following and stops again.*

MR. MCCLEERY. I like to know who's living in my house. I like to know what my boys are up to.
BEN. Ahhh.

MR. MCCLEERY *just looks at him.*

BEN. I'm not up to much, actually. I'm just visiting. I mean—I've always wanted to see Berkeley.

MR. MCCLEERY *takes a couple more steps and stops again.*

MR. MCCLEERY. You're not one of those agitators?
BEN. What?

MR. MCCLEERY. One of those outside agitators.
BEN. Oh—no sir.
MR. MCCLEERY. I hate that. I won't stand for it.

He looks at BEN *searchingly, then turns and continues up the stairs and down the hall.*

Cut to:

Int. rooming house— BEN's *room—Night. Pan the room in a circle, seeing a sink in one corner, a bed, a bureau, a table, a lamp, a chair, a window that overlooks a Berkeley street—ending on a closeup of* BEN, *standing in the middle of it, looking lost.*

Cut to:

Ext. Wendell Hall—Quadrangle—Dawn. Dawn. The campus is empty except for BEN *who, dressed carefully in his black suit, sits on a bench in the quadrangle outside of Wendell Hall.*

Ext. Wendell Hall quandrangle—series of dissolve (or cuts)—Day. During which BEN *remains static while the quadrangle and the area around him fill up with students; walking, talking, hurrying to class, strolling, sitting, reading, handing out petitions, etc.*

Ext. campus building—Day—Long shot. ELAINE *comes out. She walks, carrying her books, in* BEN's *direction.*

Shot— BEN. *He sees her and stiffens.*

Shot— ELAINE. *Approaching from the distance.*

Shot— BEN. *He stands.*

Shot— ELAINE. *As she walks, she is joined by another girl with whom she converses as they walk.*

Shot— BEN *watching. He takes a step forward.*

Shot— ELAINE *and girl. As they approach, they are joined by a tall boy with a beard.*

Shot— BEN. *He starts toward them, falters, straightens himself.*

Shot— ELAINE, *girl, boy. They are getting quite near. Suddenly they are joined by three African exchange students, in tribal robes. They all greet each other and continue to walk toward us.*

Shot— BEN. *He looks at the massed group moving toward him, horror taking over his face. He starts forward. As he passes* ELAINE *and her friends he seems to take a deep breath and hold it.*

She stops and slowly turns to look in his direction. Her companions also stop. BEN *changes his direction and makes a circle to his left as though he has just changed his mind. He looks at her. He does not stop walking. He makes a slow circle around her as he speaks.*

BEN. ELAINE. Hey—what a surprise *(not quite looking at her)*. Say—I thought I remembered that you were going to school up here—well—we'll have to get together sometime—I'll be up here myself for a little while.

Shot— BEN's *POV.* ELAINE *and the others staring at him.*

Shot— BEN.

BEN—it certainly has been nice—I think I'm late—yes, I am—

He turns and walks away from them. They stand still watching him go. He starts to walk faster and faster. They watch him as he gets further and further away and then breaks into a run. He disappears in the distance.

Sound: Footsteps running, a door opening and closing, footsteps running upstairs, a door opening and slamming.

Cut to:

Int. rooming house— BEN's *room—Day.* BEN *leans with his back against the closed door, breathing heavily.*

Dissolve to:

Ext. various campus locations—Day—Series of shots. BEN *following and watching* ELAINE.

Dissolve to:

Int. Telegraph Street restaurant—Day. BEN *is sitting at a table by the window through which we can see the street. He is drinking a beer. Other tables are filled with students having animated discussions.* BEN *starts to pour some beer from the bottle into the glass. He stops as he sees something through the window. He leans forward.*

ELAINE *comes out of a bookstore across the street. She crosses the street and moves to a bus stop. He stands, fumbles in his pocket for money, puts a dollar on the table and rushes out.*

Cut to:

Ext. Restaurant Telegraph Street—Day. BEN *comes out of the door just as* ELAINE *gets into a bus and the doors close behind her.*

The bus starts off, BEN *runs after it. The bus gets to the next corner and stops for a red light.* BEN *catches up with it, runs to the front door and knocks on the door. The door opens and he climbs in.*

Int. bus no. 1—Day—Shot— ELAINE. *She is seated next to an older lady by the window immediately in front of the rear exit door. She keeps looking out the window, almost holding her breath as she hears:*

BEN's VOICE *(getting closer as he moves past people toward her)*. Excuse me—I'm sorry—I wonder if I could get by—excuse me—

There is a pause and then, immediately behind her:

BEN's VOICE *(cheerfully)*. Well—how about this for a coincidence.

New angle. BEN's *face is right behind* ELAINE, *between her and the older lady sitting next to her.* BEN *is standing on the steps to the rear exit door.* ELAINE *continues to look out the window.*

BEN *(leaning in a little)*. I was wondering where you were headed.

ELAINE *doesn't answer. The lady sitting next to* ELAINE *takes a look at her, turns around and looks at* BEN, *then looks at* ELAINE *again.*

ELAINE. I'm meeting someone.
BEN. Ah. Where?

She doesn't answer.

BEN. Where are you meeting this person?
ELAINE. At the Zoo.
BEN. The Zoo. They have a pretty good one here, do they?
ELAINE. I don't know. I've never seen it.
BEN. Oh. Well, I haven't either. I might just ride out there with you.

Hold on them riding.
Cut to:

Ext. zoo—Day. BEN *and* ELAINE *are walking along in front of one of the outside animal cages. Ben is walking a step or two behind* ELAINE. *He is darting glances to the right and left.*

BEN. Is that him over there?
ELAINE. No.
BEN. Where did he say he was going to meet you?
ELAINE. I thought he said by the monkey house.
BEN. Oh.

She stops. BEN *stops.*

ELAINE. Benjamin—I would like to know what you're doing here.

BEN. Here? In Berkeley?

ELAINE. Yes.

BEN. Well, I have this very pleasant room on Carter Street—and I've been getting to some classes—

ELAINE. But you're not enrolled.

BEN. No. I just sit in. They don't seem to mind. They've been very congenial about it.

She looks at him and starts to shake her head.

ELAINE. Benjamin—you're—I don't know what to say—you're—

BEN. Maybe we could get together some time and talk about it.

ELAINE. —really incredible—

BEN. Here he comes.

ELAINE. What?

BEN. I've got a real feeling that this is the fellow.

ELAINE *looks. A good-looking young man is striding briskly toward them. It is* CARL SMITH.

CARL *(waving).* Elaine!

BEN. He certainly is a good walker.

CARL *strides up to them. He takes the pipe out of his mouth and puts it in his pocket. He reaches out and takes* ELAINE'S *hands.*

CARL. Am I late? I'm sorry.

BEN. We thought you said by the monkey house.

CARL *frowns and looks up over* ELAINE'S *shoulder at* BEN. BEN *smiles.*

ELAINE. This is Benjamin Braddock. Carl Smith. Benjamin rode here with me on the bus.

CARL. Glad to meet you, Ben.

BEN *steps forward and grasps* CARL'S *hand.*

BEN. Great meeting you, Carl.

CARL *steps back and puts an arm around* ELAINE'S *shoulder. The three of them look at each other for a moment.*

BEN. Swell seeing you. Have a good time.

BEN *turns and starts walking back the way he came.* CARL *and* ELAINE *turn and go in the opposite direction.* BEN *stops after a few steps and walks over to one of the cages. He grips the rail with his hand and looks back at:*

*Shot—*CARL *and* ELAINE. *Walking away, his arm over her shoulder, his other hand gesturing with the pipe in it as he talks.*

*Shot—*BEN. *As he watches them go. His artificial smile disappears. The agony is such that he has to steady himself with his hand on the rail. He turns his face away, toward the cage. There is an animal in it, staring at* BEN. *They look at each other. There is a box—an automatic device with a recorded description of the animal—that begins to deliver its recorded message.*

Dissolve to:

*Int. rooming house—*BEN'S *room and hallway—Day—Shot—* BEN. *He runs to the bed and puts the covers back into place. He goes to the window sill, picks up an empty beer can, crosses to the bureau, opens a bureau drawer. He crosses to the wastepaper basket under the sink, bends down and takes a newspaper out of it. He crosses to the chair and sits down. He holds the newspaper in front of him. It is hopelessly crumpled. He gets up, crosses to the bureau, opens a drawer and takes out a traveling iron. He kneels down, puts the newspaper on the floor and tries to straighten it out with the iron.*

There is a knock on the door. He rises, puts the iron back in the drawer as quietly and quickly as he can, then back to the chair, sits down and holds the newspaper on his lap.

There is another knock. BEN *crosses to the door and opens it.* ELAINE *is standing in the hall.*

ELAINE. I want to ask you a question and then I'm going.

BEN. Come in.

ELAINE. No. I want to know why you're here in Berkeley.

BEN. Because—I am.

ELAINE. Is it because I'm here?

BEN. What do you think?

ELAINE. I think it is.

BEN *nods.*

ELAINE. I said I think it is.

BEN. *All right then! Yes!*

ELAINE. Well, I want you to leave.

BEN. Well—I love you.

ELAINE *(looking down).* How could you do that, Benjamin?

BEN *moves in behind her and puts his hand on her arm.*

ELAINE. Do you just hate everything? How could you possibly rape my...

BEN. What?

ELAINE. I don't understand—

BEN. Did you say rape her?

ELAINE—how you—how anyone—could do a thing like that.

BEN. What did she say?

ELAINE *(holding his arm)*. Let me go.

BEN. You've got to tell me what she said.

He touches her hair.

ELAINE. Why?

BEN. Because it isn't true.

ELAINE. I have to go now.

BEN *pushes her down softly onto the bed. He kneels alongside of her.*

BEN. Tell me.

BEN *sits next to her and puts his hand on her shoulder.*

ELAINE. She said she was having a drink in the hotel with a friend. You waited for her in the parking lot and told her she was too drunk to drive home and that you would get her a room for the night.

BEN. Then what?

ELAINE. Then you took her upstairs and you raped her.

BEN. Elaine—that is not what happened.

She puts her hands on his shoulder.

ELAINE. Please let me go.

BEN. All right—but listen to me. What happened was there was this party at my parents. I drove your mother home—then we went upstairs to see your portrait—

ELAINE *tightens her arms around his neck.*

ELAINE. Don't tell me—

BEN—and when we got up in the room she started taking her clothes off—and—

ELAINE. Benjamin—this is my *mother*!

BEN—suddenly there she was without any clothes on—I mean really naked—

BEN *is almost lying on top of her.* ELAINE *screams—a long, loud scream.* BEN *looks at her. He leaps off the bed and runs to the sink. He fills a glass with water and brings it to* ELAINE. *He starts toward the door.*

Sound of footsteps on the stairway and in the hall. BEN *goes to the closet, opens the door, takes a jacket from a hanger and puts it on.*

Sound: A knock on the door.

MR. MCCLEERY'S VOICE. What's going on in there?

ELAINE *sits up and drinks the water.* BEN *looks at her then goes to the door and opens it.*

BEN. Oh—hello, Mr. McCleery.

MR. MCCLEERY. Who screamed?

BEN. It's all right, Mr. McCleery.

MR. MCCLEERY. Screaming isn't all right. Not in *my* house it isn't.

BEN. It was just a visitor. But it's all right now.

Several boys are gathering in the hallway trying to see into the room. BEN *edges through the door into the hallway.*

Int. rooming house hallway—Day.

MR. MCCLEERY. What did you do to her?

BEN. Look—she's all right. She's upset and she screamed. But she's okay now.

A BOY. Shall I get the cops?

BEN. What?

A BOY. I'll get the cops.

He starts for the stairs.

BEN. Hey—wait a minute. Now damn it—look.

He opens the door a little way. They all try to see in.

BEN. See—she's just having some water. Now there's no need for the cops or anything.

MR. MCCLEERY. All right, boys—I think you can get back to your rooms. I don't think we'll have any more of this agitation. Will we, Braddock?

BEN. No, sir.

The boys start back to their rooms. MR. MCCLEERY *and* BEN *stand and look at each other for a few seconds.*

MR. MCCLEERY. I want you out of here.

MR. MCCLEERY *turns away and walks down the hall and starts down the stairs.*

BEN. Mr. McCleery?

MR. MCCLEERY. You heard me. Out of here.

BEN. What for?

MR. MCCLEERY *(going down the stairs).* Because I don't like you.

MR. MCCLEERY *disappears down the stairs.* BEN *turns and goes back into the room.*

Int. rooming house—BEN's room—Day. ELAINE *is standing at the sink. She is putting water on her face.* BEN *goes to the closet and takes out his suitcase and carries it to the bed.*

ELAINE. I'm sorry I screamed.

BEN *opens the suitcase.*

ELAINE. Benjamin, when you came up here, what did you think was going to happen between us?

BEN. Elaine—right now I don't feel like talking much. I'm sorry about everything but I think I'll just do this now.

He stands, looking into the empty suitcase.

ELAINE. Can I just sit here while you're packing?
BEN. If you want.

ELAINE *sits in the chair. She watches him as he goes to the bureau, takes some shirts from a drawer and puts them in the suitcase, then goes back to the bureau. He gets down on his knees and looks under the bureau.*

ELAINE. What are you looking for?
BEN. My belt.
ELAINE. Don't you have it on?
BEN. No. I have two. I have one and then I have another. The other one is the one I'm looking for. *(he reaches under the bureau).* What's this? *(he brings out a marble).* It's from my grandmother.
ELAINE. That marble?
BEN. The belt I'm looking for was from my grandmother.
ELAINE. Oh.

BEN *takes the marble to the suitcase and packs it.*

ELAINE. What are you going to do now?
BEN. I don't know.

He goes back to the bureau, gets some socks and underwear and carries them to the suitcase.

ELAINE. Are you going home?
BEN. No.
ELAINE. Well—*where are you going?*

He goes back to the bureau, opens a drawer, takes out some T-shirts and the beer can and carries them to the suitcase.

BEN. Elaine—you're going to have to stop asking me that.

He packs the T-shirts, then carries the beer can back to the bureau and puts it back in the drawer, takes some ties from the drawer and crosses to the suitcase. ELAINE *gets up, goes to the door and opens it.*

ELAINE. I don't want you to leave tomorrow.
BEN. I don't understand.
ELAINE. I don't want you to go anywhere until you have a definite plan.
BEN. But Elaine—
ELAINE. Goodbye.

She walks out, shutting the door behind her. He crosses to the window.

Ext. rooming house street—Day. Past BEN, *through the window, we see* ELAINE *walking away. She walks the length of the street and disappears.*

Dissolve to:

Int. rooming house— BEN's *room—Night.* BEN *asleep in his bed. Suddenly he sits up.*

*Shot—*ELAINE. *Standing in the darkness by the door.*

BEN. What's happening?

He gets out of the bed.

ELAINE. Benjamin?
BEN. What?
ELAINE *(taking a step forward).* Will you kiss me!

He goes to her and they kiss.

BEN. Will you marry me?

She shakes her head.

BEN. You won't?
ELAINE. I don't know.
BEN. But you might.
ELAINE. I might.
BEN. Is that so? You might marry me?
ELAINE. Yes.
BEN. When?
ELAINE. I don't know.
BEN. How about tomorrow? I don't mean to be pushy but—
ELAINE. I don't know. I don't know what's happening.
BEN. You mean you're confused?

She nods.

BEN. Well—look—don't be confused. We're getting married.
ELAINE. I don't see how we can.
BEN. We just can.
ELAINE. I have to go back now.

She goes to the door.

BEN. Elaine—are you serious about this?
ELAINE. I'll think about it.
BEN. You really will?
ELAINE. Yes.

She opens the door and steps into the hall. He goes to the door.

BEN. Well—let's get together sometime.

He closes the door.

BEN. Good God!

Dissolve to:

Int. rooming house downstairs hall—Day—Close-up of telegram addressed to MR. BENJAMIN BRADDOCK. *Sound: footsteps descending stairs. Someone whistling. The footsteps and whistling get nearer and stop. Hands come in and pick up telegram, open the envelope and unfold the telegram. It reads:*

Leave Berkeley immediately or serious repeat serious trouble will result.—Mrs. G.L. ROBINSON

Pan up to BEN. *He crumples the telegram in his hand.*

Cut to:

Ext. campus near classroom building—Day. Close on BEN'S *hand fiddling with the crumpled telegram. Students are moving quickly from building to building.* BEN *is walking alongside* ELAINE.

BEN. We could go down and get our blood tests tomorrow.
ELAINE. Tomorrow?
BEN. Or this afternoon. It's a good day for it.
ELAINE. Benjamin—I haven't even said I'll marry you yet.
BEN. We'll need our Birth Certificates. I happen to have mine with me. Where's yours?

They move up the steps of a classroom building. BEN *pushes through a lot of students to keep up with* ELAINE.

Cut to:

Int. classroom building corridor—Day. They walk down a corridor. On each side are open doors to classrooms with students filing into each of them.

ELAINE. I just don't think it would work.
BEN. Why wouldn't it?

A bell rings. ELAINE *turns into one of the doors.* BEN *is left in the hall. He looks around. All the doors in the classrooms close. He leans against the wall.*

Another angle— BEN. *Standing poised by the door. The bell rings. The classroom doors open and students start to file out.* ELAINE *comes out of the classroom.*

BEN. Why wouldn't it?
ELAINE. I just don't think it would...

ELAINE *starts walking down the corridor towards the exit door.* BEN *follows her, moving out of the way of the other students.*

Cut to:

Int. gymnasium—Day. ELAINE *and twenty other girls are in basketball uniforms. Two teams of girls are playing basketball.* ELAINE *sits on the bench, watching.* BEN *stands behind her. The girls are shouting and clapping and jumping up and down.*

BEN. Tomorrow then—can we get our blood tests tomorrow morning?

She turns and looks at him.

ELAINE. Why don't you just drag me off if you want to marry me so much?
BEN. Why don't I just drag you off? All right—I will. Right after we get the blood tests.
ELAINE. Well—I have to see Carl first.
BEN. Carl who?

ELAINE *jumps up, applauding a shot.*

BEN. Carl who?
ELAINE. Carl Smith. He's a medical student. We've known him for years.
BEN. Who—that guy at the Zoo?
ELAINE. Yes.
BEN. Why do you have to see him?
ELAINE. Well—I said I might marry him.

ELAINE *and several other girls run onto the court as a number of girls run off the court to the bench.*

BEN *(yelling after her).* You *what?*

Cut to:

Int. Library—Day. BEN *is seated across a study table from* ELAINE. *There are many other students scattered around the room.*

BEN. How did he do it? Did he get down on his knees? He didn't get down on his knees, I hope.
ELAINE. No, Benjamin.
BEN. Well, what did he say? I'm curious.
ELAINE. He said he thought we'd make a pretty good team.
BEN. Oh no. He said that.
ELAINE. Shhhh.
BEN. Where did he do it?

She starts to get up.

BEN. I'd like to know where it happened?

She starts to move away.

BEN. It wasn't in his car, was it?

Cut to:

Ext. Wendell Hall—Day. BEN *and* ELAINE *are standing at the entrance.*

BEN. Are we getting married tomorrow?

ELAINE. No.

BEN. The day after tomorrow?

ELAINE. I don't know. Maybe we are and maybe we aren't.

She goes through the doorway into Wendell Hall. BEN *remains standing in exactly the same position. After a few moments the door opens and* ELAINE *comes out, steps quickly to* BEN, *kisses him, then runs back inside.* BEN *turns and starts away from the door. The door opens again.* BEN *turns back and takes a step toward the door, smiling expectantly. A tall bearded man comes out and goes past* BEN. BEN *breaks up.*

Cut to:

Ext. Berkeley street—Day. Through the window of a hippy jewelry store we see a saleswoman modeling a ring for BEN. *He nods, she takes it off, puts it in a box and gives it to him. He pays for it and exits past camera, whistling.*

Int. rooming house—downstairs—Night. BEN *enters carrying four oddly shaped boxes and some flowers.*

Int. rooming house stairs and BEN's *room—Night.* BEN *is whistling happily as he runs up the stairs two at a time. He opens the door to his room and steps in. The room is dark. The figure of a man is silhouetted against the window.* BEN *freezes just inside the door. There is a long pause.*

MR. ROBINSON (*clearing his throat*). Do you want to try and tell me why you did it?

BEN. Mr. Robinson?

MR. ROBINSON. Do you have a special grudge against me? Do you feel a particularly strong resentment for me?

BEN. No, it's not that at all—

MR. ROBINSON. Is there something I've said that's caused this contempt? Or is it just the things I stand for that you despise?

BEN. It was nothing to do with you, sir.

MR. ROBINSON. Well, Ben, it was quite a bit to do with me.

BEN *takes a step forward.*

BEN. Now look—please—

MR. ROBINSON. Ben, I think we're two civilized human beings. Do you think it's necessary to threaten each other?

BEN. I am not threatening you.

MR. ROBINSON. Do you want to unclench your fists, please? Thank you. I can see in the dark, you know. I've been here quite a while.

BEN. I am trying to tell you I have no personal feelings about you, Mr. Robinson. I am trying to tell you I do not resent you.

MR. ROBINSON. You don't respect me terribly much either, do you?

BEN. No, I don't.

MR. ROBINSON. Well, I don't think we have a whole lot to say to each other, Ben. I do think you should know the consequences of what you've done. I do think you should know that my wife and I are getting a divorce soon.

BEN. But why?

MR. ROBINSON. Why?

BEN. It shouldn't make any difference what happened.

MR. ROBINSON. That's quite a statement.

BEN. Listen to me. We got—we got into bed with each other. But it was nothing. It was nothing at all. We might—we might just as well have been shaking hands.

MR. ROBINSON. Shaking hands. Well, that's not saying much for my wife, is it?

BEN. You miss the point.

MR. ROBINSON. Don't shout at me, Ben.

BEN. The point is—I don't love your wife. I love your daughter, sir.

MR. ROBINSON. Well—I'm sure you think you do, Ben, but after a few times in bed with Elaine I feel quite sure you'd get over that as quickly as you—

BEN. HUH?

MR. ROBINSON. I think we've talked about this enough. I don't know how far I can go, Ben. I don't know if I can prosecute or not, but I think maybe I can. In the light of what's happened I think maybe I can get you behind bars if you ever look at my daughter again. I have seen Elaine and I have spent the afternoon taking steps to insure...

MR. ROBINSON *climbs across the bed to get to the door.* BEN *takes a step toward him.*

MR. ROBINSON. Stay away from me, Ben!

MR. ROBINSON *stands at the door.*

MR. ROBINSON. I don't want to mince words with you. As far as Elaine's concerned you're to get her out of your filthy mind right now. Is that perfectly clear to you? That's all, Ben. You'll pardon me if *I* don't shake hands with you.

MR. ROBINSON *opens the door and starts into the hall.*

MR. ROBINSON. I think you are filth.

MR. ROBINSON *turns back from the hall.*

MR. ROBINSON. I think you are scum.

MR. ROBINSON *starts down the stairs.* MR. MC-CLEERY *is standing on the stairway, listening.*

MR. ROBINSON. You are a *degenerate*!

MR. ROBINSON *turns and goes down the stairs, past* MR. MCCLEERY *who looks up at* BEN.

Shot— BEN. *He walks to the door, looks out into the hall at* MR. MCCLEERY, *then shuts the door.* BEN *goes to the window and looks out.*

Ext. rooming house street—night—what he sees.

On the street below, MR. ROBINSON *getting into a cab.*

Int. rooming house— BEN'S *room—Night— Shot—* BEN. *He runs out of his room.*

Int. rooming house hall and stairs—Night. BEN *runs down the stairs.* MR. MCCLEERY *is standing by the pay phone.*

BEN. Mr. McCleery—do you have some change? I need to use the phone?

MR. MCCLEERY. I want you out of here.

BEN *(takes out some money)*. Look—I'll give you ten dollars for a dime—I'll give you twenty—for God's sake, will you let me use that phone?

MR. MCCLEERY. I am going to call the police now.

BEN. Could I make one phone call first?

MR. MCCLEERY. Get out!

BEN *stuffs the money back in his pocket and runs down the stairs and out of the building. Through the door we see him run down the street and out of sight.*

Cut to:

Int. Wendell Hall—Day—Close-up—Lady Receptionist #2.

LADY RECEPTIONIST #2. *(hanging up phone)*. Elaine Robinson has left school.

Cut to:

Close-up— BEN. BEN *reacting.*

LADY RECEPTIONIST #2. Her roommate is coming down with a note for you.

Int. Wendell Hall—Corridor—Day—Long shot. The elevator at the end of the hall opens and a fat girl walks toward us with an envelope in her hand. She walks into camera.

Cut to:

Ext. road no. 1 to Los Angeles—Day. BEN *driving his car (right to left). Sound: an envelope being ripped open.*

ELAINE'S VOICE *(over)*. Dear Benajmin—I promise you someday I will write a long letter about everything but right now I can't think and all I can say to you is please forgive me

because I know what I am doing is the best thing for you. My father is so upset you've got to understand. I love you, but it would never work out.

Ext. street no. 2—near ROBINSON *house— Night.* BEN'S *car is parked two blocks from the* ROBINSON *house.* BEN *has just left the car and is making his way to the* ROBINSON *backyard.*

Ext. ROBINSON *backyard—Night.* BEN *climbs a fence into the backyard and moves to the house. He looks up at* ELAINE'S *bedroom window.*

BEN *(a whispered shout)*. Elaine—Elaine—

He picks up a pebble and throws it at the window.

Angle on BEN. *He moves to the back door, takes off his shoes, puts them into his jacket pockets, tries the back door. It opens and he goes in.*

Int. Sunroom—Night. There are no lights. BEN *moves through the house into the hall and up the stairway.*

Int. ROBINSON *upstairs hall—Night.* BEN *goes to the door of* ELAINE'S *room and looks in. There is a light on in the room and the sound of someone moving around. He goes in.*

BEN. Elaine?

Int. ELAINE'S *room—Night. As* BEN *moves further into the room,* MRS. ROBINSON, *carrying some of* ELAINE'S *clothes, comes out of* ELAINE'S *closet and moves past* BEN.

MRS. ROBINSON. Hello, Benjamin.

She does not stop, but walks calmly past him into the hall.

Int. ROBINSON *upstairs hall and* MRS. ROBINSON'S *room—Night.* BEN *follows her through the hall into* MRS. ROBINSON'S *room.*

BEN. Where is she?

Int. MRS. ROBINSON'S *room—Night.* MRS. ROBINSON, *without stopping, puts* ELAINE'S *clothes down next to a half-packed open suitcase on her bed and moves to a telephone on the night table. She lifts the receiver and dials zero.* BEN *follows.*

MRS. ROBINSON. Hello. Get me the police, please.

BEN. Where is Elaine?

MRS. ROBINSON. I'll be with you in a moment, Benjamin *(into phone)*. Do you have a patrol car in the vicinity of twelve hundred Glenview Road? We have a burglar here.

Good. Just a second. I'll ask him. *(to* BEN*)*. Are you armed? *(into phone)*. No—I don't believe he is. Thank you.

She hangs up.

BEN. What have you done to her?

MRS. ROBINSON. I think we have everything quite under control now, Benjamin. Would you like a quick drink before you go?

She picks up a glass from the night table and takes a drink.

BEN. You can't stop me from seeing her, Mrs. Robinson. I'll find her.

MRS. ROBINSON. I'm sorry we won't be able to invite you to the wedding, Benjamin, but the arrangements have been so rushed—

BEN. What the hell have you done!

Sound of several cars turning into the driveway.

MRS. ROBINSON. Ahh. I don't think you'll have time for that drink after all.

BEN. I'll find her.

MRS. ROBINSON. I don't think so.

The cars have reached the top of the driveway. Sound of the squeal of brakes and car doors opening.

Int. ROBINSON *halls—Night.* BEN *dives head first into the hall, scrambles to his feet and runs to the back of the house.*

Ext. ROBINSON *backyard—Night.* BEN *comes through the back door, runs to the back fence and vaults it. Lights start to go on in the house behind him.*

Ext. street—Night. BEN*, driving rapidly. He jams on the brakes and stops the car in the middle of the street. Cars, honking move around him as he sits, staring ahead.*

BEN. Wedding! God damn it—wedding!

People are yelling at him from the cars going by.

MR. ROBINSON'S VOICE. Carl—I think you and Elaine will make a good team.

CARL'S VOICE. Your father's right, Elaine. You and I will make a darned good team.

BEN *swings the car around in a U-turn and speeds off in the other direction.*

Ext. road no. 6—to Berkeley—Night (becoming day). Series of shots.

BEN *driving rapidly (left to right) past the landmarks established on the previous drive to Berkeley.*

WOMAN'S VOICE. We have two Carl Smiths. Is it Carl with a "C" or a "K"?

BEN'S VOICE. I'm afraid I don't know.

WOMAN'S VOICE. The Karl Smith with a "K" teaches History of Advertising—

BEN'S VOICE. And the other?

WOMAN'S VOICE. The one with the "C", Carl Smith Junior, is in our medical school. He lives at Gamma Delta Tau.

Ext. Fraternity house—Day. BEN *pulls up in front of the Gamma Delta Tau House. He gets out of the car. He is haggard, tired and unshaven. The car is mud-spattered.*

Int. Fraternity house—Hall and dining room—Day. BEN *enters the hall. Through a door can be seen a dozen or so fraternity brothers seated at a table chowing down. It is breakfast.* BEN *walks into the dining room.*

Int. Fraternity dining room—Day. The fraternity brothers are eating and talking noisily.

BEN. Say fellows—

They stop eating and turn toward him.

BEN. Do any of you fellows know where Carl Smith is?

FRAT BROTHER #1. He took off in the middle of the night to get married.

He goes back to his breakfast.

FRAT BROTHER #2. Probably one step ahead of the shotgun.

BEN. Do you happen to know where he's getting married? I'm supposed to be there.

FRAT BROTHER #2. Why don't you ask Carter?

BEN. Would you happen to know where I might find him?

FRAT BROTHER #2. He's probably still in the sack. He's *always* in the sack.

They start to laugh.

FRAT BROTHER #3. Or in the can.

They all laugh a great deal. BEN *gives a polite smile.*

Cut to:

Int. Fraternity washroom—Day. A large steam-filled room with a row of fraternity brothers in front of a row of sinks, brushing, combing, shaving, etc. BEN *is standing at the door.*

MAN AT SINK NO. 1. Hey, Carter—where's the Make Out King getting married?

CARTER'S VOICE *(echo sound)*. Santa Barbara.

BEN *(calling in the direction of* CARTER'S *voice)*. You don't happen to know exactly where the Make Out King is getting married, do you? I'm supposed to be there.

CARTER'S VOICE. I don't know. Maybe at his old man's home.

MAN AT SINK NO. 2. You going to the wedding?

BEN. Yes.

MAN AT SINK NO. 2. Give the bride a message for me. Tell her to act surprised.

A great deal of laughter follows this gem.

Cut to:

Ext. road no. 1 to Santa Barbara—Day. BEN *driving (right to left). The laughter from the previous scene can still be heard for a moment.*

BEN *is exhausted-looking. He opens the windows, turns the radio on and rubs his eyes.*

Ext. various roads to Santa Barbara—Day. Sequence of shots. The car, moving speedily (right to left) south on the Highway to Santa Barbara.

Ext. freeway exit and gas station—Day. Shot the car leaving the freeway under a Santa Barbara sign. The car swings onto an off ramp and down to a street, turns into a gas station and stops near the office. BEN *gets out of the car and runs into the office.*

Int. gas station office—Day. The clock on the office wall reads 2:05. The gas station ATTENDANT *is sitting reading a stock car magazine.*

BEN. Do you have a phone?

The ATTENDANT *points.* BEN *reaches for the phone book hanging under the pay phone.*

Shot—bringing phone book up into focus. The front of it says Santa Barbara Telephone Directory. BEN *opens it to the S's. His finger runs down to the Smiths. There is at least half a page of them.*

Shot—The page. BEN's *finger runs up and down and stops at the name: Smith, Carl W., M.D.*

Shot— BEN. *He inserts a dime and dials. The* ATTENDANT *watches him. Sound of buzzing from the phone. It clicks open.*

Shot—tight on BEN.

WOMAN'S VOICE. 657-2036.

BEN. Hello—who is this?

WOMAN'S VOICE. This is Dr. Smith's answering service.

BEN. Is the doctor anywhere?

WOMAN'S VOICE. I'm afraid the doctor can't be reached right now. If you'd like to leave your—

BEN. I have to know where he is.

WOMAN'S VOICE. Well—you see—the doctor is at his son's wedding, but I'm sure it's over by now. He should be checking in any moment—

BEN. Listen to me. I am Dr. Smith's brother—Reverend Smith—and I am supposed to perform the ceremony. I just got in—from—Portland—and I've forgotten what church—you see?

Shot—The ATTENDANT. *The* ATTENDANT *puts down his magazine and stares.*

Shot—tight on BEN.

WOMAN'S VOICE. Oh. Well—I'm not sure— but you might try the First Presbyterian. That's on Allan Street.

BEN. Thank you.

WOMAN'S VOICE. I certainly hope you—

Shot— BEN. BEN *hangs up the phone. He turns to the* ATTENDANT.

BEN. Allan Street. Where is it?

ATTENDANT *(suspiciously).* Six blocks up— three blocks over.

BEN *runs out of the office. The* ATTENDANT *goes to the door.*

Ext. gas station—Day—Shot of BEN *getting into the car. The* ATTENDANT *is in the b.g.*

ATTENDANT. You need any gas, Father?

BEN. I'm not a priest—I'm a minister.

The car drives out of the station.

Ext. Santa Barbara street—Day. The car comes toward us through the traffic. It stops in the intersection to make the turn.

Shot—Int. car. Sound. The engine failing. BEN *looks down.*

Shot—the gas gauge. The needle is on "E".

Shot— BEN. *He pumps the gas pedal.*

Shot—the car. It makes the turn and rolls to a stop by the curb.

Shot— BEN. *He jumps out of the car, leaving the door open, and starts to run down the street.*

Ext. street near church—shot—with BEN *as he runs. He looks up ahead on the other side of the street.*

Ext. church—what he sees. The First Presbyterian Church.

Ext. street in front of church—Day (2:15 PM)—Shot of BEN. *Running across the street. He stops for a moment and looks around. There are a number of cars parked in front of the church. Among them is* MRS. ROBINSON's *car.* BEN *runs by it and up the steps to the front doors of the church.*

Ext. church—Day—Shot of BEN. *He pulls at the doors. They are locked. Through the glass doors, we can see to the front of the church where the wedding ceremony is taking place.*

Ext. side of church—Day—Shot of BEN, *running around the side of the church. There are glass windows and doors through which, as he runs, we can see the ceremony continuing.*

Ext. back of church—Day, BEN *runs, looking for an entrance. He goes all the way around the church and stops at a side door. He opens the door and goes in.*

Int. church hall and stairs—Day. BEN *is in a hall. A flight of stairs is in front of him. He runs up the stairs.*

Int. church—balcony—Day. The balcony is between two huge windows, one of which looks out on the lawn outside, the other looks into the interior of the church where the ceremony is taking place. The sun is coming through the window. BEN *stops and looks through the inside window. The minister is just closing the book. He says something and* CARL *and* ELAINE *kiss.*

BEN. Oh, Jesus—God—no—

He puts his hands up against the glass and slumps. The minister shakes hands with CARL, *then takes* ELAINE's *hand. The organ music starts to thunder.*

BEN *(straightening).* No!

He moves to the center of the window and begins to pound on the glass.

BEN. Elaine—Elaine!

BEN's *shadow is thrown across the celebrants. They all turn around and look up at him.*

Int. church—day—shot from front of church. BEN *like a trapped moth, beating on the window and yelling soundlessly.*

*Shot—*MRS. ROBINSON. *She looks up at* BEN *with a small, triumphant smile.*

*Shot—*MR. ROBINSON *looking up at* BEN.

*Shot—*CARL *looking up at* BEN.

*Shot—*ELAINE *looking up at* BEN. *She moves down the aisle toward him, dazed.*

Shot—All of them. MR. ROBINSON, CARL, *and* MRS. ROBINSON *are moving toward* ELAINE. *The organ is playing loudly.* BEN's *voice can be heard shouting* ELAINE's *name. The pounding on the glass can be heard.*

CARL. Who is that guy? What's he doing?
MR. ROBINSON. I'll take care of him.
MRS. ROBINSON. He's too late.

The other guests are adlibbing their confusion.

*Shot—*ELAINE. *She turns back toward her mother, father and Carl as they come toward her.*

*Close-up—*ELAINE *looking at them. All sound stops, except for* BEN's *voice in the distance shouting "ELAINE ELAINE ELAINE."*

ELAINE's *POV—*CARL. *Frozen frame.*

ELAINE's *POV—*MR. ROBINSON. *Frozen frame.*

ELAINE's *POV.—*MRS. ROBINSON. *Frozen frame.*

*Shot—*ELAINE. *Her face turning quickly to look up at* BEN.

ELAINE's *POV—*BEN. *Frozen frame. His face twisted with passion, his body spread-eagled against the glass.*

*Close-up—*ELAINE *looking up at* BEN.

ELAINE *(screaming).* Ben!

The sound of the organ and the guests' voices starts again.

Int. church vestibule—stairs—day—shot— BEN. *He starts to go back down the stairs. He reaches the bottom of the stairs and goes through a door which leads into the vestibule of the church.*

Int. Church vestibule—Day. MR. ROBINSON *is waiting for* BEN, *crouching, his arms spread. Behind him is* ELAINE. BEN *moves toward them.* MR. ROBINSON *grabs* BEN *around the waist.* BEN *twists away.* MR. ROBINSON *grabs* BEN's *collar and tears his jacket half off.* BEN *turns and hits* MR. ROBINSON *in the face.* MR. ROBINSON *falls down.* BEN *moves to* ELAINE *and grabs her hand. He pulls her toward the doors.*

BEN. Come on—don't faint.

Shot—the organist. His back to the action, clawing away at the organ obliviously.

Shot—the door. A man in clerical garb is guarding the door. BEN *and* ELAINE *move toward the door.*

BEN. Get out of my way!

CARL *steps in and grabs* BEN *from behind.* BEN *breaks* CARL's *hold and picks up a gold cross off a nearby stand. He begins to swing it, advancing toward* CARL. CARL *backs up toward the other guests.*

New angle. MRS. ROBINSON *steps to* ELAINE. *She reaches out and takes* ELAINE's *wrist.*

MRS. ROBINSON. Elaine — it's too late.

ELAINE *pulls her hand away.*

ELAINE. Not for *me.*

Shot — BEN. *He turns toward the man standing in front of the door and raises the cross over his head.*

BEN. *Move!*

The man moves away from the door. ELAINE *steps forward and opens the door. She and* BEN *go out.*

Ext. front of church — Day. BEN *jams the cross through the handles of the door. He grabs* ELAINE's *wrist.*

BEN. Run, Elaine, Run!

They start to run. ELAINE *trips and falls.* BEN *helps her up and they continue to run.*

Int. church vestibule — Day. From inside the church vestibule. Through the glass doors, we can see ELAINE *and* BEN *running down the street. The wedding party members are tugging furiously at the jammed doors.* MRS. ROBINSON *turns toward us and calmly begins to put on her gloves.*

Ext. street in front of church — Day. BEN *and* ELAINE *running along the sidewalk.* BEN *holds her hand and is pulling her. She still holds her flowers. They run to a bus that is just closing its doors.*

Shot — BEN. *He bangs on the closed door of the bus. The door opens.* BEN *climbs the step into the bus and pulls* ELAINE *up after him. The doors close.*

Int. bus no. 2 — Day — Shot of BEN, ELAINE *and* DRIVER. BEN *holds out a dollar bill.*

BEN. How much?
DRIVER. Where do you want to go?
BEN. To the end.

The DRIVER *takes the bill and gives* BEN *some change.* BEN *turns and pulls* ELAINE *along to the back of the bus. He pushes her into one of the seats and sits beside her.* BEN *looks toward the front of the bus.*

BEN's *POV. He sees the driver and the passengers, all turned around in their seats and looking back at them.*

Shot — BEN.

BEN. Let's go. Let's get this bus moving!

Shot — the DRIVER. *He turns and starts the bus.*

Shot — BEN *and* ELAINE. *They are breathing heavily.*

ELAINE. Benjamin?
BEN. What?

She takes his hand.

Ext. street in front of church — Day. Through the window in the back of the bus the church can be seen receding in the distance. There seem to be a number of men dressed in black running around in the street in front of it.

Fade out.

The end.

BUTCH CASSIDY
AND THE SUNDANCE KID

Screenplay by William Goldman

BUTCH CASSIDY	Paul Newman
THE SUNDANCE KID	Robert Redford
ETTA	Katherine Ross
GARRIS	Strother Martin
BIKE SALESMAN	Henry Jones
SHERIFF BLEDSOE	Jeff Corey
AGNES	Cloris Leachman
HARVEY LOGAN	Ted Cassidy
MARSHAL	Kenneth Mars

Screenplay by William Goldman
Produced by John Foreman for TC Fox/Campanile, 1969
Directed by George Roy Hill
Cinematography by Conrad Hall
Music by Burt Bacharach

Winner of the Academy Award for Best Story and Screenplay in 1969 based on material not previously published or produced, as well as the Writers Guild Award for Best Drama written directly for the screen that year, Mr. Goldman's script is a model of the male bond that exists in many a genre other than the Western form that it takes here. No traditional Western is this; rather, a set piece, like an outdoor drawing room comedy featuring two pals: not in the tradition of Quirt and Flagg or Spencer Tracy and Clark Gable fighting and brawling over dames and running afoul of the law from time to time, but two friends, linked in a common, albeit unlawful enterprise; close and trusting yet not knowing very much about each other.

Born in Chicago in 1931, Mr. Goldman graduated from Oberlin College in 1952 and received his master's degree from Columbia University in 1956. He turned to writing novels by 1957, and in that year he had his first published, *The Temple of Gold,* which was soon followed by works like *Marathon Man* and *Magic.* His screenplay credits are varied and numerous. *Harper* (1966) and *All the President's Men* (1976) are among the most notable. Mr. Goldman won an Academy Award for the latter script, which gives him two at this point, including *Butch Cassidy and the Sundance Kid.*

Flip, tongue-in-cheek, insouciant, this script provided an opportunity for Mr. Newman and Mr. Redford, two of the most successful male stars in American cinema, and their resourceful director, Mr. Hill, to stage their gallows-humor "folk ballet" in a manner that allowed them not only to utilize the freedom in style and range permissible in the Western genre but also to make an ironic, almost nihilistic, comment on that decade of the sixties, so notable for its disenchantment with American institutions and conventional middle-class beliefs.

Mr. Goldman provided that opportunity because his script prepared for it in his screen directions, with his sophisticated comments and suggestions for the "musical interludes" and the use of songs as "emotional connections" with the scenes, for example. His awareness of the value of music for emotional and dramatic impact and for its contribution to the style of a movie is unusual for a screenwriter. It is no accident, in a way, that Mr. Bacharach, in writing his splendid song, "Raindrops Keep Falling on My Head," won an Academy Award for its appearance in the picture.

Interesting, too, is Mr. Goldman's use of "Who *are* those guys?", a question posed more than once during the chase sequence, when the posse pursuing them implacably and doggedly stays on their tail.

This question, I believe, means more than simply a determined posse ready to pursue them to hell and gone. It reflects a number of things for me. For one, Mr. Harriman, the railroad magnate behind this no-nonsense posse, represents middle-class virtue and business, no longer willing to condone the forays of a Butch Cassidy in a West that was closing its frontier. In this sense, Butch and the Sundance Kid mirror a kind of a last hurrah of the frontier, where fate is catching up with them and they know it.

Perhaps that loaded question also reflects the demise of the Western, which has faltered in number and has almost disappeared from our cinema menu over the last decade and a half.

Fatalistic, accepting their eventual bloody demise, living in the present, blotting out their past, and foregoing any future, Butch and the Sundance Kid, as Mr. Goldman envisioned them, readily mirror much of the prevailing mood of that era of the sixties for a large segment of American youth at that time. Looking back at it now, almost two decades later, I find the film, despite its obvious box-office cleverness, more than flip, more than exploitive, and not only genuinely creative on the part of its author and all the others who contributed in that way but reflecting an important current in American history that often comes to the surface in times of discontent, when we find ourselves identifying in some small way with bandit native folk heroes who thumb their noses at what they consider to be a somewhat tainted law and order.

Let me add one small note on the creative script-filmmaking process here. As I have commented elsewhere, this work also had changes and/or deletions effected for the sake of climax rhythm in the last few scenes of the completed film. The whole sequence of the movie-within-the-movie scene on pages 384 and 385 in the screenplay was either omitted from the shooting or deleted after it was filmed—quite clearly because it held up the inexorable climax of the film. This most frequently occurs within the climax scenes of films simply because a filmed story takes on a life of its own once created and makes its own rhythmic logic.

Fade in on almost the entire screen in black shadow. The upper right corner is the only color, and that is a white that almost stings to look at it—it is the white heat of the afternoon sun, and the shadow, we come to realize, is the side of some building together with the shadow of that building on the ground. If we don't know quite what it is that we're seeing at this point, that's all right. Camera holds on the shot, after a moment the shadow of a man begins to fill the upper right corner. As the shadow lengthens,

Cut to:

A man, idly walking around a corner of the building. He is BUTCH CASSIDY and hard to pin down. Thirty-five and bright, he has brown hair, but most people, if asked to describe him, would remember him blond. He speaks well and quickly and has been all his life a leader of men; but if you asked him, he would be damned if he could tell you why.

Cut to:

BUTCH, stopping by a window, giving it a glance.

Cut to:

The window. It is heavily and magnificently barred.

Cut to:

BUTCH, scowling briefly at the bars. He moves in toward the window to look through, and as he does, there begins a series of very quick cuts. (BUTCH, it might be noted here, is casing the bank, and what he is doing as his eyes flick from place to place inside is probing the place for weaknesses. But if we don't know quite what it is that he's doing at this point, that's all right too.)

Cut to:

A door. It is thick and solid metal and strong.

Cut to:

Paper money, being counted by ten skilled fingers.

Cut to:

A gun in a holster, belonging to a uniformed man in a guard's uniform.

Cut to:

A window high up on one wall. It is, if anything, more heavily and magnificently barred than the first.

Cut to:

The door of a big safe. It is behind shining bars and it is the kind of safe that has a time lock and—

Cut to:

BUTCH, eyes expertly flicking from place to place. Then he starts to walk around the bank again, and he isn't happy.

Cut to:

A bank guard. It is closing time now and he is slamming metal plates into place, the sound loud and sharp and final. The camera pulls back to reveal BUTCH, watching the guard work.

BUTCH. What was the matter with that old bank this town used to have? It was beautiful.

GUARD. (continuing to slam things shut). People kept robbing it.

Cut to:

BUTCH, who starts to walk away across the street toward a barn of a building with a sign outside: "Macon's Saloon." In the middle of the street he turns and stares back at the bank. It is new, and ugly, and squat, and functional, and built like a tank.

Cut to:

Close-up—BUTCH.

BUTCH (yelling back to the guard). That's a small price to pay for beauty.

And from this close-up of BUTCH—

Dissolve to:

Close-up—a MUSTACHED MAN. Pull back to reveal MACON's saloon. It is a barn of a place, without much decoration, and it is all but empty now, giving an even greater impression of size. Almost the only action in the place comes from a game of blackjack in which the MUSTACHED MAN is dealing (There are other tables set up ready for play, chips and cards neatly placed, but this is afternoon now, the sun slants in through windows, and the other tables are empty.)

Cut to:

The blackjack game. The MUSTACHED MAN is dealing to a PLAYER.

PLAYER. Hit me.

The MUSTACHED MAN flicks a card.

PLAYER. Over.

He pushes back from the table. Hesitates. Then—

PLAYER. Gimme credit, Mr. Macon?

Cut to:

JOHN MACON. *He is a well-dressed, good-looking man in a big, rugged way. Not yet thirty, he gives the strong impression of power and maturity—he has come a long way through a tough world and he has come fast. He is a man who, at all times, knows whereof he speaks.*

MACON (*shaking his head "no"*). You know my rules, Tom.

He turns now, looks at the MUSTACHED MAN.

MACON. You just about cleaned everybody, fella—I don't think you lost since you got the deal.

Cut to:

THE MUSTACHED MAN. *He says nothing.*

Cut to:

MACON.

MACON. What's the secret of your success?

Cut to:

THE MUSTACHED MAN.

MUSTACHED MAN. Prayer.

Cut to:

MACON. *And he isn't smiling.*

MACON. Let's just you and me play.

Cut to:

MACON *and* THE MUSTACHED MAN. THE MUSTACHED MAN *deals quickly, with no excess motion. The betting and the flicking out of the cards goes fast.*

MACON. Hit me. (*he gets another card*) Again. (*another card comes fast*) Too much.

As the MUSTACHED MAN *starts to take in the money—*

Cut to:

MACON. *Smiling now.*

MACON. You're what's too much, fella—whatever it is you're doing. You're one helluva cardplayer, and I know, because *I'm* one helluva cardplayer, and *I* can't even spot how you're cheating.

Cut to:

THE MUSTACHED MAN, *doing his best to ignore what has just been said. He continues to carefully stack his winnings into even piles.*

Cut to:

MACON, *on his feet. He wears guns, and his big hands are near them, relaxed and ready.*

Cut to:

MACON *and* THE MUSTACHED MAN.

MACON (*pointing to the money*). That stays—you go.
MUSTACHED MAN. What if I stay?

His reply is not arrogant—just factual.

MACON. You won't.

Cut to:

THE MUSTACHED MAN. *He sits almost sadly, slumped in his chair. His head is down. Now—*

Cut to:

BUTCH, *tearing up to the card table, talking as he comes—*

BUTCH. —we look a little short of brotherly love around here—

Cut to:

MACON, *standing there, his hands by his guns.*

MACON. You with this garbage, get yourselves out of here—

Cut to:

BUTCH *and* THE MUSTACHED MAN. BUTCH *is pulling at the* MUSTACHED MAN, *who does not budge. As he pulls, he talks to* MACON—

BUTCH. Yessir, thank you sir, we were just on our way and—

Urgently now—to the MUSTACHED MAN, *who will not move—*

BUTCH. Will you come on?

Cut to:

BUTCH, *dropping down now beside the* MUSTACHED MAN. *This next is whispered and fast—*

MUSTACHED MAN. —I wasn't cheating—
BUTCH (*trying to budge the other man*). —move —
MUSTACHED MAN. —I wasn't cheating —

Cut to:

MACON, *getting a little impatient now—*

MACON. You can die—no one's immune—you can *both* die—

Cut to:

BUTCH *and the* MUSTACHED MAN. *Lower and faster even than before—*

BUTCH. —you hear that? —now you got him mad at me—

MUSTACHED MAN. —if he invites us to stay, then we'll go—

BUTCH. —*we were gonna leave anyway*—

MUSTACHED MAN. —*he's gotta invite us to stick around!*—

Cut to:

Close-up—the MUSTACHED MAN. *And here there will be a series of quick cuts, as his eyes take in everything around him. This will be not dissimilar in style to the moment with* BUTCH *casing the bank. While the cuts are going on, the following dialogue will continue overlapping and low between* BUTCH *and the* MUSTACHED MAN. *The cuts will include the following:*

A. MACON'S *hands.*

B. A window and sun streaming in and does it hit anybody's eyes.

C. The area behind the MUSTACHED MAN *and is there anyone dangerous there.*

D. MACON'S *eyes.*

E. The area to the side of the MUSTACHED MAN *and is there room to move.*

To repeat: while these quick cuts take place (and if we don't know what they're for, again, that's all right), camera returns constantly to the MUSTACHED MAN *in close-up, with* BUTCH *beside him, moving in and out, both of them talking fast.*

BUTCH. —he'll draw on you—he's ready now and you don't know how fast he is—

MUSTACHED MAN. —that's just what I want to hear—

BUTCH. —face it—he don't look like he intends to lose—

MUSTACHED MAN. —you're really building up my confidence—

BUTCH. —well I'm over the hill—it can happen to you—every day you get older—that's a law—

THE MUSTACHED MAN *is clearly not leaving and as* BUTCH *realizes this*—

Cut to:

BUTCH, *rising, moving to* MACON.

BUTCH. What would you think about maybe inviting us to stick around.

MACON. *What?*

BUTCH. —you don't have to mean it or any-thing—but if you'd just please invite us to stick around I promise you we'll go and—

MACON *gestures sharply for* BUTCH *to get the hell back out of the way and*—

Cut to:

BUTCH. *He hesitates a moment, glancing down at the* MUSTACHED MAN *who still sits slumped in his chair.* BUTCH *shakes his head, then moves back out of the way.*

BUTCH *(softly).* Can't help you, Sundance.

Camera zooms in on MACON *as the last word echoes. It registers, that word, and now* MACON *has a secret he tries desperately to keep behind his eyes: the man is terrified.*

Cut to:

THE SUNDANCE KID, *for that is the name of the* MUSTACHED MAN. *He sits slumped a moment more, his head down. Then he slowly raises his head. His eyes dazzle. He looks dead into* MACON'S *eyes. Still staring, he stands. He too wears guns.*

Cut to:

MACON. *A brave man doing his best, he stands still and does not look away.*

Cut to:

SUNDANCE. *He says nothing.*

Cut to:

MACON, *and now the panic is slowly starting to seep out.*

MACON. I didn't know you were the Sun-dance Kid when I said you were cheating.

Cut to:

SUNDANCE. *He says nothing. His eyes are on* MACON'S *hands now.*

Cut to:

MACON'S *hands, still close to his guns.*

Cut to:

SUNDANCE. *He says nothing. He just waits, stares.*

Cut to:

MACON.

MACON *(the words burst out of him).* If I draw on you you'll kill me.

Cut to:

SUNDANCE.

SUNDANCE. There is that possibility.

Cut to:

BUTCH, *moving in on* MACON *now.*

BUTCH. No sir, you'd just be killing your-self. *(urging now)* So invite us to stick around, why don't you?

Cut to:

MACON. *He starts to speak, stops, and—*

Cut to: BUTCH.

BUTCH. —you can do it—easy—come on, come on—

Cut to:

SUNDANCE. *The man does not make unneces-sary motions: he stands now as before, silent and staring, eyes bright, ready.*

Cut to:

MACON.

MACON *(he can barely get the words out).* . . . stick around why don't you? . . .

Cut to:

BUTCH *and* SUNDANCE.

BUTCH. Thanks but we got to be going.

And as they move together along the path of gambling tables toward the door—

Cut to:

MACON, *watching them go.*

MACON. Kid? *(a little louder now)* Hey how good are you?

Cut to:

BUTCH *and* SUNDANCE. SUNDANCE *makes no move, no reaction to having heard* MACON's *words.*

BUTCH. Don't just stand here, show the man—

And he unexpectedly grabs some poker chips from a table, flips them high and—

Cut to:

The poker chips, red and blue, and spinning prettily, and—

Cut to:

SUNDANCE, *diving left and dropping and long before the move is done the guns are out and roaring and as the terrible noise sounds—*

Cut to:

All the poker chips, and maybe one of them falls untouched through the noise, but all the others, all of them, shatter, and—

Cut to:

JOHN MACON, *breathing the biggest sigh of relief anyone ever saw and—*

Cut to:

SUNDANCE, *his guns quiet now, and—*

Cut to:

BUTCH, *staring at the one poker chip that lays intact on the floor, indicates it to* SUNDANCE, *as they move to exit.*

BUTCH. Like I been telling you—over the hill.

And they are gone.

Dissolve to:

Main title sequence. This is a series of shots which, for the first time, really open up the story visually. Up until now, the scenes have been "western" but they haven't attempted to include any of that incredible feeling of awesome size this kind of picture ought honestly to have. Now, in this series of cuts—some with BUTCH *and* SUNDANCE, *riding, some without—we get it all. There is a feeling of time passing, of distance, of changing terrain, all of it leading to the culminating shots when the credits end, and the effect by then should be considerable, for by then we will be at Hole-in-the-Wall. A list of shots might include:*

Clouds. They are white, just like clouds ought to be, and they are fluffy, and they hang there in the sky, and pull back to reveal BUTCH *and* SUNDANCE, *riding along, above the clouds, which spread out below them, filling a canyon. As* BUTCH *and* SUNDANCE *begin riding down into the clouds—*

Cut to:

A small herd of deer, startled and scared, veering one way, then another, then gone as BUTCH *and* SUNDANCE *come riding down.*

Cut to:

The sun, dying. BUTCH *and* SUNDANCE *sit by a low fire, eating quietly.*

Cut to:

A snake. It is hot and sunny and it makes its quick way toward a lake. As it starts to swim—

Cut to:

BUTCH *and* SUNDANCE *riding slowly through the heat, skirting the edge of the lake, continu-ing on. They started their ride high up some-where, they are now just as clearly down low. There is heat and dry rock and blazing sun and—*

Cut to:

A flock of birds, flying up at a slow angle, and as they continue to soar, in the distance, there are mountains, and on top of the mountains, snow.

Cut to:

BUTCH *and* SUNDANCE, *starting a long climb now, working their way up a canyon. It is not easy riding and they take their time and—*

Cut to:

A bend in a stream, as the first cool sun rays begin to bounce off. Then—

Cut to:

BUTCH *and* SUNDANCE, *saddling their horses as the dawn brightens. Their breakfast fire is already beginning to flicker away; they have been up awhile.*

Cut to:

A mountain stream bed. It rises toward a distant crest and—

Cut to:

BUTCH *and* SUNDANCE, *working their way carefully up along the stream bed, toward the crest.*

Cut to:

Another angle—

BUTCH *and* SUNDANCE, *riding along the crest, picking up their pace a little now because they are getting there and—*

Cut to:

A rock formation that is strangely shaped, almost like a gated entrance to something, which it is, the entrance to Hole-in-the-Wall and now—

Cut to:

Hole-in-the-Wall. It is a sloping green valley, concave in shape, its upper rim coming in direct contact with a series of enormously high cliffs which rise almost vertically. At the bottom of the valley are a series of small lakes and streams.

Cut to:

BUTCH *and* SUNDANCE, *in the gated entrance made by the rock formation.*

Cut to:

Close-up— BUTCH *and* SUNDANCE, *staring out at all the desolate isolation.*

BUTCH. Ahhhhh; home.

And they start to ride down into the valley.

Cut to:

BUTCH *and* SUNDANCE *riding. As they move along, several of the cliffs behind them become momentarily visible, which is of interest for only one reason: the cliffs are filled with caves and every so often an armed lookout appears from a cave and signals and* BUTCH, *without ever breaking the rhythm of his speech, signals back.*

BUTCH. Y'know, every time I see Hole-in-the-Wall again . . .

Pan to the valley and the cliffs, glorious and desolate, breathtaking and lonely.

BUTCH'S VOICE *(o.s.)*. . . . it's like seeing it fresh, for the first time . . .

Cut to:

BUTCH, *riding along,* SUNDANCE *beside him.*

BUTCH. . . . and whenever that happens I ask myself the same question: how can I be so damn stupid as to keep coming back here?

SUNDANCE *has heard this kind of speech before from* BUTCH.

SUNDANCE. What's your idea this time?

Cut to:

Close-up— BUTCH.

BUTCH. Bolivia!

Cut to:

SUNDANCE. *He gives* BUTCH *a look.*

SUNDANCE. What's Bolivia?

Cut to:

BUTCH *and* SUNDANCE.

BUTCH. Bolivia's a country, stupid—in Central or South America, one or the other.

SUNDANCE. Why don't we just go to Mexico?

BUTCH. 'Cause all they got in Mexico is sweat and they sell plenty of that back here. Now listen: if we'd been in business during the California gold rush, where would we have gone to operate? California, right? Well, when I say Bolivia, you think California because they're falling into it down there—silver mines, tin, gold; payrolls so big we'd strain our backs stealing 'em—

Cut to:

SUNDANCE. *He looks at* BUTCH, *shakes his head.*

SUNDANCE. You just keep thinking, Butch; that's what you're good at.

Cut to:

BUTCH.

BUTCH. I got vision and the rest of the world wears bifocals.

Cut to:

A shot of the base of the valley. Several plain cabins are visible. Outside the cabins there are a considerable number of men and horses.

Cut to:

BUTCH *and* SUNDANCE *riding up.*

BUTCH *(calling out, waving).* Hey, News—

Cut to:

NEWS CARVER, *a slender man of thirty. He is terribly busy taking care of his horse and makes no answer.*

Cut to:

BUTCH *and* SUNDANCE, *pulling up beside him.*

BUTCH. News, what're you doing?

NEWS *(looking up, suddenly smiling).* Oh, hi Butch. Nothing, nothing. Hello there, Sundance.

BUTCH. Sure y'are. You're getting ready to do something. What?

Cut to:

NEWS. *He is not happy and his words, when they come, come fast.*

NEWS. Just fixing to rob the Union Pacific Flyer, Butch, that's all we had in mind.

Cut to:

BUTCH *and* SUNDANCE. BUTCH *dismounts.* SUNDANCE *stays still, watching.*

BUTCH *(as he gets down).* You got everything I told you wrong—when I left I said we *might* hit the Flyer, but even if we did, it wasn't this run but the one after, the return. Now Sundance and me been out checking the bank situation and—

HARVEY LOGAN'S VOICE *(o.s.).* No banks.

BUTCH *(looking around, genuinely confused).* What?

Cut to:

HARVEY LOGAN, *in the doorway to one of the cabins. He is a big man, thick and powerful. He was, in reality, a terrible man, vicious and frightening, and some of that should show.*

LOGAN. The Flyer, Butch.

Cut to:

BUTCH, *looking around at his men as he talks and explaining, as a good teacher might—*

BUTCH. Now how many times have I told you people: banks are better than trains. You can rely on a bank—they don't move. They stay put and you always know there's money inside and my orders were—

Cut to:

LOGAN, *moving away from the cabin toward* BUTCH.

LOGAN. New orders been give.

BUTCH. Harvey, I run things here.

LOGAN. Use to you did. Me now. *(pointing off suddenly)* This don't concern you.

Cut to:

SUNDANCE, *silent, seated on his horse, looking down at them all.*

Cut to:

BUTCH *and* LOGAN.

LOGAN. Tell him to stay out.

BUTCH. He goes his own way, like always.

Then he suddenly whirls to face the gang of men who stand bunched, watching. BUTCH *moves toward them, talking as he goes—*

BUTCH. What's the matter with you people?—before I came here you were starving and you know it. You weren't even a gang—*I* formed you. News—News—read that damn clipping—

Cut to:

NEWS, *reaching into his pockets.*

NEWS. Which one?

Cut to:

BUTCH, *hurrying to him.*

BUTCH. Any of 'em.

NEWS *has taken out a batch of news clippings. Unfolding the first—*

NEWS. This here's from the Salt Lake Herald—*(he begins to read)* "Butch Cassidy's Wild Bunch struck again today, looting the—"

BUTCH. That's enough right there. "Butch Cassidy's Wild Bunch."—Hear that? That's you and that's me. Harvey gonna plan for you all? Harvey gonna do your thinking and run things and—

He turns back to NEWS, *who has kept right on reading throughout* BUTCH's *speech.*

BUTCH. News, you can shut up now.

Cut to:

NEWS. *He looks up at* BUTCH *for a moment.*

NEWS. Not til I come to the good part. *(reading away again)* "Also known to have participated in the holdup are Flat Nose Curry and News Carver." *(folding up the clipping now)* I just love hearing my name in the papers.

NOTE: *As indicated,* NEWS *continues to read from the clipping while* BUTCH *talks. What he reads goes like this:*

NEWS. "Butch Cassidy's Wild Bunch struck again today, looting the Montpelier Idaho bank over close to twenty thousand dollars. Cassidy's gang, all notorious outlaws and desperadoes of the first water, camped outside of Ogden while they planned their robbery. Cassidy and the Sundance Kid had half a dozen outlaws with them on their foray. Harvey Logan was one."

From here, NEWS *is back into the regular dialogue scene with* BUTCH. *If the above is too short, more can be added; if, as seems likely, it runs too long, it can obviously stand cutting.*

Cut to:

BUTCH *and his men.*

BUTCH. Now let's just forget about Harvey taking over. Okay, Flat Nose?

FLAT NOSE CURRY *has been nicknamed for obvious reasons.*

FLAT NOSE CURRY. You always told us anyone could challenge you—
BUTCH. That's 'cause I figured nobody'd do it.

Cut to:

LOGAN, *smiling, starting toward* BUTCH *again.*

LOGAN. Figured wrong, Butch.

Cut to:

BUTCH *and his men.*

BUTCH *(a little desperate now).* You can't want Logan—
NEWS. —at least he's with us, Butch—you been spending a lot of time gone—

Cut to:

Close-up— BUTCH.

BUTCH. That's 'cause everything's changing now—it's all going new on us—

Cut to:

LOGAN.

LOGAN. Guns or knives, Butch?

Cut to:

BUTCH. *Going rapidly on, doing his best to ignore* LOGAN.

BUTCH. —everything's harder than it used to be—you got to plan more, you got to prepare, you got to be damn sure what you're doing or you're dead—

Cut to:

LOGAN, *moving in front of* BUTCH *now.*

LOGAN. Guns or knives?
BUTCH. Neither.
LOGAN. *Pick!*
BUTCH. I don't want to shoot with you, Harvey.

Cut to:

LOGAN, *smiling.*

LOGAN. Whatever you say, Butch.

And suddenly a knife is in his hand and—

Cut to:

The men, and with the appearance of the knife they start to get really excited, and from here on in that excitement only builds as they surge toward LOGAN *who is calmly taking off his shirt.* BUTCH *moves to* SUNDANCE.

Cut to:

SUNDANCE *on his horse, waiting quietly as* BUTCH *approaches.* BUTCH *is doing his best to cover how he feels.*

BUTCH. Maybe there's a way to make a profit on this—bet on Logan.
SUNDANCE. I would, but who'd bet on you?
BUTCH. I made this gang. You know I did. Now look at 'em.

Cut to:

The gang, clustered around LOGAN. *He is stripped to the waist and his body is brutal. Suddenly he calls out—*

LOGAN. Sundance—when we're done, if he's dead, you're welcome to stay.

Cut to:

BUTCH *and* SUNDANCE. *Looking out at* LOGAN. BUTCH *speaks quietly to* SUNDANCE.

BUTCH. Listen, I'm not a sore loser or any-thing, but when we're done, if I'm dead, kill him.

SUNDANCE *(to Logan, but in answer to Butch).* Love to.

Cut to:

BUTCH. *He fidgets a moment, then starts the long walk back toward* LOGAN. LOGAN *is younger and faster and stronger and* BUTCH *knows it, and knowing it doesn't make the walk any pleasanter. Still he moves forward, un-armed as yet, toward the other man.*

Cut to:

LOGAN, *watching him come. In the sun his body glistens.*

Cut to:

BUTCH, *moving through the gang toward* LOGAN. *He is unarmed and a knife is offered him by one of the gang.*

BUTCH. Not yet. *(moving up to Logan now)* Not til Harvey and me get all the rules straight.

LOGAN. *Rules? In a knife fight? No rules!*

As he finishes speaking BUTCH *delivers the most aesthetically exquisite kick in the balls in the history of the modern American cinema.*

Cut to:

LOGAN. *For a moment he just stands there. Then he makes an absolutely indescribable sound and, as the look on his face moves from disbelief to displeasure he sinks slowly to his knees.*

Cut to:

BUTCH. *He goes on as if nothing whatsoever had happened.*

BUTCH. Well, if there aren't going to be any rules, I guess we might as well get this fight started. Somebody say "one-two-three-go."

Cut to:

SUNDANCE.

SUNDANCE *(like a shot).* One-two-three-go.

Cut to:

LOGAN. *He is green now, and still on his knees.* BUTCH *approaches, nods, locks his hands together and, as if swinging a baseball bat, delivers a stunning blow to* LOGAN's *jaw.* LOGAN *falls and lies there.*

Cut to:

FLAT NOSE CURRY *and several others, all hurrying to* BUTCH.

FLAT NOSE. I was sure rooting for you, Butch.

BUTCH *(with great earnestness).* I know, Flat Nose. That's what sustained me in my time of trouble. *(looking around).* News? Now what's all this about the Flyer?

Cut to:

NEWS *as he moves to* BUTCH.

NEWS. Harvey said we'd hit 'em both, this run and the return. He said no one'd ever done that yet to the Flyer so no matter what we got the first time, they'd be sure to figure the return was safe and load it up with money.

BUTCH. Harvey thought that up?

NEWS. Yessir, he did.

BUTCH. Well I'll tell you something: that's just what we'll do.

Cut to:

LOGAN, *who is still out, as* BUTCH *drops to his knees beside him.*

BUTCH *(slapping Logan's cheeks).* Good thinking, Harvey.

Cut to:

SUNDANCE, *and we don't know quite what he's doing. But he is dressed differently from the preceding, and the sun is at a different angle, so we do know this is a different time, perhaps a different place. There is a, for the moment, unidentified and continuing roar and as it goes on, it becomes clear that* SUNDANCE *isn't paying any attention to it. But whatever it is he is paying attention to, he is concentrating com-pletely, almost like an Olympic high jumper before attempting a seven-foot leap.* SUNDANCE *continues his intense concentration a moment more because whatever he is about to do is damn dangerous and then his quick body is in motion and—*

Cut to:

Another angle— SUNDANCE *running and—*

Cut to:

A passing train, curving below the rock from which SUNDANCE *hurls himself. The train is not far below the level of the rock, so the drop isn't dangerous—what's dangerous is that the thing is moving like hell and if he lands wrong* SUNDANCE *is going to roll off and die and—*

Cut to:

SUNDANCE, *landing wrong, but not completely, and he scrabbles his body back onto the center of the top of the train car and then—*

Cut to:

*Close-up—*SUNDANCE, *sweating and happy to be breathing. He stays where he is for a moment, getting collected, before standing and starting his precarious way up toward the engine.*

Cut to:

SUNDANCE, *moving along. (When this kind of thing is done in movies, it's by John Wayne and it's easy apple pie. Well it isn't easy, you can get killed up there, and that is very much in* SUNDANCE'*s mind as he makes his way).*

Cut to:

Inside the engine. The ENGINEER *and the* FIREMAN *are working. The* ENGINEER *is fifty and spare, almost a New England type. The* FIREMAN *is small, but with tremendous arms and shoulders and would speak a lot clearer if he had more teeth.*

Cut to:

The empty tracks ahead. The landscape whizzing by on either side. All very peaceful and S.O.P. and—

Cut to:

THE ENGINEER. *Taut, and without a word, his hands start to raise as we—*

Cut to:

SUNDANCE, *quickly inside the engine, guns ready.*

Cut to:

The three of them. The ENGINEER *has the responsibility of the train, and he acquits himself throughout as well as he can, considering the fact that he is always aware that he is liable to get killed at anytime. The* FIREMAN, *frightened at first, stays close to the* ENGINEER. *Gradually, as the scene goes on, he gains confidence.*

ENGINEER *(low and clipped).* You want it stopped?

SUNDANCE *nods once.*

ENGINEER. Where?
SUNDANCE. Here would be fine.

Cut to:

THE ENGINEER, *starting to slow the train.*

Cut to:

THE FIREMAN *looking at* SUNDANCE, *maybe gathering courage to say something and—*

Cut to:

THE ENGINEER, *making a quick move for a gun down out of the way and—*

Cut to:

SUNDANCE, *on top of him like a shot, grabbing the gun away, and—*

Cut to:

SUNDANCE *and the* ENGINEER. *The* ENGINEER *is almost panting and he can't stop.*

ENGINEER. That wasn't so smart of me.
SUNDANCE. Not very.
ENGINEER. I don't want any trouble.
SUNDANCE. It looks that way.

Cut to:

THE ENGINEER. *He starts to say something more, decides against it, turns and works on stopping the train and—*

Cut to:

A shot of the tracks from inside the engine. In the distance a figure can be seen standing in the center of the tracks.

Cut to:

SUNDANCE, *as the toothless* FIREMAN *goes to him and points out—*

FIREMAN. I bet that's old Butch himself.

SUNDANCE *gives him a look.*

FIREMAN. Oh, you wouldn't remember me, but I worked the Great Northern Express when you hit it near Wagner.

Cut to:

THE ENGINEER, *watching them.*

ENGINEER. Shut up, Gummy.
FIREMAN. He ain't gonna shoot us—hell, if he was gonna shoot us, he'd a shot us when you tried to shoot him, right, Kid?

Cut to:

SUNDANCE. *He says nothing.*

Cut to:

The head of a train passenger, as it appears from a window, looks around, trying to see why the train is stopping. This is shot from the engine, so that when other heads appear, as they will soon, they will form an almost endless line of heads sticking out.

Cut to:

THE FIREMAN, *looking back toward the passengers, as another head sticks out, then another and another.*

FIREMAN. I'd like to tell you it was engine trouble folks, but we're being held up by the Wild Bunch and The Sundance Kid would like for you all to stay in your seats—so stick your heads in.

Cut to:

The passenger cars. More heads are sticking out now, all of them turning and babbling and asking questions of one another.

Cut to:

THE FIREMAN, *shouting to the heads.*

FIREMAN. Stick your heads in . . . stick your heads in . . .

Cut to:

The passenger cars, with all the heads sticking out like turtles now, babbling and jabbering and—

Cut to:

SUNDANCE, *firing. The bullets are not intended to kill. Just to come close. And they do. Very.*

Cut to:

All conceivable heads, disappearing in unison back inside the cars and—

Cut to:

SUNDANCE *and the* FIREMAN, *as* SUNDANCE *starts out of the engine.*

FIREMAN *(roaring with laughter).* That sure was a sight, I'm here to tell you.
SUNDANCE. You sure are.

And he drops to the ground, starts moving along the passenger cars. Behind him, the FIREMAN *clambers to the ground. During this, other members of the gang are visible, some of them standing, guns drawn, in the doorways of the passenger cars. The* FIREMAN *hurries along, falling into step with* SUNDANCE, *who looks down at the little man a moment, then slowly shakes his head.*

FIREMAN. Thought I'd watch.
SUNDANCE. Bring the kids why don't you?

Cut to:

THE ENGINEER. *He grins gummily.*

Cut to:

Ext. Express car. BUTCH, *gun in hand, is banging at the door. While the following dialogue goes on, other members of the gang can be seen planting dynamite beneath the car.*

BUTCH *(he is clearly a little frayed).* You're just gonna get yourself blown up so open the door!
VOICE *(o.s., from inside the car).* I can't do that on account of I work for Mr. E. H. Harriman of the Union Pacific Railroad and he entrusted me—

BUTCH *has been hearing a lot of this these last few minutes.*

BUTCH. Will you shut up with that E. H. Harriman business and open the door.

Cut to:

SUNDANCE, *moving up to* BUTCH. *The* FIREMAN *is half a pace behind.*

BUTCH *(as Sundance approaches).* They got a patriot on their side.
FIREMAN. That's young Woodcock; he's awful dedicated.
NEWS *(hurrying to Butch).* Dynamite's ready.

BUTCH *nods.* NEWS *goes.*

BUTCH. Woodcock?

Cut to:

*Int. Express car—*WOODCOCK. *He stands pressed against the door. Behind him is a good-sized safe.* WOODCOCK *is a young man with a soft western accent, an unexceptional but pleasant face. His sandy hair is slightly receding and he is right now scared to death and it shows. But his voice—words well chosen, spoken calmly—belies that fact.*

WOODCOCK. Yes sir?
BUTCH'S VOICE *(o.s.).* You know who we are?
WOODCOCK. You're the Wild Bunch, Mr. Cassidy. I understand that, but you gotta understand that Mr. E. H. Harriman himself of the Union Pacific Railroad gimme this job and I never had such responsibility before and since he entrusted me to get the money through, I got to do my best, don't you see?

Cut to:

*Ext. Express car—*BUTCH *and* SUNDANCE.

BUTCH. Your best doesn't include getting killed.

Cut to:

WOODCOCK—*Inside. His eyes are closed now as he presses hard against the door.*

WOODCOCK. Mr. E. H. Harriman himself, he had the confidence in me—
BUTCH'S VOICE *(o.s.).* Open the door. Or that's it.

WOODCOCK *makes no move.*

Cut to:

BUTCH—*Outside.*

BUTCH. Ya think he'd die for you, ya lousy amateur?

There is no answer from inside the car.

BUTCH. *Now, Woodcock!*

Cut to:

WOODCOCK —*Inside, huddled up, waiting for the blast.*

WOODCOCK. I work for Mr. E. H. Harriman of the Union Pacific Railroad—

Cut to:

Ext. Railroad car exploding, one wall just ripped away.

Cut to:

WOODCOCK's *body hurtling through the air, crashing down.*

Cut to:

BUTCH *and* SUNDANCE, *followed by the rest of the gang pouring into the car. While* SUNDANCE *heads for the same*

Cut to:

BUTCH *going to* WOODCOCK, *who is alive and crawling and a little bloody.*

BUTCH. You okay?

WOODCOCK *makes a nod. As* BUTCH *helps* WOODCOCK *to get comfortable—*

Cut to:

SUNDANCE *kneeling beside the safe ouside the car, deftly wedging several sticks of dynamite into place, lighting them, then backing off fast and—*

Cut to:

The safe. There is a muffled explosion and the door bursts neatly open.

Cut to:

SUNDANCE *as* BUTCH *approaches.* BUTCH *looks at the beautifully-blown safe.*

BUTCH. Dammitall, why is everything we're good at illegal?

Cut to:

NEWS, *taking money from the same.*

Cut to:

BUTCH *and* SUNDANCE *watching him.*

BUTCH. Hurry it up; give us our shares.
NEWS. There ain't what I'd call a fortune in here, Butch.
BUTCH. Just so we come out ahead, News; that's the main thing.

Cut to:

A young, competent MARSHAL—*night. Pull back to reveal a crowd of citizens standing in a street, looking up at the* MARSHAL. *It is dusk. The* MARSHAL *is speaking in a very businesslike tone—without much emotion.*

MARSHAL. All right; they just robbed the Flyer outside our town, and that makes it our responsibility to get after them—

Cut to:

The second floor porch of a building down the street. The building is Fanny Porter's, and it was as well known as any brothel-saloon of the period. Seated on the porch, listening to the MARSHAL *talk, are* BUTCH *and* SUNDANCE. *They are sprawled comfortably, hats pulled down. Between them on the table are two large steins and a bucket of beer. They are both a little buzzed.*

MARSHAL'S VOICE *(o.s.)* —now you'll have to bring your own horses—

Cut to:

THE MARSHAL *and the crowd.*

MARSHAL. —how many of you can bring your own guns?—

Cut to:

The crowd. No one can. No hands are raised.

Cut to:

THE MARSHAL.

MARSHAL. Okay. Then how many of you want me to supply you with guns?

Cut to:

The crowd. No hands are raised.

Cut to:

THE MARSHAL. *It is beginning to dawn on him now that he is not getting through to his audience.*

MARSHAL. Come on now—it's up to us to do something.

Cut to:

THE MARSHAL *and the crowd.*

FIRST CITIZEN. What's the point? They're probably half way to Hole in the Wall already.
MARSHAL. That's why we've got to hurry—we can head them off—
SECOND CITIZEN *(aghast).* —head 'em off? —you crazy? —we do that and they'll kill us.

There is general vocal agreement on this point from the crowd.

Cut to:

BUTCH *and* SUNDANCE—*on the porch.*

BUTCH *(beaming).* I just eat this up with a spoon.

SUNDANCE *nods; as they fill their steins with more beer—*

Cut to:

FANNY PORTER *entering from a door behind them. It isn't easy running a successful brothel and she shows the strain.*

FANNY *(moving up behind Butch and Sundance).* All right, you two; I want you at my party.

She gestures to the open door through which she entered and—

Cut to:

The scene through the door. ONE YOUNG MAN *is by a piano with* HALF A DOZEN GIRLS. *A song of the period is being sung. A home-made sign—* "REMEMBER THE MAINE" *—is amateurishly strung along one wall.*

FANNY'S VOICE *(o.s.).* I'm losing my piano player—he's going off to fight in the Spanish-American War.

Cut to:

FANNY.

FANNY *(as she exits).* I'm giving him a send-off, so come on.

Cut to:

BUTCH *and* SUNDANCE. *They each take a long drink from their steins—* BUTCH *is really buzzed by this time—then they turn and glance back through the door.*

Cut to:

THE PIANO PLAYER. *He is sitting on top of the piano now, the girls grouped around him, looking up at his face.*

Cut to:

BUTCH *and* SUNDANCE, *staring inside.*

BUTCH. Y'know, when I was a kid, I always figured on being a hero when I grew up.
SUNDANCE. Too late now.
BUTCH. You didn't have to say that—what'd you have to say that for?

As he drains his glass—

Cut to:

THE YOUNG MARSHAL *still trying to gather his posse. He is a clever man and he is using psychology now.*

MARSHAL. Listen—it's *my* job to go fight them—you want me to go off alone and fight the Wild Bunch, fine with me—*you want your kids* to know you let me do that? Fine with me, but I don't think that's what *you* want, is it?

Cut to:

THE CROWD. *There is no negative outcry whatsoever.*

Cut to:

BUTCH, *whirling in his chair, grabbing* SUNDANCE, *excited—*

BUTCH. Hey-hey—let's enlist and go fight the Spanish—you and me in the war—

SUNDANCE *just gives him a look.*

BUTCH. —listen, we got a lot going for us: experience, maturity, leadership. Hell, I bet we'd end up officers—I'd be Major Parker—

Cut to:

SUNDANCE.

SUNDANCE. Parker?

Cut to:

BUTCH *and* SUNDANCE.

BUTCH. That's my real name—Robert Leroy Parker.
SUNDANCE. Mine's Longbaugh.
BUTCH. —long what?
SUNDANCE. Harry Longbaugh.
BUTCH. You'd be Major Longbaugh then; what do you say?

Cut to:

SUNDANCE.

SUNDANCE. You just keep thinking, Butch; that's what you're good at.

Cut to:

BUTCH.

BUTCH *(into his beer)*. I got vision and the rest of the world wears bifocals.

Cut to:

THE MARSHAL, *and he is mad.*

MARSHAL. You gonna go through life with your heads down? You gonna travel with your tail between your legs? You gonna shake at every sound you can't see what's makin' it? *What do you say?*

A NEW AND DIFFERENT VOICE *(o.s.)* I say boys and girls

As the voice goes on—

Cut to:

THE SPEAKER. *He is a* SALESMAN *and in a minute we will find out what he's selling.*

SALESMAN. —friends and enemies—*(big)*— Meet—the—*future.*

As he says the word "future"—

Cut to:

A brand new dazzling bicycle.

A VOICE FROM THE CROWD *(o.s.)*. The future what?

Cut to:

THE SALESMAN, *moving up alongside the* MARSHAL.

SALESMAN *(the man has leather lungs)*. The future mode of transportation for the weary western world.

MARSHAL. Now just what in the hell do you think you're doing?

SALESMAN. You got the crowd together— that's half my work—I just figured I'd sell a little and—

MARSHAL. Well I'm trying to raise a posse if you don't mind—

SALESMAN. I got a short presentation—*(to the crowd)*—the horse is dead! *(to the* MARSHAL*)* —you'll see—this item sells it-self—*(to the crowd)* Soon the eye will see nothing but silk-ribboned bicycle paths stretching to infinity.

MARSHAL *(to crowd)*. You gonna listen to him or you gonna come with me?

Cut to:

THE CROWD.

A CITIZEN. How much those things cost?

Cut to:

SALESMAN, *mounting his machine.*

SALESMAN. An indecently paltry amount. *(starting to ride)*. A bicycle is cheaper to buy than a horse, cheaper to maintain, as fast over short distances and I promise you this—

And now he removes both hands from the bars—

SALESMAN. —the pleasures it provides can be equalled only by the love of your lady.

Cut to:

A BLONDE GIRL, *moving up behind* BUTCH. *She has worked at* FANNY'S *for a while but is still young enough so it doesn't show.*

GIRL. Fanny says for you to come right now to her party.

BUTCH *nods, stands.* THE GIRL *comes into his arms.*

GIRL. You ever going to make an honest woman of me, Butch?

BUTCH. There aren't enough hours in the day.

Cut to:

SUNDANCE. *He stands too.*

SUNDANCE. I think I'll get saddled up and go looking for a woman too.

Cut to:

BUTCH, *moving away with the blonde.*

BUTCH. Good hunting.

Cut to:

SUNDANCE.

SUNDANCE. Shouldn't be too hard; I'm not picky. Just so she's pretty and sweet and quiet and smart and refined . . .

As he begins his list of qualifications—

Dissolve to:

ETTA PLACE—*Twilight. As* SUNDANCE'S *list is spoken, her face, at first faint, comes more and more clear. She is very much as described—she is in her middle twenties, and has dark hair pulled back tight into a bun. She wears neat, starched clothing, and it is impossible to tell what her figure might be like. The camera pulls back to reveal that she is in a schoolhouse, and it is twilight. There isn't really enough light to work, but she works anyway, sitting at her desk, grading papers. From somewhere outside the schoolhouse comes a night sound, and it startles her.*

Cut to:

The window and the night beyond. Nothing moves.

Cut to:

ETTA. *There is a clock on her desk. She glances at it, brings the papers into a neat pile, and gets up, goes to the door. As she opens it—*

Cut to:

The doorway, and ETTA *is turning off the inside light, moving into the dark night, quickly closing and locking the door and hurrying now around a corner of the building.*

Cut to:

A small house—night. She almost runs to it. The night is very dark and there is wind. The house is set off by itself behind the school. It is a one-story affair, obviously the kind of place built by the town to house the schoolmistress.

Cut to:

ETTA, *entering her small house. Closing the front door she moves across the tiny living room into the bedroom, undressing as she goes.*

Cut to:

Another angle— ETTA, *entering the bedroom, pulling off her blouse. There is a small light by the bed and as she gets it on, in this shadow-light, it is clear that she is really a terribly pretty thing. She wear a white slip and it contrasts nicely with her sun-darkened skin. She has a fuller body than she showed before. She begins to take off her skirt and is almost done before she whirls and freezes and damn near screams and—*

Cut to:

SUNDANCE, *gun in his lap, seated happily in a corner of the room, watching.*

SUNDANCE *(gesturing with his gun)*. Keep going, teacher lady.

Cut to:

ETTA. *She does not move.*

Cut to:

SUNDANCE.

SUNDANCE. It's all right, don't mind me—

And now he gestures with his gun again—

SUNDANCE. —keep right on going.

Cut to:

ETTA. *She makes a nod, then nervously manages to undo her skirt and as it slips to the floor—*

Cut to:

SUNDANCE. *He is enjoying himself.*

SUNDANCE. Don't stop on my account.

Cut to:

The two of them. She stares at him a moment, then begins to take off her slip. As she does so—

SUNDANCE. I'll tell you something, teacher lady—you're not so bad. Outside you're all stiff and starchy and prim, but underneath it all, not so bad.

Her slip is off now and her body, is also revealed to him. It is a splendid body.

SUNDANCE. Okay. Let down your hair.

Cut to:

ETTA. *She hesitates a moment before reaching back behind her head with both hands. Her fingers work quickly and in a moment her hair tumbles down over her shoulders.*

Cut to:

SUNDANCE, *watching appreciatively.*

SUNDANCE. Shake your head.

Cut to:

ETTA. *She shakes her head and her hair loosens up, covering her shoulders now, thick and gloriously black.*

Cut to:

SUNDANCE. *He tilts his head a moment, carefully examining the girl.*

Cut to:

ETTA, *as she stands there. She looks wild.*

Cut to:

SUNDANCE. *Slowly he begins to rise from the chair and move across the silent room toward her.*

Cut to:

ETTA, *not looking away, watching him come.*

Cut to:

SUNDANCE, *very close to her now. Beside them is the bed.*

Cut to:

ETTA, *unafraid, she stares at him.*

ETTA. Do you know what I wish?
SUNDANCE. What?
ETTA. That you'd once get here on time.

And her arms go around him, her mouth finds his, and locked, they fall toward the bed. As their bodies fall—

Cut to:

BUTCH's *head, just his head—gliding past a window at dawn. He might be a balloon floating by, for that is the impression his floating head gives. As his head goes by,* BUTCH *whispers a few words, much in the style of the melodrama villains of the time.*

BUTCH. You're mine, Etta Place; mine do you hear me?

The camera pulls back to reveal SUNDANCE *and* ETTA *asleep in bed. As her name is called out,* ETTA *stirs.*

Cut to:

BUTCH, *as his head glides by another window, then disappears a moment before reappearing again, floating gracefully past another window as, from inside, we watch his disembodied head circling the house.*

Cut to:

ETTA, *eyes open now, not entirely certain of the vision that confronts her and—*

Cut to:

BUTCH, *as he passes the window by the bed again.*

BUTCH. Mine I tell you; *mine!*

Cut to:

ETTA, *as she gives a laugh, grabs a robe and—*

Cut to:

The front door of the house, opening and ETTA *standing there. It is a beautiful early morning, barely dawn, and she turns, smiling, as around a corner of the house comes* BUTCH. *He is riding a bicycle, which accounts for the gliding impression he has been giving.*

BUTCH *(pulling up beside her).* Meet—the—future.

And he gestures for her to get on the cross bar.

ETTA. Do you know what you're doing?
BUTCH. Theoretically.

Cut to:

BUTCH, *pushing off after* ETTA *has hesitatingly gotten on the bike. It's downhill but it's still precarious at first and they almost tumble until he gets the hang of it, but once he's got it, he never loses it, and as they begin to pick up speed we are into:*

Musical Interlude Number One.

There are going to be three of them before the film is over. This, the first, is a song sung while BUTCH *and* ETTA *ride the bike. The song will be sung by male voices, and the feel of it is terribly contemporary, because in fact, the sound of the songs of this period are shockingly close in feel to the popular music of today.*

What we hear will not be a song like "Bicycle Built for Two". The song will be poignant and pretty as hell and, like the songs, for example, in "The Graduate", they will make an emotional comment on the scene, not a literal one; they will have an emotional connection with the scene, not a literal one.

Cut to:

BUTCH *and* ETTA, *spinning along, through a stunning aspen grove just after dawn, the sun slanting across them as they go and—*

Cut to:

BUTCH *and* ETTA, *with* BUTCH *swerving skillfully through a close packed bunch of aspen, almost like a halfback in heavy traffic, and after he has completed the move he says something that makes* ETTA *smile, then something else that makes her laugh and as she starts to break up—*

Cut to:

*Close-up—*ETTA, *laughing, as we pull back to reveal* ETTA, *seated high on the branch of a tree, watching down below as* BUTCH *rides around and around and—*

Cut to:

BUTCH, *starting warily to stunt, not all that sure at first that he can really do it well, but in a minute he is riding with his back to the handlebars, slowly, then faster, and—*

Cut to:

ETTA, *applauding, and as she does—*

Cut to:

BUTCH, *trying a lunatic move, a headstand on the handlebars as the bike spins steadily down along a road lined with wooden fences. Now—*

Cut to:

ETTA, *watching fascinated as in the distance,* BUTCH *begins to actually do the handstand, and—*

Cut to:

BUTCH, *handstand completed, riding gracefully into a wooden fence and getting pitched on his ass over the thing to the ground and—*

Cut to:

ETTA, *roaring, as we—*

Cut to:

BUTCH, *muttering, getting to his feet, looking around for his derby, seeing it, but not seeing something else which we now—*

Cut to:

A large bull, and it has large horns, and it is moving toward BUTCH, *who glances around, as we—*

Cut to:

ETTA, *crying out and—*

Cut to:

BUTCH, *running like a mad bastard with the bull behind him and as it closes the gap* BUTCH *tears for the wooden fence, diving back to safety.*

Cut to:

The bull, staring balefully through the fence.

Cut to:

BUTCH, *staring angrily back through the fence at the beast.*

Cut to:

A stream. The sun starting to bounce off it as BUTCH *and* ETTA *come riding across, their feet up in the air and it is a reflection shot we have been looking at and now, as the song starts to climax—*

Cut to:

A quiet town, no one moving, the shops empty—

Cut to:

BUTCH *and* ETTA, *spinning by, as seen from inside the empty shops.*

Cut to:

Animals scattering, chipmunks, badgers, as BUTCH *and* ETTA *come sailing along and as they do—*

Cut to:

A BOY, *maybe ten, staring after them through a wood fence, and the bicycle rivets him, and he calls out and* A GIRL, *maybe nine, runs up, and he points out to* BUTCH *and* ETTA *gliding by, and as he points he imitates riding and—*

Cut to:

BUTCH *and* ETTA *riding along the road with the wooden fences lining one side and the* BOY *and* GIRL *chasing after them and the thing is, the girl is faster because after awhile the boys slows and stops, but the girl keeps right on running, not closing the gap but not losing ground either. Then she too starts to tire. She stops. She makes a little wave after the bike.*

Cut to:

Another angle— BUTCH *and* ETTA, *back in the trees again, the brighter light hitting them, the whole thing lovely and fresh.*

Cut to:

Close-up— BUTCH *and* ETTA, *riding along. The song ends.*

Cut to:

BUTCH *and* ETTA, *as he begins slowly now to ride back toward her house.*

ETTA. You've come to get him for the Flyer?

BUTCH *(nods).* And not a day too soon—I'm broke already.

ETTA. Why is there never any money, Butch?

Cut to:

BUTCH.

BUTCH. I swear, Etta, I don't know; I've been working like a dog all my life and I can't get a penny ahead.

Cut to:

ETTA.

ETTA. Sundance says it's because you're a soft touch and you're always taking expensive vacations and buying drinks for everybody and you're a rotten gambler.

Cut to:

BUTCH.

BUTCH. Well, I guess that has something to do with it.

Cut to:

BUTCH *and* ETTA, *as they pedal along.*

ETTA. And after the Flyer?

BUTCH. Sundance tell you about Bolivia?

ETTA *nods.*

BUTCH. You think I'm crazy too?
ETTA *(she means this).* Not with what they're finding in the ground down there; and if you happen to be a thief.
BUTCH. You're like me, Etta—
ETTA *(she has heard this before).* —sure, sure, sure; I got vision and the rest of the world wears bifocals.

BUTCH *laughs, leans forward, kisses her gently on the cheek. She looks at him for a moment. Then—*

ETTA. Butch? Do you ever wonder if I'd met you first if we'd been the ones to get involved?

Cut to:

BUTCH.

BUTCH. We are involved, Etta; don't you know that?

Cut to:

ETTA. *He has said this last straight and for a moment now she is absolutely uncertain of herself. Then—*

Cut to:

BUTCH.

BUTCH. I mean, you're riding on my bicycle—in certain Arabian countries that's the same as being married.

Cut to:

ETTA. *She breaks out with a laugh, holds him very tight and—*

SUNDANCE'S VOICE *(o.s.).* Hey—

Cut to:

Ext. ETTA's *house—* SUNDANCE*—Day—standing in the doorway.*

SUNDANCE. What're you doing?

Cut to:

BUTCH *and* SUNDANCE *and* ETTA, *as* BUTCH *rides close to the house.*

BUTCH. Just stealing your woman.
SUNDANCE. Take her, take her.
BUTCH. You're a romantic bastard; I'll give you that.
ETTA *(whispering to Butch).* I love that man; do you know why?
BUTCH. No. Why?

ETTA *(ruefully).* I was sort of hoping you did; I sure as hell don't.

And on her words, there begins a series of quick cuts, all adding up to the very clear impression that what is happening now is that The Flyer is being stopped a second time. Among the flash impressions are:

A. SUNDANCE *moving along the train top.*

B. The Flyer's gigantic wheels starting to slow.

C. Several outlaws jumping into position between the cars, guns drawn and ready.

D. A train conductor standing very still, his hands raised.

E. A car full of passengers sitting deadly quiet and nervous as hell and now—

Cut to:

Ext. Express car, as BUTCH *approaches. Behind him now comes* SUNDANCE.

BUTCH. Okay, okay, open up.

A VOICE *(o.s., from inside the car).* I work for Mr. E. H. Harriman—
BUTCH *(delighted).* Hey, Woodcock.

Cut to:

WOODCOCK*—inside the car. He is banged up and bandaged, but mobile, and sort of happy to hear from* BUTCH *again too.*

WOODCOCK. Hi, Butch.

Cut to:

BUTCH, *outside the car.*

BUTCH. You okay? That's wonderful—let's have a look at you—

Cut to:

WOODCOCK*—inside, and he isn't buying.*

WOODCOCK. Now Butch, you got to have more respect for me than to think I'd fall for that—

Cut to:

BUTCH*—outside.*

BUTCH. You can't want to get blown up again—

WOODCOCK'S VOICE *(o.s.).* Butch, if it was only my money you know there's no one I'd rather have steal it, but I am still in the employ of Mr. E. H. Harr—

A NEW VOICE *(o.s., and very loud).* Start this train!

Cut to:

AN ELEPHANT OF A WOMAN, *standing on the stairs of the nearest passenger car. She drops heavily to the ground and bulls her way toward* BUTCH *and* SUNDANCE.

VERY LARGE WOMAN (*as she comes*). I'm a grandmother and a female and I've got my rights!

Cut to:

BUTCH, *watching her come.*

BUTCH. I got troubles of my own, lady, so—
VERY LARGE WOMAN. You don't frighten me—no man frightens me—

Cut to:

SUNDANCE *as the woman pushes by him to get at* BUTCH. *There is a strange expression on* SUNDANCE's *face and it is hard to tell just what it is. But what is isn't is a smile.*

SUNDANCE. We got no time for this.

Cut to:

WOODCOCK—*inside the car pressed against the door, listening.*

VERY LARGE WOMAN'S VOICE (*o.s.*). You may cow the others but I remain unafraid—I've fought against whisky, I've fought against gambling, I can fight against you—

BUTCH'S VOICE (*o.s., whispered almost*). Sundance, will you put your guns down—

SUNDANCE'S VOICE (*o.s.*). I'm telling you, we got no time—

BUTCH'S VOICE (*o.s.*) —but what's the point to violence—

SUNDANCE'S VOICE (*o.s.*)—it's the only thing that Woodcock understands. (*louder now*). Woodcock?

WOODCOCK. I hear you.

VERY LARGE WOMAN'S VOICE (*o.s., almost incoherently*). —no—no—

WOODCOCK. What are you going to do to her?

SUNDANCE'S VOICE (*o.s.*). Whatever you force me to.

WOODCOCK. Well leave her alone!—you're after the money—the money's in here—

VERY LARGE WOMAN'S VOICE (*o.s., she is frightened now*). —please—all I want is the train to start—somebody please—

SUNDANCE'S VOICE (*o.s.*) Open the door Woodcock, or tell her good-bye.

WOODCOCK (*torn, enormously upset*). But I got my job to do.

SUNDANCE'S VOICE (*o.s.*). And I got mine.

VERY LARGE WOMAN'S VOICE (*o.s.*)—help me—please—

Cut to:

BUTCH, SUNDANCE *and the* VERY LARGE WOMAN—*outside the train.* SUNDANCE *holds her firmly, his hand over her mouth. Both his guns are in their holsters.* BUTCH *goes on with his imitation of the woman, just as he's been doing.*

BUTCH.—oh dear God won't someone do something?—

Cut to:

WOODCOCK—*inside, anguished.*

WOODCOCK. Nobody kills innocent people.
SUNDANCE'S VOICE (*o.s.*). You do, Woodcock—she's on your conscience, not mine—

And now there is the sound of a gun being cocked—

Cut to:

BUTCH *outside, going on magnificently.*

BUTCH. Our Father who art in heaven—

Cut to:

Close-up— WOODCOCK.

WOODCOCK. *Stop*!

And as he throws the door open—

Cut to:

BUTCH *and* SUNDANCE *and the* VERY LARGE WOMAN—*outside the train, standing there and—*

Cut to:

WOODCOCK *shaking his head as he realizes he has been had.*

WOODCOCK. How'm I ever gonna explain this to poor Mr. Harriman?

Cut to:

BUTCH *and* SUNDANCE, *getting into the car;* SUNDANCE *carries a box of dynamite sticks and as they are inside they both stop dead.*

BUTCH. Woodcock—what did you have to go and get something like that for?

Cut to:

WOODCOCK, *standing beside the biggest rail-road safe anyone ever saw.*

WOODCOCK. I'm sorry Butch, but you blew that last one so easy I just hadda do something.

Cut to:

BUTCH *and* SUNDANCE, *as* BUTCH *indicates the box of dynamite.*

BUTCH. Gimme that and get some more.

And as he reaches for the dynamite —

Cut to:

BUTCH *working quickly, efficiently inside the railroad car. He is beginning to perspire now as he continues to wedge in the dynamite.*

Cut to:

The safe, really loaded up with dynamite now and —

Cut to:

The central dynamite fuse. As BUTCH *lights it, it begins to sizzle and burn toward the dynamite sticks and —*

Cut to:

BUTCH, *getting the hell out of there and fast. Then —*

Cut to:

The safe, just before a cataclysmic explosion rocks it. For a moment there is just the flash of blinding light, then deafening sound. The whole goddam railroad car has been blasted away to its foundation and as the sound diminishes, something fills the air: money.

Cut to:

A view of the sky, as pieces of paper money flutter this way and that in the breeze.

Cut to:

BUTCH *and* SUNDANCE, *as* SUNDANCE *starts to laugh.*

SUNDANCE. Think you used enough dynamite there, Butch?

Cut to:

The money, fluttering this way and that on the breeze. It seems to fill the air. Then —

Cut to:

THE GANG, *starting off after the money, some of them crawling across the ground, others are jumping into the air, trying to clutch the fluttering bills.*

Cut to:

BUTCH, *starting to laugh at his own stupidity and —*

Cut to:

SUNDANCE, *roaring and —*

Cut to:

THE GANG, *pursuing the money as the wind blows it along. They might almost be a convention of butterfly collectors as they scrabble around, jumping and crawling and turning and —*

Cut to:

BUTCH, *as slowly his laughter dies. He is looking off at something.*

Cut to:

Train engine pulling single car in the distance. It might be noted here that whatever color the Flyer's cars are, this single car is something very distinctly different.

Cut to:

BUTCH, *still looking off at the engine and the strange single car.* SUNDANCE *is beside him now and they both watch. Around them, members of the gang still scramble around gathering up bits and pieces of money.*

Cut to:

The engine pulling the single car, drawing closer and closer and —

Cut to:

BUTCH *and* SUNDANCE, *watching it come.*

BUTCH. Now what in the hell is that?

Cut to:

The car, drawing closer, and now there is music under it all, nervous and fast, but not loud, not yet, as the train and the single car continue to come toward camera.

Cut to:

BUTCH *and* SUNDANCE, *looking at each other in absolute bewilderment.*

Cut to:

The car. It is still some ways off but the music is faster now and starting to get loud as the car continues to come toward camera, steadily and swiftly, and the music builds and builds and then without warning we are into: the longest traveling shot in the history of the world. The camera starts to move toward the car. As the camera starts, the car stops and just waits there, and the music is louder than ever now as the camera picks up speed, moving toward the car which stands dead still on the tracks as the camera comes and comes and now the camera is really moving, going like a goddam shot toward the car and the car still waits, and now the music is starting to deafen and Craig Breedlove must be driving the camera as it roars toward the car, close now, really close, right up almost on top of the goddamn car and just as it seems as if it's going to smash right into the side of the car, the entire side of the car swings open and down, and the camera recoils, like a human face would recoil after receiving a terrible blow, and out of the car right into the eye of the camera comes riding—THE SUPERPOSSE. The SUPERPOSSE consists of perhaps a half dozen men. Taken as a group, they look, act, and are, in any and all ways, formidable.

Cut to:

BUTCH and SUNDANCE.

BUTCH. Whatever they're selling, I don't want it—

And he spins, shouts to the men gathering up the money—

BUTCH. Leave it!

Cut to:

THE SUPERPOSSE, riding like hell. They are still a good distance away.

Cut to:

SUNDANCE, vaulting onto his horse, grabbing BUTCH's horse's reins and leading the animal over to BUTCH who is in the midst of his men, stinging them to leave the money and take off.

Cut to:

THE SUPERPOSSE, at a distance, but closer now. One of them reaches for a rifle.

Cut to:

BUTCH, dragging men away from the money which still lies scattered thick across the ground. Gradually, most of the gang commence to run for their horses, but NEWS and FLAT NOSE still chase the money.

BUTCH (to NEWS and FLAT NOSE). Ya crazy fools—

He gestures wildly toward the SUPERPOSSE—

BUTCH. —ya think they been sent here to help us?

As NEWS and FLAT NOSE mutter "coming", "right away", "just one sec", etc., BUTCH gets the hell on his horse and—

Cut to:

THE SUPERPOSSE, all of them with rifles out now and—

Cut to:

SUNDANCE, riding. Several members of the gang form close beside him. Several shots ring out. SUNDANCE stops, looks back, and—

Cut to:

NEWS and FLAT NOSE, and FLAT NOSE isn't moving anymore. NEWS, severely damaged, does his best to crawl. There is another shot. NEWS lies still.

Cut to:

SUNDANCE, as BUTCH rides up to him. SUNDANCE is staring back and BUTCH follows his stare.

Cut to:

NEWS and FLAT NOSE, dead.

Cut to:

THE SUPERPOSSE bunched tight together.

Cut to:

BUTCH and SUNDANCE, watching motionless for a moment. Then—

SUNDANCE. Butch?
BUTCH. What?
SUNDANCE. They're very good.

And with that they take off and—

Cut to:

BUTCH and SUNDANCE, catching up with the rest of the Gang; then—

Cut to:

A camera shot from an enormous height. It is as if two great black centipedes were racing. In front, THE WILD BUNCH, moving like crazy. Behind them, THE SUPERPOSSE, not losing ground. The terrain ahead of them is flat. On either side lie hills.

Cut to:

THE WILD BUNCH, still from above but lower down. The sound of the horses is loud and for a moment, that is the only sound. Then BUTCH's voice is heard—

BUTCH (shouting it out). Scatter!

And like a sunburst, THE WILD BUNCH *fragments, every man taking a different direction, except* BUTCH *and* SUNDANCE, *who ride together.*

Cut to:

BUTCH *and* SUNDANCE, *reaching the crest of a hill.* SUNDANCE *is first and as he gets to the top he pauses just for a moment, glancing back.* BUTCH *is just a step or two behind, almost to the top himself.*

BUTCH. How many of 'em are following us?

SUNDANCE. All of 'em.

BUTCH *(stunned).* All of 'em?

He is beside SUNDANCE *now at the top of the hill and he too pauses, looking back.*

Cut to:

THE SUPERPOSSE, *still bunched, coming after them. In the distance and safe, the rest of the gang rides away.*

Cut to:

BUTCH, *furious, pointing out the rest of his men —*

BUTCH. What's the matter with those guys?

Cut to:

SUNDANCE, *taking off,* BUTCH *a step behind.*

Cut to:

THE SUPERPOSSE. *They just keep coming.*

Cut to:

BUTCH *and* SUNDANCE, *riding just as fast as they can.*

Cut to:

THE SUPERPOSSE. *They are going at exactly the same pace as before. They are all in the same position in the pack. Nothing has changed. They are like a machine.*

Cut to:

BUTCH *and* SUNDANCE, *going, if anything, faster than before. But the strain is beginning to tell. The sun was high when this began. Now there are shadows. And on their faces, strain.*

Cut to:

THE SUPERPOSSE, *coming on, more like a machine than ever.*

Cut to:

BUTCH *and* SUNDANCE. *The are approaching a spot where several trails are indicated. At the*

last moment they veer left, following the least likely path.

Cut to:

Another angle — BUTCH *and* SUNDANCE *riding on. The shadows are deeper now. So is their strain.*

Cut to:

Another angle — BUTCH *and* SUNDANCE. *Abruptly they halt.*

BUTCH. I think we lost 'em. Do you think we lost 'em?
SUNDANCE. No.
BUTCH. Neither do I.

And they are off again, riding flat out.

Cut to:

A watering place. SUNDANCE *stands beside his horse.* BUTCH *sits slumped astride his. As the animals drink —*

SUNDANCE. Horses aren't good for much more.
BUTCH. Me too. *(as Sundance remounts).* We just got to get to Fanny's, that's all. Once we get to Fanny's we'll be fine.

Cut to:

FANNY PORTER—*Night, in her brothel, looking concerned.*

FANNY. Trouble?

BUTCH *and* SUNDANCE *move into the shot.* BUTCH *nods.*

BUTCH. Bring me Sweetface.

Cut to:

A long swirling shot, that moves and moves across the main floor of the brothel to the stairs. No one is ever still — BUTCH *and* SUNDANCE *make their steady way to the stairs throughout the shot, and the rest of the activity spins around them.* SUNDANCE, *to a bartender who has come running up:*

SUNDANCE. —get our horses —they're out back—

BUTCH *is talking to* SWEETFACE *now.* SWEETFACE *has the visage of an aging cherub, soft and pink. Compared to him, Cuddles Zacall looks like Mike Mazurki.*

BUTCH. —listen you dirty old man—I know you're a lying thief and so do you but who'd ever think it to look at you, so move yourself out front fast—

SUNDANCE *(to the bartender—almost at the stairs).* —feed 'em good and get 'em out of sight—

BUTCH *(he is on the stairs now—to* SWEETFACE*).* —you seen us ride through town not ten minutes ago—you do this right I'll get you an old dog to kick—

And as he and SUNDANCE *take the stairs two at a time, the swirling shot ends and we—*

Cut to:

An absolutely glorious tangle of long blonde hair. Pull back to reveal a room upstairs. There are whiskey bottles and glasses on a table. SUNDANCE *stands by the curtained window, looking out.* BUTCH *is in a chair, locked in a tight embrace with the owner of the blonde hair. Her name is* AGNES *and we met her already when she came to get* BUTCH *to come to the piano player's party.* AGNES *is no Phi Beta Kappa from Bryn Mawr.*

Cut to:

BUTCH, *as the embrace ends. Eyes still closed, he gently rubs his cheek against* AGNES'. *Holding her close, he speaks in a soft tone.*

BUTCH. Do you realize you're driving me crazy looking out that window? I swear to you, Sweetface can handle this easy. He wouldn't dare louse it up—he's that scared of me.

Cut to:

SUNDANCE, *still watching out the window.*

Cut to:

The view outside the window—Night. SWEETFACE *is visible across the street, whittling intently. It is dusk now, with the sun about to die.*

BUTCH'S VOICE *(o.s.).* How can I give Agnes the concentration she deserves with you with your nose all the time out the window?

Cut to:

Int. Brothel bedroom—Night. SUNDANCE *has not moved from the window.* BUTCH *is still fondling Agnes.*

AGNES. You're really something, Butch, you know that?

BUTCH. Could you be a little more specific there, Agnes?

Cut to:

The view outside the window. SWEETFACE *looks up quickly, then just as quickly he is back to his whittling. There is a pause. Then the*

SUPERPOSSE *is visible. The second they appear—*

Cut to:

Int. Room.

SUNDANCE'S VOICE *(o.s., sharp).* Butch!

BUTCH *moves to the window and looks out.* AGNES *is still very much in his arms.*

Cut to:

Ext. Street. The SUPERPOSSE *comes to a halt.* SWEETFACE *looks up.*

BUTCH'S VOICE *(o.s.).* Okay, Sweetface— give 'em the smile.

SWEETFACE *smiles. Then he stands and moves toward the* SUPERPOSSE *with his hand cupped to an ear, indicating a hearing infirmity.*

Cut to:

BUTCH, SUNDANCE *and* AGNES *watching.*

BUTCH. I swear if he told *me* I rode out of town ten minutes ago, I'd believe him.

Cut to:

Ext. Street. SWEETFACE *is nodding now and pointing down the street.* THE SUPERPOSSE *moves off.* SWEETFACE *sits back down and begins whittling again.*

Cut to:

Int. room. BUTCH *gives a genuine sigh of relief and even* SUNDANCE *relaxes.* AGNES *discreetly begins to undress.* SUNDANCE *takes notice of this.*

SUNDANCE *(as he goes to the door).* No, no, don't ask me to stay.

And as he closes the door—

Cut to:

AGNES, *continuing to undress. As she does, she speaks of her feelings for* BUTCH. *Two things are a little odd about the moment: (1) they are across the room from each other, and not in bed, as the tone of her talk might logically indicate, and (2) there is a definite rote quality to* AGNES' *words.*

AGNES. You're the only real man I ever met, Butch—it's not just because you got all that money to spend on people—it's you—

Cut to:

BUTCH, *while this is going on. He is doing his best to get his damn boots off.*

AGNES *(o.s.)* — the way you're always looking to see am I happy or not — a lot of the other girls — they might want you for when you got money to spend on people — me, I don't care for clothes and money and jewels and furs and —

She stops because from outside there is the unmistakable sound of horses' hooves coming closer and closer and —

Cut to:

SUNDANCE, *throwing the door of the room open, tearing across to the window, and as* BUTCH *joins him — zoom to* SWEETFACE, *surrounded by the* SUPERPOSSE. *As they draw their guns, without a second's pause, he points dead at the window where* BUTCH *and* SUNDANCE *are hiding, and as he does —*

Cut to:

BUTCH *and* SUNDANCE — *Night, silhouetted against the glow left by the sun as they race across a flat rooftop. They jump to a lower building, tear across that, and —*

Cut to:

BUTCH *and* SUNDANCE, *with the camera at ground level, pointed up as their two bodies fall, thud heavily to the ground.*

Cut to:

SUNDANCE, *on his feet, helping* BUTCH, *then the two of them taking off around a corner and —*

Cut to:

BUTCH *and* SUNDANCE, *racing toward the next corner of the building, reaching it, stopping dead*

Cut to:

Member of the SUPERPOSSE — *back to them — rifle in hand — the reason for their halt. He guards the* SUPERPOSSE'S *horses which are in background.*

Cut to:

BUTCH *and* SUNDANCE, *as they dive for him.* BUTCH *hits him around the middle, pinioning his arms, while* SUNDANCE *clobbers the* GUARD'S *head with the butt of his pistol. The* GUARD *falls without a sound.*

Cut to:

SUNDANCE, *moving off in one direction, beckoning for* BUTCH.

SUNDANCE. Our horses are over here —

Cut to:

BUTCH.

BUTCH. Get 'em, then get me.

And he breaks into a run toward the SUPERPOSSE'S *horses.*

Cut to:

The horses, as BUTCH *reaches them. They are enormous animals and they do not move as he comes up. Quickly he goes from one to the next, untying each in turn until they are all freed. Then —*

BUTCH *(his voice urgent, but not loud).* Okay, move.

The horses stand there.

BUTCH. Move I told you.

He leads one horse a few steps. Louder now —

BUTCH. It's okay, go on now, go on.

The horses do not budge. Louder than before —

BUTCH. Get out of here!

The horses stay where they are.

BUTCH *(big).* Ya fatheaded beasts get gone!

Cut to:

SUNDANCE, *riding up, leading* BUTCH'S *horse.*

SUNDANCE. You're the fatheaded beast — quit shouting.

BUTCH *mounts, about to take off. He glances back one time.*

Cut to:

The SUPERPOSSE'S *horses. They stand very still, waiting.*

Cut to:

BUTCH *and* SUNDANCE.

BUTCH *(shaking his head).* Somebody sure trained 'em.

Cut to:

Another angle — BUTCH *and* SUNDANCE, *riding off, top speed into the early darkness.*

Cut to:

Some woods — Night. Above, a little moon. BUTCH *and* SUNDANCE *ride by.*

Cut to:

More woods. Thicker. It is dark here. BUTCH *and* SUNDANCE *appear, riding slowly. It is ugly riding, the branches of trees constantly whipping out at them.*

Cut to:

Deeper woods. The trees are attacking them now as they ride slowly past, doing their best to protect themselves.

Cut to:

Darkness. The woods are still very deep. Abruptly BUTCH *reins up.*

BUTCH. Why are we killing ourselves? It's night. What if they're not even after us?
SUNDANCE. What if they are?

And he rides on without pausing. BUTCH *rides after him.*

Cut to:

BUTCH *and* SUNDANCE *riding. Their faces are cut now, their clothes torn.*

Cut to:

A clearing—Night. SUNDANCE *rides into it first, stops.*

SUNDANCE. Which way?
BUTCH *(stopping beside him).* Hell, it doesn't matter—I don't know where we've been and I've just been there. So they can't be following us. We're safe.
SUNDANCE. You really think so?
BUTCH. I will if you will.

He rides off. SUNDANCE *rides after him.*

Cut to:

Their two horses, riderless. Camera pulls back to reveal the crest of a hill. The horses are safely tied. It is still very much night. At the crest of the hill, BUTCH *and* SUNDANCE *sit, staring out the way they came. For a moment nothing is said. Then—*

BUTCH. How long you figure we been watching?
SUNDANCE. Awhile.
BUTCH. How much longer before you think they're not after us?
SUNDANCE. A while longer.
BUTCH. How come you're always so talkative?
SUNDANCE. Born blabby.

Cut to:

BUTCH. *He smiles, stands, stretches.*

BUTCH. I haven't rode so much since I quit rustling. That's a miserable occupation; dusk to dawn, dusk to dawn, no sleep, rotten food—*(and suddenly his tone changes—)* Hey—
SUNDANCE *(as Butch crouches down beside him).* I see it.

Cut to:

A long shot of the deep wood—Night, through which they have just come. And now, for the first time, the SUPERPOSSE *begins to take on an almost phantom quality. For what we see, very faintly in the distance, is a slowly moving glow. The glow never stops moving. It never moves fast, but it keeps coming toward them.*

BUTCH'S VOICE *(o.s., whispering).* Torches, you think?
SUNDANCE'S VOICE *(o.s.)* Maybe. Maybe lanterns.
BUTCH'S VOICE *(o.s.)* That's our path they're following.
SUNDANCE'S VOICE *(o.s.)* Dead on it.
BUTCH'S VOICE *(o.s.)* I couldn't do that. Could you do that? How can they do that?

Cut to:

Close-up— BUTCH'S *face, worried. His words are the first mention of what will become a litany.*

BUTCH. Who *are* those guys?

Cut to:

BUTCH *and* SUNDANCE, *riding.*

Cut to:

The glow behind them in the woods. It just keeps on coming.

Cut to:

Ext. Trail— BUTCH *and* SUNDANCE, *riding side by side, talking as they go. They have been going over and over this.*

SUNDANCE. —you sure this'll work?
BUTCH. Positive.
SUNDANCE. You were positive Sweetface was scared of you.
BUTCH. This'll work.

Cut to:

The trail where it divides. BUTCH *and* SUNDANCE *come riding into view, side by side still, and* SUNDANCE *takes a deep breath, times his move, then switches horses, clambering on behind* BUTCH. *When the trail divides,* BUTCH *and* SUNDANCE *on one horse go off one way, while* SUNDANCE'S *horse is supposed to take the other way, only the horse starts to follow them.* SUNDANCE *takes a swipe at it with his hat and both shout for the animal to take off.*

Cut to:

SUNDANCE'S *horse, stopping.*

Cut to:

BUTCH *and* SUNDANCE, *riding on.*

Cut to:

SUNDANCE'S *horse. It takes the other trail. It runs into the darkness and is gone.*

Cut to:

BUTCH, *pacing. Pull back to reveal the crest of another hill. This one more rock-like than the one preceding, as the terrain is starting to change.* SUNDANCE *rests on his haunches, staring back down the way they've come. The one horse is in the b.g. It is still dark, but getting close to dawn now.*

BUTCH *(continuing his nervous movement).* Once they divide up, we'll take 'em; no trouble at all, right?
SUNDANCE. Maybe.
BUTCH. For a gunman you're one helluva pessimist.
SUNDANCE. All the laughing boys are gone.

And with that he snaps his fingers, points—

Cut to:

The view of the SUPERPOSSE, *coming steadily ahead.*

BUTCH'S VOICE *(o.s.).* They should get to where we split any time now.

The glow of the SUPERPOSSE *stops.*
SUNDANCE'S VOICE *(o.s.).* They're there.
BUTCH'S VOICE *(o.s.).* I wonder how many'll come our way—I wish we had rifles—they got rifles—but what the hell, we got surprise going for us, right?—

The glow of the SUPERPOSSE *separates now. One glow begins moving toward camera. The other begins going in a different direction.*

Cut to:

BUTCH, *up and pacing again. He takes out his guns, starts to check them over as he moves.*

BUTCH. —so far they're doing what we want, so do you think this is a good place to try and take 'em?—down closer to the trail maybe or—

SUNDANCE'S VOICE *(o.s., big).* Dammit.

As BUTCH *whirls—*

Cut to:

The SUPERPOSSE. *Slowly, the two glows are moving back together again. They join up, and now there is but a single glow again, and again slowly, relentlessly, the glow begins moving toward the camera.*

Cut to:

Close-up— SUNDANCE. *For the first time now he is worried, and it shows.*

SUNDANCE. Who *are* those guys?

Cut to:

The glow of the SUPERPOSSE, *as it continues to move slowly toward them—*

Cut to:

SHERIFF RAY BLEDSOE, *asleep in his bed. He is in a small room connected to a small jail. One window looks out at rocky terrain.*

Cut to:

BUTCH *and* SUNDANCE, *entering.* BLEDSOE *stirs, sees them, then suddenly erupts from his bed.*

BLEDSOE. What are you doing here?
BUTCH. Easy Ray—
BLEDSOE *(riding roughshod through anything* BUTCH *starts to say to him).* —hell easy—just because we been friends doesn't give you the right—what do you think would happen to me if I was seen together—I'm too old to hunt up another job. *(glaring hard at them)* At least have the decency to draw your guns. *(* BUTCH *and* SUNDANCE *draw)* You promised you'd never come into my territory—

BUTCH—and we kept our word, didn't we, Ray?
SUNDANCE. —we never pulled off anything near you—
BUTCH. everybody in the business we told, "leave old Ray Bledsoe alone"—
SUNDANCE. —we been good to you, Ray—
BUTCH. —now you be good to us—help us enlist in the Army and fight the Spanish.
BLEDSOE. You are known outlaws.
SUNDANCE. We'd quit.
BLEDSOE *(exploding).* You woke me up to tell me you reformed?
SUNDANCE. It's the truth, Ray, I swear.
BUTCH. No; let's not lie to Ray. We haven't come close to reforming. We never will. *(he is desperately honest now)* It's just—my country's at war and I'm not getting any younger and I'm sick of my life Ray.
BLEDSOE *(there is a pause. Then—)* BULL!

BUTCH. All right. There's a certain situation that's come up and—it could work, Ray—

a lot of guys like us have joined up; we could too if you'd help us—either fake us through or tell the government how we changed—they got to believe you; hell, you never done a dishonest thing yet and what are you, sixty?

BLEDSOE. You've done too much for amnesty and you're too well known to disguise; you should have got yourselves killed a long time ago when you had the chance.

SUNDANCE. We're asking for your help, Ray!

BLEDSOE. Something's got you panicked and it's too late. You may be the biggest thing ever to hit this area, but in the long run, you're just two-bit outlaws. I never met a soul more affable than you, Butch, or faster than the Kid, but you're still nothing but a couple two-bit outlaws on the dodge.

BUTCH. Don't you get it, Ray—*something's out there*. We can maybe outrun 'em awhile longer but then if you could—

BLEDSOE. —you just want to hide out til it's old times again, but it's over. It's over, don't you get that? It's over and you're both gonna die bloody, and all you can do is choose where. *(softer now)* I'm sorry. I'm getting mean in my old age. Shut me up, Sundance.

Cut to:

The glow of the SUPERPOSSE, *seen in the distance.*

Cut to:

SUNDANCE, *the gag in his hands.*

Cut to:

BUTCH, *reaching the rear door, opening it, going out. A moment later,* SUNDANCE *follows him.*

Cut to:

BLEDSOE, *staring after them, moved. Camera holds on the old man a moment. Then—*

Cut to:

The sun, and it is blinding.

Cut to:

BUTCH *and* SUNDANCE, *riding the one horse and riding as fast as they can, considering the terrain, which is a narrow path bordered on both sides by enormous boulders. This is mountainous territory starting now and the horse slips, rights itself, and they continue to move with no slowing of pace until we—*

Cut to:

A mountain stream—Day. BUTCH and SUNDANCE *ride across it, then double back al-* *most immediately into the stream and ride in the water for awhile. Then they move out of the stream, and almost immediately double back again, recrossing it surprisingly, picking up the pace now, and then—*

Cut to:

Narrow trail—BUTCH and SUNDANCE—Day, *seated on the horse. They are motionless and so is the animal as they all three wait in a narrow part of the all but invisible path they have been following. Now—*

Cut to:

Close-up—BUTCH and SUNDANCE. *This shot takes a long long time, as they wait, hardly breathing, and listening for the least conceivable sound. First there is nothing. Then, as their ears get accustomed, there is wind. The wind picks up. It dies. It starts up again and BUTCH and SUNDANCE still wait, motionless, wanting to be sure they are safe and through the wind another sound begins to drum in now; faint but always growing, it is the hooves of the* SUPERPOSSE *and—*

Cut to:

BUTCH and SUNDANCE'S *horse, starting off in overdrive and—*

Cut to:

BUTCH and SUNDANCE, *going as fast as they can along a difficult trail. They are more worried than before and they neither of them bother to hide it as they work their horse along as best they can and—*

Cut to:

BUTCH and SUNDANCE, *making a difficult cut on their horse, moving into an area that is bounded by boulders and it's miserable terrain to ride through but they keep on going, sweaty and beat and—*

Cut to:

Another angle—BUTCH and SUNDANCE, *riding along faster than before, trying another change of direction, then another, never slowing for a second and—*

Cut to:

Another angle—BUTCH and SUNDANCE, *seated motionless on their horse again. This is another long, long, listening shot only they are breathing a little harder now from their efforts and it's hard to get perfectly quiet but they make it and then as before, there is no sound, nothing. Then, again as before, there is wind. Then the wind dies. Then as it starts to build again there* comes the sound right behind them of a rock slipping down and the sound means the SUPERPOSSE *has them dead but* BUTCH *jerks around desperately getting his guns out and* SUNDANCE'*s are already free and he fires and fires and as the sound explodes off the boulders—*

Cut to:

A little dead lizard. It has caused the sound they'd heard, the little rock rolling a little way and—

Cut to:

BUTCH *and* SUNDANCE, *looking at each other, both of them with their guns out, and there isn't anything to say, because they are both of them scared and they know it and it shows.* SUNDANCE *puts his guns back.* BUTCH *does the same. They look away from each other and start to ride.*

Cut to:

Ext. Boulder area—The horse, riderless. It stands still, drinking water from a small stream as we pull back to reveal BUTCH *exhausted, lying half in, half out of the water, rubbing his face with a bandana.*

BUTCH *(as he lies there).* You're just wasting your energy doing that.

Cut to:

SUNDANCE. *He is climbing a large boulder to get a view of the countryside.*

Cut to:

BUTCH, *lying in the water, shouting up.*

BUTCH. They can't follow us over rocks.

Cut to:

SUNDANCE, *on top of the boulder now, staring out.*

SUNDANCE. Tell them that.

Cut to:

BUTCH. *He struggles to his feet and begins walking to the boulder where* SUNDANCE *is. As he moves, he starts going faster, running now across the ground and when he reaches the boulder he leaps onto it, scratching his way up alongside* SUNDANCE.

Cut to:

Rocky terrain—A long, long shot, with the blinding sun bouncing off rocks making everything hard to see. But there, in the great dis-

tance, is the SUPERPOSSE. *Looking at them is like looking at a mirage.*

Cut to:

BUTCH *and* SUNDANCE, *squinting, shielding their eyes, trying desperately to see.*

Cut to:

Mirage shot. It is very hard to make out what is going on, but perhaps all the SUPERPOSSE, *save one man, are on horseback, and perhaps that one man is on his haunches, staring at the ground.*

Cut to:

BUTCH *and* SUNDANCE, *squinting out.*

BUTCH *(genially).* They're beginning to get on my nerves. *(not so genially)* Who are those guys?

SUNDANCE. You remember when you and Etta and me went to Denver last summer for a vacation?

Cut to:

*Close-up—*BUTCH. *He is absolutely stupefied by the question.*

BUTCH. Now there's a really important topic, considering our situation—I'm sure glad you brought that up—

Cut to:

*Close-up—*SUNDANCE. *He is as pensive right here as* BUTCH *is agitated.*

SUNDANCE. That night we went gambling, remember?

Cut to:

BUTCH *and* SUNDANCE.

BUTCH. Sure, Kid, I remember. We ate supper at the hotel first. I had the roast beef and Etta ordered chicken and if I could only remember what you had I'd die a happy man.
SUNDANCE *(ignoring Butch; going right on).* Look out there—

And as he points—

Cut to:

Mirage shot. It is still very hard to make anything out with clarity, but it appears that all the SUPERPOSSE *are still on horseback, save one, who is still on his haunches, staring at the ground.*

SUNDANCE'S VOICE *(o.s.).* We got to talking with some gambler that night. And he told us about the Indian. A full blooded Indian except he called himself with an English name. Sir somebody—

BUTCH'S VOICE *(o.s.)*. Lord Baltimore.

SUNDANCE'S VOICE *(o.s.)*. That's right. He called himself Lord Baltimore and he could track anybody. Over anything. Day or night.

Cut to:

BUTCH *and* SUNDANCE, *lying on the boulder, staring out.*

BUTCH. So?

SUNDANCE. That guy on the ground—I think it's him—

Cut to:

Mirage shot. They appear to be almost statues.

Cut to:

Mirage shot—The man on the ground. It is as if BUTCH *and* SUNDANCE *are straining their eyes to the point of pain trying to see clearly. The Man on the Ground might indeed be an Indian—but the sun bouncing off the rocks is just too strong, the distance just too great. During this—*

BUTCH'S VOICE *(o.s.)*. I can't quite see him clear.

SUNDANCE'S VOICE *(o.s.)*. Me either. But it might be.

Cut to:

BUTCH *and* SUNDANCE. SUNDANCE *still stares out.* BUTCH *turns to him.*

BUTCH. Except he works out of Oklahoma—Lord Baltimore's strictly an Oklahoma man and I don't know where we are but it isn't Oklahoma, so it couldn't be him, it couldn't be him.

SUNDANCE *(nodding)*. I guess.

Cut to:

Mirage shot—The man on the ground. He stands slowly, then gestures dead in the direction of BUTCH *and* SUNDANCE. *As he does—*

SUNDANCE'S VOICE *(o.s.)*. But whoever he is, he sure the hell is somebody.

The Man on the Ground mounts. The SUPERPOSSE *begins to move forward again, steadily, inevitably, and—*

Cut to:

Ext. Canyon trail— BUTCH *and* SUNDANCE*— Day, both of them on the one horse riding as fast as they can.*

Cut to:

Very high shot, of a trail leading through a canyon. The terrain now is wilder, rockier, increasingly isolated, increasingly beautiful. Below now, BUTCH *and* SUNDANCE *can be made out. Camera pulls back to reveal* THE SUPER-POSSE *behind them closer now, moving as steadily and smoothly as a machine.*

Cut to:

BUTCH *and* SUNDANCE, *on the horse.* BUTCH *is going on nervous energy now and it shows. They come to a break in the rocks and he stares back, we know at what.*

BUTCH. Damn them anyway. Aren't they hungry?—aren't they tired?

SUNDANCE. Got to be.

BUTCH *(anger building)*. Then why don't they slow down? Hell, they could speed up and that'd be fine too—it'd be a change. They don't even break formation—*(shouting)* Do something!

Cut to:

Mirage shot. The SUPERPOSSE *moves on as before.*

SUNDANCE'S VOICE *(o.s.)*. They're like their horses—somebody sure trained 'em . . .

Cut to:

An extremely rocky area—Day.

Cut to:

BUTCH *and* SUNDANCE. SUNDANCE *leads the horse now as they scramble along as fast as they can. When the terrain allows for it, they run.*

Cut to:

BUTCH *and* SUNDANCE, *running, until without warning* BUTCH *trips and falls heavily down.*

BUTCH *(grabbing the rock that tripped him)*. Ya stupid rock!

And he smashes it down against a boulder—

Cut to:

BUTCH *and* SUNDANCE, *walking, terribly out of breath. Their faces drip sweat.*

SUNDANCE. Butch?

BUTCH. What?

SUNDANCE. Who's the best lawman?

BUTCH. Best how? you mean toughest or easiest to bribe?

SUNDANCE. Toughest.

BUTCH *(without hesitation)*. Joe Lefors.

SUNDANCE *(nodding)*. Got to be.

BUTCH. Why?—(*answering the question himself*) You crazy? Joe Lefors never leaves Missouri—never, and you know it.

SUNDANCE. But he wears a white straw skimmer, doesn't he? That's how you know it's Joe Lefors, by that white straw skimmer.

Cut to:

Mirage shot.

SUNDANCE'S VOICE *(o.s.).* Well? That guy in the middle . . .?

The SUPERPOSSE *is too far away to tell anything exactly. But the man in the middle does appear to be wearing a hat that might indeed be white, that might be made of straw.*

Cut to:

BUTCH *and* SUNDANCE, *wedged between some rocks, staring out at the* SUPERPOSSE—

BUTCH *(almost a whisper now).* Who are those guys?

Cut to:

A shot of the terrain—Day. It is even rougher now, verging on the mountainous. And really very beautiful.

Cut to:

BUTCH *and* SUNDANCE, *stumbling along, leading the horse. The way they are taking is the flattest way possible, but now, more and more, there are paths that lead up into the mountains.*

Cut to:

Another angle— BUTCH *and* SUNDANCE, *making their way. They are completely exhausted now, beat down to the ground. Their clothes are ragged and torn and so are they. They pause for a moment, gulping down air, pulling it into their lungs and*

Cut to:

Mirage shot. The SUPERPOSSE *is moving on foot now, their horses following along behind them. But they move fast and seemingly without effort, as if in a dream.*

Cut to:

BUTCH *and* SUNDANCE, *glancing back, pushing on.*

Cut to:

A shot of the mountains. It's later in the afternoon now.

Cut to:

BUTCH *and* SUNDANCE, *sending their horse the way they have been going while they cut off and up, into the mountains.*

Cut to:

The horse, going.

Cut to:

BUTCH *and* SUNDANCE, *moving up higher into the mountains.*

Cut to:

The two of them, making their way. They are following a fairly wide path and making good time. Below them, a mountain stream is occasionally visible.

Cut to.

BUTCH *and* SUNDANCE, *catching their breath a moment, glancing back the way they came.*

BUTCH. I figure they followed the horse, don't you?

SUNDANCE. No.

Cut to:

The path, far below them. The SUPERPOSSE *moves into view, on foot.*

Cut to:

BUTCH *and* SUNDANCE, *watching as the* SUPERPOSSE *becomes visible.*

BUTCH. If you're so smart, why aren't you rich?

Cut to:

The SUPERPOSSE. *They move on foot as they moved on horseback: bunched together, silently, without strain.*

Cut to:

BUTCH *and* SUNDANCE, *going like sixty.*

Cut to:

The path they are following as it curves along. Below, the stream is widening and going faster, something it continues to do. Shadows are starting to lengthen. Soon, dusk.

Cut to:

BUTCH *and* SUNDANCE, *doing their best. The path is narrower now, but still wide enough for them both to move side by side and they force themselves along it.*

Cut to:

The path, curving up. They race along it, then begin to slow as the path starts to narrow.

Cut to:

Another angle—The path. They are moving Indian file now, SUNDANCE *leading.*

Cut to:

A shot of the two of them from the stream below. At this distance, perhaps fifty feet, as they move through sunlight and shadow, they seem very, very, small.

Cut to:

The path, widening now, and they pick up the pace.

Cut to:

Another angle—The path, widening more, and now they are both of them running flat out, heedless of where they are and—

Cut to:

The sun, just starting to edge down over the mountains and—

Cut to:

The stream, quite wide and fast now, and still in sunlight, while all around it there is shadow; the effect is stunning as it swirls around and around—

Cut to:

The path—At dusk, ending.

Cut to:

BUTCH *and* SUNDANCE, *standing there, just standing there gaping at the dead end the path has led them into.*

BUTCH *and* SUNDANCE *(together).* DAMMIT!

Cut to:

A long shot—the two of them, standing there stunned, the sound echoing over and over and—

Cut to:

BUTCH *and* SUNDANCE, *whirling, starting back the way they came and—*

Cut to:

The SUPERPOSSE, *moving up toward them.*

Cut to:

BUTCH *and* SUNDANCE, *watching them come.*

BUTCH. What I figure is we can fight or we can give. *(Sundance nods).* If we give, we go to jail.

Cut to:

*Close-up—*SUNDANCE, *shaking his head.*

SUNDANCE *(with all the meaning in the world).* I been there already.

Cut to:

BUTCH, *nodding in agreement.*

BUTCH. Me too. If we fight they can stay right where they are and starve us out—

He glances up now and—

Cut to:

The mountain above them. High up, there are open flat places where a man could fire down on them.

BUTCH'S VOICE *(o.s.)*—or they could go for position and shoot us—

Cut to:

BUTCH *and* SUNDANCE.

BUTCH.—or they could start a little rock slide and get us that way. What else could they do?

SUNDANCE. They could surrender to us but I don't think we oughtta count on that.

Cut to:

BUTCH. *He laughs, but the moment won't hold.*

BUTCH *(flat and down).* What're we gonna do?

Cut to:

BUTCH *and* SUNDANCE.

SUNDANCE. You always been the brains, Butch; you'll think of something.

BUTCH. Well that takes a load off; for awhile there I was worried.

He looks back down the way they came and—

Cut to:

The SUPERPOSSE. *The man in the white hat is gesturing and now the* SUPERPOSSE *begins to split, some of them moving onto a higher path that leads above where* BUTCH *and* SUNDANCE *are.*

Cut to:

BUTCH *and* SUNDANCE, *watching them climb.*

SUNDANCE. They're going for position all right.

SUNDANCE *takes out his guns, starts to examine them with great care.*

SUNDANCE. We better get ready.

BUTCH (*getting his guns ready*). The next time I say let's go somewhere like Bolivia, let's go somewhere like Bolivia.

SUNDANCE. Next time.

Cut to:

The SUPERPOSSE. *They continue to make their way up, moving quickly and silently across the mountain.*

Cut to:

SUNDANCE.

SUNDANCE (*watching them get into position*). You ready, Butch?

BUTCH'S VOICE (*o.s.*). NO!

And as SUNDANCE *turns—the camera zooms to close-up of* BUTCH. *He is smiling.*

BUTCH. We'll jump!

Cut to:

The stream below. It is fifty feet down and going very fast.

Cut to:

BUTCH *and* SUNDANCE.

SUNDANCE. Like hell we will.

BUTCH *is really excited now—all this next is overlapping and goes like a shot.*

BUTCH. No, no, it's gonna be okay—just so it's deep enough we don't get squished to death—they'll never follow us—

SUNDANCE. —how do you know?

BUTCH. —would you make that jump if you didn't have to?—

SUNDANCE. —I have to and I'm not gonna—

BUTCH —it's the only way. Otherwise we're dead. They'll have to go all the way back down the way we came. Come on—

SUNDANCE (*looking up the mountain*). —just a couple decent shots—that's all I want—

BUTCH —*come on*—

SUNDANCE. — no —

BUTCH. —we got to—

SUNDANCE. —*no* —

BUTCH. —yes—

SUNDANCE. —get away from me—

BUTCH. —why?—

SUNDANCE. —I wanna fight 'em—

BUTCH. —they'll kill us—

SUNDANCE. —maybe—

BUTCH. —you wanna die?—

SUNDANCE. —don't you?—

BUTCH. —I'll jump first—

SUNDANCE. —no—

BUTCH—okay, you jump first—

SUNDANCE. —*no* I said—

BUTCH (*big*). What'sa matter with you?

SUNDANCE (*bigger*). I can't swim!

Blind mad, wildly embarrassed, he just stands there—

Cut to:

BUTCH, *starting to roar.*

Cut to:

SUNDANCE, *anger building.*

Cut to:

BUTCH.

BUTCH. You stupid fool, the fall'll probably kill you.

Cut to:

SUNDANCE, *starting to laugh now and—*

Cut to:

The two of them. BUTCH *whips off his gun belt, takes hold of one end, holds the other out.* SUNDANCE *takes it, wraps it once tight around his hand. They move to the edge of the path and step off.*

Cut to:

Another angle – BUTCH *and* SUNDANCE, *falling through the twilight.*

Cut to:

The biggest splash ever recorded.

Cut to:

The stream—Dusk, going like hell. Then—

Cut to:

BUTCH *and* SUNDANCE, *alive in the water. Music begins, the same music that went on during* BUTCH *and* ETTA'S *bicycle ride, and as the music picks up, so does the speed of the current as it carries them along, spinning and turning and—*

Cut to:

The SUPERPOSSE, *frozen in the twilight in the mountains. As they stand there—*

Cut to:

Ext. Stream— BUTCH *and* SUNDANCE—*Twilight, from high above, swirling happily along. Hold on* BUTCH *and* SUNDANCE *in the twilight; they move in and out of shadow, sputtering and coughing, holding tight to the gun belt and as the music hits a climax, they are swirled safely out of sight . . .*

Fade out.

Fade in:

ETTA's place — On her doorstep — Late night.
ETTA's arms are locked around her legs; her
chin rests on her knees. She looks half dead.

Cut to:

Close-up — ETTA. She just sits there waiting,
hunched over, motionless. One gets the feeling
she was born in that position, and when she
dies, she will never have moved.

Cut to:

The night. It is too dark to make anything out
clearly until we —

Cut to:

BUTCH *and* SUNDANCE, *moving out of the*
darkness toward ETTA. *They have come a long*
way now, and there is nothing left. They manage
to keep walking.

Cut to:

ETTA, *rising as they close the gap. Without a*
word she moves to meet them and her arms go
around them both. They stand that way a mo-
ment, ETTA *and her men. Then —*

ETTA. The papers said they had you.
SUNDANCE. Was it Lefors did they say?
ETTA *(a little hesitant nod).* Joe Lefors? . . .
I think that was the name . . .
SUNDANCE. And their tracker?
ETTA. Tracker?
BUTCH. Was it Lord Baltimore?
ETTA. I think so . . . the paper's inside.

BUTCH *hurries into the house. For a moment,*
ETTA *holds just* SUNDANCE, *but their game has*
never been to show anything, no matter what,
so she drops her arms.

SUNDANCE. Got enough to feed us?
ETTA. Don't you know I do?

Cut to:

ETTA, *turning. She starts toward the front*
door. With her back to SUNDANCE —

ETTA. They rumored you were dead and —

Cut to:

SUNDANCE.

SUNDANCE. — don't make a big thing out of
it.

Cut to:

ETTA. *She nods once, continues silently to-*
ward the house. Then —

Cut to:

SUNDANCE, *watching as* ETTA *moves away.*

SUNDANCE. No . . . it's okay; make a big
thing out of it.

Cut to:

ETTA, *starting to whirl toward him but before*
the move is half done he has her and she com-
pletes the spin with his arms already around her
and it's dark, and they don't embrace for long,
but still, we can see it; they care for each other.
They care.

Cut to:

Int. ETTA's *house —* BUTCH *— Night, sitting at*
the dining table, looking at a paper.

BUTCH *(calling out).* Hey-it was Lefors and
Baltimore and you know who else?

Cut to:

SUNDANCE *and* ETTA, *entering.* ETTA *goes to*
stove where a large pot is simmering and proba-
bly has been for days. She reaches for plates and
during this —

Cut to:

BUTCH *and* SUNDANCE.

BUTCH *(reading: the names are enormously*
impressive to him). Jeff Carr, George Hiatt,
T.T. Kelliher—
SUNDANCE *(the names register on him too; as*
he sits across from Butch). We lucked out, getting away, you know that?

BUTCH *nods.*

SUNDANCE. Now why would those guys join
up and take after us?
BUTCH *(folding the paper away).* Forget it—
a bunch like that won't keep together long.

Cut to:

ETTA, *concentrating very hard on fixing their*
food.

ETTA. You didn't finish the article, Butch—
they're hired til you're dead.

Cut to:

BUTCH *and* SUNDANCE, *stunned.*

Cut to:

ETTA. *She looks at them briefly, nods.*

Cut to:

BUTCH *and* SUNDANCE.

SUNDANCE. Who by?

Cut to:

ETTA, *piling food onto two plates, being very careful not to spill.*

ETTA. Mr. E. H. Harriman of the Union Pacific Railroad. He resents the way you've been picking on him so he outfitted a special train and hired some special employees—you've spent the last few days avoiding them—it's really sort of flattering, if you want to think about it that way.

Cut to:

BUTCH *and* SUNDANCE *and* ETTA.

BUTCH. Hell, a setup like that's costing him more'n we ever took—

ETTA. Apparently he can afford it.

Cut to:

*Close-up—*BUTCH, *wild and upset and angry.*

BUTCH. That crazy Harriman—it's bad business—how long do you think I'd stay in operation if every time I pulled a job it cost me money?—if he'd just give me what he's spending to make me stop robbing him, I'd stop robbing him—he probably inherited every penny he's got; those inherited guys, what do they know?

Cut to:

SUNDANCE *and* ETTA.
SUNDANCE. You say they're hired permanent?
ETTA. No, no, no—just til they kill you.

She brings food to table and—

Cut to:

SUNDANCE, *up fast, moving to door—he is upset now too—*
SUNDANCE. That means they're still after us, Butch—it's gonna be like yesterday all over again—they'll show here sooner or later—

Cut to:

BUTCH.
BUTCH. I vote for later.

And as he begins ravenously to eat—

Cut to:

Two plates, rapidly emptying of food.

Cut to:

ETTA. *sitting on the front steps while behind her at the table, Butch and Sundance eat.*

SUNDANCE. Hey Etta—

Very pensive, she stares out, in the same waiting position as when they came back. Now she rises—

ETTA. I'll get you some more.

Cut to:

BUTCH *and* SUNDANCE, *as* ETTA *takes their plates, goes to stove.*

SUNDANCE. Butch and me been talking and wherever the hell Bolivia is, that's where we're off to.

Cut to:

ETTA, *at the stove. She nods, says nothing.*

Cut to:

BUTCH *and* SUNDANCE *and* ETTA.
BUTCH. We're just gonna hide out til it's safe and maybe keep our hand in a little—if that lousy Harriman wants to spend some money tracking us down, let's let him really spend some money.
SUNDANCE. Butch speaks some Spanish—
BUTCH. You know, I can wrestle with a menu okay.

Cut to:

SUNDANCE.

SUNDANCE *(to Etta).* You speak it good. And it'd be good cover for us going with a woman—no one expects it—we can travel safer. So what I'm saying is, if you want to come with us, I won't stop you, but the minute you start to whine or make a nuisance, I don't care where we are, I'm dumping you flat.

Cut to:

BUTCH.
BUTCH. Don't sugarcoat it like that, Sundance—tell her straight—

Cut to:

*Close-up—*ETTA. *For a moment, she says nothing. Then, starting soft, building as she goes—*

ETTA. I'm twenty-six, and I'm single, and I teach school, and except for being twenty-six and single and a librarian, that's the bottom of the pit. And the only excitement I've ever known is sitting in the room with me now. So I'll go with you, and I won't whine, and I'll sew your socks and stitch you when you're wounded, and anything you ask of me I'll do, except one thing: I won't watch you die. I'll miss that scene if you don't mind . . .

Hold on ETTA's *lovely face a moment—*

Dissolve to:

A small suitcase. Camera pulls back to reveal ETTA, *dressed for travel. The house is dark as she picks up the suitcase, goes to door, looks around her little home one final time, then—*

Cut to:

BUTCH *and* SUNDANCE—*Night, waiting outside.* ETTA *goes to* SUNDANCE *who reaches for her bag.* BUTCH *takes a final glance around and as he turns his head, camera pans to the night and everything existing in it. It is a gigantic, long pan shot and everything the camera touches has its own beauty and as the camera continues its way, it goes by* ETTA'S *dark house and there, leaning against the side of the house is* BUTCH'S *bike and the second the camera hits it—zoom to* BUTCH, *close-up, bawling it out at the top of his lungs—*

BUTCH. *The future's all yours, ya lousy bicycles!*

as his words echo—

Cut to:

The bike, as the camera continues its move. As it goes, the night darkens, until we are for one second looking at a black screen and then there is a bright white flash and we are beginning—

Musical Interlude Number Two.

Like the first, this does not make a literal connection with the action on screen; again, the two connect emotionally, and as a matter-of-fact, since what takes place on screen is happy and "up," the song here will more than likely be a poignant one. Among the moments cut to here are:

The bright white flash mentioned above—this is the flash from a portrait photographer's camera and as the flash ends, SUNDANCE *and* ETTA *are visible, both of them dressed as elegantly in formal attire, standing side-by-side. Then there is another shot.*

A. BUTCH, *is seen, similarly dressed.*

Then there is another shot:

B. The three of them. And as the photographer escorts them cordially to the door of his studio, the door opens and we see—

*Ext. New York City street—At the turn of the century—*ETTA, BUTCH *and* SUNDANCE—*Day. And that's why they are happy during this, because they've never been there before and it's new and so incredibly different—the buildings loom gigantic and the streets seem jammed and there are streetcars and horse-drawn carriages*

and drummers on the sidewalk hawking medals and silly games and flags waving from the building windows and men with sandwich boards advertising things like lunch and watch repairing and—

An umbrella—In the rain, and as we pull back, we see the three of them hurrying under it and then there are more umbrellas as we continue to pull back and the whole street is hurrying along trying to beat the rain and—

Ext. New York street— BUTCH *and* SUNDANCE *and* ETTA—*A sunny day, veering down the street in a shiny black car with red wheels.* SUNDANCE *is driving, and as a horse-drawn carriage passes them, we go to—*

Ext. Tiffany's—Day. It was in Union Square at this time, and there were streetcar tracks in front and the sign said "Tiffany & Company" and more often than not, there were horse-drawn carriages lined up and from here we are—

Int. Tiffany's. BUTCH *is selecting* ETTA *a ring and she is touched; he sees the price of the ring, whispers to her and she surreptitiously goes into her purse, but she doesn't have enough so she glances at* SUNDANCE *who hands her some money she passes on to* BUTCH *who casually pays for the ring and the next thing we see is—*

A Highly Untrustworthy Face, clearly the face of a man who makes a somewhat shadowy living, and the Untrustworthy Face doesn't look happy and as we pull back, we see why, because now we are in a shooting gallery of the period and the Untrustworthy Face runs the gallery and the reason he isn't happy is that BUTCH *and* SUNDANCE *are firing, and as they fire, targets go down, and as the targets fall,* ETTA *wins toys and prizes, more and more of them, as we move from* BUTCH *and* SUNDANCE *firing to the Untrustworthy Face stunned and starting to perspire, to* ETTA, *the pile of prizes in her arms continues to grow.* ETTA *cannot help laughing, and as* BUTCH *and* SUNDANCE *continue to upset the balance of payments in the shooting gallery, we see—*

Int. A terribly elegant restaurant. There are headwaiters and musicians and BUTCH *and* SUNDANCE *and* ETTA *are eating. They are wonderfully well-dressed and the whole look of the three of them fits right in with their surroundings, and then* SUNDANCE *and* ETTA *are dancing, and they do it well, as well as any other dancers on the floor, and as they continue to spin and turn, we see a number of things very quickly, and they all share one thing: elegance. A fine red wine is poured into a fragile goblet; a headwaiter bows; a silver tray cover is pulled up, revealing a beautifully cooked game bird, and the feeling of splendor and elegance builds along with the music until the interlude ends and we —*

Cut to:

A small patch of sand. A pair of boots walk onto the patch, stand there. Then another pair of boots move up to the first; finally, a pair of shoes encasing a lady's feet move up and stop. There is moment's pause before we pull back to reveal BUTCH *and* SUNDANCE *and* ETTA, *standing on what might be called a street in a pit of a town that in no way resembles the French Riviera — horrid little low adobe huts stretch out and an occasional pig grunts by; we are in Bolivia.* BUTCH *glances at* SUNDANCE *who is close to a homeric anger. In the distance, a stagecoach pulls away.*

BUTCH *(to Etta).* Just think: fifty years ago there was nothing here.

SUNDANCE *gives* BUTCH *a look.*

BUTCH. It's not as bad as it might be — you get more for your money in Bolivia than anywhere — I checked —
SUNDANCE — what could they sell here you could possible want to buy? —

Cut to:

The Bolivian street — Day. It really is terrible. You wouldn't wish the place on your mother-in-law.

Cut to:

BUTCH *and* SUNDANCE.

BUTCH. All Bolivia can't look this way —
SUNDANCE. How do *you* know? — this might be the garden spot of the whole country — people may travel hundreds of miles just to get right where we're standing now — this might be the Atlantic City, New Jersey of all Bolivia, for all *you* know —
BUTCH. I know as much about Bolivia as you do about Atlantic City, New Jersey, I'll tell you that much —
SUNDANCE. You do? I was born in New Jersey; I was brought up there, so —

Cut to:

BUTCH, *genuinely surprised.*

BUTCH. You're from the East? I didn't know that.

Cut to:

SUNDANCE.

SUNDANCE. The total tonnage of what you don't know is enough —

Cut to:

ETTA, *moving to them, doing her best to pacify —*

ETTA. I'm not sure we're accomplishing as much as we might. Now, if —
SUNDANCE. Listen: your job is to back me up because *you'd starve without me.*
ETTA *(biting the words out).* I — shall — commit — that — to — memory.
SUNDANCE *(to Butch now).* And you — your job is to shut up.

Cut to:

BUTCH, *moving to* ETTA.

BUTCH *(softly; consoling).* He'll feel a lot better once we robbed a couple banks.

Cut to:

SUNDANCE, *staring around him.*

SUNDANCE. *Bolivia!*

Cut to:

Ext. A small bank in a different, bigger town — Day. The bank is on the town's busiest street — a few people straggle by. Pull back to reveal BUTCH *and* SUNDANCE *casually watching the bank from across the street.*

BUTCH *(as they start toward the bank).* Now, when we get inside, remember, the first thing we do is head straight for the —
SUNDANCE. — I know how to rob a bank — don't tell me how to rob a bank —
BUTCH. Boy, a few dark clouds appear on your horizon, you just go all to pieces.

Int. The Bank, as BUTCH *and* SUNDANCE *appear in the doorway.*

Cut to:

BUTCH *and* SUNDANCE, *peering around, trying to get their bearings.*

Cut to:

A Large Armed Guard, watching them. He is seated but now stands, begins moving forward.

Cut to:

BUTCH *and* SUNDANCE, *watching the* GUARD *approach, both of them ready.*

Cut to:

THE ARMED GUARD. *He stops. There is a pause. Then —*

ARMED GUARD. Buenos dias; le puedo servir?

Cut to:

BUTCH *and* SUNDANCE. SUNDANCE *looks at* BUTCH, *waiting for him to say something.* BUTCH *just stands there, stunned. Then—*

Cut to:

Int. A cheap hotel room. BUTCH *and* SUNDANCE *and* ETTA *sit, huddled together.* ETTA *is teaching them Spanish.*

ETTA. All right, pay attention now. This is a robbery: esto es un robo.
BUTCH. Esto es un robo.
ETTA *(to Sundance).* We're supposed to be doing unison recitation.
SUNDANCE. I don't know why I have to do any of this—he's the one claimed he knew the damn language—
ETTA. We've gone over this before—your line of work requires a specialized vocabulary—
BUTCH. That's right—I got nervous—I didn't know the words—shoot me.
SUNDANCE. You've had worse ideas lately—

Cut to:

ETTA. *She means what she's saying—*

ETTA. I simply cannot tolerate this kind of outburst—*both together now*—this is a robbery: esto es un robo.

Cut to:

BUTCH *and* SUNDANCE.

BUTCH *and* SUNDANCE *(together—Sundance a trifle sullenly).* Esto es un robo.

Cut to:

ETTA. *Throughout, her vocal intonations are of the same machinelike quality achieved by Berlitz instructors.*

ETTA. Raise your hands: manos arriba.

Cut to:

BUTCH *and* SUNDANCE *and* ETTA—*Day. They are walking along a hot, quiet street now. The lesson goes right on.*

BUTCH *and* SUNDANCE *(together).* Manos Arriba.
ETTA. Raise them!: Arriba!

BUTCH *and* SUNDANCE *(together).* Arriba!

Cut to:

*Close-up—*ETTA.

ETTA. All of you—back against the wall.

Pull back to reveal BUTCH *and* SUNDANCE *and* ETTA, *eating in a crummy restaurant.*

BUTCH *(doing his best).* Todos ustedes—arrismense a la pared.

ETTA *(to Sundance now).* Give me the money.

Cut to:

*Close-up—*SUNDANCE. *It's on the tip of his tongue. Pull back to reveal* SUNDANCE *and* ETTA *in bed.*

SUNDANCE. What was that again?

ETTA *(impatient).* Give me the money.

SUNDANCE *embraces* ETTA *suddenly. He's all over her, nuzzling her, holding her to him—*

ETTA. That's not going to work and we're going to stay up all night til you get this—*give me the money. (she knocks on the wall by the bed)* You still thinking in there?

BUTCH'S VOICE *(o.s.).* What the hell else is there to do?

ETTA *(to the wall).* Try this one: Where's the safe? Open it.

Cut to:

BUTCH—*in the next room. He is rapidly running his finger down a crib sheet.*

BUTCH. That's a hard one—just lemme think now— *(and he's found it on his sheet).* Donde esta la caja? Abrala.
ETTA'S VOICE *(o.s.).* That's very good, Butch.

Cut to:

ETTA *and* SUNDANCE *in bed.*

BUTCH'S VOICE *(o.s.).* You're just a good teacher, Etta.
ETTA. For the last time: give me the money.

Cut to:

SUNDANCE. *The answer is so close now it's killing him.*

Cut to:

ETTA.

ETTA. You'd starve without me.

Dissolve to:

A Bolivian street—Day. Pull back to reveal BUTCH *and* SUNDANCE *and* ETTA. ETTA *is looking out the window. She is dressed, purse in hand.*

ETTA. Someplace out there must sell horses. I'll get the best I can with what we've got left. *(she goes to the door)* But don't expect much. *(as she exits)* And don't stop—begin at the beginning and go right through: This is a robbery.

And on these words—

Cut to:

The same armed guard as before. As before, he speaks—

GUARD. Buenos dias, le puedo—

SUNDANCE's *gun hits him once on the head and as he falls senseless—pull back to reveal* BUTCH *and* SUNDANCE *in the bank, guns drawn—*

BUTCH. Esto es . . . es . . . *(yanks out his crib sheet)* Robo!

Cut to:

Everyone in the bank. Before BUTCH *can even finish, they all quietly raise their hands and back quickly against the wall.*

Cut to:

BUTCH, *jumpy as hell—reading, first more or less to himself making sure he's got it right, then out loud.*

BUTCH *(to himself)*. Raise your hands. *(out loud)*. Manos arriba.

Cut to:

SUNDANCE, *moving nervously among the people in the bank, frisking them for weapons as he goes.*

SUNDANCE. They got 'em up—skip on down—

Cut to:

BUTCH, *reading.*

BUTCH *(to himself)*. Raise them! *(out loud)* Arriba!

Cut to:

SUNDANCE.

SUNDANCE. Skip—on—down!

Cut to:

BUTCH.

BUTCH *(to himself)*. Back against the wall. *(out loud)* Arrimense a la pared.

Cut to:

SUNDANCE.

SUNDANCE. *They're-against-the-wall-already!*

Cut to:

BUTCH, *furious.*

BUTCH. *Don't you know enough not to criticize someone who's doing his best?* *(going to Sundance, shoving the paper at him)* Here— you're so damn smart, *you* read—

Cut to:

The Bank People, standing quietly confused, hands raised, looking at each other.

Cut to:

BUTCH *and* SUNDANCE, *each of them carrying small bags of money, tearing out of the bank and—*

Cut to:

ETTA, *in the shadows by a building. She is dressed in men's clothing and she waits expectantly, staring out of the shadows. She holds the reins of three horses, none of them much worth looking at. As* BUTCH *and* SUNDANCE *come running into view, she quickly mounts her horse, leads the other two toward them and—*

Cut to:

People from the bank, pouring out onto the street, looking around, then starting to call out:

BANK PEOPLE. Bandidos—*Bandidos Yanqui—*

Cut to:

BUTCH *and* SUNDANCE *and* ETTA, *riding just as fast as their horses will go out of town and—*

Cut to:

Half a dozen Bank People, running into the office of the local constabulary— "corregidors" they were called.

BANK PEOPLE *jabbering to the* CHIEF COR-REGIDOR—*a lean, uniformed officer.*

BANK PEOPLE. —*Bandidos Yanqui— Bandidos Yanqui—*

Cut to:

*Ext. Bolivian countryside—*BUTCH *and* SUNDANCE *and* ETTA, *riding on, except all the horses are rotten and already starting to show strain. The three keep riding full out and—*

Cut to:

*Int. Constabulary—*THE CHIEF CORREGIDOR, *racing into a room where* THREE ASSISTANTS *sit playing cards.*

CHIEF CORREGIDOR—Bandidos Yanqui—

And as the men quickly stand—

Cut to:

Ext. Bolivian countryside— THE FOUR CORREGIDORS, *riding out of town. Their horses are fresh and powerful-looking and there is no question that they look competent as hell and—*

Cut to:

THE FOUR CORREGIDORS, *in open country now, riding quickly and well and—*

Cut to:

The terrain—there are rocks and groves of trees now as THE FOUR CORREGIDORS *continue their efficient way and—*

Cut to:

THE FOUR CORREGIDORS *riding like hell in one direction, a no-nonsense quartet, and as a terrible barrage tears into them, a hat flies off, their horses rear in sudden panic, and* THE THREE ASSISTANTS *take off without a moment's hesitation, back in the opposite direction, back the way they came. The* CHIEF CORREGIDOR *hesitates for only a moment, but when another barrage of bullets sounds, he takes off in the same direction as his men: away.*

Cut to:

BUTCH *and* SUNDANCE *and Etta, staring after the disappearing* CORREGIDORS.

BUTCH *(gesturing after them).* Isn't that a beautiful sight? *(a note of triumph)* We're back in business, boys and girls—it's just like the old days!

And with these words we begin— Musical Interlude Number Three. *This accompanies a series of South American robberies. There is dialogue in and out, and it is entirely possible that the song, for example, would be entitled "Bandidos Yanqui" and would be loud and rhythmic, like one would expect a Spanish-titled song to be. But not necessarily—again, here as before, the connection is not literal between scene and song: the song might be a simple Quaker-type tune extolling the virtues of labor. Or any number of other notions. In any case, the robberies go like this:*

Cut to:

Int. Bank #2—Two Bolivian Bank Clerks. Their hands are raised, their backs against a wall, and they are watching as, in the b.g., BUTCH *and* SUNDANCE *busily rob the bank.*

FIRST BANK CLERK *(whispering to the Second Clerk).* Bandidos Yanqui.

THE SECOND CLERK *looks blank. The* FIRST CLERK *repeats, a little louder.*

FIRST BANK CLERK. Bandidos Yanqui.

The SECOND CLERK *just shrugs—he's never heard of them.*

Cut to:

Int. Bank #3—an elegantly dressed bank executive, moving toward an enormous bank vault. As he goes, he gestures about proudly, showing off his bank.

Cut to:

BUTCH *and* SUNDANCE, *dressed extremely well.* SUNDANCE *carries a satchel and both he and* BUTCH *are clearly very impressed with the quality of the bank they are depositing their money into. As they approach the vault door,* BUTCH *gestures and* SUNDANCE *hands the* BANK EXECUTIVE *their satchel. The* BANK EXECUTIVE *smiles and—*

Cut to:

The vault door, swinging open.

Cut to:

BUTCH *and* SUNDANCE *and the* BANK EXECUTIVE.

BANK EXECUTIVE *(still smiling).* So you see how foolish your fears were?

SUNDANCE *(as they enter the vault).* No one could get in here, that's for sure.

And suddenly there is a gun in his hand and—

Cut to:

THE BANK EXECUTIVE.

BANK EXECUTIVE. Who are you?

Cut to:

BUTCH, *happily scooping up money, stuffing it into their satchel—*

BUTCH. We're from the Red Cross.

Cut to:

Int. Bank #4—Two Bolivian Bank Clerks. (Note: Not *the same two as before). Their hands are raised, their backs against a wall, and they are watching as, in the b.g.,* BUTCH *and* SUNDANCE *busily rob the bank.*

FIRST BANK CLERK *whispering to the* SECOND CLERK *as he nods toward* BUTCH *and* SUNDANCE.

FIRST BANK CLERK. Bandidos Yanqui.
SECOND BANK CLERK (*interested—he's heard of them*). Si?
FIRST BANK CLERK. Si.

Cut to:

Ext. Bolivian countryside—A Band of Corregidors, riding like crazy in one direction before getting blasted. They immediately wheel around and take off like hell back the way they came and—

Cut to:

*Int. Bank #5—*BUTCH, *robbing a bank alone—it is a very small place and there is but a single* TELLER.

BUTCH (*stuffing a little money into a bag*), C'mon, there's gotta be more around here—
TELLER. No, Senor
BUTCH. Where's the rest?
TELLER. Senor, I swear—

Cut to:

SUNDANCE, *moving like a streak across the bank, launching into a dive, and* BUTCH *turns, but too late, as* SUNDANCE *knocks him sprawling, grabs his gun and the bag of money.*

Cut to:

BUTCH, *blind mad, starting slowly to rise as we—*

Cut to:

SUNDANCE, *covering* BUTCH *while he barks orders to a group of* CUSTOMERS *lined against a far wall—*

SUNDANCE. —get the Corregidors—*the Corregidors—*

As one of the Customers runs off—

Cut to:

THE TELLER, *as* SUNDANCE *hands him back what* BUTCH *stole.*

SUNDANCE. Rest of the money safe?

THE TELLER *nods, pats an innocent-looking drawer—*

Cut to:

BUTCH, *hurrying to the drawer as* SUNDANCE *whirls, covers the stunned* TELLER *and the* CUSTOMERS.

BUTCH. We do nice work.

Cut to:

THE CUSTOMERS, *lined up, their hands raised, watching as, in the b.g.,* BUTCH *and* SUNDANCE *rob the bank.*

FIRST CUSTOMER (*whispering to the man beside him*). Bandidos Yanqui.

SECOND CUSTOMER *raises his hands a little bit higher in the air, turns and whispers to the man beside him.*

SECOND CUSTOMER. Bandidos Yanqui.

THIRD CUSTOMER *immediately turns, and whispers to the man beside him—*

THIRD CUSTOMER. Bandidos Yanqui—

And as the whisper moves down along the row, with the steady repeated whisper of "Bandidos Yanqui," The Third Musical Interlude ends.

Cut to:

BUTCH *and* SUNDANCE *and* ETTA—*Night, dining in as nice a restaurant as Bolivia has to offer. It is early evening, a lovely night, and the restaurant offers a fine view of the street.* BUTCH *and* SUNDANCE *are looking just a little older now; not much, just a little.*

BUTCH (*raising a glass*). I'd like to propose a toast to Bolivian law enforcement.

They drink. A waiter appears, with a large tray of food, puts it down nearby.

Cut to:

BUTCH *and* ETTA, *watching as the waiter sets about serving them. The food looks really good.*

BUTCH (*to Etta*). I don't know that we'd ever eat out in places like this without you—you're ugly and you're mean, but you're good cover
ETTA. You'll turn my head with talk like that—

And as she glances to SUNDANCE—

Cut to:

SUNDANCE, *only he isn't there now, just an empty chair, and then quick—*

Cut to:

BUTCH *and* ETTA, *looking around confused and—*

Cut to:

SUNDANCE, *and he is doing something very strange: his body pressed flat, he is standing against the closest wall of the restaurant, hiding, and he cannot take his eyes from the street.*

Cut to:

The Street—Night. It is dark, but not too dark to make out Three Men moving by the restaurant. The man in the middle wears a white straw skimmer. Zoom to BUTCH, *frantically saddling up his horse.*

Cut to:

SUNDANCE *and* ETTA, *watching him. This is a dimly lit stable, and* SUNDANCE *guards the door.* ETTA *moves between them.*

SUNDANCE. —I say let's go find him—let's get it done—

BUTCH. We might lose—we just saw two men with him—he might have twenty, we don't know—

ETTA. You don't even know for sure it was Lefors—

BUTCH. I'm a helluva guesser.

ETTA. He can't arrest you here—there are laws against that. And he can't take you back either.

SUNDANCE. He's not about to take anybody back—he's going to finish us right here. He's just gonna wait until we pull another job and then hunt us down like before, and if he misses us, he'll wait for the next job and get us then. So let's finish it now, Butch, one way or the other.

Cut to:

BUTCH, *and he is smiling.*

BUTCH. He's waiting for us, right? Well, let him—we'll drive him crazy—we'll outlast the bastard—we'll go straight!

And on the word "straight" —

Cut to:

Close-up— PERCY GARRIS*—Day.*

GARRIS. So ya want jobs—

The camera pulls back to reveal GARRIS *standing on the steps in front of his office at the Concordia Tin Mines, high in the Bolivian mountains. He is a flinty banty rooster of a man, with an incongruously mellifluous voice.*

GARRIS. —you're from the U.S. of A. and you're seeking after employment. Well, you couldn't have picked a more out of the way place in all Bolivia, I'll tell you that.

Cut to:

BUTCH *and* SUNDANCE, *standing at the foot of the steps below him.*

BUTCH. We're awful interested in learning about mining without any of those big city distractions.

Cut to:

GARRIS.

GARRIS. Ordinarily you got to wait to work for Percy Garris, but this ain't ordinarily, bingo.

It might be mentioned here that GARRIS *is a world class tobacco spitter, and his speech is punctuated with the words "dammy" or "bingo," depending on his accuracy.*

Cut to:

BUTCH *and* SUNDANCE.

BUTCH. Then there are jobs?

Cut to:

GARRIS. *advancing on them.*

GARRIS. Yes there are jobs, there are lotsa jobs, don't you wanna know why?

SUNDANCE. Okay. Why?

GARRIS. Dammy—cause I can't promise to pay you, don't you wanna know why?

BUTCH. Okay. Why?

Cut to:

GARRIS.

GARRIS. On account of the payroll thieves, fellow citizens, that's why, bingo. Every mine around gets its payroll from La Paz and every mine around gets its payroll held up—

Cut to:

BUTCH *and* SUNDANCE, *as* GARRIS *moves toward them again.*

GARRIS. Some say it's Bolivian bandits, some say the Bandidos Yanqui, can you hit anything?

And he points to their guns.

SUNDANCE. Sometimes.

GARRIS. Hit that—

And he pitches a plug of tobacco a good distance away.

Cut to:

SUNDANCE, *stepping back, getting ready to draw. Then—*

GARRIS'S VOICE (o.s.). No, no—(and he moves into view). —I just want to know if you can shoot.

He grabs one of SUNDANCE'S *pistols from its holster, shoves it to* SUNDANCE.

GARRIS. Shoot.

SUNDANCE *grabs the gun, fires, and—*

Cut to:

The tobacco plug, undisturbed as the shot misses.

Cut to:

BUTCH, *stunned, looking at* SUNDANCE.

Cut to:

SUNDANCE *and* GARRIS.

SUNDANCE. Can I move?
GARRIS *(confused)*. Move? What the hell you mean, move?

But before the words are half finished—

Cut to:

SUNDANCE, *dropping, drawing, firing, all in one motion and as his gun erupts—*

Cut to:

The tobacco plug, obliterated.

Cut to:

SUNDANCE, *rising.*

SUNDANCE *(explaining; simply)*. I'm better when I move.

Cut to:

BUTCH *and* SUNDANCE *and Garris.*

GARRIS *(he is not unimpressed)*. Considering that I'm desperate, and you're just what I'm looking for, on top of which you stem from the U.S. of A., we'll start in the morning.
BUTCH. You mean you're hiring us?
SUNDANCE *(as excited as Butch)*. We got jobs?
GARRIS *(nodding)*. Payroll guards.

And as the occupation is named—

Cut to:

Ext. Mountain trail—Three men on muleback, riding down the mountain. GARRIS *rides ahead, singing "Sweet Betsy from Pike" in a loud and lovely voice.* BUTCH *and* SUNDANCE *lag behind.*

Cut to:

BUTCH *and* SUNDANCE. *They have never done this kind of thing before and are both in a sweat, anticipating attack.*

BUTCH *(low and tense)*. I think they're in those rocks up ahead—

SUNDANCE *points to the other side of the trail.*

SUNDANCE. No—the shrubs—*(a whisper)*. Butch, I see them moving—

Cut to:

GARRIS, *glancing balefully around at the two of them.*

Cut to:

BUTCH *and* SUNDANCE, *riding nervously on.*

BUTCH. I'm telling you they're in the rocks—
SUNDANCE. You take the rocks, I'll take the shrubs—

Cut to:

The rock-shrub area, as BUTCH *and* SUNDANCE *ride slowly through—* GARRIS *has ridden through it already and has stopped up ahead of them, still glaring back.*

Cut to:

GARRIS.

GARRIS. Will you two beginners cut it out!

Cut to:

BUTCH *and* SUNDANCE, *riding up to him.*

BUTCH. We're just trying to watch out for ambush, Mr. Garris.
SUNDANCE. We've never done this kind of work before—we want to get it right—
GARRIS *(exploding)*. Morons!—I got morons on my team!—nobody's gonna rob us going *down* the mountain—we got no money going *down* the mountain—when we get the money, on the way back, *then* you can sweat!

Cut to:

Four payroll bags being pushed across a counter. Camera pulls back to reveal GARRIS *in a bank by the counter, signing for the payroll money as* BUTCH *and* SUNDANCE *stand aside, watching him.*

GARRIS *(taking the bags)*. Jones—gimme a hand with these—
SUNDANCE *(whispered)*. Which are you, Smith or Jones?
BUTCH *(shrugging)*. Live.

And as he starts toward GARRIS—

Cut to:

The three of them, riding out of La Paz, starting back up toward the mountains.

Cut to:

BUTCH *and* SUNDANCE *and* GARRIS—*in the mountains now.* GARRIS *rides with the payroll* bags. BUTCH and SUNDANCE are more nervous than ever, whirling and turning as they ride.

GARRIS. 'Bout a half hour more we can start to worry.

He points to an enormous rock a considerable distance up ahead of them.

GARRIS. Once we pass that rock.
SUNDANCE. They might try something here.
GARRIS (shaking his head). Better cover up there.

They are riding through an area with smaller rocks and boulders around them, and BUTCH *and* SUNDANCE *finger their guns constantly on the alert.* GARRIS *rides calmly ahead.*

GARRIS. Got to relax, you fellas; got to get used to Bolivian ways; got to go easy, dammy, like I do—

Cut to:

BUTCH *and* SUNDANCE, *continuing their constant straining around.*

Cut to:

GARRIS.

GARRIS (chattering on). —course you probably think I'm crazy but I'm not—bingo— I'm colorful; that's what happens to you when you live ten years alone in Bolivia—you get colorful—

And as a sudden unexpected blast of gunfire starts—

Cut to:

BUTCH *and* SUNDANCE *and* GARRIS, *rolling off their mules.*

Cut to:

The area around them, as more shots ring out. No one is visible.

Cut to:

BUTCH *and* SUNDANCE, *wedged together behind one rock as the firing at them continues.*

BUTCH. It's not us so it must be the Bolivians.

Cut to:

The area around them. Still more shots pour down, narrowly missing them, but still no one is seen.

Cut to:

BUTCH *and* SUNDANCE, *wedged behind the rock.* BUTCH's *face is visible.* SUNDANCE's, *behind him, is not.*

SUNDANCE. Butch . . .

BUTCH *is trying desperately to locate where the firing is coming from.*

BUTCH. What?
SUNDANCE. *Butch!*
BUTCH. I'm right beside you—(suddenly Sundance hits him on the back) Hey— (as SUNDANCE hits him again) Cut it out!

SUNDANCE *turns and we see his face now. He is terribly moved.*

SUNDANCE. What are we doing here? (Butch says nothing) You got to tell me—I got to know—what are we doing?—I'm not sure anymore—are we outlaws?—you're smart Butch so you tell me—
BUTCH (and now he is moved, too) We're outlaws. Outlaws, I don't know why. Cause we're good at it. I been one since I was fifteen and my wife left me on account of it and she took our kids on account of it and I'm not sure anymore either.

Cut to:

Close-up— SUNDANCE.

SUNDANCE. You had a family? I didn't know that.

Cut to:

Close-up— BUTCH. *He says nothing.*

Cut to:

SUNDANCE.

SUNDANCE. Let's find Garris and get the hell out of here.

He gestures toward a neighboring rock and as the firing continues—

Cut to:

BUTCH *and* SUNDANCE, *diving from their rock to* GARRIS', *rolling over and up and—*

Cut to:

GARRIS, *dead. The payroll bags are beside him.*

Cut to:

BUTCH *and* SUNDANCE. *They hover over* GARRIS *for just a moment until firing increases in intensity. Then* SUNDANCE *grabs for a payroll bag, brings out a knife and as he begins to slit the bag—*

Cut to:

The rock behind which they are hiding. The firing continues. Suddenly a payroll bag comes flying out from behind the rock and soaring high into the air.

Cut to:

The payroll bag. It arcs down and as it hits, coins come spilling out through a cut in the side.

Cut to:

The second of the four bags, flying through the air, landing and—

Cut to:

The third and fourth bags, and while they are still in the air—

Cut to:

BUTCH *and* SUNDANCE, *breaking from cover and running away like crazy down the mountain. A few scattered shots land near them as they continue to run away . . .*

Dissolve to:

A large pile of coins, and, beside it, several smaller piles. The camera pulls back to reveal half a dozen armed BOLIVIAN BANDITS. They sit silently on their haunches watching as one of them, the LEADER, carefully divides up the money. The only sound is that of the coins falling.

Cut to:

BUTCH *and* SUNDANCE, *moving onto a flat piece of ground, a bit above the bandits. They stand still, their guns in their holsters.*

Cut to:

THE LEADER. *He glances up, sees them. He makes no move to draw, but points instead.*

Cut to:

BUTCH *and* SUNDANCE, *motionless and still as the other bandits look up at them.*

Cut to:

THE BANDITS, *waiting, still on their haunches. There is no sound.*

Cut to:

BUTCH *and* SUNDANCE.

SUNDANCE. Tell him we were hired to take it back—it's our job—tell him the money isn't ours.
BUTCH. El dinero . . . no es nuestro . . .
SUNDANCE. Tell him we need it.
BUTCH. El dinero . . . lo nececitamos . . .

Cut to:

THE LEADER. *He cannot believe what he is hearing.*

Cut to:

BUTCH *and* SUNDANCE *and* THE BANDITS. *No one makes a move.*

SUNDANCE. Leave the money and go.
BUTCH. Dejon el dinero y vayanse.
LEADER. Dejon el dinero y vayanse?
BUTCH. Si.

Cut to:

THE BANDIT LEADER. *Slowly he stands.*

Cut to:

BUTCH *and* SUNDANCE.

BUTCH. What do you think?
SUNDANCE. Not so good. Try telling him again, it's not our money.
BUTCH. El dinero . . . no es nuestro.
SUNDANCE. *No es nuestro.*

Cut to:

THE BANDITS. *A second man stands now. Then a third. Still no sound.*

Cut to:

BUTCH *and* SUNDANCE.

SUNDANCE. Can you take the two on the right?
BUTCH. Listen, there's something I think you ought to know—I've never shot anybody.
SUNDANCE. This is one helluva time to tell me.

Cut to:

THE BANDITS. *They are all standing now. Silent.*

Cut to:

BUTCH *and* SUNDANCE.

SUNDANCE. —try the two on the right—I'll work my way over if I can—go for the guy, dead center—that way if you miss a little you'll still hit something—

Cut to:

Close-up— SUNDANCE.

SUNDANCE. —you got a wife and kids and you never shot a soul— *(bewildered; almost sad)* I just don't understand anything anymore.

Cut to:

THE BANDITS. *The* LEADER *is saying something to his men but the words aren't clear.*

Cut to:

BUTCH *and* SUNDANCE.

SUNDANCE. Please go. *Please.* Por favor.

Cut to:

THE BANDITS.

THE LEADER. Por favor? *(it strikes him funny)* Por favor?

And he goes for his guns and—

Cut to:

BUTCH *and* SUNDANCE, *drawing and firing.* SUNDANCE *first,* BUTCH *after him and*

Cut to:

The bloodbath. Camera stays on the BANDITS *and in the next sixty seconds the action freezes sixty times and the first sound that we hear is the deafening blast of gunfire as* BUTCH *and* SUNDANCE's *bullets thud home and from left to right, the* BANDITS *start to die. And the left to right move is the first move the camera makes, panning across the dying men, some of them with their guns still in their holsters, and then as the gunfire ends, another sound begins, just as loud and just as terrifying and this sound is a scream. It doesn't come from any one bandit, it isn't even connected in any actual way with any one man, but it is the loudest scream anyone ever heard and it peaks almost immediately and then it really starts to build as the blood starts pouring from the* BANDITS, *from their chests, mouths, eyes. And once the left to right move is over, the camera begins its second move, and the direction of the second move is down, as gradually, the* BANDITS, *no longer able to stand, start slipping gracelessly to earth. And every second the action freezes them in their final trip, and the scream keeps them company, and even though the trip is short, it still takes time for all six to slip and stagger and crumble awkwardly to their knees and beyond, toppling sideways and backwards and forwards, but always down, colliding finally with the hard earth which is red now with their blood as it leaves their dying bodies and as the scream ends, the blood continues to drain ceaselessly into the ground . . .*

Cut to:

BUTCH *and* SUNDANCE, *staring at the holocaust.* BUTCH *is shattered;* SUNDANCE *is numb.*

SUNDANCE *(very quiet).* Well, we've gone straight, what'll we try now?

Cut to:

Ext. Concordia Mines—Night. GARRIS' *mule moves into view.* GARRIS *is strapped to it. As the mule comes close to camera, the payroll bags are visible, strapped tight to* GARRIS' *body. As the mule moves on—*

Cut to:

ETTA—*by the fire—night. She is pouring coffee. Camera pulls back to reveal a campsite. It is night and it is cold.* SUNDANCE *sits near the fire, finishing a plate of food. He nods when* ETTA *puts his coffee down beside him.*

Cut to:

ETTA, *moving to* BUTCH *with another cup of coffee. He sits off by himself.*

Cut to:

BUTCH, *as* ETTA *comes up. He and* SUNDANCE *both look a little older now. Not much. Just a little.*

ETTA *(as she gives him his coffee).* Done? *(Butch nods)* I'll take your plate then.

She picks it up—the food is untouched.

ETTA. Full? *(Butch nods again).* Good.

She starts away. As she does—

Cut to:

ETTA.

ETTA. There's other ways of going straight, you know.

Cut to:

BUTCH. *He makes no reply.*

Cut to:

ETTA, *pouring coffee for herself, sitting beside* SUNDANCE.

ETTA. There's other ways of going straight, you know. *(she sips her coffee)* There's farming—we've got the money; we could buy a little place.
SUNDANCE. I don't know how to farm.
ETTA. What about a ranch, then?
BUTCH'S VOICE *(o.s.).* Closest we ever came to ranch work was back in our rustling days—

Cut to:

BUTCH.

BUTCH. We weren't much at it even then, and it's hard. The hours are brutal. No, you got to be a kid to start a ranch.

Cut to:

ETTA.

ETTA. It was a silly idea; sorry.

Cut to:

SUNDANCE, *watching the fire.*

Cut to:

BUTCH, *watching the night.*

Cut to:

ETTA, *sipping her coffee. After a moment, she closes her eyes . . .*

Dissolve to:

The Campsite. The fire is out now; it is very late and very cold—when they speak, the three of them, you can see their breath white in the darkness. SUNDANCE *and* ETTA *lie under one blanket, their backs to each other.* BUTCH, *wrapped in a blanket, is off by himself. This scene is written for the camera to be in constant motion, moving above the three people lying below; sometimes it comes down close to them, sometimes it rises away. But it never stops moving*

ETTA *(wide awake).* Hey?
SUNDANCE *(wide awake too).* Hmm?
ETTA. Maybe I might go back ahead of you.
SUNDANCE. You mean home?
ETTA. I was thinking of it.
SUNDANCE *(he doesn't want her to go).* Whatever you want, Etta.
ETTA. Then maybe I'll go.
SUNDANCE *(to Butch).* Hey?
BUTCH *(he is also awake).* Hmm?
SUNDANCE. Etta's thinking of maybe going home ahead of us.
BUTCH *(he doesn't want her to go either).* Whatever she wants.
ETTA. I'll go then.
BUTCH. Hey?
ETTA. Hmm?
BUTCH. Remember what you said once about leaving us?
ETTA *(she remembers).* No; what did I say?
BUTCH. That you wouldn't stick around to watch us die.
ETTA. Now Butch you know I never said anything like that.
BUTCH. Then that's not why you're going?
ETTA *(of course it is).* Of course it isn't.
BUTCH. I didn't think it was . . .

And now, as the camera moves to the night, it holds for just a moment on the silent darkness. Then, as a very distinct hissing sound becomes increasingly audible—

Cut to:

The faint flickering image of an evil-looking man. Camera pulls back to reveal a makeshift movie theater—it is really nothing more than a large-sized tent—on the edge of a decent-sized Bolivian town. The theater is crammed with Bolivian peasants, all of them hissing the evil-looking man on the screen. Seated among the Bolivians are BUTCH *and* SUNDANCE *and* ETTA. *The hissing stops suddenly, turns to a gasp and*

Cut to:

The Screen. An innocent, beautiful, helpless young Girl is totally unaware that the evil-looking Man is creeping up behind her.

Cut to:

BUTCH *and* SUNDANCE *and* ETTA. BUTCH *and* SUNDANCE *are drinking more than a little.* ETTA *is dressed for travel. She looks weary.*

ETTA *(opening her purse, consulting a time-piece).* I ought to get over to the station—
SUNDANCE. We'll walk you.
ETTA. It's just down the street.

The hissing grows louder and—

Cut to:

The Screen. The evil-looking Man is carrying the Girl across a moor.

Cut to:

BUTCH *and* SUNDANCE *and* ETTA.

BUTCH. Listen, if there's one thing about us, we got manners—
ETTA *(firmly).* It's just down the street. *(softer)* Really.

There are cheers from the audience now so—

Cut to:

The Screen. A blond handsome man appears, begins chasing the evil-looking Man and Girl. The title comes on reading: "The Cliff" and then the evil-looking Man is visible, holding the Girl over a precipice. Then another title comes on reading: "In the Nick of Time."

SUNDANCE'S VOICE *(o.s., while the title is on).* These guys can't read English.
BUTCH'S VOICE *(o.s.)* These guys can't read Spanish.

Cut to:

The Audience, cheering wildly now.

Cut to:

BUTCH *and* SUNDANCE *and* ETTA, *watching the screen as the Hero and Villain struggle on the precipice. The Hero falls, clutches the edge* with his fingertips. The Villain stomps on them but the Hero fights his way back, and now it is the Villain's turn to fall and clutch the edge. The Hero does his best to save him, but too late. The Villain falls to eternity. The cheering is tumultuous. During all this—

ETTA. They just ship them straight down from America—they're supposed to be very popular up there now.

BUTCH. Hey, you'll write to us, won't you?

On the screen, the Hero holds the Girl. Then the title: "The End". Then a plain white light beams onto the screen as the next picture is gotten ready.

Cut to:

ETTA, *nodding, slowly starting to stand.*

ETTA. There's something I'd like to say to you both—

Cut to:

BUTCH *and* SUNDANCE, *looking at her.*

Cut to:

BUTCH *and* SUNDANCE *and* ETTA, *with* ETTA *on her feet now.*

ETTA *(catching their look).* Oh, you thought I was going to be sentimental and embarrass you, admit it. *(shaking her head)* All these years and we don't know each other at all.

She starts to go, stops suddenly, as the next one reeler begins and the title "The Wild Bunch" flickers on the screen.

Cut to:

BUTCH *and* SUNDANCE, *riveted.*

Cut to:

A Title reading: "The Wild Bunch Are All Dead Now But Once They Ruled The West". This is followed by a picture of a gang of men in shadow watching the approach of an oncoming train.

Cut to:

The Audience, starting to hiss.

Cut to:

The Screen, and a title reading: "Ruthless Evil Men, They Stopped At Nothing" followed by a close-up of the gang. (Note: in this "movie", all the actors should be dressed as the real people were dressed, and they should look like the real people as much as possible.)

Cut to:

The Audience, hissing louder now.

Cut to:

BUTCH *and* SUNDANCE.

BUTCH *(to Sundance).* Did it say we're dead? We're not dead.

Cut to:

*The Screen, and a title reading, "Their Leaders Were Butch Cassidy and The Sundance Kid." This is followed by a shot of "*BUTCH AND SUNDANCE*" grappling with a small child.*

Cut to:

The Audience, as suddenly the hissing doubles in volume and—

Cut to:

*The Screen, as "*BUTCH *and* SUNDANCE*" are tying the child to the railroad tracks in order to stop the oncoming train and—*

Cut to:

BUTCH *and* SUNDANCE.

SUNDANCE. —we didn't do that—never—
BUTCH. —damn right we didn't—Etta—you tell 'em—

And as he glances around for her—

Cut to:

*Close-up—*ETTA*—Night. She is just leaving the theater now and this is the first of a series of shots of her—all of them walking shots as she moves away and into the night—all of them close and getting closer.*

Cut to:

*Int. Tent Theater—*BUTCH *and* SUNDANCE*—Night.* BUTCH *whirls back to the screen as suddenly the audience is cheering like crazy and—*

Cut to:

The Screen, as the SUPERPOSSE *appears. The cheering sound grows louder as the "*SUPERPOSSE*" take out guns and begin firing.*

Cut to:

The Screen and BUTCH *and* SUNDANCE *watching it.*

BUTCH *(as "Harvey Logan" is gunned down)* Hey that's Harvey— *(grabbing Sundance now)* They didn't get Harvey then—you think they got him later?

SUNDANCE. —I don't know, I don't know— *(as News Carver is shot)* —they just got "News"—

He turns quickly, glancing back to where ETTA *exited.*

Cut to:

Close-up—ETTA. *Walking. The sound of the crowd inside the theater is terribly loud in the night. She continues to move away.*

Cut to:

Int. Tent Theater—BUTCH *and* SUNDANCE *watching the screen.*

BUTCH (*as "Flat Nose" Curry dies*) —there goes "Flat Nose"—my God, they're getting everybody.—

The Audience is screaming now and BUTCH *turns on them*—

BUTCH. Shut up, you people—

Cut to:

Close-up—SUNDANCE.

SUNDANCE (*riveted on the screen*). Butch—

Cut to:

BUTCH *and* SUNDANCE.

SUNDANCE (*grabbing* BUTCH *now*) Look—they're coming after us!

Cut to:

*The Screen, as the "*SUPERPOSSE*" takes off after "*BUTCH *and* SUNDANCE*".*

Cut to:

BUTCH, *turning again to the screaming audience*—

BUTCH. This isn't how it was— it wasn't like that—shut up—

Cut to:

*The Screen. The "*SUPERPOSSE*" is closing the gap on "*BUTCH *and* SUNDANCE*".*

Cut to:

BUTCH *and* SUNDANCE, *staring at the screen and*—

Cut to:

*The Screen, as "*THE SUPERPOSSE*" draws nearer, nearer and*

Cut to:

BUTCH *and* SUNDANCE, *on their feet now, caught up in the action on screen, talking softly, almost in spite of themselves*—

BUTCH. —They'll never get you—
SUNDANCE. —move—you can do it—move

BUTCH—come on you guys—
SUNDANCE. —all the way—
BUTCH *and* SUNDANCE (*together*). —come-on-you-guys—

But on the screen, the SUPERPOSSE *continues to close in.*

Cut to:

A series of shots. And this next sequence consists of quick cuts to:

A. BUTCH *and* SUNDANCE, *watching the screen.*

B. *The action on the screen.*

C. *The Audience, cheering wildly, the sound always building.*

D. ETTA, *walking away, her face always growing as the camera comes closer and closer to her.*

On the screen, the SUPERPOSSE *forces* BUTCH *and* SUNDANCE *into a corner where they can't ride any more and* BUTCH *and* SUNDANCE *get off their horses and try to climb to safety up the rocks that have cornered them, but the* SUPERPOSSE *is too quick for them, too smart, and before* BUTCH *and* SUNDANCE *are halfway up the rocks, the* SUPERPOSSE *is already firing and the audience is screaming itself crazy as* BUTCH *gets winged and the explosive nature of the sound carries through the night to* ETTA, *who continues her walk away from it all, and on screen now,* BUTCH *is hit again,* SUNDANCE *too, and they slip and slide down the rocks as the* SUPERPOSSE *continues to fire on them.* BUTCH *is dead as he slides to earth. As* SUNDANCE *dies,* ETTA*'s stunning face fills the screen. Hold on* ETTA . . hold . .

Fade out.

Fade in on.

Ext. Jungle trail—Shot from above, a mule train moving slowly along. It is a payroll train and the four men that accompany it are armed. The trail is narrow, the going, slow. The sun is blistering.

Cut to:

A section of jungle. Foliage is terribly thick and nothing is visible beyond it. Then, something moves and—

Cut to:

BUTCH *and* SUNDANCE, *crouched in the jungle beside the trail. They both look older now. Not a little. A lot.* BUTCH *is nervous, continually swatting away flies.*

BUTCH *(whispering—the payroll train is close)*. No more of this jungle work for me.

SUNDANCE *(whispering back)*. You're getting to be an old maid.

Cut to:

The four Payroll Guards. They stand tight together, arms raised. SUNDANCE *covers them while in the background,* BUTCH *gathers up the payroll money. The Guards look at each other, silently mouth the words "Bandidos Yanqui" and stand very still.*

Cut to:

BUTCH, *as he works away.*

BUTCH. You can keep your old maid remarks to yourself, if you don't mind,—Hey, c'mere.

Cut to:

SUNDANCE, *moving to* BUTCH, *always watching the Guards.*

SUNDANCE. What?

BUTCH. Whoever owns this Alpoco Mine must be a millionaire—*(he points to the payroll—it is big)* we'll never be able to carry it all.

He reaches for the nearest mule—it is a large, silver-gray animal. They start to work, transferring payroll bags to mule.

BUTCH. If it isn't one thing, it's another.

Cut to:

The Mule, loaded with the payroll. BUTCH *starts to lead it off.*

BUTCH *(as he goes)*. Tell them not to move.

SUNDANCE. What's the word?

BUTCH *(to the guards)*. Quietos.

And he disappears into the jungle.

SUNDANCE *(to the guards)*. Quietos.

Cut to:

The Four Guards. They are alone with their mules now. Sweat pours down their faces. They do not move . . .

Dissolve to:

*A Street in a small town—*BUTCH *and* SUNDANCE, *walking along. They lead two mules, the large silver-grey one and one other. The silvery-grey mule carries the payroll money which has been adequately concealed beneath a blanket.*

SUNDANCE. There's better cover in the jungle.

BUTCH. Look—I gotta right to my opinion and my opinion is there's snakes in the jungle, so I'll work in the mountains and I'll work in the cities, but from now on, jungle work is *out.*

BUTCH. This must be San Vicento, you think?

SUNDANCE *(nods)*. Isn't there supposed to be a good place to eat here?

Cut to:

A Small White-haired Man. He owns the restaurant. Pull back to reveal BUTCH *and* SUNDANCE, *talking to him.*

BUTCH *(miming eating)*. Comer? Si?

WHITE-HAIRED MAN *(gestures toward a patio)*. Si.

BUTCH *and* SUNDANCE *start off in the direction the man indicated, leading their mules. The man smiles as they go. Then his smile abruptly dies and—*

Cut to:

The silver-gray mule. It is branded.

Cut to:

*Int. tiny restaurant—*BUTCH *and* SUNDANCE, *seated alone, starting to eat.*

Cut to:

Ext. Restaurant—The silver-grey mule. Pull back to reveal the restaurant owner and two POLICEMEN *peering from behind cover at the mule.*

RESTAURANT OWNER *(whispering as he points to the mules)*. El mulo es de Alpoca Mines.

FIRST POLICEMAN. Cierto?

RESTAURANT OWNER *(raising his right hand)*. Si.

The FIRST POLICEMAN *whispers something to the* SECOND, *who moves off quickly.*

*Int. Restaurant—*BUTCH *and* SUNDANCE. BUTCH *takes a bite of food, throws his fork down, stands.* SUNDANCE *manages to continue to swallow the stuff.*

BUTCH. The Specialty of the House and it's still moving.

SUNDANCE. Bitch, bitch, bitch.

Cut to:

The Doorway of the tiny restaurant. BUTCH *moves into it and stands there in the sunlight until a shot almost takes his head off and—*

Cut to:

BUTCH, *diving down back inside the room.* SUNDANCE *is crouched, guns ready.*

BUTCH. That settles it—this place gets no more of my business.

Cut to:

SUNDANCE, *moving around the room, from window to window.*

Cut to:

The view outside the window. There is a wall that surrounds the restaurant with just the open patio in between. Beyond the wall, no one is visible.

Cut to:

A view from above. Spaced around the wall are close to TWENTY POLICEMEN, *all of them armed.*

Cut to:

*Int. Restaurant—*BUTCH, *moving close alongside* SUNDANCE *as he completes his move around the tiny room.*

BUTCH. What do you think?
SUNDANCE. Can't tell.
BUTCH. I bet it's just one guy.

SUNDANCE *takes off his hat, raises it to a window. As he does this—*

Cut to:

Ext. Restaurant—Half a dozen policemen, rising up behind the wall, blasting away.

Cut to:

BUTCH *and* SUNDANCE.

SUNDANCE *(pulling his hat back).* Don't you get sick of being right all the time?

Cut to:

The window, as seen from beyond the wall. Again the hat appears and again, half a dozen policemen rise and fire and—

Cut to:

A neighboring window, and SUNDANCE *framed there, firing back and—*

Cut to:

A tall policeman, spinning and falling, lying quiet on the ground.

Cut to:

The mules, in the far corner of the patio. The sound of gunfire increases steadily. The mules stand motionless.

Cut to:

The tall policeman, lying on the ground. Then—Pull back to reveal several other policemen, lying sprawled out too.

Cut to:

*Int. Restaurant—*BUTCH *and* SUNDANCE. *It has been all shot up. The tables are turned over for protection.* BUTCH *is crouched behind one window,* SUNDANCE *behind another.*

SUNDANCE *(loading his pistols).* This is all I got left.
BUTCH. Me too—*(he starts to crawl along the floor to a different window)*—now we can either stay here until we run out and get killed, or we can go get some more.

He points.

Cut to:

The mules, all the way across the patio from the tiny restaurant.

Cut to:

BUTCH *and* SUNDANCE, *crouched by a window, staring at the animals. The Silver-Grey Mule is behind the smaller pack mule.*

SUNDANCE. Which one's got the bullets?
BUTCH. The little one.
SUNDANCE *(starting to crawl toward the door).* I'll go.

Cut to:

BUTCH.

BUTCH. This is no time for bravery: I'll let you.

Cut to:

The patio. From where they are, the mules are a long, long way

Cut to:

Inside the room. SUNDANCE *is by the door now.* BUTCH, *across the floor, watches him.*

BUTCH. Hey?

SUNDANCE *glances at him.*

BUTCH. I gotta be the one to go.
SUNDANCE. Why you?
BUTCH. I could never give you cover. You can cover me.

SUNDANCE *says nothing.*

BUTCH. I'm right. You see that, don't you?

Cut to:

*Close-up—*SUNDANCE.

SUNDANCE. You go.

Cut to:

*Close-up—*BUTCH.

BUTCH. Why am I so damn smart all the time?

And as he shakes his head—

Cut to:

The patio, and, far across, the mules.

Cut to:

The Head Policeman, rifle in hand, staring in at the room where BUTCH *and* SUNDANCE *are.*

Cut to:

Inside the Room. BUTCH *and* SUNDANCE *stand by the door. Silently,* BUTCH *hands* SUNDANCE *his pistols.*

Cut to:

Ext. Restaurant and Patio—The Head Policeman, staring in across the patio toward where BUTCH *and* SUNDANCE *are. Then, as he watches, the door to the room silently opens. The Head Policeman raises his rifle, aims it dead at the door.*

Cut to:

The door, completely open now.

Cut to:

The Head Policeman, waiting. Then—

Cut to:

SUNDANCE, *vaulting through a shattered window, moving out into the sunlight of the patio, two guns in his hands, two more in his holsters, and as he comes he fires, and starts to turn and as the first turn happens—*

Cut to:

BUTCH, *barrelassing out the door.*

Cut to:

SUNDANCE, *now, firing with both guns, turning around and around, firing as he spins and maybe he wasn't the greatest gunman that ever lived but then again, maybe he was and—*

Cut to:

BUTCH, *running like hell then diving to the ground, rolling up and running again and—*

Cut to:

The Head Policeman with SUNDANCE *in the b.g. He is about to fire when suddenly* SUNDANCE *changes the direction of his turn and*

the Head Policeman has to drop for safety behind the wall.

Cut to:

BUTCH, *streaking, diving again, then up, and the bullets landing around him aren't even close as—*

Cut to:

SUNDANCE, *whirling and spinning, continuing to fire and—*

Cut to:

Several policemen, dropping for safety behind the wall and—

Cut to:

BUTCH, *really moving now, dodging, diving, up again and—*

Cut to:

SUNDANCE, *flinging away one gun, grabbing another from his holster, continuing to turn and fire and—*

Cut to:

Two policemen, falling wounded to the ground and—

Cut to:

BUTCH, *letting out a notch, then launching into another dive forward and—*

Cut to:

SUNDANCE, *whirling, but you never know which way he's going to spin and—*

Cut to:

The Head Policeman, cursing, forced to drop for safety behind the wall and—

Cut to:

BUTCH, *racing to the mules, and then he is there, grabbing at the near mule for ammunition and—*

Cut to:

SUNDANCE, *throwing the second gun away, reaching into his holster for another, continuing to spin and fire and—*

Cut to:

BUTCH. *He has the ammunition now and—*

Cut to:

Another policeman, screaming as he falls and—

Cut to:

BUTCH, *his arms loaded, tearing away from the mules and they're still not even coming close to him as they fire and the mules are behind him now as he runs and cuts and cuts again, going full out and—*

Cut to:

The Head Policeman, cursing incoherently at what is happening and—

Cut to:

SUNDANCE, *whirling faster than ever and—*

Cut to:

BUTCH, *dodging and cutting and as a pattern of bullets rips into his body he somersaults and lies there, pouring blood and—*

Cut to:

SUNDANCE, *running toward him and—*

Cut to:

All the policemen rising up behind the wall now, firing, and—

Cut to:

SUNDANCE, *as he falls.*

Cut to:

BUTCH, *crawling.*

Cut to:

SUNDANCE, *half up now, going the best he can, and—*

Cut to:

The policemen, pumping bullets and—

Cut to:

SUNDANCE, *his left arm hanging, going for* BUTCH, *starting to pull him toward the safety of the room and it's not far away but bullets are landing all over now, and first one of them is hit again, then the other, and—*

Cut to:

Inside the room, as BUTCH *and* SUNDANCE *come falling through the door and lie there. The firing continues.* SUNDANCE *manages to get the door shut and then there is no sound except for their agonized breathing. They are both wounded terribly, but that fact never for a moment enters into their conversation, either here or later.*

BUTCH *pushes himself up into a sitting position* . . .

BUTCH. . . . I thought you were gonna cover me . . .

SUNDANCE *(sitting now too)*. . . . I thought you were gonna run . . . if I'd known you were just gonna stroll along—

BUTCH. Stroll!

They are both doing what they can with their wounds now—muttering to themselves as we:

Cut to:

Ext. Restaurant and Patio—The Head Policeman, standing nervously at attention, saluting. Pull back to reveal over a hundred members of the Bolivian Cavalry. A Young Captain rides at their head; beside him is the Policeman who had been dispatched earlier.

HEAD POLICEMAN. Mi Capitan.

The CAPTAIN *is a young energetic man, handsome and volatile—he dismounts rapidly while behind him, his troops remain on horseback. As he looks around—*

CAPTAIN. El enimigo?

The Head Policeman points to the small room where BUTCH *and* SUNDANCE *are. The* CAPTAIN *glances at it briefly, then back to the* HEAD POLICEMAN.

CAPTAIN. Cuantos hombres?

HEAD POLICEMAN *(holding up two fingers)*. Dos.

CAPTAIN *(furious)*. Dos hombres?

HEAD POLICEMAN *(trying to get a word in)*. Capitan, por favor—

CAPTAIN. *Dos hombres?*

HEAD POLICEMAN. —Bandidos—*Bandidos Yanqui*—

CAPTAIN *pointing at the room where* BUTCH *and* SUNDANCE *are.*

CAPTAIN. Bandidos Yanqui?

HEAD POLICEMAN Si, mi Capitan.

Cut to:

*Close-up—*THE CAPTAIN.

CAPTAIN. Ahhhhhhhhhh . . .

Cut to:

The Cavalry, dismounting, beginning to move into position around the outside of the patio and—

Cut to:

*Int. Restaurant and Patio—*BUTCH *and* SUNDANCE *watching; quick glimpses of the running cavalrymen are visible. They are still bleeding as badly as before.*

Cut to:

The sun, crimson red and falling. There is a sharp metallic sound and—

Cut to:

One of the four sides of the patio. The Troops are sharply slipping their bayonets onto their rifles. THE CAPTAIN *moves quickly along his men, making sure that everyone and everything is ready, and as he turns a corner—*

Cut to:

Another wall lined with Troops. As the CAPTAIN *approaches, this Group snaps on its bayonets, and again there is the sharp metallic sound. As the* CAPTAIN *continues his efficient military way—*

Cut to:

BUTCH *and* SUNDANCE, *crouched close together by a window, peering out toward the setting sun.*

BUTCH. I got a great idea where we should go next.
SUNDANCE. Well I don't wanna hear it.
BUTCH. You'll change your mind once I tell you—
SUNDANCE. Shut up.
BUTCH. Okay; okay.
SUNDANCE. It was your great ideas got us here.
BUTCH. Forget about it . . .
SUNDANCE. I never want to hear another of your great ideas, all right?
BUTCH. All right.
SUNDANCE. Good.
BUTCH. Australia.

Cut to:

SUNDANCE. *He just looks at* BUTCH.

Cut to:

BUTCH.

BUTCH. I figured secretly you wanted to know so I told you: Australia.

Cut to:

BUTCH *and* SUNDANCE.

SUNDANCE. That's your great idea?
BUTCH. The latest in a long line.
SUNDANCE *(exploding with everything he has left)*. Australia's no better than here!
BUTCH. That's all you know.
SUNDANCE. Name me one thing.
BUTCH. They speak English in Australia.
SUNDANCE. They do?
BUTCH. That's right, smart guy, so we wouldn't be foreigners. And they ride horses.

And they got thousands of miles to hide out in—and a good climate, nice beaches, you could learn to swim—
SUNDANCE. Swimming's not important, what about the banks?
BUTCH. Easy, ripe and luscious.
SUNDANCE. The banks or the women?
BUTCH. Once we get the one we'll get the other.
SUNDANCE. It's a long way, though, isn't it?
BUTCH *(shouting it out)*. Everything always gotta be perfect with you!
SUNDANCE. I just don't wanna get there and find out it stinks, that's all.

Cut to:

BUTCH.

BUTCH. Will you at least think about?

Cut to:

SUNDANCE. *He considers this a moment.*

SUNDANCE. All right, I'll think about it.

Cut to:

Extreme close-up— BUTCH *and* SUNDANCE.

BUTCH. Now after we—*(and suddenly he stops)*—wait a minute—
SUNDANCE. What?
BUTCH. You didn't see Lefors out there?
SUNDANCE. Lefors? No.
BUTCH. Good. For a minute I thought we were in trouble.

Cut to:

THE CAPTAIN. *He nods and as he does, one group of men begins to load their weapons, the bullets slipping into the chambers and—*

Cut to:

The sun dying. There is the continuing sound of rifles loading and . . .

Cut to:

THE CAPTAIN, *moving almost into a run around the perimeter of the walls, making sure everything is ready, and as the men stand taut—*

Cut to:

Close-up— BUTCH *and* SUNDANCE, *listening as the sounds come to them, the metallic sounds of the military, and then the* CAPTAIN's *voice is heard, starting to call out one word, over and over and—*

Cut to:

Close-up— THE CAPTAIN. *Over and over as he gestures forward toward the tiny room where* BUTCH *and* SUNDANCE *are:*

CAPTAIN. *—ataque—ataque—ataque—*

Cut to:

One group of men, vaulting the wall, moving forward and quickly.

Cut to:

Another group of men and another, all of them vaulting the wall and starting to run and—

Cut to:

Close-up— BUTCH *and* SUNDANCE. *The camera freezes them. And as it does, a tremendous fusilage of shots is heard, then another, even louder, and more and more shots, building its tempo and sound. The shots continue to sound.* BUTCH *and* SUNDANCE *remain frozen.*

Final fade-out.

THE END

SOUNDER

Screenplay by Lonne Elder III

NATHAN LEE MORGAN	Paul Winfield
REBECCA MORGAN	Cicely Tyson
DAVID LEE MORGAN	Kevin Hooks
MRS. BOATWRIGHT	Carmen Matthews
SHERIFF YOUNG	James Best
IKE	Taj Mahal

Screenplay by Lonne Elder III
Produced by Radnitz/Mattel Productions for Twentieth Century-Fox, 1972
Produced by Robert B. Radnitz
Directed by Martin Ritt
Cinematography by John Alonzo
Music by Taj Mahal

Nominated for both an Academy Award and a Writers Guild Award in 1972, Mr. Elder's screenplay, as adapted from the novel by William H. Armstrong, is a model of the scriptwriter's craft in its elemental spareness. Mr. Elder is noted for the intensity of feeling and warmth of his language, which gives one the feeling of prose poetry.

Born in Americus, Georgia, on December 26, 1931, Mr. Elder received his education at the New Jersey State University and at the Yale University School of Drama at New Haven. Mr. Elder won numerous awards for his exceptional play *Ceremonies in Dark Old Men* after it was produced in New York by the Negro Ensemble Company in 1969. This play was subsequently followed by his distinguished screenplay for *Sounder* in 1972.

Like *Meet John Doe,* Mr. Elder's screenplay deals with America's great depression of the 1930s. As Robert Riskin's *Meet John Doe* deals with the plight of the poor and hungry, urban, white workingman in the cities, Mr. Elder's work deals with a poor, rural black family in the South at that time, the Morgans, trying to eke a Spartan living out of the soil, always frightfully close to starvation.

Mr. Elder's work is also a populist work in the sense that *Meet John Doe* is. Each in its own way deals with hope for the future in a democratic society. *Sounder,* of course, deals with it in the hunger for education expressed by Morgan's boy and by his supporting family as well.

This hunger for education to break out of the cycle of poverty of a deprived rural black class is beautifully realized. Mr. Elder mirrors black life as it must really have been in that society. The story has a strong feeling of veracity and unfolds without sentimentality, without rancor toward white society, without adornment—realistic yet suffused with warmth, humanity, and hope. The rural, agricultural, and hunting experience, the closeness to the land, the strong filial ties, a black experience in the South just a few generations away from slavery amidst the company-town mentality of patronization by whites all are beautifully realized with a simplicity of style that is almost biblical.

Fade in. Before titles. Ext. hunting woods—Landsdown County—Night. It is a clear but cold Autumn night at some time in the nineteen thirties. The Landsdown Woods are an assortment of various elements of nature; quiet water streams, rushing rivers, heavy brushland, small trees, and the more dominant, great tall pines. NATHAN LEE MORGAN, *a Black man in his late thirties or early forties, treks deep into the woods with his eleven year old son,* DAVID LEE, *and his hound dog,* SOUNDER. NATHAN LEE *is a well built, strong manner of a man with a deliberate and quiet manner—* DAVID LEE, *like his father is tall and strong with big, bright active eyes.* SOUNDER, *their hound dog, is a mixture of red-bone hound and bulldog, with great square jaws.*

TITLES BEGIN.

NATHAN LEE *carries an old rifle, and a burlap sack thrown across his shoulder—* DAVID LEE *walks with a lantern as* SOUNDER *tracks ahead of them. They keep moving until they come upon a quiet river stream—*

Ext. river stream—Night. They walk along the edges of the river, with deliberation. It is obvious that they have walked this route many times. They reach a cut-off point and circle back into the woods, and pick-up a pathway—.

Ext. pathway—Night. They pick up speed in close approach to a weeded area and stop. DAVID *looks about in disappointment.* SOUNDER *scratches the earth—* NATHAN *looks out into the darkness with a nagging expression on his face—*

TITLES INTERRUPTED.

DAVID LEE. There ain't no possums in this woods tonight, Daddy.

NATHAN LEE. Looks that way, son. Guess the cold done drove most of 'em down to the big water country—but if there's one left out here—we gotta find him.

DAVID LEE. It's cold, Daddy!

NATHAN LEE. Here, put my jacket over you.

NATHAN *takes his jacket off and drapes it over the boy's frame as* SOUNDER *begins to scratch and whine with intensity. He moves to stand over the dog.*

NATHAN LEE. You all right, boy?

Suddenly SOUNDER'S *voice lets out and he breaks away in a burst of speed.* NATHAN *and* DAVID *react quickly and take up the chase behind him.*

TITLES BEGIN AGAIN.

As SOUNDER *makes his way through the woods—* NATHAN *and* DAVID *rush behind him, following the great unique sound of the dog's voice. It is a sound that bounces—soulful, louder and clearer than any purebred redbone. It is spaced with precision, bouncing from slope to slope like a rubber ball, filling up the night with music as though the branches of all the trees were being pulled across silver strings.*

Ext.—The base of the tree where the possum has taken refuge—Night. SOUNDER *arrives and makes a leap to climb the tree as* NATHAN *and* DAVID *rush on to the scene.* NATHAN *looks up and points to the spot where the possum is. He puts his rifle down near him, and* DAVID *assists him in the shaking of the tree as* SOUNDER *makes his leaps upward to the rhythm of the sound coming from his voice. The possum gives way to the force and falls to the ground.* SOUNDER *charges for the animal—* NATHAN *quickly picks up his rifle and aims for the animal. He fires into blank darkness and misses. The possum recovers from the fall and scampers into thick brushland, with* SOUNDER *in close pursuit.*

Ext.—The area of the thick brushland—Night. SOUNDER *cannot overcome the briar thickness of the brushland—but the possum with his smaller size manages to elude the dog.*

Ext.—The edges of the brushland area—Night. SOUNDER *comes out of the brush area, whining in frustration as* NATHAN *and* DAVID *approach him.* NATHAN *immediately realizes that the possum has gotten away.*

END OF TITLES:

NATHAN LEE *(slams his rifle to the ground).* Dammit! And I remember the time when a bull couldn't a stopped him from gettin' that possum!

DAVID LEE *kneels down and caresses* SOUNDER'S *frame.* NATHAN *realizes that* DAVID *is disturbed over his harshness.*

NATHAN LEE. Come here, son—

DAVID LEE *goes to his father, who kneels to him, and puts both of his huge hands on the boy's shoulders.*

NATHAN LEE. It's all right. He did his job—I just got foolish for a minute.

He gives the boy a quick embrace and rises to his feet—

NATHAN LEE. If anybody's to blame, it's me—I oughta nailed him when I took that shot.

DAVID LEE. It was too dark, Daddy.

NATHAN LEE. Yeah. We better git back to the house now.

NATHAN *puts his hand on* SOUNDER's *neck, gives him an affectionate rub. They gather their equipment and head for home. They move out of the brush area on to a pathway.*

Ext. road and cabin—Night. This area of the road is about ten hundred feet from the front yard of the cabin. The yard is wide, and stretches out to the very edges of the road which comes to a horseshoe deadend about two hundred feet at the far end of their cabin.

NATHAN LEE. In all the years me and Sounder been tracking down possums and coons in these woods—he ain't tore one of 'em up yet....He always brought 'em back whole and healthy....And that's the difference between a hound dog that's dirty and mean, to one that's great like ol' SOUNDER here.

Ext.—The cabin's front yard—Night. They move through the yard, up the steps, on to the porch, and open the door to the house.

Int.—The Kitchen-Sitting Room—Night. NATHAN, DAVID, *and* SOUNDER *step into the cabin. It is an old house but it is the home of the Morgan family so it is kept neat and clean at all times. To one side of the area is a kitchen table, a wood stove, and an old beat-up cabinet. To the other side are two old rockers, an old dresser, and one or two pieces of other old living room furniture—there are three portals in this area; the backdoor in the kitchen section which leads to the backyard, and two in the sitting room which leads to the children's and* NATHAN *and* REBECCA's *rooms.*

REBECCA MORGAN, *an attractive brown-skin woman in her thirties, sits in a rocker by the stove alone, picking kernels out of walnut shells with a bent hairpin. She looks up to* NATHAN *as he stands just inside the door, and looks down at her.*

NATHAN LEE. We cornered one, but he got away.

He does not wait for a response from her—he, DAVID *and* SOUNDER *keep moving across the floor, and on out the back door.* REBECCA's *eyes slowly trail their backs out the door. Her eyes just hang there after they have moved out of sight.*

Int. The Shed—Night. The shed is medium in size and old like the house. There is a long wide table running along side the right wall. There are hanging nails on all of the walls and along

side the table. The various pieces of archaic farm equipment are all neatly put in organized places. NATHAN, DAVID *and* SOUNDER *enter the shed.* NATHAN *hangs the burlap sack on one of the wall nails, and places the rifle down on the table—* DAVID *does likewise with the lantern.*

NATHAN LEE. Bet you're a tired little fellow, David Lee.

NATHAN *takes the lantern apart and begins to clean it—and* DAVID LEE *picks up a small can of oil and puts it on top of the table.*

DAVID LEE. Yes, sir...

NATHAN LEE. You oughta be tired, too, Sounder. That possum shore whipped the hell outta you tonight!

He laughs behind his own remark as he finishes the business with the lantern and picks up his rifle.

DAVID LEE. He beat you, too, Daddy, and you had a big ol' shootin' rifle.

NATHAN LEE *(serious)*. Boy, you don't make funny with your daddy, like that.

His father has caught him off guard—he was only joking—he doesn't understand the attitude—he doesn't know what to say—he turns and walks away.

NATHAN LEE. David Lee...

DAVID LEE *(stops and turns)*. Yes, sir...

NATHAN LEE. You had a rough time out there tonight—so you stay home from that school tomorrow.

DAVID LEE. I wanna go—the trip don't bother me none.

NATHAN LEE. You learnin' anything at that school?

DAVID LEE. Yes, sir—I learn to write a little bit, and I can read a lot—

DAVID LEE *looks on him for a moment, and then softly nods his head—*

NATHAN LEE. Readin' must be somethin' powerful, huh, son?

DAVID LEE. Yes, sir...

NATHAN LEE *slams the rifle closed, moves towards the exit and steps hastily out into the backyard—* DAVID LEE *and* SOUNDER *follow him—*

Ext. the backyard—Night. The backyard spreads out in the form of a jagged horseshoe, surrounded by low levels of grass—at the far end is a pathway, running about three hundred feet away to where the tall grass grows. The shed sits to the far left edge and more to the right edge is a waterwell. To the right of the waterwell is a woodpile. Up against the house to the right of the steps to the back door are two wash tubs with homemade scrubbing boards. NATHAN *keeps walking directly to the waterwell, reaches it and lowers the bucket down into the well, brings the bucket of water up, scoops up with a dipper, drinks, and tries to look out over the plains and hills from the back of his house.*

NATHAN LEE. When the fall comes in these parts, the Night moon runs away like a rabbit—you could stay out here lookin' all night, and not see a thing out yonder.

DAVID LEE. We goin' huntin' again tomorrow?

NATHAN LEE. Yep. I guess you must wonder why, though, what with the luck we havin', but like I always say—

DAVID LEE. "You lose some of the time, what you always go afta, but you lose all the time what you don't go afta!"

NATHAN LEE. Now who says I didn't lay my mark on you, boy!

They both laugh as REBECCA *steps out into the backyard from the house, and moves swiftly towards them.*

REBECCA. David Lee, it's time for you to get to bed!

DAVID LEE. Goodnight...

He starts moving away towards the house.

NATHAN LEE. Night, son!

REBECCA. And don't wake up Josie Mae and Earl!

They watch DAVID LEE *enter the house—then* NATHAN LEE *looks to* SOUNDER *as they begin to move for the house.*

NATHAN LEE. Your bedtime too, hound dog.

SOUNDER *hops up on him—he strokes the dog's back, and then pushes him away.*

NATHAN LEE. Off you go, boy!

SOUNDER *scampers away around the side of the house.*

REBECCA. I bet you could use a hot cup of coffee, Nathan Lee.

NATHAN LEE. I shore could, Miss Rebecca.

They start back into the house.

Ext. front of the house—Night. SOUNDER *crawls just under the front porch and lies down on a burlap sack for his night's sleep.*

Int. the children's room—Night. DAVID LEE *has taken some of the walnuts and is sitting up in the bed.* EARL *and* JOSIE MAE, *their sister, are fast asleep across from them.* EARL *is a sprightly*

little boy about eight years of age who has the kind of round face that gives one the impression that he is forever smiling. DAVID LEE *grabs his book and starts to read.*

Int. kitchen-sitting room—Night. NATHAN *and* REBECCA *enter the house through the back door—* NATHAN *stops at the table in the kitchen area as* REBECCA *moves directly to the doorway of the children's room—just before she gets to the door, she notices that the bowl of walnuts on the floor by the rocker has been disturbed—she snatches the bowl up from the floor and looks to* NATHAN—

REBECCA. The boy done went into my walnuts! I skin my fingers to the bone to pick two pounds that's worth almost nothin' at the commissary and he done took almost half of what I pick!

NATHAN LEE. The boy is hungry, Rebecca.

His words cut through her frustration—she puts down the bowl on an old dresser next to the door that leads to the children's room and just stands there for a moment—she and NATHAN, *looking directly on each other—after a moment she moves across the floor and nestles into the embrace of his arms—he holds her close to him for a moment and then they break the embrace—*

NATHAN LEE. Dammit!

He moves halfway across the floor and stops as REBECCA *goes to the stove to prepare his coffee—*

REBECCA. We been through these off-seasons before—we made it.

NATHAN LEE. What we make it to? The next season to work ourselves to death, share croppin' for ol' man Howard, so he can get richer and we can't even eat when the croppin' time is done?

His coffee is ready—she puts it on the table—he moves to it and sits and takes a sip with the frustration still nagging him. She stands over him from behind and puts her hand on his strong neck for a moment and then she moves for the children's room and enters—he drinks his coffee—

Int. REBECCA *and* NATHAN's *bedroom—Night.* REBECCA *enters, unrobes and crawls into bed—she lies there for awhile in thought, turns over to position herself and then she hears the back door SLAM. She raises her head for a moment and then she decides to get up. She puts her clothes back on hurriedly and moves out of the room.*

Int. kitchen-sitting room—Night. REBECCA *moves with directness through the room, on out the door to the backyard.*

Ext. the backyard—Night. REBECCA *stands in the middle of the backyard, looking about in the darkened area.*

REBECCA *(softly)*. Nathan?

There is not a sound—then she moves hastily around the side of the house to the front yard.

Ext. the front yard—Night. She looks down under the edge of the porch to see SOUNDER *fast asleep. She turns and tries to see through the darkness down the road—she slowly moves up on the porch and stands in the doorway looking out into the night. She begins to hum—the kind of hum to relax the nerves—to move the thoughts away from the mind—thoughts that were plaguing her.*

Dissolve to:

Int. the Morgans' kitchen—Day. It is about six a.m. the following morning and hot food is piping on the stove.

Int. the children's room—Day. DAVID LEE *awakes first and catches the aroma of the food floating into their room. He jumps out of bed and arouses* JOSIE MAE *and* EARL.

DAVID LEE. Come on y'all, git up, somethin's cookin' in the kitchen! Come on, Earl!

They all jump into their clothes and rush for the kitchen.

Int. the kitchen—Day. They head straight for the stove where DAVID *takes the lid off one of the pots and then the other.*

EARL. What's in there, David!?
DAVID LEE. Sausage and hambones!

EARL *tries to put his hand in one of the pots but* DAVID *slaps it away.*

DAVID LEE. Don't do that!
JOSIE MAE. Where did it come from!?

JOSIE MAE *is a tall, pretty girl for her nine years—with a sort of brooding air about her.*

DAVID LEE. Come on!

DAVID *sees* SOUNDER *through the front-door screen, scratching to get in—he hurriedly lets the dog in, and they all dash out the back door.*

Ext. the backyard—Day. REBECCA *is hanging out wash on the clothes line as the children rush toward her.*

DAVID LEE. Mama, there's hot meat on the stove!

REBECCA. That's right!
DAVID LEE. Where did it come from, Mama?
REBECCA. Where all meat come from—now git yourself washed up and be snappy about it—you got six miles ahead of you to that school.

She heads for the kitchen while the children proceed to wash up at the well.

Int. the kitchen—Day. REBECCA *enters the kitchen and immediately starts preparing breakfast as* NATHAN *is awakened and is standing in the doorway to the kitchen from their room. She notices him and stops her work for a moment.*

REBECCA. Good mornin', Nathan.
NATHAN LEE. Mornin'...
REBECCA. You ready to eat?
NATHAN LEE. I'll wait till after the children.

She goes back to preparing the food as she moves into the kitchen to put together some scraps of food for SOUNDER.

NATHAN LEE. How's the weather out there?
REBECCA. Little chilly.
NATHAN LEE. Hope it don't freeze out our baseball game today!

Ext. the backyard—Day. The children meet NATHAN *as he is coming out of the house and they are about to enter.*

CHILDREN. Mornin', Daddy!
NATHAN LEE. Mornin' back atcha!

They rush on past him into the house as he smiles.

NATHAN LEE. Don't forget to save me some!

He stops in the center of the yard and looks about.

NATHAN LEE. Sounder!

SOUNDER *comes running toward him from the field in back of the shed.* NATHAN *bends to a pan on the ground and puts the scraps of food in it as* SOUNDER *arrives and begins to eat.* NATHAN *rises and looks on, pleasingly.*

NATHAN LEE. That oughta put you in good shape for tonight!

Int. the kitchen—Day. The children are at the table eating as REBECCA *is about to return to her laundry work in the backyard.*

REBECCA. Don't take all day at that table, David Lee.

JOSIE MAE. Mama, when kin me and Earl go to school with David Lee?

REBECCA. Maybe soon—

She moves out of the door—

Ext. the backyard—Day. Out in the backyard, NATHAN *is chopping wood with* SOUNDER *nearby him as* REBECCA *returns to hanging out the wash. She starts that nervous hum of hers, and occasionally glances over to him at the woodpile. He lifts his head for a moment and calls out to her.*

NATHAN LEE. The one thing we got plenty of is wood!

She stops her work and just looks on him with concern when DAVID, JOSIE *and* EARL *dash out into the yard, breaking her trend of thought.*

DAVID LEE. Ready to go, Mama!

REBECCA. Tuck that shirt in, David Lee.

He moves toward her, cramming the shirt down into his pants.

REBECCA. You got two shirts on?

DAVID LEE. Yes mam...

REBECCA. When you get outta that school, you come right on back home, y'all gon' have to take this laundry work I done for Miss Boatwright today.

She gives him a quick hug and kiss. He rushes over to his father.

DAVID LEE. 'Bye, Daddy...

They shake hands...

NATHAN LEE. 'Bye, son...

He takes off with JOSIE MAE, EARL *and* SOUNDER.

REBECCA *starts back toward the clothesline, and as if to make a decision, she stops and turns to him.*

REBECCA. Where was it you went last night, Nathan?

He rises from his chopping position and faces her directly.

NATHAN LEE. I went where I had to go, Rebecca. My children was hungry.

As if to say the conversation is over, he immediately goes back to chopping wood. She gives him a long but soft look and then finally returns to her work.

Ext. the road—Day. DAVID LEE *rides in the back of the wagon of a white farmer, who is giving him a lift part of the way.*

DAVID LEE *runs a distance of the road—sits and rests on the side of the road for a few minutes—walks at a slow pace for a while.*

The boy climbs up into the wagon of a black farmer—The wagon pulls away.

He makes the final dash up the road.

Ext. school yard—Day. He speeds around the side of the building, and enters through a back door.

Int. school hallway—Day. He rushes down the short hallway until he comes to a door, and enters.

Int. classroom of the school—Day. This is a Southern White school where they segregate off into a far corner one or two black children they allow to attend the school.

DAVID LEE *enters the room in an exhausted state as he stops just inside the door.*

All eyes are upon him, including a black boy and girl who are segregated off in the back corner of the room. The teacher picks up his clock from the desk and looks at it.

DAVID LEE. I'm sorry, Mr. Clay...

MR. CLAY. You are one hour late...

DAVID LEE. Yessir...

MR. CLAY. Well, take your seat.

DAVID LEE, *with all eyes still upon him, moves carefully to a chair in the far corner—sits next to the black boy and girl.* MR. CLAY *takes up his book from the desk, and looks out on the class—*

MR. CLAY. Now where were we before we were interrupted—Oh yeah, Huckleberry Finn, chapter thirty-four! This chapter is called: WE CHEER UP JIM! Here we go: "Tom says: What's the vittles for? Going to feed the dogs? The colored boy kind of smiled around gradually over his face, and says: Yes, Mars Sid, a dog. Cur'us dog, too. Does you want to go en look at 'im?"

Close angle— DAVID *and other two children. The teacher's words can hardly be heard as he continues with the reading—as the* CHILDREN's *faces hold mixed expressions of confusion, pain, and mostly boredom. A head shaking, pathetic moment—*

Ext. front of MRS. BOATWRIGHT's *house— Day. It is a medium size one-family house, painted gray—trimmed in white around the edges of the frame—the yard is surrounded by well-kept hedges—the yard is mostly green grass and flower beds—with walkways leading to the front and back of the house. The children* and the dog move into the yard from the residential street—

Ext. side of the house—Day. They walk around the side of the house to a back door. The boys put the basket down— DAVID *knocks on the door—after a moment,* MRS. BOATWRIGHT, *a tall, attractive white woman in her early forties, opens the screen door.*

DAVID LEE. We brought your laundry, Miss Boatwright.

MRS. BOATWRIGHT. Come in, children.

They enter the house, leaving SOUNDER *in the backyard.*

Int. MRS. BOATWRIGHT'S *kitchen—Day.* DAVID *and* EARL *stop in the middle of the floor, holding the basket.*

MRS. BOATWRIGHT. Put it right up on this table, boys.

The two boys lift the basket up on the table. She looks through the clothes for a moment.

MRS. BOATWRIGHT. You tell Rebecca ain't a Chinaman in all this world can beat her ironing.

She reaches into her pocket and pulls out some change, picks out some and passes it on to DAVID.

MRS. BOATWRIGHT. This is for your mama's work, and here's something for the three of you.

DAVID LEE. Thank you, Miss Boatwright.

JOSIE MAE & EARL. Thank you, Miss Boatwright.

MRS. BOATWRIGHT. Oh, by the way, David, I have the book I promised you.

She moves for another room as the children all look to each other—she returns immediately with the book, and hands it to DAVID LEE—

MRS. BOATWRIGHT. It's about the Three Musketeers.

DAVID LEE. Thank you, Miss Boatwright.

MRS. BOATWRIGHT. When you read it— we'll talk about it...

DAVID LEE. Yes mam...We gotta go, Miss Boatwright...

MRS. BOATWRIGHT. Tell Rebecca I said 'hi', now...

The children turn and walk out of the back door—

Ext. outside of MRS. BOATWRIGHT'S *back door—Day.* MRS. BOATWRIGHT *is in the doorway as* DAVID, EARL *and* SOUNDER *move ahead*

of JOSIE MAE, *who stops and turns to* MRS. BOATWRIGHT—

JOSIE MAE. What's a Chinaman, Miss Boatwright?

Before MRS. BOATWRIGHT *can struggle up a response—*

DAVID LEE. Come on, Josie Mae! We gotta hurry!

JOSIE MAE *turns and catches up with them— they all rush around and out of* MRS. BOATWRIGHT'S *yard—*

Ext. the country—Day. They run up the road and into a field—continue on across the field and over a slope until they can see crowds of people at a make-shift baseball diamond where two teams of black sharecroppers are engaged in a heated baseball contest. They keep moving on into the crowd—

Ext. the baseball diamond area—Day. Men, women and children are standing around, loudly rooting for their team as the three children make their way through the crowd to find their mother. NATHAN LEE *is pitching on the mound for his team. He throws a pitch—the Batter misses it—*

DAVID LEE. Look at Daddy throw that ball!

They keep moving until they spot their mother, who is seated on a bench with another woman. They rush to her.

WOMAN. Rebecca, your children git bigger by the hour!

REBECCA. It's the good livin' that do it, Harriet!

She smiles as the children approach her. DAVID LEE *hands her the money.*

DAVID LEE. Miss Boatwright gave me this book and all of us a nickel apiece!

REBECCA *holds her hand out with palm up as if to say "hand it over"—the three children pass the money on to her—*

DAVID LEE. Who's winning, Mama?

REBECCA. Nobody yet—it's all tied up.

The ballgame goes on as they shout and root for NATHAN'S *team.* NATHAN *is putting on quite a pitching performance in the close, exciting game.*

NATHAN'S *team is at bat—there are two out—a man at second and a man at bat. The man at bat hits a ground ball to the second baseman, the ball trickles away from his glove into the outfield—he quickly retrieves the ball and tries to make a play at First Base, but the Batter is called safe—meanwhile the runner on Second has moved past Third Base and is attempting to score—the first baseman throws the ball to the catcher at Home Plate as the runner slides into Home. It is a close play and the umpire makes the decision to call the runner safe. An uproar takes place as the other team shows its displeasure over the umpire's call—but the people who are rooting for* NATHAN's *team shout and scream in ecstasy. After a short time, order is restored.*

Ext. on the road away from the baseball diamond—Day. NATHAN *and his family are on their way home, accompanied by a guitar-playing friend named* IKE. *As he plays he sings one of those basic black back-country blues. He finishes the song and gives out with a big laugh and boasts—*

IKE. If they heard me sing like this up North I'd be richer than the man I sharecrop for.

NATHAN LEE. And if they saw me *pitch* the way I did today—they'd hire me just to strike out Babe Ruth!

NATHAN *and* IKE *give out with a big laugh.* REBECCA *just smiles.*

Ext. road and church—Day. They pass a white church on the road. A number of people are standing in the yard of the church and some are entering. DAVID *watches with inquisitiveness.*

DAVID LEE. What do they do in the white churches, Mama?

REBECCA. Same as we—they pray.

IKE. You know, one time by mistake I went into a white church down in Row County and to this day I don't know how'n the devil I got outta that church alive.

NATHAN LEE. They probly thought you was crazy.

IKE. I guess so—but I went home and did me some praying to the Lord. I said, Lord, I went into this white church down in Row and all I want you to tell me is how I ever got outta there in one piece.

NATHAN LEE. What did the Lord tell you, Ike?

IKE. He said, I don't know, Ike—you doin' better'n me, I been tryin' to git in there for 200 years and ain't make it yet!

IKE *bursts out in loud laughter, joined by* NATHAN, REBECCA *and the children—*

REBECCA. If there ever was a devil in this county, Ike, you is it!

NATHAN LEE. Ike, you could make a song outta that!

IKE. I believe I'll do just what you say, speed ball!

They keep moving and come to a stop at a crossroad.

IKE. Well, this is where I havta say goodnight to y'all—it's been fun, Miss Rebecca.

REBECCA. Us too, Ike.

IKE. It's a good, warm night comin' up, Nathan—you goin' to the woods?

NATHAN LEE. Oh, yeh—possums and coons better hide deep from us tonight!

IKE *moves away from them—As they continue on home they can hear him singing to himself—*

Ext. about three hundred feet away from the MORGAN's *cabin—Day. The darks has set well as the family approach the house.* SOUNDER *starts to growl—the children stop, and* DAVID LEE *turns his head to* NATHAN *and* REBECCA—

DAVID LEE. There's two men in front of our house, Daddy.

They all stop—and can see the shadowy figures of two men, standing in their yard, and a Pick-Up Truck parked off the road toward the other side of the cabin.

DAVID LEE. Who is they?

REBECCA. Children, come here...

The children move back— NATHAN LEE *looks behind himself and across the fields as if he would like to make a dash for it—but* REBECCA's *eyes follow every physical, and mental motion he makes.*

NATHAN LEE. We better see who they is...

They begin to move slowly toward the house with deliberate caution, with the two men becoming more visibly identifiable with their shotguns dropped to their sides. They move into the yard and stop about twelve feet from the two men.

Ext. the front yard—Day. SHERIFF YOUNG *steps out of the front door of their house. The two groups do not speak for a moment—they merely stare at each other—the* MORGAN *family with inquiring and fretful eyes.*

SHERIFF YOUNG. We been in your house, Nathan—

NATHAN *and* REBECCA *look to each other with knowing glances.*

SHERIFF YOUNG. We found what we was lookin' for.

He moves away from the door and stops at the edge of the porch—

SHERIFF YOUNG. You took some food and stuff from the James' Smoke House last night so me and my deputies here gon' hafta take you to the County house.

SHERIFF YOUNG *nor the* DEPUTIES *make a physical move toward* NATHAN. *There is a long moment of tense silence. For a second,* NATHAN *seems to want to make a desperate break and run, but* REBECCA *holds him by the arm with all the strength her hand can afford.*

SHERIFF YOUNG. Okay, boys...

The DEPUTIES *move in and take* NATHAN *by the arms from both sides and put handcuffs on him.*

EARL. What they doin', Mama?
REBECCA. Be quiet, son...

EARL *falls into his mother's embrace—suddenly,* SOUNDER's *voice rips into the atmosphere, and for the first time the* DEPUTIES *draw their shotguns to waist level—*

SHERIFF YOUNG. Shut that mongrel up!

DAVID *runs to* SOUNDER *and tempers him as the sound fades to a growl—the dog frantically scratches the earth as* DAVID *holds on to him—*

SHERIFF YOUNG. Git that truck up close here, and quick!

One of the DEPUTIES *moves out in a hurry to fetch the vehicle as* SHERIFF YOUNG *moves down the steps into the yard and looks to* DAVID, *holding* SOUNDER.

SHERIFF YOUNG. Now boy, if you love that dog, you better keep a good, strong hold on him

The sound of the truck is heard moving up close to the house, and stopping. REBECCA *moves away from* JOSIE MAE *and* EARL, *and stops directly in the face of* SHERIFF YOUNG.

REBECCA. You been knowin' Nathan for a long time, Sheriff Young, and you know what kind of man he is, and you know the trouble we face in these off-seasons.

The SHERIFF *cannot look her in the face—he walks away from her and everyone, and just looks out over the fields—then finally he motions with his hand to the two* DEPUTIES, *standing at* NATHAN's *side to put him into the truck. They lift him up into the truck as* JOSIE MAE, *standing up on the porch with* EARL, *starts to cry softly as* REBECCA *moves to the edge of the vehicle, real close to* NATHAN's *face. She kisses*

him lightly on the mouth, and then they just look on each other for awhile, in a way they knew and loved each other so well. Then in a physical, tough manner, REBECCA *turns away and walks up on the porch with* JOSIE MAE *and* EARL.

One DEPUTY *gets in the back of the truck with* NATHAN, *and the other sits at the wheel—as* SHERIFF YOUNG *climbs up and sits next to him.*

SHERIFF YOUNG. Alright, let's go!

The truck starts to pull away— DAVID *lets go of his grip on* SOUNDER, *and makes a dash out into the road.*

DAVID LEE. Don't take my Daddy! Please don't take my Daddy!
REBECCA. David, come back here!

SOUNDER *lets out with his voice, and charges past* DAVID *for the truck on the road.*

Ext. the road—Day. The DEPUTY *in the back of the truck aims his shotgun as* SOUNDER *leaps for the truck—the thunder from the* DEPUTY's *shotgun is the only sound that can be heard in the entire valley—* SOUNDER *falls to the road.*

Ext. the porch—Day. REBECCA *rushes down from the porch to the edge of the yard.*

REBECCA. David!

Ext. The Road—Day. DAVID *keeps running in the direction of the truck and* SOUNDER.

He sees SOUNDER *rise and fall, give out with a faint yelp, and circle into the field. He moves in the direction of the house, falling, and floundering with the hind part of his body, staying up—moving from side to side.*

DAVID *arrives at the spot where the animal was cut down, stops with his eyes deadpan on the truck as it fades from his view. He looks down on a huge blot of blood in the sand— reaches down and digs his fingers into it—lifts his hand up and frowns—looks out into the field to track the dog's movements—then makes his way back to the cabin.*

Ext. the front yard—Day. DAVID *trots back to the front yard—* REBECCA *is at the edge of the yard—* JOSIE MAE *and* EARL *are still on the porch—* DAVID *keeps moving on around the house—* REBECCA *stares down the road—in her background, the figure of* DAVID *and the lighted lantern can be seen faintly, crawling under the house.* JOSIE MAE *and* EARL *come down from the porch, and stop just behind their mother.*

JOSIE MAE. Mama, why did they take Daddy away?

REBECCA (*pause*). Because he cared so damn much about you and me, child.

JOSIE MAE. Is he gon' be gone long?

REBECCA (*pause*). Might be...

Ext. under the house—Day. DAVID LEE, *with the lantern, crawls about under the house looking for* SOUNDER.

DAVID LEE. Sounder...Sounder...

He stops and looks all around him with a pained expression on his face— SOUNDER *is not under the house...*

Int. the kitchen—Day. The following morning REBECCA *pours the walnuts from the bowl into a paper bag and proceeds to tie the bag up as* DAVID LEE *looks on.* JOSIE MAE *and* EARL *enter.*

REBECCA. Josie Mae, I'm goin' into town for awhile to see about your Daddy—David Lee is gon' be in charge here, so you and Earl do just like he tells you.

She steps out of the front door with DAVID— JOSIE MAE *and* EARL *watch them move through the yard, and on to the road leading away from the house.*

Ext. the road near house—Day. REBECCA *and* DAVID LEE *slowly move along up the road.*

REBECCA. Watch the fire—don't go too far lookin' for Sounder, and warm up some of that corn mush for y'all to eat. If anybody comes to the house that's a stranger to you— don't say nothin'.

They come to a halt at a short distance from the house—and then she looks softly down on the boy for a moment.

DAVID LEE. 'Bye, Mama...

REBECCA. 'Bye, son—I won't be gone long.

The mother and son move away on the road with their backs to each other. DAVID LEE *picks up speed and runs.*

Int. Kitchen—Day. As JOSIE MAE *and* EARL *look on,* DAVID LEE *completes building a fire in the wood stove.*

He warms up and serves corn mush to his sister and brother.

Exts. backyard, under cabin, road, fields and woodlands—Day. DAVID LEE *chops wood at the woodpile—takes up a few chunks into his arms and heads back into the house.*

He crawls under the cabin, searching about carefully, looking for the dog.

The boy charges up the road away from the house and then cuts off into the field.

He spirals the brown stalk land in ever-widening circles, searching the fence-rows— and then he comes to the edge of the woodlands.

DAVID LEE *searches under the jack oaks and cottonwoods, but* SOUNDER *is not there. He stands in one spot, looking about the woods in painful confusion.*

Ext. Landsdown Main Street—Day. REBECCA *moves into town, picking up the main street, crosses the town square, moving in the direction of* SHERIFF YOUNG'S *office which is adjacent to the County Court House.*

Int. SHERIFF'S *Office—Day.* SHERIFF YOUNG *is seated behind his desk—a* DEPUTY *is sitting at a table across the room.* REBECCA *enters and stands before the* SHERIFF'S *desk.*

SHERIFF YOUNG. Howya do, Rebecca. I sorta been expectin' you this mornin'.

REBECCA. I wanta see Nathan.

SHERIFF YOUNG. I wish I could, Rebecca, but I can't let you.

REBECCA. I don't understand that, Sheriff Young.

SHERIFF YOUNG. It's the rules and I gotta follow 'em. No visitin' 'cept holidays and Sunday—and no womenfolk anytime.

REBECCA. You mean to tell me I can't see my own husband?

SHERIFF YOUNG. That's the way they do things here in Landsdown. I just follow orders.

REBECCA. I got to see my husband, Sheriff Young!

SHERIFF YOUNG. I'd like to help you, Rebecca. But all that would do, is git us both in trouble.

REBECCA. Will they give him a trial?

SHERIFF YOUNG. Shore thing—next week sometime, and as soon as I git the day, I'll ride out and let you know 'bout it.

REBECCA. You gotta low-life job, mister sheriff!

REBECCA *turns and storms out of the* SHERIFF'S *office and onto the street.*

Ext. street—Day. REBECCA *walks in haste and anger away from the* SHERIFF'S *office on the main street of Landsdown.*

Ext. commissary. She even moves past the commissary—stops and calms herself for a moment, turns around and enters the store.

Int. The commissary store—Day. She moves directly to the counter where an elderly man stands behind the counter. MR. HOWARD, *the owner of the store and farm owner the* MORGAN

family share-crops for. She puts the bag of walnuts up on the counter.

MR. HOWARD. Rebecca, you jest the one I
wanta see.

REBECCA. I brought these walnuts to trade.

*He looks into the bag—then empties the wal-
nuts onto a weighing scale—looks to her...*

MR. HOWARD. That's one dollar an' twenty
cents.

REBECCA. I wanta get some things.

MR. HOWARD. I hope it ain't a lot, 'cause I
can't give you no more credit till the croppin'
season gits back, that is if Na—

REBECCA. I didn't say nothin' 'bout credit,
Mr. Howard.

MR. HOWARD. Whatcha wanta order?

REBECCA. I need some nutmeg, flour, eggs,
sugar, and...

*A few minutes later, he puts her last article up
on the counter.*

MR. HOWARD. Now what I wanta talk to you
'bout is Nathan. He oughtn' done what he did:
sneakin' into the James' place and takin' they
goods. That looks bad on me. I been good to
y'all—didn't I go to all that trouble to get the
people of Landsdown to let your David Lee
go to they school? Didn't I?

With the mood she's in, REBECCA *does not
have anything to say to this man concerning*
NATHAN, DAVID LEE *or that damn school. For a
moment he waits for her to say something and
then he goes on—*

MR. HOWARD. And another thing; with
Nathan stuck in jail and all, how you gon'
crop for me when the spring season comes,
huh?

*She still can't find words to say to this man,
but tries. He is impatient, and a little snap
cracks in his voice.*

MR. HOWARD. Dammit, I'm talkin' to you,
woman! I gotta farm to think about and I need
answers.

REBECCA *(pause)*. The season is a long way
off, Mr. Howard, and by that time, Nathan
oughta be home. If he ain't, believe me—the
children and me—we will grow the crops. We
have to because we owe you all that money—
Mr. Howard.

*What she has just said about the money they
owe is a frustrated thought in* HOWARD'S *mind as
he looks to her helplessly.*

Ext. porch steps of the MORGAN'S *cabin—
Day.* DAVID LEE, JOSIE MAE *and* EARL *are sitting
on the steps, looking out on the road.*

JOSIE MAE. Do you think Sounder is dead,
David Lee?

EARL. Will he stay dead?

DAVID LEE. He ain't dead, now stop askin'
crazy questions!

JOSIE MAE. You don't havta get mad 'cause
you didn't find the ol' dog!

JOSIE'S *words hit him hard. He looks to her for
a moment with a pained expression—turns his
eyes back to the road where he spots someone
coming up the road toward the house from an
unidentifiable distance.*

Ext. the yard—Day. DAVID LEE *stops in the
middle of the yard with his eyes dead set on the
approaching figure.*

DAVID LEE. Somebody's comin' here...

JOSIE MAE *and* EARL *move down from the
stoop and stand behind* DAVID LEE, *their eyes
dead set on the road.*

DAVID LEE. It's Mama!

The children run out to greet her.

JOSIE MAE & Earl. Hi, Mama!

*They all reach her as she lays some of the
packages down on the ground.*

REBECCA. Hi, Children—here, take some
of these packages.

*The children relieve her of all of the pack-
ages, and they start moving through the yard for
the house.*

DAVID LEE. Did you see Daddy?

REBECCA. No, son. We havta wait 'til the
holiday comes—anyway, they won't let womenfolk see their men no time.

DAVID LEE. Can I go when the holiday
comes?

REBECCA. You sure can, son...

*They step up on the porch and move into the
house.*

*Int. sitting room-kitchen—Day. They enter
the house and start putting the packages on the
table.*

REBECCA. Any sign of Sounder?

DAVID LEE. No mam—I looked all over.

REBECCA. I think maybe he was scraped on
the head by that shot. I don't think he's dead—
just gone somewhere to heal himself.

*She takes out of one of the bags flour, cocoa,
and a small bottle of vanilla flavoring.* EARL

takes out from one of the bags an empty cardboard box.

EARL. Nothin' in here, Mama.

REBECCA. I'm goin' use it to put a cake in
and I'm gon' let David Lee take it to your
daddy!

As the children help their MOTHER *put the
things away.*

DAVID LEE. Mama...Make a chocolate
cake...Daddy likes things that's chocolate!
(smile).

*Int. mezzanine section, court room—Day. It
is a small section provided for "colored only"—*
REBECCA *is seated with* DAVID LEE *and* IKE—*A
few other black people are seated about in this
area, overlooking the main courtroom.*

COURT CLERK. Defendant will rise and
come before the bench.

*They don't even bother to sit—they stand just
inside the entrance and watch in intense silence.* NATHAN *moves slowly before the* JUDGE's
bench and stops.

JUDGE. Nathan Lee Morgan, you have been
found guilty of unlawful trespass and robbery—do you have anything to say before
sentence is passed?

NATHAN LEE *(almost in a whisper)*. No,
sir...

JUDGE. It is the judgment of this court that
you be remanded to the custody of the sheriff
of this county and that you be taken forthwith
to serve a term of one year at hard labor at
such county labor camp as shall be hereafter
designated. Next case, please...

*They watch two guards lead him from the
courtroom in handcuffs.* DAVID *looks on sadly
as* REBECCA *cringes at the sight of the Guards
taking him away.*

*Ext. Court House Square—Day. From the top
of the Court House building,* REBECCA, DAVID
LEE *and* IKE *can be seen, slowly walking across
the square, moving farther and farther away.*

Ext. backyard—Day. REBECCA *hangs out
clothes—* DAVID LEE *draws water from the well—*
JOSIE MAE *wrings the water out of the clothes—*
EARL *pours water into the wash tub.*

Ext. schoolyard—Day. DAVID LEE, *on his
way to school, is late again—enters the schoolyard, and dashes into the building.*

Ext. woods—Day. DAVID LEE *roams about
the woods, alone in the hope that he might come
upon* SOUNDER.

Int. the kitchen—Day. DAVID LEE *reads from
"The Three Musketeers" to* REBECCA, JOSIE
MAY *and* EARL. *It is very funny—they laugh.*

Int. the shed—Day. DAVID LEE, *in the shed,
takes his father's baseball glove down from the
wall—puts the glove on—holds it up, and then
slaps his fist into the pocket several times—stops
and looks off into blank space—He keeps looking straight ahead as if he can visually see his
father off from a long distance.*

Ext. Landsdown, Main Street—Day. Sunday,
REBECCA *and the children—* DAVID LEE *carrying
the cake box, make their way down the street—
people are moving back and forth in their Sunday dress. They move into the Square at the
Court House.*

*Ext. Court House Square—Day. At the
square, they come to a halt as* REBECCA *looks up
at the clock on top of the Court House building.
It is about ten minutes to twelve noon. They
continue on around to the back of the building—*

*Ext. back of building—Day. They stop in front
of a huge back entrance and look up to the small
windows with prison bars. A number of Black
people are moving into the area, milling about
and waiting as* REBECCA *and the children are.*

REBECCA. Be sure to ask your daddy to tell
you what camp they goin' to send him to. And
whatever you do in there, David Lee, act
perkish, and don't grieve him.

*The clock above the Court House strikes
twelve times. They listen with intensity until the
twelfth stroke.*

REBECCA. Allright, son, that's it—now
don't forget what I told you.

DAVID LEE *moves through the doorway with
the other people—*

*Int. the corridors and stairways of the build-
ing—Day.* DAVID *follows the other people down
the corridor and then up a group of stairs—then
down another corridor. They line up at a huge
steel door.* DAVID *touches the* MAN *in front of
him on the arm—*

DAVID LEE. This where you go visit,
mister?

MAN. Yeah...

*Int. admittance area—Day. The door swings
open and a red-faced Guard at a table just inside
the door begins to admit people.* DAVID's *turn
comes and the Guard stops him.*

GUARD. Whatcha got there, boy?

DAVID. A cake for my Daddy.

GUARD. Well, you put it on this table here'n wait 'til I check it.

DAVID puts the cake on the table just inside the door as the Guard sits at the table.

GUARD. Can't be too careful, boy, jest might have a steel file or hacksaw in it.

The GUARD opens the box, pulls from his pocket a switchblade knife and with slow deliberation punctures knife holes in about fifteen different places in the cake. After he is done, he closes the box and rises.

GUARD. What's your daddy's name?
DAVID LEE. Nathan Lee Morgan...

The GUARD checks his list on the table—

GUARD. Okay, boy, fourth cell down there on your left.

DAVID moves inside—

Int. corridor of jail cells—Day. DAVID LEE moves along the corridor, looking from one side to the other at the men sitting on cots and standing behind iron gates. He comes to NATHAN's cell and there is his father, standing with his hands on the bars.

NATHAN LEE. Well, looka here...
DAVID LEE. Hi, Daddy...
NATHAN LEE. Hi to you, son...

He extends his hands and they shake—and then he draws the boy close and embraces him—

DAVID LEE. Mama is outside with Josie Mae and Earl.
NATHAN LEE. They is!? It shore is good to see you, boy!

Finally DAVID passes the box with the cake on to him.

DAVID LEE. This was a real cake before the man at the door put all these holes in it.

NATHAN *takes the box and immediately opens it—*

NATHAN LEE. Aw, don't make no difference, son. If I know your mama, a few knife holes ain't gon' destroy the soul she put into this cake. Come on, have a piece with your daddy.

NATHAN *breaks a piece for himself and passes another on to DAVID. DAVID takes a bite out of the cake.*

DAVID LEE. We didn't find Sounder yet.
NATHAN LEE. He'll show up one day.
DAVID LEE. Do you think he's dead, Daddy?

NATHAN LEE. Naww—he'll come back to you, soon as his wounds heal. This cake shore is tasty, son.

He walks away from the cell door and moves to the window of his cell, looks up with his back to DAVID.

NATHAN LEE. It's a shame they won't let 'em come in here. If I had the strength I'd knock down these damn walls—if I could just git my arms 'round your mama right now—is they on this side of us, son?
DAVID LEE. I think so...

NATHAN *jumps up to the window a couple of times until his hands can get a grip around the bars of the small window—he strains and pulls, trying to get his eyes up to the window level—*

NATHAN LEE. Dammit! I'm gon' see 'em if I have to break my arms!

NATHAN *finally gets his eyes up to the window—he looks down—he can see them—*

NATHAN LEE. I can see them! I can see them!

His arms give way and he drops back to the floor on his feet—he moves slowly to DAVID and takes him by the arms through the bars of the cell

NATHAN LEE. Son, don't ever let yourself get caught in a place like this.

There is a moment of agonizing silence as they look at each other—

DAVID LEE. Can you say what camp they gon' send you to, Daddy?
NATHAN LEE. I don't know, son—they won't tell us things like that—but I don't want y'all to come here no more.
DAVID LEE. Why, Daddy; you won't be here?
NATHAN LEE. Just do like I tell you—I'll get word to you through the visitin' preacher.
GUARD'S VOICE. Visitin' over!

People start filing out but DAVID remains in front of the cell, looking on his father—

GUARD'S VOICE. Come on, boy!
NATHAN LEE. Go, son...

NATHAN *and DAVID shake hands and then DAVID slowly moves away from the cell, sporadically looking back over his shoulder toward his father until he moves through the cell block door—the door slams behind him—*

Ext. back of the Court House building—Day. DAVID steps out into the Court House yard where they are waiting for him—his feelings bound in confusion, and his face flooded in tears—he runs to his mother's arms. She embraces him long and deep.

Int. Church—Day. REBECCA and the children attend services at the Church—everyone is standing—they are in the midst of a song, led by the Pastor of the Church.

Like everything else in Landsdown for Black People, it is an old disinherited structure with creaky, movable chairs for the worshippers to sit in—there are two high windows on both sides.

The Pastor reads the verses of the song in the traditional, dramatic Black Preacher's fashion, and the congregation repeats the verses musically.

Song:

Ext. Church—Day. Coffee, cold drinks, cookies and fruit are being served to a laughing, chattering crowd of church goers—inside a woman is at the piano, playing rhythmic uptempo gospel songs. IKE is there also.

REBECCA, with HARRIET in line behind her, and the children are moving up to the table to be served.

HARRIET. If this wasn't a church, I'd do me a dance to that music she's playin'.
REBECCA. Why don't you try it, Harriet, and just see what everybody would do.
HARRIET. Now, Rebecca, I may be a country woman, but I ain't no fool.

REBECCA and HARRIET take coffee and cookies at the table while the children take fruit. They move across the floor for a corner to sit—HARRIET does a little moving dance step as they arrive to the corner and sit.

REBECCA. You determined to get that dance in.
HARRIET. Well, you can't blame a girl for tryin' if the feelin' hits her.

REBECCA notices the PREACHER talking to a group of women across the floor.

REBECCA. If I don't go over there and butt in, I ain't gon' ever get to talk to the Preacher about Nathan.

She rises and moves across the floor. DAVID LEE watches closely as his mother approaches the PREACHER and gets his attention by touching him on the arm, and they move off to a more secluded spot in the Church. DAVID rises and moves to join their company.

PREACHER. No, I ain't got no word yet, Rebecca. I went to the courthouse yesterday to see 'bout it, but they just won't tell me nothin' about what labor camp Nathan was sent to. I'm sorry, Rebecca.
REBECCA. It's a shame, Reverend. It's a damn shame.
PREACHER. I hope you don't take to bitterness, Sister Morgan. I tell you like I tell all the women in this church who got the same trouble you got. No matter what the trial or what the misery is, I tell 'em to stay with God.
REBECCA. Yeah, he'll crawl into my bed tonight, lie close to my body and keep me warm—and rectify the evil in the men who live over us in this valley.
PREACHER. It's not that simple, Sister Rebecca—the Lord works in mysterious ways—we come into this life with nothin' and we'll leave it with nothing.
REBECCA. Is that a blessing, Reverend?

Her words jar and disturb the PREACHER.

Ext. front of the MORGANS' cabin—Night. REBECCA and the children are just about to enter the yard, when DAVID LEE stops and pulls on his mother's arm.

DAVID LEE. Mama, did you hear that?!

REBECCA, JOSIE MAE and EARL come to a halt on his words.

REBECCA. What is it, David Lee?
DAVID LEE. Listen, Mama...

They stand quietly for a moment—and then they hear the sound of a faint whine coming from the direction of the porch—the whine becomes louder—

DAVID LEE. Mama, I hear Sounder!

He takes off in the direction of the porch—

Ext. the porch—Night. DAVID stops just at the top of the porch, and there, scratching at the door and wagging his tail, is SOUNDER. The side of his head where the shot scraped him is discolored and hairless—the top of his eye is scarred causing it to be half closed, and what's left of his ear on the same side, sticks straight out. Upon seeing DAVID LEE, he raises his good ear and whines. DAVID rushes to grab him.

DAVID LEE. You come back, boy! I just knowed it! I just knowed you'd come back!

REBECCA, JOSIE MAE and EARL arrive at the porch—REBECCA kneels, looks on the bad sight of the dog and strokes his back—

REBECCA. Poor creature...

DAVID LEE. He'll be allright, Mama. I'll make him allright.

Ext. the backyard—Day. The next morning, DAVID LEE *feeds* SOUNDER *as* EARL *stands by looking on.*

DAVID LEE. He eats all right—his throat ain't scarred.

EARL. Then why don't he holler like he usta.

DAVID LEE. He will... *(to* EARL*).* Come on, git down and act like a possum.

EARL. I don't look like no possum!

DAVID LEE. Act like one!

After a moment of hesitation, EARL *gets down on his hands and knees—*

DAVID LEE. Git him, boy!

EARL *jumps to his feet quickly and backs away across the yard—*

EARL. Don't tell that dog to git me!

SOUNDER *merely turns to* DAVID LEE *and gives out with a few muffled whines—*

DAVID LEE. I guess I'll havta work harder to git him back like he usta be.

EARL. Why don't you try and git you a new dog?

DAVID LEE *takes off after* EARL—*who turns, breaks and runs out into the back field—*

Ext. crop field—Day. REBECCA, DAVID LEE, JOSIE MAE *and* EARL *are in the field, working; planting, hoeing and cultivating the soil—* SOUNDER *trots about the field in the vicinity of* DAVID LEE—

Ext. the field—Day. REBECCA *is looking on about three hundred feet away as* DAVID LEE *runs about with* SOUNDER *in open field, trying to work him back into physical shape—he halfway picks the dog up—drops him to the ground, takes off and runs but* SOUNDER *does not follow him. He comes back to the dog and ruffles him affectionately—takes off and runs again—this time,* SOUNDER *takes off after him.* REBECCA *and* DAVID *look to each other and smile broadly— success!! He caresses and hugs the dog—they move toward* REBECCA, *join her, and they start walking back toward the house—and then the rains come—they and the dog take off in speed with huge raindrops splattering against their faces and bodies. From the field, as they make a run for it, their figures become smaller as they near the backyard and the doorway to their home...*

Ext. MRS. BOATWRIGHT's *backyard—Day. A bright sunny day—*DAVID LEE *is just about to quit for the day in some gardening work he is doing for* MRS. BOATWRIGHT. *He moves to the side of the house to put some equipment away when the lady approaches him—*

MRS. BOATWRIGHT. David, you never cease to amaze me at how good you are in taking care of my garden.

DAVID LEE. My father taught me...

MRS. BOATWRIGHT. Would you like to have a cool drink, David?

DAVID LEE. No, thank you—I gotta go do some work in the field today.

DAVID *starts to walk away and then decides to stop, turns to her as she is heading back into the house—*

DAVID LEE. Miss Boatwright—

MRS. BOATWRIGHT *(stops, turns).* Yes, David...

DAVID LEE. Will you help me to find out what camp they sent my father to?

MRS. BOATWRIGHT. The courthouse has rules about things like that, David—but I'll ask around town about it.

He looks on her with an expression of disappointment, turns and walks away.

DAVID LEE. See you tomorrow, Miss Boatwright.

MRS. BOATWRIGHT. David!

DAVID LEE *(turns to her).* Yes, ma'am...?

MRS. BOATWRIGHT. I'll *find* out where your daddy is for you.

DAVID LEE *(smiles).* Thank you, Miss Boatwright! *(turns and runs away).*

MRS. BOATWRIGHT. Don't mention this to anyone! You hear me, David!

He just keeps running—

Ext. front yard, back yard, back field—Day. DAVID LEE, *at top speed, runs into the front yard from the road, on around the side of the house— through the back yard and on into the field in the back of the house, heading for the crop field.*

Ext. the crop field—Day.

REBECCA, JOSIE MAE *and* EARL *are working the field as* DAVID LEE *comes running towards them—*

DAVID LEE. Mama! Mama! Miss Boatwright, say she gon' help me find where Daddy is!

REBECCA. Good! But you don't have to tell the whole valley 'bout it! You'll get that woman in trouble!

Int. Court Clerk's Office—Day. CHARLIE DAVID, *the Court Clerk, is standing behind his desk—* MRS. BOATWRIGHT *is seated in a chair before his desk. There are two windows in the small office, a coat rack in the corner diagonally behind his desk, three chairs, another small working desk, and a row of file cabinets against the wall—*

CHARLIE. I can't do it, Rita—that's the policy here on colored prisoners, and I ain't about to change it, not even for a friend like you.

MRS. BOATWRIGHT. Charlie, just because a man and his family are colored, you—

CHARLIE. Now look, Rita, I don't make the rules—you puttin' yourself on a limb, comin' here, askin' me to do a thing like this. And I be damn if I'm going to jeopardize my job because you are in love with a little colored boy!

The phone on his desk rings—he picks up the receiver to his ear and sits down—

CHARLIE. County Clerk's office, Charlie Davis speaking… Yes, sir… You bet your life, sir… Yes, sir, I'll be right there.

He puts the receiver down—jumps up, goes to the rack and gets his coat and starts to fix his tie—

CHARLIE. That was Judge Elliot on the phone and when Judge Elliot calls, I jump! Good day, Rita.

He moves to the door, to the waiting area and opens it to leave— DAVID LEE *can be seen standing in the background of* CHARLIE—

MRS. BOATWRIGHT. But, Charlie—
CHARLIE. No! N - O, NO!

Just like that he is gone. MRS. BOATWRIGHT *stands in the middle of the floor in a moment of frustration, with* DAVID LEE *looking on from the alcove. She thinks for a moment and then looks to the file cabinets against the wall.* DAVID *stands in the doorway as she decides to go to the file cabinets. She checks the outer notation on each one of the cabinets until she comes to the one that reads: PRISONER CASES. She quickly opens the cabinet drawer and hurriedly fingers through the files until she finds the file with* NATHAN LEE MORGAN's *name on it. She goes through it until she has gotten the information she wants and just as she is about to put it back,* CHARLIE DAVIS *has returned and has caught her in his files. She looks cheaply to him, slips the file back into its place, closes the cabinet drawer and backs away from the file cabinet. He moves past* DAVID LEE *into the office on to*

the file cabinet where she was, opens it enough for him to tell that she has disturbed the one single file of NATHAN LEE MORGAN. *He slams the file drawer back shut and turns to her.*

CHARLIE. I see you found what you was lookin' for.

MRS. BOATWRIGHT. I did look, Charlie, but I—

CHARLIE. No buts, Rita!

MRS. BOATWRIGHT. Charlie, you have no legal right not to let this boy know where his father is! You hear that, you and this whole damn court house; what you are doing is wrong!

CHARLIE. Don't tell me about what's wrong. You come into my office as a friend and steal city files! I could have you arrested for that—and if you give out that information to anybody, that's exactly what I'm going to do—and I'll tell everybody in this town how you got the information and who you got it for! You won't have a friend left in this county to bring you a piece of candy!

MRS. BOATWRIGHT. You would do that, wouldn't you?

CHARLIE. You getting the point, Mrs. Boatwright.

MRS. BOATWRIGHT *gives him a hard and long look with the feeling that he means what he says—*

MRS. BOATWRIGHT. Let's get out of here, David Lee.

She turns and moves out of the office, through the door, with DAVID LEE *following—*

Ext. Court House steps—Day. MRS. BOATWRIGHT *and* DAVID *are slowly descending the Court House steps, and on towards her automobile, parked about a hundred feet away. She is about to open the door of the car, when* DAVID LEE *stops—*

DAVID LEE. You know where my father is, don't you, Miss Boatwright?

MRS. BOATWRIGHT *(pause).* No, he was wrong, David, I didn't find out.

DAVID LEE. But I saw you—you looked in there, and you found out, Miss Boatwright.

MRS. BOATWRIGHT. If I tell you I didn't, David, that's what I mean.

DAVID LEE. But, Miss Boatwright, you—

MRS. BOATWRIGHT. I don't know a damn thing, now stop bothering me about it!

She gets into the car as he shuffles his feet about on the ground with his head turned slightly down, remaining in one place—

MRS. BOATWRIGHT. Come, I'll take you home.

DAVID LEE. I'll walk...

MRS. BOATWRIGHT. Don't pout now, David, it's a long trip.

DAVID LEE. I'm used to it.

MRS. BOATWRIGHT. Well, you can't say I didn't try.

DAVID LEE *watches her drive off and away— and then he slowly starts walking away...*

Ext. backyard—Day. DAVID LEE *at the well draws up a pail of water and pours it into a container for* SOUNDER *who is standing beside him, anxiously waiting for the water. As* SOUNDER *drinks the water,* DAVID *turns around to see* MRS. BOATWRIGHT *standing in the middle of the yard.*

MRS. BOATWRIGHT. Hello, David...

DAVID LEE. Hi, Mrs. Boatwright...*(pause).* I'm sorry 'bout the way I acted the other day, Miss Boatwright.

MRS. BOATWRIGHT. There's nothin' to be sorry about, David—where's your mother?

REBECCA. Right here, Miss Boatwright.

REBECCA *is standing in the doorway of the shed—* MRS. BOATWRIGHT *doesn't quite know how to begin—the two women just look to each other for awhile—then—*

MRS. BOATWRIGHT. The camp Nathan is at is called Wishbone Labor Camp. It's in Nolan Town!

REBECCA *lets the news soak in for a moment—* DAVID LEE *has a big smile on his face.* REBECCA *moves from the doorway and stands directly before* MRS. BOATWRIGHT.

REBECCA. Miss Boatwright—you shore is a crazy actin' woman sometime!

She bursts out laughing and kicks up her leg— DAVID *picks up the laughing, then* MRS. BOATWRIGHT. EARL *and* JOSIE MAE *arrive and stop at the corner of the house—can't quite make out what this crazy laughing is all about but they move to the center of the yard with them and join in with the laughing. After a short while the laughter comes to a sudden stop—sudden, absolute silence—*

JOSIE MAE. Mama, what was we laughin' for?

REBECCA. At the way you ask funny questions, Josie Mae!

Int. the kitchen-sitting room—Day. In the house, REBECCA *and all the children are gathered around* MRS. BOATWRIGHT *at the table*

with a map spread out as she scans it carefully with a pencil—

MRS. BOATWRIGHT. We go from "A-2"— now let me see where we go from here...

REBECCA. Trouble, Miss Boatwright?

MRS. BOATWRIGHT. Oh, no, these maps are easy to read.

But she is having trouble locating the place as her pencil moves about in several confusing spots on the map-like having to find a bigger town's indicating alphabet and number in order to search about at random to locate a smaller town—but finally—

MRS. BOATWRIGHT. There it is, right there!

She makes a marker with the pencil and holds it down on the place—everybody leans over the map as close as possible to see the little area she has made a circle around— DAVID *straightens up—*

DAVID LEE. How do you get there, Miss Boatwright?

Everybody straightens up to get MRS. BOATWRIGHT'S *directions. She holds the map up as they look on.*

MRS. BOATWRIGHT. Now they have numbers and letters on here to tell you where to look on the map, but Nolan Town is not under a number but we know it's in Northern Landsdown—the number for Northern Landsdown is: "h7", but since Landsdown is the largest county, it actually stretches over into "a2" but "a2" is—Am I making myself clear?

REBECCA. It's clear, Miss Boatwright—it's so clear, you don't havta go any further— thank you—when the time comes for us to find that place, we will—won't we, children?

ALL THE CHILDREN. RIGHTTTTTTT!

Ext. crop field—Day. REBECCA *and* DAVID LEE *are hoeing as* JOSIE MAE *and* EARL *run up and down the grooves planting seeds.* REBECCA *and* DAVID *complete their hoeing and plop down on the ground out of exhaustion as* JOSIE *and* EARL *move toward them, seeding the last grooves of earth.*

Int. the sitting room—Night. REBECCA *is sitting in her rocker, knitting, when* DAVID LEE *comes out of his room—She turns and looks to him—*

REBECCA. Can't sleep?

DAVID LEE. No, ma'am...*(pause).* Mama, I wanted Mrs. Boatwright to find out where Daddy is, so me and Sounder can go see him.

REBECCA. So did I. I figured when the time got right, we could all take a day or two and walk up there, but it's not the kind of long trip for a child to take alone.

DAVID LEE. I can do it, Mama—you know that. In the Bible stories you read to us, everybody's always goin' on a long journey. Jacob goes into a strange land where his uncle is and he don't even know where he lives, but he finds him. Everybody finds what they supposed to find.

REBECCA. But you'll be away from home for days—what will you do when the dark comes, where will you sleep? I can't send you away from here like that!

DAVID LEE. Mama, don't I always do what you say—every time I go to the fields to plant the corn, to Miss Boatwright's and the woods—you tell me what to do and I do it, and you don't worry.

REBECCA *(pause)*. No, I don't and I oughtn't not to after the way you've taken over since they took him away—and I would like for you to see 'im so you can come back and tell me about 'im. *(pause)*. The field's all planted, so I guess I can spare you for a little while. When do you wanta leave?

REBECCA *gets up from the rocker and starts putting her knitting away in the dresser—*

DAVID LEE. Can I go day after tomorrow?

REBECCA. Yes, son. You better get back to bed.

DAVID LEE. Good night, Mama...

REBECCA. Good night...

He turns, moves out of sight into his room. REBECCA *gets up from the rocker, puts her knitting away, picks up the map* MRS. BOATWRIGHT *left, off the dresser, and spreads it on the table to the light of the lantern. She can't make sense of the map—she folds it back up and shoves it to the side—looks across the room in thought.*

Int. kitchen-sitting room—Early Morning. Two days later, a little after daybreak, DAVID *is all set to make the journey with* SOUNDER— DAVID *is at the table—* IKE *is standing over him as he writes on a piece of paper—* REBECCA *and the other children are looking on—*

IKE. Now ofta you go by Nolan, the first road you come to is Jordan road—keep walkin' on that road and you'll run right into it. It's a long trip, David Lee, so good luck to you.

DAVID LEE. Thank you, Mr. Ike...

They all turn around and move out the front door—

Ext. front of the house—Day. They move out the house and down into the yard and stop.

REBECCA. I wish you wouldn't take the dog with you, David—he's likely to be a burden to you.

DAVID LEE. I got to, Mama. I know Daddy wants to see him.

REBECCA *passes on to him a big brown bag of food—*

REBECCA. Here's your food—now you go straight to that place—if you need to rest, go into a church or railroad station—but don't go into nobody's house, you hear me?

DAVID LEE. Yes, mam...

REBECCA. Ask your daddy to give you some word about when he'll be comin' home—and tell 'im we love him.

IKE. Tell 'im I said, "Hi", too, David.

REBECCA *pulls him into her arms—*

REBECCA. Good luck to you, son...*(releases him)*. Allright now, get movin', you losin' daylight.

DAVID *gives quick embraces to* JOSIE MAE *and* EARL—*and then he and* SOUNDER *hit the road—* JOSIE MAE *and* EARL, *follow him part the way—* REBECCA *moves back up on the porch, stops and turns in time to see* DAVID *bidding* JOSIE MAE *and* EARL *"goodbye"—* JOSIE MAE *and* EARL *move back toward the house, and then the boy and dog slowly fade from her view...*

Ext. sharecroppers' cabin—Day. DAVID LEE *and* SOUNDER *walk the road. They pass a cabin, where another family is working.*

Int. railway station—Night. DAVID *and* SOUNDER *are in a small cubby hole of the station with a sign overhead that reads: "Colored Waiting Room." He is looking over an old newspaper as a man in a chair across from him is fast asleep and snoring—finally he too falls asleep.*

Ext. stream pond—Day. DAVID *goes in the water to cool off and refresh.*

Ext. a migratory camp—Day. DAVID *and* SOUNDER *come upon a sign in front of a migratory farm with a sign that advertises: "Fruit pickers and sorters needed."*

Ext. Sorting Area—Day. DAVID *works sorting fruit for part of the day and after he is done they have a bite to eat—*

Ext. the road—Day. Back on the road as DAVID LEE *and* SOUNDER *continue their journey. They move through an area with landscapes and mountains, the size and shape that* DAVID *has never seen. At one point, he stops and looks on in wonder and admiration.*

Ext. The front of a house—Day. DAVID LEE *washes a car as* SOUNDER *looks on. A man pays him—he goes over the piece of paper with* IKE'S *directions, and then they move on—*

Ext. the road—Night. DAVID *and* SOUNDER *approach the camp. He moves close to a sign that reads: WISHBONE LABOR CAMP, NOLAN COUNTY.*

They move on farther along the barbed wire barricade of the camp and then they come to a halt when DAVID *sees two lights and wide barbed wire gate entrance with two guards just inside the gate. They move off the road down a sloped hill just beneath the entrance of the camp. They lie down on the grass to sleep.*

Ext. the slope off the road—Day. It is early morning as DAVID *is awakened by the voices of the guards and the motor of a truck.*

TRUCK DRIVER'S VOICE. Whatcha got for me today!?

GUARD'S VOICE. Same bunch you had yesterday!

TRUCK DRIVER'S VOICE. Well, I'll take what I kin git!

DAVID *hears the truck motor into the grounds of the compound. He and* SOUNDER *crawl up to the edge of the slope so they can see. Finally he decides to walk across the road to the gate where the guard is—*

Ext. labor camp gate—Day. DAVID *and* SOUNDER *approach the gate and stop—one of the guards sees them and walks over—*

DAVID LEE. Mister, can you visit anybody here?

GUARD. Gotta wait 'til visitin' days.

DAVID LEE. When's that?

GUARD. Sunday.

DAVID LEE. Do you know my daddy, Nathan Lee Morgan?

GUARD. Never heard of 'im. We gotta lotta men here...

The sound of the truck, approaching—

GUARD. All right, boy, outta the way, truck's comin'...

He opens the gate as DAVID *and* SOUNDER *scatter back across the road—the* OTHER GUARD *calls out—*

OTHER GUARD. Section J comin' through!

GUARD. Let 'er roll!

The truck motors through the gate and stops just outside as the GUARD *makes his final check of the men.* DAVID, *from where he is standing, also checks it thoroughly to see if his* FATHER *is*

on the truck. A number of trucks roar through the gate and DAVID *checks them all thoroughly, but his father is not on any of them. Finally the last truck comes out—*

OTHER GUARD. Last one comin' atcha!

GUARD. Let me have it!

The truck pulls to a halt just outside the gate, and DAVID *eyes the men on the truck carefully as the* GUARD *makes his check—*

DAVID LEE. He gotta be on this one, Sounder, it's the last truck.

There are not too many men on this truck which makes it quite easy for DAVID *to see that his father is not on it. Then where is he? The boy thinks to himself as he sees the truck move away up the road. The truck is moving no more than about twenty miles an hour—* DAVID LEE *makes a decision and takes off after the truck, running—*

Ext. a farm—Day. A half hour later, the truck with the convicts pull into a huge farm area—the TWO GUARDS *jump down from the truck and herd the men into a group while a third guard gets out of the cab—and they distribute farm equipment to the men. A picket fence stretches the area where the men work.*

Ext. the road—Day. Some minutes later DAVID LEE *and* SOUNDER, *walking, approach the farm area where the convicts are, moving along the road outside of the fence.*

They stop— DAVID *watches the men work and the guards covering them from distances of about three hundred feet in a half moon formation, spread out.* DAVID *decides and moves to the fence to question the men. When he gets to the edge of the road next to the fence, one of the guards spots him and starts moving over—*

DAVID LEE. Mister...?

CONVICT. Boy, where did you come from?

DAVID LEE. I wanta find out 'bout my Daddy. Is he here?

CONVICT. Can't you see that guard comin'—git!

GUARD. Whatcha doin' here, boy, move!

DAVID *hurriedly gets back across the road with* SOUNDER *and watches the guard as he moves the men back.* DAVID *looks on in frustration, trying to figure out what his next move will be. The guard moves away from the men and walks up to another guard to engage him in a conversation—while the two guards are rapping with each other,* DAVID *decides to make a desperate try of it—*

DAVID LEE. Okay, Sounder, let's go!

DAVID LEE and SOUNDER *dash across the road, and slip under the fence into the farm area—*

Ext. the farm—Day. DAVID LEE and SOUNDER *turn on all the speed they can muster, heading directly for the group of Convicts—They get there—*

DAVID LEE. Please tell me, mister! Is Nathan Lee Morgan here!?
CONVICT. There is nobody name Morgan! Now get away from here before you git us in trouble!

SOUNDER *lets out a growl at one of the Guards who is now charging toward them.* DAVID *takes off in a circle with the Guard in pursuit of him, away from the direction of the road—* SOUNDER *is close behind him—They circle back into the direction of the road and zoom past the group of Convicts—* DAVID *is running at electrifying speed.* DAVID *and* SOUNDER *are making tracks with the Guard still after the boy. They come to the fence and quickly slip through, but* DAVID'S *hand falls on a broken bottle with gashing force—he leaps up and continues on across the road and into an open field. The Guard stops at the edge of the road and gives up the chase—*

Ext. field—Day. DAVID *and* SOUNDER *are still running with great speed.* DAVID *looks back over his shoulder to see if the Guard is still after him. They slow down when they approach an old abandoned barn—*

Int. the barn—Day. He staggers into the barn and drops his body against one of the walls to catch his breath. SOUNDER *hobbles in and nestles beside him.*

Dissolve to:

Ext. the road—Day. DAVID, *holding his hand, sits on the road with the dog—puts his hand up before his eyes—it is practically covered in blood. A pain strikes him, causing him to grimace for a moment—looks about the area—They rise and start out once again—*

DAVID LEE. Sorry, Sounder, but we lost. Better keep movin' though, 'til we find somebody to tell us how to get back home.

Ext. road and school. They come upon a large Schoolhouse with the name over it: Borderdale School. They stop when DAVID *sees a number of Black Children playing on the grounds—climbing on little ladders and swinging on swings. He notices a water pump on the grounds, looks at his blood-covered hand—hesitates for a moment and then decides to enter the grounds—*

Ext. school grounds—Day. DAVID *and* SOUNDER *head straight for the pump and just as they arrive at the pump a group of Children gathers around them—*

#1 CHILD. You new here?
#2 CHILD. You comin' here to school?
#1 CHILD. What's wrong with that dog?

Two dogs near the edge of the Schoolhouse bark at SOUNDER—*he merely whines and scratches back at them but their barking intensifies until a young, attractive black female teacher interferes—*

CAMILLE. Come on now, get away from here!

The two dogs gallop off as do the Children—they scatter away from around DAVID *and* SOUNDER. *The* TEACHER *walks over to* DAVID *and stops—*

DAVID LEE. I just wanta wash my hand. It's got blood where I hurt it.
CAMILLE. You don't live around here, do you?
DAVID LEE. No, mam...I come from way back there. Me and my dog was tryin' to find my daddy and we got lost.
CAMILLE. Is he here in Borderdale?
DAVID LEE. I don't know, he's in a prison camp.
CAMILLE. Here, you put your hand under the water and I'll pump for you.

She pumps and DAVID *puts his hand under the cool, flowing water—*

CAMILLE. My name is Camille—Camille Johnson and I'm the Supervisor of this school. What's your name?
DAVID LEE. David Lee Morgan. My dog's name is Sounder. *(takes his hand out from under the water).* That feels better.
CAMILLE. Let me see it...

She takes his hand into hers—pulls a kerchief from her pocket and dries the water off—

CAMILLE. Your hand needs medicine on it. You better come with me into the school so I can put something on it—

Int. a classroom in the school—Day. She applies some medication to his wound—he winces for a moment—and then she begins to wrap it in a bandage— DAVID *keeps looking about the room, admiring its cleanliness, the long blackboard, the strong, steady student chairs—*

CAMILLE. You keep looking around, David. Don't you go to school?
DAVID LEE. Sometime, but not like this.

CAMILLE. It's a good thing your hand did not become infected—how did you cut it like this?

DAVID LEE. Me and Sounder went to this prison camp to see my Daddy and the police guard runs us away and I fell on some glass.

CAMILLE. Did your mother know you were going to see your father?

DAVID LEE. Uh huh...

CAMILLE (*completes the bandaging*). That does it.

DAVID LEE. Thank you, Miss Johnson.

CAMILLE. I don't live far from here. You and your dog can come home with me and have yourself a hot meal and then we'll talk about how to get you back home.

Dissolve to:

Ext. CAMILLE's *place—Day.* DAVID *walks about* CAMILLE's *quaint, neat little home with his eyes lit up as he looks around and about—*

DAVID LEE. You got a pretty house, Miss Johnson!

CAMILLE. I try...

Int. CAMILLE's—*Day. They enter.* DAVID *spots the many books she has on a shelf—he moves to the shelf as she stands next to him—*

DAVID LEE. You got a lotta books, too. (*scanning the books*). You got any books with people in 'em like Huckleberry Finn?

She turns in a quick, reflex motion, directly to the boy—

CAMILLE. Hell, no!

DAVID *breaks out in a big smile because he is glad to know that she has no books like Huckleberry Finn. She returns his smile, and puts her finger on one of the books—*

CAMILLE. Here, let me tell you something about the books on this shelf: This one's about a man whose name was Crispus Attucks. He fought in a war to help this country to become the United States. And this one is about a woman who helped to free slaves. Her name was Harriet Tubman, and...

Int. CAMILLE's *kitchen—Night.* CAMILLE *finishes washing the dishes—moves for the sitting room as* DAVID *trails her—*

DAVID LEE. And you say all them people is dead now?

CAMILLE. That's right—

Int. CAMILLE's *sitting room—Night. She moves into the room with* DAVID *following her—*

CAMILLE. They lived a long time ago—before you and I were born.

DAVID LEE. Where is Africa, Miss Johnson?

She moves to her desk and pulls out a drawer—

CAMILLE. Come here and I'll show you.

She opens the desk drawer—gets down on the floor and spreads the map out. DAVID *sits down next to her as she goes over the map.*

CAMILLE. Here it is, right here.

DAVID LEE. That's where we come from first?

CAMILLE. That's where we came from first.

She rises from the floor and puts the map back into the desk drawer as DAVID *moves to the book shelf—*

DAVID LEE. And the other people you told me 'bout, they is all colored folk?

CAMILLE. Colored.

DAVID LEE. Don't you teach in your school 'bout folk who ain't dead?

CAMILLE. Sure—

She moves to the shelf next to him and takes a book from it—

CAMILLE. Here's one by a man that's very much alive.

DAVID LEE. What's his name?

CAMILLE. Dr. William E. B. Dubois. (*fingers through the book*).

DAVID LEE. What he talk 'bout?

CAMILLE. Why don't you sit and I'll read you something he said.

She sits in a chair at the desk and he takes a place on the floor just beneath her, waiting anxiously for her to begin the reading—

CAMILLE. (*reads from the book*). THE LONGING OF BLACK MEN MUST HAVE RESPECT —(*she diverts*). Which means that a man and a woman are human and must be treated that way—(*she returns to the text*). THE RICH AND BITTER DEPTH OF THEIR EXPERIENCE, THE UNKNOWN TREASURES OF THEIR INNER LIFE —

As she reads, DAVID's *mind and imagination take to drawing pictures and images of what he can apply to his intuitive understanding of what she is reading to him—*

CAMILLE's *voiceover*
—THE STRANGE ENDINGS OF NATURE THEY HAVE SEEN, MAY GIVE THE WORLD NEW POINTS

OF VIEW AND MAKE THEIR LOVING, LIVING, AND DOING PRECIOUS TO ALL HUMAN

DAVID's *images*
The night in the woods with his father and SOUNDER. *The shouting and laughter after the baseball game —*

Voice over
HEARTS. AND TO THEMSELVES IN THESE DAYS THAT TRY THEIR SOULS

DAVID's *images*
HE, JOSIE *and* EARL, *running and playing in the field.*

Voice over
THE CHANCE TO SOAR IN THE DIM BLUE AIR ABOVE SMOKE IS TO THEIR

DAVID's *images*
His visit with his father at the County Jail house —

Voice over
FINER SPIRITS BOON AND GUERDON FOR WHAT THEY LOSE ON EARTH BY BEING BLACK.

DAVID's *images*
His mother, with her head thrown back, her eyes aglitter and laughing.

CAMILLE *has finished reading — she places the book down on the desk as he looks on her from the floor with tenderness —*

DAVID LEE. You're a friendly lady, Miss Johnson.
CAMILLE. And you're a tired little boy. I'll make up the cot and you must get some sleep.

She moves into the corner to prepare a place for him in the sitting room.

DAVID LEE. What about Sounder?
CAMILLE. He'll get his place too — now off with your clothes and into bed.

DAVID *unclothes himself and crawls into the bed as* CAMILLE *stands over him —*

CAMILLE. Now don't you think it's time you told me all about yourself?
DAVID LEE. I have a mother and her name is Rebecca — My father's name is Nathan Lee Morgan, and...

Int. school room class — Full angle — Day. CAMILLE *is standing in front of her desk before an overfilled class room.* DAVID LEE *is seated in a chair against a wall on one side of the room.*

CAMILLE. Anyone here know what chapter that story was from?

A boy rises with abrupt and fast confidence —

BOY #1. Chapter twenty-six!
CAMILLE. Twenty-six!? The text has but six chapters!
BOY #1. That's what I meant, Miss Johnson. Take away the two in front and all you got left is a six!

The class room breaks out in a gusto of laughter —

CAMILLE. Now you know I'm not going to have the laughing!

The laughing dies sharply and quickly — CAMILLE *smiles to herself —*

CAMILLE. I'll get back to you later, Mr. Twenty-six. Let's not stop now, we have to keep this mood moving. The story has to come from one of the text books we've already read in class, or it has to be a true story of your own. Let's get it going now — we don't have that much time left...

She moves around and sits at her desk — after some indecision on the part of all of the Children, one boy finally rises from his chair —

CLARENCE. I got a story, Miss Johnson — It's a true story that happened to me.

CLARENCE *is a soft eyed boy about eleven or twelve years of age. He behaves as if he's not too sure, he wants to tell his story —*

CAMILLE. You know that the class is going to challenge your story, don't you, Clarence?
CLARENCE. Yes, Miss Johnson...
CAMILLE. Go on...
CLARENCE *(hesitates).* Me and my little sister, went down to the water hole, last Saturday —

A GIRL *rises and interrupts him —*

GIRL #1. You're doin' somethin' wrong already — You didn't tell us the name of your sister...
CLARENCE *(pause).* My sister's name is... *(pause)* — Me and my sister, Laura, went down to the water hole last Saturday and we was playin' 'long the edge of the water and Laura slipped and fell in the water. I started to run back home, but I turned around, ran back, dove into the water and got her out before she could drown...

No one says anything — CLARENCE *just stands there, looking around the room, waiting for someone to utter something —*

CAMILLE. How was your sister after you pulled her out of the water?

CLARENCE. She was dirty and wet...

Swing to:

Close angle – GIRL #1.

GIRL #1. What were you doin', runnin' away from the water?!

Swing back to:

Close angle – CLARENCE.

CLARENCE. I was goin' home to get my daddy.

Quick to:

Close angle – BOY #1.

BOY #1. What made you stop and go back!?

Quick to:

Close angle – CLARENCE.

CLARENCE. Cause if I hadda ran home, by the time I got back, my sister woulda drowned.

Quick back to:

Close angle – GIRL #1

GIRL #1. How come you didn't know that at first?

Moves back to:

Close angle – CLARENCE.

CLARENCE. I was scared!

Quick move to:

Angle – BOY #2.

BOY #2. Hold it! Clarence story ain't true! Me and Clarence been to the river a lotta times, and I know, he can't swim!

Moves to:

Close angle – CAMILLE.

She is somewhat thrown – hesitates but must follow through, delicately –

CAMILLE. Clarence, would you tell us a story that was not true, after telling us it was?

Pulls to:

Cross half angle – Class room.

CLARENCE. No, Miss Johnson...
CAMILLE. Can you swim?
CLARENCE *(pause)*. Yes mam...

Swing to:

Angle – BOY #2.

BOY #2. Clarence, you know you can't swim! Everytime I tried to show you, you fell down, and I had to always pull you out!

Swing to:

Close angle – CAMILLE.

CAMILLE. Is that true, Clarence?

Moves to:

Close angle – CLARENCE.

CLARENCE *(pause)*. Yes mam...But when I saw my sister 'bout to drown in the water, I tried because I wasn't scared no more! I was just swimming and kickin'! I don't know how I was doin' it! But I was, cause my sister was drowning! She was drowning!

Pulls to:

Full angle – class room. CLARENCE *sits – the class is silent –*

Moves to:

Close angle – DAVID LEE.

DAVID LEE *has been deeply involved in everything that has taken place in the room. As he sits, he is split with indecision as to whether he should rise and say something or to remain in his place. But he makes a sudden decision, and rises –*

DAVID LEE. I believe Clarence's story...

Pulls to:

Full angle – Class Room.

All eyes turn to David Lee –

CAMILLE. You want to come forward and tell us why, David?

He hesitates for a moment – he moves and stands before the class –

DAVID LEE. Some people came and took my daddy away and other people said we couldn't work the farm. But we had to, 'cause we didn't wanna lose our farm. We planted the crops and they grew. I believe his story 'cause his story is about what he did when he had to do somethin'. He didn't know how to swim but he had to or else his sister woulda drowned. That's how he did it...

He looks around to CAMILLE, *and then he moves back to the place where he was, and sits – and then the class room breaks out in applause –*

Moves to:

Angle – CLARENCE.

He is happy to know that his story has finally been accepted as the truth—

Swings to:

Close face angle— DAVID LEE.

His face too is beaming with laughter—

Ext. front of Borderdale School—Day. CAMILLE *and* DAVID LEE *exit from the school house—* DAVID *is filled with excitement over his adventure in the class room. They are joined by* SOUNDER *who is impatiently waiting for* DAVID. DAVID LEE *strokes the dog a few times, and they keep moving on out of the school yard—*

CAMILLE. Well, how did you like the class, David?

DAVID LEE. It was the best thing I ever been to, Miss Johnson!

They move out of the school yard towards town.

Int. CAMILLE's *place—Night.* CAMILLE *is busying herself, sweeping, dusting furniture items, putting things in place, etc.—* DAVID LEE *is following her about the place, helping her where ever he can—His spirits are very high at the moment.* SOUNDER *is crouched in a corner, looking on the activity—*

DAVID LEE. . . . So me and Sounder, ran right by the men that was the prisoners, and crawled under the fence! That's when I cut my hand on the glass. It hurt like mad! But I kept runnin', and then I didn't feel no more hurtin' 'till I stopped runnin'! *(pause)*. Why was that, Miss Johnson?

CAMILLE. Because all you could think of, was getting away from the guard.

DAVID LEE. Oh. . .*(pause)*. You right, that's all that was worryin' me right then. . .

CAMILLE. You know; that was a good thing you did for Clarence, in class today. I believed his story, but I was afraid the other children wouldn't. . .

DAVID LEE. He was real scared nobody would believe him—I could tell, even when he first stood up.

CAMILLE. You could? How?

DAVID LEE. I been like that myself, when I thought nobody was gonna believe me. . . *(pause)*. You wanna hear another story?!

CAMILLE. Not now, David, it's time for bed. You have a long trip ahead of you in the morning. . .

A thought grips the boy, and he moves to the window, and stares out into the darkness, as CAMILLE *starts to make the bed for him—she*

stops for a moment, and looks up and over at him at the window—

CAMILLE. What are you looking at out there? There's nothing to see.

DAVID LEE. My daddy likes to look into the dark, even when there ain't nothin' to see—it's what you hear he say.

CAMILLE *notices and feels that his mood has changed.*

CAMILLE. You think about your father a lot, don't you?

DAVID LEE. Yes mam. . .

CAMILLE. Well, you shouldn't worry about him too much, David.

DAVID LEE. What do I tell my mama when I get home. I didn't find him and that's what I wanted to do.

CAMILLE. But you did all you could, David. Not many little boys could've gone on such a journey as you did.

DAVID LEE. But where is my daddy!?

CAMILLE. I can't answer that for you—but it's no fault of your own that you don't know where your father is, now. You tell me what you did that kept you from finding your father? *(pause)*. Come on, tell me. . .?

DAVID LEE *(pause)*. Nothin'. . .

CAMILLE. And so you did your job, right?

DAVID LEE *(pause)*. Yes, mam. . .

CAMILLE. Whewwww! You sure keep my mind jumping, boy!

DAVID LEE. What do that mean?

CAMILLE. Means you keep me using my head, and that's good!

She returns to making up the bed.

DAVID LEE *(pause)*. Miss Johnson. . .Do you think I can come back here, and you let me study school with the other children?

The question stops her work—and then she momentarily struggles for an answer for the boy—she sits down on the bed as he turns back to gazing out of the window. She looks on him for a moment, rises, moves to the window, puts her arm around his shoulder—and they both look out of the window into the blank darkness—

Ext. front of the house—road—Day. JOSIE MAE *is on the porch with* EARL *when she spots* DAVID *and* SOUNDER *on the road, rushing toward the house.*

JOSIE MAE. Mama! Mama!

She and EARL *rush out to the road to meet them—* REBECCA *moves out of the front door behind them.* DAVID *is carrying two books given to him by* CAMILLE. *They all reach him about the same time.*

JOSIE & EARL. Hi, David! Sounder!

REBECCA. What happened to you? I've been worried out of my life. What's wrong with your hand, son?

DAVID LEE. I cut it on some glass and we got lost, Mama.

REBECCA. Did you find your father?

DAVID LEE. Didn't see 'im, Mama. The other men there say they didn't know Daddy.

REBECCA. I guess they musta sent 'im to another camp.

They all start moving for the house.

REBECCA . What's that you carryin'?

DAVID LEE. Some books Miss Johnson gave me.

REBECCA. Who's Miss Johnson?

DAVID LEE. Miss Johnson is a teacher, and...

They move on through the yard.

Int. kitchen-sitting room—Day. They enter— DAVID *and the other children sit at the table—* REBECCA *begins to prepare something for the boy to eat.*

DAVID LEE. So when I left, she gave me these books.

REBECCA. Miss Johnson must be a real kindly lady.

DAVID LEE. She is, Mama...*(pause)*. When the fall comes, she wants me to come to her school.

REBECCA. How can you do that? You don't live anywhere near that school.

DAVID LEE. She says I can come live with her while school goin' on, and come back home every time there ain't no school.

REBECCA. But who's gonna help me here with the house and in the field?

She puts some food on the table before him— he hesitates before eating—she is about to exit through the back door—stops in the doorway and turns back to him.

REBECCA. If your father is back by then it's all right with me if it'll be all right with him...

REBECCA *moves out just like that, leaving the boy thrown and bewildered for a moment—he looks in the direction of his mother's room for awhile and then slowly starts to eat, with his appetite practically gone—* JOSIE MAE *and* EARL *on the other side of the table are staring at him.*

DAVID LEE. Whatcha starin' at?

JOSIE MAE. Tell us some more 'bout the trip!

Exts. cornfield—weighing station—Day. A hot, mid-July day—late afternoon— REBECCA, DAVID LEE, JOSIE MAE *and* EARL *are working the mill.*

DAVID LEE *points with his fingers in giving out assignments to* JOSIE MAE *and* EARL. *They run across the fields to a particular row of corn, with croker sacks in their hands.*

JOSIE MAE *and* EARL *are behind* REBECCA, *picking the corn in armfuls—run back to the stationary place where they left their croker sacks, and drop the corn into the sacks.*

Ext. cornfield—Day. A white man in a wagon rolls in the aisle between the rows of corn—stops the wagon at each sack, where REBECCA *and* DAVID LEE *load the corn up on the wagon.*

Ext. weighing station—Day. The wagon rolls up to the weighing station on MR. HOWARD'S *premises and comes to a halt—* REBECCA *and* DAVID LEE *climb down from the wagon.* MR. HOWARD *is there.*

REBECCA *and* DAVID LEE *unload the sacks from the wagon, and put them down on the scale, while the man who was driving the wagon writes down the weight numbers on a piece of paper.*

Int. the kitchen—Night. REBECCA, JOSIE MAE *and* EARL *are gathered around* DAVID LEE *as he slowly completes writing a letter—he sits back to read it.*

DAVID LEE *(reads)*. "Dear Miss Johnson. How are you? I am doing okay. I told my mama, my brother and my sister about you, and they like you too. I can't make this letter too long because I have work to do. Bless you, David Lee Morgan"

They all look to each other with big triumphant smiles of pride on their faces.

REBECCA. Son, you sure write a good fine letter!

Ext. the woods—Day. DAVID LEE *walks through the woods with a book in his hand—he stops, sits down at the base of a tree, when suddenly he reacts as if he hears something—he rises and rushes away—he runs, stops and looks around him, in search of someone, and then he takes off again at—high speed along a pathway of the woods. His speed builds and builds, and suddenly he breaks the woods, and the night, into high grass field.*

Ext. grass field—Day. It is broad daylight, and the sun is shining— DAVID LEE *wipes his eyes and looks about the field of high grass—he* hears a voice and takes off running until he breaks the high grass into open field.

Ext. open field. He sees his father, with SOUNDER at his side, standing about three hundred feet away from him, smiling. He rushes to his father—they embrace and then they start to run across the open field, the three of them. They run and they run, keeping pace with each other, as their speed increases. DAVID LEE drops his book, stops to pick it up—After he straightens up with the book to continue the running, he stops in his tracks—his father and SOUNDER are nowhere to be seen—he looks out over the entire field—they are not there.

Int. children's room—Night. DAVID LEE wakes up—he looks to EARL and JOSIE MAE, and then into the empty darkness of the room, and wonders; where did the dream come from—where did it go to—

Ext. the porch—Day. Later the same day, DAVID LEE is lying on his stomach, reading from one of his books. REBECCA is doing some sewing—SOUNDER comes from around the side of the house, hobbling back and forth to the road and back.

REBECCA. What's wrong with him, David?
DAVID LEE. It's the heat.
REBECCA. It's when the heat is so bad, dogs go crazy.
DAVID LEE. He won't go mad—he's just lookin' for a cooler spot.

REBECCA sees a lone figure upon the landscape way out from the house emerge as a speck and slowly grow into a ripply form through the heat waves—JOSIE MAE and EARL come from around the house and sit down in the yard.

REBECCA. Who's that to be fightin' scorchin' heat out in open land like that?

SOUNDER moves about restlessly in the yard—and then suddenly the voice of the great coon hound breaks the sultry August deadness—and dashes across the road toward the figure. REBECCA jumps to her feet.

REBECCA. He's gone mad! Stop him, David!

DAVID LEE takes off after SOUNDER—his voice is ringing at a peak as he keeps moving until he arrives at the figure. REBECCA sees the man kneel and take the dog into his arms, and now the light hits at the top of her mind.

REBECCA. Oh my God, it's Nathan! It's Nathan!!!

She drops everything and charges off the porch with JOSIE MAE and EARL, making haste behind her.

Medium angle—REBECCA, JOSIE MAE and EARL—Porch POV. As they dash across the road and into the field, almost in one physical motion.

Quick pull to:

Full long angle—MORGAN family—Porch POV. DAVID LEE falls into his father's arms—REBECCA embraces and holds him close to her—JOSIE MAE and EARL move into his embrace—SOUNDER moves back and forth around them—DAVID LEE jumps up and down with joy—They start moving toward the house—NATHAN moves with an accented limp in his right leg, and then they stop.

Smash to:

Ext. the field—close face angle—DAVID LEE—Day.

DAVID LEE. What's wrong with your leg, Daddy?

Close face angle—NATHAN LEE.

NATHAN LEE. Got it hurt in a dynamite blast, son. The dirty dogs had no more use for me, so they let me have time off my sentence, and let me come home.

Pull to:

Full angle—Everyone.

REBECCA. The most important thing is that you're home! (pause). We was gonna have cold eatin' tonight, 'cause of the heat, but now, I'm goin' to cook!
NATHAN LEE. Well, let's get to it, Miss Rebecca, 'cause I been waitin' too long a time, for your good cookin'!

They move out of the field, and across the road for their home.

Int. kitchen—Night. NATHAN and the children are at the table just after eating as REBECCA is busying herself in the area, cleaning up.

NATHAN LEE. All I can say, Rebecca, is that was some meal! Thank you!

She stops her work, turns to him and smiles.

REBECCA. I'm glad you liked it, Nathan.

She returns to her work.

REBECCA. Alright, children, it was your bedtime two hours ago—let's get a move on you...

JOSIE MAE *and* EARL *rise and move around the table to their father.*

JOSIE MAE. Goodnight, Daddy...
NATHAN LEE. Goodnight to you, little pretty girl.

He kisses her on the face and then EARL *moves to him.*

EARL. Night, Daddy...
NATHAN LEE. Goodnight, son...

He embraces EARL—*and then the two children move for their room, with* REBECCA *accompanying them.*

NATHAN LEE. Son, that was some trip you went on...
DAVID LEE. Where was you, Daddy?
NATHAN LEE. That musta been afta they sent me to this place call Clayburn. That was the hardest workin' camp they sent me to. The work was so hard, you had to look for somethin' to laugh about to keep from feelin' the whole pain in your body. Like one time, it was in the middle of the day, and there weren't no sun—you hear that?
DAVID LEE. Where did the sun go to, Daddy?
NATHAN LEE. Into the clouds and behind the mountains.
DAVID LEE. What happened afta that?
NATHAN LEE. The rains started to come, and the prisoners were scared to run 'cause they had to wait for guards to round us up, and tell us when to move—but we didn't mind the rain comin' 'cause it meant we would git a little rest—we just stood there, watchin' the guards and they weapons get wet, and that made us all feel kinda good for a minute. I was laughin' all over inside—a minute, that's all, but what a minute it was!

He laughs— DAVID LEE *laughs along with him—the laughter trails off.*

DAVID LEE. Daddy, I'm so glad you home!

NATHAN *reaches across the table and shakes the boy's head with his hand.*

NATHAN LEE. And me too, son! You shore done got to be such a big little man!
DAVID LEE. We goin' huntin' again, Daddy!?
NATHAN LEE. You bet we is!
DAVID LEE. I cleaned and oiled all your stuff while you was gone...

REBECCA *re-enters from the children's room, crosses for her room, stops at the door, and turns to them.*

REBECCA. Your time now, David Lee...

She enters the room— DAVID LEE *rises from the table, moves to his father, and extends his hand out to him for a shake—they shake hands.*

DAVID LEE. Goodnight, Daddy...
NATHAN LEE. Goodnight to you, son...

DAVID LEE *moves for his room, stops and turns back to his father.*

DAVID LEE. Daddy, you home now...that's all I want—I don't want nothin' else...
NATHAN LEE. Come here, son...

DAVID LEE *moves closer to him—* NATHAN *takes the boy into his arms, and holds him close. He releases him—the boy smiles, turns and moves into his room.* NATHAN *looks on the door for awhile where the boy has entered, rises from the table and moves into his room.*

Int. NATHAN *and* REBECCA's *room—Close face angle—* DAVID LEE—*Day. An expression of soft thoughts and affection.*

Pulls to:

Angle— NATHAN LEE—DAVID LEE *POV.* NATHAN *is in bed, asleep. He turns over and as he does, his eyes catch sight of* DAVID LEE—*He props himself on his elbow to come out of the sleep as he looks to the boy.*

NATHAN LEE. Mornin', son...
DAVID LEE. Mornin', Daddy...

Moves to:

Full angle— NATHAN *and* DAVID LEE.

NATHAN LEE. Where's everybody?
DAVID LEE. They gone to the field...
NATHAN LEE. Guess I can't just lay here, then.

He lifts himself up and sits on the edge of the bed, rubs his hand through his hair—reflects, looking down on the floor.

Close face angle— DAVID LEE. *As he looks to his father with affection—*

Pulls quick to:

Full angle—room. DAVID LEE *crosses to a chair, takes up his father's trousers and shirt off a chair and his shoes from the floor and passes them on to him at the bed.*

NATHAN LEE. Thank you, son...

He begins to slowly put on his clothes—

DAVID LEE. You feel alright today, Daddy?
NATHAN LEE. Great, son—not like wakin' up in jail. For a minute or two, didn't quite

know where I was, but when I saw your face lookin' down on me, made me know right away the day was gonna be a good one, and it all belonged to me!

Close half angle— NATHAN LEE. *As he smiles down to the boy—*

Cut to:

Close angle— DAVID LEE. *As he returns his father's smile—*

Pulls to:

Full angle—room. As they both exit from the room— NATHAN LEE *leading the way—*

Int. sitting room-kitchen—Full angle—Day. They keep moving to the kitchen area.

DAVID LEE. Mama left somethin' for you to eat on the stove—

They arrive at the stove— NATHAN *takes the cover off a pan to take a look.*

NATHAN LEE. Smells good, too!

He turns away from the stove, and they move out the backdoor for the backyard.

Ext. The backyard—Full angle—Day. Just as they step out into the yard, they are immediately greeted by SOUNDER.

NATHAN LEE. Hi there, big boy!

SOUNDER *leaps all over him—He wrestles playfully with the dog.*

NATHAN LEE. They thought one little ol' shot gun was gonna stop you—you showed huh, boy!

SOUNDER *continues to paw all over him.*

NATHAN LEE. Down boy! That's enough!

SOUNDER *turns to* DAVID *who kneels to stroke and caress him as* NATHAN *moves to the water well, and begins to wash up.*

DAVID LEE. Daddy, when is we goin' huntin'?

NATHAN LEE. Soon—but it won't be too much huntin' you'll be doin', 'cordin' to a good little story your mama told me last night—you'll be goin' away from here, won't you?

Quick move to:

Close face angle— DAVID LEE. NATHAN'S *question seems to stab the boy, and he sinks into a troublesome silence.*

Pulls back to:

Full angle— NATHAN— DAVID *POV. He waits a moment for the boy to reply, then moves for the shed and enters—* DAVID LEE *looks on the blank door of the shed where* NATHAN *has entered— He rises from the ground and he and* SOUNDER *move into the shed.*

Int. shed—Angle— NATHAN—*Their POV— Day.* DAVID LEE *and* SOUNDER *enter and stop just inside the door.* NATHAN *is going over his equipment.*

NATHAN LEE. You kept my stuff in real good shape, son.

He takes up his baseball glove and a ball— tries the glove out in his hand—then tosses the ball to DAVID. DAVID *catches it—* NATHAN *picks up his bat—*

NATHAN LEE. Come on, son, throw a couple to me!

He moves briskly out of the shed back into the yard— DAVID *and* SOUNDER *run out behind him—*

Ext. backyard—Full angle—Day. NATHAN *moves to the house end of the yard—* DAVID *takes a position at the field end.*

NATHAN LEE. Alright, chunk it to me!

DAVID *throws the ball softly and it lands in* NATHAN'S *glove. He throws the ball back to* DAVID— DAVID *catches it in his bare hand.*

NATHAN LEE. Let me have one with a little steam on it, now!

DAVID *rears back and fires a hard one at him. It pops into his glove.*

NATHAN LEE. Boy, that was a mean curve you just threw!

DAVID *rears back once again, and throws a hard one.*

NATHAN LEE. That's enough for now, son. I better eat so we can get out to the field and help your mama before she come lookin' for us, and you know how tough your mama can get!

Ext. cornfield—Day. REBECCA, JOSIE MAE, *and* EARL *are working the field when* MR. HOWARD *drives out in his truck—He gets out and approaches them.*

MR. HOWARD *(smiling).* Hi ya, Rebecca...
REBECCA *(the cynical truth).* Tired.
MR. HOWARD *(looks about the field).* Somebody told me Nathan was back. How is he?

REBECCA. Why don't you pay him a visit, Mr. Howard—he'll tell you all about it.

MR. HOWARD. I'll do that, Rebecca...I'll do just that...

MR. HOWARD moves back to his truck and drives off. As they watch the truck move away—

Ext. cornfield—Day. They all turn to see NATHAN *limping toward them with* SOUNDER *and* DAVID LEE. *They wait until they arrive—*

NATHAN LEE. What did he want?

REBECCA. To invite you to his house—the two of you could just sit under the shade tree, drink ice cold whiskey, and just shoot the breeze!

NATHAN LEE. Did you tell 'im I was too busy for that kinda stuff?

He puts his arms around her shoulders, and draws her close to him—The children stand by with big wide open smiles on their faces—

NATHAN LEE. Dammit! It shore feels good to be back home!

He releases her—walks about twelve feet away—inspects some of the corn—looks about over the field—

NATHAN LEE. Y'all did some good job with the crop.

He turns and walks back to them—

NATHAN LEE. Well, let's get to work!

REBECCA. You sure you feel up to it, Nathan?

NATHAN LEE. Yeah. I feel real up to it right now. Come on, David Lee, you and me'll do the loading.

REBECCA *and the other children start in with the picking, but* REBECCA *watches* NATHAN *with concern as he,* DAVID LEE *and* SOUNDER *move through the field—finally, she returns her full attention to the work—*

NATHAN LEE. I'm real proud of how you helped your mama to keep this place goin', David Lee.

DAVID LEE. Thank you, Daddy...

They come to a group of corn-filled sacks alongside the wagon and stop.

NATHAN LEE. I'll lift up the back end, and you just hold on to the front end for me.

He lifts up the back end of the sack— DAVID LEE *takes hold of the front, tied end, and they struggle to get it up on the wagon, with* NATHAN *grunting and groaning. The same thing happens with the second sack—*

NATHAN LEE. Wheeew! This is some hard work, but it beats goin' to jail.

DAVID LEE. You won't be goin' to jail again, will you, Daddy?

NATHAN LEE. No, son—they'd have to kill me before I'd let 'em do that to me again!

He realizes he has said the wrong thing from the worried look on the boy's face.

NATHAN LEE. Nobody's goin' to jail, and nobody's gittin' hurt. Come on, let's get this one up on the wagon.

NATHAN *reaches down for the bag—his leg gives way on him and he falls on his behind—*

DAVID LEE. You hurt, Daddy!?

NATHAN LEE. No, no, I'm allright, son...This damn leg just won't act right no more!

He tries to get up right away but the leg is in such pain, he can't make it—

DAVID LEE. Mama! Mama!

REBECCA *and the other children come running toward them—*

REBECCA. What's wrong, Nathan?

DAVID LEE. He can't get up, Mama!

NATHAN LEE. This done happen before. It ain't nothin'—I just have to wait a minute or two.

REBECCA. Is there something I can do to help you?

NATHAN LEE. Yeah, just stay where you is...

He supports himself on his right arm and slowly pushes himself up to where he can stand on his foot—

NATHAN LEE. There, you see!?

REBECCA. I see, allright—It's time for us to get out of this field.

NATHAN LEE. I just got out here!

REBECCA. It's lunchtime, and I wanna have a talk with you, Nathan Lee. Come on, children...

She turns briskly and moves off with JOSIE MAE *and* EARL *following—*

NATHAN LEE. Woman worries too much for me.

He slowly starts to limp away with SOUNDER *but* DAVID LEE *remains standing where he is—*

Close face angle— DAVID LEE. *There is worry and concern in his face as he watches his father strain to walk on the injured leg—*

Pulls to:

Full angle – NATHAN LEE, SOUNDER *and*
DAVID LEE. *As* NATHAN *stops and turns to*
DAVID LEE –

NATHAN LEE. You comin with us, son?

After a bit of hesitation, DAVID LEE *slowly
moves toward his father, who has now turned
and is moving farther out of the field* –

Ext. front of the house – *Full angle* – *Everyone* – *Day.* REBECCA *is sitting on the porch, cutting string beans,* JOSIE MAY *and* EARL *are
playing hop scotch* – DAVID LEE *is tossing the
baseball to his father as* IKE *enters the yard* – *He
has a white envelope in his hand* – SOUNDER *is
standing near* NATHAN.

NATHAN LEE. Hi ya doin' there, Ike?

IKE. Any time it's Saturday and I don't hafta
do any work, I'm doin' okay!

NATHAN LEE. Whatcha got there?

IKE. Seems this piece of mail came to Mr.
Howard's place this mornin' and he had me to
bring it over here.

NATHAN LEE. Well, let me have it.

IKE. Don't belong to you! It's for the little
important man, here!

He hands it to DAVID LEE – DAVID LEE *does
not look at the envelope as he takes it* – *Everyone's attention is to* DAVID LEE *and the letter
now* –

NATHAN LEE. Well, son, who is it from?

DAVID LEE *hesitates for a moment, then holds
the letter up to read* –

DAVID LEE *(pause)*. From Miss Johnson –

NATHAN LEE. Well, ain't you gon' open and
read it for us?

*He looks directly to his father, and then to his
mother* – *walks to the steps and sits. They all
gather closer to him as he takes his time, opening the envelope. When it is opened* – *he seems
not to want to read it* –

DAVID LEE *(reads)*. Dear David, if you are
coming to school here, be sure to bring some
warm clothes. The school term will begin
September 8th, but it would be good for you
to be here by the 4th or 5th of the month. I do
hope everything is fine and you will be here.
Give my "hello" to your family. Yours truly,
Miss Camille Johnson...

NATHAN LEE. September 4 – how far away
is that?

REBECCA. 'Bout a week...

With directness, NATHAN LEE *moves toward
the wagon in front of the yard* – *stops and turns* –

NATHAN LEE. Come on, children, let's go!

Moves on to the wagon –

Pulls to:

Wider angle – *Include edge of road and
wagon.* NATHAN *climbs up on the wagon and
SOUNDER leaps up behind him as* JOSIE MAE
and EARL *follow.* DAVID LEE *steps down into the
yard and merely looks on* –

REBECCA. Where you goin'!?

NATHAN LEE. To the commissary to get this
boy some clothes! I'm gon' get everybody
somethin'!

REBECCA. But, Nathan –

NATHAN LEE. Don't tell me nothin' 'bout
what we owe ol' man Howard! I'll do the
owing, and let him worry 'bout the collecting! Come on, David Lee!

DAVID LEE *does not move from where he is
standing.*

NATHAN LEE. Did you hear me, boy? Come
on!

DAVID LEE *moves slowly to the wagon, stops
and looks up to his father* –

Close face angle – DAVID LEE.

DAVID LEE. You just came back home,
Daddy. I don't wanna leave right now – I
wanna stay home and be with you.

NATHAN LEE. And I wanta be with you, too,
but this school is somethin' that's good for
you – somethin' you need, like good air to
breathe, and I want you to have it, boy, and
that's the way it's gonna be!

DAVID LEE. But, Daddy, you need me here
to help you in the field – Daddy, your leg is
hurt – you can't work like you used to. Who's
gonna help you!? Who's gonna do the work,
Daddy?!

NATHAN LEE *(grabs him by one arm)*. Let me
tell you somethin', boy! I don't care if both of
my legs was cut off! I can do more work in
that field, than you could in a hundred years!

DAVID LEE. I won't go, Daddy! I won't go!

NATHAN LEE. Now wait justa minute! You
don't tell me what you ain't gonna do! I tell
you! I say, you goin' to that school, you goin'!
You hear me!

*He releases the boy, climbs back up on the
wagon, and looks down to him* –

Pulls to:

Wider angle – *Include wagon, children and*
SOUNDER.

Close face angle – DAVID LEE. *With a look of
confused sadness* –

DAVID LEE. Daddy, don't make me go away from you.

Quick move to:

Angle— NATHAN LEE. *The boy's words have rendered him speechless—he doesn't quite know what to do or say for the moment.*

Moves to:

Full angle—front of the house. DAVID LEE *turns and runs out into the field—*

NATHAN LEE. David!

The boy keeps running— NATHAN *climbs down from the wagon and goes after him—*

NATHAN LEE. David Lee, come back here!

REBECCA *rushes down from the porch and moves for* NATHAN—

REBECCA. Nathan!

NATHAN LEE *stops in his tracks, his back to her—*

Pulls to:

Angle— REBECCA— NATHAN's *POV.*

REBECCA. Please, leave him be, Nathan! He missed you in a grave way while you was gone—he sweated and worried to find out where they holdin' you—went on that long journey—you come home, and it's a natural thing for him to wanta hold on to you now.

Medium close angle— NATHAN LEE. *As he takes a long hard look to her—turns, and moves out into the field to find the boy—* SOUNDER *follows him—*

Moves to:

Close face angle— REBECCA. *As she watches him move out into the field—*

Ext. the cornfield—Angle— NATHAN LEE— *Day. As he moves about the field in search of* DAVID—*He moves into various areas—farther and farther into the field.*

NATHAN LEE. David! David Lee!

He gets no response to his call—He moves on and on about the field in search of the boy—

NATHAN LEE. David! You hear me callin' you!?

He moves on even farther, and finally he spots the boy, sitting on a high lump of earth with his face down between his legs, crying— NATHAN *stops, and then slowly moves to the boy and sits beside him—*

NATHAN LEE. Son, will you listen to me for a minute?

After a minute's hesitation, DAVID *slowly raises his head, and looks up to his father—*

NATHAN LEE. You know, son; when I got this leg hurt, I was down in a rock quarry, and all of a sudden, there was this dynamite blast comin' at me with the kind of force to kill ten men, but I got outta the way of most of them rock, quicker'n the lightnin' in God's mind—'cause I made it up in my head, just that quick to beat the death that was comin' at me. And that's what I'm gonna do with this trouble in my leg. I'm gon' beat it. That's all that's left for me to do. That's what I want you to do. I want you to beat the life they got laid out for you in this valley.

DAVID LEE *looks directly at him and then turns away.*

NATHAN LEE. I was watchin' your sister and brother out here the other day, and I said to myself, these is just children—they ain't got no business out here in this hot sun...As for me and your mama; we been in this field so long, we ain't never known anything else.

DAVID LEE *is looking straight out and away from him.* NATHAN *waits as* DAVID *hesitates—finally the boy holds his hands up before his eyes—he drops his hands, rises and moves away from his father—stops about five feet away. About three rows away, the white man is driving through the field in a truck—They watch the truck move on—*

NATHAN LEE. There ain't nothin' here but people like them bastards that sent me away, and tried to kill me. Son, please don't get too used to this place. I'm gonna love you wherever you is. Me, your mama, Josie Mae and Earl, we gonna love you even more. We gonna be at that school to see you every chance we get.

Close face angle— NATHAN LEE.

Cut to:

Close face angle— DAVID LEE. *As they look to each other—their eyes drawing them closer to each other, and then* DAVID *rushes into his father's waiting arms—*

NATHAN LEE. I love you, son! Don't ever think I don't love you! *(pause).* We gon' get to be friends?

DAVID LEE. Yes, Daddy! Yes!

NATHAN *holds the boy out from him—They just look to each other as* DAVID *wipes his eyes and calms down. They start moving out of the field—*

Pulls to:

Longer angle— NATHAN *and* DAVID LEE. *As they make their way out of the field—*

Int. the children's room—Full angle—Day. DAVID LEE *is packing a bag with* SOUNDER *near by him as* JOSIE MAE *and* EARL *look on—when he is done, he closes the bag on to* EARL—

DAVID LEE. Allright, get a move on you, bag boy!

EARL *drops the bag on the floor—*

EARL. You carry your own bag!
JOSIE MAE. I'll carry it, David...

EARL *quickly picks the bag back up—*

EARL. Naw, I'm carryin' it!
DAVID LEE. Thank you, Josie Mae.
JOSIE MAE. For what?
DAVID LEE. For Earl helpin' me out with my bag!

He laughs as they all move out of the room—

Ext. front of the house—Day. As the children exit from the house, REBECCA *is at the wagon, looking on* NATHAN *as he loads a box of* DAVID'S *things on the wagon—they approach him, and he takes the bag from* EARL *and loads it up on the wagon.* NATHAN *climbs up to the reins,* SOUNDER *hops up on the wagon, and then* REBECCA *takes* DAVID *into her arms—*

REBECCA. Be good and be smart, little boy.

DAVID LEE. Yes, ma'm...

She releases him. He embraces JOSIE MAE *and* EARL—*climbs on the wagon behind his father.*

NATHAN LEE. I oughta be gettin' back here by tomorrow night some time...Gitttt!

The wagon rolls away— DAVID *turns back to wave—*

DAVID LEE. BYE...!
ALL. BYE...!

REBECCA *keeps her eyes on the wagon for awhile, and then, she and the children turn and slowly move into the house—*

Ext. the wagon—Day. As the wagon rolls up the road, DAVID LEE *reaches back and ruffles* SOUNDER *about the neck—looks out over the field, and all the places he is familiar with— turns to his father—*

DAVID LEE. You know somethin', Daddy?
NATHAN LEE. What's that, son?
DAVID LEE. I'm gon miss this ol' raggedy place.

NATHAN *is worried for a moment—but* DAVID *breaks out in a big grin as if he's about to get to the punchline of a joke—*

DAVID LEE. But I ain't gon worry 'bout it!

The father and son break out in a gusto of laughter as the wagon rolls along up the road...

Fade out.

Finis.

ON GOLDEN POND

Screenplay by Ernest Thompson

NORMAN THAYER, JR.	Henry Fonda
ETHEL THAYER	Katharine Hepburn
CHELSEA	Jane Fonda
BILL RAY	Doug McKeon
BILLY RAY, JR.	Dabney Coleman

Screenplay by Ernest Thompson, adapted from his play *On Golden Pond*
Produced by ITC/IPC; Bruce Gilbert, for Universal, 1979
Directed by Mark Rydell
Edited by Robert L. Wolfe
Cinematography by Peter R. Norman
Music by Dave Grusin

Winner of the 1981 Academy Award for Best Screenplay Based on Material from Another Medium, as well as the Writers Guild Award for Outstanding Achievement for "a Drama adapted from Another Medium," as adapted by Mr. Thompson from his play, this script probes deeply and tenderly, albeit sentimentally, into family relationships in a manner that enables the superb cast, directed by Mark Rydell, to bring out all the warmth and humanity inherent in the work.

Born in Vermont in 1949, Mr. Thompson studied theater in a number of universities around the country and became an actor before writing plays. *On Golden Pond* was his first full-length play. It opened on February 28, 1979, in New York at the New Apollo Theatre and was well received. It ran for one hundred and fifty-six performances. An earlier play, *The Westside Waltz,* was revised for its star, Katharine Hepburn, who took it on tour and then to New York during the 1981–82 season.

Laced with laconic wit, which serves its sentiment well, particularly in the role of Norman Thayer, Jr., as played by Henry Fonda, Mr. Thompson, in this screenplay (also his first), has fashioned a comparatively rare study of old age in cinema. Thayer, who at seventy-nine is preoccupied with his mortality and acutely aware of death hovering over him, yet manages to keep his dignity as a human being in the face of it.

Thayer's bond with his wife, brilliantly played by Katharine Hepburn, is a moving affirmation of the value of love and affection in marriage at the last moments of life.

Particularly moving, perhaps even more so, is the development of the relationship between Thayer and his daughter, as played by Jane Fonda, which Mr. Thompson turns his story on. The estrangement between father and daughter and their eventual reconciliation and understanding of each other's deepest feeling adds poignancy and utmost veracity to Mr. Thompson's depiction of this special family.

What stays with you in the screenplay, as well as the picture, of course, is the passing on of love as an indestructible force, a bond that goes on past and beyond death, which we can all leave for those who remain behind as in the legacy, for example, that Thayer leaves to the boy, Billy. That and the unity of human love, of life and death, and of nature itself. As Mr. Thompson notes in his last scene of the screenplay, as they observe two loons soar away from Golden Pond " . . . the camera draws back and we see Norman and Ethel (Thayer) like the last summer flowers on the shore. Solitary figures. Not sad, but peaceful and hopeful and proud..."

Fade in. *Aerial shot—Day. From high above, we see rural New England, all green and gray, laced with black and brown winding roads and blue rivers, and blue ponds, little drab towns highlighted with the inevitable white church.*

And then the lake—Day. Golden Pond, shimmering like a sapphire against the deep green forest.

Ext. road—Day. A late-model Buick, modest color and style, cruises along this country highway. It passes a small farm where a farmer is erecting a new section of fence.

Ext. road—Day. A signpost with a charming collection of information, pointing out the direction to Golden Pond, as well as other points of interest. The Buick turns off the highway onto a smaller tar road.

Ext. hill—Day. An open meadow, ablaze with wild flowers, blueberry bushes just budding. The Buick stops at the meadow's edge. We see the lake shining down below.

Int. car—Day. ETHEL THAYER *is at the wheel. She is sixty-nine, full of life and energy, feisty. Beside her is* NORMAN THAYER, JR., *seventy-nine, gray and faded. He stares out the car window without emotion, but* ETHEL *is aglow with enthusiasm and excitement. She looks at* NORMAN *and smiles. The car moves on.*

Ext. village—Day. A cluster of ancient houses, a gas station, where a teenaged boy is carefully painting the single pump. The Buick drives slowly by.

Ext. village—Day. The General Store. A woman sweeps the sidewalk. A man is nailing up a sign announcing "Summer Hours." A small marina, new boats piled up. The Buick crosses a tiny bridge. We see a channel, bordered by houses, opening onto the lake.

Ext. lake—Day. The camera pans down to it and across its surface, and we see the lake's personalities:

Ext. cove—Day. The water is calm and relaxed, golden where the sun hits the shallowest parts.

Ext. peninsula—Day. Little waves lap the scraggly shore.

Ext. open sea—Day. Bigger waves, angrier, white-capped, bouncing hard against white-topped rocks, red and black buoys bobbing in the swells.

Ext. shoreline—Day. God's greenest trees, towering high, bending occasionally to the water. Rolling along behind them is the Buick.

Ext. shoreline—Day. A length of sandy beach, a scrubby swamp.

Ext. houses—Day. Little modern things, with lots of glass, too close together. Two young men are mooring out a sailboat.

Ext. cabins—Day. Old, delicate ones with docks piled on the banks. An old man struggles with a section of dock.

Ext. estate—Day. A sprawling place, with tennis courts and manicured lawns. Several men are working, pruning trees.

Ext. Camp Koochakiyi—Day. Little cabins and dining hall. Float and docks on the beach, boats and canoes being painted.

Ext. cottages—Day. The originals, some boarded up now, others in various stages of ready: docks in place, an occasional boat.

Ext. Thayer house—Day. A wonderful rustic place, two stories high, rambling porch, a widow's watch. On the bank are piled sections of a dock, and a float with a diving board. The yard is covered with pine needles. The board storm doors have been taken off the front of the house and now lean on the porch. There's an old washtub in the back, full of dirt, where later flowers will grow.

The Buick pulls into the yard. ETHEL *jumps out,* NORMAN *follows slowly.* ETHEL *dashes round the side of the house down to the dock, making Loon calls. From the distance the Loons answer.* ETHEL *turns to* NORMAN *who stands at the side of the house watching bemused.*

ETHEL. Norman. The Loons. They heard me! Hello Golden Pond. We're here.

NORMAN *fumbles with keys, and opens the door.* ETHEL *follows.*

Int. house—Day. NORMAN *and* ETHEL, *step into the living room.*

NORMAN *and* ETHEL *step into the living room.*

It is large, high-ceilinged, comfortable-looking. There's a cheery glow from the lake, which can be seen through the large windows. The room is practically alive with character and history. Its furniture, eclectic and interesting, is mostly hidden now by dust covers, and there are porch chairs and tables piled up inside as well.

On the walls we see an amazing chronicle of a family. Hundreds of photographs, diplomas and 4-H ribbons, and drawings, and yellowed newspaper clippings.

The whole room, indeed, as we'll see, the whole house, is a huge album of memories.

There are old fishing hats on a rack, and old jackets, fishpoles, boat cushions, anchors, a water ski, knickknacks galore, pine cones, stuffed fish, and the like, and hundreds of wonderful books, collections of Dumas and Twain and Dickens and Defoe and Stevenson and other masters of the ilk.

ETHEL. Just look at this place.

NORMAN. It's a mess, isn't it?

ETHEL. Just take a minute. Be all shipshape again.

She pulls off her jacket, puts on a marvelous, dilapidated old thing and steps outside. NORMAN *studies the room, seemingly confused, as though staring at an old friend he can't quite place. He wanders to the fishpoles.*

On the wall is a photo of NORMAN *as a younger man holding two large fish.* NORMAN *stares at the picture. Beside it is a clipping whose headline reads, "Professor Thayer Retires." It is dated 1966.*

NORMAN. Huh.

NORMAN *wanders across the room. We see an aluminum canoe near the porch door, the name "Gertrude" emblazed on its bow.*

NORMAN *opens the wooden front door. He pushes the screen door, but instead of swinging open, it falls over onto the porch.* NORMAN *regards it for a moment, then steps back into the living room.*

He looks about. He lifts a dust cover and finds a fifties-style telephone on a small table. He lifts the receiver and listens.

NORMAN *(continuing; calling).* The phone works! *(to himself).* At least I think it does. *(he dials "O").* Hello? Hello? Hello?

He is distracted by a photo of himself and ETHEL *when they were both much younger.*

NORMAN *(continuing).* Who the hell is that? *(he calls).* Who the hell is in this picture here?

No answer.

NORMAN *(continuing).* Who the hell *is* that? Hello? Who is this? . . . The operator! What do you want? . . . You called, you must want something . . . Oh, wait a minute. I did call you, but you never answered . . . Well . . . How *are* you? . . . How nice. Listen. This is Norman Thayer, Jr. over on Golden Pond, and I have something I'd like you to do. Call me up. Can you do that? . . . I want to check my phone and make certain it still rings. It hasn't been rung all winter, and it may have lost its whatsis. Do you have my number? . . . I have

no idea, it has a nine in it, that's all I know . . . Well, it's in the book, you must have a book . . . Norman Thayer, Jr. Let's give it a try, shall we?

NORMAN *hangs up. He stares at the phone expectantly. A moment passes. He squints at the photo.*

NORMAN *(continuing).* Who the hell is that?

We hear a knock at the door. NORMAN *is startled. He calls to the kitchen.*

NORMAN *(continuing).* Someone's at the door!

Ext. back stoop—Day. ETHEL *stands on the step, arms full of logs.*

ETHEL. It's me, you old poop.

She waits impatiently until at last NORMAN *opens the door.*

NORMAN. Well, look at you.

ETHEL. Yes, quite a sight, aren't I?

Int. living room—Day. ETHEL *marches in,* NORMAN *follows. He watches while she dumps her load of logs, and straightens up a bit.*

ETHEL. Norman, it's so beautiful. Everything's just waking up. Little tiny birds, little tiny leaves. I saw a whole patch of little tiny flowers out by the old cellar hole. I forgot what they're called, little tiny yellow things.

NORMAN. What were you doing out there in the woods?

ETHEL. Getting firewood, what do you think I was doing? What happened to the screen door?

NORMAN. It fell over.

ETHEL. How?

NORMAN. I pushed it.

ETHEL. What do you mean?

NORMAN. I pushed the door and the door fell over.

ETHEL. It's not supposed to do that when you push it.

NORMAN. I didn't think so. I'll fix it later.

ETHEL. You might have closed the big door. Now we'll be swatting black flies for the next two days.

She swings it shut. NORMAN *takes a hat off the rack and puts it on. He studies himself in the mirror.*

NORMAN. How do you like this hat?

ETHEL. Stunning. Do you want to help me with the dust covers?

NORMAN. I don't have anything else to do.

She pulls the sheet off the sofa. He reluctantly removes a cover from a chair and begins to fold it carefully.

ETHEL. I met a very nice couple.

NORMAN. What? . . . Where?

ETHEL. In the woods.

NORMAN. A couple of people.

ETHEL. No. A couple of antelope. Of course a couple of people. Migliore was their name, I believe.

NORMAN. Migliore? What sort of name is that.

ETHEL. I don't know, dear. Italian, probably. They're up from Boston.

NORMAN. Middle age means the middle, Ethel, the middle of life. People don't live to be 150.

ETHEL. We're at the far edge of middle age, that's all.

NORMAN. We're not, you know. We're not middle aged. You're old, and I'm ancient.

ETHEL *(approaching irritated)*. Oh, pooh, you're in your seventies, and I'm in my sixties.

NORMAN. Just barely on both counts.

ETHEL. Are we going to spend the afternoon quibbling about this?

NORMAN. We can if you like.

ETHEL. The Migliore's whatever their age group, have invited us to dinner, sometime. Wouldn't that be nice?

NORMAN. I don't know. I'm not sure my stomach is ready for rigatoni and that sort of thing.

She scowls at him. She carries an old hand-made table up to the front door.

NORMAN *(continuing)*. How's that table? A bit heavy?

ETHEL. Lord, yes. My father built this table in 1917. The first summer I went to Camp Koochakiyi.

NORMAN *tries on another hat.*

NORMAN. What do you think of this one?

ETHEL. Quite a sight. Oh, no, poor Elmer has had a terrible fall.

NORMAN. Who's poor Elmer?

ETHEL. Elmer, my dolly. He fell into the fireplace.

NORMAN. Well, he should be more careful.

ETHEL. Poor little Elmer. The life you've had. Did you know he turned sixty-five this spring?

NORMAN. No, I must say I wasn't aware of that.

He tries on more hats, one of which he'll wear for the rest of the scene.

ETHEL. My father got him for me on my fourth birthday. I wanted a red scooter, but my father said red scooters were excessive and contrary to the ways of the Lord. He told me I'd understand when I got older. Well, I'm a lot older now and I'm afraid I still don't understand. But he gave me Elmer. And Elmer and I, the times we've had. He was my first true love, you know.

NORMAN. I've known all along I wasn't the first in line.

ETHEL. No, you were a rather cheap substitute for my darling Elmer. And now he's had a fall, poor dear.

NORMAN. Maybe he was trying to kill himself. Maybe he wants to be cremated. Probably got cancer or termites or something.

ETHEL. Are you hungry, darling?

NORMAN. No. It wouldn't be a bad way to go, huh? A quick front flip off the mantel, a bit of a kick at the last minute, and end up right in the fire. Nothing to it.

ETHEL. Shut up, Norman!

NORMAN. When my number's up, do that for me, would you? Prop me up on the mantel and point out which way is down. I may even try for a full gainer with a half twist.

ETHEL. Norman Thayer, will you shut up? Your fascination with dying is beginning to frazzle my good humor.

NORMAN. It's not a fascination. It just crosses my mind now and then.

ETHEL. Every five minutes. Don't you have anything else to think about?

NORMAN. Nothing quite as interesting.

ETHEL. Well, what's stopping you? Why don't you take your dive and get it over with? See what it's like?

NORMAN. And leave you alone with Elmer? You must be mad.

ETHEL. Oh, for pity's sake. Come along with me and let's get the canoe off the porch.

She opens the enclosed porch.

Int. porch—Day.

ETHEL. All right. Grab an end.

NORMAN *takes one end, she lifts the other.*

Ext. house. They plod slowly down the steps.

NORMAN. This is not our canoe. It's way too heavy.

The phone rings.

ETHEL. Well, what do you know? The phone's ringing.

NORMAN. Who the hell is it?

ETHEL. I don't know, dear.

She sets her end down. NORMAN *sets down his. Phone rings again.*

NORMAN. *I'll* get it. Maybe it's St. Peter. You take the canoe on down.

He hurries back to the house. ETHEL *drags the canoe.*

Int. living room. The phone rings. NORMAN *enters. He pauses a moment to regain his breath. He lifts the receiver.*

NORMAN. Hello? Who is this? . . . The operator! What do you want? . . . Oh, to check the ring. Of course. Does it work?

Ext. porch—Day. NORMAN *carries the phone onto the porch and watches as* ETHEL *gathers up paddles and cushions, puts the binoculars around her neck and carries them all down to the canoe.*

NORMAN. Yes, I guess it did ring here. Thank you . . . I beg your pardon? . . . Oh. Thank you.

He hangs up the phone and leaves it on the porch. He ambles down the bank shaking his head.

NORMAN *(continuing).* She said to have a nice day. What a strange thing to say. What did she think I was going to do? Well, the phone works.

ETHEL. That's good.

Ext. dock—Late afternoon. He sits on a rock and watches ETHEL *move sections of dock.*

ETHEL. Oh, guess who else I ran into?

NORMAN. You ran into someone else? The woods are full of people. What's this place coming to?

ETHEL. It was only Charlie.

NORMAN. Who's Charlie?

ETHEL. *Charlie,* Norman. The mailman. He said he'd come round and put in our dock for us.

NORMAN. I'll put in the dock.

ETHEL. You won't put in the dock.

NORMAN. Why not?

ETHEL. Because you're too old.

NORMAN. I'm not old at all. I'm middle-aged.

ETHEL. Charlie says our boat's all ready and he'll bring it on Saturday!

NORMAN. I remember Charlie when he was just a little fellow. He used to laugh at anything. I thought then he was a bit deficient.

ETHEL. Chelsea had such a crush on him. Remember, Norman?

NORMAN. Yes. I could never understand that.

He pulls himself up and studies the beached float.

NORMAN *(continuing).* Remember Chelsea trying to be on the diving team at school? Ha, ha, ha. *(he holds out his hands).* She was about this wide.

He climbs up on the diving board. He may take a jump or two while they talk.

ETHEL. Tsk. She wasn't any such thing. She had a few fat years, that's all.

NORMAN. I should say so. It's no wonder she could never do a back flip. No center of gravity.

ETHEL. Well, she tried . . . She only did it to please you, anyway.

NORMAN. I know.

ETHEL. Oh, Norman. Wouldn't it be nice if I could persuade her to come and spend a few days this summer?

NORMAN *(after a moment).* Mmm. Want to go up to the house and play a quick game of Parcheesi?

ETHEL. Not now, Norman. We've got the whole summer for you to try to win back the fortune you lost to me last year.

NORMAN. Heh heh.

ETHEL. I hope you thought about your tactics over the winter.

NORMAN. Heh heh.

ETHEL. Pretty shoddy, some of those moves of yours.

NORMAN. Heh heh.

The two of them stare out at the lake.

ETHEL *(continuing).* Isn't it beautiful, Norman?

He steps to her and puts his arm around her.

NORMAN. Yes.

ETHEL. Let's take a quick ride, shall we? First ride of the year.

NORMAN. It's a little cold for that sort of thing, isn't it?

ETHEL. Come on.

She pushes the canoe into the water and holds the bow. He hesitates, but finally begins to climb in. The canoe rocks and NORMAN *stumbles.*

NORMAN. Good God.

ETHEL. Well, watch yourself.

NORMAN. I think you're trying to kill me.

ETHEL. I've thought about it.

At last he settles in. ETHEL *hands him a paddle, then climbs aboard, and they're off.*

Ext. lake—Late afternoon. NORMAN *and* ETHEL *in the canoe. She is paddling energet-*

ically in the bow. He is faking it in the stern. The canoe, consequently, is veering crookedly.

ETHEL. Are you paddling, Norman?
NORMAN. Of course I'm paddling.
ETHEL. Then you're not steering. Do you want me to take the stern?
NORMAN. I most certainly do not.

He tries a little harder. The canoe glides along by other cottages.

ETHEL. Charlie says he doesn't expect Miss Appley to make it up this summer.
NORMAN. Who's Miss Appley?
ETHEL. *Miss Appley,* Norman, who lives in there with Miss Tate. They're both in their nineties. They were up here together when I was a teenager. Wearing their neckties, and singing in the gazebo. Holding hands. What a marvelous love affair, if that's what it is.
NORMAN. Yes.
ETHEL. Can you imagine being together so long?
NORMAN. No.
ETHEL. Thanks a lot. Charlie says Miss Appley is just too frail and Miss Tate won't come without her. It's sad, isn't it?
NORMAN. Yes.

NORMAN *and* ETHEL *paddle up the shore. A fish breaks the water.*

ETHEL. Norman! Look at the fish! My word. It's going to be a good summer. My father always said if the fish start jumping in May it's a good sign. We'll have to go to the village and get your license.
NORMAN. I don't think I'll be doing any fishing this time around.
ETHEL. All right, Norman . . .
NORMAN. No point in wasting the money. You'd think they'd give the license free to an old case like me. It's not as though I'd come out here and deplete the entire bass population or anything.
ETHEL. You always catch your share. You always have.
NORMAN. Well, that's all behind me now.
ETHEL. All right, Norman.

They paddle without speaking for a moment. Suddenly Ethel's attention is caught by something. She shrieks.

ETHEL *(continuing).* Norman!
NORMAN. Good God! What is it?
ETHEL. The loons! I've spotted the loons!

She scrambles back in the canoe to retrieve the binoculars.

ETHEL *(continuing).* Oh, my goodness. They're so lovely. Here. Look.

He takes the glasses and trains them on the water.

ETHEL *(continuing).* Do you see them?
NORMAN. No. Oh. Oh, my goodness. There they are.
ETHEL. Aren't they beautiful?
NORMAN. They're huge! I've never seen such big loons in my life.
ETHEL. Those are boats, you poop. Come in closer.

He lowers the glasses. We see two loons, huge and black. They swim close to each other.

ETHEL *(continuing).* A husband and a wife. I think they're looking at us.
NORMAN. Yes. They are.

He waves.

ETHEL. They're talking.
NORMAN. I can't make out what they're saying. Can you read beaks?
ETHEL. Look! They're kissing. My word.
NORMAN. How wonderful.

Another angle — on the loons. They do indeed seem to be kissing. But suddenly they look around, wary. We hear the sound of a motorboat, loud and threatening.

Another angle. Now we see the boat, a runabout, sleek and fast, a young couple aboard.

They head right at the Loons, who look at the boat, and disappear. The boat zooms right over the spot where the Loons had been.

On the canoe

ETHEL. My God! What are they doing?

Another angle. Now the speedboat continues and heads right at the canoe. NORMAN paddles like mad. At last the boat veers.

The young man and young woman wave pleasantly and speed off.

Now the wake of the boat rolls toward the canoe.

NORMAN *(raises his middle finger in a vulgar gesture, shouting).* Buzz off!!

ETHEL *imitates his gesture.*

ETHEL. That's right; Buzz off!
NORMAN *(shocked).* Ethel! What are you doing?
ETHEL. What do you mean?
NORMAN. Don't do that!

ETHEL. Why not? You did it!

NORMAN *turns the canoe about to face the waves.*

NORMAN. Never mind, I'll explain later.

He and ETHEL *are rocked violently by the waves, but they ride it out.*

Another angle. The Loons have now surfaced. One of them calls angrily.

ETHEL (o.s.) You're absolutely right. They should be ashamed of themselves!

On the lake. The water is almost golden in the late afternoon sun.

ETHEL. Norman. Look at our house. Isn't it beautiful?
NORMAN. Yes . . . which one is it?
ETHEL. You're such a poop. It's the one with the birch tree, as you very well know.
NORMAN. Oh, yes, that's right.

They drift for a moment, looking at the distant house, and the Loons. A pastoral picture.
ETHEL. Norman, do you realize this is our forty-eighth summer on Golden Pond.
NORMAN. Hmmm. Probably our last.
ETHEL. Oh, shut up.

She splashes him with her paddle.

A series of long dissolves between nature shots indicating the passage of time.

Ext. dock—Day. ETHEL *is repainting "Thayer" on the metal mailbox. In the b.g. we see* NORMAN *on the porch reading a paper.*

We see a boat approaching. In it is CHARLIE MARTIN, *a local, simple and good-hearted. He is towing the "Thayer Four," a grand old mahogany speedboat.*

ETHEL. My God, Norman! Charlie's brought the boat. Come down and say hello.
NORMAN. You say hello for me.
ETHEL. Oh, come on.
NORMAN *(snapping).* No.

CHARLIE *draws up to the dock and ties the Thayer Four.*

ETHEL. Oh, Charlie, you've done a beautiful job.
CHARLIE. Thank you, Ethel.
ETHEL. Hello, Thayer Four. You look wonderful.
NORMAN *(from porch).* Make sure he ties it up right.
ETHEL. Oh, shut up.
CHARLIE. Hello, Norman.

NORMAN *nods hello.*

ETHEL. Come on down, Norman, we'll go for a ride.
NORMAN. No, thank you.
ETHEL. So enthusiastic, isn't he?

CHARLIE *laughs.*

ETHEL *(continuing).* I love your laugh, Charlie.
CHARLIE. Thank you, Ethel.

NORMAN *steps down toward them.*

NORMAN. He's got the whatsie on the wrong side. The thing you tie the boat to. That's not where we put the boat. It's all wrong.

ETHEL *and* CHARLIE *look at the dock and at each other.*

CHARLIE. He's right.

He lifts the piece out.

ETHEL *(to* NORMAN*).* Well. You should have been down here helping instead of sitting on the porch being disagreeable.
NORMAN. I can see that now.

He looks around, feeling rather smug. He looks at ETHEL's *paintwork.*

NORMAN *(continuing).* You spelled our name wrong.
ETHEL. What.

She actually looks at the mailbox, then back at NORMAN *who smiles slyly.* ETHEL *shakes her head.*

Int. living room—Night. NORMAN *and* ETHEL *are playing Parcheesi.* ETHEL *throws the dice.*

ETHEL. Look at that. Eleven! *(she moves).* Five—six—seven—eight—nine—ten—eleven. Puts me right on your man. How about that?
NORMAN *(challenging).* Where were you?
ETHEL. Oh, don't give me that.

NORMAN *glowers at her.*

NORMAN.   *Five*—six—seven—eight—nine—ten—eleven. Damn it!

ETHEL *smiles at him.*

Int. living room—Day. NORMAN *is hunched over a newspaper, scanning the classified ads with a magnifying glass. He nods his head and calls.*

NORMAN. Here's one. Listen. "Driver wanted for occasional chaufferring and errands, five days a week. Pay negotiable." Sound about right?

No answer.

NORMAN *(continuing).* "Experience required." Well, I guess I've had enough experience. I've driven enough cars, God knows. *(he calls).* How many cars would you say I've had?

No answer.

NORMAN *(continuing).* Twenty probably, if you don't count the Nash. Twenty cars and one Nash. Sounds like experience to me. *(he calls).* I think I'll give these people a call. Huh?

No answer.

NORMAN *(continuing).* There's no number. How do you like that? For God's sake. It's so typical. They want a man for a job and yet they don't list a number. Well, I hope those errands weren't too crucial. Good God!

There is a knock at the door. NORMAN *looks up, startled. He stands and calls.*

NORMAN *(continuing).* Someone's at the door.

Ext. back stoop—Day.

ETHEL *stands on the step, a berry bucket in each hand. In the washtub behind her we see little plants growing.*

ETHEL. It's me, you poop. Open up.

The door opens and NORMAN *ushers her in.*

Int. back entryway—Day.

NORMAN. Where have you been?

ETHEL. Out picking berries. There are oodles and oodles of little strawberries along the old town road. Look.

NORMAN. How nice.

ETHEL. What on earth you're doing in here on a morning like this is beyond me.

NORMAN *(carrying his papers).* Oh, I've been quite busy. I've been looking through yesterday's paper for gainful employment.

ETHEL. Here we go again.

She shakes her head and disappears into the kitchen.

NORMAN. Very good prospects, I think. Chauffeurs, yardwork. The Dairy Divine wants an ice cream dipper. I think I could do something like that, don't you?

He realizes she's not in the room. He looks about, irritated, then heads for the kitchen.

Int. kitchen—Day. ETHEL *is busily dumping her berries into a large bowl.*

NORMAN *enters.*

NORMAN. Oh, here you are. What do you think?

ETHEL. What are you going to do if you call and someone says, "Come on over and start tomorrow"?

NORMAN. Go on over and start tomorrow.

ETHEL. Oh, for the love of God. Whatever is the matter with you? Why don't you take a bucket and go pick us another quart of strawberries? I'll fix us up a scrumptious shortcake for lunch.

NORMAN. You want me to pick strawberries?

ETHEL. Yes. Do I have to put an ad in the paper?

NORMAN. I'm not sure I know how to pick strawberries.

ETHEL. There's really nothing to it, Norman. You bend over and you pick them. Come on.

NORMAN. Bend over? Where are they?

ETHEL. On the ground, where they belong.

NORMAN. The last time we picked blueberries they were on a bush. Didn't have to bend over at all.

ETHEL. Well, these are strawberries. They're on the ground.

She leads him out.

Ext. house—Day. ETHEL *leads* NORMAN *down the stoop and into the yard. We hear a motorboat.* NORMAN *looks at the lake.*

NORMAN. Oh. Here comes what's-his-name. He'll be bringing the paper, you know. I wouldn't want to miss any career opportunities just because I was off looking for strawberries.

ETHEL *(leading him along).* I'll pay you, Norman. It could be the beginning of something big. You may become a major strawberry picker.

NORMAN. Not if I have to be bending over all the time. I think you're trying to kill me.

ETHEL. I've thought about it.

NORMAN. You needn't bother. I'm on borrowed time as it is.

ETHEL. Would you please take your cheery personality and get out of here?

NORMAN. I hope you'll be prepared to massage my bent back this evening.

ETHEL *(kissing him).* With pleasure.

She gives him a push and he steps away, mumbling.

NORMAN. Maybe I could lie down to pick the berries.

He seems confused as he turns and trudges into the woods. ETHEL *watches, concerned, but glad to have gotten him into motion. She looks at the lake, heads down to it.*

Ext. dock—Day. ETHEL *moves toward the house as* CHARLIE *roars up in his boat. He waves. And cuts his motor.*

CHARLIE *(shouting)*. Morning, Ethel.

ETHEL *(shouting)*. Come on up and have some coffee. You can take five minutes off. I'll write you a note and you can send it to the Postmaster General.

CHARLIE *loves this. He laughs and clambers out of the boat. He holds a small package and a packet of mail, from which he pulls a letter.*

CHARLIE. You got a letter from Chelsea. The rest is just bills and junk like that.

He heads up the bank.

Ext. porch—Day. CHARLIE *pulls open the door, but it falls over on him. He sets down the mail and props the door against the wall.*

CHARLIE *(calling)*. Uh-oh. I think I broke your door.

ETHEL *(from the kitchen)*. Oh, no, it's been that way for a month now. Norman is supposed to fix it, but I'm afraid it's not high on his list of priorities.

Which makes CHARLIE *laugh. They step inside.*

Ext. forest—Day. NORMAN *is standing at the end of the lane with his berry bucket. He slaps at a mosquito. He steps into the woods, then quickly steps back to the lane, unsettled. He tries again. Into the woods, a little further this time. He stops, stares up at a huge tree as though surprised to find it there. He seems ready to cry.*

Int. living room—Day. CHARLIE *stands by the fireplace, not totally comfortable in the Thayer home. He looks at the photos, and smiles.*

On the photos. One of NORMAN *as a younger man, in his bathing suit, on the diving board.*

One of the daughter, CHELSEA, *plump, but pretty. Also on the diving board. He picks it up.*

On CHARLIE. *He gazes at the photo with great interest.*

ETHEL *(o.s.)* Come and get a biscuit, Charlie.

He fumbles with the picture and puts it back. He steps into the kitchen.

Int. kitchen—Day. ETHEL *is setting out coffee and biscuits.* CHARLIE *hands* ETHEL *the letter from* CHELSEA. ETHEL *slips it into her pocket.*

CHARLIE. You know, they lost a little girl in Purgatory Cove. She was visiting her grandparents, you know, the McCreas up on the point . . .

ETHEL. Of course . . .

CHARLIE. Yuh . . . She sailed her little sailboat right into Purgatory Cove, and went up on the rocks and drownded. I felt just awful.

ETHEL. Oh, dear, dear. Isn't that tragic? Poor Mrs. McCrea.

CHARLIE. Yuh. Count your blessings.

CHARLIE *takes a biscuit and sits at the table.* ETHEL *looks at him fondly and sits beside him.*

ETHEL. How's your mother, Charlie?

CHARLIE. My mother?

ETHEL. Yes.

CHARLIE. She's holding her own. *(he sits and roars with laughter).* She fell down, you know, a couple of months ago.

ETHEL. Oh. I didn't know.

CHARLIE. Yuh, a couple of months ago, right on her rump, when she was out helping clean up town common with the Ladies Auxiliary. She was having a tug-a-war with a dead juniper bush, and she won, or lost, depending on how you look at it. *(he laughs).* But, if you'll pardon the expression, she's one old lady who really believes in busting her ass for the community.

They both roar with laughter. Suddenly the door opens and NORMAN *enters. They stop laughing.*

CHARLIE *(continuing)*. Hi, Norman.

ETHEL. Hello, Norman. What are you doing back already? You've barely left.

NORMAN. So? I moved fast. I ran all the way, picked without stopping, and ran all the way back.

ETHEL *(going to him)*. Let me see what you've got.

NORMAN. I'll just dump them in with yours.

He starts for the sink. ETHEL *grabs for the bucket, it tumbles to the floor and bounces.*

ETHEL. You didn't get a single strawberry. What's the matter with you?

NORMAN. I must have eaten them all.

An awkward moment as the three exchange looks.

NORMAN *(continuing)*. No mail today, Charlie?

CHARLIE. Holy Mackinoly! I left it on the porch.

NORMAN. How about bringing it in? Could you do that?

CHARLIE. You bet.

He exits. ETHEL *stares at* NORMAN.

ETHEL. Would you like a glass of milk, Norman?

NORMAN. No!

ETHEL. I'll get you one.

NORMAN *follows* CHARLIE *into the living room.*

Int. living room—Day.

NORMAN. I see you broke the screen door, Charlie.

CHARLIE. Oh, well, it's just missing its little thingamabobbers for the hinges. I could bring you a couple from town tomorrow.

NORMAN. No, just be careful next time.

CHARLIE *hands the package and packet of mail to* NORMAN, *who goes back into the kitchen.* CHARLIE *follows.*

Int. kitchen. NORMAN *sits and studies the package.* ETHEL *sets a glass of milk by him.*

ETHEL. Here, Norman, drink this.

NORMAN. Thank you, nurse.

ETHEL. Sit down, Charlie, and finish your coffee.

He looks uncomfortably at NORMAN, *then sits.*

ETHEL *(continuing).* What have you got there, Norman?

NORMAN. I have no idea. I can't open it. Here, could you bite this, please?

He hands it to CHARLIE, *who laughs and pulls it open.*

ETHEL. Ah. It's your medicine.

NORMAN. Oh, goody, what a swell surprise.

ETHEL *(to* CHARLIE*).* It's nothing serious. Just for his palpitations.

NORMAN. That's right, Charlie, I have occasional heart throbs.

ETHEL. We got a letter from Chelsea.

NORMAN. Oh?

He hides in his newpaper. ETHEL *busies herself with the letter. A moment passes,* CHARLIE *feels slightly left out.*

CHARLIE. Well, how is old Chelsea?

NORMAN *doesn't answer.* ETHEL *doesn't look up.*

ETHEL. Mm-mmm.

NORMAN. Look at the goddam Orioles. Baltimore has always been a sneaky town.

ETHEL. Norman! She says she's coming for your birthday.

NORMAN. Really? How nice.

ETHEL. Yes. And she's bringing her friend. *(to* CHARLIE*).* She has the nicest boyfriend.

CHARLIE. Oh.

He half laughs.

ETHEL. They're coming together and then they're going on to Europe for awhile.

NORMAN. Ohhh. Well, I don't want crowds of people here on my birthday. I don't want crowds of people watching me turn older.

ETHEL. Oh, pooh. There'll be just the three of us. Is three a crowd?

NORMAN. That's what they say.

CHARLIE. That's right. Three's a crowd. *(laughs).* What happened to her husband?

ETHEL. Wait a minute. It's not that Freddie person. This is a different boyfriend altogether.

NORMAN. What the hell is going on? Detroit has disappeared, Good God!

ETHEL. What is it, Norman?

NORMAN. Detroit is gone. Three weeks ago they looked like a contender, and now this stupid paper has them missing.

CHARLIE. What happened to her husband?

ETHEL. What did you say, Charlie?

CHARLIE. I wondered what happened to Chelsea's husband.

ETHEL. He didn't work out. *(reading).* She says she's in love. With a dentist.

NORMAN. Oh, really? Does her boyfriend know about this?

ETHEL. That is her boyfriend. Her new boyfriend is a dentist.

CHARLIE. That's interesting.

NORMAN. That's who she's bringing here? A dentist?

ETHEL. Yes.

NORMAN. Oh, God, he'll be staring at our teeth all the time. Why does she have such a fascination with Jewish people?

ETHEL. Who said this one is Jewish?

NORMAN. He's a dentist, isn't he? Name one dentist who isn't Jewish.

ETHEL. Your brother.

NORMAN. My brother is deceased. Name me one living dentist who isn't Jewish.

ETHEL. Oh, for Lord's sake.

CHARLIE. I didn't want anyone else . . . How old will you be?

NORMAN. When?

CHARLIE. On your birthday.

NORMAN. One hundred three.

CHARLIE. Miss Appley was ninety-seven in May. Isn't that amazing?

NORMAN. Yes.

CHARLIE. She died, you know.

NORMAN. No.

CHARLIE. Yuh. Last Tuesday. We got a call in case any mail comes up.

NORMAN. They gave you a forwarding address for Miss Appley?

CHARLIE *roars at this.* ETHEL *enters.*

ETHEL. What's so funny?

NORMAN. One of the lesbians expired.

Which sends CHARLIE *into paroxysms of laughter.*

ETHEL. Oh, Norman. *(to* CHARLIE*).* Which one?

CHARLIE. Miss Appley.

ETHEL. Oh, dear. Well, she had a good, full life.

NORMAN. Charlie says she was ninety-seven.

ETHEL. Really? How wonderful.

NORMAN. Puts us all to shame, doesn't it? There's something to be said for a deviant lifestyle.

CHARLIE *(standing and laughing).* I always liked those old ladies, but I sure used to wonder what the heck was going on in there. Well, thanks for the coffee, Ethel. You still make the best biscuits on the lake.

ETHEL. Thank you, dear. You must come round when Chelsea's here.

CHARLIE. Oh, yuh. I haven't seen her in a long time. Well . . .

ETHEL. Norman, Charlie's leaving.

NORMAN. Good. 'Bye.

CHARLIE. Goodbye.

NORMAN. Watch out for that screen door.

ETHEL *leads* CHARLIE *out of the kitchen.*

ETHEL. He's such a poop, isn't he?

Ext. house — Day. ETHEL *and* CHARLIE *walk across the porch and down the bank.*

ETHEL. Seen our loons out there today?

CHARLIE. Yuh. Out by Honey Island. They're teaching their baby to fly.

ETHEL. Oh. Isn't that exciting?

Ext. dock — Day. CHARLIE *climbs into his boat.*

CHARLIE. Yuh. Well, see you next time.

He starts his motor and pulls away. ETHEL *waves, and looks out at the lake. She heads back to the house.*

Ext. porch — Day. NORMAN *steps out with the newspaper folded to the classifieds.*

ETHEL. Norman, isn't that exciting? Teaching their baby to fly.

NORMAN. Listen to this. "Retired people sought for handbill delivery. Some walking involved." I should call, I can walk.

ETHEL. Is that why you came rushing back here? To read those goddam ads?

NORMAN *throws down the paper. He glares at* ETHEL.

NORMAN. Do you want to know why I came back so fast? I got to the end of our lane and I couldn't remember where the old town road was. I went a little way into the woods and nothing looked familiar, not one damn tree. And it scared me half to death. So I came running back here to you, to see your pretty face, and to feel that I was safe. That I was still me.

He puts his face in his hands. ETHEL *is shocked by this, but she rallies quickly. She sits by him and rubs his back.*

ETHEL. You're safe, you old poop. And you're definitely still you, still picking on poor Charlie. After lunch, after we gobble up all the strawberries, we'll take ourselves to the old town road. We'll remember it all, my darling, we've walked it a thousand thousand times. *(she pauses, trying to find the right words).* Listen to me mister, you're my knight in shining armor and don't you forget it. We're going to get right back on that horse. I'm going to be right behind you holding on tight, and away we're going to go, go, go!

NORMAN. I don't like horses.

They look at each other.

NORMAN *(continuing).* You *are* a *pretty* old dame, aren't you?

She hugs him.

NORMAN *(continuing).* What are you doing with a dotty old son of a bitch like me?

ETHEL. I haven't the vaguest idea.

She holds him close. They stare out at the lake.

A series of long dissolves between nature shots indicating the passage of time.

Ext. channel — Day. ETHEL *drives the Thayer Four slowly along the channel while* NORMAN *sits glumly in the passenger seat.*

Ext. marina—Day. ETHEL *draws the boat up to the marina dock.* NORMAN *holds onto the pier while* ETHEL *jumps out.*

ETHEL. Do you want to stay and watch the boat while I run up to the store?
NORMAN. I think I'm qualified to watch the boat.
ETHEL. Well, come with me if you want.
NORMAN. No, thank you very much.

ETHEL *shrugs and turns to* SUMNER TODD, *a teenaged gas station attendant. His friend, also a teenager, loafs nearby.*

ETHEL. Hello, Sumner.
SUMNER. 'Morning, Mrs. Thayer.
ETHEL. Could you fill us up, dear?
SUMNER. Oh, sure.
ETHEL. Norman will help you.

SUMNER *looks over at* NORMAN *without enthusiasm as* ETHEL *walks quickly up the shore.*

Ext. marina—Day. NORMAN *watches* SUMNER *closely. He looks at the pump and shakes his head.*

NORMAN. Do you know how much gas cost when I was your age? Twelve cents a gallon.
SUMNER *(looks at his friend, then at the sky).* Is that a fact? I didn't even know they had gas back then.

The other boy giggles and SUMNER *smiles.*

NORMAN *(looks from one to the other).* What are you, a couple of nitwits? You think it's funny being old? My whole goddam body's fallin' apart. Sometimes I can't even go to the bathroom when I want to, but I'm still a man, let me tell you. I can take on either one of you punks.

He steps toward them, ready to fight, when ETHEL *arrives with a bag of groceries. The boys look at her, relieved to be rescued.* NORMAN *climbs quickly into the driver's seat. He helps* ETHEL *into the boat.*

NORMAN *(continuing).* I'll drive home.
ETHEL. Are you sure?
NORMAN *(snapping).* Yes! If I take a wrong turn and end up in Michigan or somewhere, you be sure and tell me.

ETHEL *sees no point in arguing. She sits and waves at* SUMNER *who pushes them away from the dock. The boys stand openmouthed, watching them go.*

Ext. lake—Day. NORMAN *has a look of great intensity in his eyes.* ETHEL *looks nervous.*

ETHEL. You remember, don't you, to go outside the flag?

He doesn't seem to hear. He heads for the inside of a buoy that is some distance from the shore.

ETHEL *(continuing).* Norman, you fool. Go outside the flag!

We see rocks jutting up between the flag and land. The boat is racing toward them.

ETHEL *(continuing; scared now).* Norman, turn the boat!

But NORMAN *is looking stubborn. He bears down on the rocks, and only at the last minute does he turn the boat and travel alongside them. His face shows nothing as he now speeds to the outside of the flag.* ETHEL *looks more than a little undone.*

A series of long dissolves between nature shots indicating the passage of time.

Int. living room—Dusk. ETHEL *is bustling about, excited, wearing her usual grubbies. She hangs a sign which reads, "Happy Birthday, Norman." On the wall across from it is one saying, "Welcome Home, Chelsea."*

Int. bedroom—Dusk. NORMAN *is standing at the mirror tying his tie. He scowls at his reflection and pulls at his collar, which seems oddly large for him. We hear the loons call.*

Ext. porch—Dusk. ETHEL *rushes to the door and pushes it. Down it falls.*

ETHEL. Oh, Norman, for God's sake.

She steps out, closing the big door, and moving the screen door. She rushes down to the dock.

Ext. dock—Dusk. ETHEL *stands at the end, in the golden glow of sunset.*

ETHEL. Yoo-hooo, loo-oons! Looony loo-oons! Yoo-hooo!

The loons answer. ETHEL *is delighted.*

Ext. widow's watch—Dusk. NORMAN *is standing on the balcony looking down at* ETHEL, *amused.*

NORMAN. I don't think you should do that in front of Chelsea's companion.
ETHEL. Oh, pooh, I'm just talking to my friends. My, my, look at you. You have on a tie.
NORMAN. Yes. I know. I put it there. Do I look all right? I haven't overdressed, have I?

ETHEL. You look sexy! I'm going to have to do some pretty fast maneuvers to catch up with you.

NORMAN. I have other ties. You could come as Miss Appley.

ETHEL. Thanks a lot.

She goes inside.

Int. living room—Evening. NORMAN *comes down the stairs.*

NORMAN. "Welcome Home, Chelsea." I see my birthday wasn't cause enough for a celebration.

ETHEL. Oh, stop. I just want our little girl to feel welcome, that's all.

NORMAN *(rechecking his tie at the hallway mirror).* Uh-huh.

ETHEL. Wouldn't it be nice if we could all get along this time.

NORMAN. Uh-huh. Where the hell are they? I'm getting older by the minute.

ETHEL. They said they'll be here when they get here.

NORMAN. Is that what they said? That's a hell of an attitude. No wonder we have no grandchildren.

ETHEL. What would we do with grandchildren?

NORMAN. Toss them on our knees. We're the last of the Thayers, you know. End of the line for a damn good name.

ETHEL. Well, we'll take it out in style.

Their attention is caught by the sound of a car. We see headlights through the window. NORMAN *and* ETHEL *look at each other.*

ETHEL *(continuing).* Oh, no! They're here! And I'm not dressed. I look like an old character.

NORMAN. Well, run upstairs and change if it makes you feel better.

ETHEL. Will you be nice to them?

NORMAN. Sure. I'll explain to them the risk involved in arriving late for an old man's birthday party.

We hear a voice calling.

CHELSEA *(o.s.).* Hey! Anybody home?

ETHEL. Too late!

ETHEL *opens the back door and rushes out.*

Ext. house—Evening. CHELSEA THAYER WAYNE *steps toward the house. She is forty-two, attractive, restless, with* NORMAN'S *humor. She grins at* ETHEL. *Behind her a car is turning around in the growing darkness.*

CHELSEA. Heeeey.

ETHEL *(stepping to her).* Hey yourself.

After the briefest pause they embrace.

CHELSEA. Mommy.

ETHEL. Dear little girl . . . Chelsea.

CHELSEA *looks to the house. We see* NORMAN *at the screen door peering out.* CHELSEA *walks up the steps and inside.* ETHEL *follows.*

Int. living room—Evening. CHELSEA *smiles at* NORMAN, *then steps to him and hugs him awkwardly. He is embarrassed, surprised. He tries to respond.* CHELSEA *steps back.*

CHELSEA. Hello, Norman. Happy birthday.

NORMAN. Look at you. Look at this little fat girl, Ethel.

CHELSEA, *who is not fat. looks quickly at her body.*

ETHEL. Oh, stop it. You're thin as a rail. Isn't she, Norman?

NORMAN. Oh, sure.

A moment of adjustment. ETHEL *jumps in.*

ETHEL. Dear Chelsea. I'm so glad you're home.

CHELSEA. I thought we'd never get here. We rented a car that explodes every forty miles.

NORMAN. You rented a car?

CHELSEA. Yes. In Boston.

NORMAN. Huh. What sort of car is it?

CHELSEA. Oh. I don't know. Red, I think.

ETHEL. Ooh! A red car!

NORMAN. No. I meant—what sort of make is it?

CHELSEA. Um. I don't know.

ETHEL. She doesn't know, dear. It doesn't matter.

NORMAN. Of course it doesn't matter. I was just curious.

CHELSEA. Well, I should have looked, I guess. It's um, very ugly, and it breaks down a lot.

NORMAN. Ugly and it breaks down a lot. That sounds like a Nash.

An awkward moment.

CHELSEA. Yeah. Well . . .

She looks about, smiles at her "Welcome Home" sign.

ETHEL *(stepping in).* Where's your friend? You did bring your friend, didn't you?

CHELSEA. I knew I was forgetting something.

She steps to the door.

NORMAN. That's still on then?

CHELSEA. As far as I know. (*she calls out*). Come on in, no one's going to bite you. Mommy and Norman, this is Billy Ray.

In walks BILLY RAY, *thirteen and sassy and full of life, a bit shy and defensive, lousy posture. He smiles.*

BILLY. How ya doin'?

He grabs NORMAN'S *hand.* NORMAN *stares at him, shocked at first.* ETHEL *loves it.*

NORMAN. You seem awfully young to be a dentist.
CHELSEA. This is Billy Ray, Jr.
NORMAN. Oh. I'm Norman Thayer, Jr. Where's . . . ?
CHELSEA. His father is out trying to park the car.
ETHEL (*taking* BILLY'S *hand*). Well, what a great surprise. You can call me Ethel, Billy, and you can call Norman Norman.
CHELSEA. I like your logic, Mommy. I'm going to see if Bill's driven into the lake.

She exits. ETHEL *steps to the door to watch.*

ETHEL. It's so dark outside. It never used to be this dark.

NORMAN *is staring down poor* BILLY.

BILLY. I hear you turned eighty today.
NORMAN. Is that what you heard?
BILLY. Yeah. That's really old.
NORMAN. Oh? You should meet my father.
BILLY. Your father's still alive?
NORMAN. No, but you should meet him.

ETHEL *steps to them.*

ETHEL. Isn't this fun? Norman, why don't we put Billy in Chelsea's old room and then he can look out at the lake in the morning.
NORMAN. Why don't we put him out on the float and he can look at the lake all night long.
BILLY. I'd like that.
ETHEL. I'm afraid you'd be eaten alive by all the bugs.
NORMAN. So?
ETHEL. Norman, take him up and we'll show him where everything is.
NORMAN. Come on, boy, grab your bag.

NORMAN *scowls at* ETHEL, *but leads* BILLY *upstairs.*

BILLY. I just had a birthday, too. I turned thirteen two weeks ago.
NORMAN. Oh? We're practically twins.

ETHEL *turns as* CHELSEA *enters.*

CHELSEA. He will be right here. He thought he had to lock the car.

ETHEL. I'm so glad you're here.
CHELSEA. Norman looks very old.
ETHEL. Well . . . I don't know.
CHELSEA (*quickly*). You look great though.
ETHEL. Thank you. So do you. I love your hair like that.
CHELSEA (*surprised, she touches her hair*). You do? Um. How's his mind? Is he remembering things any better?

NORMAN *has appeared on the landing. He stops when he hears this.*

ETHEL. Oh, he's all right.
NORMAN. Come on, Billy, I'll show you the bathroom, if I can remember where it is.

He disappears again. CHELSEA *looks at* ETHEL *and smiles.*

CHELSEA. He hasn't changed too much, has he?
ETHEL. Nope. Still impossible. It means so much to him to have you here.
CHELSEA. Yeah. Great. Now he's got someone to pick on.
ETHEL. Oh, stop. Thank you for coming.
CHELSEA. Thank you for inviting me.

BILL *enters carrying a load of suitcases.*

CHELSEA. Look at you. You made it. This is my mother. Mommy, Bill Ray.
ETHEL. How do you do?
BILL. Hi. I think I saw a bear.
ETHEL. Oh, you wouldn't have seen a bear out here this time of year. There *are* a lot of very nasty moths flying around, though.
BILL. This was kind of big for a moth.
CHELSEA. If you want a real scare you've got to meet my father.

BILLY *comes crashing down the stairs.* NORMAN *follows.*

BILLY. Dad, they do have indoor plumbing.
BILL. Oh. Good.
BILLY. Chelsea was just bullshitting us.
BILL. Billy!
CHELSEA (*to* ETHEL). I always try to paint a rustic picture of life on Golden Pond.
ETHEL. Oh, it's rustic all right.
BILL. It's lovely though. Lovely rusticity.

He looks up as NORMAN *approaches.*

NORMAN. We've been peeing indoors for forty years.
BILL. You must be Norman.
NORMAN. Yes, I must be. Who are you?
BILL. Bill Ray.
NORMAN. Bill Ray? The dentist?
BILL. Yes.

NORMAN. Want to see my teeth?

He bares them.

ETHEL. Norman!

BILL *(undaunted)*. I just want to tell you, sir, how glad I am to be here. Chelsea's told us so much about you and your wife and your wonderful house on the lake, and I'm very pleased she's brought us here.

This fine sentiment is greeted by a typical NORMAN *silence, which makes* BILL *feel like a bigger fool than he should.*

NORMAN. I'm frankly surprised Chelsea could find the way.

ETHEL. She's here now, Norman, that's the important thing.

NORMAN. Do you visit your folks, young man?

BILL. No. My parents have both passed away.

NORMAN. I see. Then you have a good excuse, don't you?

ETHEL *(sweetly)*. Norman . . .

CHELSEA. Norman. Please . . .

NORMAN. What? Am I not allowed to speak to our guest? Is that it? *(to* BILL*)*. They're afraid I'm going to embarrass them.

CHELSEA. Well. I'm going down and say hello to the lake. Anyone like to come?

BILLY. Me. I've never seen anyone say hello to a lake.

CHELSEA. Then this will be a valuable experience for you, wise guy. It's always my first order of business when I get to Golden Pond. Coming, Mommy?

ETHEL. Yes. Want to take the boat?

BILLY. All right!

CHELSEA. Let's go, Bill.

BILL. Where? Outside?

CHELSEA. That's where the lake is. Coming, Norman?

NORMAN. No. I think I'll just sit here and enjoy the quiet.

BILL *(quickly)*. I'll stay, too.

NORMAN. With Bill.

CHELSEA *and* ETHEL *exchange a glance.* CHELSEA *shrugs and opens the door.*

CHELSEA. The screen door's fallen down.

ETHEL. Really? Norman will fix it.

NORMAN *makes a face.* BILLY *follows the women outside leaving* NORMAN *staring at* BILL, *who feels more than a little uncomfortable.*

BILL. I love your house.

NORMAN. Thank you. It's not for sale.

BILL. Oh, no, I wasn't thinking about buying it, I just like it. It has a charming *ambience*.

A word he clearly likes using.

NORMAN *looks at him, less than impressed.* BILL *tries again.*

BILL *(continuing)*. How does it feel to turn eighty?

NORMAN *(scowling at him)*. It feels twice as bad as it did turning forty.

BILL. Well, I know what that's like. I turned forty five year ago. I'm forty-five now . . . *(pause)* . . . Norman.

NORMAN. Yes?

BILL. May I call you Norman?

NORMAN. I believe you just did.

BILL. I don't want to press. What shall I call your wife?

NORMAN. How about Ethel? That's her name. Ethel Thayer. Thounth like I'm lithping, doethn't it? Ethel Thayer. That almost kept her from marrying me. She wanted me to change my last name to hers.

BILL. What was that?

NORMAN. I don't remember. Ethel's all you need to know. That's the name she goes by.

BILL. I never knew. Chelsea always calls her Mommy.

NORMAN. There's a reason for that.

BILL. But she calls you Norman.

NORMAN. There's a reason for that, too, I *am* her father, but not her daddy. Ethel is her mommy, and I'm Norman.

BILL. Oh.

The conversation screeches to a halt. NORMAN *stands.*

NORMAN. I think I'll start a new book. See if I can finish it before I'm finished myself.

He steps to the shelves.

NORMAN *(continuing)*. Maybe a novelette. Maybe something out of *Reader's Digest Abridged*. Here's *Treasure Island*. Ever read it?

BILL. Yes, it's great. I'd recommend it.

NORMAN. No need for that. I've read it, too. But my mind is going so it'll all be new to me. Has that son of yours read this book?

BILL. I . . . don't think so.

NORMAN. Your son hasn't read *Treasure Island*?

BILL. No. But I intend to have him read it. His mother's been the real force in his life lately and now I'm trying to . . . eradicate some of the . . . dishevelment.

He looks to NORMAN *to see what sort of impression he's registered. None apparently.* NORMAN *has settled down and is reading his book.*

BILL *(continuing)*. Yeah, things are coming together pretty nicely for me now, and I'm feeling very good about myself. Meeting Chelsea was a major . . . thing. We have a very kinetic relationship, very positive. I'm sure you'd be pleased.

NORMAN *looks up from his book.*

NORMAN. What do you charge for a filling?
BILL. Huh?
NORMAN. You're a dentist, aren't you? What do you charge for a filling?
BILL. Um. Forty dollars, generally.
NORMAN. Forty dollars! Good God.

He returns to his book.

BILL. Um. Norman . . . *(quickly).* We'd like to sleep together if it's all right with you.
NORMAN. What do you mean?
BILL. We'd like to sleep together, in the same room, in the same bed, if you don't find that offensive.
NORMAN. All three of you?
BILL. Oh, no! Just two.
NORMAN. You and Billy?
NORMAN. Would you like the room where I first violated her mother, or would you be interested in the master bedroom?
BILL. Um . . .
NORMAN. Ethel and your son and I could all sleep out back and you could do it right here on the hearth. Like that idea?
BILL *(having heard enough)*. You're having a good time, aren't you?
NORMAN. Hmmmm?
BILL. Chelsea told me all about you, about how you like to have a good old time with people's heads. She does it, too, sometimes, and sometimes I can get into it, sometimes not. I just want you to know I'm very good at recognizing *crap* when I hear it. You know, it's not imperative that you and I be friends, but it might be *nice*. I'm sure you're a fascinating person, and I'm sure it would be fascinating to get to know you. That's obviously not an easy task. But, it's all right, you go ahead and be as *poopy* as you want, to quote Chelsea, and I'll be as receptive and pleasant as I can. I just want you to bear in mind while you're jerking me around and I'm feeling like a real asshole that I know precisely what you're up to and that I can take only so much of it. Okay? Good.

He pauses, waits for a reaction. NORMAN *has been listening very intently.*

BILL *(continuing)*. Now, what's the bottom line on the illicit sex question?
NORMAN. Very good. That was a good speech. Bottom line, huh? You're a bottom-line man. All right. Here's the bottom line: oh-kay.
BILL. Huh?
NORMAN. You seem like a nice man. A bit verbose perhaps, but nice.
BILL. Thank you.
NORMAN. And you're right about me. I *am* fascinating.
BILL. I'm sure you are.
NORMAN. Tell me something. What goes on in an kinetic relationship exactly? Other than what we've just discussed.
BILL. Oh, the usual. We play tennis, go out dancing, we talk to each other.
NORMAN. I've never taken Ethel dancing. I've always felt badly about that. I think she would have liked it, she's the type, you know.
BILL. It's not too late.
NORMAN. That's what you think. My mind and my body are having a great race to see who can poop out first. I'd put my money on the body, but you never know . . . Here, now, I didn't mean to weight down our conversation. Let's go back to talking about sex. Anything you want to know, just ask me.
BILL. Well, I do want to make sure I have this little matter clear. Chelsea and I *can* sleep together, right?
NORMAN. Sure. Please do. Just don't let Ethel catch you.

Now BILL *is right back to being confused.* BILLY *bounds in the door.*

BILLY. Dad! I paddled a canoe. It's a boat just like the Indians had.
NORMAN. Actually the Indians used a different grade of aluminum.
BILLY. Chelsea wants you to come down, Dad. She and Ethel *are going skinny-dipping.*
BILL. Skinny-dipping?
NORMAN. Go ahead. Permissiveness runs rampant here on Golden Pond.

BILL *heads for the door, stops.*

BILL. Oh . . . Are there any bears around these parts.
NORMAN. Oh, sure. Black bears and grizzlies. One came along here last month and ate an old lesbian.

BILL *looks a bit horrified.*

BILLY. Come on, Dad, he's bullshitting you.

With little confidence BILL *steps out.*

Ext. house—Night. BILL *tiptoes along the porch, down into the darkness. He's convinced there's a bear behind every tree. Suddenly he notices* BILLY *beside him.*

BILL. Where do you think you're going?

BILLY *(grinning)*. Skinny-dipping with Chelsea.

BILL. Oh no, you're not. You're going back in the house and talk to Mr. Thayer.

BILLY. Bullshit! I'm not goin' in there with that old turkey. He gives me the creeps. What if he dies.

BILL *(grabbing him)*. Listen, buster, you behave yourself. Do you understand? Or I'm going to send you right back to your mother. Is that what you want? . . . Is it?

BILLY *stands silent.*

BILL *(continuing)*. Now go on inside and talk to him, maybe you'll learn something.

BILLY *turns and walks back to the house. And* BILL *moves toward the lake. He stops when he hears the sound of* ETHEL *and* CHELSEA *skinny-dipping. Not quite ready to confront their nudity, he settles nervously in a lawn chair.*

Ext. lake—Night. ETHEL *and* CHELSEA *are indeed skinny-dipping. Their heads bob on the water.*

CHELSEA. Remember when I was about nine and I came down and caught you and Norman skinny-dipping.

ETHEL. No, I don't think I remember that.

CHELSEA. I had that big flashlight and I shone it on Norman when he was standing on the diving board all naked. Then he started screaming at me that I was a spy and he sent me to my room for the rest of the year or something. It took me a long time to get over *that.*

ETHEL. It took Norman a long time before he'd go skinny-dipping again. I remember. He wouldn't get out of the water until I went up and made sure you were asleep. I was so mad at him for yelling at you, I let him float down here for an hour or so.

CHELSEA. Good.

She and ETHEL *look at each other and laugh.*

Int. living room—Night. NORMAN *is watching* BILLY *who is pretending to be interested in the fish poles. A moment passes.*

BILLY. You going skinny-dipping?

NORMAN. Nope. You?

BILLY. Naw. I try to be selective about who I flash in front of.

NORMAN *(not following)*. Oh.

BILLY. Chelsea says you're a real heavy-duty fisherman. She calls you *the old man of the sea.*

NORMAN. Ah. I've caught a few. You fish?

BILLY. Nah.

NORMAN. Want to go sometime?

BILLY. I don't know . . .

NORMAN. Well . . . We'll see. What do you think of your father?

BILLY. He's not bad . . .

BILLY *and* NORMAN *state at each other a moment.*

NORMAN. Why do you stand with your shoulders all bent like that?

BILLY. I have a lot on my mind.

NORMAN. I see. What do you do out there in California? I mean, what does one do for recreation when one is thirteen and not in school?

BILLY. Cruise chicks.

NORMAN. Hmmm?

BILLY. Meet 'em. Girls. Try to pick them up.

NORMAN. And what do you do with them when you have them?

BILLY. Suck face.

NORMAN. I beg your pardon?

BILLY. You know—kiss. Suck face—kiss.

NORMAN. Oh.

He looks from BILLY *to the book, which he stills holds.*

NORMAN *(continuing)*. Have you ever read this book, *Treasure Island*?

BILLY. No.

NORMAN. Go read it.

BILLY. Now?

NORMAN. Go on. Read the first chapter and give me a report on it in the morning.

BILLY. I thought we were going to have a party.

NORMAN. I'll call you when the party's underway, if it ever is. Go on.

BILLY *looks at* NORMAN *sideways. But there's something in* NORMAN's *authority that* BILLY *responds to favorably.*

Ext. house—Night. BILL *is still seated on the lawn chair.* ETHEL *steps the bank, dressed in a robe.*

ETHEL. Hey.

BILL *(startled)*. Acch!

ETHEL. Come on down, dear. Chelsea's still in the water. No one should ever skinny-dip alone.

She leads him toward the dock. He stops, scared.

BILL. What's that?

ETHEL. That's a lawn chair. Come on.

Int. living room—Night. NORMAN *looks up casually as* ETHEL *enters.*

ETHEL. Well, we've got Bill in the swim of things.

NORMAN. I thought you'd be nude.

ETHEL. Nope. Sorry. I didn't want to overwhelm our guest on his first night. He's nice isn't he?

NORMAN. Yes. Forty dollars a filling.

ETHEL. Forty dollars?

NORMAN. That's enough to keep you off sweets.

ETHEL. He'd be quite a catch wouldn't he?

NORMAN. He said they wanted to sleep together.

ETHEL. Why not? They're big people.

NORMAN. Yes.

ETHEL. You and I did didn't we?

NORMAN. Did we?

ETHEL. Have you been picking on him?

NORMAN. Yes. He finds me fascinating.

ETHEL. I'm sure.

She sits on the arm of his chair.

ETHEL *(continuing; proceeding carefully).* Norman. Norman, Chelsea wants us to do something. For her. She wants to leave Billy with us for a month.

NORMAN. Which Billy?

ETHEL. Tsk. The little one. Billy. Bill is supposed to have him for the summer and he'd be miserable in Europe. Bill seems very nice, and Chelsea needs someone nice. Couldn't we do that for her?

NORMAN. What would we do with the boy? What would I say to him?

ETHEL. You'd think of something. Let's do it. Let's say we'll do it and give Chelsea some happiness.

NORMAN *looks fully prepared to say no, but he nods.*

NORMAN. All right.

ETHEL. You're such a poop. We're going to have a splendid time, the three of us, aren't we?

NORMAN. I don't know. We might.

ETHEL. You really are the sweetest man in the world. And I'm the only one who knows.

Int. living room—Closeup—Cake with candles. Widen as ETHEL *carries a beautiful candle-covered cake to the table.* ETHEL, CHELSEA, BILLY *and* BILL *sing to* NORMAN:

ETHEL, BILLY, CHELSEA AND BILL. Happy birthday, dear Norman, Happy birthday to you.

NORMAN *hates it. But he's pleased. He rises, takes a deep breath and blows out the candles. Everyone applauds.*

NORMAN. I suppose you expect *me* to sing something now. Well, I'm not about to. I've been trying all day to draw some profound conclusion about living four score years. And I haven't thought of anything. I'm surprised I got here so fast. *(he looks at* ETHEL*).* But I am glad I got to spend so much time with this beautiful woman. What's your name again?

He smiles as ETHEL *shakes her head. He turns to the others.*

NORMAN *(continuing).* And I certainly want to thank all of your people for coming all the way here from Disneyland to witness this historic event.

Ext. Thayer dock—Day. BILL *stands in his designer jeans and Lacoste shirt and Adidas, proudly watching* CHELSEA *backstroking smoothly toward the float.* CHARLIE's *boat appears.*

Ext. float—Day. CHELSEA *climbs onto the float and waves as* CHARLIE *pulls alongside. They look at each other for a moment.*

CHARLIE. Well, Holy Mackinoly. Look at you. Chelsea Mackinelsea.

CHELSEA. Charlie Mackinarlie.

CHARLIE *(laughing).* Doy, it's good to see you. You've held up good.

CHELSEA. Thanks. So have you.

She turns to BILL *and shouts.*

CHELSEA *(continuing).* Bill, this is my old friend, Charlie, the mailman.

BILL. Hi, there.

CHARLIE. Hullo.

CHARLIE *reaches his hand to* CHELSEA.

CHARLIE *(continuing).* Want a ride?

CHELSEA *smiles and steps into the boat. They move slowly toward the dock.*

BILL *(smiles).* So, you actually deliver the mail by boat. What an incredible tradition.

CHELSEA. Charlie is a legend on this lake. He gets the mail through no matter what. Isn't that right, Charlie?

CHARLIE. Yuh, I guess so.

BILL *(gazing out at the lake)*. It must be a bitch in the winter.

Now CHARLIE *laughs and brings the boat to a smooth stop by the dock.*

CHARLIE. Oh, yuh, in the winter I have a hell of a time. Of course there's nobody on the lake to deliver to so I get done a lot faster.

BILL *puts a foot up on* CHARLIE'*s boat.*

BILL. You've got a great setup here. Well, you're a lucky man.

He helps CHELSEA *from the boat.*

CHARLIE *(looking at* CHELSEA*)*. You're a lucky man, too.
BILL. Yes, I guess I am.

The bow of the boat is now drifting from the dock. BILL *finds himself being stretched.*

BILL *(continuing)*. Um. What do you do at a time like this?
CHARLIE. I generally just fall into the lake.
BILL. Oh, yes.

And he does. CHARLIE *and* CHELSEA *laugh.* CHELSEA *pulls* BILL *to her and kisses him.* CHARLIE *watches, interested.*

Int. living room—Night. NORMAN, ETHEL, BILL *and* BILLY *are playing Parcheesi.* CHELSEA *sits across the room scanning the newspaper.* BILL *rolls the dice.*

BILL. Two threes. What does that mean?
NORMAN *(patronizing)*. It means doubles. Which always gives you 14, you see.
BILL. Oh. Okay. *(he moves)*. 7, 12, 13, 14. Right? I seem to have landed where you are. What does that mean?
NORMAN. It means you send me home and you get 20 more, for God's sake.
BILLY. All right, Dadders!
BILL. That's good, huh?
ETHEL. Excellent. You're a natural.
NORMAN. I'm starting to regret teaching you this game.
BILL. Hey, Chels, I'm a Parcheesi pro.

CHELSA *nods.*

NORMAN. Chelsea has never liked playing games. We don't know why. Probably she doesn't like losing.
CHELSEA. I tend to panic when the competition is too intense.
NORMAN. And what is that supposed to mean?
CHELSEA. Nothing.

ETHEL *(trying to keep it light)*. We play serious Parcheesi around here. I let Norman win every week or so to keep up his spirits.
NORMAN. Ha, ha, ha.
CHELSEA *(her goat gotten, she challenges* NORMAN*)*. What I want to know is why do you *like* playing games?
NORMAN. What?
CHELSEA. You seem to like beating people. I just wonder why.

NORMAN *and* CHELSEA *glare at each other, until he at last turns and smiles at* BILL.

NORMAN. You get another chance, Bill. You get another roll of the dice.

\ *Ext. gazebo—Dawn. Mist hovers over the lake in the early morning light.* CHELSEA *sits wrapped in a blanket, staring at the lake.* ETHEL *steps down the bank in her robe, two cups of coffee in her hands. She watches a moment.*

ETHEL. Having fun? That's why you came to camp—to have fun.

CHELSEA *tries to smile.*

ETHEL *(continuing)*. What's the matter with you?
CHELSEA. Nothing.

She looks at the lake; a moment passes.

CHELSEA *(continuing)*. I don't think I've ever grown up on Golden Pond. Do you understand?
ETHEL *(trying to)*. I don't think so.
CHELSEA. It doesn't matter. I act like a big person everywhere else. I'm in charge of Los Angeles; but I come back here and I feel like a little fat girl.
ETHEL. It's only because your father said that.
CHELSEA. My father is a goddam bastard . . . poop!
ETHEL *(automatic reflex)*. Watch your language, young lady.
CHELSEA. Are you going to make me wash my mouth out with soap? That was a rather bizarre custom. Do you know that I have spent my whole life answering to Norman? Even when I'm 3,000 miles away and never see him, I still find myself answering to him. *(really mad now, she shouts)*. Norman is a goddam poop!
ETHEL. Oh, for Lord's sake. Here we go again. You had a miserable childhood. Your father was overbearing, your mother ignored you. What else is new? You have this unpleasant chip on your shoulder which is very unattractive. You stay away for years at a time. You only come home when I beg you to and

then all you can do is be disagreeable about the past. What is the point? Don't you think everyone looks back on his childhood with some bitterness or regret about something? It doesn't have to ruin your life. You are a big girl now, aren't you tired of it all? . . . Life marches by, Chelsea. I suggest you get on with it.

ETHEL *turns and marches up the bank, leaving* CHELSEA *to sit alone, staring at the lake.*

Ext. house—Day. BILL *is setting the suitcases into the trunk.* NORMAN, ETHEL *and* BILLY *and* CHELSEA *stand nearby.*

ETHEL. Have a wonderful time. And don't worry. Billy will take good care of us.
CHELSEA. Okay.
NORMAN. Don't go getting involved with any foreigners.
CHELSEA. Right.
BILL *(to* BILLY). You gonna be all right?
BILLY. Oh sure.
BILL *(hugging* BILLY). Behave yourself.
BILLY. Okay. You guys behave, too.
CHELSEA. Okay.

She kisses BILLY.

BILL. 'Bye Norman. Work on your Parcheesi game.
NORMAN. Ha, ha, ha.
CHELSEA. Good luck, everybody.

The car drives down the lane, everyone waving. BILLY *turns to* NORMAN *and* ETHEL.

BILLY. I just want you guys to know I'm not about to take any crap from you.

He heads for the lake. NORMAN *looks at* ETHEL.

Ext. lake—Day. BILLY *picks up a pine cone and tosses it at a tree.* ETHEL *surveys the situation and opts for something decisive.*

ETHEL. All right, gentlemen. It's a beautiful day. We're going fishing.
NORMAN. What? Doing what?
ETHEL. Fishing, dear. You remember fishing. Come on, you can show Billy what life is all about on Golden Pond. Come on, Billy.
BILLY. Bull—shit.
ETHEL *(stopping)*. Does that mean you can't wait to get out there or it's not your cup of tea?
BILLY. It's bullshit. That's all. I'll do what I want to do when I want to do it. Okay?
ETHEL *(nodding)*. Come on, Norman. Let's get ready.

She marches up the steps and into the house. NORMAN *follows. He stops.*

NORMAN. You like that word, don't you? Bullshit.
BILLY. Yeah.
NORMAN *(thinking about it)*. It's a good word.

He continues into the house.

Int. master bedroom—Day. NORMAN *is making a great production out of donning his old fishing vest, examining himself in the mirror.* ETHEL *has changed her clothes and sits at her vanity, putting on her hat. In her mirror she sees* BILLY *coming up the stairs.*

ETHEL *(whispering)*. Okay, Grandpa. Do your stuff.

NORMAN *looks from* ETHEL *to the doorway as* BILLY *appears.*

NORMAN. Pretty slick, huh?

BILLY *shrugs.* NORMAN *reaches into the closet, pulls out another smaller fishing vest and throws it on the bed.*

NORMAN *(continuing)*. Look at this. This was Chelsea's when she was about your age. She caught some pretty respectable fish wearing this.
BILLY. I'm surprised you kept it if it's Chelsea's. Since you obviously don't like her.
BILLY *(continuing)*. Hey, you know, uh, I might not stick around here. I might just haul my ass out to Wyoming or Puerto Rico or one of those places.

NORMAN *and* ETHEL *share a look.*

BILLY *(continuing)*. Listen, I mean, I know I'm just being *dumped* here, which is like my middle name. You turkeys don't *want* me.
NORMAN. Bullshit. *(pause)*. I'm 67 years older than you. How do you know what I want.
BILLY. Well . . . you didn't say. If you don't *say*, how's anybody supposed to know anything?

NORMAN *stares at him a moment, his feelings hit.*

NORMAN. Okay. We're going fishing now. We *want* you to go along. If you *want* to come with us, I suggest you get your ass down to the dock in two minutes. Okay, Mrs. Turkey, let's go.

ETHEL *takes his arm and they walk out of the room.*

Ext. dock—Day. ETHEL *is sitting in the boat.* NORMAN *stands holding it. He looks up at the house, waiting. He nods when* BILLY *comes sauntering down, wearing* CHELSEA's *fishing vest, and carrying one of* NORMAN's *hats.*

BILLY. I thought I just might sort of come along and see what this bullshit is all about.

BILLY *climbs in and* NORMAN *starts the motor.* ETHEL *turns to* BILLY.

ETHEL. You look very handsome in that vest.

BILLY *is embarrassed, but pleased. He pulls the hat down over his eyes, playing it cool.*

BILLY. How fast does this old tub go anyway?

NORMAN *scowls at him, then revs the engine. The Thayer Four zooms away, sending* BILLY *sprawling. He grins.*

BILLY *(continuing).* All right!

Ext. Lake – Day. NORMAN, BILLY, ETHEL *in the Thayer Four.* NORMAN *has his fishing gear spread before him.* BILLY *holds a pole, looking almost interested.* NORMAN *hands* BILLY *a worm.* ETHEL *holds a parasol and book and tries to be interested.*

NORMAN. All right. Hold this.

BILLY *takes it, not without some trepidation.*

NORMAN *(continuing).* That's a worm.
BILLY. I guess I know that.
NORMAN. Good. Just don't tell the fish. As far as they're concerned that's filet mignon. Now. Put it on your hook.

BILLY *thinks about it, then drapes the worm over the curve of the hook.*

NORMAN *(continuing).* This is not going to be easy. Here's what you do. You start with the worm's head. You can tell this is the head because he's smiling at you, see? And you slowly stick the hook into the guy's neck and work it up through the body.

BILLY *watches, horrified.*

BILLY. Gross me out.

Ext. lake – Day. NORMAN *is busily concentrating on his fishing.* BILLY *watches him and mimics his demeanor. He sits perfectly still and scowls at the water.*

ETHEL. Why is it taking so long, Norman?

NORMAN *glares at her incredulously. Suddenly* BILLY's *pole is bent.*

BILLY. Norman! What's going on!
NORMAN. You've got a bite.
ETHEL. Ooh! A bite! How wonderful!

BILLY. What do you mean?
NORMAN. A fish is biting your worm.

BILLY. No shit. Here.

He passes the pole to NORMAN, *who passes it back to him.*

NORMAN. Bring it in. The fish! Bring it in!

BILLY *panics. He sets down the pole and begins pulling in the line, hand over hand.*

NORMAN *(continuing).* With the reel, for God's sake!

Now BILLY *reels in.*

BILLY. This is San Frantastic.

He cranks like mad and at last brings out of the water a small but mighty sunfish.

BILLY *(continuing).* Hey, wow. Look at that. I caught that. Me. I caught a fish. Can you believe it?
ETHEL. It's wonderful, Billy. Congratulations.
NORMAN *(unimpressed).* It's only a sunfish.
BILLY. Only a sunfish! This is a beautiful fish, man. Look at it.

He swings the fish through the air, and hits NORMAN's *face, a move which goes unappreciated.* NORMAN *grabs the fish, unhooks it and throws it back into the lake.* BILLY *is horrified.*

BILLY. What are you doin', man?
NORMAN. I don't allow sunfish in my home. We're looking for trout, boy.

BILLY *looks stricken.*

ETHEL. Oh, well, don't worry about it, dear, there are plenty more where that one came from. Aren't there, Norman?
NORMAN. How the hell would I know? I think we should go in!
ETHEL. Norman . . .
NORMAN *(firmly).* We'll go in. Now!

He starts reeling in. BILLY *looks a bit hurt.*

ETHEL. Well, there'll be plenty of other chances to go fishing, won't there, Norman?
NORMAN. Maybe.

Ext. lake – Dawn. Fish are breaking the surface of the lake in early morning feeding.

Ext. house – Day (early morning). NORMAN *trudges down to the dock where he's surprised to find* BILLY *waiting with the boat ready.*

BILLY. Let's go, Captain Turkey. Look out, fish, here we come!
NORMAN. Shhh. You'll wake up the old lady.

But BILLY *gestures with his head and we see* ETHEL *walk down the bank carrying her sewing basket and her old doll.*

NORMAN *(continuing).* Oh, well. Look at you. You're not coming with us, are you?
ETHEL. No. You don't have to worry. You two go on and have a good time, and don't be mean to the fish.
NORMAN. All right. Goodbye, woman.

NORMAN *starts the engine and the boat speeds away from the back.*

Ext. dock—Day (morning). ETHEL *sits with Elmer. She watches the boat move in the distance through her binoculars, then begins sewing the doll.*

ETHEL. Well, Elmer, looks like we've been deserted. *(she pauses, looks at the doll wistfully).* Remember how we used to sit down here and wait for Dad and watch the fishing boats from Golden Pond Hotel. And they'd ring the bell to call them in for supper. All gone, Elmer. That time is all gone . . . They say the lake is dying, but I don't believe it . . . Remember how I used to sit you down here on the dock, Elmer, when I'd head off to Camp Koochakiyi, when I was a little girl? And I'd wave goodbye, and you always waved back, didn't you, Elmer?
(she sings).

> I can see the birds
> Way up in the sky
> From my tent on the bank
> Of the lake
> At Camp Koochakiyi,
> Camp Koochakiyi,

(she thinks about it).
What a terrible song.

Ext. lake—Day. BILLY *and* NORMAN *sit silently fishing.*

BILLY. I don't think there's any trout in this lake.

NORMAN *stares at the boy, thinking hard.*

NORMAN. Can I trust you to keep a secret?
BILLY. Yeah.
NORMAN. If I take you to a certain place on this lake where the trout are humungus, will you promise not to tell anybody?
BILLY. Who'm I gonna tell?
NORMAN. Promise?
BILLY. Okay. I promise. No bullshit.
NORMAN. All right. Pull up the anchor.

NORMAN *is very serious about this. He sets down his gear and starts the boat.*

Ext. lake—Day. The Thayer Four cruises along a deserted stretch of lake, swings in a circle, then stops. NORMAN *looks about to ensure that no one has followed them.* BILLY *looks about, too, skeptical.*

BILLY. This is it?
NORMAN. This is it. *(NORMAN and BILLY prepare to fish).* You have to be patient when you fish for trout, boy. There is a trout living in this cove, who weighs ten pounds if he weighs an ounce. I first saw him four or five years ago, and I hooked him two years ago, and last year, too, but he's . . . *(he yells at the water)* a crafty old son-of-a-bitch! *(to the trout)* This is your last chance, Walter! I named him Walter because he reminds me of Ethel's brother, because . . . *(to the fish)* he's fat and lazy and ugly! *(BILLY loves all this.* NORMAN *nods at him).* Where's your line? Are you on the bottom? If your line's floating you're on the bottom, and that won't do you any good. Bring it up, bring it up, for Christ's sake.
BILLY. Okay, man, don't yell at me! Who do you think you are, Long John Silver?
NORMAN. I'm sorry.
BILLY. It's okay.

They sit for a minute. NORMAN *looks at* BILLY, *searching for something to say.*

NORMAN. You having fun?
BILLY. Yeah.
NORMAN. That's good. Now isn't this better than "cruising chicks"?
BILLY. No.
NORMAN. No, I suppose not. *(he thinks about it).* You planning on getting married one of these days?
BILLY. No way, Jose. I just want to suck face, man.

NORMAN *nods. He fiddles with his line, thinking he has a bite, deciding he doesn't.*

BILLY *(continuing).* How old were you the first time you did it with Ethel?
NORMAN. I beg your pardon? Did what?
BILLY. You know what I'm talking about.

NORMAN *stares at* BILLY, *trying to think of an answer.*

NORMAN. It's not a good idea to talk too much out here. Scare the fish away. If the sons of bitches are even here.

NORMAN *looks around, irritated. Suddenly we hear the putt-putt of a small outboard motor.*

ETHEL *(o.s.) whistles a greeting.*

NORMAN *and* BILLY *turn to see* ETHEL *approaching in their skiff.*

NORMAN. For God's sake! What the hell are you doing here?
ETHEL *(holding up a basket).* Shhh . . . I brought you lunch.

ETHEL *paddles to them.*

NORMAN. How the hell did you find us?
ETHEL. Shhh . . . you'll scare the fish.
BILLY *(whispering).* This is supposed to be a secret fishing place.
ETHEL. Just a lucky guess.

She smiles and holds out the basket.

NORMAN. We don't need any lunch. We've got more important things going on here.
ETHEL. Take the basket, you poop. Billy might be hungry.

ETHEL *sets the basket into the boat.*

ETHEL *(continuing).* Have a nice lunch. I'll see you both later.
NORMAN. Goodbye!
BILLY. Thanks, Ethel.

She starts the motor and moves off. NORMAN *casually opens the basket.*

NORMAN. Might as well see what she brought.

The two of them set down their poles and attack the sandwiches voraciously. A moment passes while they feast. Suddenly NORMAN'S *pole is bent double and yanked into the air. He lunges and grabs it just in time.*

NORMAN *(continuing).* Ah ha. Ah *ha!* Hold on, you son of a bitch!

We see the trout break the water, flipping in the air.

NORMAN *(continuing).* He's not Walter, but he's related. *(to the fish)* He's an ugly old son of a bitch!

NORMAN *is now standing, reeling like mad.* BILLY *stands, too, thrilled.*

NORMAN *(continuing).* Get the net, boy! We're going to have trout for dinner tonight.

He pulls the large fish out of the water.

NORMAN *(continuing).* Get the net under him. That a boy.

BILLY *nets the trout a 3-pounder.*

NORMAN. *This* is a trout. See? A rainbow trout.

NORMAN *is genuinely excited. He punches* BILLY.

NORMAN *(continuing).* Good work, kid.

Int. dining room—Dusk. ETHEL *enters with a platter, on which lies the trout all cooked and yummy looking. She sets it down in front of her two tired fishermen.*

NORMAN. Well, look what you've done. Look at what this beautiful woman has done, Billy.
BILLY. San frantastic.
ETHEL. Did you boys have a good time out there today?
BILLY. It was a trip.
NORMAN. He's right. It was a trip.
ETHEL *(smiling).* Well, that's good. Isn't it?

Ext. float—Day. BILLY *is perched backwards at the end of the diving board.* NORMAN *sits in the canoe nearby.* ETHEL *is swimming a circle around them on an air mattress.*

NORMAN *(rather strongly).* Now go *up* this time, not just back. *Up* and back. Come on.

BILLY *looks hesitant.*

NORMAN *(continuing).* Come on, there's nothing to be scared of. The back flip is one of the *easiest* dives.
BILLY. Then you do it.

NORMAN *looks challenged. He starts peeling off his shirt.*

ETHEL *(from the water).* Norman Thayer, stay where you are!

He scowls at ETHEL. BILLY *loves it. He covers his mouth and pretends to giggle.*

NORMAN. Dive, boy.

BILLY *does. He goes up all right, but doesn't turn all the way. He lands rather face-first. He surfaces and punches the water.*

BILLY. Ouch! *(sounding like* NORMAN*).* For God's sake!
NORMAN. That wasn't it.
BILLY. Thanks for telling me.

BILLY *climbs back up on the float.* ETHEL *swims alongside the canoe.*

ETHEL. Norman, we're going to have him for a month. I don't think you should kill him the first week.

NORMAN *scowls at her.*

Ext. house—Late afternoon. NORMAN *is sitting on a chair watching* BILLY *clean an enor-*

mous pile of fish. ETHEL *can be seen in the b.g. gathering kindling. They all wear sweaters.*

BILLY. We caught eight million fish. Are you sure none of these is Walter?

NORMAN. Yep. Walter is humungus! Those fish you got there are just little mothas.

BILLY. Well, they're disgusting little mothas.

NORMAN. You got something against fish guts boy?

BILLY *makes a face.*

BILLY. Can I ask you something? How did you get Ethel anyway?

NORMAN. What? I sent away for her. Two box tops from Quaker Oats.

BILLY. Don't bullshit me man . . .

NORMAN. I met Ethel when I was a principal and she was a substitute teacher. She was about the prettiest thing I'd ever seen. So I told her she made my heart go pitter-pat. She fell in love with me immediately.

ETHEL, *having overheard the end of* NOR-MAN'S *conversation, moves forward carrying a bunch of kindling.*

ETHEL. Hah! . . .

BILLY. Is that really the way Norman got you Ethel?

ETHEL. Don't be silly. Norman didn't get me at all, I won him in a contest. He was the booby prize! Has he got you cleaning those stupid fish?

NORMAN. That's right . . . he cleans the stupid ones and I clean the smart ones. Fortunately, the smart ones are too smart to get caught. That's why they're in schools . . . Ha, ha, ha!

ETHEL *and* BILLY *share a look. She hands* NORMAN *the kindling.*

ETHEL. Come in Norman and get a fire going. It's going to be a bit nippy tonight.

NORMAN *extends the kindling to* BILLY.

NORMAN. Do you hear that boy . . . get a fire going!

ETHEL. For God's sake Norman, Billy doesn't have to do all your chores.

NORMAN *shakes his head as he walks to the house with the wood.*

NORMAN. What is the point of having a dwarf if he doesn't do chores?

ETHEL *now shakes her head and looks at* BILLY *who smiles.*

Int. living room—Late Afternoon. NORMAN *is methodically lighting a fire, a pile of newspapers on the hearth beside him.* BILLY *enters carrying a fish bucket as* NORMAN *struggles to light a match.*

NORMAN. Damn it.

BILLY *(whispering).* Got the matches backwards. Want me to do it?

NORMAN. I think I know how to light a fire, for Christ's sake!

BILLY *shrugs. Sets down the bucket and steps onto the porch.*

Now NORMAN *has the paper ignited. He fans the fire and stands and watches it with satisfaction. He looks around for* BILLY. *Heads for the porch.*

Ext. porch—Late afternoon. BILLY *sits reading as* NORMAN *steps out.*

NORMAN. What are you reading?

BILLY *(not looking up).* A Tale Of Two Cities.

NORMAN. Ah . . . Tres bien, tres bien.

NORMAN *looks at* BILLY *for a moment trying to think of something to say. Suddenly,* ETHEL *yells from inside.*

ETHEL *(o.s.).* Norman, for God's sake! You've set the house on fire!

Pandemonium as NORMAN *and* BILLY *rush inside.*

Int. living room—Late afternoon. The newspapers on the hearth are ablaze. ETHEL *is frantically trying to stomp out the flames.*

NORMAN. What the hell is going on?

ETHEL. Get a bucket Norman!

NORMAN. What?

But BILLY *races by him and grabs the fish bucket. He throws the water and the clean fish onto the fire, extinguishing it.*

NORMAN. For God's sake! You made a hell of a mess!

BILLY. What? Don't yell at me man.

ETHEL *(overlapping).* Norman!

NORMAN. I guess it's not safe to have me around here is it? *(he looks to* BILLY*).* What are you staring at me for? You little son of a bitch!

BILLY *looks ready to punch him. Instead, he storms out, knocking down the screen door.* NORMAN *marches up the stairs, leaving* ETHEL *to look after them both, upset. She bends and returns the fish to the bucket, then steps to the stairway, and calls:*

ETHEL. Norman. I'd still appreciate your making a fire when you get a chance.

No answer. She steps outside.

Ext. dock—Late afternoon. BILLY *stands staring at the lake, troubled.* ETHEL *comes down the bank.*

ETHEL. You mustn't let Norman upset you, dear.

BILLY. Sure.

ETHEL. He is not yelling at you . . . you know.

BILLY. It sounds like he is yelling at me.

ETHEL. No. He is yelling at life.

BILLY. What the heck does that mean?

ETHEL. Well, he's like an old lion. And he has to remind himself that he can still roar.

BILLY. Oh.

ETHEL. Sometimes you have to look hard at a person and remember that he is doing the best he can. He is just trying to find his way. That's all. Just like you.

BILLY *stands silently for a moment, thinking.*

BILLY. You could come out fishing with us anytime, you know. If you get lonely.

ETHEL. Well, no, I've never liked fishing. It always seemed like the dead fish were staring at me.

BILLY. We don't just fish, you know.

ETHEL. No?

BILLY. Nope. We have a pretty good old time. Norman makes me practice my French, and I make him tell me stories. We've got a real kinetic thing going.

ETHEL. That's wonderful.

BILLY. Oh, yeah. And you don't have to worry about him. I keep an eye on him.

ETHEL *smiles.*

Int. living room—Night. NORMAN *is fastidiously minding the fire, anything flammable moved well out of danger. He looks at* ETHEL *and* BILLY, *who sit reading.*

NORMAN. Um. Did you want to play Parcheesi, or not? . . . It's all right, we don't have to.

ETHEL *and* BILLY *look at him, amused.*

NORMAN *(continuing).* Unless you want to. It doesn't matter. If you'd rather not play a game. It's not important.

ETHEL *and* BILLY *look at each other and smile.*

ETHEL. Set it up, buster, and prepare to lose your shirt.

Ext. gazebo—Early Evening. ETHEL *is busily crocheting. She feels something and brushes at her neck . . . then again. We see* NORMAN *behind the gazebo railing. A mischievous look in his eye and he tickles* ETHEL *with a long piece of grass. She grins.*

ETHEL. Oh, Norman. For God's sake.

NORMAN. How is my little Petunia?

She looks at him surprised, but pleased. BILLY *calls from the dock.*

BILLY. Hey, I was wondering if I could take a little spin in the Thayer Four.

NORMAN. Absolutely not.

BILLY. I know how to drive.

ETHEL. I think it would be all right. Don't you, Norman?

NORMAN. Good God! Can you be careful.

BILLY. Oh sure!

He hops into the boat. NORMAN *climbs up over the gazebo rail.*

ETHEL. Norman!

NORMAN *sits beside her and puts his arm around her.*

ETHEL *(continuing).* Well it has finally happened. You have lost your marbles.

Ext. lake—Early evening. BILLY *drives the Thayer Four away from the house, straight out past the point and out of sight.*

Ext. lake—Early evening. BILLY *drives the boat in great looping circles and figure eights, cutting and weaving, bouncing wildly on the waves, having a marvelous time.*

Int. living room—Day. ETHEL *scowls as* NORMAN *loads fishing gear onto an already overburdened* BILLY.

NORMAN. I'll get the rest . . .

He picks up a small net and exits. ETHEL *shakes her head.*

ETHEL. You two will be sorry. The loons have been calling for rain all night. "Rain, rain, send us the rain."

BILLY. That's what the loons said? Huh?

He smiles and shakes his head. We hear NORMAN *call:*

NORMAN *(o.s.).* Allons, debut!

BILLY. Je viens! *(to* ETHEL*).* That's French, you know. It means, "I'm coming."

ETHEL. Ah. I'll get la porte.

She carefully opens the screen door and is amazed to discover its hinges are operable.

ETHEL *(continuing)*. I don't believe it!

BILLY. Yeah . . . Norman and I fixed the mutha.

Ext. dock—Day. NORMAN *waits impatiently in the boat as* ETHEL *and* BILLY *trudge down with their loads.* ETHEL *casts a wary look at the sky.*

NORMAN. Hey, boy, grab my chair, would you?

ETHEL. Norman. For God's sake, his hands are full.

NORMAN. So? He's got teeth, doesn't he?

ETHEL. Norman, get the chair.

Grumbling, NORMAN *does. He and* BILLY *pile into the boat.*

ETHEL *(continuing)*. You two be careful out there. And don't be gone long, or you'll miss dinner.

NORMAN. Then we'll just have to eat raw fish like the Orientals do. *(to* BILLY*)* Of course you'll never get any taller. *(to* ETHEL*)* Goodbye, woman.

BILLY. Goodbye, woman.

They motor away from the dock.

Ext. lake—Late afternoon. The sky is growing dark as the Thayer Four cuts across the water. NORMAN *stops the boat at the entrance to a rocky cove.*

NORMAN. This is about the only place we haven't looked for this stupid son a bitch fish. We might as well give it a try, huh?

He turns the boat and slowly maneuvers into the cove.

NORMAN *(continuing)*. They call this Purgatory Cove, boy. See those rocks? They eat boats.

BILLY *looks around skeptically.*

BILLY. Do you know the way?

NORMAN. Of course I know the way. I've been on this lake 48 years, for Christ's sake. Now you get up on the deck and tell me where the rocks are.

BILLY *does, with some trepidation.* NORMAN *moves the boat forward slowly and carefully.*

BILLY. Um. There's a rock coming up, Norman.

NORMAN. Which side?

BILLY. Uh, right!

NORMAN. Starboard, boy.

BILLY. Okay, starboard.

NORMAN *turns the boat.*

BILLY. Another one. On the left. Um. Shit. *Port!*

NORMAN *turns the boat. Now they are into the cove. We see rocks breaking the surface, or lying green and ominous just below. The boat zig zags along as* BILLY *shouts directions.*

BILLY. Port! Port. Starboard. No, port!

At last they reach the center of the cove, and NORMAN *cuts the motor.*

NORMAN. Now doesn't this look like the ideal hiding place for a *(he shouts)* crafty old son of a bitch?

BILLY *looks around at the cove, still and eerie looking in the fading light.*

NORMAN *(continuing)*. Well? The fish aren't going to just jump up into the boat, you know, Get it in gear, turkey.

BILLY *readies his fish pole. He and* NORMAN *sit fishing quietly, reflecting the somberness of the weather.* NORMAN *looks at the sky pensively.*

NORMAN *(continuing)*. It's getting dark, Chelsea.

BILLY. Who you calling Chelsea? I'm Billy. Come on, man.

NORMAN *looks at him, nods.*

BILLY *(continuing)*. Are you okay?

NORMAN. Of course I'm okay.

BILLY. Okay. We better hurry up and catch Walter, huh? I'm not going to be here much longer.

NORMAN. Neither am I.

BILLY. I'll miss you, Norman.

NORMAN. What?

BILLY. Life really sucks sometimes, doesn't it?

They grow quiet again, each lost in his thoughts. BILLY *idly cranks his reel and feels something pulling on his line.*

BILLY *(continuing)*. Norman! Shit! I got the mutha! I got him!

He cranks like mad, while NORMAN *watches.*

BILLY *(continuing)*. Get the net, Norman! Get it in gear, turkey!

NORMAN *grabs the net. He stands by while* BILLY *excitedly reels in, struggling with his catch. He peers over the side.*

BILLY *(continuing)*. What the heck is that?

BILLY *reaches into the water and pulls out the body of a loon, obviously dead for some time.*

BILLY *(continuing)*. Good God. It's a dead loon, Norman. The poor thing. *(he makes a face)* Phew! It stinks, too.

But he stands staring at it, fascinated.

NORMAN. Put it back.
BILLY. What? It's dead.
NORMAN. Put it back.

BILLY *carefully drops the bird into the water, and watches it float away from the boat.* NORMAN *returns to his own end of the Thayer Four, and sits silently.* BILLY *seems shaken by what's happened. The sky grows steadily darker.*

BILLY *(quietly)*. Norman, are you afraid of dying?
NORMAN. What?
BILLY *(persisting)*. Are you afraid to die?
NORMAN. What the hell kind of question is that?
BILLY. I was just wondering, that's all.
NORMAN *(muttering)*. Well, I don't know why everybody has to talk about everything all the time.

He stares at the water, looks up at the sky, then back at BILLY. *He smiles.*

NORMAN. Let's go home, boy.

He reels in, and pulls up the anchor. BILLY *reels in, and looks around nervously as the darkness closes in.*

BILLY. Are you sure we're going to be able to get out of here?
NORMAN. What? Of course we are. Now get on the deck.

NORMAN *starts the motor and looks at* BILLY, *who moves reluctantly onto the deck.* NORMAN *senses* BILLY'S *fear.*

NORMAN *(continuing)*. Hey. Get back here. I forgot you're a hot shot boat driver. You take the wheel and I'll navigate.
BILLY. Yeah?

He climbs back into the boat as NORMAN *pulls himself onto the deck.*

BILLY *(continuing)*. I'm not afraid, you know.
NORMAN. I know. Now you just take us real slow and do what I tell you.

BILLY *moves the boat forward.* NORMAN *points as he gives commands.*

NORMAN *(continuing)*. All right. Starboard. Go port. That a boy. Good. Now. The other way. Very good. Okay. Starboard again.

The boat zig zags along. The visibility gets worse and worse, and NORMAN *has to squint at the darkness, struggling to see the way.*

NORMAN *(continuing)*. Port, Billy. Port! Good boy.

Suddenly ahead of the boat there looms a whole series of rocks, with seemingly no passageway.

NORMAN *(continuing)*. Good God! Reverse! Full throttle in reverse!

BILLY *panics. He hits the throttle in forward, and the boat races ahead.*

NORMAN *(continuing)*. Reverse!

But it's too late. The boat slams into a rock, sending NORMAN *flying into the water.* BILLY *hits the windshield and is thrown back as the Thayer Four rolls onto its side. We see a huge gash on the bottom. Water pours through it, as the grand old boat quickly fills and starts to sink.* NORMAN *splashes in the water, bleeding profusely from a scalp wound.*

NORMAN. Chelsea! Chelsea!

BILLY *swims toward* NORMAN, *calling.*

BILLY. Norman! Norman!

At last he reaches NORMAN. *He grabs him.*

BILLY *(continuing)*. Norman! I screwed up. I'm sorry.

But NORMAN *is in no condition for conversation. His face is covered with blood from the gash in his scalp. He looks at* BILLY, *then closes his eyes.* BILLY *pushes him through the water, looking for safety.* NORMAN *is clearly too heavy for the boy, but* BILLY *forges on. At last he spots a rock jutting out of the water, jagged and slippery. He drags* NORMAN *to it, and tries to push him onto it, but* NORMAN *is practically deadweight, and it takes all of* BILLY'S *remaining strength to force* NORMAN *onto the rock.* BILLY *shakes him.*

BILLY. Come on, Norman. You gotta live, man.

BILLY *is crying. He slides back into the water, exhausted.* NORMAN *lies still for a moment, then finally begins to regain his senses. He hears splashing near him as* BILLY *struggles to stay above water.*

NORMAN. Billy? Billy?

He drops into the water, hanging onto the rock, and he reaches for the boy. With a great lunge he grabs BILLY *and pulls him back to the rock, and holds him there.*

Ext. marina—Dusk. ETHEL'S *car screeches to a halt. She jumps out.*

Int. CHARLIE'S *boathouse—dusk.* CHARLIE *is tinkering with a motor at his workbench as* ETHEL *enters.*

ETHEL. Come on, Charlie, we're going for a boat ride.

CHARLIE. Huh?

ETHEL. They're out on the lake. They should have been back before dark. Let's go!

She heads across the boathouse to CHARLIE'S *boat moored in its slip.* CHARLIE *grabs his slicker and follows her. They climb into the boat and move off.*

Ext. lake—Night. BILLY *and* NORMAN *cling to each other, and to the rock, both exhausted.*

Ext. lake—Night. CHARLIE'S *boat clips across the lake,* ETHEL *shining a spotlight back and forth across the water.* CHARLIE *stops the boat.*

CHARLIE. Ethel, we've been back and forth here three times. They must have pulled up somewhere.

ETHEL *peers into the darkness. She shines the light on the entrance to Purgatory Cove.*

ETHEL. You don't think he went in there, do you?

CHARLIE. He's not that crazy.

ETHEL. Yes, he is. Let's go.

CHARLIE. I'm not going to drive my boat into Purgatory Cove.

ETHEL. Then I'll drive. Here; Hold this.

She thrusts the spotlight into his hands, and takes the wheel. The boat moves carefully into the cove.

Ext. lake—Night. BILLY *and* NORMAN *are now on opposite sides of the rock, arms interlocked.*

BILLY. Maybe I should try swimming to shore.

NORMAN *shakes his head, too tired to answer.* BILLY *grips him tighter.*

Ext. lake—Night. ETHEL *steers the boat past the rocks, while* CHARLIE *tries to find them with his light.*

CHARLIE. Left, Ethel. Now *right!* Oh, my God.

He can barely watch, but the boat winds along. Suddenly they hit something.

CHARLIE *(continuing).* Uh, oh.

He shines the light on the water.

CHARLIE. Holy Mackinoly.

We see a section of the Thayer Four floating in the water. ETHEL *sees it too. She shouts.*

ETHEL. Norman Thayer! Where the hell are you?

ETHEL *maneuvers forward, and* CHARLIE *slowly passes the light across the path. A dark mass looms ahead of them.* ETHEL *brings the boat closer and we see* NORMAN *and* BILLY *just barely hanging onto the rock.*

ETHEL. There they are. Take the wheel, Charlie.

She suddenly jumps into the water, and swims to the rock.

NORMAN *(weakly).* Ethel. You shouldn't be out here in this sort of weather.

She hugs him to her. She pulls BILLY *up and hugs him, too.*

ETHEL. You poops. You goddam poops.

CHARLIE *maneuvers his boat alongside.*

Ext. lake—Dawn. Golden Pond is calm. The morning sun glistens on the water.

Int. living room—Day. NORMAN *and* BILLY *sit at a table concentrating on a jigsaw puzzle.* NORMAN *wears a small bandage on his forehead.* ETHEL *steps in from the kitchen carrying her berry buckets.*

ETHEL. I'm off to get some berries. Will you two be all right?

They appear too busy to respond other than to nod or wave her off. She nods.

ETHEL *(continuing).* Bye, then.

She exits through the kitchen. As soon as the back door slams, BILLY *and* NORMAN *spring into action. They grab fishing vests and hats and gear, and scramble out the door.*

Ext. dock—Day. BILLY *and* NORMAN *rush down the bank to the dock until they are stopped dead in their tracks by* ETHEL'S *voice.*

ETHEL *(o.s.).* Hey!

BILLY *and* NORMAN *look up innocently as* ETHEL *approaches.*

ETHEL. And where are you juvenile delinquents off to?

BILLY *and* NORMAN *smile stupidly at her.*

ETHEL *(continuing, to* NORMAN*).* I thought you were in too much pain to exert yourself.

NORMAN. What? Well, I am. I'm only doing this for Billy—give the poor boy another chance to catch a fish. We've been doing goddam jigsaw puzzles for a week.

ETHEL. Mm-hmm. You'll be staying in our cove, won't you?

NORMAN. Tsk. There are no trout left in our cove.

ETHEL. We have enough trout in the fridge to last us six years.

BILLY. But we don't have Walter.

NORMAN. Never mind. We'll stay in the damn cove.

NORMAN *steps to her and grabs her, and kisses her.*

Ext. Blueberry Hill—Day. High above the lake. ETHEL *stands, picking berries. After a moment she begins to sing.*

ETHEL.
I can see the trees and the hills beyond,
from my tent on the bank
of the lake called Golden Pond,
On Golden Pond.

Ext. road—Day. A car rounds a bend and stops. CHELSEA *steps out and breathes in the warm air. She stares down at the lake, looking more buoyant than we've seen her. She hears* ETHEL's *voice and moves toward her, intrigued.*

Ext. Blueberry Hill—Day. ETHEL *is dancing a little Indian dance.*

ETHEL.
We are the girls from Camp Koochakiyi,
you can tell who we are by
the gleam in our eyes.
Our minds are clear
and our hearts are strong,
we are dancing here but we
won't be long . . .

CHELSEA *climbs down quickly behind her.* ETHEL's *dance grows.*

ETHEL *(continuing).*
There will soon be deer
where there are now fawns,
And we'll remember our years
on Golden Pond . . .

CHELSEA *joins in.*

CHELSEA AND ETHEL. On Golden Pond.

ETHEL *turns, startled.*

CHELSEA *(continuing).* How.

ETHEL. How did you get here?

CHELSEA. I rented a car. A Volare. Made by Plymouth.

CHELSEA *looks at* ETHEL *then at her jacket.*

CHELSEA. Look at you. You've had that coat as long as I can remember.

ETHEL. Looks it, doesn't it?

CHELSEA. It looks great.

CHELSEA *and* ETHEL *hug each other.*

ETHEL. You're in a huggy mood today. What's the matter?

CHELSEA. You look different.

ETHEL. You mean old. Like my coat.

CHELSEA. I don't know.

ETHEL. That's what happens if you live long enough. You get old.

CHELSEA. How does it make you feel?

ETHEL. Well, it doesn't make me feel like jumping up and down.

CHELSEA. It makes me goddamn mad!

ETHEL. They're not digging my grave yet. Well, how was your trip?

CHELSEA. Not bad.

ETHEL. Ah.

CHELSEA. How's the kid? Still got him or did you drown him?

ETHEL. We still got him. He's right out there fishing with his best buddy. You can see them.

CHELSEA *peers out at the lake, a wistful look in her eyes.*

CHELSEA. Where's the Thayer Four?

ETHEL. Oh, Charlie's fixing it. Norman and Billy tried to drive it through a rock in Purgatory Cove.

CHELSEA. Did they get hurt?

ETHEL. Norman got a bump on his forehead, which he's been playing to the hilt, but they're both fine, thank God. Do you still have Bill or did you drown him?

CHELSEA. Still got him. But he had to get back to the coast. He had a mouth that needed looking into. *(she smiles).* Have Norman and Billy gotten along all right?

ETHEL. Billy is the happiest thing that's happened to Norman since Roosevelt. I should have rented him a 13-year-old boy years ago.

CHELSEA. You could have traded me in. Billy reminds me of myself out there. Way back when. Except I think he makes a better son than I did.

ETHEL. Well, you made a very nice daughter.

CHELSEA. Isn't that cute the way they're so buddy-buddy? How come it's so easy?

ETHEL. What do you mean?

CHELSEA. Why wasn't the old son of a bitch ever my friend?

ETHEL. You're sounding very childish. Of course he was your friend . . . he's your father.

CHELSEA. I like your logic, but it's bullshit!

ETHEL. Oh, dear. You're such a nice person, can't you think of anything nice to say?

CHELSEA. Um. I married Bill in Brussels.

ETHEL. You did what in Brussels?

CHELSEA. I married Bill.

ETHEL. Does it count in this country?

CHELSEA. Fraid so.

ETHEL *(hugging her)*. Well, bless you. Congratulations.

CHELSEA. Nothing to it.

ETHEL. Norman will be so pleased.

CHELSEA. Yeah, right. What do you think he's going to say, "Hey, Chelsea, *fantastic.* I'm so *glad* you're finally getting your life together, and I'm so *proud* of you"?

ETHEL. I doubt it, but he *will* be happy for you.

CHELSEA. No, he won't. You know why? Because he doesn't really care. He cares about Norman Thayer, Jr., but he doesn't care about *me* . . . and he doesn't care about *you* either. He's a selfish *son of a bitch! (she yells at the lake).* You old son of a bitch!

ETHEL, stunned by all this, slaps CHELSEA's face.

ETHEL. That old son of a bitch happens to be my husband.

Now CHELSEA is stunned. She turns and runs headlong down the hill.

Ext. woods—Day. CHELSEA runs along the shore. She reaches a little point of land, runs onto a huge rock, and flings herself into Golden Pond.

Ext. lake—Day. CHELSEA stays under the water for a moment, then surfaces, spitting out a spray of water.

CHELSEA. Well, shit.

Ext. lake—Day. BILLY is struggling to reel in his line. NORMAN watches skeptically.

BILLY. Shit! Oh, wow, man!

NORMAN. It's only a sunfish, don't get excited.

BILLY. This is only a sunfish? It's doing a pretty good trout impression. Get the net!

NORMAN. Are you doubting the word of a genius? There are no respectable trout in this cove. I chased them out years ago.

At which point the fish breaks the water, a huge trout.

BILLY. What is that then?

NORMAN. That is a trout. *(he scrambles for the net).* Good God! It's Walter! What the hell are you doing *here,* you son of a bitch?

He scoops the fish into the net, and he and BILLY fall over each other landing the fish on the boat's floor.

BILLY. We caught Walter!

NORMAN. *We caught Walter.* The son of a bitch!

Ext. dock—Day. CHELSEA is sitting on the dock, hair and shorts still wet, shoes gone. She looks at the lake through binoculars. She lowers the glasses as ETHEL steps onto the dock. An awkward moment passes.

ETHEL. I brought your car.

CHELSEA. Thank you. *(after a moment).* I'm sorry.

ETHEL. I'm sorry, too. But you're wrong, you know. Your father *does* care. Deeply. It's true he's an absolute mutt when it comes to telling anybody, but I know he'd walk through fire for me, and he would for you, too. And if you can't see that, then you're not looking close enough.

CHELSEA *(after a beat).* I don't even know him.

ETHEL. Well, he'll be here in a minute, I'll be glad to introduce you.

CHELSEA. Right. Maybe someday we can try to be friends.

ETHEL. Chelsea, Norman is 80 years old. He has heart palpitations and a problem remembering things. When exactly do you expect this friendship to begin?

CHELSEA. I don't know. I'm afraid of him.

ETHEL. Well, he's afraid of you. You should get along fine. *(she pauses).* Here he comes. Talk to him.

She turns and marches up the bank, leaving CHELSEA to gaze nervously out as NORMAN's boat approaches the dock.

Ext. Shore—Day. CHELSEA is wading in the shallow water, studying the little pebbles that glisten in the sun. She looks up as BILLY and NORMAN approach the dock. BILLY spots CHELSEA. He jumps from the boat to the dock, and smiles at her. She looks at BILLY in surprise. He seems taller, his posture improved, his face ruddy. They look at each other a moment, then he jumps into the water. He and CHELSEA embrace.

BILLY. Look at you.

CHELSEA. Hi, kid.

BILLY. Where's the dentist?

CHELSEA. He had to go back. He'll call you tonight. Hello, Norman.

NORMAN *(sitting in the boat)*. Well, well, well.

BILLY. Chelsea, we caught Walter! Do you know who Walter is?

CHELSEA. I have a feeling he's a fish.

BILLY. Yes. A humungus fish. And we caught him! We *caught him*!

CHELSEA. Well? Let me see him.

NORMAN. We let him go.

BILLY. Yeah, we let him go.

CHELSEA. I think I've heard this story before.

BILLY. No, it's true. We figures if he's lived this long we should let him keep on living.

He climbs up the bank.

BILLY *(continuing)*. I've got to tell Ethel we caught him. *(he grins at NORMAN)*. We caught the son of a bitch!

BILLY *runs off.* CHELSEA *looks at* NORMAN. *She has to squint in the bright sun.*

CHELSEA. Got yourself a friend, huh?

NORMAN. He's all right. It hasn't been too difficult.

He starts to climb out of the boat.

CHELSEA. How's your forehead?

NORMAN. What? This? *(he touches the bandage)*. Oh, not too bad. A lot of pain, nothing to worry about.

CHELSEA. Norman, I want to talk to you.

NORMAN *(sitting back down)*. What seems to be the problem?

CHELSEA. There's no problem. I just . . . want to talk to you. I, um . . . I was thinking, it occurred to me that maybe you and I should have the kind of relationship we're supposed to have.

NORMAN. What kind of relationship is that?

CHELSEA. Well, you know, like a father and a daughter.

NORMAN. Oh. Just in the nick of time, huh? Worried about the will, are you? I'm leaving everything to you, except what I'm taking with me.

CHELSEA. Oh, stop it. I don't want anything. It just seems like you and I have been mad at each other for too long.

NORMAN. Oh? I didn't know we were mad, I thought we just didn't like each other.

This hits CHELSEA *hard enough. She wades a little deeper, trying to regroup.*

CHELSEA. I want to be your friend.

NORMAN *(hit himself)*. Oh. Does this mean you might come around more often? It would mean a lot to your mother.

CHELSEA. I'll come around more often.

NORMAN *nods.* CHELSEA *nods. They both work at not looking at each other.*

NORMAN. Well . . .

CHELSEA. Yep. Oh. Yeah. By the way, I got married in Brussels.

NORMAN. You did? In Brussels? Ah ha.

CHELSEA. Yes. It's the best thing that's ever happened to me. He makes me very happy.

NORMAN. Well, good. Does he speak English?

CHELSEA. Tsk. I married Bill.

NORMAN. Bill? Oh, Bill! Ah. *(he thinks about it, smiles at her)*. Well. I'm glad, Chelsea. That's um . . . San Frantastic.

CHELSEA *(surprised)*. What?

NORMAN. Billy going to live with you?

CHELSEA. Yes.

NORMAN. Good. Isn't that something? Good for you.

He smiles at her. A moment passes.

NORMAN. Oh, you know, I've got him doing a back flip. Just like a pro.

CHELSEA. Oh, yeah? That's great.

NORMAN. You want me to get him down here and show you?

CHELSEA. Um, no thanks, not right now.

NORMAN. Okay. Oh, that's right, you never were a great back-flipper, were you?

CHELSEA. No, I was never a great one. I was too fat, remember?

NORMAN *(laughing)*. Ha, ha, yes I do remember that now. Oh, well, I guess it's probably easier for a boy anyway.

CHELSEA. I beg your pardon? Would you like to see me *do* a back flip?

CHELSEA *starts heading out toward the float.*

NORMAN. What?

CHELSEA. I'm going to do a goddam back flip.

Now she swims. NORMAN *watches confused.*

NORMAN. Chelsea, you don't have to . . .

CHELSEA *(interrupting)*. I *want* to do it. It's part of my growing-up process. Come on, coach, let's go.

She swims to the raft. NORMAN *turns the boat and rows after her.*

Ext. float—Day. CHELSEA *stands on the diving board, back to the water, looking intense, and scared.* NORMAN *sits in the boat near her.*

NORMAN. Be sure to go up and not just back. Up and back.

CHELSEA *looks at him, a little girl.*

CHELSEA. I'm scared.

NORMAN. There's nothing to be scared of. The back flip is one of the easiest dives of all.

CHELSEA. But I'm scared anyway.

NORMAN. Then don't do it. It doesn't matter if you don't do the stupid dive. It's not important.

CHELSEA *stares at him, hearing the message she would have liked to hear 30 years ago. She half smiles, and then throws herself up and back and does a flip. Not perfect, but passable.*

After a moment, she surfaces, amazed at herself. NORMAN *stands in the boat and claps. He shouts at the house.*

NORMAN. She did it! Chelsea did a back flip!

Ext. porch. ETHEL *and* BILLY *stand clapping.*

Ext. house—Day. CHELSEA, ETHEL *and* BILLY *stand by* CHELSEA'S *car.*

CHELSEA. You could come out, you know. Instead of going to Florida.

ETHEL. Well, we'll discuss it. If I can get Norman to accept the fact that Los Angeles is part of the United States, it shouldn't be too much trouble.

They turn as NORMAN *marches out carrying a fish pole.*

ETHEL *(continuing).* Norman, what are you doing now?

NORMAN *(handing the pole to* BILLY*).* Here, cool breeze. In case you want to take a break from cruising.

BILLY. Wow. Thank you, Captain.

ETHEL. Norman, he can't take that stupid thing on the plane.

CHELSEA. Yes, he can.

NORMAN *looks at* CHELSEA *gratefully.*

NORMAN. I've got something for you, too.

He fishes in his pocket and pulls out a medal, which he hangs around CHELSEA'S *neck.*

NORMAN *(continuing).* You know what this is?

CHELSEA. Yes.

NORMAN. University of Pennsylvania diving finals. 1921. Second place.

CHELSEA. Thank you. *(she's touched).* Now I can retire.

NORMAN. Show it to your new husband. Maybe he'll give us a discount on dental work.

BILLY *shakes* NORMAN'S *hand.*

BILLY. I'll see ya, ya nitwit.

NORMAN. Okay.

BILLY *hugs him, which is a shock to* NORMAN, *but he hugs him, too.* BILLY *steps to Ethel.*

BILLY. Well, goodbye, woman.

They embrace.

ETHEL. Goodbye, dear.

CHELSEA *stands by* NORMAN.

CHELSEA. Um. 'Bye. Norman. Dad.

With a what-the-hell, NORMAN *grabs and hugs her, too.*

Int. living room—Night. NORMAN *watches as* ETHEL *packs up the Parcheesi game.*

NORMAN. What are you, quitting? Let's play "Loser drives home".

ETHEL. Tsk. You owe me four million dollars

NORMAN. Double or nothing.

She smiles, shakes her head. She puts the board back down and sits across from NORMAN. *They look like two gunfighters ready to square off.*

Ext. shore—Day. NORMAN *watches* CHARLIE *haul up the last section of dock.*

CHARLIE. Unh. Well. Another summer, huh, Norman?

NORMAN. Yep. Now wait a minute. You better get that section all the way up the bank.

CHARLIE *shakes his head and strains to lift the thing higher.* NORMAN *waves him on.*

NORMAN *(continuing).* That's it, come on. I don't want to get back here next year and find out my damn dock has floated away. That's a good boy.

CHARLIE *wipes his brow. He climbs into his boat.*

CHARLIE. We'll see you next summer, Norman.

NORMAN. Okay, Charlie. You take care of yourself.

CHARLIE. You bet.

He starts the motor and roars off. NORMAN *stands watching* CHARLIE'S *boat skim across the water.*

ETHEL *(o.s.).* Norman. Come on, dear.

He turns and walks up the bank.

Ext. porch—Day. ETHEL *is on the porch. There are two boxes beside her.*

ETHEL. Let's get these last boxes to the car and be gone.

NORMAN. Oh, for God's sake.

He starts to lift one box, she takes the other.

ETHEL. It's not too heavy, is it?

NORMAN. Of course it's not too heavy. Good God, this is heavy! *(he takes a few steps).* You're trying to kill me.

ETHEL. I've thought about it. Put it down if it's too much trouble.

NORMAN. What the hell do you have in here?

ETHEL. My mother's china. Put it down, Norman.

NORMAN. Your mother never liked me.

He's clearly in pain.

ETHEL. Of course she did. Put the box down. Dammit!

He drops the box with a terrible crash. NORMAN *falls down after it.* ETHEL *drops her box and rushes to help him. He lies clutching himself as she holds him to her.*

ETHEL *(continuing).* Oh, my God. Norman! Where's your medicine? Oh God!

She rushes to the back of the house. NORMAN *lies still, gasping in pain.* ETHEL *runs back. She wrestles with the medicine bottle.*

ETHEL *(continuing).* Whoever designed these caps is a madman.

At last she has it open. She cradles NORMAN's *head.*

ETHEL *(continuing).* Here. Put this under your tongue.

NORMAN. What is it?

ETHEL. Nitroglycerin. Put it under your tongue.

NORMAN. You must be mad. I'll blow up.

ETHEL. Do it, dammit.

He does. She watches as he closes his eyes.

ETHEL *(continuing).* Dear God, don't take him now. You don't want him, he's a poop. Norman? Norman!

NORMAN *(his eyes closed).* Maybe you should call a doctor. We can afford it.

ETHEL *(jumping up).* Oh, yes. I should have done that. Dear God.

She rushes onto the porch and into the house.

Int. living room—Day. The furniture is all stacked and covered again. ETHEL *finds the telephone and dials "O."*

ETHEL. Hello, hello. Dear God.

She steps back out the door, carrying the phone.

Ext. porch—Day.

ETHEL. How are you feeling, Norman?

NORMAN. Oh, pretty good. How are you?

ETHEL. How's the pain, dammit?

NORMAN. Pretty good, as pain goes.

ETHEL. Is the medicine doing anything?

NORMAN. No.

ETHEL. Why don't they answer the phone?

NORMAN. Who'd you call?

ETHEL. The stupid operator. Hello? Hello, hello, hello, hello, hello, hello! Whatever is the matter with her?

NORMAN. She's slow.

ETHEL. How do you feel now?

NORMAN. I don't know.

ETHEL. Are you planning to die? Is that what you're up to? Well, while I'm waiting for this moron to answer the phone, let me say something to you, Norman Thayer, Junior. I would rather you didn't.

NORMAN. Really?

ETHEL. Yes! This stupid, stupid woman. I'm going to have to call the hospital directly. *(she heads back to the door, muttering).* The phone book, where's the phone book?

NORMAN. Ethel?

ETHEL *(fearing the worst).* Yes. What is it?

NORMAN. Come here.

ETHEL *drops the phone, rushes to him, kneels by him.*

ETHEL. Oh, God. Yes, Norman, my darling.

NORMAN. Ethel.

ETHEL. Yes. I'm here, Norman.

NORMAN. Ethel.

ETHEL. Yes, yes, yes.

NORMAN. Ethel.

ETHEL. What is it?

NORMAN. Ethel. I think I'm feeling all right now.

ETHEL. Oh, God. *(she clutches him to her).* Are you serious?

NORMAN. My heart stopped hurting. Maybe I'm dead.

ETHEL. Oh, Norman. Oh, thank God. I love you so much.

NORMAN. Now my heart's starting to hurt again. Sorry about your mother's china.

ETHEL. Why did you strain yourself? You know better.

NORMAN. I was showing off. Trying to turn you on.

ETHEL. Well, you succeeded. There's no need for you to try that sort of thing again.

NORMAN. Good.

She holds him and they don't move for a long time. She gazes out at the lake.

On the lake. The lake looks more golden than ever, with dabs of yellow and red reflecting in the water.

ETHEL *(o.s.)*. Norman. This is the first time I've really felt we're going to die.

NORMAN *(o.s.)*. I've known it all along.

On NORMAN *and* ETHEL.

ETHEL. When I looked at you lying on the ground I could actually see you dead. I could see you in your blue suit and a white starched shirt, lying in Thomas' Funeral Parlor on Bradshaw Street.

NORMAN. How did I look?

ETHEL. Not good, Norman. You've been talking about dying ever since I met you. But today was the first time I've really felt it.

NORMAN. How does it feel?

ETHEL. It feels . . . Odd. Cold, I guess. But not that bad, really. Almost comforting, not so frightening, not such a bad place to go. I don't know.

She looks at him, looks away. He reaches up and pulls her head to him. She smiles at him, leans against him. After a moment he pulls himself up.

NORMAN. Well? Don't you want to say goodbye to the lake?

ETHEL. Are you sure you're strong enough?

NORMAN. I think so. If I fall over face first in the water, you'll know I wasn't.

ETHEL. Well, be careful, for God's sake. I'm only good for one near miss a day.

He steps to her, takes her in his arms.

NORMAN. Hello, there.

ETHEL. Hi.

NORMAN. Want to dance? Or would you rather just suck face?

ETHEL. You really are a case, you know.

They move down to the water's edge. The loons call.

ETHEL *(continuing)*. Norman! The loons! They've come 'round to say goodbye.

NORMAN. How nice.

On the lake. The two loons light on the water for a moment, then rise again and soar away.

On NORMAN *and* ETHEL. *They watch the loons.*

ETHEL. Just the two of them now. Little baby's all grown up and moved to Los Angeles or somewhere.

NORMAN. Yes.

ETHEL. Hello, Golden Pond. We've come to say goodbye.

They stare out at the lake. The camera draws back and we see NORMAN *and* ETHEL, *like the last summer flowers on the shore. Solitary figures. Not sad, but peaceful and hopeful and proud. The camera draws back, away, above them. They become smaller and smaller, but still visible and bright on the golden pond.*

Fade out.

The end.

ARTHUR

Screenplay by Steve Gordon

ARTHUR	Dudley Moore
HOBSON	John Gielgud
LINDA	Liza Minnelli
MARTHA	Geraldine Fitzgerald
SUSAN	Jill Eikenberry
MR. JOHNSON	Stephen Elliott

Screenplay by Steve Gordon
Produced by Robert Greenhut for Warner/Orion, 1980
Directed by Steve Gordon
Cinematography by Fred Schuler
Music by Burt Bacharach

Winner of the Writers Guild Award in 1981 for Best American Comedy, and nominated for an Academy Award that same year, this scintillating screenplay by the late Steve Gordon, writer-director of *Arthur*, is much in the tradition of those marvelous comedies of the thirties with their bizarre, funny characters—perhaps a modernized version of *My Man Godfrey*, written by Morrie Ryskind and Eric Hatch, to which it bears kinship in so many ways, despite possessing two butlers as major characters who are as disparate as any you might likely come across. Godfrey is as gentle and sweet as (Sir John Gielgud's) Hobson is caustic and pungently witty. But both are alike in their love of their masters. And both never lose sight of that.

Arthur, as written by Mr. Gordon, is a superb creation. This poor little rich boy, who belatedly comes of age—to a point, when he finds the right woman—is beautifully realized. This script was passed over many times by studios in Mr. Gordon's first frustrating attempts to get it financed and produced. "Who could possibly sympathize with a rich irresponsible drunk and a girl who goes around shoplifting?" he was told in being rejected again and again. Of course it happened—the picture was produced and became a real winner in the best of the word-of-mouth tradition.

This final screenplay and the film that emerged after shooting is as excellent an example of fine tuning from script to print as you might ever observe, for those of you who wish to get into this aspect of film writing and directing when the screenwriter and the director can be one and the same creative person.

To do so, of course, you will have to have the script beside you as you run a videotape of the film. The reshaping of bits of dialogue, the movement of scenes from one spot in the script to another, as in the episode where Arthur takes his turn around the racetrack he has rented for the day, shifted from earlier, as it is in the script, to much later on in the film as shot, where it becomes more effective and more meaningful. Also, the scene on the veranda that occurs between Arthur and Linda (Liza Minnelli) during the party for his engagement to the other woman, in the script is likewise changed for the better when it is shifted to the stables, not so much for the transformation of location but for the emphasis on Arthur and Linda's love for each other. As in so many other fine comedies, the coming down to the wire, so to speak, to the climax and resolution of the story makes certain rhythms necessary. To accomplish that, one must let that rhythm take over above all, and one must learn how to be spare and ruthless in cutting down and cutting out material that gets in the way. *Arthur* accomplishes that very well in the changes that were made down the stretch from the final script, and the screenplay is worth studying to get the feel of it.

Suffice it to say, we are outraged, surprised, delighted, and feel warm toward this couple, Arthur and Linda, let alone Hobson—toward all the cockeyed people in this story, once it runs its merry, witty path.

Mr. Gordon's untimely death at the age of forty-two, shortly after the successful emergence of *Arthur*, is a loss to cinema, a brilliant career as a writer-director nipped in the bud. Prior to *Arthur*, he was involved in but one feature film, *The One and Only*, which he wrote and coproduced (1978).

At least we have *Arthur*.

Ext.: Lexington Avenue around 52nd Street—Night. Late. Not much traffic. A couple of very attractive hookers stand on the corner. Tired. Yawning. It's been a long night. One looks at her watch. The other lights a cigarette. Suddenly! The biggest Rolls Royce limousine in the world screeches to a halt in front of them. The back window of the limo goes down. The head that sticks out of that window is that of Arthur Bach. He is in his mid-thirties. Good looking. He wears a tuxedo. He is rip roaring drunk. He holds a bottle of scotch in one hand which he drinks from, from time to time. This is an outrageous man. Every night is New Year's Eve. Everything is at the top and hysterically funny to him.

ARTHUR *(very drunk and slurring his words).* Girls! Girls! Hello girls! Would the more attractive of you please step forward? *(he laughs a huge drunken laugh)* God . . . that's funny! *(settles down)* Actually . . . you're both very attractive. Would the one who thinks *I'm* attractive please step forward? Uh . . . as quickly as possible. Time is money . . .

One of the girls approaches the car. In the front seat, the driver in full chauffeur's dress stares straight ahead. This is BITTERMAN, *a black man in his forties. The back seat of the limo has a bar, TV set, a refrigerator and almost every device known for mixing a drink. The girl is* GLORIA.

GLORIA. What did you have in mind?
ARTHUR. VD! I'm really into penicillin! *(he laughs)* Now . . . that's funny!

GLORIA *stares at him.*
ARTHUR. I know this is last minute. *(he laughs)* Ahh . . . I finally heard someone laughing. Oh . . . it was me. What I have in mind . . . is spending the evening with a stranger who loves me.
GLORIA. It's going to cost you a hundred dollars.
ARTHUR. Oh yeah . . . what time do you get off work? *(he laughs)* I'm kidding. If you laugh a little I throw in nylons and Hershey bars. Let's make it two hundred. But I will ask you to Simonize my car.

GLORIA *stares at him.*

ARTHUR *(looking at her staring).* Tell me . . . has there been a death in your family? This is funny stuff here.
GLORIA. Who are you?
ARTHUR. I'm rich. That's who I am. Get in the car.

GLORIA *takes a look at the other hooker who has been watching. She shrugs. She hesitantly gets into the car.* ARTHUR *pushes a button to talk to the driver.*

ARTHUR *(to* BITTERMAN*).* Bitterman, give her friend a hundred dollars. She came in second.

BITTERMAN *gets out of the car. He approaches the other hooker and gives her a hundred dollars.*

GIRL *(to* BITTERMAN*).* Who is that guy?
BITTERMAN. I'd rather not say.
GIRL. I think I know. I've seen his picture in the paper. That's Arthur Bach . . . isn't it?
BITTERMAN. Uh . . . what if it is?
GIRL. Is there something wrong with him?
BITTERMAN. Yes.

The credits start. Under the credits, BITTERMAN *gets back into the car and starts the engine. The huge Rolls turns right on 49th Street and continues west. It turns right on Park. The credits stop.*

Cut to:

Int.: Back seat—Limousine. ARTHUR *drinks.* GLORIA *sits.*

ARTHUR. Permit me to introduce myself.

He reaches up to his head to doff his top hat but it isn't on his head.

ARTHUR. Where the hell is my hat?
GLORIA. It's on the floor.
ARTHUR. I hate it when that happens. I am Arthur.
GLORIA. I'm Gloria. What are you drinking?
ARTHUR. Scotch. Would you like some?
GLORIA. Why not?
ARTHUR. You're with me and you can ask that question? We also have cocaine, marijuana, vodka, gin and some prune danish.
GLORIA. Scotch. You are funny.
ARTHUR. I know. *(he laughs).* Sometimes I just think funny things.

ARTHUR *mixes her a drink.*

GLORIA. What do you do for a living?
ARTHUR. I race cars. I play tennis . . . I fondle women . . . but I get weekends off and I'm my own boss.

ARTHUR *makes a toast.*

ARTHUR *(toasting).* Here's to us . . . and to all the little people who made this possible.
GLORIA. Are you into anything kinky?

ARTHUR. Nah. What good are whips and chains when you're dating a turtle?

GLORIA *laughs.*

ARTHUR *(Cont.)* I really am the funniest person I know.

Cut back to:

Ext.: limo rolling up Park Avenue. Credits again roll. As the credits continue we hear the conversation from the limo.

GLORIA *(o.c.)* Are we going to your place?

ARTHUR *(o.c.)* Of course not! We just met! Whatever happened to dinner? Whatever happened to dancing? Whatever happened to Doris Day for Christ's sakes? *(to* BITTERMAN*)* Bitterman . . . the Plaza and step on it.

BITTERMAN *(o.c.)* Sir . . . if I may say so . . .

ARTHUR. Bitterman . . . don't talk . . . just drive.

GLORIA *(o.c.)* Can I have another drink?

ARTHUR *(o.c.)* Yes! Isn't this fun! Isn't fun the best thing to have! Don't you wish you were me! I know I do. Go through the park, Bitterman! You know I love the park!

The limo turns left on 72nd and goes through the park. It is a lovely night. The city is glowing. There is little traffic. The credits end as the limo pulls up to

Cut to:

Ext.: The Plaza—Night. The limo glides to a stop. BITTERMAN *gets out of the car and opens the back door.* GLORIA *gets out.* ARTHUR *falls out of the car and onto the curb. He laughs heartily at this.*

ARTHUR *(on the curb laughing).* I fell out of the goddamned car! Is that funny!

BITTERMAN *is helping him up.*

BITTERMAN. Are you hurt, sir?

ARTHUR. Bitterman! I fell out of the car! Is that the funniest thing ever! Ahh . . . you had to be there.

BITTERMAN. You are quite amusing, sir.

ARTHUR. Well then laugh it up, Bitterman.

BITTERMAN *laughs.*

Cut to:

Int.: The Oak Room. GLORIA *stands at the entrance.*

CAPTAIN. I'm sorry Madam . . . we have no . . .

ARTHUR *stumbles in.*

ARTHUR. It's alright Raymond . . . she's with me.

CAPTAIN. Mr. Bach! So good to see you!

He shakes ARTHUR'S *hand.*

ARTHUR. If only someone I knew felt that way.

CAPTAIN. We have your regular table.

They start to follow the captain. Many people stare at GLORIA *who obviously doesn't belong here.* ARTHUR *sees this. He puts his arm around her.*

ARTHUR *(to* GLORIA*)* They're used to seeing me with the turtle.

They wend their way through the Oak Room. ARTHUR *staggers. A white-haired prosperous-looking gentleman seated along the way with his wife, a rather portly bejeweled dowager. This is* ARTHUR'S *uncle and aunt,* PETER *and* PEARL BACH. ARTHUR *moves towards them.*

ARTHUR. Uncle Peter! And Aunt Pearl!

PETER *(rising to greet him).* Arthur . . . you're looking well . . .

ARTHUR *kisses his aunt on the cheek.*

ARTHUR. Aunt Pearl . . . may I say you are looking younger every day. *(to* GLORIA*)* Doesn't Aunt Pearl look wonderful, darling?

GLORIA. She looks great.

PEARL. Arthur . . . I don't believe we've had the pleasure of meeting this young woman. Would you introduce us?

ARTHUR. How stupid of me! Princess Gloria . . . may I introduce my Aunt and Uncle . . . Peter and Pearl Bach.

GLORIA. How are you?

PEARL. Princess? did you say princess, Arthur?

ARTHUR. Yes.

He gets very close to his Aunt's face. She wishes he would not do this. His breath is all scotch.

ARTHUR. There is a *very* small country in the West Indies. I mean small.

PEARL *(hating him this close).* I see. Thank you.

ARTHUR. It's terribly small. Tiny little country. Rhode Island could beat the crap out of it in a war. That's how small it is.

PEARL. Small . . .

ARTHUR. Very little. It's 85 cents in a cab from one end of the country to the other. I'm talking small here.

PETER. We understand it's small, Arthur.

ARTHUR *leans up to receive this comment to his Uncle. He goes back right next to Pearl's face for his next drunken speech.*

ARTHUR. They recently had the whole country carpeted. This is not a big place.

PETER. We understand that it's small, Arthur. We also understand that you are very drunk. Why don't we meet again when you're sober?

He stops. He looks down at them.

ARTHUR *(sadly)*. Right. I'm sorry. I can't help it.

PETER. Grow up, Arthur. You'd make a fine adult.

Cut to:

Int.: Oak Room— ARTHUR's *table—Night.* ARTHUR *and* GLORIA *are seated. A* WAITER *approaches the table.*

WAITER. How are you, Mr. Bach.

ARTHUR. Scotch. *(to* GLORIA*)* I hate small talk.

WAITER. The usual for you.

GLORIA. I'll have a steak, medium, shrimp cocktail, baked potato and a Bud. I'll walk it off.

ARTHUR. And hurry up with that drink. I'm due at an Alcoholics Anonymous meeting in an hour.

The WAITER *and* GLORIA *laugh.*

ARTHUR. Everybody loves me.

The waiter withdraws.

GLORIA. How rich are you?

ARTHUR. All I can tell you is . . . I wish I had a dime for every dime I have. The service here is terrible. Where the hell is my drink?

GLORIA. We just ordered.

ARTHUR. That's always their excuse.

GLORIA. Are you married?

ARTHUR. There's only one woman for me and I can't stand her. Her name is Susan. I can't tell you her last name because that would be indiscreet. Johnson. Susan Johnson. My father wants me to marry her . . . but I'm not going to! You're the only woman at this table.

The waiter returns with a bottle of beer and a glass of scotch. He places the bottle in front of GLORIA *and the glass in front of* ARTHUR.

ARTHUR *(to the waiter)*. Sure . . . you bring her a whole bottle . . . me you bring a glass.

The waiter chuckles and withdraws.

ARTHUR. Aren't waiters wonderful? You ask them for things and they bring them.

Same principle as Santa Claus. Tell me about yourself.

GLORIA. You mean . . . why am I a hooker?

ARTHUR. Are you a hooker? Jesus . . . I forgot. I just thought I was doing great with you. Okay . . . why are you a hooker?

GLORIA. My mother died when I was six.

ARTHUR *bangs on the table.*

ARTHUR. Son of a bitch! Don't they know what they do to kids!

GLORIA. My father raped me when I was 12.

ARTHUR. So . . . you had six relatively good years. I'm sorry. Listen . . . my father screwed me too. Do you like me?

GLORIA. You're cute.

ARTHUR. I know that. Do you like me?

GLORIA. Yes.

ARTHUR. Well Princess . . . we're going to have fun. Tonight is New Year's Eve! Third time this week! Is my hat on my head?

GLORIA. No.

ARTHUR. I hate that. Here's to you.

Cut to:

Int.: ARTHUR's *gigantic bedroom. This is a triplex apartment.* ARTHUR's *room features an enormous bed. Among the original paintings, there are also pictures of Willie Mays and Reggie Jackson. The picture of Mays is enormous and takes up the entire wall across from* ARTHUR's *bed. One of the chairs in the room is an enormous throne with a red carpet leading to it. This is a crazed man. Half boy. Half man . . . who can't make up his mind.* GLORIA *and* ARTHUR *lie in bed sleeping. A set of electric trains circle around an enormous miniature landscape behind the bed.* GLORIA *starts to wake. She rolls into* ARTHUR.

ARTHUR *(feeling his head)*. Oooh . . . oooh . . . *(he sees* GLORIA*)* Hello darling . . . good morning . . . did you sleep well?

GLORIA. Fine.

ARTHUR. Good. Who are you?

GLORIA. Gloria.

ARTHUR. I'm Arthur. I meet more people here. What do you do, Gloria? I'll bet we're both naked.

GLORIA. I'm a hooker.

ARTHUR. Another conquest. I remember now. I'm very fond of you . . . right?

GLORIA. You were last night.

ARTHUR. Yeah! Can I have a free kiss?

GLORIA. Yeah.

He kisses her. The door to the bedroom opens and a very stiff, determined, formal man enters in a well-tailored suit. This is HOBSON. *A career servant, but a man with great breeding and* taste. *He is also the driest, most sarcastic person ever.* HOBSON *has great distaste for everything. Every word* HOBSON *utters is clipped, precise and possibly damaging. He has great distaste, apparently, for the antics of his master.* HOBSON *is about 60. He carries orange juice and aspirins on a tray as he enters. He enters on the kiss.*

HOBSON *(observing the kiss)*. Please stop that.

ARTHUR *and* GLORIA *look up.* ARTHUR *is glad to see him. It is obvious that he has real affection for the older man.*

ARTHUR. Hobson! Good to see you!

Each word of HOBSON's *is clipped, precise and alone from the other words.*

HOBSON. Thank you so much. I have taken the liberty of anticipating your condition . . . and I have brought orange juice, coffee and aspirins. Or . . . do you have to throw up?

ARTHUR *(downing the aspirins)*. No . . . Gloria . . . I would like you to meet Hobson. My best friend in the world.

HOBSON. I relish the compliment. It is thrilling to meet you, Gloria.

GLORIA. Hi.

HOBSON *moves towards the drapes to open them.*

HOBSON. Yes. You obviously have a wonderful economy with words, Gloria. *(mutters)* A total illiterate. *(to Gloria)* I look forward to your next syllable with great eagerness.

He has completed opening the drapes.

HOBSON. You . . . , as we all can see . . . it is a lovely day . . . which would indicate that the night is over. Gloria . . . I have arranged breakfast for you on the East Patio.

ARTHUR. You have to get to know him.

HOBSON *reaches into the closet and pulls out a robe. He hands it to* GLORIA.

HOBSON. This is a robe. Please put it on. You may dress in the bedroom to your right as you leave the elevator. I have placed your footgear and your blouse and your various undergarments in there. There was no time for dry cleaning. Say goodby to her, Arthur.

ARTHUR. Hobson . . . must you treat our guest so badly?

HOBSON *(to* GLORIA*)*. I can only pray that I have not offended you. If I have . . . a thousand pardons. Perhaps some day . . . I can introduce you to the New York Giants. Arthur, your father wants to see you at noon.

(to Gloria) It would be wonderful of you to leave. Your breakfast is waiting.

ARTHUR *(to* GLORIA*)*. You'd better go.

GLORIA *stands. As she passes* HOBSON *she stops and looks at him for a moment.*

GLORIA. What's the matter old man? Don't you like sex?

HOBSON. I adore sex. Now go suck your coffee.

GLORIA *(to* ARTHUR*)*. It's been a kick.

ARTHUR. I love you. Want to make a quick thousand dollars?

GLORIA. Yeah.

ARTHUR. Smile. It'll get me through the day.

GLORIA *(smiling)*. You're a very nice man. I can use the money. I have a sick kid . . . and . . .

HOBSON. Of course. *(to* GLORIA*)* And we have the matched set of luggage . . . the trip to Acapulco . . . and the dinner service for eight. Congratulations . . . and thank you for playing . . . Schtup the rich playboy. And now . . . you really must go.

GLORIA *steps into the elevator.*

GLORIA *(to* ARTHUR*)*. Ten thousand dollars! I'm going to tell you something that I've never told to anybody in my life . . .

The elevator doors close.

ARTHUR. Hobson . . . you treated her like trash.

HOBSON. Yes. May I suggest that you get your ass out of bed? Your father is enormously upset. Please get dressed. Drink your coffee.

ARTHUR *laughs. He crosses to the throne in his bedroom.*

HOBSON *(looking into the bed)*. Many pubic hairs . . .

ARTHUR *sits in his throne.* HOBSON *brings him a newspaper, gives* ARTHUR *the sports section and keeps page one for himself.*

ARTHUR. Hobson . . .

HOBSON. Yes?

ARTHUR. You know what I'm going to do?

HOBSON. No, I don't.

ARTHUR. I'm going to take a bath.

HOBSON. I'll alert the media.

ARTHUR. Do you want to run the bath for me?

HOBSON. It is what I live for.

ARTHUR *rises from his throne. He exits into the bathroom.* HOBSON *sits on the throne, opens the paper.*

HOBSON. Maybe you'd like me to come in there and wash your dick for you . . . you little shit.

Cut to:

Int.: huge bathroom—Day. It is the biggest bathroom in the world. Every appointment is perfect. An enormous tub. The floor is marble. And he is in the huge bathtub, ARTHUR *is happy and singing. Next to* ARTHUR, *on the wall, is an intercom system for every room in the large old apartment.* ARTHUR *wears his top hat in the tub. The water runs.*

ARTHUR *(in the tub, singing).*
You'd better watch out.
You'd better not cry.
You'd better not pout.
I'm telling you why.
Santa Claus is coming to town . . .

He pushes a button on the wall. This connects him with HOBSON'S *room.*

HOBSON *(o.c.).* Yes?

ARTHUR *loves* HOBSON. *He smiles as he does the rest and laughs at* HOBSON'S *sarcasm and wit. These two have been at it a long time.*

ARTHUR *(smiling).* Hobson . . . this is Arthur.

HOBSON *(o.c.).* How delightful to hear from you.

ARTHUR. I'm in the bathtub. What are you doing?

HOBSON. I'm in bed with the lovely Gloria. I'll be with you in a moment.

ARTHUR. How about a pitcher of martinis?

HOBSON *(o.c.).* No, thank you.

ARTHUR *(laughing).* I'm not facing my father sober. If you don't bring them I'll have someone else do it.

HOBSON *(o.c.).* I'll bring them. Say goodbye.

ARTHUR. Goodbye.

HOBSON *rings off.* ARTHUR *laughs. He's having a good time.*

ARTHUR *(to himself).* He treats me like a kid.

He starts to sing again.

ARTHUR. He knows when you are sleeping.
He knows when you're awake.
He knows when you've been bad or good.

He pauses. The next line is spoken.

ARTHUR. He's a peeping tom for Christ sakes!

ARTHUR *watches television and plays with boats in the bathtub. He laughs. He pushes another button. A female voice answers. This is* GRETTA, *the cook.*

GRETTA *(o.c.).* Gretta here.

ARTHUR. Gretta . . . good morning . . . this is Mr. Bach. I'm in the bathtub.

GRETTA *(o.c.).* Yes, sir.

ARTHUR. I won't be having any breakfast this morning.

GRETTA *(o.c.).* Yes, sir.

ARTHUR. I'm not really hungry this morning. Secondly . . . I'm a little on edge. My father wants to see me. I don't get along with him that well. He hates me.

GRETTA *(o.c.).* Yes, sir.

HOBSON *enters. He carries a pitcher of martinis and a glass. He hands them to* ARTHUR *in the tub. He starts to exit.*

ARTHUR *(into the wall phone).* Well, I really have to go, Gretta.

GRETTA *(o.c.).* Yes, sir.

ARTHUR *unplugs* GRETTA'S *button. He pours himself a martini.*

HOBSON. You know, Arthur . . . your father is going to demand that you marry Susan.

HOBSON *starts to exit.*

ARTHUR. I don't care what he demands. Stay with me a minute, Hobson. You know how I hate to be alone.

HOBSON. Yes. Bathing is a lonely business.

ARTHUR. Except for fish . . .

HOBSON. I beg your pardon. Did you say "except for fish?"

ARTHUR. Yes. Fish all bathe together. Although they do tend to eat one another. I often think that fish must get tired of seafood. What are your thoughts, Hobson?

HOBSON. Pardon me . . .

HOBSON *picks up a big sponge, hits* ARTHUR *on the head with it.* ARTHUR *laughs.*

HOBSON. Your father is going to demand that you marry Susan. Please refrain from talking about fish! Shall I hit you again?

ARTHUR. Please.

HOBSON *hits him again.* ARTHUR *laughs like a child.*

ARTHUR. I love you, Hobson. No one else ever hits me over the head in the bathtub. I'm not marrying Susan.

HOBSON *throws the sponge into the tub. It floats along.*

HOBSON *(kneeling down to Arthur, more serious).* Why not? She's a lovely girl.

ARTHUR. Hobson . . . I've decided to marry Gloria. Where else would I find a woman who makes 10,000 dollars a night? *(he laughs)* Is that funny?

HOBSON *points to the sponge floating in the tub.* ARTHUR *hands it to him.* HOBSON *hits him over the head.*

HOBSON. Arthur . . . I don't want you to be alone.

ARTHUR. I'll never be alone. I have you. Isn't life wonderful, Hobson!

HOBSON. Yes, Arthur. It is. Do your armpits.

ARTHUR *(drinking).* A hot bath is . . . wonderful! Girls are wonderful!

HOBSON. Yes. Imagine how wonderful a girl who bathes would be. Get dressed.

ARTHUR. Jesus, Hobson . . . every time a plane leaves the ground it's going somewhere else! Isn't it all wonderful? Am I boring you, Hobson?

HOBSON. Let's say that I am less than titillated. Why don't you write a book entitled crap that I have talked about?

HOBSON *exits.* ARTHUR *lies alone in the tub.*

ARTHUR. How can I get married? Who would take care of him?

Cut to:

Ext.: The Bach Building—Day. ARTHUR's *limo is parked in front,* BITTERMAN *at the wheel. A large plaque on the building says "*THE BACH BUILDING.*"*

Cut to:

Int.: the reception area of the office of STANFORD BACH—*Day.* ARTHUR *sits with a drink with* HOBSON *in the reception area of the office of* STANFORD BACH.

ARTHUR *(in a low voice).* I hate it here.

HOBSON. Of course you hate it. People work here. Here, read this magazine. There are many pictures.

ARTHUR. Look how nobody ever smiles here. Why doesn't anybody ever smile here?

HOBSON. They smile at lunchtime. Lower your voice, Arthur. And sit up.

ARTHUR *does so.*

HOBSON. And stop being so nervous. Later . . . we'll get ice cream.

MRS. STREET *calls from her desk.*

MRS. STREET. Mr. Bach . . . your father will see you now.

ARTHUR *(rising).* Come on, Hobson.

MRS. STREET. He wants to see you alone.

ARTHUR *(nervous).* Oh.

ARTHUR *exits into his father's office. An executive enters the room, picks up a phone.*

EXECUTIVE *(to Hobson).* He gets all that money. And he pays his family back by being a stinking drunk. It's enough to make you sick.

HOBSON. I really wouldn't know, sir. I'm just a servant. On the other hand . . . go screw yourself.

EXECUTIVE *(into the phone).* Hello . . . Betty. . . .

Cut to:

Int.: STANFORD BACH's *enormous office—Day.* STANFORD BACH *sits behind his gigantic desk. Trim. Tough. About 55. Good looking. Smart. And not the nicest man.* ARTHUR *stands in the middle of the office.* MR. BACH *looks up from his reading and they face each other. On the wall and desks are pictures of* STANFORD BACH *with practically every luminary of the past thirty years. Roosevelt, Truman, Kennedy, Nixon, Ford and others. The whole office speaks of power. This is a powerful man. There is a long pause as* ARTHUR *and his father face each other.*

MR. BACH *(finally).* Sit down, Arthur.

ARTHUR. How long will this take, sir?

MR. BACH *(reading).* I don't know. Do you have any pressing appointments?

ARTHUR. No.

MR. BACH. I wouldn't think so. Sit down please.

ARTHUR *sits on a couch rather distant from his father. His father continues to read the report in his hands.*

MR. BACH. *(cont.)* Pardon me for a moment, Arthur. I have to read this. It's important.

ARTHUR. Father . . .

MR. BACH *(reading).* Yes, Arthur . . .

ARTHUR. It's good to see you.

MR. BACH. Really, Arthur?

ARTHUR. Yes. Somehow . . . no matter what . . . it's always good to see you. I don't know why. I tell people I hate you.

MR. BACH *(smiling).* You've always been honest. It's good to see you too, Arthur . . . Let me read this . . .

ARTHUR. I used to hide in your closet . . .

MR. BACH. Pardon?

ARTHUR. I just remembered . . . I used to hide in your closet.

MR. BACH. Why?

ARTHUR. You went to work and your clothes stayed home. Remember that huge closet in your bedroom in Harrison? Before I was sent away? I used to hide in there.

MR. BACH. From what?

ARTHUR. Lions . . . tigers . . . Indians . . . the main thing was . . . nobody could see me . . . and I used to put on your suits . . . and your shirts . . . and your ties . . . and I would become you . . . and I would want to come home from work and play with my son Arthur . . .

MR. BACH. You're too gentle to live in this world, Arthur . . .

ARTHUR. Yes. May I get a drink?

MR. BACH. Help yourself.

ARTHUR *rises. He crosses to the elaborate bar and prepares himself a drink. He drinks.* MR. BACH *puts down what he is reading and picks up a rather large folder. He pulls out several press clippings.*

MR. BACH. The press has a good time with you, Arthur . . . millionaire drunk playboy.

ARTHUR. Yes . . .

MR. BACH. You're the weakest man I've ever known! I despise your weakness!

ARTHUR *(pouring himself a drink).* What weakness?

MR. BACH *rises. He starts to cross to* ARTHUR *at the bar.*

MR. BACH *(on the cross).* Arthur . . . I'm afraid we have to talk.

ARTHUR *(almost to himself).* I'll be good. I'll be good.

MR. BACH *reaches* ARTHUR *at the bar. He pours himself a drink.*

MR. BACH. Arthur . . . surely you realize that we can't let you go on like this . . .

ARTHUR. Yes. Shall we sit down and discuss this? I'm glad we're talking. I have been excessive.

ARTHUR *crosses to the couch. His father follows.*

ARTHUR *(almost to himself).* I'm in such trouble. . . .

MR. BACH. You're going to marry Susan Johnson. One month from today. We want this marriage, Arthur. We want your children. If you do nothing else with your life . . . you're going to father a Bach!

ARTHUR *crosses back to the bar. His father sits on the couch.*

ARTHUR *(on the cross).* Excuse me a moment. *(to himself)* This is big trouble.

He turns to his father.

ARTHUR *(cont.).* I'm not going to marry her. I've told you that a thousand times.

MR. BACH. Fine. Arthur . . . if that is your decision, then the family has no choice. I'm sorry, Arthur . . . very sorry, but as of this moment, you are cut off.

ARTHUR *(very nervous).* Do you mean . . . cut off from you and grandmother and the family?

MR. BACH *shakes his head no.*

ARTHUR. So you mean that I'm cut off from the uh . . . the . . . uh . . .

MR. BACH. The money, Arthur.

ARTHUR. May I have another drink? I don't need it . . . but it's something to hold in my hand.

MR. BACH. Your grandmother and I have had the papers drawn up. We want this marriage, Arthur. I want it. Burt Johnson wants it.

ARTHUR. Burt Johnson is a criminal!

MR. BACH. We all are, Arthur. And as you know, we usually get what we want.

ARTHUR *(drawing himself up).* So . . . that's it, is it? I marry a woman I don't love . . . or lose the money? Well, father . . . I'd rather starve. And I will.

ARTHUR *starts for the door.*

ARTHUR *(cont.).* I'll get married when I fall in love with somebody.

MR. BACH. Fine. I respect your integrity. You just lost 750 million dollars.

There is a long silence.

ARTHUR. Actually . . . Susan is a very nice girl.

MR. BACH. Very nice.

ARTHUR. Have you ever seen her when the light hits her face just right? She looks very beautiful. Of course, you can't depend on that light. And she does wonderful things with a chicken. I love a chicken made at home.

MR. BACH *(overlapping).* The wedding's one month from today. The invitations will be mailed tonight.

ARTHUR *(overlapping).* I love that Susan.

MR. BACH *goes to his desk and opens a drawer. He crosses back to* ARTHUR. *He carries a ring box.*

MR. BACH. Arthur . . . this is the engagement ring your grandfather gave to your grandmother. She wants you to give it to Susan.

He opens the box, revealing an enormous exquisite diamond ring.

ARTHUR *(looking at the ring)*. This is to marry one girl? Father—please don't do this to me.

MR. BACH. Arthur, I've waited for you to grow up. I can't wait any longer. There will be an engagement party at our summer house in Southampton next Wednesday. Everything is taken care of, Arthur. All you have to do is show up . . .

ARTHUR. You win, father. Congratulations.

MR. BACH. I had every intention of winning. Congratulations to you, Arthur. You're going to be a wealthy man for the rest of your life.

ARTHUR. Good

Cut to:

Ext.: speedway—Day. The sound of a racing car going through gears.

One car races around the track. It is ARTHUR *in a jazzy little open race car speeding around the track. Alone. Very fast.* HOBSON *stands to one side of the track with the owner of the speedway. They are the only people on the track.*

OWNER. Very few people would rent this track just for themselves . . .

HOBSON. Yes . . . it's the only way he is assured of winning.

ARTHUR *pulls up in front of* HOBSON.

ARTHUR. Want to take her for a spin, Hobson?

HOBSON. No, thank you.

OWNER *(to Hobson)*. Call me whenever you need the track.

The OWNER *leaves.* HOBSON *joins* ARTHUR.

ARTHUR. Say ready—set—go!

HOBSON. I'd rather not.

ARTHUR. How is it—in all my years of racing, I've never won a race.

HOBSON. Yes . . . I feel strongly that you are one of the few men in the history of the Grand Prix to be arrested for drunk driving.

ARTHUR. Hobson . . . do you know how miserable I am?

HOBSON. You're miserable? I have all this and I'm on a salary.

ARTHUR *pulls out a bottle of scotch, takes a swig.*

ARTHUR. You know the worst part of being me?

HOBSON. I would imagine your breath.

ARTHUR *smiles at* HOBSON.

ARTHUR. Let me be unhappy, will you? The worst part is . . . I never got to meet her.

HOBSON. Who?

ARTHUR. The girl I never met.

HOBSON. I am not confused.

ARTHUR *takes off, drives for fifty yards. Fast. He stops.*

ARTHUR. You know, Hobson . . . I could love somebody. I never got to love anybody! What do I have to live for? I'm a failure at everything I do. I'm just in everyone's way.

HOBSON. Yes. Step outside the car for a moment.

ARTHUR *climbs out of the car.*

HOBSON *(cont.)*. Would you remove your helmet, please

ARTHUR. Why?

HOBSON. Please . . .

ARTHUR *removes his helmet.*

HOBSON. And the goggles . . .

ARTHUR. Why?

HOBSON. Please . . .

HOBSON *slaps him hard across the face.*

HOBSON. You spoiled little bastard. You're a man who has everything! But that's not enough! Is it? You feel unloved, Arthur? Welcome to the world. Everyone is unloved! Now stop feeling sorry for yourself. And incidentally, I love you. Did I hurt you?

ARTHUR *starts to cry.*

HOBSON. Now . . . that's a good idea. Crying is a wonderful release.

ARTHUR *(crying)*. I hate to cry in front of you.

HOBSON. You did when you were little. . . . Get it out. Marry Susan, Arthur. Poor drunks do not find love, Arthur. Poor drunks have very few teeth. They urinate outdoors. They freeze to death in the summer. I can't bear to think of you that way.

ARTHUR. Me neither.

HOBSON. Arthur . . . you're being asked to be 35 when you've never been 27. It really is very unfair.

Cut to:

Int.: Bergdorf Goodman Men's Department— Main Floor—Day. ARTHUR *stands by a counter buying some shirts.* HOBSON *stands wearily by.*

ARTHUR. I'll take three dozen of these shirts. Assorted colors. *(to Hobson)* I hate my father.

HOBSON. Then purchase four dozen.

ARTHUR. Four dozen. And I want 14 of those sweaters, all green.

SALESLADY. All green?

ARTHUR. I don't wear sweaters. Give her the card, Hobson. Send them to my address.

Behind ARTHUR *and* HOBSON, LINDA MAROLLA *is browsing among the ties. She looks around. Then quickly stuffs one of the ties into her satchel.* ARTHUR *and* HOBSON *see this. As does a man on the floor who, if we don't know it already, will turn out to be the security guard. The girl, after her crime, nonchalantly looks around.*

Angle on ARTHUR *and* HOBSON *near the shirts.* HOBSON *has completed filling out the card to buy the shirts and sweaters.* ARTHUR *is strangely excited by what he has seen.*

ARTHUR *(whispering to Hobson).* Hobson! Did you see that!?

HOBSON. Yes.

ARTHUR *(very excited).* She stole that tie! It's a perfect crime! Girls don't wear ties. *(pause)* Although . . . some do. It's not a perfect crime! But, it's a good crime.

HOBSON. Yes. If she murdered the tie . . . it would be a perfect crime. Why are you so happy about this?

THE GIRL, LINDA, *starts to walk slowly toward the Fifth Avenue exit of the store. Following her is the security guard. Following him are* ARTHUR *and* HOBSON. ARTHUR *is totally intrigued with the whole thing.*

ARTHUR *(whispering).* I think the guy following her is the security guard! We've got to be calm! Isn't she beautiful! Jesus!

HOBSON. May I ask . . . what we have to do with this?

ARTHUR. Look at her! If she's willing to do this for a tie . . . imagine what she'd do for a suit! I love that she's walking slow. I'd be running . . . wouldn't you?

They've stopped at the cosmetic counter. ARTHUR *toys with a powder compact.*

HOBSON. If you're not going to purchase that compact, please put it back.

Cut to:

Ext.: Bergdorf Goodman—Day. The Fifth Avenue exit. LINDA *exits the building. The security guard exits a few moments later.* ARTHUR *and* HOBSON *follow. The caravan travels a block or so before the security guard stops* LINDA.

SECURITY GUARD *(showing her his badge).* I beg your pardon, Miss. I'm the security guard in the store.

LINDA *(most definitely from New York).* Yeah? Trust me . . . you don't need the badge. No customer would be wearing that jacket. Well, whattya want?

ARTHUR *and* HOBSON *are watching the confrontation along with a small group of spectators.*

SECURITY GUARD. I'm afraid I'm going to have to look in your bag, Miss. I saw you put something in it.

LINDA *takes out a pencil and pad.*

LINDA. You got trouble, mister! You're never going to work on the East Coast again. What's your name?

Angle on ARTHUR *and* HOBSON *watching.*

ARTHUR. She's sensational! I love her!

HOBSON *(bored).* She does have a certain Eleanor Roosevelt quality.

Angle on LINDA *and the security guard.*

LINDA *(writing).* Chester Manning. Okay. What's your address, Chester?

SECURITY GUARD. Uh . . . Miss . . .

LINDA *(screaming).* What's the address, Chester! *(louder)* Let's have it! I'm not playing games with you!

SECURITY GUARD. Look! I saw you put a a tie in that bag!

LINDA *(furious).* What did you say? *(to the crowd)* Somebody call a cop. Chester . . . I don't want you to move out of my sight. Get your hands off me.

His hands are nowhere near her.

ARTHUR *steps forward.*

ARTHUR *(to the security guard).* Uh . . . Chester . . . I'm Arthur Bach . . . I think I can straighten this out.

SECURITY GUARD. Hello, Mr. Bach. You really should stay out of this.

LINDA. Well . . . he's in it, Chester. Tell him, Alfred.

ARTHUR. Uh . . . I know this young woman. In fact . . . we were shopping together.

LINDA. Right. Where the hell have you been?

SECURITY GUARD. She's a friend of yours, Mr. Bach?

LINDA. He just said that, Chester. You're such a schmuck, Chester.

ARTHUR. He's just doing his job, darling.

LINDA. Well . . . this whole thing is being handled badly. You're lucky he showed up, Chester.

ARTHUR. I asked her to pick out a tie for me. I was going to put it on my bill at the shirt counter.

LINDA. And you didn't pay for it? Chester . . . what can I say? I had no idea.

ARTHUR *starts to reach into* LINDA's *satchel.*

ARTHUR *(to Linda).* May I look at the tie?
LINDA. Of course. I hope you like it.

ARTHUR *pulls out the tie.*

ARTHUR. I love it. Thank you. You're really wonderful.

ARTHUR *grabs her and kisses her fully on the lips. After the kiss,* LINDA *looks at him menacingly.*

LINDA *(after the kiss).* Not in front of all these people, dear. They might think you're an animal.
SECURITY GUARD. Mr. Bach . . . you understand that it's my job to . . .
ARTHUR. And you did it well. I'll mention it to Mr. Peterson when I see him.
LINDA. Me too.
ARTHUR. Would you ask the woman at the shirt counter to put this on my bill?

The security guard goes back into the store. The small crowd disperses.

HOBSON *joins them.* LINDA *and* ARTHUR *look at each other for a beat.* ARTHUR *is smiling a huge almost grotesque smile.*

ARTHUR. Were you scared?
LINDA. Yes Why are you smiling like that?

ARTHUR *continues to smile at her.*

LINDA *(cont.).* I see. You're a little strange. But cute. *(to* HOBSON*)* How are you? *(to* ARTHUR*)* So . . . have a safe trip home . . . thank you . . . I'm going to walk to the bus stop now . . .
ARTHUR. I don't know your name.
LINDA. I know. A lot of people would walk with me.

They start to walk to a bus stop on Fifth. As they walk:

ARTHUR. Why did you steal the tie?
LINDA. I don't know. I'm a wonderful person. I'm serious. *(to* HOBSON*)* I'll be with you in a minute. He's starting to get on my nerves.

They arrive at the bus stop.

LINDA *(to* ARTHUR*).* Could you stop smiling like that? So far I'm talking to your teeth. *(she looks at* HOBSON *again)* Is he with us?
ARTHUR. My name is Arthur and this is Mr. Hobson.
HOBSON. Good afternoon.
LINDA *(to* ARTHUR*)* Good afternoon? My name is Linda. I'd like to thank you. You did a nice thing. That was an interesting kiss. Is that the way you kiss your wife?

The bus pulls up.

ARTHUR. I'm not married.

The bus pulls away.

LINDA. Keep smiling. 688-5549. Don't expect big things on the first date.
HOBSON. Yes . . . Well . . . it has been a distinct pleasure meeting you. We really must be going, Arthur. Thank you for a memorable afternoon. Usually one must go to a bowling alley to meet a woman of your stature.
LINDA *(to* ARTHUR*).* Wouldn't it be funny if he called me?
HOBSON. Yes . . . Arthur . . . I see no reason to prolong this conversation. Unless we start planning to knock over a fruit stand later this evening. *(to* LINDA*)* Good luck in prison.
LINDA *(to* ARTHUR*).* What does he do?
ARTHUR. He helps me.
LINDA. What do you do?
ARTHUR. Nothing.
LINDA *(to* HOBSON*).* You got a good job.
ARTHUR. Who was the tie for?
LINDA. A guy. Look how he stopped smiling. My father. It's his birthday. You're cuter than I am. 688-5549. . . . Look how nobody writes it down.

A bus rolls up.

ARTHUR. Don't get on that bus!
LINDA. Okay. Take it easy

The bus pulls away. She puts her hand on his shoulder. She feels his suit.

LINDA. Silk?
ARTHUR. Silk.
LINDA. Very nice . . .
ARTHUR. This tie needs a box. I mean you can't just give an unwrapped gift.

He giftwraps the tie by unwrapping one of his shirts and putting the tie in the empty box.

LINDA. You're really nice.
ARTHUR. The nicest.
LINDA. Are the . . . uh . . . pants silk?
ARTHUR. Silk.
LINDA. We're talking eight . . . nine hundred dollars here, right?

HOBSON. Oh dear . . .

ARTHUR. I really don't know.

LINDA *(as casual as possible)*. What's your last name, Arthur?

ARTHUR. Bach.

LINDA. You're the son of . . .

ARTHUR. Stanford Bach.

LINDA *(overlapping)*. Stanford Bach . . .

LINDA puts a cigarette in her mouth.

LINDA. Got a light?

ARTHUR *reaches into his pocket. He pulls out the ring box.*

ARTHUR. Here. you want a ring?

LINDA. What the hell is this?

HOBSON *(grabbing it)*. I'm afraid there's been some mistake.

BITTERMAN *in the limo pulls up.* LINDA *sees this.*

LINDA. Why are you carrying around that ring?

ARTHUR. I'm having it cleaned for my grandmother.

LINDA. Right. At a car wash? A Rockefeller would mug for this ring.

ARTHUR. What are you doing tomorrow night?

LINDA. I don't know. I have plans for tomorrow night. What should I wear?

HOBSON. Steal something casual.

LINDA *(to* ARTHUR*)*. I like him.

HOBSON. Likewise I'm sure.

ARTHUR. I'll have Bitterman drive you home.

LINDA. No . . . Bitterman doesn't have to drive me home. *(waves)* Hi, Bitterman. You know . . . I really don't take the bus ever . . . but it's so hard to get a cab . . . I'm sure we know a lot of the same people.

ARTHUR *(opening the door to the limo)*. Shhhh. Get in. You just tell Bitterman where to take you. And make sure he gets your address and phone number. *(to* BITTERMAN*)* Take good care of her.

He closes the door. The car drives off.

ARTHUR. Come on, Hobson. She's terrific.

HOBSON. Yes . . . So much better than an arsonist.

Cut to:

Ext.: Small apartment complex in Queens— Afternoon. The limo approaches LINDA*'s address.* BITTERMAN *has to blow the horn because three kids are playing softball in the middle of the street. The limo continues to the address.*

The kids run alongside the car. They stop in front of LINDA*'s building.*

LINDA. You'd think they'd never seen a car before. Could you children please allow us our privacy. Please.

BITTERMAN. I believe this is the address, Madam.

LINDA. Yes, it is. Thank you very much.

BITTERMAN. Not at all.

LINDA. Uh . . . Bitterman . . . could I just sit here until one of my neighbors walks by? . . . I just want one person to see me get out of this.

BITTERMAN *(smiling)*. I understand.

LINDA. Good. So . . . Bitterman . . . have you been with Mr. Bach long?

BITTERMAN. Many years.

LINDA. That long? Smart. Nobody wants a chauffeur who's been with a lot of different families. They might be talkers. Do you drive Mr. Bach to his dates? It's none of my business. Do you?

BITTERMAN. Madam, I really . . .

LINDA. Of course. That's confidential information. Good, Bitterman. Who is the ring for? Give me a break, will you, Bitterman?

BITTERMAN. I am not at liberty . . .

LINDA. Alright! Here comes Mrs. Nesbit. This should kill her.

A lady walks near the limo.

BITTERMAN. Don't touch the door. Let me do it. Mrs. Nesbit should get the entire treatment.

LINDA. Yeah. Hurry up.

BITTERMAN *gets out of the car. He walks to the rear door.* MRS. NESBIT*'s attention has already been caught by the limo.* BITTERMAN *lets* LINDA *out.*

LINDA *(casually exiting the limo)*. Thank you, Bitterman. Hello Mrs. Nesbit.

BITTERMAN. Will that be all, Madam?

LINDA. I think so.

BITTERMAN *doffs his cap and re-enters the limo. He drives off.*

LINDA. Have a nice evening, Mrs. Nesbit.

MRS. NESBIT. Linda, what is this?

LINDA. A way of life, Mrs. Nesbit. Just another way of life.

She walks into her building.

Int.: LINDA*'s apartment—Early evening.* RALPH, LINDA*'s father, sits at the dining table playing solitaire. He is attired in a tee shirt.* LINDA *enters. She is radiating happiness. She carries the shirt box.*

RALPH. Marie called you . . . I didn't find a job . . . the Mets won . . . the Yankees lost . . . a guy in Staten Island killed his wife and three kids. It's raining in Detroit. Why are you so happy?

LINDA. Come here. I want you to see something.

RALPH. I can't imagine what.

LINDA. Right. Would you come here?

RALPH *crosses to the living room.* LINDA *hands him the box and kisses him.*

LINDA *(kissing him)*. Happy birthday, dad!

RALPH. Is it my birthday? I forgot.

LINDA. Right. Every year you forget. Like a priest forgets Easter. Open it, you phoney.

RALPH. Bergdorf's?

LINDA. And Goodman.

RALPH *(shaking it)*. Could be a big tie . . .

LINDA. It is a tie.

RALPH. Then guessing would be out of the question.

He opens it.

RALPH. It is a tie!

LINDA. Surprise!

She kisses him again.

RALPH. I love it. It goes with everything I have. I hope you like it. If I don't get a job soon . . . you may get it back for your birthday.

LINDA. Dad . . . shut up. A funny thing happened today.

RALPH. Yeah?

LINDA. Yeah. You know why girls marry badly?

RALPH. Is this a joke? Are these Polish girls?

LINDA. No. The reason is . . . there are so many girls and there are so few princes.

RALPH. You met a prince?

LINDA. I met a nice guy. With my help, he could become a prince.

RALPH. Who is he?

LINDA. Just this guy.

RALPH. What does he do?

LINDA. Nothing.

RALPH. Another beauty. How does he make a living?

She starts toward the kitchen.

LINDA. Look . . . I have to make dinner.

RALPH. I take it this bum is going to call you.

LINDA. He's a millionaire.

RALPH. You have my permission to marry him.

Cut to:

Ext.: Madison Avenue in the 60's—Day. ARTHUR *is at the wheel of a beautiful Lamborghini convertible. The top is down. He glides into a space in front of a plant store. He is excited like a child.*

Int.: plant store—Day. The owner, an older man with a Jewish accent, comes around to wait on ARTHUR. ARTHUR *is at the top.*

ARTHUR *(to the owner)*. I love your place! Plants really make a place look great!

OWNER *(Jewish accent)*. Yeah. A plant store looks better den a delicatessen . . . because a delicatessen is hanging salamis. What's your problem?

ARTHUR *smiles. He likes this man already. He puts his hand on the owner's shoulder. The owner looks at the hand.*

ARTHUR. Listen . . . here's the thing. I met this girl!

OWNER. Good. Roses. Yellow. She'll drop dead. She'll love them.

ARTHUR. Okay. Yellow roses. Two dozen. I think something else would be nice, too.

OWNER. Red roses. With the yellow . . . she won't know what hit her. You'll be aces with her. You're a nice boy.

ARTHUR. Right. Two dozen red. You know what happened?

OWNER. No. I don't.

ARTHUR. A couple of days ago, I met her outside Bergdorf's.

OWNER. Good. Good.

ARTHUR. And I can't stop thinking about her! Are you married?

OWNER. Once. She's alive.

ARTHUR. Did you ever feel that way?

OWNER. I felt dat way this morning. I got Joe Namath's sex life . . . only it's all with the same lady. Why am I telling you this?

ARTHUR. What's that?

OWNER. A yucca plant.

ARTHUR. I'll take it.

OWNER. How many?

ARTHUR. Four.

OWNER. Where were you when I was selling cars?

ARTHUR *(grabbing his arm)*. How did you know when you first fell in love? I mean . . . how does anybody know?

OWNER. I was on a train. It came from Washington. It went to New York.

ARTHUR. I love this! Yeah? Yeah? What's that?

OWNER. A fern. You need five. A girl got on the train. Skinny. Gave me a smile. By Baltimore I was a dead duck.

ARTHUR. Did you whistle a lot? I find that I whistle.

OWNER. I whistled.

ARTHUR. Did you feel funny? I feel funny.

OWNER. No. You may have a cold.

ARTHUR *writes down the address and hands him a credit card.*

ARTHUR. Send that stuff and anything else you can think of to this address. Here's the name. And send two dozen roses to your wife. The skinny one from the train.

OWNER. You're the rich one? The one who drinks?

ARTHUR. Yeah.

OWNER. How does it feel to have all that money?

ARTHUR. It feels great.

Cut to:

Ext.: rooftop cafe—Dusk. ARTHUR AND LINDA *seated at a table on a rooftop atop Rockefeller Center. The spires of St. Patrick's are in the b.g. Three wandering musicians are playing.*

ARTHUR. What do you do? I never asked you.

LINDA. I'm going to be an actress. I mean, I'm studying to be an actress. But I work as a waitress. A lot of talented girls do that.

ARTHUR. What's that like?

LINDA. Well, it's interesting. Yesterday a man walked in and pulled out . . .

The musicians have crossed to their table. The violinist leans in playing. They stop talking. He finishes and moves away. They clap.

LINDA. Anyway, this guy walks in and pulls out . . .

Now the accordionist moves in and continues playing where the violinist left off.

LINDA *(interjecting).* A gun!

ARTHUR. Thank God.

They laugh, toast and drink.

Cut to:

Ext.: midtown Manhattan—Night. LINDA *and* ARTHUR *speed through the night in* ARTHUR'S *convertible.*

ARTHUR *(screaming to be heard).* Isn't this terrific!

LINDA. Yeah. Terrific. I'm freezing my ass off. Watch where you're going! Jesus!

ARTHUR. Was that dinner sensational?

LINDA. I could make that same soup for less than a dollar.

They stop at a traffic light. ARTHUR *hands her a rose.*

ARTHUR. Here's a rose. I stole it from the restaurant.

LINDA. Thank you.

ARTHUR. If you're cold . . . I'll put the top up.

LINDA. Nah. It's your toy. Play with it. Are you cute . . .

ARTHUR. Where do you want to go?

LINDA. I'll get out wherever you have the accident.

ARTHUR. I've never taken care of anyone . . . everyone's always taken care of me . . . but if you got sick . . . or anything . . . I would take care of you.

LINDA. Then I'll get sick.

The car goes forward.

Cut to:

Int.: penny arcade—Night. One of those bears in a penny arcade that groans and goes the other way when it gets hit. Pull back to see ARTHUR *and* LINDA *engrossed in shooting the bear.* ARTHUR *has the gun. They are in a cheap penny arcade.*

LINDA. When do I get a turn?

ARTHUR. Shhh! Don't you realize I'm after a new world's record? After only 12 games— I've got 80 coupons!

LINDA. I knew it would be different spending an evening with a millionaire.

ARTHUR. I'm 17 for 17. This is where you really have to have it in the clutch.

He shoots.

Angle on the bear. Groaning and turning.

ARTHUR. Two more . . . I'm 20 for 20 and it's 35 more coupons. *(to everyone around)* Could we have some quiet please?

LINDA. You nut! Can you come to dinner next Tuesday?

ARTHUR *looks at her. Goes back to his gun.*

ARTHUR. No . . . uh . . . no . . . you see . . .

He shoots.

Angle on the bear. It groans and turns.

ARTHUR. That's 19 for 19! Uh . . . I'm going to be out of town.

An old man stands nearby watching them.

LINDA. Oh. I get it . . . it's one thing to take a waitress to Coney Island and shoot a bear, but you wouldn't be caught dead eating at my house, right? If you think you're slumming, hot shot, take me home.

ARTHUR. What time do we eat?

LINDA. How's seven o'clock Tuesday?

ARTHUR. Fine. Now can I shoot my bear?

LINDA. So shoot the bear. Look at him with his gun.

Angle on the bear. He keeps going. He has not been hit.

ARTHUR. I missed!

LINDA. Sure you missed. Go shoot a bear with a beautiful girl standing next to you. Let's get out of here. Are you cute . . .

The man with the coupons approaches.

ARTHUR *(to the man)*. Nineteen.

COUPON MAN. For nineteen you get fifteen coupons.

Angle on ARTHUR *and* LINDA *walking through the arcade.*

Int.: penny arcade—prize counter—Night. ARTHUR *and* LINDA *arrive at the prize counter.*

ARTHUR *(to the prize man)*. What can I get for 95 coupons?

PRIZE MAN. An International Beauty Pageant doll . . .

He shows them the doll.

LINDA. If you wind it up does it have sex with an international beauty pageant judge?

PRIZE MAN. . . . or two back scratchers or three Roman warriors or a skull cup.

ARTHUR *(pointing to another prize)*. What's that?

PRIZE MAN. It's a mophead. But it's 120 coupons.

ARTHUR. Oh no. I've got to get that for you.

LINDA *produces 40 coupons.*

LINDA *(to the prize man)*. We'll take the mophead. *(to Arthur)*. I'll be honest. On the way back from the bathroom I shot a duck.

ARTHUR. Are we great together! *(to the man)*. One mophead.

ARTHUR *hands the mophead to* LINDA.

ARTHUR. Take care of this.

LINDA. Take care of it? I just named it.

ARTHUR. What?

LINDA. For my grandmother on my mother's side . . . Arthur.

Cut to:

Ext.: ARTHUR's *car outside* LINDA's *apartment—Night.*

ARTHUR. Goodnight.

LINDA. Goodnight? Are you out of your mind? I don't know what they do on Park Avenue . . . maybe you just rub each other's money . . . but here we kiss each other.

ARTHUR. Well . . .

He kisses her lightly on the cheek.

LINDA. What the hell was that? That was a kiss to make a boo boo better. Arthur . . . is there a woman in your life? Are you in love with somebody? Tell me now. Because this is big for me . . .

ARTHUR. I don't love anybody else.

LINDA. Then kiss me, you jerk. The lips. Kiss the lips.

They kiss passionately.

ARTHUR. That's the first thing I've ever done that I like better than drinking.

LINDA. Wait. I'll show you stuff you'll like better than heroin. See you next Tuesday. Dinner.

LINDA *gets out of the car. She gets back in.*

LINDA. I like this rose better than all the other roses you sent me. God forbid you should date a a girl with hayfever. I had fun. So did you.

Cut to:

Ext. A gorgeous Townhouse on Sutton Place—Day. ARTHUR's *convertible pulls up.*

Int.: Dining room of the spacious old apartment—Day. Seated at the dining room table with a drink is ARTHUR's *grandmother,* MARTHA. *She is old. But a tough, old dowager. The absolute matriarch of the family. In the room is a birdcage. It is a talkative, whistling parrot,* OSCAR. MARTHA *speaks in dulcet, high-pitched tones.* ARTHUR *enters the room. He rushes to kiss his grandmother. These two are fond of each other.*

ARTHUR *(kissing her)*. Martha! you look great!

MARTHA *(sweet, almost Eleanor Roosevelt)*. How very kind of you to visit me, Arthur. Don't you love the roses? You have always been my favorite grandchild. But . . . then . . . you are my only grandchild.

She laughs. The quiet laugh of an older woman. But long.

MARTHA. *(cont.)* That's quite funny . . . don't you think?

ARTHUR. Yes.

He sits.

MARTHA. Then do an old woman a favor and laugh.

ARTHUR *laughs.*

MARTHA. *(cont.)* Thank you. Excuse me . . . I'm going to sneeze.

MARTHA *does not change her expression for a few moments. She takes out her handkerchief and looks calmly across the table at* ARTHUR. *Finally, she starts to get the first sign of a sneeze.*

MARTHA. *(cont.)* Huh! Huh! Huh!

She finally sneezes. The sneeze is not audible. Not a sound.

ARTHUR. Did you do it?

MARTHA. Yes. Now . . . how about a drink? I could use another one myself.

The bird starts to carry on.

MARTHA. Oh, Oscar . . . shut up!

ARTHUR. Scotch.

MARTHA. I'll call Harriet.

MARTHA *suddenly starts to get lower and lower at the table.*

MARTHA. The buzzer is under the table.

ARTHUR. Of course. I remember. It might be smarter to keep Harriet under the table.

MARTHA *is getting lower and lower. She is almost out of sight.*

MARTHA. When you get to my age, Arthur . . . you can be set in your ways, too. I seem to have gotten shorter over the years.

There is finally the sound of a buzzer from the kitchen.

MARTHA. There!

The kitchen door opens and a black maid enters. This is HARRIET. HARRIET *goes directly to* MARTHA *and pulls her up from her almost prone position.*

MARTHA *(after being pulled up).* Gin and tonic for me. Scotch on the rocks for my grandson.

HARRIET *exits into the kitchen.*

ARTHUR. I've come to you to ask you a favor, Martha.

MARTHA *starts to get lower and lower at the table again.*

MARTHA. Peanuts. I forgot to tell her peanuts. What kind of favor, Arthur?

ARTHUR. I don't want to marry Susan Johnson.

MARTHA *is getting lower and lower at the table.*

MARTHA *(almost prone again).* I don't know why. She's a lovely girl. Where is that buzzer?

MARTHA *is just about out of sight.* ARTHUR *is talking to an empty chair.*

ARTHUR. Martha . . . why don't we just take the table away and sit around the buzzer?

Finally there is the sound of the buzzer from the kitchen. HARRIET *appears from the kitchen. She goes to* MARTHA. *She picks her up.*

MARTHA *(to Harriet).* Peanuts. You may serve us in the drawing room.

HARRIET *goes back into the kitchen.* ARTHUR *and* MARTHA *rise.*

MARTHA. I must get away from this bird. *(to the bird)* You are a pain in the ass, Oscar. Goodby.

Int.: MARTHA's *enormous drawing room— Day.* MARTHA's *hand rips open brown paper covering a painting. A Vermeer is revealed.*

MARTHA. This Vermeer just came today, Arthur. It's called "Woman Admiring Pearls." Isn't it lovely? The dealer jerked me around on the price . . . but what the hell. You live once.

ARTHUR. Martha . . .

MARTHA. What's the matter, Arthur?

ARTHUR. I can't marry Susan Johnson.

MARTHA. Really?

ARTHUR. See . . . I met this girl . . .

MARTHA. You're a charming boy, Arthur. Unfortunately . . . every time you have an erection . . . it makes the papers. Goodness, I sound like a dime novel.

HARRIET *enters with drinks and peanuts.*

MARTHA. Peanuts! Isn't my grandson handsome, Harriet?

HARRIET. Yes.

MARTHA. Thank you, Harriet.

HARRIET *exits.*

MARTHA. Is it wonderful to be promiscuous, Arthur?

ARTHUR. At your age, Martha, it just might be dangerous.

MARTHA. Who is she? The one you met?

ARTHUR. I don't know. She lives in Queens. She's nobody.

MARTHA. I see. Don't make any mistakes, Arthur. You're too old to be poor. You don't know how. We are ruthless people. Don't screw with us.

She hugs him.

MARTHA. I love you, Arthur. And if you don't marry Susan, I'll cut you off without a cent.

ARTHUR. You're a scary old broad, Martha.

MARTHA. Yes. And you are a delightful child, Arthur. Marry Susan and cheat with the nobody from Queens. Do you like the Rembrandt?

Cut to:

Int. ARTHUR's *bedroom—Early evening.* ARTHUR *is getting dressed. He picks up the phone. He dials.*

Intercut—A two-way conversation with LINDA *in her living room—* ARTHUR *in his bedroom.*

ARTHUR *(into the phone).* Hello . . . Linda . . . how are you?

LINDA. Fine. I got off work early. Do you like lasagna?

ARTHUR. Yes.

LINDA. Thank God!

ARTHUR. Uh . . . Linda . . . listen . . . I know this is last minute . . . but . . . something's come up . . . I can't make it tonight.

LINDA. Fine. No problem.

ARTHUR. I've got the flu.

LINDA. Gee, that's tough. Stay in touch.

ARTHUR. Linda, listen . . . the truth is . . . I'm getting engaged tonight. The easiest thing in the world would be to lie to you, but I do like you and . . .

LINDA. Look! No sweat! We had some laughs. Good luck.

ARTHUR. Right. I wanted to tell you the other night.

LINDA. Don't worry about it. I really have to go.

Cut to:

Int. LINDA's *apartment—Early evening. On* LINDA. RALPH *is next to her.*

RALPH. What is it! What is it! Why can't he come?

LINDA. Forget it, Dad. Our millionaire can't come. He's getting engaged.

RALPH *sits at the table. He starts to weep.*

RALPH *(weeping).* Oh no! There goes everything! There goes the Buick, there goes Florida, there goes my heart!

LINDA. Can I get you anything?

RALPH *(crying).* I'll be okay. I just want to be alone for a minute. That's all.

LINDA. You'll be fine.

RALPH. That's easy for you to say. You're young.

Cut to:

Int.: ARTHUR's *bedroom—Early evening.* ARTHUR *in his bedroom.* BITTERMAN *enters.*

BITTERMAN. Shall I get the car, Mr. Bach?

ARTHUR. No, Bitterman. Tonight . . . I'll drive myself. How often does a young man get engaged? Where's Hobson?

BITTERMAN. Mr. Hobson was tired, sir. He is resting.

ARTHUR. He's been tired quite a bit lately . . . Bitterman . . .

BITTERMAN. I'm sure he's fine, sir.

Cut to:

Int.: HOBSON's *bedroom—Early evening.* HOBSON *lies in bed. He doesn't look well. He takes a pill, grimaces in pain. There is a knock on the door.* HOBSON *hides the pill bottle.*

HOBSON. Come in.

ARTHUR *enters. He carries a drink. He sits in a chair across from the bed.*

ARTHUR. What's wrong with you?

HOBSON. I told you, I have a cold.

ARTHUR. Then sneeze.

HOBSON. Arthur . . . stop looking at me like that. *(playfully)* All I have is this little pain in the left side of my chest.

ARTHUR. Stop it!

HOBSON *(a mock heart attack).* Uh . . . uh . . .

HOBSON *does his mock death scene. He closes his eyes and dies.*

ARTHUR. Will you cut it out!

HOBSON *opens his eyes.*

HOBSON. Actually . . . I didn't want to tell you . . . there's this tumor in my head. Did your lights go off?

ARTHUR *(smiling).* Hobson . . . just talk to me.

HOBSON. With a tumor in my head?

He reaches for his head.

HOBSON. Ahhh! Ahhh! There are three books . . . this is important . . .

ARTHUR. Yeah?

HOBSON. Take them back to the library . . .

HOBSON *again dies.* ARTHUR *laughs.* HOBSON *opens his eyes.*

HOBSON. I have a cold. Go get engaged.

ARTHUR *rises.*

ARTHUR. I told Linda that I was getting engaged.
HOBSON. I don't know why. A little tart like that could save you a fortune in prostitutes.

ARTHUR *suddenly becomes furious.*

ARTHUR. Look old man! Don't you ever talk that way about her again! She's the best person I know! Goddamn it! Why are you such a snob?

ARTHUR *exits the room and slams the door. One moment later he opens the door.*

ARTHUR *(softly).* Hobson, I raised my voice to you. I've never done that before.
HOBSON. That's quite alright. You know . . . you may be growing up. And I'm sorry for what I said about Linda.
ARTHUR. You want anything?
HOBSON. I want to be younger.
ARTHUR. I'm sorry. It's your job to be older. I'll go get engaged now.

ARTHUR *exits. We stay on* HOBSON. *He is in pain. He is sick.*

Cut to:

Ext.: West Side Highway—Early evening. ARTHUR *drives a spiffy little Packard convertible. He's really whipping along the road. The top is down. He drinks from a bottle of scotch in a paper bag as he drives.*

Int.: convertible—Early evening. ARTHUR *drinking and driving.*

ARTHUR *(singing).* He's making a list,
Checking it twice.
Gonna find out who's naughty
and nice,
Santa Claus . . .

He stops singing. He reflects on the song. He's drunk. He talks to himself.

ARTHUR. It would be impossible for one old man in a red suit to deliver all those toys to all those kids in one night. I don't buy it! *(pause)* Damn it . . . I do buy it.

Cut to:

Ext.: a huge driveway—Early evening. The driveway leads to a huge mansion in upstate New York. ARTHUR'S *convertible zips up the driveway. He turns off the motor. He drinks one last gulp from his bottle of scotch.*

Cut to:

Int.: large foyer of mansion—Early evening. The doorbell rings. A rather stiff older butler answers it. ARTHUR *enters. He is happy drunk.*

BUTLER *(stiff).* Good evening, Mr. Bach.
ARTHUR. Good evening, Mr. Butler. I'm here to get engaged.

ARTHUR *enters.*

ARTHUR *(yelling up the marble staircase).* Susan! Susan!
BUTLER. Miss Susan is expecting you. She's dressing. I'll tell her that you're here.
ARTHUR. Tell her it's Chief Inspector Flanigan, homicide. That should get her down here. Nothing . . . Offer to take my coat.
BUTLER. You don't have a coat.
ARTHUR. Well offer to take my tie.

The BUTLER *stares.*

ARTHUR. Just a little joke. Take the rest of the week off. You're obviously under a lot of tension.
BUTLER. Would you care to wait in the library?
ARTHUR. Yes, I would . . . The bathroom is out of the question. Another little joke.

ARTHUR *laughs. The* BUTLER *stares.*

BUTLER. Follow me, please.

ARTHUR *follows the* BUTLER *into the library.*

ARTHUR. I'm a little nervous. I'm getting engaged.

Int. Library—Evening. ARTHUR *and the* BUTLER *enter the beautifully appointed library. There are stuffed fish and moose heads on the walls.* MR. JOHNSON *is obviously a sportsman.*

BUTLER. You may wait here.
ARTHUR. Right.
BUTLER. Would you care for anything while you wait?
ARTHUR. Do you have today's Pravda? I like to keep up with Russia.
BUTLER. No.
ARTHUR. Then fill a glass with scotch. Are you sure you want to be a nightclub comic?

The BUTLER *goes to the bar and mixes* ARTHUR *a drink.* ARTHUR *picks up the phone.*

ARTHUR *(into the phone).* Marty . . . he's pouring a scotch. I'll get back to you. No, you bring the potato salad.

He hangs up. The BUTLER *brings him a drink.*

ARTHUR. Thank you. I'm glad we had this time together. You're a funny guy.

The BUTLER *bows.*

ARTHUR *(holding his neck, as if in pain).* You got that too? Terrible, isn't it?

The BUTLER *exits.* ARTHUR *drinks and looks around. He looks at the moose.*

ARTHUR *(to the moose head).* This must be awfully embarrassing for you.

MR. BURT JOHNSON *enters.* SUSAN's *father. He is dressed impeccably but there is something menacing about him. A time bomb ready to go off. The man is a killer.*

MR. JOHNSON. Hello, Arthur. Haven't seen much of you lately.

ARTHUR. Hello, Mr. Johnson. The reason you haven't seen much of me is because I usually pick Susan up at her apartment in town. And you live here. Have a drink.

MR. JOHNSON. I never drink. No one in my family drinks.

ARTHUR. That's great! I bet you've never run out of ice in your whole life.

MR. JOHNSON. I don't drink because drinking affects your decision making.

ARTHUR. You may be right. I can't decide. Just a little humor.

ARTHUR *stands on one side of the moose.* MR. JOHNSON *on the other.*

ARTHUR. Where's the rest of this moose?

MR. JOHNSON. Arthur . . . I think we should get to know one another . . .

ARTHUR. I do too. That's why I had you come over today. *(he laughs)*

MR. JOHNSON *stares at him.*

ARTHUR *(to the moose).* This is a tough room. But I don't have to tell you. *(to* MR. JOHNSON.*)* You must have hated this moose.

MR. JOHNSON. Why don't we forget the moose for a moment?

ARTHUR. Somehow it's not an easy moose to forget.

MR. JOHNSON. I didn't inherit money like you did, Arthur. I started with nothing. And yet . . . I was a millionaire when I was 18. Anybody stood in my way . . . got hurt.

ARTHUR *glances at the moose. He nods.*

MR. JOHNSON. When I was 11 years old . . . I killed a man.

ARTHUR. Well . . . when you're 11 . . . you probably don't even know there's a law against that. *(he laughs)* Is Susan here?

MR. JOHNSON. I knew what I was doing. We were very poor. He came to our house to steal food . . .

ARTHUR. Well . . . he was asking for it.

MR. JOHNSON *(strange, loud).* I took a knife! I killed him in our kitchen!

ARTHUR. All I can say is . . . you're under arrest. No. I'm joking. I'll have another drink.

ARTHUR *moves to the bar.*

ARTHUR. You probably ate out that night. I mean . . . with that man lying in your kitchen.

He drinks a drink quickly.

MR. JOHNSON. You seem to find humor in everything.

ARTHUR. Sorry.

MR. JOHNSON *comes very close to* ARTHUR's *face. Nose to nose. He speaks louder. More menacingly.*

MR. JOHNSON. Arthur . . . do you know what I consider to be my most precious possession?

ARTHUR. No.

MR. JOHNSON. My daughter! She is my gold! She is my treasure!

ARTHUR. She's very nice.

MR. JOHNSON. I protect what is mine, Arthur. I do it in an ugly way! I'm from the gutter.

ARTHUR. I understand. The gutter. You seem upset . . .

MR. JOHNSON. Susan loves you, Arthur. And I want you to make her happy!

ARTHUR. You can count on it.

MR. JOHNSON. I *insist* that you make her happy!

ARTHUR. Listen . . . uh . . . what happens . . . I mean . . . this is just hypothetical . . . if I don't make her happy? *(fast)* Which is out of the question! I swear she'll be happy. But . . . let's just say . . . I make her cranky? For cranky . . . I guess you would probably just break my ankles . . .

MR. JOHNSON. You'll make her happy. I don't like your drinking. It makes you unreasonable. And I want you to work. Your father and I have talked about it. I want you to work for me.

MR. JOHNSON *puts his arm around* ARTHUR.

ARTHUR. Is this it? She's not happy already?

MR. JOHNSON *(laughingly)*. Arthur . . . Susan loves you. So I love you, too. You'll find me a friend.

ARTHUR. That's really nice. Now what if I told you I'd like to go into your kitchen and have a little snack?

MR. JOHNSON *laughs.* ARTHUR *laughs. They exit.*

Cut to:

Int.: Barbetta's Restaurant—Night. ARTHUR *and* SUSAN *sit at a table.* SUSAN *is pretty. Bright. Serious. Knows what she wants. She wants* ARTHUR. SUSAN *eats her fish.* ARTHUR *has only a glass of scotch in front of him. No food.* ARTHUR *is drunk and nervous.*

SUSAN. This poached bass is wonderful. May I give you some?

ARTHUR. No, thanks. You want some of my scotch? They do it beautifully here.

SUSAN. Why don't you eat something?

ARTHUR. I don't want to put anything suspicious into my body. And I'm not hungry.

SUSAN. What's the matter, Arthur?

ARTHUR. Are you looking at me lovingly?

SUSAN. Yes. Arthur . . . don't you get it? You can get drunk . . . you can throw up . . . you can forget to call me for months . . . you can't lose with me. I know you too well. And I'm much stronger than you are.

She takes his hand.

SUSAN. I know how alone you are. I hate how alone you are. I've cried because you're so alone. Don't be afraid, Arthur. You're never going to be alone again.

ARTHUR. Waiter!

A WAITER *comes to the table.*

ARTHUR. I'll have another one. *(to Susan)* You want another fish?

SUSAN. Don't drink any more, Arthur.

ARTHUR. Don't be the sheriff. *(to the waiter).* I'm Arthur Bach. Millionaire drunk. A smart waiter could spend the rest of his life in Florida from this one dinner. Know what I mean? Don't be a stranger.

The WAITER *withdraws.*

ARTHUR. Susan . . . you're such an asshole! This is what I am! Everyone who drinks is not a poet! Some of us drink because we're not poets!

SUSAN. A real woman could stop you from drinking.

ARTHUR. It would have to be a real big woman.

SUSAN *reaches for* ARTHUR's *hand.*

SUSAN. Arthur . . . will you take my hand?

ARTHUR. That would leave you with one. Sorry. Here's the hand.

They hold hands.

SUSAN. I love you, Arthur.

ARTHUR. Good. I have to talk to the waiter now.

The WAITER *puts another drink in front of* ARTHUR.

ARTHUR *(to the waiter).* My doctor has told me that I have to drink ten of these an hour.

WAITER. I understand, Mr. Bach.

The WAITER *chuckles and withdraws.* ARTHUR *pulls out the ring box and puts it on the table.*

ARTHUR. This is the ring that my grandfather gave to my grandmother. Then . . . he died and . . . subsequently, she gave it to me . . .

SUSAN. I'll always love you, Arthur.

ARTHUR. Actually, she gave it to my father who then gave it to me in his office about a week ago. It's just a great ring, isn't it?

SUSAN. It's a beautiful ring. It's a magical night.

ARTHUR. Yes. Do you have any objection to naming a child Vladimir? Even a girl?

There is a huge silence. SUSAN *stares at* ARTHUR *lovingly. Soon* ARTHUR *takes the ring box and begins to throw it up and down.*

SUSAN. Ask me, Arthur.

ARTHUR. Will you marry me, Susan? Take the weekend if you want.

SUSAN. Yes.

ARTHUR. Congratulations!

SUSAN. You put it on, Arthur.

He puts the ring on her finger after several misses.

ARTHUR. Would you mind if I took you home now? I have a terrible headache.

Cut to:

Ext.: LINDA's *apartment in Queens—3:00 in the morning.* ARTHUR's *convertible weaves to a stop. He staggers out of the car.*

ARTHUR *(a whispered scream to nobody).* Linda! Linda! This must be her building.

He rings the bell of an apartment. While he waits:

ARTHUR. I hope it's not late. Who am I talking to?

A fat, dragon-lady in curlers answers the door. She wears a robe.

LADY *(screaming)*. What do you want?

ARTHUR *almost falls over backward from her scream.*

ARTHUR *(very drunk)*. I'm very sorry to disturb you, Madam. I'm looking for Linda. I hope I have the wrong house. No offense.

LADY *(at the top of her lungs)*. My husband has a gun!

ARTHUR *(again, almost falling over from her)*. I'm sure he does, madam. For all I know he shot it while you screamed. Do you suppose you could scream in a lower tone. Some people around here are trying to sleep. Do you know where Linda Marolla lives?

ARTHUR *covers his ears.*

LADY *(screaming)* Why do you want to know! *(to her husband behind her)* Perry! Come here!

Her husband, a huge man, comes to the door.

LADY *(a shout)*. Perry! He wants to know where Linda lives!

PERRY. She lives in 2478. Apartment A. Next door.

His wife belts him in the face.

LADY *(belting her husband)*. You tell a stranger that? Don't you think you should ask him who he is?

PERRY *(calm)*. He looks okay.

ARTHUR. Thanks, Perry. Hey, Perry . . . come here.

PERRY *steps closer to* ARTHUR.

ARTHUR. She's terrible, Perry! Does she always hit you like that?

PERRY. Yeah. What can I do?

ARTHUR. Perry . . . hit her back. She's going to kill you.

ARTHUR *pats* PERRY *on the back.*

ARTHUR. Get in there, Perry. Give her a shot. Jesus.

PERRY *goes back in the house.* ARTHUR *starts to walk next door to the next building. He looks for the address.*

ARTHUR. 2478 . . .

He bumps into a hedge.

ARTHUR. Pardon me. Oh . . . you're a hedge.

Int.: hall outside LINDA's *apartment—Night. He comes to* LINDA's *door. He rings the bell. He waits.*

ARTHUR. Linda! Linda! I know you're in there. Linda! Linda!

From inside the apartment we hear RALPH's *voice.*

RALPH *(o.c.)*. Who is it?

ARTHUR. Arthur Bach.

RALPH *opens the door.* LINDA *is standing in the background in a night shirt.* ARTHUR *shakes* RALPH's *hand.*

ARTHUR *(to Ralph)*. You must be Linda's father.

RALPH. Yeah. It's kind of late. Although I wasn't sleeping. *(very charming)*. Nice meeting you.

ARTHUR. Hi Linda. Could I come in? Don't you hate Perry's wife?

LINDA. Let him in.

Int.: LINDA's *apartment—Night.* ARTHUR *enters the apartment. He walks directly over to* LINDA. *On the cross he knocks over a letter holder. Holder and letters fall to the floor.*

ARTHUR. Oh, I'm so sorry, Linda.

RALPH. It happens.

LINDA *and* ARTHUR *sit on the floor to pick up the letters.*

LINDA. What the hell is the matter with you? Nobody knocks on a door at three in the morning! You're so drunk you can hardly stand up. You're totally obnoxious! And you're engaged!

ARTHUR *is attempting to fix the broken letter holder. He lays it, in pieces, in* LINDA's *lap..*

LINDA. Can it! You haven't met my father. Arthur . . . this is Ralph. Arthur is the schmuck I met at Bergdorf's.

ARTHUR. Hi, Ralph.

RALPH. Hi Arthur. Let me help you up. I wish you'd been here last night. Nobody can cook like my Linda. This little lady is quite remarkable. Her take home is $88.29 a week.

ARTHUR. I'm sure it mounts up.

RALPH. And yet she's managed to take this apartment from nothing and turn it into what you're looking at now. I'm just so damn proud of her. She cooks. She sews . . .

ARTHUR. She steals.

LINDA. Shut up! Okay, hot shot, this better be good. What do you want?

ARTHUR. I have to talk to you. Can we go into your bedroom?

LINDA. Don't be silly. Why should you have to travel? I'll send my father to a movie and we can have sex right here.

RALPH *(laughing)*. She's funny.

ARTHUR. I'm not talking about sex. I just have to talk to you without your father around. Where's your mother?

LINDA. She's dead. You happy?

RALPH. Linda's bedroom is over here, son.

He leads ARTHUR *towards* LINDA's *room.*

RALPH. When you get a chance, I'd like to talk to you about an idea I have for drive-in restaurants.

LINDA. Dad, don't you understand what's going on here? He's playing with us. We're a novelty to him. He's a rich, spoiled playboy. Who got engaged tonight. And I'm not the stag party. Goodnight.

She exits, slams the bedroom door.

RALPH *(to* ARTHUR*)*. She's highstrung, but she's a very nice girl. Would you like to go into her bedroom?

ARTHUR. No. She seems a bit upset.

ARTHUR *starts to leave. He falls.* RALPH *helps him up.*

RALPH. Take care of yourself. We need each other.

RALPH *helps* ARTHUR *to the front door.*

ARTHUR. You're a very nice man, Ralph. You're a very nice man. Thank you.

RALPH. Thank you. Goodnight.

ARTHUR *leaves.* RALPH *returns to the living room.*

RALPH. Millions!

Cut to:

Ext.: Bach's Southampton mansion—tennis courts—Day. We watch ARTHUR *and* MR. BACH *play a point which* MR. BACH *wins. Then they meet at the net.*

MR. BACH. Arthur . . . Burt told me you went to see a young woman after your date with Susan the other night.

ARTHUR *(picking up a can of tennis balls)*. Don't worry about it, father. *(he drinks from the can)* Fuzzy drink. I want the money. I'll never see her again.

He looks around. The house. The beach. The pool. The grounds.

ARTHUR. We really are rich, aren't we?

MR. BACH. Yes. Yes, we are.

ARTHUR. If the poor people knew about this . . . they'd be even madder than they are.

MR. BACH. But they don't know about this.

ARTHUR. I love the money. I love having everything!

He hits a tennis ball over the fence.

ARTHUR. Everything!

He hits another tennis ball over the fence.

ARTHUR. I want it all.

He turns to his father.

ARTHUR. Don't worry about me marrying Susan. Now serve.

MR. BACH *goes back to the service line. He serves.* ARTHUR *hits a blistering winner.*

MR. BACH. Nice shot, Arthur! I didn't know you were that good.

ARTHUR. I have a tendency to let you win. Serve.

Cut to:

Ext.: LINDA's *house—Early afternoon. The limo pulls up,* BITTERMAN *at the wheel.* HOBSON *exits the car and starts to walk towards* LINDA's *door.*

Int.: LINDA's *apartment—Early afternoon.* RALPH *sits at the kitchen table clad in his undershirt playing solitaire. The doorbell rings.* RALPH *crosses to answer it.*

RALPH *(to Hobson)*. Yeah?

HOBSON. Good afternoon.

RALPH. Good afternoon?

HOBSON. Yes . . . Pardon me for ringing without a prior appointment, but could you tell me if Linda Marolla is receiving callers?

RALPH. Is she what?

HOBSON. Yes . . . to put it briefly . . . is she here?

RALPH. Who wants to know?

HOBSON. A person with very little patience, my good man. Is she here?

RALPH. Yeah.

HOBSON. Then would you be good enough to fetch her? May I come in? If you and your undershirt could take two paces back I could enter this dwelling.

RALPH *goes to the bedroom.* HOBSON *enters the house. He looks around.*

HOBSON *(to himself)*. How revolting . . .

LINDA *and* RALPH *enter from the bedroom.*

LINDA. Look who's here. The British Tonto. If you're here to apologize for that jerk you work for, forget it! I'm dating a doctor.

HOBSON. Very well. Then I shall leave.

LINDA. Actually, I went to a doctor. I had a little kick in the side. A little gas. How you been? How's Arthur?

RALPH *(to* HOBSON*)*. You know, ever since I met that Arthur . . . I just liked him. I just hope that these two wonderful kids can get together.

HOBSON *(to* LINDA*)*. Who is this person?

LINDA. He's my father.

RALPH. Yes, I . . .

HOBSON *(to* RALPH*)*. Try not to speak. Could you get me a cup of tea? I should like to speak to Linda.

RALPH. Sure.

He exits to the kitchen. He listens.

HOBSON. The tea is in the top cupboard on the right.

RALPH. That's right.

LINDA. Would you care to sit down?

HOBSON *(looking at the furniture)*. Where? There is an engagement party tonight at Arthur's father's house in Southampton. Here is the address. Perhaps you should attend.

LINDA. Why? Are all the ones he passed up coming?

HOBSON. Young woman . . . this is a tie you cannot steal. I'm afraid this is a tie you are going to have to work for.

RALPH *peeks out.* HOBSON *waves him off.*

LINDA. Are you inviting me to Arthur's engagement party?

HOBSON. My dear child . . .

LINDA. Look . . . why don't I skip the engagement party and just go with them on the honeymoon.

HOBSON. This is not an invitation. However, if there is one thing that old gentlemen can still do—they can still spot young gentlemen in love. Please go to the party.

He coughs.

LINDA. Are you okay?

HOBSON. Yes, I'm fine.

He sits down.

LINDA. Does Arthur know you're here?

HOBSON. No. Arthur is far too fine a person to be involved in something as devious as this. This is best left to scalawags such as myself. And perhaps you.

LINDA. Listen . . . we're two of the nicest scalawags I know. You really watch out for him, don't you?

HOBSON *coughs.*

HOBSON. Yes. And it's a job that I can recommend highly. I have something for you.

He crosses to the kitchen area and gives her a box.

LINDA. What is this?

HOBSON. If I told you it would ruin the surprise, wouldn't it? Don't open it.

RALPH. I have your tea.

HOBSON. I despise tea. Now would you please go to the bathroom and get two aspirins. They're on the top shelf to the left. Behind the untouched shaving cream.

RALPH. How does he know that?

RALPH *exits.* HOBSON *coughs again.*

LINDA. That sounds bad. Have you seen a doctor?

HOBSON. Yes. And he has seen me.

LINDA. I see. Thank you. I think Arthur has a good friend. May I kiss you on the cheek?

HOBSON. Is it something you feel strongly about?

LINDA. Yes.

HOBSON *nods.* LINDA *kisses him.*

LINDA. What about the aspirins?

HOBSON. The aspirins are for you, my dear.

He exits. LINDA *opens the box. In the box is a dress, shoes, etc. and a note.* RALPH *enters with the aspirins.*

RALPH. Where did he go? What's all that?

LINDA *takes the aspirins and tea from* RALPH.

Cut to:

Int.: Bach summer mansion—living room—Night. Angle on MARTHA *dancing. Pull back to reveal* MARTHA *dancing with* ARTHUR *in the Bach's enormous Southampton living room. People everywhere watching, drinking, dancing.*

Angle on SUSAN *dancing.*

Pull back to reveal SUSAN *dancing with* MR. BACH.

Angle on ARTHUR *dancing.*

The band continues playing.

Cut to:

Ext.: Bach summer mansion—driveway—Night. Parking attendants are parking the cars of the very rich as they arrive at the door of the summer mansion in their expensive cars. The guests are attired in summer tuxedos and gowns.

Angle on a cab rolling up to the mansion. LINDA *gets out of the cab. She looks at the house. The cab pulls away.* LINDA *stands by herself. The house is aglow.*

LINDA. Oh my God . . .

Cut to:

Int.: Bach summer mansion—foyer—Night. A butler stands by the door. He opens the door and LINDA *enters. The band plays.*

LINDA. Hi.
BUTLER. Good evening. May I have your name, please?

LINDA *assumes a posture as if she's been doing this her whole life.*

LINDA. Ms. Marolla.
BUTLER. You're not on the list . . .
LINDA. You're new, aren't you?
BUTLER. No.
LINDA. My good man . . . I am on no list. I recently arrived from Panama for the singular purpose of congratulating Arthur on his nuptials. Now you may take my wrap.
BUTLER. If you would just wait a moment . . .

GOVERNOR BRADLEY *walks by the door. She grabs his arm.*

LINDA. Governor Bradley . . . how are you? *(to the butler).* Please return to your post. Anyone could walk in.

Int.: Bach summer mansion—living room—Night. The party.

LINDA *(to Governor Bradley).* You're looking well. It's Linda.
GOVERNOR BRADLEY. How are you? Linda . . .
LINDA. Well . . . it's been run . . . run . . . run . . . ever since the tennis in Monaco. Oh—all the best people are here.
GOVERNOR BRADLEY. It's good to see you, Linda.
LINDA *(sotto, to the Governor).* Father wants you to announce for your next term—soon. Now I want you all to mingle. I really must fly. *(to the Governor's wife).* Keep in touch, Ruth.

LINDA *goes into the crowd to find* ARTHUR. *She walks into another room. Disappears. A moment later she emerges on the arm of a dowager.*

LINDA. Don't worry about your son. It's just a phase he's going through. As far as your sister-in law is concerned, what does she know from suffering? . . . It's over there.

The dowager leaves. A young gentleman approaches LINDA. *Drink in hand. Nice looking, young rich social person.* PRESTON.

PRESTON. Hello.

The band continues to play in the background.

LINDA. Good evening.
PRESTON. Don't you hate these things?
LINDA. Despise them.
PRESTON. It's terribly hard to begin any sort of relationship at a party like this.
LINDA. So true. And yet . . . one must meet one's friends somewhere. And Arty insisted that I come.
PRESTON. Oh. Are you good friends with Arthur?
LINDA *(laughing).* For ages. I'm so pleased that he finally found the right woman. Where is she?
PRESTON. Over there. Isn't she just beautiful?
LINDA. Of course she is. Why would Arthur marry a dog?
PRESTON. Pardon?
LINDA. Nothing at all.

The music stops.

Angle on ARTHUR. *A waiter comes by with a tray of drinks.* ARTHUR *takes the tray.*

ARTHUR. God knows when I'll see you again.

The waiter goes into the crowd. SUSAN *comes over to* ARTHUR.

SUSAN. Arthur . . . will you play something?

The crowd murmurs.

GUESTS. Yes!
ANOTHER GUEST. Play something, Arthur!
ANOTHER GUEST. Will you sing, Arthur?

They move to the piano. LINDA, *with* PRESTON, *watches* ARTHUR *doing his turn at the piano.*

ARTHUR *(fiddling with the keys).* This is all very nice . . . if only I knew how to play the piano. Well . . . as you know . . . songs come and go . . . but I love the classics . . . I hope you all like this . . .

He plays a very classical introduction with a great flourish. Then:

ARTHUR *(singing slowly with great feeling).* You'd better watch out . . .
You'd better not cry . . .

The crowd laughs. ARTHUR *nods his recognition.*

ARTHUR *(with great feeling).*
You'd better not pout . . .
I'm telling you why . . .
Santa Claus is coming to town . . .
GUEST. How do you feel about getting married, Arthur?
ARTHUR *(singing).* Blue Moon . . .

The crowd laughs. ARTHUR *isn't kidding.*

ARTHUR. You saw me standing alone.
Without a song in my heart,
Without a dream of my own . . .
SUSAN. Thanks a lot. That's flattering.
ARTHUR *(singing)* If you knew Susan like I knew Susan . . .

ARTHUR *sees* LINDA *talking to* PRESTON.

ARTHUR. Oh . . . oh . . . I need a drink.

He rises from the piano, goes looking for a drink. The band starts to play again.

Angle on LINDA *and* PRESTON. ARTHUR *is approaching now.* LINDA *sees him.*

LINDA. Tell me your entire name, darling.
PRESTON. Preston Langly.

For ARTHUR's *benefit* LINDA *squeezes* PRESTON's *hand and laughs flirtatiously.*

LINDA *(laughing).* Oh Preston! Really! If you don't remember when we met! Honestly! *(lower)* Put your arm around me, Preston.
PRESTON. Of course.

PRESTON *does so.* ARTHUR *is now close enough for* LINDA *to talk to him conversationally.* ARTHUR *is surprised, amused, perhaps a little frightened to see her. He looks back to* SUSAN. PRESTON's *arm is around* LINDA.

ARTHUR. Linda! You're here!
LINDA *(formally).* So true, Arthur, join us.

She extends her hand which ARTHUR *takes.* ARTHUR *can't get over her.*

LINDA. Congratulations. Father sends his regards.

ARTHUR *and* LINDA *are playing a game only for them.*

ARTHUR *(equally as formal).* Does he?
LINDA. Yes he does. *(to* PRESTON*).* Wednesday night may be difficult for me.
PRESTON. What?
ARTHUR. You're looking wonderful, my dear . . .
LINDA. Don't I? Thank you . . .
PRESTON. Wednesday?

ARTHUR. It's difficult for her that night, Preston . . . isn't that the night you and your father usually attend the ballet, darling?
LINDA. Yes.
PRESTON. Actually . . . I feel foolish, but I don't recall ever . . .

LINDA *smacks* PRESTON *playfully but hard on the arm.*

LINDA. Preston . . . would you be a darling and get me a gin and tonic?
ARTHUR. Scotch for me, Preston.
PRESTON *(to Linda).* Wait here for me.
LINDA. If it takes forever.

PRESTON *exits.* ARTHUR *looks at* LINDA *for a long time. He starts to laugh. So does she.*

ARTHUR. What are you doing here? And why are you talking like that?
LINDA. I was in the neighborhood. It took me two busses, two trains and a cab to get me in the neighborhood . . . but what the hell. *(looking around)* Nice place. I like a living room you can land a plane in.
ARTHUR. There's a lot more of it. Like a tour?
LINDA. I've seen bedrooms. Don't be a lover. Be a person.
ARTHUR. You make me happy.
LINDA. You're looking at me like my father looks at a pot roast. Blink a little.
ARTHUR. Right.

PRESTON *arrives with drinks.*

LINDA. Thank you, Preston.
ARTHUR. Thank you, Preston.

PRESTON *waits. After a moment:*

LINDA *(to Preston).* 290 East 73rd Street. Apartment 15D. I think it'll look better if you leave first.

PRESTON *goes.*

LINDA. Where's Mr. Hobson?
ARTHUR. He's in the city. Why?
LINDA. Just looking for a familiar face.
ARTHUR. Come with me.
LINDA. Where? So far . . . Susan isn't thrilled with me.

She looks over at SUSAN *who is staring at them.* ARTHUR *and* LINDA *make their way through the crowd to a door that leads to a veranda overlooking the ocean.*

Cut to:

Ext.: Bach summer mansion—veranda— Night. ARTHUR *and* LINDA *arriving on the ve-*

randa. It's a beautiful night. The ocean is in the distance.

ARTHUR. That's the ocean.

LINDA. Thank you. Do you wish you were a sailor?

ARTHUR. Yes.

LINDA. I knew that.

ARTHUR. Also a pirate.

LINDA. I knew that too.

ARTHUR. And also a chiropractor.

LINDA. That I didn't know.

ARTHUR *puts his hands on her shoulders.*

ARTHUR. What are you doing here?

LINDA. We're very fond of each other. Did you know that?

ARTHUR. I want to be with you. I mean . . . alone . . . you know what I mean?

LINDA. No. I'm real stupid. Look, hot pants . . . I came to this party to give you one more shot at me. Don't blow it. *(softer).* Arthur . . . I've never been happier than this moment.

SUSAN *and* MARTHA *appear on the veranda.* ARTHUR *quickly takes his hands off* LINDA's *shoulders.* SUSAN *and* MARTHA *come over to where* ARTHUR *and* LINDA *are standing.*

MARTHA. Isn't it a little bit cold out here, Arthur? Oh . . . I don't believe I've met your friend.

ARTHUR. Linda . . . this is my grandmother . . . Martha Bach, and my fiancee, Susan Johnson. This is Linda Marolla.

SUSAN. Nice to meet you, Linda.

LINDA. Love your ring . . .

SUSAN. This is the ring that Arthur's grandfather gave to Martha many years ago.

She squeezes MARTHA's *hand.*

SUSAN. I'll always treasure it.

LINDA. You should always insure it.

There is a forced laugh from ARTHUR *and* MARTHA.

MARTHA. What an adorable retort, my dear. Your friend is adorable, Arthur.

ARTHUR. Yes . . . anyway, Linda . . . tell Harold the next time I'm in Boston . . . we'll spend some real time together. *(to* MARTHA *and* SUSAN) Harold is Linda's husband. I met him in prep school.

LINDA *is appalled by this.*

SUSAN. Is Harold here?

ARTHUR. No, Susan. Harold is in Boston. You know . . . it is cold out here and . . .

LINDA. Harold is quite ill.

ARTHUR *gives* LINDA *a stern look.*

SUSAN. What's wrong with him?

ARTHUR. It's really nothing. I just spoke to Harold last week.

LINDA. Harold's eyes are failing.

SUSAN. I'm so sorry.

LINDA. Last week he stepped on our cat. The man can't see.

She starts crying. ARTHUR *puts his arm around her.*

ARTHUR. I'm sorry. I'm so sorry, Linda.

LINDA. Listen . . . we'll be okay. Both boys are doing poorly in school. It's not easy living with a man who is going to be sightless.

MARTHA. Arthur . . . why don't you and Susan go back to the party. I'd like to talk to Linda.

ARTHUR. What about?

MARTHA. Harold.

ARTHUR *(to* LINDA). I'll see you before you leave?

LINDA. Go back to your party.

SUSAN *and* ARTHUR *exit.* LINDA *is crying.*

MARTHA. Linda . . . I know who you are. Burt Johnson, Susan's father, knows who you are. It is hopeless, my dear. We don't lose to people like you . . .

LINDA *(crying).* People like me? I just . . .

MARTHA. I know. And it is a very romantic notion . . . but I'm afraid Arthur will marry Susan and you will go back to . . . which borough do you come from?

LINDA. Queens.

MARTHA. Yes. I'm sorry.

LINDA *(furious).* Look! Don't be so sorry! I'm not losing here! Everybody's losing here! That means you too, Martha! So far I'm the only person at this party I'd want to meet. Goodnight. And try some makeup.

Int.: Bach summer mansion—living room— Night. ARTHUR *and* SUSAN *walk in from the veranda.* MR. JOHNSON *approaches them.*

MR. JOHNSON. Susan! Arthur!

He joins them.

SUSAN. My two favorite guys.

MR. JOHNSON. Mind if I borrow your young fellow for a minute, Susan?

SUSAN. Not too long.

He kisses SUSAN, *then strolls with* ARTHUR. *In the background we see* LINDA *storm in from the veranda and cross to the front door. She exits.*

MR. JOHNSON. I don't want you to see that girl again.

ARTHUR. Uh . . . I really should say good-night to my guest.

MR. JOHNSON. Don't.

ARTHUR. Don't ever tell me what to do again . . . okay? I don't like it . . . Burt.

ARTHUR goes to the door and exits. BURT *goes to a servant and whispers something.*

Cut to:

Ext.: Bach summer mansion—driveway—Night. LINDA *stands alone in the driveway waiting for her cab. She is crying. In the background we see* ARTHUR *exit the house. He comes over to* LINDA.

ARTHUR *(to the parking attendant).* Get my car, will you?

ATTENDANT. Right away, Mr. Bach.

LINDA *(to the attendant).* How about my cab.

ATTENDANT. Ten minutes.

They stand in silence.

LINDA. Why do I have a Harold?

ARTHUR. You mean—old, blind Harold! You come to my engagement party uninvited. . . .

LINDA. I've gone to better places uninvited . . .

ARTHUR's *car arrives.*

LINDA. Now get in your Donald Duck car and leave.

ARTHUR. Get in the car.

LINDA. Screw you!

ARTHUR. When I was a kid I used to play baseball over there.

LINDA. So?

ARTHUR. I wanted you to see it.

LINDA. Show Susan. Were you good?

ARTHUR. No. I played with Hobson.

LINDA. He's a nice man.

ARTHUR. How do you know?

LINDA. I just know.

ARTHUR. You're ruining my life.

LINDA. Big deal.

ARTHUR. Let's not talk.

LINDA. You got it.

They get in the car. ARTHUR *pulls the top down. They drive off.*

Cut to:

Ext.: Plaza Hotel—Night. They pull up front.

LINDA. This isn't home.

ARTHUR. One drink.

LINDA. One.

Dissolve to:

Int.: Plaza Hotel—Elevator—Night. ARTHUR *and* LINDA *stand in the elevator. Three other people are in the elevator with them.*

LINDA *(smashed).* I love that bar downstairs. Where are we?

ARTHUR *(equally smashed).* We're in an elevator.

LINDA *laughs hysterically. The people in the elevator react.*

LINDA. God . . . you're funny! Who are these people?

ARTHUR. These are the other people who are riding on this elevator. *(introducing them)* This is Mr. Furguson . . . his wife Margaret . . . and of course you remember Janice.

LINDA *shakes hands all around. The people are bewildered.*

LINDA. Where are we going?

ARTHUR. My family has a suite in this hotel. *(nudging and winking at one of the passengers)* I have to get a shirt I left there.

LINDA *(to the passengers).* He's engaged. *(nudging and winking at another passenger)* But . . . we like each other.

The elevator doors open and they exit.

Cut to:

Int.: Huge ornate Plaza Hotel suite—living room—Night.

LINDA *(smashed).* I love that bar downstairs. Where are we?

ARTHUR *(making drinks).* This is a suite my family keeps at the hotel.

LINDA *grunts toward the bar, indicating that she wants a drink.* ARTHUR *grunts back.*

LINDA. Were we recently in an elevator?

ARTHUR. Yes.

LINDA. So . . . basically . . . we're in the same hotel . . . only on a higher floor . . . is that it?

ARTHUR. Yes. We came here to make love.

LINDA. You got a fat chance hot shot . . . although . . . you shouldn't give up.

ARTHUR *(holding Linda's foot, ad lib, doing a shoe salesman bit)* This is much too tight. We just got a shipment in from Florence . . . Florence! Bring in the six-inch heel.

LINDA *(toasting).* Well . . . here's to you and Susan . . . and me and Harold . . .

ARTHUR. The bed is in the next room. We call it the bedroom.

LINDA. Really? So this room is just for foreplay . . . I'm drunk.

LINDA. Just what the world needs. A chauvinist lush. You know . . . I hate it when the man I'm with has an engagement party earlier in the evening . . .

ARTHUR. Jesus! Will you stop harping on that! That was hours ago! Linda . . . let's just take off our clothes and lie down . . . we don't have to do anything.

LINDA. You're pathetic. You're not even good at this! *(she touches his face)* You have the face of a boy who shaves. Do you love her at all? Susan?

ARTHUR. I like her a lot. Want to see how I kiss her?

LINDA. Yeah.

They lean forward.

ARTHUR. You're Susan. I'm kissing you good night.

LINDA. I know my part.

He kisses her lightly on the lips.

LINDA. I see. It's not as bad as you think.

They are close together.

ARTHUR. Now . . . would you like to see how I once screwed a nurse in Philadelphia?

LINDA *(laughing).* Yeah. You got slides?

ARTHUR. Linda, I'm crazy about you!

LINDA. Arthur, take me to the bedroom.

They exit into the bedroom.

Int.: Plaza Hotel suite—Night. ARTHUR *is lying on the bed.* LINDA *walks around the room.*

LINDA *(looking around).* Look at this room! It's not easy to feel cheap here.

LINDA *walks to the window and looks out.*

LINDA. New York . . . is all lit up.

ARTHUR. You were expecting Pittsburgh?

LINDA. It looks like a gigantic Christmas tree. Central Park lake looks that big. *(she gestures)* I feel like we're a young couple from the Midwest on our first trip to New York.

ARTHUR *(lying back on the bed).* Come here.

LINDA *goes to the bed and lies next to him. He puts his arms around her. They lie like that for a beat.*

LINDA. What are we waiting for?

ARTHUR. The other girl will be here in a minute. You didn't think this was going to be you and me, did you? You'll like her.

LINDA *laughs.*

LINDA *(laughing).* Why do I feel so comfortable with you?

ARTHUR. Because we are that couple from the Midwest. And we're very nice people.

He kisses her. Light at first. Then it quickly turns to passion.

ARTHUR *(breathing heavily).* You're a nice girl . . . but you don't turn me on physically.

LINDA. You're not going to marry that girl. And you know it.

ARTHUR *kisses her again.*

ARTHUR. Let's not talk anymore. Okay?

LINDA. I know you're not going to marry her.

ARTHUR. She's talking. Linda . . . let's not talk.

He rolls over and kisses her again. After the kiss:

LINDA. Let's talk for a second . . .

ARTHUR. I'm having sex here! Do you mind!

LINDA. Why would you marry a woman you don't love?

ARTHUR. I have to. Can I help you with that?

LINDA. What do you mean . . . you have to?

ARTHUR. Could we talk about this later?

LINDA. Just tell me what you mean . . . you *have* to?

ARTHUR. My family is forcing me to marry her.

LINDA. You asshole! Nobody gets married like that! That hasn't happened since 1850!

ARTHUR. They'll cut me off if I don't! Without a cent!

LINDA. So! You'll get a job like everybody else! How much money is it?

ARTHUR. 750 million dollars.

LINDA. Try it with her for a few years. Maybe it'll work out.

ARTHUR. Linda . . . you see this suite? I have to be in suites like this.

LINDA. Why?

ARTHUR. Because . . . that's who I am. I'm Arthur Bach. I've got nothing but the money.

LINDA. Me. You got me.

ARTHUR *(touching her face).* Yeah. We have each other. How would you like to share the money with me?

LINDA. What do you mean?

ARTHUR. I mean, we can always be together. We can have anything we want.

LINDA. Including Susan?

ARTHUR. Yes. I have to marry Susan. Grow up, Linda. This is life.

LINDA. We're not that nice young couple from the Midwest, are we? I'll get a cab.

LINDA *crosses to the door.* ARTHUR *sits on the bed. She stops.*

LINDA. You can't have everything, Arthur. If you get the potato you don't get a vegetable.

ARTHUR. Would you turn down this money?

LINDA. Are you crazy? Of course not! I steal ties for Christ sakes! But when you look for a mistress . . . make it a mistress! She should speak French and give back rubs. Don't come to me. I want to get married. What do I know about being a mistress? You'd get me an apartment and I'd want to know if it's near a good school.

ARTHUR. Goodby, Linda.

LINDA. Don't pout. You're lovely. I'll remember you the rest of my life.

LINDA *exits. The phone rings.* ARTHUR *picks it up.*

ARTHUR *(into the phone).* Hello . . . Bitterman . . . oh no. *(he looks at his watch)* I'll meet you there in an hour.

Int.: Hobson's hospital room—Day. HOBSON *lies in bed. He looks very much worse than the last time we saw him. He wears a hospital robe. He reads a book.* BITTERMAN *and* ARTHUR *enter the room.*

HOBSON *(looking up).* Oh my goodness! Is there no place I can go to get away from you?

BITTERMAN. I had to tell him, Mr. Hobson.

ARTHUR *walks over to the bed. He reaches out for* HOBSON'S *hand and holds it.*

HOBSON. Promise me that when I die . . . you will not conduct a seance and try to contact me. I do not relish coming from another world to tell you where your underwear is.

ARTHUR *(smiling, holding his hand).* You're not going to die.

HOBSON. Really? Excellent. I would appreciate it . . . on your next trip . . . if you would bring presents

ARTHUR. Bitterman . . .

BITTERMAN *exits the room.*

HOBSON *(to* ARTHUR).* What did you do?

ARTHUR. Santa Claus is coming to town.

BITTERMAN *enters with his arms totally loaded with things. They are all wrapped. He puts them down near the bed.*

HOBSON *(to* ARTHUR).* And you didn't drink?

ARTHUR *(snaps his fingers).* I forgot!

HOBSON. I should die more often.

ARTHUR. I'm not going to let you die.

HOBSON. How reassuring. Arthur . . . I promise you that this is real. I am not a brave person. In fact, I'm frightened. I'm frightened to close my eyes and go to sleep because I may never open them again. It will hurt you to be with me.

ARTHUR. Who else do you have? You old fart! I swear to you that we'll walk out of this place together. Stop talking.

BITTERMAN. Yes. Save your strength.

ARTHUR. It's not that. He's boring.

HOBSON *smiles. A* YOUNG DOCTOR *enters the room.*

DOCTOR. How are you feeling, Mr. Hobson?

HOBSON. I'm not quite sure. Ask me at the funeral. *(to Arthur)* First they tell you you are expiring and then they inquire about your health.

DOCTOR *(to* BITTERMAN *and* ARTHUR).* Would you excuse us for a moment?

ARTHUR. Of course *(to* HOBSON)* We'll be in the hallway.

They exit.

DOCTOR *(to* HOBSON).* Now, would you relax . . . please.

Cut to:

Int.: hospital corridor—Day. ARTHUR *and* BITTERMAN *stand in the hallway outside* HOBSON'S *room.* ARTHUR *stands with his hand against the wall looking down.*

ARTHUR. Are you okay, Bitterman?

BITTERMAN. Yes, sir. Would you like me to get you some scotch, sir?

ARTHUR. No. We'll get through this, Bitterman.

BITTERMAN. Yes, sir. It's very hard. I'm glad to have you here, sir.

ARTHUR. Bitterman . . . do me a favor. Go back to the house and call my father and Mr. Johnson and Miss Susan. Tell them what's happened. The wedding will have to wait. And then bring me some clothes here.

BITTERMAN. Yes, sir.

BITTERMAN *walks toward the elevators. The* DOCTOR *now exits from the room.*

ARTHUR. Doctor . . . I'm . . . family . . . what is it?

DOCTOR. I'm sorry. It's lymphoma. *(off Arthur's reaction)* A cancer of the lymph glands.

ARTHUR. Is there an operation that . . .

DOCTOR. It's too far advanced for surgery. I'm sorry.

ARTHUR. Are you saying that he . . .

DOCTOR. Yes. I'm afraid it's terminal. I'm very sorry. We can keep him out of pain.

ARTHUR *(louder)*. Doctor . . . do you know who I am?

DOCTOR. No, I don't.

ARTHUR. I'm Arthur Bach. My father is Stanford Bach. Half this hospital was built on a donation from my family.

DOCTOR. I know who you are.

ARTHUR. Good. Then you know that I don't care what this costs.

DOCTOR. I'm sorry. This isn't a financial problem.

The DOCTOR *walks away from* ARTHUR.

Int.: HOBSON'*s hospital room—Day.* ARTHUR *enters.*

ARTHUR *(to Hobson)*. Let's open the presents.

ARTHUR *walks over to* HOBSON'*s bed. He puts all the presents on the other bed. He begins to unwrap one.*

HOBSON. I'm sorry, Arthur . . .

ARTHUR. For what?

HOBSON. You know what.

ARTHUR *unwraps the first present. It is a basketball.*

HOBSON *(very dry)*. Why . . . it's a basketball.

ARTHUR. What the hell. I knew you didn't have one. We'll put this over here.

ARTHUR *puts the basketball on the other bed.*

HOBSON. Yes. If I feel the urge to dribble . . . I can call the nurse. *(smiling)* You really are funny.

ARTHUR *starts to unwrap the next present.*

ARTHUR *(while unwrapping)*. Do you remember playing catch with me when I was a kid?

HOBSON *(very dry)*. Yes. What fun we had.

He unwraps a huge toy locomotive. An engine. Big.

HOBSON. Yes. You purchased a choo-choo.

HOBSON *starts to laugh.* ARTHUR *begins laughing.*

ARTHUR *(laughing)*. Look . . . the wheels go around.

HOBSON *(laughing)*. I'm very pleased.

ARTHUR *puts the engine on the tray table. He starts to unwrap another present.*

ARTHUR. Do you remember playing hide and seek with me? I would hide. You never found me.

HOBSON. Did you know I never looked?

ARTHUR. Come on . . .

HOBSON. I looked a little . . .

ARTHUR *unwraps a large Texas ten-gallon hat. He unwraps another one.*

ARTHUR. One for you and one for me. Put it on.

HOBSON. I don't wish to put it on. I'll put it on. *(he puts it on)* If I start to die . . . please take this off my head. This is not how I wish to be remembered.

ARTHUR *(with hat on)*. Aren't these great? And I've got guns and holsters for both of us. *(Texan accent)* Just in town for supplies . . . pardner . . .

HOBSON. I'm frightened, Arthur. Give me my basketball.

ARTHUR *does so.*

ARTHUR. I know. And I'm going to take care of you.

Cut to:

Int.: HOBSON'*s hospital room—Early morning. It is seven days later. Angle on the door. The door opens. An orderly walks in with a tray of food for* HOBSON.

Pan the room. ARTHUR *is sleeping in another bed next to* HOBSON. ARTHUR *rises and takes the tray from the orderly.*

ARTHUR. I'll take that.

The room now has bookshelves, paintings and other things of HOBSON'*s.*

ORDERLY. Mr. Bach . . . you look terrible . . . You haven't slept in a week.

ARTHUR. We didn't have a good night. He was up.

ORDERLY. I got the kippers and eggs. I'm going to be fired.

ARTHUR. No you won't.

He hands the orderly a large bill.

ARTHUR. Listen . . . for lunch . . . I want the trout almandine from Lutece. Tell Henri it's for me.

ORDERLY. He shouldn't be eating this stuff.

ARTHUR. I don't want his last meal to be jello. Thank you. I'll see you later.

HOBSON *wakes up.* ARTHUR *stands by his bed with the tray.*

ARTHUR. Okay . . . we got kippers and eggs . . . we got toast . . . we got orange juice . . . we got blueberry cakes . . . we got great coffee.

HOBSON (*weakly*). You know, Arthur . . . I'm very glad you're here.

ARTHUR. Eat something. You know what this costs? I got chefs working at six in the morning all over town.

He feeds HOBSON *a bite of egg.* HOBSON *refuses it.*

HOBSON. You look awful, Arthur.

ARTHUR. You've just never seen me sober. Eat. Come on . . . you used to make me eat . . .

HOBSON. Arthur . . .

ARTHUR. What?

HOBSON. It's not so bad. You don't have to be so frightened of it.

ARTHUR. What?

HOBSON. Dying. It seems natural . . . even comforting now.

ARTHUR. You're even teaching me how to die?

HOBSON. I'm through teaching you, Arthur. You've grown up. Arthur . . .

ARTHUR. What?

HOBSON. You can do anything with your life that you want to.

ARTHUR. What does that mean?

HOBSON. Figure it out. Seen Linda Marolla lately?

ARTHUR. Linda Marolla? Why would you ask about her?

HOBSON. I don't know what I'm saying. I'm dying.

ARTHUR. You want me to read you some Shakespeare? Hamlet was in trouble when we left off.

HOBSON. No, Arthur. . . .

ARTHUR. Yeah?

HOBSON. You're a good son.

Int.: ARTHUR'S *apartment—* HOBSON'S *room Day.* ARTHUR *looks around* HOBSON'S *room. He sits in a chair facing a chess set. He moves a piece. He looks to the empty chair opposite. After a moment he gets up, crosses to the door.*

Int.: ARTHUR'S *apartment—hall outside* HOBSON'S *room—Day.* ARTHUR *locks* HOBSON'S *door.*

Cut to:

Ext.: St. Bartholomew's—Day. We hear the sound of church bells ringing. St. Bartholomew's.

*Int.: St. Bartholomew's—Day. The entire church is filled with wedding guests. The minis-*ter *and a huge choir are in place at the front of the church. They are all waiting for* ARTHUR.

Cut to:

Ext.: St. Bartholomew's steps—Day. MR. BACH *and* MR. JOHNSON *are walking up the steps.* MR. BACH *looks at his watch.*

MR. JOHNSON. I want you to know . . . that if he doesn't show up for this wedding . . . I'm going to kill him.

MR. BACH. Don't worry about it. I've talked to Arthur every day. Since Hobson's death, Arthur has stopped drinking . . . he's anxious to work . . . he's become a responsible citizen. He'll be a good husband.

Cut to:

Int.: LINDA'S *apartment—Day. The doorbell rings.* LINDA *crosses to answer it.* ARTHUR *is at the door in top hat and tails. He is incredibly drunk and furious. She opens the door.*

ARTHUR (*mad and drunk*). God damn you!

LINDA. Oh Jesus. What are you doing here? Are you doing a musical?

ARTHUR. I'm getting married in thirty minutes. You're not invited.

LINDA. Are you dangerous?

ARTHUR. I came here to tell you a few things! Later . . . I'm marrying Susan. Who it turns out . . . I'm crazy about! Get me a drink.

LINDA. Go screw yourself.

ARTHUR. I thought you'd say that! That's so like you.

He hits her in the arm. She punches him in the stomach.

ARTHUR (*a little in pain*). You know . . . when I hit you in the arm . . . it's just an indication that I don't like you. But when you hit me in the stomach . . . it really hurts.

LINDA (*more conversational*). I'm sorry. I've been working out.

ARTHUR (*conversational*). Oh really. Did you join a club?

LINDA. No. Just some jogging . . . watching what I eat . . .

ARTHUR (*furious again*). God damn you! I've been going through hell and you've been watching what you eat! I despise you!

He hits her in the arm.

ARTHUR. Now be careful.

LINDA *hits him in the stomach.* ARTHUR *doubles over.*

ARTHUR. You don't understand about hitting friends.

He sits down on the sofa.

ARTHUR. Hobson died three weeks ago. He weighed less than a hundred pounds.

LINDA *sits on the sofa.*

LINDA. I wish you had called me.
ARTHUR. I do too. You'd be amazed how few people I love.
LINDA. You love me?
ARTHUR. You stupid asshole! I don't love you! How could I love you? I'm marrying Susan who is no bargain either, but who has never hit me in the stomach.

He hits her in the arm. She hits him in the stomach. He doubles up.

ARTHUR. You're not a kind person.
LINDA. Do you love me?
ARTHUR *(still doubled over).* Very much. I have a tendency to love the person who is maiming me. I hate you!
LINDA. Come on. This is important. You're getting married soon. Do you love me? I won't tell anyone.
ARTHUR. Love you? Let me tell you something . . . it will help you pass the time while you're watching what you eat. I was a kid . . . growing up . . . I went to school. I was rich. I drank. I was happy. I screwed the upstairs maid. I didn't have you bothering me! Then I got bigger. I went to Europe. I drank. I was rich. I was happy.

He stands up.

ARTHUR. That was before I met you! Then . . . I got bigger. I drank. I met you! Now . . . I drink. I screw nobody! I may lose all my money! And for what? Forget it! *(losing control)* Yes! Yes! I love you! Oh shit! My life is in the toilet! I can't marry Susan. Oh shit! I'm going to be poor!
LINDA *(holding him).* It's not so bad.
ARTHUR. Have you ever been rich?
LINDA. No.
ARTHUR. Then you know nothing about being poor. I have to go tell Susan I'm not marrying her. Do you love me?
LINDA. Somebody has to. Hobson told me.
ARTHUR. What?
LINDA. Who do you think dressed me for your engagement party?
ARTHUR. He's still helping me.

Cut to:

Ext.: St. Bartholomew's—Day. ARTHUR's *limo pulling up in front of the church.* BITTERMAN *gets out of the car to let* ARTHUR

out. ARTHUR *and* LINDA *are necking in the back seat.*

BITTERMAN. Your wedding, sir.
ARTHUR. God. What am I going to tell her, Bitterman? Women hate this kind of crap.
BITTERMAN. Sir . . . if I may say so . . . you are doing a very courageous thing. Just tell her the truth.
LINDA. Look! Get in there! What do you want for dinner tonight?
ARTHUR. I can't. I just can't.
BITTERMAN. Get in there! Right now!
ARTHUR. Bitterman . . . who do you think you are—Hobson?
BITTERMAN. Yeah . . . get your ass in there.
ARTHUR. Yes, Mr. Bitterman. Thank you *(to Linda)* You understand . . . that if I'm killed . . . I can't marry you either.
LINDA. Just make sure you come back to this car single.
BITTERMAN. Good luck, sir. I'm sure that wherever Mr. Hobson is . . . he's enjoying this.
ARTHUR. Yeah. You have to be dead to enjoy this.

He walks up the steps to the church.

Cut to:

Int.: St. Bartholomew's—Day. ARTHUR *entering the back of the church. All the guests turn to look at him.* ARTHUR *starts to walk down the aisle. He stops at one of the guests.*

ARTHUR *(whispering).* Pardon me . . . I'm Arthur Bach . . . the groom . . .
GUEST. Yes. Congratulations!
ARTHUR. Thank you. Thank you very much. I wonder if you could tell me where the wedding party is?
GUEST. They're in that room over there.
ARTHUR. Thank you.

ARTHUR *continues to walk down the aisle.*

ANOTHER GUEST. Good luck, Arthur.
ARTHUR. That's very kind. Thank you.

ARTHUR *cuts through an aisle on his way to the vestibule, tripping over guests as he goes.*

Int.: St. Bartholomew's—vestibule—Day. ARTHUR *enters.* SUSAN *and the wedding party are there.* SUSAN *in her wedding gown.*

ARTHUR *(to everyone).* Hi! Sorry I'm late. Ahhh . . . Susan . . . just the one I want to talk to. Nice dress.
SUSAN. Arthur . . . the ceremony . . .
ARTHUR. Darling . . . just let's talk for a moment away from these people.

ARTHUR *guides* SUSAN *over to the side of the vestibule.*

ARTHUR *(barely audible).* Susan . . . I don't love you.
SUSAN. What?
ARTHUR *(a little louder).* I don't love you.
SUSAN. What darling?
ARTHUR *(loud).* I don't love you.
SUSAN. Arthur . . . you're drunk . . . you're frightened . . .
ARTHUR. Yes . . . I'm both of those . . . but *(very quietly)* I am in love with another woman.
SUSAN. What, Arthur?
ARTHUR *(a little louder).* I am in love with another woman.
SUSAN. I can't hear you.
ARTHUR *(loud).* I am in love with another woman and . . .

SUSAN *starts to weep.* ARTHUR *puts his arms around her.*

ARTHUR. Susan . . . the one innocent person in all of this has been you . . . I'm so sorry . . . I . . .
SUSAN. Shut up! Just shut up, Arthur! Daddy!

MR. JOHNSON *enters the vestibule, joins them.*

ARTHUR. Oh, hi Mr. Johnson! I was just telling Susan that . . .

Int.: St. Bartholomew's—Main Chapel—Day. The assembled guests sit quietly awaiting the ceremony. We hear an off-stage roar.

MR. JOHNSON *(o.c.).* You son of a bitch!

We hear a man being hit and falling against the wall.

The guests at the wedding start to murmur. We hear another roar.

MR. JOHNSON *(o.c.).* I'll kill you!

Cut to:

Ext.: St. Bartholomew's steps—Day. LINDA *and* BITTERMAN *standing on the steps of the church. A lady comes out of the church.*

LINDA *(to the lady).* What's going on in there?
LADY. I really don't know. It seems someone is murdering the groom. I'm going home.

LINDA *looks at* BITTERMAN.

LINDA. I'm going in there, Bitterman!

Int.: St. Bartholomew's—Main Chapel—Day. LINDA *enters the church. As she does, everyone* looks back to see the bride. The organ starts playing "Here Comes the Bride." LINDA *waves at the organ player to stop.* LINDA *starts to walk down the aisle.*

LINDA *(to the same guest that Arthur talked to).* Pardon me . . . I'm with the wedding party . . . where are they? I'm late . . . from out of town.
GUEST. They're in that room over there.
LINDA. Thank you. Isn't everything just lovely?

She starts to walk down the aisle.

LINDA *(to a guest).* I'm late. I'm from out of town. Isn't everything just lovely?

There is another roar off stage. It is MR. JOHNSON's *voice. Another body hits a wall.*

MR. JOHNSON *(o.c.).* I'm going to strangle you!
LINDA. Arthur was probably just nervous.

LINDA *passes through the same aisle on the way to the vestibule. She opens the door.*

Int.: St. Bartholomew's—vestibule—Day. ARTHUR *is on the floor.* MR. JOHNSON *stands over him.*

MR. JOHNSON. Come on, come on, stand up, son. I'm going to kill you with my bare hands.
SUSAN. Here's your ring, Arthur. I hope you're happy.

LINDA *enters.*

ARTHUR *(from the floor).* Hi, Linda! I think you know everyone. This is Susan's father.

LINDA *runs to* ARTHUR. *She leans over him.*

LINDA. Oh my God! you're really hurt!
ARTHUR. I've got him right where I want him.
LINDA *(to Mr. Johnson)* Look . . . animal . . . it's over. He doesn't love your daughter. I'm sorry. It happens. He loves me.
SUSAN. What about Harold?
LINDA. Harold . . . you poor thing.

MR. JOHNSON *goes to* LINDA *and pushes her aside hard.*

MR. JOHNSON. Is this the slut that you disgraced my daughter for!
ARTHUR. Slut? . . . Slut? . . .

ARTHUR *gets up. He rushes at* MR. JOHNSON. *He hits him hard.* MR. JOHNSON *doesn't flinch. He belts* ARTHUR *very hard.* ARTHUR *goes down.* LINDA *bends over him.*

LINDA. Arthur . . . God . . . are you alive? *(to Mr. Johnson).* You bastard!

MR. JOHNSON. Get away from me, slut!

LINDA. Can you move, Arthur? Can you move?

ARTHUR. No. You see, he knocked me out.

SUSAN *tries to stop* MR. JOHNSON.

SUSAN. Stop it, Daddy! He's not worth it.

MR. JOHNSON. Susan, get out of here! Everybody out!

SUSAN *and the bridesmaids leave.* MR. JOHNSON *advances on* ARTHUR. *He picks up a knife.*

ARTHUR *(to Linda).* He's taking the knife out of the cheese.

LINDA. He's taking the knife out of the cheese.

ARTHUR. Do you think he wants some cheese?

LINDA. No. I think we better get out of here.

ARTHUR. I can't move!

LINDA. We gotta get out of here.

MARTHA *and* MR. BACH *enter the vestibule.*

MARTHA. Stop it this instant!

MR. BACH. What the hell is going on here?

MR. JOHNSON. Stay out of this, Martha! I'm going to kill him!

MARTHA *slaps* BURT *hard across the face.*

MARTHA. Don't screw with me, Burt! You'll find yourself doing business with no one in this country!

MR. JOHNSON. Arthur . . . some day . . .

MARTHA. Forget it, Burt! You're talking to a Bach! Now get out of here! The wedding is off! I'll explain to the guests.

ARTHUR *saunters over to* BURT JOHNSON.

ARTHUR. You're just lucky she stopped it, Burt.

MR. JOHNSON *exits.*

ARTHUR. Martha, if I may, I'd like to explain to our guests.

He exits.

MARTHA *(to Mr. Bach).* He's your son. Why didn't you do something?

MR. BACH. Well, Mom . . . I . . .

MARTHA. Shut up, Stanford!

LINDA *giggles.*

MARTHA. Shut up, Marolla!

LINDA. Right, Martha. You did good, Martha.

Cut to:

Int.: St. Bartholomew's — Main Chapel — Day. ARTHUR *staggers out of the vestibule. His tux is torn. His face is bleeding. He tries for dignity.*

ARTHUR. Ladies and gentlemen . . . I'm sorry. As you probably have surmised by now . . . there will be no wedding. The bride has had second thoughts . . . and has decided not to marry me. Most of you know me . . . can you blame her? It would have been a beautiful wedding . . . and I am truly sorry. But there should be love, even at a beautiful wedding. I won't be seeing most of you anymore because I'm going to be poor. I'll miss you. And now . . . there is a good chance that I should go to a hospital.

ARTHUR *faints.*

Cut to:

Ext.: St. Bartholomew's — steps — Day. The last guest exits the church.

Int.: St. Bartholemew's — Main Chapel — Day. MARTHA *is seated at the back of the church. From her POV two tiny people stand in the front of the church. It is* ARTHUR *and* LINDA. *They can't see her.* LINDA *starts to take a cloth to* ARTHUR'S *face.*

LINDA. Okay . . . this has some iodine on it . . . so it may hurt a little.

ARTHUR. No. . . .

LINDA. Look . . . if it doesn't hurt . . . it won't help.

ARTHUR. I'll yell if it hurts . . . and you'll stop . . . okay?

LINDA *(swabbing his face).* You must really love me. 750 million dollars.

ARTHUR. If it was 800 million . . . I really would have had to think twice. That hurts!

LINDA. I told you it would hurt!

ARTHUR. That hurts! I hate that! Stop it!

LINDA *kisses him.*

LINDA. I won't do it anymore. We're in a church. Would I lie to you?

She kisses him. Then she quickly swabs his face one more time.

ARTHUR. Why did you do that?

LINDA. Because I hate an infection.

They stand and look at each other. They are in an empty church. They cannot see MARTHA *who watches from a distance.*

LINDA. We're in a church. Do you promise to love me . . . obey me . . . and be a good boy?

ARTHUR. I do. Do you promise never to put that stuff on my face again?

LINDA. I do, and I promise you on my word of honor, you couldn't do better. I am terrific.

ARTHUR. We'll be great! We'll be one of those poor couples on the subway . . . who hold hands . . . how much is the subway?

LINDA. Sixty cents. If you spit . . . it's a 500 dollar fine.

ARTHUR. Then I won't spit.

LINDA. None of the really good people do.

ARTHUR. I'll get a job! That's what I'll do! I'll get a job! I'll work! Gee . . . this is going to be great!

LINDA. Good. Look how excited he is . . .

ARTHUR. I'll come home from work . . . You'll be ironing . . . we'll eat some disgusting cheap food . . .

LINDA. We'll be a couple.

MARTHA *(from the back of the church).* Arthur!

LINDA. Who's that?

ARTHUR. I think we're in trouble.

LINDA. It's Martha!

ARTHUR. What are you doing back there, Martha?

MARTHA. Getting older, Arthur, and watching you. It is quite obvious that you two are in love.

LINDA. We are.

MARTHA. Yes. Love has triumphed over money. How I pity you, Arthur. And you too, Marolla.

ARTHUR. Martha . . . I'm going to get a job . . . I'm going to . . .

MARTHA. You are going to play at being poor, Arthur. I assure you that you will soon tire of it. You know, Marolla, money is a drug. Once you have it you can never forget it. It is more pleasurable to name a yacht than a child. I know. I've done both. Arthur will die without the money.

LINDA. Then I'll be a widow, because we're getting married.

MARTHA. I see. Goodby, Arthur. I shall never see you again.

She starts to walk towards the exit.

ARTHUR *(to Linda).* It's just too bad Martha will never see her great-grandchildren, isn't it, darling?

LINDA. Yes, it is.

ARTHUR. They'll be beautiful children . . . poor but beautiful. What do you think our son will grow up to be, darling?

LINDA. Well, my father was a welder.

ARTHUR. A welder . . . that would be nice. Or a barber. Whatever he wants to be.

LINDA. Right. You know what a sanitation worker makes these days?

MARTHA. Stop! That is out of the question! There is no such thing as a working-class Bach!

LINDA *(to* ARTHUR*).* Do we have her?

ARTHUR. We got her.

MARTHA. Perhaps with a certain allowance each year . . .

ARTHUR. No.

MARTHA. No?

LINDA. We had her.

ARTHUR. No allowance, Martha. The one great lesson I think we can take out of this is that money is a curse. It took me a long time to learn that, Martha. But I've grown up. I'm a responsible person now.

He turns to look at LINDA. MARTHA *can't see. He is cross-eyed.*

ARTHUR. Money has screwed me up my whole life. I just want my kids to have the advantages of growing up normally. We'd just like to raise a well-adjusted barber or welder. We don't want your money, Martha.

MARTHA. You are so full of crap, Arthur.

ARTHUR. Really? Try me, Martha. I don't want an allowance.

MARTHA. Very well.

MARTHA *starts to exit.*

LINDA. Asshole! You blew the allowance!

ARTHUR. She'll be back. I am a direct descendant of one of the greatest bargainers who ever lived. I'm a Bach! I'm doing business. She'll be back.

LINDA. Or we raise a barber.

ARTHUR. Right.

MARTHA *turns.*

MARTHA. Alright! What do you want, Arthur!

ARTHUR. You know what I want, Martha! Everything! Everything I was born for. I want all the money!

MARTHA. But you have disgraced the family.

LINDA. Don't look now, Martha, but we are the family.

They all laugh.

MARTHA. I want a Bach in the White House in 45 years.

LINDA. We'll get on it right away.

ARTHUR. That takes money, Martha.

MARTHA. Yes. It does.

ARTHUR. Plenty of money.

MARTHA. I know.

ARTHUR. How much money, Martha?

MARTHA. 750 million dollars.

LINDA. That should do it.

MARTHA. You have your money, Arthur. Do something about his drinking, Marolla.

MARTHA *exits.*

Cut to:

Ext.: St. Bartholomew's—Day. RALPH *is running up the steps as* MARTHA *is walking down.*

RALPH. Pardon me. Is Linda Marolla in there?

MARTHA. Yes. Who are you?

RALPH. I'm Linda's father.

MARTHA. Oh dear Lord . . . Mr. Marolla, I have just given your daughter 750 million dollars.

RALPH. I see.

Cut to:

Int.: St. Bartholomew's—Main Chapel—Day. LINDA *and* ARTHUR.

ARTHUR. Let's go. We got nine months.

They exit the church.

Ext.: St. Bartholomew's—steps—Day. BITTERMAN *is slapping* RALPH *who has fainted on the steps.* LINDA *and* ARTHUR *go to them.*

ARTHUR. *(to* BITTERMAN*)* What happened, Bitterman?

BITTERMAN.. I don't know, sir. He keeps mumbling something about Buicks, Florida and fast food restaurants.

ARTHUR, LINDA *and* BITTERMAN *carry* RALPH *to the limo. They get in.*

Fade out.

THE CANDIDATE

Original screenplay by Jeremy Larner

BILL MCKAY	Robert Redford
LUCAS	Peter Boyle
JARMON	Don Porter
KLEIN	Allen Garfield
NANCY	Karen Carlson
JENKIN	Quinn Redeker
HENDERSON	Morgan Upton
CORLISS	Michael Lerner
STARKEY	Kenneth Tobey
JOHN J. MCKAY	Melvyn Douglas

Written by Jeremy Larner
Produced by Walter Coblenz for Warner Bros., 1972
Directed by Michael Ritchie
Cinematography by V. J. Kemper, A.S.C.
Production designed by Gene Callahan
Director of Photography: John Korty
Editors: Richard A. Harris, Robert Estrin
Sound Mixer: Gene Cantamessa
Production Assistant: Michael Britton
Titles: Don Record
Associate Producer: Nelson Rising
Music by John Rubinstein
Costume Designer: Patricia Norris
Set Decorator: Patrizia von Brandenstein
Makeup: Gary Liddiard
Script Supervisor: Lillian MacNeill
Casting: Hoyt Bowers
Location Manager: Ward Wardman
Assistant Director: Michael Daves
Publicist: Vernon White

Winner of the Academy Award for Best Original Screenplay produced in 1972, Mr. Jeremy Larner's screenplay is rather unusual in that there have been just a handful of political films that have been made in Hollywood. Furthermore, this political film is even more unique in that it addresses itself more to our political processes in America—the how of elections in America in modern times with its special media needs. Compare it with *Meet John Doe* as written by Robert Riskin over thirty years before. It will prove interesting.

Born in Orleans, New York, on March 20, 1937, Mr. Larner was educated at Brandeis University, where he received a bachelor of arts in 1958. After attending the University of California at Berkeley in 1959, Mr. Larner—a novelist and journalist—got involved in politics to the extent of being presidential candidate Eugene McCarthy's principal speechwriter in 1968. (He later wrote a book about the experience, *Nobody Knows,* Macmillan, 1970.)

In depicting a decent, idealistic, and well-meaning liberal in the person of McKay, played by Robert Redford, who becomes a candidate for senator in California and wants to be his own man, Mr. Larner has his character discover that it is difficult to keep one's ideals and ideas without compromising them when you have to get into the political meat grinder, television campaigning. His compromises turn out to be less than that when he discovers as well the bewildering and morally indefensible thicket of political effluvia, as represented by TV commercials and the like, which made his moral stands seem stupid, vapid, and nonsensical, when one subjected them to intense scrutiny.

Mr. Larner has McKay beating his conservative opponent. But what kind of a person does he turn out to be doing it?

This is one of the disturbing questions raised by Mr. Larner's screenplay. The film's emphasis on the media electioneering is the heart of its content and effectiveness, for in raising those disturbing questions, it makes us realize that they are far from being solved. Each succeeeding campaign for the presidency, the highest office in our land, seems to be taking us further down the road to sloganeering, posturing, and meaningless debating, which seem to be rated more on performance than content, where watchers do not seem to care so much what is being said or not said but the way that it is said or not said. Who won? That seems to be the end result of it.

In this film, it is not important to weigh the issues. The stands taken by the candidates, whatever your political persuasion, do not really matter in the context of Mr. Larner's work. Indirectly addressing itself to the utilization of the media in our political processes, his screenplay most effectively makes us realize that this is a problem we should and must solve. If McKay winds up bewildered, anxious, and somewhat cynical on the eve of his taking office, as he says to Lucas, his campaign mentor and director, ". . . what do we do now?," we can only hope that things get better for him once he gets to the floor of the Senate.

Fade in. Int. Baltimore Hotel ballroom ("Regency Hyatt House")—Election night.

Girls in straw hats—their eyes shining—chanting "We want Neil! We want Neil!"

Behind them, above empty platform and bare podium, a huge poster of Candidate's face, with the slogan: "Neil Atkinson—a fresh hope."

Int. suite in same hotel. Pull back from TV to discover actual face of Candidate, watching grimly. On the arm of his chair, his wife, in neat suit and hat. On the floor at his feet, several of his children, in suits, short pants, frock dresses, sit solemnly watching.

All around them: People moving—reporters, staff visitors in constant motion. Sound of TV returns mixed with constant talking, greeting, phones ringing. People drinking, eating hors d'oeuvres as they chatter, nodding and looking toward the center of the suite, where Candidate sits with his back to them.

Door to corridor is open—people going in and out. Grave young men in suits (Candidate's staff) now and then going up to whisper in his ear—but Candidate does not react.

HOWARD KLEIN—*the celebrated political commercial maker—roving around the room—now and then turning to murmur to the two assistants who follow him. Klein stands talking fiercely among three or four others in suits on phones in the back of the room. As a friend passes, Klein taps him lightly on the back; the man turns, Klein scowls and shrugs.*

Suits gather again around Candidate. This time he gets to his feet, and all at once reporters are racing for the door.

Int. corridor. Suits take Candidate down hall and into another room. Door closes. One last staff man tries to enter but is firmly closed out. Hubbub of voices reaches a new intensity.

VOICES. —They want him to concede.
—Too early . . .
—hasn't got a chance . . .
—get on the eleven o'clock . . .

Door opens and Candidate strides out into corridor, Aides following. One of them plucks at his arm and gets him to stop, talks urgently very close to his face. Reporters push up behind them; in background, TV camera and light strut.

Suddenly Candidate lashes out and hits the Aide in the chest, sending him backwards into the pack.

Camera in angle of door follows Candidate as he strides calmly into suite again, sits down once more in front of TV.

Klein, following, mutters, ". . . shoulda done that six weeks ago!"

Klein goes to TV, switches through several channels: Crowds in ballrooms, girls chalking on blackboards, announcers' faces.

Candidate gets up slowly; and this time everyone rushes for door.

From doorway: Candidate moving down hall in a throng, Aides leading people out of the way.

Violence at the elevator as reporters jam in and are shoved out.

Int. ballroom. Young girls in straw hats leaping up and down ecstatically.

Candidate is at podium on stage. He wears a determined smile, but his wife and children look forlorn.

CANDIDATE. They said when we got into this thing we didn't have a chance.

Girls and boys cheering, their faces radiant.

CANDIDATE. They said there was nothing we could do.

More cheers.

CANDIDATE. And now the count has gone against us, whatever that means. Well, I'm not sorry. I hope you're not sorry—

Shouts of "No! No!" Grief-stricken faces, cheering through tears, etc.

CANDIDATE'S VOICE.
I think we've proved our point. We may have lost our personal campaign—that's not important.

Camera discovers. MARVIN LUCAS *looking bored among a cluster of well-dressed older men who whisper among themselves.*

VOICES.—You hear about Philadelphia?
—What time is it?
My golf clubs in your car!

A man is whispering to LUCAS—*he nods, steps back.* KLEIN *moves up beside* LUCAS. *They stand side by side, arms folded. Candidate still talking, but we can't hear his voice.*

KLEIN. Big Luke!

LUCAS (*still looking ahead*). Have a good night?

KLEIN. Two out of three. Not bad for an off-year election.

LUCAS *raises eyebrows. Aide whispers to* KLEIN. *General buzzing.*

KLEIN (*to Lucas*). Glad this is one campaign you weren't running?

LUCAS. It was in the cards. Helluva guy, though.

His aide is pulling KLEIN *away.*

KLEIN. . . . nice guys . . .

LUCAS *(turning away; we see he is carrying briefcase and coat).* He never had a chance.

CANDIDATE *(voice in again).* What really matters is that the crusade started by the people in this room—and by so many more, young and old, rich and poor, black and white, all over the state of Maryland—ladies and gentlemen, that campaign is a winner! It is going to go on.

KLEIN. Wait a minute! *(he brushes off his aide and follows after Lucas)*

CANDIDATE *(keeps talking over cheers—with manic cheerfulness).* We will keep going till we lick the conditions that brought us into this.

Cheers and shouts.

Ext. hotel lobby. KLEIN *catches up with* LUCAS.

KLEIN. What's your hurry? I'll walk you out.

KLEIN *and* LUCAS *cross lobby.*

KLEIN. We were supposed to have a drink with Forbes.

LUCAS. He wants to talk about California. Tell Forbes I won't have anything to say for at least a week.

Ext. front of hotel (rain)—Doorman with big umbrella.

CANDIDATE'S VOICE *(amplified).* We'll be back and next time, by golly—

LUCAS *and* KLEIN *emerge from revolving door.*

CANDIDATE'S VOICE. We're going to win!
KLEIN. What . . . you got someone in California?
LUCAS. I doubt it.

Doorman blows whistle for cab as LUCAS *stands under umbrella.*

KLEIN. Democrats out there might as well nominate Jarmon, they're all so afraid of him.
LUCAS *(looking up the street).* You never know.

LUCAS *pulls out crumpled clippings—hands one to* KLEIN, *who smooths it out on his knee.* LUCAS *grabs* KLEIN'S *arm and pulls hand with clipping under the umbrella.*

Close-up—Newsweek clipping. Title, "Then and Now". First picture: Young blond boy on father's shoulders, holding up V-for-Victory sign. Second picture: young man sitting at desk,

surrounded by women and children with signs proclaiming "Save our Parks."

KLEIN. The son?
LUCAS. I knew him at Stanford.
KLEIN. McKay's son. I saw this stuff. The legal aid bit.

Cab pulls up.

KLEIN. It doesn't prove he's got kishkes.

LUCAS *gets into cab.*

KLEIN. Nobody's gonna beat Jarmon!
LUCAS. Tell me something else I don't know.

Cab roars off into the night.

Close-up—Credit card (Int. airport counter) getting zapped.

Int. plane in flight. Stewardess on plane speaking to LUCAS. *He extinguishes cigar without taking his eyes off her face.*

Ext. plane landing in San Diego. Begin titles.

Int. Hertz counter. Credit card getting zapped again for car rental.

Ext. road. LUCAS *riding freeway in shiny rented red convertible. More titles. People staring as he rides through rundown farm town, finally pulls up in front of shabby storefront. Sign:* LEGAL ASSISTANCE.

Int. garage. Long shot: LUCAS *has pulled in drive and sits watching from car as—* BILL MCKAY *and three of his staff men stand with mechanic in front of hydraulic lift.* JAIME *is arguing with the mechanic, translating from Spanish for* MCKAY.

WILSON *waiting off to the side with his briefcase.*

MCKAY *naturally takes the role of leader; we sense he can be tough and even arrogant in a good cause. The others defer to him. He wears a nondescript suit, shirt open at the neck, loafers and a Navaho bracelet. He's 33-35 years old.*

PETE WILSON *is a chubby young lawyer of about 25, smart and ambitious.*

JAIME *is an office assistant, a radical, 19 years old, who goes to a community college at night.*

DAVID *is another assistant, an "Anglo," very polite and idealistic.*

The mechanic, like JAIME *a Chicano, leans sullen and stolid against their old, wood-sided station wagon. On the side of the wagon is painted:* COMMUNITY LEGAL SERVICES— CALL *383-1776.*

As LUCAS *approaches—*

MCKAY. What are these "occupation charges" he keeps talking about?
JAIME. He means storage charges.

MCKAY *begins to laugh.* LUCAS *comes up smiling as though he were sharing in the joke.*

MCKAY. It's not enough just to sock us three times what it's worth, he wants us to pay him for not giving the damn car back! *(as McKay talks, he turns around, looks right at Lucas, doesn't recognize him, and turns back)*

LUCAS. Bill McKay.
MCKAY *(turning).* Yeah? . . . Marvin Lucas! Grew a beard, huh?

LUCAS *nods, with a little smile.*

MCKAY. Will you excuse us?
LUCAS. I'll wait.

JAIME *is arguing in Spanish again—appealing for solidarity.*

MCKAY *(turns back to others, then—over his shoulder).* Newsweek, right?
WILSON *(to McKay).* This had to happen the day I get thrown out of superior court.
MCKAY *(to Jaime).* Ask him if he's ever heard of a license renewal hearing.
DAVID. Hey, can we do that?
MCKAY *(to Wilson).* What did you say about superior court?
WILSON. He wouldn't hear it, Bill. He never let us get started. Said it's all a federal matter now.
MCKAY. Pete, this watershed thing is too important. You've got to get back there with a petition.
WILSON. Christ, Bill, we had three months' worth of briefs!

DAVID *politely approaches* LUCAS.

MCKAY. I don't care! A petition is the only way.
DAVID. Anything I can help you with?
LUCAS. No, I'll wait for McKay.
WILSON. Okay, we'll try it. But these courts just aren't gonna move.
MCKAY. They'll move.
DAVID *(to Lucas again).* What was it about?
LUCAS. Senator.

MCKAY *hearing this, bursts out laughing, startling his friends.*

MCKAY *crossing street to phone booth,* LUCAS *following.*

LUCAS. You have thought about it?
MCKAY. You know what I see?
LUCAS. A stampede of 18-year-old breasts?
MCKAY *(going to booth).* I see a bunch of party hacks reacting to some magazine stories.
LUCAS. Of course I talked to some people—

MCKAY *makes a face as he slides door closed.*

Int. MCKAY's *office.* MCKAY *sits with his feet up on an old wooden desk covered with papers.* LUCAS *leans against the side of the desk, arms folded.* WILSON *sits in a chair, carefully listening.*

*Lots of action in the background: young staff people (*JANICE, DAVID, JAIME*) running mimeo machine, handling phone calls, grabbing papers from an old file cabinet.* BARBARA, *a lawyer about* WILSON's *age, sits interviewing a grape picker and his wife, who holds a child in her lap.*
The furniture is makeshift; the walls are covered with an impasto of posters, clippings, photos, and leaflets—prominent among them the black eagle of the United Farm Workers.
MCKAY *and others are eating from a pile of take-out burgers and fries wrapped in grease paper.*

LUCAS. What do you think of Jarmon?
MCKAY. Smooth character.
LUCAS. Don't you think someone ought to take him on?
MCKAY. Some big-time Democrat.

JAIME *comes over to grab a hamburger.*

LUCAS. They're all afraid of him.
MCKAY. I guess you're up against it then.
LUCAS. Unless we get something new. Someone who has something he believes in.
MCKAY. Whatever that means.
LUCAS. Someone who can go one on one with Jarmon—spend a year telling people what he thinks is important.
MCKAY. Not that way he doesn't. Not in any political campaign.

JAIME *snickers.* WILSON *shushes him.*

LUCAS. It doesn't have to work that way.
MCKAY. Hey, don't tell me how it works. I watched my Dad for 20 years.
LUCAS. That was no good, huh?
MCKAY. It was good for him. He loved it. He got to be Governor John J. McKay. What good it did for anyone else I never knew.
LUCAS *(aware of the others).* But I'm not talking about him. I'm talking about a man who can call his own shots.

A beat passes.

JAIME *(taking the opportunity).* I want to tell you something, man.

LUCAS. Okay.

JAIME. What you call politics . . . politics is bullshit.

LUCAS. I was wondering what it was.

An awkward silence. BARBARA *comes over.* MCKAY *gets to his feet.*

BARBARA. Hey, what's going on—oh. *(she sees their expressions and cuts herself off)*

MCKAY. I have to stop by the house for an hour. *(to Janice)* Did Nancy leave the car for me?

JANICE. Nope.

LUCAS. I can drop you off.

MCKAY *nods but doesn't move for the door.* LUCAS *senses he wants a word with his friends.*

LUCAS. I'll wait outside.

LUCAS *goes out.*

MCKAY—*gathering up his papers and stuffing them in briefcase—looks to* WILSON.

MCKAY. Well?

WILSON. If you could really do it your own way . . .

MCKAY. Yeah?

WILSON. He's got a point.

MCKAY. That's what bothers me.

JAIME *is shaking his head.*

Int. MCKAY *house. Day. A cheerful, young married-modern living room. Books, records, flowers, hi-fi, littered coffee-tables, etc.*

Cameras and leather cases lie on round wooden dining table, where NANCY *sits assembling a lens apparatus.*

From NANCY's *POV.:* MCKAY *and* LUCAS *enter,* LUCAS *talking.*

NANCY *rises to meet them. She is a tall, beautiful blonde, who handles herself with poise and humor and a sense of her own attractions. By nature she is a winner, whose only problem is that she doesn't understand what's eating her husband.*

LUCAS *(entering)*. . . . of course you could go on for a hundred years, filing law suits in the sticks—or you could take a year and lay out a real position for yourself in this state—

MCKAY. Nancy, this is Marvin Lucas. My wife Nancy.

NANCY. Hi.

MCKAY *(moving toward bar)*. Want a beer?

LUCAS *(to Nancy).* Don't let us interrupt you.

NANCY. Not at all.

NANCY *goes back to work—starting to photograph a still-life she has set up against a white screen. But she is listening.*

LUCAS. The contacts, for example. You'll meet people who know how to get things done—people you can call on for money. Even if you go back to your legal assistance operation, that doesn't run on hamburgers. It's a matter of resources—

MCKAY *grabs two cans of beer, a box of crackers, and a can of nuts, throws them on the coffee table.*

MCKAY. Listen. I just spent this weekend working straight on through, twenty hours a day. I didn't earn a dime, but I loved every little moment. Why do I need what you're offering? I'm happy.

LUCAS. You're happy?

MCKAY. Yes!

LUCAS. Clams are happy. But what did you accomplish?

MCKAY. You want a list?

LUCAS. You saved some trees. You got a clinic opened. Does that make you feel good? Meanwhile Jarmon sits on his committees and carves up the land, the oil, the taxes— Have you ever seen him? Have you ever seen him operate?

MCKAY. Marvin.

NANCY *has put on her zoom lens. From across the room, she snaps* MCKAY.

LUCAS. Yeah?

MCKAY. What's in it for you?

LUCAS. Oh, an air card, a phone card and a thousand bucks a week.

MCKAY. And that's all?

LUCAS *shrugs, with his little smile.* NANCY *raises her camera again and snaps* LUCAS—*to* MCKAY's *amusement. He turns to her.*

MCKAY. Marvin wants me to go into politics.

NANCY. What else is new? *(pauses)* For what office?

LUCAS. Senator.

NANCY *lowers her camera. She immediately moves toward them, grabbing glass bowls from sideboard.*

NANCY. Well, why not? If he put his mind to it.

She dumps crackers and nuts into bowls.

NANCY *(to* MCKAY, *teasingly).* But that means you'd have to register. *(to Lucas)* He never has, you know.

She sits down between them.

LUCAS. I hope he keeps that a secret.
MCKAY *(mumbling).* No reason to.
NANCY. Unless you took it seriously.

There is a beat as LUCAS *takes in their exchange—and them. Then he gets back on his subject.*

LUCAS. The point is you can go with the things you believe in.
MCKAY. And get my ass served up on a platter.
LUCAS. That's up to you. *(begins to scribble in matchbook)* For openers, you've got credibility. And you've got the name—
MCKAY. What do you mean the name? You're not going to bring my father into this.
LUCAS. Okay. We won't.
NANCY. He's got the looks.
LUCAS. Right.
NANCY. And he's got the power.
MCKAY. What does that mean?
NANCY. You know what it means . . . don't you?
MCKAY. No.
NANCY *(giggles, gets up).* Well. If you'll excuse me, gentlemen, I've got to remove some film from my bathtub before it rots.

NANCY *goes out,* LUCAS *watching her leave with appreciation. He waits, still smiling, for* MCKAY *to speak.*

MCKAY. You're saying I can say what I want, do what I want, go where I please . . .
LUCAS. That's right. Here's your guarantee. *(hands him matchbook. He has written: "You lose.")*
MCKAY. I lose.
LUCAS. That's it. You're free, McKay. You can't win, so say what you like. It's between you and the public.

A beat. MCKAY *holds the matchbook.*

LUCAS. The question is whether you can put your ass on the line.
MCKAY. The question is whether it's worth it.

LUCAS *gets to his feet.*

LUCAS. Well—thanks for the beer.
MCKAY. I'll walk you out.

NANCY *comes in with a tray—beer in glasses, cheese, bread.*

NANCY. Oh, are you leaving?

LUCAS. Are you sorry?
NANCY. I'll wait and see.

Ext. MCKAY *house. Day. A big old frame house, which they have renovated, sitting high on a hill. From below, near* LUCAS' *car, we see* MCKAY *and* LUCAS *emerge and cross porch, come down steps and toward camera.* LUCAS *gets into car. There is a feeling that one of them is about to speak, but neither does.* LUCAS *drives off.*

Ext. barbecue. Somewhere in Orange County. Day. Close-up of SENATOR CROCKER JARMON *in the middle of a speech, every inch the genial and distinguished orator.*

JARMON. . . . but I remember this. I remember my Mom and Dad went through the 1930's without welfare, without poverty programs—in fact, none of us kids had a social worker! How did we do it? Ladies, excuse me, but we worked our butts off!

Laughter and applause. Pan over crowd. Beef turning on spits. Band and bandstand. Around edges, state cops with folded arms, security men standing on tops of cars.

JARMON. Now lately I hear that the idea of hard work has gone out of fashion. Why work, when big government is supposed to take care of everything? Some folks want Washington to become the world's biggest insurance company—they want it to insure our health, our homes, and even our incomes.

Camera picks out MCKAY. *He is watching people applauding: families, young people with clean cut hair—the light of belief shining in their eyes.*

JARMON. But I want to tell you something, good people. Crocker Jarmon still believes that individuals are responsible for themselves!

Applause. JARMON'S *wife sitting behind him, watching devoutly.*

JARMON. And so does the vast majority of the American people!

Applause.

JARMON. That's why we're going to tell Big Brother to get lost!
Now if people are really sick, really helpless, they deserve—and as long as I am around they are going to get—all the help we can give them.
But there is no reason on God's earth why you have to share your paycheck with welfare chiselers!

Applause. MCKAY *moving around—watching, frowning.*

JARMON. The solution to welfare is not more welfare, it's more enterprise, more industry and more jobs.

Now there are those who say to industry, don't build, don't develop, don't cut a single tree or you will destroy our watershed and so on. But I know this: when it's time for building *we will build,* because *building means jobs* —and we will find a way to love Mother Nature and preserve her *without going to extremes.*

Do you think I'm mean?

Shouts of "No! No!"

JARMON. Well, if I am, I've spent 18 years in the Senate being a meanie.

And if need be, I'll spend another 18 years working to keep this country healthy and growing and moving forward into the future!

Big cheers as JARMON *ends speech, his wife comes up to him, etc.*

JARMON *making his way through crowd— shaking hands.*

Further back: MCKAY *pushing his way through at another angle.*

JARMON. So long . . . thanks for coming . . . You did, huh, you devil! I wish I could, but you know—the old ball and chain! *(nods toward wife, who is smiling along behind him).*

MCKAY *comes into frame. Man with vest grabs Jarmon.*

VEST. Good to see you again, Senator!

AIDE *(whispers in Jarmon's ear).* Harry Rich.

JARMON. Good to see you, Harry! How's business!

WOMAN. Senator Jarmon, remember my little Toddy—*(holding up her son).*

JARMON. Hello, Toddy. *(picks up boy).* He's an ugly little cuss! What's that?

TODDY. My Daddy says he wants you to be Vice President.

JARMON *(hands him back).* Get this child to a violin!

MCKAY *(forcing his way in).* Hello, remember me?

JARMON. Sure do, son! How's the old throwing arm?

Two old ladies pluck at JARMON.

JARMON. Not in public, ladies. I'm a married man!

They love it.

MCKAY. No. It's Bill McKay.

JARMON. Well, of course! How are you, son! Last time I saw you, you were a little monkey sitting in someone's lap. How's old John J.?

MCKAY. I don't know.

JARMON *(pats McKay on the back and turns away).* Well, just tell him the old Crock says hello! *(reaching for more hands).* Put her there! Not too hard!

JARMON *is swept along among the crowd of his admirers, leaving* MCKAY *staring after him.*

Int. MCKAY's *office.* MCKAY *sitting on top of his desk in short-sleeved shirt and khaki pants. He is brightly lit for TV.*

MCKAY *(head down, reading statement).* Today at 4:30 P.M. I filed the papers to enter my name in the Democratic primary as a candidate for the U. S. Senate. *(lifts head)* Any questions?

VOICE. Why are you doing this?

MCKAY. I'm doing this because . . . I don't think the incumbent is really in touch with how most people live and what they need. That's what I tried to do as a lawyer, and that's what I hope I can go on doing as a candidate.

VOICE. How do you feel about welfare?

MCKAY. We subsidize trains, we subsidize planes, why not subsidize people?

VOICE # 2. What about bussing?

MCKAY. I'm for it.

VOICE # 3. What would you do about property taxes?

MCKAY. I don't know.

Quick cut—Reporter (voice #3) standing next to LUCAS *guffaws.*

Pull back: We see two TV cameras and REPORTERS *just behind them.*

VOICE #3 *(same reporter).* Mr. McKay, what makes you think you have a chance?

View of MCKAY *switches to TV monitor.*

MCKAY. That's not the point.

VOICE #1. What's the point?

VOICE #2. Can you win the primary?

VOICE #3. What's your platform?

MCKAY. What do you mean "platform"?

QUIET VOICE *(TV Producer).* Bill, would you mind moving over there with your office staff?

TV camera in—Blurry pan to the office staff standing crowded in the other half of the room— NANCY *among them.*

MCKAY. No. Sorry. Any more questions?

Camera snaps back as MCKAY *rises and walks forward, toward camera, breaking the frame.*

VOICE #4. Why won't you stand with your staff?

MCKAY. They're not responsible for me.

Staff applauds raucously.

Monitor is snapped off—Pull back— KLEIN'S *face.*

KLEIN. I dig it. It's raw, but I eat it up.

Pull back to reveal: Int. KLEIN'S *office—Day.*

KLEIN *snaps off* MCKAY *on monitor.*

LUCAS *standing,* MCKAY *sitting in corner, wearing suit. Movieolas and video equipment around the room. Photographs of politicians with* KLEIN; *election posters. Outside: view of New York buildings.*

KLEIN. There's a lot of work to do, my man but I get the feeling you know where you're going.

Phone buzzes; KLEIN *snaps buttons, picks it up.*

MCKAY *(with a shrug).* I don't.

KLEIN *(into phone)*. . . . Honey, I told you a party of five. One more and we have to use another car, so we blow the whole conversation. *(hangs up)*

LUCAS. Bill is concerned about what kind of control we'll have over which commercials go on the tube, etcetera . . .

Good-looking secretary (LISA*) comes in with papers, puts them in front of* KLEIN *and stands there taking it all in.*

KLEIN *(to* MCKAY*).* Now Luke knows this— he knows I checked you out. The bottom line is I like what you stand for. You got balls, or I'd never take you on. *(signs papers)* I take my crew and get you doing your thing. And that's it. *(to Lisa)* Thanks, honey.

KLEIN *(to* MCKAY*).* You just get it on with the people, and let me worry about the cameras. I come back in a week, show you my stuff, and you can see for yourself if I sold you out.

LISA *leaves.* KLEIN *opens one drawer, then another, as he continues.*

KLEIN *comes up with a paper bag and a silver hammer—upends bag and dumps lollypops all over his desk.*

KLEIN *throws bag away.*

MCKAY. Then I have the final say.

KLEIN. If you don't like what you see pull it. It's your money, my friend. Is that fair?

KLEIN *cracks the lollypops with the hammer.*

MCKAY *(leaning back and watching).* We'll see.

KLEIN. But let me tell you one thing.

KLEIN *pops lollypop slivers into his mouth.*

MCKAY. Tell me one thing.

KLEIN. You just might make it, my man. Because the people are gonna look at our stuff and see a guy who has guts. And they're gonna look at the Crock and think maybe he can't get it up anymore.

MCKAY. That's what it's all about, huh?

KLEIN *stops with hand to mouth, glances at* MCKAY.

KLEIN. Forget I even said it. Just look at this.

KLEIN *flips on tape machine.*
On the monitor, we see the U. S. Senate seal. Pan down to: JARMON, *leaning against a big smooth desk, holding his glasses in his hand— flanked by flags in flag-stands.*
Phone buzzes.

KLEIN *(into phone).* Klein. Keep talking.

JARMON. My friends, the issue is whether we hold onto the most successful philosophy in the history of mankind—or whether we trade it in for a collectivist state.

KLEIN. Stop right there!

KLEIN *throws switch and freezes frame.*

KLEIN *(into phone).* You're on your own, baby. *(hangs up)* You see what I mean, Luke? He works from a staged pose. But how many politicians you ever see who can look straight into the camera and not come off shifty-eyed?

Starts machine.

JARMON. It's the work of free individuals, the foresight and daring of free enterprise, that has made this nation great . . .

KLEIN. Corny, right? But it's just what he wants. The man's a master. Watch.

TV camera tightens on JARMON.

Phone buzzes.

JARMON. But we will not continue in greatness unless we resolve to protect our way of life . . .

VOICE OVER. Crocker Jarmon—he's been good for California . . .

JARMON *(voice in).* Think about it, my friends . . .

QUIET TV VOICE. The preceding was a political message paid for by the Committee to Re-elect Crocker Jarmon.

KLEIN. The guy gets away with a hard-sell! *(into phone)* Sorry, Norm. I'm being much too frank because I love you, but that's it. *(snaps buttons)* Come in here, honey. *(to MCKAY)* We're gonna label him Geritol, you'll do the I'm-my-own-man-bit. But first we're gonna have to cut the hair and 86 the side-burns. Now look at this!

KLEIN *snaps on movie projector.*

Girl comes in.

On movie screen: montage of younger JARMON *talking to people at picnic—in front of drug store—running along pushing his grand-son on a bike.*

KLEIN. This was twelve years ago. Jarmon's doing the man-of-the-people number. The guy can go any way he wants.

VOICE OVER. Crocker Jarmon—people can talk to him.

KLEIN *freezes frame.*

KLEIN *(to MCKAY).* You see, the guy has sincerity. There's nothing new in the world. Except for you.

LUCAS *(to MCKAY).* The idea is to get you in completely natural situations.

KLEIN *(to girl).* Would you hold the calls for five minutes, honey.

Int. MCKAY *house—early evening.*

MCKAY *lets himself in the back door. Sound from hi-fi: Mozart early piano sonata, played by Glenn Gould.*

Dark kitchen: MCKAY *opens refrigerator and is revealed in its light. He leans against the door and stands staring in.*

NANCY'S VOICE. Bill?

MCKAY *closes the refrigerator door.*

MCKAY. Yah.

MCKAY's *footsteps echo on the board floor as he crosses the dark living room toward the bedroom.*

NANCY *sits at her dressing table in an alcove, in her slip and heels.* MCKAY *walks into the shot.*

NANCY. We don't have much time. Want to hand me that earring?

MCKAY. How 'bout a walk on the beach?

NANCY. In your tux?

MCKAY. We could talk or something.

NANCY. We could talk on the way to the banquet.

MCKAY. Or we could not go to the banquet.

NANCY *(spinning around).* Bill, don't do this!

MCKAY *gives up—flops on the bed.*

NANCY *glances over with some alarm.*

NANCY. Oh, they cut your hair!

MCKAY *doesn't answer.*

NANCY. Let me see.

NANCY *walks around and sits beside him on the bed—starts to run her hands through his hair—because she is really pleased—and she wants to placate him.*

NANCY. Oh, I like it. I like it, Bill.

The music stops, sound of record arm ejecting and clicking off.

MCKAY *grabs her hand—gives her a fierce look—he wants something real.*

NANCY *stops.*

MCKAY *grabs her—roughly pulls her down to him.*

She starts to resist, to shove herself away.

NANCY. Oh, Bill!

He pulls her down again.

NANCY *(as she gives in, responding to him).* You *are* crazy.

Ext.: San Diego hotel—Cars pulling into circular drive.

Int. hotel lobby—Same night. People passing through to ballroom. Glimpses of Hubert Humphrey, George McGovern. LUCAS *hurries forward as he sees* MCKAY *and* NANCY *come through outer doors. (* MCKAY *wears rented tux,* NANCY *in dress from previous scene looks hand-some and composed.)*

LUCAS. Hello, hello, how are *you?*

MCKAY. Can I go home now?

LUCAS. Your husband is one of the great wits. *(to MCKAY)* I wrote up a few pages, just as a suggestion. *(shows him typed sheets)* Maybe we ought to go down to the coffee shop and look 'em over.

MCKAY, *grinning, pulls index card out of his pocket.*

MCKAY. Got it all right here.

LUCAS *(raising eyebrows).* Oh? Then it's on to the ballroom.

Int.: hotel ballroom—Democratic Fund-Raising Dinner. People eating at numbered ta-

bles. Up on stage: MCKAY *comes in late, takes his place wih about 30 others eating on dais, including* JESSE UNRUH, SAM YORTY, JOHN TUNNEY. *The* M.C., *a well-known stand-up comedian, is at the podium.*

Ladies and gentlemen, you know while the last candidate was speaking, you all saw that gentleman leaning over and whispering in my ear? That man was the Sanitation Director of San Dimas. Let's hear it for him.

—NANCY *in audience at table with* LUCAS.

Scattered laughter and applause—Tight on distingushed man in dinner jacket, laughing, eating it up.

M. C. And to think of it, ladies and gentlemen, after an ovation like that, this man was complaining about the food! What a nerve! I told him last week the Republicans paid 100 dollars a plate for the very same food!

Applause.

M.C. Of course, it was fresh then.

Laugh.

M.C. Let's see, now, we have one more candidate for Senator, the only guy his age in the whole state of California who has already had experience in higher office. He used to get his diapers changed there. *(as the audience laughs)* No . . . no . . . I don't mean that. He's a fresh new talent. Really he is. They discovered him on a stool at Schwab's.

Seriously, folks, you better watch out, he fires from the hip! And he's hip when he fires—Bill McKay!

MCKAY *moves to the podium, fumbling in his pocket but not coming up with his index card. He hesitates, then—*

MCKAY *(rapidly).* I guess it is a bit funny, isn't it? But you know, when you think about it, the whole idea of two guys making decisions for twenty million people—that's pretty funny . . .

Some people titter, but MCKAY *goes right on.*

MCKAY. Still, you can't laugh too much—when you think what's at stake.

The fact is that in the next few elections we will decide what it's going to be like to live in this country—whether people will have more power to shape their own lives—or whether we will lose that power—or whether, in fact, we will even survive. *(Voice is heard—"That's enough!"—TV lights go off.)* But anyone can say that much. The hard part is the details, how you get people involved. I wish I had ten

years to think it over. But I think these issues have to be raised right now. Because we're getting further away—we're losing control—our lives are more and more determined by forces that overwhelm the individual. *(takes a breath)* I don't know if you can raise these questions in a political campaign. I don't know if people are ready to listen. But I'm going to try. I hope you'll support that effort. Or at least give me the benefit of the doubt.

Abruptly he stops—and sits down.
The audience hesitates—giggles are heard. Then they applaud, most of them.—As if to say, he is peculiar, but charming.

LUCAS *in the audience shakes his head—then smiles.*

Int.: lobby space—Near entrance to ballroom. Affluent, middle-class banqueters passing out. Some reclaiming fur wraps at coat check booth to side. Others passing through receiving line of the candidates and their wives.

MCKAY *and* NANCY *are the stars of the line, a beautiful couple.* MCKAY *is uncomfortable and a little slow, but impressive in his way of really looking at people.* NANCY *loves it, she is radiant, well aware that people are marvelling at her.*

Close-up on one girl in the line. The girl—with dark hair and glasses, handsome in a different way from NANCY, *younger, more intense—seems to gather herself as she approaches him.*

THE GIRL *takes* MCKAY'S *hand and gives him a look of terrific intensity. She turns his hand over and squeezes it.* MCKAY *is startled. But she passes on, and he greets the next person.*

NANCY. So nice to meet you. It's good of you to come.

WELCH, *a stocky man with big sideburns, grabs* MCKAY'S *elbow as he shakes hands and holds on.*

WELCH. Hey, Bill! Brad Welch. Riverview Elementary. Remember the time we stole all the shoes and socks and threw 'em in the septic tank? I never woulda thought my old buddy would be goin' for the U.S. Senate!

MCKAY. As I remember it, you laid my head open with a rock.

WELCH. Oh boy, those were the days!

MCKAY. Yeah. But I don't remember us being friends.

WELCH'S *expression drops into a dubious frown. Just then* NANCY *turns and bestows upon* WELCH *a gorgeous smile.*

NANCY. So nice of you to come.

WELCH *(shaking hands)*. Hey! Great to be here.

Int.: campaign car. Near Monterey Beach— Day. MCKAY, LUCAS, JENKIN *and* CORLISS *approaching the beach. Through the rear window, we can see the station wagon with* KLEIN *and his camera crew.*

JENKIN. We got a stand down over there.

CORLISS *(peering through his glasses)*. I think there's a crowd . . .

MCKAY. I don't want to drive up in this tank. Just stop it here, okay?

The others reach to stop him, but LUCAS *indicates they should leave him alone.* MCKAY *gets out and walks down to the beach.*

LUCAS. He's right.

CORLISS. Sure he's right!

JENKIN. I don't know what good this does.

LUCAS. It's good for him.

Beach—pier area. LUCAS *et al get out of car— see* MCKAY *walk up to young people on beach— surfer-types rather than hippies—some pretty strange and strung-out.* DAVID *and other campaign workers are giving out popsicles, buttons, and one-page mimeo'd leaflets.* DAVID *shrugs off a panhandler.*

DAVID *(through portable electric megaphone)*. Here he is. Here's Bill McKay.

MCKAY *won't take megaphone or step up on speaker's box. He just starts talking.*

MCKAY *(to redheaded girl)*. Hi, Red.

GIRL *(amused)*. Hi.

MCKAY. I'm here because I'm running for Senator, like it says in the leaflet.

Some kids stop, some go on walking or talking. Constant noise of voices, yelling, planes overhead, etc.

MCKAY. I wanted to come here because I used to hang out around here a few years ago.

Dubious laughter— MCKAY *grins.*

MCKAY. In those days you could swim here. *(gestures toward factories emitting smoke in background)* Before they turned the harbor into a chemistry set.

In those days there used to be another beach—right over there—*(gestures towards rows of cars)* where that parking lot is.

Anyhow, coming out here—that used to be special. Today it's not so special.

VOICE. You got pan-handled!

MCKAY. Right. I did. I look around this beach, and you know what I see?

VOICE. Freaks!

Cheers.

MCKAY. I see lost people.

Awkward silence. But the crowd is growing— more people stopping to listen.

LOUD KID. It's your middle-class values, man!

MCKAY. What does that mean?

LOUD KID. Total horseshit!

Cheers again.

MCKAY. Maybe it's that. Maybe it's just sad. I mean when middle-class sixteen-year-olds come up and ask for a hand-out, that's *pathetic*! It shows you something has gone wrong with the whole set-up.

VOICE. No kiddin!

Laughter.

High angle—from "Jolly Rogue" restaurant balcony on the pier. We see KLEIN'S *hand-held camera team film* MCKAY *from the back of the crowd.*

Reverse angle—On the balcony. KLEIN *and* LUCAS.

KLEIN. He's wasting our time.

LUCAS. It's *his* time. He'll get there.

KLEIN. I thought his wife was supposed to be here. Have you seen the wife?

LUCAS. I checked her out.

KLEIN. Is she gonna give us trouble?

LUCAS. She's perfect.

Back to MCKAY.

MCKAY. That's what this drug thing is all about. We let people get lost.

Kids murmuring.

MCKAY. We won't solve it by calling in the cops.

VOICE. Right on!

MCKAY. But we can solve it by making a society where everyone has useful work.

They are silent.

MCKAY. I guess I am middle class, in a way.

VOICE. Really!

MCKAY. Really, yeah. I didn't find that out today. I found that out working with people who are trying to make sure their kids have something to eat tomorrow morning.

There's no reason for anyone in this country to go hungry—and there's no reason for anyone to get lost. Because there is just too damn much to *do*!

For instance, if we had a *real* Job Corps, you could start right here and rebuild the whole damn place.

You could take some of those gas and oil taxes and clean up the harbor—get some real law enforcement on that sewage dump across the bay—and rip out that damn pavement!

Meanwhile we could take the freeway money and work out a way to get around that wouldn't trash the air and take up the space we need to live in.

And instead of building atomic reactors we could clean up every river in this state; instead of drilling for oil, we could have an ocean that wouldn't stick to your body or poison the fish!

For the first time—some real cheers. MCKAY *talks right through his cheers, too.*

MCKAY. And we could take the billions of dollars that're spent on guns . . .*(more cheers)*. . . and use them to build schools *(boos)*. . . and pay decent salaries to get better teachers *(boos)*. . . and fire the Board of Regents *(cheers)*. . . so that everyone can get the kind of education he needs to stand up and *do something* . . .

So he won't be lost, and he won't think it's bitchin' to be a panhandler. (MCKAY *grins)* And so middle-aged middle-class guys like me can walk the streets safely again. Right?

Kids respond.

MCKAY. I guess that's it. Thanks for listening.

MCKAY *turns and walks to the car.*

Close-up— MCKAY's *face—as if on TV.*

VOICE (ARTHUR FLEISCHER). Don't you think your lack of experience will damage your credibility as a candidate?

MCKAY. Well, up to now my work has been entirely involved with serving the public. So I don't think it hurts that I haven't been a politician. As for credibility, as I understand it, that depends on whether you mean what you say.

VOICE (WALLY HENDERSON). You say you wouldn't draw the line in Vietnam. Well then, just where do you propose to stand up against the Communists?

MCKAY *(he grins . . . shakes his head)*. I . . . uh . . . really that depends on the circumstances. There's no set answer for that one.

LUCAS. Hold on now! That's honest all right but it leaves us nowhere.

Pull back to reveal

Int.: den in home of big backer. A heavy-faced man who sits in a big chair with a brooding expression. MCKAY *sits on bar stool facing group of aides assembled by* LUCAS. *Including:* WALLY HENDERSON *(fat man who is to be Press Secretary), 27-year-old* PAUL CORLISS *(short, bespectacled, buck-toothed bright little wise-ass who will become the speechwriter),* RICH JENKIN *(lean, dogged law student who will serve as head of advance),* DAVID, *from* MCKAY's *legal assistance office (who will often appear carrying* MCKAY's *briefcase), and* ARTHUR FLEISCHER, *professor in his 40's on leave of absence from UCLA.*

LUCAS *sits on back of couch opposite* MCKAY. *His shoes rest on the couch cushions. Near him sits* JIM PILE, *a professional gag writer.*

MCKAY. It's not a serious question!

HENDERSON. It's exactly what you're gonna get asked tomorrow in Long Beach.

CORLISS. It sure is!

LUCAS. Have you got an answer for him, Cory?

CORLISS. He could say Japan or India, countries with certain kinds of governments which legitimately request our help—

LUCAS. You're speech-writing! This isn't the Cow Palace, it's a local TV interview!

HENDERSON *(to* MCKAY). A lot of people in this state still expect an invasion in Pasadena.

GAG WRITER. Then we'll fight 'em in the Rose Bowl.

Silence. No one laughs.

LUCAS. That's not funny, Jim.

CORLISS. Frankly, I don't think this is a gag writer situation.

The GAG WRITER *crouches with his head in his hands.*

GAG WRITER *(moaning)*. Oooo, I feel so awful.

FLEISCHER. He could refer them to our foreign policy position paper.

HENDERSON. *What* position paper?

FLEISCHER. The draft should be ready in two weeks.

GAG WRITER *(spins around, hands up)*. I got it! *(they all turn to look at him)*. McKay says . . . he sure as hell won't let 'em land on the beach at Santa Monica. The parking problem is bad enough already!

A pause . . . then MCKAY *laughs . . . and one by one, his staff follow suit.*

LUCAS. Okay, that's it. Never hurts to toss one off.

FLEISCHER. But does he really want to say *that*?

LUCAS. Next question.

DAVID. What about legalized abortion?

CORLISS. Good question.

MCKAY. I'm all for it. A woman should have that right.

LUCAS. Wait a minute, Bill. You can't put it that way.

MCKAY. That's what I think.

LUCAS. That's not gonna be understood without one hell of a long explanation. How about this, for the time being: just say it's worth studying.

MCKAY *(hesitates)*. Okay. I'll think about it.

CORLISS *looks to* LUCAS, *who nods.*

CORLISS. Mr. McKay, we notice your father hasn't said a word about your campaign. Is he sitting it out?

MCKAY *(stunned for a moment)*. Let's have that again.

CORLISS. Is your father sitting out—

MCKAY. I'm running on my own hook.

EVERYONE. —Now wait. —Wait a second. Bill. —That'll never do. —Listen. —Hold on.

MCKAY *gets up, with a dirty look towards* LUCAS, *and goes out.*

BIG BACKER. How the hell are we supposed to raise any money?

LUCAS. Okay, that's all for now, fellas—

CORLISS *moves to follow* MCKAY.

LUCAS *(sharply)*. I said that's all for now!

Ext.: Ford Motor Company—Milpitas, California. Around 5:00 P.M. Workers (hard hats) filing out with lunch pails, going home.

MCKAY *standing stiffly trying to greet workers one by one as they come through gates. Obviously a great effort.*

MCKAY. Hello, I'm Bill McKay . . . I'm Bill Mc— . . . Bill McKay, running for Senator . . .

Now and then someone shakes hands, looking puzzled. Most of the workers brush on by without looking up.

KLEIN's *crew is inconspicuously filming.*

HENDERSON, JENKIN, DAVID *stand off to side watching.*

DAVID *is trying to pass out leaflets which no one will take. Finally a young worker takes one, and, looking* DAVID *in the eye, crumples it up and throws it on the ground.*

A WORKER *finally stops—a man with a dead pan face.*

WORKER. What're you trying to do?

MCKAY. Just talk to you.

WORKER. What about?

MCKAY. Well, about how the economy throws everything on the back of the working man. Why interest rates and rents and food costs go up faster than your paychecks.

WORKER. Yeah, that's very interesting.

He stands staring at MCKAY *without changing expression. Other workers still going by— some stop for a second, look, move on.*

KLEIN *in the background with his crew.*

KLEIN's *man still filming—* KLEIN *shifting him for better angles.*

MCKAY. Most people think you've got it made because you've got a union.

WORKER. They do?

MCKAY. But you still get laid off.

WORKER. Yeah. Well, I got to go now.

WORKER *shakes hands with* MCKAY *and walks off, impossible to tell what he's thinking.*

Long shot. MCKAY *goes on trying to shake hands. Some women cross the street to say hello—perhaps on a dare.* MCKAY *shakes hands with them and with a baby—and we see the women laughing and giggling.* MCKAY *can't help laughing himself.* KLEIN *moves his cameraman in closer.*

Ext.: MCKAY *campaign headquarters—Abandoned movie theater—Night.*

Int.: victory party going on in lobby. CHEERLEADERS *in straw hats dancing and singing.*

On stairs to mezzanine: MCKAY *and* NANCY *lit up by TV lights. Now and then people move behind them waving, holding up signs, etc.*

TV REPORTER. Walter, we're out here in California with young Bill McKay, who has, on the strength of his name it seems, assumed a strong lead over a field of unknown candidates for the Democratic Senatorial nomination.

Now, Mr. McKay, your victory was predicted. Was it any surprise to you?

MCKAY. Everything that happens is a surprise to me.

TV REPORTER. I know you've heard this before, but can Crocker Jarmon be beat?

MCKAY. I don't know why not. He's been in the Senate 18 years without tackling any of the problems this country faces.

TV REPORTER. Let's bring your beautiful wife into it. How do you feel, Mrs. McKay?

NANCY. Very proud of the way people are responding to the issues Bill has raised.

TV REPORTER. But do you feel that the kind of response you've had is sufficient to —

TV lights suddenly switch off.

TV REPORTER. — glub, glub, glub, I guess that's it, folks.

JENKIN *and* FLEISCHER *standing right behind them — pounce on* MCKAY. *Some women descend on* NANCY.

JENKIN. Bill, you've got to get on the phone to Mrs. York. She won't give a dime unless you ask her in person.

FLEISCHER. She's under the impression you're a well-spring of political wisdom.

Lobby. Aides begin to move MCKAY *past desks, tables covered with food and drink as people stand talking.*

A few people grab at MCKAY.

BOY VOLUNTEER *(well-dressed)*. Hit 'em on repression, man. Get it right up front.

HENDERSON *pushes through, comes up close to* MCKAY, *shoving aside* JENKIN *and* FLEISCHER.

HENDERSON *(whispering)*. Natalie Wood is here.

MCKAY *is shoved up to* NATALIE WOOD, *as the crowd parts around them. They begin a friendly but awkward talk about what kind of yogurt they prefer. A radio man is thrusting a mike, trying to catch it.* FLEISCHER *squeezes in behind* NATALIE.

FLEISCHER. Natalie . . . do you remember me? Arthur Fleischer? The peace seminar at Santa Barbara?

NATALIE WOOD *(smiling vaguely)*. Oh, yes . . .

FLEISCHER. I'm handling the foreign policy aspects of the campaign.

HENDERSON *(from behind Fleischer)*. Oh, Arthur . . . Arthur . . . will you come here a moment? *(Henderson hauls him away.)*

LUCAS *and* DAVID *have appeared at* MCKAY'S *elbow.*

DAVID. We have to get going now, Bill.

MCKAY *(to* NATALIE WOOD*)*. I'm sorry.

MCKAY *begins backing away, people still reaching for his hand.* DAVID *is fencing people off. Suddenly* MCKAY *breaks away from him and moves through a cluster of people into tight shot with* THE GIRL.

MCKAY. How are you?

The GIRL *puts her hand on his shoulder and says something into his ear.*

MCKAY *(he nods)*. I know.

Pull back: MCKAY *turning to join* NANCY, *who is guided up to him, as people at party turn and watch them go up the staircase.*

On the other side of the staircase.

KLEIN *grabs* LUCAS *as he is about to move up to meet* MCKAY *at top.*

KLEIN. Did you contact Starkey?

LUCAS. Forget it. He just won't go for the kid.

KLEIN. What about getting the old man into it?

LUCAS. Not yet.

KLEIN. He wants to win, doesn't he?

LUCAS. He'll be all right.

Int.: LUCAS' *office in wings of mezzanine.* MCKAY *holding phone;* LUCAS *standing by;* NANCY *sitting on desk,* BIG BACKER *on bench;* HENDERSON *guarding open door, through which we can see the party still holding.*

MCKAY *(into phone)*. Well, it was good to talk to you. I'll do that. Thanks again. I hope so, too. *(hangs up)* That's that. She's sending a check.

LUCAS. If the rest of you don't mind for a second —

WOMAN *(coming up)*. Mr. McKay, I'm your captain down in San Pedro.

HENDERSON *has left door and people are coming in.*

LUCAS *pulls* MCKAY *into bathroom.*

Int.: made-over janitor's washroom. MCKAY *sitting on toilet seat,* LUCAS *on rim of mop basin.*

LUCAS *(frowning intently)*. Have you seen the breakdown?

MCKAY *(drink in hand)*. You want me to look at this now?

LUCAS. Yeah, look here.

LUCAS *hands him a sheet of paper, tries to kneel down beside him, but there is not quite enough room for him to crouch between toilet and wall. He almost tips over, puts hand on floor to steady himself.* LUCAS *bumps into* MCKAY, *who spills some of his drink on the paper.*

MCKAY. I'm sorry.

LUCAS. You can still read it.

MCKAY. Wait. I've got it.

MCKAY *reaches for paper towel, tries to wipe off paper.*

LUCAS. I'm disappointed a little.

MCKAY. I got 47 per cent of the primary field.

LUCAS. Yeah, but when you look at the printout here, it projects to only 32 per cent in the election.

MCKAY *(stunned).* What are you saying?

LUCAS. I'm saying that if these figures hold till November it'll be Jarmon 68, McKay 32.

MCKAY. You told me I was supposed to lose.

LUCAS. Now I'm telling you you're going to get wiped out.

MCKAY. That wasn't part of the deal.

The doorknob jiggles. Both of them stare at it. It jiggles again.

LUCAS. Someone is in here!

Knob jiggles, door rattles.

MCKAY. Get lost!

MAN'S VOICE *(over party noises).* Sorry, guys.

MCKAY. Okay, I'll go home.

LUCAS. You can't do that.

MCKAY. Why not?

LUCAS. You're the Democratic nominee for Senator.

MCKAY. That sounds like a death sentence. Change or die, is that it?

LUCAS. *(gently).* No no no. It's just that up to now you're reaching only the people who already agree with you. We have to go after the rest.

MCKAY. What does that mean?

Tapping on the door.

LUCAS. We have to do more in terms of TV, for one thing.

MCKAY. Like what?

MAN'S VOICE *(at top of his lungs).* All right, you guys, we know you're in there!

LUCAS *kicks the door. Wham!*

LUCAS. Get your ass away from there!

Laughter outside. Giggling.

WOMAN'S VOICE. Just listen to the man!

LUCAS *(to McKay).* There's a lot of things. We haven't even started. *(More pounding.)* Goddamn it!

MCKAY *(rising).* Hey, Luke? Can't we talk it over in the morning?

LUCAS. I'll go along to Pasadena. We can talk in the car.

MCKAY. We have to work it out.

LUCAS *shrugs.*

LUCAS. We will.

More pounding.

Int.: KLEIN'S *office. Curtains pulled—Day. Monitor screen—a row of three screens showing different cuts of* KLEIN'S *footage on* MCKAY. KLEIN *presses buttons and we see—*

Montage: KLEIN'S *commercials.*

MCKAY *in "street situations" talking to kids on the Monterey Beach, cops in a cruiser, workers at the Ford Plant, black people in Watts, old people, housewives at supermarket and in front of Ford plant.*

In the Monterey footage and in the Ford plant footage, it is amazing how different things look through KLEIN'S *camera. The kids on the beach seem to be pushing eagerly to talk to* MCKAY. *The worker at the Ford plant seems to be the front man for a thronging crowd; his talk with* MCKAY *seems serious and significant. In each scene we get only fragments of what* MCKAY *is saying, but he comes off casual, informal, and working very hard. Each one ends with a freeze frame.*

HEAVY VOICE OVER.. . . Bill McKay. He talks to people. *All* the people. He's tougher. He's got more energy. And nobody owns him.

Lights on. KLEIN, LUCAS, MCKAY, PR *man,* HENDERSON, CORLISS.

KLEIN. What'd I tell ya!

HENDERSON. Sensational!

CORLISS *(little guy has huge cigar).* I think they're awfully good, Howard.

LUCAS. Thanks, Howard. It comes at a good time.

MCKAY. Just for the hell of it, what happened to the stuff where I talk about health clinics?

KLEIN. You want health clinics?

MCKAY. Yeah.

KLEIN. I'll give you health clinics!

KLEIN *snaps in tape reel. Lights out.*

Tape of MCKAY *in hospital waiting room, talking to* TWO LARGE BLACK LADIES, *holding babies on their laps.*

MCKAY. It took you three hours to get here? I think that's unacceptable. If we can get to the moon we can put a clinic near every sick child in this state.

Babies squirming: KLEIN *freezes frame on mothers' faces: worn out and without expression.*

KLEIN'S VOICE. You see, they're not responding.

MCKAY'S VOICE. What about what I'm saying?

KLEIN'S VOICE. What about it?

The tape continues. MCKAY *reaches out to pat baby, but baby jerks away and mother smacks baby's head.*

Close-up — MCKAY *winces, recovers.*

MCKAY. That'll make more jobs, too. We can start training people for health careers right in their communities.

KLEIN *freezes frame on* MCKAY *with an odd, forced smile.*

KLEIN'S VOICE. Grim scene, baby. You're off into other issues now, you look uptight and uncool, no one's listening and no one's digging you.

MCKAY. But aside from that, it's a great bit.

Int.: campaign headquarters — Late at night. A few workers moving around; TV set on. MCKAY *slumped in chair holding beer bottle. Glazed eyes fixed on TV. Everything he says here is blurred by fatigue.*

Chart on wall:

	JARMON	*McKAY*	UNDECIDED
JULY	58%	36%	6%
AUG	54%	39%	7%
SEPT			

On TV: Reporter standing with JARMON *on football field. LA Rams working out in background.*

LUCAS *comes in. He also looks tired.* MCKAY *motions toward the TV screen.*

ANNOUNCER (VAN AMBERG). . . . Despite the continued dryness and the threat of new fires, it was politics as usual around the state today. Crocker Jarmon took his campaign to Long Beach, where he visited the Rams on their practice field, and had a present for the coach.

JARMON. Derek, I was presenting the coach with a copy of *Life* Magazine, because they have it here in this issue, on the newsstands today, how much it meant when I went down to the locker room with my little grandson Dickie and we found all of those big tough guys down on their knees —

MCKAY. Shooting craps!

JARMON. — in a simple moment of prayer —

MCKAY *sprawls forward and snaps off the set — on which* JARMON'S *image lingers, and slowly fades . . .*

LUCAS. You better get some sleep.

MCKAY *(stares — blinks eyes).* This TV stuff . . . It's not working. I'm not talking to anyone and I'm not saying anything.

LUCAS. The point is you're showing your face. That's what we have to sell first.

MCKAY. Sell!

LUCAS. Exposure. You might want to take a little glance at these polls Klein had done in key counties — in every one you're up 3-4 points.

MCKAY *takes sheets.*

MCKAY. Well . . . You know what I'm gonna do?

LUCAS. Learn something about economics?

MCKAY. I'm gonna challenge Jarmon to a crap-shoot. Crap-shoot is a matter of individual enterprise. Crap-shoot made this country great.

LUCAS. God made this country great.

MCKAY. God shoots crap. *(Lucas repeats with him)* My little grandson saw him.

They stare glassy-eyed.

Int.: plane, L.A. Airport. (Plane is on the ground.) A football flies across the aisle. We discover the ball is moving between HENDERSON *and* MCKAY, *who sits next to* LUCAS. JENKIN, *the head advance man, suddenly comes up the steps and into the plane, rushes up the aisle.*

JENKIN. Bill! We've got to get off — right now!

MCKAY. What about that lunch in San Diego?

JENKIN. There's a forest fire in Malibu. It's perfect!

Cut to: aerial shot of forest fire as seen from helicopter.

Closer shot of helicopter — as LOU HURLEY *broadcasts.*

HURLEY. Here we are looking down from the Hurley-bird on a major brush fire fanned by gale force Santa Ana winds. We can see homes being evacuated in a thirty square mile area on either side of the Santa Monica mountain range. . . .

Cut to: MCKAY, LUCAS, JENKIN *and* HENDERSON *riding in car. Fire as seen from car. Radio helicopter hovering.*

JENKIN. About 400 homes have been burnt out already. There's fire all the way from Tarzana to Calabasas. The press is all over the place—swing up there, Wally, there's a copter up over the ridge, I think it's CBS—that means the wire service guys will be there too.

LUCAS. We can hit 'em on three points. Federal disaster insurance, the watershed stuff, and the fire prevention program.

MCKAY. Watershed. I want to do the watershed. Fires like this come from neglect.

LUCAS. But disaster insurance is *now*. These people are losing their homes, their possessions—and the insurance companies won't underwrite 'em.

MCKAY. And that damn Jarmon has been against the federal government getting into it.

HENDERSON. Hey, wait a minute! Don't make this an issue thing. It's gonna look as if you're trying to make political capital out of a fire.

MCKAY. I'm not going to make capital—it's something I've been talking about for years!

The car pulls into a clearing. Flames and smoke in background. Press vehicles, fire trucks, reporters, firemen.

As they get out of the car—

HENDERSON. Just don't beat 'em over the head with it.

LUCAS. OK, start with the watershed stuff and go into the insurance—

MCKAY. OK, OK . . .

JENKIN. Over here, Bill!

MCKAY *shakes hands with firemen etc. Reporters cluster around* MCKAY, *including one TV crew.*

REPORTER. You want to make a statement?

Some reporters are thrusting recorder microphones.

MCKAY. Yeah, I feel sick when I look at this. It's the result of something we've been talking about—what happens when you erode the watershed by indiscriminate road-building and developing, so you lose the root system that holds the water in the ground, and your brush dries out—

Sound of helicopter. A shadow comes over them.

REPORTER 2. There he is!

Radio men lower mikes.

TV REPORTER *(to crew)*. All right—that's it!

The crew hustles off toward the helicopter, along with other reporters.

Long shot: Helicopter landing, through the smoke.

Close-up: MCKAY, LUCAS, HENDERSON, JENKIN—*standing abandoned.*

LUCAS. You know who that is?

MCKAY. Yeah. Smokey the Bear.

SENATOR JARMON *climbs briskly out of his helicopter along with* JARMON'S MANAGER *and* PRESS SECRETARY.

LUCAS. Go right up to him.

HENDERSON. Hit him on the debate.

MCKAY *pushes through reporters, who crowd close after him with mikes.*

MCKAY. Mr. Jarmon!

JARMON *is startled for just an instant—reacts quickly, reaches to shake hands.*

JARMON. Well, how are you, son?

JARMON *holds on to* MCKAY'S *hand and beams over* MCKAY'S *shoulder towards the TV camera.*

MCKAY. I just wanted to tell you I'm still waiting for a chance to debate.

Close-up: JARMON. *He gives* MCKAY *a wink.*

JARMON *(under his breath, away from mikes).* Don't blame you a bit. *(moving right on)* Well, how ya doin', Jack, I see you got your wet suit on!

JARMON *is shaking hands with Fire Chief, Policemen, etc. His Press Secretary moves him toward helicopter with fire showing in background.*

JARMON'S MANAGER. Gentlemen, if you'll just step back a bit, the Senator has an announcement.

Reporters grudgingly move back a few steps, as TV camera is carried forward, lights are focused on JARMON.

JARMON. I'll make this very brief. First of all, I've been on the phone to the President, and one hour from now the President will declare Malibu a national disaster area. This means the Red Cross will be moving in, and the Governor will be calling up the National Guard within 30 minutes. There is a heroic effort being made here, and I am assured that within the next 24 hours this fire will be checked.

Now our concern is to make absolutely certain such disasters can't happen in the future.

That's why I'm very happy Mr. McKay took the trouble to be on hand for this announcement. As soon as I leave here, I will fly back to Washington to introduce the Jarmon Watershed Bill, which will include provisions for federally-financed disaster insurance.

Quick cut: JARMON'S MANAGER *smugly nodding.*

Pan, and we see he is nodding across to LUCAS, *who smiles grimly. Next to* LUCAS, MCKAY *is stunned; he mouths the words "son of a bitch!"*

JARMON. I think I can guarantee swift passage of that bill through the Senate Finance committee, since I happen to be Chairman of that committee. So we're doing all we can, and I want to add my personal thanks to the brave volunteers who have risked their lives to save the homes of their neighbors. Goodbye, good luck, and God bless you!

JARMON *waves, turns around, and gets into his helicopter.*

MCKAY *watches as the helicopter dramatically lifts off.*

Reporters turn again to MCKAY—*except for the TV crew, seen in the background packing up their equipment.*

REPORTERS. —What's your reaction, Mr. McKay?
—Will you back the Jarmon Bill?
—Do you have a statement?

MCKAY *stands baffled and speechless.*

REPORTER 2 *(cutting through). Will* you back the Jarmon Bill?

MCKAY *(biting off his words).* It's an emergency. I welcome any action at all.

MCKAY *abruptly turns away, rushes off with his staff.*

Motel pool—Same night. 2:00 A.M. Everything dark, including the water.

MCKAY, *in bathing suit, with a towel around his neck, slides open the glass doorway to his room, carefully eases door closed.*

POV—Other side of pool. MCKAY *slips into dark pool and swims up and down.*

Close-up. His face is relaxed, the feeling is loose, sensual, smooth, quiet. MCKAY *hangs from the low diving board, catching his breath. He sees someone swimming toward him from the other end. We see as she gets nearer that it is a blonde, a young girl, about 16-17 . . . and naked.*

She treads water right in front of him. She grins.

BLONDE. Did you go to Van Nuys High School?
MCKAY. No.
BLONDE. Oh. Then you don't know Pinky King.
MCKAY. Sorry.
BLONDE. Oh. I thought you went to Van Nuys High School.

Int.: San Fernando Valley Shopping Center—Canoga Park—Day. MCKAY *standing at microphone on little platform with local pols jammed around him at bottom of pit.*

Above him, a crowd packed and milling on three levels of shopping areas. Balloons are suspended from railings.

Behind the crowd, store facades stretch away on three levels. Escalators cross dizzyingly.

The speakers are placed so that MCKAY'S *words come with a couple of echoes. The visual and auditory effects of this scene are hallucinatory—a glimpse of a modern "Inferno".*

Zoom in: MCKAY *on platform staggers, as if overwhelmed—trying to orient himself.*

MCKAY. Mr. Jarmon says he's taking his case to the people. *(Echo: the people . . . the people . . .)* Then why does he refuse to meet me in open debate?

Claque in front of MCKAY *breaks into cheers when he pauses. They are fitted out with banners and hats.*

Camera rotates to people on higher levels— cheering, milling, walking off, throwing peanuts at floating balloons.

MCKAY. Mr. Jarmon says the economy is moving again. *(Echo) Mr. Jarmon says . . . Mr. Jarmon says . . .)* Then why is my office down in San Diego County . . . *(my office . . . my office . . .)* full of people looking for work? *(full of people . . . full of people . . .)* I say there's a better way. *(a better way . . . a better way . . .)* we have to retool a great deal of our industry—build mass transit—and things people can use—things that make our lives better—things that last longer than five minutes . . .

Big buzz comes on mike. Man in MCKAY *hat and flag shirt jumps up and grapples with microphone.* MCKAY *again steps back—dizzy.*

NBC News camera catches MCKAY *being led through enthusiastic crowd.*

TV camera POV: MCKAY *being moved—eye level—kids jumping up and down to get in front of lens. Hands being held up and waved, blotting out scene.*

Ext. Shopping Center— MCKAY's *new campaign bus—Day. New bus is painted red, white and blue—fitted out with gigantic photo of* MCKAY. *Large printed letters:* THE BETTER WAY.

MCKAY *waving to crowd, getting into bus, crowd holds up signs, V-fingers, etc.—pressing in, pressing in.*

From inside the bus: bodies of staff and press jamming bus aisle. Crowd outside seen through reflections on bus and store windows—all heightening effect of claustrophobia.

MCKAY *looks sick as bus pulls out.* HENDERSON *hands him a sandwich.*

HENDERSON. Jenkin got 500 farmers over in a high school gym in Bakersfield. They're furious up there about the whole farm program, and Jarmon was the one who got it through committee.

MCKAY *stares at sandwich—puts it in his pocket.*

Int.: H.S. gym, Bakersfield—Day. Camera scanning rows of empty metal chairs. Here and there a hard-faced farmer leans intently forward in his chair, dead-panned. No more than 20 in the whole place.

MCKAY *(voice over).* . . . *I wasn't a farmer myself, but I've been in the fields, and I think I know how you feel . . .*

Row of reporters leaning against brick wall in back of gym, whispering and laughing. Phones installed along folding tables ignored, except by LUCAS *who kneels, talking intensely on one phone.*

MCKAY *(voice over).* A better way. And that way is to subsidize the small farmer directly, rather than pay the huge agricultural combine to wipe him out . . .

Long shot—from rear.

MCKAY *all alone up in front of gym, under the basket, speaking to 20 farmers scattered in sea of empty chairs.*

MCKAY. Are there any questions? I'd be happy to respond to anything on your minds.

Silence.

MCKAY. Any comments? Suggestions? Dirty jokes?

One solitary farmer starts to laugh. He laughs a slow, honking laugh which echoes to the roof. Honk . . . honk . . . honk.

Int.: H.S. locker room—Immediately afterwards. Coke machine, pay phone. MCKAY *and* LUCAS *alone.* MCKAY *in shirtsleeves is rummaging through the pockets of his coat—comes up with sandwich.*

MCKAY. Goddamn that Jenkin. Why didn't he call? Why didn't he pick up that phone and say no one's there?

LUCAS. He was probably trying to get through. Listen, Bill—

MCKAY. And where is he now? Off with some farmer's daughter.

HENDERSON *rushes in.*

HENDERSON. Did you hear about Evans and Novack?

LUCAS. I'm just about to tell him that. Now will you get out of here, Wally?

HENDERSON. It's gonna be in every paper in the state tomorrow morning.

LUCAS. Just please leave us alone.

HENDERSON. It has to be counteracted now, or we're dead. These guys want to see the candidate. They've got to file in half an hour and they want a statement.

LUCAS *(pushing him toward door).* The statement is, it's not true, and we'll have more tomorrow. The candidate is not going to comment till tomorrow. And that's it.

MCKAY *is tearing away at sandwich, deliberately not saying a word.*

HENDERSON *(pompously).* That's not good enough, Luke.

LUCAS *(really exasperated).* You think I'm going to pull the old man out of my back pocket? Now get out and tell 'em what you can!

HENDERSON *leaves.*

LUCAS *(slamming door).* And don't come back!

Bill, those giants of journalism Evans and Novack have written a column saying your dad is really for Jarmon. It's coming out tomorrow morning.

I'll get more in a minute. *(moving to pay phone on wall)* This afternoon Tom Brokaw took his crew up to that cabin of John J's . . .

MCKAY *moves to coke machine, fishing for dime.*

LUCAS *(on phone).* Operator, I want to place a call to Los Angeles on the following credit card—314-8726—yes, that *is* a legitimate number!

LUCAS *hits clicker.*

HENDERSON *charges in again.*

HENDERSON *(to Lucas).* We got through to Brokaw and he confirmed it.

MCKAY *is jiggling handle—pushes coin release.*

LUCAS. Yeah, you're just half an hour behind me. Please get out of here, Wally.

HENDERSON *shrugs, leaves.*

LUCAS. Hey, are you there? Okay, operator, I'll call collect.
MCKAY. Can't you put a man on the door? Use one of your brilliant advance-men.

DAVID *rushes in.*

DAVID. All the reporters are on the bus.
LUCAS. Okay, start the bus, right?
DAVID. Right.
LUCAS. And drive 'em right over a cliff. *(into phone).* Now where the hell did you go! Oh, sorry. I wasn't "cursing" you, operator. Okay, I'll wait. *(to McKay)* Apparently John J. refused to say one thing or another. But that makes it look true. We'll get a look at that on the 6:00 o'clock news.

DAVID *stands there.*

LUCAS. Just go outside and watch the door a moment, will you David?
DAVID. Just talk to me straight, man.

DAVID *goes out.*

LUCAS *(into phone).* Okay, honey, are you ready? *(starts giving number)*

MCKAY *slams the coke machine.*

LUCAS *grabs his arm—stretching phone cord.*

A JANITOR *comes in—to tape a cut finger. As he tapes, he stands between* MCKAY *and* LUCAS, *looking from one to the other, utterly baffled.*

LUCAS. Bill. You're gonna have to go up and talk to him. It's the only way.
MCKAY *(shakes his head).* We don't use him. I told you that from the beginning.
LUCAS. Then we might as well announce you're quitting.
MCKAY. Announce whatever you like.

MCKAY *starts hitting machine slowly and methodically.*

LUCAS *(to operator).* Is that a trunk busy or a line busy! Operator? Operator? Damn! *(slams down phone)*

MCKAY. I'm gonna knock this mother into little pieces.

LUCAS *stands in his way.*

LUCAS. All we need is a simple statement of support.
MCKAY. I'm not gonna do it, Luke. Will you please get out of my way?
LUCAS. Even a straight denial would hold us for a week or two.

MCKAY *looks at him blankly.*

MCKAY. I can't think.

KID *sticks his head in.*

KID. Anyone want a coke?
MCKAY *(violently).* No!

Int.: MCKAY HOUSE. MCKAY *comes in the front door and stops short. Photographer's lights are set up on a stand.* TWO MEN *stand there.*

MCKAY. What are you doing in my house?
WRITER. I'm having an affair with your wife.
MCKAY. Huh?
WRITER. She said if you came in I should say I was a writer from *Parade*. But you don't believe that.

NANCY *emerges from bedroom in riding pants, with crop and felt riding helmet.*

NANCY. Oh Bill, this is Mr. Shearer, Bill, and this is Mr. Scott.
MCKAY *(shaking hands).* From *Parade*.
WRITER. I trust this is the beginning of a life-long affinity.
MCKAY. It's the beginning of something, anyhow. Can you excuse us a minute, gentlemen?
WRITER. Certainly, certainly.

MCKAY *and* NANCY *step to the side.*

MCKAY. What's going on?
NANCY. They want to photograph me riding.
MCKAY. You haven't worn that stuff in years.
NANCY. You haven't worn that dark suit in years.

MCKAY *starts to walk away, turns back to her.*

MCKAY. Just not in the house, Nancy. Get those guys out of the house.
NANCY. I was doing it for you.

NANCY *starts to cry, turns away, walks back into the kitchen.*

Parade guys turn their backs.

MCKAY *follows her into kitchen—takes her loosely in his arms, comforts her awkwardly. We* can see by the way he touches her he is irritated and put off. Blue bottles with buttons, nuts, raisins, etc. sit in frame against window—shine in the late afternoon sun.

MCKAY. Take it easy now—take it easy . . .
NANCY. It isn't that, it isn't that . . .

She turns to him helplessly crying without making a sound.

Ext.: road in Sierra Mountains. Day. MCKAY *driving, makes a turn . . . comes upon—*

Ext.: hunting lodge. Big Lincoln parked outside.

Int.: hunting lodge. Knock on door and MCKAY *enters, dressed in jeans, boots, old hat and jacket.*

MCKAY. Johnny.
HOUSE BOY. Lo', Mr. McKay.

We see a tall old man standing with a beer glass in his hand, watching the color TV. Behind him, a stuffed bear, standing with his claws stretched up to the ceiling.

JOHN J. Hello, Bud, what the hell.
MCKAY. Right, right.
JOHN J. *(hardly glancing over)*. Bud, you know Mrs. Ford.

She is in her late 40's—still has a strong body but her face is puffy and over made up. She wears a tight Chinese dress like a hostess at a Beverly Hills Chinese restaurant. Sound of football game on TV.

MCKAY. Hello, Mabel.
MABEL. Hello, Bud.
JOHN J. Get this man a beer.

MCKAY *stands by his father—who is still watching the game.* HOUSE BOY *comes and brings him a can of beer and an empty beer glass on a tray.* MCKAY *takes the can only.*

MCKAY. Thanks.

FROM TV. . . and so the field goal fails, the Raiders have the ball first and ten on their own twenty, the score still tied ten-all, and while we're waiting for the offense to get on the field, here's a word from the automobile of champions!

HOUSE BOY. You're welcome, Mr. McKay. Nice to see you.

JOHN J. *stretches, raps* MCKAY *a devastating slap on the back.*

JOHN J. Well, how are ya, Bud!

JOHN J. *flops back in easy chair.*

MCKAY *takes off his hat and tosses it on the bear—flops down on the rug.*

Both of them are facing TV. We can see MCKAY'S *face in reflected color light,* JOHN J.'S *face back in the dark. Now and then* JOHN J. *raises glass—catching light—or* MCKAY *drinks from can.*

MCKAY. How's it going?
JOHN J. Oh, the old knee kicks up once in a while.
MCKAY. When it rains, I guess.

Big play on TV.

JOHN J. How's that?
MCKAY. Your knee hurts when it rains.
JOHN J. You think that's it, huh?
MCKAY. Yeah.

*Commercial—*JOHN J. *snaps channels by remote control—ratcheting snap, snap, snap to another game.*

JOHN J. See your mother?
MCKAY. About a month ago. She's started playing golf.
JOHN J. She has, huh? How is she?
MCKAY. She's fine.
JOHN J. Woman'll bury me yet.
MCKAY. Wouldn't be surprised.
JOHN J. You wouldn't, huh?

*Another commercial—*JOHN J. *sits up.*

JOHN J. Hey, Mabel, you know old Bud is running for U.S. Senate?
MABEL. That's very good, Bud.
JOHN J. Get him a real drink, Mabel. He needs a drink.
MCKAY. No thanks, Mabel.
JOHN J. Well, get him something, Mabel. Tell Johnny to make him a sandwich or something. A man running for Senator has got to want *something*. Right, Bud?

MCKAY *just looks at him.*

We can see the old man grinning in the dark.

Ext.: woods. The two MCKAYS *are walking in heavy brush.* DOG *following.* JOHN J. *wears hunting cap and carries shotgun.*

MCKAY. It's just a matter of a statement.
JOHN J. *(holding up his gun)*. Sure you don't want to go back for the other one?
MCKAY. You don't have to do anything.
JOHN J. Bear to the right here. Watch it.
MCKAY. As a matter of fact, I really wish you wouldn't.
JOHN J. Wouldn't what?
MCKAY. Do anything.
JOHN J. Slow down now. Can you feel it?
MCKAY. Feel what?

JOHN J. Tell me something, Bud. What's it like to run a campaign in this state these days?

MCKAY. I wouldn't know.

JOHN J. *laughs—keeps looking from side to side.*

MCKAY. Did you really run your own campaign?

JOHN J. Shit, yes! What do you take me for?

MCKAY *(shaking his head)*. I guess I just don't—

JOHN J. I hear your advance work is unbelievable.

MCKAY *laughs.*

JOHN J. *(shouts).* Hold it!

A jackrabbit— JOHN J. *blasts away. Ka—Bam—Bam!*

The rabbit leaps in the air—falls.

Silence. JOHN J., *with an air of satisfaction, opens the gun across his knees and knocks out the empty shells.*

MCKAY *stands rigid.*

MCKAY. Will you do it?

Ext.: Alameda "Swap Meet" Outdoor Market—Day. MCKAY *walking through stalls—greeting people, getting good response. Obviously he is known now, and having a good time. Vendors calling to him, giving him fruit. Hippies giving peace sign—one hands him a flower. Lady holds up baby—* MCKAY *chucks it under chin but won't take it.*

Ext.: men's room—Market. MCKAY *entering with* CORLISS *close behind, carrying newspaper.*

CORLISS. I don't know what you said to your dad, but that sure was a snappy denial.

MCKAY. Excuse me. *(goes to urinal)*

HENDERSON *and* JENKIN—*standing guard outside door.*

HENDERSON. Hey, Rich! We got a sneak on the Field Poll. We're only 8 points behind.

JENKIN. If we can pick up one point a week . . .

HENDERSON. One point a week.

Int.: men's room. MCKAY *stands, pissing all alone at end of long row of urinals.* CORLISS *leaning casually against wall near door.*

Toilet door opens— A MAN WITH GLASSES *comes out. The man sees* MCKAY *and gives him elaborate take—goes over and stands almost in front of him as he pisses.*

MAN. You know, this is a heaven-sent opportunity. There's something I've been meaning to tell you, McKay. You are shit, and what's more, you know you're shit! Your father was shit before you. In fact, you come from a long line of total shits.

CORLISS. Now hold on!

MAN *(quickly holds up hand palm out, in elegant "hold" gesture)* Very well then.

MCKAY *has zipped up pants and quickly washed his hands.*

MAN. Between the two of us, McKay. Am I right, Or am I right?

MCKAY, *laughing to himself, dashes his wadded paper towel into the trash basket.*

Ext.: Swap Meet Market again. Mob pushing and tugging at MCKAY. *Girl opening shirt—"Sign me!" Kids grabbing at his clothes.* MCKAY *with fixed grin trying to get away with all his might.*

A HUGE MAN *hands* MCKAY *a hot dog in one hand and a Coke in another—then slugs him in the jaw.*

The screen goes black as MCKAY *falls.*

Ext.: campus—Day. MCKAY *has finished talk and is being put into car. Crowd of* STUDENTS *following along—most passively watching—some yelling "Right On" and waving fingers. Other waving fists and heckling. Right in front of car* THREE STUDENTS *waiting with big signs:*

IMMEDIATE
UNCONDITIONAL
WITHDRAWAL

They poke signs in MCKAY's *face.*

SIGN CARRIER. What do you say, McKay?

MCKAY. Keep the heat on!

MCKAY *ducks into car.*

Int.: car. MCKAY *suddenly finds himself alone in back seat with* NANCY—*who is well dressed and wearing hat. There is a beat as they look at one another.*

NANCY. Hello, Bill.

MCKAY. Hi, Kid. How are you?

MCKAY *leans over then to kiss her—but students are gleefully banging on window: "Come on out,* MCKAY".

Through windshield—we see them trying to climb on hood.

DAVID *is driving—* HENDERSON, JENKIN *and* CORLISS *jammed in front seat.*

JENKIN *(grabbing wheel).* Turn right, dammit!

Car swings right—cops appear waving them on, and they are clear.

NANCY *(by way of explanation)*. We're going to a women's club.
HENDERSON *(turning around)*. Next stop is that women's club, Bill!

The four guys in front seat make show of talking among themselves for the rest of the scene.

NANCY. You look tired.
MCKAY. I'm okay.
NANCY. Is it like . . . what you thought?

They are in a jam on the freeway. Stop and go driving. People in other cars jab each other to look at them, wave fingers, etc. MCKAY *returns signs, slouches down, contemplates his knees.* CORLISS *up front doing a lot of waving and grinning.*

MCKAY. When the faces start to move in on you . . . it's like a bad dream.
NANCY. I know what you mean. I can't go to a supermarket.

NANCY *has cigarette in mouth—trying to scrape match.* HENDERSON *reaches back with lighter.*

MCKAY. I guess you get it too.

For the first time, they exchange a smile.

NANCY. When you speak—are you saying what you meant to say?
MCKAY *(making a real effort)*. Well, you try.
NANCY. Yes, but Bill, you're getting somewhere. It's something I can feel.

She means well, but she's lost him. MCKAY *leans back with a fixed smile.*

JENKIN *(to others in front)*. So we come into Sacramento with 23 press and there's Cooley to meet us in a VW!
NANCY. Bill?

MCKAY *reaches for* NANCY's *hand and gets lighted cigarette instead. Gives a little grunt of pain.*

NANCY. Oh, Bill!

Guys in front seat turn around.

HENDERSON. You okay, Bill?
MCKAY. Yeah, yeah, it's okay. *(motioning them to turn around)*
HENDERSON. Burnt your hand, huh? *(then turns to front)*
NANCY. Maybe I have something for it.

NANCY *rummages in purse.*

NANCY. If I can only find it . . .

She stops rummaging—because she sees he isn't listening. MCKAY *is sucking hand, staring out window, brooding. They are moving now— passing oil wells.*

NANCY, *her hand in purse, stares at* MCKAY. *Slowly she closes her purse.*

Ext.: women's club—garden party—Women mobbing MCKAY. *Hundreds of ladies wearing hats press around him.*

THE CHAIRLADY *clutches microphone.*

CHAIRLADY. Ladies . . . Ladies. If we can just simmer down and keep our blood pressure under control, Mr. McKay has something very important he wants to talk to us about.
MCKAY *(gravely)*. First of all I want to say . . . I'm sorry I ate all the shrimp.

Hysterical laughter.

Ext.: Watts—Day. MCKAY *on a staged walking tour, trailed by staff,* KLEIN's *camera crew, and a dozen reporters. A huge black football star alongside* MCKAY, *dressed in a full-length multicolored suede coat.*

JENKIN *(backing up in front of them)*. Gentlemen, this way, if you please. We will proceed five blocks to our Watts Headquarters!

Jostling, bumping—various cameramen try to get close to MCKAY. MCKAY *is trailed by small group of* BLACK PEOPLE—*in both Afro and conventional dress—wearing* MCKAY *buttons.*

CORLISS *is passing out a mimeo'd statement to reporters. They take it without looking at it.*

CORLISS. I'll ask you just one question: Could Jarmon walk through Watts?

Reporter shrugs. Another reporter has gotten up to MCKAY.

REPORTER #2. Is your father going to join the campaign?
MCKAY. Whether he does or not, I'll tell you what's basic for the ghetto. It's a scandal there's no hospital here and no on-the-job training for medical aides—
REPORTER #3. When would he come, if he does come?
MCKAY. There's no housing program, no public transportation, no birth control center—
BLACK FOOTBALL STAR. Tell it, brother!
REPORTER *(arrogantly)*. So what else is new?

MCKAY *stops—he would like to punch the guy.*

People in street mostly stare. MCKAY *shakes a few hands in passing. Bursts of wild laughter.*

JENKIN. Right around this corner, gentlemen. There will be a cook-out in the park at 3 p.m.
BLACK LADY *(flatly).* What's a cook-out?

MUSCULAR BLACK MAN *in T-shirt, cut-off shorts and sandals, breaks through to* MCKAY, *wild look in his eyes. He is pulling a little dog on a leash.*

MAN WITH DOG. Hey, brother!
MCKAY *(with reserve).* How you doin'?
MAN WITH DOG *(jiving, exaggerated voice and face).* Bill McKay! You the gol-den wonder of the West!
MCKAY. Oh, I wouldn't say that.
MAN WITH DOG. But what about my dog, huh?
HENDERSON. That's a nice dog.

MAN *suddenly turns to* HENDERSON *with hands outstretched.*

MAN. Give me five, man!
HENDERSON. Huh?

CORLISS *comes up and slaps the man's hands.*

MAN. That's my man! But looky here—

Jumps back to MCKAY.

MAN. What about my dog, huh? What do you think of my dog?
BLACK FOOTBALL STAR. Get out of here, man.
MAN *(exaggerated take).* Hooo hooo! What have we here?

A moment of tension between these two very different black men—then caravan moves on, leaving the man with his dog glaring in puzzled hostility.

Passing youth holds up three fingers.

REPORTER #2. What's that mean?
MCKAY. Peace and up yours!
HENDERSON. Hey, look at that!

Long shot—three little black boys—shooting baskets in a playground

HENDERSON. You used to play ball, didn't you, Bill?. . . . Go on, Bill, just shoot a few!

Photographers begin charging ahead.

From Boys' POV

Mob of white people bearing down on them.

The boys run.

Int.: MCKAY's *headquarters—Night. Across the back of the room stretches a huge photo with a slogan—* MCKAY: *"The Better Way".*

Working area: Desks, phones, papers, mimeo machines, partitions, papers all over, posters, maps, charts on wall. Same chart as seen before, now up to date.

	JARMON	*McKAY*	UNDECIDED
JULY	58%	36%	6%
AUG	54%	39%	7%
SEPT	49%	40%	11%
OCT			

Most of the lights are out. Small clusters of staff are quietly sitting on desks and talking.

Balcony area: Near TV monitors.

CORLISS *is arguing with a* LARGE GIRL *about* MCKAY.

CORLISS.. . . for example, he still hasn't come out with a welfare program. If only he would . . .
LARGE GIRL. You're so dense! Really! Don't you see, the man *cannot fake what he doesn't feel.*
CORLISS. I'm talking about the *purely political* problem of reassuring the suburban mentality.
LARGE GIRL. When his instinct tells him it's time to share his feelings on welfare, he will, that's all!
CORLISS. Hell, I've been holding this 8 point program for 3 weeks!
LARGE GIRL. Why don't you hold a 3 point program for 8 weeks!

LUCAS, MCKAY *come in—staff crowds around them.*

THE GIRL *is trailing behind—stops in doorway and leans there, never taking her eyes off* MCKAY.

HENDERSON *(from TV).* It's coming on now!

Everyone crowds around TV.

Tight on tube: the face of HOWARD K. SMITH *on ABC-TV.*

HOWARD K. SMITH. A television commercial is a way of selling a product. A political candidate's bid for our votes is supposed to be a higher order of expression, with moral implications for the kind of people we are and want to become.
Increasingly in this country, candidates are merging the two, selling themselves like underarm deodorant in commercials just long enough to pound in some mindless slogan . . . cheapening candidate and voter alike.

But in the California Senate Race, young Bill McKay seemed different. He conspicuously rejected the machine type politics by which his father won office and fame . . . abhorred those slick hit and run commercials . . . ran a campaign refreshing in frankness and directness.

If the polls are right, it was working. Without commercials, without support from any large newspaper, McKay has got to where his veteran opponent, Crocker Jarmon, can feel the younger man's hot breath on his neck.

But now with a month to go, McKay's ways have visibly changed. Those early hard statements are turning into mush. Specific policies dissolve into old generalities. The Madison Avenue commercial has taken over as his standard means of persuasion.

Quick cut: CORLISS *gives the screen a long loud raspberry.*

SMITH. Voters are asked to choose a detergent: socco salesmanship, no moral considerations involved.

Once again it appears virtue is too great a strain for the long campaign haul.

Immediate reaction from staff.

STAFF. . . . What kind of shit?
. . . I can't believe my ears!
. . . Typical liberal cop-out!
. . . They got to him! Jarmon bought him off!

MCKAY *speaks only to* LUCAS—*as they move toward* LUCAS' *office—partitioned off in wings.*

MCKAY. I want to talk to you.
LUCAS. Don't take it seriously.
MCKAY. I do take it seriously.
LUCAS. It won't hurt us.

CORLISS *grabs* MCKAY *as* LUCAS *goes on into his office.*

CORLISS. Wait a minute, Bill! No one's gonna listen to that. He gives us a boost when he says we're pulling even. That's all the average voter will get from it.

LYNN *(passing).* How about the people who give us money?

CORLISS *follows her arguing as* MCKAY *goes into* LUCAS' *office and shuts door.*

Int.: LUCAS' *office.* LUCAS *is on the phone—suddenly grinning.*

LUCAS. He did! Well, how do you like—That's just . . . ducky. I agree. I agree. Let's just hope we don't get killed. Right! Back to you in the morning. *(jams down phone—waits)*

Jarmon's agreed to debate. He obviously thinks he's going to wipe the floor with you.
MCKAY. He won't wipe the floor.
LUCAS. As far as the campaign goes, you know, it's all been your decision. I've never gone behind your back.

Phones start ringing. LUCAS *pokes his head out door.*

LUCAS. Lynn! Lynn, get in here!

LYNN *comes.*

LYNN. Yes, my lord?
LUCAS. Get on the board, honey, and cut off everything coming in here. Jarmon's agreed to debate. I don't want a thing for 15 minutes.
LYNN. The board is plugged through for the night.
LUCAS. Well, find Harry and get him to re-plug it!
LYNN *(shrugs).* Whatever you say. *(goes out)*
LUCAS. Now listen. I've got to get in there and negotiate this thing tomorrow morning. We gotta pick a panel of questioners. And I gotta make sure you're sitting down.

LUCAS *rapidly starts jotting things down—as* MCKAY *stares grimly.*

LUCAS. Lighting, make-up, ground rules, moderator, panel, time of night—
MCKAY. Why sitting down?
LUCAS. The man comes on like your father. We have to avoid any hand-shaking stunts like he pulled at that damn fire. He'll try to make you look like a kid.
MCKAY. I don't give a damn. I don't want a panel either. I just want to get up there and say what I came to say.
LUCAS. We'll go over it. But you can't say too much on TV.
MCKAY. I thought the point was to say what I wanted.
LUCAS. It is. In the right way at the right time.
MCKAY. We never talked about any right time!
LUCAS. We didn't have to—because you know it as well as I do.
MCKAY. Don't tell me what I know.
LUCAS. Don't make me. *(picks up phone)* Get me Spivack at NBC.

MCKAY *grabs the phone.*

MCKAY. Let's get this straight!
LUCAS. Get *what* straight!
MCKAY. I want to know just what the hell this campaign is!

LUCAS *(with a sigh)*. Look. We've come up 14 points since this thing began. That's why Jarmon is debating you. Do you know what that means? The man is scared! And the reason why he's scared is that for the first time in this campaign you're getting through!

MCKAY *reacts—he is nonplussed.*

LUCAS. Now we're not back at the beginning. My job is not explaining any more. My job right now is to keep you from looking like you're sitting in Jarmon's lap. Now if you feel I'm not doing the job, tell me to shove off. Any time . . .

MCKAY *is stymied—stands there glowering.*

LYNN *(opening door)*. Have you got Spivack?
LUCAS *(picking up another phone)*. Bob? Hold on.
MCKAY *(very low)*. From here on out, no promises.
LUCAS *(lower)*. I never asked you to make any promises.

MCKAY *glares.* LUCAS *returns his glare.*

From behind LYNN—CORLISS, DAVID, HENDERSON, *and* JENKIN *rush into room. Another phone rings and* CORLISS *grabs it.*

HENDERSON. We got to get goin' on this thing right away. Better get on the horn and get everybody in here.
LUCAS *(hand over mouthpiece)*. Lynn! Get Fleischer in here for a briefing session at 11:00 tonight. Hear that, Cory? Get Klein on the phone and tell him to start earning his money. Wally, phone up those three guys on our lawyers committee, and I'll get 'em going on the negotiations.

People start moving in and out. MCKAY *can't stop the action. The whole staff is going wild with calls and bulletins.* MCKAY *sinks into an armchair as bodies rush past him.*

CORLISS *(on phone)*. That's right. It's all over now but the shouting.

Another phone rings.

MCKAY. I think that's for me.
LYNN. I'll tell them you're not here.

MCKAY *sees a large photo of himself leaning on the floor on its side. He sees himself throwing a football. He leans sideways to look into his own eyes—as the action rages around him.*

Ext.: plane landing in Oakland Airport—Day.

Int.: plane. Passengers pulling out hand baggage, getting on coats, bumping in aisles. MCKAY *is up front with a few reporters pressing behind him.*

HENDERSON *in rear of plane conferring with Stewardess #1.*

JENKIN *(announcing from front of plane)*. The McKay party will disembark at this end and proceed to the South parking lot.

Passengers move toward front.

HENDERSON. Okay, everybody, the McKay party off at the back.

Some passengers turn around, bumping into others.

JENKIN. Excuse me, Wally—we've got it covered.

STEWARDESS #2 *whispers to* JENKIN *from behind.*

STEWARDESS #2. The door won't open.
HENDERSON. Wait a minute, Rich.
JENKIN. Will you hold it, please, ladies and gentlemen, until we get this squared away.

Passengers are thoroughly confused. Sound of baby crying. Reporters start to crowd MCKAY.

REPORTER #1. How will you prepare for the debate?
REPORTER #2. Have you seen Jarmon's crime ads?
REPORTER #3. Do you think Jarmon is playing the backlash?
MCKAY *(answering woman reporter's earlier question)*. . . . typical California boyhood. We got juiced up every Saturday night and stole hubcaps.
ANNOUNCEMENT OVER P.A. *(Stewardess #2)*. We cannot de-plane until all passengers have resumed their seats.
REPORTER #1. What the hell is going on?
LADY. I'm not with McKay! I just want to get outta here!

Big confusion. LUCAS *and* CORLISS *jerk* MCKAY *into cockpit.*

JENKIN'S VOICE. Ladies and gentlemen, I am informed there will be a slight delay.

Tight angle in cockpit.

PILOT. This isn't any cocktail lounge!
LUCAS. Now look. There's no point even mentioning an ad like that. As far as the shooting thing in Oakland goes, you have compassion for all concerned, but you're waiting to hear the details. Now the reason

you're vulnerable on this stuff is that you just haven't established yourself on crime. Right?

PILOT. You'll have to get out of here, gentlemen.

LUCAS. In a second, officer.

CORLISS. This is Bill McKay.

PILOT. I don't care if it's Henry Fonda!

LUCAS. Give him that damn program, Cory.

CORLISS *hands* MCKAY *a typewritten script.* MCKAY *calmly looks it over.*

LUCAS. This is your crime program. You have to give it at the lunch speech today and you have to get it in the papers tomorrow.

MCKAY. Crime's not an issue, it's a symptom.

CORLISS. Hey, that's a good line!

LUCAS. Yeah, for when you write your book. The point now is to hit that 5-point prevention and enforcement stuff. Part of the better way.

MCKAY *(to pilot as he moves off).* Better way to screw 'em all!

PILOT *is totally bewildered—looks to* LUCAS.

LUCAS. I agree, I agree.

Int.: Fairmont Hotel corridor—Night of the debate. MCKAY *coming toward elevator with* LUCAS, CORLISS, FLEISCHER. LUCAS *carries briefing book for debate.*

MCKAY *(quiet and concentrated).* You think it's okay on the health insurance stuff?

They go into elevator.

CORLISS. It's terrific stuff. Jarmon'll be left nowhere if you say it just that way.

MCKAY. Let me check those figures.

LUCAS *hands him book.*

LUCAS. It's number 23.

MCKAY *stands holding open book but looking at* VERY OLD MAN *who is standing shyly in a corner of elevator watching him.* FLEISCHER *leans over* MCKAY'S *shoulder, opens his mouth to speak, but* MCKAY *closes book.*

LUCAS. Want to go over it again?

MCKAY *(handing back the book).* No, I got it.

FLEISCHER. I still don't know if that's what you really want to say.

MCKAY, *ignoring* FLEISCHER, *carefully shakes the old man's hand.*

MCKAY. Hi. How are you?

OLD MAN *(beaming).* I remember your Dad.

MCKAY. I bet you do.

The elevator stops, doors slide open, and they all get out.

LUCAS. The main thing is to say only what we came to say—no matter what the questions are.

MCKAY *(mildly).* When this is all over, I'm going out on the desert—by myself. Maybe stay there.

FLEISCHER *looks amazed to hear such talk at a time like this.*

LUCAS. Good idea! Hey, wait a second! Change ties with me!

MCKAY, *almost in a trance—starts to undo his tie—then hesitates.*

MCKAY. Why? . . . never mind.

He goes ahead and changes.

LUCAS. Here.

CORLISS *looks on approvingly, assessing the change of ties. They move into the lobby, still re-tying their ties.*

Int.: Tiny make-up room at studio. HOWARD KLEIN *personally supervising make-up man making up* MCKAY—*and whispering instructions to* MCKAY *on handling himself. He is whispering because a female reporter is sitting behind him, with her notebook open.* LUCAS *and* KLEIN'S *secretary* LISA *also sit watching.*

KLEIN. Look now, you'll be sitting on the right. Keep looking at Jarmon all the time he's talking. Try to keep your eyes steady, don't blink. Don't look up, or your eyes glaze and you look like a moron. And when you're not gesturing, keep your fingers *interlaced*!

KLEIN *tries to adjust* MCKAY'S *hands.* MCKAY *slaps away his fingers.*

KLEIN. I'm just trying to help, okay? Now do it!

In the tension of perfect silence, monitor views of JARMON *and* MCKAY, *brooding, waiting. Silence continues as we see—*

An overhead view of JARMON *and* MCKAY *sitting on separate chairs, facing a moderator and three-man panel.*

A series of shots moving in on key people in TV studio. Everyone in position for debate— KLEIN *and* LUCAS *together in control booth, flanked by stacks of TV monitors.* DAVID *sitting with* JAIME *in spectator's balcony.* NANCY *watching with* HENDERSON *from private screening room among other spectators.*

Close-up: TV DIRECTOR *(Michael Ritchie), getting ready to cue in cameras. Director raises his hand.*

DIRECTOR *(as cameras move in on key people, silently, nervously waiting).* Five seconds . . . four seconds . . . three seconds . . . two . . . one . . . Move in and cue Van.

VAN AMBERG *(Voice over, as we see faces of* MCKAY *and* JARMON. MCKAY *seems perfectly composed.)* Tonight! Senator Crocker Jarmon faces William McKay, his challenger in the race for the U.S. Senate seat from the State of California. The Jarmon-McKay Debate!

Good evening, I'm Van Amberg, ABC. I'll be your moderator for tonight's debate. We have three of California's best-known broadcast journalists on our panel. They are, Rollin Post, Ken Jones, and Morey Green. We'll begin our questioning now with Morey Green.

PANELIST—MOREY GREEN. Mr. McKay, at the beginning of your campaign, you favored bussing to achieve integration in the schools. Lately, you seem to be against it. Which is it?

MCKAY. Well, we can't let a school bus carry all the burdens of our society. The main question is still, how do we get a first-rate education for each and every child? We can't afford inferior education anywhere—and we should always try to preserve the concept of the neighborhood school in achieving this.

Quick cuts: KLEIN *sneaking a grin to* LUCAS. JAIME *leans toward* DAVID *in balcony— "Aw, shit!"*

PANELIST—KEN JONES. Gentlemen, is pollution a political issue in this campaign—or is this one subject you both can agree on?

JARMON. Of course it's not political. Now let's look at that oil spill that fouled our beaches. Now I warned about that oil spill, I testified, I hollered about stronger regulations. But we needed the oil, and we weren't careful enough about how we went in and got it. So I end up in the shower along with everyone else, trying to scrub the oil out of my old grey hair. *(relaxed and effusive)* Now, when it comes to smog, we are bucking the dream of every private citizen in his own automobile. So, we had to take on the battle of installing devices. In fact, we can now say, as the result of our Herculean labors, that we are turning the corner on smog here in California.

MODERATOR. Mr. McKay.

MCKAY. Well, I don't think we can see the corner, much less turn it.

Quick cut: LUCAS *and* KLEIN *laughing at their own pre-set line.*

MCKAY. I won't say it's a matter of Republicans or Democrats, but it's politics all right, when politicians put the needs of the polluters over the needs of the public. Now we have the money to do this job—we don't have to raise taxes one cent. We just have to have the leadership to get the job done.

JARMON *looks smugly irritated.*

PANELIST—ROLLIE POST. Mr. McKay, what do you think of legalized abortion?

MCKAY. Well, this is a matter that affects not only women, but all of us. We can't tolerate leadership that shuts its eyes to the problem. And it certainly deserves a lot more study than it's been getting.

Quick cuts: LUCAS *grinning,* JAIME *shaking his head.*

MODERATOR. Senator Jarmon.

JARMON. Well, I'm an old fashioned guy when it comes to this . . . and I don't care who knows it. I say human life is sacrosanct, it is God-given and we must have control over just how and when we let people take it away.

PANELIST—ROLLIE POST. Mr. McKay, up until recently, the public opinion polls have shown Senator Jarmon substantially ahead, and now you're reportedly closing the gap, though you're still behind. Now what effect will the public opinion polls have on your campaign?

MCKAY. I'm the underdog, so I don't believe in polls.

A laugh from the panel—again, LUCAS *and* KLEIN *are pleased with the pre-set answer.*

MCKAY. I wouldn't believe in 'em anyhow. You can't trim what you say to suit someone's poll.

PANELIST—MOREY GREEN. Mr. McKay, your opponent has implied that you have nothing to say about crime. Do you?

MCKAY. I have put out a five point program on prevention and enforcement—

Quick cut: CORLISS *in studio audience beams.*

MCKAY. And that program spells out in detail the training and equipment of the men who enforce our laws. And we must give them every means to handle crimes against person and property with speed, with effectiveness and safety. In addition we've got to set up the kind of system that stops crime before it has a chance to start.

MODERATOR. Senator Jarmon?

JARMON *(He begins to show his disgust, his voice is too harsh and loud.)* Well, of course, it's easy for anyone to come into it at this time and say anything that might capitalize—to pretend you have all the answers—to a situation you may have helped encourage—indirectly, that is.

MCKAY *watches calmly—permits himself a hint of a smile.*

JARMON. The question is, where do you draw the line? For some people their idea of getting tough is longer suspended sentences. Let's just think where crime comes from. Studies have proved it's this whole attitude of permissiveness. Well, let's face it! This attitude has given us some real bums to contend with. Our society has gone soft as . . . soft as an old banana!

JARMON *is losing his cool—* LUCAS *and* KLEIN *look delighted.*

PANELIST—KEN JONES. Senator Jarmon, at the beginning of your campaign, your supporters were predicting a record-breaking victory margin. Do you still go along with that?

JARMON *(struggling to recover an easier delivery).* Well now, Ken, I've played on too many losing football teams where we thought we had it won to . . .

MCKAY *checks a smile.*

JARMON *(hastily).* Of course, I've played on many more winning occasions.

JARMON *forces a laugh—* MCKAY *grins right back at him.*

JARMON. But I have learned never to predict whether you're gonna win or lose or what that point spread's gonna be. If the people have faith in you, and think that faith will be reflected, well, that's fine.

PANELIST—MOREY GREEN. Mr. McKay, there's been a—

JARMON *(jumping in harshly).* But you don't predict.

A little ripple of laughter in the studio. The panelists shift uneasily.

MODERATOR. Thank you, Senator. Gentlemen, relax for just a moment while we pause for this message.

MCKAY *smiles gravely.*

Control booth— KLEIN *slugs* LUCAS' *arm.*

KLEIN. What did I tell you? He's got balls in both hands!

LUCAS. Just wait, wait.

NANCY *and* HENDERSON.

HENDERSON. We got it!

NANCY *(smiling with delight).* Shhh.

Long shot—panelists stretching. JARMON's CAMPAIGN MANAGER *crosses the set to him, whispers urgently—hands* JARMON *a notecard.*

JARMON, *frowning, studies the notecard.*

MCKAY *sees* JARMON *staring grimly into space, fingering the card.*

Voice of TV director gives countdown again.

On a monitor: The faces of MCKAY *and* JARMON *are flickeringly superimposed as cameras focus in for the finish.*

MODERATOR. We come now to our concluding statements. The order was picked by a flip of the coin, and Senator Jarmon will go first. Senator Jarmon.

JARMON *(grimly composing himself, glowering into the camera).* To me, this country was never stronger. But the test of a strong country is how it faces its difficulties. Now and then, when I hear the barking and the baying of those who would knock our system down, I am reminded of the last days of the great Roman Empire.

They argued about what vices they could legalize, and what happened was an onslaught that nearly spelled the end of civilization.

MCKAY *is listening soberly. We stay on his face—watch it harden as* JARMON *continues.*

JARMON. Now I'm not suggesting that is what will happen if the people of California in their wisdom do not send me back to the Senate. I just promise you this. That as your Senator in Washington, I will continue to stand up for the philosophy of individualism and self-reliance that made this country great—and is more than ever called for if we are to face the future with faith and confidence.

Close on JARMON's *stern face.*

JARMON. I have that hope, because I believe in America. I believe that our greatest moment . . . is yet to come. Thank you.

Pan across panel to MCKAY, *who sits thoughtfully, staring at his tightly interlaced hands.*

MODERATOR. Mr. McKay, you now have one minute to sum up.

MCKAY *remains looking downward, doesn't speak.*

Close-up: LUCAS, *focussing intently on* MCKAY, *willing him to finish the job.*

MODERATOR. Mr. McKay.

MCKAY. In the beginning . . . *(he checks himself angrily, abandons his text.)* I think it's important to note what subjects we have not discussed.

Reaction: LUCAS, *who catches it right away, and takes a step forward, as if he'd like to grab* MCKAY *and stop him.*

MCKAY *(getting into it, with passion).* We've completely ignored the fact that this is a society divided by fear, hatred and violence.

Reaction: JARMON, *who comes alert, sensing an opportunity.*

MCKAY. And until we talk about what this society really is, then I don't know . . how we're going to change it.
We haven't discussed the rot that destroys our cities. We have all the resources we need to check it, but we don't use them. And we haven't discussed why not.

Reaction: LUCAS *and* KLEIN, *scowling.*

MCKAY. We haven't discussed race in this country, we haven't discussed poverty. In short, we haven't discussed any of the sicknesses that may yet . . . *(he fumbles)* send this country up in flames.
And we better do it. We better get it out in the open and confront it—before it's too late!
MODERATOR. Gentlemen—
JARMON. Just a moment, please!

LUCAS *and* KLEIN. KLEIN *smacks his fist into his hand.*

KLEIN. You had to do it, didn't you!

The camera swoops around the set, as everyone tries to talk at once.

JARMON *(prevailing over other voices, as camera settles on him).* I never dreamed that my opponent would stoop to encourage violence! I very seriously doubt that any man who would do that—
MCKAY. That's not what I said!
MODERATOR. Gentlemen, gentlemen . . .

A babble of voices as we zoom in on LUCAS *and* KLEIN. KLEIN *walks away in disgust;* LUCAS *remains staring in shock.*

MODERATOR *(turning to camera).* This has been the Jarmon-McKay debate, coming to you from—

Abrupt cut to—

Int.: tiny make-up room. Silence. Make-up man is swabbing off MCKAY's *make-up—as people begin to crush in.*

CORLISS. You were great, Bill. You touched all the bases.
FEMALE REPORTER. I thought you were splendid!
CORLISS. See, that 5-point program works, it works right in.
MCKAY. You liked it, huh?

MCKAY *remains impassive—shell-shocked—not sure yet what he's done.*

HENDERSON. Hey, Bill, your wife's waiting in the lounge. Should she stay here or go back to the hotel?
MCKAY *(hesitates).* I'll be out in a minute.
HENDERSON. You'll be out in a minute, huh? *(pushes close and speaks in low voice).* Quite a show.
MCKAY. What does that mean?
HENDERSON. What does it mean? I don't know.

DAVID *and* JAIME *enter.*

DAVID. Hey, Bill, that ending really took care of business!

DAVID *slaps* MCKAY's *hand.*

MCKAY. Hey! Jaime!

They fumble a revolutionary handshake. JAIME *can't look at* MCKAY—*tries to smile—turns and leaves.*

REPORTER. Mr. McKay, how would you assess the impact of tonight's debate?
MCKAY. I don't know, you saw it. *(stands up)* Where's my jacket?
DAVID. I got it.

Outside room— KLEIN *and* LUCAS, *coming along corridor with their heads down, trying to keep their voices low.* KLEIN *is furious;* LUCAS *simply depressed.* (LUCAS *is still carrying* Issues *book.)*

KLEIN. He took 23 out of 24 bits, kept us beating our meat for a whole year and all the time he was waiting behind a bush to unzip himself.
LUCAS. He probably doesn't see it that way.
KLEIN. He damn well will when I'm through with him.
LUCAS. Don't say a word, Howard.

KLEIN. Oh no, Luke, not after I brought Jarmon down from 20 points to 4! He says what he wants; I say what I want!

KLEIN *shoves into make-up room.*

LUCAS *(grabbing Klein's shoulder).* Goddammit, I feel just as bad as you do—

JOHN J. MCKAY *suddenly appears.*

JOHN J. Where is that son of mine?

LUCAS *hauls* KLEIN *out of the way.*

JOHN J. Hey, Bud!

People fall back to let him through—reporters move in behind him. JOHN J. *shoves right up to* MCKAY, *embraces him with his left arm, shakes his hand with his right—with professional heartiness. Photographers flash.* KLEIN *starts shoving* LUCAS *in ribs.*

KLEIN. A goddamn endorsement!

JOHN J. Hello, Bud. I think the old Crock looked a little sick—until the end, when he kind of turned it on you.

MCKAY *(still in shock).* I just wonder if anyone understood what I was trying to do.

JOHN J. Don't worry, son. It won't make any difference.

LUCAS. You see, Howard—
KLEIN. Shut up!

NANCY *appears in doorway.*

JOHN J. Now look at this gorgeous female creature!

JOHN J. *rushes over and embraces* NANCY. *Photographers flash again.* NANCY *clings to* JOHN J., *giving it her Sunday smile, turning this way and that to give the cameras their angles, clearly triumphant and ready to celebrate. She cocks her head to* MCKAY, *as if to say, "come on over!"*

MCKAY'S *reaction: negative.*

JOHN J. We're all goin' over to Big Sullivan's! I got 'em a liquor license and now they have to pay for it!

Everyone roars. JOHN J. *moves out the door with* NANCY *and everyone follows. As* MCKAY *goes out, he gives* LUCAS *a searching look.* LUCAS *smiles uncomfortably.*

LUCAS. What the hell. Forget it.

MCKAY *nods, stunned and bewildered.*

Int.: immense auditorium—Night—Spotlighted. Red plush curtains. LITTLE BOY *steps out to loud applause, carrying soap box. He puts down his box, climbs on it. More applause.*

Boy has mop of long blond hair, and is dressed in Little Lord Fauntleroy suit.

BOY. Ladies and gentlemen! Aren't I somethin'? I think I ought to be Senator. Then this state will be a really swell place for kids to play. Right, Dad?

HEAVY VOICE. *Right, son!*

Freeze frame. Super: Paid for by the Committee to Re-elect Senator Crocker Jarmon.

KLEIN'S *face (Int.:* KLEIN'S *office—Day. He is smoking cigar with phone cradled in his neck).*

KLEIN. I love it, we're gettin' to him. The Crock is worried. Now, look. We don't have any time to do new stuff, but I'll tell you what. I got the way to handle it. I'm gonna re-cut some of the old stuff and give you 30 seconds of McKay the statesman. . . . That's a guarantee! Right, Luke.

Throws the phone in its cradle with a solid clunk.

30 seconds of MCKAY *the statesman. Footage cut from previous commercials. The effect is tighter, stronger, more solid.*

Int.: hotel room—Night. JOHN J. *waiting for Bill with* FLOYD STARKEY, *the big Teamster leader.* LUCAS *pacing around: his secretary,* LYNN, *sitting quietly.*

LUCAS. I'm sure he'll be along in a minute, Mr. Starkey.

JOHN J. Keep in mind that Floyd has to get to a meeting at the local on Mission Street at 7:30 tomorrow morning.

LUCAS. Bill was telling me how he appreciates your effort in coming here, Mr. Starkey.

STARKEY. Hell of a way of showing it.

CORLISS *looks into room as if he expects to see* MCKAY *there.* LUCAS *lifts his eyebrows;* CORLISS *shrugs.*

LUCAS. He was probably held up on the freeway.

LYNN *(mischievously).* No, I saw him in the hotel.

LUCAS *looks daggers at her, but* JOHN J. *breaks out laughing.*

JOHN J. Some things are more important than an election.

LUCAS *grins.*

STARKEY. I don't know what the hell you mean by that.

STARKEY *gestures with his head to* JOHN J.

STARKEY. John . . . *(he takes him aside)* I'm telling you, John, I'm just about getting to the point where it's not worth it.

JOHN J. You think not, huh?

STARKEY. He's gonna get his ass kicked.

JOHN J. He's not gonna get his ass kicked.

STARKEY. Oh, yeah?

JOHN J. He's cute.

Corridor outside room. LUCAS *pacing in the corridor—sees* MCKAY *coming around a corner. As* LUCAS *starts toward him—* THE GIRL *appears, walking about fifteen feet behind* MCKAY. MCKAY *passes* LUCAS *without looking at him—turns into the room.* THE GIRL *too passes looking straight ahead, her face set and proud.* LUCAS *takes a speculative peek at her ass as she goes—then follows* MCKAY *into the room.*

In the room.

LUCAS. Bill, this is Floyd Starkey. He has to leave in a few minutes because a hundred thousand Teamsters in this state are waiting to hear what he has to say.

MCKAY *(crosses room and sits down without shaking hands—leaving Starkey standing).* Sorry I'm late.

JOHN J. This is a man who can do you a lot of good, Bud.

MCKAY. Uh-huh.

STARKEY. And you could do us some good, if you get to Washington.

MCKAY. You didn't do much good trying to break up the farm workers.

STARKEY. Oh yeah? *(working to swallow his hostility)* That isn't how I would put it. *(pause—looks over to John J., who shrugs cheerfully, as if to say, "I warned you")* There's no point chewing over our differences, though. When we get right down to it, you might find we have a lot in common.

MCKAY *(remaining seated).* I don't think we have shit in common.

Tense pause—then JOHN J. *laughs, and one by one everyone laughs, including* STARKEY—*and finally* MCKAY *himself has to smile. Without knowing why, he has lost it.*

Ext.: deserted beach—Long shot—(heavy fog, perhaps rain). MCKAY *running hard.*

Cut to:

Steep sand dune or bluff—seen from below. MCKAY *comes diving over the top of the bluff head first, literally risking his neck. He comes rolling, sliding down into the camera and past—all the way to the beach, one hundred feet down.*

White screen—which turns out to be Kleig lights over auditorium.

VOICE OVER. . . . and I give you the man—

Pan down to discover STARKEY—*as he turns to the wings with his arm outstretched.*

STARKEY. The man who will be the next Senator from this great state of California, Bill McKay!

A thunderous ovation—as MCKAY, *with a little nod from* LUCAS—*leaves the wings and comes walking out on the stage.*

In front of him a roaring crowd, a TV crew, cheerleaders with MCKAY *hats and short skirts. Behind him, a row of dignitaries—including* JOHN J. *and* NANCY—*who rise to applaud.*

MCKAY *takes the podium—and looks around him, somewhat dazed.*

The crowd begins a chant: "We want Bill, we want Bill . . ."

MCKAY *breaks into a confident grin. For the first time in the campaign, he raises his arms to the crowd.*

LUCAS, *in the wings, is smiling with intense satisfaction.*

MCKAY *begins what will be his first real stump speech.*

MCKAY *(as noise dies away).* Thank you. Thank you . . . Good to see you all. I had nothing else to do tonight, so I thought I'd drop by. *(gets a laugh and stops for it, as he will throughout, having learned at last to milk his lines)*

MCKAY. Seriously, it's nice to talk to an audience of working people . . . because I can congratulate you on having jobs. *(smaller laugh)* You do have jobs, don't you? *(laugh)* How many are out of work? *(a few hands up)* How many have relatives out of work? *(many hands)* Well, the unemployment figure for this state is eight per cent! And that's just the official figure. Really it's closer to twelve per cent. And I say that's unacceptable.

Think of it: the biggest, richest, most powerful country in all the world cannot keep its full work force working. It cannot tend all its sick people. It cannot feed all its hungry people or decently house its poor people. It cannot educate everyone who needs an education.

I say there has got to be a better way! *(applause—more chanting)* And to me that's what this election is all about.

Because the time has passed when you can turn your back on the fundamental needs of the people!

MCKAY *waits—and the audience realizes this is a big applause line.*

Pan to STARKEY *and others applauding.*

Side view— MCKAY, *scratching an itch under his ribs.*

MCKAY. And don't think you can distract them any more by playing off the young against the old, the black against the white, the poor against the less poor. *(he pauses—soberly gathers himself)* I think the time has come when the American people realize we are all in this together. *(Patriotic music begins to swell on soundtrack.)* We sink or swim together. And, I say to you maybe . . . I say to you just maybe . . . that is the way it should be—a test of our courage, of our compassion, our faith in ourselves and our faith in our country.

We see believing, glowing faces, people choked with tears.

Applause. MCKAY *gauges it, decides to relax them before ending pitch.*

MCKAY. No candidate can come before you and say that he's got all the answers.
Crocker Jarmon says that he has the answers. Does he?

Cries of "No! No!" MCKAY *grins.*

In the audience, find PETE WILSON, *the young lawyer from* MCKAY's *legal aid office, nodding shrewdly as he listens.*

MCKAY. All a man can say is, here I am. And that's what I say to you tonight. Here I am—I'm willing to give it all I've got. *(he raises a fist and shouts—as the music reaches a crescendo).* Let's make a beginning!

The crowd goes wild.

Long shot: STARKEY *raising* MCKAY's *arm, like a winning boxer's—and as* MCKAY *walks off, begins once more to lead the chant—"We want Bill! We want Bill!"*

Int. backstage, same auditorium. MCKAY *party pushing their way toward exit door.* NANCY *and* JOHN J. *moving on ahead as* MCKAY *stalls in heavier traffic—all shaking hands.* PETE WILSON *suddenly appears and stops* MCKAY.

WILSON. Bill, I gotta tell you something.
MCKAY. Pete! Hey! What's happening back at the office?

MCKAY *shakes his hand;* WILSON *holds on.*

WILSON. Well, some of the guys are down on you, but we know that. Look, Bill, I was there in the beginning. I know what this is costing you.

MCKAY *braces himself.*

WILSON. And I saw something out there tonight. Believe me, this is effective. Really, I can feel it—you can go all the way! Look, you and I both know this is bullshit, but the point is they're believing it!

PETE *waits for an answer, but* MCKAY *is stunned.*

MCKAY. Yeah, Pete, good to see you . . .

JENKIN. Hey, Bill, come on.

MCKAY, *uncomfortable, moves off quickly and runs right into cheerleader doing bump with big* MCKAY *photo-pin on her panties.*

WILSON *is shocked not to get a soul-to-soul reaction. He stands staring after* MCKAY *as* MCKAY *is moved through revolving door. Then a shrewd smile appears;* WILSON *nods his head. He is telling himself he understands—he is the only one.*

Montage: MCKAY *giving stump speech in six different places. Senior Citizens' Park—Watts Headquarters—Shopping center—Women's club—Hotel ballroom—Roof of car—Courthouse steps—High school Homecoming parade . . .*

Glimpses of NANCY *in background . . .*

Echo effects: "A better way . . . a better way . . ."

Audience sounds feeding in seemingly at random, inappropriate, not connected with what he is sayng: Laughter, applause, cheers, boos, yelling.

MCKAY. . . . can't tend all its sick people . . . can't feed all its hungry people . . . Ladies and gentlemen, there has got to be . . .
That's what this election is all about . . .
. . . got to be a better way . . . better way . . . a better way!
It won't be decided by the newspapers . . . or by TV commercials . . .
It's time to take government back for the people . . . the people . . . the people . . .
Because I think . . . the time has passed . . . the time has passed . . . has passed . . .
. . . the problem will not go away . . . the people will not go away . . .
. . . if you don't give them . . . give them . . . a test of our courage . . . our compassion

. . . our faith in ourselves . . . our way of life . . . There has got to be a better way . . . a better way!

Final words, "A better way . . . a better way!" echo louder as montage slows and fades.

Close-up— MCKAY—through car window— Day.

MCKAY *(babbling dreamily).* Ladies and gents, the time has passed, the time has passed, got to be a better way, I say to you, can't any longer, oh no, can't any longer play off black against old, young against poor. This country cannot house its houseless, feed its foodless. *(MCKAY makes babbling noise with his tongue; LUCAS in front seat glances around.)* They are demanding a government of the people, peopled by people. Our faith. Our compassion. Our courage on the grid-iron. *(a noise with his lips)* The basic indifference that made this country great! And on election day, we won't run away, vote once, vote twice, for BILL MCKAY!. . . . you middle-class Honkies!

HENDERSON, *driving, turns around.*

MCKAY *stares back at him—raises both hands making V-sign with fingers.*

Pull back. The car is crossing Golden Gate Bridge.

Ext.: station wagon racing along streets in rain—Day—Oakland. LUCAS *in back seat with* MCKAY, *his hand on* JENKIN's *shoulder as he drives.*

LUCAS. Goddammit, losing 15 minutes of free air time is like throwing away $80,000. Go on, fella! Go! I don't care what you do!

Long shot. The car swings down left hand lane, past long line of cars waiting at red light, HENDERSON *leaning out right hand window.*

HENDERSON. Okay so far, okay so far . . .

JENKIN *very nervous. They whip through red light and past traffic cop.*

HENDERSON. Excuse us, officer.

Int.: lobby of TV station. Two uniformed receptionists, one black, one white, sitting at desk by elevators.

LUCAS, JENKIN, MCKAY, DAVID *(carrying briefcase) and* HENDERSON *dash in and run to elevators.* JENKIN *pushes button three-four times.*

RECEPTIONIST #1. Excuse me, but you can't go up there.

LUCAS. This is Bill McKay.

RECEPTIONIST #1. I don't care who it is, we have to phone your names up.

LUCAS. We're doing an interview upstairs.

Meanwhile, in background OFFICE BOY *rushes up, dressed in smock.*

OFFICE BOY. Mr. McKay, you're doing a great job. Right on, man!

MCKAY. Thanks.

OFFICE BOY. My girl would kill me if I didn't get your autograph.

MCKAY *scrawls autograph.*

RECEPTIONIST #2. If you gentlemen will just take a chair, we'll be happy to send up your names.

LUCAS *picks up a chair.*

LUCAS. We'll take this one, okay?

Receptionists advance on them.

RECEPTIONIST #2. Gentlemen, we're just doing our job.

Elevator door opens and MCKAY's *party rushes in.* LUCAS *backs in brandishing chair.*

RECEPTIONISTS *(trying to get at them).* You can't do that! It's the rules!

LUCAS. Back, back, I say!

OFFICE BOY. Oh, wow!

Doors close and open. MCKAY's *party rush out—they are upstairs—dash down corridors— run into stagehand coming out of swinging doors with red light flashing overhead.*

STAGEHAND *(as they pass).* You're too late.

Int.: taping studio with small office set, which grips are beginning to disassemble. Behind it, the regular 6 o'clock news set—the "Anchor Men" getting into position. MCKAY's *party confronted by* STUDIO MANAGER, *with clipboard.*

MANAGER. Mr. Lucas.

LUCAS. We'll go right on.

MANAGER. We're not gonna reassemble it, I'm sorry. *(to MCKAY)* Hello, Mr. McKay.

MCKAY. We'll play it as is, if that's okay.

MCKAY *walks onto set.*

MANAGER. It's up to you. We don't have time for more than one take on this.

LUCAS. Over on the right, Bill! The right!

MCKAY *moves.* MANAGER *is signalling to camera and to engineer in booth.*

LUCAS. Everybody off the floor now. Come on!

HENDERSON. Okay, everybody off the floor!

They file into production booth, watch through slanted glass window.

ENGINEER *(into mike)*. Ready, number one? Tape rolling, okay, GO!

MCKAY *(leaning back on set)*. This is Bill McKay. I want to say a few words about the crisis—

The sound boom is lowered beside him, and MCKAY *cracks up.*

MANAGER. Cut! Take it from the top!

ENGINEER. Ready, tape rolling, go!
MCKAY. This is Bill McKay. I want to say a few words about the crisis in health . . . in health . . .

MCKAY *cracks up again.* LUCAS, *in booth, breaks into a laugh.*

MANAGER. I fail to see the humor.
LUCAS. Hold it just one second, okay?

Through the glass, we see LUCAS *go out on set and talk to* MCKAY. *Whispering, amplified through overhead microphone:*

LUCAS. Take it easy, Bill. Grim up.
MANAGER *(leaning into mike)*. This is it, gentlemen.

LUCAS *kneels down behind camera.*

ENGINEER. Tape rolling, ready, GO!
MCKAY. This is Bill—

He cracks up immediately.

LUCAS *jumps up and tries to grab* MCKAY's *shoulders. Manager comes rushing out on floor.*

MCKAY *(twisting away, unable to stop laughing)*. Just a minute, wait a minute.
MANAGER. That's just about enough, gentlemen.
LUCAS. Can you give us thirty seconds?
MANAGER. There's nothing I can do.
MCKAY. No, I got it. I got it.

But once more he is laughing uncontrollably. Manager stands staring at him, shaking his head.

Anaheim Stadium, Night rally. JARMON *addressing a large crowd of older and better-dressed people.*

JARMON. Now I know it's fashionable to weep for criminals. But sometimes the person weeping the loudest is the one who's taken the fullest advantage of all this system has to offer.

You know who I mean?

Cries of "McKay! Baby Bill!"

JARMON. Let me say one thing to him about our country. The United States of America is the most successful country in the history of mankind.
Is it worth respecting?

Crowd: "Yes!"

Is it worth defending?

Crowd: "Yes!"

Then above all we must obey our laws and honor the men who enforce them!

Ovation for JARMON. *He raises his arms in front of a huge poster of himself. Backers appear on his left and right.*

Pull back to find BILL STOUT *of CBS at rear of hall, turning away from the cheering crowd to speak into his microphone—as he appears on a TV set.*

STOUT. . . . and that's the scene here at Anaheim, Walter, a scene of confidence and celebration, as Crocker Jarmon proves once more he hasn't lost his velvet touch.

Int.: suite at Fairmont Hotel, San Francisco, Day—with a view of the city out the windows at every angle.

JENKIN, HENDERSON, *and six advance men.*

JENKIN. Now listen, guys, these last few days are going to be murder. When you see your event is running off-schedule even by five minutes, you've got to contact me—and nobody else—by phone or radio. Got that? Now let's run through this motorcade stuff.

HENDERSON *and* JENKIN *prop cardboard map of Montgomery Street against the lamp.*

JENKIN. Now here we have a four block area on Montgomery Street. Damn!

Map falls down. They put it up again.

JENKIN. This is the entire run of the parade, because it's the only place in Northern California where we have the right-sized buildings old enough to get the windows open for the ticker tape. Now we are going to come through at exactly 12:04, because that's when people are coming down on their lunch breaks.

As JENKIN *talks—an* OLD BLACK WAITER *in a white coat wheels in carts with covered plates.* THE ADVANCE MEN *start lifting the metal plate lids—revealing platters of prime ribs.*

JENKIN. When they pop out of their elevators and hit that street, they've got to see activity and commotion—and in the middle of that activity and commotion, the happy teeth of Bill McKay bearing down on them.

ADVANCE MAN #1. Who had the medium rare?

We make sure of this in two ways.

One, we stall cars blocking adjacent streets. *(indicating on map with pointer)*

HENDERSON. Hold a medium for me.

Two, we send a sound truck up and down Montgomery Street for half an hour before McKay arrives.

Wally, will you pass out the assignment sheets. You're each of you timed down to the minute, or else we blow the parade!

Wally!

Clanking of platters.

ADVANCE MAN #2. There's one medium missing.

HENDERSON. The one with the asparagus is mine!

HENDERSON *passes out the sheets as fast as he can. No one looks at them.*

ADVANCE MAN #2. That's not asparagus!

JENKIN. Then there's the ticker tape. We have it set up for . . . when?

ADVANCE MAN #3. For 12:15!

JENKIN. No, no, no! That's exactly what I'm talking about. Timing is critical. 12:05. The union people are set to start dropping it.

ADVANCE MAN #1. Is that the end cut?

JENKIN. It goes up here. Now are you guys listening!

ADVANCE MAN #2. The medium has the julienne potatoes. We're listening!

JENKIN. First you got your dixieland band on a flatbed. Then in the first car we got Lucas and Assemblyman Whatsisname and the Mayor.

ADVANCE MAN #1. The Mayor won't be there.

JENKIN Thanks for telling me! *(nervous laugh)* Now the second car is open and in it we have McKay and Nancy and no one else.

HENDERSON. I say it's spinach, and I say the hell with it!

JENKIN. Third car is key press, set up by our ace press secretary, Wally Henderson.

HENDERSON. You got it, Jenkin! But this isn't my plate.

JENKIN. Now the procession moves at exactly three miles an hour. We got twenty minutes to cover those three blocks by 12:24. Right?

ADVANCE MAN #1. Wally, you ordered it. I heard you!

ADVANCE MAN #2. Wait a minute! Let's get one thing straight!

Everybody stops and turns to him.

ADVANCE MAN #2. Who has the medium rare?

Ext.: Montgomery Street—various angles— Ticker tape parade.

1. Standard TV shots—Dixieland band, paper coming down, long shot from above.

2. Office workers dumping wastebaskets out windows.

3. JENKIN *standing with stopwatch. Behind him—cars honking behind car stalled lengthwise across street.*

*Close-up—*MCKAY *and* NANCY, *smiling, waving.* NANCY *looks glamorous, and is having a great time looking as if she feels this is how things should be.*

Their POV. Paper coming down, people cheering. MCKAY—*with his now professional grin—is shaking hands left and right. At the same time, he seems surprised at what is happening.*

Int. MCKAY *headquarters—election eve— About 5 P.M.*

Staff and volunteers crowd stage. Final chart:

	JARMON	*McKAY*	UNDECIDED
JULY	58%	36%	6%
AUG	54%	39%	7%
SEPT	49%	40%	11%
OCT	46%	42%	12%
NOV			

MCKAY *next to* LUCAS *leaning against desk on back wall.* MCKAY *is talking. Back of crowd: people standing on chairs, craning to see. Other people looking down from balcony.*

MCKAY. . . . you believed in what we're doing . . .

SHOUTS FROM BACK. Louder! Louder!

JENKIN. Will you please be quiet!

MCKAY. Without you we couldn't have done a thing, and win or lose, I want you to know we've been honored to have you.

LUCAS *climbs up on desk. Cries of "Big Luke"—"Cool Hand".*

LUCAS *(holding up V-sign and draws cheers).* All right, that's enough.

Luckily for Bill, he hasn't gotten to know some of you the way I have. Otherwise, he'd see what a miracle this campaign really is!

Hoots and jeers. Cries of "right on" and "off him". Laughter. LUCAS *holds up his hands again.*

LUCAS. And let's not kid ourselves, what we got here in this room is essentially a bunch of lazy dilettantes!

LUCAS *gets a hand.* MCKAY *is grinning.*

LUCAS. The polls say we are now within 3 points! *(applause)* We haven't made too many converts, but we sure have made a lot of undecided . . .
So I'll leave you with a final word before you hit the slopes and beaches. Get out the vote tomorrow—give us one more long day's work. Stay off the hard stuff—and leave your number at the desk.

The workers cheer him—and themselves.

Ext. sidewalk in front of headquarters—People waiting for MCKAY *to emerge.*

CORY *stands talking with* LARGE GIRL, *as* FEMALE REPORTER *avidly scribbles it down.*

LARGE GIRL. . . it's obvious you don't know him in the slightest. This campaign is not about what he says or doesn't say. The point is that just by getting up in front of us and letting us do our thing, he's given us freedom. That's why he never tells us what to do. He accepts us, you see, and then it's up to us to find out who we are—

Excitement: MCKAY *coming out.*

CORLISS. You have a nice mouth.

He rushes off toward MCKAY.

LARGE GIRL. Pig!

CORLISS *pushes up to* MCKAY. *People shoving in all around.*

CORLISS. Bill, I got to tell you! The feeling hit me today! Fantastic vibes man! We got a winner!
HENDERSON. The feeling hit me too!

Short young CORLISS *and big fat* HENDERSON *embrace and break into a dance.*

Int. MCKAY'S *bedroom—Night. Windows open. Cricket outside.* MCKAY *is undressing as* NANCY *watches from the bed.*
A matchbook falls from MCKAY'S *shirt pocket. He picks it up and stares at it.*

NANCY. What's that?
MCKAY. Nothing.

He chucks it toward wastebasket, misses. NANCY *picks it up.*

NANCY *(reading).* "You lose". Now what's that?
MCKAY. An early return.

MCKAY *gives one of his political grins.* NANCY *is uncomfortable.*

NANCY. I'm tired, aren't you?

MCKAY *nods, looking at her sadly now and with appreciation of the fact that she, too, wishes to avoid any sort of showdown.*
The phone rings. MCKAY *answers and stands listening.*

MCKAY. Sorry.

He hangs up and stands holding an undershirt, transfixed, completely lost in thought.
NANCY *sits up and watches him.*
MCKAY *at last reaches over and puts the phone off its cradle.*

NANCY. Bill?
MCKAY. Hmmm?
NANCY. Do you wish you were somewhere else?
MCKAY. I feel like I just came up from eight months in the New York subway.

He turns then and puts down his undershirt.

NANCY. I guess we had better go to bed. *(flops over on her tummy)* Oh, I feel so stiff!

MCKAY *straddles her, delicately lowers her nightgown halfway and begins gently rubbing her back.*

MCKAY. It was his last wish that Nancy have a back rub.
NANCY. It feels good.

MCKAY'S *hands—working harder, mechanically squeezing and pounding.*

Close-up— MCKAY'S *eyes are dull and groggy.*

Pull back to side: NANCY *lies silent and motionless as he works with small grunts. Shot is held past the point where we would expect a cut.*
MCKAY *stops—droops forward for a moment, his head almost touching her bare back. Then he pulls back and carefully climbs off of her.*
MCKAY *pads toward bathroom—stops and looks back at her.*

From MCKAY'S *POV.* NANCY *is lying perfectly still, her head turned away, her blond hair fanned out on the pillow.*

From the other side—we see that her eyes are wide open.

Black screen. Sound of phone ringing. MCKAY—*groggy—snaps on light and picks up phone.*

JENKIN'S VOICE. Bill!
MCKAY. Yeah?
JENKIN. Bill, are you still in bed! Bill, you got to get out and vote by seven A.M., or you're not gonna make the afternoon papers!
MCKAY. What time is it?

Polling booth. BILL & NANCY MCKAY *emerging fresh and smiling. A reporter puts his mike in* MCKAY's *face.*

REPORTER. What do you think of the weather?

Row of apartment house doorknobs. JARMON *workers putting voting slates on doorknobs. They wear raincoats and carry umbrellas.*

Ext. MCKAY *headquarters. "MCKAY: The Better Way" on marquee.*

TV REPORTER *in raincoat huddles under marquee.*

TV REPORTER. Walter, it's raining today on election day all over the state, and here at McKay headquarters there is frantic concern to get their voters to the polls. Generally, they believe a large turn-out is to their man's advantage. Hundreds of volunteers are going out to knock on doors—

Apartment house doorknobs. The hands of McKay workers rip off Jarmon's slate cards, replace them with McKay slate cards.

Ext. nursing home. JARMON WORKER *pushing old man in wheelchair into* JARMON *van.*

RADIO VOICE *(over).* . . *Crocker Jarmon has authored 76 other pieces of major legislation.*

Pan up past poster of Jarmon on side of van to discover—radio commercial coming from speakers on top of van.

RADIO VOICE *(continues).* What has Bill McKay accomplished?
Nothing much, but his father was Governor.
The preceding was paid for by the Committee to Save America.

Bum lying with bottle in alley. A young worker with McKay slate approaches, pulls him to his feet, leads him away.

JOHN J. MCKAY *emerging from his house in Los Angeles—moves toward his car as reporters close in on him.*

REPORTER. Guess there's no point in asking you who you've voted for?
JOHN J. *(laughing).* You wouldn't really want me to say that, would you?

REPORTER. I hear it's raining in the Southern part of the state.
JOHN J. It is?
REPORTER. How would you say this will affect your son's chances?
JOHN J. It might help a great deal—keep the enemy indoors!

SENATOR CLAUDE JARMON *emerging from polling place at fire station with* MRS. JARMON.

JARMON. It's going to be a great day for America!
PHOTOGRAPHER. Kiss her!
JARMON. That's the best suggestion I've heard all morning.

Freeze as JARMON *kisses his wife.*

Long shot. Int. MCKAY *headquarters.* LUCAS *wandering among phone banks, stopping here and there to comment.*

LUCAS. Are the phones working in East L.A.? Are you double-sure? Well, check again. Is everything all right at the hotel?
LYNN. Don't you have anywhere to go?
LUCAS. Look, I have to make sure that things happen here.
LYNN. You're driving everyone crazy!
LUCAS. There's a lot of details!
LYNN. Well, why don't you go clean your beard?

Int. JARMON *house.* JARMON *walks grimly down a long oak staircase, past stained glass windows. Without breaking stride, he checks his watch. The only sound is his footfalls.* MRS. JARMON *sits at the bottom of the stairs—looking up at him. He walks past her without a word.*

Ext.: polling place. Suburban school. Interviewer with housewife.

HOUSEWIFE. Of course the women on my block voted for McKay just on the basis of looks.
REPORTER. What about yourself?
HOUSEWIFE. I was taught that "handsome is as handsome does."

TV screen: Int.: San Francisco TV studio. VAN AMBERG *is interviewing* PIPE SMOKING POLLSTER.

NEWSCASTER *(VAN AMBERG).* I'm talking with Dr. Benjamin Dwight, who in the last three elections has predicted every major race in California hours before the polls close. Would you mind, Dr. Dwight, describing your technique?
Dwight *(striving for boredom).* We pick the key precincts in Los Angeles County, George,

and we interview voters on their way from the polls.

Cut to:

10 quick cuts. Six different types of Californians telling interviewers that they voted for Jarmon; four for McKay.

Ext. bus driver sitting in bus.

INTERVIEWER'S *voice*. You say you're an independent?

DRIVER. That's right.

INTERVIEWER'S VOICE. Would you mind telling us who you voted for in the Senate race?

DRIVER. Not at all. I'll tell you who I voted for. You see, I don't wait till the last minute to make up my mind.

INTERVIEWER'S VOICE. Who is it then?

DRIVER. None of this electioneering stuff has the slightest effect on me. *(tapping his head)* I know what I know.

Cut to:

INTERVIEWER'S VOICE. Will you tell us then, who you voted for?

DRIVER. I'll tell the world.

INTERVIEWER'S VOICE. Just . . . when . . . will you tell the world?

DRIVER. When I'm good and ready, that's when!

Cut to:

Int.: hotel room—LUCAS, KLEIN, CORLISS, HENDERSON, FLEISCHER *watching TV, keeping score of key counties.*

THEIR VOICES. . . Don't go in there—he's sleeping.

. . . Plenty of time yet.

. . . Well, we blew John J.'s county.

. . . No, that was the other county.

Cut to:

TV screen: Newscaster & the pollster again.

NEWSCASTER. And based on your interviews, what is your projection for the Senate race?

DWIGHT *(removing pipe, leans forward dramatically)*. Crocker Jarmon by 8 per cent!

Hotel room. LUCAS, *furious, leaps out of his chair.*

LUCAS. What kind of shit is this? The polls don't close for an hour!

FLEISCHER *(disdainfully)*. That doesn't change anyone's mind.

LUCAS. No, schmuck, it doesn't change their minds. They just stay home!

Int.: hotel ballroom. Crowd chanting for MCKAY.

All-white Hotel Room. Begin with TV screen, as VAN AMBERG *tells about results beginning to come in, trouble with voting machines, etc. Pan across to find* MCKAY'S *key staff—one by one, talking quietly on phones or among themselves—*CORLISS, FLEISCHER, HENDERSON, JENKIN, DAVID . . . *as we move across two white-covered beds, finally reaching* KLEIN, *hunched over, watching intently, and* LUCAS, *sprawled on a bed, worn out, yet not taking his eyes from the TV.*

The crowd in the ballroom—as seen on TV— quietly waiting. Floating balloons. Announcer's face comes in over them, with election results displayed underneath. MCKAY *has a slight lead.*

ANNOUNCER. The polls closed just twenty minutes ago, but as you can see, we already have some early returns . . .

Another hotel room, with a cocktail party going on. JOHN J. MCKAY *and* STARKEY *are having an enjoyable conversation—not heard in the general babble.* LUCAS *drinks a glass of champagne, smiles nervously.* FLEISCHER *is playing with a balloon on a string.*

Another TV—same announcer.

ANNOUNCER. . . with seven per cent of the vote tabulated, the challenger Bill McKay still clings to a narrow lead . . .

Crowd in ballroom cheering.

ANNOUNCER. . . however, we still have only scattered returns from the southland . . .

Some people in ballroom are beginning to dance.

Same announcer later—with much higher vote totals beneath him.

ANNOUNCER. . . Jarmon's margin in the South may not be sufficient to offset McKay's surprising strength in the North . . .

The crowd in the ballroom is beginning to chant: "We Want Bill!"

ANNOUNCER.. . . We may be able to call this one any moment!

Quick cut: KLEIN, *crowing like a rooster, grabs* LUCAS' *hand and pumps it violently.*

Back to ballroom—crowd is going wild, chanting and yelling.

BILL STOUT *stands among them, getting jostled, trying to make himself heard.*

BILL STOUT. Roger, as this upset becomes more and more evident with every passing minute, the people gathered here in the ball-rom, are getting ready to tear the roof off. . . .

As he talks, Stout's image is transferred to a TV set. Pan away, to another TV set.

VAN AMBERG.. . . our ABC computer has just declared young Bill McKay the winner . . .

Continue pan, past TV camera crew, find MCKAY *in an armchair, his face grave and expressionless, just like the face of the defeated candidate in the opening sequence.*

On the arm of MCKAY's *chair,* NANCY *sits, radiant, talking to news reporter.*

NANCY. . . I think Georgetown would certainly be a fine place to live, or Chevy Chase. . . .

It is obvious that they are going to be together now.

KLEIN *(to Lucas).* Five of six tonight, baby!

LUCAS, *grinning, walks into the next room of the suite, where* JOHN J. *is having a ball, shaking hands and greeting people.*

The hallway is thronged with people trying to get in, including all the people we have seen before in the campaign, staff, cheerleaders, film stars, rapturous girls in straw hats, and money people.

JENKIN *is at the door, trying to keep people out and direct traffic.* FLEISCHER *rushes past him, popping his balloon.*

FLEISCHER. We did it!

JENKIN *shakes his head in disgust.*

JENKIN *(to Henderson).* Wally, will you get those people back. We're going to clear the hall and bring him down in one minute.

JOHN J. *walks through the crush, makes his way into the other room, where* MCKAY *still sits glumly pondering, bends down over his son.*

JOHN J. Son, you're a politician.

A long look between father and son. MCKAY *looks baffled, as if he would like to smile, but can't.* JOHN J. *breaks out in a big-toothed grin—then laughs, up close, in* MCKAY's *face.*

MCKAY, *without smiling, gets to his feet.*

VOICE. Here he comes!

MCKAY's *POV—as he moves through the door of the suite—past* DAVID, *who has a full-out grin on his face—as the hallway churns behind him.*

MCKAY *sees hands reaching for him—he follows* LUCAS *through the crowd down the hallway. The noise is deafening as everyone tries to speak to* MCKAY *as he passes.*

Hands, faces press in upon him. A brief glimpse of THE GIRL, *who watches him silently as he passes her.*

LUCAS *is calling out something about "the undecideds!"—laughing that they went his way.* MCKAY *follows* LUCAS' *back.* MCKAY's *face looks blank.* KLEIN *and other staffers press close behind him.*

Suddenly MCKAY *glances sharply around him, as if looking for a way out. He presses forward and grabs* LUCAS.

MCKAY. I want to talk to you.

LUCAS. Okay. Later.

MCKAY. Now! I want to talk to you now!

LUCAS. Okay.

LUCAS *pulls* MCKAY *off to the side, around a corner, through swinging doors and into a freight elevator.*

Door closes on pack trying to follow.

Int. freight elevator. MCKAY *and* LUCAS *are crowded up against burlap wall padding by huge metal cart, loaded with dirty dishes, which takes up most of the elevator.*

A BUS BOY *is crowded up against the opposite wall. He eyes them suspiciously.*

LUCAS *(to* MCKAY*).* Well?

BUS BOY. Hey! You guys ain't supposed to be in here.

MCKAY *and* LUCAS *exit from the elevator—go through a door, around a corner and down a corridor to a room which* LUCAS *unlocks.*

Int. LUCAS' *empty hotel room—the white room, where earlier he was watching returns. Dishes, ashtrays, etc. scattered around. Small suitcase standing on desk by door.*

Noise of key in lock. LUCAS *and* MCKAY *hurry into room. In the interval while door is open, we hear far-off crowd noises.*

LUCAS *(grinning).* Okay, they saw you go with me, so we have about sixty seconds of privacy before they come looking for you. So what's on your mind? . . . Senator.

Long pause—noises louder.

Camera cuts back and forth from MCKAY *to* LUCAS. MCKAY *leans against desk.*

MCKAY. I don't know.

Banging on door.

LUCAS *(shrugs).* Okay. I gotta get out there.

LUCAS *opens door a crack.*

MCKAY. Marvin!
LUCAS. What? *(glancing at watch)*

LUCAS *tries to hold the door closed. Noise of people shouting. They shove the door part open and we can see them clamoring to get in.*

MCKAY. What do we do now?
LUCAS. *(to the people outside)* Wait a minute! Wait a minute! *(back to* MCKAY*)* What?
MCKAY. What do we— *(we see his mouth say "do now?"—)*

But the words are lost as the crowd streams past LUCAS—*who shows by the expression on his face that he has not understood what* MCKAY *is saying.*

MCKAY'*s POV*—LUCAS *shrugs, smiling, as the people push past him and bear down on* MCKAY *like a tidal wave.*

From the end of the room—The crowd of well-wishers and reporters quickly surround MCKAY *and lead him out.*

The door closes behind them with a little click. Voices out. Silence.

Patriotic music faintly begins to swell as we—

Hold on—the empty white hotel room.

The white room fades.

The End.